Then password

BreakonThrough

Evidence

Evidence

A Problem-Based and Comparative Approach

THIRD EDITION

Peter Nicolas

JEFFREY & SUSAN BROTMAN PROFESSOR OF LAW
UNIVERSITY OF WASHINGTON SCHOOL OF LAW

CAROLINA ACADEMIC PRESS
Durham, North Carolina

ISBN 978-1-61163-095-4
LCCN 2011938053

CAROLINA ACADEMIC PRESS
700 Kent Street
Durham, North Carolina 27701
Telephone (919) 489-7486
Fax (919) 493-5668
www.cap-press.com

Printed in the United States of America

To my family —
Mom, Dad, Mike & Alex

Contents

Table of Principal Cases

Table of Federal Rules of Evidence

Preface to the Third Edition

In the three years since the second edition of this textbook went to press, two key developments—the restyling of the Federal Rules of Evidence and a series of U.S. Supreme Court decisions clarifying the relationship between the Confrontation Clause and the admission of hearsay evidence against criminal defendants—compelled me to produce a new edition of the textbook and its accompanying statutory supplement.

On December 1, 2011, a restyled version of the Federal Rules of Evidence went into effect. The purpose of the restyling of the rules was both to make them easier to understand and to ensure consistent style and terminology throughout. According to the Advisory Committee Notes, the changes are intended to be stylistic only, and are not intended to make any substantive changes.

In addition to revising the text of the rules in the statutory supplement to reflect these changes, all references to the rules have been updated throughout the textbook to be consistent with the new language. Pre-restyling cases have been annotated (with a combination of brackets and editorial footnotes), as have references to the pre-restyling rule numbers and sub-sections in cases in the textbook as well as in the Advisory Committee Notes and legislative history in the statutory supplement.

This new edition of the textbook contains a completely overhauled section on the Confrontation Clause that incorporates edited versions of the U.S. Supreme Court's most recent decisions—*Melendez-Diaz v. Massachusetts*, *Michigan v. Bryant*, and *Bullcoming v. New Mexico*—as well as in-depth coverage of lower court decisions grappling with the many open questions that the Supreme Court has yet to answer.

This new edition also expands on the second edition's inclusion of state rules of evidence (and cases interpreting the same) that differ significantly from the federal rules. The expansion is both in terms of the number of rules for which comparative materials are included, as well as the number of states whose rules are included. These materials greatly facilitate discussion of the policies underlying the rules of evidence, and also take on greater importance with the restyling of the federal rules, since virtually no state rule now tracks the language of the restyled federal rules.

In addition, this textbook has been updated throughout to include recent cases grappling with a number of modern social and technological issues that arise in applying the rules of evidence. Examples include edited cases addressing such questions as:

- The admissibility of evidence that the accused is in a same-sex relationship when challenged on Rule 403 grounds;
- The admissibility of electronic evidence—including evidence found on social networking websites—when challenged on authentication or best evidence grounds; and
- The admissibility of evidence that a juror made racially biased comments when challenged on Rule 606 grounds.

Finally, in an effort to lighten things up just a little bit, this new edition contains a series of cartoons by cartoonist-attorney Stu Rees that illustrate a number of the cases and doctrines. The cartoons are not only funny, but sufficiently memorable to help students commit certain doctrines to memory.

In making all of these changes, I was guided by one of the reasons that I decided to write an evidence textbook in the first place: the desire to have a textbook that was short enough to teach from cover-to-cover in a typical evidence course. Accordingly, rather than simply adding the new materials (which would have expanded the book by almost 200 pages in length), I generally followed a rule of "one in, one out." In other words, for every new page of material added, a page of old material was removed. The result is not only a textbook that continues to be manageable in length, but also one in which all included materials have survived a "hard look" review.

In putting this new edition of the textbook and its accompanying statutory supplement together, I am indebted to my student assistants—Erin Adam, Amy Alexander, Chris Olah, and Walter Smith—who meticulously proofread them from cover-to-cover. I also wish to thank the many students and faculty that use the textbook at law schools throughout the country who have contacted me with helpful suggestions. Finally, I wish to thank the students to whom I teach evidence each year at the University of Washington, upon whom I rely to test out new materials before incorporating them into new editions of the textbook.

Peter Nicolas
Seattle, Washington
December 2011

Preface to the Second Edition

There have been a number of important developments in the law of evidence since the first edition of this textbook was published in 2005. This new edition incorporates these changes while at the same time adding several new features.

When the first edition of this book went to press, the United States Supreme Court had just issued its landmark decision in *Crawford v. Washington*, which completely re-theorized the relationship between hearsay evidence and the Confrontation Clause. This new edition incorporates key post-*Crawford* decisions, including the Supreme Court's 2006 decision in *Davis v. Washington* and its 2008 decision in *Giles v. California*, as well as several new problems designed to help students navigate the nuances of these decisions.

Since the first edition was published, Federal Rules of Evidence 404, 408, 606, and 609 have been amended, Federal Rule 502 (addressing waiver of the attorney-client privilege and the work-product doctrine) has been enacted into law, and an amendment to Federal Rule 804(b)(3) has been proposed. All of these changes have been incorporated into this new edition of the textbook.

This new edition of the textbook also explores in greater depth the application of the rules of evidence in the modern era in which much evidence is in an electronic form. Accordingly, many of the cases and problems involve the application of the rules of evidence to e-mail messages, chat room conversations, information contained on personal digital assistants (PDAs), and the like.

The problem-based approach of the first edition is not only maintained, but expanded, in this new edition. Twenty-four new in-depth problems have been added, bringing the total number of problems in the book to 114.

A key feature of this new edition is the inclusion of selected state rules of evidence and cases interpreting the same that differ significantly from the Federal Rules of Evidence. These comparative materials are focused on those Federal Rules of Evidence and decisions interpreting the same that are viewed by many commentators as resting on questionable rationales or policies, and are designed to facilitate class discussion about those underlying rationales and policies.

With these changes comes a new title designed to reflect them, with the new edition of the textbook being *Evidence: A Problem-Based and Comparative Approach*.

In putting this new edition of the textbook together, I am indebted to my student assistants, La Rond Baker, Alexander Casey, Blythe Chandler, Jason Voss, and Jennifer Heidt White, who meticulously proofread the new edition from cover-to-cover. I also wish to thank the students in my Autumn 2008 evidence course, who gave these new materials a trial run and provided me with valuable feedback as I prepared the materials for press.

Peter Nicolas
Seattle, Washington
January 2009

Preface to the First Edition

One of the biggest challenges facing those who teach the rules of evidence—and by extension those who write textbooks on the subject—is striking the proper balance between the amount of reading assigned to students and the breadth and depth of coverage. The Federal Rules of Evidence—around which this textbook is organized—consist of 67 separate rules, most of which contain multiple sub-rules as well as interpretive ambiguities. While devoting a large number of credit hours to the course in evidence might be the ideal solution for some, the reality is that at most American law schools, no more than three or four credit hours are devoted to the subject. Thus, a major goal of mine in undertaking this project was to provide teachers and students of evidence with a book that comprehensively covers the rules of evidence yet is short enough that it can realistically be taught in three semester hours.

This textbook is comprehensive in that it covers virtually every single one of the federal rules of evidence. Some textbooks attempt to solve the length-coverage dilemma by omitting coverage of those rules deemed to be "less important." Yet what may as a general matter be unimportant may be of critical importance in any given case that a student may encounter in the future, and lack of exposure to those rules when learning the rules of evidence as a student is likely to translate into lack of awareness when practicing. Accordingly, in my evidence course as well as in this textbook, I cover rules that are typically neglected, such as the so-called "minor" exceptions to the hearsay rule, the rules governing the calling and interrogation of witnesses by judges, and the parent-child and clergy-communicant privileges. My decision to do so is reinforced by stories from former students who have surprised opposing counsel and judges alike by successfully invoking such often-ignored rules.

Yet in providing broad coverage, I did not want to sacrifice depth of coverage. Thus, the textbook digs deep into the nuances of the rules of evidence, raising and attempting to answer such questions as: How does one authenticate an e-mail message? Is a remedial measure undertaken by a third party subject to exclusion under Rule 407? Does the adverse spousal testimony privilege apply in civil cases? When a rule of evidence references state law in cases with multi-state contacts, to *which* state's law is it referring? Does forensic handwriting analysis satisfy *Daubert*? Is a billboard a "writing" subject to the strictures of the best evidence rule? Can the dying declaration exception to the hearsay rule be invoked in *attempted* murder cases?

By using a balanced mix of cases, problems, textual narrative, and explanatory notes, the textbook is able to provide broad and deep coverage of the rules of evidence without sacrificing brevity. Chapter 1, as an example, contains just six edited cases but has eleven problems, forty-three explanatory notes, and several pages of textual narrative. Learning to read judicial decisions is an important skill, which is why there are several edited cases in each chapter, yet it is but one of many skills that students must master. Moreover, cases are an inefficient vehicle for conveying large amounts of information. Accordingly, cases are used sparingly, and when used, are carefully chosen and rigorously edited.

The approach used in most sections of the textbook thus proceeds as follows. First, students are given several pages of introductory narrative designed to introduce them to the rule covered in that section, including its history and underlying policy justifications. That narrative is followed by a problem or series of problems, designed for use in class as a vehicle for raising and addressing the conceptual ambiguities that arise in interpreting and applying the rule. Resources for answering those questions are provided by the materials following the problems, usually a case or two followed by a series of explanatory notes.

The extensive use of problems throughout the textbook—ninety in-depth problems in all, or on average about two or three for each class hour—allows students to master the *application* of the rules of evidence. By the time law students take the course in evidence, most of them have learned how to read cases and to recite the holdings of those cases. Yet many students find it difficult to apply those principles when presented with alternative factual scenarios. These problems thus provide students with ample opportunity to hone their skills in applying the rules of evidence and to receive feedback on the same.

The topics in the textbook are organized in the order in which I normally teach them, but the chapters are sufficiently independent of one another that they can be taught in a different sequence without difficulty. Chapter 1 introduces the basic concepts of relevance and prejudice. Chapter 2, which covers the rules governing authentication of evidence, logically follows from Chapter 1's discussion of conditional relevance. Chapter 3 then introduces the categorical rules—such as those addressing character evidence, subsequent remedial measures, and the like—that refine the concepts of relevance and prejudice introduced in Chapter 1. The focus of Chapter 4 is on witnesses, examining the rules governing their competency, qualification, and examination. Chapter 5 turns to privileges, with a focus on the attorney-client, spousal, psychotherapist-patient, parent-child, and clergy-communicant privileges. The next two chapters cover the two sets of rules that express a preference for what is thought to be superior evidence, the best evidence rule in Chapter 6 followed by the hearsay rule, its exceptions, and the Confrontation Clause in Chapter 7. The following two chapters examine two methods of shortcutting normal methods of proof, with Chapter 8 focusing on the rules governing judicial notice and Chapter 9 examining evidentiary presumptions. Chapter 10 examines the various methods of impeaching and rehabilitating witnesses, and finally, Chapter 11 examines the rules governing appellate review of evidentiary rulings.

Throughout, the textbook incorporates recent changes in substantive law as well as changes in technology that raise special challenges in applying the rules of evidence. The book includes the Supreme Court's 2004 decision in *Crawford v. Washington*, which redefined the relationship between the hearsay rule and the Confrontation Clause, as well as notes on post-*Crawford* developments in the lower courts. The book also examines proposed changes to Rules 404, 408, 606, and 609 that are being considered as this book goes to press in early 2005. The book includes an enriched section on scientific evidence that considers the application of the Supreme Court's decision in *Daubert v. Merrell Dow Pharmaceuticals, Inc.* to a variety of forms of expert testimony, including DNA analysis, fingerprint analysis, handwriting analysis, and polygraph testing, as well as to expert testimony on eyewitness reliability and battered woman syndrome. In addition, the textbook considers the rules of evidence in a modern context by considering their application to electronic evidence, such as e-mail messages, postings on the Internet, and output generated by global positioning system devices and computers.

In putting this textbook together, I am indebted to several student assistants who provided extraordinary assistance in researching and proofreading the book. Two student assistants in particular—Matthew Koenigs and Elizabeth A. Tutmarc—were involved in the project from start to finish, each researching several chapters of the book and each meticulously proofreading the entire book. In addition, student assistants Matthew W. Daley, Kyla C.E. Grogan, and Sarah Shirey each played a key role in researching individual chapters of the book. I also wish to thank Ms. Tutmarc and my secretarial assistant, Wendy Condiotty, who together played a crucial role in researching and editing the separate statutory supplement for this textbook. Finally I wish to thank the students in my Autumn 2004 evidence course, who gave these materials a trial run and provided me with valuable feedback as I prepared the materials for press.

Peter Nicolas
Seattle, Washington
January 2005

Acknowledgments

I am grateful to the following sources for permission to reprint excerpts of their work:

American Law Institute, Restatement (Third) of the Law Governing Lawyers §69 cmt. e (2000). Copyright © 2000 by the American Law Institute. Reprinted with permission. All rights reserved.

1 Attorney-Client Privilege in the United States §5:2 (2d ed. 2004). Copyright © 2004 by West, a Thomson business. Reprinted with permission. All rights reserved.

Mike Strong, Map of Sairey Gamp Elementary School Enhanced Drug Penalty Area. Copyright © 2005 by Mike Strong. Reprinted with permission. All rights reserved.

2 Wigmore on Evidence, §§282a, 302, 303 (Chadbourn rev. 1979). Copyright © 1979, by James H. Chadbourn. Reprinted with permission from Aspen Publishers. All rights reserved.

3 Wigmore on Evidence, §§767, 773 (Chadbourn rev. 1970). Copyright © 1970, by James H. Chadbourn. Reprinted with permission from Aspen Publishers. All rights reserved.

4 Wigmore on Evidence, §§1177, 1182 (Chadbourn rev. 1972). Copyright © 1972, by James H. Chadbourn. Reprinted with permission from Aspen Publishers. All rights reserved.

5 Wigmore on Evidence, §1439 (Chadbourn rev. 1974). Copyright © 1974, by James H. Chadbourn. Reprinted with permission from Aspen Publishers. All rights reserved.

6 Wigmore on Evidence, §1871 (Chadbourn rev. 1976). Copyright © 1976, by James H. Chadbourn. Reprinted with permission from Aspen Publishers. All rights reserved.

7 Wigmore on Evidence, §2153 (Chadbourn rev. 1978). Copyright © 1978, by James H. Chadbourn. Reprinted with permission from Aspen Publishers. All rights reserved.

8 Wigmore on Evidence, §§2292, 2327 (McNaughton rev. 1961). Copyright © 1961, by John T. McNaughton. Reprinted with permission from Aspen Publishers. All rights reserved.

9 Wigmore on Evidence, §§2569, 2570 (Chadbourn rev. 1981). Copyright © 1981, by James H. Chadbourn. Reprinted with permission from Aspen Publishers. All rights reserved.

Evidence

Chapter 1

Relevance

A. Rule 402: The Gateway to Admissibility

While one may attribute a variety of purposes to conducting criminal and civil trials, one purpose seems paramount: to resolve disputed questions about an event or series of events that took place in the past. Thus, for example, in a murder trial, an overriding purpose is to determine whether the accused caused the victim's death, and if so, with what intent. And in a civil trial involving a claim that someone breached a contract, an over-riding purpose may be to determine whether a contract was made, what its terms were, and the extent to which the party complied with those terms.

To assist, or perhaps more accurately, to persuade, the person or people responsible for resolving these disputed questions (known as the trier of fact, who will often be a jury but sometimes a judge), the competing parties in a formal trial will present a great deal of information, known as evidence. The trier of fact will then use that information to re-solve the disputed questions.

Of course, it is not only in the course of formal trials that people go through the process of examining information to determine what happened at some point in the past. Before civil or criminal litigation is initiated, the person or entity contemplating litigation will en-gage in a similar process of examining information to figure out what happened. Thus, for example, when a dead body is discovered, government officials examine a variety of clues to figure out who was responsible for causing the person's death before filing criminal charges.

Moreover, although we are an ever increasingly litigious society, not every effort to determine what happened in the past will make its way into a court of law. In our every-day life, we frequently sift through information to resolve disputes over what happened in the past. Consider, for example, the rather classic problem of misplacing your keys. Immediately several thoughts come to your mind, first and foremost, "Where did I last see them?" If you remember that you saw them three hours ago, when you opened the door to your office, in your mind you rather naturally start to catalogue the various places that you have visited between the time that you opened your office door and the present mo-ment: your office, Susan's office, the snack bar, the restroom. You instinctively return to all of those places in search of your keys, and if you don't find them, you ask other peo-ple who were also at those places—such as Susan and the snack bar attendant—whether they know anything about the whereabouts of your keys.

Why is it that in searching for your keys, you rather naturally go only to those places that you remember visiting between now and the last time you recall seeing the keys? The answer seems so obvious that it hardly seems worth mention: to look elsewhere would serve no purpose in your quest to find your keys. Absent information (evidence) suggesting that some other person picked up your keys and put them somewhere else (information that you might discover by speaking with Susan or the snack bar attendant), or information (often in the form of a reminder by someone else) that you visited some other place that you had forgotten about, it simply makes no sense to look anywhere else.

Before cluttering your mind with legal jargon, take a crack at the following problem, which, like the mystery of the misplaced keys, is unlikely to work its way into a courtroom, although the punishment imposed on the offending party may rival that imposed by a court of law.

Problem 1-1: The Case of the Missing Cheesecake

The inhabitants of the Smith household — Tom, Susan, Lisa, David, and Robert — have insatiable appetites for sweets. Accordingly, on the kitchen table there is always some sort of cake or pie. In the Smith household, it is considered taboo to eat the last slice of cake or pie without replacing it with another cake or pie.

Early on Wednesday morning, Tom ate the last slice of a cherry pie, which he promptly replaced with a cheesecake. Yet later that afternoon, when Tom returned to the kitchen, he saw that every slice of the cheesecake was gone but there was no replacement! Outraged, he has called on you to investigate the matter. In your investigation, the following facts come to your attention:

1. Susan was out of town from Tuesday morning through Wednesday night.

2. Lisa is lactose intolerant.

3. David has blue eyes and blond hair.

4. Lisa tells you that she saw Robert eat the last slice of cheesecake.

5. The last time this happened, it turned out that David was the culprit.

6. Lisa despises Robert.

7. It was raining all day on Wednesday.

In conducting your investigation, which of these facts would matter to you?

As the previous examples suggest, when trying to resolve questions about events taking place in our everyday lives, we instinctively draw a sharp line between those pieces of information that seem to matter and those that do not. It should thus come as little surprise that when such questions are to be resolved in the courtroom, a similar line is drawn between information that matters and information that does not matter. In particular, Federal Rule 402 provides as follows:

Relevant evidence is admissible unless any of the following provides otherwise:

- the United States Constitution;
- a federal statute;
- these rules; or
- other rules prescribed by the Supreme Court.

Irrelevant evidence is not admissible.

We can set aside for the moment the formal definition of the word "relevant" as well as the difficulties attendant in determining relevancy, accepting for now that it roughly means "information that matters." What is important to note for the moment is that Rule

402 really contains two rules, or more precisely, an absolute rule and a rebuttable presumption.

The absolute rule is found in the second sentence of Rule 402: information that does not matter is not admissible. The rule is absolute and admits no exceptions: if some piece of information does not matter, it cannot be admitted into evidence and thus cannot be presented to the trier of fact. This part of Rule 402 aligns with our intuition in resolving questions in our everyday lives: our minds reject information that does not matter in the same way that Rule 402 excludes such evidence.

The rebuttable presumption is found in the first sentence of Rule 402: information that matters is admissible, unless there is some *other* reason to exclude it. The presumptive admissibility of such evidence, like the absolute rule excluding evidence that does not matter, is consistent with our intuition in resolving questions in our everyday lives. Yet the proviso allowing for the exclusion of such evidence when another rule of evidence "provides otherwise" is what sets apart Rule 402 and thus, fact-finding in the courtroom generally from fact-finding in our everyday lives. Much of the study of the rules of evidence is devoted to learning about those circumstances in which another rule of evidence "provides otherwise."

In this sense, Rule 402 serves as an initial gateway on a road to admissibility through which every piece of evidence must pass before making its way to the trier of fact. The absolute rule contained in Rule 402 makes it both the start and the end of the road for evidence that is deemed not to matter. Such evidence is dead on arrival, and no other rule can revive it. Evidence that matters can make it through the Rule 402 gateway, but it must travel a long journey down a road and survive a series of situations in which another rule of evidence "provides otherwise" before ultimately making its way before the trier of fact.

Notes and Questions

1. What purpose is served by the absolute rule contained in Rule 402? After all, as discussed in the text, this rule should align with the natural intuition of rational individuals. To the extent that information is not relevant, won't jurors disregard such information in the same way that they would when resolving questions in their everyday lives?

2. The Advisory Committee Note to Rule 402 cites to James Bradley Thayer's Preliminary Treatise on Evidence at the Common Law 264 (1898). There, Thayer wrote:

> There is a principle—not so much a rule of evidence as a presupposition involved in the very conception of a rational system of evidence ...—which forbids receiving anything irrelevant, not logically probative....

> There is another precept which should be laid down as preliminary, in stating the law of evidence; namely, that unless excluded by some rule or principle of law, all that is logically probative is admissible. This general admissibility, however, of what is logically probative is not, like the former principle, a necessary presupposition in a rational system of evidence; there are many exceptions to it.

3. Technically, of course, it is unnecessary for Rule 402 to state that relevant evidence is subject to exclusion if the United States Constitution so requires, for the Constitution would always trump the rule. Rather, as the Advisory Committee's Note points out, it serves as a reminder that the exclusionary rule and other constitutional rules must be considered separate and apart from the rules of evidence, as the rule itself "makes no attempt to spell out the constitutional considerations which impose basic limitations upon the admissibility of relevant evidence."

B. Defining Relevance: Rule 401

Thus far, we have defined "relevant" evidence loosely as "information that matters." But how do you determine whether something matters? Rule 401 sets forth a formal definition of "relevant evidence" as follows:

Evidence is relevant if:

(a) it has any tendency to make a fact more or less probable than it would be without the evidence; and

(b) the fact is of consequence in determining the action.

The definition of relevance is best conceptualized as containing two separate requirements, materiality and probative worth, both of which must be satisfied for evidence to be deemed "relevant."

The Advisory Committee's Note to Rule 401 points out that Rule 401's requirement of "materiality" is represented in the Rule's text by Rule 401(b)'s requirement that the fact be "of consequence in determining the action." What does it mean to be "of consequence in determining the action"? To say that a piece of evidence is of consequence to the determination of the action means that it is somehow significant. What does it mean to be significant?

In the context of solving mysteries in our own lives, such as determining who took the last slice of cheesecake, there is only one thing that is significant: who took the cheesecake? Yet when dealing with formal judicial proceedings, what is significant are the elements of the claims raised or offenses charged and those of any valid defenses that have been raised, which can be determined only by reference to the underlying substantive law and the parties' pleadings. Evidence is material only if it is offered to prove or disprove an element of a legally cognizable claim, offense, or defense that has been raised in the parties' pleadings. Thus, for example, in a workers' compensation case, evidence offered by the employer of the employee's negligence would be immaterial, as contributory negligence is typically not a valid defense under the workers' compensation laws of most states.

Even if evidence is offered to prove or disprove a material fact, it is relevant only if it is probative of that fact. In other words, only if it tends to prove or disprove the point for which it is offered. How persuasive need it be to be deemed relevant? Not very, for the probative-worth prong of Rule 401 — set forth in Rule 401(a) — provides that evidence is relevant if "it has *any* tendency to make a fact more or less probable than it would be without the evidence" (emphasis added). In the words of McCormick, as quoted by the Advisory Committee, "A brick is not a wall," with "brick" referring to a piece of evidence and "wall" referring to the standard by which the evidence presented must collectively persuade the trier of fact of the elements of a claim, offense, or defense. In this sense, there is a critical distinction between the sufficiency of an item of evidence, standing alone, to satisfy the party's burden of proof on an element of a claim, offense, or defense, and its admissibility. Under Rule 401, the evidence need not be sufficient to be admissible; it need only have some tendency, however slight, to support the party's claim with respect to that element.

Because the requirements of materiality and probative worth are independent requirements, the failure to satisfy either requirement is fatal to a claim of relevancy. Thus no matter how high the probative worth of a piece of evidence may be, if it is probative of something that is unrelated to an element of a claim, offense, or defense in the case, it is not admissible.

There are further complications in dealing with both the materiality and probative-worth prongs of relevance. But before delving into these, take a stab at the following problems to make sure that you grasp the basic concepts.

Problem 1-2: Statutory Rape

Lisa, a nineteen-year-old female, is indicted on charges of violating her state's statutory rape law in connection with a sexual encounter that she is alleged to have had with Tom, a fifteen-year-old male. The statute provides that "[a] person is guilty of statutory rape in the first degree if he or she is over the age of eighteen (18) years and engages in sexual penetration with another person under the age of sixteen (16) years." Lisa wishes to introduce evidence that (a) she believed that Tom was sixteen years old; and (b) that in any event, Tom consented. Specifically, she would like to testify that when she asked him how old he was, he told her that he was sixteen, and also that she believed him to be sixteen years old because he drove a car, and under state law, only those aged sixteen years and older are licensed to drive cars.

Is the evidence that Lisa wishes to offer material? Is it probative?

Problem 1-3: One Too Many for the Road

Kevin is indicted on charges of driving a motor vehicle while intoxicated. The prosecution wishes to offer into evidence the testimony of the arresting officers, who if permitted would testify that: (a) they pulled Kevin over after they noticed his car swerving back and forth over the yellow line; (b) when they approached Kevin, he smelled of alcohol; (c) they found a bottle of vodka in Kevin's car that was about half-empty; and (d) he could not walk a straight line when asked to do so by the officers.

Kevin's attorney argues that none of the proffered evidence is relevant, contending that there are explanations for the swerving, the smell of alcohol, the half-empty bottle of vodka, and Kevin's lack of coordination that are consistent with Kevin's claim of innocence.

Construct an argument on Kevin's behalf to explain away the proffered evidence. What impact does that argument have on the relevancy of the evidence offered by the prosecution?

Notes and Questions

1. In general, statutory rape laws do not recognize as defenses either consent of the victim or a mistaken belief that the victim was above the required age. *See generally* Colin Campbell, Annotation, *Mistake or Lack of Information as to Victim's Age as Defense to Statutory Rape*, 46 A.L.R.5th 499 (1997) (mistaken belief as to victim's age not usually a recognized defense in statutory rape); 65 Am.Jur.2d *Rape* §84 (2011) (consent not a valid defense in statutory rape). However, some statutes do recognize a defense for a mistaken belief that the victim was above the required age, *see, e.g.*, 18 U.S.C. §2243(c)(1) (reasonable belief that person with whom defendant engaged in a sexual act was 16 years or older an affirmative defense to federal crime of engaging in sexual act with a minor), in which case evidence that would affect the defendant's belief in the victim's age would be relevant.

2. On the immateriality of contributory negligence in workers' compensation cases and the rationale for not allowing such a defense, *see Hough v. Pacific Ins. Co.*, 927 P.2d 858, 864–65 (Haw. 1996); *Snyder v. General Paper Corp.*, 152 N.W.2d 743, 748 (Minn. 1967).

3. A federal statute, 18 U.S.C. § 842(i)(1), makes it a crime for a person convicted of a felony to possess an "explosive" which has been shipped or transported in or which affects interstate commerce. In a prosecution under that statute, can the defendant offer evidence that the dynamite that was found in his possession was no longer capable of exploding? *See United States v. Markey*, 393 F.3d 1132, 1135–36 (10th Cir. 2004) (noting that "[t]o determine what evidence is relevant, we first turn to the elements of the offense," and concluding that the term "explosive" as used in the statute refers only to "a device's intended and usual use—not its actual capability").

4. Although the Advisory Committee Note to Rule 401 eschews use of the common law term "materiality," many courts continue to use the term in applying Rule 401 and describe it as distinct from the requirement of probative worth:

> Although the Federal Rules of Evidence do not define relevancy in terms of materiality, the concept of materiality is embodied in Rule 401 insofar as relevancy is defined as a relationship between certain evidence and a "fact ... of consequence [in determining] the action." Thus, although evidence may tend to make the existence of a fact more probable or less probable than it would be without the evidence, the evidence is not relevant unless the fact to be proved or disproved is material. Whether a fact is material is determined by the substantive law which governs the action.

United States v. Shomo, 786 F.2d 981, 985 (10th Cir. 1986).

5. On the relationship between admissibility and sufficiency, consider the following:

> Under our system, molded by the tradition of jury trial and predominantly oral proof, a party offers his evidence not *en masse*, but item by item. An item of evidence, being but a single link in the chain of proof, need not prove conclusively the proposition for which it is offered. It need not ever make that proposition appear more probable than not. Whether the entire body of one party's evidence is sufficient to go to the jury is one question. Whether a particular item of evidence is relevant to his case is quite another. It is enough if the item could reasonably show that a fact is slightly more probable than it would appear without that evidence. Even after the probative force of the evidence is spent, the proposition for which it is offered still can seem quite improbable. Thus, the common objection that the inference for which the fact is offered "does not necessarily follow" is untenable. It poses a standard of conclusiveness that very few single items of circumstantial evidence ever could meet. A brick is not a wall.

1 McCormick, Evidence § 185, at 278 (5th ed. 1999).

6. Inherent in the low threshold for admissibility under Rule 401 is the possibility that there may well be alternative explanations for an item of evidence consistent with innocence. Yet such arguments go only to the weight to be given to the evidence, not its admissibility. *See, e.g., United States v. Maravilla*, 907 F.2d 216, 221 (1st Cir. 1990) ("Obviously, the fact that Dominguez owned a gun makes his guilt somewhat more probable than if he did not own a gun. The fact that he might have had a good reason, consistent with innocence, for owning a gun, makes the evidence less probative, not irrelevant."); *United States v. Viserto*, 596 F.2d 531, 536 (2d Cir. 1979) (evidence that the defendants, who lacked legitimate occupations, possessed a large amount of cash relevant in trial for en-

gaging in a narcotics conspiracy); *State v. Hampton*, 855 P.2d 621, 623 (Or. 1993) ("The possibility that an inconsistent or contradictory inference may reasonably be drawn from the offered item of evidence does not destroy that item's relevancy so long as the inference desired by the proponent is also a reasonable one.").

C. Inferential Relevance

Although the materiality prong of relevance requires a connection to some element of a claim, offense, or defense, that connection need not be a direct one. Rather, evidence is material if it is logically related, either directly or through a chain of inferences, to an element of a claim, offense, or defense. Thus, although motive is not a necessary element of the crime of murder, evidence of motive or the lack thereof is nonetheless relevant, as the fact that the defendant had a motive to commit a murder does have some tendency to make it more likely that the defendant in fact committed the acts constituting the elements of murder, while the absence of a motive has some tendency to make it less likely that the defendant committed such acts. Similarly, while leaving one's fingerprints at the scene of a murder is not an element of murder, the fact that the defendant's fingerprints were found at the scene of the crime does have some tendency to make it more likely that the defendant played a part in the murder.

Yet when dealing with evidence the relevance of which is dependent on a chain of inferences from that piece of evidence to an element of a claim, offense, or defense in the case, a court must carefully examine each intermediate inference, for the relevance of the evidence is dependent upon the soundness of each of the intermediate links. Consider this as you look at the following problem and the cases that follow.

Problem 1-4: Tampering with Evidence

Tom, an attorney at a law firm, is on trial on charges of murdering his coworker, Diego. A great deal of evidence tends to show that Diego had learned that Tom was overbilling clients and had confronted him about it. The evidence includes e-mail messages that Diego sent to Tom as well as a face-to-face confrontation that another coworker, Marie, overheard. There is also evidence that as the police investigation began to focus on Tom, Tom attempted to delete the e-mail messages from Diego from his computer and he approached Marie and urged her not to tell the police about the conversation she had overheard.

Is the evidence that Diego was threatening to expose Tom's billing practices relevant in the murder trial? How about the evidence that Tom attempted to delete the e-mail messages? How about his conversation with Marie?

United States v. Dillon
870 F.2d 1125 (6th Cir. 1989)

MERRITT, Circuit Judge.

Appellant Thomas J. Dillon was indicted for, and convicted of, various drug offenses....

He appeals on [the ground] that the District Court erred by admitting evidence of his flight and by giving the jury an instruction on flight....

EVIDENCE OF FLIGHT

Flight evidence comes in as an admission of guilt by conduct. Cleary, *McCormick on Evidence* § 271, at 803 (3d ed.1984). The Supreme Court has expressed scepticism as to its value:

> [W]e have consistently doubted the probative value in criminal trials of evidence that the accused fled the scene of an actual or supposed crime. In *Alberty v. United States*, 162 U.S. 499, 511, this Court said: "… it is not universally true that a man, who is conscious that he has done a wrong, 'will pursue a certain course not in harmony with the conduct of a man who is conscious of having done an act which is innocent, right and proper,' since it is a matter of common knowledge that men who are entirely innocent do sometimes fly from the scene of a crime through fear of being apprehended as the guilty parties, or from an unwillingness to appear as witnesses. Nor is it true as an accepted axiom of criminal law that 'the wicked flee when no man pursueth, but the righteous are as bold as a lion.'"

Wong Sun v. United States, 371 U.S. 471, 483 n. 10 (1963). Where evidence of flight has genuine probative value, however, it is "generally admissible as evidence of guilt, and … juries are given the power to determine 'how much weight should be given to such evidence.'" *United States v. Touchstone*, 726 F.2d 1116, 1119 (6th Cir. 1984). The task for a District Court in determining whether to admit evidence of flight, thus, is to determine whether the proferred [sic] evidence in fact tends to prove guilt and not merely the terror that may befall an innocent person confronted by the criminal justice system, and whether the evidence, even if probative of guilt, is so prejudicial that its admission offends Fed.R.Evid. 403. Our task is to review those determinations for an abuse of discretion.

The Fifth Circuit has devised a four-step analysis of flight evidence that, as many courts have recognized, allows an orderly inquiry into the inferences proposed by evidence of flight. According to this formulation, the probative value of flight evidence

> depends upon the degree of confidence with which four inferences can be drawn: (1) from the defendant's behavior to flight; (2) from flight to consciousness of guilt; (3) from consciousness of guilt to consciousness of guilt concerning the crime charged; and (4) from consciousness of guilt concerning the crime charged to actual guilt of the crime charged.

United States v. Myers, 550 F.2d 1036, 1049 (5th Cir. 1977). All four inferences must be "reasonabl[y] support[ed]" by the evidence.

In the present case, Dillon was charged with, and convicted of, supplying Edward Knezevich with cocaine between December 1982 and March 26, 1983. Knezevich obtained a pound of cocaine from Dillon on the latter date and sold it, through a pre-arranged deal, to Sheila Bezotsky. Bezotsky was cooperating with the FBI, and Knezevich was arrested when he delivered the cocaine to her. All those events took place in Columbus, where Dillon then lived.

Knezevich was eventually convicted for his role in this deal. After his conviction he was subpoenaed to testify before a Grand Jury. On December 19, 1984, Knezevich told Dillon that he would testify the next day before a Grand Jury, and that he intended to tell the truth about Dillon's role in the cocaine deal. Knezevich also testified that, as part of his agreement with the government, he would attempt to contact Dillon, wearing a hidden tape recorder, on December 20; that he had tried to find Dillon; and that he had failed to find him.

Dillon's ex-wife testified that Dillon did not keep his engagement to take custody of their children, on Christmas day. She also testified that, ever since that day and for the next two years, Dillon contacted her only by phone, and that she had no way of knowing whether he was in Columbus or not.

Dillon was arrested in Florida in June 1987. The FBI agent who arrested him testified that he was living there under an assumed name. There is no evidence that he denied to the FBI agent arresting him that he was Thomas Dillon. He was indicted on the present charges on July 30, 1987.

At trial, the government attempted to prove that Dillon had fled Columbus after learning about Knezevich's planned Grand Jury testimony, and that such a flight proved Dillon's awareness of his guilt of the crimes charged. Dillon preserved his appeal from the admission of evidence of flight by timely objections at trial. He seeks to persuade this Court that his departure from Columbus came at least two years after the alleged offense and well before the indictment was filed, so that he had "nothing to flee from." To accept this argument we would have to ignore the crucial fact that the government adduced evidence suggesting that Dillon fled Columbus within days after hearing from a co-conspirator that the co-conspirator was about to implicate Dillon in a big cocaine deal in Grand Jury testimony. The real question before us is whether the evidence, *including* Dillon's December 19 conversation with Knezevich, his unexplained failure to keep his Christmas plans with his children, and his subsequent phone rather than personal contacts with his ex-wife, are sufficiently probative of a guilty conscience to overcome the prejudice it entails. We conclude that the four *Myers* inferences are all adequately supported by the evidence introduced at Dillon's trial.

The first question is whether the evidence supports the inference that there has been a "flight" in the first place. The *Myers* court found that no such inference was allowable where the jury could infer flight only by resort to "conjecture and speculation." We believe that the evidence before Dillon's jury allowed a sound inference, not merely a speculative one, that he had fled. Dillon's ex-wife testified that, only six days after hearing from Knezevich about the latter's planned Grand Jury testimony, he broke an important family commitment and from then on contacted her by phone from an undisclosed location. He was arrested in Florida, where he was living under an assumed name. We do not believe it would be unreasonable for a jury to infer from these undisputed facts that Dillon fled Columbus soon after his conversation with Knezevich.

In this case, the second and third inferences — (2) that the defendant is afflicted with a guilty consciousness (3) of the crime charged — involve examination of two interrelated factors: immediacy and the defendant's knowledge that he is in trouble with the law. For flight evidence to be admissible, the timing of flight must itself indicate the sudden onset or the sudden *increase* of fear in the defendant's mind that he or she will face apprehension for, accusation of, or conviction of the crime charged. Flight immediately after the crime charged, of course, will tend to prove guilt of that crime. But the mental crisis that precipitates flight may fail to occur immediately after the crime, only to erupt much later, when the defendant learns that he or she is charged with the crime and sought for it.

We reject Dillon's argument that these cases allow introduction of evidence of a postponed flight only when that flight occurs after the defendant learns of the charges against him or her. Rather, these cases recognize that flight may be proven where it occurs after any event which would tend to spark a sharp impulse of fear of prosecution or conviction in a guilty mind. This might occur long after the defendant learns of the charges, as it did in *Touchstone*, where defendants did not flee until the heat of trial became unbearable. And it can occur long before the defendant learns of the charges: for instance, when flight occurs after the defendant is served, himself, with a subpoena to appear before a Grand Jury. Indeed, the "commencement of an investigation" may substitute for accusation as the precipitating event.

Dillon argues that he departed Columbus a year and nine months after the crime at the earliest, that the indictment was issued after his arrest, and that nothing in the interim constitutes notice of the sort that courts have recognized as a substitute for immediacy-after-the-crime. This reasoning ignores the December 19 conversation with Knezevich and urges a wooden and literalistic reading of the case law. Common sense on this question is loud and clear: a guilty defendant is almost as unequivocally put on notice of his peril by a convicted co-conspirator who is on the verge of testifying before a Grand Jury about their common crime, as he would be by hearing from someone that he is charged and sought. We see no flaws in an inference from such notice to the defendant's guilty consciousness of the crime charged.

Dillon raises no argument that the fourth *Myers* inference—from guilty consciousness to actual guilt—is unsupported by record evidence. We, therefore, hold that the District Court did not abuse its discretion in admitting evidence of flight at Dillon's trial....

State v. Wisdom

24 S.W. 1047 (Mo. 1894)

GANTT, P.J.

The defendant was indicted, together with one John Willard, for murder in the first degree of Edward Drexler, in the city of St. Louis, on the 24th day of April, 1892, by beating and wounding him on the head with an iron bar, and that Willard was present, aiding and abetting the murder....

In the course of the examination of the witness Hill, he was asked to tell what happened down at the morgue by the dead body of Mr. Drexler, when the witness Willard and defendant were there, prior to the inquest. This was objected to as immaterial. The objection was overruled. The witness answered that "they told us to put our hands on Mr. Drexler;" and that he and Willard did so, but defendant would not do it. Officer McGrath corroborated this statement. Defendant objected to McGrath's statement, but assigned no reason. The action of the court in this regard is now assigned as error. Who it was that told them to put their hands on Mr. Drexler's dead body does not appear. The request to touch the body was evidently prompted by the old superstition of the ordeal of the bier in Europe in the middle ages, which taught that the body of a murdered man would bleed freshly when touched by his murderer, and hence it was resorted to as means of ascertaining the guilt or innocence of a person suspected of a murder. This superstition has not been confined to one nation or people. It obtained among the Germans prior to the twelfth century, and is recorded in the Nibelungenlied, a great epic poem of that century, in the incident in which the murdered Siegfried is laid on his bier, and Hagen is called on to prove his innocence by going to the corpse, but at his approach the dead chief's wounds bleed afresh. That it dominated the English mind is attested by the passage of Matthew Paris that when Henry II. died at Chinon, in 1189, his son and successor came to view his body, and, as he drew near, immediately the blood flowed from the nostrils of the dead king, as if his spirit was so indignant at the approach of the one who caused his death that his blood thus protested to God. And Shakespeare voices the same superstition in Richard III., (act 1, sc. 2,) thus:

> O, gentlemen, see, see! dead Henry's wounds
> Open their congealed mouths, and bleed afresh.

—And so does Dr. Warren, in Diary of a Late Physician, (volume 3, p. 327). That it was a prevalent belief in Africa and Australia, in another form, see 17 Enc. Brit. pp. 818, 819. This superstition has come to this country with the emigration from other lands, and, although a creature of the imagination, it does to a considerable degree affect the opinions of a large class of our people. It is true, it was not shown that defendant believed that touching this body would cause any evidence of guilt to appear, or that he entertained any fear of possible consequences; but it was simply a test proposed by some bystander, and it was offered as showing the manner in which the three suspects conducted themselves when it was proposed. Clarke v. State, 78 Ala. 474; Chamberlayne's Best, Ev. p. 488. While defendant had a perfect right to decline, either because of his instinctive repugnance to the unpleasant task, or because no one had a right to subject him to the test, and his refusal might not prejudice him in the minds of a rational jury, on the other hand, a consciousness of guilt might have influenced him to refuse to undergo the proposed test, however unreasonable it was, and it is one of the circumstances of the case that the jury could weigh. The jury could consider that, while it was a superstitious test, still defendant might have been more or less affected by it, as many intelligent people are by equally baseless notions, as shown by their conduct and movements. It often happens that a case must be established by a number of facts, any one of which, by itself, would be of little weight, but all of which, taken together, would prove the issue....

Notes and Questions

1. As with relevance generally, the fact that an inference is weak in that the evidence can be interpreted in multiple ways, some consistent with the evidentiary hypothesis of the proponent of the evidence and others inconsistent with that hypothesis, bears only on the weight to be given to the evidence and does not bear on its relevance. *E.g., United States v. Carmona*, 873 F.2d 569, 572 (2d Cir. 1989). Thus, even though there might be an explanation for flight that is consistent with innocence (as posited by the Supreme Court in the *Wong Sun* decision, cited in *Dillon*), that should not impact the relevancy determination, which requires only a tendency to prove the point for which it is offered. Yet the *Dillon* Court, citing *Myers*, holds that the four inferences must be "reasonably supported." This, as we will soon see, is an application not of Rule 401 but rather of Rule 403, which is referred to in the *Dillon* case. *See United States v. Quattrone*, 441 F.3d 153, 188 (2d Cir. 2006) ("so long as a chain of inferences leads the trier of fact to conclude that the proffered submission affects the mix of material information, the evidence cannot be excluded at the threshold relevance inquiry.... drawn out inferential chains do not defeat relevance but subject challenged evidence to Rule 403 considerations"); *United States v. Ravich*, 421 F.2d 1196, 1204 n.10 (2d Cir. 1970) ("The length of the chain of inferences necessary to connect the evidence with the ultimate fact to be proved necessarily lessens the probative value of the evidence, and may therefore render it more susceptible to exclusion as unduly confusing, prejudicial, or time-consuming, but it does not render the evidence irrelevant.").

2. Construct the evidential hypothesis—that is, the chain of inferences—necessary to make the evidence offered by the prosecution in *Wisdom* relevant. Does this chain of inferences require that the "test" itself be accurate? If the defendant *had* touched the body when asked to do so and it did not bleed afresh, could *he* offer that into evidence? What would be his evidentiary hypothesis?

3. A federal statute, 18 U.S.C. § 1546(a), makes it a crime to use a false alien registration card (also known as a "green card"). To successfully prosecute a defendant under the statute, the government must show: (1) that he used or attempted to use a green card; (2) that the card is false; and (3) that the defendant knew that the card is false. *See United States v. Amaya-Manzanares*, 377 F.3d 39, 43 (1st Cir. 2004). In such a prosecution, is evidence that the defendant unlawfully entered the United States relevant? Consider the following:

> The most straightforward reason for relevance is that Amaya's status as an unlawful entrant who has not upgraded his status makes it more likely that he acquired the forged green card by buying it from someone who was obviously not a government agent authorized to issue it. This might be conceived of as motive evidence (one who is an unlawful entrant has a motive to buy a forged green card) or mechanically (someone with Amaya's status would have been rebuffed if he had sought a green card from the INS and so had to resort to the black market).
>
> Either way, if Amaya bought the green card on the black market, this practically assures that Amaya knew the card he acquired was forged rather than valid. It is not simply the possession of a forged document that creates a strong inference of knowledge that it is false; someone with a single forged $20 bill in his wallet may as easily be a victim rather than a perpetrator. Rather, it is the *added* proof (that Amaya's status prevented him from getting a valid green card from the INS) which greatly increases the chances that he engaged in a transaction that by its nature would also have led him to believe that the document he had obtained was not valid.

Id. at 44.

4. Logicians distinguish between deductive and inductive arguments. In a deductive argument, the stated premises, if true, *necessarily* lead to a particular conclusion. For a deductive argument to be sound, its premises must be true *and* it must be logically impossible for the conclusion to be false given the truth of the premises. In contrast, in an inductive argument, even if the premises are true, the conclusion does not necessarily follow, but only follows with some degree of probability.

Most arguments are inductive, and Rule 401 — with its focus on probabilities rather than certainties — readily allows for such arguments. Consider the argument that guilt can be inferred from flight. One could attempt to construct a deductive argument as follows: *If a person flees when sought by the police, then he must be guilty; the defendant fled when sought by the police; therefore, the defendant is guilty.* We know that the first premise is not true: some people flee from the police for reasons other than guilt. Yet we know that at least *some* people in fact flee from the police because they are in fact guilty, and can thus construct an inductive argument as follows: *Some people who flee when sought by the police do so because they are guilty; the defendant fled when sought by the police; therefore, there is some likelihood that the defendant is guilty.*

On the differences between inductive and deductive arguments, *see generally* Ian Hacking, An Introduction to Probability and Inductive Logic 1–22 (2001).

5. Should you feel uncomfortable with the use of arguments based on probabilities, consider that much of what we think is certain is not as certain as we might believe:

> We are all convinced that the sun will rise to-morrow....

[I]f we are asked why we believe that the sun will rise to-morrow, we shall naturally answer, 'Because it always has risen every day.' We have a firm belief that it will rise in the future, because it has risen in the past. If we are challenged as to why we believe that it will continue to rise as heretofore, we may appeal to the laws of motion....

The interesting doubt is as to whether the laws of motion will remain in operation to-morrow....

The *only* reason for believing that the laws of motion will remain in operation is that they have operated hitherto, so far as our knowledge of the past enables us to judge.... But the real question is: Do *any* number of cases of a law being fulfilled in the past afford evidence that it will be fulfilled in the future? If not, it becomes plain that we have no ground whatever for expecting the sun to rise to-morrow, or for expecting the bread we shall eat at our next meal not to poison us, or for any of the other scarcely conscious expectations that control our daily lives. It is to be observed that all such expectations are only *probable*; thus we have not to seek for a proof that they *must* be fulfilled, but only for some reason in favour of the view that they are *likely* to be fulfilled....

It has been argued that we have reason to know that the future will resemble the past, because what was the future has constantly become the past, and has always been found to resemble the past, so that we really have experience of the future.... But such an argument really begs the very question at issue. We have experience of past futures, but not of future futures, and the question is: Will future futures resemble past futures?

....

Thus we must either accept the inductive principle on the ground of its intrinsic evidence, or forgo all justification of our expectations about the future. If the principle is unsound, we have no reason to expect the sun to rise to-morrow, to expect bread to be more nourishing than a stone, or to expect that if we throw ourselves off the roof we shall fall. When we see what looks like our best friend approaching us, we shall have no reason to suppose that his body is not inhabited by the mind of our worst enemy or of some total stranger. All our conduct is based upon associations which have worked in the past, and which we therefore regard as likely to work in the future; and this likelihood is dependent for its validity upon the inductive principle.

Bertrand Russell, The Problems of Philosophy, Chapter VI: On Induction (1912).

D. Determining Relevance

Having defined the concept of materiality, the determination whether something is material seems pretty straightforward: one need only examine the elements of the underlying claims and defenses to determine what qualifies as material. But how does one determine whether something satisfies the probative-worth prong of the relevance definition? How does one know that a motive to murder someone increases the likelihood that one did in fact murder that person? That the act of fleeing has any tendency to suggest that the person might be guilty?

The Advisory Committee Note to Rule 401 provides the following guidance:

Does the item of evidence tend to prove the matter sought to be proved? Whether the relationship exists depends upon principles evolved by experience or science, applied logically to the situation at hand.

This raises the question, "Whose experience?" This turns on who it is that determines relevance. Rule 104(a) answers this question, providing in pertinent part that:

The court must decide any preliminary question about whether a witness is qualified, a privilege exists, or evidence is admissible.

Thus, it is the trial court judge alone, relying on his or her own experience and knowledge of the world, who will decide questions of relevance, including the question whether a piece of evidence has "any tendency" to make something more or less probable. *See, e.g., United States v. Curtin*, 489 F.3d 935, 948 (9th Cir. 2007) (en banc); *United States v. Williams*, 545 F.2d 47, 50 (8th Cir. 1976). This is so even though the inquiry may involve findings that are factual in nature. *See* Advisory Committee's Note to Rule 104(a).

Although judges as a group have some common experiences and knowledge, like all people, their experiences, knowledge, and worldviews are not uniform. To what extent can this impact the relevancy determination? Moreover, what impact does a judge's ruling that an item of evidence is or is not relevant on a particular point have outside of the courtroom? Consider this as you examine the next problem and the notes that follow.

Problem 1-5: Same-Sex Sexual Assault and Child Molestation

Robert is on trial on charges of sexually assaulting John. At Robert's trial, the prosecution seeks to introduce evidence that Robert owns non-pornographic gay-oriented publications such as *Out* and *The Advocate* that depict and discuss relationships among adult males.

Is the evidence relevant? Would evidence that John is gay, if offered by the defense, be relevant? How, if at all, would your answer differ if John is a young child?

Notes and Questions

1. On the admissibility of evidence that the defendant is gay in a child molestation case involving a victim of the same gender, *compare State v. Taylor*, 663 So. 2d 336, 340–341 (La. Ct. App. 1995) (holding that defendant's sexual orientation has "some relevance" in that it shows that he is interested in having sex with another male), *with State v. Rushing*, 541 N.W. 2d 155, 162 (Wis. Ct. App. 1995) ("[h]aving a homosexual encounter with a consenting adult is completely different from assaulting a sleeping child"). On the admissibility of evidence of sexual orientation generally, *see* Peter Nicolas, *"They Say He's Gay": The Admissibility of Evidence of Sexual Orientation*, 37 Ga. L. Rev. 793 (2003).

2. In a suit alleging sexual harassment of one female employee by another female employee based on sexual desire, is evidence offered by the defense that the alleged perpetrator was in a long-term, heterosexual relationship relevant? *Compare Pedroza v. Cintas Corp. No. 2*, 397 F.3d 1063, 1069 n.2 (8th Cir. 2005) ("We disagree with Straw regarding the inferences that may flow from the facts that she had children and had been in a long-

term relationship with a man. These facts tend to prove only that Straw was not strictly homosexual. They do not preclude a jury from finding that Straw was motivated by some degree of homosexual desire towards Pedroza. It would be naive and artificial for us to conclude otherwise."), *with id.* at 1071 (Colloton, J., concurring) ("A long-term heterosexual relationship is *relevant* to whether Straw acted out of homosexual desire—that is, it has a 'tendency' to make the existence of homosexual desire less probable than if, say, Straw had been in a long-term homosexual relationship—but it is by no means conclusive on the point.").

3. Note that in deciding issues of admissibility under Rule 104(a), the trial court can receive evidence pro and con on a particular issue. *See* Advisory Committee's Note to Rule 104(a). Thus, the judge's knowledge can be enhanced by information offered to her by the parties.

4. Rule 104(a) provides that "[i]n so deciding, the court is not bound by evidence rules, except those on privilege." Furthermore, Rule 104(c) generally provides for determinations on the admissibility of evidence to be conducted out of the hearing of the jury. What do these two provisions, in combination, suggest about the policies behind the rules of evidence in general? Behind the rules of privilege in particular?

5. On the impact of relevancy rulings on behavior outside of the courtroom, consider the following passage:

> To allow prosecutors to parade before the jury snippets from a defendant's library ... would compel *all* persons to choose the contents of their libraries with considerable care; for it is the innocent, and not just the guilty, who are sometimes the subject of good-faith prosecutions.

Guam v. Shymanovitz, 157 F.3d 1154, 1159 (9th Cir. 1998).

The efficacy of this passage is reconsidered in Chapter 3 in *United States v. Curtin.*

6. Even if the judge decides to admit evidence because he determines that it is material and that it has probative worth, the jury is ultimately free to determine what weight to give to it, and the parties remain free to introduce evidence before the jury relevant to the weight to be given to a particular piece of evidence. *See* Fed. R. Evid. 104(e) ("This rule does not limit a party's right to introduce before the jury evidence that is relevant to the weight or credibility of other evidence."); *see also* Advisory Committee Note to Rule 104(c) ("[n]ot infrequently the same evidence which is relevant to the issue of establishment of fulfillment of a condition precedent to admissibility is also relevant to weight or credibility"). In contrast, if the judge deems the evidence not to be relevant, the jury never gets a chance to evaluate its weight. Given that the jury remains free to ultimately weigh evidence that is admitted, should a judge dealing with an item of evidence that is of dubious probative worth err on the side of admitting it? Or are there countervailing concerns that suggest a more cautious approach?

E. Conditional Relevance

As discussed in the previous section, Rule 104(a) provides that, in general, it is the role of the trial court judge alone to determine the admissibility of evidence, which includes the determination whether an item of evidence is material and has probative worth as required by Rule 401.

Yet the general rule set forth in Rule 104(a) is qualified by Rule 104(b), which provides in pertinent part that:

> When the relevance of evidence depends on whether a fact exists, proof must be introduced sufficient to support a finding that the fact does exist.

The Advisory Committee Note to Rule 104(b) provides two examples of what is typically referred to as "conditional relevancy":

> In some situations, the relevancy of an item of evidence, in the large sense, depends upon the existence of a particular preliminary fact. Thus when a spoken statement is relied upon to prove notice to X, it is without probative value unless X heard it. Or if a letter purporting to be from Y is relied upon to establish an admission by him, it has no probative value unless Y wrote or authorized it.

To be sure, testimony that a statement was made, if heard by X, would be probative in showing that X was on notice of whatever was contained in the statement. Yet it would have no probative worth if the statement was made under circumstances in which X could not possibly have heard it. Thus, the relevancy of the evidence that the statement was made is conditionally relevant on there being evidence that X heard the statement.

The concept of conditional relevancy is best understood by thinking about the condition of fact and the conditionally relevant piece of evidence as each being one blade of a pair of scissors. For the purpose of cutting something, one blade of a pair of scissors alone serves no purpose.

One might wonder, "So what's the big deal?" In this situation, you just have the judge decide one more thing: in addition to determining whether the evidence is material and whether it has probative worth, the judge can also decide whether there is sufficient evidence to satisfy the condition or conditions of fact on which the relevancy of the conditionally relevant piece of evidence is based.

The answer, as indicated in the Advisory Committee Note to Rule 104(b), is that to allow that would substantially undercut the right to trial by jury:

> If preliminary questions of conditional relevancy were determined solely by the judge, as provided in subdivision (a), the functioning of the jury as a trier of fact would be greatly restricted and in some cases virtually destroyed. These are appropriate questions for juries.

Rule 104(b) contemplates a shared role between the judge and the jury when it comes to issues of conditional relevancy. Unlike relevancy issues governed by Rule 104(a), in which the judge must be personally persuaded, for issues governed by Rule 104(b), the judge plays only a screening role. In this role, the judge need not be persuaded of the fulfillment of the condition of fact on which the relevancy of the evidence is based (for to so require would be to usurp the jury's role in finding facts); he need only determine that a reasonable jury could so find. In the words of the Supreme Court:

> [T]he trial court neither weighs credibility nor makes a finding that the [proponent] has proved the conditional fact.... The court simply examines all the evidence in the case and decides whether the jury could reasonably find the conditional fact ... by a preponderance of the evidence.

Huddleston v. United States, 485 U.S. 681, 690 (1988). *See also* Advisory Committee Note to Rule 104(b) ("The judge makes a preliminary determination whether the foundation evidence is sufficient to support a finding of fulfillment of the condition. If so, the item is admitted.").

Note that Rule 104(b) does not even dictate the *order* in which the conditionally relevant evidence and the evidence of the conditional facts are introduced. The rule provides that "[t]he court may admit the proposed evidence on the condition that the proof be introduced later." This flexibility in the order of proof is in recognition of the practical problems that would arise under a more rigid rule:

> So far, then, as concerns the time of its introduction in evidence, one might expect a rule requiring such a fact *not to be given in evidence until the connecting facts*, by reason of which it becomes relevant, have first been put in evidence.
>
> No such rule, however, would be practicable; for those same connecting facts would themselves often be irrelevant apart from the fact in question; in other words, the relevancy appears only when all are considered together. Now it is obviously impossible to present all the facts at precisely the same moment or in the testimony of a single witness. Hence, some of the connected facts must be allowed to be presented before the others, even though the former, standing alone, are irrelevant. Thus the fundamental rule, universally accepted, is that with reference to facts whose relevancy depends upon others, *the order of presentation is left to the discretion of the party himself*, subject of course to the general discretion of the trial court ... in controlling the order of evidence.... The possibility that the other facts may not be made good is a necessary risk to be taken; and in case of a failure to make them good, the subsequent striking out of the evidence now offered is regarded as an adequate remedy....

6 Wigmore, Evidence § 1871, at 664–65 (Chadbourn rev. ed. 1976).

We will see the distinction between Rules 104(a) and 104(b) arise in the application of several different rules of evidence. For now, it is sufficient that you understand their application to Rules 401 and 402. To do so, take a stab at the following problem.

Problem 1-6: Green Baseball Cap

> David is on trial on charges of robbing a magazine vendor at gunpoint. Ellen, an eyewitness to the crime, testifies for the prosecution that the person who committed the robbery was wearing a green baseball cap. On cross-examination, David's attorney tries to establish that Ellen was too far away to accurately make out the color of the baseball cap, but Ellen stands by her testimony. The judge thinks that Ellen is lying. The prosecution then calls Lisa, David's housekeeper, who would testify that David owns a green baseball cap. David's attorney objects.
>
> *Is Ellen's testimony relevant? How about Lisa's testimony? Based on the rules you have studied so far, will the judge exclude Lisa's testimony? What if Ellen admits on cross-examination that she is color-blind?*

Notes and Questions

1. If a party opposes the admission of an item of conditionally relevant evidence that has been admitted subject to subsequent proof of the conditions of fact, it is the responsibility of that party to move to strike the evidence if the proponent of the evidence fails

to introduce the promised evidence. *Huddleston v. United States*, 485 U.S. 681, 690 & n.7 (1988).

2. What purpose is served by the judge playing a screening role? If the evidence is such that a jury could not reasonably find the conditions of fact, won't jurors just ignore the evidence whose relevance is conditioned on proof of those facts?

F. Pragmatic Relevance: Rule 403

[handwritten: Risk of not submitting or submitting]

By now, you have probably figured out that it does not take very much to satisfy the requirements of Rules 401 and 402. A clever attorney will in most cases be able to come up with a plausible hypothesis for why a given piece of evidence is relevant within the meaning of Rule 401. However, the low threshold for admissibility set forth in Rules 401 and 402 creates a risk that evidence may make it before the jury that is marginally relevant but that possesses a danger of being overvalued or misused by the jury. Indeed, it is possible that the proponent of the evidence might actually identify a formal, legal issue to which the evidence is marginally relevant as a mere pretext for getting the evidence before the jury in the hopes that it will be overvalued or otherwise misused by the jury. Rule 403 addresses this concern, providing that:

> The court may exclude relevant evidence if its probative value is substantially outweighed by a danger of one or more of the following: unfair prejudice, confusing the issues, misleading the jury, undue delay, wasting time, or needlessly presenting cumulative evidence.

Thus, even though evidence having the slightest of probative value ("any tendency") may satisfy the requirements of Rules 401 and 402, it may nonetheless be subject to exclusion under Rule 403. Rule 403 thus calls for a form of cost-benefit analysis in which the trial court balances the "benefit" of the evidence (its probative worth) against the "costs" of admitting the evidence (time and risks of confusion and misuse). Thus, how *much* of a tendency evidence has to prove or disprove a point takes on an importance under Rule 403 that was lacking under Rules 401 and 402.

Evidence possessing such benefits and costs poses an accuracy dilemma: there is a concern that the verdict will be less accurate if the evidence is excluded (because relevant evidence will not be put before the jury), and a countervailing concern that the verdict will be less accurate if the evidence is allowed in (because it may be misunderstood or misused). The court's task in applying Rule 403 is to decide which risk is more tolerable.

Note, however, that although Rule 403 to some degree offsets the liberal standard of admissibility set forth in Rules 401 and 402, it nonetheless tilts the scales in *favor* of admitting relevant evidence. Under Rule 403, evidence can be excluded only if its probative worth is "substantially outweighed" by one of the Rule 403 dangers. Thus, Rule 403 poses no bar to admissibility where benefits and costs are in equipoise, or even where costs only somewhat exceed benefits.

Of course, it is much easier to state the rule than it is to apply it. The benefits and costs of admitting an item of evidence cannot readily be quantified, and so the balancing process is to some degree qualitative and subjective. To better understand Rule 403 in practice, consider the following problems and the cases that follow.

Problem 1-7: I Killed Sally

Steve is on trial for second-degree murder in connection with the death of Sally. At trial, the prosecution seeks to offer testimony by Bob, who would testify that shortly after Sally's death, Steve said to him, "I killed Sally so that I could get the insurance money." Steve's attorney objects.

Is Bob's testimony relevant? If so, is it nonetheless subject to exclusion under Rule 403?

Problem 1-8: Sexual Assault, Child Molestation, and Grand Theft Auto

In each of the following scenarios, assess the relevancy of the proffered evidence and consider whether it should be excluded under Rule 403:

(a) Defendant, a male, is on trial on charges of sexually assaulting an adult male. The prosecution seeks to offer into evidence non-pornographic gay-oriented publications such as *Out* and *The Advocate* that depict and discuss relationships among adult males found in the defendant's house.

(b) Defendant, a male, is on trial on charges of sexually assaulting an adult male. The prosecution seeks to offer pornographic gay magazines found in the defendant's house.

(c) Defendant, a male school bus driver, is charged with molesting a young boy who rides on the bus. The prosecution seeks to offer into evidence pornographic gay magazines found in the defendant's house.

(d) Defendant, a male school bus driver, is charged with molesting a young boy who rides on the bus. The prosecution seeks to offer into evidence magazines that depict sexual acts between adult males and young boys.

(e) Defendant, a male, is on trial on charges of sexually assaulting an adult woman. The prosecution seeks to offer into evidence copies of *Playboy* magazine found in the defendant's house.

(f) Defendant, a male, is on trial on charges of sexually assaulting an adult woman. The prosecution seeks to offer into evidence magazines depicting heterosexual rape scenes found in the defendant's house.

(g) Defendant is on trial on charges of stealing a new Mini Cooper. The prosecution seeks to offer into evidence a copy of *Car & Driver* magazine with a cover story about the Mini Cooper found in the defendant's house.

Problem 1-9: Pornographic Photographs

William is on trial on charges of knowingly possessing child pornography, in violation of 18 U.S.C. §2252(a)(4)(B). The photographs were found on the hard drive of William's computer. William's sole defense is that he was not knowingly in possession of the materials because they were downloaded onto his computer by one of his roommates who had access to the computer. He is thus willing to stipulate to the fact that the photographs are pornographic depictions of children within the meaning of the statute. At trial, the government seeks to offer copies of the photographs into evidence.

Are the photographs relevant? If so, are they nonetheless subject to exclusion under Rule 403?

Problem 1-10: Videotape

Tom, a nine-year-old boy, is run over and killed by a drunk driver. Tom's parents bring a wrongful death action against the driver. At trial, the attorney for Tom's parents seeks to offer into evidence a videotape of Tom playing catch with his father.

Is the videotape relevant? If so, is it nonetheless subject to exclusion under Rule 403?

Problem 1-11: He's Not From Around Here ...

Structures, Inc. was hired by a state university in Texas to construct a new dormitory. While working on the construction project, one of Structures' employees, Lucero, was severely injured when an aerial lift tipped over and fell on him. He brings suit against Structures for damages resulting from his injuries. Included in his claim for damages are lost future earnings measured at United States wage levels. At trial, Structures seeks to offer evidence that Lucero is a Mexican citizen who is in the United States without proper documentation.

Is Lucero's undocumented status relevant? If so, should it nonetheless be excluded as unfairly prejudicial?

Problem 1-12: Hate Crime

Donald is on trial for threatening to injure a group of African Americans who were having a picnic in a state-owned park if they did not leave the park. Charges are brought against him under 18 U.S.C. § 245(b)(2)(B), which makes it a crime for a person to interfere with other people's federally protected rights on account of their race. At trial, the prosecution seeks to offer into evidence white supremacist literature found at Donald's house.

Is the evidence relevant? If so, is it nonetheless subject to exclusion under Rule 403?

Old Chief v. United States
519 U.S. 172 (1997)

Justice SOUTER delivered the opinion of the Court....

I

In 1993, petitioner, Old Chief, was arrested after a fracas involving at least one gunshot. The ensuing federal charges included not only assault with a dangerous weapon and using a firearm in relation to a crime of violence but violation of 18 U.S.C. § 922(g)(1). This statute makes it unlawful for anyone "who has been convicted in any court of, a crime punishable by imprisonment for a term exceeding one year" to "possess in or affecting commerce, any firearm...." "[A] crime punishable by imprisonment for a term exceeding one year" is defined to exclude "any Federal or State offenses pertaining to antitrust violations, unfair trade practices, restraints of trade, or other similar offenses relating to the regulation of business practices" and "any State offense classified by the laws of the State as a misdemeanor and punishable by a term of imprisonment of two years or less." § 921(a)(20).

The earlier crime charged in the indictment against Old Chief was assault causing serious bodily injury. Before trial, he moved for an order requiring the Government "to refrain from mentioning—by reading the Indictment, during jury selection, in opening statement, or closing argument—and to refrain from offering into evidence or soliciting any testimony from any witness regarding the prior criminal convictions of the Defendant, *except* to state that the Defendant has been convicted of a crime punishable by imprisonment exceeding one (1) year." He said that revealing the name and nature of his prior assault conviction would unfairly tax the jury's capacity to hold the Government to its burden of proof beyond a reasonable doubt on current charges of assault, possession, and violence with a firearm, and he offered to "solve the problem here by stipulating, agreeing and requesting the Court to instruct the jury that he has been convicted of a crime punishable by imprisonment exceeding one (1) yea[r]." He argued that the offer to stipulate to the fact of the prior conviction rendered evidence of the name and nature of the offense inadmissible under Rule 403 of the Federal Rules of Evidence, the danger being that unfair prejudice from that evidence would substantially outweigh its probative value....

The Assistant United States Attorney refused to join in a stipulation, insisting on his right to prove his case his own way, and the District Court agreed, ruling orally that, "If he doesn't want to stipulate, he doesn't have to." At trial, over renewed objection, the Government introduced the order of judgment and commitment for Old Chief's prior conviction. This document disclosed that on December 18, 1988, he "did knowingly and unlawfully assault Rory Dean Fenner, said assault resulting in serious bodily injury," for which Old Chief was sentenced to five years' imprisonment. The jury found Old Chief guilty on all counts, and he appealed.

[The Ninth Circuit affirmed the district court.]

We granted Old Chief's petition for writ of certiorari.... We now reverse the judgment of the Ninth Circuit.

II

A

As a threshold matter, there is Old Chief's erroneous argument that the name of his prior offense as contained in the record of conviction is irrelevant to the prior-conviction element, and for that reason inadmissible under Rule 402 of the Federal Rules of Evidence.... To be sure, the fact that Old Chief's prior conviction was for assault resulting in serious bodily injury rather than, say, for theft was not itself an ultimate fact, as if the statute had specifically required proof of injurious assault. But its demonstration was a step on one evidentiary route to the ultimate fact, since it served to place Old Chief within a particular sub-class of offenders for whom firearms possession is outlawed by § 922(g)(1). A documentary record of the conviction for that named offense was thus relevant evidence in making Old Chief's § 922(g)(1) status more probable than it would have been without the evidence.

Nor was its evidentiary relevance under Rule 401 affected by the availability of alternative proofs of the element to which it went, such as an admission by Old Chief that he had been convicted of a crime "punishable by imprisonment for a term exceeding one year" within the meaning of the statute. The 1972 Advisory Committee Notes to Rule 401 make this point directly:

> "The fact to which the evidence is directed need not be in dispute. While situations will arise which call for the exclusion of evidence offered to prove a point conceded by the opponent, the ruling should be made on the basis of such considerations as waste of time and undue prejudice (see Rule 403), rather than under any general requirement that evidence is admissible only if directed to matters in dispute." Advisory Committee's Notes on Fed. Rule Evid. 401.

If, then, relevant evidence is inadmissible in the presence of other evidence related to it, its exclusion must rest not on the ground that the other evidence has rendered it "irrelevant," but on its character as unfairly prejudicial, cumulative or the like, its relevance notwithstanding.

B

The principal issue is the scope of a trial judge's discretion under Rule 403.... Old Chief relies on the danger of unfair prejudice....

1

The term "unfair prejudice," as to a criminal defendant, speaks to the capacity of some concededly relevant evidence to lure the factfinder into declaring guilt on a ground different from proof specific to the offense charged.... So, the Committee Notes to Rule 403 explain, "'Unfair prejudice' within its context means an undue tendency to suggest decision on an improper basis, commonly, though not necessarily, an emotional one." Advisory Committee's Notes on Fed. Rule Evid. 403.

Such improper grounds certainly include the one that Old Chief points to here: generalizing a defendant's earlier bad act into bad character and taking that as raising the odds that he did the later bad act now charged (or, worse, as calling for preventive conviction even if he should happen to be innocent momentarily).... Justice Jackson described how the law has handled this risk:

> "Courts that follow the common-law tradition almost unanimously have come to disallow resort by the prosecution to any kind of evidence of a defendant's evil character to establish a probability of his guilt.... The state may not show defendant's prior trouble with the law, specific criminal acts, or ill name among his neighbors, even though such facts might logically be persuasive that he is by propensity a probable perpetrator of the crime. The inquiry is not rejected because character is irrelevant; on the contrary, it is said to weigh too much with the jury and to so overpersuade them as to prejudge one with a bad general record and deny him a fair opportunity to defend against a particular charge...."
> *Michelson v. United States*, 335 U.S. 469, 475–476 (1948).

Rule of Evidence 404(b)[(1)]* reflects this common-law tradition by addressing propensity reasoning directly.... There is, accordingly, no question that propensity would be an "improper basis" for conviction and that evidence of a prior conviction is subject to analysis under Rule 403 for relative probative value and for prejudicial risk of misuse as propensity evidence.

As for the analytical method to be used in Rule 403 balancing, two basic possibilities present themselves. An item of evidence might be viewed as an island, with estimates of its own probative value and unfairly prejudicial risk the sole reference points in deciding

---

* Editor's Note: Rule 404(b)(1) provides as follows: "***Prohibited Uses.*** Evidence of a crime, wrong, or other act is not admissible to prove a person's character in order to show that on a particular occasion the person acted in accordance with the character."

whether the danger substantially outweighs the value and whether the evidence ought to be excluded. Or the question of admissibility might be seen as inviting further comparisons to take account of the full evidentiary context of the case as the court understands it when the ruling must be made. This second approach would start out like the first but be ready to go further. On objection, the court would decide whether a particular item of evidence raised a danger of unfair prejudice. If it did, the judge would go on to evaluate the degrees of probative value and unfair prejudice not only for the item in question but for any actually available substitutes as well. If an alternative were found to have substantially the same or greater probative value but a lower danger of unfair prejudice, sound judicial discretion would discount the value of the item first offered and exclude it if its discounted probative value were substantially outweighed by unfairly prejudicial risk. As we will explain later on, the judge would have to make these calculations with an appreciation of the offering party's need for evidentiary richness and narrative integrity in presenting a case, and the mere fact that two pieces of evidence might go to the same point would not, of course, necessarily mean that only one of them might come in. It would only mean that a judge applying Rule 403 could reasonably apply some discount to the probative value of an item of evidence when faced with less risky alternative proof going to the same point. Even under this second approach, as we explain below, a defendant's Rule 403 objection offering to concede a point generally cannot prevail over the Government's choice to offer evidence showing guilt and all the circumstances surrounding the offense.[7]

The first understanding of the Rule is open to a very telling objection. That reading would leave the party offering evidence with the option to structure a trial in whatever way would produce the maximum unfair prejudice consistent with relevance. He could choose the available alternative carrying the greatest threat of improper influence, despite the availability of less prejudicial but equally probative evidence. The worst he would have to fear would be a ruling sustaining a Rule 403 objection, and if that occurred, he could simply fall back to offering substitute evidence. This would be a strange rule. It would be very odd for the law of evidence to recognize the danger of unfair prejudice only to confer such a degree of autonomy on the party subject to temptation, and the Rules of Evidence are not so odd.

Rather, a reading of the companions to Rule 403, and of the commentaries that went with them to Congress, makes it clear that what counts as the Rule 403 "probative value" of an item of evidence, as distinct from its Rule 401 "relevance," may be calculated by comparing evidentiary alternatives. The Committee Notes to Rule 401 explicitly say that a party's concession is pertinent to the court's discretion to exclude evidence on the point conceded. Such a concession, according to the Notes, will sometimes "call for the exclusion of evidence offered to prove [the] point conceded by the opponent...." Advisory Committee's Notes on Fed. Rule Evid. 401. As already mentioned, the Notes make it clear that such rulings should be made not on the basis of Rule 401 relevance but on "such considerations as waste of time and undue prejudice (see Rule 403)...." *Ibid.* The Notes to Rule 403 then take up the point by stating that when a court considers "whether to exclude on grounds of unfair prejudice," the "availability of other means of proof may ... be an appropriate factor." Advisory Committee's Notes on Fed. Rule Evid. 403.... Thus the notes leave no question that when Rule 403 confers discretion by providing that ev-

---

7. While our discussion has been general because of the general wording of Rule 403, our holding is limited to cases involving proof of felon status. On appellate review of a Rule 403 decision, a defendant must establish abuse of discretion, a standard that is not satisfied by a mere showing of some alternative means of proof that the prosecution in its broad discretion chose not to rely upon.

idence "may" be excluded, the discretionary judgment may be informed not only by assessing an evidentiary item's twin tendencies, but by placing the result of that assessment alongside similar assessments of evidentiary alternatives....

2

In dealing with the specific problem raised by § 922(g)(1) and its prior-conviction element, there can be no question that evidence of the name or nature of the prior offense generally carries a risk of unfair prejudice to the defendant. That risk will vary from case to case, for the reasons already given, but will be substantial whenever the official record offered by the Government would be arresting enough to lure a juror into a sequence of bad character reasoning. Where a prior conviction was for a gun crime or one similar to other charges in a pending case the risk of unfair prejudice would be especially obvious, and Old Chief sensibly worried that the prejudicial effect of his prior assault conviction, significant enough with respect to the current gun charges alone, would take on added weight from the related assault charge against him.

The District Court was also presented with alternative, relevant, admissible evidence of the prior conviction by Old Chief's offer to stipulate....

Old Chief's proffered admission would, in fact, have been not merely relevant but seemingly conclusive evidence of the element. The statutory language in which the prior-conviction requirement is couched shows no congressional concern with the specific name or nature of the prior offense beyond what is necessary to place it within the broad category of qualifying felonies, and Old Chief clearly meant to admit that his felony did qualify, by stipulating "that the Government has proven one of the essential elements of the offense." As a consequence, although the name of the prior offense may have been technically relevant, it addressed no detail in the definition of the prior-conviction element that would not have been covered by the stipulation or admission. Logic, then, seems to side with Old Chief.

3

There is, however, one more question to be considered before deciding whether Old Chief's offer was to supply evidentiary value at least equivalent to what the Government's own evidence carried. In arguing that the stipulation or admission would not have carried equivalent value, the Government invokes the familiar, standard rule that the prosecution is entitled to prove its case by evidence of its own choice, or, more exactly, that a criminal defendant may not stipulate or admit his way out of the full evidentiary force of the case as the Government chooses to present it....

This is unquestionably true as a general matter. The "fair and legitimate weight" of conventional evidence showing individual thoughts and acts amounting to a crime reflects the fact that making a case with testimony and tangible things not only satisfies the formal definition of an offense, but tells a colorful story with descriptive richness. Unlike an abstract premise, whose force depends on going precisely to a particular step in a course of reasoning, a piece of evidence may address any number of separate elements, striking hard just because it shows so much at once; the account of a shooting that establishes capacity and causation may tell just as much about the triggerman's motive and intent. Evidence thus has force beyond any linear scheme of reasoning, and as its pieces come together a narrative gains momentum, with power not only to support conclusions but to sustain the willingness of jurors to draw the inferences, whatever they may be, necessary to reach an honest verdict. This persuasive power of the concrete and particular is often essential to the capacity of jurors to satisfy the obligations that the law places on them.

Jury duty is usually unsought and sometimes resisted, and it may be as difficult for one juror suddenly to face the findings that can send another human being to prison, as it is for another to hold out conscientiously for acquittal. When a juror's duty does seem hard, the evidentiary account of what a defendant has thought and done can accomplish what no set of abstract statements ever could, not just to prove a fact but to establish its human significance, and so to implicate the law's moral underpinnings and a juror's obligation to sit in judgment. Thus, the prosecution may fairly seek to place its evidence before the jurors, as much to tell a story of guiltiness as to support an inference of guilt, to convince the jurors that a guilty verdict would be morally reasonable as much as to point to the discrete elements of a defendant's legal fault.

But there is something even more to the prosecution's interest in resisting efforts to replace the evidence of its choice with admissions and stipulations, for beyond the power of conventional evidence to support allegations and give life to the moral underpinnings of law's claims, there lies the need for evidence in all its particularity to satisfy the jurors' expectations about what proper proof should be. Some such demands they bring with them to the courthouse, assuming, for example, that a charge of using a firearm to commit an offense will be proven by introducing a gun in evidence. A prosecutor who fails to produce one, or some good reason for his failure, has something to be concerned about. "If [jurors'] expectations are not satisfied, triers of fact may penalize the party who disappoints them by drawing a negative inference against that party." Saltzburg, A Special Aspect of Relevance: Countering Negative Inferences Associated with the Absence of Evidence, 66 Calif. L.Rev. 1011, 1019 (1978). Expectations may also arise in jurors' minds simply from the experience of a trial itself. The use of witnesses to describe a train of events naturally related can raise the prospect of learning about every ingredient of that natural sequence the same way. If suddenly the prosecution presents some occurrence in the series differently, as by announcing a stipulation or admission, the effect may be like saying, "never mind what's behind the door," and jurors may well wonder what they are being kept from knowing. A party seemingly responsible for cloaking something has reason for apprehension, and the prosecution with its burden of proof may prudently demur at a defense request to interrupt the flow of evidence telling the story in the usual way.

In sum, the accepted rule that the prosecution is entitled to prove its case free from any defendant's option to stipulate the evidence away rests on good sense. A syllogism is not a story, and a naked proposition in a courtroom may be no match for the robust evidence that would be used to prove it. People who hear a story interrupted by gaps of abstraction may be puzzled at the missing chapters, and jurors asked to rest a momentous decision on the story's truth can feel put upon at being asked to take responsibility knowing that more could be said than they have heard. A convincing tale can be told with economy, but when economy becomes a break in the natural sequence of narrative evidence, an assurance that the missing link is really there is never more than second best.

4

This recognition that the prosecution with its burden of persuasion needs evidentiary depth to tell a continuous story has, however, virtually no application when the point at issue is a defendant's legal status, dependent on some judgment rendered wholly independently of the concrete events of later criminal behavior charged against him. As in this case, the choice of evidence for such an element is usually not between eventful narrative and abstract proposition, but between propositions of slightly varying abstraction, either a record saying that conviction for some crime occurred at a certain time or a statement admitting the same thing without naming the particular offense. The issue of substituting one statement for the other normally arises only when the record of conviction would not be admissible for any purpose beyond proving status, so that excluding it would not deprive the prosecution of evidence with multiple utility; if, indeed, there were a justification for receiving evidence of the nature of prior acts on some issue other than status.... Nor can it be argued that the events behind the prior conviction are proper nourishment for the jurors' sense of obligation to vindicate the public interest. The issue is not whether concrete details of the prior crime should come to the jurors' attention but whether the name or general character of that crime is to be disclosed. Congress, however, has made it plain that distinctions among generic felonies do not count for this purpose; the fact of the qualifying conviction is alone what matters under the statute. "A defendant falls within the category simply by virtue of past conviction for any [qualifying] crime ranging from possession of short lobsters, *see* 16 U.S.C. § 3372, to the most aggravated murder." *Tavares*, 21 F.3d, at 4. The most the jury needs to know is that the conviction admitted by the defendant falls within the class of crimes that Congress thought should bar a convict from possessing a gun, and this point may be made readily in a defendant's admission and underscored in the court's jury instructions. Finally, the most obvious reason that the general presumption that the prosecution may choose its evidence is so remote from application here is that proof of the defendant's status goes to an element entirely outside the natural sequence of what the defendant is charged with thinking and doing to commit the current offense. Proving status without telling exactly why that status was imposed leaves no gap in the story of a defendant's subsequent criminality, and its demonstration by stipulation or admission neither displaces a chapter from a continuous sequence of conventional evidence nor comes across as an officious substitution, to confuse or offend or provoke reproach.

Given these peculiarities of the element of felony-convict status and of admissions and the like when used to prove it, there is no cognizable difference between the evidentiary significance of an admission and of the legitimately probative component of the official record the prosecution would prefer to place in evidence. For purposes of the Rule 403 weighing of the probative against the prejudicial, the functions of the competing evidence are distinguishable only by the risk inherent in the one and wholly absent from the other. In this case, as in any other in which the prior conviction is for an offense likely to support conviction on some improper ground, the only reasonable conclusion was that the risk of unfair prejudice did substantially outweigh the discounted probative value of the record of conviction, and it was an abuse of discretion to admit the record when an admission was available.[8] What we have said shows why this will be the general rule when proof of convict status is at issue, just as the prosecutor's choice will generally survive a Rule 403 analysis when a defendant seeks to force the substitution of an admission for evidence creating a coherent narrative of his thoughts and actions in perpetrating the offense for which he is being tried....

---

8. There may be yet other means of proof besides a formal admission on the record that, with a proper objection, will obligate a district court to exclude evidence of the name of the offense. A redacted record of conviction is the one most frequently mentioned. Any alternative will, of course, require some jury instruction to explain it (just as it will require some discretion when the indictment is read). A redacted judgment in this case, for example, would presumably have revealed to the jury that Old Chief was previously convicted in federal court and sentenced to more than a year's imprisonment, but it would not have shown whether his previous conviction was for one of the business offenses that do not count, under § 921(a)(20). Hence, an instruction, with the defendant's consent, would be necessary to make clear that the redacted judgment was enough to satisfy the status element remaining in the case. The Government might, indeed, propose such a redacted judgment for the trial court to weigh against a defendant's offer to admit, as indeed the Government might do even if the defendant's admission had been received into evidence.

[The dissenting opinion of Justice O'Connor is omitted.]

Campbell v. Keystone Aerial Surveys, Inc.

138 F.3d 996 (5th Cir. 1998)

BENAVIDES, Circuit Judge:

On May 28, 1994, a Cessna 320E airplane crashed into the wall of a canyon near Battle Mountain, Nevada. Steve Fish, the pilot, and Thomas Campbell were killed in the accident. The pilot was employed by Keystone Aerial Surveys, Inc. ("Keystone"), and Campbell was conducting aerial magnetic surveys for Keystone. This appeal arises out of a wrongful death and survival action brought by Melva Campbell, Thomas Campbell's widow, and his five children, against Keystone....

IV.

Appellants also appeal the district court's refusal to admit evidence of the suicide of Campbell's son, Thomas Moises Campbell, and evidence regarding the condition of Campbell's body after the crash.

A.

A little more than a year after his father's death, Thomas Moises Campbell ("Thomas") committed suicide. In a suicide note, Thomas referred to his father's death and said that he was "going to visit him." Although the Campbells did not assert a cause of action on behalf of Thomas's estate, they did urge that evidence of his suicide should be admitted to show the degree of mental anguish that the other members of the family had suffered as a result of Campbell's death. Noting the potential for this evidence to inflame the jury and confuse the issues, the district court ruled that no mention could be made of the fact that Thomas had taken his own life.

The risk that the jury would confuse the mental anguish suffered by family members as a result of young Thomas's suicide with that resulting from Campbell's death was substantial. *See* Fed.R.Evid. 403. By contrast, the probative value of this evidence to show the degree of mental anguish suffered by other family members as a result of Campbell's death was tenuous. Moreover, the Campbells did not assert mental anguish on behalf of Thomas's estate. Under these circumstances, we conclude that the district court acted within its discretion under Rule 403 in refusing to admit evidence relating to Thomas's suicide.

B.

The district court also refused to admit evidence relating to the condition of Campbell's remains. Campbell was decapitated in the accident, and his body was badly burned. The Campbells specifically challenge the district court's exclusion of photographs of the crash site showing Campbell's remains, a coroner's report, which contained photographs of Campbell's remains, and the videotaped deposition testimony of George Franklin Hobbs, an undersheriff in the Lander County Sheriff's Department, who reviewed photographs showing the condition of the bodies found at the crash site. The Campbells argue that this evidence was relevant to show the extent of the mental anguish suffered by members of Campbell's family. Mrs. Campbell and Marisol Campbell, Campbell's oldest daughter, apparently saw photographs of the crash site and Campbell's remains.

Keystone argues that because there was no dispute as to the manner of Campbell's death and the Campbells did not pursue a claim for conscious pain and suffering on behalf of Campbell's estate, the excluded evidence had no probative value and was therefore inadmissible under Federal Rule of Evidence 402. We disagree. Evidence is relevant if it has "any tendency to make [a fact] more or less probable than it would be without the evidence." Fed.R.Evid. 401[(a)]. We have little doubt that the knowledge that their husband and father was decapitated and badly burned in the accident added to the Campbells' mental anguish.

Keystone argues that, even if this evidence was relevant, the district court properly refused to admit it under Rule 403 because its probative value was substantially outweighed by its unduly prejudicial nature and its tendency to inflame the jury. "Because Rule 403 requires the exclusion of relevant evidence, it is an extraordinary measure that should be used sparingly." *United States v. Morris*, 79 F.3d 409, 411 (5th Cir. 1996) (citing *United States v. Pace*, 10 F.3d 1106, 1115 (5th Cir. 1993); *United States v. McRae*, 593 F.2d 700, 707 (5th Cir. 1979)). Nevertheless, "[a] district court has broad discretion in assessing admissibility under Rule 403," and we review only for an abuse of that discretion. *Id.*

We turn first to the district court's exclusion of photographs of Campbell's remains. The Advisory Committee's Note to Rule 403 specifically notes the risk that proffered evidence will "induc[e] a decision on a purely emotional basis" as a circumstance that may require the exclusion of relevant evidence under Rule 403. Fed.R.Evid. 403 advisory committee's note. This circuit has explained that "[p]hotographs of the victim bleeding profusely are classic examples of such evidence." *Jackson v. Firestone Tire & Rubber Co.*, 788 F.2d 1070, 1085 (5th Cir. 1986); *see also Gomez v. Ahitow*, 29 F.3d 1128, 1139 (7th Cir. 1994) (holding that the district court erred in admitting "gruesome" photographs of victim's body); *Ferrier v. Duckworth*, 902 F.2d 545 (7th Cir. 1990) (holding that the district court erred in admitting enlarged photographs of a pool of the victim's blood). The balance does not always weigh against the admission of such evidence, however, as evidenced by numerous decisions in this circuit upholding the district court's decision to admit such evidence. *See In re Air Crash Disaster Near New Orleans*, 767 F.2d 1151 (5th Cir. 1985) (holding that the district court did not abuse its discretion in admitting photographs of the bodies of plane crash victims with third degree burns where conscious pain and suffering was an issue); *United States v. Bowers*, 660 F.2d 527, 529–30 (5th Cir. 1981) (holding that the prejudice inherent in color photographs of a child's lacerated heart in a criminal prosecution for the child's death did not substantially outweigh the probative value of the evidence to show cruel and excessive physical force); *United States v. Kaiser*, 545 F.2d 467, 476 (5th Cir. 1977) (holding that admission of photographs of murder scene was not an abuse of discretion).

In this case, the photographs that the Campbells sought to introduce created some risk that the jury's decision would be based on a visceral response to the images presented. Although the evidence had some probative value, it was within the district court's discretion to exclude the evidence after weighing that probative value against the risks of presenting these photographs to the jury. Accordingly, we find that the district court did not abuse its discretion in excluding the photographic evidence of Campbell's remains.

To the extent that the district court's ruling precluded any testimony regarding the condition of Campbell's remains, however, that ruling was an abuse of discretion. As discussed above, the facts that Campbell was decapitated and his body burned were probative of the mental anguish suffered by members of his family. Moreover, any prejudice from the testimony regarding the bare facts of the condition of his body would not give rise to "undue" prejudice under Rule 403. Likewise, testimony alone would not have the same potential to inflame the jury that the photographic depictions of Campbell's remains might have....

United States v. Caldwell

586 F.3d 338 (5th Cir. 2009)

GARWOOD, Circuit Judge:

Defendant-appellant, Arkon Christopher Caldwell, appeals his convictions of one count of knowing possession, on or about November 7, 2005, of material transported in interstate commerce involving the sexual exploitation of minors, in violation of 18 U.S.C. § 2252(a)(4)(B), (b)(2), and of one count of the knowing receipt, from on or about February 4, 2005, to on or about November 7, 2005, of materials transported in interstate commerce involving the sexual exploitation of minors, in violation of 18 U.S.C. § 2252(a)(2), (b)(1)....

During the Government's case-in-chief, it offered and published to the jury three short clips taken from over an hour's worth of child pornography. It introduced one video of child pornography, which lasted three minutes and thirty-two seconds. That video was not itself published to the jury. However, the court allowed the Government to publish to the jury a short excerpt of that video over the defendant's objection. Then, the Government introduced and published to the jury excerpts from two more child pornography videos found on the defendant's computer. These excerpts lasted thirty-four (or twenty-three) seconds and thirty-one seconds, respectively. The Government's evidence showed that one of these videos had been opened and previewed approximately half an hour before the agents arrived on November 7, 2005. All three of these brief video excerpts were entered into evidence and published to the jury over the defendant's Rule 403 objection.

The defense argued that because it had stipulated that the videos contained child pornography, under *Old Chief v. United States,* the Government did not need to publish the videos to the jury. The stipulation (which was read to the jury) states:

> "The government and the defense have stipulated that the 17 videos listed in Government's Exhibit 37 were found in the shared or incomplete LimeWire folders on the hard drive of the computer belonging to Arkon Caldwell and seized by George O'Campo on November 7, 2005 from 1910-B Humphrey [Caldwell's residence], which is located on Fort Bliss, Texas, and is also located within the Western District of Texas. That these videos were transported to that computer in interstate or foreign commerce, that is, through the internet via LimeWire.
>
> It is further stipulated that these 17 videos contain visual depictions of minors under the age of 18, engaging in sexually explicit conduct, and that the parties have no evidence to suggest that actual minors were not used in the creation of those videos, and that the videos do show the minors engaged in sexually explicit conduct."

....

While all relevant evidence tends to prejudice the party against whom it is offered, Rule 403 excludes relevant evidence when the probative value of that evidence is *substantially* outweighed by the *unfairly* prejudicial nature of the evidence. When one party stipulates to a disputed fact, the stipulation conclusively proves that fact. Any additional evidence offered to prove that fact, while still relevant, could potentially violate Rule 403.

Old Chief addresses the admissibility under Rule 403 of additional relevant evidence in light of a stipulation.... [T]he Court begins its analysis with the general rule: the criminal defendant cannot stipulate his way out of the full evidentiary force of the Government's case. The Court concludes by reversing the conviction as an exception to the general rule because the defendant's legal status (felon) is not part of the Government's narrative or story. A foundation of the *Old Chief* decision seems to turn on the contribution of the challenged evidence to the overall narrative of the Government's case ("Evidence thus has force beyond any linear scheme of reasoning, and as its pieces come together a narrative gains momentum, with power not only to support conclusions but to sustain the willingness of jurors to draw inferences, whatever they may be, necessary to reach an honest verdict.").

Unlike *Old Chief*, child pornography is graphic evidence that has force beyond simple linear schemes of reasoning. It comes together with the remaining evidence to form a narrative to gain momentum to support jurors' inferences regarding the defendant's guilt. It provides the flesh and blood for the jury to see the exploitation of children. The general, conclusory language of the stipulation that the videos "contain visual depictions of minors under the age of eighteen, engaging in sexually explicit conduct" does not have the same evidentiary value as actually seeing the particular explicit conduct of the specific minors. Jurors have expectations as to the narrative that will unfold in the courtroom. If those expectations are not met, jurors may very well punish the party who disappoints by drawing a negative inference. For example, jurors expect to see a gun in the case of a person charged with using a firearm to commit a crime. Likewise, the actual videos exploiting children in a child pornography case form the narrative that falls within the general rule stated in *Old Chief*. Moreover, the specific videos published — one of which the evidence showed was opened and previewed the morning of the search — reflected how likely it was that the defendant knew that the video depicted child pornography (which knowledge the stipulation did not mention). We cannot say the trial court abused its discretion when it showed the jury three short excerpts from three of the seventeen different videos of child pornography on defendant's computer....

Kalispell v. Miller

230 P.3d 792 (Mont. 2010)

Justice PATRICIA O. COTTER delivered the Opinion of the Court.

. . . .

On February 9, 2008, Miller, a probation and parole officer, and her lesbian partner Benware, along with a friend and co-worker of Benware's, Amanda Dumke, spent an evening drinking at a local bar in Kalispell. After several drinks, Benware threw a beer bottle at Miller and was evicted by the barkeep for disorderly behavior. Miller and Dumke remained at the bar but Dumke grew concerned about Benware and called to check on her. This conversation caused Dumke significant concern and at 9:51 p.m., she called the Kalispell Police Department (KPD), asking that they conduct a "welfare check" on Benware. Dumke explained that Benware, a lawful gun owner, was "playing" with her gun and was very upset. The KPD agreed to dispatch officers immediately. However, when Dumke told Miller she had called the KPD, Miller feared that Benware might lose her job at the Flathead County Sheriff's Department Animal Control Unit; therefore, at 10:06 p.m., Miller called the KPD dispatcher, identified herself as a probation and parole officer, and told the dispatcher that Dumke's call had been a prank and Benware was with them at the bar.

Meanwhile, when an intoxicated Benware arrived home after being expelled from the bar, she took several prescription sleeping pills and then left in her car, intending to get a soft drink. As a result, she was not at home when the KPD arrived to check on her. While KPD officers were still at Benware's residence, dispatch called the officers and informed them that the requested welfare check had been a prank. The officers left Benware's home and suspended their efforts to find Benware. Unbeknownst to the officers, Miller, or Dumke at that time, Benware had had an automobile accident at approximately 9:54 p.m., which passersby had reported to the Flathead County Sheriff's Department. This accident occurred approximately 12 minutes before Miller told the KPD dispatcher that Benware was at the bar with her.

On February 25, 2008, the City of Kalispell charged Miller with misdemeanor obstructing a peace officer based on Miller's untruthful claim that Dumke's call had been a hoax and that Benware was with them. A jury trial was held in June 2008, at the conclusion of which the jury convicted Miller of the charged offense. Miller appealed to the District Court arguing that the Trial Court erred in allowing multiple references to Miller's homosexuality into evidence. . . .

Miller maintains on appeal that the Trial Court erred in allowing repeated references to her homosexuality during the trial. Relying on *State v. Ford*, 926 P.2d 245 (1996), and extra-jurisdictional cases, she claims her sexual orientation is unrelated to the elements of the charged crime and therefore it was irrelevant. She further opines that admission of this evidence was highly prejudicial, had no probative value, and constituted reversible error. Miller had suggested to the Trial Court during pretrial discussion of motions that the relationship between Miller and Benware be characterized as "close" or "best" friends to the jury.

The City argued to the Trial Court that characterizing the women's relationship as anything other than what it was—an intimate homosexual relationship—was to lie and mislead the jury. It argued that knowledge that the women were intimate partners put both Benware's and Miller's conduct during that evening in context.

The Trial Court denied Miller's pretrial motion to exclude evidence of homosexuality, noting that had Miller and Benware been a man and a woman, the nature of their relationship would be relevant and admissible. The District Court affirmed the Trial Court's ruling concluding that "[t]he salient aspect of the evidence is the romantic nature of the relationship—not whether it was lesbian or heterosexual."

While the Trial Court and the District Court equated homosexuality and heterosexuality for purposes of legal analysis, we conclude it was prejudicial error to do so under the circumstances presented here. Society does not yet view homosexuality or bisexuality in the same manner as it views heterosexuality. Because there remains strong potential that a juror will be prejudiced against a homosexual or bisexual individual, courts must safeguard against such potential prejudice.

In *Ford*, Ford was charged with sexual intercourse without consent with another man. At trial, Ford testified that he was bisexual. The jury returned a guilty verdict and Ford appealed, in part, on grounds that the district court erroneously overruled his objections to the admissibility of evidence of his bisexuality. While we affirmed the district court in *Ford*, noting that Ford's sexuality "was relevant to, and probative of an essential issue in this case," we also cautioned:

> There is, unquestionably, the potential for prejudice in this situation. There will be, on virtually every jury, people who would find the lifestyle and sexual preferences of a homosexual or bisexual person offensive. . . . [O]ur criminal justice system must take the necessary precautions to assure that people are convicted based on evidence of guilt, and not on the basis of some inflammatory personal

trait. Therefore, we caution prosecutors and district courts not to assume, based on this opinion, that evidence of a defendant's sexual preference would be admissible under most circumstances.

Ford, 926 P.2d at 250.

Unlike the situation in *Ford*, where Ford's sexual orientation was squarely at issue, Miller's sexual orientation and the existence of an intimate relationship with Benware was not probative or relevant evidence vis-à-vis the crime with which Miller was charged. As Miller suggested before trial, if the State was concerned that the jury understand Miller's motive for calling off the KPD welfare check, it could have simply explained that the two women were good friends. There was no need to make repeated references throughout the trial to the homosexual nature of their relationship—either as an element of the crime or to establish context. As we noted in *Ford*, if there is no need for purposes of proof of a crime to introduce to the jury a potentially "inflammatory personal trait," then it may well be error to do so. Under the circumstances of this case, we conclude that introduction of the nature of the parties' sexual relationship was an abuse of the Trial Court's discretion....

Justice BRIAN MORRIS dissents.

The Court overreaches in its search for prejudice and perpetuates the stereotypes from which it professes to protect Miller. I disagree with the Court's conclusion that the municipal court improperly admitted evidence of Miller's intimate relationship with Benware. The State's allegedly prejudicial remarks emphasized the intimate nature of the relationship between Miller and Benware in order to demonstrate that Miller had a motive to make the call in order to protect Benware. The State's characterization of the relationship did not emphasize its same sex nature. The State instead focused on the length and intimacy of the relationship between Miller and Benware.

The State argued that the long-term intimate nature of the relationship between Miller and Benware proved qualitatively different than a mere friendship to demonstrate Miller's motive to protect Benware. The Court appears to concede that evidence regarding the nature of the relationship would have been relevant and admissible had the relationship been a heterosexual one. Yet the Court concludes that such evidence should have been inadmissible here solely because it concerned a same sex relationship.

Miller used *voir dire* in an effort to uncover any potential for prejudice arising from Miller's sexual orientation and her relationship with Benware. Miller's counsel questioned the jury exhaustively about same sex relationships and the potential for prejudice against a lesbian defendant. Miller's counsel failed to unearth any potential prejudice during *voir dire*. I would not assume that any unspoken prejudice among the potential jurors rose to the level of a potential juror being more likely to convict Miller for misdemeanor obstruction of a peace officer due to the fact that Miller and Benware had established an intimate relationship for thirteen years....

Notes and Questions

1. Why do you suppose that the prosecutor in *Old Chief* was so intent on introducing the evidence of the defendant's prior felony conviction? Is it possible that the prosecution was hoping that the jury might on its own use the evidence to draw the propensity inference forbidden by Rule 404(b)(1)? Was it likely that the prosecutors in *Caldwell* and *Kalispell* were similarly motivated by the possibility that the jurors might make improper use of the evidence?

2. It is important to remember in applying Rule 403 that mere prejudice alone is insufficient to justify exclusion. "Virtually all evidence is designed to be prejudicial (i.e., to help one side's case and to hurt the other's); therefore, Rule 403 concerns itself not with prejudice per se but with *unfair* prejudice." *United States v. Winchenbach*, 197 F.3d 548, 559 (1st Cir. 1999); *accord Costantino v. David M. Herzog, M.D., P.C.*, 203 F.3d 164, 174–75 (2d Cir. 2000). As *Old Chief* points out, evidence is unfairly prejudicial where it has a tendency to lead the jury to decide the case based on something other than proof specific to the case before it.

3. In general, what is the relevance of photographs of the victim's body in a murder case? Courts have held that they are relevant to show, *inter alia*, the nature and extent of injuries and the cause of death, *United States v. Greatwalker*, 356 F.3d 908, 912–13 (8th Cir. 2004), the fact of death (corpus delicti), *United States v. Fleming*, 594 F.2d 598, 607–08 (7th Cir. 1979), and to prove the intent with which the defendant killed the victim, *Willingham v. Mullin*, 296 F.3d 917, 928 (10th Cir. 2002). *See generally United States v. Rezaq*, 134 F.3d 1121, 1137 (D.C. Cir. 1998).

4. What is the risk of prejudice to the defendant if such photographs are admitted? After all, such photographs don't necessarily prove that the *defendant* committed the crime, only that someone did. In other words, unlike the evidence subject to exclusion in *Old Chief*, which the jury would know with certainty related directly to the defendant, such photographic evidence should only matter if the defendant in fact committed the crime. Consider the following as an explanation:

> "Blood will have blood," WILLIAM SHAKESPEARE, MACBETH, Act 3, sc. 4; accordingly, photographs of gore may inappropriately dispose a jury to exact retribution.

United States v. Rezaq, 134 F.3d 1121, 1138 (D.C. Cir. 1998).

When one considers the emotional responses of anger and fear that the jurors might have after exposure to such photographs, coupled with the fact that their only choice is to convict or acquit the defendant and an unspoken presumption they might have that the person charged likely had some connection to the crime, this may very well be a valid concern.

5. To successfully prosecute a hate crime, prosecutors have to prove that the crime was committed because of animus based on a particular characteristic of the victim, making it necessary to introduce evidence that might shed light on the defendant's biases against people possessing that characteristic. *See, e.g., United States v. Allen*, 341 F.3d 870, 885–88 (9th Cir. 2003).

6. While much of the discussion of Rule 403 focuses on evidence that may elicit an emotional reaction in jurors, it is not just emotional reactions that Rule 403 is concerned with. As the Advisory Committee Note points out, "'Unfair prejudice' within its context means an undue tendency to suggest decision on an improper basis, commonly, *though not necessarily*, an emotional one" (emphasis added). Take, for example, the evidence at issue in *Old Chief*. The concern there was that the jury might infer from the fact that the defendant committed an assault in the past that he has a propensity to commit assaults and thus that he had some tendency to commit an assault on this occasion. Of course, that isn't emotional, is it? Indeed, there is great logical appeal to such an argument, and one could construct an *inductive* argument supporting it, as follows: *One who has committed assaults in the past is more likely to commit assaults in the future than someone who has not committed assaults in the past; the defendant has committed an assault in the past; therefore, the defendant is more likely to have committed an assault in this instance.* The risk of

such evidence, however, is not that it is illogical or that it may evoke an emotional response, but rather that jurors might overvalue the evidence, giving it *more* weight than they should. Indeed, in their minds, the jurors may compose a *deductive* argument, as follows: *Once a criminal, always a criminal; the defendant committed a crime once before; therefore, the defendant committed the crime charged on this occasion.* While there likely is *some* connection between prior and future criminal activity, jurors are not perfect logicians, and there is a risk that they may overvalue the degree to which past and future criminal activity is correlated, potentially allowing it to drown out other relevant evidence.

7. Rule 403 is applicable even when dealing with conditionally relevant evidence. Thus, even though Rule 104(b) calls for the admission of conditionally relevant evidence so long as there is sufficient evidence for the jury to find the conditions satisfied, where that conditionally relevant evidence raises any of the Rule 403 dangers, the court can exclude the evidence. *See Huddleston v. United States*, 485 U.S. 681, 691 (1988). Thus, Rule 403 to some extent transfers back to the trial court judge some of the authority that Rule 104(b) reserves for the jury.

8. Often, trial courts conflate their analysis under Rules 401 and 402 with that under Rule 403. *See generally* Peter Nicolas, *De Novo Review in Deferential Robes?: A Deconstruction of the Standard of Review of Evidentiary Errors in the Federal System*, 54 Syracuse L. Rev. 531, 541–42 (2004). Yet to exclude evidence under Rule 403 means something very different than to exclude evidence under Rules 401 and 402. Consider the following in connection with Problem 1-5:

> Although Rule 403 remains at the judge's disposal to keep out evidence with low probative worth and a high tendency to prejudice the jury, holding the evidence to be relevant under Rule 401 but excludable under Rule 403 sends a very different message to society than does merely excluding the evidence as irrelevant under Rule 401. The former stigmatizes gay people by sending a message that there is some truth to the link between the evidence and the point that it is being offered to prove, but that it is being excluded only because the jury may make improper use of the evidence. The latter approach, on the other hand, refuses to even credit the stigmatizing claim. While exclusion of evidence under Rule 403 is concerned with the message that admitting the evidence will send to the jury and a judgment about the capacity of the jury, exclusion pursuant to Rule 401 is concerned with the message that will be sent to society at large. Thus, while some judges merge their analysis of evidence under Rules 401 and 403, which rule they ultimately employ to exclude the evidence makes an enormous difference in the message that their judgment sends to society.

Peter Nicolas, *"They Say He's Gay": The Admissibility of Evidence of Sexual Orientation*, 37 Ga. L. Rev. 793, 848–49 (2003).

9. Don't we sometimes *want* jurors to use their emotions? Don't they necessarily need to do so to determine pain and suffering and other emotional damages? *See* Eric Posner, *Law and Emotions*, 89 Geo. L.J. 1977, 2000 (2001) (arguing that evoking jurors' emotions does not improve their ability to determine pain and suffering damages, but conceding that the issue is an arguable one).

10. For an analysis of Rule 403 from a law and economics perspective, *see* Richard A. Posner, Frontiers of Legal Theory 386–389 (2001).

11. Subject to only one exception (discussed in Chapter 10), evidence that satisfies the requirements of every other federal rule of evidence is still subject to exclusion under

Rule 403. Accordingly, Rule 403 should always be considered a last stop in determining the admissibility of any item of evidence. *See Forrest v. Beloit Corp.*, 424 F.3d 344, 355 (3d Cir. 2005) ("Rule 403 is an '"umbrella rule" spanning the whole of the Federal Rules of Evidence,' and as such trial judges must apply Rule 403 'in tandem with other Federal Rules under which evidence would be admissible.'") (quoting *Coleman v. Home Depot, Inc.*, 306 F.3d 1333, 1343 (3d Cir. 2002)).

12. In a prosecution for unlawful possession of a firearm by an unlawful user of a controlled substance, a violation of 18 U.S.C. §922(g)(3), is it relevant that a copy of *High Times* magazine—a publication about marijuana growing and use—was found in the defendant's house? Is it unfairly prejudicial? *See United States v. Patterson*, 431 F.3d 832, 839–40 (5th Cir. 2005) (holding that it is relevant in that it "show[s] that it was more probable that [the defendant] used marijuana" and not unfairly prejudicial). In what way is such evidence different from any of the evidence offered in Problem 1-8?

13. Note that unfair prejudice is not the only basis for excluding evidence under Rule 403; evidence is also subject to exclusion where its probative worth is outweighed by the dangers of confusion of the issues, or misleading the jury, or by considerations of undue delay, waste of time, or needless presentation of cumulative evidence. As with the danger of unfair prejudice, these likewise involve a balancing of benefits and costs by the trial court. *See, e.g.*, *United States v. Williams*, 81 F.3d 1434, 1443 (7th Cir. 1996) ("Evidence is 'cumulative' when it adds very little to the probative force of the other evidence in the case, so that if it were admitted its contribution to the determination of truth would be outweighed by its contribution to the length of the trial, with all the potential for confusion, as well as prejudice to other litigants, who must wait longer for their trial, that a long trial creates.").

I weigh the "probative value" vs. the "prejudicial effect" vs. "how I feel". Usually, "how I feel" wins.

G. Rule 105: An Alternative to Exclusion

It is often the case that an item of evidence may be admissible for one purpose yet inadmissible for another. Thus in *Old Chief*, evidence of the defendant's prior conviction was admissible for the purpose of proving the element of being a felon in possession of a firearm yet inadmissible for drawing a character inference from criminal activity on a prior occasion to criminal activity on a future occasion. Similarly, in a case involving multiple plaintiffs or defendants, it may turn out that a piece of evidence is admissible only against some parties but not others. In such circumstances, are the court's only choices to exclude or admit the evidence?

Not necessarily. Rule 105 addresses this situation, and provides as follows:

> If the court admits evidence that is admissible against a party or for a purpose — but not against another party or for another purpose — the court, on timely request, must restrict the evidence to its proper scope and instruct the jury accordingly.

The possibility of giving a limiting instruction under Rule 105 must always be considered as an alternative to outright exclusion under Rule 403 when the basis for exclusion is unfair prejudice. *See* Advisory Committee Note to Rule 403 ("In reaching a decision whether to exclude on grounds of unfair prejudice, consideration should be given to the probable effectiveness or lack of effectiveness of a limiting instruction."); Advisory Committee Note to Rule 105 ("The availability and effectiveness of this practice must be taken into consideration in reaching a decision whether to exclude for unfair prejudice under Rule 403.").

A limiting instruction involves the judge telling jurors that they may use the evidence only for one purpose but not for another, with the instruction sometimes being given at the time the evidence is introduced, sometimes just before the jury deliberates, and sometimes on both occasions.

Notes and Questions

1. In her dissent in *Old Chief*, Justice O'Connor suggested that the problem in the case could have been addressed by a limiting instruction to the jury to use the evidence only as proof of the element of being a felon in possession and not for the purpose of drawing a character inference. Are you persuaded that such an instruction would have been effective? Consider the following:

> We are not nearly so sanguine concerning the efficacy of jury instructions in curing the prejudice caused by the introduction of other crimes evidence. To tell a jury to ignore the defendant's prior convictions in determining whether he or she committed the offense being tried is to ask human beings to act with a measure of dispassion and exactitude well beyond mortal capacities. In such cases, it becomes particularly unrealistic to expect effective execution of the "mental gymnastic" required by limiting instructions, and "the naive assumption that prejudicial effects can be overcome by instructions to jury" becomes more clearly than ever "unmitigated fiction," *Krulewitch v. United States*, 336 U.S. 440, 453 (1949) (Jackson, J., concurring). As the Third Circuit has observed, once evidence of prior crimes reaches the jury, "it is most difficult, if not impossible, to assume continued integrity of the presumption of innocence. A drop of ink cannot be removed from a glass of milk."

(handwritten) Can't unring the bell

United States v. Daniels, 770 F.2d 1111, 1118 (D.C. Cir. 1985).

2. Notwithstanding the skepticism expressed by the *Daniels* court, courts generally do entertain the presumption that juries in fact heed limiting instructions. *See, e.g., United States v. Cruz*, 326 F.3d 392, 397 (3d Cir. 2003); *United States v. Ebner*, 782 F.2d 1120, 1126 (2d Cir. 1986). Consider the following defense of such a presumption:

> The rule that juries are presumed to follow their instructions is a pragmatic one, rooted less in the absolute certitude that the presumption is true than in the belief that it represents a reasonable practical accommodation of the interests of the state and the defendant in the criminal justice process.

Richardson v. Marsh, 481 U.S. 200, 211 (1987).

However, at some point in a criminal case the presumption can be overcome and the instruction deemed to be constitutionally ineffective. *See Bruton v. United States*, 391 U.S. 123 (1968).

H. Rule of Completeness

United States v. Lopez-Medina
596 F.3d 716 (10th Cir. 2010)

O'BRIEN, Circuit Judge.

. . . .

Lopez-Medina and Lopez-Ahumado were charged with possession with intent to distribute 500 grams or more of methamphetamine, in violation of 21 U.S.C. §841(a)(1), and aiding and abetting the same based on the drugs found in the pickup truck (Count I). Lopez-Ahumado was also charged with possession with intent to distribute 50 grams or more of methamphetamine, also in violation of 21 U.S.C. §841(a)(1), based on the drugs discovered in the Clearfield apartment (Count II).

Lopez-Ahumado pled guilty to Count I. In a statement submitted to the court in advance of his guilty plea, Lopez-Ahumado stated:

> I stipulate and agree that the following facts accurately describe my conduct. They provide a basis for the Court to accept my guilty plea and for calculating the sentence in my case:

> On August 5, 2005, I, Rogelio Lopez-Ahumado, knowingly aided & abetted Gerardo Lopez-Medina in jointly possessing, with intent to distribute, 4.833 kilograms of mixture and substance containing methamphetamine (4.63 kilograms actual methamphetamine) which was located in Lopez-Medina's vehicle parked near 607 South 1000 East, Clearfield, Utah.

> On August 5, 2005, I also knowingly possessed, with intent to distribute, 444.4 grams of mixture and substance containing methamphetamine (426.6 grams actual methamphetamine) that was located in my apartment at 607 South 1000 East, Apartment E, Clearfield, Utah.

Lopez-Ahumado admitted to these facts at his change of plea hearing. In his plea agreement, the government agreed to request a downward departure at sentencing if Lopez-Ahumado provided substantial assistance to the government "in the prosecution of others involved in Controlled Substance Offenses." Lopez-Ahumado did not assist the government and was sentenced to 262 months imprisonment. Lopez-Medina proceeded to trial....

Prior to trial, the government filed a motion in limine informing the court defense counsel had represented to the government that Lopez-Medina's defense would be that the government had already convicted the guilty individual, Lopez-Ahumado, and Lopez-Medina was merely an innocent bystander. The government stated it did not plan to call Lopez-Ahumado as a witness in its case-in-chief due to his refusal to answer questions. The government asked the court to prohibit Lopez-Medina from introducing the fact of Lopez-Ahumado's conviction through other witness' testimony on the grounds it was irrelevant and inadmissible hearsay. The government argued if "the Court allow[ed] [Lopez-Ahumado's] conviction to come in as an exception to the hearsay rule, the government should be allowed under the rule of completeness to put in [Lopez-Ahumado's] factual statement in support of his guilty plea" to prevent the jury from assuming Lopez-Ahumado admitted sole responsibility for the crime.

At the pretrial conference, both parties said they did not intend to call Lopez-Ahumado as a witness. The government repeated its objection to the admission of testimony relating to Lopez-Ahumado's conviction but stated if defense counsel "wants to put in the conviction ... as long as the government is allowed to give the rest of the story, that he has admitted to aiding and assisting [Lopez-Medina] in distributing meth, we have no problem." The court responded: "I will let [defense counsel bring out Lopez-Ahumado's plea and conviction], but then I'm going to let the government point out that this guy also said ... that he knowingly aided and abetted [Lopez-Medina]."....

Defense counsel ... argued if the factual allocution was admitted, Lopez-Ahumado's entire plea agreement should be admitted so he could point out Lopez-Ahumado had been offered the possibility of a reduction in sentence if he gave substantial assistance to the government. The court denied this request....

[On appeal, Lopez-Medina challenges the trial court's admission of Lopez-Ahumado's factual allocution.]

The rule of completeness is a common law doctrine partially codified in Rule 106 of the Federal Rules of Evidence.... While Rule 106* applies only to writings and recorded statements, we have held "the rule of completeness embodied in Rule 106 is '"substantially applicable to oral testimony," as well by virtue of Fed.R.Evid. 611(a)....'"

The government contends the court correctly admitted the fact allocution pursuant to the rule of completeness because it clarified that Lopez-Ahumado had admitted to jointly possessing the drugs found in the truck and did not take sole responsibility for the crime....

"The purpose of Rule 106 is to prevent a party from misleading the jury by allowing into the record relevant portions of a writing or recorded statement which clarify or explain the part already received." "The rule of completeness, however, does not necessarily require admission of [an entire statement, writing or recording.] Rather, only those portions which are 'relevant to an issue in the case' and necessary 'to clarify or explain the portion already received' need to be admitted." "In determining whether a disputed portion of a statement must be admitted [under the rule of completeness], the trial court should con-

---

* Editor's Note: Rule 106 provides: "If a party introduces all or part of a writing or recorded statement, an adverse party may require the introduction, at that time, of any other part—or any other writing or recorded statement—that in fairness ought to be considered at the same time."

sider whether '(1) it explains the admitted evidence, (2) places the admitted evidence in context, (3) avoids misleading the jury, and (4) insures fair and impartial understanding of the evidence.'"

The fact allocation satisfies this four-part test. It is clear from the record that, as the government predicted, Lopez-Medina tried to pin the crime entirely on Lopez-Ahumado. The government objected to any reference to Lopez-Ahumado's conviction as irrelevant and inadmissible hearsay. Defense counsel stated he wanted the jury to know Lopez-Ahumado was convicted because he wanted the jury to hear the full story. The fact allocation explains the basis for Lopez-Ahumado's guilty plea and places that evidence in context. It avoids misleading the jury into believing Lopez-Ahumado accepted sole responsibility for possessing the drugs found in the truck and ensures that the jury understood Lopez-Ahumado's guilty plea did not relieve Lopez-Medina of potential liability.

Even if the fact allocation would be subject to a hearsay objection, that does not block its use when it is needed to provide context for a statement already admitted. *See* Christopher B. Mueller & Laird C. Kirkpatrick, Federal Evidence § 1:43 (3d ed. 2007); *see also, e.g., United States v. Bucci*, 525 F.3d 116, 133 (1st Cir.2008) (the rule of completeness "may be invoked to facilitate the introduction of otherwise inadmissible evidence"); *United States v. Sutton*, 801 F.2d 1346, 1368 (D.C.Cir.1986) (noting every major rule of exclusion, with the exception of Rule 106, includes the proviso "except as otherwise provided by these rules" and stating "Rule 106 can adequately fulfill its function only by permitting the admission of some otherwise inadmissible evidence when the court finds in fairness that the proffered evidence should be considered contemporaneously"); *but see United States v. Guevara*, 277 F.3d 111, 127 (2d Cir.2001) (Rule 106 does not make admissible what is otherwise inadmissible), *rev'd on other grounds on rehearing*, 298 F.3d 124 (2d Cir.2002). Thus, the court did not err in admitting the fact allocation pursuant to the rule of completeness.

Lopez-Medina argues if the fact allocation was properly admitted under the rule of completeness, that same rule should have allowed him to introduce the government's promise it would seek a downward variance if Lopez-Ahumado provided substantial assistance in the prosecution of others. The rule of completeness connects with Rule 403 of the Rules of Evidence.... The district court acted within its discretion in excluding the government's promise under Rule 403 because it does not satisfy the four-part test outlined above.

The fact the government promised to seek a lower sentence in exchange for Lopez-Ahumado's substantial assistance does not explain either the fact of Lopez-Ahumado's plea or the factual basis for his plea. In the statement he submitted to the court in advance of his guilty plea, Lopez-Ahumado admitted to possessing with intent to distribute the methamphetamine found in the pickup truck and the methamphetamine found in the Clearfield apartment. Presumably he pled guilty to one count to avoid proceeding to trial and facing a possible (even likely) conviction on two counts. The fact Lopez-Ahumado did not assist the government suggests the government's promise to seek a downward variance in exchange for such assistance was not the reason he pled guilty. And there is no reason to believe the government's promise altered the facts to which Lopez-Ahumado admitted. Admitting the government's promise would not have ensured a fair and impartial understanding of the evidence which is the purpose of the rule of completeness. Actually, it would have had quite the opposite effect—misleading the jury by suggesting the government's offer motivated Lopez-Ahumado's guilty plea, when, in fact, it did not....

Notes and Questions

1. According to the Advisory Committee, "[f]or practical reasons," Rule 106 encompasses only writings and recordings, and does not apply to testimony about oral statements. What are the practical reasons for so limiting the rule? In any event, as indicated by the court in *Lopez-Medina*, some courts invoke Rule 611(a)(1)—which provides that "[t]he court should exercise reasonable control over the mode and order of examining witnesses and presenting evidence so as to ... make those procedures effective for determining the truth"—to extend the rule of completeness to encompass oral statements. *See, e.g., United States v. Li*, 55 F.3d 325, 329 (7th Cir. 1995); *United States v. Mussaleen*, 35 F.3d 692, 696 (2d Cir. 1994). Rule 611(a)(1) is examined in closer detail in Chapter 4.

2. As the *Lopez-Medina* court indicates, lower courts are split on the question whether Rule 106 can be invoked to admit otherwise inadmissible evidence, or if it merely alters the order of proof but is limited to evidence that would be otherwise admissible. If Rule 106 does not allow for the admission of otherwise inadmissible evidence, does the misleading nature of the evidence stripped of its context call for exclusion of the evidence under Rule 403? *See United States v. LeFevour*, 798 F.2d 977, 981 (7th Cir. 1986) ("If otherwise inadmissible evidence is necessary to correct a misleading impression, then either it is admissible for this limited purpose by force of Rule 106 ... or, if it is inadmissible ... the misleading evidence must be excluded too.").

3. In contrast to the federal scheme, consider the following provisions of the Texas Rules of Evidence:

Texas Rule 106. Remainder of or Related Writings or Recorded Statements

When a writing or recorded statement or part thereof is introduced by a party, an adverse party may at that time introduce any other part or any other writing or recorded statement which ought in fairness to be considered contemporaneously with it. "Writing or recorded statement" includes depositions.

Texas Rule 107. Rule of Optional Completeness

When part of an act, declaration, conversation, writing or recorded statement is given in evidence by one party, the whole on the same subject may be inquired into by the other, and any other act, declaration, writing or recorded statement which is necessary to make it fully understood or to explain the same may also be given in evidence, as when a letter is read, all letters on the same subject between the same parties may be given. "Writing or recorded statement" includes depositions.

Does the scheme set forth in the Texas Rules of Evidence resolve the ambiguity in Federal Rule 106 discussed in note 2? *See Wright v. State*, 28 S.W.3d 526, 535–36 (Tex. Crim. App. 2000) (describing Texas Rule 106 as merely an interruption rule but Texas Rule 107 as a rule of admissibility).

I. Relevance of Probabilistic Evidence

We have seen that to be relevant, evidence need not prove or disprove the point for which it is being offered with any particular threshold of certainty: *any* tendency to prove or disprove the point suffices. Of course, such evidence, standing alone, would not be sufficient proof, but there is, as we know, a distinction between sufficiency and admissibility.

Typically, evidence does not come with a probability attached to it, but sometimes it does, as the following cases demonstrate. Such evidence can be very useful, but it sometimes presents dangers that require analysis under Rule 403.

People v. Collins
438 P.2d 33 (Cal. 1968)

[handwritten annotation: Math Not admissible]

SULLIVAN, Justice.

We deal here with the novel question whether evidence of mathematical probability has been properly introduced and used by the prosecution in a criminal case. While we discern no inherent incompatibility between the disciplines of law and mathematics and intend no general disapproval or disparagement of the latter as an auxiliary in the fact-finding processes of the former, we cannot uphold the technique employed in the instant case. As we explain in detail *infra*, the testimony as to mathematical probability infected the case with fatal error and distorted the jury's traditional role of determining guilt or innocence according to long-settled rules. Mathematics, a veritable sorcerer in our computerized society, while assisting the trier of fact in the search for truth, must not cast a spell over him. We conclude that on the record before us defendant should not have had his guilt determined by the odds and that he is entitled to a new trial. We reverse the judgment.

A jury found defendant Malcolm Ricardo Collins and his wife defendant Janet Louise Collins guilty of second degree robbery (Pen.Code, §§ 211, 211a, 1157). Malcolm appeals from the judgment of conviction. Janet has not appealed.[1]

On June 18, 1964, about 11:30 a.m. Mrs. Juanita Brooks, who had been shopping, was walking home along an alley in the San Pedro area of the City of Los Angeles. She was pulling behind her a wicker basket carryall containing groceries and had her purse on top of the packages. She was using a cane. As she stooped down to pick up an empty carton, she was suddenly pushed to the ground by a person whom she neither saw nor heard approach. She was stunned by the fall and felt some pain. She managed to look up and saw a young woman running from the scene. According to Mrs. Brooks the latter appeared to weigh about 145 pounds, was wearing "something dark," and had hair "between a dark blond and a light blond," but lighter than the color of defendant Janet Collins' hair as it appeared at trial. Immediately after the incident, Mrs. Brooks discovered that her purse, containing between $35 and $40, was missing.

About the same time as the robbery, John Bass, who lived on the street at the end of the alley, was in front of his house watering his lawn. His attention was attracted by "a lot of crying and screaming" coming from the alley. As he looked in that direction, he saw a woman run out of the alley and enter a yellow automobile parked across the street from him. He was unable to give the make of the car. The car started off immediately and pulled wide around another parked vehicle so that in the narrow street it passed within six feet of Bass. The latter then saw that it was being driven by a male Negro, wearing a mustache and beard. At the trial Bass identified defendant as the driver of the yellow automobile. However, an attempt was made to impeach his identification by his admission that at the preliminary hearing he testified to an uncertain identification at the police lineup shortly after the attack on Mrs. Brooks, when defendant was beardless.

---

1. Hereafter, the term "defendant" is intended to apply only to Malcolm, but the term "defendants" to Malcolm and Janet.

In his testimony Bass described the woman who ran from the alley as a Caucasian, slightly over five feet tall, of ordinary build, with her hair in a dark blond ponytail, and wearing dark clothing. He further testified that her ponytail was "just like" one which Janet had in a police photograph taken on June 22, 1964.

On the day of the robbery, Janet was employed as a housemaid in San Pedro. Her employer testified that she had arrived for work at 8:50 a.m. and that defendant had picked her up in a light yellow car[2] about 11:30 a.m. On that day, according to the witness, Janet was wearing her hair in a blonde ponytail but lighter in color than it appeared at trial.[3]

There was evidence from which it could be inferred that defendants had ample time to drive from Janet's place of employment and participate in the robbery. Defendants testified, however, that they went directly from her employer's house to the home of friends, where they remained for several hours....

Officer Kinsey interrogated defendants separately on June 23 while they were in custody and testified to their statements.... According to the officer, Malcolm stated that he sometimes wore a beard but that he did not wear a beard on June 18 (the day of the robbery), having shaved it off on June 2, 1964.[5] He also explained two receipts for traffic fines totaling $35 paid on June 19, which receipts had been found on his person, by saying that he used funds won in a gambling game at a labor hall. Janet, on the other hand, said that the $35 used to pay the fines had come from her earnings.[6]

....

At the seven-day trial the prosecution experienced some difficulty in establishing the identities of the perpetrators of the crime. The victim could not identify Janet and had never seen defendant. The identification by the witness Bass, who observed the girl run out of the alley and get into the automobile, was incomplete as to Janet and may have been weakened as to defendant. There was also evidence, introduced by the defense, that Janet had worn light-colored clothing on the day in question, but both the victim and Bass testified that the girl they observed had worn dark clothing.

In an apparent attempt to bolster the identifications, the prosecutor called an instructor of mathematics at a state college. Through this witness he sought to establish that, assuming the robbery was committed by a Caucasian woman with a blond ponytail who left the scene accompanied by a Negro with a beard and mustache, there was an overwhelming probability that the crime was committed by any couple answering such distinctive char-

---

2. Other witnesses variously described the car as yellow, as yellow with an off-white top, and yellow with an egg-shell white top. The car was also described as being medium to large in size. Defendant drove a car at or near the times in question which was a Lincoln with a yellow body and a white top.

3. There are inferences which may be drawn from the evidence that Janet attempted to alter the appearance of her hair after June 18. Janet denies that she cut, colored or bleached her hair at any time after June 18, and a number of witnesses supported her testimony.

5. Evidence as to defendant's beard and mustache is conflicting. Defense witnesses appeared to support defendant's claims that he had shaved his beard on June 2. There was testimony that on June 19 when defendant appeared in court to pay fines on another matter he was bearded. By June 22 the beard had been removed.

6. The source of the $35, being essentially the same amount as the $35 to $40 reported by the victim as having been in her purse when taken from her the day before the fines were paid, was a significant factor in the prosecution's case. Other evidence disclosed that defendant and Janet were married on June 2, 1964, at which time they had only $12, a portion of which was spent on a trip to Tiajuana [sic]. Since the marriage defendant had not worked, and Janet's earnings were not more than $12 a week, if that much.

acteristics. The witness testified, in substance, to the "product rule," which states that the probability of the joint occurrence of a number of *mutually independent* events is equal to the product of the individual probabilities that each of the events will occur.[8] *Without presenting any statistical evidence whatsoever in support of the probabilities for the factors selected*, the prosecutor then proceeded to have the witness *assume*[9] probability factors for the various characteristics which he deemed to be shared by the guilty couple and all other couples answering to such distinctive characteristics.[10]

Applying the product rule to his own factors the prosecutor arrived at a probability that there was but one chance in 12 million that any couple possessed the distinctive characteristics of the defendants. Accordingly, under this theory, it was to be inferred that there could be but one chance in 12 million that defendants were innocent and that another equally distinctive couple actually committed the robbery. Expanding on what he had thus purported to suggest as a hypothesis, the prosecutor offered the completely unfounded and improper testimonial assertion that, in his opinion, the factors he had assigned were "conservative estimates" and that, in reality "the chances of anyone else besides these defendants being there, * * * having every similarity, * * * is somewhat like one in a billion."

Objections were timely made to the mathematician's testimony on the grounds that it was immaterial, that it invaded the province of the jury, and that it was based on unfounded assumptions. The objections were "temporarily overruled" and the evidence admitted subject to a motion to strike. When that motion was made at the conclusion of the direct examination, the court denied it, stating that the testimony had been received only for the "purpose of illustrating the mathematical probabilities of various matters, the possibilities for them occurring or re-occurring."

Both defendants took the stand in their own behalf. They denied any knowledge of or participation in the crime and stated that after Malcolm called for Janet at her employer's

---

8. In the example employed for illustrative purposes at the trial, the probability of rolling one die and coming up with a "2" is $1/6$, that is, any one of the six faces of a die has one chance in six of landing face up on any particular roll. The probability of rolling two "2's" in succession is $1/6 \times 1/6$, or $1/36$, that is, on only one occasion out of 36 double rolls (or the roll of two dice), will the selected number land face up on each roll or die.

9. His argument to the jury was based on the same gratuitous assumptions or on similar assumptions which he invited the jury to make.

10. Although the prosecutor insisted that the factors he used were only for illustrative purposes — to demonstrate how the probability of the occurrence of mutually independent factors affected the probability that they would occur together — he nevertheless attempted to use factors which he personally related to the distinctive characteristics of defendants. In his argument to the jury he invited the jurors to apply their own factors, and asked defense counsel to suggest what the latter would deem as reasonable. The prosecutor himself proposed the individual probabilities set out in the table below. Although the transcript of the examination of the mathematics instructor and the information volunteered by the prosecutor at that time create some uncertainty as to precisely which of the characteristics the prosecutor assigned to the individual probabilities, he restated in his argument to the jury that they should be as follows:

Characteristic	Individual Probability
A. Partly yellow automobile	$1/10$
B. Man with mustache	$1/4$
C. Girl with ponytail	$1/10$
D. Girl with blond hair	$1/3$
E. Negro man with beard	$1/10$
F. Interracial couple in car	$1/1000$

In his brief on appeal defendant agrees that the foregoing appeared on a table presented in the trial court.

house they went directly to a friend's house in Los Angeles where they remained for some time. According to this testimony defendants were not near the scene of the robbery when it occurred. Defendant's friends testified to a visit by them "in the middle of June" although she could not recall the precise date....

As we shall explain, the prosecution's introduction and use of mathematical probability statistics injected two fundamental prejudicial errors into the case: (1) The testimony itself lacked an adequate foundation both in evidence and in statistical theory; and (2) the testimony and the manner in which the prosecution used it distracted the jury from its proper and requisite function of weighing the evidence on the issue of guilt, encouraged the jurors to rely upon an engaging but logically irrelevant expert demonstration, foreclosed the possibility of an effective defense by an attorney apparently unschooled in mathematical refinements, and placed the jurors and defense counsel at a disadvantage in sifting relevant fact from inapplicable theory.

We initially consider the defects in the testimony itself. As we have indicated, the specific technique presented through the mathematician's testimony and advanced by the prosecutor to measure the probabilities in question suffered from two basic and pervasive defects—an inadequate evidentiary foundation and an inadequate proof of statistical independence. First, as to the foundation requirement, we find the record devoid of any evidence relating to any of the six individual probability factors used by the prosecutor and ascribed by him to the six characteristics as we have set them out in footnote 10, *ante*. To put it another way, the prosecution produced no evidence whatsoever showing, or from which it could be in any way inferred, that only one out of every ten cars which might have been at the scene of the robbery was partly yellow, that only one out of every four men who might have been there wore a mustache, that only one out of every ten girls who might have been there wore a ponytail, or that any of the other individual probability factors listed were even roughly accurate.[12]

The bare, inescapable fact is that the prosecution made no attempt to offer any such evidence. Instead, through leading questions having perfunctorily elicited from the witness the response that the latter could not assign a probability factor for the characteristics involved,[13] the prosecutor himself suggested what the various probabilities should be and these became the basis of the witness' testimony (see fn. 10, ante). It is a curious circumstance of this adventure in proof that the prosecutor not only made his own assertions of these factors in the hope that they were "conservative" but also in later argument to the jury invited the jurors to substitute their "estimates" should they wish to do so. We can hardly conceive of a more fatal gap in the prosecution's scheme of proof. A foundation for the admissibility of the witness' testimony was never even attempted to be laid, let alone established. His testimony was neither made to rest on his own testimonial knowledge nor presented by proper hypothetical questions based upon valid data in the record....

---

12. We seriously doubt that such evidence could ever be compiled since no statistician could possibly determine after the fact which cars, or which individuals, "might" have been present at the scene of the robbery; certainly there is no reason to suppose that the human and automotive populations of San Pedro, California, include all potential culprits—or, conversely, that all members of these populations are proper candidates for inclusion. Thus the sample from which the relevant probabilities would have to be derived is itself undeterminable. (See generally, Yaman, Statistics, An Introductory Analysis (1964), ch. I.)

13. The prosecutor asked the mathematics instructor: "Now, let me see if you can be of some help to us with some independent factors, and you have some paper you may use. Your specialty does not equip you, I suppose, to give us some probability of such things as a yellow car as contrasted with any other kind of car, does it? * * * I appreciate the fact that you can't assign a probability for a car being yellow as contrasted to some other car, can you? A. No, I couldn't."

But, as we have indicated, there was another glaring defect in the prosecution's technique, namely an inadequate proof of the statistical independence of the six factors. No proof was presented that the characteristics selected were mutually independent, even though the witness himself acknowledged that such condition was essential to the proper application of the "product rule" or "multiplication rule." (See Note, supra, Duke L.J. 665, 669–670, fn. 25.)[14] To the extent that the traits or characteristics were not mutually independent (e.g. Negroes with beards and men with mustaches obviously represent overlapping categories[15]), the "product rule" would inevitably yield a wholly erroneous and exaggerated result even if all of the individual components had been determined with precision. (Siegel, Nonparametric Statistics for the Behavioral Sciences (1956) 19; see generally Harmon, Modern Factor Analysis (1960).)

In the instant case, therefore, because of the aforementioned two defects — the inadequate evidentiary foundation and the inadequate proof of statistical independence — the technique employed by the prosecutor could only lead to wild conjecture without demonstrated relevancy to the issues presented. It acquired no redeeming quality from the prosecutor's statement that it was being used only "for illustrative purposes" since, as we shall point out, the prosecutor's subsequent utilization of the mathematical testimony was not confined within such limits.

We now turn to the second fundamental error caused by the probability testimony. Quite apart from our foregoing objections to the specific technique employed by the prosecution to estimate the probability in question, we think that the entire enterprise upon which the prosecution embarked, and which was directed to the objective of measuring the likelihood of a random couple possessing the characteristics allegedly distinguishing the robbers, was gravely misguided. At best, it might yield an estimate as to how infrequently bearded Negroes drive yellow cars in the company of blonde females with ponytails.

The prosecution's approach, however, could furnish the jury with absolutely no guidance on the crucial issue: *Of the admittedly few such couples, which one, if any, was guilty of committing this robbery?* Probability theory necessarily remains silent on that question, since no mathematical equation can prove beyond a reasonable doubt (1) that the guilty couple *in fact* possessed the characteristics described by the People's witnesses, or even (2) that only *one* couple possessing those distinctive characteristics could be found in the entire Los Angeles area.

As to the first inherent failing we observe that the prosecution's theory of probability rested on the assumption that the witnesses called by the People had conclusively established that the guilty couple possessed the precise characteristics relied upon by the pros-

---

14. It is there stated that: "A trait is said to be independent of a second trait when the occurrence or non-occurrence of one does not affect the probability of the occurrence of the other trait. The multiplication rule cannot be used without some degree of error where the traits are not independent." (Citing Huntsberger, Elements of Statistical Inference (1961) 77; Kingston & Kirk, The Use of Statistics in Criminalistics (1964) 55 J.Crim.L., C. & P.S. 516.) (Note, supra, Duke L.J. fn. 25, p. 670.)

15. Assuming *arguendo* that factors B and E (see fn. 10, ante), were correctly estimated, nevertheless it is still arguable that most Negro men with beards *also* have mustaches (exhibit 3 herein, for instance, shows defendant with both a mustache and a beard, indeed in a hirsute continuum); if so, there is no basis for multiplying $1/4$ by $1/10$ to estimate the proportion of Negroes who wear beards *and* mustaches. Again, the prosecution's technique could *never* be meaningfully applied, since its accurate use would call for information as to the degree of interdependence among the six individual factors. (See Yamane, op. cit. supra.) Such information cannot be compiled, however, since the relevant sample necessarily remains unknown. (See fn. 10, ante.)

ecution. But no mathematical formula could ever establish beyond a reasonable doubt that the prosecution's witnesses correctly observed and accurately described the distinctive features which were employed to link defendants to the crime. (See 2 Wigmore on Evidence (3d ed. 1940) §478.) Conceivably, for example, the guilty couple might have included a light-skinned Negress with bleached hair rather than a Caucasian blonde; or the driver of the car might have been wearing a false beard as a disguise; or the prosecution's witnesses might simply have been unreliable.[16]

The foregoing risks of error permeate the prosecution's circumstantial case. Traditionally, the jury weighs such risks in evaluating the credibility and probative value of trial testimony, but the likelihood of human error or of falsification obviously cannot be quantified; that likelihood must therefore be excluded from any effort to assign a *number* to the probability of guilt or innocence. Confronted with an equation which purports to yield a numerical index of probable guilt, few juries could resist the temptation to accord disproportionate weight to that index; only an exceptional juror, and indeed only a defense attorney schooled in mathematics, could successfully keep in mind the fact that the probability computed by the prosecution can represent, *at best*, the likelihood that a random couple would share the characteristics testified to by the People's witnesses— *not necessarily the characteristics of the actually guilty couple.*

As to the second inherent failing in the prosecution's approach, even assuming that the first failing could be discounted, the most a mathematical computation could *ever* yield would be a measure of the probability that a random couple would possess the distinctive features in question. In the present case, for example, the prosecution attempted to compute the probability that a random couple would include a bearded Negro, a blonde girl with a ponytail, and a partly yellow car; the prosecution urged that this probability was no more than one in 12 million. Even accepting this conclusion as arithmetically accurate, however, one still could not conclude that the Collinses were probably *the* guilty couple. On the contrary, as we explain in the Appendix, the prosecution's figures actually imply a likelihood of over 40 percent that the Collinses could be "duplicated" by at least *one other couple who might equally have committed the San Pedro robbery.* Urging that the Collinses be convicted on the basis of evidence which logically establishes no more than this seems as indefensible as arguing for the conviction of X on the ground that a witness saw either X or X's twin commit the crime.

Again, few defense attorneys, and certainly few jurors, could be expected to comprehend this basic flaw in the prosecution's analysis. Conceivably even the prosecutor erroneously believed that his equation established a high probability that *no* other bearded Negro in the Los Angeles area drove a yellow car accompanied by a ponytailed blonde. In any event, although his technique could demonstrate no such thing, he solemnly told the jury that he had supplied mathematical proof of guilt.

Sensing the novelty of that notion, the prosecutor told the jurors that the traditional idea of proof beyond a reasonable doubt represented "the most hackneyed, stereotyped, trite, misunderstood concept in criminal law." He sought to reconcile the jury to the risk that, under his "new math" approach to criminal jurisprudence, "on some rare occasion

---

16. In the instant case, for instance, the victim could not state whether the girl had a ponytail, although the victim observed the girl as she ran away. The witness Bass, on the other hand, was sure that the girl whom he saw had a ponytail. The demonstration engaged in by the prosecutor also leaves no room for the possibility, although perhaps a small one, that the girl whom the victim and the witness observed was, in fact, the same girl.

* * * an innocent person may be convicted." "Without taking that risk," the prosecution continued, "life would be intolerable * * * because * * * there would be immunity for the Collinses, for people who chose not to be employed to go down and push old ladies down and take their money and be immune because how could we ever be sure they are the ones who did it?"

In essence this argument of the prosecutor was calculated to persuade the jury to convict defendants whether or not they were convinced of their guilt to a moral certainty and beyond a reasonable doubt. (Pen.Code, § 1096.) Undoubtedly the jurors were unduly impressed by the mystique of the mathematical demonstration but were unable to assess its relevancy or value. Although we make no appraisal of the proper applications of mathematical techniques in the proof of facts ... we have strong feelings that such applications, particularly in a criminal case, must be critically examined in view of the substantial unfairness to a defendant which may result from ill conceived techniques with which the trier of fact is not technically equipped to cope. (See State v. Sneed, supra, 414 P.2d 858; Note, supra, Duke L.J. 665.) We feel that the technique employed in the case before us falls into the latter category.

We conclude that the court erred in admitting over defendant's objection the evidence pertaining to the mathematical theory of probability and in denying defendant's motion to strike such evidence. The case was apparently a close one. The jury began its deliberations at 2:46 p.m. on November 24, 1964, and retired for the night at 7:46 p.m.; the parties stipulated that a juror could be excused for illness and that a verdict could be reached by the remaining 11 jurors; the jury resumed deliberations the next morning at 8:40 a.m. and returned verdicts at 11:58 a.m. after five ballots had been taken. In the light of the closeness of the case, which as we have said was a circumstantial one, there is a reasonable likelihood that the result would have been more favorable to defendant if the prosecution had not urged the jury to render a probabilistic verdict. In any event, we think that under the circumstances the "trial by mathematics" so distorted the role of the jury and so disadvantaged counsel for the defense, as to constitute in itself a miscarriage of justice. After an examination of the entire cause, including the evidence, we are of the opinion that it is reasonably probable that a result more favorable to defendant would have been reached in the absence of the above error. (People v. Watson (1956) 46 Cal.2d 818, 836.) The judgment against defendant must therefore be reversed....

APPENDIX

If "Pr" represents the probability that a certain distinctive combination of characteristics, hereinafter designated "C," will occur jointly in a random couple, then the probability that C will *not* occur in a random couple is $(1 - Pr)$. Applying the product rule (see fn. 8, ante), the probability that C will occur in *none* of N couples chosen at random is $(1 - Pr)^N$, so that the probability of C occurring in *at least one* of N random couples is $[1 - (1 - Pr)^N]$.

Given a particular couple selected from a random set of N, the probability of C occurring in that couple (i.e., Pr), multiplied by the probability of C occurring in none of the remaining N-1 couples (i.e., $(1 - Pr)^{N-1}$), yields the probability that C will occur in the selected couple and in no other. Thus the probability of C occurring in any particular couple, and in that couple alone, is $[(Pr) \times (1 - Pr)^{N-1}]$. Since this is true for each of the N couples, the probability that C will occur in precisely *one* of the N couples, without regard to which one, is $[(Pr) \times (1 - Pr)^{N-1}]$ added N times, because the probability of the occurrence of one of several *mutually exclusive* events is equal to the *sum* of the individual probabilities. Thus the probability of C occurring in *exactly one* of N random couples (*any* one, but *only* one) is $[(N) \times (Pr) \times (1 - Pr)^{N-1}]$.

By subtracting the probability that C will occur in *exactly one* couple from the probability that C will occur in *at least one* couple, one obtains the probability that C will occur in *more than one* couple: $[1 - (1 - Pr)^N - [(N) \times (Pr) \times (1 - Pr)^{N-1}]$. Dividing this difference by the probability that C will occur in at least one couple (i.e., dividing the difference by $[1 - (1 - Pr)^N]$) then yields *the probability that C will occur more than once in a group of N couples in which C occurs at least once.*

Turning to the case in which C represents the characteristics which distinguish a bearded Negro accompanied by a ponytailed blonde in a yellow car, the prosecution sought to establish that the probability of C occurring in a random couple was 1/12,000,000 — i.e., that $Pr = 1/12,000,000$. Treating this conclusion as accurate, it follows that, in a population of N random couples, the probability of C occurring *exactly once* is $[(N) \times (1/12,000,000) \times (1 - 1/12,000,000)^{N-1}]$. Subtracting this product from $[1 - (1 - 1/12,000,000)^N]$, the probability of C occurring in *at least one* couple, and dividing the resulting difference by $[1 - (1 - 1/12,000,000)^N]$, the probability that C will occur in at least one couple, yields the probability that C will occur more than once in a group of N random couples of which at least one couple (namely, the one seen by the witnesses) possesses characteristics C. In other words, the probability of *another* such couple in a population of N is the quotient A/B, where A designates the numerator $[1 - (1 - 1/12,000,000)^N]$ − $[(N) \times 1/12,000,000) \times (1 - 1/12,000,000)^{N-1})$, and B designates the denominator $[1 - (1 - 1/12,000,000)^N]$.

N, which represents the total number of all couples who might conceivably have been at the scene of the San Pedro robbery, is not determinable, a fact which suggests yet another basic difficulty with the use of probability theory in establishing identity. One of the imponderables in determining N may well be the number of N-type couples in which a single person may participate. Such considerations make it evident that N, in the area adjoining the robbery, is in excess of several million; as N assumes values of such magnitude, the quotient A/B computed as above, representing the probability of a second couple as distinctive as the one described by the prosecution's witnesses, soon exceeds 4/10. Indeed, as N approaches 12 million, this probability quotient rises to approximately 41 percent. We note parenthetically that if $1/N = Pr$, then as N increases indefinitely, the quotient in question approaches a limit of $(e - 2)/(e - 1)$, where "e" represents the transcendental number (approximately 2.71828) familiar in mathematics and physics.

Hence, even if we should accept the prosecution's figures without question, we would derive a probability of over 40 percent that the couple observed by the witnesses could be "duplicated" by at least one other equally distinctive interracial couple in the area, including a Negro with a beard and mustache, driving a partly yellow car in the company of a blonde with a ponytail. Thus the prosecution's computations, far from establishing beyond a reasonable doubt that the Collinses were the couple described by the prosecution's witnesses, imply a very substantial likelihood that the area contained *more than one* such couple, and that a couple *other* than the Collinses was the one observed at the scene of the robbery. (See generally: Hoel, Introduction to Mathematical Statistics (3d ed. 1962); Hodges & Leymann, Basic Concepts of Probability and Statistics (1964); Lindgren & McElrath, Introduction to Probability and Statistics (1959).)

[The dissenting opinion of Justice McComb is omitted.]

The culprit had big eyes, big ears, and big teeth. Statistically, the chance of it being anyone other than the defendant is only one in 12 million.

United States v. Chischilly
30 F.3d 1144 (9th Cir. 1994)

CHOY, Circuit Judge:

On July 2, 1992, appellant Daniel Chischilly ("Chischilly") was convicted by a jury in the United States District Court for the District of Arizona of aggravated sexual abuse and murder in violation of 18 U.S.C. §§ 1111, 1153 and 2241(b)(1). Chischilly appeals, challenging ... the admission of testimony relating to Chischilly's DNA test results....

BACKGROUND

....

Following completion of the competency hearing, Chischilly learned from the Government that FBI tests had established a match between his blood sample and semen found on the victim's clothing. Chischilly filed a motion in limine ... to examine the admissibility of this identification evidence.... [T]he district court denied Chischilly's motion in limine....

According to the testimony of Government witnesses, DNA analysis conducted by the FBI later indicated a match between a sample of Chischilly's blood and sperm found on the victim. A Government expert witness, Dr. Chakraborty, further testified that one in 2563 would be a "conservative estimate" of the probability of a similar match between the DNA of a randomly selected American Indian and either the evidentiary sample or the defendant's DNA....

DISCUSSION

IV. Admission of DNA Test Results

[The Court first addressed the defendant's objection under Rule 702, which is discussed in Chapter 4.]

Of particular concern is where the Government seeks to present probability testimony derived from statistical analysis, the third main phase of DNA profiling. Numerous hazards attend the courtroom presentation of statistical evidence of any sort.[17] Accordingly, Rule 403 requires judicial vigilance against the risk that such evidence will inordinately distract the jury from or skew its perception of other, potentially exculpatory evidence lacking not so much probative force as scientific gloss.

With regard to DNA evidence, there are two general tendencies that should be guarded against: (1) that the jury will accept the DNA evidence as a statement of source probability (i.e., the likelihood that the defendant is the source of the evidentiary sample); and (2) that once the jury settles on a source probability, even if correctly, it will equate source with guilt, ignoring the possibility of non-criminal reasons for the evidentiary link between the defendant and the victim. As to the second concern, there is little chance in this case that the jury could have mistakenly equated source probability with guilt because it is clear that the evidentiary sample was criminally linked with the victim. The presence of sperm in the circumstances of this case undermined Chischilly's claim of innocence, as well as any hapless bystander or good samaritan defense, by clearly establishing a causal, and not merely a casual, link between the crime and the evidentiary sample.[20]

The first concern is somewhat more complex. The FBI matching statistic does not represent source probability. Rather, the test results reflect the statistical probability that a match would occur between a randomly selected member of the database group and either the evidentiary sample or the defendant. To illustrate, suppose the FBI's evidence establishes that there is a one in 10,000 chance of a random match. The jury might equate this likelihood with source probability by believing that there is a one in 10,000 chance that the evidentiary sample did not come from the defendant. This equation of random match probability with source probability is known as the prosecutor's fallacy.

There is also a corresponding defense fallacy. Suppose there were 10,000,000 members of the group represented in the database used. The defense may claim that there is then only a one in 1,000 (10,000/10,000,000) chance that the evidentiary sample came from the defendant because 1,000 matches would occur if the entire population were tested. This claim resembles the prosecutor's fallacy in making an illogical leap, but differs in *understating* the tendency of a reported match to strengthen source probability and narrow the group of potential suspects. Lying somewhere between the two, the real source probability will reflect the relative strength of circumstantial evidence connecting the defendant and other persons with matching DNA to the scene of the crime.

---

17. For a similar instance outside the context of DNA profiling, see *People v. Collins*, 438 P.2d 33 (1968) (rejecting assumptions about the statistical probability of a couple other than the defendants having committed the crime being 1 in 12 million where several of the probabilities multiplied together, including hair and eye color, were obviously interdependent).

20. We recognize that sperm found inside the victim could also be consistent with recent consensual sexual activity as well as sexual assault. However, the jury could reasonably have concluded that the additional presence of sperm on Ms. Tso's recently removed bra and the forcefully disheveled state in which she was found substantially ruled out the former possibility.

Often acute even for Caucasian suspects, these pitfalls become more perilous where the defendant is a member of a substructured population, such as Navajo Indians. Under-representation of persons of like ethnicity in the profile data bases and questionable assumptions of allelic independence[24] may inflate the odds against a random match with the defendant's sample. In such a situation the jury may be ill-suited to discount properly the probative value of DNA profiling statistics.

Geographic factors may further increase the potential of prejudice from the FBI's database selection. Although "the fact that certain alleles occur more frequently in the Navajos than they do in European and West African populations is of little consequence for a crime committed in Boston, where few Navajos reside," this fact is of considerable consequence for a crime committed on a reservation in Arizona, where many Navajos make their home. In such instances, the troubling possibility arises with singular force that the product rule, founded on the questionable premise of allelic independence at different test sites, will understate the random probability that some other nearby resident with a similar genetic profile could have been the source of the sample found on the victim.

On the other side of the Rule 403 ledger, statistical evidence derived from sample processing and match analysis, properly documented and performed in compliance with established, peer-reviewed laboratory protocols, is certainly probative of the defendant's guilt or innocence. Where the district court provides careful oversight, the potential prejudice of the DNA evidence can be reduced to the point where this probative value outweighs it.

In this case, the district court provided such oversight, the prosecution was careful to frame the evidence properly and the defense was adequately equipped to contest its validity. Confronted with an unusually informed, capable and zealous challenge from the defense, the Government was careful to frame the DNA profiling statistics presented at trial as the probability of a random match, not the probability of the defendant's innocence that is the crux of the prosecutor's fallacy. . . .

In sum, we conclude that the district court did not abuse its discretion in admitting the DNA evidence in this case.... [T]he potential prejudicial effect in this case did not outweigh the probative value of the evidence under Rule 403....

[The dissenting opinion of Judge Noonan is omitted.]

Notes and Questions

1. What are the problems with the evidence presented in *Collins*? Are they problems of relevance, Rule 403 risks, sufficiency of the evidence to support a verdict, or some combination of all of these? Assuming that the prosecution could provide accurate values for each of the six factors and that the factors were statistically independent, would the evidence be relevant? Would it be admissible? Would it be sufficient, standing alone, to support a conviction? Would the other evidence presented in the case, standing alone, be sufficient to support a conviction? Even if the prosecution could solve some of the methodological problems, wouldn't the statistical evidence only be conditionally relevant? On what would its relevancy be conditioned (in this regard, consider why it is that the prosecution chose the factors that it did)?

---

24. "Allelic independence" refers to the absence of correlation between the inheritance of an allele controlling one genetic characteristic, such as eye color, with the inheritance of other alleles governing other traits and occurring at other loci.

2. In what ways is the DNA evidence at issue in *Chischilly* similar to the evidence at issue in *Collins*? In what ways do they differ? What explains the differing outcomes in the two cases?

3. Why might DNA evidence take on an aura of infallibility in a way that other evidence might not? Consider the following:

> We are also cognizant of the likelihood that DNA evidence may confuse or over-whelm the jury. The differences between DNA profiling and traditional modes of forensic analysis substantially increase this likelihood. Fingerprint, foot print, handwriting, and bite mark evidence, for example, are easily comprehensible to the jury because they are taken from everyday life. The least experienced juror has observed a fingerprint, footprint, or bite mark, on many different occasions long before he or she enters the courtroom. And the fact that handwriting tends to vary from person to person is evident from grade school. DNA profiling evidence, on the other hand, is totally alien to most jurors. The specter of bands on an autorad is no more familiar to the average juror than the innermost workings of the stealth bomber.

> Also, unlike voice, handwriting, footprint, fingerprint or bite mark evidence, neither the DNA evidence nor the faceless laboratory technicians who performed the critical laboratory tests and procedures are present in the courtroom for independent credibility evaluation by the jury. DNA evidence is invisible to the naked eye, so bringing the used agarose gel to court would be pointless. In the words of one appellate court, DNA evidence, "unlike that presented with fingerprint, footprint or bite mark evidence, is highly technical, incapable of observation, and requires the jury to either accept or reject the scientist's conclusions that it can be done." The juror's almost complete dependence on the testimony of the expert and her inability to independently evaluate the accuracy of the DNA profiling results thus weighs against admissibility.

Government of Virgin Islands v. Byers, 941 F. Supp. 513, 527 (D.V.I. 1996).

4. Is there really a difference between formal probabilistic evidence and other forms of evidence, such as eyewitness testimony of what occurred? Consider the following:

> "All evidence is probabilistic—statistical evidence merely explicitly so," because nothing with which the law deals is metaphysically certain. Statistical evidence is merely probabilistic evidence coded in numbers rather than words. "Nothing about the nature of litigation in general, or the criminal process in particular, makes anathema of additional information, whether or not that knowledge has numbers attached. After all, even eyewitnesses are testifying only to probabilities (though they obscure the methods by which they generate those probabilities)—often rather lower probabilities than statistical work insists on." An eyewitness does not usurp the jury's function if he testifies that he is *positive* that he saw the defendant strike a match, and it would make no difference if he said that he is "99 percent" positive.

United States v. Veysey, 334 F.3d 600, 605–06 (7th Cir. 2003).

5. Is it possible that the preference for evidence that does not come with probabilities attached to it is due to a desire to mask the inherent uncertainty in determining guilt or innocence? *See* Charles R. Nesson, *Reasonable Doubt and Permissive Inferences: The Value of Complexity*, 92 Harv. L. Rev. 1187, 1198–1199 (1979) (so arguing).

6. The Supreme Court has described the requirement in criminal cases of proof of each element beyond a reasonable doubt as only a finding of *probable* guilt:

[T]he beyond a reasonable doubt standard is itself probabilistic. "[I]n a judicial proceeding in which there is a dispute about the facts of some earlier event, the factfinder cannot acquire unassailably accurate knowledge of what happened. Instead, all the factfinder can acquire is a belief of what *probably* happened." *In re Winship*, 397 U.S., at 370 (Harlan, J., concurring).

Victor v. Nebraska, 511 U.S. 1, 14 (1994).

7. Although no quantifiable degree of certainty is attached to the beyond a reasonable doubt standard in criminal cases, *see United States v. Hall*, 854 F.2d 1036, 1043–45 (7th Cir. 1988) (Posner, J., concurring), the typical standard in civil cases—a preponderance of the evidence—is readily quantifiable: anything more than 50 percent certainty suffices. Does this mean that statistical evidence tending to show that a defendant in a civil case is liable should be sufficient, standing alone, to support a verdict? Consider the following:

> Judges, and commentators on the law of evidence, have been troubled by cases in which the plaintiff has established a probability that only minutely exceeds 50 percent that his version of what happened is correct. The concern is illuminated by the much-discussed bus hypothetical. Suppose that the plaintiff is hit by a bus, and it is known that 51 percent of the buses on the road where the plaintiff was hit are owned by Bus Company A and 49 percent by Company B. The plaintiff sues A and asks for judgment on the basis of this statistic alone (we can ignore the other elements of liability besides causation by assuming they have all been satisfied, as in this case); he tenders no other evidence. If the defendant also puts in no evidence, should a jury be allowed to award judgment to the plaintiff? The law's answer is "no." Our hypothetical case is a variant of *Smith v. Rapid Transit*, 317 Mass. 469, 58 N.E.2d 754 (1945), where the court held that it "was not enough" "that perhaps the mathematical chances somewhat favor the proposition that a bus of the defendant caused the accident." *Id.* at 755. *Kaminsky v. Hertz Corp.*, 94 Mich.App. 356, 288 N.W.2d 426 (1979), is sometimes cited as being contrary to *Smith*, but this is not an accurate reading. Besides the fact that the corresponding percentages were 90 percent and 10 percent, there was nonstatistical evidence pointing to the defendant's ownership of the truck that had caused the accident.
>
> *Smith* and *Kaminsky* involve explicitly probabilistic evidence. But as all evidence is probabilistic in the sense of lacking absolute certainty, all evidence can be expressed in probabilistic terms, and so the problem or dilemma presented by those cases is general. The eyewitness might say that he was "99 percent sure" that he had seen the defendant, and jurors appraising his testimony might reckon some different probability that he was correct. What powers the intuition that the plaintiff should lose the bus case is not the explicitly probabilistic nature of the evidence, but the evidentiary significance of missing evidence. If the 51/49 statistic is the plaintiff's only evidence, and he does not show that it was infeasible for him to obtain any additional evidence, the inference to be drawn is not that there is a 51 percent probability that it was a bus owned by A that hit the plaintiff. It is that the plaintiff either investigated and discovered that the bus was actually owned by B (and B might not have been negligent and so not liable even if a cause of the accident, or might be judgment-proof and so not worth suing), or that he simply has not bothered to conduct an investigation. If the first alternative is true, he should of course lose; and since it *may* be true, the probability that the plaintiff was hit by a bus owned by A is *less* than 51 percent and

the plaintiff has failed to carry his burden of proof. If the second alternative is true—the plaintiff just hasn't conducted an investigation—he still should lose. A court shouldn't be required to expend its scarce resources of time and effort on a case until the plaintiff has conducted a sufficient investigation to make reasonably clear that an expenditure of public resources is likely to yield a significant social benefit. This principle is implicit in the law's decision to place the burden of producing evidence on the plaintiff rather than on the defendant. Suppose it would cost the court system $10,000 to try even a barebones case. This expenditure would be worthless from the standpoint of deterring accidents should it turn out that the bus was owned by B. It makes sense for the court to require some advance investigation by the plaintiff in order to increase the probability that a commitment of judicial resources would be worthwhile.

Howard v. Wal-Mart Stores, Inc., 160 F.3d 358, 359–60 (7th Cir. 1998).

Note that such statistical evidence, although insufficient to determine culpability, can be used to apportion damages among defendants who have been shown to be culpable:

But if both bus companies had been determined to be negligent, so that the only issue was which had hit the plaintiff, then in many states the 51/49 ratio of A's to B's buses would be enough for a judgment against A—indeed against A and B.

United States v. Veysey, 334 F.3d 600, 605 (7th Cir. 2003).

Chapter 2

Authentication

A. Introduction

In everyday life, most people have a tendency to take things at face value. If one receives a letter that is signed "Maria Robertson," one assumes that the letter *is* from Maria Robertson. If one receives a phone call from someone who identifies himself as "Robert Brandt," one assumes that the person calling *is* Robert Brandt. If one is shown a photograph that depicts William Jones standing in the lobby of a particular bank, one assumes that William Jones *was* in the lobby of that bank at a particular point in time.

Yet given the high stakes involved in most criminal and civil trials, the rules of evidence can ill afford such complacency and refuse to take things at face value. Thus, a fundamental prerequisite to the admission of all forms of physical evidence, including writings, recordings, photographs and objects, and for some forms of testimonial evidence, is that the evidence be authenticated or identified (or in the common parlance of lawyers and judges, that one "lay the foundation" for admitting the evidence).

In this regard, the rules greet every piece of evidence with a skeptical eye. They thus ask, how do we *know* that Maria Robertson wrote this letter? How do we *know* that the person who called was really Robert Brandt? How do we *know* that William Jones was in fact in the bank lobby?

The standard for authenticating evidence is set forth in Rule 901(a), which provides that "[t]o satisfy the requirement of authenticating or identifying an item of evidence, the proponent must produce evidence sufficient to support a finding that the item is what the proponent claims it is." It is followed in Rule 901(b) by a list of ten specific methods of authenticating evidence that the rule stresses "are examples only — not a complete list — of evidence that satisfies the requirement" set forth in Rule 901(a). This in turn is followed in Rule 902 by a list of twelve types of evidence for which the rules let their guard down and take at face value, deeming them to be "self-authenticating."

Note that Rule 901(a) is not actually the *source* of the authentication requirement, but rather assumes the existence of such a requirement and proceeds to explain how that requirement can be satisfied. What, then, is the source of the requirement? Moreover, whose role is it to determine the authenticity of an item of evidence: the judge, the jury, or both? If both are to play a role, what if they disagree?

The following case addresses these threshold questions. It is then followed by a series of cases and problems that consider the application of the authentication requirement to various types of evidence.

Ricketts v. City of Hartford
74 F.3d 1397 (2d Cir. 1996)

MAHONEY, Circuit Judge:

Plaintiff-appellant Weldon L. Ricketts appeals from a judgment entered October 15, 1993 in the United States District Court for the District of Connecticut, Alfred V. Covello, *Judge,* that dismissed Ricketts' complaint charging numerous deprivations of his constitutional rights in violation of 42 U.S.C. § 1983, and from an order entered April 6, 1994 that denied Ricketts' motion for a new trial. . . .

On August 12, 1987, numerous police officers (nearly all white, except for one Hispanic and one black) were engaged in a lengthy chase of Timothy Moore, a black man suspected of an assault and attempted robbery, through the streets of Hartford, Connecticut. The chase passed through a soccer field, where Ricketts, also black, coached a soccer team of black youths. Just after passing through the soccer field, the police caught up with Moore and attempted to subdue him. After a series of events, described entirely differently by each side to this litigation, both Moore and Ricketts were arrested. . . .

Ricketts, who claimed that he believed that the officers were trying to kill Moore, moved towards the officers and asked them why they were beating Moore. . . .

Either just as Ricketts arrived, or after an exchange with the officers, or after Ricketts was told or threatened repeatedly not to interfere with Moore's arrest, several officers turned upon Ricketts and wrestled him to the ground. . . .

Ricketts claimed that when he approached the officers and asked them why they were beating Moore, one officer, Davis, grabbed Ricketts across his neck from behind with a baton, preventing him from breathing. . . .

The tape recording of the officers' radio transmissions reveals that someone said: "Run him over." Ricketts contends that the voice belonged to Davis (the tape also reveals that the police dispatcher said "[d]on't give up, Rob," which is Davis' nickname), but Davis denied saying this, or even hearing it at the time of the chase. . . .

After Davis testified, Ricketts sought to introduce the tape recording of the police officers and police dispatcher that contains the statement (apparently referring to Moore): "Run him over." Ricketts claims that Davis made this statement, and shortly thereafter became the chief aggressor against Ricketts. After listening to the tape in camera, the district court excluded it from evidence, ruling that Ricketts had failed to authenticate that Davis was the unidentified officer. . . .

Specifically, the court stated: "The court heard Davis testify extensively. After listening to the tape the court was not satisfied that the voice on the tape was that of Davis."

Three provisions of the Federal Rules of Evidence are implicated. [The court proceeds to quote the full text of Federal Rules 901(a), 104(a), and 104(b).]

Finally, an advisory committee note to Rule 901 states that: "Authentication and identification represent a special aspect of relevancy. . . . This requirement of showing authenticity or identity falls in the category of relevancy dependent upon fulfillment of a condition of fact and is governed by the procedure set forth in Rule 104(b)."

We explained the interaction of these rules in *United States v. Sliker,* 751 F.2d 477, 496–500 (2d Cir. 1984). . . . In determining that the question of authentication was primarily for the jury to determine, we undertook an examination of the relevant rules:

[S]ubsection (a) [of Fed.R.Evid. 104] governs questions concerning the competency of evidence, i.e., evidence which is relevant but may be subject to exclusion by virtue of some principle of the law of evidence, leaving it for the judge to resolve factual issues in connection with these principles.... Removing factual issues related to determining whether evidence is competent from the jury is based on recognition that the typical juror is intent mainly on reaching a verdict in accord with what he believes to be true in the case he is called upon to decide, and is not concerned with the long term policies of evidence law.

Subsection (b) provides different treatment for situations in which the *relevancy* (i.e., probative value) of evidence, rather than its *competency,* depends upon the existence of a prior fact....

The requirement that a given piece of evidence be what its proponent claims does not reflect some special evidentiary policy like hearsay rules or privileges.... Authentication is perhaps the purest example of a rule respecting relevance: evidence admitted as something can have *no* probative value unless that is what it really is. *Cf.* Notes of Advisory Committee to Rule 901(a). Thus, the Notes of the Advisory Committee accompanying Rule 901 state that questions concerning authentication are governed by the procedures in Rule 104(b).

Under Rule 104(b), the trial judge may make a preliminary determination as to the prior fact and admit the evidence....

The judge's preliminary determination does not, however, finally establish the authenticity of the tape. As with other matters under Rule 104(b), only the jury can finally decide that issue....

F.R.E. 901(a) requires "evidence sufficient to support a finding that the [item] is what [the] proponent claims," but does not definitively establish the nature or quantum of proof that is required. Subsection (b) provides illustrations of what will suffice. Subsection (b)(5)*[deals] specifically with the question of voice identification.... [The defendant] argues that the opinion referred to [in subsection (b)(5)] must be that of a witness and not that of the trier of the fact, and the Notes of the Advisory Committee suggest that this is so, as does Judge Weinstein, 5 [Jack B. Weinstein and Margaret A. Berger,] Weinstein's Evidence, ¶¶ 901(b)(5)[01], [02] [(1982)]. However, subsection (b)(5) is only an illustration and several of the other illustrations do not require opinion testimony and leave it to the jury to make its own comparison.... We thus see no reason in principle why, in a case like this, where the person whose voice on a tape [that] is to be identified has testified, the jury cannot itself make the comparison....

Sliker, 751 F.2d at 498–500....

While *Sliker* did not entirely remove a judge's ability to exclude a tape on authentication grounds, the judge's discretion to do so is limited to a determination whether "'sufficient proof has been introduced so that a reasonable juror could find in favor of authenticity or identification.'"....

---

* Editor's Note: Rule 901(b)(5) provides as follows: "*Opinion About a Voice.* An opinion identifying a person's voice—whether heard firsthand or through mechanical or electronic transmission or recording—based on hearing the voice at any time under circumstances that connect it with the alleged speaker."

The district court's determination that it "was not satisfied that the voice on the tape was that of Davis" is inconsistent with these principles. So long as a jury is entitled to reach a contrary conclusion, it must be given the opportunity to do so.... Although we do not have the benefit of having heard Davis testify, given ... that the jury did hear him testify, we believe that the district court erred in excluding the tape on authentication grounds without making a finding that no rational juror could have concluded that Davis made the statement at issue....

[The opinion of Judge Godbold, concurring in part and dissenting in part, is omitted.]

Notes and Questions

1. Rule 901 as interpreted in *Ricketts* and countless other cases like it significantly constrains the judge's role in the authentication process. For what purpose is the judge's role in this regard so narrowly constrained? Moreover, given how low the standard is set for getting the issue of authenticity past the judge and to the jury, why bother to have the judge play *any* role? If proof of authenticity of an item of evidence is so weak or unbelievable that "no rational juror" would believe in its authenticity, won't the jury disregard the evidence anyway? If not, what does that say about the rationality of jurors?

2. How different would the voice on the tape have to be from that of the defendant's live testimony for a court to conclude that "no rational juror" could find that the two voices were one in the same? Is it enough that the voice on the tape is a high-pitched female voice, while the defendant's voice is a low-pitched male voice? Or could a rational juror find the two voices to be one in the same even in that instance?

3. Note the *Sliker* court's unwillingness to be constrained by the specific text of the illustrations set forth in Rule 901(b), reasoning that although Rule 901(b)(5) appears to contemplate opinion testimony by a *witness* who has heard the alleged speaker's voice at some other point in time, comparison by the *jury* is an acceptable alternative. In one sense, this is consistent with the Advisory Committee's Note to that rule, which states that "[t]he examples are not intended as an exclusive enumeration of allowable methods but are meant to guide and suggest, leaving room for growth and development in this area of the law." Does this mean that the illustrations place *no* constraints on judicial creativity in this regard? For example, could a judge deem the requirement of authenticity satisfied by a document that otherwise fits Rule 901(b)(8) but is nineteen years old? Sixteen years old? If the illustrations do impose some constraints, what are those constraints?

4. Suppose that there were no tape recording of the statements made in *Ricketts*, but only testimony by a bystander who was present and heard "someone" make the alleged statement. Could such a bystander serve as an authenticating witness even if she was not familiar with Davis's voice at the time the statement was made?

> For voice identifications, Rule 901(b)(5) requires only the "hearing [of] the voice at any time under circumstances [that] connect[] it with the alleged speaker." Rule 901 was satisfied in this case. The government established that Duran had both tellers' undivided attention during the robbery while Duran shouted many commands, demanded money, and threatened the occupants of the bank. Both tellers also had the opportunity during Duran's first trial to hear Duran speak. Both tellers testified, based on their observations of Duran's unusual voice and accent, that his was the voice of the robber. Accordingly, we conclude that the district court did not abuse its discretion because a sufficient foundation supported the admission of the tellers' voice identifications of Duran.

United States v. Duran, 4 F.3d 800, 802 (9th Cir. 1993). *But see United States v. Jones*, 600 F.3d 847, 858 (7th Cir. 2010) ("Courts should examine what actually transpired at the court proceeding in question to ensure that the defendant actually spoke enough to give a listener minimal familiarity with his or her voice. There may well be situations in which a defendant said so little that a listener could not claim the minimal familiarity our case law requires; and in such a situation, a court would be justified in finding that the voice identification was not admissible.")

Of course, in this situation, as with most situations involving testimony by a witness that an unrecorded voice that they heard was that of a particular person, the jury has no ability to compare the voices. What, then, is the finding that the jury is to make, and in turn, what is the preliminary finding that the trial court must make?

5. A judge's determination that an item of evidence has satisfied Rule 901 means only that the trier of fact will be permitted to consider the evidence (assuming it is not subject to exclusion under some other rule of evidence); it does not prevent a party from raising questions about its authenticity before the trier of fact. *See, e.g., United States v. Tin Yat Chin*, 371 F.3d 31, 38 (2d Cir. 2004) ("Once Rule 901's requirements are satisfied, 'the evidence's persuasive force is left to the jury.'... the other party then remains free to challenge the reliability of the evidence, to minimize its importance, or to argue alternative interpretations of its meaning, but these and similar other challenges go to the *weight* of the evidence—not to its *admissibility*.").

6. Assuming that the voice on the tape *is* that of Davis, why does that matter in this case? Note that on the tape, Davis is allegedly talking about running over Moore, not Ricketts, and it is Ricketts, not Moore, who is the plaintiff in this case. Does Davis thus have another potential objection to the admission of the tape? Does Ricketts have a good response?

B. Authentication of Physical Objects

Problem 2-1: Coke and Guns

During a raid on Martin's apartment pursuant to a search warrant, police officers Torres and Smith seized a number of plastic bags containing a white, powdery substance and a semi-automatic gun that Martin had on his person. Upon seizing the gun, Officer Smith noticed that the serial number on it had been scratched off and noticed another set of scratches on one side of the gun that appeared to be a "figure 8" pattern. After Martin was arrested, Officer Torres delivered both the gun and the plastic bags to an evidence locker at the police station. Officer Richardson later checked out the items and delivered them to the state crime laboratory for ballistics and chemical testing, and after the testing was completed, Officer Peters delivered them back to the evidence locker.

Martin was indicted on charges of possessing cocaine with intent to distribute and with unlawful possession of a firearm. At trial, the government sought to offer both the plastic bags and the gun into evidence. The defense objected, contended that the evidence was not admissible because the government had not introduced any evidence to prove that these were the items seized from Martin's apartment.

*How should the court rule? If the defense is correct, what must the government
do to overcome the objection?*

United States v. Cardenas
864 F.2d 1528 (10th Cir. 1989)

BRORBY, Circuit Judge....

On July 9, 1987, Martin Cardenas and Julian Rivera-Chacon were arrested in the underground parking lot in the area of the (then) Regent Hotel located in Albuquerque, New Mexico. Lawrence Villas also was arrested and indicted along with Rivera-Chacon and Cardenas....

Officers Montoya, Gunter and Garcia of the Bernalillo Police Department, Officer Mares of the Socorro County Sheriff's Office, and Special Agent Ortiz of the United States Bureau of Alcohol, Firearms and Tobacco, were all present. Lieutenant Lundy, searching Rivera-Chacon, found a gun hidden in his boot. Officer Garcia, conducting a full inventory search of Cardenas' truck, discovered a .25 caliber handgun behind a potato chip bag in an open dashboard compartment on the driver's side of the car; the open compartment was inches from the steering wheel, within an effortless reach of Cardenas. Under the front seat, Garcia found a brown paper bag containing a plastic sack with a white substance inside. Garcia handed the brown paper bag containing the plastic sack, and the .25 caliber handgun to Officer Gunter. From this moment, Officer Gunter had sole physical custody of this evidence.

Officer Mares testified that Gunter showed him a plastic sack containing a white substance. Mares was too busy to inspect the substance. He testified that he did not see a brown paper bag, nor did he see Garcia give the substance to Gunter. In addition, at trial Officer Mares could not absolutely identify the plastic sack containing the white substance as the plastic sack that Gunter displayed at the scene; however, he did state that the plastic sack exhibited at trial in every respect resembled the sack displayed to him at the arrest. No field test was performed on the substance. Officer Garcia accompanied Gunter to the station with the seized evidence. At the station, Mares assisted Gunter in tagging the evidence. Gunter then, unobserved, carried the *sealed* evidence bags to the evidence room on the third floor of the station. The evidence technician testified that no brown paper bag was submitted to her; that she is obligated to accept any evidence given her; and that ultimately the police officers decide what is evidence and what is not.

Since Officer Gunter committed suicide one month prior to the trial, he was not available to testify.

I.

Defendant alleges that the plastic sack containing cocaine was improperly admitted into evidence on [the ground that] the government failed to provide a sufficient chain of custody....

Controlling the admission or exclusion of real evidence at trial[is] Fed.R.Evid. Rule 901(a)....

The condition precedent to the admission of real evidence is met by providing the proper foundation. If the proffered evidence is unique, readily identifiable and relatively resistant to change, the foundation need only consist of testimony that the evidence is what its proponent claims. However, when the evidence, as here, is not readily identifiable and is susceptible to alteration by tampering or contamination, the trial court requires a more stringent foundation "entailing a 'chain of custody' of the item with *sufficient completeness* to render it *improbable* that the original item has either been exchanged with another or been contaminated or tampered with."

.... Before admitting or excluding real evidence, the trial court must consider the nature of the evidence, and the surrounding circumstances, including presentation, custody and probability of tampering or alteration. If, after considering these factors, the trial court determines that the evidence is substantially in the same condition as when the crime was committed, the court may admit it.

The cocaine, not uniquely identifiable, requires a sufficient chain of custody to support its admission. However, the chain of custody need not be perfect for the evidence to be admissible. The well-established rule in this circuit is that deficiencies in the chain of custody go to the weight of the evidence, not its admissibility; once admitted, the jury evaluates the defects and, based on its evaluation, may accept or disregard the evidence.

On appeal, defendant alleges that there was an insufficient chain of custody to support the trial court's admission of the cocaine since Officer Gunter, who had custody of it from the time of its initial seizure until he delivered it to the evidence room, was unavailable to testify. Based on this, defendant contends that the cocaine should not have been admitted since there was a "substantial break in the chain."

From the moment Officer Garcia seized the cocaine from Cardenas' truck, its whereabouts were accounted for. Testimony at trial by Officers Garcia and Mares shows that there was no substantial break in the chain. Upon seizing the cocaine, Officer Garcia handed it to Officer Gunter who, in turn, displayed it to Officer Mares. Admittedly Officer Mares could not absolutely identify the plastic sack containing white powder offered at trial as that seized from the truck. However, given that the plastic sack was not uniquely identifiable and considering his testimony that the evidence at trial in every respect resembled the evidence seized from the truck, the lack of absolute identification does not amount to an insufficient chain of custody. *See United States v. Brewer*, 630 F.2d 795, 802 (10th Cir. 1980) (lack of positive identification went to weight of evidence). After the arrests, Officers Garcia and Gunter drove directly to the police station where Gunter, in the presence of Mares, tagged and sealed the evidence. Officer Gunter then walked up three flights to the evidence room, delivered the evidence, tagged and sealed, to the evidence technician who secured it for testing. This was the only moment Officer Gunter was alone with the evidence; however, considering the brevity of time, the fact that the evidence was already tagged and sealed, and defendant's lack of any evidence of tampering or alteration at this point in the chain of custody, we do not consider it a substantial break resulting in alteration. The trial court need not rule out *every* possibility that the evidence underwent alteration; it need only find that the reasonable probability is that the evidence has not been altered in any material aspect.

The fact that Officer Gunter was not available to testify is not determinative of the admissibility of the cocaine since the whereabouts of the cocaine was accounted for from its original seizure from Cardenas' truck until it was offered as evidence at trial. There is no rule that the prosecution must produce *all* persons who had custody of the evidence to testify at trial. Defendant's allegation as to the insufficiency of the chain of custody is unpersuasive....

United States v. Abreu
952 F.2d 1458 (1st Cir. 1992)

BOWNES, Senior Circuit Judge....

Count XIV charged defendant with possession of one Boito double barrel 12 gauge shotgun, serial number 145266, having a barrel approximately 12¾ inches in length and an overall length of approximately 22 inches. Defendant was charged with failure to register the shotgun in the National Firearms Registration and Transfer Record, a violation under 26 U.S.C. §§ 5861(d) and 5871 and 18 U.S.C. § 2....

[Defendant] claims that the admission of the shotgun into evidence was erroneous because of foundation problems and in particular because of gaps in the chain of custody....

In determining whether the evidence is admissible [under Rule 901(a)], the trial court "must conclude that it was reasonably probable that the evidence had not been altered since the occurrence of the crime."

The evidence in question is properly admitted if it is readily identifiable by a unique feature or other identifying mark. On the other hand, if the offered evidence is of the type that is not readily identifiable or is susceptible to alteration, a testimonial tracing of the chain of custody is necessary. The purpose of testimonial tracing is to render it improbable that the original item either has been exchanged with another or has been tampered with or contaminated....

Even though there may be gaps in the chain of custody for a certain piece of evidence, such gaps factor into the weight given to the evidence rather than its admissibility....

The shotgun was seized by BATF Special Agent Brian Glynn (Glynn) during the raid of the Third Avenue apartment. During trial, he was able to identify the shotgun as the same one he seized by identifying the evidence tag which was placed on the gun at the time of its seizure and by his signature which appeared on the tag. Agent Glynn, however, inaccurately described the firearm as an "S.S. Christy" shotgun. The gun was an S.S. Kresge shotgun. He was unable to locate a serial number on the shotgun or the evidence tag. He did state, however, that the shotgun was in substantially the same condition as when he seized it.

Special Agent David Sherman of the Providence office of the BATF was involved in the investigation of the defendant's organization. After defendant's arrest and the seizure of the drugs, drug paraphernalia and firearms, Sherman measured the seized shotgun, in his Providence office. Sherman testified that the shotgun was in substantially the same condition as when he measured it and identified it as a "Boito, 12-gauge shotgun, made for S.S. Kresge Company, serial number 145266." He also testified that just prior to his measurement, it had been kept in the evidence vault. He further stated that he checked the registration of the shotgun with the Firearms Registration and Transfer record at the BATF and found that it was unregistered. During his testimony, Detective Walter Williams of the Bureau of Criminal Identification of the Providence Police Department also identified the shotgun by its model and serial number.

Defendant argues that the discrepancy in Agent Glynn's named description of the gun indicated a lost gun or missing link in the chain of custody. A foundation for the identification of the gun had, however, already been laid by Agent Glynn's identification of the evidence tag which he placed on the gun. The error in Glynn's testimony was mitigated by Agent Sherman's and Detective Williams' clear identification of the gun and testimonial tracing of the chain of custody from the seizure to trial. We also note that "Christy" and "Kresge" sound alike.

The admission of the shotgun satisfied Federal Rule of Evidence 901(a). There was no abuse of discretion, and we will not disturb the trial court's ruling on this issue.

Defendant was free to argue to the jury that they could accord less weight to the shotgun because Glynn incorrectly named the gun. This, however, is a different issue than admissibility of evidence. It is the province of the jury to decide the appropriate weight to give to specific evidence....

Notes and Questions

1. What distinguishes evidence for which a showing of the chain of custody is necessary from evidence for which no such showing is necessary?

2. When evidence of a chain of custody from seizure to trial is necessary, what justifies allowing for *any* break in the chain of custody? If every person in the chain of custody testifies, the jury has the ability to assess their credibility and to take that into account in deciding whether to believe that the evidence is really what the proponent purports it to be, to wit, evidence seized from the defendant. But suppose that in *Cardenas*, Officer Gunter swapped the plastic sack seized from the defendants with another plastic sack. If he does not testify before the jury, how is the jury to assess his credibility, and in turn, whether the evidence is what the government purports it to be? *See, e.g., United States v. King*, 356 F.3d 774, 779 (7th Cir. 2004) ("Without any evidence of tampering or other interference, there is a presumption of regularity when evidence is within official custody."). *Accord United States v. Rawlins*, 606 F.3d 73, 85 (3rd Cir. 2010). The evidentiary effect of presumptions is discussed in Chapter 9.

3. Recall that the jury remains free to take breaks in the chain of custody into account in weighing the evidence. How are jurors likely to react to such breaks in the chain? Do you suppose that defense counsel will raise the issue before the jury? Are these sufficient incentives for the government to maintain and produce evidence of a complete chain of custody?

C. Authentication of Written Documents

Problem 2-2: The Threatening Note

David Burns is on trial on charges related to threats he allegedly made to Lisa Golden. At trial, the government seeks to offer into evidence a handwritten note that Lisa received. The note reads, "If you value your life, you will put your rare coins and diamond brooch in the trash bin at the end of your driveway tonight."

Although the people from whom Lisa bought the rare coins and the diamond brooch are aware of the fact that she is in possession of those items, she bought the coins and the diamond brooch from two different people, and according to her, the only persons to whom she has disclosed these joint purchases are her mother and David. In addition, the note did not have a clean tear on the top, and a notepad found in David's house has a remnant of a page that appears to be a match for the tear at the top of the note.

David objects to the admission of the note, contending that the government has made no showing that he is the author of the note.

Explain the various ways in which the government may go about providing the necessary foundation for identifying David as the author of the note. What if the note said "broach" instead of "brooch"? What if instead the note were typewritten?

United States v. Scott
270 F.3d 30 (1st Cir. 2001)

LYNCH, Circuit Judge.

Identity theft is said to be among this country's fastest growing crimes. In the 1990's and earlier, Alan Scott, a former paralegal handy with documents, apparently enhanced his income through an extensive array of white collar crimes using the identities of others....

[A] jury convicted Scott of conspiring to make and of making false claims to an agency of the United States, 18 U.S.C. §§ 286, 287 (1994). Scott filed twenty false income tax returns with the IRS for the tax year 1996 seeking tax refunds in the names of at least twelve people....

James Donahue, an IRS agent, testified that certain documents in evidence were in Scott's handwriting. Donahue had followed Scott through a number of IRS investigations over a number of years, beginning when Donahue participated in the 1989 search. Donahue testified on voir dire that during this time he had seen examples of Scott's handwriting that included three to five letters, five to ten court pleadings, signature cards to open three bank accounts in Scott's name, fifty or sixty checks and deposit slips for those accounts, five to ten money orders, applications to file tax returns electronically, two driver's licenses, a pilot's license, and five to ten forms Scott had signed as part of booking procedures at police stations, among others. Donahue also saw Scott sign a document in his presence: a fingerprint card at the marshal's office during an earlier investigation.

Scott made two objections to Donahue's testimony as a whole, which he renewed after the voir dire. First, he objected that Donahue had acquired familiarity with Scott's handwriting "for purposes of the litigation,"* and thus could not testify as a lay witness under Federal Rule of Evidence 901(b)(2). Second, he objected that despite Donahue's exposure to Scott's handwriting Donahue nevertheless lacked sufficient familiarity with that handwriting to testify. The district court overruled Scott's objections, but required Donahue to refer to the documents in general terms in order to avoid undue prejudice to Scott. The jury was not told that the documents providing the basis for Donahue's familiarity came from earlier investigations, arrests, and seizures.

Donahue then identified Scott's signature and handwriting on various documents which the government had previously introduced as found in Scott's possession. These documents included a birth certificate in the name of Ralph Swoboda, a list of names, which included Scott's codefendants, the purported signature of Randy LaPlante on Western Union forms, an application for a copy of Daniel Richard Brogan's birth certificate, and similar papers....

In admitting the testimony, the district court relied on Federal Rule of Evidence 701**
....

---

* Editor's Note: This phrase in the rule was restyled in 2011 to read: "acquired for the current litigation."

** Editor's Note: Rule 701 provides as follows: "If a witness is not testifying as an expert, testimony in the form of an opinion is limited to one that is: (a) rationally based on the witness's perception; (b) helpful to clearly understanding the witness's testimony or to determining a fact in issue; and (c) not based on scientific, technical, or other specialized knowledge within the scope of Rule 702."

The district court distinguished Rule 901 as dealing only with authentication as a condition precedent to the admissibility of evidence, and therefore not with evidence that had already been admitted. The court reasoned in the alternative that if Rule 901 did apply, Rule 901(b)(2)* (on which Scott relied) would nevertheless permit admission....

Scott argues primarily that the correct rule for considering admissibility of such handwriting authentication or identification evidence is Rule 901(b)(2), and that the evidence was inadmissible because Donahue came to know Scott's handwriting through his criminal investigation of Scott.

Rule 901(b) illustrates two ways of authenticating or identifying through the testimony of a witness the handwriting on a document as being written by a particular person. The handwriting may be identified through a lay witness who has familiarity with the alleged author's handwriting and who did not acquire that familiarity for purposes of the litigation. Fed.R.Evid. 901(b)(2). Alternatively, the handwriting may be identified as the alleged author's handwriting by an expert, who lacks such familiarity except as acquired for purposes of the litigation but has the requisite expertise and who compares the sample with specimens which have been authenticated.[13] Fed.R.Evid. 901(b)(3); *see also* Fed.R.Evid. 901(b)(2) advisory committee's note ("Testimony based upon familiarity acquired for purposes of the litigation is reserved to the expert....").

The district court ruled that Rule 701 governed and that Rule 901 did not apply.[14] This is an issue of law we review de novo. We hold that both rules must be satisfied.

The essence of the district court's reasoning was that the documents that contained the handwriting had already been admitted into evidence. As such, they had, of course, been authenticated or identified. Fed.R.Evid. 901(a). Authentication refers to evidence that tends to prove that a document is what its proponent claims it to be. The documents were earlier authenticated as documents found in the search of Scott's car or home, and admitted as such. The handwriting on those documents was not previously authenticated as evidence that tended to prove that the handwriting was Scott's. To prove that point, the evidence had to comply with Rule 901.[15]

Whether Donahue's testimony satisfied Rule 901 depends on the purpose of the requirement that the familiarity of a lay opinion witness with handwriting may not be "acquired for purposes of the litigation." This limitation is properly understood in light of the common law tradition with which Rule 901(b)(2) and Rule 901(b)(3) break. English courts, and early American courts, placed strict limits on testimony concerning identification of handwriting by its style, called "comparison of hands." 7 J. Wigmore, *Evidence* § 1991, at 253 (Chadbourn rev.1978). Professor Wigmore explains that when this rule was at its strictest, no witness was permitted to identify handwriting in a criminal case unless the witness had seen the document in question written or signed. Over time, however, courts came to permit handwriting identification based on ever-looser degrees of

---

* Editor's Note: Rule 901(b)(2) provides as follows: "**Nonexpert Opinion About Handwriting.** A nonexpert's opinion that handwriting is genuine, based on a familiarity with it that was not acquired for the current litigation."

13. Alternatively, the trier of fact may do this directly. Fed.R.Evid. 901(b)(3).

14. There may be situations in which Rule 901(b)(2) is satisfied, but Rule 701 is not—that is, in which an identification might not be helpful to the jury even though based on properly acquired familiarity.

15. An alternate rationale would lead to the same result: even if Donahue's testimony was not authentication within the meaning of Rule 901, we think that Rule 701's requirement that lay opinion testimony be helpful to the jury would be best read in light of the limits Rule 901(b)(2) places on lay opinion testimony regarding handwriting.

familiarity: one who had seen the alleged author sign other documents, or one who had seen samples of writing known to be by that author over a period of time, could give such testimony. *Id.* §§ 1992–1993, at 257–62.

Rule 901(b)(2) retains only one vestige of the common law rule. A lay witness may not enter court, see for the first time two samples of handwriting, and identify the contested sample as written by the same person as the previously authenticated sample; the result is the same, moreover, if the witness compared the two samples before entering the courtroom. After all, such a comparison could be made as easily by the jury as by the witness. Therefore, lay witness testimony without familiarity would not be helpful to the jury and would be prohibited by Rule 701 even if Rule 901 did not exist.

This case involves no such situation. Donahue became familiar with Scott's handwriting over the course of several years, and he did so not for the purpose of testifying, but instead for the purpose of solving a crime. Scott was perfectly entitled to argue to the jury that Donahue's interest in securing a conviction colored Donahue's perception of Scott's handwriting. That possibility, however, did not require the district court to exclude the evidence under Rule 901(b)(2).

We may dispense quickly with Scott's remaining objections to Donahue's testimony. Scott makes a different argument that Donahue was not sufficiently familiar with Scott's signature to testify. This fact-bound ruling is reviewed for abuse of discretion. It is true that Donahue conceded that he saw Scott sign his name only once. Other categories of experience can, however, demonstrate familiarity, such as seeing signatures on writings purporting to be those of the alleged author when the circumstances would indicate that they were genuine. The rule for which Scott seems to contend—not only a strict requirement that the witness see the alleged author in the act of signature, but also a further demand that this occur multiple times—is far too strict. *See United States v. Standing Soldier*, 538 F.2d 196, 202 (8th Cir. 1976) (permitting authentication testimony on the basis of a single exposure to an uncontested signature and a single exposure to a contested one). In this case, there was enough familiarity on the part of the witness to admit the testimony. Scott's arguments go rather to the weight of the evidence. Scott took advantage of this, and cross-examined the agent on the paucity of actual sightings of Scott endorsing his signature. Accordingly, there was no abuse of discretion and no error....

United States v. Jones
107 F.3d 1147 (6th Cir. 1997)

MOORE, Circuit Judge....

Appellant Kathleen Jones stole a credit card application from the mailbox of her son-in-law's aunt and uncle, fraudulently applied for the credit card under their names, and made twenty charges on the credit card between July 8, 1991, and July 21, 1991, for ATM withdrawals and hotel visits. The total amount charged on the credit card was $3,748.08. Jones was convicted of one count of mail fraud, in violation of 18 U.S.C. § 1341; two counts of using a fictitious or false name in order to carry on a scheme to defraud by mail, in violation of 18 U.S.C. § 1342; one count of using an unauthorized access device, in violation of 18 U.S.C. § 1029(a)(2); one count of possessing stolen mail, in violation of 18 U.S.C. § 1708; and one count of obstruction of correspondence, in violation of 18 U.S.C. § 1702.

One of the government's primary arguments at trial was that Jones's signature was on: (1) the credit card application; (2) a post-office box registration form for the post-office box to which the card was sent; and (3) two Howard Johnson's motel registration forms, which contained the fraudulently procured Visa number at issue. To prove that these items contained Jones's signature, Grant Sperry, a forensic document analyst for the United States Postal Service, testified as an expert witness for the government. He compared the three signatures at issue with documents purportedly written by Jones and concluded that her signature was on all of the documents. The parties stipulated to the admissibility of two of the writings used by Sperry, Government Exhibit 11, known business writings of defendant, and Government Exhibit 12, handwriting exemplars obtained by postal inspectors. The defendant, however, refused to stipulate to the admissibility of a third document used by Sperry, a card allegedly sent by Jones to Bruce Cronin, whose son is married to Jones's daughter. The card was admitted into evidence through Cronin, who testified that while he was not familiar with Jones's signature, he knew the card was sent by Jones based on its content. . . .

Appellant asserts that the district court erred by allowing into evidence the card allegedly written by Jones to Cronin because it had not been properly authenticated. According to her, because Cronin was a non-expert who was unfamiliar with Jones's handwriting, he could not testify regarding the genuineness of the card. . . .

It is clear that Rule 901(b)(2) does not apply, because Cronin himself admitted that he was not familiar with Jones's handwriting. Appellee argues, however, and we are convinced, that Rule 901(b)(4)* applies. "[A] document . . . may be shown to have emanated from a particular person by virtue of its disclosing knowledge of facts known peculiarly to him. . . ." Fed.R.Evid. 901(b)(4) advisory committee's note. In *Maldonado-Rivera*, the Second Circuit stated:

> In accordance with Rule 901(b)(4), "the contents of a writing may be used to aid in determining the identity of the declarant," *United States v. Wilson*, 532 F.2d 641, 644 (8th Cir.), *cert. denied*, 429 U.S. 846 (1976), if, for example, the writing "deal[s] with a matter sufficiently obscure or particularly within the knowledge of the persons corresponding so that the contents of the [writing] were not a matter of common knowledge[.]" 5 J. Weinstein & M. Berger, *Weinstein's Evidence*, ¶ 901(b)(4)[01], at 901–49 (1990).

922 F.2d at 957. *See also United States v. Newton*, 891 F.2d 944, 947 (1st Cir. 1989) (concluding that a document which contained statements "from which it could be inferred that [the defendant] authored the document" was properly authenticated). In the present case, Cronin expressed the opinion that the card was written by Jones because the card was signed "Kathie Jones" and because the card contained references to Cronin's daughter-in-law and granddaughter that no one else could have written. In light of this testimony, we conclude that the district court did not abuse its discretion by finding that the card allegedly written by Jones to Cronin met the authentication requirements in Rule 901. . . .

[The opinion of Judge Krupansky, concurring in part and dissenting in part, is omitted.]

Notes and Questions

1. Is *Scott's* holding that a lay witness who has familiarized himself with a person's handwriting for the purposes of the litigation cannot serve to authenticate the document

---

* Editor's Note: Rule 901(b)(4) provides as follows: "*Distinctive Characteristics and the Like.* The appearance, contents, substance, internal patterns, or other distinctive characteristics of the item, taken together with all the circumstances."

as being written by that person inconsistent with the opening sentence of Rule 901(b) that it sets forth "examples only — not a complete list — of evidence that satisfies the requirement"? Or is *Scott* interpreting (and Rule 901(b)(2) effectively codifying) some *other* provision of the rules of evidence?

2. Although both lay and expert witnesses are often called to authenticate handwriting in accordance with Rules 901(b)(2) and 901(b)(3), a party need not call *any* witnesses in order to authenticate handwriting. As indicated in footnote 13 of *Scott*, Rule 901(b)(3) permits handwriting to be authenticated by having the trier of fact itself compare the handwriting on the document in question with another document that contains handwriting known to belong to the person alleged to be the author of the disputed document. *See, e.g., United States v. Saadey*, 393 F.3d 669, 679–80 (6th Cir. 2005).

3. The subject of expert testimony generally, and expert testimony on handwriting identification specifically, is addressed in Chapter 4.

4. In *Jones*, the contents of the card were deemed to be authenticated by testimony that "no one else" had knowledge of the information contained therein. What if more than one person, although admittedly a small pool of individuals, had knowledge of the information contained therein? Consider the following:

> [T]he information in each of the purported records, although not secret by any means, was not widely held.... Wigmore states that when information is in the sole possession of a person, and a document purportedly written by that person contains that information, there is sufficient evidence of the authenticity of the document. 7 Wigmore § 2148 at 745 (3d ed. 1940) Although Wigmore maintained that so long as more than one person had the information the inference of authenticity was devoid of all force, *id.* at 746, we believe that the better rule is that the inference does not vanish but rather diminishes as more people know the information contained in the documents. *See* 5 J. Weinstein & M. Berger, *Weinstein's Evidence* ¶ 901(b)(4)[01] at 901–49 (1982 ed. & Supp.) ("The force of the inference decreases as the number of people who know the details and may have written the letter increases.") Although we do not know precisely how many people had the information contained in the proffered evidence, we suspect, as noted above, that the number is small. Therefore, the nature of the information in the documents further supports their authenticity.

McQueeney v. Wilmington Trust Co., 779 F.2d 916, 929–930 (3d Cir. 1985).

5. In addition to substance within a letter that is peculiarly within the knowledge of a person or small group of persons, stylistic characteristics of a writing — such as peculiar spelling errors that are consistent with errors in writings known to be written by a person — can be used to identify that person as the author of a writing. *See United States v. Clifford*, 704 F.2d 86, 90–91 (3d Cir. 1983).

6. A special application of Rule 901(b)(4) is the reply doctrine:

> When a letter is received by due course of mail, purporting to come in answer from the person to whom a prior letter has been sent, there are furnished thereby, over and above mere contents showing knowledge of facts in general, three circumstances evidencing the letter's genuineness: First, the tenor of the letter as a reply to the first indicates a knowledge of the tenor of the first. Second, the habitual accuracy of the mails, in delivering a letter to the person addressed and to no other person, indicates that no other person was likely to have received the first letter and to have known its contents. Third, the time of the arrival, in due course, lessens the possibility that the letter, having been received by the right per-

son but left unanswered, came subsequently into a different person's hands and was answered by him.

7 Wigmore, Evidence § 2153, at 752 (Chadbourn rev. 1978). *Accord United States v. Reilly*, 33 F.3d 1396, 1407–08 (3d Cir. 1994).

7. Can you trace typewritten documents to a particular person in the same way that you can trace handwritten ones? Consider the following:

[I]n view of the scientific development of the study of documents by microscopy and other arts, the authorship of typewritten documents can often be traced with certainty to the specific machine used; so that this mode of authentication does not then differ in principle from that of using the handwriting.

7 Wigmore, Evidence § 2149, at 748 (Chadbourn rev. 1978). *Accord Commonwealth v. Gipe*, 84 A. 2d 366, 367–68 (Pa. 1951). But even if you trace the document to a specific *typewriter*, does that suffice to link it to a particular *person*? If not, what additional evidence would be needed?

United States v. Kairys

782 F.2d 1374 (7th Cir. 1986)

CUMMINGS, Chief Judge....

Statement of the Case and Facts

Denaturalization proceedings were commenced against Kairys on August 13, 1980, by the United States Justice Department. The government brought three pertinent counts against him under § 340(a) of the Immigration and Nationality Act of 1952. Count I charged willful misrepresentation or concealment of a material fact in defendant's petition for naturalization; Count II charged illegal procurement of naturalization because defendant's service as a Nazi camp guard made him ineligible for a visa; and Count III charged illegal procurement of citizenship due to willful misrepresentations in obtaining his visa. The district court entered an order under Count II revoking Kairys' citizenship....

The main issue at trial was the defendant's identity—was Kairys the person the government claimed him to be? The defendant contends that he is Liudas Kairys born in Kuanas, Lithuania, on December 20, 1924. As a child he moved to Svilionys, Lithuania, where he completed four years of grammar school. His schooling continued in Svencionys, Lithuania, and he then completed three years of secondary education in Vilnius, Lithuania. Defendant asserts that between 1940 and 1942 he worked on a farm in Radviliskis, Lithuania, and that in 1942 he was captured and sent to the Hammerstein prisoner of war (POW) camp. The defendant claims he was a forced laborer in various locations throughout Lithuania and Poland for the remainder of the war.

The government, on the other hand, maintains that the defendant is Liudvikas Kairys born in Svilionys, then Polish, on December 24, 1920. He joined the Lithuanian army, which merged with the Russian army in 1939. The government contends that some time before March of 1940 Kairys moved to Vilnius, Lithuania, and obtained Lithuanian citizenship.[6] During the German invasion of Poland, Kairys was captured and placed in the Hammerstein POW camp. In June of 1942 he was recruited by the Nazis and sent to training

---

6. The necessity of Kairys' obtaining Lithuanian citizenship relates to the dispute over his birthplace. If Kairys was born in Kuanas, he would have been a Lithuanian citizen by birth. If, however, he was born in Svilionys, his 1920 birth would not be sufficient for citizenship because Svilionys was under Polish sovereignty at that time.

camp at Trawniki, Poland. In March of 1943 Kairys was transferred to the Treblinka labor camp in Poland to serve as a Nazi camp guard, where he remained until the camp was closed in July 1944 when the Russians advanced into Poland. At some point during his service he was promoted to *Oberwachmann* of his Nazi guard unit....

Kairys' argument focuses on the accuracy and admissibility of a *Personalbogen*, which is a German Waffen Schutzstaffel (SS) identity card. The government relied in part on the *Personalbogen* to establish its version of the defendant's identity. The district court admitted the *Personalbogen* under Federal Rule of Evidence 901(b)(8). The defendant argues that the admission of the document was error, claiming that it is a forgery fraught with inaccuracies, erasures, inconsistencies, and unexplained problems. The government counters that the defendant failed to produce any substantive evidence that the document was anything other than what it was purported to be — the defendant's Nazi SS personnel card.

A. *Admissibility*

Federal Rule of Evidence 901(b)(8) governs the admissibility of ancient documents. The Rule states that a document is admissible if it "(A) is in [a] condition [that] create[s] no suspicion [about] its authenticity[;] (B) was in a place where[], if authentic, [it] would likely be[;] and (C) [is at least] 20 years [old when] offered." The question of whether evidence is suspicious and therefore inadmissible is a matter of the trial court's discretion. We see no error here.

Although the Rule requires that the document be free of suspicion, that suspicion goes not to the content of the document, but rather to whether the document is what it purports to be.... In other words, the issue of admissibility is whether the document is a *Personalbogen* from the German SS records located in the Soviet Union archives and is over 20 years old. Whether the contents of the document correctly identify the defendant goes to its weight and is a matter for the trier of fact; it is not relevant to the threshold determination of its admissibility.

The defendant does argue that a question was raised about whether the document was actually an original *Personalbogen*. First, the defendant raises general allegations that the Soviet Union routinely disseminates forged documents as part of propaganda campaigns. Next the defendant contends that the thumbprint ink was "unusual" and that it could have been placed on the document by mechanical means. But government witnesses testified that the only likely way for the print to appear on the *Personalbogen* was from the defendant's pressing his thumb to the paper. Additionally, the defendant notes that the government failed to establish the proper chain of custody from Treblinka to the Soviet archives. However, it is not necessary to show a chain of custody for ancient documents. Rule 901(b)(8) merely requires that the document be found in a place where, if authentic, it would likely be. All that is left, then, is the vague allegation that the Soviet Union regularly releases forged documents. That is not sufficient to make the document suspicious for purposes of admissibility.

There was sufficient evidence in the record that the document was a German SS *Personalbogen*. It matched other authenticated *Personalbogens* in form; it was found in the Soviet Union archives, the depository for German SS documents; and its paper fiber was consistent with that of documents more than 20 years old. Its admission was not error....

Notes and Questions

1. Evidence that satisfies the standard set forth in Rule 901(b)(8) automatically falls within an exception to the rule against hearsay. *See* Federal Rule of Evidence 803(16) (excluding

from the hearsay rule "[a] statement in a document that is at least 20 years old and whose authenticity is established."). What is the justification for treating older documents differently? The rationale at common law was necessity: after a sufficiently long period of time, most of the people who eyewitnessed the document being written or who could identify the author's handwriting will have died. Over time, the common law steadily reduced the age necessary for a document to be deemed "ancient," from 50 to 40 and eventually to 30 years. *See* 7 Wigmore, Evidence § 2137, 2138, at 721–24 (Chadbourn rev. 1978). Yet Rule 901(b)(8) reduces the period still further to 20 years, explaining that with this shift comes "some shift of emphasis from the probable unavailability of witnesses to the unlikeliness of a still viable fraud after the lapse of time." Advisory Committee Note to Rule 901(b)(8); *see also* Advisory Committee Note to Rule 803(16) ("age affords assurance that the writing antedates the present controversy"). However, a number of states still retain the common law period of 30 years. *See, e.g.,* La. Code Evid. Ann. Art. 901(B)(8); Pa. R. Evid. 901(b)(8); Tenn. R. Evid. 901(b)(8).

2. How does one satisfy the prerequisite of Rule 901(b)(8)(C) that the document "is at least 20 years old when offered"? Is the date that appears on the face of the document, standing alone, sufficient? If not, what more is required? *See* 7 Wigmore, Evidence § 2138, at 725 (Chadbourn rev. 1978) ("The *purporting* date is of itself not determinative; for anybody may have forged the written date but yesterday. Accordingly, this existence of the document 30 years ago must be somehow shown."). *See also Halliburton Energy Services, Inc. v. NL Industries,* 648 F. Supp. 2d 840, 894 n.63 (S.D. Tex. 2009) (listing various ways of proving age, including "visible marks of aging and archaic styles of penmanship, spelling or phraseology," and noting that "the contents of a document might permit an inference as to its age, as where the document refers to events or persons contemporaneous with its creation") (quoting 31 Charles A. Wright & Victor Gold, Federal Practice and Procedure § 7113 (2000)).

3. Can an audiotape qualify as an ancient document? *See Penguin Books U.S.A., Inc. v. New Christian Church,* 262 F. Supp. 2d 251, 264 (S.D.N.Y. 2003) ("The term 'ancient document' generally encompasses written items such as wills, deeds, contracts, newspapers, publications, letters, office memoranda, ledger books, scientific reports, inscriptions, and the like. Wright & Miller, § 7113(b)(8). The tapes, therefore, are not 'ancient documents' as that term is used in the relevant evidentiary rules, nor do they contain a 'compilation' of any 'data,' rather they are simply alleged to be recordings of [people speaking with one another].").

D. Authentication of Audio Recordings, Photographs, and Video Recordings

Problem 2-3: A Picture Is Worth a Thousand Words ...

Michael is on trial on charges of robbing two different banks, First National and Federal Savings & Loan. The First National robbery, which took place during business hours, was witnessed by a number of bank customers and employees. Moreover, an automatic camera took a photograph that depicted Michael pointing a gun at a teller.

The Federal Savings & Loan robbery, which took place in the middle of the night, was not witnessed by anyone, but a bank camera took a photograph depicting Michael attaching an explosive device to the bank's safe.

The prosecution seeks to offer into evidence the photographs from both of the banks' automated cameras. The defense objects on the ground that the photographs have not been authenticated.

What options does the government have for authenticating the photographs? Are they the same options for both photographs?

Problem 2-4: The Secret Recording

David is on trial on charges of unlawful distribution of cocaine. The government seeks to offer into evidence a tape recording of a conversation between Robert, an undercover agent of the Drug Enforcement Agency, and David in which David offered to sell Robert cocaine. David objects on the ground that the tape has not been authenticated.

What options does the government have for authenticating the tape?

United States v. Rembert

863 F.2d 1023 (D.C. Cir. 1988)

SENTELLE, Circuit Judge. . . .

Rembert's convictions arise from crime sprees occurring on July 7 and 26, 1987. On July 7, according to the testimony of victim witness Mary Simon, she drove to a Signet Bank in Falls Church, Virginia, at approximately 10:30 p.m. As she attempted to use her bank card in the automatic teller machine ("ATM"), a man armed with a knife reached into the open window of her car, grabbed her by the neck, and threatened to kill her if she did not give him her ATM code number. . . .

A second victim witness, Andrea McGee, testified that on Sunday, July 26, 1987, in the midafternoon, she drove her automobile to an ATM machine in Washington, D.C. After she discovered the machine was out of order, she accidentally drove her car into the wall of the bank, where it became stuck. Two men, one of whom she later identified at a line-up and in court as appellant, and a third man not further involved in the incident, assisted in freeing her vehicle. The men identified as appellant and his companion then told her that they had missed their bus while helping her, and asked her to drive them to a bus stop. However, once in the car and under way, one of them threatened her with a butcher's knife and told her to drive to Virginia. The other man, identified as appellant, rifled through her purse. Once in Virginia, the assailants ordered her to stop at a bank, where appellant's companion took her bank card and demanded her code number in order to obtain money. With some difficulty, he extracted $10 from the machine. Appellant's companion then took over the driving, and the two forced her to accompany them to another bank. At that bank they spotted a male customer, later identified as John Lynn, attempting to use the ATM machine. Appellant jumped from the car with the knife and began stabbing Lynn. Appellant's companion demanded and obtained Lynn's wallet, keys, and card code. After unsuccessfully attempting to steal Lynn's car, the assailants fled the scene in McGee's car, appellant driving, and forced her to accompany them to a Seat Pleasant, Maryland, branch of Sovran Bank, where they unsuccessfully attempted to use

Lynn's ATM card.[2] After taking her purse, they finally returned McGee to Washington, D.C., where they abandoned her and her vehicle near the point of her abduction.

In addition to positive eyewitness identifications of Rembert by the two women victims and Lynn, the prosecution offered at trial evidence that each had identified Rembert in line-ups and that Simon had identified appellant in a series of photographs taken by a closed-circuit surveillance video camera at the Seat Pleasant bank where the two assailants took McGee. These photographs were received into evidence....

[A]ppellant's sole assignment of error concerns the admission of the photographic evidence from the video recorder at the Sovran Bank in Seat Pleasant, Maryland. The sole authenticating witness for the photos was Katie Wohlfarth, a supervisor in the loss control division of the bank, who testified that she was in charge of investigating questioned activities through the ATM machines. She testified that the machine-maintained records at the Seat Pleasant branch showed an unusual pattern of use associated with John Lynn's ATM card on July 26, 1987, at approximately 8:00 p.m. The machine's records indicated that the card had been entered ten times on that occasion and was retained by the machine on the tenth attempt. She further testified that video cameras are maintained at each of the three ATM machines at the Seat Pleasant location. A video recorder taped the view from each camera in sequence, rotating to the next camera, taking a photograph every three seconds. This videotaping process imprints the date and time at which the pictures were made on the resultant photographs. She then identified a strip of pictures which was admitted into evidence over Rembert's objection. She further testified that she had viewed the original videotape and the resultant photographs and that the photographs were fair and accurate depictions of what was on the videotape. The imprinted date and times on the photographs ranged from 8:04:22 p.m. until 8:13:30 p.m. on July 26, 1987. On cross examination, she testified that she had no personal knowledge of the events that transpired at the Seat Pleasant location on that date, and could not say from her own knowledge whether the photographs fairly and accurately depicted the scene and events at that time and place or not.

Appellant argues that photographs are admitted under two theories of authentication, and that the foundation offered by the prosecution in the present case meets neither theory. He first presents the classic model of illustrative or "pictorial testimony" use of photographs as evidence. Under this theory, a sponsoring witness (whether or not he is the photographer) who has personal knowledge of the scene depicted testifies that the photograph fairly and accurately portrays that scene. Obviously this model was not followed in Rembert's trial.

Appellant next argues that the only other basis for the introduction of photographic evidence is the "silent witness" model, under which the admissibility of a photograph is based on the reliability of the process by which it is made. This model is most often associated with the introduction of x-rays, where obviously no witness has viewed the scene portrayed. Appellant persuasively contends that the foundational evidence of the witness Wohlfarth does not meet that description. Her testimony did not really speak to the reliability of the process. She testified rather as a custodian of the records without supplying evidence as to the type of camera used, its general reliability, the quality of its product, the purpose of its employment, the process by which it is focused, or the general reliability of the entire system.

Appellant is undoubtedly correct that the evidence in this case does not meet either of those two models. He is further correct that those models are adopted in the Federal Rules

---

2. Lynn had supplied a false code, which later resulted in an ATM machine rejecting, and ultimately retaining the card.

of Evidence under the Authentication and Identification heading of Rule 901. Fed.R.Evid. 901(b)(1) (testimony that a matter is what it is claimed to be); 901(b)(9) (evidence describing a process or system used to produce a result and showing that the process or system produces an accurate result). But this does not close our inquiry. Rule 901 expressly prefaces the two subsections set forth above by the language that they function "[b]y way of illustration only, and not by way of limitation,"* thereby leaving room for the general application of Rule 901(a)....

As we have already held in a case also dealing with photographic evidence, "[a]uthentication and identification are specialized aspects of relevancy that are necessary conditions precedent to admissibility." *United States v. Blackwell*, 694 F.2d 1325, 1330 (D.C. Cir. 1982) (citations omitted). The *Blackwell* case involved a prosecution for unlawful possession of firearms. The photographs in question depicted the defendant holding a firearm, apparently the same as one of the guns seized at the time of his arrest. The prosecution had obtained the photographs as the result of a search of the same room in which the firearms were found. No witness could testify as to when the photographs were made, where they were made, by what process, or whether they fairly and accurately depicted any particular scene on any particular date. The detective who conducted the search did testify that the details of the pictured weapon and the background interior were similar to the details of the weapon and room in question. We applied the same authentication and identification analysis as we would have with reference to the contents of any documentary evidence. That is, we required only that "the proponent of documentary evidence make a showing sufficient to permit a reasonable juror to find that the evidence is what its proponent claims."....

These same principles apply to the photographic evidence in the instant case. Appellant correctly states the two traditional bases for the admission of the photographic evidence, but the uses of photography have not stood still and neither should the law. Nor has the law on the use of photographic evidence remained unaffected by the changes in society. For example, in *United States v. Stearns*, 550 F.2d 1167 (9th Cir. 1977), Judge (now Justice) Kennedy wrote for the Ninth Circuit in a case in which the trial court had admitted certain photographs of a boat taken on the open seas. The defendants in that case were charged with stealing a boat named the *Sea Wind*. As part of a factually involved trial, the defendants contended that they had taken *Sea Wind* only to protect the vessel and at a time when their own vessel, the *Iola*, was disabled. Details within the photograph showed the rigging of the *Sea Wind* in the foreground (as if the photograph were taken from that vessel) and the *Iola* under full sail in the background. Other details in companion photographs provided circumstantial evidence of the date of the taking of the photographs as being after the time of the alleged disability of the *Iola*. In upholding the trial court's admission of the evidence, Judge Kennedy wrote: "Even if direct testimony as to foundation matters is absent ... the contents of a photograph itself, together with such other circumstantial or indirect evidence as bears upon the issue, may serve to explain and authenticate a photograph sufficiently to justify its admission into evidence."

Other courts, both federal and state, have likewise modernized their standards for admissibility of photographic evidence. In *United States v. Taylor*, 530 F.2d 639 (5th Cir. 1976), for example, the trial court had admitted into evidence in a bank robbery trial contact prints made from a film taken by the bank camera after the victim bank employees had been locked in a vault. The bank camera was in the business area of the bank

---

* Editor's Note: This phrase in the rule was restyled in 2011 to read: "The following are examples only—not a complete list—of evidence that satisfies the requirement...."

so that none of the witnesses could testify as to the accuracy of the scene depicted at the time of the taking of the prints. The only foundational evidence was introduced by government witnesses not present at the time of the robbery, who testified as to the manner in which the film was installed in the camera, how the camera was activated, the removal of the film immediately after the robbery, the chain of possession, and the method of development. The Fifth Circuit held that admission of that evidence on that foundation was within the discretion of the district court and that the district court did not abuse its discretion....

Consistent with our decision in *Blackwell* and the teachings of our sister circuits and the courts of the several states, we conclude that the contents of photographic evidence to be admitted into evidence need not be merely illustrative, but can be admitted as evidence independent of the testimony of any witness as to the events depicted, upon a foundation sufficient to meet the requirements of Federal Rule of Evidence 901(a). In this case the circumstantial evidence provided by the victim witnesses as to the occurrences at the ATM machines, together with the testimony of Wohlfarth as to the loading of the cameras and the security of the film, coupled with the internal indicia of date, place, and event depicted in the evidence itself provide ample support for the District Court's exercise of its discretion. Just as the Ninth Circuit held that the contents alone provided sufficient circumstantial evidence for the authentication of the photographs in *Stearns*, so do the contents of the photos in the instant case supply any further need for authentication that the contact prints from the ATM machine may require on the present record....

United States v. Tropeano
252 F.3d 653 (2d Cir. 2001)

WINTER, Circuit Judge....

David Barroso, Jr., appeals from a conviction after a jury trial before Judge Scheindlin. He was found guilty of conspiring to commit securities and wire fraud, in violation of 18 U.S.C. § 371....

The evidence showed that Barroso and his co-defendants, Marlon and Frederick Tropeano, conspired to defraud four customers of the brokerage firm at which they were employed.... Marlon and Frederick Tropeano pleaded guilty a few days prior to the commencement of the trial. Barroso went to trial, his primary defense being that he was duped by the Tropeano brothers into unknowingly facilitating their crimes....

The government introduced five taped telephone conversations in which Barroso, among other things, urged employees of a transferee brokerage to execute and settle sales from a transferred account quickly. He also lied regarding his authority to transfer the customer accounts, and his tales were not always ones that would have been told by an innocent dupe. In particular, he is recorded as bolstering his claim of power over an account by claiming to know the owner and to be a friend of the owner's son. The account owner testified that he had no son and had never met Barroso, much less authorized him to transfer his account. Barroso's boasting of a personal relationship with an account owner and his non-existent son in order to support a claim of authority over an account unequivocally undermined any plausible defense that he was duped into facilitating what he believed to be an innocent scheme....

Barroso ... challenges the admission of the audiotapes on the ground that the government failed as a matter of law to establish the tapes' authenticity. As noted, the audiotapes recorded telephone conversations between Barroso and other brokers. The district court admitted the tapes, over defense objection, after the brokers testified that they had listened to the tapes before trial and that they were fair and accurate recordings of their conversations....

[The court cites Rule 901(b)(1) (Testimony of a Witness with Knowledge) and 901(b)(5) (Opinion About a Voice).] In Barroso's case, the brokers who authenticated the tapes had firsthand knowledge of the conversations and each identified the voices on the tapes.

Barroso, however, argues that the government also needed to establish a chain of custody for the tapes, relying upon *United States v. Fuentes*, 563 F.2d 527 (2d Cir. 1977). In *Fuentes*, we upheld the admission of tapes as sufficiently authenticated by evidence of an unbroken chain of custody. However, our upholding the authentication of tapes by establishing a chain of custody in the absence of testimony by a contemporaneous witness to the recorded conversations does not imply, as appellant suggests, that such a witness cannot provide equally sufficient authentication without proof of a chain of custody. Indeed, appellant's position is contrary to the plain language of Rule 901. Finally, *Fuentes* also noted that "this Circuit has never expressly adopted a rigid standard for determining the admissibility of tape recordings." The district court therefore did not abuse its discretion in admitting the tapes.

Authentication of course merely renders the tapes admissible, leaving the issue of their ultimate reliability to the jury. Barroso was free to challenge the tapes' reliability by, for example, cross-examination of the brokers concerning their familiarity with Barroso's voice and the tape recording system. Any doubts raised by such a challenge would, however, go to the weight to be given to the tapes by the jury, not to their admissibility....

Notes and Questions

1. Was it necessary for the government in the *Rembert* case to expand the ways in which photographs can be authenticated, or were there more straightforward options available?

2. Are the risks that an audiotape might be altered sufficient to justify a higher standard for admissibility? A number of courts hold that in recognition of the fact that "recorded evidence is likely to have a strong impression upon a jury and is susceptible to alteration ... the government [must] 'produce clear and convincing evidence of authenticity and accuracy' as a foundation for the admission of such recordings." *United States v. Ruggiero*, 928 F.2d 1289, 1303 (2d Cir. 1991) (internal quotations omitted). *Accord United States v. Westmoreland*, 312 F.3d 302, 310–11 (7th Cir. 2002). Is such a requirement consistent with Rules 901 and 104(b)? Or are the courts in imposing this standard relying on a different rule? Are the risks associated with an audiotape any different from the risks associated with missing links in a chain of custody of fungible physical evidence?

E. Authentication of Telephone Conversations

Problem 2-5: The Threatening Call

Assume the same facts as in Problem 2-2, except that instead of receiving a note, Lisa receives a telephone call in which the caller states, "This is David Burns. If you value your life, you will put your rare coins and diamond brooch in the trash bin at the end of your driveway tonight."

What can the government do to provide the necessary foundation for identifying David as the caller?

United States v. Khan
53 F.3d 507 (2d Cir. 1995)

MINER, Circuit Judge.

Defendants-appellants Deborah Williams, Rosaly Saba Khalil, Lancaster Lo and Gilbert Ross appeal from judgments of conviction and sentence entered on November 10, 1993, in the United States District Court for the Southern District of New York (Martin, J.) following a jury trial.... All defendants-appellants were convicted of conspiring to participate in, and participating in, a racketeering enterprise designed to defraud the New York State Medicaid system, in violation of 18 U.S.C. § 1962(c) and (d), and mail fraud, in violation of 18 U.S.C. § 1341, and each defendant-appellant, with the exception of Ross, was convicted of money laundering, in violation of 18 U.S.C. § 1956(a)(1)(A)(i)....

Williams argues that the substance of two telephone conversations that she had with DSS representatives, and reports of those calls, were admitted improperly at trial. We find that the district court did not abuse its discretion in receiving this evidence because there was adequate circumstantial evidence to establish its reliability.

The first telephone call involved Virginia Hale, a DSS representative. Hale testified that, on June 26, 1990, DSS received a provider enrollment application from Williams. Williams does not challenge the fact that she signed and submitted the form, which included a telephone number where she could be contacted. Hale placed a call to that number, which turned out to be one of the Khan clinics, and left a message for Williams to call her back. Later that day, Hale received a telephone call from a woman who identified herself as Williams, and who confirmed the address where the Medicaid checks were to be sent and provided information about one of the clinics. The person also stated that she would check with her "partner" to see if the clinic at which she would be working was certified in New York State. Hale made a written record of the conversation.

The second phone call was described by Anna Graham, who worked with Hale at DSS. Graham testified that on June 28, 1990, she received and made a written record of a telephone call from a woman who identified herself as Williams. During the conversation, the woman stated that the clinic would be licensed as a private office, and that she wanted to enroll as an individual provider.

Williams objected to the admission of the testimony, claiming that there was an insufficient foundation to demonstrate that she was the person making the calls.... While a mere assertion of identity by a person talking on the telephone is not in itself sufficient to authenticate that person's identity, some additional evidence, which "need not fall in[to] any set pattern," may provide the necessary foundation. Fed.R.Evid. 901(b)(6), Advisory Committee notes, example 6. "[S]elf-identification of *the person called* at a place where he reasonably could be expected to be has long been regarded as sufficient" for authentication purposes. *O'Neal v. Morgan*, 637 F.2d 846, 850 (2d Cir. 1980). On the other hand, self-identification by a person *who makes a call*, alone, is insufficient for authentication purposes.... In this case, it is alleged that Williams made the telephone call. Hence, the question becomes whether the circumstances adequately established that Williams was more likely than not the caller. We believe that they do.

First, the calls in question were made in response to a call by Hale to a number that Williams had provided. Hale left a message for Williams and received a return telephone call the same day. Usually, people provide telephone numbers where they reasonably believe they can receive a message. Hence, the circumstances indicate that Williams believed she would receive messages that were left at that location. Second, during this period, there is no question that Williams was seeking the Medicaid provider number that she eventually received, indicating her strong interest in returning the call. Third, the caller provided Williams' father's address as the address to which Medicaid payments should be sent. These circumstances provide a sufficient basis to admit the telephone calls....

First State Bank of Denton v. Maryland Casualty Co.
918 F.2d 38 (5th Cir. 1990)

JERRY E. SMITH, Circuit Judge....

The Millses' residence, which was insured by the Maryland Casualty Company, was completely destroyed by fire. Pursuant to Texas law, the policy provided that in case of total loss, Mills would receive $133,000, the entire face amount of the policy. After inspecting the site, however, the insurance company concluded that the fire was set intentionally and thus refused to make any payment on the policy.

The Millses brought suit to recover on their policy, but both of them died before the trial. The First State Bank of Denton continued the claim as executor. At trial, the insurance company introduced evidence showing that the Millses' house was unoccupied for several weeks prior to the fire but that a neighbor had seen a light in the home a few hours before the flames struck. The company also introduced the testimony of a witness who, right before the fire started, saw a pickup truck leaving the road which accesses the residence. Only Mills and his wife had a key to the house, and Mills owned a pickup truck.

The insurance company also showed that Mills was in financial trouble, as he had bought a second home before he had sold his first. For two years, Mills had attempted to sell his first home, but it had enkindled little interest; because of poor market conditions, the value of the home now was significantly less than the face value of the Millses' policy.

The company concluded by introducing evidence showing that Mills was not at his new home at the time of the fire. About fifteen minutes after the fire began, a police dispatcher attempted to contact Mills at his new residence to notify him of the fire. The dispatcher testified that when she called Mills there, at 1:00 a.m., an unidentified person replied that Mr. Mills was not home....

Under the plain language of rule 901(b)(6),* when a person places a call to a listed number, and the answering party identifies himself as the expected party, the call is properly authenticated. What is different about the present case is that the person who answered the phone did not identify himself as Mr. Mills; rather, he simply identified the residence as "the Millses' residence." The plaintiff contends that this does not fit within the illustration and that the phone call thus was unauthenticated.

---

* Editor's Note: Rule 901(b)(6) provides as follows: "*Evidence About a Telephone Conversation.* For a telephone conversation, evidence that a call was made to the number assigned at the time to: (**A**) a particular person, if circumstances, including self-identification, show that the person answering was the one called; or (**B**) a particular business, if the call was made to a business and the call related to business reasonably transacted over the telephone."

What plaintiff ignores is that the illustrations are not exclusive, but are intended only to provide clear examples of properly authenticated evidence. All that is necessary in authenticating a phone call is that the proponent offer "sufficient authentication to make a *prima facie* case that would allow the issue of identity to be decided by the jury." *United States v. Register*, 496 F.2d 1072, 1077 (5th Cir. 1974).

The plaintiff's position, in demanding that the person answering the phone himself be the defendant, implicitly treats the authentication requirement as requiring an admission by a party opponent. This ignores the true reason for requiring the self-identification: The primary authentication occurs because the phone company usually is accurate. "The calling of a number assigned by the telephone company reasonably supports the assumption that the listing is correct and that the number is the one reached." Rule 901, advisory committee note example (6).

The self-identification supports this maxim by showing that the correct number was dialed. "In such a situation the accuracy of the telephone system, the probable absence of motive to falsify and the lack of opportunity for premeditated fraud all tend to support the conclusion that the self-identification of the speaker is reliable." E. Cleary, *McCormick on Evidence* § 226 at 698 (3d ed. 1984); *accord Register*, 496 F.2d at 1076–77.

The evidence in this case meets the *prima facie* standard established in *Register*. The dispatcher who called the Millses' residence on the night of the fire testified that she correctly dialed the Millses' number and that when she asked whether she had reached the Millses' residence, the person replied that "[t]his is the Millses' residence." Furthermore, when she asked whether Mr. Mills was home, the person answered, "J.T. Mills is not at home."

While the evidence does raise potential hearsay problems, it was sufficiently reliable for authentication. There is little doubt that the dispatcher actually reached Mills's home. The trial court thus did not abuse its discretion by overruling the authentication objection....

Notes and Questions

1. Can telephone company records be offered to prove that a conversation took place between two individuals? Consider the following:

> Records that reflect calls to and from telephone numbers associated with the participants in a criminal scheme permit the inference that the participants were in telephonic contact with one another; and where, as here, the timing and frequency of the calls coincide with key events in the scheme, one may reasonably infer that the participants were consulting one another in regard to those events. Of course, it is theoretically possible that persons other than the defendants were parties to the telephone calls at issue in this case, and even if the defendants themselves were conversing, they were not necessarily speaking about the scheme to defraud Motorola. But it would have been reasonable for the jury to infer that these calls reflected conversations between Adeniji and her co-defendants about the nuts and bolts of the effort to defraud Motorola.

United States v. Adeniji, 221 F.3d 1020, 1030 (7th Cir. 2000). Is such a holding consistent with Rule 901(b)(6)? *See Smith v. United States*, 380 F. Supp. 2d 973, 976 (N.D. Ill. 2005) ("[T]hat Rule applies to telephone conversations, not the records of the calls themselves. Records that reflect calls between telephones registered to alleged members of a conspiracy permit the inference of the conspiracy.").

F. Authentication of Electronic Communications: E-Mail and the Internet

Problem 2-6: The Threatening E-mail

Assume the same facts as in Problem 2-2, except that instead of receiving a note, Lisa receives an e-mail message that read as follows:

> From: David Burns (david87@coldmail.com)
> Sent: Sat. 1/3/2012 8:54 AM
> To: Lisa Golden (lisa26@coldmail.com)
>
> Lisa—
>
> If you value your life, you will put your rare coins and diamond broach in the trash bin at the end of your driveway tonight.
>
> —David

What can the government do to provide the necessary foundation for identifying David as the sender of the e-mail message?

Problem 2-7: The Chat Room

Mark is indicted on charges that he sexually assaulted Tom. Mark admits that he had sexual intercourse with Tom, but defends on the ground that it was consensual. The incident at issue took place after the two began speaking to one another online in a chat room and decided to meet in person at Mark's house.

During its case-in-reply, the defense seeks to offer, over a prosecution objection, testimony by Steve, a close friend of Tom. If permitted, Steve would testify that on the evening in question, he was in the same chat room as Tom and Mark, and that he received an instant message from a user named "Tom25" that read: "As I type, I am chatting with this guy named Mark. I'm going to meet him at his house tonight, and I plan to have sex with him before leaving!" Steve would further testify that shortly thereafter, he received a phone call, and when he answered, the person on the other end said, "Did you get my instant message about Mark? I'm heading over there right now!"

What can the defense do to provide the necessary foundation for identifying Tom as the author of the instant message that Steve received?

Griffin v. State
19 A.3d 415 (Md. 2011)

BATTAGLIA, J.

In this case, we are tasked with determining the appropriate way to authenticate, for evidential purposes, electronically stored information printed from a social networking website, in particular, MySpace.

Antoine Levar Griffin, Petitioner, seeks reversal of his convictions in the Circuit Court for Cecil County, contending that the trial judge abused his discretion in admitting, without proper authentication, what the State alleged were several pages printed from Griffin's girlfriend's MySpace profile. The Court of Special Appeals determined that the trial judge did not abuse his discretion, and we granted Griffin's Petition for Writ of Certiorari....

Griffin was charged in numerous counts with the shooting death, on April 24, 2005, of Darvell Guest at Ferrari's Bar in Perryville, in Cecil County. During his trial, the State sought to introduce Griffin's girlfriend's, Jessica Barber's, MySpace profile to demonstrate that, prior to trial, Ms. Barber had allegedly threatened another witness called by the State. The printed pages contained a MySpace profile in the name of "Sistasouljah," describing a 23 year-old female from Port Deposit, listing her birthday as "10/02/1983" and containing a photograph of an embracing couple. The printed pages also contained the following blurb:

FREE BOOZY!!!! JUST REMEMBER SNITCHES GET STITCHES!! U KNOW WHO YOU ARE!!

When Ms. Barber had taken the stand after being called by the State, she was not questioned about the pages allegedly printed from her MySpace profile.

Instead, the State attempted to authenticate the pages, as belonging to Ms. Barber, through the testimony of Sergeant John Cook, the lead investigator in the case. Defense counsel objected to the admission of the pages allegedly printed from Ms. Barber's MySpace profile, because the State could not sufficiently establish a "connection" between the profile and posting and Ms. Barber....

Defense counsel was permitted to voir dire Sergeant Cook, outside of the presence of the jury, as follows:

[Defense Counsel]: How do you know that this is her [MySpace] page?....

[Sergeant Cook]: Through the photograph of her and Boozy on the front, through the reference to Boozy, [ ] the reference [to] the children, and [ ] her birth date indicated on the form.

....

Whether the MySpace printout represents that which it purports to be, not only a MySpace profile created by Ms. Barber, but also upon which she had posted, "FREE BOOZY!!!! JUST REMEMBER SNITCHES GET STITCHES!! U KNOW WHO YOU ARE!!," is the issue before us....

Anyone can create a MySpace profile at no cost, as long as that person has an email address and claims to be over the age of fourteen ...

After a profile is established, the user may invite others to access her profile, as a "friend," who if the user accepts the befriending, can access her profile pages without further ado....

Although a social networking site generally requires a unique username and password for the user to both establish a profile and access it, posting on the site by those that befriend the user does not.

The identity of who generated the profile may be confounding, because "a person observing the online profile of a user with whom the observer is unacquainted has no idea whether the profile is legitimate." The concern arises because anyone can create a fictitious account and masquerade under another person's name or can gain access to another's account by obtaining the user's username and password....

The potential for fabricating or tampering with electronically stored information on a social networking site, thus poses significant challenges from the standpoint of authentication of printouts of the site, as in the present case. Authentication, nevertheless, is generally governed by Maryland Rule 5-901, which provides:

> (a) **General provision.** The requirement of authentication or identification as a condition precedent to admissibility is satisfied by evidence sufficient to support a finding that the matter in question is what its proponent claims.

Potential methods of authentication are illustrated in Rule 5-901(b). The most germane to the present inquiry are Rules 5-901(b)(1) and 5-901(b)(4), which state:

> (b) **Illustrations.** By way of illustration only, and not by way of limitation, the following are examples of authentication or identification conforming with the requirements of this Rule:
>
> (1) Testimony of witness with knowledge. Testimony of a witness with knowledge that the offered evidence is what it is claimed to be.[11]
>
> * * *
>
> (4) Circumstantial evidence. Circumstantial evidence, such as appearance, contents, substance, internal patterns, location, or other distinctive characteristics, that the offered evidence is what it is claimed to be.

. . . .

In the present case, Griffin argues that the State did not appropriately, for evidentiary purposes, authenticate the pages allegedly printed from Jessica Barber's MySpace profile, because the State failed to offer any extrinsic evidence describing MySpace, as well as indicating how Sergeant Cook obtained the pages in question and adequately linking both the profile and the "snitches get stitches" posting to Ms. Barber. The State counters that the photograph, personal information, and references to freeing "Boozy" were sufficient to enable the finder of fact to believe that the pages printed from MySpace were indeed Ms. Barber's.

We agree with Griffin and disagree with the State regarding whether the trial judge abused his discretion in admitting the MySpace profile as appropriately authenticated, with Jessica Barber as its creator and user, as well as the author of the "snitches get stitches" posting, based upon the inadequate foundation laid. We differ from our colleagues on the Court of Special Appeals, who gave short shrift to the concern that "someone other than the alleged author may have accessed the account and posted the message in question." While the intermediate appellate court determined that the pages allegedly printed from Ms. Barber's MySpace profile contained sufficient indicia of reliability, because the printout "featured a photograph of Ms. Barber and [Petitioner] in an embrace," and also contained the "user's birth date and identified her boyfriend as 'Boozy,'" the court failed to acknowledge the possibility or likelihood that another user could have created the profile in issue or authored the "snitches get stitches" posting.

We agree with Griffin that the trial judge abused his discretion in admitting the MySpace evidence pursuant to Rule 5-901(b)(4), because the picture of Ms. Barber, coupled with her birth date and location, were not sufficient "distinctive characteristics" on a MySpace profile to authenticate its printout, given the prospect that someone other than Ms. Barber could have not only created the site, but also posted the "snitches get stitches" comment. The potential for abuse and manipulation of a social networking site

---

11. We add this section to highlight that a witness with knowledge, such as Ms. Barber, could be asked whether the MySpace profile was hers and whether its contents were authored by her; she, however, was not subject to such inquiry when she was called by the State.

by someone other than its purported creator and/or user leads to our conclusion that a printout of an image from such a site requires a greater degree of authentication than merely identifying the date of birth of the creator and her visage in a photograph on the site in order to reflect that Ms. Barber was its creator and the author of the "snitches get stitches" language.

In so holding, we recognize that other courts, called upon to consider authentication of electronically stored information on social networking sites, have suggested greater scrutiny because of the heightened possibility for manipulation by other than the true user or poster. In *Commonwealth v. Williams,* 926 N.E.2d 1162 (2010), the Supreme Judicial Court of Massachusetts considered the admission, over the defendant's objection, of instant messages a witness had received "at her account at MySpace." In the case, the defendant was convicted of the shooting death of Izaah Tucker, as well as other offenses. The witness, Ashlei Noyes, testified that she had spent the evening of the murder socializing with the defendant and that he had been carrying a handgun. She further testified that the defendant's brother had contacted her "four times on her MySpace account between February 9, 2007, and February 12, 2007," urging her "not to testify or to claim a lack of memory regarding the events of the night of the murder." At trial, Noyes testified that the defendant's brother, Jesse Williams, had a picture of himself on his MySpace account and that his MySpace screen name or pseudonym was "doit4it." She testified that she had received the messages from Williams, and the document printed from her MySpace account indicated that the messages were in fact sent by a user with the screen name "doit4it," depicting a picture of Williams.

The Supreme Judicial Court of Massachusetts determined that there was an inadequate foundation laid to authenticate the MySpace messages, because the State failed to offer any evidence regarding who had access to the MySpace page and whether another author, other than Williams, could have virtually-penned the messages....

The court emphasized that the State failed to demonstrate a sufficient connection between the messages printed from Williams's alleged MySpace account and Williams himself, with reference, for example, to Williams's use of an exclusive username and password to which only he had access....

Similarly, in *People v. Lenihan,* 911 N.Y.S.2d 588 (N.Y.Sup.Ct.2010), Lenihan challenged his second degree murder conviction because he was not permitted to cross-examine two witnesses called by the State on the basis of photographs his mother had printed from MySpace, allegedly depicting the witnesses and the victim making hand gestures and wearing clothing that suggested an affiliation with the "Crips" gang. The trial judge precluded Lenihan from confronting the witnesses with the MySpace photographs, reasoning that "[i]n light of the ability to 'photo shop,' edit photographs on the computer," Lenihan could not adequately authenticate the photographs.

In *United States v. Jackson,* 208 F.3d 633 (7th Cir.2000), Jackson was charged with mail and wire fraud and obstruction of justice after making false claims of racial harassment against the United Parcel Service in connection with an elaborate scheme in which she sent packages containing racial epithets to herself and to several prominent African-Americans purportedly from "racist elements" within UPS. At trial, Jackson sought to introduce website postings from "the Euro-American Student Union and Storm Front," in which the white supremacist groups gloated about Jackson's case and took credit for the UPS mailings. The court determined that the trial judge was justified in excluding the evidence because it lacked an appropriate foundation, namely that Jackson had failed to show that the web postings by the white supremacist groups who took responsibility for the racist mailings "actually were posted by the groups, as opposed to being slipped onto the groups' websites by Jackson herself, who was a skilled computer user."

The State refers us, however, to *In the Interest of F.P.*, 878 A.2d 91 (Pa.Super.Ct.2005), in which the Pennsylvania intermediate appellate court considered whether instant messages were properly authenticated pursuant to Pennsylvania Rule of Evidence 901(b)(4), providing that a document may be authenticated by distinctive characteristics or circumstantial evidence. In the case, involving an assault, the victim, Z.G., testified that the defendant had attacked him because he believed that Z.G. had stolen a DVD from him. The hearing judge, over defendant's objection, admitted instant messages from a user with the screen name "Icp4Life30" to and between "WHITEBOY Z 404." Z.G. testified that his screen name was "WHITEBOY Z 404" and that he had printed the instant messages from his computer. In the transcript of the instant messages, moreover, Z.G. asked "who is this," and the defendant replied, using his first name. Throughout the transcripts, the defendant threatened Z.G. with physical violence because Z.G. "stole off [him]." On appeal, the court determined that the instant messages were properly authenticated through the testimony of Z.G. and also because "Icp4Life30" had referred to himself by first name, repeatedly accused Z.G. of stealing from him, and referenced the fact that Z.G. had told high school administrators about the threats, such that the instant messages contained distinctive characteristics and content linking them to the defendant. *In the Interest of F.P.* is unpersuasive in the context of a social networking site, because the authentication of instant messages by the recipient who identifies his own "distinctive characteristics" and his having received the messages, is distinguishable from the authentication of a profile and posting printed from MySpace, by one who is neither a creator nor user of the specific profile.[13]

. . . .

In so doing, we should not be heard to suggest that printouts from social networking sites should never be admitted. Possible avenues to explore to properly authenticate a profile or posting printed from a social networking site, will, in all probability, continue to develop as the efforts to evidentially utilize information from the sites increases. A number of authentication opportunities come to mind, however.

The first, and perhaps most obvious method would be to ask the purported creator if she indeed created the profile and also if she added the posting in question, i.e. "[t]estimony of a witness with knowledge that the offered evidence is what it is claimed to be." Rule 5-901(b)(1). The second option may be to search the computer of the person who allegedly created the profile and posting and examine the computer's internet history and hard drive to determine whether that computer was used to originate the social networking profile and posting in question. One commentator . . . notes that, "[s]ince a user unwittingly leaves an evidentiary trail on her computer simply by using it, her computer will provide evidence of her web usage."

A third method may be to obtain information directly from the social networking website that links the establishment of the profile to the person who allegedly created it and also links the posting sought to be introduced to the person who initiated it. . . .[15]

---

13. We further note that authentication concerns attendant to e-mails, instant messaging correspondence, and text messages differ significantly from those involving a MySpace profile and posting printout, because such correspondences [are] sent directly from one party to an intended recipient or recipients, rather than published for all to see.

15. Federally, some of the uncertainty involving evidence printed from social networking sites has been addressed by embracing the notion of "conditional relevancy," pursuant to Federal Rule 104(b). . . . In this way, the trier of fact could weigh the reliability of the MySpace evidence against the possibil-

HARRELL, J., dissenting in which MURPHY, J., joins.

I dissent from the Majority Opinion's holding that "the picture of Ms. Barber, coupled with her birth date and location, were not sufficient 'distinctive characteristics' on a MySpace profile to authenticate its [redacted] printout...."

Maryland Rule 5-901 ("Requirement of authentication or identification") derives from and is similar materially to Federal Rule of Evidence 901. Thus, federal cases construing the federal rule are almost direct authority impacting on our construction of a Maryland analog rule. In construing and applying Federal Rule 901, federal courts have held almost unanimously that "a document is properly authenticated if a *reasonable juror could find in favor of authenticity.*" Although, to date, we have not enunciated such a standard, because I think that the "reasonable juror" standard is consistent with Maryland Rule 5-901 — requiring only "evidence *sufficient to support a finding* that the matter in question is what its proponent claims" (emphasis added) — I would adopt it.

Applying that standard to the present case, a reasonable juror could conclude, based on the presence on the MySpace profile of (1) a picture of a person appearing to Sergeant Cook to be Ms. Barber posing with the defendant, her boyfriend; (2) a birth date matching Ms. Barber's; (3) a description of the purported creator of the MySpace profile as being a twenty-three year old from Port Deposit; and (4) references to freeing "Boozy" (a nickname for the defendant), that the redacted printed pages of the MySpace profile contained information posted by Ms. Barber.

I am not unmindful of the Majority Opinion's analysis relating to the concern that someone other than Ms. Barber could access or create the account and post the threatening message. The record, however, suggests no motive to do so. The technological heebie jeebies discussed in the Majority Opinion go, in my opinion, however, not to the admissibility of the print-outs under Rule 5-901, but rather to the weight to be given the evidence by the trier of fact.

It has been said that the "purpose of authentication is to ... filter untrustworthy evidence." *Phillip M. Adams & Assocs., L.L.C. v. Dell, Inc.,* 621 F.Supp.2d 1173, 1184 (D.Utah 2009). Like many filters that are unable to remove completely all impurities, Rule 5-901 does not act to disallow any and all evidence that may have "impurities" (i.e., in this case, evidence that could have come, conceivably, from a source other than the purported source). As long as a reasonable juror could conclude that the proffered evidence is what its proponent purports it to be, the evidence should be admitted. The potentialities that are of concern to the Majority Opinion are fit subjects for cross-examination or rebuttal testimony and go properly to the weight the fact-finder may give the print-outs. Accordingly, I dissent....

Commonwealth v. Purdy

945 N.E.2d 372 (Mass. 2011)

GANTS, J.

The defendant was convicted of deriving support from the earnings of a prostitute ... and maintaining a house of prostitution.... On appeal, the defendant challenges the admission of ten electronic mail (e-mail) exchanges that he claims were not properly authenticated....

---

ity that an imposter generated the material in question. Maryland Rule 5-104(b) establishes a nearly identical protocol; we, however, have not been asked in this case to address the efficacy of the Rule 5-104(b) protocol.

The defendant owned and operated the About Hair Salon (salon) in Harvard Square in Cambridge, which was simultaneously a hair salon, antique store, art studio, and massage parlor. The gist of the Commonwealth's case was that the massage business the defendant ran provided sexual services as "extras" to the massages....

The police executed a search warrant of the salon on October 7, 2005, and during the course of that search seized a desktop computer. After the defendant received Miranda warnings and waived his rights, he told Detective Joseph Murphy of the Cambridge police department, in response to his questions, that the desktop computer was his and that he used it. He also provided, from his own memory, the passwords needed to access programs on the computer....

Detective Murphy made an exact copy of the hard drive of the defendant's computer and, in searching it, located numerous e-mails, of which ten e-mail exchanges were admitted in evidence. These e-mails were sent from an e-mail account that the defendant acknowledged during his testimony that he used, with an e-mail address that contained the defendant's first and last names....

Among the e-mail exchanges admitted in evidence was one that was initiated from the defendant's e-mail address and signed with the defendant's name and the address of the salon, and had the "header," "personal assistant with benefits?." The author wrote that he was "seeking a personal secretary with an open mind, who ... knows where to keep her nose and where not." In response to a reply from a recipient, the author described himself as a "working artist, as well [as an] entrepreneur, small business guy, hairstylist, art and antiques dealer, [and] massage therapist," and added, "and I operate a service." In a later e-mail in this exchange, also from the defendant's e-mail address, the author asserted that potential earnings could range from $200 to $2,000 per week.

A separate e-mail was entitled "massage" and was sent from the defendant's e-mail address and signed with the defendant's first name. The author describes a "blond girl" who is "fairly new and so a little nervous," and states: "If you are gentle and kind to her I'm sure you're going to have a very good time." He adds, "She has beautiful breasts and she will allow light touching. It is ok, but no other touching." The recipient of the e-mail responded that he wanted an "unhurried session" with a "gal who will treat me right[,] be slow [,] gentle and very friendly within her limits." An e-mail from the defendant's e-mail address and signed with the defendant's first initial replied, "I will make sure you are treated well."

....

The computer was located in the area of the salon that was devoted to the sale of antiques, near the massage room, and the defendant testified that it was always on and that other people in the salon, particularly the masseuses, knew the passwords to his computer and used the computer frequently. He testified that they used his e-mail account to play pranks on him, and that they answered e-mails in his name. Asked about each e-mail individually, the defendant asserted that most of the e-mails in evidence were pranks and he was unsure what the others were....

The defendant argues that the judge erred in admitting the ten e-mail exchanges because the evidence was insufficient to authenticate them as having been authored by him. "The requirement of authentication ... as a condition precedent to admissibility is satisfied by evidence sufficient to support a finding that the matter in question is what its proponent claims." Mass. G. Evid. § 901(a) (2011). See also Fed.R.Evid. § 901(a) (2010) (same). "The role of the trial judge in jury cases is to determine whether there is evidence sufficient, if believed, to convince the jury by a preponderance of the evidence that the item in question is what the proponent claims it to be. If so, the evidence should be admitted, if it is otherwise admissible." Here, because the relevance and admissibility of the communications depended on their being authored by the defendant, the judge was required to determine whether the evidence was sufficient for a reasonable jury to find by a preponderance of the evidence that the defendant authored the e-mails. Evidence may be authenticated by direct or circumstantial evidence, including its "[a]ppearance, contents, substance, internal patterns, or other distinctive characteristics." Mass. G. Evid. §901(b)(1), (4). Fed.R.Evid. §901(b)(1), (4).

Here, the defense moved in limine to preclude the Commonwealth from introducing the e-mails in evidence. Defense counsel represented that the defendant shared his computer with others at the salon and that he denied authoring the e-mails, but did not challenge the prosecutor's representation that the e-mails she sought to offer were taken from the hard drive of the computer owned by the defendant and were signed with the defendant's first name or his first initial. The judge denied the motion in limine based on the prosecutor's unrebutted representation. At the time the e-mails were offered and admitted in evidence, the Commonwealth not only had provided evidence to support its representations but also had elicited evidence from Detective Murphy that the defendant knew and provided from memory all the passwords necessary to access the computer's programs, and that the e-mails originated from an e-mail address that the defendant used and that bore his name.[6] The Commonwealth, however, did not furnish direct evidence that the defendant had authored any of the ten e-mails admitted in evidence; there was no testimony that anyone observed him typing any of the e-mails or that anyone had discussed any of the e-mails with him. The defendant contends this evidence is insufficient to establish that the e-mails were what the Commonwealth claimed them to be, that is, e-mails authored by the defendant. We disagree, and we conclude that the evidence was sufficient to authenticate the e-mails as having been authored by the defendant.

A judge making a determination concerning the authenticity of a communication sought to be introduced in evidence may look to "confirming circumstances" that would allow a reasonable jury to conclude that this evidence is what its proponent claims it to be. In the context of telephone conversations, where a witness has received a telephone call and cannot identify the caller's voice, evidence that the caller identified himself as the defendant is not sufficient to authenticate the conversation. But other "confirming circumstances" may provide sufficient evidence that the defendant was the caller. Thus, a witness who lived in the same home as the victim was allowed to testify about the statements made by a caller who claimed to be the defendant, where she had previously answered other telephone calls from a person who identified himself as the defendant, the behavior of the victim and defendant on these previous occasions corroborated the identity of the caller, telephone records showed that a call had been placed from the defendant's telephone number to the victim's residence around the time of the call in question, and the defendant said he had telephoned the victim's residence that day. Similarly, where a witness placed a telephone call to a "land-line" telephone number located in an apartment in which the defendant was the only male resident, where the male answering the telephone had the same voice as the male who had answered previous telephone calls to that telephone number, and where the male provided information during the telephone call that confirmed his identity as the defendant, the telephone call was sufficiently authenticated and properly admitted in evidence.

---

6. The Commonwealth also provided evidence through the testimony of Detective Murphy that the printed e-mails offered in evidence were accurate reproductions of the original electronic evidence extracted from the defendant's computer.

In the context of written letters, where a witness has received a letter and cannot identify the writer's handwriting or signature, evidence that the writer identified himself as a particular individual is not sufficient to authenticate the letter. But where a witness identified the handwriting in a letter as that of the defendant, or where the letter was received as a reply to a letter sent by the witness to a particular addressee, or where other confirming circumstances are present, a letter can be authenticated and properly admitted in evidence.

While e-mails and other forms of electronic communication present their own opportunities for false claims of authorship, the basic principles of authentication are the same. See *United States v. Safavian*, 435 F.Supp.2d 36, 41 (D.D.C.2006) ("The *possibility* of alteration does not and cannot be the basis for excluding e-mails as unidentified or unauthenticated as a matter of course, any more than it can be the rationale for excluding paper documents" [emphasis in original]); *Simon v. State*, 279 Ga.App. 844, 847 (2006) ("e-mail offers unique opportunities for fabrication [but] it is held to the same standards of authentication as other similar evidence"). Evidence that the defendant's name is written as the author of an e-mail or that the electronic communication originates from an e-mail or a social networking Web site such as Facebook or MySpace that bears the defendant's name is not sufficient alone to authenticate the electronic communication as having been authored or sent by the defendant. See *Commonwealth v. Williams*, 456 Mass. 857, 868–869, 926 N.E.2d 1162 (2010). There must be some "confirming circumstances" sufficient for a reasonable jury to find by a preponderance of the evidence that the defendant authored the e-mails.

Here there were adequate "confirming circumstances" to meet this threshold: in addition to the e-mails having originated from an account bearing the defendant's name and acknowledged to be used by the defendant, the e-mails were found on the hard drive of the computer that the defendant acknowledged he owned, and to which he supplied all necessary passwords. While this was sufficient to authenticate the e-mails in the absence of persuasive evidence of fraud, tampering, or "hacking," there was additional evidence of the defendant's authorship of most of the e-mails. At least one e-mail contained an attached photograph of the defendant, and in another, the author described the unusual set of services provided by the salon when he characterized himself, among other things, as a "hairstylist, art and antiques dealer, [and] massage therapist."[7] The defendant's uncorroborated testimony that others used his computer regularly and that he did not author the e-mails was relevant to the weight, not the admissibility, of these messages. . . .

---

7. The confirming circumstances in this case are stronger than those in *Commonwealth v. Williams*, 456 Mass. 857, 868–869, 926 N.E.2d 1162 (2010), where we concluded that messages sent from the MySpace Web page of the defendant's brother were not properly authenticated as having been authored by the defendant's brother. In that case, we noted that there was no testimony regarding how secure a MySpace Web page is, who can access it, or whether codes are needed for such access. Moreover, "while the foundational testimony established that the messages were sent by someone with access to [the defendant's brother's] MySpace Web page," the author of the messages did not identify himself with the name of the defendant's brother (or any other name). Unlike in *Commonwealth v. Williams*, where the messages could have been sent from any computer or device with access to the Internet and there was no evidence of how authorship might have been limited, the e-mails in this case were found on a computer belonging to the defendant and for which passwords were required.

While we noted in *Commonwealth v. Williams* that the Commonwealth did not offer expert testimony that the defendant's brother was the only person who could communicate from that Web page, we do not suggest that expert testimony or exclusive access is necessary to authenticate the authorship of an e-mail. Nor do we suggest that password protection is necessary to authenticate the authorship of an e-mail, even though there was such protection here.

Notes and Questions

1. Sometimes, individuals will engage in a combination of online and offline activities such that their offline activity can serve to authenticate their online identities. Thus, for example, if a person using a particular chat room handle describes himself and agrees to meet with another person he is communicating with in the chat room at a particular time and location, and someone fitting that description shows up at that particular location at the appointed time, it tends to authenticate that person as the author of the online chat room communications. *See, e.g., United States v. Tank*, 200 F.3d 627, 630–31 (9th Cir. 2000).

2. Consider the following argument *against* treating electronic evidence differently from traditional forms of evidence:

> [A]ppellant would have us create a whole new body of law just to deal with e-mails or instant messages. The argument is that e-mails or text messages are inherently unreliable because of their relative anonymity and the fact that while an electronic message can be traced to a particular computer, it can rarely be connected to a specific author with any certainty. Unless the purported author is actually witnessed sending the e-mail, there is always the possibility it is not from whom it claims. As appellant correctly points out, anybody with the right password can gain access to another's e-mail account and send a message ostensibly from that person. However, the same uncertainties exist with traditional written documents. A signature can be forged; a letter can be typed on another's typewriter; distinct letterhead stationary can be copied or stolen. We believe that e-mail messages and similar forms of electronic communication can be properly authenticated within the existing framework [for authenticating non-electronic evidence]. We see no justification for constructing unique rules for admissibility of electronic communications such as instant messages; they are to be evaluated on a case-by-case basis as any other document to determine whether or not there has been an adequate foundational showing of their relevance and authenticity.

In re F.P., 878 A.2d 91, 95–96 (Pa. Super. Ct. 2005). Are you persuaded? Or do the concerns raised by the majority in *Griffin* counsel in favor of a more cautious approach?

3. Can a computer file qualify as an "ancient document" if it is sufficiently old? *See* Advisory Committee Note to Rule 901(b)(8) ("The familiar ancient document rule of the common law is extended to include data stored electronically or by other similar means. Since the importance of appearance diminishes in this situation, the importance of custody or place where found increases correspondingly. This expansion is necessary in view of the widespread use of methods of storing data in forms other than conventional written records.").

G. Shortcuts for Authenticating Evidence

As demonstrated by the materials in this chapter, the formal process of authenticating evidence can be a somewhat time-consuming process. While this process may be unavoidable, it is sometimes possible to avoid the requirements of Rule 901 altogether for evidence that is deemed to be "self-authenticating."

Rule 902 sets forth a list of 12 categories of evidence that are deemed to be "self-authenticating," meaning that "they require no extrinsic evidence of authenticity in order to be admitted." These categories, many of which have detailed technical requirements, include: certain domestic and foreign public documents, certified copies of public records, official publications, newspapers and periodicals, trade inscriptions and the like, acknowledge documents, commercial paper, and certified business records.

The rationale for dispensing with the normal requirement of authentication for these types of evidence is a judgment that the likelihood that the evidence will be something other than what its proponent purports it to be is sufficiently minimal as to be outweighed by the costs of requiring the parties to comply with Rule 901. Of course, only the requirement of a preliminary showing of authenticity is dispensed with: the jury must still be persuaded of the authenticity of the evidence, and the opposing party remains free to dispute authenticity before the jury.

Even if evidence is not self-authenticating under Rule 902, the formal process of authentication can be avoided if the parties stipulate to its authenticity. While this is purely voluntary, opposing parties have a mutual interest in doing so for evidence whose authenticity is unquestioned in that it saves time and money for both.

Finally, in civil cases, the Federal Rules of Civil Procedure provide a number of methods of short-circuiting the authentication process. For example, in a request for admissions filed pursuant to Federal Rule of Civil Procedure 36, a party can ask an opposing party to admit to authenticity of particular items of evidence, with an unreasonable refusal to do so subjecting the opposing party to financial sanctions.

Accordingly, before putting each piece of evidence through the expensive and time-consuming formal process of authentication, parties should try to take advantage of the alternatives available under Rule 902, and in civil cases, under the various provisions of the Federal Rules of Civil Procedure.

Chapter 3

Relevance and Prejudice Refined

It probably has struck you by now that Rules 401 through 403 lack the precision necessary to ensure predictability and consistent application across all judges and cases. However, the rules must of necessity be written in general terms to accommodate the variety of relevancy issues that are likely to arise, and unless one were willing to write a rule to address every possible scenario that might arise (were that even possible), some degree of unpredictability and inconsistency are necessary costs.

Yet there is a middle ground between these two extremes, one that the drafters of the federal rules of evidence opted for. Recognizing that "some situations recur with sufficient frequency to create patterns susceptible of treatment by specific rules," Advisory Committee Note to Rule 401, the drafters developed a set of rules—Rules 404 through 415—that refine the concepts of relevance and prejudice as applied to particular types of evidence when offered for specific purposes and in some instances provide bright-line rules regarding admissibility.

Some of these rules merely represent an application of the principles of Rules 401 through 403, with the balancing being done by the drafters of the rules instead of each individual judge to ensure consistent and predictable application. But in some instances they go further, excluding relevant evidence to further substantive policies that transcend the individual case and the truth-seeking process. As you will soon discover, understanding the policies that underlie each rule is important, for courts often use these policies as an aid in interpreting the rules.

These rules typically identify a category of evidence and call for its exclusion when offered for a particular purpose or by a particular party but not when offered for other purposes or by other parties. It is, however, important to remember that even if such evidence is not excluded by one of the categorical rules (because, say, it is offered for some purpose not forbidden by the rule), it may nonetheless be subject to exclusion under Rule 403, or at the very least, call for a limiting instruction under Rule 105. In other words, notwithstanding these specific rules, the general rules remain pertinent even when dealing with evidence of the sort covered by these rules.

A. Evidence of Character

Suppose that you are asked to determine whether an individual is guilty of murder or assault. In determining whether he is guilty or innocent of the crime charged, might it not be useful to know generally or specifically about past instances of violent behavior on his part? Of course, the fact that he has been violent in the past does not necessarily mean that he was in fact violent on some future occasion (people don't always act in conformity with their propensities), but to be relevant it need only have some tendency to prove the point for which it is offered, and surely there is some correlation between past violent behavior and future violent behavior, at least enough to pass muster under Rules 401 and 402.

Yet Rule 404 in two places raises a general bar to the use of such so-called propensity evidence. Rule 404(a)(1) provides that "[e]vidence of a person's character or character trait is not admissible to prove that on a particular occasion the person acted in accordance with the character or trait," and Rule 404(b)(1) provides that "[e]vidence of a crime, wrong, or other act is not admissible to prove a person's character in order to show that on a particular occasion the person acted in accordance with the character." The rule to this extent codifies the antecedent common law and is grounded in the same rationale:

> The State may not show defendant's prior trouble with the law, specific criminal acts, or ill name among his neighbors, even though such facts might logically be persuasive that he is by propensity a probable perpetrator of the crime. The inquiry is not rejected because character is irrelevant; on the contrary, it is said to weigh too much with the jury and to so overpersuade them as to prejudge one with a bad general record and deny him a fair opportunity to defend against a particular charge. The overriding policy of excluding such evidence, despite its admitted probative value, is the practical experience that its disallowance tends to prevent confusion of issues, unfair surprise and undue prejudice.

Michelson v. United States, 335 U.S. 469, 475–476 (1948).

However, this bar is not as absolute as it might seem. First, a number of explicit exceptions in Rule 404(a) allow for the admission of evidence of character to prove action in conformity therewith under certain circumstances. Second, because Rule 404(b)(1) only bars evidence of other crimes, wrongs, or acts when offered to prove a person's character and to in turn show that on a particular occasion the person acted in accordance with that character, such evidence when offered for other purposes is not barred by the rule (a point explicitly made in Rule 404(b)(2)). Third, together Rules 404 and 406 bar only "character" evidence while allowing for the admission of "habit" evidence: to the extent that evidence is deemed more like the latter than the former, Rule 404 poses no bar to its admission. Finally, there are special rules set forth in Rules 412 through 415 that address the admissibility of character evidence in sex offense cases and that differ substantially from the general principle set forth in Rule 404.

1. Character of Accused and Victim

The general bar of Rule 404 coupled with three exceptions set forth in Rule 404(a)(2) give criminal defendants control over whether either evidence of their own character traits or those of the alleged victim can be offered by either side for the purpose of showing action in conformity therewith (subject to important caveats in sex offense cases, discussed below).

Under normal circumstances, Rule 404 bars the prosecution from introducing evidence of the defendant's character for the purpose of showing action in conformity therewith. Thus, for example, in an assault or murder case, Rule 404 bars the prosecution from introducing evidence of the defendant's violent character for the purpose of showing that he was violent on the occasion at issue. Similarly, in such a case, Rule 404 also bars the prosecution from introducing evidence of the victim's peaceful character offered for the purpose of showing that the defendant was the likely aggressor.

However, Rules 404(a)(2)(A) and 404(a)(2)(B), respectively, give the defendant in a criminal case the option of introducing evidence of "pertinent" character traits of himself or the victim. Yet this privilege does not come without cost. While Rule 404 normally bars the prosecution from introducing character evidence, once the defendant opens the door to such evidence by way of the exceptions set forth in Rules 404(a)(2)(A) or 404(a)(2)(B), those same exceptions give the prosecution the ability to introduce character evidence to rebut that offered by the defendant. Moreover, Rule 404(a)(2)(C) provides that, in some instances, the defendant can, without even introducing character evidence, open the door to the prosecution's use of character evidence.

The following problem and the notes that follow are designed to help you to understand these explicit exceptions to Rule 404. Set aside for the moment concerns about the form of the character evidence; we will come to that soon enough. For now, try to master when Rule 404 allows for character evidence and when it does not.

Problem 3-1: Violent or Non-Violent?

Mary is on trial on charges that she assaulted Rebecca using a deadly weapon. Mary claims that she acted in self-defense. Assume that Mary does not testify at the trial.

(a) Can the prosecution, during its case-in-chief, offer evidence of Mary's violent character? Of Rebecca's non-violent character?

(b) Can the defense, during its case-in-reply, offer evidence of Mary's peaceful character? Of Rebecca's violent character?

(c) Can the defense, during its case-in-reply, offer evidence of Mary's character for honesty? Her character for temperance? How about her character for law-abidingness?

(d) Assume that the defense offers only evidence of Rebecca's violent character. Can the prosecution in its case-in-rebuttal introduce evidence of Rebecca's non-violent character? How about of Mary's violent character?

(e) Assume that the defense offers no character evidence, but does call a witness to the assault who testifies that Rebecca started the fight. Can the prosecution in its case-in-rebuttal offer evidence of Rebecca's non-violent character?

(f) How, if at all, would your answers to the previous questions change in a civil action for battery brought by Rebecca against Mary in connection with these same facts? How, if at all, would your answers change if this were a murder prosecution?

Problem 3-2: Violent or Non-Violent Revisited

Assume the same facts as in Problem 3-1, except that the proceedings are taking place in a state court in Iowa. Iowa's version of Federal Rule 404 provides in pertinent part as follows:

a. Character evidence generally. Evidence of a person's character or a trait of the person's character is not admissible for the purpose of proving that the person acted in conformity therewith on a particular occasion, except:

(1) Character of accused. Evidence of a pertinent trait of the person's character offered by an accused, or by the prosecution to rebut the same.

(2) Character of victim.

(A) In criminal cases. Subject to rule 5.412, evidence of a pertinent trait of character of the victim of the crime offered by an accused, or by the prosecution to rebut the same, or evidence of a character trait of peacefulness of the victim offered by the prosecution in any case where the victim is unavailable to testify due to death or physical or mental incapacity to rebut evidence that the victim was the first aggressor.

(B) In civil cases. Evidence of character for violence of the victim of assaultive conduct offered on the issue of self defense by a party accused of the assaultive conduct, or evidence of peaceable character to rebut the same.

Iowa R. Evid. 5.404.

In what ways would your answers to the questions set forth in Problem 3-1 differ if you were applying the Iowa rule? As a matter of policy, which rule do you prefer, and why?

Notes and Questions

1. The exceptions in Rules 404(a)(2)(A) and 404(a)(2)(B) allow for evidence of a "pertinent" trait of character. What does it mean to be "pertinent"? The cases interpret this as the equivalent of "relevant," meaning that it must have some tendency to prove or disprove an element of the offenses charged or defenses claimed. *See, e.g., United States v. John*, 309 F.3d 298, 303 (5th 2002); *United States v. Angelini*, 678 F.2d 380, 381 (1st Cir. 1982). Thus, where some violent act is an element of an offense or defense, a person's character for violence will certainly be pertinent. Yet the concept tolerates more general evidence of character, and thus evidence of a trait of "law-abidingness" will almost always be pertinent. *See In re Sealed Case*, 352 F.3d 409, 412 (D.C. Cir. 2003); *United States v. Diaz*, 961 F.2d 1417, 1419 (9th Cir. 1992); *Angelini*, 678 F.2d at 381; *United States v. Hewitt*, 634 F.2d 277, 279 (5th Cir. 1981). However, character for truthfulness is generally deemed to be pertinent only if the crime itself involves an element of dishonesty or false statement, such as criminal fraud. *See In re Sealed Case*, 352 F.3d at 412; *Hewitt*, 634 F.2d at 279. With regard to character of the victim, it typically arises in self-defense cases and involves evidence of the victim's violent or non-violent character. *See United States v. Smith*, 230 F.3d 300, 307 (7th Cir. 2000); *United States v. Weise*, 89 F.3d 502, 504 (8th Cir. 1996).

2. What is the definition of "character"? The Advisory Committee Note to Rule 406, in differentiating it from "habit," defines it as "a generalized description of one's disposition, or of one's disposition in respect to a general trait, such as honesty, temperance, or peacefulness."

3. When the defendant introduces character evidence about either himself or the victim, that does not open the door to *any* character evidence about that individual. Rather, as the exceptions point out, the prosecution's right to rebut is only with "evidence of the *same* trait of character." *See United States v. Reed*, 700 F.2d 638, 645 (11th Cir. 1983).

4. Prior to December 1, 2000, when the defendant invoked Rule 404(a)(2)(B) to attack the victim's character, the prosecution could only respond by offering offsetting evidence about the *victim's* character. Under an amendment that took effect on December

1, 2000, however, the defendant, by attacking the victim's character, also opens himself up to an attack of his *own* character on that same trait. According to the Advisory Committee:

> The amendment makes clear that the accused cannot attack the alleged victim's character and yet remain shielded from the disclosure of equally relevant evidence concerning the same character trait of the accused. For example, in a murder case with a claim of self-defense, the accused, to bolster this defense, might offer evidence of the alleged victim's violent disposition. If the government has evidence that the accused has a violent character, but is not allowed to offer this evidence as part of its rebuttal, the jury has only part of the information it needs for an informed assessment of the probabilities as to who was the initial aggressor.

Advisory Committee's Note to 2000 Amendment to Rule 404.

It is important to keep in mind that many *state* versions of Rule 404 still track the language of the earlier version of the federal rule.

5. In a joint trial of two defendants, if one defendant introduces character evidence of the victim, is the prosecution entitled to introduce character evidence as to *both* defendants or only the one who introduced the character evidence? *See United States v. Herder*, 59 Fed. Appx. 257, 268–69 (10th Cir. 2003) (discussing but not deciding the issue).

6. In one narrow situation, the prosecution is allowed to introduce evidence of the victim's character even if the defendant has not introduced any character evidence. Rule 404(a)(2)(C) provides that, "in a homicide case, the prosecutor may offer evidence of the alleged victim's trait of peacefulness to rebut evidence that the victim was the first aggressor," and the Advisory Committee Note makes clear that this exception applies to such a claim "however proved." What justifies such an exception in this circumstance?

7. Can the exceptions set forth in Rules 404(a)(2)(A) and 404(a)(2)(B) be invoked in *civil* cases? Until relatively recently, the answer to this question was unclear, with some courts holding that they could never be invoked in civil cases, *see, e.g., S.E.C. v. Towers Financial Corp.*, 966 F. Supp. 203, 204–05 (S.D.N.Y. 1997), and others holding that they could be invoked in those civil cases in which the conduct that forms the basis for the action is criminal in nature, such as civil actions for assault and battery, *see, e.g., Perrin v. Anderson*, 784 F.2d 1040, 1044 (10th Cir. 1986); *Carson v. Polley*, 689 F.2d 562, 575–76 (5th Cir. 1982). However, amendments to Rule 404 that took effect in 2006 make clear that the exceptions set forth in these two sub-sections can be invoked only in criminal cases. *See* Advisory Committee's Note to 2006 Amendment to Rule 404.

8. Note that even if the evidence fits within one of the exceptions, the court still has authority to exclude the evidence under Rule 403. *See United States v. Schatzle*, 901 F.2d 252, 256 (2d Cir. 1990).

9. Is it always clear who is the "victim" of a crime? When a defendant is being prosecuted for jury tampering, is the juror who was being tampered with a victim? *See United States v. Bailey*, 834 F.2d 218, 228–29 (1st Cir. 1987) (holding that it is the government, not the juror, who is the victim in such a case).

10. Another explicit exception, set forth in Rule 404(a)(3), provides that "[e]vidence of a witness's character may be admitted under Rules 607, 608, and 609." Because this exception is better understood in connection with the rules that it cross-references, it will be addressed in Chapter 10, which examines the rules governing impeachment of witnesses.

Evidence of my prior defecation on the lawn is inadmissible to prove this current charge of defecation!

stus.com

2. Character as an Element of a Crime, Claim, or Defense

In very rare instances, an individual's character is actually an *element* of a crime, claim, or defense. In other words, a party must prove something about an individual's character in order to succeed on her claim or defense. If the substantive law so requires, it would make little sense for the rules of evidence to bar the use of character evidence, and indeed such evidence is viewed as falling outside the general ban imposed by Rule 404. The Advisory Committee's Note to Rule 404 indicates that the rule has "no provision on the subject," and such evidence is said to fall outside the scope of the rule because the evidence of character is not being offered for the purpose forbidden by Rule 404 — to show action in conformity therewith on some particular occasion — but rather is being offered for its own sake, to prove that the person has such a character.

One instance in which character arises as an element is in defamation cases, where the statement that is alleged to be defamatory is about an individual's character and truth has been raised as a defense. In such a case, character is a necessary element of the defense of truth, and Rule 404 poses no bar to evidence of that character. *E.g., Schafer v. Time, Inc.*, 142 F.3d 1361, 1371–73 (11th Cir. 1998); *Longmire v. Alabama State Univ.*, 151 F.R.D. 414, 419 (M.D.Ala. 1992).

A second instance in which character arises as an element is in criminal prosecutions in which entrapment is raised as a defense. Part of the prosecution's burden when such a defense is raised is to show that the defendant was predisposed to commit such a crime, which involves evidence of the defendant's character. *E.g., United States v. Thomas*, 134 F.3d 975, 978–80 (9th Cir. 1998); *United States v. Murzyn*, 631 F.2d 525, 529 n.2 (7th Cir. 1980).

A third instance in which character arises as an element is in a tort action for negligent entrustment. In such a suit, the claim is that the defendant was negligent in allowing a careless individual to operate their vehicle or other equipment, and evidence of the individual's character for carelessness is thus necessary to prove an element of the claim. *E.g.*, *Crawford v. Yellow Cab Co.*, 572 F. Supp. 1205, 1209–10 (N.D. Ill. 1983).

There are a handful of other instances in which character is an element of a crime, claim, or defense, but they are exceedingly rare.

Notes and Questions

1. Note that unlike the case when invoking the exceptions set forth in Rules 404(a)(2)(A) and 404(a)(2)(B), there is no distinction between civil and criminal cases when the character evidence is being offered because character is an element of a crime, claim, or defense. Do you see why this is so?

3. Proving Character and Challenging Such Proof

Assuming that evidence of a person's character is admissible for one of the reasons discussed above, how would one go about proving it? Prior to the codification of the rules of evidence, where evidence of character was offered for the purpose of showing action in conformity therewith, only one method of proving character was recognized:

> When the defendant elects to initiate a character inquiry.... Not only is he permitted to call witnesses to testify from hearsay, but indeed such a witness is not allowed to base his testimony on anything but hearsay. What commonly is called "character evidence" is only such when "character" is employed as a synonym for "reputation." The witness may not testify about defendant's specific acts or courses of conduct or his possession of a particular disposition or of benign mental and moral traits; nor can he testify that his own acquaintance, observation, and knowledge of defendant leads to his own independent opinion that defendant possesses a good general or specific character, inconsistent with commission of acts charged. The witness is, however, allowed to summarize what he has heard in the community, although much of it may have been said by persons less qualified to judge than himself. The evidence which the law permits is not as to the personality of defendant but only as to the shadow his daily life has cast in his neighborhood.... While courts have recognized logical grounds for criticism of this type of opinion-based-on-hearsay testimony, it is said to be justified by "overwhelming considerations of practical convenience" in avoiding innumerable collateral issues which, if it were attempted to prove character by direct testimony, would complicate and confuse the trial, distract the minds of jurymen and befog the chief issues in the litigation.

Michelson v. United States, 335 U.S. 469, 477–78 (1948).

Rule 405, which sets forth the permissible means of proving character, deviates from this common law tradition only in one sense: it allows evidence of character to be offered not only by way of testimony as to reputation, but also in the form of an opinion, on the theory that reputation evidence is usually just opinion in disguise. However, Rule 405 maintains the common law rule barring the use of evidence of specific instances of prior conduct as a means of proving character.

Thus, for example, if a party seeks to prove that someone has a violent character, he can call a witness to testify that the individual is known as a violent person (reputation), or to testify that, in the witness' opinion, the individual is violent (opinion). However, the party *cannot* introduce evidence of prior instances of violent conduct by the individual as a means of proving that he has a propensity for violence.

This may strike you as rather a strange rule: it allows each side to parade before the jury people who will testify to the individual's reputation or give their own opinions on the matter, but keeps out what is likely the most potent proof of the individual's character. The Advisory Committee recognized this problem, but struck this balance for the same reasons that the common law did. In the words of the Advisory Committee:

> Of the three methods of proving character provided by the rule, evidence of specific instances of conduct is the most convincing. At the same time it possesses the greatest capacity to arouse prejudice, to confuse, to surprise, and to consume time.

However, Rule 405 does allow for reference to specific instances of conduct in two situations. First, Rule 405(b) provides that when character is an essential element of a charge, claim, or defense, proof of character *may* be made not only through the use of reputation and opinion evidence, but also with evidence of specific instances of the person's conduct. Since proving character is a central issue in this instance and not a side-show, the Advisory Committee, consistent with the common law, *see United States v. Manos*, 848 F.2d 1427, 1431 n.4 (7th Cir. 1988), viewed this as a situation "deserving of a searching inquiry."

Second, Rule 405(a) provides that, when a witness gives reputation or opinion testimony about an individual's character, "[o]n cross-examination of the character witness, the court may allow an inquiry into relevant specific instances of the person's conduct." What purpose is served by this exception, and what risks does it pose? Consider these questions as you answer the following problem and read the cases that follow it.

Problem 3-3: Violent or Non-Violent Revisited (Again!)

Assume the same facts as in Problem 3-1. Assume further that the court rules that, pursuant to Rule 404, the defense, during its case-in-reply, may offer evidence of Mary's peaceful character and of Rebecca's violent character.

(a) Can the defense offer evidence of Mary's peaceful character by calling Rhonda, a friend of Mary's, who if permitted would testify that, in her opinion, Mary is a peaceful person?

(b) Can the defense offer evidence of Rebecca's violent character by calling Donald, a long-time neighbor of Rebecca's, who if permitted would testify that Rebecca has a reputation in the neighborhood for being a violent person?

(c) Can the defense offer evidence of Rebecca's violent character by calling Tom, who if permitted would testify that he once saw Rebecca punch another person in the face?

(d) Assuming that the evidence set forth in sub-part (a) is admitted, can the prosecution ask Rhonda on cross-examination, "Did you know that Mary broke another woman's nose in a bar fight two years ago?"

(e) How, if at all, would your answers to the above questions differ if the case were being adjudicated in Florida, whose version of Federal Rule 405 provides as follows:

Florida Evidence Code § 90.405. Methods of proving character.

(1) Reputation. When evidence of the character of a person or of a trait of that person's character is admissible, proof may be made by testimony about that person's reputation.

(2) Specific instances of conduct. When character or a trait of character of a person is an essential element of a charge, claim, or defense, proof may be made of specific instances of that person's conduct.

United States v. Hewitt
663 F.2d 1381 (11th Cir. 1981)

VANCE, Circuit Judge:

Bobby Gene Chesser and Samuel B. Hewitt appeal their convictions after trial by jury of aiding and abetting the use of an explosive to commit a felony in violation of 18 U.S.C. §§ 2, 844(h). Hewitt also was convicted of two counts of mail fraud in violation of 18 U.S.C. § 1341....

Hewitt alleges that the trial judge committed reversible error in allowing the prosecutor to cross-examine one of Hewitt's reputation witnesses improperly. At trial, Hewitt called four reputation witnesses, each of whom testified to Hewitt's good reputation in the community. The prosecution cross-examined each of the four witnesses by asking them whether they had heard that Hewitt had been indicted, arrested, and was to go to trial in Muscogee County Superior Court on two counts of theft of air conditioning units. The first three reputation witnesses testified that they had heard of the impending trial, but that their assessment of Hewitt's reputation in the community was unaltered. The fourth reputation witness, Diane Gibbons, stated that she had not heard of the impending trial....

The Supreme Court established long ago in *Michelson v. United States*, 335 U.S. 469, 478–79 (1948), that a reputation witness for the defense may be cross-examined as to whether he has heard of certain facts that tend to reflect negatively on defendant's reputation. This line of cross-examination is allowed for the very specific purpose of impeaching the witness' credibility. If the reputation witness has not heard of a fact that is likely to have caused a negative community impression of the defendant, the government has shown that the witness' knowledge of defendant's reputation is shallow and unreliable. If the reputation witness has heard of this fact but nevertheless testifies that the defendant's reputation is good, then the government has shown that the witness is either lying or is applying a lowered standard by which he assesses the defendant's good reputation....

United States v. Krapp
815 F.2d 1183 (8th Cir. 1987)

ROSS, Circuit Judge.

Patricia E. Krapp appeals her conviction of three counts of making false record entries with intent to mislead, deceive or defraud the United States in violation of 18 U.S.C. § 2073....

I.

Krapp was the postmaster of the Pocahontas, Iowa post office from November 1983 to February 1986. An investigation by United States Postal Inspectors in January 1986 revealed a shortage of 100 coils of 22 cent stamps ($2200) at the Pocahontas post office. Krapp admitted to the inspectors that she had discovered the shortage in late November or early December 1985, but had failed to accurately reflect the shortage on certain postal forms and reports which she was required to fill out in connection with her duties as postmaster. Krapp stated that she did not report the shortage because she was investigating the incident and because she lacked expertise in filling out the postal forms. Krapp was charged with three counts of making false record entries with intent to defraud the United States.

II.

At trial, Krapp presented a character witness who testified that Krapp had a reputation as "an honest, trustworthy person." On cross-examination the Assistant United States Attorney asked the witness "Are you aware that Pat Krapp's husband with her knowledge omitted cash income that he had on his—on their tax returns?" Before the witness answered, Krapp's attorney objected to the question and moved for a mistrial on the basis that the question was improper. Although refusing to grant a mistrial, the trial court sustained the objection and admonished the jury to disregard the question. Krapp now argues that a mistrial should have been granted because the question was asked without good faith and served only to prejudice the jury....

This court has previously recognized the possible prejudicial impact of "did you know" type impeachment questions if they have no basis in fact. In *Gross*, we noted:

> "The rule permitting the cross-examiner to ask the character witness whether he 'has heard' of other particular crimes of accused involving the same trait is pregnant with possibilities of destructive prejudice. The mere asking by a respected official of such a question, however answered, may well suggest to the jury that the imputation is true."

Further, "[u]nless circumscribed by rules of fairness and grounded in demonstrated good faith on the part of the prosecution, the result could be most prejudicial to the defendant and make for a miscarriage of justice."

When asked by the trial judge outside the hearing of the jury what his good faith basis was for asking the question, the prosecutor stated that the notes of one of the postal inspectors reflected that Krapp had told the inspector that her husband received cash income which he did not report on their tax return. Further, the prosecutor had seen the tax returns and he believed them to be joint returns. Krapp replied that the postal inspector's notes concerned her 1985 tax return which the prosecutor knew had not been filed.

The trial court, in sustaining Krapp's objection, stated that he was not impugning any bad faith on the part of the prosecutor in asking the question, but found that the prejudicial effect of the question outweighed its probative value. We also make no determination as to whether the question was asked in good faith, although we find the issue to be a close one. Instead, we determine that even if the question were improper, when viewed in the context of the whole trial it was not so offensive as to warrant a mistrial....

However, we admonish the Assistant United States Attorney for asking Krapp's character witness about the Krapps' tax returns in front of the jury without first raising the matter with the trial judge. Before an attempt at impeachment of a character witness with "did you know" type questions such as this, the trial judge should have the opportunity, out of the hearing of the jury, to rule on the propriety of the questions. By failing to raise the matter first with the trial judge, the Assistant United States Attorney created the risk of mistrial after substantial time had been invested in the trial....

Notes and Questions

1. Before a witness can give reputation or opinion testimony about someone's character, he must demonstrate that he is qualified to give such testimony. This he can do by "showing such acquaintance with the defendant, the community in which he has lived and the circles in which he has moved, as to speak with authority of the terms in which generally he is regarded." *Michelson v. United States*, 335 U.S. 469, 478 (1948).

2. The *Michelson* opinion refers to testimony as to a person's reputation as a form of hearsay evidence. We will closely examine the hearsay doctrine in great detail, but it is worth noting at this juncture that Rule 803(21) creates an exception to the rule against hearsay for "reputation among a person's associates or in the community concerning the person's character."

3. What sort of limiting instruction is to be given to the jury in such a case? In *Michelson*, the trial court used the following instruction:

> I instruct the jury that what is happening now is this: the defendant has called character witnesses, and the basis for the evidence given by those character witnesses is the reputation of the defendant in the community, and since the defendant tenders the issue of his reputation the prosecution may ask the witness if she has heard of various incidents in his career. I say to you that regardless of her answer you are not to assume that the incidents asked about actually took place. All that is happening is that this witness' standard of opinion of the reputation of the defendant is being tested. Is that clear?

Michelson v. United States, 335 U.S. 469, 472 n.3 (1948). *See also* 1A Fed. Jury Prac. & Instr. § 11.15 (5th ed. 2003) (setting forth standard limiting instruction analogous to that given by the trial court judge in *Michelson*).

What is your answer to the judge's question to the jury? Is not the gist of the instruction that the jury is to judge the credibility of the witness based on that witness knowing or not knowing of an event that the jury is instructed not to conclude actually took place? How likely are jurors to understand the instruction? To follow it even if they do understand it?

4. Ultimately, even if there exists a good-faith basis for asking such a question, the court retains the ability to exclude the evidence under Rule 403. *E.g.*, *United States v. Bush*, 58 F.3d 482, 489 n.8 (9th Cir. 1995).

5. Note that Rule 405(a) does not require that the person have actually been arrested, charged, or convicted for the conduct at issue. Nonetheless, the fact that none of that occurred may bear on the court's willingness to allow the questioning.

6. What exactly is the risk of allowing questions that lack a factual basis? Consider the following explanation:

> The prosecutor could not have asked Goggin "Isn't it true that in the evenings Finley is a female impersonator who fleeces customers in seedy bars?" unless he had information to that effect. The answer "I've never heard anything of the sort", followed by a change of subject, leaves things dangling. Trials are not occasions for character assassination.... Denial of a serious accusation, without follow-up, leaves an impression that may be unwarranted.

United States v. Finley, 934 F.2d 837, 840 (7th Cir. 1991).

7. Courts have rather unanimously held that constitutional limitations bar the use of Rule 405(a) to ask reputation and opinion witnesses questions regarding the very conduct for which the defendant is on trial. *E.g., United States v. Shwayder*, 312 F.3d 1109, 1120 (9th Cir. 2002); *United States v. Russo*, 110 F.3d 948, 952 (2d Cir. 1997).

8. At common law, because only reputation and not opinion testimony was permitted, there were strict rules regarding the form of the question asked of the witness:

> Since the whole inquiry ... is calculated to ascertain the general talk of people about defendant, rather than the witness' own knowledge of him, the form of inquiry, "Have you heard?" has general approval, and "Do you know?" is not allowed.

Michelson, 335 U.S. at 482.

As current law has altered the common law to allow for opinion as well as reputation testimony, this sort of quibbling objection is no longer relevant in the federal courts. *See* Advisory Committee Note to Rule 405; *United States v. Scholl*, 166 F.3d 964, 974 (9th Cir. 1999); *SEC v. Peters*, 978 F.2d 1162, 1169 (10th Cir. 1992). However, because some states retain the common law rule limiting such evidence to reputation evidence, *see, e.g.*, Florida Stat. § 90.405(1), the form of the question may matter in some state courts.

Moreover, even in federal court, the distinction between opinion and reputation testimony matters when cross-examining a character witness:

> Evidence Rule 405(a) has not effected a merger between reputation and opinion evidence. The reference in the rule's second sentence to cross examination on 'relevant specific instances of [the person's] conduct' is to instances of conduct relevant to the type of testimony offered on direct examination. Thus an opinion witness can be cross examined only on matters bearing on his own opinion, while a reputation witness can only be examined on matters reasonably proximate to the time of the alleged offense and likely to have been known to the relevant community at that time.

United States v. Curtis, 644 F.2d 263, 269 (3d Cir. 1981).

4. Evidence of Other Crimes, Wrongs, or Acts Used for "Other Purposes"

Recall the warning at the start of the chapter about the categorical rules of exclusion: they identify a category of evidence and call for its exclusion when offered for a particular forbidden purpose but not when offered for other purposes. Rule 404(b) is explicit in this regard. While Rule 404(b)(1), as we have seen, provides that "[e]vidence of a crime, wrong, or other act is not admissible to prove a person's character in order to show that on a particular occasion the person acted in accordance with the character," Rule 404(b)(2) states that such evidence may be admissible for *another* purpose, and then provides a list that includes the use of such evidence to prove "motive, opportunity, intent, preparation, plan, knowledge, identity, absence of mistake, or lack of accident." The list is meant to be illustrative only and not exhaustive, and thus Rules 404(b)(1) and 404(b)(2) together stand for the proposition that evidence of other crimes, wrongs, or acts is barred *only* if its relevancy is based on drawing an inference from the other conduct to a propensity to engage in the conduct to a conclusion that the defendant engaged in the conduct on the occasion at issue.

Of course, even if the evidence of other crimes, wrongs, or acts is offered for some other purpose, there remains a substantial risk that the jury may nonetheless draw the forbidden propensity inference. Indeed, as with any other evidence that is relevant for both a permissible and a forbidden purpose, there is a risk that the proponent of the evidence may very well be hoping that the jury will use it for the forbidden purpose. Things may be further complicated by the fact that there may even be uncertainty as to whether the other crimes, wrongs, or acts actually took place. What is the role of the trial court with respect to these issues?

Problem 3-4: Drugs, Not Hugs

Betty is on trial on charges of possession of cocaine with intent to distribute the same. At trial, the government seeks to offer into evidence Betty's prior convictions for (a) possession of cocaine with intent to distribute the same; (b) possession of marijuana with intent to distribute the same; (c) possession of cocaine; and (d) possession of marijuana. The defense objects to the evidence on the ground that it is improper character evidence.

How should the prosecution respond, and how will the court likely rule?

Problem 3-5: Clowning Around

Paul is on trial on charges of armed bank robbery. During the bank robbery at issue, the robber wore a clown suit, forced the tellers to strip naked and lie face down after they handed over their money, and left a rose on the back of each teller. At trial, the government seeks to offer the testimony of a former acquaintance of Paul's, who would testify that he robbed a different bank with Paul eight years earlier, and that during that robbery, Paul wore a clown suit, forced the tellers to strip naked and lie face down, and left a rose on the back of each teller (an incident for which Paul was never charged or convicted). The defense objects to the evidence on the ground that it is improper character evidence.

How should the prosecution respond, and how will the court likely rule? Suppose instead that after Paul was arrested for the bank robbery at issue, someone wearing a clown suit robbed another bank, forced the tellers to strip naked, and left roses on their backs. Could Paul offer the details of that incident into evidence?

Problem 3-6: What Are the Odds?

Defendant is on trial on charges of murdering her third child, who drowned in the family's swimming pool. The prosecution wishes to introduce evidence that on previous occasions, two of the defendant's other children also drowned in the swimming pool. The defense argues that the evidence of the prior drowning incidents is not admissible absent the introduction of evidence sufficient for the jury to find that the defendant caused the prior deaths, but the state disagrees, contending that the mere fact that all three of the defendant's children have died in the same way is probative of her guilt for the crime charged.

Is the evidence admissible under Rule 404(b)?

Huddleston v. United States
485 U.S. 681 (1988)

Chief Justice REHNQUIST delivered the opinion of the Court....

Petitioner, Guy Rufus Huddleston, was charged with one count of selling stolen goods in interstate commerce, 18 U.S.C. § 2315, and one count of possessing stolen property in interstate commerce, 18 U.S.C. § 659. The two counts related to two portions of a shipment of stolen Memorex videocassette tapes that petitioner was alleged to have possessed and sold, knowing that they were stolen.

The evidence at trial showed that a trailer containing over 32,000 blank Memorex videocassette tapes with a manufacturing cost of $4.53 per tape was stolen from the Overnight Express yard in South Holland, Illinois, sometime between April 11 and 15, 1985. On April 17, 1985, petitioner contacted Karen Curry, the manager of the Magic Rent-to-Own in Ypsilanti, Michigan, seeking her assistance in selling a large number of blank Memorex videocassette tapes. After assuring Curry that the tapes were not stolen, he told her he wished to sell them in lots of at least 500 at $2.75 to $3 per tape. Curry subsequently arranged for the sale of a total of 5,000 tapes, which petitioner delivered to the various purchasers — who apparently believed the sales were legitimate.

There was no dispute that the tapes which petitioner sold were stolen; the only material issue at trial was whether petitioner knew they were stolen. The District Court allowed the Government to introduce evidence of "similar acts" under Rule 404(b), concluding that such evidence had "clear relevance as to [petitioner's knowledge]." The first piece of similar act evidence offered by the Government was the testimony of Paul Toney, a record store owner. He testified that in February 1985, petitioner offered to sell new 12" black and white televisions for $28 apiece. According to Toney, petitioner indicated that he could obtain several thousand of these televisions. Petitioner and Toney eventually traveled to the Magic Rent-to-Own, where Toney purchased 20 of the televisions. Several days later, Toney purchased 18 more televisions.

The second piece of similar act evidence was the testimony of Robert Nelson, an undercover FBI agent posing as a buyer for an appliance store. Nelson testified that in May 1985, petitioner offered to sell him a large quantity of Amana appliances — 28 refrigerators, 2 ranges, and 40 icemakers. Nelson agreed to pay $8,000 for the appliances. Petitioner was arrested shortly after he arrived at the parking lot where he and Nelson had agreed to transfer the appliances. A truck containing the appliances was stopped a short distance from the parking lot, and Leroy Wesby, who was driving the truck, was also arrested. It was determined that the appliances had a value of approximately $20,000 and were part of a shipment that had been stolen.

Petitioner testified that the Memorex tapes, the televisions, and the appliances had all been provided by Leroy Wesby, who had represented that all of the merchandise was obtained legitimately. Petitioner stated that he had sold 6,500 Memorex tapes for Wesby on a commission basis. Petitioner maintained that all of the sales for Wesby had been on a commission basis and that he had no knowledge that any of the goods were stolen.

In closing, the prosecution explained that petitioner was not on trial for his dealings with the appliances or the televisions. The District Court instructed the jury that the similar acts evidence was to be used only to establish petitioner's knowledge, and not to prove his character. The jury convicted petitioner on the possession count only....

We granted certiorari to resolve a conflict among the Courts of Appeals as to whether the trial court must make a preliminary finding before "similar act" and other Rule 404(b) evidence is submitted to the jury. We conclude that such evidence should be admitted if there is sufficient evidence to support a finding by the jury that the defendant committed the similar act.

Federal Rule of Evidence 404(b)—which applies in both civil and criminal cases—generally prohibits the introduction of evidence of extrinsic acts that might adversely reflect on the actor's character, unless that evidence bears upon a relevant issue in the case such as motive, opportunity, or knowledge. Extrinsic acts evidence may be critical to the establishment of the truth as to a disputed issue, especially when that issue involves the actor's state of mind and the only means of ascertaining that mental state is by drawing inferences from conduct. The actor in the instant case was a criminal defendant, and the act in question was "similar" to the one with which he was charged. Our use of these terms is not meant to suggest that our analysis is limited to such circumstances.

Before this Court, petitioner argues that the District Court erred in admitting Toney's testimony as to petitioner's sale of the televisions.[3] The threshold inquiry a court must make before admitting similar acts evidence under Rule 404(b) is whether that evidence is probative of a material issue other than character. The Government's theory of relevance was that the televisions were stolen, and proof that petitioner had engaged in a series of sales of stolen merchandise from the same suspicious source would be strong evidence that he was aware that each of these items, including the Memorex tapes, was stolen. As such, the sale of the televisions was a "similar act" only if the televisions were stolen. Petitioner acknowledges that this evidence was admitted for the proper purpose of showing his knowledge that the Memorex tapes were stolen. He asserts, however, that the evidence should not have been admitted because the Government failed to prove to the District Court that the televisions were in fact stolen.

Petitioner argues from the premise that evidence of similar acts has a grave potential for causing improper prejudice. For instance, the jury may choose to punish the defendant for the similar rather than the charged act, or the jury may infer that the defendant is an evil person inclined to violate the law. Because of this danger, petitioner maintains, the jury ought not to be exposed to similar act evidence until the trial court has heard the evidence and made a determination under Federal Rule of Evidence 104(a) that the defendant committed the similar act.... According to petitioner, the trial court must make this preliminary finding by at least a preponderance of the evidence.

We reject petitioner's position, for it is inconsistent with the structure of the Rules of Evidence and with the plain language of Rule 404(b). Article IV of the Rules of Evidence deals with the relevancy of evidence. Rules 401 and 402 establish the broad principle that relevant evidence—evidence that makes the existence of any fact at issue more or less probable—is admissible unless the Rules provide otherwise. Rule 403 allows the trial judge to exclude relevant evidence if, among other things, "its probative value is substantially outweighed by [a] danger of [...] unfair prejudice." Rules 404 through 412 address specific types of evidence that have generated problems. Generally, these latter Rules do not flatly prohibit the introduction of such evidence but instead limit the purpose for which it may be introduced. Rule 404(b), for example, protects against the introduction of extrinsic act evidence when that evidence is offered solely to prove character. The text

---

3. Petitioner does not dispute that Nelson's testimony concerning the Amana appliances was properly admitted under Rule 404(b).

contains no intimation, however, that any preliminary showing is necessary before such evidence may be introduced for a proper purpose. If offered for such a proper purpose, the evidence is subject only to general strictures limiting admissibility such as Rules 402 and 403.

Petitioner's reading of Rule 404(b) as mandating a preliminary finding by the trial court that the act in question occurred not only superimposes a level of judicial oversight that is nowhere apparent from the language of that provision, but it is simply inconsistent with the legislative history behind Rule 404(b). The Advisory Committee specifically declined to offer any "mechanical solution" to the admission of evidence under 404(b). Advisory Committee's Notes on Fed.Rule Evid. 404(b). Rather, the Committee indicated that the trial court should assess such evidence under the usual rules for admissibility: "The determination must be made whether the danger of undue prejudice outweighs the probative value of the evidence in view of the availability of other means of proof and other factors appropriate for making decisions of this kind under Rule 403." *Ibid.*; see also S.Rep. No. 93-1277, p. 25 (1974) ("[I]t is anticipated that with respect to permissible uses for such evidence, the trial judge may exclude it only on the basis of those considerations set forth in Rule 403, *i.e.* prejudice, confusion or waste of time").

Petitioner's suggestion that a preliminary finding is necessary to protect the defendant from the potential for unfair prejudice is also belied by the Reports of the House of Representatives and the Senate. The House made clear that the version of Rule 404(b) which became law was intended to "plac[e] greater emphasis on admissibility than did the final Court version." H.R.Rep. No. 93-650, p. 7 (1973). The Senate echoed this theme: "[T]he use of the discretionary word 'may' with respect to the admissibility of evidence of crimes, wrongs, or other acts is not intended to confer any arbitrary discretion on the trial judge." S.Rep. No. 93-1277, *supra*, at 24. Thus, Congress was not nearly so concerned with the potential prejudicial effect of Rule 404(b) evidence as it was with ensuring that restrictions would not be placed on the admission of such evidence.

We conclude that a preliminary finding by the court that the Government has proved the act by a preponderance of the evidence is not called for under Rule 104(a). This is not to say, however, that the Government may parade past the jury a litany of potentially prejudicial similar acts that have been established or connected to the defendant only by unsubstantiated innuendo. Evidence is admissible under Rule 404(b) only if it is relevant.... In the Rule 404(b) context, similar act evidence is relevant only if the jury can reasonably conclude that the act occurred and that the defendant was the actor. See *United States v. Beechum*, 582 F.2d 898, 912–913 (CA5 1978) (en banc). In the instant case, the evidence that petitioner was selling the televisions was relevant under the Government's theory only if the jury could reasonably find that the televisions were stolen.

Such questions of relevance conditioned on a fact are dealt with under Federal Rule of Evidence 104(b).... In determining whether the Government has introduced sufficient evidence to meet Rule 104(b), the trial court neither weighs credibility nor makes a finding that the Government has proved the conditional fact by a preponderance of the evidence. The court simply examines all the evidence in the case and decides whether the jury could reasonably find the conditional fact—here, that the televisions were stolen—by a preponderance of the evidence. The trial court has traditionally exercised the broadest sort of discretion in controlling the order of proof at trial, and we see nothing in the Rules of Evidence that would change this practice. Often the trial court may decide to allow the proponent to introduce evidence concerning a similar act, and at a later point in the trial assess whether sufficient evidence has been offered to permit the jury to make the requisite finding.[7] If the proponent has failed to meet this minimal standard of proof, the trial court must instruct the jury to disregard the evidence.

We emphasize that in assessing the sufficiency of the evidence under Rule 104(b), the trial court must consider all evidence presented to the jury. "[I]ndividual pieces of evidence, insufficient in themselves to prove a point, may in cumulation prove it. The sum of an evidentiary presentation may well be greater than its constituent parts." *Bourjaily v. United States*, 483 U.S. 171, 179–180 (1987). In assessing whether the evidence was sufficient to support a finding that the televisions were stolen, the court here was required to consider not only the direct evidence on that point—the low price of the televisions, the large quantity offered for sale, and petitioner's inability to produce a bill of sale— but also the evidence concerning petitioner's involvement in the sales of other stolen merchandise obtained from Wesby, such as the Memorex tapes and the Amana appliances. Given this evidence, the jury reasonably could have concluded that the televisions were stolen, and the trial court therefore properly allowed the evidence to go to the jury.

We share petitioner's concern that unduly prejudicial evidence might be introduced under Rule 404(b). See *Michelson v. United States*, 335 U.S. 469, 475–476 (1948). We think, however, that the protection against such unfair prejudice emanates not from a requirement of a preliminary finding by the trial court, but rather from four other sources: first, from the requirement of Rule 404(b) that the evidence be offered for a proper purpose; second, from the relevancy requirement of Rule 402—as enforced through Rule 104(b); third, from the assessment the trial court must make under Rule 403 to determine whether the probative value of the similar acts evidence is substantially outweighed by its potential for unfair prejudice, see Advisory Committee's Notes on Fed.Rule Evid. 404(b); S.Rep. No. 93-1277, at 25; and fourth, from Federal Rule of Evidence 105, which provides that the trial court shall, upon request, instruct the jury that the similar acts evidence is to be considered only for the proper purpose for which it was admitted....

State v. Terrazas
944 P.2d 1194 (Ariz. 1997)

MOELLER, Justice....

Evidence of prior bad acts committed by a defendant is usually inadmissible at trial. However, evidence of prior bad acts may be admissible to establish "motive, intent, absence of mistake or accident, identity and common scheme or plan." The issue presented in this case is by what standard these prior bad acts must be proved to be admissible against the defendant in a criminal case.

The first case to set forth the standard in Arizona was *State v. Hughes*. In *Hughes*, this court noted that the overwhelming majority of other states required the proof to be "clear," or "clear and convincing," or that there must be "substantial proof" that the other crime was committed by the defendant. The court stated that, whether the standard is given by

---

7. "When an item of evidence is conditionally relevant, it is often not possible for the offeror to prove the fact upon which relevance is conditioned at the time the evidence is offered. In such cases it is customary to permit him to introduce the evidence and 'connect it up' later. Rule 104(b) continues this practice, specifically authorizing the judge to admit the evidence 'subject to' proof of the preliminary fact. It is, of course, not the responsibility of the judge sua sponte to insure that the foundation evidence is offered; the objector must move to strike the evidence if at the close of the trial the offeror has failed to satisfy the condition." 21 C. Wright & K. Graham, Federal Practice and Procedure § 5054, pp. 269–270 (1977).

any of these phrases, "the test appears to be that the proof both as to the commission of another crime and its commission by the defendant, must be by 'substantial evidence sufficient to take the case to a jury.'" This court has subsequently cited and followed *Hughes*.

In 1977, Arizona adopted the Federal Rules of Evidence. Even so, "we are not bound by the United States Supreme Court's non-constitutional construction of the Federal Rules of Evidence when we construe the Arizona Rules of Evidence." The United States Supreme Court interpreted the standard of proof required to allow evidence of prior bad acts under Federal Rules of Evidence 104(b) in *Huddleston*. The standard adopted by the Supreme Court differs from the standard set forth in *Hughes*. *Huddleston* only requires a jury to be able to find the conditional fact by a preponderance of the evidence. *Hughes* requires the judge to find the conditional fact by "substantial evidence sufficient to take the case to a jury." Because both *Huddleston* and *Hughes* have been cited by this court, a question has arisen as to which standard should now be used in Arizona. We clarify that we did not adopt the preponderance standard set forth in *Huddleston*. Rather, we adhere to *Hughes* and clarify that, for prior bad acts to be admissible in a criminal case, the profferer must prove **by clear and convincing evidence** that the prior bad acts were committed and that the defendant committed the acts....

Many other courts require clear and convincing proof of evidence of prior bad acts (both that the act occurred and that the defendant committed the act) before they will allow the evidence to be admitted.

However, a number of states have chosen to apply a "preponderance"-type standard. Additionally, one state applies the standard of "beyond a reasonable doubt."

We believe there are important reasons to apply a clear and convincing standard, rather than some lesser standard, to evidence of prior bad acts. Such evidence is quite capable of having an impact beyond its relevance to the crime charged and may influence the jury's decision on issues other than those on which it was received, despite cautionary instructions from the judge. Studies confirm that the introduction of a defendant's prior bad acts "can easily tip the balance against the defendant." Because of the high probability of prejudice from the admission of prior bad acts, the court must ensure that the evidence against the defendant directly establishes "that the defendant took part in the collateral act, and to shield the accused from prejudicial evidence based upon 'highly circumstantial inferences.'" Applying the standard of "clear and convincing evidence" establishes a "clear, recognizable standard for courts and lawyers and is consistent with the due process owed under the federal and state constitutions." To allow a lesser standard in a criminal case is to open too large a possibility of prejudice.... Therefore, before admitting evidence of prior bad acts, trial judges must find that there is clear and convincing proof both as to the commission of the other bad act and that the defendant committed the act....

[The opinion of Vice Chief Justice Jones, specially concurring, is omitted.]

MARTONE, Justice, dissenting....

Although we are not bound by Supreme Court cases when we construe the Arizona Rules of Evidence, they are "instructive" and "persuasive.".... Because the language is the same, we should achieve consistency with the Federal Rules of Evidence absent a compelling reason to the contrary.

The majority imposes the higher clear and convincing standard because of a fear of prejudice. But "the protection against such unfair prejudice emanates not from a requirement of a preliminary factual finding by the trial court" but from the four *Huddleston* factors....

Logic, too, counsels against engrafting a clear and convincing standard onto Rule 104(b). Rule 104(b) applies to both criminal and civil cases. If "evidence sufficient to support a finding of the fulfillment of the condition"* means evidence proved by clear and convincing evidence, then the standard for *admissibility* in civil cases would be higher than the ultimate burden of proof. This makes no sense. Nor would it make sense to use a different standard in civil cases: the common language of Rule 104(b) — "evidence sufficient to support a finding" — would then have two different meanings.

It is analytically unsound to transpose a proof standard to an admissibility setting. That a higher burden of proof exists in the criminal context does not alter this reality. The admissibility standard "is unrelated to the burden of proof on the substantive issues, be it a criminal case or a civil case." The ultimate burden of persuasion has nothing to do with the threshold question of admissibility. "[T]here is no logical connection between the standard appropriate in the two situations."

Nothing in the Rules of Evidence requires, or even suggests, the application of a clear and convincing standard to questions of admissibility. The only justification the majority offers is its fear of prejudice. But that arises from its overly cautious approach to the admission of "other act" evidence, a view not shared by those who drafted the Federal and Arizona Rules of Evidence. I respectfully dissent.

United States v. Carroll
207 F.3d 465 (8th Cir. 2000)

BOWMAN, Circuit Judge....

I.

Carroll has been convicted of armed robbery previously. In 1988, he robbed a bank using a firearm. He pleaded guilty in 1989 and was sentenced to a substantial prison term. He entered supervised release on September 6, 1996. On July 30, 1998, Carroll and an accomplice, Kevin Carroll, robbed the St. Louis Community Credit Union, the crime at issue in this appeal. During Gerald Carroll's trial, the United States sought to introduce evidence of his prior conviction under Federal Rule of Evidence 404(b).... Like all other evidence, evidence admissible under Rule 404(b) is still subject to analysis under Rule 403, which allows admission unless the evidence's unfair prejudice substantially outweighs its probative value. Over objection, the District Court determined that the evidence of Carroll's prior conviction was "admissible for purposes of showing a plan or pattern ... a melding basically of that, plus identity." The District Court instructed the jury that it could use the Rule 404(b) evidence "to help [it] decide whether the similarity between the acts previously committed and the ones charged in this case suggest that the same person committed all of them." We review for abuse of discretion.

The case law discusses two circumstances in which prior bad acts can be used to show a "plan or pattern." In some circumstances, a defendant's prior bad acts are part of a broader plan or scheme relevant to the charged offense. "For example, when a criminal steals a car to use it in a robbery, the automobile theft can be proved in a prosecution for the robbery." 1 McCormick on Evidence § 190, at 660–61 (John W. Strong ed., 5th ed.1999). If the evidence merely shows the full context of the charged crime, it is "intrinsic evidence" not governed by Rule 404(b). Evidence of past acts may also be admitted under

---

* Editor's Note: When Federal Rule 104(b) was restyled in 2011, the quoted phrase was replaced with the phrase "proof must be introduced sufficient to support a finding that the fact does exist."

Rule 404(b) as direct proof of a charged crime that includes a plan or scheme element, or evidence might serve both intrinsic and direct-proof purposes. In other circumstances, where the "pattern and characteristics of the crimes [are] so unusual and distinctive as to be like a signature," 1 McCormick on Evidence § 190, at 663, evidence of a defendant's prior crimes is admissible to prove that it was indeed the defendant that committed the charged crime. In these cases, the evidence goes to identity. These "plan" and "identity" uses of Rule 404(b) evidence are distinct from each other and from use of prior acts to show knowledge and intent. In drug distribution cases, for example, knowledge and intent are often contested facts proven in part through prior bad acts.

We reject the theory that Carroll's ten-year-old conviction was admissible as part of a broad criminal undertaking including both the prior offense and the charged offense. "The victims were different, and the events were far apart in time. Absent more specific linkage, such evidence is relevant to 'plan' or 'preparation' only insofar as it tends to prove a propensity to commit crimes, which Rule 404(b) prohibits." *LeCompte*, 99 F.3d at 278. The fact that Carroll was incarcerated in the interim period only reinforces the conclusion that the events are not part of the same criminal undertaking.

The District Court's jury instruction demonstrates that the evidence was admitted to show identity. If the conduct underlying Carroll's prior conviction and his current charged offense both involved a unique set of "signature facts," then his prior conviction would be admissible to show that the same person committed both crimes. But unless the robberies are "sufficiently idiosyncratic" to make them "clearly distinctive from the thousands of other bank robberies committed each year," evidence of the prior crime is "nothing more than the character evidence that Rule 404(b) prohibits."

In sum, in order to admit Rule 404(b) identity evidence on the signature facts or *modus operandi* theory, the District Court must make a threshold determination that, based solely on the evidence comparing the past acts and the charged offense, a reasonable juror could conclude that the same person committed both crimes. Two factors are relevant in analyzing the question. The first is the distinctiveness of the facts that make the crimes unique and the second is the proximity of the crimes in space and time. After reviewing the evidence in this case, we believe that the prior bank robbery and the credit union robbery charged here are too generic and remote from one another to permit a reasonable inference of identity.

First, the characteristics shared by the two robberies are too common to form a *modus operandi* that uniquely identifies Carroll as the perpetrator. All the United States can argue is that, in both crimes, the perpetrator wore a nylon stocking mask, carried a gun, and vaulted over the counter to put the bank's money in a bag.

We must initially determine the frame of reference against which to measure the uniqueness of the crimes. As the question of how often a particular crime is committed in a particular way is ultimately factual, it might be appropriate, in some cases, for the District Court to take evidence on the matter in, for example, deciding a motion in limine. In other cases, the *modus operandi* or other characteristics of the prior crime and the crime currently charged may be so distinctive as to self-evidently permit a reasonable inference of identity between the perpetrator of the first and the perpetrator of the second. In the present case, we simply use a set of data readily before us. Based merely on the descriptions of bank robberies available in the published federal appellate reporters, which are incomplete in detail and refer only to a subset of all bank robberies committed, it is amply clear that the signature facts relied upon by the government in this case occur frequently, even in combination. The bank robbery cases finding signature facts have reported much less common features, such as distinguishing costumes or equipment, *see, e.g., Robinson*, 161 F.3d at 468 (orange ski mask and "distinctive" duffel bag), unusual methods, *see, e.g., United States v. Moore*, 115 F.3d 1348, 1355 (7th Cir. 1997) (robbers entered bank thirty to sixty minutes before robbery and politely asked for a job application or directions), or distinctive use of a weapon, *see, e.g., Smith*, 103 F.3d at 603 (robbers brandished knives and held them vertically during robbery).

Further, examination of the closeness of the robberies, geographically and in time, supports the conclusion that the crimes are not sufficiently related to allow an inference of identity. The two financial institutions here, while not in the same neighborhood, are both in the St. Louis area, relatively close to each other. But the crimes occurred ten years apart. This is not a case, as in *Robinson*, 161 F.3d at 468 (ten days apart), *Smith*, 103 F.3d at 603 (one month apart), or *Moore*, 115 F.3d at 1355 ("a few months" apart), where it could be inferred from the temporal and geographic proximity of the two robberies, along with other facts, that the same individuals committed them both. The government, citing *United States v. Alaniz*, 148 F.3d 929 (8th Cir.), *cert. denied*, 525 U.S. 1047 (1998), asserts that the intervening period is irrelevant because Carroll was incarcerated for most of that time. *Alaniz* dealt with the use of prior drug crimes to show the defendant's mental state with respect to a new drug conspiracy, a much different use from the signature-facts identity theory advanced in this case. Perhaps Carroll's incarceration undercuts the significance of the ten-year delay to some extent, but certainly not enough to permit an inference of identity.

Based on the generic nature of the crimes and on the ten years that passed between them, we conclude that the prior conviction was not relevant to prove identity through *modus operandi* because no substantial inference of identity reasonably could be made. Our criminal justice system has long forbidden juries from convicting an individual, not for facts which prove the charged offense, but for prior acts that, at best, show a criminal propensity. It was therefore an abuse of discretion to admit evidence of the prior bank robbery committed by Carroll, for that robbery is not relevant to any question other than Carroll's propensity to rob banks....

United States v. Chavis
429 F.3d 662 (7th Cir. 2005)

MANION, Circuit Judge.

A federal jury convicted Andrew Chavis on charges of both conspiracy and possession of crack cocaine with intent to distribute. Chavis appeals, asserting that his conviction cannot stand because the district court improperly admitted certain evidence....

I.

In November 2002, the DEA began investigating illegal drug distribution in Rockford, Illinois. This investigation relied on Robert and Rosa Flemons, both of whom had pleaded guilty to dealing crack cocaine but had chosen to cooperate with the government. As part of the cooperation agreement, the DEA provided the Flemonses with money to make purchases from suspected drug dealers while the DEA monitored the transactions....

On November 22, the DEA decided to shut down the drug conspiracy. To that end, [DEA Agent Doug] Hopkins instructed the Flemonses to set up one more drug deal with [Alex "Alley Cat"] Thompson. Meanwhile, the local police continued surveillance on Thompson, who met and picked up [Frank] Jefferson in his white Chrysler. At first, Jefferson had trouble reaching Chavis on Chavis's cell phone to tell him that he needed more crack.... Jefferson finally set up a meeting with Chavis in a liquor store parking lot near Capitol Cleaners to obtain the drugs.

Jefferson and Thompson reached the parking lot first, and the police continued to observe their activities, watching them through binoculars. After approximately twenty minutes, Chavis and his girlfriend, Sidra Moses, pulled up in Moses's Oldsmobile. Jefferson then left Thompson's Chrysler and entered the back seat of Moses's car. Detective Robert Veruchi, one of the local police assisting the DEA's surveillance, saw Chavis, sitting in the front passenger seat, appear to give something to Jefferson. After observing this apparent hand-off, the police then approached and surrounded the car, ordering the occupants out.

When Chavis left the front seat of the car, a cell phone and a pager dropped onto the ground. Chavis agreed to a police pat-down, which turned up $1,128 in Chavis's right front pocket and $3,525 in his left rear pocket. Police found on Jefferson a cell phone, crack cocaine, and $1,239 in cash. DEA Agent Hopkins also discovered a baggie containing crack cocaine on the floor of the car near where Jefferson had been sitting. While they were being taken into custody, Jefferson and Chavis turned on each other, each yelling to the other: "You set me up." Once they arrived at the police station, Chavis shouted to Moses: "Don't talk. Don't say nothing, baby. They got nothing." Chavis told the police that Jefferson had handed a bag of cocaine to him in the car, and that he (Chavis) threw it back at Jefferson just as the police came up....

At trial, Jefferson, local police, and DEA agents all testified about the drug ring and Chavis's involvement in it. Chavis attempted to exclude several pieces of evidence, including a prior conviction for possession of cocaine with intent to distribute.... The district court proceeded to analyze the disputed evidence pursuant to Fed.R.Evid. 404(b), concluding that the prior conviction was admissible as it was being used to show Chavis's intent rather than propensity....

II.

....

Chavis first contends that the district court improperly admitted evidence relating to his 1997 conviction for possession of crack cocaine with intent to distribute. For a specific intent crime, like the ones charged in this case, intent is a required element of the offense, which the government must prove beyond a reasonable doubt. *See Best*, 250 F.3d at 1091. "We have repeatedly held that when a defendant is charged with a specific intent crime, the government may introduce evidence of other acts to prove intent." *Id.; see also Jones*, 389 F.3d at 756; *United States v. Macedo*, 406 F.3d 778, 793 (7th Cir. 2005). However, we also recognize that the permissible use of prior convictions to prove intent may have the potentially impermissible side effect of allowing the jury to infer propensity.

Understanding the difficulty in distinguishing between the legitimate use of prior convictions as evidence of intent and the illegitimate use to show propensity, we have held: "the government must affirmatively show why a particular prior conviction tends to show the more forward-looking fact of purpose, design, or volition to commit the new crime." *Jones*, 389 F.3d at 757. In other words, a prior conviction introduced solely for its own sake is propensity evidence, but a prior conviction shown to have some additional relevance can qualify as intent evidence. Of course, the devil lies in the details of what must be shown for the conviction to attain legitimacy.

This court has held in several cases that a theory of defense that calls into question intent can supply the additional relevance. In *Jones* we noted, "a prior conviction may be relevant to show intent if the defendant concedes that he possessed the drugs but denies that he planned to distribute them, or if he denies knowing that the substance was contraband." *Id.* at 757–58; *see also Puckett,* 405 F.3d at 596 ("evidence of a prior conviction … is especially relevant and probative" when defendant conceded that he had possession of a large amount of cocaine, but claimed it was for personal use). Each of the examples in *Jones* sketches a case in which the defendant himself opens the door to the use of the conviction by asserting that he lacked the requisite intent for the crime. In another recent case, we allowed the admission of the convictions to respond to the defense theory that the defendant did not have any intent to enter into a conspiracy to distribute drugs because he was "simply present at the airport by happenstance." *See Macedo,* 406 F.3d at 793. "This theory, coupled with the government's need to prove an essential element of the case, i.e., that the defendant acted with the requisite specific intent, supports the district court's decision to admit the prior bad acts." *Id.* In *United States v. Kreiser,* 15 F.3d 635, 640 (7th Cir. 1994), this court held that "the 1984 cocaine transactions show that Kreiser was familiar with the cocaine business and was not some hapless fool mistakenly caught up in some overzealous enforcement action." Such a defense theory provides the additional relevance necessary for a prior conviction to satisfy Rule 404(b) as intent evidence.

Turning to Chavis's case, we find that the prior conviction was used as evidence of his intent to engage in a conspiracy to possess drugs with an intent to distribute rather than to show his propensity to commit this crime. Chavis presented a defense that he was simply in the wrong place at the wrong time. He claimed no intent to distribute drugs because he was completely innocent. This is nearly identical to *Macedo.* By portraying himself as a clueless bystander, Chavis himself gave the prior conviction the requisite relevance to satisfy Rule 404(b). Given the defense theory and the government's obligation to prove specific intent, the district court did not abuse its discretion in determining that the prior conviction went to intent and not propensity....

CUDAHY, Circuit Judge, concurring.

I do not agree that evidence of Chavis's 1997 conviction of a drug crime was admissible to show intent (or, as the government has also argued, knowledge). Chavis's defense was that although he was present at the scene of the drug sale, he did not supply the drugs at issue to Jefferson or Thompson. As the majority puts it, Chavis claimed that "he was simply in the wrong place at the wrong time." His defense, then, is that the drugs were not his, not that he did not realize that drugs were involved. Although "[a] prior conviction may be relevant to show intent if the defendant concedes that he possessed the drugs but denies that he planned to distribute them, or if he denies knowing that the substance was contraband," neither of those scenarios is presented here. *United States v. Jones,* 389 F.3d 753, 757–58 (7th Cir. 2004). The analysis would be different, and intent or knowledge as discrete issues might be implicated, if Chavis had admitted to involvement in the transfer but asserted that he thought the stuff transferred was not crack cocaine but cough drops.

The government describes Chavis's defense as an assertion "that he just happened to stumble upon the scene of a drug deal, and that someone just happened to hand him crack cocaine, but that he never intended to possess or distribute the crack." This description is an attempt to shoehorn the prior conviction into the intent or knowledge exception by painting his defense (the drugs weren't mine) as a lack of intent (I had them, but I wasn't going to sell them) or a mistake (I thought they were cough drops). But again, Chavis never claimed that he had mistakenly sold anything or that he was unaware of what crack cocaine looked like. As in *Jones,* the government here has failed to articulate how the prior conviction established specific intent or some other state of mind as a concept discrete from Chavis's propensity to commit drug crimes.

This, I think, is the essential point. To meet the test of Rule 404(b), there must be a showing that an issue has been joined as to intent, or another of the 404(b) categories, discrete from a showing of mere propensity. It is not enough that one or more of these categories (like specific intent) be a formal element of the crime. These categories must be discretely placed in issue to be a basis of 404(b) relevance. If not, the only plausible reason for introducing prior conviction evidence is to show propensity. The prior convictions tell the jury in fairly blatant terms that a defendant is not to be believed when he says the drugs were not his because he has done it before. This evidence, then, violates basic principles of criminal justice....

Notes and Questions

1. Suppose that the other acts evidence consists of conduct for which the person was tried and acquitted. In *Dowling v. United States*, 493 U.S. 342 (1990), the Supreme Court rejected arguments that introducing evidence of prior conduct for which a criminal defendant was tried and acquitted under Rule 404(b)(2) is barred by the Double Jeopardy and Due Process Clauses and by the doctrine of collateral estoppel. The rationale, according to the court, was the difference in the burden of proof involved in convicting someone and the burden of proof required for evidence admitted under Rule 404(b)(2):

> For present purposes, we assume for the sake of argument that Dowling's acquittal established that there was a reasonable doubt as to whether Dowling was the masked man who entered Vena Henry's home with Delroy Christian two weeks after the First Pennsylvania Bank robbery. But to introduce evidence on this point at the bank robbery trial, the Government did not have to demonstrate that Dowling was the man who entered the home beyond a reasonable doubt: the Government sought to introduce Henry's testimony under Rule 404(b), and, as mentioned earlier, in *Huddleston v. United States*, we held that "[i]n the Rule 404(b) context, similar act evidence is relevant only if the jury can reasonably conclude that the act occurred and that the defendant was the actor." Because a jury might reasonably conclude that Dowling was the masked man who entered Henry's home, even if it did not believe beyond a reasonable doubt that Dowling committed the crimes charged at the first trial, the collateral-estoppel component of the Double Jeopardy Clause is inapposite.

Dowling, 493 U.S. at 348–49.

2. If evidence of conduct for which the defendant has been acquitted is admitted under Rule 404(b)(2), is the defendant entitled to introduce evidence to the jury that he was acquitted? Although the lower court judge in the *Dowling* case informed the jury that the defendant had been acquitted of the prior offenses, *see Dowling*, 493 U.S. at 345–346, some lower courts have held that a defendant is not so entitled, reasoning as follows:

> There are two primary reasons why a judgment of acquittal is not generally admissible to rebut inferences that may be drawn from evidence that was the basis of a previous trial. First, judgments of acquittal are hearsay. Second, judgments of acquittal are not generally relevant, because they do not prove innocence; they simply show that the government did not meet its burden of proving guilt beyond a reasonable doubt.

United States v. Wells, 347 F.3d 280, 286 (8th Cir. 2003) (quoting *Prince v. A.L. Lockhart*, 971 F.2d 118, 122 (8th Cir. 1992). The first ground, dealing with hearsay, will be discussed later in the book. Do you agree with the second ground, to wit, that such evidence is not relevant? *Compare United States v. Bailey*, 319 F.3d 514, 517–18 (D.C. Cir. 2003) (dicta suggesting that it may fall within an exception to the hearsay rule and that it may be relevant to rebut a likely mistaken jury inference that the defendant was convicted for the conduct). How about evidence that the defendant was never prosecuted? *See Bailey*, 319 F.3d at 518 (holding it is admissible because it poses no hearsay problem and is relevant to rebut a likely mistaken jury inference).

3. As the *Huddleston* Court points out, Rule 404(b) applies in both criminal and civil cases. Note that this sets it apart from the Rule 404(a)(2) exceptions, which can be invoked only in criminal cases. However, there is one important difference between civil and criminal cases: in criminal cases, the defendant is entitled upon request of advance notice, usually pretrial, of the prosecution's plan to introduce such evidence to reduce surprise and to promote pretrial resolution of questions of admissibility. *See* Fed. R. Evid. 404(b)(2); Advisory Committee's Note to 1991 Amendment to Rule 404.

Admitting Rule 404(b) evidence offered by the prosecution without notice to the defense is considered a serious error that can result in the reversal of a conviction tainted by such error. *See, e.g., United States v. Carrasco*, 381 F.3d 1237, 1240–41 (11th Cir. 2004); *United States v. Vega*, 188 F.3d 1150, 1155 (9th Cir. 1999); *United States v. Spinner*, 152 F.3d 950, 961 (D.C. Cir. 1998) (alternative holding). *But see United States v. White*, 405 F.3d 208, 213 n.3 (4th Cir. 2005) (finding the error to be harmless in light of the other evidence properly admitted at trial). Note, however, Rule 404(b)(2)(A) states only that "reasonable notice" is required, without specifying how far in advance of trial notice must be given. What constitutes "reasonable notice"? *See United States v. Perez-Tosta*, 36 F.3d 1552, 1561–62 (11th Cir. 1994) (holding that whether notice is reasonable turns on when the government learned or reasonably should have learned of the evidence, the extent to which the defendant would suffer prejudice from abbreviated notice, and the importance of the evidence to the government's case).

4. Note that Rule 404(b)(1) refers to "other act[s]," and is not limited to *bad* acts. Thus, it is possible for a party to introduce evidence of other, lawful acts where relevant for some reason other than propensity. *See Ansell v. Green Acres Contracting Co., Inc.*, 347 F.3d 515, 520 (3d Cir. 2003) (in an age discrimination case, admitting evidence that employer hired other people of the same age to negate claim of discriminatory intent). *Accord United States v. Curtin*, 489 F.3d 935, 943 n.3 (9th Cir. 2007).

5. Not every type of "other act" is an "other act" within the meaning of Rule 404(b):

> "background" evidence.... often referred to as "*res gestae*," does not implicate Rule 404(b). However ... the "background circumstances exception" to the general exclusion of other act evidence is not an open ended basis to admit any and all other act evidence the proponent wishes to introduce. Rather the very definition of what constitutes background evidence contains inherent limitations.... background or *res gestae* evidence consists of those other acts that are inextricably intertwined with the charged offense or those acts, the telling of which is necessary to complete the story of the charged offense.
>
> Proper background evidence has a causal, temporal or spatial connection with the charged offense. Typically, such evidence is a prelude to the charged offense, is directly probative of the charged offense, arises from the same events as the charged offense, forms an integral part of a witness's testimony, or completes the story of the charged offense.

United States v. Hardy, 228 F.3d 745, 748 (6th Cir. 2000). What are the practical effects of deeming such acts not to be "other act[s]" within the meaning of Rule 404(b)(1)?

See United States v. Bowie, 232 F.3d 923, 928 (D.C. Cir. 2000) ("treating evidence as inextricably intertwined not only bypasses Rule 404(b) and its attendant notice requirement, but also carries the implicit finding that the evidence is admissible for all purposes notwithstanding its bearing on character, thus eliminating the defense's entitlement, upon request, to a jury instruction"). Such evidence, however, is nonetheless subject to exclusion pursuant to Federal Rule 403. *See United States v. Holt*, 460 F.3d 934, 937–38 (7th Cir. 2006).

6. As the *Huddleston* Court reminds us, Rule 404(b)(2) does not provide that such evidence is automatically admissible; it only clarifies that it is not subject to exclusion under Rule 404. Thus, such evidence is admissible only if it is relevant under Rules 401 and 402 and not subject to exclusion under Rule 403. Accordingly, such evidence might nonetheless be subject to exclusion when its probative worth on the *legitimate* point for which it is offered is rather low while the risk of the jury using it to draw an improper propensity inference is high.

7. Recall that even though Rule 404(a)(2)(B) allows a defendant who claims self-defense to introduce evidence of the victim's violent character to show action in conformity therewith, Rule 405 limits him to introducing reputation and opinion evidence. However, in such cases, it is sometimes possible to invoke Rule 404(b)(2) to introduce evidence of specific prior instances of violent behavior by the victim, not for the purpose of showing action in conformity therewith, but instead for showing that the defendant's reaction when confronted by the victim was reasonable in light of his knowledge of the victim's past specific acts of violence. *E.g., Government of Virgin Islands v. Carino*, 631 F.2d 226, 229–30 (3d Cir. 1980). Such prior instances of conduct are relevant to such a defense, however, only if the defendant *knew* of the prior instances at the time he was confronted by the victim. *United States v. Smith*, 230 F.3d 300, 307–08 (7th Cir. 2000).

8. What is the theoretical justification for admitting evidence of prior acts as proof of intent in some other instance? Consider the following:

> The argument here is purely from the point of view of the doctrine of chances— the instinctive recognition of that logical process which eliminates the element of innocent intent by multiplying instances of the same result until it is perceived that this element cannot explain them all ... similar results do not usually occur through abnormal causes; and the recurrence of a similar result (here in the shape of an unlawful act) tends (increasingly with each instance) to negative accident or inadvertence or self-defense or good faith or other innocent mental state, and tends to establish (provisionally, at least, though not certainly) the presence of the normal, i.e., criminal intent accompanying such an act....

2 Wigmore, Evidence § 302, at 241 (Chadbourn rev. 1979).

9. For evidence of prior acts to be relevant on the issue of intent, there must be similarity between the other acts and the charged act. *United States v. Queen*, 132 F.3d 991, 996 (4th Cir. 1997); *see also* 2 Wigmore, Evidence § 302, at 241 (Chadbourn rev. 1979) ("Since it is the improbability of a like result being repeated by mere chance that carries probative weight, the essence of this probative effect is the likeness of each instance."). They need not be *identical*, however, and in the context of drug distribution cases, courts typically hold that the type of drug distributed need not be the same. *E.g., United States v. Gibson*, 170 F.3d 673, 679 (7th Cir. 1999). The circuits are split, however, on whether evidence of prior instances of drug possession is relevant in a case in which the individual is charged with distribution. *See generally United States v. Haywood*, 280 F.3d 715 (6th Cir. 2002).

10. As a general matter, the more remote in time a prior crime, wrong, or act is, the less probative it is of an individual's intent, knowledge, and the like at a later time when he is alleged to have committed a similar crime, wrong, or act, and thus the less likely it is that a court will admit it under Rule 404(b). *See, e.g., United States v. Verduzco,* 373 F.3d 1022, 1027 (9th Cir. 2004); *United States v. Williams,* 308 F.3d 833, 837 (8th Cir. 2002). Yet there is no bright-line rule requiring a court to exclude evidence of prior acts after a certain period of time has elapsed, with the importance of the prior event's age depending on the theory of admissibility and the similarity of the prior event to the charged crime. *See United States v. Strong,* 415 F.3d 902, 905–06 (8th Cir. 2005); *United States v. Johnson,* 132 F.3d 1279, 1283 (9th Cir. 1997). As indicated in *Carroll,* some courts hold that in determining the remoteness of a prior crime, the relevant date for determining the age of the prior act is the date when the individual was released from incarceration for committing that offense. Are you persuaded that this date is more significant than the date on which the prior offense occurred?

11. Does Rule 404(b) allow for the introduction of evidence of crimes, wrongs, or acts performed *subsequent* to the one charged? For example, if a defendant is on trial for bank robbery, is evidence that he committed a *subsequent* robbery using a similar modus operandi admissible? Rule 404(b) draws no distinction between prior and subsequent acts; so long as the evidence of subsequent conduct is relevant for the purpose for which it is offered, it is potentially admissible. *E.g., United States v. Anifowoshe,* 307 F.3d 643, 646–48 (7th Cir. 2002).

12. Can a criminal defendant introduce evidence under Rule 404(b)(2) to suggest that someone other than the defendant committed the crime? For example, if a defendant is on trial for bank robbery, can he introduce evidence of other bank robberies using the same distinctive modus operandi committed by someone else? Typically referred to as "reverse 404(b) evidence," evidence of someone else's conduct that tends to negate the defendant's guilt is admissible under Rule 404(b). *E.g., United States v. Wilson,* 307 F.3d 596, 601 (7th Cir. 2002); *United States v. Lucas,* 357 F.3d 599, 605 (6th Cir. 2004); *United States v. Stevens,* 935 F.2d 1380, 1401–06 (3d Cir. 1991).

Is such evidence as likely to be excluded by Rule 403 as is evidence offered by the government under Rule 404(b)? *See United States v. Seals,* 419 F.3d 600, 606–07 (7th Cir. 2005) (holding that "'because prejudice to the defendant is not a factor'.... the defense is not held to as rigorous of a standard as the government in introducing reverse 404(b) evidence").

13. In what way does the evidence of other acts in Problem 3-6 differ from other acts evidence in the materials we have examined thus far? Should that matter? Consider the following:

> It will be seen that the strength of the foregoing kind of inference does not rest exclusively on a given person's connection with the prior injurious transactions. It is possible to negative accident or inadvertence, and to infer deliberate human intent, without forming any conclusion as to the personality of the doer. Thus, if one morning after a high wind, A's cellar window is found broken, the pieces lying inside, he may well assume the probability that the force of the wind blew the glass in; but if, on the next morning and the next, he again finds a window broken in the same way, though no high wind prevailed the night before, he gives up the hypothesis of the force of the wind as the explanation, and concludes that a deliberate human effort was the highly probable cause of the breakage, although he can form no notion whatever of the personality of the doer.
>
> Thus it is thus clear that innocent intent—accident, inadvertence, or the like— may be negatived by *anonymous instances* of the previous occurrence of the same

or a similar thing. After the defendant's connection with the deed charged is assumed or proved, his innocent intent may be negatived by such instances, which may have force for that purpose, though they are not connected with the defendant....

2 Wigmore, Evidence § 303, at 247–48 (Chadbourn rev. 1979).

14. Would admitting the evidence of the prior deaths in Problem 3-6, absent sufficient evidence to support a finding that the defendant committed those acts, be consistent with *Huddleston*? Recall that in *Huddleston*, the Court held that "similar act evidence is relevant only if the jury can reasonably conclude that the act occurred *and that the defendant was the actor*." *Huddleston*, 485 U.S. at 689 (emphasis added). *See* Edward J. Imwinkelreid, *"Where There's Smoke, There's Fire": Should the Judge or the Jury Decide the Question of Whether the Accused Committed an Alleged Uncharged Crime Proffered Under Federal Rule of Evidence 404?*, 42 St. Louis U. L. J. 813, 836–44 (1998). Would it be enough to satisfy *Huddleston* that at the time each of the other children drowned, the mother was the only person around? *See State v. Norlin*, 951 P.2d 1131, 1133–36 (Wash. 1998) (holding that state equivalent of Rule 404(b) requires that other acts be connected to the defendant by a preponderance of the evidence, but finding that evidence that the defendant was alone with victim during prior instances when he was injured could suffice). In upholding a state court conviction challenged on constitutional grounds, the U.S. Supreme Court in *Estelle v. McGuire*, 502 U.S. 62 (1991), appeared to recognize the relevance of such evidence:

> When offered to show that certain injuries are a product of child abuse, rather than accident, evidence of prior injuries is relevant even though it does not purport to prove the identity of the person who might have inflicted those injuries.

Estelle, 502 U.S. at 68. However, the Court did make a point of stressing that there was evidence sufficient under *Huddleston* for the jury to find that the defendant did commit the other acts. *Id.* at 73–74.

United States v. Curtin

489 F.3d 935 (9th Cir. 2007) (en banc)

TROTT, Circuit Judge:

....

I

....

[After communicating online and making plans to have sex with an undercover officer posing as a 14-year-old girl named "Christy," Kevin Eric Curtin arranged to meet her in a bowling alley.]

On that Sunday, the police officer whose picture was sent to Curtin waited in the bowling alley as a decoy, dressed in the clothes that Christy indicated she would be wearing.... Curtin entered the bowling alley at 1:45 p.m. and walked toward the area where the decoy officer was sitting. He walked past her and then turned and walked past her again, looking at her each time. Curtin then left the area where the decoy was sitting and went to the back of the bowling alley, where he used his personal digital assistant. At the request of law enforcement officers, a casino security guard approached Curtin and asked for identification. Curtin showed the guard a United States passport and subsequently left the bowling alley area of the casino.

Curtin reentered the bowling alley at approximately 2:05 p.m. He looked around and again walked to the area where the decoy officer was sitting. After less than a minute, he moved closer to her, looking in her direction the entire time. He stopped behind the officer, and she turned and said "hi" to him. Whether he said "hi" in return is disputed.

Curtin then left the bowling alley and started getting into a van, at which point law enforcement officers stopped and asked him for identification.... In a voluntary statement, he stated that he had traveled by car to Las Vegas for meetings. He explained that he was at the bowling alley to meet a female friend he had met on the internet. He admitted to using the screen name and email address used to contact Christy. Curtin explained that he often enters chat rooms and "role play[s]" as if he is engaged in "daddy/daughter" type conversations, and that he expected Christy to be a thirty- to forty-year-old woman pretending to be a girl.

Curtin was then arrested by the Las Vegas police. The personal digital assistant, which was taken from him at the time of his arrest, contained in the form of text over 140 stories about adults having sex with children....

Curtin was indicted on one count of travel with intent to engage in a sexual act with a juvenile, in violation of 18 U.S.C. § 2423(b), and one count of coercion and enticement, in violation of 18 U.S.C. § 2422(b).

II

A.

Prior to the trial, it became clear that the only disputed issue in this case would be Curtin's subjective intent: did he intend to hook up sexually with a minor, or with a 30- to 40-year-old woman who liked to engage in sex acts while pretending she was a child having incestuous sex with her daddy?

....

B.

Confronted with Curtin's aggressive incest-fantasy-intent defense—to sexually play daddy/daughter incest, not with a minor but with an adult—and facing the traditional demanding burden of proof beyond a reasonable doubt, the government offered as part of its case-in-chief stories contained on Curtin's personal digital assistant, or "PDA." These stories were offered in evidence for two equally germane purposes: (1) to prove that Curtin harbored the subjective intent made unlawful by law, and (2) to rebut in anticipation Curtin's lack-of-intent defense that the daughter in his daddy/daughter sexual fantasy was an adult pretending to be a child....

D.

On the second day of trial, the government offered two of the stories, "My Little Sister" and "Love for the World," to show modus operandi, intent, preparation, and knowledge.... The stories were neither circulated nor read to the jury.

The technician who extracted the stories from Curtin's PDA testified that both stories were about a father having sex with his young daughter and the daughter's enjoyment of the experience. However, when the government sought to introduce a third story, "Melanie's Busy Day," the district court stopped the questioning. The court allowed the government to ask general questions, such as whether the stories related to sex between a minor and an adult, but did not unconditionally admit them. Recognizing the potentially prejudicial nature of the stories, and acknowledging Curtin's argument based on Rule 404(a) that the evidence constituted inadmissible character or propensity evidence, the court held that a story could be entered into evidence only if it tied into Curtin's intent, knowledge, preparation, or modus operandi; in other words, if it had some relevance to the charges....

The government then asked the court to make a preliminary legal determination about the admissibility of the remaining stories. The government argued that "Melanie's Busy Day" was admissible to show intent, modus operandi, preparation, and knowledge because it had language similar to that used by Curtin in his email to Christy, namely, language concerning oral sex and a child masturbating. The government argued that "Missing Big Brother," which discussed how the adult did not want to hurt the child during sex, also was admissible for intent, modus operandi, preparation, and knowledge. The government made similar arguments with regard to seventeen other stories....

Eventually, after more argument and extensive offers of proof, but without reading the stories in their entirety, the district court agreed to admit with limiting instructions five of the stories: "My Little Sister" (which involved incest and the impregnation of a nine-year-old girl), "Love for the World" (which involved incest), "Melanie's Busy Day" (which involved an eleven-year-old girl initiating sex with, among others, her father and her teacher), "Restrictions" (same), and "Daddy's Lessons" (same).

E.

Curtin contends here, as he did at trial, that (1) the five stories amounted to inadmissible character evidence, introduced only to show propensity in violation of Rule 404(a) of the Federal Rules of Evidence, and (2) that the probative value of the stories was exceeded by their potential prejudice, in violation of Rule 403.... the government argues that the stories were properly admitted under Rule 404(b), not as general bad character or propensity evidence, but as evidence of acts tending to prove Curtin's intent. Finally, the government asserts that the admission of the stories did not violate Rule 403.

Curtin objected also to the admission of the stories in the district court, relying, *inter alia*, on *Guam v. Shymanovitz*, 157 F.3d 1154 (9th Cir.1998) (as amended). *Shymanovitz* was a middle-school guidance counselor who was charged with sexually and physically abusing several of the boys under his supervision. Both *Shymanovitz* and this appeal address whether sexually explicit reading material is admissible under Rule 404(b). We concluded in *Shymanovitz* that the magazine articles failed to constitute a Rule 404(b) "bad act." "[P]ossession of lawful reading material is simply not the type of conduct contemplated by Rule 404(b)."

. . . .

III

. . . .

D.

The Relevancy of Curtin's Stories

Under the precise circumstances of this case, and given the nature of the defense, was Curtin's immediate possession in his PDA of material involving sexual contact with minors relevant? Our answer is "yes." *To the extent* that the stories involved sexual activity between adults and children, his possession of that material was "evidence having any tendency to make the existence of any fact that is of consequence to the determination of the action more probable or less probable than it would be without the evidence." Fed.R.Evid. 401....*

Curtin's possession in his PDA of this material at the time of his intended encounter with Christy clearly illuminated his thoughts and his subjective intent to carry out his daddy/daughter sexual initiation escapades with a juvenile, not an adult. Any lingering question of relevancy was put to rest by Curtin's defense that it was all a fantasy to be consummated with an adult. The similarities between the email conversations and the content of the stories were readily apparent.

Moreover, the relevancy of the disputed evidence in this case has another dimension. This was not a case where the defense, relying on the government's burden of proof, simply contended that the government's evidence fell short of demonstrating the required intent beyond a reasonable doubt. Here, the defense was not merely arguing that the intent had not been proved, but rather that Curtin harbored a completely different intent than the intent required to convict; and the defense set out aggressively to establish this innocent intent in the minds of the jurors....

Curtin's defense makes the stuff in Curtin's possession all the more relevant because this is where the battle lines were drawn—what was in Curtin's mind as he traveled to meet Christy. Consequently, the stories were not of marginal relevance, the stories were at the core of the only material fact the defense sought to dispute. The nature of the defense heightened the probative value of the stories because they not only tended to prove Curtin's intent, but to demonstrate also that his aggressive defense was not credible. Thus, the evidence was probative both of Curtin's intent and the credibility of his innocence defense....

To further illustrate the relevancy of Curtin's recent PDA downloads, what would we certainly hold if the evidence in question was Curtin's possession of stories in his PDA consisting of role playing daddy/daughter incest with female adults—not minors—and the district court had excluded the stories as "irrelevant"? Curtin would have attempted to admit the stories into evidence to demonstrate that he had intended to meet an adult. Without a doubt, a convicted Curtin would assert on appeal that the content of the stories shed light on his subjective intent and—as counsel put it to the jurors—his "thoughts" as he communicated with "christy13," and as he traveled interstate with the stories in his pocket to meet her; and there is no doubt that we would agree. Why? Because the stories would have a "tendency to make the existence of any fact that is of consequence to the determination of the action more probable or less probable than it would be without the evidence." Fed.R.Evid. 401. Such stories would corroborate his claim of adult incest fantasy. How else could he do that without evidence of "other acts," as they are called? Conversely, the absence of such adult stories, coupled with the presence of stories wherein children are the objects of the sexual appetites of adults, is equally relevant to prove the government's case and to confront Curtin's defense.

In Internet "sting" cases such as this involving claims of entrapment, the issue of what a defendant's state of mind was immediately prior to his contact with a sexual target purporting to be a minor is routinely a serious point of contention. We call the issue one of "predisposition," and it is primarily a question of fact....

Thus, contextual and circumstantial evidence becomes acutely relevant to a defendant's material state of mind "prior to his contact" with the object of his sexual attention....

---

* Editor's Note: The quoted language differs slightly from the current text of Rule 401, which was restyled in 2011.

IV

Shymanovitz

We come now to the central question of whether there is something about relevant literature per se such that, as held by *Shymanovitz* and then followed by the panel in this case, "'possession of lawful reading material is simply not the kind of conduct contemplated by Rule 404(b).'" After reviewing the controlling Rules as previously explained in this opinion, and the case law arising from Rules 401 and 404, we conclude that no such blanket exclusion or privilege exists.... Moreover, we find nothing in the Constitution or in the First Amendment's guarantees of free press and free speech that would support such an exclusion or privilege. It is not surprising that the panel in *Shymanovitz* cited to no authority in support of its declaration regarding literature—none exists. Not only is there no precedent to support this holding in *Shymanovitz*, but the Supreme Court has held on many occasions in other contexts that opinions and other information that otherwise might be entitled to First Amendment protection are not immune from discovery and use as evidence in court, as long as they are relevant to an issue in a given case.

In 1989, for example, Wisconsin successfully prosecuted Todd Mitchell for aggravated battery and theft. His sentence was enhanced on the ground that he had intentionally selected his victim because of the victim's race. To provide evidentiary support for this "hate crimes" enhancement, the prosecution introduced evidence that prior to the beating, the defendant and his accomplices had discussed the racially charged movie "Mississippi Burning" and they expressed an intent to "[move] on some white people." Mitchell challenged the sentencing enhancement in the Wisconsin Supreme Court on First Amendment grounds, arguing that the enhancement statute was overbroad because the evidentiary use of his speech would necessarily chill the freedom of expression protected by our Bill of Rights. Mitchell's argument prevailed in that forum, and the First Amendment issue made its way to the United States Supreme Court, which reversed and remanded to state court. In so doing, the Court said:

> The First Amendment, moreover, does not prohibit the evidentiary use of speech to establish the elements of a crime or to prove motive or intent. Evidence of a defendant's previous declarations or statements is commonly admitted in criminal trials subject to evidentiary rules dealing with relevancy, reliability, and the like.

. . . .

This said, our holding here should not be interpreted as a holding (1) that the simple possession of any book or written materials generically similar to a charged crime is automatically admissible against the possessor defendant, or (2) that all pornography or obscenity in the possession of a defendant in these cases is admissible without undergoing the scrutiny required of Rules 401 and 403. In this respect, our holdings are properly limited to the facts of this case. For example, a book such as *The Great Train Robbery* would not necessarily be relevant and admissible in a run-of-the-mill theft case. On the other hand, if the crime charged happened to be theft of a money shipment from a train, then possession of the book might possibly be relevant—depending upon the precise facts and circumstances of the case. All we hold today is (1) that the information in the stories in Curtin's possession in Las Vegas when he intended to contact Christy was relevant in *this* case, (2) that the First Amendment provides no bar to its use as evidence under these circumstances, and (3) that the district court properly exercised its discretion in so concluding. In this connection, we note that Curtin is not being prosecuted for possession of literature, but for crossing a state line with the intent to engage in sexual acts with a minor. We are confident in the ability of our trial judges to discern the difference between relevant and irrelevant written or graphic materials and that our holding will not inappropriately impinge upon or chill anyone's legitimate First Amendment rights to possess books or other written materials.

V

Rule 403

Curtin contends that the district court abused its discretion pursuant to Rule 403 by admitting his stories in evidence.... The government disputes this contention and defends the court's exercise of its responsibility pursuant to Rule 403.

Our principal problem with the government's defense is that the district court did not read every word of the five disputed stories in preparation for making its balancing decision.... Instead, as the court went about the task of determining the admissibility of this evidence, the court read only two of the stories in full, Exhibit 7a "My Little Sister" and Exhibit 7b "Love for the World," plus blue highlighted excerpts — called "snippets" — from the other three. As for the other three stories, including "Melanie's Busy Day," the court asked for an offer of proof, which was delivered by the government....

This troubling circumstance raises a question primarily of procedure or process rather than substance: Was the trial court in this case required to have read every word of these stories when exercising its balancing discretion pursuant to Rule 403 to determine whether their potential for undue prejudice substantially outweighed their probative value? Our answer here is in the affirmative. The inflammatory nature and reprehensible nature of these abhorrent stories, although generally relevant, is such that a district court making a Rule 403 decision must know precisely what is in the stories in order for its weighing discretion to be properly exercised and entitled to deference on appeal. We see no other way for a court to make this important decision involving prejudice and redundancy, especially when the stories are such that a court finds itself unable to read all of them. In this context, reliance on an offer of proof simply is not enough.

The record in this case demonstrates why this must be the rule. Lurking in unread paragraph 9 of "Melanie's Busy Day," Exhibit 7C, is a particularly graphic description of "Melanie" engaged in sexual acts of mutual oral copulation with, and masturbation of, a dog. The acts described are enough to sour the stomach. Under no circumstances was this part of Exhibit 7C admissible with respect to any issue in this case. Had the district court read Exhibit 7C, the court would no doubt have spotted this excrescence and required that it be edited out of the exhibit as both irrelevant and dangerously prejudicial....

[W]e hold as a matter of law that a court does not properly exercise its balancing discretion under Rule 403 when it fails to place on the scales and personally examine and evaluate *all* that it must weigh.... Here, given the depraved and patently prejudicial nature of the irrelevant evidence in Exhibit 7C that the court overlooked, we are unable to conclude—as the government would have us do—that this error was harmless.

The record shows that in all other respects, the court was sensitive to Rule 403 and went to great lengths to protect the defendant's rights. The court pared down the government's attempt to offer 144 stories to just 5, and the court held the government's feet to the fire on the limited specific purpose for which the evidence was being admitted, correctly instructing the jury in the process as required by Rule 105....

KLEINFELD, Circuit Judge, with whom PREGERSON, KOZINSKI, THOMAS, and BERZON, Circuit Judges, join, concurring:

....

We ought to be wary when the government wants to use what people read against them. Our freedom to read and think requires a high wall restricting official scrutiny. The government (or others) can smear people by revealing what books they buy and borrow from the library, what magazines they purchase at the newsstand, what movies they rent at the video store, and what they look at on the internet. And not just for smut. Can the government introduce a defendant's copy of *The Monkey Wrench Gang*, *Lolita*, or *Junky*, to prove intent? DVDs of *The Thomas Crown Affair* to prove intent to rob a bank, or *Dirty Harry* to prove intent to deprive someone of civil rights? *Huckleberry Finn* (with quotes out of context) to prove hate crime motivation? In the 1950s, people with leftist books sometimes shelved them spine to the wall, out of fear that visitors would see and report them. Perhaps these days they would shelve *Huckleberry Finn* or *The Monkey Wrench Gang* spine to the wall. Readers should not have to hide what they read to be safe from the government....

The Constitution has long protected our private papers and thoughts, even those entirely lacking in social value.... So, in *Stanley v. Georgia*, the Supreme Court held the First Amendment prohibits the government from policing the private possession of obscenity. *Stanley* was decided on the basis that the material was obscene, not merely pornographic, so as a matter of law the First Amendment protects private reading material even if the material itself is not protected speech because it is obscene.

Fantasy is constitutionally protected. "Whatever the power of the state to control public dissemination of ideas inimical to the public morality, it cannot constitutionally premise legislation on the desirability of controlling a person's private thoughts." Likewise, in *Jacobson v. United States* "the Supreme Court held a person's inclinations and 'fantasies ... are his own and beyond the reach of government.'"

Based on *Stanley* and *Jacobson*, Curtin had a First Amendment right to possess and read the disgusting stories he downloaded from the internet and to fantasize about the criminal sexual conduct they describe. He emphatically did not have a right to attempt to persuade a person under 18 to have sex with him or to travel from California to Nevada "for the purpose" of having sex with a person under 18. The trial court should have managed the admission of evidence so as to allow the government to prove Curtin's intent and purpose, but protect him from being convicted for his execrable taste in reading material and repulsive fantasies....

The stories should have been excluded (and reading matter generally ought to be excluded) for lack of relevance. That is what we held in *Guam v. Shymanovitz*, and there is no good reason to overrule our own precedent.

This is not to say that all reading material is irrelevant in all circumstances. *Shymanovitz* does not create a rigid barrier against the introduction of reading material. Sometimes literature may be relevant and the probative value of evidence a defendant possessed certain reading material may exceed the prejudicial effect of admission. If a person is accused of planting a sophisticated bomb on a train, his possession of an instruction manual and the train schedule might tend to prove his guilt. Likewise, evidence that an accused contract killer owns a copy of *Hit Man: A Technical Manual for Independent Contractors* has been held to be sufficiently probative to outweigh any unfair prejudice.

But Curtin's stories are not a how-to manual. They are fantasy. Fantasy is not reality. It is generally the case that, as *Shymanovitz* holds, "[t]he mere possession of reading material that describes a particular type of activity makes it neither more nor less likely that a defendant would intentionally engage in the conduct described and thus fails to meet the test of relevancy under Rule 401." Barring exceptional circumstances, such as instructions for committing a crime otherwise hard to accomplish, used against one who accomplished it, what people read or fantasize should not be used to prove what they intend to do. *Shymanovitz* explained that the possession of male homosexual pornography tended to prove that the defendant "had an interest in looking at gay male pornography, reading gay male erotica, or perhaps even, reading erotic stories about men engaging in sex with underage boys." It did not prove "that he actually engaged in, or even had a propensity to engage in, any sexual conduct of any kind."

The majority errs by confusing fantasy with intent.... The statutes at issue in this case, like most criminal statutes, require intent, not mere fantasy. The link between fantasy and intent is too tenuous for fantasy to be probative. People commonly fantasize about doing things they have no intention of actually doing, or even firmly intend not to do. One may fantasize about riding a motorcycle across the country, but firmly intend never to do it because of the time, physical exertion and discomfort, and risk of injury. People go to psychiatrists for treatment of troubling fantasies that they want to avoid acting on, such as suicide. Johnny Cash probably could not have written *Folsom Prison Blues* without imagining himself a murderer imprisoned for life — "I shot a man in Reno, just to watch him die" — but there is no reason to suppose that he ever intended murder in real life.

No doubt some people commit sex crimes because they want to turn their fantasies into reality, but most people with criminal fantasies probably refrain from acting on them, because they know it would be wrong, or because they do not want to risk the penalties. And some people probably commit sex crimes without fantasizing about them at all, because their minds are addled by drugs or alcohol....

In this case, there are two additional reasons why Rule 401 was not satisfied. First, there was no evidence that Curtin had read the stories used against him.... The prosecutor never asked Curtin whether he actually read the five stories admitted. And we cannot assume he did, because of the volume of material.... Curtin had to plow through 2,998 single-spaced pages of this garbage to have read them all, three times the length of *War and Peace*. The content of the stories cannot be relevant to show what was in Curtin's mind without foundation to support an inference that he read them.

Second, the stories describe a different fantasy from what Curtin was charged with intending to do. All five stories admitted into evidence were about incest.... Curtin was not charged with incest. He was charged with traveling in interstate commerce with the intent of sexually abusing a person under 18. If christy13 were real, sex with her would be a crime, but it would not be incest. Even if proving a person's sexual fantasy were relevant to show an intention to carry it out, a doubtful proposition, it would not be relevant to show conduct quite different from the fantasy.

Wisconsin v. Mitchell, the majority's primary authority for overruling *Shymanovitz*, does not stand for the proposition that a person's reading material, by itself, can be used to prove a criminal purpose. Mitchell's viewing of *Mississippi Burning* did not prove he was racially motivated; it was his discussion with friends, where he clearly rejected the movie's message, that did so....

Even if we assume, *arguendo*, that the stories were relevant to support an inference of intent, they would still have to be excluded under Federal Rules of Evidence 403 and 404....

Perverse sexual desire is a trait of character. Using a person's perverse sexual fantasies to prove action in conformity therewith is exactly what subsection (a)[(1)] of Rule 404 prohibits. The exceptions in subsection (b)[(2)] ... are not a meaningless litany that deletes subsection (a). The stories admitted against Curtin were not a guide, fictional or otherwise, to arranging a tryst for sex with a minor. They shed no light on his motives, intentions, or plans. Good prosecution proves that the defendant committed the crime. Bad prosecution proves that the defendant is so repulsive he ought to be convicted whether he committed it or not. Rule 404(a)[(1)] prevents this sort of bad prosecution. We held in *Shymanovitz* that "possession of lawful reading material is simply not the type of conduct contemplated by Rule 404(b)," and we should follow our precedent. A jury is entitled to decide the truth, without having the window it looks through covered with slime....

The stories would have to be excluded in this case even if the judge had read them. Rule 403 "prohibits evidence whose 'probative value is substantially outweighed by [a] danger of [...] unfair prejudice.'"

. . . .

Prejudice is "unfair" if it has [ ] "an undue tendency to suggest decision on an improper basis, commonly, though not necessarily, an emotional one." Even normal biological functions induce disgust when exposed to public view. Perverse sexual fantasies generate even more intense disgust. "We accept without need of extensive argument that implications of child molestation, homosexuality, and abuse of women unfairly prejudice a defendant."

. . . .

Curtin's stories were used to make him disgusting to the jury. They portray every variety of incest. "[I]ncest has had a rare power to disgust." Their strong tendency to produce disgust outweighs any probative value they might have to prove an intention to have (non-incestuous) sex with a person under 18. I disagree with the majority's suggestion that the district court can cure this unfair prejudice by redacting parts of the stories, including the bestiality in one of the stories. Excluding this material might make the stories marginally less nauseating, and thus marginally less prejudicial. But it would also make the stories appear more relevant than they actually are, and thus amplify the prejudice of admitting them at all....

The law of evidence affects what kind of a country we live in. Fantasies and dreams are not intentions, or close to them. The reading material people get from libraries, bookstores, newsstands, and the internet should generally not be used to prove that they intended to do what it portrays, because such evidentiary use "would compel *all* persons to choose the contents of their libraries with considerable care; for it is the innocent, and not just the guilty, who are sometimes the subject of good-faith prosecutions." However repulsive a person's dreams or fantasies may be, they offer little support for an inference of an intention to act on them....

[The concurring opinions of Judges McKeown and Wardlaw are omitted.]

5. Character Evidence in Sexual Assault and Child Molestation Cases

Problem 3-7: He Said, She Said

Bill is on trial on charges that he sexually assaulted Linda. The incident at issue took place when Bill took Linda home after having taken her out to dinner on what was their first date. Bill does not dispute the fact that he had sexual intercourse with Linda, but claims that the act was consensual. At trial, Bill wishes to offer testimony by Megan that Linda has a reputation for being promiscuous and testimony by Tom that before Bill went on a date with Linda, he told Bill that Linda had sex with him when he took her home from dinner on their first date. The prosecution wishes to introduce evidence by Marie and Dawn, who would each testify that Bill tried to sexually assault them after they went out to dinner together, as well as testimony by Anna that Bill has a reputation as being rough with the ladies.

Based solely on the principles that you have studied under Rules 401 through 405, consider how a court might address the admissibility of the evidence proffered by the parties.

If evidence in sexual assault cases were treated no differently than evidence in other cases, you might expect that Bill might have some success in getting evidence about Linda admitted while the prosecution might run into difficulty getting evidence about Bill admitted.

Consider first the testimony by Megan that Linda has a reputation for being promiscuous. Recall that Rule 404(a)(2)(B) allows the accused in a criminal case to provide evidence of a pertinent trait of character of the victim for the purpose of showing action in conformity therewith. Is evidence of the victim's alleged promiscuity "pertinent"? A defendant might argue that such evidence is relevant because the fact that the victim consented to sexual intercourse on first dates on other occasions has some tendency to support the defendant's contention that the victim consented on the occasion at issue, an argument that was historically accepted by courts in the United States. *See generally* 1A Wigmore, Evidence § 62, at 1260–1264 (Tillers rev. 1983). To be sure, the probative value of such evidence might be rather low, but Rule 401 requires only a tendency, however slight, to support the proposition for which the evidence is offered.

Tom's testimony would not be admissible under Rule 404(a)(2)(B), for where evidence of character is admissible, Rule 405 would only allow evidence by way of reputation or opinion and not evidence of specific instances of conduct. However, Bill might argue that such evidence is admissible under Rule 404(b)(2) for the purpose of supporting a mistake of fact defense, to wit, that based on his *knowledge* of prior instances in which Linda consented to sexual intercourse on a first date, he *reasonably believed* that she was consenting on the occasion in question.

To the extent that the prosecution sought to offer any of its evidence to prove that Bill had a sexually violent character and that he acted in conformity with that trait, it would all be inadmissible under Rule 404. Indeed, such evidence would be inadmissible even if Bill offered evidence of Linda's promiscuous character, for even under the 2000 amendment to Rule 404(a)(2)(B)(ii), the prosecution can in such instances only rebut with evidence of the *same* trait of character of the accused, not a different trait. Only if Bill offered evidence under Rule 404(a)(2)(A) that he had a sexually non-violent character could the prosecution rebut with evidence of his sexually violent character, and even then only Anna's reputation testimony would be admissible (although on cross-examination of Bill's character witnesses, the prosecution could inquire about the witnesses' knowledge of the incidents involving Marie and Dawn). The only way to get the evidence of the prior incidents involving Marie and Dawn admitted would be to argue that they were somehow relevant for some reason other than for showing action in conformity therewith, such as intent, modus operandi, or for other reasons not forbidden under Rule 404(b). Historically, however, courts were reluctant to admit such evidence under Rule 404(b). *See* 2 Wigmore, Evidence § 357, at 334–342 (Chadbourn rev. 1979).

However, evidence in both civil and criminal cases involving allegations of sexual misconduct *is* treated differently from evidence in other cases. With regard to evidence about the victim, Rule 412, subject to certain exceptions, bars in such cases any evidence offered to prove her "sexual predisposition" or to prove that she engaged in "other sexual behavior." In cases involving alleged sexual misconduct, Rule 412 thus creates an exception to the exception set forth in Rule 404(a)(2)(B) as well as an exception to Rule 404(b)(2). The Advisory Committee explained the rationale for the rule as follows:

> The rule aims to safeguard the alleged victim against the invasion of privacy, potential embarrassment and sexual stereotyping that is associated with public disclosure of intimate sexual details and the infusion of sexual innuendo into the factfinding process. By affording victims protection in most instances, the rule also encourages victims of sexual misconduct to institute and to participate in legal proceedings against alleged offenders.

Advisory Committee's Note to Rule 412.

With regard to evidence about defendants in sexual assault cases, Rules 413 through 415, enacted by Congress in 1994, represent a dramatic departure from Rule 404. Collectively, the three rules provide that, in civil and criminal cases involving sexual assault or child molestation, evidence that the defendant engaged in other such conduct "may be considered on any matter to which it is relevant." The legislative history makes clear that "any" really means "any," and that such other acts can even be admitted to show "the defendant's *propensity* to commit sexual assault or child molestation offenses." The rationale for the new rules was described as follows:

> The proposed reform is critical to the protection of the public from rapists and child molesters, and is justified by the distinctive characteristics of the cases it will affect. In child molestation cases, for example, a history of similar acts tends to be exceptionally probative because it shows an unusual disposition of the defendant—a sexual or sadosexual interest in children—that simply does not exist in ordinary people. Moreover, such cases require reliance on child victims whose credibility can readily be attacked in the absence of substantial corroboration. In such cases, there is a compelling public interest in admitting all significant evidence that will illumine the credibility of the charge and any denial by the defense.

> Similarly, adult-victim sexual assault cases are distinctive, and often turn on difficult credibility determinations. Alleged consent by the victim is rarely an issue in prosecutions for other violent crimes—the accused mugger does not claim that the victim freely handed over [his] wallet as a gift—but the defendant in a rape case often contends that the victim engaged in consensual sex and then falsely accused him. Knowledge that the defendant has committed rapes on other occasions is frequently critical in assessing the relative plausibility of these claims and accurately deciding cases that would otherwise become unresolvable swearing matches.

> The practical effect of the new rules is to put evidence of uncharged offenses in sexual assault and child molestation cases on the same footing as other types of relevant evidence that are not subject to a special exclusionary rule. The presumption is in favor of admission. The underlying legislative judgment is that the evidence admissible pursuant to the proposed rules is typically relevant and pro-

bative, and that its probative value is normally not outweighed by any risk of prejudice or other adverse effects.

Floor Statement of the Principal House Sponsor, Representative Susan Molinari, Concerning the Prior Crimes Evidence Rules for Sexual Assault and Child Molestation Cases (Cong.Rec. H8991-92, Aug. 21, 1994).

Are you persuaded that there are distinctive reasons why evidence about victims and defendants should be treated differently in sexual assault cases than in all other cases? That the collective impact of Rules 412 through 415 is fair to criminal defendants? Consider these questions as you examine the materials that follow.

Problem 3-8: He Said, She Said Redux

Dennis is on trial on charges that he sexually assaulted Nancy. The evidence presented by the prosecution at trial showed that Nancy was examined at a sexual assault trauma center on the night in question and that she had lacerations and heavy bruising on her body. Dennis concedes that they had sexual intercourse earlier that evening, but claims that it was consensual, and that he is not responsible for her physical injuries. To support his defense, Dennis seeks to offer the following into evidence:

(1) His own testimony that he has engaged in sexual intercourse with Nancy several times in the past year.

(2) Testimony by Nancy's neighbor that, shortly after she saw Dennis leave Nancy's apartment, she saw another man knock on her door, saw Nancy open the door and start "making out" with him, and then saw Nancy walk into the apartment with him.

(3) Testimony by Lisa, who hangs out at the same bar as Nancy does, that Nancy regularly leaves the bar each night with a different guy and regularly reports the next day that she had sexual intercourse with the guy.

(4) Testimony by Anne, an acquaintance of Nancy's, who would testify that earlier that evening, when they were at a bar and Dennis walked by, Nancy said to her "I want that man in my bed tonight!"

(5) Testimony that on two previous occasions, Nancy has accused men of sexually assaulting her but later retracted those accusations after being confronted with inconsistencies in her story.

Notes and Questions

1. The Advisory Committee Note to Rule 412(a) indicates that the bar on evidence of "other sexual behavior" is broadly defined to bar not only evidence of actual sexual contact, but also any evidence of activities that imply such contact, including evidence of use of contraception, birth of an illegitimate child, or of a sexually transmitted disease, and even evidence regarding the victim's fantasies or dreams. The bar on evidence of "sexual predisposition" covers any evidence that might have a sexual connotation, including evidence of the victim's dress, speech, or lifestyle. The definition is broadly construed by courts to effectuate the policies underlying the rule. *E.g., Wolak v. Spucci*, 217 F.3d 157, 160 (2d Cir. 2000) (evidence that the victim watched pornography barred by the rule). *See also United States v. Tail*, 459 F.3d 854, 859 (8th Cir. 2006) (Rule 412 bars

evidence that the victim tested positive for Hepatitis B). Does the definition of "sexual pre-disposition" include evidence of a victim's sexual orientation? *See* Peter Nicolas, *"They Say He's Gay": The Admissibility of Evidence of Sexual Orientation*, 37 Ga. L. Rev. 793, 821–22 (2003).

2. Rule 412 only applies in cases "involving alleged sexual misconduct." The Advisory Committee notes make clear that this includes rape, sexual battery, and sexual harass-ment cases but not defamation cases, but beyond that the parameters are unclear. Would it, for example, include a murder case in which the defendant claims he acted in self-de-fense to repel an unwanted sexual assault by the victim? *See id.* at 823–24.

3. Rule 412(b)(1)(A) creates an exception to Rule 412 in criminal cases for "evidence of specific instances of a victim's sexual behavior, if offered to prove that someone other than the defendant was the source of semen, injury, or other physical evidence." How-ever, the courts have narrowly interpreted this exception to apply only if the *prosecution* has introduced into evidence the existence of injuries or semen. *See United States v. Richards*, 118 F.3d 622, 623–24 (8th Cir. 1997); *see also* Advisory Committee Note to Rule 412(b) ("Where the prosecution has directly or indirectly asserted that the physical evidence originated with the accused, the defendant must be afforded an opportunity to prove that another person was responsible."). What is the rationale for so limiting the exception?

4. Rule 412(b)(1)(B) creates an exception to Rule 412 in criminal cases for "evidence of specific instances of a victim's sexual behavior with respect to the person accused of the sexual misconduct, if offered by the defendant to prove consent or if offered by the pros-ecutor." What is the justification for treating prior instances of sexual behavior with the accused differently from prior instances of sexual behavior with third persons? Is the ex-ception as broad as the definition of "sexual behavior," such that it would likewise cover the victim's fantasies and dreams regarding the defendant? *See* Advisory Committee Note to Rule 412(b) ("Admissible pursuant to this exception might be evidence of prior in-stances of sexual activities between the alleged victim and the accused, as well as statements in which the alleged victim expressed an intent to engage in sexual intercourse with the accused, or voiced sexual fantasies involving the specific accused."). Why might such ev-idence ever be offered by the prosecution? *See id.* ("In a prosecution for child sexual abuse … evidence of uncharged sexual activity between the accused and the alleged vic-tim offered by the prosecution may be admissible pursuant to Rule 404(b) to show a pat-tern of behavior.").

5. Does Rule 412 bar the prosecution from introducing evidence of a victim's virgin-ity? Is it a fair reading of the phrase "sexual behavior" to include within its scope a fail-ure or refusal to engage in sexual behavior? Is such an interpretation consistent with the policies behind Rule 412? Consider the following:

> One of the purposes of the rule is to encourage the victims of sexual crimes to come forward, free from the fear that their sexual history will be gratuitously exposed in court. This policy would be undermined if the government were free to produce such evidence … the prohibition on evidence of "sexual behavior" in-cludes chaste sexual behavior. If the defendant in such a case is prohibited from playing on the potential prejudices of a jury by introducing evidence of the al-leged victim's promiscuity, the government should also be forbidden to play on potential prejudices by introducing evidence of the alleged victim's chastity.

United States v. Blue Bird, 372 F.3d 989, 995 (8th Cir. 2004), *implied overruling on other grounds recognized by Harris v. Chand*, 506 F.3d 1135, 1139 n.2 (8th Cir. 2007).

6. Rule 412(b)(1)(C) creates an exception to Rule 412 in criminal cases for "evidence whose exclusion would violate the defendant's constitutional rights." Strictly speaking, of course, such an exception is superfluous since the Constitution would in any event trump an inconsistent rule of evidence.

7. Suppose that a criminal defendant seeks to invoke one of the exceptions set forth in Rule 412(b)(1), offering, for example, evidence of specific prior instances of sexual behavior between himself and the victim to prove consent under Rule 412(b)(1)(B). If the victim denies that any such prior consensual sexual behavior took place, what sort of finding must the judge make? *See* Advisory Committee Note to 1994 Amendment to Rule 412(c) ("One substantive change made in subdivision (c) is the elimination of the following sentence: 'Notwithstanding subdivision (b) of Rule 104, if the relevancy of the evidence which the accused seeks to offer in trial depends upon the fulfillment of a condition of fact, the court, at the hearing in chambers or at a subsequent hearing in chambers scheduled for such purpose, shall accept evidence on the issue of whether such condition of fact is fulfilled and shall determine such issue.' On its face, this language would appear to authorize a trial judge to exclude evidence of past sexual conduct between an alleged victim and an accused or a defendant in a civil case based upon the judge's belief that such past acts did not occur. Such an authorization raises questions of invasion of the right to a jury trial under the Sixth and Seventh Amendments."). *See also United States v. Platero*, 72 F.3d 806, 813–14 (10th Cir. 1995) (describing this as a question of conditional relevancy governed by Rule 104(b)).

8. Can a defendant circumvent Rule 412 by arguing that the evidence of the victim's reputation and prior instances of sexual conduct is being offered for the purpose of showing the defendant's reasonable belief that she consented based on his knowledge of her promiscuous character? *See Doe v. United States*, 666 F.2d 43, 47–48 (4th Cir. 1981) (leaving open the possibility that such evidence might be admissible where necessary to preserve the defendant's constitutional rights).

9. Is evidence that the victim has previously made false accusations of sexual assault subject to exclusion under Rule 412? False accusations are not evidence of "sexual behavior" or "sexual predisposition," are they? The Advisory Committee Note to Rule 412 indicates that Rule 412 poses no bar, but that the evidence must still satisfy Rule 404. Would evidence of specific prior instances of false accusations be admissible under Rules 404 and 405?

10. Although Rule 412 applies in both civil and criminal cases, in civil cases, evidence offered to prove the alleged sexual behavior or sexual predisposition need not fit one of the specific exceptions set forth in Rule 412(b)(1) to be admissible. Rather, such evidence is admissible under Rule 412(b)(2) "if its probative value substantially outweighs the danger of harm to any victim and of unfair prejudice to any party." Although similar to the default approach of Rule 403 that would apply in the absence of Rule 412, the balancing test set forth in Rule 412(b)(2) differs in three ways that make it a more stringent test: the burden is on the proponent of the evidence rather than the opponent; it requires that probative value substantially outweigh dangers instead of merely not being substantially outweighed by dangers; and it includes on the dangers side the harm to any victim and not just the harm to the parties. *See* Advisory Committee Note to Rule 412(b).

11. Note that when an exception to Rule 412 applies, usually it allows *only* for evidence in the form of specific instances of conduct. The Advisory Committee Note to Rule 412(b) explains: "Subdivisions (b)(1)(A) and (b)(1)(B) require proof in the form of specific instances of sexual behavior in recognition of the limited probative value and dubious reliability of evidence of reputation or evidence in the form of an opinion." What does this suggest about Rules 404 and 405?

12. Rule 412(c) requires that a party seeking to offer evidence under one of the exceptions in Rule 412(b) must generally file a written motion at least 14 days before trial. It further provides that such hearings shall be conducted out of public view and that the papers related to the matter shall be kept under seal unless otherwise ordered by the court. The rationale for this provision is to ensure that the privacy of the victim is preserved in cases in which the court rules that the evidence does not fit within an exception.

13. Even if evidence fits within an exception to Rule 412, it may nonetheless be subject to exclusion under other rules. *See* Advisory Committee Note to Rule 412(b) ("In a criminal case, evidence may be admitted under subdivision (b)(1) pursuant to three possible exceptions, provided the evidence also satisfies other requirements for admissibility specified in the Federal Rules of Evidence, including Rule 403.").

Problem 3-9: He Said, She Said Redux II

Assume the same facts as in Problem 3-8. Assess the admissibility of the following evidence offered by the prosecution to support its case:

(1) Testimony by Wendy that Dennis sexually assaulted her two years ago after he brought her home from a dinner date. Wendy never reported the incident to the authorities.

(2) Testimony by Danielle that Dennis has a reputation for being "rough with the ladies."

Johnson v. Elk Lake School District
283 F.3d 138 (3d Cir. 2002)

BECKER, Chief Judge.

This case arises out of plaintiff Betsy Sue Johnson's claim that her guidance counselor Wayne Stevens sexually harassed and abused her while she was a high school student in the Elk Lake School District. Johnson sought damages from Stevens in the District Court for the Middle District of Pennsylvania, claiming violations of 42 U.S.C. § 1983 and state tort law. Johnson also sought damages from the School District, the Elk Lake School Board, and District Superintendent Charlotte Slocum (to whom we shall collectively refer as "the Administration"), claiming that they too were liable under § 1983 for having failed to prevent Stevens's abuse....

I. Facts and Procedural History

Johnson entered the Elk Lake School District high school as a freshman in September 1991. Sometime in November or December of that year Johnson began making regular visits to Stevens's office to discuss family difficulties. Johnson contends that shortly thereafter, in December 1991, Stevens began sexually harassing and abusing her. She alleges that for the next two years Stevens repeatedly sent her letters, roses, cards, and other suggestive correspondence, attempted on numerous occasions to hug and kiss her without her consent, and at one point fondled her breasts and vagina....

III. Exclusion of Radwanski's Testimony Under Rule 415

A. The Incident

During the course of the trial, Johnson attempted to introduce the testimony of Karen Radwanski, a teacher's associate in the high school's restaurant training program and a friend of Stevens, regarding an incident in which Stevens allegedly sexually assaulted her in the office of another teacher, Tony Blaisure. Radwanski had just walked into the office carrying lunch when Stevens allegedly picked her up and threw her over his shoulder. According to Radwanski, who was wearing a skirt at the time, Stevens's hand went up her skirt and touched her in the crotch area while he raised her off the floor. Stevens soon let her down to the floor and the two of them, along with Blaisure, proceeded to sit down and eat lunch together.

Whether Stevens's alleged touching of Radwanski's crotch was intentional or accidental is unclear from the record, as Radwanski offered somewhat inconsistent accounts of the incident....

C. History and Background of Rules 413–15

Federal Rules of Evidence 413–15 are relatively recent additions to the Rules, adopted by Congress as part of the Violent Crime Control and Law Enforcement Act of 1994. Pub.L. No. 103-322, 108 Stat. 1796 (1994).... Rules 413–15 establish exceptions to the general prohibition on character evidence in cases involving sexual assault and child molestation. Rules 413 and 414 apply to criminal proceedings, while Rule 415 applies to civil trials.

Ever since their initial proposal, Rules 413–15 have been met with hostility by the legal establishment.... Although Congress bypassed the ordinary rulemaking procedures when adopting Rules 413–15, the enacting legislation provided the Judicial Conference 150 days within which to make and submit alternative recommendations on the rules to Congress. The Judicial Conference's Advisory Committee on Evidence Rules, with what it noted was "highly unusual unanimity," ardently opposed the new rules, fearing that they "could diminish significantly the protections that have safeguarded persons accused in criminal cases and parties in civil cases against undue prejudice." *Judicial Conference Report*, 159 F.R.D. at 53. Embracing the views of the Advisory Committee, the Conference recommended that Congress "reconsider its policy determinations underlying Evidence Rules 413–415" or, in the alternative, adopt amendments to Rules 404 and 405 proposed by the Advisory Committee. *Id.* at 54. Congress rejected both alternatives, and the rules stand today as originally enacted.

D. Standards for Admission of Evidence under Rule 415

In order for evidence of a past act to be admitted under Rule 415, the District Court must determine whether the act satisfies the applicable definition [of "sexual assault"] ... provided by Rule 413(d)....

Although the language of Rule 413(d) is ambiguous ... the legislative history of Rules 413–15 indicates that Congress intended to allow admission not only of prior convictions for sexual offenses, but also of uncharged conduct....

While uncharged conduct is admissible under Rule 415, some limits, of course, need to be placed on its admissibility in order to ensure that the plaintiff may not "parade past the jury a litany of potentially prejudicial similar acts that have been established or connected to the defendant only by unsubstantiated innuendo." *Huddleston v. United States*, 485 U.S. 681, 689 (1988). At the same time, for reasons of judicial efficiency and economy, the district court cannot be expected to conduct a "trial within a trial" to determine the veracity of the proffered evidence. So exactly what must a district court do before deciding whether to admit or exclude evidence of prior sexual assaults under Rules 413–15? The texts of Rules 413–15 are silent on this issue, and the Supreme Court has never answered this question in the specific context of these rules. The Supreme Court has, however, in *Huddleston*, considered the same issue in the context of Federal Rule of Evidence 404(b)....

In *Huddleston*, ... the Court identified Rule 104(b), which governs the relevancy of evidence conditioned on fact, as the applicable safeguard against the risk of introducing prejudicial unsubstantiated evidence.

Huddleston identified Rule 104(b) as appropriate because the question of the defendant's commission of the past act "was simply one of conditional relevancy—the relevancy of the bad act is conditioned on the defendant's having committed it." *Federal Rules of Evidence Manual* 388–89 (Stephen A. Saltzburg et al. eds., 7th ed. 1998). Under Rule 104(b), no preliminary finding is required; rather, the trial "court simply examines all the evidence in the case and decides whether the jury could reasonably find the conditional fact—[whether the defendant committed the prior act]—by a preponderance of the evidence." *Huddleston*, 485 U.S. at 690....

In part because of the similarity between Rules 404(b) and Rules 413–15—both allow the admission of past acts, including uncharged conduct, albeit for different purposes—the few courts and commentators that have considered the issue have concluded that *Huddleston*'s standard for screening uncharged conduct applies to Rules 413–15. *See United States v. Enjady*, 134 F.3d 1427, 1433 (10th Cir. 1998); 2 *Weinstein's Federal Evidence*, § 413.03[1], at 413–7. As explained in the margin, we find this position somewhat problematic in light of the difference between the types of evidence that are likely to be introduced under Rules 404(b) and 413–15....[8] Were it within our power to select the better rule, therefore, we would be inclined to adopt the more exacting standard for the admission of past act evidence rejected by the Court in *Huddleston*: a preponderance of the evidence finding under Rule 104(a). We find ourselves constrained from doing so, however, by the texts of Rules 413–15 as well as by their legislative history, which indicates that Congress intended that the *Huddleston* standard apply in this context.

As noted above, the texts of Rules 413–15 are silent as to the appropriate standard for admitting evidence of past acts of sexual assault. Following the Court's reasoning in *Huddleston*, this silence alone is an important reason for not imposing a Rule 104(a) requirement on evidence introduced under Rules 413–15. In interpreting Rule 404(b), the *Huddleston* Court considered it important that Rule 404(b)'s "text contains no intimation ... that any preliminary showing is necessary," and that such a requirement was "nowhere apparent from the language of" the rule. 485 U.S. at 687–88, 108 S.Ct. 1496. Similarly, Rules 413–15 do not contain any language indicating that a preliminary finding is necessary.

---

8. In our view, because of the severe social stigma attached to crimes of sexual assault and child molestation, evidence of these past acts poses a higher risk, on the whole, of influencing the jury to punish the defendant for the similar act rather than the charged act than the type of evidence that is often introduced under Rule 404(b).... In light of this higher risk of unfair prejudice, we think the need to guard against the introduction of unsubstantiated evidence is greater, and would be best addressed by requiring the trial court to make a finding by a preponderance of the evidence under Rule 104(a).

To be sure, certain past acts likely to be introduced under Rule 404(b) are similarly, if not more highly, stigmatized—such as murders or assaults and batteries—and thereby present a significant risk of inappropriate punishment. However, many, if not most, of the past acts introduced under Rule 404(b)—e.g., burglaries, thefts, etc.—are not as potentially inflammatory as offenses of sexual assault or child molestation. On the whole, therefore, we believe that the risk of unfair prejudice is less in the Rule 404(b) context than in the context of Rules 413–15.

Moreover, just as in *Huddleston* the Court noted that the legislative history counseled against imposing a Rule 104(a) finding requirement on evidence introduced under Rule 404(b), *see* 485 U.S. at 688, the legislative history of Rules 413–15 points to the same conclusion in this context....

As such, a trial court considering evidence offered under Rule 415 must decide under Rule 104(b) whether a reasonable jury could find by a preponderance of the evidence that the past act was ["sexual assault"] under Rule 413(d)'s definition and that it was committed by the defendant.

Even if a trial court is satisfied that the proffered past act evidence satisfies Rule 104(b), however, it may still exclude it under Federal Rule of Evidence 403.... Initially, there was some doubt as to whether Rule 403's balancing inquiry was at all applicable to Rules 413–15....[12]

It appears from the legislative history of Rules 413–15, however, that ... Congress did not intend for the admission of past sexual offense evidence to be mandatory; rather, Congress contemplated that Rule 403 would apply to Rules 413–15. *See, e.g.,* 140 Cong. Rec. 24,799 (1994) (Statement of Sen. Dole) ("[T]he general standards of the rules of evidence will continue to apply [to Rules 413–15], including ... the court's authority under rule 403 to exclude evidence whose probative value is substantially outweighed by its prejudicial effect.").[13]

Having concluded that Rule 403 is applicable to Rules 413–15, we now turn to the manner in which the balancing inquiry ought to be performed. Relying on the legislative history, a number of courts and commentators have concluded that Rule 403 should be applied to Rules 413–15 with a thumb on the scale in favor of admissibility....

In our view, this characterization of the role of Rule 403 is overly simplified. It makes sense when the past act sought to be introduced under Rules 413–15 is demonstrated with specificity, *see Enjady*, 134 F.3d at 1433 (identifying "how clearly the prior act has been proved" as a factor to be considered in assessing the probative value of evidence of past sexual assaults), and is sufficiently similar to the type of sexual assault allegedly committed by the defendant. *See United States v. Guardia*, 135 F.3d 1326, 1331 (10th Cir. 1998) (noting that "the similarity of the prior acts" to the acts at issue in the case is a factor to be considered in determining their probative value). In these archetypal cases, where the propensity inference that can be drawn from the past act evidence is greatest, Congress surely intended for the probative value of the evidence to outweigh its prejudicial effect, and, conversely, did not want Rule 403 factors such as undue delay, waste of time, confusion of the issues, etc., to justify exclusion....

In other cases, however, where the past act is not substantially similar to the act for which the defendant is being tried, and/or where the past act cannot be demonstrated with sufficient specificity, the propensity inference provided by the past act is weaker, and no presumption in favor of admissibility is warranted. Where a past act cannot be shown with reasonable certainty, its probative value is reduced and it may prejudice the defendant unfairly, confuse the issues, mislead the jury, and result in undue delay and wasted time—all reasons for excluding evidence under Rule 403. The same can be said of evidence of

---

12. While we express no view on the matter, we note that a policy of mandatory admission, particularly in the criminal context, has been thought to raise serious constitutional concerns under the Due Process Clause. *See Enjady*, 134 F.3d at 1430; *Judicial Conference Report*, 159 F.R.D. at 53.

13. While we again express no view on the matter, we note that the presence of the Rule 403 safeguard has served to assuage the concerns of at least one of our sister courts of appeals, the Tenth Circuit, regarding the constitutionality of Rules 413–15 under the Due Process Clause. *See Enjady*, 134 F.3d at 1433.

past acts that are dissimilar to the act for which the defendant is being tried; in particular, the introduction of dissimilar past acts runs the risk of confusing the issues in the trial and wasting valuable time. Also relevant to the Rule 403 balancing analysis are the additional factors recognized by the Tenth Circuit in *Guardia*: "the closeness in time of the prior acts to the charged acts, the frequency of the prior acts, the presence or lack of intervening events, and the need for evidence beyond the testimony of the defendant and alleged victim." 135 F.3d at 1330 (internal citations omitted).

Finally, it bears repeating that despite these general guidelines, the Rule 403 balancing inquiry is, at its core, an essentially discretionary one that gives the trial court significant latitude to exclude evidence. *See Elcock v. Kmart Corp.*, 233 F.3d 734, 754 (3d Cir. 2000).

E. Discussion

....

The District Court correctly noted that in order for the touching incident to qualify as ["sexual assault"] ... under Rule 413(d)'s definition ... requires that the touching have been done intentionally. As described in Part I, *supra*, Radwanski gave conflicting descriptions of the incident. In one account she implied that Stevens's hand merely brushed by her crotch as he lifted her off the ground; in another she indicated that his hand lingered on her crotch for a moment or two. When asked during her deposition whether she thought the touching incident was intentional, Radwanski replied, "I guess maybe at the time it didn't feel right, but I guess the greater part of me not wanting to think anything just was like, you know, just shrugged it off, no big deal."[15]

In deciding to exclude Radwanski's testimony, the District Court did not indicate what standard for admission it was applying to the evidence. In keeping with *Huddleston*, the Court was not obliged to hold an *in limine* hearing, as requested by Johnson, or make a formal finding under Rule 104(a) when excluding the evidence.[16] Under *Huddleston*, the Court needed only to ask itself whether a jury could reasonably find by a preponderance of the evidence that Stevens committed the act intentionally, provided that the Court was satisfied that the evidence need not be excluded under Rule 403. Although the Court did not say so explicitly, it appears to us that the Court concluded that Radwanski's testimony did not satisfy Rule 403, and it accordingly — and appropriately — bypassed the *Huddleston* reasonable jury determination.

The basis for the Court's Rule 403 determination seems to have been that Radwanski's equivocal testimony was insufficiently specific as to the intentionality of Stevens's conduct. The District Court stated, "I think there's insufficient evidence that the touching was in any way intentional....". Lacking more specific evidence of intentionality, the Court apparently concluded that the probative value of the evidence was slight and was outweighed by Rule 403's concerns of prejudice, undue delay, waste of time, etc. This judg-

---

15. We are aware that victims of sexual assault are often hesitant to report their assailants for a variety of reasons. *See* United States Department of Justice, Bureau of Justice Statistics, *National Crime Victimization Survey* (2000) (noting that in 1999 "rape or sexual assault was [the violent crime] least often reported to law enforcement (28%)"). Indeed, for this reason we do not place too much emphasis on the fact that Radwanski did not report the touching incident to the state police when they interviewed her in response to Johnson's criminal complaint against Stevens, a factor relied on by the District Court.

16. Although an *in limine* hearing is not required, district courts might find this a useful technique for considering the admission of evidence proffered under Rule 415. Moreover, while a formal "finding" under Rule 104(a) is not required, it would be helpful to our reviewing function if district courts would state explicitly their reasons for admitting or excluding evidence under Rules 413–15....

ment appears to us to be sound given the equivocal nature of Radwanski's testimony as regarding the intentionality of Stevens's conduct.

Additionally, we find the exclusion of the evidence justifiable for a reason not stressed by the District Court: the differences between Stevens's alleged assaults of Radwanski and Johnson. The former occurred in another teacher's office with that teacher present, involved an adult co-worker of Stevens, and consisted of a bizarre incident in which Stevens lifted Radwanski off the ground and placed her on his shoulders. The latter is said to have taken place with no one else present in Stevens's office, involved a minor to whom Stevens served as guidance counselor, and allegedly involved Stevens making more direct sexual advances upon a much younger female. In our view, these dissimilarities reduced significantly the probative value of Radwanski's testimony. The case law is in accord. *See, e.g., Doe ex rel. Rudy-Glanzer v. Glanzer*, 232 F.3d 1258, 1269–70 (9th Cir. 2000) (upholding exclusion of prior sexual assault evidence as too dissimilar because of age difference between victims and the dissimilar circumstances of the alleged misconduct).

We also consider it relevant that the alleged touching of Radwanski appears to have been an isolated incident. Although Johnson presented evidence of rumors of Stevens acting inappropriately around female students in her attempt to attach § 1983 liability to the Administration ... during her trial against Stevens she did not attempt to present any other evidence of offenses of sexual assault allegedly perpetrated by Stevens besides the lone incident with Radwanski. While the isolated nature of the incident alone would probably not be enough to warrant excluding it, we nevertheless consider it a relevant factor supporting the District Court's decision. *See Guardia*, 135 F.3d at 1331 (recognizing "the frequency of the prior acts" as a factor in determining the evidence's probative value).

In sum, the uncertainty of the testimony regarding intentionality, the dissimilarities between the similar and alleged acts, and the isolated nature of the Radwanski incident reduced significantly the probative value of Radwanski's testimony. Given this reduced probative value, any presumption in favor of admissibility was unwarranted, and the District Court's exclusion of the evidence can be justified on grounds that its introduction might have prejudiced Stevens unfairly, misled the jury, confused the issues, and wasted valuable trial time. Accordingly, we cannot say that the Court abused its discretion in excluding Radwanski's testimony....

Notes and Questions

1. Do Rules 413 through 415, like Rule 404(b), allow for the admission of evidence of acts that occurred *subsequent* to the one charged? *See United States v. Sioux*, 362 F.3d 1241, 1244–46 (2004) (holding that they do).

2. Do Rules 413 through 415 allow for the admission of reputation or opinion evidence regarding the defendant's propensity to commit sexual assaults or child molestation? To what extent, if any, does the text or structure of the rules answer that question?

3. To be admitted under Rules 413 through 415, the conduct must fall within the scope of the phrases "sexual assault" and "child molestation" as defined by those rules. As it turns out, not all sexually suggestive acts—not even those involving physical contact—fall within the scope of those phrases. *See United States v. Blue Bird*, 372 F.3d 989, 992–94 (8th Cir. 2004), *implied overruling on other grounds recognized by Harris v. Chand*, 506 F.3d 1135, 1139 n.2 (8th Cir. 2007).

4. Note that although most states have a rule equivalent to Rule 412, only a minority of states have rules equivalent to Rules 413 through 415. Are there good reasons to adopt the former rule but not the latter group of rules?

5. Note that in any case in which a party intends to invoke Rules 413–415, they must disclose the proposed evidence to the other party in advance of trial. *See* Rule 413(b), 414(b), 415(b).

6. Can Rules 413–415 be invoked to introduce evidence of sexual assaults or acts of child molestation that took place outside of the United States? What is to be made of the definitions of "sexual assault" and "child molestation" in these rules as being a crime under federal or state law? Does that mean that the event had to be *subject* to those laws, or only that it was the *sort* of conduct prohibited under those laws?

7. Rules 413 and 414 apply only in criminal cases in which the defendant is "accused," respectively, of "a sexual assault" or "child molestation." Does this mean that the rule can only be invoked in cases in which the defendant is indicted for such crimes, or does it more broadly apply in cases in which the defendant has been verbally "accused" of sexual assault or child molestation during the course of an investigation into a separate criminal offense? *See United States v. Courtright*, 632 F.3d 363, 368 (7th Cir. 2011) (concluding that Rule 413 can only be invoked in a case in which the accused has been indicted for sexual assault).

8. Given that Rules 413–415 explicitly *endorse* the relevance of the propensity argument where other acts of sexual assault or child molestation are concerned, what dangers are to be guarded against in conducting Rule 403 balancing? Consider the following:

> Rule 413 affects the Rule 403 analysis of past sexual offenses introduced in sexual assault cases.... Rule 404(b) identifies the propensity inference as improper in all circumstances, and Rule 413 makes an exception to that rule when past sexual offenses are introduced in sexual assault cases.... Because Rule 413 identifies this propensity inference as proper, the chance that the jury will rely on that inference can no longer be labeled as "unfair" for purposes of the Rule 403 analysis. While Rule 403 remains the same, a court's Rule 403 analysis of prior conduct differs if the evidence falls under Rule 404(b) versus Rule 413; in the former analysis, the rule has decreed that the propensity inference is too dangerous, while in the latter, the propensity inference is permitted for what it is worth.

> That said, evidence of prior sexual offenses may still pose significant dangers against which the district court must diligently guard. Even if the evidence does not create unfair prejudice solely because it rests on propensity, it may still risk a decision on the basis of something like passion or bias—that is, an improper basis. Even though Congress has made the propensity inference permissible, it has not said that evidence falling within Rule 413 is *per se* non-prejudicial. To the contrary, a jury might use such evidence, for example, to convict a defendant because it is appalled by a prior crime the defendant committed rather than persuaded that he committed the crime charged. Or a jury, uncertain of guilt, may convict a defendant because they think the defendant is a bad person generally deserving of punishment. We mention these dangers only as examples; our list does not purport to be exhaustive. Rule 403 remains an important safeguard against the admission of prejudicial evidence, and courts enjoy wide discretion in applying the rule. When exercising that discretion, however, courts must recognize that, for Rule 413 evidence, the propensity inference must be viewed differently.

United States v. Rogers, 587 F.3d 816, 822–23 (7th Cir. 2009).

9. What justifies treating the crimes of sexual assault and child molestation differently from all other crimes, both with regard to evidence about the defendant and the victim? Do you agree with the suggestion in the *Johnson* decision that there are reasons to be even *more* restrictive about evidence regarding the defendant's prior acts in cases involving sexual assault and child molestation? Assuming that both the relevance and prejudice of prior acts are greater in this context than in other contexts, which is greater relative to the baseline?

10. Is the overall effect of Rules 412 through 415 so unfair as to deny defendants their due process rights? *See United States v. Withorn*, 204 F.3d 790, 796 (8th Cir. 2000) (holding that the rules in combination are not so unfair as to violate due process). *But see State v. Cox*, 781 N.W.2d 757 (Iowa 2010) (holding Iowa analogue to Federal Rule 413 unconstitutional under the due process clause of the Iowa constitution as applied to the situation in which evidence of prior incidents involving a different victim is admitted to show propensity).

B. Evidence of Habit

In stark contrast to Rule 404's general declaration that evidence of a person's character is not admissible to prove action in conformity therewith, Rule 406 states that evidence of an individual's habit or an organization's routine practice *is* potentially admissible to prove action in conformity therewith (subject, of course, like virtually all other evidence, to exclusion under Rule 403).

This immediately raises two questions, one practical and the other jurisprudential, although the two questions to some extent merge into one. First, *how* does one distinguish evidence of character from evidence of habit? Second, *why* distinguish between evidence of character on the one hand and evidence of habit on the other? In other words, what justifies a general rule barring the former while freely admitting the latter?

The Advisory Committee Note to Rule 406, quoting McCormick, attempts to distinguish character from habit:

> Character and habit are close akin. Character is a generalized description of one's disposition, or of one's disposition in respect to a general trait, such as honesty, temperance, or peacefulness. 'Habit,' in modern usage, both lay and psychological, is more specific. It describes one's regular response to a repeated specific situation. If we speak of character for care, we think of the person's tendency to act prudently in all the varying situations of life, in business, family life, in handling automobiles and in walking across the street. A habit, on the other hand, is the person's regular practice of meeting a particular kind of situation with a specific type of conduct, such as the habit of going down a particular stairway two stairs at a time, or of giving the hand-signal for a left turn, or of alighting from railway cars while they are moving. The doing of the habitual acts may become semi-automatic.

The Advisory Committee goes on to indicate that the key factors in determining whether behavior rises to the status of habit are "adequacy of sampling and uniformity of response," but concedes that it is not possible to delineate a precise formula and that there will be differences of opinion on whether something constitutes evidence of character or evidence of habit.

With regard to the *reason* for distinguishing evidence of character from that of habit, the Advisory Committee again quotes McCormick:

> Character may be thought of as the sum of one's habits though doubtless it is more than this. But unquestionably the uniformity of one's response to habit is far greater than the consistency with which one's conduct conforms to character or disposition. Even though character comes in only exceptionally as evidence of an act, surely any sensible man in investigating whether X did a particular act would be greatly helped in his inquiry by evidence as to whether he was in the habit of doing it.

Given the stark difference in the admissibility of character and habit evidence, you can imagine that there is significant litigation over whether evidence constitutes character or habit evidence. The materials that follow are designed to help you to make that distinction.

Problem 3-10: Who Ran the Light?

Late one evening, David and Paul crashed into one another at the intersection of Fifth & Main. Given the time of night, there were no other witnesses to the accident, and each driver maintains that the light was green in his favor. Paul has sued David for damages arising out of the accident and David has counter-claimed for the same.

At trial, Paul seeks to introduce evidence that in the past 10 years, David has received three tickets for running red lights, two tickets for speeding, and one ticket for reckless driving. David in turn seeks to introduce evidence that in the past 10 years, Paul has received eight tickets for running red lights.

Is the evidence offered by either party admissible?

Problem 3-11: Seat Belt Snafu

While driving a car manufactured by Specific Motors, William Farmington is killed on December 5, 2011, when the car skids off the road and crashes into a tree. William's spouse, Tina Farmington, brings a wrongful death action against Specific Motors in federal court, invoking that court's diversity jurisdiction. The evidence is undisputed that William's seat belt was not fastened around him when his body was discovered at the accident scene. The plaintiff's theory, however, is that the belt buckle had a defect known as "false latching" that caused it to appear to the person wearing it as though it was latched, but that would result in unbuckling as soon as pressure was exerted on it, such as would occur in an accident. Specific Motors defends on the ground that there is no evidence that William was wearing his seat belt at the time of the accident.

Tina seeks to offer, over Specific Motors' objection, the following testimony:

(1) Her own testimony that she drove with William at least 3 times per week for the last 10 years, and that he always put his seat belt on before the car was started, regardless of the length of the trip and regardless of whether he was the driver or the passenger.

(2) Testimony by a co-worker that in his opinion, William was an "extremely cautious" driver.

Is the evidence offered by Tina admissible?

United States v. Yazzie

188 F.3d 1178 (10th Cir. 1999)

JOHN C. PORFILIO, Circuit Judge.

Raymond Jones and Alfred Yazzie challenge their convictions for second-degree murder and aiding and abetting second-degree murder [of Thomas Briggs, also known as Eagle]....

III. Evidentiary Issues

A. Character Evidence

At trial, the strength and credibility of Mr. Jones' and Mr. Yazzie's claim of self-defense rested on portraying Eagle as a violent man, one habitually instigating fights and carrying a knife or a gun.... Jones now targets the [district] court's limitation of the testimony of two of their witnesses on the ground its interpretation unduly constricted Fed.R.Evid. 406 and impeded their defense....

The two witnesses ... were Chuck Cowen, the manager of an Albuquerque bar, and Teresa Meyers-Johnson, the owner of a tribal smoke shop who had lived with Briggs for a year. Prior to their testifying, defense counsel made an offer of the evidence they would provide: their opinion of Briggs as a violent person, his reputation as a violent person, and his habits of regularly carrying a gun and knife and routinely starting fights. Over the government's objecting to "this nonsense about habit," the court agreed to hear their testimony initially without the jury present to decide whether there was sufficient foundation to permit the testimony to establish Briggs' habits to prove his violent character.

First, Mr. Cowen related he knew Briggs for five years, until about six months before his death, observing him daily in his bar. Mr. Cowen stated "routinely, daily," Briggs intimidated, scared, and threatened people in the bar.

> He would always get in a fight, he would fight people that he could bully. He would push them around. If people stood up to him, he would hit them. He would just—beat them until he got what he wanted out of them. Either they were subdued or they were submissive to him.

Mr. Cowen described Briggs' introducing himself to new patrons by removing his shirt to display his tattoos and pulling down his lower lip to reveal the obscene tattoo. Mr. Cowen stated he repeatedly caught Briggs in the bathroom intravenously injecting drugs but feared reporting him to the police because Briggs threatened to kill him if he did. Further, he testified Mr. Briggs routinely carried a large knife although weapons were prohibited in the bar.

The government objected the testimony was too remote in time, especially given the more recent statement of the Zia bartender that Briggs was charming and polite. It relied broadly on the proviso in the advisory committee's note to Rule 406 about using "intemperate 'habits' " as proof of drunkenness in accident cases "to show habit or assault." The court then questioned the witness, clarifying the statement Briggs had a fight everyday, expressing its concern over whether the evidence, in fact, more properly reflected specific acts proving character. Pursuing that distinction, the court asked,

> The Court: Mr. Cowen, did he beat up everybody in the bar?

The Witness: No, he didn't.

The Court: What happened to the other people....

The Witness: Some people he—he picked on the weak people.

The Court: Okay. So he would come into the bar and then he would eventually ... get into a fight because he would seek out the weak people?

The Witness: Yes, he would look for somebody that he could threaten first. If they didn't agree with him, then he'd fight them.

The Court: I think that's character evidence. *If he beat up everybody he met, that would be habit.* So he didn't—his character—and he can testify as to the violent character of Mr. Briggs.

The court also ruled the evidence of Briggs' use of drugs and selling stolen goods constituted character evidence and agreed with the government's request to prohibit Mr. Cowen from testifying about any specific acts. Consequently, Mr. Cowen simply told the jury Briggs had a reputation of being a bully and "a very violent man," and wore a foot-long knife in his belt or in his boot.

The government similarly objected to the second witness, Ms. Myers-Johnson, proffered for the same purposes. It asserted such habit evidence is inadmissible "with respect to [Jones'] self-defense claim. He can only bring in reputation for violence, that's it." Reluctantly, the court followed the same procedure, excusing the jury for counsel to voir dire the witness....

She, too, testified Briggs regularly picked fights, manipulated and intimidated people and carried a gun, either a small gun behind his jacket or a larger one under his arm. Ms. Myers-Johnson stated Briggs threatened her daily, knowing she did not want to remain in the relationship. She stated Briggs went to bars every day, told people he confronted he was a member of the Banditos, although he was not, and often stole the motorcycle of individuals he met and overcame. She also described Briggs' pulling down his lower lip in salutation.

However, the court ruled the testimony about this behavior, even if revealing habit, was irrelevant to Briggs' propensity for violence,[23] necessarily rejecting defense counsel's explanation the conduct was a manifestation "intertwined with the violence that's intrinsic to our defense." However, it nonetheless concluded Briggs' putting a gun in his belt each morning qualified as evidence of habit. Ms. Myers-Johnson then told the jury Briggs was a "very violent man," known by others for his aggressiveness. She also testified Briggs always carried a gun and was left-handed.

Persisting in their characterization of the excluded evidence, Jones maintains the district court abused its discretion in unduly limiting his presentation of a defense. The essence of his claim, portraying the victim as aggressor, predicated defendants' theory of self-defense. Thus, Jones insists, the evidence of habit was essential to establish Briggs routinely was the aggressor in encounters he provoked....

[B]ecause character evidence is highly susceptible to these enumerated shortcomings [in Rule 403], it is categorically excluded under Fed.R.Evid. 404 *except* in three instances. One such exception, subsection (a)(2)[(B)], figures here. While 404(a)(2)[(B)] permits evidence of the victim's character, Fed.R.Evid. 405 limits the permissible methods of proof.

---

23. The court observed, "You haven't told me how it is relevant to this case. If the man had a habit of brushing his teeth every morning, it's not relevant to this case."

There is ample precedent defining the circumstances and bounds for admitting evidence of a victim's violent character to prove a claim of self-defense.... In each case, Fed.R.Evid. 405 limited the reach of Fed.R.Evid. 404(a)(2)[(B)].

However, these limitations do not burden proof of habit. Habit, one's "regular practice of meeting a particular kind of situation with a specific type of conduct," Fed.R.Evid. 406 advisory committee's note, is admissible to show a person acted "in [accordance] with the habit or routine practice.".... Habit evidence may offer a backdoor to proving character for, although evidence an individual routinely acted in a particular manner may be offered to show he *acted* in conformity on an occasion, those routine practices may also coalesce to provide specific instances proving character. A habit of routinely accosting others may, thus, provide potent evidence the individual similarly acted in conformity and may have been the aggressor in a particular instance. Indeed, "[c]haracter may be thought of as the sum of one's habits," Fed.R.Evid. 406 advisory committee's note. Thus, this potential of establishing the forbidden ultimate fact, proof of action in conformity with one's *character*, makes its admission highly discretionary and potentially troublesome.

Certainly, the district court was well versed in these distinctions and exercised its discretion to admit defendants' evidence of Briggs' reflexive action of placing a gun in his waistband or knife in his boot, recognizing the uniformity of this response established its habitual nature. However, to the third proffer, that Briggs routinely started fights, picking on weak people he met in bars and beating them up, the court balked, excluding that evidence because it did not represent a sufficiently semi-automatic reaction, it was, instead, evidence of character. Although Jones may be correct in stating that Rule 406 does not require an individual "to act in a given way every minute" in every situation,[26] "[t]he extent to which instances must be multiplied and consistency of behavior maintained in order to rise to the status of habit inevitably gives rise to differences of opinion." Fed.R.Evid. 406, advisory committee's note. Resolving those differences resides within the trial court's sound exercise of discretion. Under the circumstances here, we cannot say exclusion of the evidence was an abuse of that discretion....

Notes and Questions

1. Rule 406 provides for the admission of evidence of habit or routine practice "regardless of whether it is corroborated or whether there was an eyewitness." This is a deviation from the common law, which permitted evidence of habit only if there were no eyewitnesses and required corroboration for evidence of the routine practice of an organization. States whose comparable rules are modeled after the common law may, however, continue to have either or both of these requirements. Would such a rule be justified on the ground that eyewitness testimony of what actually happened on a particular occasion is superior to evidence about what *likely* happened based on prior behavior? In *Meyer v. United States*, 638 F.2d 155 (10th Cir. 1980), a patient brought suit alleging that her dentist failed to warn her of the potential risks of undergoing a particular procedure. The dentist could not specifically remember whether he had given her a warning, but testified to his habit of doing so. The court rejected any claim that the patient's eyewitness testimony was superior to the evidence of habit:

---

26. In fact, the advisory committee's note to Rule 406 offers examples of habits but recognizes "precise standards" do not delineate when a particular behavior matures into a habit although two factors predominate: adequacy of sampling and uniformity of response.

The plaintiff does not take the position that the habit evidence was inadmissible. Nevertheless, she claims that it is not to be preferred over the positive evidence of the plaintiff that she was not warned inasmuch as the court did not find that her testimony was lacking in truthfulness.

We disagree with the argument as to the weight to be given to testimony of habit. Our conclusion is that it does not stand in a special light nor is it to be referred to a second-class category which automatically carries little weight. If it is admissible, the weight to be given to it is dependent on the particular circumstances....

Such evidence, when substantial, supports an inference by the trier of the facts that the habit was conformed with on a particular occasion. This is true regardless of whether the individual relying on habit had a recollection of conforming with it on a particular occasion, even though the plaintiff in the case directly contradicts such conformity with the habit.

Meyer, 638 F.2d at 158.

2. In what *form* may evidence of habit be given? While the rule as originally drafted indicated that evidence of habit or routine practice could be given either by way of opinion testimony or by evidence of specific instances of conduct, Congress deleted this provision, believing that it should be left to the courts to deal with on a case-by-case basis. By contrast, some states specify the form in which habit evidence may be given. *Compare* Arkansas Rule of Evidence 406(b) ("Habit or routine practice may be proved by testimony in the form of an opinion or by specific instances of conduct sufficient in number to warrant a finding that the habit existed or that the practice was routine."), *with* Maine Rule of Evidence 406(b) ("Habit or routine practice may be proved by specific instances of conduct sufficient in number to warrant a finding that the habit existed or that the practice was routine.").

3. Because organizations often consist of a large number of individuals and/or engage in a large number of transactions, evidence of routine practice can be particularly valuable in cases in which it is unlikely that anyone remembers the transaction itself or the individuals involved in it. *See United States v. West*, 22 F.3d 586, 592 n.19 (5th Cir. 1994).

4. Numerous instances of conduct, standing alone, cannot be sufficient to deem it to be habitual conduct, can they? After all, another requirement of habit evidence is uniformity of response, and that "requires some comparison of the number of instances in which any such conduct occurs with the number in which no such conduct took place," doesn't it? *See Wilson v. Volkswagen of America, Inc.*, 561 F.2d 494, 511–12 (4th Cir. 1977). Or at some point is the number of instances sufficient to imply uniformity? If so, how many instances are sufficient? *See generally Fort Hall Landowners Alliance, Inc. v. Bureau of Indian Affairs*, 407 F. Supp. 2d 1220, 1226–28 (D. Idaho 2006) (holding that numerous instances of conduct alone is insufficient in the abstract to establish habit or routine practice, and requiring a comparison between the number of instances in which the allegedly habitual or routine conduct occurred with those instances in which it did not occur).

5. Typically, habit evidence is offered in an effort to prove what an individual actually did on a particular occasion in question. Can it also be offered in an effort to prove what an individual *likely* would have done had circumstances been different? *See Williams v. Security National Bank of Sioux City*, 358 F. Supp. 2d 782, 814 (N.D. Iowa 2005) ("[T]here is no greater leap of faith involved in relying on 'habit' evidence to prove an instance of *probable conduct* under *hypothetically similar circumstances*, than is involved in using 'habit' evidence to prove *actual conduct* under *actually similar circumstances*, as expressly sanctioned by Rule 406. In either case, the jury must use 'habit' evidence as a predictor of conduct in similar circumstances.").

C. Subsequent Remedial Measures

Suppose that while walking through a supermarket, you suddenly slip and fall on the floor, sustaining severe injuries to your back. As it turns out, an employee had just mopped the floor and it was still wet when you walked over it, although there was no sign warning you that the floor was wet. Shortly thereafter, you bring a lawsuit against the supermarket, claiming that they were negligent in maintaining the floor in that condition without a warning.

Suppose that in the course of preparing your case for trial, your attorney discovers that, at some point after you fell, the supermarket purchased yellow warning signs and established a policy requiring that employees must put them up whenever they mop the floor. Would the fact that the store developed such a policy be relevant to your claim that they were negligent in failing to do so before? Would evidence of the policy be admissible in your case?

The first sentence of Rule 407 categorically bars the use of evidence of subsequent remedial measures when offered to prove negligence, culpable conduct, a defect in a product or its design, or the need for a warning or instruction. The Advisory Committee Note provides two justifications for the rule. The first justification given is that such evidence is of questionable probative worth in that such conduct is equally consistent with the absence of negligence or culpable conduct. The Advisory Committee concedes, however, that under the liberal theory of relevancy set forth in Rules 401 and 402, this ground alone would be an insufficient basis for excluding the evidence. The Committee thus explains that the more persuasive justification for the rule is to encourage, or at least not to discourage, people from taking steps to improve safety. (To be sure, the strength of this policy rationale is at least a debatable one: small-time defendants likely don't even know about Rule 407 and thus their behavior is unlikely to be influenced by it, while major corporations have a natural incentive to solve problems to avoid the risk of other people becoming injured and bringing suit.)

Like Rule 404, evidence of subsequent remedial measures may be admissible if offered for some purpose *other than* the forbidden purpose; in the case of Rule 407, that would mean for some purpose other than to show negligence or culpable conduct. The second sentence of Rule 407 makes this point explicitly:

> But the court may admit this evidence for another purpose, such as impeachment or — if disputed — proving ownership, control, or the feasibility of precautionary measures.

Of course, like evidence admitted under Rule 404(b)(2), evidence admitted pursuant to the second sentence of Rule 407 might be used by the jury not only for the permissible purposes set forth in that sentence, but also for the forbidden purpose set forth in the first sentence, and courts retain the ability to exclude such evidence under Rule 403.

Prior to a 1997 amendment to Rule 407, the first sentence of the rule read as follows:

> When, after an event, measures are taken which, if taken previously, would have made the injury or harm less likely to occur, evidence of the subsequent measures is not admissible to prove negligence or culpable conduct in connection with the event.

This language, which is still used in many state analogues to Rule 407, led to two interpretive ambiguities that divided the lower federal courts. First, did the rule apply only in negligence cases or did it also extend to product liability actions? And second, did the word "event" refer to the date that a product was manufactured or designed or the date on which the injury or harm occurred? As to the first issue, language added by the 1997 amendment makes clear that the rule applies in both negligence and strict liability actions. As to the second issue, language was added to make clear that the pivotal date for determining the rule's application is the date when injury occurs, not the date that a product was designed or manufactured. Thus, "[e]vidence of measures taken by the defendant prior to the 'event' causing 'injury or harm' do not fall within the exclusionary scope of Rule 407 even if they occurred after the manufacture or design of the product." Advisory Committee Note to 1997 Amendment to Rule 407. It is important to keep in mind, however, that since many state versions of the rule continue to use language similar to the pre-1997 federal rule, the interpretation of some state analogues to Rule 407 may continue to contain these conceptual ambiguities.

The 1997 amendments notwithstanding, there remain a number of important questions that arise in applying Rule 407. First, what sorts of things qualify as "measures"? Second, the rule refers to measures that "are taken"—taken by whom? Third, to what extent does the *Erie* doctrine require a federal court in diversity cases to apply *state* law on the question of admitting evidence of subsequent remedial measures when that law differs from the federal rule? And finally, what safeguards exist to ensure that parties do not use the second sentence of Rule 407 to undermine the policy of the first sentence?

Problem 3-12: Road Work

Pete, a laborer on a road construction crew, is injured when his leg is crushed by a piece of machinery operated by one of his fellow employees. The day after the incident, the construction company fires the employee who was operating the machinery and installs emergency shut-off switches on the outside of the machinery.

In a suit by Pete against the construction company for negligence on a theory of respondeat superior, would evidence of either of the construction company's actions on the day after the incident be admissible? Would a report by the company's risk manager suggesting that the emergency shut-off switches be added to the machinery be admissible? What if the shut-off switches were added by the construction company after the State Department of Occupational Safety & Hazards issued regulations requiring that they be installed on such machinery? Would the evidence of what the construction company did be admissible in a suit brought by Pete against the manufacturer?

Problem 3-13: Slip and Fall

Recall the facts of the slip-and-fall incident from the introduction to this section. Assume that the suit is filed in a federal district court in Rhode Island, invoking that court's diversity jurisdiction. Rhode Island's version of Rule 407 differs significantly from the federal rule, providing as follows:

> When, after an event, measures are taken which, if taken previously, would have made the event less likely to occur, evidence of the subsequent measures is admissible.

Would evidence of the new policy of putting up yellow warning signs be admissible in the case?

Diehl v. Blaw-Knox
360 F.3d 426 (3d Cir. 2004)

SMITH, Circuit Judge.

This products liability case, arising under the law of Pennsylvania, presents a question of admissibility under Federal Rule of Evidence 407 of remedial measures offered by a plaintiff to establish that a product is defective. Timothy Diehl was severely injured when his legs became trapped under the rear wheels of a machine manufactured by Blaw-Knox. Mr. Diehl and his wife sued Blaw-Knox, alleging that the machine was defective....

I.

On May 24, 1999, Timothy Diehl was severely injured while working as a laborer on a road crew for IA Construction, Inc. ("IA"). On the day of the accident, the road crew was using a machine called a "road widener" to extend the shoulder of a road. Manufactured by Blaw-Knox in 1970, the road widener is used to deposit and spread material to one side of the roadway. The road widener is usually followed by laborers who must perform a number of tasks, including removing excess material that is inadvertently left on the paved portion of the roadway; removing stones that become lodged in the material; leveling off the material that has been spread; and straightening the outer edge of the deposited material. The laborers are then followed by a roller to press the material.

On the day of the accident, Mr. Diehl was working as one of the laborers behind the road widener. The road widener had come to a stop, and then began to move in reverse. Mr. Diehl, who was working within "a couple of feet" of the road widener, was not aware that the machine was reversing toward him. One of the exposed wheels struck Mr. Diehl's right ankle, trapping and crushing his lower leg.

The Diehls' theory of the case was that the road widener was defective in design for three reasons: (1) it lacked a bumper or any other enclosure of the rear wheels; (2) the back-up alarm was inaudible, particularly because it was placed on the front of the machine; and (3) it lacked proper warnings. The Diehls sought to introduce testimony by an IA mechanic that, shortly after the accident, the mechanic modified the road widener by (1) installing a rear bumper/guard that enclosed the rear tires; (2) relocating the back-up alarm to the rear of the machine; and (3) placing warning signs on the rear of the machine (the "IA redesign"). According to the mechanic's testimony, the IA redesign was done in response to the accident and for the purpose of preventing similar accidents. Significantly, IA is not a party to this lawsuit.

Blaw-Knox filed a motion in limine prior to trial to prohibit the Diehls from introducing evidence of the IA redesign. The Diehls filed their own motion in limine seeking an order allowing them to introduce evidence of the IA redesign at trial. The District Court granted Blaw-Knox's motion and denied the Diehls' motion, ruling that the IA redesign was a subsequent remedial measure inadmissible under Fed.R.Evid. 407....

II.

The primary issue in this case is whether Fed.R.Evid. 407 excludes evidence of subsequent remedial measures taken by a non-party such as IA.... "Rule 407 rests on the strong public policy of encouraging manufacturers to 'make improvements for greater safety.'" *Stecyk*, 295 F.3d at 415 (quoting *Kelly v. Crown Equip. Co.*, 970 F.2d 1273, 1276 (3d Cir. 1992)); *see also* Fed.R.Evid. 407 advisory committee's note ("The other, and more impressive, ground for exclusion rests on a social policy of encouraging people to take, or at least not discouraging them from taking, steps in furtherance of added safety."). The Rule recognizes that manufacturers will be discouraged from improving the safety of their products if such changes can be introduced as evidence that their previous designs were defective.

This policy is not implicated where the evidence concerns remedial measures taken by an individual or entity that is not a party to the lawsuit. The admission of remedial measures by a non-party necessarily will not expose that non-party to liability, and therefore will not discourage the non-party from taking the remedial measures in the first place. It is noteworthy that each of the circuits to address this issue has concluded that Rule 407 does not apply to subsequent remedial measures taken by a non-party.

The able District Judge declined to follow these authorities, observing that the text of Rule 407 makes no exception for subsequent remedial measures taken by a non-party. This is true enough, but the Advisory Committee's notes to Rule 407 state that the rule "incorporates conventional doctrine which excludes evidence of subsequent remedial measures as proof of an admission of fault." Prior to the enactment of Rule 407, conventional doctrine in this circuit was that the rule excluding evidence of repairs made after an accident was not applicable to repairs made by a non-party. The Advisory Committee's reference to "an admission of fault" reinforces this limitation: it hardly makes sense to speak of a party's fault being "admitted" by someone other than the party. Furthermore, the Advisory Committee was well aware of the courts' consistent interpretation of the rule. The notes to the 1997 amendment of Rule 407 — making the rule applicable to products liability actions — cite with approval the First Circuit's opinion in *Raymond v. Raymond Corp.* The court in *Raymond* expressly ruled that "there is no rationale for excluding third party subsequent repairs under the Rule." 938 F.2d at 1524.

Because Rule 407 does not apply to evidence of subsequent remedial measures taken by a non-party, it was error for the District Court to exclude evidence of the IA redesign under that rule.

. . . .

Bush v. Michelin Tire Corporation
963 F. Supp. 1436 (W.D. Ky. 1996)

HEYBURN, District Judge

. . . .

This products liability action arises from an accident that occurred when Plaintiffs attempted to mount a 16-inch Michelin LT tire on a 16½ inch rim manufactured by the Kelsey-Hayes Company. Plaintiffs were not trained mechanics or tire experts. On October 9, 1990, they put four new 16-inch Bridgestone tires on one of their vehicles. The removed Michelin tires were probably in substantially used condition and possibly not fit for extended highway use. After replacing the older Michelin LT tires with the Bridgestones, Plaintiffs decided to use one of these removed tires as a spare. Plaintiffs were apparently aware of the statement "MOUNT ONLY ON APPROVED 16-INCH RIMS" on the tire. Whether this statement adequately warned Plaintiffs of the potential dangers involved in mismatching 16-inch tires with 16½-inch rims is a central issue of this case.

Plaintiffs found a rim lying around their farm. They were unaware of where it came from, how long it had been there or how it had been used previously. We have learned since that Kelsey-Hayes manufactured the rim in December 1972; Michelin manufactured the tire in December 1985. Plaintiffs attempted to mount the old tire on the old rim. Plaintiffs knew that a 16 inch tire should be mounted on a 16 inch rim, so they searched the rim to determine the rim's size. The tire rim was stamped with a designation "16.5 x 6.00." Plaintiffs saw this designation but could not determine what it meant with respect to size. Raymond Bush proceeded to compare the found rim with one of the 16" rims used for the new Bridgestone tires. Concluding that the found rim and the 16-inch rim were compatible, Raymond Bush mounted the used 16-inch Michelin LT tire onto the rim.

Plaintiffs had already mounted the new tires on the existing rims without difficulty. Raymond encountered no difficulty in mounting the spare tire onto the rim. He then rolled it to Morris Bush for inflation. Morris noted that the maximum inflation pressure was 65 psi. He noted no warnings. His first attempt to inflate the tire was unsuccessful; it failed to seat. He then deflated the tire, resoaped it and repositioned it upon the rim. During his second attempt to inflate the tire, it exploded. He was seriously injured....

V.

C. Defendant's subsequent bead design

Plaintiffs wish to introduce evidence that in 1991 Defendant made its 21-strand bead standard in all of its 16-inch tires. Plaintiffs contend that the bead design adopted in 1991 is the same as or similar to the one Defendants began testing in 1984, and is, therefore, relevant to show the unreasonableness of the earlier decision and the feasibility of the safer one. Defendants say that the evidence is excluded by FRE 407 ("Subsequent Remedial Measures")....

Plaintiffs argue that the subsequent bead design should come in under the FRE 407 exception, which allows subsequent remedial measures to be admitted if they go to the feasibility of the design and if feasibility is controverted. Defendant says that it does not intend to contest feasibility and that, therefore, evidence going to it is irrelevant.

Plaintiff argues that because Defendant discusses the complexity and expense of adopting the 21-strand bead, it is essentially contesting feasibility. However, several other courts have concluded that discussing the trade-offs in taking precautionary measures does not necessarily place feasibility in issue. *See, e.g., Gauthier v. A.M.F., Inc.*, 788 F.2d 634, 638 (9th Cir. 1986); *see also Flaminio v. Honda Motor Co.*, 733 F.2d 463, 468 (7th Cir. 1984). In *Gauthier*, the defendant argued that although the safer design was feasible, the risks were not significant enough to offset the increased complexity of the design and the resulting consumer frustration. *Gauthier*, 788 F.2d at 638. Similarly, in this case, Defendant should be able to discuss the trade-offs in order to argue that its design was not unreasonably dangerous. If plaintiffs in products liability cases were allowed to introduce subsequent remedial measures whenever a defendant was forced to argue about the trade-offs of alternative designs, the "feasibility" exception to FRE 407 would swallow the rule. *See Flaminio*, 733 F.2d at 468.

"Feasibility" is relevant to a strict liability case because if no alternative design existed at the time of manufacture, then a jury may consider whether the existing design meets the industry standard. Even if a new design is "feasible," a defendant might still suggest that it made a logical decision not to implement it and that the existing design was reasonably safe for its intended uses. Typically, "feasibility" concerns the ability of a manufacturer or designer to overcome technological and scientific obstacles in marketing a product. From that prospective, feasibility is not disputed in this case. The design existed in 1983. It could be mass produced. The only remaining issues concern why Defendants chose not to use the design on all of its tires in 1983. This question raises issues of testing and cost compared to the urgency of the need for the change or the significance of the misuse as well as other relevant factors.

All these issues may be argued without reference to the 1991 standard design change. Excluding the evidence of the change only prevents Plaintiff from arguing that because the design was changed in 1991, the 1984 design must have been defective. This is precisely the type of argument which FRE 407 by its language and its policy seeks to bar.

Evidence of subsequent design changes has marginal relevance as to whether a product was defective at a previous time, particularly when a defendant does not contest the feasibility of the change. FRE 407 expressly rejects the inference that fault is admitted when remedial measures are taken. The reason is that in this case and in other cases, actions taken long after an event are equally consistent with the injuries occurring by accident or by contributory negligence as they are a result of a defective product. For these reasons, the Court believes that where Defendants will stipulate to feasibility, as is the case here, introduction of a subsequent standard design change should be prohibited. *See* *Raymond v. Raymond Corp.*, 938 F.2d 1518, 1523 (1st Cir. 1991).

Nevertheless, the Court is concerned that Defendants' argument may directly or indirectly imply that to change the design standard in 1984 was impractical. Such an argument would too closely question feasibility. To avoid this unfairness, the Court will require Defendants to tender a written proffer explaining why the design existing in 1983 or 1984 was not used in all tire models. Defendants may lay out the reasons for not adopting the new design and it may assert that the existing design was acceptable. The Court will consider whether the proffer avoids contesting feasibility before finally excluding the evidence of a subsequent design change. Assuming that such evidence is excluded, the Court nevertheless reserves the right to admit evidence of subsequent design changes if Defendants appear to be arguing feasibility either directly or indirectly....

Sims v. Great American Life Ins. Co.
469 F.3d 870 (10th Cir. 2006)

TYMKOVICH, Circuit Judge.

Lawrence Sims died when the speeding car he was driving sailed off a rural road. Prior to his untimely death, he had obtained life insurance from Great American Life Insurance Company. Sims's wife made a claim on this policy, but after an investigation Great American denied the claim under its non-accidental death provision concluding that Sims committed suicide. Mrs. Sims then filed suit against Great American alleging breach of contract and bad faith for its failure to pay her husband's life insurance policy. A jury found the death was accidental and awarded Mrs. Sims $1.4 million in compensatory and punitive damages....

At the heart of Great American's appeal is its argument that the Federal Rules of Evidence govern questions of admissibility in federal diversity cases, irrespective of the existence of conflicting state statutes. This argument rests on the proposition that the doctrine set forth in *Erie R.R. v. Tompkins*, 304 U.S. 64 (1938), is inapplicable to these Rules. Based on this premise, Great American asserts that the district court improperly applied state law, as opposed to the Federal Rules of Evidence, to exclude [certain evidence].

We are persuaded that the Federal Rules of Evidence are not governed by the *Erie* doctrine. Having said that, concepts of federalism still guide our understanding of the interplay between the Federal Rules and state law. Although we do not ground our holding in *Erie*, we conclude that state substantive policy directs the admissibility of evidence under the relevancy considerations of Rule 401.

1. *Erie* and Federal Rules of Evidence

This case presents us with a classic civil procedure question—in the face of a conflicting state statute, when does a federal court sitting in diversity apply federal law? This question, of course, invokes the Supreme Court's seminal decision in *Erie Railroad v. Tompkins* and the landmark trilogy which followed. *See Guar. Trust Co. v. York*, 326 U.S. 99 (1945) (creating the outcome determination test); *Byrd v. Blue Ridge Rural Elec. Coop.*, 356 U.S. 525 (1958) (holding that the outcome determination test is not dispositive in the face of countervailing federal interests); *Hanna v. Plumer*, 380 U.S. 460 (1965) (holding *Erie* inapplicable to the Federal Rules of Civil Procedure). Collectively, the "broad command" flowing from these cases requires federal courts "to apply state substantive law and federal procedural law." *Hanna*, 380 U.S. at 465. However, the sweep of this broad command is limited—only federal common law is governed by the *Erie* doctrine; congressional acts and the Federal Constitution fall outside its scope. As the *Erie* court famously stated:

> *Except in matters governed by the Federal Constitution or by acts of Congress*, the law to be applied in any case is the law of the state.... There is no federal general common law. Congress has no power to declare substantive rules of common law applicable in a state whether they be local in their nature or "general," be they commercial law or a part of the law of torts.

Erie, 304 U.S. at 78 (emphasis added). This seemingly simple rule, however, has a surprisingly complex application when the federal rule at issue is one of the Federal Rules of Evidence.

Great American argues that the Federal Rules of Evidence are an "act of Congress," not federal common law, and therefore outside the purview of *Erie*. Accordingly, when applying these Rules, Great American continues, federal diversity courts should not look to *Erie* but instead should apply the test formulated in *Stewart Org., Inc. v. Ricoh Corp.*, 487 U.S. 22 (1988), which governs the application of a federal statute to a diversity case. Following *Stewart*, a court asks whether the evidentiary rule is both (1) "sufficiently broad to control the issue before the Court," and (2) "a valid exercise of Congress' authority under the Constitution." To be a valid exercise of congressional authority, the federal rule must be "capable of classification" as a procedural rule. If the rule satisfies both conditions, absent other considerations, the federal evidentiary rule applies.

A brief review of the origins of the Federal Rules of Evidence shows that *Stewart* provides the starting point in determining the admissibility of evidence in this case.

a. *Origin of Federal Rules of Evidence*

Great American's argument rises or falls on the premise that the Federal Rules of Evidence are a product of congressional action. Our review of the relevant history reveals this to be so.

Prior to the enactment of the Federal Rules of Evidence, Federal Rule of Civil Procedure 43(a) governed evidentiary matters in federal courts. Under Rule 43, federal courts typically applied state evidentiary law to questions regarding the admissibility of evidence. But in 1972, the Supreme Court started drafting an independent set of rules governing the admissibility of evidence in federal courts: the Federal Rules of Evidence.

At the time the Supreme Court was considering the Rules of Evidence, Congress passed a statute requiring congressional approval before the Court could promulgate not only these

Rules but also amendments that had been proposed in 1972 to the already promulgated Federal Rules of Civil and Criminal Procedure. *See* Act of March 30, 1973, Pub.L. No. 93-12, 87 Stat. 9. Congress's concern, in large part, was based on a desire to protect substantive state law. In this way, Congress became intricately involved in formulating the Federal Rules of Evidence, and the Rules themselves became an act of Congress.[2] *See* Act of Jan. 2, 1975, Pub.L. No. 93-595, 88 Stat.1926. Remembering that *Erie* limits its holding to federal common law and excepts congressional actions, this history makes clear that *Erie* does not apply to the original Federal Rules of Evidence.

Nor can we find that Congress otherwise explicitly limited the applicability of the Federal Rules of Evidence in the face of conflicting state law. Two statutes normally limit the effect of evidentiary and procedural rules, the Rules Enabling Act[3] and the Rules of Decision Act.[4] But these laws do not govern the Federal Rules of Evidence as originally enacted. The Rules Enabling Act proscribes the ability of the Supreme Court to alter substantive rights. Here, with the original enactment of the Federal Rules of Evidence, it was Congress, not the Supreme Court, creating the Rules. Under the Rules of Decision Act, state law provides for the rule of decision in civil cases except where Congress or the Constitution provides otherwise. Again, we are dealing with a congressional act. Put simply, there is nothing in these Acts that limits the scope of the Federal Rules of Evidence as originally enacted.[5]

. . . .

b. Federal Court Application of Erie Doctrine to Federal Rules of Evidence

We recognize that numerous federal diversity courts have grappled with this tricky issue and reached an opposite conclusion. These courts, such as the district court below, suggest we limit application of the Federal Rules of Evidence to those matters not implicating substantive state policy. . . .

Under their approach, federal courts apply the *Stewart* analysis *only if* the conflicting *state evidentiary rule* is procedural. If, however, the state evidentiary rule is substantive, these courts have held that *Erie* controls and state law prevails over conflicting federal evidentiary rules. State substantive rules, then, are governed by an *Erie* analysis. . . .

---

2. The Act of March 30, 1973 required congressional approval only for the Supreme Court orders in late 1972. Those orders proposed the original Federal Rules of Evidence as well as certain amendments to both the Federal Rules of Civil Procedure and the Federal Rules of Criminal Procedure. Congress did not extend this Act to apply to all future amendments of the Federal Rules. Instead, under the current system, amendments are made pursuant to a process whereby the Supreme Court approves a change to the Rules and notifies Congress of such change. If Congress fails to act, the amended rule goes into effect. In short, since 1975, amendments to the Federal Rules have not been promulgated by an act of Congress. As discussed below, our analysis focuses on Rule 401. Because this Rule has remained unamended since 1975, we need not analyze the effect of *Erie* on evidentiary rules amended since that time.

3. The Rules Enabling Act, granting the Supreme Court "the power to prescribe general rules of practice and procedure and rules of evidence for cases in" federal courts, simultaneously prohibits the Supreme Court from proscribing any rule of procedure or practice for cases in the federal courts that shall "abridge, enlarge or modify any substantive right." 28 U.S.C. § 2072. This Act has been used to limit the reach of the Federal Rules of Civil Procedure.

4. The Rules of Decision Act provides that state law, "except where the Constitution or treaties of the United States or Acts of Congress otherwise require or provide, shall be regarded as rules of decision in civil actions" in the federal courts. 28 U.S.C. § 1652.

5. Again, we note that a number of the Federal Rules of Evidence have been amended since 1975. We do not address how these amendments affect the reach of either the Rules Enabling Act or the Rules of Decision Act.

Yet, as previously explained, this *Erie* approach turns *Stewart* on its head. *Stewart* requires the court to look first at the *federal evidentiary rule*. If that rule is arguably procedural, it governs even when a state substantive law is on point. Simply put, because *Erie* is inapplicable, we must first look to the Federal Rules of Evidence.

c. Tenth Circuit Approach

Our precedent suggests that where a conflict exists between the Federal Rules of Evidence and state law, we apply the Federal Rules unless the state law reflects substantive concerns or policies....

In our most noteworthy and extensive discussion of this issue, *Moe v. Avions Marcel Dassault-Breguet Aviation*, 727 F.2d 917, 930–33 (10th Cir. 1984), we addressed the applicability of the Federal Rule of Evidence governing subsequent remedial measures. We held that state law rather than Rule 407 prevails, thus rejecting the notion that the "admissibility of evidence in diversity actions is governed exclusively by federal law—that is, the Federal Rules of Evidence." We employed instead an *Erie* analysis and categorized the state law as one of substance, not procedure. In doing so, we stated such distinction was necessary to effect the twin goals of *Erie*—(1) uniformity, and (2) prevention of forum-shopping....

We are careful to point out, however, that the court's discussion regarding the application of the Federal Rules of Evidence was dicta.... Indeed, one judge in a concurring opinion refused to join the court's *Erie* discussion....

d. Effect of Rule 401

Although the *Moe* court's reasoning is tempting, we are persuaded that *Erie* is inapplicable to the Federal Rules of Evidence. We recognize, of course, that a federal court's apparently unchecked ability to apply the Federal Rules of Evidence without any regard for state substantive policy creates considerable tension with notions of federalism. But this tension is overstated. Congress did not give federal courts unbridled discretion to preempt state substantive law on all arguably procedural matters. Instead, the Rules of Evidence expressly provide for the application of state law in numerous circumstances. *See* Fed. R. Evid. 302 (presumptions); *id.* 501 (privileges); *id.* 601 (competency of witnesses).

Most pertinent to this case, Rule 401 protects against incursion into state substantive policy as part of its admissibility assessment. Rule 401 defines relevant evidence as "evidence having any tendency to make the existence of any fact *that is of consequence* to the determination of the action *more probable or less probable* than it would be without the evidence" (emphasis added).*

This definition requires a dual inquiry: (1) whether the evidence is *probative* or factually relevant to the proposition asserted (i.e., whether the evidence tends to make the existence of that fact more or less probable), and (2) whether the proposition for which the evidence is offered is *properly* provable in the case (i.e., the fact is material—of consequence—to the question of state law). The first inquiry is a procedural question of evidence law and the second is a substantive question regarding the materiality of the evidence....

Where a state law excludes certain evidence in order to effect substantive policy considerations, Rule 401 acts to exclude the evidence since the proposition for which the evidence is submitted is not properly provable and, therefore, irrelevant to the claim.[8] For

---

* Editor's Note: The quoted language differs slightly from the current text of Rule 401, which was restyled in 2011.

8. We would be presented with a different case where state law admits certain evidence, but a Federal Rule of Evidence directly on point excludes the same evidence. In such a case the Federal Rule likely

example, state law defines the elements and defenses of a cause of action in a diversity case. If, in such a case, a defendant proffers evidence supporting a defense that is no longer permitted by state statute, that proffer is of no consequence to the action and therefore not properly provable.

In sum, although we find that the Federal Rules of Evidence are not subject to *Erie's* substance/procedure distinction, this distinction still has meaning in making evidentiary determinations in federal diversity cases....

[The opinion of Judge Hartz, concurring in part and dissenting in part, is omitted.]

Notes and Questions

1. If a subsequent remedial measure is taken pursuant to a government mandate, is evidence that such a measure was taken by a party barred by Rule 407? Would the policies underlying the rule be hampered if such evidence were to be admitted? *See O'Dell v. Hercules, Inc.*, 904 F.2d 1194, 1204 (8th Cir. 1990) (holding that Rule 407 only applies to subsequent remedial measures that are voluntarily undertaken).

2. The word "measures" is broadly defined in the Advisory Committee Note to Rule 407 to include "subsequent repairs, installation of safety devices, changes in company rules, and discharge of employees." It is often the case that, after a workplace injury occurs, an employer will conduct a post-accident investigation to determine what went wrong and to suggest subsequent changes. Is such a report subject to exclusion under Rule 407? Most courts considering the matter hold that they are not subject to exclusion, although to the extent that they make reference to remedial measures that were taken post-accident, they are subject to redaction. *E.g., McFarlane v. Caterpillar, Inc.*, 974 F.2d 176, 181–82 (D.C. Cir. 1992); *Rocky Mountain Helicopters, Inc. v. Bell Helicopters*, 805 F.2d 907, 918–19 (10th Cir. 1986). Do you agree that such an interpretation is consistent with the policies that underlie Rule 407? Aren't such investigations often a necessary pre-cursor to any remedial measures being taken, and won't such an interpretation deter such investigations from taking place? *See Green v. Baca*, 226 F.R.D. 624, 635 n.14 (C.D. Cal. 2005) (assuming without deciding that such a report would constitute a "measure" within the meaning of Rule 407).

3. For a rare case in which evidence of a subsequent remedial measure was successfully used to show ownership or control, *see Clausen v. Sea-3, Inc.*, 21 F.3d 1181, 1190–92 (1st Cir. 1994).

4. Like the exception for feasibility, the exception for impeachment can swallow the rule if not carefully administered by trial courts in conjunction with Rule 403. For an excellent review of the cases addressing the impeachment exception, *see* Douglas R. Richmond, *Subsequent Remedial Measures and the Problem of Impeachment*, 13 No. 5 Practical Litigator 35 (2002).

5. Can Rule 407 be invoked in a criminal case, or only in civil cases? *See United States v. Wittig*, 425 F. Supp. 2d 1196, 1233 (D. Kan. 2006) (holding that it can be invoked only in civil cases); *United States v. Gallagher*, 1990 WL 52722, at *1–2 (E.D. Penn. Apr. 24, 1990) (same). Is such an interpretation consistent with the policies underlying the rule?

---

controls. This is because Federal Rule of Evidence 402 [provides that relevant evidence is admissible unless excluded by "these rules"].

6. Does the Tenth Circuit's decision in *Sims* overrule its earlier decision in *Moe*, at least so far as Rule 407 is concerned? How, if at all, does the fact that Rule 407 was amended in 1997 impact your answer to that question?

D. Compromises, Payment of Medical Expenses, and Liability Insurance

Imagine that in the slip-and-fall scenario discussed in the previous section, the store manager runs up to you and says, "A doctor is on his way." You protest, saying that you aren't sure you can pay the doctor's fees and the manager responds, "Don't worry at all, we'll pay for all of his fees."

Several months later, you file your negligence action against the store, seeking $100,000 in damages. The store's owner contacts you and says, "Hey, let's not make a big deal out of this. We probably could have done a better job of posting warnings, but there's no way that you had 100 grand worth of harm. I'll give you 5 grand to drop this thing."

Notwithstanding the offer, you continue to pursue the lawsuit. During pre-trial discovery, you discover that the defendant has an insurance policy that covers any injuries caused by the negligence of his employees. At trial, you seek to introduce evidence that the store provided you with medical services, that the store's owner offered to give you $5,000, and that the store has liability insurance. Is evidence of any of these relevant? If so, is evidence of any of these admissible?

Pretty clearly, all three are relevant under the liberal theory of relevance espoused by Rule 401. The store's willingness to pay your medical bills and to pay you some money may be a tacit admission of being at least partially responsible for your injuries. Arguably, evidence that the defendant has liability insurance may have some small tendency to suggest that the defendant acted negligently. The argument would be that the defendant, knowing that any injuries he caused would be covered by insurance, had somewhat less of an incentive to exercise due care than he would in the absence of such insurance. Of course, the payment of the medical expenses may simply be a humanitarian gesture on the store's part, the offer of $5,000 may simply reflect a business decision that such a payment would be far less than the costs associated with defending even a frivolous lawsuit, and the decision to purchase insurance may simply reflect risk-aversion, but that there are alternative explanations does not change the fact that the evidence is relevant.

Nonetheless, all three types of evidence may be subject to exclusion under separate categorical rules of exclusion. First, Rule 409 bars the admission of evidence of furnishing, offering, or promising to pay medical expenses resulting from an injury when offered to prove liability for the injury. Second, Rule 408 bars the admission of evidence of offering or accepting "a valuable consideration" in compromising or attempting to compromise a claim that is disputed either as to validity or amount. Third, Rule 411 bars evidence that a person was or was not insured against liability when offered on the issue of whether the person acted negligently or otherwise wrongfully.

Each of these rules is based in part on the low probative worth of such evidence and in part on social policy grounds. The policy underlying Rule 408 is that of encouraging parties to settle their disputes, which in turn reduces court congestion and preserves judicial resources, while the policy underlying Rule 409 is to avoid discouraging people from acting on their humanitarian impulses to assist those who have been injured. The assumption, of course, is that parties would be chilled from engaging in settlement discussions or offering to pay medical expenses if they knew that evidence of these could later be used against them. The policy underlying Rule 411 is a concern that knowledge of the presence or absence of liability insurance would induce juries to decide cases on improper grounds. More specifically,

> [T]he strict exclusion of this fact ... is due ... chiefly to the assumption that a knowledge of the fact of insurance against liability will motivate the jury to be reckless in awarding damages to be paid, not by the defendant, but by a supposedly well-pursed and heartless insurance company that has already been paid for taking the risk.

2 Wigmore, Evidence § 282a, at 148 (Chadbourn rev. 1979).

Each of these rules have conceptual ambiguities, and the problems and materials that follow are designed to assist you in navigating the nuances of these rules.

Problem 3-14: NASDAQ Attack

John borrowed $100,000 from Bank of America to finance his Internet start-up company. Shortly after the NASDAQ collapsed, so did John's company. In a telephone discussion with a Bank of America representative shortly after he stopped making payments on his loan, John said "I realize that I still owe you nearly $100,000, but would you take $3,000 as I am almost bankrupt?"

In a suit brought by Bank of America against John on the contract, is evidence of what he said to the representative admissible?

Problem 3-15: Distracting Cell Phone

Tanya is riding her bicycle to school when she is hit by a car driven by David. David gets out of his car, runs up to Tanya, and says "I'm so sorry, I was on my cell phone and didn't notice the stop sign. Are you OK? Let me call my personal physician and have him come out and take a look at you, and don't worry, I'll pay his fees." David calls his doctor on the cell phone and then says to Tanya, "Say, do you think we can work this out between the two of us without getting lawyers involved? Between you and me I know I'm to blame, but I can't imagine that your harm is more than $2,000. What do you think?"

In a suit brought by Tanya against David, is evidence of what he said to her immediately after the accident admissible?

Problem 3-16: Car Accident

Christina, who is driving eastbound, collides at an intersection with Rob, who is driving southbound. Lisa is a passenger in Rob's car, and she, along with Rob, is injured in the accident. Lisa settles her claims with Christina out of court, but Rob brings suit against Christina for his injuries.

In Rob's suit against Christina, can he introduce evidence of the settlement between Lisa and Christina? How, if at all, would your answer change if Christina called Lisa as a witness, and Lisa testified that "Rob ran the red light"?

Problem 3-17: Arson

Kevin Demming is on trial on charges of having committed arson. The prosecution claims that on the evening of January 6, 2012, Kevin intentionally set on fire a commercial building that he owned. The prosecution's theory is that Kevin wanted to collect on an insurance policy that he had taken out on the property. At trial, the prosecution seeks to offer evidence that Kevin had an insurance policy that would reimburse him for the value of the property in the event it was destroyed in a fire.

Is the evidence proffered by the prosecution admissible?

United States v. Roti

484 F.3d 934 (7th Cir. 2007)

EASTERBROOK, Chief Judge.

Saddled with a judgment for more than $400,000 on account of a guarantee of his small corporation's debts, James Roti decided to hide his assets from creditors. He has been convicted of bankruptcy fraud, see 18 U.S.C. § 157, and concealing assets from the bankruptcy trustee, see 18 U.S.C. § 152. His sentence is 21 months' imprisonment. Roti concedes that he parked some assets with family members and moved others to accounts unknown to his creditors, and that he lied to his principal creditor, to the federal bankruptcy court, and to the trustee. Roti says that his lawyer Andrew Werth put him up to it, and at trial he contended that he should be acquitted because Werth managed the scheme's details....

What Roti did propose to offer is evidence that, after the fraud was uncovered, he filed suit against Werth. That suit was taken over by Roti's trustee in bankruptcy and settled for $15,000. According to Roti, the settlement shows Werth's recognition of his culpability for Roti's predicament. The district court held, however, that Fed.R.Evid. 408 barred the introduction of evidence about the settlement, and Roti's principal argument on appeal is that the decision was mistaken because Rule 408 does not apply in criminal prosecutions.

United States v. Prewitt, 34 F.3d 436 (7th Cir.1994), states that Rule 408 is limited to civil cases....

The panel in *Prewitt* deemed Rule 408 inapplicable to criminal prosecutions because its text did not specifically mention criminal litigation.... In 2006 the Supreme Court promulgated an amendment to Rule 408 demonstrating that at least the new version (which took effect on December 1, 2006) applies to criminal cases....

Note that the new Rule 408(a)(2),* by creating a partial exception for criminal cases, shows that the rest of the rule applies to both civil and criminal litigation. The Committee Note accompanying the amended Rule 408 explains that this was done because the Committee agreed with the result of *Prewitt*, which concluded that admissions of fault made in compromise of a civil securities enforcement action were admissible against the accused in a criminal action for mail fraud, but not *Prewitt*'s view that Rule 408 is wholly inapplicable to criminal prosecutions....

---

* Editor's Note: Rule 408(a)(2) excludes evidence of "conduct or a statement made during compromise negotiations about the claim — except when offered in a criminal case and when the negotiations related to a claim by a public office in the exercise of its regulatory, investigative, or enforcement authority" when offered for one of prohibited purposes set forth in Rule 408(a).

Notes and Questions

1. Particularly in the area of business transactions, it can sometimes be difficult to determine where business communications end and compromise negotiations begin, an important line given that only the latter are protected by Rule 408. It is fairly clear that communications between the parties after litigation has been threatened or commenced will be deemed to be compromise negotiations. *See Pierce v. F.R. Tripler & Co.*, 955 F.2d 820, 827 (2d Cir. 1992). But a dispute need not reach the point of threatened litigation before Rule 408 kicks in; it is enough that "an actual dispute or a difference of opinion exists" between the parties. *Affiliated Mfrs., Inc. v. ALCOA*, 56 F.3d 521, 527 (3d Cir. 1995). Is the determination whether the parties were engaged in compromise negotiations at the time the communications were made a question for the judge to decide under Rule 104(a) or for the jury to decide under Rule 104(b)? *See Pierce*, 955 F.2d at 827 (judge decides under Rule 104(a)). Note further that the language of Rule 408 is sufficiently broad to encompass unilateral offers to settle made by one party to the other.

2. Note that Rule 408 by its terms applies only if a claim is "disputed." Thus, the rule would apply in a situation in which a party concedes that he was negligent but disputes the amount of the damages. In contrast, "[t]he policy considerations which underlie the rule do not come into play when the effort is to induce a creditor to settle an admittedly due amount for a lesser sum." Advisory Committee Note to Rule 408. *See, e.g., Molinos Valle Del Cibao v. Lama*, 633 F.3d 1330, 1354 (11th Cir. 2011). Is the determination whether there was a "dispute" a question for the judge to decide under Rule 104(a) or for the jury to decide under Rule 104(b)? *See id.* (judge decides under Rule 104(a)).

3. At common law, statements of fact made during compromise negotiations were *not* subject to exclusion under the common law equivalent to Rule 408 unless the parties made clear that the statements were being made "hypothetically" or "without prejudice." Rule 408 abrogates this common law limitation, providing that evidence of "conduct or a statement made during compromise negotiations about the claim" is likewise not admissible. However, an amendment that took effect in 2006 creates an exception when such evidence is "offered in a criminal case and when the negotiations related to a claim by a public office in the exercise of its regulatory, investigative, or enforcement authority." *See* Fed. R. Evid. 408(a)(2). What is the rationale for this exception?

4. Rule 408 does not prevent documents from being admitted into evidence if otherwise admissible simply because such documents were disclosed to the other party for the first time during compromise negotiations. Until recently, the text of the rule explicitly provided that it "does not require the exclusion of any evidence otherwise discoverable merely because it is presented in the course of compromise negotiations." However, an amendment that took effect in 2006 deleted the sentence on the ground that it is "superfluous," reasoning that the rule with that sentence omitted cannot reasonably be construed to protect pre-existing information simply because it was presented to an adversary in compromise negotiations. *See* Advisory Committee's Note to 2006 Amendment to Rule 408.

5. Is the phrase "valuable consideration" limited to offers of money? *See Dimino v. New York City Transit Auth.*, 64 F. Supp. 2d 136, 162 (E.D.N.Y. 1999) (indicating that it extends to offering a formal apology and giving someone back her job).

6. Rule 408 contemplates the exclusion not only of offers to compromise, but also of completed settlements. The Advisory Committee Note to Rule 408 states in this regard:

While the rule is ordinarily phrased in terms of offers of compromise, it is apparent that a similar attitude must be taken with respect to completed compromises when offered against a party thereto. This latter situation will not, of course, ordinarily occur except when a party to the present litigation has compromised with a third person.

It seems clear, does it not, that such a broad interpretation of the rule is necessary to ensure that parties are not deterred from settling with individuals in multi-party disputes? *See generally Hudspeth v. CIR*, 914 F.2d 1207, 1213 (9th Cir. 1990).

7. Like the other categorical rules of exclusion, Rule 408 excludes evidence only when offered for certain purposes but not when offered for other purposes. Specific examples of purposes for which the rule does not bar the admission of evidence include "proving a witness's bias or prejudice, negating a contention of undue delay, or proving an effort to obstruct a criminal investigation or prosecution." *See* Federal Rule of Evidence 408(b). Similarly, Rule 411 does not apply when evidence of insurance is offered for other purposes, "such as proving a witness's bias or prejudice or proving agency, ownership, or control." Until recently, the federal courts were split on the question whether the use of statements made in compromise negotiations to impeach a witness by means of a prior inconsistent statement or through contradiction was "another purpose" permissible under Rule 408. However, an amendment to Rule 408 that took effect in 2006 prohibits using statements made in compromise negotiations for that purpose, reasoning that allowing it "would tend to swallow the exclusionary rule and would impair the public policy of promoting settlements." *See* Advisory Committee's Note to 2006 Amendment to Rule 408.

8. Even if evidence is offered for "another purpose" under Rules 408, 409, and 411, it may nonetheless be excluded under Rule 403 if the court concludes that its probative worth on the point for which it is legitimately offered is substantially outweighed by the risk that the jury may misuse it for one of the reasons forbidden by those rules. *See, e.g., Weir v. Federal Ins. Co.*, 811 F.2d 1387, 1395–96 (10th Cir. 1987). And where evidence of a settlement is offered for "another purpose," Rule 403 balancing may result in admitting only the *fact* of settlement but not the *amount*. *See, e.g., Crigger v. Fahnestock & Co., Inc.*, 2005 WL 857368, at *1–*2 (S.D.N.Y. Apr. 14, 2005) ("[e]ven if the fact of the settlement is admissible for a purpose other than proof of liability, disclosure of the settlement amount may constitute reversible error") (quoting *Weinstein's Federal Evidence* § 408.04 (2d ed. 2005)); *Green v. Baca*, 226 F.R.D. 624, 641–42 (C.D. Cal. 2005) (in suit against municipality for over-detention of plaintiff by police department, fact of prior settlements of similar suits, but not the amount of such prior settlements, admissible to prove municipality's knowledge that such over-detentions were occurring).

9. Can a party unilaterally waive the protections of Rule 408 and offer evidence of his *own* settlement offer or his own statements made in settlement negotiations? To avoid any confusion on this issue, Rule 408 was amended in 2006 to make clear that the protections of the rule cannot be waived unilaterally by a party because it protects both parties from having the fact that negotiations took place disclosed to the jury. *See* Advisory Committee's Note to 2006 Amendment to Rule 408.

10. A federal court only has jurisdiction over a diversity action if the amount in controversy exceeds $75,000. *See* 28 U.S.C. § 1332. Does Rule 408 bar a court from considering a settlement offer that one party made to the other in excess of $75,000 in determining whether the amount in controversy requirement is satisfied? Does that not involve using evidence of a settlement offer to prove the *amount* of the claim? *See Vermande v. Hyundai*

Motor America, Inc., 352 F. Supp. 2d 195, 201–02 (D.Conn. 2004) (collecting cases and relying on the purpose of Rule 408 to conclude that determining the "amount" in controversy is not the same as proving the "amount" of a claim). *Accord Rising-Moore v. Red Roof Inns, Inc.*, 435 F.3d 813, 816 (7th Cir. 2006).

11. Rule 409 is to some extent broader than Rule 408 in that it applies even where the parties cannot be said to be engaged in compromise negotiations. Yet it is narrower in that it excludes only evidence of paying or offering to pay medical expenses, but not factual statements made in the course of such a tender. The Advisory Committee Note to Rule 409 explains:

> Contrary to Rule 408, dealing with offers of compromise, the present rule does not extend to conduct or statements not a part of the act of furnishing or offering or promising to pay. This difference in treatment arises from fundamental differences in nature. Communication is essential if compromises are to be effected, and consequently broad protection of statements is needed. This is not so in cases of payments or offers or promises to pay medical expenses, where factual statements may be expected to be incidental in nature.

12. Note that Rule 411 applies not only to evidence that a person is insured against liability, but also evidence that a person is *not* insured against liability. What risks would there be if a party were allowed to inform the trier of fact that he lacked insurance coverage?

13. Rule 411 by its terms applies only to evidence that a person has or lacks *liability* insurance; it does not apply to other forms of insurance, such as casualty or property insurance. *See, e.g., Jacobs Press, Inc. v. Hartford Steam Boiler Inspection & Ins. Co.*, 107 F.3d 866, 1997 WL 90665, at *8 n.14 (4th Cir. Mar. 4, 1997). Are indemnification agreements akin to liability insurance subject to exclusion under Rule 411? *Compare D.S.C. Communications Corp. v. Next Level Communications*, 929 F. Supp. 239, 242–45 (E.D. Tex. 1996) (no), *with Kirchoff v. Flynn*, 786 F.2d 320, 324 (7th Cir. 1986) (yes). *See also Matosantos Commercial Corp. v. SCA Tissue North America, LLC*, 369 F. Supp. 2d 191, 195 (D.P.R. 2005) (holding that Rule 411 applies, reasoning that "in the eyes of the jury the fact remains that a third party, be it an insurance company or another corporation, will bear the damages instead of the defendant").

E. Pleas and Plea Discussions

Subject to limited exceptions, Rule 410 provides for the exclusion of evidence in a civil or criminal case of statements made by a criminal defendant in the course of plea discussions, evidence of certain types of pleas entered by a criminal defendant, and evidence of statements made at hearings to enter certain types of pleas. It bars such evidence only when offered against the criminal defendant who made the plea or participated in the plea discussions, although it can be invoked by that individual in criminal and civil proceedings alike.

The various provisions of Rule 410 are justified in part on social policy grounds and in part on concerns that the probative worth of such evidence is substantially outweighed by its prejudicial effect. The overarching policy rationale for the rule is to foster plea bargaining: just as Rule 408 is designed to encourage the settlement of disputes in the civil context by excluding evidence of compromises and offers to compromise, so Rule 410 is designed to encourage plea bargaining in the criminal context by excluding evidence of certain pleas as well as statements made during plea discussions.

Rule 410(a)(1) excludes evidence that a defendant entered a guilty plea that is later withdrawn. Criminal defendants have the right to withdraw guilty pleas under a variety of circumstances (such as a failure to understand the charge and potential penalties or ineffective assistance of counsel) and to insist that the issue of guilt be determined by a jury. The effectiveness of that right would be undermined if the fact that the plea was withdrawn could be brought to the jury's attention (who likely would give it undue if not conclusive weight), which in turn might deter criminal defendants from pleading guilty in the first instance.

In contrast, Rule 410 does *not* exclude evidence of a guilty plea that was *not* withdrawn. A guilty plea is a factual admission by a defendant that he committed the elements of the crime for which he pled guilty, and may be relevant evidence in a subsequent civil suit arising out of the same factual situation or in a subsequent criminal prosecution. However, Rule 410(a)(2) does exclude evidence that a defendant entered a plea of *nolo contendere*. Such a plea, although equivalent to a plea of guilty for purposes of the punishment imposed, differs in that it is not a factual admission that the defendant committed the elements of the crime but is instead a statement by the defendant that he will not contest the charge against him and will accept the punishment associated with committing such an offense. Two reasons justify exclusion of evidence of pleas of *nolo contendere*. First, because it is not a factual admission, its probative worth is diminished. Second, the very purpose of such a plea is to encourage plea bargaining in criminal cases by creating a way to accept criminal punishment for a crime without subjecting oneself to the future collateral consequences that would result from a guilty plea.

The same reasons that justify excluding evidence of pleas of *nolo contendere* or pleas of guilty that are later withdrawn justify excluding evidence of statements made during hearings in which such pleas are entered, and Rule 410(a)(3) provides for the exclusion of such evidence.

Finally, to encourage defendants to enter into plea negotiations, Rule 410(a)(4) excludes evidence of statements made during the course of "plea discussions with an attorney for the prosecuting authority" in all instances save for those that result in a plea of guilty that is not later withdrawn. The scope of this particular provision has been the subject of much litigation, as the materials that follow illustrate.

United States v. Greene
995 F.2d 793 (8th Cir. 1993)

MORRIS SHEPPARD ARNOLD, Circuit Judge.

In early 1992, Patrick Joseph Greene was indicted in federal court in Iowa on five counts of drug-related charges. At trial a few months later, he was convicted on four of those counts and acquitted on one. The trial court subsequently sentenced Mr. Greene to 120 months of imprisonment on each count, the terms to run concurrently. Mr. Greene appeals both his conviction and his sentence....

IV.

Government agents searched Mr. Greene's house in October, 1991, but did not arrest him until April, 1992. By pretrial motion, Mr. Greene sought to suppress certain statements that he made to a DEA agent at the time of the initial search and after his arrest. Mr. Greene argued that those statements were made in the course of plea negotiations and were therefore excludable under Fed.R.Crim.P. 11(e)(6)(D) and Fed.R.Evid. 410[(a)](4).

The trial court denied the motion to suppress and allowed the statements to be admitted into evidence. On appeal, Mr. Greene argues that the denial of the motion to suppress was clearly erroneous. *See, e.g., United States v. Jorgensen*, 871 F.2d 725, 728 (8th Cir. 1989).

The rules themselves limit the excludable statements to those "made ... [to] an attorney for the government," *see* Fed.R.Crim.P. 11(e)(6)(D), or "made ... [to] an attorney for the prosecuting authority," *see* Fed.R.Evid. 410[(a)](4). This circuit has extended coverage under the rules, however, to statements made to a law enforcement agent who has express authority to act for the prosecuting government attorney.... The court has also suggested that a government agent's representation that he had the authority to negotiate a plea bargain might be sufficient to bring any consequent statements by a criminal defendant within the excludability provisions of the rules....

The DEA agent who talked with Mr. Greene testified at a pretrial hearing on the motion to suppress. Mr. Greene did not testify. The DEA agent stated that it was his practice always to discuss with the prosecuting government attorney "the persons [whom] the government might like to see cooperate in the course of [an] investigation" and that the prosecuting government attorney knew of this practice. The DEA agent further stated that when he went to Mr. Greene's house in October, 1991, to execute a search warrant, he intended to "personally try to determine if Mr. Greene would want to cooperate or not" and that the prosecuting government attorney knew of this intention.

The DEA agent further said that when he actually talked with Mr. Greene, he told Mr. Greene that cooperation would be welcome but that he "could make no promises other than providing for [Mr. Greene's] cooperation and making that cooperation known to [the prosecuting government attorney] and the Court." The DEA agent specifically testified, however, that he himself did not "go up to the judge and tell him" of a witness' cooperation but that the court was customarily informed through the prosecuting government attorney. In other words, the DEA agent said, the notice to the court is "kind of built into the system."

The DEA agent then related that he had told the prosecuting government attorney that in response to his initial approach to Mr. Greene, "Mr. Greene had responded favorably to that idea." When pressed about whether the prosecuting government attorney had "agreed" that the DEA agent "should go forward, pursuing cooperation with Mr. Greene," the DEA agent described the prosecuting government attorney's remarks as "'Well, that's good news. Keep up the good work.'" The DEA agent acknowledged that he considered these remarks to amount to "approval that [he] should continue forward with [his] efforts."

The DEA agent testified that he told Mr. Greene "that if [Mr. Greene's] attorney wanted some information, he could either call" the DEA agent or the prosecuting government attorney. The DEA agent stated, however, that he "recommended" Mr. Greene's calling the prosecuting government attorney. The DEA agent flatly denied ever "meet[ing] with Mr. Greene's attorney to discuss further the possibility of cooperation and a plea." He testified that Mr. Greene's lawyer came by the DEA office "unexpected" just as the DEA agent and several others were leaving the office and that in order not to "be rude to the guy," the DEA agent "basically told him briefly the situation," in other words, "how much trouble I thought Mr. Greene was in."

Actual authority may be either express or implied. *See, e.g., Restatement (Second) of Agency* § 7 comment c at 29–30, § 8 comment a at 30 (1958). In either case, it refers to authority created by acts of a principal (here, the prosecuting government attorney) that would reasonably lead another (here, the DEA agent) to believe that the other was authorized to act for the principal. *See, e.g., Restatement (Second) of Agency* §7 at 28, §7 comment c at 29–30, §26 at 100, §26 comment a at 101, §26 comment b at 101–02 (1958). On the record before it, the trial court found that there was no actual authority given by the prosecuting government attorney to the DEA agent to negotiate a plea agreement. We have read the transcript of the hearing on the motion to suppress, and we find that such a conclusion is not clearly erroneous.

Nor, having read the transcript, do we believe that the DEA agent had any apparent authority to negotiate a plea agreement, either on account of some conduct by the prosecuting government attorney in relation to Mr. Greene, *see, e.g., Restatement (Second) of Agency* §8 at 30, §8 comment a at 30–31, §8 comment b at 31–32, §27 at 103, §27 comment a at 103–04, §27 comment b at 104–05 (1958), or because the DEA agent represented himself as having the authority to negotiate a plea agreement, *see, e.g., United States v. Lawrence*, 952 F.2d at 1037, and *Rachlin*, 723 F.2d at 1376. We therefore affirm the trial court's denial of the motion to suppress....

Notes and Questions

1. Although a plea of *nolo contendere* allows a defendant to avoid some collateral consequences of a guilty plea, it does not allow him to avoid all of them. For example, a defendant who testifies is subject to impeachment under Rule 609 based on his criminal conviction, even if based on a plea of *nolo contendere*. *E.g., Brewer v. City of Napa*, 210 F.3d 1093, 1096 (9th Cir. 2000).

2. Does Rule 410 provide for the exclusion of pleas and plea bargaining that take place in a jurisdiction outside of the United States? *See United States v. Orlandez-Gamboa*, 320 F.3d 328, 330 (2d Cir. 2003) (holding that it does not, based in part on references to federal and state procedures in Rule 410(a)(3)). Is such an interpretation consistent with the policies behind Rule 410?

3. Recall that under Rule 408, it can sometimes be difficult to determine when compromise negotiations begin. Similar difficulties arise under Rule 410(a)(4) in determining when "plea discussions" begin. Specifically, courts are divided on whether statements made in a proffer session between a defendant and the prosecuting attorney to explore cooperation constitute "plea discussions" where no specific terms of a plea are discussed. *See United States v. Stein*, 2005 WL 1377851, at *9–*14 (E.D. Pa. June 8, 2005) (collecting cases and concluding that such statements are subject to exclusion under Rule 410, reasoning that "[r]equiring an actual discussion of the terms of a plea would encourage gamesmanship, rewarding defendants who by chance or design attempt to discuss a plea in the course of their proffer" and would "require courts to draw difficult distinctions between where an admissible proffer session ended and an inadmissible plea discussion began").

4. Does Rule 410 bar only direct use of statements made during pleas or in plea discussions, or does it also bar the government from using evidence that it subsequently derives as a result of those discussions? *See United States v. Stein*, 2005 WL 1377851, at *14–*15 (E.D. Pa. June 8, 2005) (collecting cases holding that Rule 410 bars only direct use of statements).

5. Note that Rule 410, by its terms, only bars evidence of pleas and plea bargaining when offered "against the defendant who made the plea or participated in the plea discussions." Can a defendant introduce evidence that he rejected an offer by the prosecution to plead guilty to a lesser charge or to testify in exchange for immunity to show

"consciousness of innocence"? *See United States v. Biaggi*, 909 F.2d 662, 690–91 (2d Cir. 1990) (indicating that Rule 410 poses no bar to such evidence). However, opening this door comes at a price by way of an explicit exception to Rule 410: when a defendant introduces a statement made during a plea or in plea discussions, other statements made during that plea or in those plea discussions are excluded from the bar of Rule 410 "if in fairness the statements ought to be considered together." Fed. R. Evid. 410(b)(1).

6. The only other explicit exception to Rule 410 is one that allows a statement made in connection with a plea to be admitted "in a criminal proceeding for perjury or false statement, if the defendant made the statement under oath, on the record, and with counsel present." Fed. R. Evid. 410(b)(2).

7. Congress considered but rejected an amendment that would have also made an exception to Rule 410 whereby a statement made by a criminal defendant in plea negotiations or during entry of a plea that was later withdrawn could be used to impeach his credibility if at trial his testimony contradicted the statements he made during plea bargaining. *See United States v. Lawson*, 683 F.2d 688, 690–93 (2d Cir. 1982). However, the Supreme Court has held that a defendant can waive his right to invoke Rule 410 to prevent impeaching use statements made in plea negotiations by signing an agreement to that effect, *see United States v. Mezzanatto*, 513 U.S. 196, 210 (1995), something that prosecutors will sometimes require a defendant to sign as a condition of entering into plea discussions. Lower courts have held that such waivers can extend beyond impeaching use of such statements to use of such statements generally at trial. *See, e.g., United States v. Mitchell*, 633 F.3d 997, 1006 (10th Cir. 2011); *United States v. Burch*, 156 F.3d 1315, 1319 (D.C. Cir. 1998).

Chapter 4

Witness Qualification, Competency, and Examination

A. Competency of Witnesses

At common law, rules governing witness competency posed one of the most significant barriers to the admissibility of testimony by witnesses. These rules categorically barred certain types of witnesses from testifying, including parties to the action, their spouses, persons with a financial interest in the outcome of the action, individuals convicted of certain crimes, children, mentally incapacitated individuals, atheists and members of certain minor religions.

What was the justification for excluding the testimony of all of these categories of individuals? The Supreme Court explained it as follows:

> Fear of perjury was the reason for the rule ... the theory of the common law was to admit to the witness stand only those presumably honest, appreciating the sanctity of an oath, unaffected as a party by the result, and free from any of the temptations of interest. The courts were afraid to trust the intelligence of jurors.

Benson v. United States, 146 U.S. 325, 335–336 (1892). *See also* George Fisher, *The Jury's Rise as Lie Detector*, 107 Yale L.J. 575, 624–25 (1997) ("In effect, this panoply of competency rules preempted the jury's lie-detecting function by declaring certain witnesses to be likely liars as a matter of law.").

Parties and those with a financial interest in the outcome of a case were thus excluded under the common law because of the fear that their interest in having the case decided in a particular way created a high risk that they would testify falsely. Spouses of parties were disqualified from testifying in part because of a fear that they would testify falsely out of loyalty to their spouses, but also because the common law viewed husband and wife as a single person:

> Since a defendant was barred as a witness in his own behalf because of interest, it was quite natural to bar his spouse in view of the prevailing legal fiction that husband and wife were one person.

Hawkins v. United States, 358 U.S. 74, 75 (1958).

Those convicted of certain crimes, including felonies and crimes that involved fraud or deceit were deemed incompetent to testify based on a view that engaging in such conduct demonstrated untrustworthiness. Children and the mentally incapacitated were deemed incompetent to testify because they were thought to lack the ability to accurately perceive and recollect events, clearly articulate what they perceived, and appreciate the obligation to testify truthfully. And atheists and members of religions that did not believe in a higher being who would punish false swearing were deemed incompetent to testify because the absence of such belief took away one of the perceived incentives for a witness to testify truthfully.

While the common law rules of competency were successful in reducing the likelihood of perjured testimony, this was so only because the categories were so broad that they had the effect of eliminating most testimony altogether! With so many witnesses deemed incompetent to testify, it was extremely difficult for parties to prove their cases.

Over time, through a combination of legislative action and modifications in the common law, the rigid competency rules of the common law were steadily relaxed. *See, e.g., Benson v. United States*, 146 U.S. 325 (1892) (parties and other interested persons); *Rosen v. United States*, 245 U.S. 467, 472 (1918) (convicted criminals); *Funk v. United States*, 290 U.S. 371, 380–81 (1933) (spouses of parties). This shift represented a shift in philosophy on how best to determine the truth of what happened:

> [T]he truth is more likely to be arrived at by hearing the testimony of all persons of competent understanding who may seem to have knowledge of the facts involved in a case, leaving the credit and weight of such testimony to be determined by the jury or by the court, rather than by rejecting witnesses as incompetent....

Rosen v. United States, 245 U.S. 467, 471 (1918).

In effect, this more modern philosophy reflects a judgment, akin to Rule 403 balancing, that allowing testimony by less reliable witnesses will further the factfinding process more than would exclusion of such testimony altogether. This philosophy underlies Federal Rule of Evidence 601, which declares that, save for limited exceptions discussed below, "[e]very person is competent to be a witness." According to the Advisory Committee, "[i]ncluded among the grounds thus abolished are religious belief, conviction of crime, and connection with the litigation as a party or interested person or spouse of a party or interested person." Advisory Committee Note to Rule 601.

Yet, as will be seen in Chapter 10, the concerns underlying the common law rules governing competency have not disappeared but have manifested themselves elsewhere in the rules of evidence. Thus, while virtually any witness can testify, to the extent that there is reason to doubt her veracity, the rules governing impeachment of witnesses allow parties to bring those reasons to the jury's attention so as to aid it in assessing the witness' credibility. Evidence of a witness' prior convictions, her interest in the outcome of the litigation, and other facts bearing on her veracity are thus admissible along with her testimony.

There are, however, certain exceptions to the general rule that all witnesses are competent to testify in federal court. Although Rule 601, as drafted by the Advisory Committee, would have applied this general rule in all cases falling within the jurisdiction of the federal courts, Congress amended the rule to provide that, in civil cases, state law governs the witness' competency regarding claims or defenses for which state law supplies the rule of decision. Of particular concern to Congress was that Rule 601 as drafted would disregard state Dead Man's Statutes in cases substantively governed by state law. Such statutes are vestiges of the common law rule rendering persons interested in the outcome of a suit incompetent to testify, but are much narrower in that they apply only where the testimony involves a transaction or communication with a deceased person and typically involve claims against the deceased person's estate. The concern of these statutes is not only that interested persons have an incentive to testify falsely (a problem that always exists with interested persons), but that in this situation, the other party to the transaction is not able to present offsetting testimony concerning the transaction because she is dead, making it impossible for the jury to make a comparative credibility assessment. These statutes make it harder to successfully mount claims against decedents' estates where available evidence is limited, thus preserving more of a decedent's estate for her heirs.

Second, two categories of witnesses — judges and jurors — are deemed incompetent to testify in federal court in certain instances. Rule 605 provides that a judge may not testify as a witness in a trial over which he presides, while Rule 606(a) provides that a juror may not testify as a witness before the jury in the trial of the case in which the juror is sitting. In addition, Rule 606(b) renders jurors incompetent to testify to most matters occurring during jury deliberations. The rationales for these special competency rules for judges and jurors, as well as the application of Rule 601, are explored in the materials that follow.

Problem 4-1: Interstate Bicycle Accident

Bob, a citizen of Indiana, is riding a bicycle in Indiana when he is struck by a car allegedly driven by Sheila, a citizen of Kentucky. Bob brings a common law negligence claim against Sheila in federal district court in Kentucky, invoking that court's diversity jurisdiction. Assume that Kentucky has a statute that provides in pertinent part that in civil cases, "No person convicted of a felony shall be competent to testify as a witness." Indiana law on competency of witnesses tracks the first sentence of Federal Rule of Evidence 601.

At trial, Sheila's attorney seeks to offer testimony by Tom, who witnessed the accident. Tom, who was convicted of a felony five years ago, would testify that Bob "biked through the intersection when the light was red for him," and that after the accident, he heard Bob say to Sheila, "The accident is my fault; I didn't notice that the light was red for me."

Bob objects to Tom's testimony, contending that he is incompetent to testify. How will the court likely rule?

Equitable Life Assur. Soc. of U.S. v. McKay
837 F.2d 904 (9th Cir. 1988)

PREGERSON, Circuit Judge....

BACKGROUND

H. David McKay, a Washington resident, died in November 1983. At the time of his death he was married to Carolyn McKay. He had previously been married to Marjorie McKay. He had three children by his first marriage....

At the time of his death, the decedent had six life insurance policies. Decedent named his children beneficiaries of the first four policies, totaling together about $45,000. All parties agree that he intended that his children be the beneficiaries of those four policies. In May 1982, decedent purchased a fifth life insurance policy, No. 32-0333-81, for $50,000. Originally, he named his wife Carolyn as beneficiary under the policy. However, in April 1983, decedent changed the policy, making his children beneficiaries. Carolyn asserts that this was done without her knowledge. However, she signed the change of beneficiary form as a witness.

In June 1983, decedent purchased a sixth life insurance policy, No. 83-1997-39, for $100,000. According to the testimony of decedent's insurance agent, Michael Gajadhar, decedent instructed Gajadhar to make Carolyn beneficiary of the policy and Gajadhar mistakenly made decedent's children beneficiaries.

In September 1984, Carolyn McKay filed suit against Gajadhar in Washington State Superior Court for professional negligence in failing to make her sole beneficiary of the sixth policy.

In November 1984, Equitable Life filed this interpleader action in Oregon District Court to sort out the claims against its policies. Equitable Life deposited the proceeds of both the $50,000 and $100,000 dollar policies with the district court and was dismissed from the action....

The district court granted summary judgment for decedent's children, holding that there were no genuine issues of material fact because the Washington State Deadman's Statute barred the testimony of Carolyn McKay and Michael Gajadhar, the two witnesses who would testify that decedent intended Carolyn to be the beneficiary of the two policies. Carolyn McKay appeals.

DISCUSSION

....

We must first decide whether the Washington State Deadman's Statute should have been applied in this case. Because this action is an interpleader action brought under 28 U.S.C. § 1335, the federal district court was required to apply the substantive law that a court of the forum state would apply.... The Washington Deadman's Statute concerns the competency of witnesses. When state law provides the rule of decision, Fed.R.Evid. 601 requires that the competency of witnesses also be determined by state law. However, in cases in which a district court in one state is applying substantive law from another state, rule 601 does not specify under which state law competency is to be determined. That question must be resolved under the choice-of-law rules of the forum state. *Klaxon Co. v. Stentor Electric Manufacturing Co.*, 313 U.S. 487, 496 (1941) (federal courts in diversity of citizenship cases are governed by the conflict of law rules of the courts of the states in which they sit); *see Griffin v. McCoach*, 313 U.S. 498, 503 (1941) (applies the *Klaxon* rule to interpleader actions)....

The subjects of this action are two insurance policies insuring the life of a Washington resident, David McKay, entered into in Washington and contested by another Washington resident, Carolyn McKay. All the parties agree that the substantive law of Washington applies. Under Oregon law, when an Oregon court applies substantive law from another jurisdiction, it applies Oregon procedural law.... Thus, an Oregon court hearing this case would apply Washington substantive law and Oregon procedural law. Because district courts must apply the law that a court of the forum state would apply, the district court in this case was required to apply Washington substantive law and Oregon procedural law.

The question before us therefore reduces itself to whether the Washington Deadman's Statute is substantive or procedural. If it is substantive, it should be applied as Washington substantive law. If it is procedural, it should not be applied because only Oregon procedural rules should be applied. The district court found that Washington's Deadman's Statute was substantive and applied it....

We cannot ascertain how an Oregon court would answer this question. Therefore, we believe it appropriate to refer this question to the Oregon Supreme Court....

Legg v. Chopra

286 F.3d 286 (6th Cir. 2002)

SUHRHEINRICH, Circuit Judge....

I.

....

On August 18, 1999, Plaintiff brought this medical malpractice action against Dr. Chopra and University Urology, P.C. [in connection with a surgical procedure that Dr. Chopra performed on plaintiff that resulted in substantial, continued blood loss to the plaintiff]. The district court granted summary judgment to Defendants, holding that Plaintiff failed to create an issue of fact that Defendants fell below the standard of care. In so ruling, the district court refused to consider the testimony of Plaintiff's medical expert, Dr. Bernard Mittemeyer, who is licensed to practice in Texas, and therefore failed to satisfy the requirements of § 29-26-115(b), which requires that the expert be licensed to practice "in the state or a contiguous border state." ... This appeal follows.

II.

....

A.

First, Plaintiff argues that the district court mistakenly applied Fed.R.Evid. 601 and state law, and not Fed.R.Evid. 702, in deciding the evidentiary question of whether her expert was qualified to render an opinion. Plaintiff further contends that Tenn.Code Ann. § 29-26-115(b) conflicts with *Daubert v. Merrell Dow Pharm., Inc.*, 509 U.S. 579 (1993), and progeny.

In federal diversity actions, state law governs substantive issues and federal law governs procedural issues. *Erie R.R. Co. v. Tompkins*, 304 U.S. 64 (1938). Rules of evidence are deemed rules of procedure ... and therefore, the Federal Rules of Evidence, rather than state evidentiary laws, are held to apply in federal diversity proceedings....

However, some state evidentiary rules have substantive aspects, thereby defying the substance-procedure distinction and creating a potential *Erie* conflict.... State witness competency rules are often intimately intertwined with a state substantive rule. This is especially true with medical malpractice statutes, because expert testimony is usually required to establish the standard of care.... The Federal Rules of Evidence resolve this potential conflict between state and federal law on the issue of witness competency.... Rule 601 incorporates the *Erie* mandate by expressly providing that [state law governs the witness' competency regarding a claim or defense for which state law supplies the rule of decision.] Fed.R.Evid. 601.

The Tennessee statute is precisely the type of rule Fed.R.Evid. 601 addresses. It provides in part:

> **29-26-115. Claimant's burden in malpractice action — Expert testimony — Presumption of negligence — Jury instructions.** — (a) In a malpractice action, the claimant shall have the burden of proving by evidence as provided in subsection (b):
>
> (1) The recognized standard of acceptable professional practice in the profession and the specialty thereof, if any, that the defendant practices in the community in which the defendant practices or in a similar community at the time the alleged injury or wrongful action occurred;

(2) That the defendant acted with less than or failed to act with ordinary and reasonable care in accordance with such standard; and

(3) As a proximate result of the defendant's negligent [act] or omission, the plaintiff suffered injuries which would not otherwise have occurred.

(b) No person in a health care profession requiring licensure under the laws of this state shall be competent to testify in any court of law to establish the facts required to be established by subsection (a), unless the person was licensed to practice in the state or a contiguous bordering state a profession or specialty which would make person's expert testimony relevant to the specialty which would make the person's expert testimony relevant to the issues in the case and had practiced this profession or specialty in one (1) of these states during the year preceding the date that the alleged injury or wrongful act occurred. This rule shall apply to expert witnesses testifying for the defendant as rebuttal witnesses. The court may waive this subsection when it determines that the appropriate witnesses otherwise would not be available.

Tenn.Code Ann. §29-26-115 (Supp.2001). The structure of the statute reflects the intimate relationship between the standard of care and the qualification requirements of the medical expert who will establish that standard. Thus, there can be little doubt but that §29-26-115(b), via Rule 601, applies in this federal diversity action....

This does not completely end our analysis, however. Implicit in Plaintiff's argument is the assumption that Rules 601 and 702 are mutually exclusive. We do not agree with this assumption. As the foregoing discussion explains, Rule 601 deals with the witness' *competency*, which makes it essentially substantive (because it is "intimately intertwined" with the substantive law), whereas Rule 702 (as interpreted by *Daubert*) is truly a measure of *qualification*, as it is directed at the science and methodology behind the witness' testimony, and is therefore a procedural issue. Thus, we see no reason why the two rules cannot work in tandem, *because they are not in direct conflict*.... Thus, if a witness is deemed competent to testify to the substantive issue in the case, such as the standard of care, his or her testimony should then be screened by Rule 702 to determine if it is otherwise admissible expert testimony. We therefore find no conflict between Tenn.Code Ann. §29-26-115(b) and Fed.R.Evid. 702, since the first is directed at establishing the substantive issue in the case, and the second is a gatekeeping measure designed to ensure [fair administration] of the case. See Fed.R.Evid. 102.

In conclusion, we hold that the district court did not err in applying Fed.R.Evid. 601 and Tenn.Code Ann. §29-26-115(b) in its analysis....

Notes and Questions

1. Rule 601 defers to state competency rules only where state law supplies the rule of decision. Often, federal law may incorporate or "borrow" elements of state law to fill in gaps in a federal statute or federal common law cause of action. In such instances, even though reference is made to state law due to its incorporation into the federal cause of action, federal law is supplying the rule of decision in such cases, and thus the first sentence of Rule 601, declaring all witnesses to be competent, applies. *E.g.*, *Andrews v. Neer*, 253 F.3d 1052, 1062 (8th Cir. 2001).

2. Suppose that a suit filed in federal court raises both federal and state claims, and a witness, while competent to testify under the first sentence of Rule 601, would be incompetent to testify under state law. What should a court do in such a situation? Would

not a literal application of Rule 601 necessitate applying federal competency law to the federal claim and state competency law to the state claim, which could be accomplished by allowing the witness to testify but giving the jury an appropriate limiting instruction under Rule 105? *See Estate of Wooters ex rel. Klein v. Goujjane*, 305 F. Supp. 2d 280, 287 n.4 (S.D.N.Y. 2003) (raising but avoiding question). For a discussion of possible methods of resolving this question, see the discussion in Chapter 5 of the analogous problem for testimonial privileges.

3. As discussed above, one of the rationales for Dead Man's Statutes is that the dead person cannot rebut the interested person's testimony. But what if the dead person *could* rebut the interested person's testimony? Some states have chosen to allow the testimony normally barred by Dead Man's Statutes but to effectively allow the deceased to rebut that testimony. They accomplish the latter by creating a special exception to the state's hearsay rule that allows comments that the deceased had previously written or spoken to be admitted into evidence. *See, e.g.*, Conn. Gen. Stat. §52-172. No comparable exception exists, however, to the *federal* rule against hearsay. When such a case is brought in federal court, what is the result? Consider the following:

> [T]he Connecticut statute is *not* a bar to testimony but, rather, creates an exception to the state hearsay rule.... Accordingly, as the Connecticut statute (despite its title) is not a *rule of witness competency* at all, but is a mere *rule of evidence*, it is not made applicable in a diversity action in federal court under Rule 601 as federal evidence rules, including rules relating to hearsay, apply in such cases.

Maltas v. Maltas, 197 F. Supp. 2d 409, 425 (D.Md. 2002), *rev'd on other grounds*, 65 Fed. Appx. 917 (4th Cir. June 12, 2003). *See also Litif v. United States*, 682 F.Supp.2d 60, 66–67 & n.5 (D.Mass. 2010) (noting that Massachusetts rule addresses both hearsay and competency, but applying only that portion dealing with competency).

Thus, while Rule 601 calls for the federal court to apply the state's competency rules (which in a state such as Connecticut would allow the interested party to testify), the federal court is required to apply the federal hearsay rule (which does not create an exception for the statements of the deceased person, notwithstanding state law to the contrary). Does it not undermine the state's overall policy to apply only *half* of its policy? Is it likely that Congress intended this result?

4 Although Dead Man's Statutes were at the forefront of Congressional debate over Rule 601, the amended language is sweeping in its terms, and thus calls for the application of all state competency rules whenever state law provides the rule of decision. Thus, for example, federal courts, through the second sentence of Rule 601, continue to apply many of the common law competency rules that the first sentence of Rule 601 eliminated as a matter of federal competency law. *E.g., Kowalski v. Gagne*, 914 F.2d 299, 307 (1st Cir. 1990) (spouses); *Knotts v. Black & Decker, Inc.*, 204 F. Supp. 2d 1029, 1035–37 (N.D. Ohio 2002) (young children).

5. Is the second sentence of Rule 601 mandated by the *Erie* doctrine? Consider in this regard the discussion of the *Erie* doctrine with respect to Rule 407, dealing with evidence of subsequent remedial measures. In this regard, note that the substance-procedure distinction discussed by the *Legg* court is different from the substance-procedure distinction discussed by the *McKay* court: the former involves the vertical choice-of-law question, while the latter involves the horizontal choice-of-law question. Indeed, it is very possible that something could be "substantive" for *Erie* purposes (requiring that a federal court apply state law), but "procedural" for horizontal choice-of-law purposes (meaning that under the state's choice of law rules, it is the law of the forum state that governs the issue). While the vertical choice-of-law issue is a question of federal law, the horizontal choice-of-law issue is a question of state law, explaining why the *McKay* court certified the question to the Oregon Supreme Court.

6. In *McKay*, the Oregon Supreme Court answered the certified question by holding that the Washington Dead Man's Statute was procedural, and thus that Oregon competency law applied. For a discussion of the horizontal choice-of-law issues raised in that case, see *Equitable Life Assur. Soc. of the U.S. v. McKay*, 861 F.2d 221 (9th Cir. 1988).

7. Although Rule 601 eliminates the *per se* common law ban on testimony by children and mentally incapacitated persons, judges may be able to exclude such testimony under other provisions of the rules of evidence:

> What must be remembered, and is often confused, is that "competency" is a matter of status not ability. Thus, the only two groups of persons specifically rendered incompetent as witnesses by the Federal Rules of Evidence are judges (Rule 605) and jurors (Rule 606). The authority of the court to control the admissibility of the testimony of persons so impaired in some manner that they cannot give meaningful testimony is to be found outside of Rule 601. For example, the judge always has the authority under Rule 403 to balance the probative value of testimony against its prejudicial effect. Similarly, under Rule 603, the inability of a witness to take or comprehend an oath or affirmation will allow the judge to exclude that person's testimony. An argument can also be constructed that a person might be impaired to the point that he would not be able to satisfy the "personal knowledge" requirement of Rule 602.

United States v. Ramirez, 871 F.2d 582, 584 (6th Cir. 1989).

8. Rule 702, governing the prerequisites for admission of opinion testimony by expert witnesses, is discussed in greater detail below.

Problem 4-2: How Sausage Is Made

David, an African-American male, is on trial on charges of bank robbery. Assume that he is convicted, and his defense attorney moves for a new trial. Which of the following could be introduced in support of the motion in federal court?

(1) Testimony by a juror that one of the other jurors had done some background research on the defendant during the trial, discovered that the defendant had previously been convicted of bank robbery, and brought that information to the attention of the other jurors.

(2) Testimony by a juror that, notwithstanding the fact that the court admitted evidence of the defendant's prior conviction for bank robbery with a limiting instruction not to draw a propensity inference from the prior bank robbery, the jury did draw such an inference.

(3) Testimony by a juror who initially voted to acquit the defendant that one of the other jurors privately threatened him with physical violence if he refused to vote to convict.

(4) Testimony by a juror that another juror stated during deliberations that "all Black people are criminals."

(5) Testimony by a juror that he read newspaper articles during the trial that contained information about the case that was not admitted into evidence at trial, and that, had he not read the information contained in these newspaper articles, he would have voted to acquit rather than to convict David.

(6) Testimony by one juror that he saw two of his fellow jurors smoke marijuana each morning before going into the courthouse.

(7) Testimony by Mark, a bartender at a bar about one block from the court-house, that at lunchtime during each day of the trial, three of the jurors would come in and each drink about a pitcher of beer.

(8) Testimony by a juror that, after reaching an impasse during the deliberations, the jurors agreed to decide whether to acquit or convict David by flipping a coin.

How, if at all, would your answers differ under the Indiana, Minnesota, and Montana counterparts to Federal Rule 606(b) excerpted below?

Problem 4-3: An Honest Misunderstanding

In a negligence action in which the plaintiff claimed $100,000 in injuries, jurors were asked to answer two questions on a special verdict form. First, they were asked to calculate the total amount of damages suffered by the plaintiff. Second, because the defendant raised the defense of comparative negligence, jurors were asked to allocate responsibility for the plaintiff's harm between the defendant and the plaintiff in percentage terms. The jury instructions indicated that in determining total damages, the jury should not make any reduction due to the plaintiff's negligence, if any.

The jury returned a verdict for $25,000 in damages, found the defendant to be 25 percent at fault, and found the plaintiff to be 75 percent at fault. The judge then reduced the amount of damages based on the finding of comparative negligence to $6,250, entered judgment in that amount, and discharged the jury.

Because the amount of damages as determined by the jury was exactly 25 percent of the total amount claimed by the plaintiff, the plaintiff's attorney believed that the jury may have misunderstood the instructions and reduced the total damages amount to reflect the plaintiff's comparative negligence. He brings a motion for a new trial, and seeks to call the jurors to testify as to how they came up with the figure of $25,000.

Defendant's attorney objects, invoking Rule 606(b). How should the court rule?

Tanner v. United States
483 U.S. 107 (1987)

Justice O'CONNOR delivered the opinion of the Court.

Petitioners William Conover and Anthony Tanner were convicted of conspiring to defraud the United States in violation of 18 U.S.C. § 371, and of committing mail fraud in violation of 18 U.S.C. § 1341....

I

. . . .

The day before petitioners were scheduled to be sentenced, Tanner filed a motion, in which Conover subsequently joined, seeking continuance of the sentencing date, permission to interview jurors, an evidentiary hearing, and a new trial. According to an affidavit accompanying the motion, Tanner's attorney had received an unsolicited telephone call from one of the trial jurors, Vera Asbul. App. 246. Juror Asbul informed Tanner's attorney that several of the jurors consumed alcohol during the lunch breaks at various times throughout the trial, causing them to sleep through the afternoons. The District Court continued the sentencing date, ordered the parties to file memoranda, and heard argument on the motion to interview jurors. The District Court concluded that juror testimony on intoxication was inadmissible under Federal Rule of Evidence 606(b) to impeach the jury's verdict. The District Court invited petitioners to call any nonjuror witnesses, such as courtroom personnel, in support of the motion for new trial. Tanner's counsel took the stand and testified that he had observed one of the jurors "in a sort of giggly mood" at one point during the trial but did not bring this to anyone's attention at the time.

Earlier in the hearing the judge referred to a conversation between defense counsel and the judge during the trial on the possibility that jurors were sometimes falling asleep. During that extended exchange the judge twice advised counsel to immediately inform the court if they observed jurors being inattentive, and suggested measures the judge would take if he were so informed. . . .

The judge also observed that in the past courtroom employees had alerted him to problems with the jury. "Nothing was brought to my attention in this case about anyone appearing to be intoxicated," the judge stated, adding, "I saw nothing that suggested they were."

Following the hearing the District Court filed an order stating that "[o]n the basis of the admissible evidence offered I specifically find that the motions for leave to interview jurors or for an evidentiary hearing at which jurors would be witnesses is not required or appropriate." The District Court also denied the motion for new trial.

While the appeal of this case was pending before the Eleventh Circuit, petitioners filed another new trial motion based on additional evidence of jury misconduct. In another affidavit, Tanner's attorney stated that he received an unsolicited visit at his residence from a second juror, Daniel Hardy. Despite the fact that the District Court had denied petitioners' motion for leave to interview jurors, two days after Hardy's visit Tanner's attorney arranged for Hardy to be interviewed by two private investigators. The interview was transcribed, sworn to by the juror, and attached to the new trial motion. In the interview Hardy stated that he "felt like ... the jury was on one big party." Hardy indicated that seven of the jurors drank alcohol during the noon recess. Four jurors, including Hardy, consumed between them "a pitcher to three pitchers" of beer during various recesses. Of the three other jurors who were alleged to have consumed alcohol, Hardy stated that on several occasions he observed two jurors having one or two mixed drinks during the lunch recess, and one other juror, who was also the foreperson, having a liter of wine on each of three occasions. Juror Hardy also stated that he and three other jurors smoked marijuana quite regularly during the trial. Moreover, Hardy stated that during the trial he observed one juror ingest cocaine five times and another juror ingest cocaine two or three times. One juror sold a quarter pound of marijuana to another juror during the trial, and took marijuana, cocaine, and drug paraphernalia into the courthouse. Hardy noted that some of the jurors were falling asleep during the trial, and that one of the jurors described himself to Hardy as "flying." Hardy stated that before he visited Tanner's attorney at his residence, no one had contacted him concerning the jury's conduct, and Hardy had not been offered anything in return for his statement. Hardy said that he came forward "to clear my conscience" and "[b]ecause I felt ... that the people on the jury didn't have no business being on the jury. I felt ... that Mr. Tanner should have a better opportunity to get somebody that would review the facts right."

The District Court, stating that the motions "contain supplemental allegations which differ quantitatively but not qualitatively from those in the April motions," denied petitioners' motion for a new trial.

The Court of Appeals for the Eleventh Circuit affirmed. We granted certiorari to consider whether the District Court was required to hold an evidentiary hearing, including juror testimony, on juror alcohol and drug use during the trial....

II

Petitioners argue that the District Court erred in not ordering an additional evidentiary hearing at which jurors would testify concerning drug and alcohol use during the trial. Petitioners assert that, contrary to the holdings of the District Court and the Court of Appeals, juror testimony on ingestion of drugs or alcohol during the trial is not barred by Federal Rule of Evidence 606(b). Moreover, petitioners argue that whether or not authorized by Rule 606(b), an evidentiary hearing including juror testimony on drug and alcohol use is compelled by their Sixth Amendment right to trial by a competent jury.

By the beginning of this century, if not earlier, the near-universal and firmly established common-law rule in the United States flatly prohibited the admission of juror testimony to impeach a jury verdict.

Exceptions to the common-law rule were recognized only in situations in which an "extraneous influence," *Mattox v. United States*, 146 U.S. 140, 149 (1892), was alleged to have affected the jury. In *Mattox*, this Court held admissible the testimony of jurors describing how they heard and read prejudicial information not admitted into evidence. The Court allowed juror testimony on influence by outsiders in *Parker v. Gladden*, 385 U.S. 363, 365 (1966) (bailiff's comments on defendant), and *Remmer v. United States*, 347 U.S. 227, 228–230 (1954) (bribe offered to juror). See also *Smith v. Phillips*, 455 U.S. 209 (1982) (juror in criminal trial had submitted an application for employment at the District Attorney's office). In situations that did not fall into this exception for external influence, however, the Court adhered to the common-law rule against admitting juror testimony to impeach a verdict. *McDonald v. Pless*, 238 U.S. 264 (1915); *Hyde v. United States*, 225 U.S. 347, 384 (1912).

Lower courts used this external/internal distinction to identify those instances in which juror testimony impeaching a verdict would be admissible. The distinction was not based on whether the juror was literally inside or outside the jury room when the alleged irregularity took place; rather, the distinction was based on the nature of the allegation. Clearly a rigid distinction based only on whether the event took place inside or outside the jury room would have been quite unhelpful. For example, under a distinction based on location a juror could not testify concerning a newspaper read inside the jury room. Instead, of course, this has been considered an external influence about which juror testimony is admissible. Similarly, under a rigid locational distinction jurors could be regularly required to testify after the verdict as to whether they heard and comprehended the judge's instructions, since the charge to the jury takes place outside the jury room. Courts wisely have treated allegations of a juror's inability to hear or comprehend at trial as an internal matter....

Most significant for the present case, however, is the fact that lower federal courts treated allegations of the physical or mental incompetence of a juror as "internal" rather than "external" matters. In *United States v. Dioguardi*, 492 F.2d 70 (CA2 1974), the defendant Dioguardi received a letter from one of the jurors soon after the trial in which the juror explained that she had "eyes and ears that ... see things before [they] happen," but that her eyes "are only partly open" because "a curse was put upon them some years ago." Armed with this letter and the opinions of seven psychiatrists that the letter suggested that the juror was suffering from a psychological disorder, Dioguardi sought a new trial or in the alternative an evidentiary hearing on the juror's competence. The District Court denied the motion and the Court of Appeals affirmed. The Court of Appeals noted "[t]he strong policy against any post-verdict inquiry into a juror's state of mind".…

Substantial policy considerations support the common-law rule against the admission of jury testimony to impeach a verdict. As early as 1915 this Court explained the necessity of shielding jury deliberations from public scrutiny:

> "[L]et it once be established that verdicts solemnly made and publicly returned into court can be attacked and set aside on the testimony of those who took part in their publication and all verdicts could be, and many would be, followed by an inquiry in the hope of discovering something which might invalidate the finding. Jurors would be harassed and beset by the defeated party in an effort to secure from them evidence of facts which might establish misconduct sufficient to set aside a verdict. If evidence thus secured could be thus used, the result would be to make what was intended to be a private deliberation, the constant subject of public investigation—to the destruction of all frankness and freedom of discussion and conference." *McDonald v. Pless*, 238 U.S., at 267–268.

See also *Mattox v. United States*, 146 U.S. 140 (1892).…

There is little doubt that postverdict investigation into juror misconduct would in some instances lead to the invalidation of verdicts reached after irresponsible or improper juror behavior. It is not at all clear, however, that the jury system could survive such efforts to perfect it. Allegations of juror misconduct, incompetency, or inattentiveness, raised for the first time days, weeks, or months after the verdict, seriously disrupt the finality of the process. Moreover, full and frank discussion in the jury room, jurors' willingness to return an unpopular verdict, and the community's trust in a system that relies on the decisions of laypeople would all be undermined by a barrage of postverdict scrutiny of juror conduct.

Federal Rule of Evidence 606(b) is grounded in the common-law rule against admission of jury testimony to impeach a verdict and the exception for juror testimony relating to extraneous influences.…

Petitioners have presented no argument that Rule 606(b) is inapplicable to the juror affidavits and the further inquiry they sought in this case, and, in fact, there appears to be virtually no support for such a proposition. Rather, petitioners argue that substance abuse constitutes an improper "outside influence" about which jurors may testify under Rule 606(b). In our view the language of the Rule cannot easily be stretched to cover this circumstance. However severe their effect and improper their use, drugs or alcohol voluntarily ingested by a juror seems no more an "outside influence" than a virus, poorly prepared food, or a lack of sleep.

In any case, whatever ambiguity might linger in the language of Rule 606(b) as applied to juror intoxication is resolved by the legislative history of the Rule. In 1972, following criticism of a proposed rule that would have allowed considerably broader use of juror testimony to impeach verdicts, the Advisory Committee drafted the present version of Rule 606(b). This Court adopted the present version of Rule 606(b) and transmitted it to Congress.

The House Judiciary Committee described the effect of the version of Rule 606(b) transmitted by the Court as follows:

> As proposed by the Court, Rule 606(b) limited testimony by a juror in the course of an inquiry into the validity of a verdict or indictment. He could testify as to the influence of extraneous prejudicial information brought to the jury's atten-

tion (e.g. a radio newscast or a newspaper account) or an outside influence which improperly had been brought to bear upon a juror (e.g. a threat to the safety of a member of his family), but he could not testify as to other irregularities which occurred in the jury room. Under this formulation a quotient verdict could not be attacked through the testimony of [a] juror, *nor could a juror testify to the drunken condition of a fellow juror which so disabled him that he could not participate in the jury's deliberations.* H.R.Rep. No. 93-650, pp. 9–10 (1973) (emphasis supplied).

The House Judiciary Committee, persuaded that the better practice was to allow juror testimony on any "objective juror misconduct," amended the Rule so as to comport with the more expansive versions proposed by the Advisory Committee in earlier drafts, and the House passed this amended version.

The Senate Judiciary Committee did not voice any disagreement with the House's interpretation of the Rule proposed by the Court, or the version passed by the House ... With this understanding of the differences between the two versions of Rule 606(b)—an understanding identical to that of the House—the Senate decided to reject the broader House version and adopt the narrower version approved by the Court. The Senate Report explained:

> "[The House version's] extension of the ability to impeach a verdict is felt to be unwarranted and ill-advised.... [I]t deletes from the Supreme Court version the proscription against testimony 'as to any matter or statement occurring during the course of the jury's deliberations.' This deletion would have the effect of opening verdicts up to challenge on the basis of what happened during the jury's internal deliberations, for example, where a juror alleged that the jury refused to follow the trial judge's instructions or that some of the jurors did not take part in deliberations....
>
> Public policy requires a finality to litigation. And common fairness requires that absolute privacy be preserved for jurors to engage in the full and free debate necessary to the attainment of just verdicts. Jurors will not be able to function effectively if their deliberations are to be scrutinized in post-trial litigation. In the interest of protecting the jury system and the citizens who make it work, rule 606 should not permit any inquiry into the internal deliberations of the jurors."

Id., at 13–14.

The Conference Committee Report reaffirms Congress' understanding of the differences between the House and Senate versions of Rule 606(b): "[T]he House bill allows a juror to testify about objective matters occurring during the jury's deliberation, such as the misconduct of another juror or the reaching of a quotient verdict. The Senate bill does not permit juror testimony about any matter or statement occurring during the course of the jury's deliberations." H.R.Conf.Rep. No. 93-1597, p. 8 (1974). The Conference Committee adopted, and Congress enacted, the Senate version of Rule 606(b).

Thus, the legislative history demonstrates with uncommon clarity that Congress specifically understood, considered, and rejected a version of Rule 606(b) that would have allowed jurors to testify on juror conduct during deliberations, including juror intoxication. This legislative history provides strong support for the most reasonable reading of the language of Rule 606(b)—that juror intoxication is not an "outside influence" about which jurors may testify to impeach their verdict.

Finally, even if Rule 606(b) is interpreted to retain the common-law exception allowing post-verdict inquiry of juror incompetence in cases of "substantial if not wholly conclusive evidence of incompetency," *Dioguardi,* 492 F.2d, at 80, the showing made by petitioners falls far short of this standard. The affidavits and testimony presented in support of the first new trial motion suggested, at worst, that several of the jurors fell asleep at times during the afternoons. The District Court Judge appropriately considered the fact that he had "an unobstructed view" of the jury, and did not see any juror sleeping.... The juror affidavit submitted in support of the second new trial motion was obtained in clear violation of the District Court's order and the court's local rule against juror interviews, MD Fla.Rule 2.04(c); on this basis alone the District Court would have been acting within its discretion in disregarding the affidavit. In any case, although the affidavit of juror Hardy describes more dramatic instances of misconduct, Hardy's allegations of *incompetence* are meager. Hardy stated that the alcohol consumption he engaged in with three other jurors did not leave any of them intoxicated. The only allegations concerning the jurors' ability to properly consider the evidence were Hardy's observations that some jurors were "falling asleep all the time during the trial," and that his own reasoning ability was affected on one day of the trial. These allegations would not suffice to bring this case under the common-law exception allowing post-verdict inquiry when an extremely strong showing of incompetency has been made.

Petitioners also argue that the refusal to hold an additional evidentiary hearing at which jurors would testify as to their conduct "violates the sixth amendment's guarantee to a fair trial before an impartial and *competent* jury."

This Court has recognized that a defendant has a right to "a tribunal both impartial and mentally competent to afford a hearing." *Jordan v. Massachusetts*, 225 U.S. 167, 176 (1912). In this case the District Court held an evidentiary hearing in response to petitioners' first new trial motion at which the judge invited petitioners to introduce any admissible evidence in support of their allegations. At issue in this case is whether the Constitution compelled the District Court to hold an additional evidentiary hearing including one particular kind of evidence inadmissible under the Federal Rules.

As described above, long-recognized and very substantial concerns support the protection of jury deliberations from intrusive inquiry. Petitioners' Sixth Amendment interests in an unimpaired jury, on the other hand, are protected by several aspects of the trial process. The suitability of an individual for the responsibility of jury service, of course, is examined during *voir dire*. Moreover, during the trial the jury is observable by the court, by counsel, and by court personnel. Moreover, jurors are observable by each other, and may report inappropriate juror behavior to the court *before* they render a verdict. Finally, after the trial a party may seek to impeach the verdict by nonjuror evidence of misconduct. Indeed, in this case the District Court held an evidentiary hearing giving petitioners ample opportunity to produce nonjuror evidence supporting their allegations.

In light of these other sources of protection of petitioners' right to a competent jury, we conclude that the District Court did not err in deciding, based on the inadmissibility of juror testimony and the clear insufficiency of the nonjuror evidence offered by petitioners, that an additional post-verdict evidentiary hearing was unnecessary....

[The opinion by Justice Marshall, concurring in part and dissenting in part, is omitted.]

United States v. Villar

586 F.3d 76 (1st Cir. 2009)

SARIS, District Judge.

After a jury trial, Defendant-appellant Richard Villar, a Hispanic man, was convicted of bank robbery. Hours following his conviction, defense counsel received an e-mail message from one of the jurors disclosing that during deliberations another juror said, "I guess we're profiling but they cause all the trouble." When defense counsel filed a motion for a court inquiry into the validity of the verdict, the court held a hearing in which the juror was asked only to authenticate the e-mail. Concluding that an allegation of ethnically biased statements within the jury room was not, as Villar argued, an external matter open to post-verdict inquiry, the district court held that Federal Rule of Evidence 606(b) precluded the court from engaging in any further examination beyond the mere authentication of the e-mail.

Appellant now challenges the conviction on the grounds that the district court erred when it ruled that Rule 606(b) prohibited it from taking juror testimony about ethnically biased comments during the course of deliberations, and that the appellant was denied the right to due process and the right to an impartial jury in violation of the Fifth and Sixth Amendments to the Constitution....

DISCUSSION

1. *Rule 606(b)*

Contending that the juror's e-mail created a possibility that the jury was racially or ethnically biased against him, appellant asserts that the district court erred in its legal conclusion that Rule 606(b) barred any inquiry into the possibility of bias within the jury room....

Rule 606(b) contains three exceptions, two of which—"extraneous prejudicial information" and "outside influence"—are relevant to our analysis....

The key case in this area is *Tanner v. United States.*... The "external/internal distinction" employed by the *Tanner* Court is not a "locational distinction" but rather is "based on the nature of the allegation." Juror testimony about a matter characterized as "external" to the jury is admissible under Rule 606(b), while testimony about "internal" matters is barred by the Rule....

Using this framework, most courts have concluded that juror testimony about race-related statements made by deliberating jurors does not fall within either the "extraneous prejudicial information" or the "outside influence" exceptions of Rule 606(b), but does fall squarely within Rule 606(b)'s prohibition of post-verdict juror testimony.

We are persuaded by the courts that have held that Rule 606(b), by its express terms, precludes any inquiry into the validity of the verdict based on juror testimony regarding racial or ethnic comments made "during the course of deliberations."

. . . .

2. *Due Process and Sixth Amendment Rights*

Appellant's more powerful argument is that the application of Rule 606(b) to prevent juror testimony about racial or ethnic statements made in jury deliberations is unconstitutional, violating a defendant's right to due process under the Fifth Amendment, and to a trial by an impartial jury as guaranteed by the Sixth Amendment....

The Constitution guarantees a criminal defendant the right to a "fair trial by a panel of impartial, 'indifferent' jurors. The failure to accord an accused a fair hearing violates even the minimal standards of due process." One touchstone of a fair trial is an impartial trier of fact—"'a jury capable and willing to decide the case solely on the evidence before it.'"

. . . .

Tanner did not address the issue of racial bias but instead involved issues of juror competence. The Supreme Court recognized that a defendant has a Sixth Amendment right to an unimpaired jury, but concluded that, because there were "several aspects of the trial process" that could protect this right, the district court's invocation of a rule of evidence to bar juror testimony did not amount to a constitutional violation. The Court listed voir dire, observations of the jury by counsel and the court during trial, opportunities for jurors to report inappropriate juror behavior prior to rendering a verdict, and the admissibility of non-juror testimony as to wrongdoing as examples of "other sources of protection" for a defendant's Sixth Amendment rights.

After *Tanner*, courts have struggled with its application to cases involving the possibility of Sixth Amendment violations during jury deliberations. In two habeas challenges involving state court convictions, two circuits have suggested that the use of juror testimony may be appropriate in the rare case where due process and Sixth Amendment concerns are implicated. In *Shillcutt*, the Seventh Circuit held that the intent of Rule 606(b) was to preclude post-verdict juror testimony, but nonetheless proceeded to address the constitutional question:

> The rule of juror incompetency cannot be applied in such an unfair manner as to deny due process. Thus, further review may be necessary in the occasional case in order to discover the extremely rare abuse that could exist even after the court has applied the rule and determined the evidence incompetent. In short, although our scope of review is narrow at this stage, we must consider whether prejudice pervaded the jury room, whether there is a substantial probability that the alleged racial slur made a difference in the outcome of the trial.

Many courts have recognized that Rule 606(b) should not be applied dogmatically where there is a possibility of juror bias during deliberations that would violate a defendant's Sixth Amendment rights.

Recently, the Tenth Circuit held that *Tanner* precluded inquiry into claims that racist statements were made in the jury room during the trial of a Native American defendant for assaulting an officer with a dangerous weapon. Several days after the defendant was convicted, a juror reported to defense counsel that, during deliberations, the foreman insisted that "'[w]hen Indians get alcohol, they all get drunk' and that when they get drunk, they get violent." Several jurors apparently discussed the need to "send a message back to the reservation." After considering juror affidavits, the trial court held that two jurors lied during voir dire about their experiences with Native Americans and that a new trial was warranted. The Tenth Circuit reversed, asserting that it is "not necessarily in the interest of overall justice" to attempt to cure "defects" such as possible racial prejudice in the jury process....

The Tenth Circuit turned to the four protections the *Tanner* Court characterized as protective of a defendant's Sixth Amendment rights: the voir dire process, the ability of the court and counsel to observe jurors during the trial, the ability of jurors to make pre-verdict reports of misconduct, and the availability of post-verdict impeachment through non-juror evidence of misconduct. Acknowledging that at least two of *Tanner*'s listed protections might not be effective at identifying racist (as opposed to drunken) jurors, the ... court concluded that, because "jury perfection is an untenable goal," the safeguards noted in *Tanner* were sufficiently protective. The court rejected the defendant's attempt to distinguish *Tanner* on the grounds that racial bias is a more serious danger to the justice system than intoxicated jurors....

While the issue is difficult and close, we believe that the rule against juror impeachment cannot be applied so inflexibly as to bar juror testimony in those rare and grave cases where claims of racial or ethnic bias during jury deliberations implicate a defendant's right to due process and an impartial jury. In our view, the four protections relied on by the *Tanner* Court do not provide adequate safeguards in the context of racially and ethnically biased comments made during deliberations. While individual pre-trial voir dire of the jurors can help to disclose prejudice, it has shortcomings because some jurors may be reluctant to admit racial bias. In addition, visual observations of the jury by counsel and the court during trial are unlikely to identify jurors harboring racial or ethnic bias. Likewise, non-jurors are more likely to report inappropriate conduct—such as alcohol or drug use—among jurors than racial statements uttered during deliberations to which they are not privy.

Accordingly, we conclude that the district court here did have the discretion to inquire into the validity of the verdict by hearing juror testimony to determine whether ethnically biased statements were made during jury deliberations and, if so, whether there is a substantial probability that any such comments made a difference in the outcome of the trial....

Although we conclude that the district court erred when it concluded that it had no discretion to hold an inquiry into possible bias in jury deliberations, we emphasize that not every stray or isolated off-base statement made during deliberations requires a hearing at which jury testimony is taken. As courts and commentators have highlighted, the need to protect a frank and candid jury deliberation process is a strong policy consideration. Still, at the other extreme, there are certain rare and exceptional cases involving racial or ethnic prejudice that require hearing jury testimony to determine whether a defendant received a fair trial under the Sixth Amendment. The determination of whether an inquiry is necessary to vindicate a criminally accused's constitutional due process and Sixth Amendment rights is best made by the trial judge, who is most familiar with the strength of the evidence and best able to determine the probability of prejudice from an inappropriate racial or ethnic comment....

Despite our view that there is a constitutional outer limit, we stress that the policies embodied in Rule 606(b) and underscored in *Tanner* are extremely important; the rule itself is rooted in a longstanding concern about intruding into jury deliberations and the problems that would be caused if jury verdicts could be easily undermined by post-judgment comments volunteered by (or in some cases) coaxed from jurors with second thoughts. In this case, we do not say that we would necessarily have pressed for further inquiry based on the somewhat terse and perhaps ambiguous report of a single juror if the district judge had not indicated his interest in doing so but for the bar of Rule 606(b), which he deemed absolute. But, as we have said, the district judge is in the best position to make the initial judgment. If in this case he thinks further inquiry appropriate, he is free to proceed; if he thinks the passage of time alters that initial disposition, that too is within his province....

Indiana Rule of Evidence 606

Competency of Juror As Witness

....

(b) *Inquiry into Validity of Verdict or Indictment.* Upon an inquiry into the validity of a verdict or indictment, a juror may not testify as to any matter or statement occurring during the course of the jury's deliberations or to the effect of anything upon that or any other juror's mind or emotions as influencing the juror to assent to or dissent from the verdict or indictment or concerning the juror's mental processes in connection therewith, except that a juror may testify (1) to drug or alcohol use by any juror, (2) on the question of whether extraneous prejudicial information was improperly brought to the jury's attention or (3) whether any outside influence was improperly brought to bear upon any juror. A juror's affidavit or evidence of any statement by the juror concerning a matter about which the juror would be precluded from testifying may not be received for these purposes.

Minnesota Rule of Evidence 606
COMPETENCY OF JUROR AS WITNESS

....

(b) **Inquiry into validity of verdict or indictment.** Upon an inquiry into the validity of a verdict or indictment, a juror may not testify as to any matter or statement occurring during the course of the jury's deliberations or to the effect of anything upon that or any other juror's mind or emotions as influencing the juror to assent to or dissent from the verdict or indictment or concerning the juror's mental processes in connection therewith, except that a juror may testify on the question whether extraneous prejudicial information was improperly brought to the jury's attention, or whether any outside influence was improperly brought to bear upon any juror, or as to any threats of violence or violent acts brought to bear on jurors, from whatever source, to reach a verdict. Nor may a juror's affidavit or evidence of any statement by the juror concerning a matter about which the juror would be precluded from testifying be received for these purposes.

Montana Rule of Evidence 606
Competency of juror as witness

....

(b) Inquiry into validity of verdict or indictment. Upon an inquiry into the validity of a verdict or indictment, a juror may not testify as to any matter or statement occurring during the course of the jury's deliberations or to the effect of anything upon that or any other juror's mind or emotions as influencing the juror to assent or dissent from the verdict or indictment or concerning the juror's mental processes in connection therewith. Nor may a juror's affidavit or evidence of any statement by the juror concerning a matter about which the juror would be precluded from testifying be received for these purposes.

However, as an exception to this subdivision, a juror may testify and an affidavit or evidence of any kind be received as to any matter or statement concerning only the following questions, whether occurring during the course of the jury's deliberations or not: (1) whether extraneous prejudicial information was improperly brought to the jury's attention; or (2) whether any outside influence was brought to bear upon any juror; or (3) whether any juror has been induced to assent to any general or special verdict, or finding on any question submitted to them by the court, by a resort to the determination of chance.

United States v. Berber-Tinoco
510 F.3d 1083 (9th Cir. 2007)

IKUTA, Circuit Judge:

....

I

Around 10:30 on the night of February 9, 2006, Border Patrol Officers Thomas Englehorn and Robert Lenoir were positioned in their vehicles at different spots on Lyons Valley

Road between Honey Springs and Japatul Valley Road.... Two hours earlier, a seismic intrusion device had been activated. Based on their experience, the officers knew that it would take an alien crossing the border approximately two hours to get to this site....

From his position at the Japatul Fire Station off of Lyons Valley Road, Officer Engelhorn saw two vehicles, a Dodge Durango and a Ford pickup truck, approach the area.... Officer Engelhorn became suspicious when he observed the two vehicles driving "right next to each other, not more than a car or two car lengths apart, traveling at a slow rate of speed."

....

Given the alarm from the seismic intrusion device, the timing when the vehicles approached the area, and their conduct which included turning around at known loading spots, the officer believed the vehicles were loading up with illegal aliens as part of a smuggling operation. Relying on this evidence and their suspicions, the officers made an investigatory stop of the two vehicles at that point.

Berber, a passenger in one of the vehicles, was arrested and charged with unlawful re-entry into the United States after deportation in violation of 8 U.S.C. § 1326. Berber filed a motion to suppress evidence of his fingerprints and statements to the officers as the fruits of an allegedly unlawful stop....

III

Berber argues that even if we determine that the investigatory stop was based on reasonable suspicion, we must reverse the district court for violating Rule 605 of the Federal Rules of Evidence* when the judge made interjections based on his own knowledge during the suppression hearing....

Berber claims that a number of the judge's interjections violated Rule 605. First, the judge interrupted defense counsel's questions to Officer Engelhorn regarding the stop signs on Lyons Valley Road, and the following exchange took place:

> Court: Counsel, let me interrupt you for just a second. I'm really familiar with that area. So if you're doing this for my benefit, you can stop because I happen to know where that stop sign is and what's further on down at Lyons Valley.
>
> ....
>
> Defense counsel: I understand, Your Honor; however, it is important to my argument. I would like to find out from the officer.
>
> Court: The problem is you're unduly consuming time. The next stop sign beyond that is at Lawson Valley Road, which is a long ways down the road, so why don't you move on.

In subsequent cross-examination, defense counsel again asked Officer Lenoir about the stop signs on Lyons Valley Road. The officer testified that there were two stop signs, but the judge interjected, "Actually, I think there's four, counsel." The judge went on at some length:

> Court: Well, there's four. Including the whole distance of Lyons Valley Road, there's four. The area he's talking about there's one at the intersection of Lyons and Japatul, and there's one at Four Corners, which is the intersection of Honey

---

* Editor's Note: Rule 605 provides in pertinent part that "[t]he presiding judge may not testify as a witness at the trial."

Springs, Lyons Valley, and Skyline Truck Trail, and it's a distance of about seven miles between those two stretches.

If that's what you're talking about, which I think is what the officer's talking about, for my purposes, for the purposes of the hearing today, it doesn't do any good to talk about the second stop sign, or the third stop sign at Lawson Valley road, or the fourth stop sign, which is down by Skyline Truck Trail, again, down at the-almost the intersection of 94.

. . . .

Later, in summing up the evidence, the district court stated:

. . . . That's a fairly narrow road running from Japatul Valley Road to the intersection with Honey Springs, not a whole lot of traffic on that road at 10:30 at night.

. . . .

By the way, I think, [Defense Counsel], I may be mistaken on this, but I think the speed limit in California, unless otherwise posted, is 55 miles an hour. So if the vehicle is traveling between 20 and 35 miles an hour, which is a very low rate of speed in a rural area, stopping periodically along areas where the officers know that people are going to be picked up, and particularly following setting off a seismic device, I believe that that's enough to create reasonable suspicion.

. . . .

We agree that the judge violated Rule 605 when he interjected his own observations regarding the location of the stop signs along the Lyons Valley Road and the narrowness of the road from Japatul Valley Road to the intersection with Honey Springs. At the time the judge first stated these facts, they were not in the record nor were they reasonable inferences from the record. Although a closer call, the judge also violated Rule 605 when he relied on personal knowledge to conclude that no speed limit was posted on Lyons Valley Road and therefore the speed limit was 55 miles per hour. Although a court might be able to take judicial notice of a speed limit under some circumstances, *see* Fed. R. Evid. 201(b), the judge here provided a personal conjecture, rather than a judicially noticed fact. . . .

Notes and Questions

1. In explaining that Rule 606(b) does not unduly infringe on a defendant's Sixth Amendment rights, the *Tanner* Court notes the situations in which Rule 606(b) would pose no bar to the admissibility of evidence that jurors were impaired by drug and alcohol consumption. The Court indicates that, during trial, inappropriate juror behavior may be observed by the court or reported to it by counsel, court personnel, or other jurors. But although Rule 606(b) poses no bar, does Rule 606(a) prevent individual jurors from being called before the judge and asked to testify about the alleged behavior? *See United States v. Robinson*, 645 F.2d 616, 618 (8th Cir. 1981) (not a violation of Rule 606(a) because not testifying before the *jury* of which he is part, but only before the judge); *accord United States v. Day*, 830 F.2d 1099, 1104 (10th Cir. 1987). The Court also indicates that a party may impeach a verdict by introducing *nonjuror* evidence that the jurors were impaired. Note, however, that the ability to do this is substantially limited by the last sentence of Rule 606(b)(1), which states that "[t]he court may not receive a juror's affidavit or evidence of a juror's statement on these matters."

2. Absent the statements about substance abuse in the legislative history, would you classify drug and alcohol use by a juror as an outside influence? Which characterization best comports with the policies underlying Rule 606?

3. In applying Rule 606(b), courts sharply distinguish between misuse of evidence introduced at trial and information obtained by jurors outside of the trial:

> Extrinsic or extraneous influences include "publicity received and discussed in the jury room, matters considered by the jury but not admitted into evidence, and communications or other contact between jurors and outside persons." ... A prior conviction of a defendant, for example, when not admitted as evidence at trial, but which nonetheless entered into the jury's deliberations through personal knowledge of a juror, has been held to be "extraneous prejudicial information."
>
> That Rodriquez did not testify is not a fact the jurors learned through outside contact, communication, or publicity. It did not enter the jury room through an external, prohibited route. It was part of the trial, and was part of the information each juror collected. It should not have been discussed by the jury, and indeed was the subject of a jury instruction to that effect. But it was not "extraneous information," and therefore does not fall within the exception outlined in Rule 606(b).

United States v. Rodriquez, 116 F.3d 1225, 1227 (8th Cir. 1997).

What justifies treating the use of extrinsic information differently? After all, isn't a juror's use of extrinsic information often just a violation of an instruction to the jury not to consider such sources of information? In that sense, how is it any different from other failures to follow jury instructions?

4. It seems clear enough that pressure or threats placed on a juror by someone associated with a party to decide a case in a particular way would qualify as an improper outside influence. But what about pressure or threats made by *other jurors*? *Compare United States v. Roach*, 164 F.3d 403, 412–13 (8th Cir. 1998) (holding that such evidence is barred by Rule 606(b)), *with Anderson v. Miller*, 346 F.3d 315, 327 (2d Cir. 2003) (dicta suggesting that such evidence might fall within an exception to Rule 606(b)). The *Tanner* Court held that the external/internal distinction has not so much to do with where the conduct at issue took place but rather the nature of the conduct. On which side of that line does this fall? How helpful is the internal/external distinction?

5. How persuasive is the *Villar* court's attempt to distinguish *Tanner* from the case before it? Once decisions such as *Villar* become widely known, will it not likely chill juror deliberation to some extent, in that jurors will be less likely to *openly* express their racial biases? Isn't there a benefit to a system in which jurors feel free to openly express their biases to one another? After all, putting those biases on the table provides fellow jurors with the opportunity to counter those biased views, doesn't it? Are criminal defendants who are members of racial minorities best served by a system that encourages *stealth* racism?

6. An amendment to Federal Rule 606(b) that took effect in 2006 provides that a juror is allowed to testify about whether "a mistake was made in entering the verdict on the verdict form." *See* Fed. R. Evid. 606(b)(2)(C). The Advisory Committee's Note indicates that the exception is "limited to cases such as 'where the jury foreperson wrote down, in response to an interrogatory, a number different from that agreed upon by the jury, or mistakenly stated that the defendant was "guilty" when the jury had actually agreed that the defendant was not guilty.'" *See* Advisory Committee's Note to 2006

Amendment to Rule 606. Would the amendment permit testimony of the sort offered in Problem 4-3? *See id.* (explaining that the amendment would *not* cover the situation in which the figure written down by the foreman was intended to be a net rather than a gross figure).

7. Evidence that jurors did outside research during the trial, such as conducting experiments or consulting an encyclopedia, dictionary, or other reference materials, can be introduced by way of juror testimony under Rule 606(b). *E.g., Sea Hawk Seafoods, Inc. v. Alyeska Pipeline Service Co.*, 206 F.3d 900, 906 (9th Cir. 2000); *Anderson v. Ford Motor Co.*, 186 F.3d 918, 920–21 (8th Cir. 1999). Yet courts hold that Rule 606(b) bars inquiry in situations in which a juror just happens to already have specialized knowledge and shares that knowledge with other jurors. *See Hard v. Burlington Northern R. Co.*, 870 F.2d 1454, 1462 (9th Cir. 1989); Paul F. Kirgis, *The Problem of the Expert Juror*, 75 Temp. L. Rev. 493 (2002). What justifies distinguishing between the two situations? How would the *Tanner* Court answer a litigant's concern about the latter situation? *See Marquez v. City of Albuquerque*, 399 F.3d 1216, 1223–24 (10th Cir. 2005) (holding that "[a] juror's personal experience ... does not constitute 'extraneous prejudicial information'" and noting that "[t]he reason that the juror's specialized knowledge did not come to light ... was a failure [on counsel's part] to fully examine the juror during voir dire").

8. Are the policies that underlie Rule 606(b) so important that the rule should be interpreted to bar evidence that the jury failed to understand jury instructions given to them during the penalty phase of a death penalty case? *See United States v. Sampson*, 332 F. Supp. 2d 325, 326–32 (D. Mass. 2004) (collecting cases and concluding that applying Rule 606(b) is not inconsistent with the Constitution's requirement of procedures to ensure heightened reliability when a death sentence is imposed).

9. Even though Rules 606(b)(2)(A) and 606(b)(2)(B) creates exceptions to the general rule of juror incompetency for evidence about *whether* "extraneous prejudicial information was improperly brought to the jury's attention" or "an outside influence was improperly brought to bear on any juror," Rule 606(b)(1) still categorically prohibits, even in such circumstances, testimony by a juror as to "the *effect* of anything on that juror's or another juror's vote" (emphasis added). *E.g., United States v. Rutherford*, 371 F.3d 634, 644 (9th Cir. 2004). Why not extend the exception to evidence of the effect on the juror's vote? Moreover, how is a court considering a motion for a new trial supposed to determine whether the improper information or influence impacted the jury's disposition of the case without such testimony? Because Rule 606(b)(1) bars inquiry into subjective evidence of actual effect on the jury's verdict, the lower courts have held that the inquiry involves an objective inquiry that examines the nature of the information or contact at issue and determines "its probable effect on a hypothetical average jury." *Manley v. AmBase Corp.*, 337 F.3d 237, 252 (2d Cir. 2003).

10. So strong are the policies underlying Rule 606(b) that the lower courts impose a high standard to even invoke the statutory exceptions set forth in the rule:

> Despite this exception, we have nevertheless warned that "[c]ourts generally 'should be hesitant[ ] to haul jurors in after they have reached a verdict ... to probe for potential instances of bias, misconduct, or extraneous influences.'" *Neron v. Tierney*, 841 F.2d 1197, 1205 (1st Cir. 1988) (quoting *United States v. Moon*, 718 F.2d 1210, 1234 (2d Cir. 1983)). A court should only conduct such an inquiry when "reasonable grounds for investigation exist," i.e., "there is clear, strong, substantial and incontrovertible evidence that a specific, nonspeculative impropriety has occurred which could have prejudiced the trial of a defendant." *Moon*, 718 F.2d at 1234.

United States v. Connolly, 341 F.3d 16, 34 (1st Cir. 2003).

11. Although Rule 606(b) is most often encountered in situations in which an effort is made to inquire into a *verdict* by a petit jury, the text of the rule covers "an inquiry into the validity of a verdict or *indictment*," (emphasis added) and it is thus equally applicable when an effort is made to call members of a *grand* jury as witnesses. *E.g., In re Grand Jury Proceedings*, 142 F.3d 1416, 1427 (11th Cir. 1998).

12. Rule 605 bars a judge from serving as a witness in a trial over which he presides. The rule is violated not only in the highly unlikely situation in which the judge actually testifies, but also in a bench trial in which the judge, say, conducts a view of the scene of the crime or injury without notification to the parties. *E.g., Lillie v. United States*, 953 F.2d 1188, 1189–92 (10th Cir. 1992) ("When a judge engages in off-the-record fact gathering, he essentially has become a witness in the case."). It is the only rule to provide that a party need not make an objection to preserve a claim that it was violated on appeal. Do you see why this is so?

13. The concept of judicial notice, referenced at the end of the excerpt from the *Berber-Tinoco* opinion, is examined in detail in Chapter 8.

14. Because Rule 605 only deems a judge to be incompetent as a witness in a trial over which he presides, it follows that a judge is in all other cases competent to serve as a fact or character witness. *E.g., United States v. Munoz-Franco*, 203 F. Supp. 2d 102, 106 (D.P.R. 2002). However, where a judge is called as a *character* witness, a court may exercise its discretion under Rule 403 to exclude such testimony where there is a risk that the jury would give the testimony undue weight because of the judge's position. *Id.* at 106–111 (excluding evidence where it is cumulative and judge called as a witness was the presiding judge in a courtroom next to the one in which trial was held).

15. What is the relationship between Rule 601 on the one hand and Rules 605 and 606 on the other? In other words, suppose the case is a civil action or proceeding in which state law supplies the rule of decision, the competency of the judge or a juror to testify arises, and the equivalent state rules of competency are materially different from Federal Rules 605 and 606. Does the general command of the second sentence of Rule 601 require the federal court to apply state competency law, or do the more specific commands of Rules 605 and 606 control? *See Wiedemann v. Galiano*, 722 F.2d 335, 337 (7th Cir. 1983) (holding that specific command of Rule 606 governs). *See also* 27 Charles Alan Wright & Arthur R. Miller, Federal Practice and Procedure §§ 6063, 6074 (2d ed. 1997 & Supp. 2011) (raising the issue and concluding that the specific command of Rules 605 and 606 control).

B. Oath Requirement

United States v. Ward
989 F.2d 1015 (9th Cir. 1992)

FLETCHER, Circuit Judge....

On March 29, 1990 a grand jury indicted Ward on three counts each of tax evasion and failure to file income tax returns. Ward chose to represent himself at trial. On July 9, 1990, Ward filed a "Motion to Challenge the Oath," which proposed an alternative oath that replaced the word "truth" with the phrase "fully integrated Honesty." The oath would read, "Do you affirm to speak with fully integrated Honesty, only with fully integrated Honesty and nothing but fully integrated Honesty?" For reasons we will not attempt to explain,

Ward believes that honesty is superior to truth. Magistrate Lawrence R. Leavitt ruled on August 2, 1990 that "the oath or affirmation which has been administered in courts of law throughout the United States to millions of witnesses for hundreds of years should not be required to give way to the defendant's idiosyncratic distinctions between truth and honesty." The district court overruled Ward's objections to the magistrate's order....

A three-day trial commenced on February 11, 1991. Ward made a lengthy opening statement and actively cross-examined government witnesses. At a sidebar during the second day of trial, Ward offered to take both the standard oath and his oath. The prosecutor was amenable to the compromise, but the district court refused to allow it. "This is an oath that has been used for a very long time," the district court said, "And I'm not going to establish a precedent where someone can come in and require the court to address that matter differently." At the close of the government's case on the third day of trial, Ward asked once again to testify under his oath. The judge again refused, saying "[T]he oath has been used for a very long time.... That's the oath that will be administered." Ward did not testify and presented no witnesses. The jury convicted Ward of all counts after an hour's deliberation.

Ward now appeals. He argues that the district court's insistence on an oath that violated his beliefs abridged his First Amendment right to free exercise of religion and his Fifth Amendment right to testify in his own defense....

Judges may not determine the truth or falsity of matters of faith. Even so, we must determine as a threshold matter whether Ward's beliefs are within the ambit of the First Amendment. In order for Ward to invoke "the protection of the Religion Clauses, [his] claims must be rooted in religious belief." *Wisconsin v. Yoder*, 406 U.S. 205, 215 (1972)....

In determining whether Ward's own peculiar notions are protected as religious beliefs, "[the] task is to decide whether the beliefs professed ... are sincerely held and whether they are, in [Ward's] own scheme of things, religious." ... While there can be no question that a "purely secular philosophical concern [ ]," *Callahan v. Woods*, 658 F.2d 679, 683 (9th Cir. 1981), is not encompassed by the free exercise clause, we conclude that the "generous functional (and even idiosyncratic) definition [of religion and religious beliefs in the] free exercise [context]," *Grove v. Mead School District*, 753 F.2d 1528, 1537 (9th Cir.) (Canby, J., concurring), *cert. denied*, 474 U.S. 826 (1985), includes Ward's system of principles.

To the extent that the free exercise clause does not protect "so-called religions which ... are obviously shams and absurdities and whose members are patently devoid of religious sincerity," *Callahan*, 658 F.2d at 683, the focus of the judicial inquiry is not definitional, but rather devotional. That is, is Ward sincere? Are his beliefs held with the strength of traditional religious convictions? Ward does not describe his beliefs in terms ordinarily used in discussions of theology or cosmology (although he at one point uses the term "atheistic"), but he clearly attempts to express a moral or ethical sense of right and wrong. Ward's actions are evidence of the strength of his beliefs. He strongly professes innocence of the crimes charged, yet he preferred to risk conviction and incarceration rather than abandon his version of the oath. Compelling him to testify under the "truth" oath would, he says, "profoundly violate" his "freedom of belief" and run counter to the "convictions that are the central theme of all his published books and writings for the past 22 years." This is the sincerity of true religious conviction. We conclude that Ward professes beliefs that are protected by the First Amendment.

The court's interest in administering its precise form of oath must yield to Ward's First Amendment rights. To begin with, there is no constitutionally or statutorily required form of oath. Federal Rule of Evidence 603 requires only that a witness [give an oath or affirmation to testify truthfully in a form designed to impress that duty on the witness's conscience.] The advisory committee notes to Rule 603 explain that "the rule is designed to afford the flexibility required in dealing with religious adults, atheists, conscientious objectors, mental defectives, and children. Affirmation is simply a solemn undertaking to tell the truth; no special verbal formula is required." This rule represents no break with the common law....

> All that the common law requires is a form or statement which impresses upon the mind and conscience of a witness the necessity for telling the truth. Thus, defendant's privilege to testify may not be denied him solely because he would not accede to a form of oath or affirmation not required by the common law.... [A]ll the district judge need do is to make inquiry as to what form of oath or affirmation would not offend defendant's religious beliefs but would give rise to a duty to speak the truth.

U.S. v. Looper, 419 F.2d 1405, 1407 (4th Cir. 1969)....

While oaths including the familiar "truth, whole truth, and nothing but the truth" formulation date back at least to the seventeenth century, the principle that the form of the oath must be crafted in a way that is meaningful to the witness also predates our constitution. In *Omichund v. Barker*, 1 Atk. 22, 45 (1744), Lord Chief Judge Willes wrote, "It would be absurd for [a non-Christian witness] to swear according to the Christian oath, which he does not believe; and therefore, out of necessity, he must be allowed to swear according to his own notion of an oath."

This case has an odd twist in that the defendant offered to take the traditional "truth" oath, but only if he were permitted to also take his "fully integrated honesty" oath. In Ward's view, as best we can state it, only his oath expressed a commitment to the abstract purity of absolute "fully integrated honesty" that must be extracted from anyone before that person's word can be relied upon. The standard "truth" oath was so much surplusage—distasteful, wrong, but not necessarily a mortal sin to take.

His own oath superimposed on the traditional one would have taken nothing away from the commitment to tell the truth under penalties of perjury and, indeed, in the defendant's mind imposed upon him a higher duty. Under these circumstances the district court clearly abused its discretion in refusing the oath and preventing the defendant's testimony. We do not have a case where the witness offers to swear only to a cleverly worded oath that creates loopholes for falsehood or attempts to create a safe harbor for perjury as in *United States v. Fowler*, 605 F.2d 181, 185 (5th Cir. 1979), where the court properly refused testimony from a defendant who would not say so much as "I state that I will tell the truth in my testimony," and was willing to say only "I am a truthful man" or "I would not tell a lie to stay out of jail." Ward's "attempt[ ] to express a moral or ethical sense of right and wrong," *Welsh*, 398 U.S. at 340, coupled with the de rigueur fervor, brings his beliefs squarely within those safeguarded by the free exercise clause....

POOLE, Circuit Judge, dissenting....

It is axiomatic that even the most sincere of beliefs is not entitled to the protection of the Free Exercise clause unless it is rooted in religion....

I believe that Ward's objection to the oath ordinarily required of witnesses by Fed.R.Evid. 603 amounts to nothing more than a philosophical predilection....

Even were I to give Ward the benefit of the doubt and ascribe religious significance to his "ultimate concern" with the merits of the word "honesty," I would still decline to require the district court to accommodate his objection. The district court must modify the oath to reflect genuinely held objections to it, but the court must also satisfy itself that the witness has committed himself to speak the truth. It is not enough that the witness says he knows of his obligation to do so; there must be a promise based on the awareness that failure to be honest is punishable under our law.... Ward's proposed alternative oath does not contain an acknowledgment of the *duty* to speak truthfully and does not ensure that the defendant is aware of the cost of dishonesty....

Notes and Questions

1. How critical is it in *Ward* that the defendant was willing to take *both* his preferred oath *and* the standard oath? Would the defendant's preferred oath, standing alone, satisfy the requirements of Rule 603?

2. As the Advisory Committee Note to Rule 603 indicates, the rule's flexibility is designed not only to accommodate religious beliefs, but also to ensure that the oath can be administered to children and the mentally incapacitated in a manner that makes sense to them. Thus, for example, Rule 603 can be satisfied in this context by a colloquy between the judge and the witness that establishes that the witness "appreciated the difference between truth and falsehood and that he knew it would be improper to lie...." *United States v. Thai*, 29 F.3d 785, 811–12 (2d Cir. 1994).

3. Although Rule 603 indicates that a witness will make the required declaration by oath or affirmation, and although the Advisory Committee Note to Rule 603 defines the word "affirmation" as a "solemn undertaking," a witness cannot be required to use the words "solemnly" or "affirm" if he objects to those on religious grounds; it is enough that he declare that he will testify truthfully and that he understands his obligation to do so. *See Ferguson v. CIR*, 921 F.2d 588, 588–91 (5th Cir. 1991).

4. Some witnesses require the aid of an interpreter to testify in court. Such interpreters are required to take a more particular "oath or affirmation to make a true translation" under Rule 604.

C. Direct and Cross-Examination of Witnesses

In a typical case, each party takes turns presenting his case. The proponent—the party who bears the burden of persuasion (the government in a criminal case and the plaintiff in a civil case)—will go first, presenting his case-in-chief. In general, the proponent has a great degree of control over the order of his case: he may generally call his witnesses and introduce documentary and physical evidence in the order that he wishes, and he need not present evidence in any sort of topical or chronological order. He must, however, during his case-in-chief present sufficient evidence to establish each of the elements of the claims or offenses.

After the proponent presents his case-in-chief, the opposing party will present his case-in-reply. Like the party bearing the burden of persuasion, the opposing party also has substantial control over the order in which he will present his case. During his case-in-reply, a party needs to present whatever evidence he can to cast doubt on the elements of the plaintiff's claim, as well as sufficient evidence to establish the elements of any affirmative defenses.

Once the opposing party has completed his case-in-reply, the initial party will get a chance to present his case-in-rebuttal. The case-in-rebuttal is much narrower than the case-in-chief, its only purpose being to meet the evidence introduced by the opposing party during his case-in-reply. Thus, for example, he may call witnesses calculated to impeach the credibility of witnesses called by the opposing party during his case-in-reply, introduce evidence to rehabilitate the credibility of any of his witnesses whose credibility was impeached during the case-in-reply, or introduce evidence calculated to cast doubt on the elements of any of the affirmative defenses raised during the opposing party's case-in-reply.

Once the case-in-rebuttal is completed, the opposing party has an opportunity to present his case-in-rejoinder. The case-in-rejoinder is much narrower than the case-in-reply, its only purpose being to meet the evidence introduced by the proponent during his case-in-rebuttal. Further rebuttal and rejoinder stages may follow as necessary.

Within each case, the examination of each individual witness also typically proceeds in a series of narrowing phases that are somewhat analogous to the phases of the parties' cases. First, the witness is subject to direct examination by the party who called him as a witness. It is expected that during direct examination of a witness, the calling party will obtain all of the witness' testimony in his favor. Thus, just as a party during his case-in-chief must introduce all the evidence he needs to establish the elements of the claim or offense, so a party calling a witness on direct examination needs to ask all the questions that he has of that witness.

Once a calling party has completed direct examination of his witness, the opposing party has the opportunity to cross-examine the witness. While at English common law, cross-examination could delve into any matter relevant in the case, U.S. practice as a general rule limits the scope of cross-examination to matters testified to on direct examination plus any matters bearing on the witness' credibility. Under this general rule, if the cross-examining party has a use for a witness that extends to matters not raised by the calling party on direct examination, then the cross-examining party should call the witness himself during his case-in-reply rather than trying to build his case in the middle of the calling party's case-in-chief. Once cross-examination is completed, it may be followed by narrower rounds of re-direct and re-cross examination designed to clarify testimony from the prior round and to rebut any false impressions that might have been created by the questioning in the prior round.

As a general rule, witnesses do not just get up on the stand and tell their stories. Rather, examination of a witness typically proceeds in a somewhat cumbersome question-and-answer form:

> May not the witness narrate his knowledge in *continuous speech* and without the interruption of questions?

> It is obvious that this method, on the one hand, has often the advantage of preserving continuity and clearness of thought for the witness himself and of saving time for all parties concerned.... On the other hand, continuous narration has the disadvantage of risking the witness' interjection of irrelevant and inadmissible matter (chiefly hearsay) without any opportunity for the opponent to know beforehand in time to object and to prevent it. The latter reason has prevailed increasingly during the past century in the United States, so that the general if not the universal practice is for the witness to narrate, on the direct examination, only by *giving answers to questions framed by counsel.*

3 Wigmore, Evidence § 767, at 148–49 (Chadbourn rev. 1970).

In addition to being conducted in question-and-answer form, questioning generally proceeds by the use of non-leading questions. What are leading questions and why are they forbidden as a general rule?

> The essential test of a leading question is whether it so suggests to the witness the specific tenor of the reply desired by counsel that such a reply is likely to be given irrespective of an actual memory. The evil to be avoided is that of supplying a false memory for the witness.

United States v. Durham, 319 F.2d 590, 592 (4th Cir. 1963). *Accord* 3 Wigmore, Evidence §769, at 154–55 (Chadbourn rev. 1970).

Although all that has been said thus far is true as a general matter, there are exceptions. Sometimes parties *will* be required to call their witnesses in a particular order. Sometimes cross-examination *will* be permitted that goes beyond the scope of direct examination. Sometimes witnesses *will* give a narrative rather than testifying in question-and-answer form. And sometimes leading questions *will* be allowed.

Rather than establishing hard-and-fast rules to govern the mode and order of examining witnesses and presenting evidence, Rule 611(a) vests trial courts with broad discretion over such matters, providing us follows:

> The court should exercise reasonable control over the mode and order of examining witnesses and presenting evidence so as to:
>
> (1) make those procedures effective for determining the truth;
>
> (2) avoid wasting time; and
>
> (3) protect witnesses from harassment or undue embarrassment.

Rule 611(a) empowers trial courts to require that evidence be presented in some sort of chronological or topical order, to require that witnesses testify in a particular order, to decide whether and to what extent re-direct and re-cross examination of witnesses will be permitted, or to allow a party to re-open her case when she has inadvertently failed to introduce any evidence on a particular element.

Similarly, a trial court has discretion to allow a witness to testify in narrative form rather than in question-and-answer form. *E.g., United States v. Pless*, 982 F.2d 1118, 1123 (7th Cir. 1992). Thus, a party who is proceeding *pro se* need not be required to ask and answer his own questions! *But see United States v. Nivica*, 887 F.2d 1110, 1120 (1st Cir. 1989) (requiring *pro se* defendant to do just that!). Rule 611(a) also gives trial courts discretion to impose time limits on the presentation of evidence and to check abusive behavior by attorneys against witnesses.

Rule 611(b) governs the appropriate scope of cross-examination. As initially proposed by the Advisory Committee, Rule 611(b) would have allowed for questioning on any relevant matter on cross-examination, without regard to the scope of the direct examination, subject to the trial court's discretion to limit cross-examination that exceeded the scope of direct examination. One rationale for such a rule was convenience for the witness, as it eliminates the need for him to return later to be examined by opposing counsel on those points. Yet another rationale for the proposal was to eliminate disputes over whether or not something fell within the scope of the direct examination:

> Obviously, the wide-open rule presents little or no opportunity for dispute in its application. The restrictive practice in all its forms, on the other hand, is productive in many court rooms, of continual bickering over the choice of the numerous variations of the 'scope of the direct' criterion, and of their application

to particular cross-questions. These controversies are often reventilated on appeal, and reversals for error in their determination are frequent.

Advisory Committee Note to Rule 611(b).

Congress, however, chose to reverse the Advisory Committee's proposal, providing for a general rule in the first sentence that cross-examination should be limited to the scope of the direct examination and matters affecting the witness' credibility, but giving the trial court discretion in the second sentence to permit inquiry on cross-examination that goes beyond the scope of the direct examination.

Rule 611(c) governs the use of leading questions. It provides as follows:

> Leading questions should not be used on direct examination except as necessary to develop the witness's testimony. Ordinarily, the court should allow leading questions:
>
> (1) on cross-examination; and
>
> (2) when a party calls a hostile witness, an adverse party, or a witness identified with an adverse party.

Thus, as a general rule, leading questions are barred on direct examination but permitted on cross-examination. What justifies treating the two situations differently as a general matter?

> The typical situation in which the witness' presumable bias removes all danger of improper suggestion is that of an *opponent's witness, under cross-examination.* The purpose of the cross-examination is to sift his testimony and weaken its force, in short, to discredit the direct testimony. Thus, not only the presumable bias of the witness for the opponent's cause, but also his sense of reluctance to become the instrument of his own discrediting, deprive him of any inclination to accept the cross-examiner's suggestions unless the truth forces him to.

3 Wigmore, Evidence § 773, at 165 (Chadbourn rev. 1970).

However, neither the ability to use leading questions on cross-examination nor the bar on the use of leading questions on direct examination are absolute. With regard to cross-examination, a proviso to Rule 611(b) provides that when the trial court exercises its discretion to allow questioning on cross-examination that goes beyond the scope of the direct examination, questioning shall proceed "as if on direct examination," meaning that leading questions are allowed only in the instances in which they would be allowed on direct examination. The reason for this is that, absent the proviso, the cross-examining party would have had to call that individual as a witness during his own case and would have had to proceed through the use of non-leading questions, and the result should be no different where, for convenience, he is allowed to ask the questions on cross-examination. Moreover, as the Advisory Committee note to Rule 611(c) explains:

> The purpose of the qualification "ordinarily" is to furnish a basis for denying the use of leading questions when the cross-examination is cross-examination in form only and not in fact, as for example the "cross-examination" of a party by his own counsel after being called by the opponent (savoring more of re-direct) or of an insured defendant who proves to be friendly to the plaintiff.

Advisory Committee Note to Rule 611(c).

With regard to direct examination (including cross-examination that proceeds "as if on direct examination"), several exceptions to the bar on leading questions are recognized. First, courts will often allow the use of leading questions on undisputed preliminary matters, such as the witness' name, age, occupation, and residence. For example, although the question, "Your name is Martha Jones, right?" is a leading question, there is no risk of undue suggestion with regard to such matters.

Second, leading questions can be used where a party calls as a witness someone who is hostile toward that party, which includes the opposing party herself and those affiliated with that party, as well as someone who is simply unwilling to be cooperative for whatever reason. The reasons for excepting such witnesses from the bar on leading questions are analogous to the reasons for generally permitting such questions on cross-examination: the witness is unlikely to be led by the questioner's suggestions.

Third, Rule 611(c) allows for leading questions "as necessary to develop the witness's testimony." One use for this exception is where the witness is very young, mentally incapacitated, or timid. While the risk of using leading questions in such a situation seems particularly high, the alternative is not to obtain any testimony at all, and the hope is that the jury will be able to determine whether the witness is being led or not. In addition, this language also encompasses the use of leading questions to help refresh a witness' memory.

Leading questions, however, are not the only means of trying to refresh a witness' memory. The cases that follow explore other methods of refreshing a witness' memory, as well as the consequences of using written documents to refresh a witness' memory.

United States v. Riccardi
174 F.2d 883 (3d Cir. 1949)

KALODNER, Circuit Judge.

The defendant was indicted under 18 U.S.C. (1940 ed.) Sections 415 and 417 in four counts charging him with wilfully, unlawfully and feloniously having transported or having caused to be transported in interstate commerce certain chattels of the value of $5,000 or more....

[W]e are called upon to decide the propriety of the method utilized at the trial to prove what chattels the defendant obtained and transported, and their value. In short, the principal question is whether the witnesses who testified to these essentials were properly permitted to refresh their memory....

The chattels involved are numerous items of bric-a-brac, linens, silverware, and other household articles of quality and distinction. They were the property of Doris Farid es Sultaneh, and were kept in her home at Morristown, New Jersey, from which the defendant is alleged to have transported them to Arizona in a truck and station wagon. The defendant did not deny receiving some of the lady's chattels, but did deny both the quantity and quality alleged....

To prove the specific chattels involved, the government relied on the testimony of Doris Farid; to prove their value, it relied on the testimony of an expert, one Leo Berlow.

Farid testified that as the chattels were being moved from the house, she made longhand notes, and that later she copied these notes on her typewriter. Only one of the original notes was produced, and became part of the evidence of the case, a search by Farid having failed to disclose the others. The government sought to have Farid testify with respect to the chattels by using the typewritten notes for the purpose of refreshing her recollection. Although the defendant's objection was overruled, the government, on the next day of the trial, submitted to Farid lists of chattels taken out of a copy of the indictment, but from which had been deleted such information as dates and values. With the aid of these lists, the witness testified that her recollection was refreshed[4] and that she presently recognized and could identify each item. She was then permitted to read the lists aloud, and testified that she knew that the items were loaded on the truck or station wagon, as the case was. The lists were neither offered nor received in evidence.

The expert, Berlow, testified that he had visited Doris Farid's home on numerous occasions in his professional capacity as dealer in antiques, bric-a-brac, etc.; that he was very familiar with the furnishings therein, having examined the household for the purpose of buying items from Farid or selling them for her on commission. He was shown the same lists which Farid had used to refresh her recollection, and with their aid testified that he could recall the items individually, with some exceptions; that he remembered them to the extent that he could not only describe the items, but in many instances could state where in the house he had seen them; and that he could give an opinion as to their value. This he was permitted to do....

Refreshing the recollection of a witness is not an uncommon trial practice, but as a theory of evidentiary law its content and application are far from clear.... Professor Wigmore separated, broadly, what he called "past recollection recorded" from "present recollection revived," attributing much of the confusion in the cases to a failure to make this distinction and to the use of the phrase "refreshing the recollection" for both classes of testimony. The primary difference between the two classifications is the ability of the witness to testify from present knowledge: where the witness' memory is revived, and he presently recollects the facts and swears to them, he is obviously in a different position from the witness who cannot directly state the facts from present memory and who must ask the court to accept a writing for the truth of its contents because he is willing to swear, for one reason or another, that its contents are true....

The difference between present recollection revived and past recollection recorded has a demonstrable effect upon the method of proof. In the instance of past recollection recorded, the witness, by hypothesis, has no present recollection of the matter contained in the writing. Whether the record is directly admitted into evidence, or indirectly by the permissive parroting of the witness, it is nevertheless a substitute for his memory and is offered for the truth of its contents. It assumes a distinct significance as an independent probative force, and is therefore ordinarily required to meet certain standards. These requirements are the more understandable in consideration of the fact that the court is at once desirous of determining whether the writing may be safely received as a substitute for the witness' memory and for the truth of the matter therein asserted, and of affording to the trier of fact information upon which it can form a reliable judgment as to its worth for the purposes offered.

In the case of present recollection revived, the witness, by hypothesis, relates his present recollection, and under oath and subject to cross-examination asserts that it is true; his capacities for memory and perception may be attacked and tested; his determination to tell the truth investigated and revealed; protestations of lack of memory, which escape

---

4. For example, at page 140a of Appellant's Appendix:
   "The Court: Well, Madam, as you look at that list does it refresh your recollection?
   "The Witness: I lived with these things, your Honor, I know them.
   "The Court: You lived with them yourself?
   "The Witness: I did.
   "The Court: So when you look at that paper, it does refresh your recollection?
   "The Witness: Absolutely."

criticism and indeed constitute a refuge in the situation of past recollection recorded, merely undermine the probative worth of his testimony. It is in recognition of these factors that we find:

"The law of cotemporary writing or entry qualifying it as primary evidence has no application. The primary evidence here is not the writing. It was not introduced in evidence. It was not offered. The primary evidence is the oral statement of the hostile witness. It is not so important when the statement was made or by whom if it serves the purpose to refresh the mind and unfold the truth." *Hoffman v. United States*, 9 Cir., 1937, 87 F.2d 410, 411.

"When a party uses an earlier statement of his own witness to refresh the witness' memory, the only evidence recognized as such is the testimony so refreshed. * * * Anything may in fact revive a memory: a song, a scent, a photograph, an allusion, even a past statement known to be false. When a witness declares that any of these has evoked a memory, the opposite party may show, either that it has not evoked what appears to the witness as a memory, or that, although it may so appear to him, the memory is a phantom and not a reliable record of its content. When the evoking stimulus is not itself an account of the relevant occasion, no question of its truth can arise; but when it is an account of that occasion, its falsity, if raised by the opposing party, will become a relevant issue if the witness has declared that the evoked memory accords with it. * * *" *United States v. Rappy*, 2 Cir., 1947, 157 F.2d 964, 967–968, certiorari denied 329 U.S. 806....

Of course, the categories, present recollection revived and past recollection recorded, are clearest in their extremes, but they are, in practice, converging rather than parallel lines; the difference is frequently one of degree....

Properly, the burden to ascertain the state of affairs, as near as may be, devolves upon the trial judge, who should in the first instance satisfy himself as to whether the witness testifies upon a record or from his own recollection. It is upon this satisfaction that the reception of the evidence depends, for if it appear to the court that the witness is wholly dependent for the fact upon the memorandum he holds in his hand, the memorandum acquires a significance which, as stated, brings into operation certain guiding rules. Similarly, the trial judge must determine whether the device of refreshing recollection is merely a subterfuge to improperly suggest to the witness the testimony expected of him....

In the instant case, the learned trial judge determined that both Farid and the expert, Berlow, testified from present recollection. On the record, we cannot say that it was plainly not so. Both witnesses stated that they knew the chattels and could identify them. Farid, who testified that she was present and helped to pack them, said she could remember which were transported; Berlow said he could give an opinion of their value. On a number of occasions the trial judge investigated the foundations of their claim to present recollection and satisfied himself as to its bona fides.... While the defendant asserts that neither Farid nor Berlow did more, the trial judge immediately recognized that the items of property involved were so numerous that in the ordinary course of events no one would be expected to recite them without having learned a list by rote memory. On the other hand, the items were such that a person familiar with them reasonably could be expected to recognize them and tell what he knows. Under these circumstances, the District Judge might well have permitted the government, in lieu of the procedure followed, to ask Farid leading questions, directing her attention to specific items, and asking her whether she knew what happened to them. This is especially true of Berlow, who did not purport to have any knowledge of the movement of the articles. Clearly, it would have been pointless to ask him to give the value of every article he had ever seen in Farid's home. The same

result could have been achieved legitimately without the use of the lists by orally directing his attention to any specific article previously identified by Farid and asking him
whether he had seen it, presently remembered it, and could give an opinion as to its value.
By the use of lists, nothing more or different was accomplished....

In the long run, the primary issue of the case was that of credibility, and it is sufficient that the jury had as sound a basis for weighing the testimony as it would in any
other instance. The defense had at its disposal the customary opportunities and all the
necessary material to test the witness' recollection and other testimonial qualifications,
including the single original longhand list which Farid located, the typewritten lists which
she said were made at the time of the events involved, and the lists the prosecution
used....

Nutramax Laboratories, Inc. v. Twin Laboratories, Inc.
183 F.R.D. 458 (D. Md. 1998)

GRIMM, United States Magistrate Judge.

BACKGROUND

This case consists of six lawsuits, consolidated for discovery, against more than twenty
defendants involving the patents of the plaintiff, Nutramax.... Pending is the defendants'
motion to compel the production of various documents used by counsel for the plaintiff
to prepare a number of witnesses, including management officials of Nutramax, for their
depositions.... By order dated July 20, 1998, I permitted the defendants to take a series
of depositions during the first phase of discovery, for the limited purpose of developing
facts relevant to the defense that the patents at issue in this case are invalid because Nutramax allegedly marketed Cosamin—the product now covered by its patents—more
than one year before it applied for the first patent, the so called "on sale bar" defense....

During the depositions, counsel for the defendants sought to determine whether sales
of Cosamin had occurred before March 31, 1992, the critical date for purposes of the "on
sale bar" defense. Predictably, the deponents' testimony was less than what the defendants expected. To test the accuracy of their memories, counsel for the defendants asked
whether the witnesses had reviewed any documents before their depositions to assist them
in recalling the events relating to the first sale of Cosamin. Although it was acknowledged
that documents had been reviewed with counsel for Nutramax during deposition preparation, the witnesses were instructed not to answer all questions designed to discover
their identity. The basis for the instruction not to answer was Nutramax's assertion of
the work product rule.[4] Contending that Fed.R.Evid. 612 entitles them to the production
of documents used to refresh the recollection of a witness prior to a deposition, the defendants filed a motion to compel the production of the documents used to prepare the
Nutramax witnesses....

DISCUSSION

The issue presented in this case, whether Fed.R.Evid. 612 requires the production of
work product materials used to prepare a witness for a deposition, but not used during
the deposition itself to refresh the witnesses' recollection, is an important one....

---

4. While instructions not to answer questions during depositions are generally improper, a witness may be instructed not to answer a question if the answer would reveal privileged information.
See Fed.R.Civ.P. 30(d)(1); Local Discovery Guideline 5(d) (D.Md.1997); *Boyd v. University of Maryland Med. Sys.*, 173 F.R.D. 143, 144 (D.Md.1997).

In preparing to defend depositions in cases where substantial document production has taken place, no competent counsel can afford to ignore reviewing with witnesses the documents which relate to critical issues. During a deposition, counsel questioning a witness will seldom fail to ask the witness about what he or she did to prepare for the deposition, and the identity of any documents reviewed for this purpose. Most often, this inquiry is not resisted by counsel defending the deposition, because the documents have already been produced to the opposing counsel. However, where, as here, many thousands of pages of documents have been produced and counsel have analyzed them and selected a population of "critical documents" relevant to case dispositive issues, a deposition question aimed at discovering what documents were reviewed to prepare for a deposition may draw an assertion of the work product doctrine, and an instruction not to answer. In response, the deposing attorney may contend that if the witness used the documents to prepare for the deposition, then work product immunity has been waived, and Fed.R.Evid. 612 requires the production of the documents. As will be seen, there is support in the case law and treatises for both sides of this argument, and it has been recognized that there is a clear conflict between Fed.R.Civ.P. 26(b)(3), which codifies the work product doctrine, and Fed.R.Evid. 612, which has been held to apply during depositions by virtue of Fed.R.Civ.P. 30(c)....

[Rule 612] in its present form marks a substantial departure from the common law and the original version of the rules of evidence, which limited production of documents used to refresh recollection to those actually used while the witness was testifying....*

[T]he legislative history of Rule 612 is somewhat ambiguous, because the rule itself is silent with respect to whether it applies to work product materials used to refresh recollection. It does appear, however, as though the House Committee on the Judiciary did not intend the rule to operate in such a way that it would allow a "fishing expedition" into the documents a witness may have referred to in preparing for trial, nor did that committee intend for it to bar "the assertion of a privilege with respect to writings used by a witness to refresh his memory." H.Rep. No. 650, 93rd Cong., 1st Sess. (1973), *reprinted in* 1974 U.S.C.C.A.N. 7075, 7086.

Because of the apparent conflict between Evidence Rule 612 and the work product doctrine, as codified in Fed.R.Civ.P. 26(b)(3), courts have looked for various ways to harmonize the two rules. The process has produced inconsistent results, with some courts concluding that work product materials which were reviewed by a witness prior to being deposed were subject to disclosure under Rule 612, and others concluding that they were not.

As a threshold matter, three foundational elements must be met before Rule 612 is applicable with respect to documents reviewed by a witness to prepare for a deposition: (1) a witness must use a writing to refresh his or her memory; (2) for the purpose of testifying; and (3) the court must determine that, in the interest of justice, the adverse party is entitled to see the writing. The first element insures that the writing is relevant to an attempt to test the credibility of the deponent. The second element safeguards against use of Rule 612 "as a pretext for wholesale exploration of an opposing party's files" and

---

* Editor's Note: In pertinent part, Rule 612(a) states that "[t]his rule gives an adverse party certain options when a witness uses a writing to refresh memory: (1) while testifying; or (2) before testifying, if the court decides that justice requires the party to have those options," while Rule 612(b) provides that "an adverse party is entitled to have the writing produced at the hearing, to inspect it, to cross-examine the witness about it, and to introduce in evidence any portion that relates to the witness's testimony."

insures "that access is limited only to those writings which may fairly be said in part to have an impact upon the testimony of the witness," because only writings which actually influenced a witness' testimony are of utility in impeachment and cross-examination. If the first two elements are not met, then the inquiry ends, as Rule 612 is inapplicable. However, if the first two elements are met, then it safely may be concluded that the documents have been put to a testimonial use for purposes of work product doctrine analysis. Whether disclosure is required then turns on the third element of Rule 612.

The third element requires the court to apply a balancing test designed to weigh the policies underlying the work product doctrine against the need for disclosure to promote effective cross-examination and impeachment.

At either end of the spectrum, it is easy to identify the goal to be served by the balancing test. On the one hand, a court must protect against disclosure of an opposing attorney's deliberative process, legal theories, case analysis, and trial preparation. On the other, courts must not allow attorneys to "exceed decent limits of preparation." *Berkey Photo*, 74 F.R.D. at 616–17. Expressed somewhat differently, the work product doctrine protects legitimate efforts to prepare a case, which include preparation of witnesses for deposition and trial testimony. These efforts do not extend, however, to manufacturing favorable testimony, or concealing unfavorable testimony. In balancing the competing interests between disclosure and the work product rule at the third step of Rule 612 analysis, the following factors should be considered.

(1) The status of the witness. Most witnesses testify about facts within their personal knowledge, as required by Fed.R.Evid. 602. Others, however, are not so restricted. Expert witnesses, for example, may base their opinions on information supplied by others, if reliable. Fed.R.Evid. 703. Similarly, Fed.R.Civ.P. 30(b)(6) allows a party to designate a witness to testify on its behalf with respect to specified subjects. The testimony of such witnesses also is not limited to matters within their personal knowledge, but extends to "matters known or reasonably available to" the party designating the witness. Rule 30(b)(6). There is a greater need to know what materials were reviewed by expert and designee witnesses in preparation for deposition since the substance of their testimony may be based on sources beyond personal knowledge. (2) The nature of the issue in dispute. Whether a witness is testifying generally about the transactions which are the subject of the litigation, or more precisely about a subset of facts which relate to a case dispositive issue (such as a statute of limitations defense, or, as in this case, the on sale bar defense) may affect the need to know what materials were reviewed to prepare for deposition. (3) When the events took place. Whether the events about which the witness will testify took place recently, or years ago, affects the need to know what materials were reviewed. The ability of a witness to perceive, remember, and relate events is fair game for cross examination, and a deposing attorney has a legitimate need to know whether the witness is testifying from present memory, unaided by any review of extrinsic information, present memory "refreshed" by reference to other materials, or really has no present memory at all, and can only "testify" as to what is memorialized in writings prepared by the witness or others. The greater the passage of time since the events about which the witness will testify, the more likely that the witness needed to refresh his or her recollection to prepare for testimony. (4) When the documents were reviewed. As noted, Fed.R.Evid. 612 only applies to use of documents to refresh recollection for purposes of providing testimony. Thus, review of documents for purposes other than deposition or trial testimony is exempt from the rule. In complex cases, or cases involving many documents, counsel may have many occasions to review with clients documents which relate to the issues in the litigation, such as preparation of pleadings or motions, responding to Fed.R.Civ.P. 34 document

production requests, and development of case strategy. Such review is not for purposes of providing testimony. Accordingly, if a witness reviewed documents months before a deposition, for a purpose other than to prepare to testify, disclosure of the documents reviewed should not be required in response to a Rule 612 demand. The nearer the review of documents to the date of the deposition may affect whether the court concludes that the purpose was to prepare for testimony. (5) The number of documents reviewed. Whether a witness reviewed hundreds of documents, as opposed to a few critical ones, may affect the decision whether to order the disclosure of work product materials in response to a Rule 612 demand. If an attorney has culled through thousands of documents to identify a population of several hundred which are most relevant to the litigation, and the witness reviews these documents to prepare for the deposition, a court may be less inclined to order the production of such work product than if the witness reviewed a single document, or very few documents, selected by the attorney which relate to a critical issue in the case.[20] (6) Whether the witness prepared the document(s) reviewed. If the witness prepared the document(s) reviewed in preparation for the deposition, particularly if they were prepared in the ordinary course of the events underlying the dispute, and not in anticipation of litigation, there may be a greater need for disclosure than if the witness reviewed documents prepared by others. (7) Whether the documents reviewed contain, in whole or part, "pure" attorney work product, such as discussion of case strategy, theories or mental impressions, which would require redaction or favor nondisclosure. (8) Whether the documents reviewed previously have been disclosed to the party taking the deposition, as part of a Fed.R.Civ.P. 34 document production, or otherwise. It may be argued that, if the deposing attorney already has received the documents during the litigation, there is no reason to order their production a second time, for the only purpose this would serve would be to disclose, indirectly, the mental impressions of the attorney who selected the documents to review with the witness. However, the forcefulness of this argument may diminish if the documents previously produced are so voluminous or technical that the party receiving them cannot readily be expected to grasp their significance. Finding the critical documents in a population of thousands may be like looking for a needle in a haystack, even with the aid of modern technology. (9) Whether there are credible concerns regarding manipulation, concealment or destruction of evidence. If the court believes that there may have been inappropriate conduct affecting either testimonial or documentary evidence in the case, and the documents demanded under Rule 612 relate to these concerns, then disclosure may be required.

The foregoing list is illustrative, not exhaustive, and the weight to be assigned to each factor may vary on a case-by-case basis. To make the determinations required by these factors may, unavoidably, require in camera review, a process favored by the learned commentators who have addressed this issue....

State ex. rel. Polytech, Inc. v. Voorhees
895 S.W.2d 13 (Mo. 1995) (en banc)

BENTON, Judge.

Polytech, Inc., sued its broker, Sedgwick James of Missouri, Inc., for not securing sufficient insurance. During his deposition, Douglas Hazel, an officer of Polytech, admitted

---

20. The opposite result may also be reached. It is possible that the selection of a single, or very few documents, by an attorney out of a much larger population, could be viewed by the court as more revealing of the attorney's deliberative process than the selection of a few hundred out of thousands.

summarizing on one page—at Polytech counsel's request—his involvement with the broker. Hazel testified that he gave the document to Polytech's attorney and later reviewed it for his deposition.

Sedgwick requested the document; Polytech objected. Sedgwick then sought to compel disclosure because Hazel used it to prepare for his deposition....

The traditional Missouri rule is that a witness need not produce a document used to refresh recollection *before* testifying....

The alternative to the Missouri rule is the federal rule, which permits disclosure if a witness uses a writing to refresh memory before testifying.... The federal rule has caused "uncertainty" in the federal courts, with widely varying results. The federal rule weakens the attorney-client and work product privileges, both by actual disclosure and by the chilling effect of potential disclosure of documents.

The Missouri rule advances the attorney-client and work product privileges by prohibiting discretionary disclosure. When a witness uses a document to refresh recollection *while* testifying, opposing counsel may examine the part used in order to verify that the testimony is drawn "from ... memory of the facts as they occurred," not "from what [is seen] in the memorandum." *State v. Miller,* 234 Mo. 588, 137 S.W. 887, 890 (1911). "It is not the memorandum that is the evidence, but the recollection of the witness." *State v. Patton,* 255 Mo. 245, 164 S.W. 223, 226 (1914).

When a witness uses a document to refresh recollection *before* testifying, the testimony is based on personal recollection "not then aided and assisted by ... notes in hand." *State v. Miller,* 368 S.W.2d 353, 356–57 (Mo.1963). Thus, the testimony is more likely a genuine recollection, reducing the need for opposing counsel to view the document "to test its sufficiency for the purpose used." *Traber v. Hicks,* 131 Mo. 180, 32 S.W. 1145, 1147 (1895).

Several other states follow the same refreshed recollection rule as Missouri....

Illinois Rule of Evidence 612
WRITING USED TO REFRESH MEMORY

If a witness uses a writing to refresh memory for the purpose of testifying, either—

(1) while testifying, or

(2) before testifying, an adverse party is entitled to have the writing produced at the hearing, to inspect it, to cross-examine the witness thereon, and to introduce in evidence for the purpose of impeachment those portions which relate to the testimony of the witness....

Notes and Questions

1. Most federal courts interpret the phrase "subject matter of the direct examination" to include all inferences and implications arising from such testimony. *E.g., United States v. Arnott,* 704 F.2d 322, 324 (6th Cir. 1983). There is much less dispute today, however, about the definition of the phrase, for in close cases the trial court in most instances can exercise its discretion to allow the cross-examination.

2. There is some dispute over how much discretion trial courts have under Rule 611(b) to allow cross-examination beyond the scope of the direct examination. *Compare United*

States v. Lara, 181 F.3d 183, 199 (1st Cir. 1999) ("This authorization confers discretion on trial judges to disregard the first sentence of Rule 611(b) and allow cross-examination to extend into areas not explored on direct."), *with Lis v. Robert Packer Hospital*, 579 F.2d 819, 822 (3d Cir. 1978) (trial judge's statement that "I have the right to permit inquiry beyond the scope of direct examination and I do it in every case unless it causes confusion" is inconsistent with Rule 611(b), whose second sentence "clearly contemplates special circumstances").

3. Do you understand why questions regarding a witness' credibility are always permitted on cross-examination? In other words, do you see why they necessarily fall within the scope of the direct examination?

4. In the special context of a criminal defendant who chooses to testify, there is a constitutional dimension to the scope-of-the-direct rule:

> It is well established that a witness, in a single proceeding, may not testify voluntarily about a subject and then invoke the privilege against self-incrimination when questioned about the details. See *Rogers v. United States*, 340 U.S. 367, 373 (1951). The privilege is waived for the matters to which the witness testifies, and the scope of the "waiver is determined by the scope of relevant cross-examination," *Brown v. United States*, 356 U.S. 148, 154–155 (1958). "The witness himself, certainly if he is a party, determines the area of disclosure and therefore of inquiry," *id.*, at 155, 78 S.Ct. 622. Nice questions will arise, of course, about the extent of the initial testimony and whether the ensuing questions are comprehended within its scope, but for now it suffices to note the general rule.

Mitchell v. United States, 526 U.S. 314, 321–22 (1999).

5. Most states follow the federal rule in limiting cross-examination to the scope of direct examination plus matters affecting witness credibility. But a few states follow the English common law rule permitting cross-examination on any relevant matter. *See, e.g.,* Ky. R. Evid. 611(b) ("A witness may be cross-examined on any matter relevant to any issue in the case, including credibility. In the interests of justice, the trial court may limit cross-examination with respect to matters not testified to on direct examination."); Miss. R. Evid. 611(b) ("Cross-examination shall *not* be limited to the subject matter of the direct examination and matters affecting the credibility of the witness.") (emphasis added).

6. The language of Rule 611(c) is written in such permissive terms as to be described by one appellate court as not so much a rule but rather merely a precatory statement. *See Sanders v. New York City Human Resources Admin.*, 361 F.3d 749, 757 (2d Cir. 2004). Indeed, appellate courts have held that the rule gives trial courts discretion not only to allow leading questions in situations not among those suggested in the rule, but also to disallow them in those situations where the rule suggests that they should be allowed. *See United States v. Hall*, 165 F.3d 1095, 1117 (7th Cir. 1999).

7. Rule 611(a)(2), which provides that "[t]he court should exercise reasonable control over the mode and order of examining witnesses and presenting evidence so as to … avoid wasting time," empowers a trial judge to set reasonable time limits on witness testimony. *See, e.g., Akouri v. State of Florida Dept. of Transp.*, 408 F.3d 1338, 1346 (11th Cir. 2005). Does this provision also empower a trial judge to exclude the testimony of certain witnesses on the ground that a party has called too many witnesses? *See United States v. Colomb*, 419 F.3d 292, 297–303 (5th Cir. 2005) (holding that Rule 611(a)(2) does not give trial courts the authority to exclude evidence, and that the decision to exclude witnesses on this basis should be made under the strictures of Rule 403).

8. The *Riccardi* case contrasts the present recollection revived with the past recorded recollection. The latter refers to an exception to the hearsay rule, which you will examine in Chapter 7, codified in Rule 803(5). That exception is sometimes useful when efforts to revive a witness' memory using a prior writing fail to revive her memory. If the writing was written by the witness herself and certain other foundational requirements are met, the writing may be read to the jury and serve as an evidentiary substitute for the witness' testimony.

9. Before attempting to refresh a witness' memory, a foundation must first be laid showing that it is necessary (because the witness' memory is exhausted) and that the writing or other item proposed to be used would be likely to assist in refreshing the witness' memory. *Hall v. American Bakeries Co.*, 873 F.2d 1133, 1137 (8th Cir. 1989).

10. While Rule 612 allows the opposing party "to introduce in evidence any portion that relates to the witness's testimony," this is understood to be for the limited purpose of impeaching the witness' credibility by showing that the witness just parroted verbatim whatever was on the paper and that he was not in fact testifying from present memory. *See* Paul R. Rice & Neals-Erik William Delker, *A Short History of Too Little Consequence*, 191 F.R.D. 678, 695–96 (2000). In other words, it does not create an exception to the hearsay rule that allows the writing to be admitted as substantive proof of the matter asserted therein.

11. Does a court have discretion under Rule 612 to prevent disclosure of a writing that a witness uses to refresh her memory "while testifying"? *Compare Magee v. Paul Revere Life Ins. Co.*, 172 F.R.D. 627, 637 (E.D.N.Y. 1997) (holding that Rule 612(a)(1) is "phrased in mandatory language"), *with EEOC v. Continental Airlines, Inc.*, 395 F. Supp. 2d 738, 744 (N.D. Ill. 2005) (holding that it is not mandatory even in that circumstance, although "the scales generally tip in favor of disclosure").

12. If a witness examines documents during a break in her testimony, is that deemed to be "while testifying" under Rule 612(a)(1) and thus subject to mandatory disclosure or "before testifying" under Rule 612(a)(2) and thus subject to the balancing test? *See Hiskett v. Wal-Mart Stores, Inc.*, 180 F.R.D. 403, 407–08 (D.Kan. 1998) (holding that it qualifies as "before testifying," even though it occurred after witness had begun to testify).

13. How is the *Nutramax* court's holding consistent with the statement in the legislative history that Rule 612 not be interpreted to bar "the assertion of a privilege with respect to writings used by a witness to refresh his memory"? Should the legislative history be interpreted to mean that you can assert the privilege, but you won't prevail?

14. In what ways do the Illinois and Missouri counterparts to Federal Rule 612 differ from the federal rule? Which of the three strikes the appropriate balance between protecting the attorney-client and work-product privileges on the one hand and furthering the truth-seeking process on the other?

D. Personal Knowledge Requirement

Kemp v. Balboa
23 F.3d 211 (8th Cir. 1994)

FRIEDMAN, Senior Circuit Judge.

In this case, a state prisoner filed suit under 42 U.S.C. §1983 (1988), accusing a prison guard of improperly confiscating his medication used to control his epilepsy, resulting in the prisoner's having epileptic fits, which injured him. The jury found for the prisoner, but awarded him only nominal damages of $1.00 and punitive damages of the same amount. The prisoner challenges the award of only nominal damages as based upon inadmissible evidence....

I

A.   There was evidence supporting the verdict from which the jury could have found as follows:

From January 1987 to January 1990, the appellant Kemp was a prisoner in the Central Missouri Correctional Center (Center). The appellant Balboa was a correctional "utility" officer there during this time. Kemp had suffered from grand mal epilepsy since childhood. The Missouri Department of Corrections had diagnosed this condition prior to Kemp's incarceration at the Center, and the Center's medical staff knew that Kemp suffered from seizures. The Center gave Kemp a prescription of medication to control his grand mal epilepsy seizures, and the Center's medical staff dispensed Kemp's prescription medicine on a weekly basis. Kemp was permitted to keep this medication in his cell. Balboa repeatedly confiscated Kemp's epilepsy medication, and flushed it down the toilet. Balboa ignored the pleas of Kemp and a fellow inmate to return the medication.

Kemp's epileptic seizures increased in frequency, allegedly due to Balboa's confiscation of Kemp's medication. During his seizures, Kemp involuntarily bit and attempted to swallow his tongue, beat his head on the concrete floor and bled from the mouth....

C.   Vicki Maness, a licensed practical nurse at the Center, testified that Kemp failed to pick up his medication from the prison infirmary on seven separate occasions. She testified that she had reviewed portions of Kemp's medical file relating to the dispensing of medication. Kemp objected to the introduction of the medical file into evidence on the ground of surprise, because Balboa had not given the file to Kemp pursuant to a pretrial order requiring the exchange of exhibits prior to trial. Balboa then told the district court that portions of the medical file would be used only to refresh Maness' recollection, and would not be offered "as evidence." Maness read from the records three dates during June and July, 1989 on which Kemp allegedly failed to pick up his epilepsy medication from the prison infirmary.

Kemp objected repeatedly to Maness' reading of these records while she was testifying on direct examination. After the court overruled these objections, Kemp asked the court to instruct the jury that Maness was testifying from the medical records rather than her own personal knowledge, but the court denied that request. Maness then testified that Kemp failed to procure his medication on three occasions in September 1989, and one time in October 1989.

On cross examination, Maness stated she was not on duty on the days that Kemp allegedly failed to obtain his medication, and that her only knowledge of the subject came from her reviewing the medical charts, which someone else had prepared. Upon completion of the cross examination, Kemp moved to strike Maness' testimony on the ground that Maness' had no personal knowledge of Kemp's failure to pick up his medication, since her testimony was based solely on her review of Kemp's medical file. The district court denied the motion to strike....

II

A.   Unlike an expert witness, who may give his or her opinion about a matter within the witness' expertise (Fed.R.Evid. 703), a lay witness may testify only about matters within his or her personal knowledge. Rule 602 prohibits a lay witness from testifying about matters that are not within the personal knowledge of the witness. *See, e.g., United States v. Lyon*, 567 F.2d 777, 783–84 (8th Cir. 1977). Rule 602 "excludes testimony concerning matter the witness did not observe or had no opportunity to observe." *Id. See also* Fed.R.Evid. 602 advisory committee notes; and McCormick on Evidence, § 69 (4th ed.1992).

Maness was not tendered and did not testify as an expert witness. She testified only as a lay witness to present factual evidence that Kemp had failed to pick up his medication from the Center infirmary. As her testimony on cross examination brought out, however, she had no personal knowledge of these facts, since she was not on duty on the days on which she stated Kemp failed to pick up his medication. Her testimony was based not upon her personal knowledge of the facts about which she testified, but solely upon what she had read in the medical records prepared by others.

Those medical records themselves were not introduced in evidence. According to the district court and Balboa, however, the records were properly used to refresh Maness' recollection. Since Maness had no personal knowledge of the facts, however, she had no recollection that was capable of being refreshed.

When it developed on cross-examination that Maness had no personal knowledge that Kemp had failed to pick up his medication, it became apparent that Rule 602 barred that testimony and that it should not have been admitted. The district court, therefore, should have struck the testimony, as Kemp moved it to do. The court's failure to exclude that testimony was erroneous.

B.   We cannot say that that error was harmless....

Maness' testimony that Kemp had failed to pick up his medication might have lead the jury to conclude that it was Kemp's own indifference to his medical needs rather than Balboa's confiscation of his medication that was primarily the cause of Kemp's increased seizures. Indeed, based on Maness' testimony, the jury might have believed that Kemp, himself, sometimes failed to take his own medication....

The jury might have determined that, in view of Balboa's serious misconduct, but its uncertainty about how responsible Balboa was for Kemp's injuries, an appropriate recognition of the justice of Kemp's cause was to award him only nominal damages. If the jury had not had Maness' incorrectly-admitted testimony before it, it might have awarded actual, rather than only nominal, damages....

Notes and Questions

1. What sort of evidence does it take to establish that a witness has personal knowledge? Rule 602 makes clear that the witness' own testimony can suffice to establish that the witness has personal knowledge of the matters to which he is testifying ("Evidence to prove personal knowledge may consist of the witness's own testimony."). Moreover, the judge's role under Rule 602 is a limited one:

> Owens argues the district court applied the wrong standard in determining the sufficiency of the evidence of personal knowledge. Owens contends the trial court held Foster's testimony was to be admitted unless it was an "impossibility" that Foster personally perceived that Owens was his assailant. Owens rests this argument solely on the fact that the trial court's memorandum opinion quoted Judge Weinstein's quotation of Professor Morgan to this effect. The trial court's quotation also included Judge Weinstein's comment that "impossibility" was too

strong a word; that "near impossibility" or "so improbable that no reasonable person could believe" might be nearer the mark; and that "[t]he judge should admit the testimony if the jury *could* find that the witness perceived the event to which he is testifying, since credibility is a matter for the jury."

The distinctions are to some extent rhetorical flourishes designed to add emphasis to the point that it is the function of the jury, not the court, to determine credibility; that the role of the judge is to determine "not whether the witness did perceive the matter, but whether a jury or other trier of fact could reasonably believe that the witness perceived it."

United States v. Owens-El, 889 F.2d 913, 915 (9th Cir. 1989). *See also* Advisory Committee Note to Rule 602 ("It will be observed that the rule is in fact a specialized application of the provisions of Rule 104(b) on conditional relevancy."). *Compare U.S. v Hickey*, 917 F.2d 901, 904 (6th Cir. 1990) ("the threshold of Rule 602 is low.... Testimony should not be excluded for lack of personal knowledge unless no reasonable juror could believe that the witness had the ability and opportunity to perceive the event that he testifies about.").

2. As you will soon see, Rule 703 allows expert witnesses to formulate opinions and testify to those opinions even if those opinions are based on facts of which they lack personal knowledge. Rule 602's last sentence indicates that "[t]his rule does not apply to a witness's expert testimony under Rule 703," and the Advisory Committee Note to Rule 602 clarifies that "[t]he reference to Rule 703 is designed to avoid any question of conflict between the present rule and the provisions of that rule allowing an expert to express opinions based on facts of which he does not have personal knowledge."

3. We will later examine the rule against hearsay, which provides that, as a general rule, a witness cannot testify about what some other person said, wrote, or otherwise communicated. However, there are numerous exceptions to the hearsay rule that allow a witness to so testify. In this situation, the personal knowledge requirement is somewhat more complicated. A witness who testifies as to what some third person (the declarant) said or wrote, assuming that it falls within an exception to the hearsay rule, need not have personal knowledge of the subject matter of the declarant's statement, but only personal knowledge of the fact that the statement was made. Thus, if a witness testifies that a declarant touched a frying pan and screamed "Ouch, that's hot," the witness need not have personal knowledge that the pan was hot (he likely would not), but only personal knowledge that the declarant said that. The declarant, however, *usually* must have personal knowledge of the subject matter of the statement:

> Stratton and the Parnesses claim that, even if Farbar's statements otherwise qualify, they should have been excluded because Farbar lacked personal knowledge of some of the events recited. For example, Farbar says that Stratton told him that he (Stratton) had threatened Hammoud's family. However, appellants misconceive the nature of the personal knowledge requirement, *see* Fed.R.Evid. 602, in the hearsay context. When A testifies that B told him of an event, A usually has personal knowledge only of B's report. It is B who has personal knowledge of the event. Thus, the hearsay rules require that the *declarant*, B in our example, have personal knowledge of the events recounted, not that the witness have such personal knowledge. *See United States v. Lang*, 589 F.2d 92, 98 (2d Cir. 1978). Thus, Farbar could have testified to Stratton's report of the threats because the threats were within the personal knowledge of Stratton.

United States v. Stratton, 779 F.2d 820, 829–30 (2d Cir. 1985). *See also* Advisory Committee Note to Rule 602 ("This rule does not govern the situation of a witness who testifies to a hearsay statement as such, if he has personal knowledge of the making of the statement. Rules 801 and 805 would be applicable. This rule would, however, prevent him from testifying to the subject matter of the hearsay statement, as he has no personal knowledge of it.").

However, in one narrow instance, not even the declarant need have personal knowledge of the subject matter of his statement. In particular, Rule 801(d)(2), the exception to the hearsay rule for admissions of an opposing party (and certain persons associated with the same), is exempt from the requirement:

> Finally, Goins argues that the two statements, even if meeting the requirements of Rule 801(d)(2)(E), were inadmissible because the declarants were not shown to have had personal knowledge of the matters asserted.... The Advisory Committee's Notes to Rule 801(d)(2), however, confirm that the foundational requirements of Rule 602 do not apply to statements admissible as non-hearsay admissions under Rule 801(d)(2):
>
> > No guarantee of trustworthiness is required in the case of an admission. The freedom which admissions have enjoyed from ... the restrictive influences of ... the rule requiring firsthand knowledge, when taken with the apparent prevalent satisfaction with the results, calls for generous treatment of this avenue of admissibility.

United States v. Goins, 11 F.3d 441, 443–44 (4th Cir. 1993).

E. Calling and Interrogation of Witnesses by the Trial Judge

United States v. Martin
189 F.3d 547 (7th Cir. 1999)

MANION, Circuit Judge.

During Henry Martin's trial for bank robbery he asserted as part of his defense that because he was financially secure he had no motive to rob the bank. While cross-examining Martin, the prosecutor inquired about an apparent inconsistency between Martin's assertion of financial security and the indigence he claimed in the financial disclosure form which he filed to obtain a free attorney. As Martin's responses to the prosecutor were somewhat ambiguous and contradictory, the district judge questioned Martin further on some of the points raised....

After the jury was dismissed, Martin's attorney objected to the court's questioning and moved for a mistrial because the court's comments "and the tone of the court's voice with regard to the questioning of Mr. Martin may have unfairly prejudiced Mr. Martin in the eyes of the jury and may have given the jurors the impression that the court thought that Mr. Martin was lying or knew that Mr. Martin was lying."

.... We review the propriety of a judge's examination of witnesses for an abuse of discretion.... [U]nder Fed.R.Evid. 614(b), a judge generally is free to interrogate witnesses to ensure that issues are clearly presented to the jury. Along with other circuits, we have frequently reminded litigants that "'the function of a federal trial judge is not that of an umpire or of a moderator at a town meeting.'" *Collins*, 143 F.3d at 336. Rather than simply being a silent spectator, intelligent questioning by the trial judge is his prerogative. The occasional questioning of witnesses is one means a judge may use to assist a jury in understanding the evidence. Thus, a trial judge may ask those questions he deems necessary in order to clarify an important issue, as long as he remains impartial.

Because trial judges wield substantial influence over juries, a judge's discretion to question witnesses is not unfettered. A judge cannot assume the role of an advocate for either side, but he can question a witness in an effort to make the testimony clear for the jury. This should not include questions which indicate the judge's belief about a witness' honesty, especially when a criminal defendant testifies on his own behalf. Therefore, the initial inquiry in reviewing challenges to a judge's questions to a witness at trial is whether by his conduct the trial judge conveyed to the jury a bias regarding the defendant's honesty or guilt.

The second inquiry concerns whether the complaining party can show serious prejudice resulting from the trial court's comments or questions. Given the challenge before us, we must examine the entire record to determine whether the district judge displayed a bias, and if so, whether this bias affected the jury's decision. If the court's questions were partial to the prosecution and they could prejudice the jury's decision, then reversal of the conviction could be in order.

In the present case, we first note that the district judge's stated purpose for interrogating the defendant—to assure that Martin was truly indigent and that the CJA program was being run efficiently—was an important one and it certainly merited some attention. It was not, however, a concern of the jury.... Due to the possibility that the district judge might appear partisan in questioning a defendant, to avoid any claims of bias district judges should inquire into such things as appointment of counsel by questioning the defendant when the jury is not present. If a judicial inquiry is not made for the benefit of the jury, the jury has no need to observe it.

But the preservation of the integrity of the CJA program was not the only purpose served by the judge's interrogation. The subject matter of his questions concerned issues which Martin's counsel and the prosecution addressed—Martin's financial condition, the extent to which he was financed by his wife's salary, and his art collection. Martin's responses to counsel on direct examination were sometimes ambiguous and conflicted with the testimony he provided on cross-examination. In interrogating Martin, the judge sought clarification of Martin's answers to questions by both parties concerning his motive, or lack thereof, to rob the bank, which is certainly a relevant issue and a legitimate concern of the jury. For if Martin did indeed own paintings worth $30,000, he may not (as he suggested) have been as needful of money as someone without any assets. Similarly, if Martin were enjoying the benefits of his wife's salary, he may have had a diminished incentive to rob the bank. So, depending on Martin's answers, the judge's questions had the potential to assist or frustrate Martin's defense. Regardless, the questions were posed to clarify Martin's testimony, and the clarification of ambiguities is a legitimate purpose of judicial interrogation of witnesses.

As to any prejudice resulting from the questions, we note that in attempting to clarify Martin's answers, the district judge was firm, but not harsh or abusive in any way.[4] The questions were not laced with skepticism and they gave no indication as to the judge's

---

4. The record also shows that the district judge asked clarifying questions of other witnesses, including witnesses for the prosecution. Because opposing witnesses were subjected to the same scrutiny, the possibility that the judge's questioning of Martin could have been interpreted by the jury as a disapproval of Martin's testimony is minimized.

thoughts about Martin's honesty or dishonesty; rather, the truth or untruth on the subject of inquiry came from Martin's responses. Importantly, the rule concerning judicial interrogation is designed to prevent judges from conveying prejudicial messages to the jury. It is not concerned with the damaging truth that the questions might uncover. So to the extent that Martin's argument is concerned with the truth made plain by the judicial inquiry, he has no basis for complaint, especially when his earlier testimony covered the subject matter and created some conflict or confusion. The district judge's questions explored earlier contradictory answers. When a defendant gets caught in his own contradictions, he shouldn't blame the district judge for asking relevant questions.

It is also important that the district judge gave the jury a cautionary instruction immediately after it returned to the courtroom from the recess that followed Martin's testimony regarding the financial disclosure. At that point the judge stated:

> Members of the jury, you may recall that at the outset I told you that you were to consider only the evidence that is received in this case. I also instructed you that neither by any ruling or by any comment or any question which I may have posed to a witness do I mean to indicate what my opinion is as to the facts or as to what your verdict should be. And I want you to bear that in mind, especially in connection with the court's inquiry regarding Exhibit Number 14.

Trial judges have broad discretion in determining whether a cautionary instruction as opposed to a mistrial will prevent any possible prejudice. We assume that juries follow the courts' instructions. Cautionary instructions may cure or diminish any prejudice that could have resulted from the trial judge's comments or questions.[5] Thus, even assuming *arguendo* that the district judge's comments could have prejudiced the jury in any way, the court's instruction was sufficient to cure the misperception....

Notes and Questions

1. Not only do judges have the authority under Rule 614(b) to question witnesses called by the parties but they also have the authority under Rule 614(a) to call witnesses themselves.

2. Note that in *Martin*, the defendant did not object to the trial judge's questioning until after the jury was dismissed. While objections are normally supposed to be made contemporaneously with the evidence or conduct being objected to, Rule 614(c) provides that "[a] party may object to the court's calling or examining a witness either at that time or at the next opportunity when the jury is not present." The Advisory Committee Note to Rule 614(c) explains that this "is designed to relieve counsel of the embarrassment attendant upon objecting to questions by the judge in the presence of the jury, while at the same time assuring that objections are made in apt time to afford the opportunity to take possible corrective measures." However, a party must make an objection within the designated window provided or it will constitute a failure fully to preserve the claim for review on appeal. *See United States v. Godwin*, 272 F.3d 659, 679 (4th Cir. 2001).

---

5. The Second Circuit has adopted a rule that presumes once "'a judge's actions create an impression of partisanship, curative instructions will generally not save the day.'" *United States v. Matt*, 116 F.3d 971, 974 (2d Cir. 1997) (quoting *Leslie*, 103 F.3d at 1104); *see Messina*, 131 F.3d at 40; *United States v. Filani*, 74 F.3d 378, 386 (2d Cir. 1996). While we can conceive of egregious situations where curative instructions would not purge the prejudice caused by communications of bias to the jury, we believe that such cases are rare. In most instances, like the one here, the potential for prejudice from judicial questions can be removed with an appropriate instruction.

3. In what way is allowing a judge to call and interrogate witnesses less of a problem than allowing a judge to serve as a witness in a case? While Rule 605 categorically bars judges from serving as a witness in a case over which they preside, Rule 614 allows them to call and interrogate witnesses, subject only to a proviso that "[t]he authority is, of course, abused when the judge abandons his proper role and assumes that of advocate." Advisory Committee Note to Rule 614(b). Each of these two rules also differs with respect to the steps that must be taken to preserve a claim that it was violated: no objection is necessary to preserve a Rule 605 claim, while an objection, albeit a delayed one, must be made in order to preserve a Rule 614 objection.

4. Are you persuaded that where a judge oversteps the line and takes on the role of an advocate, such an error can be cured by a jury instruction? Compare the approach in *Martin* to that of the Second Circuit as described in footnote 5.

F. Opinion Testimony by Lay Witnesses

At common law, only those witnesses who qualified as experts (a topic discussed in great detail in the next section of this chapter) could testify in the form of an "opinion." Mere lay witnesses, by contrast, could testify only about facts and could not render opinions.

Rule 701 modifies the common law in this regard to some degree, allowing lay witnesses to sometimes testify in the form of an opinion. The rule provides that:

> If a witness is not testifying as an expert, testimony in the form of an opinion is limited to one that is:
>
> (a) rationally based on the witness's perception;
>
> (b) helpful to clearly understanding the witness's testimony or to determining a fact in issue; and
>
> (c) not based on scientific, technical, or other specialized knowledge within the scope of Rule 702.

Consider the following questions as you examine the materials that follow. Why does Rule 701 eliminate the strict common law fact/opinion distinction? What does it mean for a witness' testimony to be rationally based on her perceptions? To be "helpful"? Finally, what is the purpose of subsection (c), that the testimony be "not based on scientific, technical, or other specialized knowledge within the scope of Rule 702"?

Problem 4-4: Funny Lookin' and Funny Smellin'

Robert is on trial on charges that he committed arson. Tom, an acquaintance of Robert's, is called as a witness for the prosecution. Tom testifies that on the evening in question, he was taking a walk a few blocks from the alleged arson site when he bumped into Robert. If permitted, Tom would further testify that Robert seemed nervous, had a guilty look on his face, and smelled like gasoline. The defense objects, contending that the testimony does not satisfy Rule 701.

How should the court rule on the defense's objections?

Problem 4-5: "He Sounded Like a Black Man"

Daniel, an African-American male, is on trial on charges of robbing several federally insured banks. The government has a great deal of forensic evidence linking Daniel to the crime. In addition, there are a number of eyewitnesses who were present during the robberies. Although these eyewitnesses were not able to see the perpetrator's face (because he was wearing a mask), they were able to hear the perpetrator's voice, and if permitted, they would each testify that the person who robbed the bank "sounded like a black man." The defense objects, contending that the testimony does not satisfy Rule 701 and in any event violates Rule 403.

How should the court rule on the defense's objections?

Asplundh Manufacturing Division v. Benton Harbor Engineering
57 F.3d 1190 (3d Cir. 1995)

BECKER, Circuit Judge....

Rule 701 represents a movement away from the courts' historically skeptical view of lay opinion evidence. At common law, witnesses not qualifying as experts were not permitted to draw conclusions which could be characterized as opinion testimony, but rather were required to limit their testimony to facts, those things "they had seen, heard, felt, smelled, tasted, or done." Hon. Charles R. Richey, *Proposals To Eliminate the Prejudicial Effect of the Use of the Word "Expert" Under the Federal Rules [of] Evidence in Civil and Criminal Jury Trials*, 154 F.R.D. 537, 542 (1994) ("Mere opinions were considered unreliable bases for testimony.").

This rigid distinction between fact and opinion led to numerous appeals and pervasive criticism by commentators. Wigmore declared, in the first edition of his treatise, that this distinction "has done more than any one rule of procedure to reduce our litigation towards a sense of legalized gambling." 3 JOHN H. WIGMORE, EVIDENCE § 1929, at 2563 (1st ed. 1904); *see also* WILLARD L. KING & DOUGLAS PILLINGER, OPINION EVIDENCE IN ILLINOIS 8 (1942) ("The American courts have had a great struggle with a rule which appeared to require them to admit statements of fact and exclude all inferences of the witness. Such a rule is quite impossible of application: all statements contain inferences."); JAMES B. THAYER, A PRELIMINARY TREATISE ON EVIDENCE AT THE COMMON LAW 524 (1898) ("In a sense all testimony to matter of fact is opinion evidence, i.e. it is a conclusion formed from phenomena and mental impressions.").

Characteristically, however, the most eloquent criticism of this common-law restriction on lay testimony was made by Judge Learned Hand:

> Every judge of experience in the trial of causes has again and again seen the whole story garbled, because of insistence upon a form with which the witness cannot comply, since, like most men, he is unaware of the extent to which inference enters into his perceptions. He is telling the "facts" in the only way that he knows how, and the result of nagging and checking him is often to choke him altogether, which is, indeed, usually its purpose.

Central R.R. Co. v. Monahan, 11 F.2d 212, 214 (2d Cir. 1926). Judge Hand also stated:

> The truth is, as Mr. Wigmore has observed at length, that the exclusion of opinion evidence has been carried beyond reason in this country, and that it would be a large advance if courts were to admit it with freedom. The line between

opinion and fact is at best only one of degree, and ought to depend solely upon practical considerations, as, for example, the saving of time and the mentality of the witness.

These concerns about the restrictions on lay opinion testimony, combined with a more general liberalization in those rules of evidence that operated to deprive the fact-finder of relevant evidence, led to the adoption of Rule 701. The Advisory Committee Note to the rule reflects the fact that Rule 701's liberalization of the admissibility of opinion evidence is rooted in the modern trend away from fine distinctions between fact and opinion and toward greater admissibility, tempered with an understanding that the adversary process, and more specifically, cross-examination will correct any problems:

> The rule retains the traditional objective of putting the trier of fact in possession of an accurate reproduction of the event.
>
> Limitation (a) is the familiar requirement of first-hand knowledge or observation.
>
> Limitation (b) is phrased in terms of requiring testimony to be helpful in resolving issues. Witnesses often find difficulty in expressing themselves in language which is not that of an opinion or conclusion. While the courts have made concessions in certain recurring situations, necessity as a standard for permitting opinions and conclusions has proved too elusive and too unadaptable to particular situations for purposes of satisfactory judicial administration. Moreover, the practical impossibility of determining by rule what is a "fact," demonstrated by a century of litigation of the question of what is a fact for purposes of pleading under the Field Code, extends into evidence also. The rule assumes that the natural characteristics of the adversary system will generally lead to an acceptable result, since the detailed account carries more conviction than the broad assertion, and a lawyer can be expected to display his witness to the best advantage. If he fails to do so, cross-examination and argument will point up the weakness. If, despite these considerations, attempts are made to introduce meaningless assertions which amount to little more than choosing up sides, exclusion for lack of helpfulness is called for by the rule.

FED.R.EVID. 701 advisory committee's note.

The prototypical example of the type of evidence contemplated by the adoption of Rule 701 relates to the appearance of persons or things, identity, the manner of conduct, competency of a person, degrees of light or darkness, sound, size, weight, distance, and an endless number of items that cannot be described factually in words apart from inferences. The more liberal approach to lay opinion testimony of this type gained acceptance as a rule of "convenience," which allowed for "'shorthand renditions' of a total situation, or [for] statements of collective facts." 1 McCORMICK ON EVIDENCE 44 & n. 16 (4th ed. 1992); *see also* Mark McCormick, *Opinion Evidence in Iowa*, 19 DRAKE L.REV. 245, 248 (1970) (viewing this rule as allowing for a "shorthand rendering of the facts").

As recognized by Professor Saltzburg, testimony that a person was "excited" or "angry" is more evocative and understandable than a long physical description of the person's outward manifestations. STEPHEN A. SALTZBURG ET AL., FEDERAL RULES OF EVIDENCE MANUAL 1032 (6th ed. 1994). For example, a witness who testifies that an individual whom he saw staggering or lurching along the way was drunk is spared the difficulty of describing, with the precision of an orthopedist or choreographer, the person's gait, angle of walk, etc.

Perhaps the best judicial description of this type of testimony under Rule 701 is found in *United States v. Yazzie*, 976 F.2d 1252 (9th Cir. 1992). Yazzie was charged with statutory rape under a federal statute that permitted a defense of reasonable mistake as to the age of the minor. At trial, Yazzie asserted that he reasonably believed that the minor, age fifteen-and-a-half, was over the statutory age of sixteen. In support of this contention, Yazzie called several witnesses who offered to testify that, as of the date of the incident, their observations caused them to believe the minor to be between the age of sixteen and twenty. The trial court excluded this testimony as impermissible lay "opinion" and limited the witnesses' testimony to "facts," such as that the minor smoked cigarettes, wore make-up, and drove a car. The Court of Appeals reversed, stating:

> We understand Rule 701 to mean that opinions of non-experts may be admitted where the facts could not otherwise be adequately presented or described to the jury in such a way as to enable the jury to form an opinion or reach an intelligent conclusion. If it is impossible or difficult to reproduce the data observed by the witnesses, or the facts are difficult of explanation, or complex, or are of a combination of circumstances and appearances which cannot be adequately described and presented with the force and clearness as they appeared to the witness, the witness may state his impressions and opinions based upon what he observed. It is a means of conveying to the jury what the witness has seen or heard.

The court concluded that the testimony of the witnesses satisfied Rule 701's requirements:

> Here, the opinion testimony not only meets the requirements of sub-part (a) of Rule 701, but of both the alternative sub-parts of (b). The testimony helps in the understanding of the witnesses' descriptive testimony and in determining a critical fact at issue—whether it was reasonable for Yazzie to believe that the minor was sixteen or older.

> In the case before us, the jurors could not themselves assess how old the minor looked at the time of the incident: by the time of the trial, the minor was almost seventeen years old, and her appearance was undoubtedly substantially different than it had been on the night in question, a year and a half earlier. Thus, the jurors were wholly dependent on the testimony of witnesses. Yet the witnesses were permitted to testify only to the minor's describable features and behavior. Their testimony was no substitute for a clear and unequivocal statement of their opinions. It did not tell the jury that these witnesses believed the minor to be at least sixteen years old at the time of the incident.

Other examples of this type of quintessential Rule 701 opinion testimony include identification of an individual, the speed of a vehicle, the mental state or responsibility of another, whether another was healthy, the value of one's property, and other situations in which the differences between fact and opinion blur and it is difficult or cumbersome for the examiner to elicit an answer from the witness that will not be expressed in the form of an opinion. These cases, it is important to add, all meet the core definitional terms of Rule 701—the opinion is based upon personal knowledge, is rationally based thereon, and is helpful to the trier of fact....

Rule 701's requirement that the opinion be "rationally based on the [witness's] perception[]" demands more than that the witness have perceived something firsthand; rather, it requires that the witness' perception provide a truly rational basis for his or her opinion....

[The dissenting opinion of Judge Gibson is omitted.]

United States v. Rollins

544 F.3d 820 (7th Cir. 2008)

TINDER, Circuit Judge.

Beginning in August of 2004, various law enforcement agencies in southern Illinois combined their efforts to concentrate on the investigation of drug distribution and drug crimes in the Alton, Illinois, area. Their endeavors resulted in an eighteen-count, twelve-defendant federal indictment in the district court. Most of the defendants entered pleas of guilty, but a handful of them contested the charges at what turned out to be a thirteen-day jury trial. This appeal is brought by two of those trial defendants, James E. Rollins Sr. and Rudy Slack, against whom the jurors returned verdicts of guilty on the charge of conspiracy to distribute cocaine and 50 grams or more of cocaine base, that is, "crack" cocaine....

The jury trial began on January 22, 2007. More than 100 recorded telephone conversations were played during trial.... Agent McGarry testified, over objection, as to his impressions about various recorded conversations. (This testimony has become the major issue raised in this appeal.) He testified that his personal impression was that Rollins Sr. was supplying Pittman with cocaine and that Rollins Sr. was getting his cocaine from Rollins Jr. McGarry also testified that based on his involvement with the wiretaps, his impression was that John Frost was assisting with the transport of the cocaine. The agent also testified as to his impression that in conversations between Rollins Sr. and Pittman on March 14, 2005, Rollins Sr. had contacted Pittman to see if he had money available and, in a phone conversation later that day, Rollins Sr. gave Pittman his location. Agent McGarry further testified that his impression was that when Rollins Sr. and Pittman talked about "big shoes and little shoes" in a recorded conversation on March 15, 2005, they were talking about 18 ounces and 9 ounces of cocaine. Another example of the agent's "impressions" testimony concerned his statement that in an April 9, 2005, conversation in which Rollins Sr. and Rollins Jr. referred to "the band" and "the singer," the "band" was a reference to Richard Pittman and the height of the singer, 5'6", was a reference to the $5,600 that was collected from him. Agent McGarry also testified as to his impression that various other phone calls between Rollins Sr. and Pittman were conversations about drug transactions....

Both defendants contend that the district court abused its discretion in allowing Agent McGarry to testify as to his "impressions" of intercepted telephone conversations as lay opinions or inferences under Federal Rule of Evidence 701. Agent McGarry was a key government witness, testifying for two days on direct examination. During his testimony, the prosecutor asked him for his "impression" as to the meaning of portions of several dozen recorded conversations. There were also more than a dozen instances in which the prosecutor, in effect, asked Agent McGarry for his impression of a recorded conversation without using the word "impression." In responding, Agent McGarry gave his impressions that particular numbers referred to amounts of or prices for illegal drugs. He testified that certain words were code words for illegal drugs. And he interpreted various conversations to show that the alleged conspirators' activities were consistent with the charged conspiracy. For example, the prosecutor asked Agent McGarry, "Your impression of what it means for them to say they are going to go have a drink at 10:30 to 11:00 o'clock?," and Agent McGarry answered, "my impression is this call is also based on—we established surveillance at James Rollins, Senior's residence, anticipating 10:30 or 11:00 arrival of a truck driven by John Frost." The agent then explained that there was no meeting at the appointed time, law enforcement continued surveillance until the early morning hours, and then terminated surveillance because they did not believe the truck would be arriving after the appointed time....

In allowing the "impressions" testimony, the district court explained:

> [T]he cases that talk about code words talk about witnesses who rely on their years of experience as a law enforcement officer. As we discussed at the side bar, the discussion here is about the words that come about that are unique to the conversations that have occurred throughout this particular alleged conspiracy. It is clear and it has been clear to this Court throughout that these guys are making this up as they go. Sometimes they make it up in each unique conversation. The officer or the agent is testifying based on his having listened to the conversations and based on his impressions, so it is clearly 701. It is not 702.... [T]he words that are being used, quite frankly, I have not heard these words in any other telephone calls that I have heard.... [T]he testimony is not coming in based on his experience as the law enforcement officer, it is based on his experience only within this conspiracy.

Even the conspirators themselves did not always pick up right away on the meaning of these peculiarly coded conversations. During many of the conversations, one of the speakers would start talking out of the blue about "having drinks," the height of a "singer" in a "band," "work," "big shoes and little shoes" and a variety of other things that would appear at first to be virtually nonsensical. For example, as Pittman explained in his testimony, during one conversation he had with Rollins Jr., Pittman initially was puzzled when Rollins Jr. started talking about running into "his little cousin." But as the discussion continued, Pittman figured out what these confusing comments really meant: Rollins Jr. was talking about being short of cocaine. And there was no pattern or predictability to the terminology. It was helpful to the jury to have explanations from the cooperating witnesses. It was also helpful to have explanations from the investigator who became intimately familiar with the unusual manner of communicating used by these conspirators.

We find that the trial judge did not err in concluding that Agent McGarry's "impressions" testimony was rationally based on his first-hand perception of the intercepted phone calls about which he testified as well as his personal, extensive experience with this particular drug investigation. The agent listened to every intercepted conversation from February through July 2005 on the phones used by Slack, the Rollinses, Pittman and Frost. Agent McGarry testified that he became "very familiar" with the voices he heard. Law enforcement surveillance of the conspirators' activities assisted in giving meaning to various words used in the recorded conversations. The officers' observations of the conspirators' activities often confirmed that their understanding of a recorded conversation was accurate. Agent McGarry participated in the interviews of witnesses who were familiar with the defendants and the drug conspiracy and in obtaining proffers from members of the conspiracy. These bases for Agent McGarry's testimony defeat Rollins Sr.'s claim the government laid an insufficient foundation for this testimony.

We also find that the "impressions" testimony assisted the jury in understanding Agent McGarry's testimony about the intercepted conversations—what the parties to the conversations said and what they meant. This testimony also assisted the jury in determining several facts in issue, including whether the defendants knowingly and intentionally participated in the charged conspiracy and their roles and extent of their involvement in that conspiracy....

The evidence at trial in this case established that certain words had certain meanings to conversation participants at different times; the speakers were making it up as they went along. They did not employ typical drug code words.... Thus, Agent McGarry's impressions testimony was not based on any specialized knowledge gained from his law enforcement training and experience in narcotics trafficking generally. Rather, his understanding of these conversations came only as a result of the particular things he perceived from monitoring intercepted calls, observing drug transactions of these conspirators, and talking with the cooperating conspirators about this drug operation as the investigation rolled into the trial preparation phase. He had become intimately familiar with each voice on the calls, particular mannerisms of the speakers and the habits of the conspirators.

We are guided by our recent decision in *United States v. Oriedo*, 498 F.3d 593, (7th Cir.2007), in which we held that an agent's testimony about how drug dealers use baggies to package drugs was erroneously admitted as lay opinion testimony. We said that the agent's testimony "fits squarely within this court's precedent defining expert testimony by officers as to matters within their experience observing narcotics trafficking practices." In reaching this conclusion, we explained that the agent's "testimony was not limited to what he observed in the search or to other facts derived exclusively from this particular investigation; instead, he brought the wealth of his experience as a narcotics officer to bear on those observations and made connections for the jury based on that specialized knowledge." Here, though, the code words used in the intercepted conversations were unique to this conspiracy and, at times, unique to the particular intercepted conversation. As the district judge observed, the words about which Agent McGarry testified were not "words in any other telephone calls that [he] ha[d] heard." Therefore, the agent's "impressions" testimony was based on his own personal observations and perceptions derived from this particular case. Such testimony is admissible as lay opinion testimony.

In sum, Agent McGarry's "impressions" testimony was not expert testimony. It was not based on scientific, technical or other specialized knowledge within the scope of Rule 702. Instead, his testimony was lay opinion testimony....

While Agent McGarry's testimony approaches the line dividing lay opinion testimony from expert opinion testimony, we find no error in the district court's decision to allow the "impressions" testimony where, as here, it is based on the agent's perceptions derived from the investigation of this particular conspiracy. The experienced trial judge did not abuse his discretion in admitting this testimony under Rule 701....

Notes and Questions

1. In a handful of cases, both federal and state courts have approved of testimony by a lay witness that a person sounded like an African-American. *See United States v. Card*, 86 F. Supp. 2d 1115 (D.Utah 2000); *Clifford v. Commonwealth*, 7 S.W.3d 371 (Ky. 1999). These decisions viewed such testimony as falling within the collective facts doctrine. *Card*, 86 F. Supp. 2d at 1116; *Clifford*, 7 S.W.3d at 376 ("His inability to more specifically describe or to demonstrate 'how a black man sounds' merely proves the reason for the collective facts rule, *i.e.*, that it would be difficult or impossible for the witness to give such a description or demonstration"). These decisions posit that such testimony is no different from testimony permitted in previous cases that someone has a "Southern" accent, a "Boston" accent, a "French" accent, or a male or female voice. *Card*, 86 F. Supp. 2d at 1116–17; *Clifford*, 7 S.W. at 375–76. Yet the decisions have been criticized as giving insufficient consideration to the potential prejudicial impact. *See* Lis Wiehl, *"Sounding Black" in the Courtroom: Court-Sanctioned Racial Stereotyping*, 18 Harv. BlackLetter L. J. 185, 195 (2002) ("statements referring to the race of an accused can move the jury to decide the case on an improper basis"). *But see Card*, 86 F. Supp. 2d at 1119 ("the evidence is not being used to suggest that because of defendant Card's ethnic status, he was more

likely to commit the offense or was more likely to be an armed robber. Rather, the evidence is directly related to the legitimate factor of identification in the case.... The mere fact that Card is African-American, does not make the evidence prejudicial.").

2. Suppose that in a trial for, say, bank robbery, the government offers into evidence a photograph taken by a surveillance camera that appears to depict the defendant, although the defendant denies that he is the person depicted in the photograph. Is testimony by a lay witness familiar with the defendant stating her opinion that the person depicted in the photograph is the defendant "helpful" to the jury under Rule 701(b)? *See United States v. Contreras*, 536 F.3d 1167, 1170–71 (10th Cir. 2008) (holding that it is helpful if the witness has prior familiarity with the defendant's appearance, as that allows the witness to "offer[] the jury a more sophisticated identification than they could make on their own"); *United States v. Dixon*, 413 F.3d 540, 544–46 (6th Cir. 2005) (holding that it can be helpful depending on the extent of the witness's familiarity with the defendant's appearance and whether the photograph is of poor quality or shows only a partial view of the subject).

3. Not only does Rule 701(a) require that the lay witness' opinion be based on facts within his personal knowledge, but it also requires that the opinion be "rationally based" on that personal knowledge. What does this mean? *See Lynch v. City of Boston*, 180 F.3d 1, 16 (1st Cir. 1999) (holding that testimony is rationally based upon a witness' perceptions when "no irrational leaps of logic" are made from the perceptions to the opinion); *Luddock Feed Lots, Inc. v. Iowa Beef Processors*, 630 F.2d 250, 263 (5th Cir. 1980) ("the opinion ... must be one that a normal person would form from those perceptions").

4. Rule 701(c) was added as an amendment to Rule 701 in 2000. The Advisory Committee Note explains the rationale for the amendment, and also provides guidance on distinguishing between lay and expert witness testimony:

Rule 701 has been amended to eliminate the risk that the reliability requirements set forth in Rule 702 will be evaded through the simple expedient of proffering an expert in lay witness clothing. Under the amendment, a witness' testimony must be scrutinized under the rules regulating expert opinion to the extent that the witness is providing testimony based on scientific, technical, or other specialized knowledge within the scope of Rule 702. By channeling testimony that is actually expert testimony to Rule 702, the amendment also ensures that a party will not evade the expert witness disclosure requirements set forth in Fed.R.Civ.P. 26 and Fed.R.Crim.P. 16 by simply calling an expert witness in the guise of a layperson.

The amendment does not distinguish between expert and lay *witnesses*, but rather between expert and lay *testimony*. Certainly it is possible for the same witness to provide both lay and expert testimony in a single case. The amendment makes clear that any part of a witness' testimony that is based upon scientific, technical, or other specialized knowledge within the scope of Rule 702 is governed by the standards of Rule 702 and the corresponding disclosure requirements of the Civil and Criminal Rules....

The amendment incorporates the distinctions set forth in *State v. Brown*, 836 S.W.2d 530, 549 (1992), a case involving former Tennessee Rule of Evidence 701, a rule that precluded lay witness testimony based on "special knowledge." In *Brown*, the court declared that the distinction between lay and expert witness testimony is that lay testimony "results from a process of reasoning familiar in everyday life," while expert testimony "results from a process of reasoning which can be mastered only by specialists in the field." The court in *Brown* noted that a lay witness with experience could testify that a substance appeared to be blood, but that a witness would have to qualify as an expert before he could testify that bruising around the eyes is indicative of skull trauma. That is the kind of distinction made by the amendment to this Rule.

Advisory Committee Note to 2000 Amendment to Rule 701.

G. Expert Witnesses

As the Advisory Committee Note to Rule 701(c) illustrates, the rules of evidence draw a sharp distinction between lay and expert witness testimony. Experts have broader latitude in terms of the basis for and the form of their testimony, but only if both the expert and the subject matter of her testimony satisfy various prerequisites, set forth in Rule 702. First, the expert must be qualified. Second, the expert's testimony must be reliable. And third, the expert's testimony must be helpful.

The materials that follow explore each of these prerequisites in detail. As you examine these materials, consider the extent to which the three prerequisites are distinct and the extent to which they overlap with one another. In addition, consider whether you believe that generalist judges are up to the tasks that Rule 702 requires them to perform, and if not, what alternatives exist to the regime that it establishes.

1. Qualification of Expert Witnesses

Problem 4-6: Pot-Smoking Expert Witness

Mary is on trial on charges of illegally importing marijuana. To prove that the marijuana originated from outside of the United States (an element of the charged crime), the government calls Wayan as an expert witness on the identification of the origin of marijuana plants. Mary's attorney seeks to exclude the expert's testimony on the ground that Wayan is not qualified to testify as an expert. When questioned, Wayan concedes that he has no formal training or education in this field. Rather, he claims an ability to identify its origin based solely on his "experience of being around it a great deal and smoking it."

How should the court rule on the defense's objection?

Waldorf v. Shuta
142 F.3d 601 (3d Cir. 1998)

GREENBERG, Circuit Judge. . . .

This case involves an appeal and a cross appeal from a judgment of $3,005,941 entered on a jury's verdict in favor of the plaintiff, Mark Waldorf, after a deduction for a collateral source recovery, in this personal injury action. Waldorf suffered injuries rendering him a quadriplegic in a motor vehicle accident in 1982 when he was 24 years old. . . .

Waldorf also argues that he should receive a new trial because the district court improperly qualified Dennis Rizzo, who testified for the Borough at trial, as an expert witness on vocational rehabilitation. . . .

Waldorf does not dispute that vocational rehabilitation is a proper subject for expert testimony; instead, he questions whether Rizzo was qualified to testify as an expert in that area. For a court to qualify a witness to testify as an expert, Rule 702 requires the witness to have "specialized knowledge" regarding the area of testimony. The basis of this specialized knowledge "can be practical experience as well as academic training and credentials." We have interpreted the specialized knowledge requirement liberally, and have stated that this policy of liberal admissibility of expert testimony "extends to the substantive as well as the formal qualification of experts." *See, e.g., In re Paoli R.R. Yard PCB Litig.*, 35 F.3d 717, 741 (3d Cir. 1994). However, "at a minimum, a proffered expert witness ... must possess skill or knowledge greater than the average layman...." *Aloe Coal Co. v. Clark Equip. Co.*, 816 F.2d 110, 114 (3d Cir. 1987).

Even though we apply Rule 702 liberally, we have not pursued a policy of qualifying *any* proffered witness as an expert. For instance in *Aloe Coal Co.*, we held that a district court abused its discretion in allowing a tractor sales representative to testify as an expert regarding the cause of a tractor fire. In making this determination we stated:

> Drewnoski [the expert witness] was not an engineer. He had no experience in designing construction machinery. He had no knowledge or experience in determining the cause of equipment fires. He had no training as a mechanic. He never operated construction machinery in the course of business. He was a salesman, who at times prepared damage estimates.

Therefore, we held that the witness was not sufficiently qualified to give an expert opinion on the issue of causation.

Numerous district court opinions within this circuit provide examples of witnesses disallowed from providing expert testimony. For example, in *Diaz v. Johnson Matthey, Inc.*, 893 F. Supp. 358, 373 (D.N.J.1995), the plaintiff alleged that working conditions at his former job caused him to develop platinum salt allergies. In support of this allegation, the plaintiff produced a doctor who sought to testify about his condition and the possible long-term health effects of the condition. The district court held that the doctor was not qualified to testify that the plaintiff had a platinum salt allergy because his experience with such patients was limited and he had only a limited familiarity with the literature regarding the illness.

However, in considering the qualification of witnesses as experts, we stress that ordinarily an otherwise qualified witness is not disqualified merely because of a lack of academic training. For instance, in *Hammond* the district court determined that a witness could testify as an expert regarding a rollover protective structure on a tractor even though he did not have a formal degree in engineering or physics. *See* 691 F.2d at 653. In spite of his lack of formal training, the witness had experience in the field, because he worked selling automotive and mechanical equipment, including agricultural equipment, and he taught automobile repair and maintenance at a high school. We upheld his qualification as an expert, stressing that his practical experience was sufficient. *See id.*

Furthermore, in *Knight v. Otis Elevator Co.*, 596 F.2d 84, 87–88 (3d Cir. 1979), we held that an engineer who had designed safety equipment could testify as an expert regarding whether unguarded elevator control buttons were a design defect, even though he had no experience with such devices on elevators. We held that the expert's generalized knowledge about machine safety sufficiently qualified him as an expert. *See also Davis v. United States*, 865 F.2d 164, 168 (8th Cir. 1988) (permitting the testimony of a public health investigator regarding the probabilities of transmitting gonorrhea despite his lack of medical training, because the expert had practical experience regarding such cases);

Circle J Dairy, Inc. v. A.O. Smith Harvestore Prod., Inc., 790 F.2d 694, 700 (8th Cir. 1986) (holding that a witness could testify as an expert regarding the feed-related health problems of dairy cattle despite a lack of academic qualifications because of his practical experience in the area).

The district court qualified Rizzo to testify as a vocational expert in spite of his lack of any formal training in that field, and notwithstanding that his educational training culminated in a master's degree in sociology and social organization from Rutgers University in 1973. But his experience was sufficient to qualify him as an expert. After obtaining his degree, Rizzo began working for the State of New Jersey in the Division of Mental Retardation as a social worker. He worked as a case manager assisting mentally retarded individuals in "meeting their life needs" and assisting families in meeting the life needs of their mentally retarded children. From 1980 to 1983, Rizzo operated a non-profit corporation whose purpose "was to expand the availability of services in the community to individuals with disabilit[ies]." From 1983 to 1986, Rizzo was employed in a marketing job selling consumer products on college campuses. In 1986, Rizzo was unemployed for nine months, but then began to work as a social worker at the North Princeton Developmental Center. He soon became a supervisor of an 80 to 84 bed care unit which housed individuals "who had severe mobility impairment, severe psychiatric involvement,[and] a variety of different disabilities...." He worked in this facility for four years.

In 1990, Rizzo began working for the State of New Jersey in the Developmental Disabilities Council as a contract manager. In 1991, he became involved in the Council's administration of a million dollar loan pool to assist disabled New Jersey residents in starting their own businesses. In that capacity, Rizzo evaluated the capacity of disabled individuals to accomplish specific employment opportunities. Rizzo also testified that, through the course of his employment, he became familiar with studies on the work that quadriplegics can perform. Furthermore in his job experience, Rizzo utilized the New Jersey Department of Labor Statistics and the New Jersey Job Listing Book, which indicate employment opportunities available in various job categories in New Jersey. Thus, based on his experience and his familiarity with the literature in the field, the district court held that Rizzo was qualified properly as a vocational expert. The court said that "[w]hile his formal credentials may be a little thin, he certainly had sufficient substantive qualifications to be considered an expert under the liberal standard of Rule 702." *Waldorf*, 916 F. Supp. at 430.

Waldorf has a heavy burden in challenging this decision because, absent an abuse of discretion, we will not substitute our own judgment for that of the trial court regarding the admission or exclusion of expert testimony. *See Aloe Coal Co.*, 816 F.2d at 114. Of course, an abuse of discretion means much more than that the appellate court disagrees with the trial court. Rather, a trial court's determination whether to admit or exclude expert testimony will be upheld "unless manifestly erroneous." *Id.*

We hold that the district court did not abuse its discretion in qualifying Rizzo as an expert witness. Even though Rizzo did not possess formal academic training in the area of vocational rehabilitation, he did have experience in the field through his employment at the Developmental Disabilities Council in attempting to provide jobs for disabled individuals. During this time, Rizzo also became familiar with the relevant literature in the field. Even if his qualifications are, as the district court described, "a little thin," he has substantially more knowledge than an average lay person regarding employment opportunities for disabled individuals. In the circumstances, we cannot say that the district court abused its discretion in determining that Rizzo possessed the minimum qualifications necessary to testify as an expert.

Whatever doubts the district court might have had regarding Rizzo's qualifications, it is important to note that "[o]nce the trial court has determined that a witness is competent to testify as an expert, challenges to the expert's skill or knowledge go to the weight to be accorded the expert testimony rather than to its admissibility." *Fox v. Dannenberg*, 906 F.2d 1253, 1256 (8th Cir. 1990); *see also Knight*, 596 F.2d at 88. The jury heard all of the testimony regarding Rizzo's qualifications, and thus the jurors could evaluate the weight to give to Rizzo's expert opinions. Therefore, because the district court did not abuse its discretion in qualifying Rizzo as an expert witness, we will uphold its denial of Waldorf's motion for a new trial. In short, this situation is one within the discretion of the court. Thus, while we do not doubt that we would not have disturbed the court's ruling if it had excluded Rizzo as an expert witness, we cannot disturb the court's ruling qualifying him. As is so often the case in discretionary rulings involving qualification of witnesses or admission of evidence, we will affirm a reasoned decision by a district court regardless of how we might have decided the issue if we had been making the original determination....

Notes and Questions

1. For a case holding an expert to be qualified on the facts of Problem 4-6, *see United States v. Johnson*, 575 F.2d 1347, 1360–61 (5th Cir. 1978).

2. Rule 104(a) provides that "[t]he court must decide any preliminary question about whether a witness is qualified...." Whether a witness qualifies as an expert is such a determination, and it is thus the judge alone who decides whether the witness is so qualified. Yet as the *Waldorf* decision indicates, once the trial court has determined that the witness qualifies, the parties remain free to bring up the expert's qualifications before the jury as the jury ultimately decides what weight to give to the expert's testimony and may be swayed by arguments regarding his qualifications. Thus, even if a court deems a witness qualified to testify as an expert, it is in the interest of both the proponent and the opponent of that witness to bring the expert's qualifications (or lack thereof) to the jury's attention. Accordingly, even if the opposing party stipulates to the expert's qualifications as an expert, the proponent will still want to ask the expert about his qualifications on direct examination in the hopes that it will impress the jury. Similarly, if an opposing party is unsuccessful in having the trial court deem an expert unqualified, he may probe the weaknesses in the expert's qualifications on cross-examination in the hopes that the jury will take those weaknesses into account.

3. The Advisory Committee, in its note to the 2000 Amendment to Rule 702, indicated that there are risks to using the term "expert" before the jury:

> The use of the term "expert" in the Rule does not, however, mean that a jury should actually be informed that a qualified witness is testifying as an "expert." Indeed, there is much to be said for a practice that prohibits the use of the term "expert" by both the parties and the court at trial. Such a practice "ensures that trial courts do not inadvertently put their stamp of authority" on a witness's opinion, and protects against the jury's being "overwhelmed by the so-called 'experts.'"

Advisory Committee Note to 2000 Amendment to Rule 702. How can a court avoid the use of the term "expert" while at the same time carrying out the process of qualifying an expert as such before the jury? Consider the following:

> [A]s is this Court's usual practice, our instructions to the jury concerning the consideration of opinion testimony will not include the "expert" label but rather will refer to persons with specialized knowledge or skill. In addition, during or after questioning of a party's opinion witnesses, counsel are not to request the

Court to "qualify" the person as an "expert" and are not to ask the Court to allow the witness to give "expert" testimony. Rather, when counsel is finished with direct examination of the witness on his or her qualifications, counsel should simply tender the witness for examination on qualifications, and the Court will inquire of opposing counsel whether they wish to examine the witness at that point or defer examination until cross. If opposing counsel do not believe that the witness has been qualified to give an opinion under Rule 702, the appropriate means to bring that to the Court's attention is to object when such testimony is elicited, stating that the witness has not been properly qualified to give opinion testimony.

Dowe v. National Railroad Passenger Corp., 2004 WL 887410, at *6 (N.D. Ill. Apr. 26, 2004). *See also United States v. Thomas*, 797 F. Supp. 19, 24 (D.D.C. 1992) (using the phrase "opinion witness" in place of the term "expert").

2. Reliability of Expert Witness Testimony

Daubert v. Merrell Dow Pharmaceuticals, Inc.
509 U.S. 579 (1993)

Justice BLACKMUN delivered the opinion of the Court.

In this case we are called upon to determine the standard for admitting expert scientific testimony in a federal trial.

I

Petitioners Jason Daubert and Eric Schuller are minor children born with serious birth defects. They and their parents sued respondent in California state court, alleging that the birth defects had been caused by the mothers' ingestion of Bendectin, a prescription antinausea drug marketed by respondent. Respondent removed the suits to federal court on diversity grounds.

After extensive discovery, respondent moved for summary judgment, contending that Bendectin does not cause birth defects in humans and that petitioners would be unable to come forward with any admissible evidence that it does. In support of its motion, respondent submitted an affidavit of Steven H. Lamm, physician and epidemiologist, who is a well-credentialed expert on the risks from exposure to various chemical substances. Doctor Lamm stated that he had reviewed all the literature on Bendectin and human birth defects— more than 30 published studies involving over 130,000 patients. No study had found Bendectin to be a human teratogen (*i.e.*, a substance capable of causing malformations in fetuses). On the basis of this review, Doctor Lamm concluded that maternal use of Bendectin during the first trimester of pregnancy has not been shown to be a risk factor for human birth defects.

Petitioners did not (and do not) contest this characterization of the published record regarding Bendectin. Instead, they responded to respondent's motion with the testimony of eight experts of their own, each of whom also possessed impressive credentials. These experts had concluded that Bendectin can cause birth defects. Their conclusions were based upon "in vitro" (test tube) and "in vivo" (live) animal studies that found a link between Bendectin and malformations; pharmacological studies of the chemical structure of Bendectin that purported to show similarities between the structure of the drug and that of other substances known to cause birth defects; and the "reanalysis" of previously published epidemiological (human statistical) studies.

The District Court granted respondent's motion for summary judgment. The court stated that scientific evidence is admissible only if the principle upon which it is based is "'sufficiently established to have general acceptance in the field to which it belongs.'" The court concluded that petitioners' evidence did not meet this standard....

The United States Court of Appeals for the Ninth Circuit affirmed. 951 F.2d 1128 (1991). Citing *Frye v. United States*, 293 F. 1013, 1014 (1923), the court stated that expert opinion based on a scientific technique is inadmissible unless the technique is "generally accepted" as reliable in the relevant scientific community. 951 F.2d, at 1129–1130. The court declared that expert opinion based on a methodology that diverges "significantly from the procedures accepted by recognized authorities in the field ... cannot be shown to be 'generally accepted as a reliable technique.'" *Id.*, at 1130, quoting *United States v. Solomon*, 753 F.2d 1522, 1526 (CA9 1985)....

We granted certiorari in light of sharp divisions among the courts regarding the proper standard for the admission of expert testimony.

II

A

In the 70 years since its formulation in the *Frye* case, the "general acceptance" test has been the dominant standard for determining the admissibility of novel scientific evidence at trial. Although under increasing attack of late, the rule continues to be followed by a majority of courts, including the Ninth Circuit.

The *Frye* test has its origin in a short and citation-free 1923 decision concerning the admissibility of evidence derived from a systolic blood pressure deception test, a crude precursor to the polygraph machine. In what has become a famous (perhaps infamous) passage, the then Court of Appeals for the District of Columbia described the device and its operation and declared:

"Just when a scientific principle or discovery crosses the line between the experimental and demonstrable stages is difficult to define. Somewhere in this twilight zone the evidential force of the principle must be recognized, and while courts will go a long way in admitting expert testimony deduced from a well-recognized scientific principle or discovery, *the thing from which the deduction is made must be sufficiently established to have gained general acceptance in the particular field in which it belongs."*

293 F., at 1014 (emphasis added).

Because the deception test had "not yet gained such standing and scientific recognition among physiological and psychological authorities as would justify the courts in admitting expert testimony deduced from the discovery, development, and experiments thus far made," evidence of its results was ruled inadmissible. *Ibid.*

The merits of the *Frye* test have been much debated, and scholarship on its proper scope and application is legion. Petitioners' primary attack, however, is not on the content but on the continuing authority of the rule. They contend that the *Frye* test was superseded by the adoption of the Federal Rules of Evidence. We agree.

We interpret the legislatively enacted Federal Rules of Evidence as we would any statute. [The Court proceeds to quote Rule 402's general principle that all relevant evidence is admissible unless excluded by some other rule or source of law, as well as Rule 401's broad definition of "relevant evidence."] The Rule's basic standard of relevance thus is a liberal one.

Frye, of course, predated the Rules by half a century. In *United States v. Abel*, 469 U.S. 45 (1984), we considered the pertinence of background common law in interpreting the Rules of Evidence. We noted that the Rules occupy the field, *id.*, at 49, but, quoting Professor Cleary, the Reporter, explained that the common law nevertheless could serve as an aid to their application....

Here there is a specific Rule that speaks to the contested issue.... Nothing in the text of this Rule establishes "general acceptance" as an absolute prerequisite to admissibility. Nor does respondent present any clear indication that Rule 702 or the Rules as a whole were intended to incorporate a "general acceptance" standard. The drafting history makes no mention of *Frye*, and a rigid "general acceptance" requirement would be at odds with the "liberal thrust" of the Federal Rules and their "general approach of relaxing the traditional barriers to 'opinion' testimony." Given the Rules' permissive backdrop and their inclusion of a specific rule on expert testimony that does not mention "general acceptance," the assertion that the Rules somehow assimilated *Frye* is unconvincing. *Frye* made "general acceptance" the exclusive test for admitting expert scientific testimony. That austere standard, absent from, and incompatible with, the Federal Rules of Evidence, should not be applied in federal trials.[6]

B

That the *Frye* test was displaced by the Rules of Evidence does not mean, however, that the Rules themselves place no limits on the admissibility of purportedly scientific evidence. Nor is the trial judge disabled from screening such evidence. To the contrary,

---

6. Because we hold that *Frye* has been superseded and base the discussion that follows on the content of the congressionally enacted Federal Rules of Evidence, we do not address petitioners' argument that application of the *Frye* rule in this diversity case, as the application of a judge-made rule affecting substantive rights, would violate the doctrine of *Erie R. Co. v. Tompkins*, 304 U.S. 64 (1938).

under the Rules the trial judge must ensure that any and all scientific testimony or evidence admitted is not only relevant, but reliable.

The primary locus of this obligation is Rule 702, which clearly contemplates some degree of regulation of the subjects and theories about which an expert may testify.... The subject of an expert's testimony must be "scientific ... knowledge."[8] The adjective "scientific" implies a grounding in the methods and procedures of science. Similarly, the word "knowledge" connotes more than subjective belief or unsupported speculation. The term "applies to any body of known facts or to any body of ideas inferred from such facts or accepted as truths on good grounds." Webster's Third New International Dictionary 1252 (1986). Of course, it would be unreasonable to conclude that the subject of scientific testimony must be "known" to a certainty; arguably, there are no certainties in science. But, in order to qualify as "scientific knowledge," an inference or assertion must be derived by the scientific method. Proposed testimony must be supported by appropriate validation—*i.e.*, "good grounds," based on what is known. In short, the requirement that an expert's testimony pertain to "scientific knowledge" establishes a standard of evidentiary reliability.[9]

Rule 702 further requires that the evidence or testimony "[help] the trier of fact to understand the evidence or to determine a fact in issue." This condition goes primarily to relevance. "Expert testimony which does not relate to any issue in the case is not relevant and, ergo, non-helpful." The consideration has been aptly described by Judge Becker as one of "fit." "Fit" is not always obvious, and scientific validity for one purpose is not necessarily scientific validity for other, unrelated purposes. The study of the phases of the moon, for example, may provide valid scientific "knowledge" about whether a certain night was dark, and if darkness is a fact in issue, the knowledge will assist the trier of fact. However (absent creditable grounds supporting such a link), evidence that the moon was full on a certain night will not assist the trier of fact in determining whether an individual was unusually likely to have behaved irrationally on that night. Rule 702's "helpfulness" standard requires a valid scientific connection to the pertinent inquiry as a precondition to admissibility.

That these requirements are embodied in Rule 702 is not surprising. Unlike an ordinary witness, see Rule 701, an expert is permitted wide latitude to offer opinions, including those that are not based on firsthand knowledge or observation. See Rules 702 and 703. Presumably, this relaxation of the usual requirement of firsthand knowledge—a rule which represents "a 'most pervasive manifestation' of the common law insistence upon 'the most reliable sources of information,'" Advisory Committee's Notes on Fed.Rule Evid. 602—is premised on an assumption that the expert's opinion will have a reliable basis in the knowledge and experience of his discipline.

C

Faced with a proffer of expert scientific testimony, then, the trial judge must determine at the outset, pursuant to Rule 104(a),[10] whether the expert is proposing to testify

---

8. Rule 702 also applies to "technical, or other specialized knowledge." Our discussion is limited to the scientific context because that is the nature of the expertise offered here.

9. We note that scientists typically distinguish between "validity" (does the principle support what it purports to show?) and "reliability" (does application of the principle produce consistent results?). Although "the difference between accuracy, validity, and reliability may be such that each is distinct from the other by no more than a hen's kick," our reference here is to *evidentiary* reliability— that is, trustworthiness. In a case involving scientific evidence, *evidentiary reliability* will be based upon *scientific validity*.

10. .... These matters should be established by a preponderance of proof. See *Bourjaily v. United States*, 483 U.S. 171, 175–176 (1987).

to (1) scientific knowledge that (2) will assist the trier of fact to understand or determine a fact in issue.[11] This entails a preliminary assessment of whether the reasoning or methodology underlying the testimony is scientifically valid and of whether that reasoning or methodology properly can be applied to the facts in issue. We are confident that federal judges possess the capacity to undertake this review. Many factors will bear on the inquiry, and we do not presume to set out a definitive checklist or test. But some general observations are appropriate.

Ordinarily, a key question to be answered in determining whether a theory or technique is scientific knowledge that will assist the trier of fact will be whether it can be (and has been) tested. "Scientific methodology today is based on generating hypotheses and testing them to see if they can be falsified; indeed, this methodology is what distinguishes science from other fields of human inquiry."

Another pertinent consideration is whether the theory or technique has been subjected to peer review and publication. Publication (which is but one element of peer review) is not a *sine qua non* of admissibility; it does not necessarily correlate with reliability, and in some instances well-grounded but innovative theories will not have been published. Some propositions, moreover, are too particular, too new, or of too limited interest to be published. But submission to the scrutiny of the scientific community is a component of "good science," in part because it increases the likelihood that substantive flaws in methodology will be detected. The fact of publication (or lack thereof) in a peer reviewed journal thus will be a relevant, though not dispositive, consideration in assessing the scientific validity of a particular technique or methodology on which an opinion is premised.

Additionally, in the case of a particular scientific technique, the court ordinarily should consider the known or potential rate of error, and the existence and maintenance of standards controlling the technique's operation.

Finally, "general acceptance" can yet have a bearing on the inquiry. A "reliability assessment does not require, although it does permit, explicit identification of a relevant scientific community and an express determination of a particular degree of acceptance within that community." Widespread acceptance can be an important factor in ruling particular evidence admissible, and "a known technique which has been able to attract only minimal support within the community," may properly be viewed with skepticism.

The inquiry envisioned by Rule 702 is, we emphasize, a flexible one. Its overarching subject is the scientific validity and thus the evidentiary relevance and reliability—of the principles that underlie a proposed submission. The focus, of course, must be solely on principles and methodology, not on the conclusions that they generate.

Throughout, a judge assessing a proffer of expert scientific testimony under Rule 702 should also be mindful of other applicable rules. Rule 703 provides that expert opinions based on otherwise inadmissible hearsay are to be admitted only [if experts in the particular field would reasonably rely on those kinds of facts or data in forming an opinion on the subject.] Rule 706 allows the court at its discretion to procure the assistance of an expert of its own choosing. Finally, Rule 403 permits the exclusion of relevant evidence "if its probative value is substantially outweighed by [a] danger of […]unfair prejudice,

---

11. Although the *Frye* decision itself focused exclusively on "novel" scientific techniques, we do not read the requirements of Rule 702 to apply specially or exclusively to unconventional evidence. Of course, well-established propositions are less likely to be challenged than those that are novel, and they are more handily defended. Indeed, theories that are so firmly established as to have attained the status of scientific law, such as the laws of thermodynamics, properly are subject to judicial notice under Federal Rule of Evidence 201.

confus[ing] the issues, [or] misleading the jury...." Judge Weinstein has explained: "Expert evidence can be both powerful and quite misleading because of the difficulty in evaluating it. Because of this risk, the judge in weighing possible prejudice against probative force under Rule 403 of the present rules exercises more control over experts than over lay witnesses." Weinstein, 138 F.R.D., at 632.

III

We conclude by briefly addressing what appear to be two underlying concerns of the parties and *amici* in this case. Respondent expresses apprehension that abandonment of "general acceptance" as the exclusive requirement for admission will result in a "free-for-all" in which befuddled juries are confounded by absurd and irrational pseudoscientific assertions. In this regard respondent seems to us to be overly pessimistic about the capabilities of the jury and of the adversary system generally. Vigorous cross-examination, presentation of contrary evidence, and careful instruction on the burden of proof are the traditional and appropriate means of attacking shaky but admissible evidence. Additionally, in the event the trial court concludes that the scintilla of evidence presented supporting a position is insufficient to allow a reasonable juror to conclude that the position more likely than not is true, the court remains free to direct a judgment, Fed.Rule Civ.Proc. 50(a), and likewise to grant summary judgment, Fed.Rule Civ.Proc. 56. These conventional devices, rather than wholesale exclusion under an uncompromising "general acceptance" test, are the appropriate safeguards where the basis of scientific testimony meets the standards of Rule 702.

Petitioners and, to a greater extent, their *amici* exhibit a different concern. They suggest that recognition of a screening role for the judge that allows for the exclusion of "invalid" evidence will sanction a stifling and repressive scientific orthodoxy and will be inimical to the search for truth. It is true that open debate is an essential part of both legal and scientific analyses. Yet there are important differences between the quest for truth in the courtroom and the quest for truth in the laboratory. Scientific conclusions are subject to perpetual revision. Law, on the other hand, must resolve disputes finally and quickly. The scientific project is advanced by broad and wide-ranging consideration of a multitude of hypotheses, for those that are incorrect will eventually be shown to be so, and that in itself is an advance. Conjectures that are probably wrong are of little use, however, in the project of reaching a quick, final, and binding legal judgment—often of great consequence—about a particular set of events in the past. We recognize that, in practice, a gatekeeping role for the judge, no matter how flexible, inevitably on occasion will prevent the jury from learning of authentic insights and innovations. That, nevertheless, is the balance that is struck by Rules of Evidence designed not for the exhaustive search for cosmic understanding but for the particularized resolution of legal disputes.

IV

To summarize: "General acceptance" is not a necessary precondition to the admissibility of scientific evidence under the Federal Rules of Evidence, but the Rules of Evidence—especially Rule 702—do assign to the trial judge the task of ensuring that an expert's testimony both rests on a reliable foundation and is relevant to the task at hand. Pertinent evidence based on scientifically valid principles will satisfy those demands....

[The opinion of Chief Justice Rehnquist, concurring in part and dissenting in part, is omitted.]

Goeb v. Tharaldson

615 N.W.2d 800 (Minn. 2000)

BLATZ, Chief Justice

[At issue in the case is the admissibility of expert testimony offered by the plaintiffs on the question whether an insecticide was responsible for their son's injuries. One argument made in the case is that Minnesota should abandon the *Frye* test in favor of the standard set forth by the U.S. Supreme Court in *Daubert*.]

A number of arguments have been made for adopting *Daubert* in Minnesota. First, critics of the *Frye* general acceptance standard claim that it may at times exclude cutting-edge but otherwise demonstrably reliable, probative evidence, and thus represents a more conservative approach to the admissibility of scientific evidence. For example, the *Frye* standard might exclude a new, but reliable, methodology or test because of the inherent time lag between the development of a new scientific technique and its general acceptance in the field. Also, a generally accepted theory or technique, although admissible, may not always be correct.

By comparison, because *Daubert* stresses a more liberal and flexible approach to the admission of scientific testimony, it has been viewed as relaxing the barriers to the admissibility of expert evidence. However, in practice, *Daubert* does not necessarily make admissible expert evidence that was not admissible under *Frye*. One commentator has noted that "[t]he post-*Daubert* era can fairly be described as the period of 'strict scrutiny' of science by non-scientifically trained judges."

The *Frye* general acceptance standard has been criticized for other reasons, most notably that it improperly defers to scientists the legal question of admissibility of scientific evidence. Some are concerned that *Frye* " 'abdicates' judicial responsibility for determining admissibility to scientists uneducated in the law." However, in repossessing the power to determine admissibility for the courts, *Daubert* takes from scientists and confers upon judges uneducated in science the authority to determine what is scientific. This approach, which necessitates that trial judges be "amateur scientists," has also been frequently criticized.

"[S]cientists often have vigorous and sincere disagreements as to what research methodology is proper, what should be accepted as sufficient proof for the existence of a 'fact,' and whether information derived by a particular method can tell us anything useful about the subject under study." Under *Daubert*, it is the responsibility of the judiciary "to resolve disputes among respected, well-credentialed scientists about matters squarely within their expertise, in areas where there is no scientific consensus as to what is and what is not 'good science,' and occasionally to reject such expert testimony because it was not 'derived by the scientific method.' " A key assumption to this approach is that judges can not only resolve disputes among qualified scientists who have spent years immersed in their field of study, but can do so without also adopting the substantive positions of some scientists but not others.

By comparison, the *Frye* general acceptance standard ensures that the persons most qualified to assess scientific validity of a technique have the determinative voice. Although this approach is discounted by some as focusing on nose counting rather than on scientific validity, "[a]dmissibility can be based on scientific merit only if judges defer to practicing scientists' assessments of scientific merit."

Another noted criticism of *Frye* is that it can be difficult to apply because it raises additional questions such as: (1) does the court look to general acceptance of a technique or the general acceptance of the underlying scientific principle; (2) who is the relevant scientific community; and (3) what is general acceptance—a majority, or a credible minority? These types of criticisms, however, are not unique to [*Frye*] given that general acceptability is also one of the *Daubert* factors. Further, because the law is continuously evolving, answers to these questions will be set forth in case law as the issues properly present themselves....

Finally, the potential for non-uniformity in the law under *Daubert* gives us considerable cause for concern. Cases built on similar facts and offering similar scientific techniques could have widely disparate results. For example, the Fifth and Ninth Circuit Courts of Appeals have held that *Daubert* overruled the per se rule excluding polygraph evidence. As a result, each federal district court will need to consider the admissibility of polygraph evidence anew each time it is raised. While some argue that this would ensure that the courts have the flexibility to change as science evolves, this practice will also lead to greater variation in decisions at the district court level that may not be correctable at the appellate level under an abuse of discretion standard of review. In contrast, under the *Frye* ... standard, the trial judge defers to the scientific community's assessment of a given technique, and the appellate court reviews de novo the legal determination of whether the scientific methodology has obtained general acceptance in the scientific community. Thus, [*Frye*] is more apt to ensure "objective and uniform rulings" as to particular scientific methods or techniques....

Notes and Questions

1. In footnote 8 of *Daubert*, the Court noted that although Rule 702 applied not only to scientific knowledge but also to technical and other specialized knowledge, it was limiting its holding to the type of evidence at issue in the case, namely scientific knowledge. In *Kumho Tire Co., Ltd. v. Carmichael*, 526 U.S. 137 (1999), the Supreme Court extended *Daubert* to all expert testimony:

> In *Daubert*, the Court specified that it is the Rule's word "knowledge," not the words (like "scientific") that modify that word, that "establishes a standard of evidentiary reliability." 509 U.S., at 589–590. Hence, as a matter of language, the Rule applies its reliability standard to all "scientific," "technical," or "other specialized" matters within its scope. We concede that the Court in *Daubert* referred only to "scientific" knowledge. But as the Court there said, it referred to "scientific" testimony "because that [wa]s the nature of the expertise" at issue. *Id.*, at 590, n. 8.

> Neither is the evidentiary rationale that underlay the Court's basic *Daubert* "gatekeeping" determination limited to "scientific" knowledge. *Daubert* pointed out that Federal Rules 702 and 703 grant expert witnesses testimonial latitude unavailable to other witnesses on the "assumption that the expert's opinion will have a reliable basis in the knowledge and experience of his discipline." *Id.*, at 592 (pointing out that experts may testify to opinions, including those that are not based on firsthand knowledge or observation). The Rules grant that latitude to all experts, not just to "scientific" ones.

> Finally, it would prove difficult, if not impossible, for judges to administer evidentiary rules under which a gatekeeping obligation depended upon a distinction between "scientific" knowledge and "technical" or "other specialized" knowledge. There is no clear line that divides the one from the others....

Kumho Tire, 526 U.S. at 147–48.

2. Although listing several factors, the *Daubert* Court was careful to state that in doing so, it did "not presume to set out a definitive checklist or test." *Daubert*, 509 U.S. at 593. In *Kumho Tire*, the Supreme Court extended its earlier decision in *General Electric Co. v. Joiner*, 522 U.S. 136 (1997), which provided for deferential review of trial court decisions admitting or excluding expert testimony, to provide trial courts with broad discretion to decide what factors to employ in applying *Daubert*:

> We agree with the Solicitor General that "[t]he factors identified in *Daubert* may or may not be pertinent in assessing reliability, depending on the nature of the issue, the expert's particular expertise, and the subject of his testimony." The conclusion, in our view, is that we can neither rule out, nor rule in, for all cases and for all time the applicability of the factors mentioned in *Daubert*, nor can we now do so for subsets of cases categorized by category of expert or by kind of evidence. Too much depends upon the particular circumstances of the particular case at issue.

> *Daubert* itself is not to the contrary. It made clear that its list of factors was meant to be helpful, not definitive. Indeed, those factors do not all necessarily apply even in every instance in which the reliability of scientific testimony is challenged....

> The trial court must have the same kind of latitude in deciding *how* to test an expert's reliability, and to decide whether or when special briefing or other proceedings are needed to investigate reliability, as it enjoys when it decides *whether* or not that expert's relevant testimony is reliable. Our opinion in *Joiner* makes clear that a court of appeals is to apply an abuse-of-discretion standard when it "review[s] a trial court's decision to admit or exclude expert testimony." That standard applies as much to the trial court's decisions about how to determine reliability as to its ultimate conclusion.... Thus, whether *Daubert*'s specific factors are, or are not, reasonable measures of reliability in a particular case is a matter that the law grants the trial judge broad latitude to determine.

Kumho Tire, 526 U.S. at 150–153. *See also United States v. Brown*, 415 F.3d 1257, 1264 (11th Cir. 2005) ("[I]t is difficult to persuade a court of appeals to reverse a district court's judgment on *Daubert* grounds. The theme that shapes appellate review in this area is the limited nature of it.").

3. In 2000, the Advisory Committee amended Rule 702 to make explicit the reliability requirement identified in *Daubert* and *Kumho Tire*. Consistent with *Daubert* and *Kumho Tire*, the Advisory Committee indicated that the factors cited in *Daubert* were "neither exclusive nor dispositive," and catalogued some other factors invoked by lower courts:

> Courts both before and after *Daubert* have found other factors relevant in determining whether expert testimony is sufficiently reliable to be considered by the trier of fact. These factors include:

> (1) Whether experts are "proposing to testify about matters growing naturally and directly out of research they have conducted independent of the litigation, or whether they have developed their opinions expressly for purposes of testifying."

> (2) Whether the expert has unjustifiably extrapolated from an accepted premise to an unfounded conclusion.

> (3) Whether the expert has adequately accounted for obvious alternative explanations.

(4) Whether the expert "is being as careful as he would be in his regular professional work outside his paid litigation consulting."

(5) Whether the field of expertise claimed by the expert is known to reach reliable results for the type of opinion the expert would give.

All of these factors remain relevant to the determination of the reliability of expert testimony under the Rule as amended. Other factors may also be relevant. Yet no single factor is necessarily dispositive of the reliability of a particular expert's testimony.

Advisory Committee Note to 2000 Amendment to Rule 702.

4. When *Daubert* was remanded, the lower court discussed the relevance of whether the research on which the expert's opinion is based was developed independent of the litigation:

One very significant fact to be considered is whether the experts are proposing to testify about matters growing naturally and directly out of research they have conducted independent of the litigation, or whether they have developed their opinions expressly for purposes of testifying. That an expert testifies for money does not necessarily cast doubt on the reliability of his testimony, as few experts appear in court merely as an eleemosynary gesture. But in determining whether proposed expert testimony amounts to good science, we may not ignore the fact that a scientist's normal workplace is the lab or the field, not the courtroom or the lawyer's office.

That an expert testifies based on research he has conducted independent of the litigation provides important, objective proof that the research comports with the dictates of good science. For one thing, experts whose findings flow from existing research are less likely to have been biased toward a particular conclusion by the promise of remuneration; when an expert prepares reports and findings before being hired as a witness, that record will limit the degree to which he can tailor his testimony to serve a party's interests. Then, too, independent research carries its own indicia of reliability, as it is conducted, so to speak, in the usual course of business and must normally satisfy a variety of standards to attract funding and institutional support. Finally, there is usually a limited number of scientists actively conducting research on the very subject that is germane to a particular case, which provides a natural constraint on parties' ability to shop for experts who will come to the desired conclusion. That the testimony proffered by an expert is based directly on legitimate, pre-existing research unrelated to the litigation provides the most persuasive basis for concluding that the opinions he expresses were "derived by the scientific method."

Daubert v. Merrell Dow Pharmaceuticals, Inc., 43 F.3d 1311, 1317 (9th Cir. 1995).

5. The Advisory Committee Note to the 2000 Amendment to Rule 702 discusses expert witness testimony based on experience:

Nothing in this amendment is intended to suggest that experience alone—or experience in conjunction with other knowledge, skill, training or education—may not provide a sufficient foundation for expert testimony. To the contrary, the text of Rule 702 expressly contemplates that an expert may be qualified on the basis of experience. In certain fields, experience is the predominant, if not sole, basis for a great deal of reliable expert testimony.

If the witness is relying solely or primarily on experience, then the witness must explain how that experience leads to the conclusion reached, why that experience is a sufficient basis for the opinion, and how that experience is reliably applied to the facts.... The more subjective and controversial the expert's inquiry, the more likely the testimony should be excluded as unreliable.

Advisory Committee Note to 2000 Amendment to Rule 702.

Is the Note referring to expert witness qualification, expert testimony reliability, or both?

6. Does the 2000 Amendment to Rule 702 merely codify *Daubert*, or does it add additional prerequisites to Rule 702? While Rule 702(c), the requirement that "the testimony is the product of reliable principles and methods," seems to be a mere codification of *Daubert*, Rule 702(b) requires that the testimony "be based on sufficient facts or data," and Rule 702(d) requires that the principles and methods be reliably applied to the facts of the case. Or are Rules 702(b) and 702(d) merely particularized applications of Rules 401 through 403? How would these be applied in the *Collins* and *Chischilly* cases from Chapter 1?

7. Is the *Daubert/Kumho Tire* standard too flexible and appellate review of the application of that standard too deferential to ensure predictability and consistency? How does *Frye* stack up in comparison, and do the benefits that *Daubert* has over *Frye* justify the costs?

8. Suppose that a federal court is exercising diversity jurisdiction, and the law of the state in which the federal court sits has a rule governing expert witness testimony that differs from the federal rule, such as still following *Frye*, or not screening expert witness testimony for reliability at all, but leaving it to the jury to make that determination. Which rule governs the admissibility of the expert witness testimony? Does *Daubert* itself shed any light on this question? *See Schrott v. Bristol-Myers Squibb Co.*, 403 F.3d 940, 943 (7th Cir. 2005) ("It is frivolous to assert that a federal court should not have applied the federal rules governing expert witnesses, just because the case happened to be a diversity case and thus one governed by state substantive law.... Indeed, *Daubert* and later Supreme Court decisions such as *General Electric Co. v. Joiner* and *Kumho Tire Co. v. Carmichael* were all diversity tort cases.").

3. A Closer Look at *Daubert* and the Helpfulness Requirement

The materials that follow examine the application of *Daubert* in a variety of contexts that recur with a fair amount of frequency, including expert testimony on DNA analysis, fingerprint analysis, handwriting analysis, battered woman syndrome, polygraph analysis, and eyewitness reliability. In addition, several of the cases also explore the "helpfulness" prerequisite to the admissibility of expert testimony.

a. DNA Evidence

United States v. Chischilly
30 F.3d 1144 (9th Cir. 1994)

CHOY, Circuit Judge:

[Chapter 1 reproduced an excerpt from this opinion addressing a claim that DNA evidence should have been excluded under Rule 403. The following is an excerpt from the opinion addressing a claim that DNA evidence does not pass muster under Rule 702.]

In view of the "raging controversy" in the scientific community over DNA testing, Chischilly contends that the district court committed reversible error by admitting evidence of a match between his blood sample and semen found on the victim's clothing, as well as testimony regarding the random probability of such a match....

Chischilly first challenged the reliability of the Government's DNA extraction and matching procedures on the following grounds: (1) the Government's experts were either drawn from the overly narrow field of forensic scientists, a group predisposed to accept new forensic techniques, or had a career interest in testifying on behalf of the FBI; (2) contaminants could have affected some of the samples relied on by the FBI in its DNA analysis and led to unreliable results; (3) inconsistencies in the gel used by the FBI in the electrophoresis process may affect the mobility of the alleles[7] in the DNA fragments; (4) ethidium bromide, used by the FBI but not most research laboratories in gel electrophoresis, may retard the migration of DNA fragments through the electrophoretic gel; (5) the presence of additional bands on the autorads[8] interpreted in the RFLP[9] test may have indicated that the DNA samples were degraded; (6) the FBI's match criteria are subjective, imprecise, insufficiently stringent and not uniformly applied; and (7) the FBI's quality assurance program is inadequate and is subject to insufficient peer-reviewed publication.

Chischilly then questioned the FBI's statistical methods for determining the random probability of a match between his DNA sample and the relevant population and raised the following additional objections: (8) the product rule is a novel statistical procedure

---

7. An allele is "any alternative form of a gene that can occupy a particular chromosomal locus. In humans and other diploid organisms there are two alleles, one on each chromosome of a homologous pair." Dorland's Illustrated Medical Dictionary 48 (27th ed. 1988). Forensic DNA tests compare allele combinations at loci where the alleles tend to be highly variable across individuals and ethnic groups. If there is no match between the alleles from the evidence DNA and the potential suspect's DNA, the suspect is generally ruled out as the source of the evidence, unless the failure is attributable to inadequate test conditions or contaminated samples. If there is a match, analysts use the frequency of the alleles' appearance in the relevant population to calculate the probability that another person could have the same pattern of allele pairs. *See* Georgia Sargeant, *DNA Evidence Finding Stricter Scrutiny, New Uses*, Trial, Apr. 1993, at 15.

8. An autorad (a.k.a. autoradiograph) is "a radiograph of an object or tissue made by recording the radiation emitted by radioactive material within it, especially after the purposeful introduction of radioactive material." Dorland's Illustrated Medical Dictionary 172. In DNA profiling, forensic scientists employ autorads in an extraction process known as "Southern Transfer", in which DNA fragments are placed atop a gel subjected to an electric current. DNA fragments comprised of alleles are then soaked up by capillary action into a nylon membrane. The membrane is then immersed in a solution containing a radioactive probe. These probes bind to portions of the DNA fragments containing complementary sequences of allelic base pairs (e.g., a radioactive probe with the sequence CCGGACAT would target a sample strand containing the nucleotide sequence GGCCTGTA). The membrane is then placed against a sheet of X-ray film known as an autorad. The radioactive molecules in the probe expose the autorad and leave traces known as "bands" indicating the location and distance travelled by the migrating alleles through the gel. A computer then scans the autorad and measures this distance, a variable corresponding to the size of a particular allele type (larger types of alleles tend to migrate more slowly through the gel). Differences in band length at a given loci are analyzed to match or distinguish the alleles in the evidentiary DNA and the potential suspect's sample. For a fuller description of gel electrophoresis as applied to DNA forensic testing, see Lempert, *Some Caveats Concerning DNA as Criminal Identification Evidence: With Thanks to the Reverend Bayes*, 13 Cardozo L.Rev. 303, 304 n. 4 (1991) (hereinafter "*Caveats Concerning DNA*").

9. RFLP (i.e., restriction fragment length polymorphism) analysis refers to the process of cutting the evidence DNA and the potential suspect's DNA into fragments at particular loci with "restriction enzymes". The resulting restriction fragments, comprised of "alleles" (i.e., one of two forms of a gene which may occur at any given gene locus; *see* n. 7 *supra*), are subjected to gel electrophoresis, as described briefly at n. 8 *supra*.

whose reliability is not generally accepted by the scientific community; (9) substructuring[10] within the Native American and Navajo populations invalidates use of the product rule to determine the probability of a coincidental match within the FBI's I-3 database for Native American populations; and (10) the FBI's I-3 database is too small and contains too few Navajos.

Chischilly marshals an impressive body of academic commentary in support of several of his contentions and points out areas where the FBI's DNA testing and statistical procedures may warrant review and revision. Nonetheless, we conclude that under *Daubert* the district court did not abuse its discretion in admitting evidence of a DNA match and testimony regarding the probability of a coincidental match.

Challenging the motivations and impartiality of Government-retained expert witnesses, Chischilly's first objection is clearly conjectural and raises a credibility issue which the trial court was in a superior position to ours to weigh. In light of *Daubert*, Chischilly's second, third and fourth objections, regarding potential faults in the DNA sample extraction processes conducted in FBI laboratories, go to the weight to be accorded the evidence, not to its admissibility in the first instance.

The fifth objection, regarding the possible degrading of the DNA samples, is more troubling, insofar as it was based on data specific to Chischilly's DNA test and was not rebutted with especial force by experts retained by the Government. Nevertheless, Chischilly failed to demonstrate that the degradation is the result of a faulty methodology or theory as opposed to imperfect execution of laboratory techniques whose theoretical foundation is sufficiently accepted in the scientific community to pass muster under *Daubert*. *See Martinez*, 3 F.3d 1191, 1198 (8th Cir. 1993) (finding under *Daubert*'s flexible standard that "[a]n alleged error in the application of a reliable methodology should provide the basis for exclusion of the opinion only if that error negates the basis for the reliability of the principle itself"). The impact of imperfectly conducted laboratory procedures might therefore be approached more properly as an issue going not to the admissibility, but to the weight of the DNA profiling evidence.

We reach the same conclusion with respect to Chischilly's sixth objection. Chischilly presented expert testimony that other laboratories, even one in which FBI protocols are used to prepare autorads, would have declared a nonmatch when comparing Chischilly's DNA sample with the evidentiary sample. With regard to admissibility, the mere existence of scientific institutions that would interpret data more conservatively scarcely indicates a "lack of general acceptance" under *Daubert*'s fourth factor. Similarly, the testimony indicates disagreement over, not an absence of, controlling standards for purposes of the second part of *Daubert*'s third factor, focusing on whether such standards exist and are maintained. Suggesting similar treatment of Chischilly's sixth objection, *Daubert* cautions lower courts not to confuse the role of judge and jury by forgetting that "vigorous cross-examination, presentation of contrary evidence, and careful instruction on the burden of proof", rather than exclusion, "are the traditional and appropriate means of attacking shaky but admissible evidence."

In regard to the first part of *Daubert*'s third factor, the known or potential rate of error, some commentators have objected that "the potential rate of error in the forensic DNA

---

10. "Substructuring" refers to the tendency toward decreasing genetic heterogeneity and allelic independence (*see* n. 7 *supra*) exhibited by ethnically homogeneous, non-randomly mating populations; that is, a substructured population may be defined as one in which the probability of a random match between two of its members is greater than the likelihood of such a match between two members of the population at large.

typing technique is unknown." However, we note that scientific institutions have undertaken on numerous occasions in recent years to estimate error rates attending DNA profiling. In addition, some commentators have cautioned against accepting overly permissive error rates, at least for false positives, in view of the high stakes involved in a criminal trial. Nevertheless, we conclude that there was a sufficient showing of low error rates so that the third factor does not weigh against the admissibility of DNA profiling evidence.

Chischilly's seventh objection, that FBI procedures are insufficiently exposed to the light of peer review, deserves but does not withstand close attention under *Daubert*'s second factor, relating to degree of publication. We note that in a learned opinion rejecting a claim that the FBI has failed to share its DNA testing data and methodology, the California Court of Appeals has commented upon the existence of "numerous published articles on DNA analysis as performed by the FBI." *Barney*, 8 Cal.App.4th at 813. In addition, the NRC Report, frequently cited by Chischilly for its recommended improvements of the FBI's DNA analysis, is at least the functional equivalent of a publication subject to peer-review under *Daubert*'s liberally framed second factor.

Chischilly's eighth, ninth and tenth objections, aimed at the FBI's statistical techniques for determining the probability of a coincidental match, are perhaps his weightiest against admission of DNA profiling evidence in this case. However, under *Daubert*, they fail to demonstrate that the district court abused its discretion by admitting into evidence testimony regarding the results of the FBI's DNA analysis. Chischilly asserts rather persuasively and with considerable scientific backing that where an individual's DNA sample is tested against samples from a population in which persons of that individual's ethnic group are underrepresented, calculations based on the product rule[14] may tend to understate the probability that a random match would occur between the evidentiary sample and that individual's ethnic group. Chischilly called numerous experts who testified that the more homogeneous a population remains through intermarriage, the less random the relationship becomes between the coincidence of certain sequences of alleles at different test sites across the two samples (i.e., matches of nucleotide base pairs at given segments of the defendant's sample and the crime scene DNA). In analyzing the DNA evidence in this case, the FBI used its I-3 database, composed of DNA samples from Native Americans.[15] Nevertheless, Chischilly's objection remains because his distinct tribe (Navajo) may have been underrepresented in the I-3 database.

Chischilly asserts that, "[t]he scientific community is torn by controversy about the appropriateness of the FBI's databases, the effects of substructuring within their databases, and their statistical methodologies. This controversy has divided the scientific community into opposing camps." Chischilly goes on to cite studies offered by proponents of the FBI techniques and to note that "[b]oth sides of this continuing controversy find support in the journals and research, and both sides have prominent spokespeople." While perhaps support for exclusion of Chischilly's DNA test results under the superseded *Frye* test, with its requirement of general acceptance of a theory in the scientific community,

---

14. Whereas no two individuals (apart from identical twins) share the same overall DNA profile, "no individual has a unique profile *at a given locus*." *DNA Profiling* at 488. Under the product rule the probabilities of finding a match at each given locus on the samples satisfying statistical criteria for a match are multiplied together to calculate the random probability that the trace DNA found at the crime scene could have come from another member of the population represented by the defendant.

15. It is only helpful to use an ethnic-specific database when it is reasonable to assume that the perpetrator of the crime is a member of that group. Crimes occurring in areas that are populated by a particular ethnic group are typical instances in which an ethnic-specific database will be used. Use of ethnic-specific databases generally strengthens the probative value of statistical data.

these same statements take on the hue of adverse admissions under *Daubert*'s more liberal admissibility test: evidence of opposing academic camps arrayed in virtual scholarly equipoise amidst the scientific journals is scarcely an indication of the "minimal support within a community" that would give a trial court cause to view a known technique with skepticism under *Daubert*'s fourth factor.

Accordingly, we conclude that under *Daubert*, the three chief components of DNA profiling as performed in this case, sample processing, match determination and statistical analysis, pass muster under Rule 702....

[The dissenting opinion of Judge Noonan is omitted.]

b. Fingerprint and Handwriting Analysis

United States v. Crisp
324 F.3d 261 (4th Cir. 2003)

KING, Circuit Judge:

Patrick Leroy Crisp appeals multiple convictions arising from an armed bank robbery carried out in Durham, North Carolina, on June 13, 2001. Crisp maintains that his trial was tainted by the Government's presentation of inadmissible expert testimony. His appeal presents a single question: whether the disciplines of forensic fingerprint analysis and forensic handwriting analysis satisfy the criteria for expert opinion testimony under *Daubert v. Merrell Dow Pharmaceuticals, Inc.*, 509 U.S. 579 (1993)....

II.

Fingerprint and handwriting analysis have long been recognized by the courts as sound methods for making reliable identifications. Today, however, Crisp challenges the district court's decisions to permit experts in those fields to testify on behalf of the prosecution. The fingerprinting expert, Brannan, gave her opinion that a palm print lifted from the Note was that of Crisp; the handwriting expert, Currin, testified that, in his judgment, the handwriting on the Note matched Crisp's handwriting....

A.

We turn first to whether the fingerprint evidence was properly admitted against Crisp. Crisp has challenged the admission of this evidence on several grounds: His primary contention is that the premises underlying fingerprinting evidence have not been adequately tested. Crisp also maintains that there is no known rate of error for latent fingerprint identifications, that fingerprint examiners operate without a uniform threshold of certainty required for a positive identification, and that fingerprint evidence has not achieved general acceptance in the relevant scientific community.

1.

Fingerprint identification has been admissible as reliable evidence in criminal trials in this country since at least 1911. While we have not definitively assessed the admissibility of expert fingerprint identifications in the post-*Daubert* era, every Circuit that has done so has found such evidence admissible.

Upholding a district court's admission of fingerprint evidence, the Seventh Circuit emphasized in *Havvard* that the district court "properly considered the *Daubert* factors in analyzing [the defendant's] motion and concluded that fingerprinting techniques have been tested in the adversarial system, that individual results are routinely subjected to peer review for verification, and that the probability of error is exceptionally low." As here, the defendant in *Havvard* contended that "fingerprint comparisons are not reliable because the government admits that the basic premise that all fingerprints are unique remains unproven, and because there are no objective standards for defining how much of a latent fingerprint is necessary to conduct a comparison or for evaluating an individual examiner's comparison." The defendant further maintained that the district court erred in requiring him to offer some basis on which to find fingerprint analysis unreliable. The *Havvard* court, however, properly rejected this line of argument. Emphasizing that general acceptance remains an important consideration under *Daubert*, the Seventh Circuit concluded that the district court properly recognized that "establishing the reliability of fingerprint analysis was made easier by its 100 years of successful use in criminal trials, and appropriately noted that nothing presented at the hearing undermined [the expert's] testimony."

2.

In his challenge to the admissibility of the fingerprint evidence, Crisp begins with the contention that the basic premises underlying fingerprint identification have not been subjected to adequate testing. The two premises that he singles out as requiring more searching scrutiny are: (1) that no two persons share the same fingerprint; and (2) that fingerprint examiners are able to make reliable identifications on the basis of small, distorted latent fingerprint fragments. In support of his assertions, Crisp notes that the expert in this case, Brannan, was unable to reference any study establishing that no two persons share the same fingerprint; she was able only to testify that no study had ever proven this premise false. In addition, Crisp contends that the Government itself seems unsure of the reliability of fingerprint evidence: in particular, Crisp notes that the National Institute of Justice, an arm of the Department of Justice, issued a solicitation for fingerprint validation studies in March of 2000. This solicitation calls for "basic research to determine the scientific validity of individuality in friction ridge examination," and also seeks the development of standard procedures for fingerprint comparisons and for the testing of those procedures once adopted. National Institute of Justice, *Forensic Friction Ridge (Fingerprint) Examination Validation Studies* 4 (Mar.2000). Finally, though Crisp cites no studies demonstrating the unreliability of fingerprinting analysis, he brings to our attention two law review articles discussing the paucity of research into the fingerprint identification process.

Crisp next maintains that, because the basic premises behind fingerprint analysis have not been properly tested, there can be no established error rates.[4] He also asserts that fingerprint examiners operate without uniform, objective standards, noting that Brannan herself testified that there is no generally accepted standard regarding the number of points of identification necessary to make a positive identification. Finally, Crisp contends that, while fingerprint analysis has gained general acceptance among fingerprint examiners themselves, this factor should be discounted because, according to

---

4. It is true that, in *Rogers*, we found fingerprinting evidence admissible in part because, in that case, "the possibility of error was mitigated ... by having two experts independently review the evidence." Here, there was no such independent review. And although Brannan, the fingerprint expert, testified to achieving perfect scores on all of her proficiency tests, such tests may not in and of themselves establish a low error rate, since a fingerprint used for testing purposes may be clearer and more complete than a print harvested from a crime scene. For example, while the *Llera Plaza* court recognized that FBI experts were required to take proficiency tests, and that those experts scored highly on such tests, it observed that the tests themselves "presented little challenge, principally because ... the latent prints in the tests were ... of substantially greater clarity than one would normally harvest from a crime scene."

Crisp, the relevant community "is devoid of financially disinterested parties such as academics."

3.

Crisp today advocates the wholesale exclusion of a long-accepted form of expert evidence. Such a drastic step is not required of us under *Daubert*, however, and we decline to take it. The *Daubert* decision, in adding four new factors to the traditional "general acceptance" standard for expert testimony, effectively opened the courts to a broader range of opinion evidence than was previously admissible. Although *Daubert* attempted to ensure that courts screen out "junk science," it also enabled the courts to entertain new and less conventional forms of expertise. As the Court explained, the addition of the new factors would put an end to the "wholesale exclusion [of expert testimony based on scientific innovations] under an uncompromising 'general acceptance' test."

The touchstones for admissibility under *Daubert* are two: reliability and relevancy. Under *Daubert*, a trial judge need not expend scarce judicial resources reexamining a familiar form of expertise every time opinion evidence is offered. In fact, if a given theory or technique is "so firmly established as to have attained the status of scientific law," then it need not be examined at all, but instead may properly be subject to judicial notice.

While the principles underlying fingerprint identification have not attained the status of scientific law, they nonetheless bear the imprimatur of a strong general acceptance, not only in the expert community, but in the courts as well. Put simply, Crisp has provided us no reason today to believe that this general acceptance of the principles underlying fingerprint identification has, for decades, been misplaced. Accordingly, the district court was well within its discretion in accepting at face value the consensus of the expert and judicial communities that the fingerprint identification technique is reliable.

In addition to a strong expert and judicial consensus regarding the reliability of fingerprint identification, there exist the requisite "standards controlling the technique's operation." As Brannan testified, while different agencies may require different degrees of correlation before permitting a positive identification, fingerprint analysts are held to a consistent "points and characteristics" approach to identification. Analysts are also consistently subjected to testing and proficiency requirements. Brannan's testimony is entirely in keeping with the conclusions of the post-*Daubert* courts that uniform standards have been established "through professional training, peer review, presentation of conflicting evidence and double checking."

Furthermore, in *Havvard*, the Seventh Circuit determined that *Daubert*'s "known error rate" factor was satisfied because the expert had testified that the error rate for fingerprint comparison was "essentially zero." Similarly, and significantly, Brannan testified here to a negligible error rate in fingerprint identifications....

While Crisp may be correct that further research, more searching scholarly review, and the development of even more consistent professional standards is desirable, he has offered us no reason to reject outright a form of evidence that has so ably withstood the test of time.

Finally, even if we had a more concrete cause for concern as to the reliability of fingerprint identification, the Supreme Court emphasized in *Daubert* that "[v]igorous cross-examination, presentation of contrary evidence, and careful instruction on the burden of proof are the traditional and appropriate means of attacking shaky but admissible evidence."....

B.

In seeking to have his convictions vacated, Crisp also challenges the admissibility of the opinions of Currin, the handwriting expert, on grounds that are essentially identical to those on which he relied to make his case against fingerprint evidence. Crisp contends that, like fingerprinting identifications, the basic premise behind handwriting analysis is that no two persons write alike, and thus that forensic document examiners can reliably determine authorship of a particular document by comparing it with known samples. He maintains that these basic premises have not been tested, nor has an error rate been established. In addition, he asserts that handwriting experts have no numerical standards to govern their analyses and that they have not subjected themselves and their science to critical self-examination and study.

1.

While the admissibility of handwriting evidence in the post-*Daubert* world appears to be a matter of first impression for our Court, every circuit to have addressed the issue has concluded, as on the fingerprint issue, that such evidence is properly admissible.[5]

2.

The Government's handwriting expert, Thomas Currin, had twenty-four years of experience at the North Carolina SBI. On voir dire, and then on direct examination, he explained that all questioned documents that come into the SBI are analyzed first by a "questioned document examiner"; and that the initial analysis is then reviewed by another examiner. Currin discussed several studies showing the ability of qualified document examiners to identify questioned handwriting.[6] In addition, he had passed numerous proficiency tests, consistently receiving perfect scores. Currin testified to a consistent methodology of handwriting examination and identification, and he stated that the methodology "has been used not only at the level of state crime laboratories, but [also in] federal and international crime laboratories around the world." When he was questioned regarding the standards employed in questioned document examination, Currin explained that every determination of authorship "is based on the uniqueness of [certain] similarities, and it's based on the quality and the skill and the training of the document examiner."

At trial, Currin drew the jury's attention to similarities between Crisp's known handwriting exemplars and the writing on the Note. Among the similarities that he pointed out were the overall size and spacing of the letters and words in the documents; the unique shaping of the capital letter "L" in the name "Lamont"; the spacing between the capital letter "L" and the rest of the word; a peculiar shaping to the letters "o" and "n" when used in conjunction with one another; the v-like formation of the letter "u" in the word "you"; and the shape of the letter "t," including the horizontal stroke. Currin also noted that the

---

5. Certain district courts, however, have recently determined that handwriting analysis does not meet the *Daubert* standards. *See, e.g., United States v. Lewis*, 220 F. Supp. 2d 548, 554 (S.D. W.Va. 2002) (finding proficiency tests and peer review meaningless where the evidence showed that handwriting experts "*always* passed their proficiency tests, ... [and that] peers *always* agreed with each others' results" (emphasis in original)); *United States v. Brewer*, 2002 WL 596365 (N.D. Ill. 2002); *United States v. Saelee*, 162 F. Supp. 2d 1097 (D. Alaska 2001); *United States v. Hines*, 55 F. Supp. 2d 62 (D. Mass. 1999).

6. Rather than analyzing the ability of document examiners to correctly identify authorship, the studies to which Currin referred examined whether document examiners were more likely than lay people to identify authorship correctly. In one study, lay participants had a 38% error rate, while qualified document examiners had a 6% error rate.

word "tomorrow" was misspelled in the same manner on both the known exemplar and the Note. He went on to testify that, in his opinion, Crisp had authored the Note.

3.

Our analysis of *Daubert* in the context of fingerprint identification applies with equal force here: like fingerprint analysis, handwriting comparison testimony has a long history of admissibility in the courts of this country. The fact that handwriting comparison analysis has achieved widespread and lasting acceptance in the expert community gives us the assurance of reliability that *Daubert* requires. Furthermore, as with expert testimony on fingerprints, the role of the handwriting expert is primarily to draw the jury's attention to similarities between a known exemplar and a contested sample. Here, Currin merely pointed out certain unique characteristics shared by the two writings. Though he opined that Crisp authored the Note in question, the jury was nonetheless left to examine the Note and decide for itself whether it agreed with the expert.

To the extent that a given handwriting analysis is flawed or flimsy, an able defense lawyer will bring that fact to the jury's attention, both through skillful cross-examination and by presenting expert testimony of his own. But in light of Crisp's failure to offer us any reason today to doubt the reliability of handwriting analysis evidence in general, we must decline to deny our courts and juries such insights as it can offer....

MICHAEL, Circuit Judge, dissenting....

The majority excuses fingerprint and handwriting analysis from any rigorous *Daubert* scrutiny because these techniques are generally accepted and have been examined for nearly one hundred years in our adversarial system of litigation. These circumstances are not sufficient to demonstrate reliability in the aftermath of *Daubert*. To say that expert evidence is reliable because it is generally accepted is to say that it is admissible under *Daubert* because it was admissible under the old rule articulated in *Frye v. United States*, 293 F. 1013, 1014 (D.C. Cir. 1923).... Nothing in the Supreme Court's opinion in *Daubert* suggests that evidence that was admitted under Frye is grandfathered in or is free of the more exacting analysis now required.

Nor is fingerprint and handwriting analysis necessarily reliable because it has been subjected to the adversarial process of litigation.... In most criminal cases, particularly those in which the defendant is indigent, the defendant does not have access to an independent expert who could review the analyses and conclusions of the prosecution's expert. Lack of money is only one problem. Lack of independent crime laboratories is another. The great majority of crime laboratories are operated by law enforcement agencies. More important, criminal defendants do not appear to have access to experts who could challenge the basic principles and methodology of fingerprint and handwriting analysis. Our adversarial system has much to commend it, but it is not a general substitute for the specific *Daubert* inquiry....

II.

A.

At Crisp's trial the government's fingerprint identification evidence failed to satisfy any of the *Daubert* requirements for establishing scientific reliability. The first *Daubert* factor is whether the technique has been tested. The government did not offer any record of testing on the reliability of fingerprint identification. Indeed, it appears that there has not been sufficient critical testing to determine the scientific validity of the technique. Specifically, with respect to forensic fingerprint examination, there have not been any studies to establish how likely it is that partial prints taken from a crime scene will be a match for only one set of fingerprints in the world....

The second *Daubert* factor is whether the science or technique has been subjected to peer review and publication. Again, the government offered no evidence on this factor at trial. Fingerprint examiners, like other forensic scientists, have their own professional publications. But unlike typical scientific journals, the fingerprint publications do not run articles that include or prompt critique or reanalysis by other scientists. Indeed, few of the articles address the principles of fingerprint analysis and identification at all; rather, most focus on the process of lifting fingerprints from crime scenes. This lack of critical analysis in the fingerprint identification field has had a predictable effect. Unlike traditional scientific fields where criticism and vibrant exchange of ideas have led to dramatic advances, the techniques used by fingerprint analysts have changed little over the years.

The third *Daubert* factor calls for consideration of the known or potential rate of error. The government has not tested the reliability of fingerprint identification, so it ignored the error rate factor in this case. Some courts have merely assumed that the rate of error in fingerprint identification is low. And that may be. But an error rate must be demonstrated by reliable scientific studies, not by assumption. Nor is it sufficient after *Daubert* for a proponent simply to show that a particular fingerprint examiner scores well on proficiency tests. First, it is unclear whether the proficiency tests taken by the examiner in this case were representative of real life conditions. Second, where tests have attempted to imitate actual conditions, the error rates have been alarmingly high. In a 1995 test conducted by a commercial testing service, less than half of the fingerprint examiners were able to identify correctly all of the matches and eliminate the non-matches. On a similar test in 1998, less than sixty percent of the examiners were able to make all identifications and eliminations. An error rate that runs remarkably close to chance can hardly be viewed as acceptable under *Daubert*.

The fourth *Daubert* factor asks whether there are universal standards that govern the application of the technique. The government did not establish that there are such standards. Its expert asserted that her department had controlling standards, yet when pressed on the point, she admitted that the degree of similarity required to find that prints are matching "is left up to each individual examiner." ... Many fingerprint examiners testify in terms of matching points, that is, the number of similarities between the ridges in the print taken from the crime scene and the ridges in the defendant's known print. But the trend has been toward eliminating any requirement for a minimum number of matching points before an opinion can be given that a latent print and a known exemplar are attributable to the same person. There is even disagreement as to what aspects of the fingerprint the examiner should rely on. One prominent expert rejects traditional reliance on ridge characteristics and calls on examiners to look at other details such as sweat pores and ridge edges. Others, however, vehemently reject this approach, explaining that[ ]variations in these particular details are especially common because of differences in pressure, residue on the fingers, the condition of the surface on which the print is left, and processing techniques....

Further, even the safety checks that are thought to be universally accepted are not consistently followed. For example, fingerprint experts are supposed to reject as matching a pair of prints that contain even one dissimilarity. At least one expert, however, has said that when fingerprint examiners believe the prints are a match, they explain away the differences rather than discounting the match. Moreover, independent verification of a match by a second examiner is considered to be essential. Moreover, any verification that does take place is not independent in the truest sense. The reviewer is usually a supervisor or colleague in a forensic lab associated with law enforcement, so the reviewer may share the same inclinations as the original examiner....

The fifth (and final) *Daubert* factor is whether the technique has been generally accepted in the relevant scientific community. I acknowledge, of course, that the general public, which sees movies and television programs that regularly portray fingerprinting and other forensic techniques as key to crime solving, regards fingerprint identification as perfectly reliable. Moreover, several circuit courts since *Daubert* have held—without going deeply into the question—that fingerprint evidence is admissible. But "[t]he *Daubert* court did not suggest that acceptance by a legal, rather than a scientific community, would suffice." *United States v. Starzecpyzel*, 880 F. Supp. 1027, 1038 (S.D.N.Y.1995). The fingerprint examination community is certainly a proponent of the technique. That community's enthusiasm, however, must be subjected to objective scrutiny if *Daubert* is to have any meaning....

B.

....

Fingerprint identification's long history of use does not by itself support the decision to admit it. Courts began admitting fingerprint evidence early last century with relatively little scrutiny, and later courts, relying on precedent, simply followed along. To put it bluntly, the precedent of prior admission, rather than exacting scientific scrutiny, led to its universal acceptance. As a matter of fact, other forms of evidence in vogue at the time fingerprinting began to be commonly used were generally believed to be *more* credible. For example, experts in the Bertillon technique took minute measurements of the human body—including the bones in the face, arms, and feet, and the shape and size of the ears—to identify criminals.... Fingerprinting replaced the Bertillon system. But Bertillonage did not fall out of favor because anyone demonstrated its unreliability or fingerprinting's superiority. Rather, law enforcement officials found the Bertillon system too cumbersome to use and too complicated to entrust to untrained technicians. Fingerprinting, on the other hand, rose in popularity because the prints could be taken and analyzed quickly by those with little training or experience. These advantages were seen to outweigh fingerprinting's primary drawback—that it was believed to be considerably *less* reliable than the Bertillon system....

III.

Handwriting identification evidence has been greeted with more skepticism by courts in the wake of *Daubert*. Some courts have refused to admit it. Other courts have allowed testimony about the similarities between handwriting samples without permitting the expert to testify to conclusions about the authorship....

I will again run through the *Daubert* factors, considering first whether the technique of handwriting analysis has been tested ... it appears that no one has ever assessed the validity of the basic tenets of handwriting comparison, namely, that no two individuals write in precisely the same fashion and that certain characteristics of an individual's writing remain constant even when the writer attempts to disguise them. The government asserted in this case that because these premises had not been disproven, they must be true....

The next *Daubert* question is whether handwriting examination has been subjected to peer review and publication. The government did not present any evidence about peer review or critical scholarship in the field. Those within the field have failed to engage in any critical study of the basic principles and methods of handwriting analysis, and few objective outsiders have taken on this challenge. This lack of critical review has hampered the advancement of methodology in the field. Indeed, the field of handwriting analysis, unlike most other technical fields, relies primarily on texts that were written fifty to one hundred years ago. The second *Daubert* factor, peer review and publication, is not satisfied.

The next *Daubert* factor requires a look at the technique's known or potential rate of error.... The testing that has been done suggests that experts, on average, do better than non-experts at avoiding false positives, that is, in identifying someone as an author who in fact is not. On some tests, however, the best of the non-experts did as well as some of the experts. Moreover, other more challenging studies that more accurately reflect real world conditions show higher rates of error. One study found that as many as nine percent of document examiners misidentified a forgery as being written by the named author, and almost one-quarter of the examiners incorrectly concluded that a disguised writing was written by someone other than the true author.

The next *Daubert* factor focuses on whether there are standards or controls that govern the expert's analysis. In this case the government's expert asserted that handwriting examiners follow the same methodology, but he provided no listing of objective criteria that are used to form an opinion. There does not seem to be any list of universal, objective requirements for identifying an author.

The last factor is whether the technique is generally accepted in the scientific community. The general acceptance of handwriting analysis appears to come only from those within the field. And those within the field have not challenged or questioned its basic premises. More is required to meet the "general acceptance" factor.

The government did not show that there are factors beyond the *Daubert* list that credibly demonstrate the reliability of handwriting evidence. Like fingerprint experts, document examiners have long been allowed to testify in judicial proceedings. But, like the case of fingerprint evidence, there is no reason to believe that longstanding use of handwriting evidence demonstrates its reliability. The testimony of handwriting experts was initially admitted into evidence because courts saw it as no less reliable than that of lay witnesses who claimed to be able to identify the writers of documents. But that does not make handwriting analysis a reliable science.

Because the government has failed to demonstrate either that its handwriting evidence satisfies the *Daubert* factors or that it is other-wise reliable, I would reverse the district court's decision to admit it as an abuse of discretion....

c. Polygraph Evidence

United States v. Scheffer

523 U.S. 303 (1998)

Justice THOMAS announced the judgment of the Court and delivered the opinion of the Court with respect to Parts I, II-A, and II-D, and an opinion with respect to Parts II-B and II-C, in which THE CHIEF JUSTICE, Justice SCALIA, and Justice SOUTER join.

This case presents the question whether Military Rule of Evidence 707, which makes polygraph evidence inadmissible in court-martial proceedings, unconstitutionally abridges the right of accused members of the military to present a defense. We hold that it does not.

I

In March 1992, respondent Edward Scheffer, an airman stationed at March Air Force Base in California, volunteered to work as an informant on drug investigations for the Air Force Office of Special Investigations (OSI). His OSI supervisors advised him that, from time to time during the course of his undercover work, they would ask him to submit to drug testing and polygraph examinations. In early April, one of the OSI agents supervising respondent requested that he submit to a urine test. Shortly after providing the urine sample, but before the results of the test were known, respondent agreed to take a polygraph test administered by an OSI examiner. In the opinion of the examiner, the test "indicated no deception" when respondent denied using drugs since joining the Air Force.

On April 30, respondent unaccountably failed to appear for work and could not be found on the base. He was absent without leave until May 13, when an Iowa state patrolman arrested him following a routine traffic stop and held him for return to the base. OSI agents later learned that respondent's urinalysis revealed the presence of methamphetamine.

Respondent was tried by general court-martial on charges of using methamphetamine, failing to go to his appointed place of duty, wrongfully absenting himself from the base for 13 days, and, with respect to an unrelated matter, uttering 17 insufficient funds checks. He testified at trial on his own behalf, relying upon an "innocent ingestion" theory and denying that he had knowingly used drugs while working for OSI....

Respondent sought to introduce the polygraph evidence in support of his testimony that he did not knowingly use drugs. The military judge denied the motion, relying on Military Rule of Evidence 707, which provides, in relevant part:

> "(a) Notwithstanding any other provision of law, the results of a polygraph examination, the opinion of a polygraph examiner, or any reference to an offer to take, failure to take, or taking of a polygraph examination, shall not be admitted into evidence."

....

Respondent was convicted on all counts and was sentenced to a bad-conduct discharge, confinement for 30 months, total forfeiture of all pay and allowances, and reduction to the lowest enlisted grade. The Air Force Court of Criminal Appeals affirmed in all material respects, explaining that Rule 707 "does not arbitrarily limit the accused's ability to present reliable evidence."

By a 3-to-2 vote, the United States Court of Appeals for the Armed Forces reversed. Without pointing to any particular language in the Sixth Amendment, the Court of Appeals held that "[a] per se exclusion of polygraph evidence offered by an accused to rebut an attack on his credibility ... violates his Sixth Amendment right to present a defense."... We granted certiorari, and we now reverse.

II

A defendant's right to present relevant evidence is not unlimited, but rather is subject to reasonable restrictions. See *Taylor v. Illinois*, 484 U.S. 400, 410 (1988); *Rock v. Arkansas*, 483 U.S. 44, 55 (1987); *Chambers v. Mississippi*, 410 U.S. 284 (1973). A defendant's interest in presenting such evidence may thus "'bow to accommodate other legitimate interests in the criminal trial process.'" *Rock, supra*, at 55 (quoting *Chambers, supra*, at 295); accord, *Michigan v. Lucas*, 500 U.S. 145, 149 (1991). As a result, state and federal rulemakers have broad latitude under the Constitution to establish rules excluding evidence from criminal trials. Such rules do not abridge an accused's right to present a defense so long as they are not "arbitrary" or "disproportionate to the purposes they are designed to serve." *Rock, supra*, at 56; accord, *Lucas, supra*, at 151. Moreover, we have found the exclusion of evidence to be unconstitutionally arbitrary or disproportionate only where it has infringed upon a weighty interest of the accused. See *Rock, supra*, at 58; *Chambers, supra*, at 302; *Washington v. Texas*, 388 U.S. 14, 22–23 (1967).

Rule 707 serves several legitimate interests in the criminal trial process....

A

State and Federal Governments unquestionably have a legitimate interest in ensuring that reliable evidence is presented to the trier of fact in a criminal trial. Indeed, the exclusion of unreliable evidence is a principal objective of many evidentiary rules. See, *e.g.*, Fed. Rules Evid. 702, 802, 901; see also *Daubert v. Merrell Dow Pharmaceuticals, Inc.*, 509 U.S. 579, 589 (1993).

The contentions of respondent and the dissent notwithstanding, there is simply no consensus that polygraph evidence is reliable. To this day, the scientific community remains extremely polarized about the reliability of polygraph techniques. Some studies have concluded that polygraph tests overall are accurate and reliable. See, *e.g.*, S. Abrams, The Complete Polygraph Handbook 190–191 (1989) (reporting the overall accuracy rate from laboratory studies involving the common "control question technique" polygraph to be "in the range of 87 percent"). Others have found that polygraph tests assess truthfulness significantly less accurately—that scientific field studies suggest the accuracy rate of the "control question technique" polygraph is "little better than could be obtained by the toss of a coin," that is, 50 percent. See Iacono & Lykken, The Scientific Status of Research on Polygraph Techniques: The Case Against Polygraph Tests, in 1 Modern Scientific Evidence, *supra*, § 14-5.3, at 629 (hereinafter Iacono & Lykken).

This lack of scientific consensus is reflected in the disagreement among state and federal courts concerning both the admissibility and the reliability of polygraph evidence.[7] Although some Federal Courts of Appeals have abandoned the *per se* rule excluding polygraph evidence, leaving its admission or exclusion to the discretion of district courts under *Daubert*, see, *e.g.*, *United States v. Posado*, 57 F.3d 428, 434 (CA5 1995); *United States v. Cordoba*, 104 F.3d 225, 228 (CA9 1997), at least one Federal Circuit has recently reaffirmed its *per se* ban, see *United States v. Sanchez*, 118 F.3d 192, 197 (CA4 1997), and another recently noted that it has "not decided whether polygraphy has reached a sufficient state of reliability to be admissible." *United States v. Messina*, 131 F.3d 36, 42 (CA2 1997). Most States maintain *per se* rules excluding polygraph evidence. New Mexico is unique in making polygraph evidence generally admissible without the prior stipulation of the parties and without significant restriction. See N.M. Rule Evid. § 11-707.[8] What-

---

7. Until quite recently, federal and state courts were uniform in categorically ruling polygraph evidence inadmissible under the test set forth in *Frye v. United States*, 293 F. 1013 (CADC 1923), which held that scientific evidence must gain the general acceptance of the relevant expert community to be admissible. In *Daubert v. Merrell Dow Pharmaceuticals, Inc.*, 509 U.S. 579 (1993), we held that *Frye* had been superseded by the Federal Rules of Evidence and that expert testimony could be admitted if the district court deemed it both relevant and reliable.

Prior to *Daubert*, neither federal nor state courts found any Sixth Amendment obstacle to the categorical rule. Nothing in *Daubert* foreclosed, as a constitutional matter, *per se* exclusionary rules for certain types of expert or scientific evidence. It would be an odd inversion of our hierarchy of laws if altering or interpreting a rule of evidence worked a corresponding change in the meaning of the Constitution.

8. Respondent argues that because the Government—and in particular the Department of Defense—routinely uses polygraph testing, the Government must consider polygraphs reliable. Governmental use of polygraph tests, however, is primarily in the field of personnel screening, and to a lesser extent as a tool in criminal and intelligence investigations, but not as evidence at trials. Such limited, out of court uses of polygraph techniques obviously differ in character from, and carry less severe consequences than, the use of polygraphs as evidence in a criminal trial. They do not establish the reliability of polygraphs as trial evidence, and they do not invalidate reliability as a valid concern supporting Rule 707's categorical ban.

ever their approach, state and federal courts continue to express doubt about whether such evidence is reliable.

The approach taken by the President in adopting Rule 707 — excluding polygraph evidence in all military trials — is a rational and proportional means of advancing the legitimate interest in barring unreliable evidence. Although the degree of reliability of polygraph evidence may depend upon a variety of identifiable factors, there is simply no way to know in a particular case whether a polygraph examiner's conclusion is accurate, because certain doubts and uncertainties plague even the best polygraph exams. Individual jurisdictions therefore may reasonably reach differing conclusions as to whether polygraph evidence should be admitted. We cannot say, then, that presented with such widespread uncertainty, the President acted arbitrarily or disproportionately in promulgating a *per se* rule excluding all polygraph evidence.

B

It is equally clear that Rule 707 serves a second legitimate governmental interest: Preserving the court members' core function of making credibility determinations in criminal trials. A fundamental premise of our criminal trial system is that "the *jury* is the lie detector." *United States v. Barnard*, 490 F.2d 907, 912 (CA9 1973) (emphasis added), cert. denied, 416 U.S. 959 (1974). Determining the weight and credibility of witness testimony, therefore, has long been held to be the "part of every case [that] belongs to the jury, who are presumed to be fitted for it by their natural intelligence and their practical knowledge of men and the ways of men." *Aetna Life Ins. Co. v. Ward*, 140 U.S. 76, 88 (1891).

By its very nature, polygraph evidence may diminish the jury's role in making credibility determinations. The common form of polygraph test measures a variety of physiological responses to a set of questions asked by the examiner, who then interprets these physiological correlates of anxiety and offers an opinion to the jury about whether the witness — often, as in this case, the accused — was deceptive in answering questions about the very matters at issue in the trial. See 1 McCormick § 206.[9] Unlike other expert witnesses who testify about factual matters outside the jurors' knowledge, such as the analysis of fingerprints, ballistics, or DNA found at a crime scene, a polygraph expert can supply the jury only with another opinion, in addition to its own, about whether the witness was telling the truth. Jurisdictions, in promulgating rules of evidence, may legitimately be concerned about the risk that juries will give excessive weight to the opinions of a polygrapher, clothed as they are in scientific expertise and at times offering, as in respondent's case, a conclusion about the ultimate issue in the trial. Such jurisdictions may legitimately determine that the aura of infallibility attending polygraph evidence can lead jurors to abandon their duty to assess credibility and guilt. Those jurisdictions may also take into account the fact that a judge cannot determine, when ruling on a motion to admit polygraph evidence, whether a particular polygraph expert is likely to influence the jury unduly. For these reasons, the President is within his constitutional prerogative to promulgate a *per se* rule that simply excludes all such evidence....

---

9. The examiner interprets various physiological responses of the examinee, including blood pressure, perspiration, and respiration, while asking a series of questions, commonly in three categories: direct accusatory questions concerning the matter under investigation, irrelevant or neutral questions, and more general "control" questions concerning wrongdoing by the subject in general. The examiner forms an opinion of the subject's truthfulness by comparing the physiological reactions to each set of questions. See generally Giannelli & Imwinkelried 219–222; Honts & Quick, The Polygraph in 1995: Progress in Science and the Law, 71 N.D.L.Rev. 987, 990–992 (1995).

Justice KENNEDY, with whom Justice O'CONNOR, Justice GINSBURG, and Justice BREYER join, concurring in part and concurring in the judgment.

I join Parts I, II-A, and II-D of the opinion of the Court.

In my view it should have been sufficient to decide this case to observe, as the principal opinion does, that various courts and jurisdictions "may reasonably reach differing conclusions as to whether polygraph evidence should be admitted." The continuing, good-faith disagreement among experts and courts on the subject of polygraph reliability counsels against our invalidating a *per se* exclusion of polygraph results or of the fact an accused has taken or refused to take a polygraph examination. If we were to accept respondent's position, of course, our holding would bind state courts, as well as military and federal courts. Given the ongoing debate about polygraphs, I agree the rule of exclusion is not so arbitrary or disproportionate that it is unconstitutional.

I doubt, though, that the rule of *per se* exclusion is wise, and some later case might present a more compelling case for introduction of the testimony than this one does. Though the considerable discretion given to the trial court in admitting or excluding scientific evidence is not a constitutional mandate, see *Daubert v. Merrell Dow Pharmaceuticals, Inc.*, 509 U.S. 579, 587 (1993), there is some tension between that rule and our holding today. And, as Justice STEVENS points out, there is much inconsistency between the Government's extensive use of polygraphs to make vital security determinations and the argument it makes here, stressing the inaccuracy of these tests.

With all respect, moreover, it seems the principal opinion overreaches when it rests its holding on the additional ground that the jury's role in making credibility determinations is diminished when it hears polygraph evidence. I am in substantial agreement with Justice STEVENS' observation that the argument demeans and mistakes the role and competence of jurors in deciding the factual question of guilt or innocence. In the last analysis the principal opinion says it is unwise to allow the jury to hear "a conclusion about the ultimate issue in the trial." I had thought this tired argument had long since been given its deserved repose as a categorical rule of exclusion. Rule 704(a) of the Federal Rules of Evidence states [that an opinion is not objectionable just because it embraces an ultimate issue.] The Advisory Committee's Notes state:

> "The older cases often contained strictures against allowing witnesses to express opinions upon ultimate issues, as a particular aspect of the rule against opinions. The rule was unduly restrictive, difficult of application, and generally served only to deprive the trier of fact of useful information. 7 Wigmore §§ 1920, 1921; McCormick § 12. The basis usually assigned for the rule, to prevent the witness from 'usurping the province of the jury,' is aptly characterized as 'empty rhetoric.' 7 Wigmore § 1920, p. 17." Advisory Committee's Notes on Fed. Rule Evid. 704.

The principal opinion is made less convincing by its contradicting the rationale of Rule 704 and the well considered reasons the Advisory Committee recited in support of its adoption....

Justice STEVENS, dissenting....

The principal charge against the respondent in this case was that he had knowingly used methamphetamine. His principal defense was "innocent ingestion"; even if the urinalysis test conducted on April 7, 1992, correctly indicated that he did ingest the substance, he claims to have been unaware of that fact. The results of the lie detector test conducted three days later, if accurate, constitute factual evidence that his physical condition at that time was consistent with the theory of his defense and inconsistent with the theory of the prosecution. The results were also relevant because they tended to confirm the credibility of his testimony. Under Rule 707, even if the results of the polygraph test were more reliable than the results of the urinalysis, the weaker evidence is admissible and the stronger evidence is inadmissible.

Under the now discredited reasoning in a case decided 75 years ago, *Frye v. United States*, 293 F. 1013 (1923), that anomalous result would also have been reached in non-military cases tried in the federal courts. In recent years, however, we have not only repudiated *Frye*'s general approach to scientific evidence, but the federal courts have also been engaged in the process of rejecting the once-popular view that all lie detector evidence should be categorically inadmissible. Well reasoned opinions are concluding, consistently with this Court's decisions in *Daubert v. Merrell Dow Pharmaceuticals, Inc.*, 509 U.S. 579 (1993), and *General Electric Co. v. Joiner*, 522 U.S. 136 (1997), that the federal rules wisely allow district judges to exercise broad discretion when evaluating the admissibility of scientific evidence.[3] Those opinions correctly observe that the rules of evidence generally recognized in the trial of civil and criminal cases in the federal courts do not contain any blanket prohibition against the admissibility of polygraph evidence....

Reliability

There are a host of studies that place the reliability of polygraph tests at 85% to 90%. While critics of the polygraph argue that accuracy is much lower, even the studies cited by the critics place polygraph accuracy at 70%. Moreover, to the extent that the polygraph errs, studies have repeatedly shown that the polygraph is more likely to find innocent people guilty than vice versa. Thus, exculpatory polygraphs — like the one in this case — are likely to be more reliable than inculpatory ones.

Of course, within the broad category of lie detector evidence, there may be a wide variation in both the validity and the relevance of particular test results. Questions about the examiner's integrity, independence, choice of questions, or training in the detection of deliberate attempts to provoke misleading physiological responses may justify exclusion of specific evidence. But such questions are properly addressed in adversary proceedings; they fall far short of justifying a blanket exclusion of this type of expert testimony.

There is no legal requirement that expert testimony must satisfy a particular degree of reliability to be admissible.... Studies indicate that handwriting analysis, and even fingerprint identifications, may be less trustworthy than polygraph evidence in certain cases.[24]

---

3. "The per se ... rule excluding unstipulated polygraph evidence is inconsistent with the 'flexible inquiry' assigned to the trial judge by *Daubert*. This is particularly evident because *Frye*, which was overruled by *Daubert*, involved the admissibility of polygraph evidence." *United States v. Cordoba*, 104 F.3d 225, 227 (CA9 1997).

24. One study compared the accuracy of fingerprinting, handwriting analysis, polygraph tests, and eyewitness identification. The study consisted of 80 volunteers divided into 20 groups of 4. Fingerprints and handwriting samples were taken from all of the participants.

In each group of four, one person was randomly assigned the role of "perpetrator." The perpetrator was instructed to take an envelope to a building doorkeeper (who knew that he would later need to identify the perpetrator), sign a receipt, and pick up a package. After the "crime," all participants were given a polygraph examination.

The fingerprinting expert (comparing the original fingerprints with those on the envelope), the handwriting expert (comparing the original samples with the signed receipt), and the polygrapher (analyzing the tests) sought to identify the perpetrator of each group. In addition, two days after the "crime," the doorkeeper was asked to pick the picture of the perpetrator out of a set of four pictures.

The results of the study demonstrate that polygraph evidence compares favorably with other types of evidence. Excluding "inconclusive" results from each test, the fingerprinting expert resolved 100% of the cases correctly, the polygrapher resolved 95% of the cases correctly, the handwriting expert re-

And, of course, even highly dubious eyewitness testimony is, and should be, admitted and tested in the crucible of cross-examination. The Court's reliance on potential unreliability as a justification for a categorical rule of inadmissibility reveals that it is "overly pessimistic about the capabilities of the jury and of the adversary system generally. Vigorous cross-examination, presentation of contrary evidence, and careful instruction on the burden of proof are the traditional and appropriate means of attacking shaky but admissible evidence." *Daubert*, 509 U.S., at 596.

The Role of the Jury

It is the function of the jury to make credibility determinations. In my judgment evidence that tends to establish either a consciousness of guilt or a consciousness of innocence may be of assistance to the jury in making such determinations. That also was the opinion of Dean Wigmore:

> "Let the accused's whole conduct come in; and whether it tells for consciousness of guilt or for consciousness of innocence, let us take it for what it is worth, remembering that in either case it is open to varying explanations and is not to be emphasized. Let us not deprive an innocent person, falsely accused, of the inference which common sense draws from a consciousness of innocence and its natural manifestations." 2 J. Wigmore, Evidence § 293, p. 232 (J. Chadbourn rev. ed.1979).

There is, of course, some risk that some "juries will give excessive weight to the opinions of a polygrapher, clothed as they are in scientific expertise." In my judgment, however, it is much more likely that juries will be guided by the instructions of the trial judge concerning the credibility of expert as well as lay witnesses. The strong presumption that juries will follow the court's instructions, see, *e.g.*, *Richardson v. Marsh*, 481 U.S. 200, 211 (1987), applies to exculpatory as well as inculpatory evidence. Common sense suggests that the testimony of disinterested third parties that is relevant to the jury's credibility determination will assist rather than impair the jury's deliberations. As with the reliance on the potential unreliability of this type of evidence, the reliance on a fear that the average jury is not able to assess the weight of this testimony reflects a distressing lack of confidence in the intelligence of the average American....

d. Eyewitness Reliability

United States v. Lester

254 F. Supp. 2d 602 (E.D. Va. 2003)

PAYNE, District Judge.

The United States has charged Cornelius Lester with interference with commerce by force in violation of 18 U.S.C. § 1951, and possession and discharge of a firearm in furtherance of a crime of violence, in violation of 18 U.S.C. § 924(c)(1)(A)(iii), in connection with the attempted robbery of a small convenience market in Richmond, Virginia....

---

solved 94% of the cases correctly, and the eyewitness resolved only 64% of the cases correctly. Interestingly, when "inconclusive" results were included, the polygraph test was more accurate than any of the other methods: The polygrapher resolved 90% of the cases correctly, compared with 85% for the handwriting expert, 35% for the eyewitness, and 20% for the fingerprinting expert. Widacki & Horvath, An Experimental Investigation of the Relative Validity and Utility of the Polygraph Technique and Three Other Common Methods of Criminal Identification, 23 J. Forensic Sciences 596, 596–600 (1978); see also Honts & Perry 365.

STATEMENT OF FACTS

Sang Foo Yoon owns the Golden Market store located at the corner of Chestnut and 3rd Streets in the City of Richmond. On August 10, 2002, an armed man attempted to rob the store, and in the process, shot Yoon in the hand. Yoon and one of his employees, Roberta Schwartz, later identified the assailant as the defendant, Cornelius Lester....

During the daylight hours of August 10, 2002, Yoon was working behind the cashier counter. Schwartz was nearby helping a customer. While Yoon was helping a customer, a black male walked into the store, proceeded to the counter, where he stood behind the customer, pulled out a handgun, pushed the customer to the ground, and demanded that Yoon turn over the money in the store. Yoon did not comply with the robber's demand and, instead, attempted to duck behind the counter, at which point, the robber fired two shots and then fled. One of the shots struck Yoon in the left hand. At the time of the attempted robbery, three or four customers were in the store. The store is equipped with video surveillance cameras, but they were not functioning at the time of the offense.

Richmond Police Officers arrived at the scene of the crime shortly thereafter, and commenced their investigation. The responding officers found no physical evidence at the scene; and, initially, only Schwartz and another customer in the store were able to provide any information about the appearance of the perpetrator. They described the robber as a black skinned male with a short "afro" hairstyle, who was between the age of 35 and 40, and who wore a grey shirt and dark jean shorts. Yoon could not give a good description of the robber, but told the responding officer that he recognized the man as someone who previously had been in the store. Schwartz confirmed Yoon's assertion on that point.

Several days later, a customer advised Yoon and Schwartz that the man who had committed the robbery was named "Neil." On September 4, 2002, ATF investigators took over the investigation, and, on that date, they solicited a description of the perpetrator from Schwartz, who told the investigators that she recalled the assailant as being approximately 6'1" tall, weighing about 180 pounds, aged in the mid-40s, and wearing shorts and a blue short-sleeved shirt at the time of the attempted robbery. Schwartz also conveyed her belief that the assailant was a regular customer of the market whose name was Neil. Investigators also obtained a description from Yoon, who speaks and understands limited English and for whom translation was provided by his daughter. Yoon described the perpetrator as a skinny black male, approximately 5'6" tall, wearing black pants and a black T-shirt. Yoon further told officers that he had seen the robber steal a beer from the store earlier in the day on August 10, and that he believed that the robber came into the store two to three times a week.

Based on this information, the ATF investigators began to suspect that the perpetrator might be Lester and they went to his home on September 19, 2002, where they obtained from Lester relevant identifying information. Based on that information, they obtained from the Richmond Police Department a booking photograph of Lester from an earlier arrest. Using the identifying data about Lester and that photograph, ATF Agent Morella identified five other individuals whose characteristics resembled those of Lester. Morella then made a photospread by using the booking photographs of those five people and Lester.

On September 25, 2002, Morella and her partner returned to the Golden Market with the photospread and showed it to Schwartz, who, with 100% asserted confidence, identified Lester as the robber. On September 30, 2002, the investigators showed the photospread to Yoon who likewise thought Lester was the perpetrator but was somewhat uncertain because the facial fullness of Lester in the photospread was different than that of the robber. Yoon's daughter, who was translating during the interview, then reminded him that the photograph was taken at an earlier time than the robbery. Yoon then asked to view the photospread again. This time he identified Lester with 90% asserted confidence. Shortly thereafter, federal agents arrested Lester and searched his home; however, no incriminating evidence was found and Lester has made no statements....

Lester made an oral motion in limine requesting that the Court allow Dr. Cutler to testify at trial respecting the general reliability of eyewitness identification. The United States opposed the motion, thereby necessitating a hearing on whether the proposed testimony of Dr. Cutler met the requirements of Fed.R.Evid. 702 as explained in *Daubert v. Merrell Dow Pharm., Inc.*, 509 U.S. 579 (1993) and *Kumho Tire Co. v. Carmichael*, 526 U.S. 137 (1999). With the consent of both parties, the Court then held the *Daubert* hearing without any additional briefing ... the Court found Dr. Cutler's *Daubert* proffer to be insufficient, concluding that Dr. Cutler had failed to provide "any detailed explanation of the research he relies upon in coming to his various conclusions." Lacking such information, the Court could not conclude that Dr. Cutler's proffered testimony was reliable, and accordingly denied Lester's motion to admit that testimony.

On January 2, 2003, Lester, with the acquiescence of the United States, requested leave to present additional testimony from Dr. Cutler in an attempt to cure the defects identified in the December 19 Opinion. A second *Daubert* hearing was held on January 11, 2003. At the January 11 hearing, Dr. Cutler identified six factors attending the eyewitness identifications in this case that, in his view, might affect the reliability of those identifications: (1) cross-race recognition; (2) exposure time; (3) weapon focus; (4) stress experienced by the witness; (5) retention interval; and (6) the relation between the witness' confidence and accuracy. Dr. Cutler described generally the various studies that formed the basis of these opinions, and explained that his conclusions respecting the effect that these factors have on eyewitness identification generally track the results of meta-analyses and reviews of these subjects conducted by other scholars in the field.

DISCUSSION

.... Under Rule 702, a trial judge may not admit expert scientific testimony unless the proffered scientific evidence is both relevant and reliable. *Daubert v. Merrell Dow Pharm., Inc.*, 509 U.S. 579, 589–90 (1993). The reliability predicate for the admissibility of expert testimony requires that the testimony be based on scientific knowledge and be derived from, and validated by, the scientific method. *Id.* at 590. The relevance predicate for admissible expert testimony is the requirement from Rule 702 that the testimony "[help] the trier of fact to understand the evidence or to determine a fact in issue." *Id.* To this end, the scientific testimony must properly "fit" the facts of the case. That is, the trial judge must decide "'whether expert testimony proffered in the case is sufficiently tied to the facts of the case that it will aid the jury in resolving a factual dispute.'" *Id.* at 591.

In *Kumho Tire Co. v. Carmichael*, 526 U.S. 137 (1999), the Supreme Court held that trial courts are to apply the requirements of *Daubert* in considering whether to admit expert testimony in non-scientific fields as well....

At the December 11 hearing, Dr. Cutler failed to demonstrate to the Court that his opinions respecting the various factors present in this case that might affect the reliability of eyewitness identifications satisfied the reliability aspect of the *Daubert* test....

At the January 11 hearing, Dr. Cutler cured this defect. For each of the identified factors, Dr. Cutler demonstrated that his conclusions were based either upon research of his own, or upon research of others. In each instance, the research contained traditional indicia of scientific reliability: the research was conducted using the scientific method, was subject to peer-review, was published in reputable journals in most instances, and the methods and conclusions appear to enjoy general acceptance in the field of social psychology. Although the Court retains a healthy skepticism of the oftentimes malleable conclusions in the social science fields, Dr. Cutler's conclusions do satisfy the first test of *Daubert*.

The issue now ready for decision is whether the proffered testimony will satisfy the relevance component of the *Daubert* calculus by assisting the trier of fact to understand the evidence or to determine a fact in issue ... in deciding whether proffered scientific evidence will assist the trier of fact, trial courts must be mindful of both the potential for expert testimony to mislead a jury, and the court's continuing obligation under Rule 403 to exclude evidence, the probative value of which is substantially outweighed by the danger of confusing the jury. The added caution is necessary because expert testimony often carries a certain aura that might lead a jury to attach more significance to the testimony than is reasonably warranted. "Because of this risk," held the Supreme Court in Daubert, "the judge in weighing possible prejudice against probative force under Rule 403 of the present rules exercises more control over experts than over lay witnesses." 509 U.S. at 595. A trial judge, therefore, may exclude reliable scientific evidence, if the court concludes that the risk of confusing the jury is too great....

Cognizant of the balance struck in *Daubert*, the Fourth Circuit has established the following benchmark to aid the trial courts in determining whether reliable scientific evidence will actually assist the jury: "[I]n determining whether a particular expert's testimony is sufficiently helpful to the trier of fact to warrant admission into trial, the district court should consider whether the testimony presented is simply reiterating facts already 'within the common knowledge' of the jurors." *Dorsey*, 45 F.3d at 814. Evidence falling within the common knowledge of jurors, "almost by definition, can be of no assistance to a jury." *Harris*, 995 F.2d at 534.

A. Expert Testimony On The Reliability Of Eyewitness Identifications And The Relevance Facet Of Rule 702

Proffers of expert testimony on the reliability of eyewitness identification implicate the second facet of the *Daubert* analysis quite strongly. In *Harris*, a pre-*Daubert* case, the Fourth Circuit noted that such testimony may be appropriate only in a narrow range of circumstances. In *Harris*, the Fourth Circuit explained that:

> [u]ntil fairly recently, most, if not all, courts excluded expert psychological testimony on the validity of eyewitness identification. But, there has been a trend in recent years to allow such testimony under circumstances described as "narrow." ... The narrow circumstances held sufficient to support the introduction of expert testimony have varied but have included such problems as cross-racial identification, identification after a long delay, identification after observation under stress, and psychological phenomena as the feedback factor and unconscious transference.... Outside of such narrowly constrained circumstances, jurors using common sense and their faculties of observation can judge the credibility of an eyewitness identification, especially since deficiencies or inconsistencies in an eyewitness's testimony can be brought out with skillful cross-examination.

In *Harris*, the Court of Appeals applied this standard and concluded that a trial court did not err in excluding expert testimony on eyewitness reliability where the enumerated factors were not present and the eyewitness testimony was corroborated by other evidence.

The lesson of *Harris* is twofold, and entirely consistent with the Supreme Court's subsequent decision in *Daubert*. First, *Harris* teaches that trial courts should be extremely reluctant to allow testimony under Rule 702 as to conclusions that are consistent with the common knowledge of juries. In eyewitness identification cases, the Court should assess each factor about which an expert intends to testify and determine whether that factor is one about which the average juror would be aware. Second, and relatedly, trial courts should remain cognizant of the efficacy of traditional methods of trial procedure to equip the jury with information from which it may fairly assess the credibility of eyewitnesses. Skilled cross-examination and argument are more than sufficient to attack reliability where the putative defect in the identification is within the common knowledge of the jury.

Daubert's emphasis on the trial court's continuing obligation under Rule 403 further reinforces the teachings of *Harris*. Expert testimony has the potential to be substantially prejudicial because of the "aura effect" associated with such testimony. In the case of expert testimony about factors that may affect the reliability of eyewitness identification, the "aura effect" could mislead the jury into believing that the presence of such a factor renders an eyewitness identification much less reliable than it actually is. With that risk of prejudice in mind, the trial court must assess carefully the probative value of the proffered expert testimony, remaining cognizant of the common knowledge of the average juror, and mindful of the efficacy of traditional trial procedures. Only when the proffered testimony is clearly beyond the jury's common knowledge, thereby rendering traditional trial procedures ineffective in exposing the possible defect in the reliability of the identification, is it possible that evidence of the sort contemplated in this case can survive the restrictions of Rule 702.

However, even if the proponent of the expert testimony on eyewitness reliability demonstrates that the factor affecting reliability of an identification is not clearly common knowledge, the testimony may still run afoul of Rule 403 if the expert cannot adequately explain to the jury in concrete terms the degree of impact on accuracy that the factor has been demonstrated to have. Although pinpoint precision certainly is not required, some level of lucid quantification is necessary in order to allow the jury to use effectively the information the expert provides, and to assess independently the credibility of the expert. Otherwise, instead of "provid[ing] the jury with more information with which the jury can then make a more informed decision," *United States v. Hines*, 55 F. Supp. 2d 62, 72 (D.Mass.1999), the testimony and the "aura" that comes with it very well might overwhelm and confuse the jury.

For example, if Dr. Cutler were to testify that "people are more likely to misidentify persons of races other than their own," the average juror, overly-impressed by the patina that attaches to "expert" testimony, might well conclude that the task of cross-race identification is hopeless. That, at least, is the Supreme Court's concern in *Daubert*. Although quantification may cure that problem, it too can be problematic because oftentimes oral attempts to quantify create more questions than they answer. If Dr. Cutler were to testify that "a person is 1.5 times more likely to misidentify a person of another race," the average juror might have trouble grasping exactly what that means. Indeed, this particular formulation begs the question, "1.5 times what?" Confusion on a collateral issue such as this is, at a minimum, troublesome, because it creates the very real possibility that the jury will be diverted from deciding the core issues of the case.

Taken together, *Daubert*, *Kumho*, *Harris* and decisions specifically addressing the admissibility of expert testimony respecting the reliability of eyewitness identification suggest that a three-step approach is appropriate when considering whether the relevance facet of *Daubert* has been satisfied in cases where a party seeks to introduce expert testimony respecting the reliability of eyewitness identification. First, the trial court must assess the significance of eyewitness identification in the prosecution's case. Where the prosecution's case relies exclusively on the identification testimony of eyewitnesses, expert evidence could be quite probative. In cases where eyewitness identification evidence is but one of several types of evidence implicating the defendant, expert evidence on reliability of identification will be much less probative....

Second, the trial court must assess whether the factors about which the expert intends to testify are both relevant to the identifications in the case, and beyond the common knowledge of the average juror. If the trial court concludes that the testimony is either irrelevant, or falls clearly within the boundary of the average juror's common knowledge, the expert evidence would not assist the jury, and, therefore, it should be excluded under Rule 702.

Finally, the trial court must conduct the Rule 403 balancing test.... For instance, where the expert intends to testify in the broadest terms about the effect of a certain factor, without any attempt to explain in concrete terms the impact associated with that effect, the jury will be unable to use effectively the information the expert provides. And, more importantly, the lack of quantification creates an almost always unacceptable risk of misleading the jury, principally because of the "aura effect" identified in *Daubert*.

B. Admissibility Of The Proffered Testimony In This Case

With this approach in mind, the various factors about which Dr. Cutler intends to testify will now be considered. As discussed above, Dr. Cutler has identified six factors—(1) cross-race recognition; (2) exposure time; (3) weapon focus; (4) stress experienced by the witness; (5) retention interval; and (6) the relation between the witness' confidence and accuracy—present in this case that have been shown to affect the reliability of eyewitness identification, and he intends to testify about each.

Under the first step in the applicable calculus ... evidence respecting the reliability of eyewitness identification could be probative because of the fact that different witnesses have given different descriptions at different times. Furthermore, the case against Lester depends almost exclusively on the testimony of two eyewitnesses. Lester's guilt or innocence will depend largely on whether or not the jury finds testimony of these eyewitnesses to be reliable. The testimony as to each of the factors that Dr. Cutler has identified, therefore, has probative value.

Under the second phase of the inquiry, the record respecting which factors fall within the common knowledge of jurors is rather sparse. At the second *Daubert* hearing, Dr. Cutler, in a conclusory fashion, testified that, based on research and experience, he believed that his conclusions respecting the reliability of eyewitness identification are not a matter of common sense. This testimony is not particularly helpful, however, because it does not address each factor separately, and directly contradicts generally accepted judicial precepts respecting common sense as it relates to two of the factors: exposure time and retention interval. Dr. Cutler intends to testify that longer exposure times result in more reliable identifications, and that there is a significant linear relationship between retention interval and accuracy—*i.e.*, the longer the interval between the event and the identification the less reliable the identification. These highly intuitive conclusions are encompassed by the standard federal jury instructions on identification evidence....

Dr. Cutler's conclusory opinion that the factors affecting reliable eyewitness identification are beyond the common sense of jurors is insufficient to overcome the well-recognized contrary jurisprudence as to these two factors.[8]

---

8. In *United States v. Norwood*, 939 F. Supp. 1132, 1138, 1141 (D.N.J.1996), another federal district court reached the opposite conclusion regarding common knowledge as to these two factors.

However, the other four factors — the problem of cross-race recognition, the phenomenon of weapon focus, the relationship of different levels of stress on eyewitness perception, and the correlation (or lack thereof) between confidence and accuracy — do seem to fall outside the common sense of the average juror. At a minimum, it cannot be confidently said that these factors obviously would be within the common knowledge of the average juror. As a result, even the most skilled advocate could find the task of impeaching the reliability of an eyewitness based on these factors to be daunting, if not impossible. Therefore, testimony about these factors could satisfy the relevance requirements of Rule 702, and, in this case, they do.

Turning then to the third segment of the approach suggested by the applicable jurisprudence, Lester has demonstrated that only three of the four remaining factors satisfy the requirements of Rule 403. Respecting the effect of weapon focus on the reliability of eyewitness identifications, Dr. Cutler intends to explain that "[w]eapon focus refers to the eyewitness's tendency to focus his or her visual attention on the weapon. When an eyewitness does this, the eyewitness has less attention to focus on a perpetrator's facial or physical characteristics." In addition to explaining that weapon focus has a negative impact on reliability, Dr. Cutler will also quantify this impact by explaining that "[e]ffect on identification accuracy is small but significant (10% difference in accuracy)." Because Dr. Cutler quantified the impact of weapon focus, and did so with sufficient clarity, the risk that this testimony might confuse the jury does not substantially outweigh the testimony's probative value.

As to the impact of stress on the reliability of eyewitness identifications, Dr. Cutler intends to explain that "there is an inverted U shape relation between stress and the reliability of the eyewitness identification. This means that, under conditions of moderate stress, the reliability of eyewitness identifications would be expected to be higher, but under extreme levels of stress, eyewitness accuracy would decline." While this method of quantification is relative, it nonetheless provides jurors with a benchmark sufficient to allow them to make a reasoned assessment of the impact of stress on the identifications in this case. The risk of confusion, therefore, is low, and does not substantially outweigh the testimony's probative value.

About the correlation between eyewitness confidence and the accuracy of identification, Dr. Cutler intends to explain that there is only a modest correlation between confidence and accuracy: "eyewitnesses who are highly confident only somewhat more likely to be correct than eyewitnesses who are minimally confident." Although this method of quantification is admittedly not as concrete as the testimony about weapon focus and stress, Dr. Cutler ... does cabin his conclusion as to this factor sufficiently enough to avoid a substantial risk of confusion as a result of the aura effect. Moreover, this testimony does not challenge the conventional wisdom respecting the ability of an eyewitness to perceive events under certain circumstances, but merely the fact that eyewitness confidence is not always a good predictor [sic] of accuracy. This testimony, therefore, likewise satisfies the requirements of Rule 403.

Norwood is noteworthy here, not because of the court's decision respecting admissibility, but because the expert there proffered testimony as to retention interval and exposure time that is markedly different from that proffered by Dr. Cutler here. There, the expert testified that "memory decreases at a non-constant rate" over time, and respecting exposure time, the expert testified that under some circumstances, prolonged exposure time may not increase the accuracy of identification. Here, Dr. Cutler intends to testify that there is a significant linear relationship between retention interval and accuracy, and that accuracy increases as length of exposure increases. Without passing judgment on which expert is correct, this Court merely notes that the scientific conclusions in this field are highly malleable, and accordingly, highly suspect.

When explaining the effect of cross-race recognition, however, Dr. Cutler has failed to cabin his conclusions within any concrete bounds, and therefore, this testimony creates a substantial risk of confusing the jury. Dr. Cutler intends to explain that "[a] cross-racial identification is the identification of an individual of one race by an eyewitness of another race, such as an identification of a White perpetrator by a Black eyewitness[,]" and that "[e]yewitnesses are more accurate at identifying people of their own race than of other races." Dr. Cutler, however, has not attempted to quantify this impact, even in general terms. This testimony, therefore, creates a risk of confusion that substantially outweighs its probative value.

In sum, the testimony as to three of the six factors that Dr. Cutler identified satisfy the strict requirements of Rules 702 and 403, as interpreted by the Fourth Circuit in *Harris*, and the Supreme Court in *Daubert* and *Kumho*....

e. Battered Woman Syndrome

United States v. Young
316 F.3d 649 (7th Cir. 2002)

BAUER, Circuit Judge.

On March 19, 2001, the federal government charged the Defendant, Roy Young, under a three-count indictment; count 1 charged Young with kidnaping Beatrice Patrick on or about January 14 to 18, 2001, a violation of 18 U.S.C. § 1201; count 2 charged him with interstate domestic violence against Patrick on or about January 14, 2001, in violation of 18 U.S.C. §§ 2261(a)(1) and (b)(3); and finally, count 3 charged Young with unlawfully using or carrying a firearm during and in relation to the commission of a crime of violence on or about January 14, 2001, in contravention of 18 U.S.C. § 924(c)(1)(A)....

During the trial, the government called Patrick as a witness. As is not entirely uncommon with victims of domestic abuse, she denied most of the allegations against Young and recanted her story about the kidnaping and abuse. Patrick testified that she still loved Young and specifically denied that he threatened her before taking her to Indiana, that he forced her to go with him to Indiana, and that he had a gun. The government then treated Patrick as a hostile witness and introduced her grand jury testimony, in which she affirmed ... the abuse....

The government also called Dr. Ann Wolbert Burgess, a psychiatric mental health nurse specializing in crime victims, as an expert to explain Patrick's recantation. Dr. Burgess has more than forty years of nursing experience and holds a doctorate in nursing science as well as both master and bachelor of science degrees. She is a Professor of Nursing at Boston College and has written, among other things, over 114 articles in various professional journals and publications on topics including forensic nursing, rape, and domestic violence. Dr. Burgess was also the chair of a group from the National Research Council Institute of Medicine that prepared a book at Congress' request entitled *Understanding Violence Against Women*.

Young objected to Dr. Burgess' testimony, but following a full *Daubert* hearing, the court ruled that Dr. Burgess could testify. The doctor stated that victims of domestic violence commonly recant their accusations and that victims of such abuse have a limited ability to perceive means of escape. She also testified that Patrick exhibited this not uncommon behavior pattern. In forming her opinion, Dr. Burgess had reviewed FBI reports, Chicago Police Department reports detailing various confrontations between Patrick and Young, Patrick's grand jury testimony, the Order of Protection Patrick obtained against Young, the criminal history report on Young, letters between Young and Patrick, the defense counsel's notes of an interview with Patrick, and recordings of telephone conversations between Young and Patrick while Young was in pre-trial detention. Dr. Burgess also spent over an hour interviewing Patrick personally.…

The jury ultimately acquitted Young of the kidnaping charge in count 1 but convicted him of the charges in counts 2 and 3.… Young appeals the district court's decision to admit the expert testimony of Dr. Burgess.…

Young does not argue that the district court improperly qualified Dr. Burgess as an expert witness. We must determine, therefore, whether the methodology used by Dr. Burgess to arrive at her opinions was reliable and relevant to this case. Young argues that Dr. Burgess' methodology was not reliable because: a) Dr. Burgess formed her opinion before meeting with Patrick; b) Dr. Burgess reached her conclusion about Patrick based upon "anecdotal" evidence of other battered women; and c) Dr. Burgess did not interview Patrick's friends and family.

The Supreme Court laid out several factors in *Daubert* that serve as a starting point for determining whether an expert's opinion is based upon reliable methodology. The Court later made clear in *Kumho Tire*, however, that "the factors [*Daubert*] mentions do *not* constitute a 'definitive checklist or test.'" Thus, the *Daubert* inquiry must be connected to the particular facts of the case.

Among the factors to consider, the expert witness' experience in a particular field is often quite relevant in determining the reliability of her opinion. In *United States v. Allen*, this Court upheld the admission of expert testimony in a drug trafficking case by a police officer with twenty-six years of experience, thirteen of which were with the DEA. The expert in that case based his opinion not only on his extensive experience investigating over 200 drug cases but also on a full examination of the relevant police reports.

Beyond considering the reliability of the expert's opinion, we must also examine its helpfulness to the jury. On this issue, two cases from our sister Circuits are most enlightening and highly relevant. In *United States v. Alzanki*, the First Circuit upheld the defendant's conviction for holding and conspiring to hold a household employee in involuntary servitude. *United States v. Alzanki*, 54 F.3d 994, 1009 (1st Cir. 1995). In so holding, the court also affirmed the admission of expert testimony by the same Dr. Burgess who testified in Young's case, deeming it helpful to the jury.

As in Young's case, Dr. Burgess based her testimony in *Alzanki* on the patterns abuse victims generally exhibit and whether the victim in that case exhibited those patterns. The court noted that Dr. Burgess' expertise focused on victims of sexual abuse but that she also researched comparable behavior in victims of nonsexual abuse in "unequal power" relationships (i.e.—battered spouses and children). The First Circuit reviewed the admission of Dr. Burgess' testimony under an abuse of discretion standard, as we do here, and concluded that her testimony "was 'reasonably likely' to assist the jury in understanding and assessing the evidence, in that the matter at issue was highly material, somewhat technical, and beyond the realm of acquired knowledge normally possessed by lay jurors."

Similarly, in *Arcoren v. United States*, the Eighth Circuit affirmed the admission of expert testimony on "battered woman syndrome." *Arcoren v. United States*, 929 F.2d 1235, 1241 (8th Cir. 1991). Like Patrick, the victim in *Arcoren* recanted her allegations of rape and abuse after describing her ordeal to police, medical professionals, and investigators and testifying to those events before a grand jury. At the trial four months later, the victim stated that she did not remember her statements before the grand jury and that she fabricated those statements she could remember making. The government in *Arcoren*, as in *Alzanki*, called an expert psychologist who worked with battered women for ten years and with rape victims for fourteen years.

In affirming the admission of the expert testimony, the Eighth Circuit noted that a "jury naturally would be puzzled at the complete about-face [the victim] made, and would have great difficulty in determining which version of [the victim's] testimony it should believe. If there were some explanation for [the victim's] changed statements, such explanation would aid the jury in deciding which statements were credible." The court then discussed how the expert testimony, strikingly similar to that offered by Dr. Burgess in both *Alzanki* and Young's case, provides the explanation a jury needs in order to properly weigh the victim's trial testimony.

Before this Court, Young initially argued that Dr. Burgess' methodology was unreliable because she arrived at her conclusion before interviewing Patrick. To support this argument, he points only to testimony from his expert witness that failing to interview Patrick first is not sound. The jury, however, is free to credit whichever witness it sees fit. Obviously, the jury did not find Young's expert persuasive, and it is not within the province of this Court to determine otherwise.

Young also argues that *Clark v. Takata Corp.*, 192 F.3d 750 (7th Cir. 1999), demonstrates that the district court abused its discretion by admitting Dr. Burgess' testimony because she arrived at her conclusion before interviewing Patrick. *Clark*, however, is inapposite, as it dealt with whether or not the proffered expert merely assumed the fact he was being called to prove. In this case, not even Young disputes that he beat Patrick for years. The government did not offer Dr. Burgess as an expert on whether or not Young abused Patrick, but rather, as an expert on how victims such as Patrick typically respond to such abuse. Furthermore, there is no legal authority supporting the proposition that Dr. Burgess must interview Patrick before forming her expert opinion.

Young's final two arguments are as futile as the first. Next, he claims that Dr. Burgess' methodology was based upon "anecdotal" evidence of other battered women; and finally, he argues that her methodology was unsound because she did not interview Patrick's friends and family. As for "anecdotal" evidence, Dr. Burgess is a highly qualified psychiatric mental health nurse with over forty years of experience. She specializes in crime victims and has published well over 100 scholarly articles and other writings on forensic nursing, rape, and domestic violence. Her work is generally accepted in the mental health profession. Even Young's own expert agreed with Dr. Burgess that abuse victims often recant their statements to protect their abusers. Dr. Burgess' background makes it clear that she based her opinion in this case on her extensive nursing experience as well as her academic research on several hundred battered women.

Furthermore, Dr. Burgess reached her opinion after conducting a thorough and full examination of the facts in this case. We noted above the substantial evidence Dr. Burgess reviewed in forming her opinion, including police and medical reports as well as communications between Patrick and Young. And, lest we forget, Dr. Burgess also spent over an hour interviewing Patrick personally. To assert that Dr. Burgess' opinion was based on "anecdotal" evidence is patently inaccurate. That Dr. Burgess did not also interview Patrick's friends and family is of no concern; it seems unlikely that they would disprove the abuse Young dealt out to Patrick for over a decade.

Finally, given Patrick's recantation at trial, we find that Dr. Burgess' expert opinion was helpful to the jury in determining how to credit that testimony....

In a last-ditch effort, Young argues that Rule 403 of the Federal Rules of Evidence prohibits the introduction of Dr. Burgess' testimony because the prejudicial effect of asserting that Young battered Patrick outweighs the probative value of her testimony. There is no real issue disputing that Young beat Patrick during the course of their relationship and over the days at issue here. The evidence of the beatings was overwhelming, and Dr. Burgess' testimony was highly probative as to why Patrick recanted on the stand in light of her earlier statements....

Notes and Questions

1. Although the questions whether an expert is qualified and whether his testimony is reliable are two distinct inquiries, they are not completely unrelated to one another. Some courts view the extent of the expert's qualifications as a factor pertinent to the *Daubert* reliability analysis. *E.g., United States v. Mitchell*, 365 F.3d 215, 242 (3d Cir. 2004) ("[T]he binary question whether an expert is or is not qualified to testify to a particular subject is analytically distinct, under Rule 702, from the more finely textured question whether a given expert's qualifications enhance the reliability of his testimony.").

2. The Advisory Committee Note to Rule 702 explained the helpfulness requirement as follows:

> Whether the situation is a proper one for the use of expert testimony is to be determined on the basis of assisting the trier. "There is no more certain test for determining when experts may be used than the common sense inquiry whether the untrained layman would be qualified to determine intelligently and to the best possible degree the particular issue without enlightenment from those having a specialized understanding of the subject involved in the dispute." Ladd, Expert Testimony, 5 Vand.L.Rev. 414, 418 (1952). When opinions are excluded, it is because they are unhelpful and therefore superfluous and a waste of time. 7 Wigmore § 1918.

Advisory Committee Note to Rule 702.

Do the opinions always use the word "helpfulness" to refer to the same thing, or does it appear to have multiple meanings?

3. As indicated in *United States v. Lester*, expert witness testimony that satisfies the requirements of Rule 702 may nonetheless be excluded under Rule 403. May a trial court circumvent the *Daubert* analysis altogether by assuming reliability but nonetheless excluding it on the ground that its probative worth would be substantially outweighed by its prejudicial effect? *See United States v. Ramirez-Robles*, 386 F.3d 1234, 1246 (9th Cir. 2004) ("The *Daubert* hearing ... is not necessary if the proffered evidence can be excluded by Rule 403. Rule 403 and *Daubert* address different aspects of evidence and therefore act independently.").

4. Note that an expert's inability to declare with certainty that a fingerprint, handwriting, or DNA is from a particular source is not a bar to admitting her testimony, but goes instead to the weight to be given to it. *See, e.g., United States v. Mornan*, 413 F.3d 372, 381 (3d Cir. 2005) ("Handwriting experts often give their opinions in terms of probabilities rather than certainties.... We therefore find no error ... in the District Court's decision ... to allow the jury to determine what weight to give her 'less-than-certain' conclusions."); *United States v. Morrow*, 374 F. Supp. 2d 51, 65 (D.D.C. 2005) ("because PCR testing creates a sliding scale of evidence, it is improper for a court to step in and demarcate some arbitrary random match probability ratio, above which evidence will be hidden from the jury. Instead, the DNA evidence should be presented to the jury, which—after cross-examination and careful consideration—may afford it the weight that it is

due."). However, as *Lester* demonstrates, an inability to quantify that uncertainty with some degree of precision is cause for exclusion under Rule 403. *See, e.g., United States v. Frazier*, 387 F.3d 1244, 1266 (11th Cir. 2004) (en banc) ("because [the expert's] opinion was imprecise and unspecific, the members of the jury could not readily determine whether the 'expectation' of finding hair or seminal fluid was a virtual certainty, a strong probability, a possibility more likely than not, or perhaps even just a possibility. As a result, [the expert's] imprecise opinion easily could serve to confuse the jury, and might well have misled it.").

5. In *Young*, expert testimony on Battered Woman Syndrome was held to be "helpful" because it provides jurors with insight into the sometimes counter-intuitive behavior of crime victims. Other examples of expert witness testimony that helps jurors to understand such behavior in crime victims include Rape-Trauma Syndrome, Stockholm Syndrome, and Child Sexual Abuse Accommodation Syndrome (CSAAS). *See Brodit v. Cambra*, 350 F.3d 985, 991 (9th Cir. 2003) ("CSAAS describes various emotional stages, experienced by sexually abused children, that may explain their sometimes piecemeal and contradictory manner of disclosing abuse."); *United States v. Peralta*, 941 F.2d 1003, 1009 n.1 (9th Cir. 1991) ("[t]he Stockholm Syndrome has been described as 'a psychological phenomenon whereby a hostage develops positive feelings for his or her captor'"); *Mathie v. Fries*, 935 F. Supp. 1284, 1295 (E.D.N.Y. 1996) ("'rape-trauma syndrome' [describes the] ordinary responses of rape victims").

4. Bases for Expert Witness Testimony

Recall that, under Rule 602, a witness's testimony normally must be based on personal knowledge. Yet Rule 602's last sentence indicates that it "does not apply to a witness's expert testimony under Rule 703," and the Advisory Committee Note to Rule 602 clarifies states that "[t]he reference to Rule 703 is designed to avoid any question of conflict between the present rule and the provisions of that rule allowing an expert to express opinions based on facts of which he does not have personal knowledge."

The first sentence of Rule 703 provides that "[a]n expert may base an opinion on facts or data in the case that the expert has been made aware of or personally observed." As the Advisory Committee Note to Rule 703 explains, this language permits an expert to base his opinion on several different sources, individually or in combination with one another.

First, an expert may base her opinion on facts or data "personally observed" by the expert. This method is the only one that is consistent with the normal requirement of Rule 602 in that the expert's testimony is based on his first-hand observations. The paradigmatic example of this method, as noted by the Advisory Committee, is expert testimony by a patient's treating physician.

Second, an expert may base his opinion on facts or data that she "has been made aware of." This may occur in one of three different ways. First, the expert may attend the trial, hear all the testimony and evidence presented, and then render an opinion based on the evidence presented. The expert witness does not evaluate the *veracity* of the evidence presented at trial, but rather assumes its truth and renders an opinion based on that assumption.

Of course, given how high expert witness' hourly fees are, it can be very expensive for a party to have the expert personally observe the proceedings. Accordingly, a second way in which the expert can be "made aware of" the facts or data is for the attorney who calls her to present a hypothetical that summarizes the evidence already admitted, asks the expert to assume the truth of those facts, and to render an opinion based on those facts. Such questions are permitted so long as there is sufficient evidence in the record to support a jury finding of the hypothetically assumed facts. *E.g., Toucet v. Maritime Overseas Corp.*, 991 F.2d 5, 10 (1st Cir. 1993); *Newman v. Hy-Way Heat Systems, Inc.*, 789 F.2d 269, 270 (4th Cir. 1986).

Finally, an expert may render an opinion based on facts or data made known to her prior to trial. Thus, for example, a physician testifying as an expert may base his opinion on a review of the patient's medical records, conversations with the patient's treating physician, conversations with the patient himself, and medical reference books.

One challenge in dealing with this last method is that the expert's opinion may be based on evidence which itself is not admissible, either because it is hearsay, has not been authenticated, or for some other reason. Yet the second sentence of Rule 703 provides that, "[i]f experts in the particular field would reasonably rely on those kinds of facts or data in forming an opinion on the subject, they need not be admissible for the opinion to be admitted."

This in turn raises two other questions: how is reasonable reliance determined, and does Rule 703 implicitly allow for such otherwise inadmissible underlying data to be admitted into evidence? The materials that follow explore both of these questions.

United States v. Stone
222 F.R.D. 334 (E.D. Tenn. 2004)

COLLIER, District Judge....

Ms. Cantrel is a Revenue Officer with eighteen years of experience with the Internal Revenue Service ("IRS"). The prosecution sought to call Ms. Cantrel to testify as an expert witness. Anticipating the issue the prosecution filed a Trial Memorandum (Court File No. 73) and in this memorandum stated that Ms. Cantrel would be asked to testify as an expert in corporate and individual tax computation. When the issue was raised on the first day of trial, the defense indicated it had objections to Ms. Cantrel's testimony.

Defendants Charles Stone, Dora Stone, and Byron Woody were on trial for tax fraud....

According to the Trial Memorandum and her testimony at trial, Ms. Cantrel has a B.S. in accounting from the University of Tennessee at Chattanooga, eighteen years of experience as an IRS agent, and a Certified Public Accountant license from Texas. She has audited numerous individuals and corporations to compute their correct tax liability.

In their response to the Government's Trial Memorandum (Court File No. 80), Defendants argued Ms. "Cantrel cannot testify about certain inadmissible hearsay evidence — specifically her conversations with non-testifying witnesses — to form the bases of her expert opinion."

....

The Government stated in its Trial Memorandum that Ms. Cantrel would base her opinions on her conversations with non-testifying employees of Benton Manufacturing Company. During argument on this issue, counsel clarified the conversations referenced were actually statements the employees provided to IRS criminal investigator Iris Bohannan during a 1998 interview that Ms. Cantrel attended....

The starting point for analysis is Federal Rule of Evidence 703. Rule 703 allows an expert to base her opinion upon three grounds: 1) facts within her personal knowledge, 2) facts presented to her at trial; and 3) facts presented to her outside of court, but not perceived by her personally, if those facts are the type of facts reasonably relied upon by experts in her field in drawing such conclusions. The Rule also imposes upon the trial judge the obligation to determine that the probative value of the otherwise inadmissible facts or data substantially outweighs their prejudicial effect, before the trial judge should allow such underlying facts to be disclosed to the jury.

The defendants' objection relates to the third ground, *i.e.*, facts presented to Ms. Cantrel outside of court. The rule now allows an expert to base her opinion on otherwise inadmissible evidence. However, such otherwise inadmissible evidence does not thereby become admissible. Rule 703 explicitly provides that otherwise inadmissible facts or data upon which an opinion is based do not themselves become automatically admissible simply because the expert relied upon them.

For such evidence the Rule imposes upon the trial judge a number of obligations to both ensure the expert is offering proper testimony and to safeguard the quality of information received by the fact finder. In essence, the Rule requires the Court to perform a gate keeping function.

> When an expert witness's proposed testimony is based wholly or in part on facts or data that the witness obtained outside the court room through a method other than personal perception, the trial court must make a preliminary determination whether the facts on which the witness relied are of a type that experts in the witness's field of expertise reasonably rely on in reaching such opinions.

4 Jack B. Weinstein & Margaret A. Berger, *Weinstein's Federal Evidence*, § 703.04[1] (Joseph M. McLaughlin, ed., Matthew Bender 2d ed.2004)....

1. The otherwise inadmissible facts or data must be type reasonably relied upon in field

The next obligation imposed upon the trial court is the obligation to determine that the inadmissible facts or data are of the type reasonably relied upon by experts in the particular field.... "It is not sufficient for the court simply to ascertain that other experts do in fact rely on that type of data. Rather, the court must make an independent assessment, based on a factual showing, that the material in question is sufficiently reliable for experts in that field to rely on it." 4 Jack B. Weinstein & Margaret A. Berger, *Weinstein's Federal Evidence*, § 703.04[2] (Joseph M. McLaughlin, ed., Matthew Bender 2d ed.2004). In particular the Rule goes much further than just obviating the need to introduce the otherwise admissible underlying facts or data. Under the current rule an expert opinion may be predicated solely on inadmissible evidence such as hearsay....

2. Court must make Rule 104(a) determination

Moreover, in cases where the expert seeks to give testimony based upon otherwise inadmissible evidence, an obligation is imposed upon the trial court to determine, pursuant to Rule 104(a), both that the facts or data relied upon by the expert are of a type relied upon by experts in the particular field and that such reliance is reasonable. In *Sphere Drake Insurance PLC v. Trisko*, 226 F.3d 951, 955 (8th Cir. 2000), the expert investigator testified he routinely relied on statements of informants as an investigating police officer. On that basis the Eighth Circuit stated he was permitted to rely on informant statements in forming his expert opinion. Other courts are in agreement that the trial court may consider the expert's own testimony concerning the types of data that are reasonably relied upon by experts in his field. In addition to relying on the experts [*sic*] own testimony, the trial court may rely upon other sources of information it deems reliable, such as the testimony of other experts. The court may consult learned treatises. And in appropriate cases the court may take judicial notice regarding the types of data that are reasonably relied upon by experts in the field.

3. Court must scrutinize specific facts relied upon by expert

Another obligation placed upon the trial court is the duty to carefully scrutinize the specific facts relied upon by the expert to ensure that the expert's reliance is reasonable in the particular case.... As a matter of logic the greater reliance by the expert on inadmissible facts that the court finds to be untrustworthy, the less likely it is that the reliance is reasonable....

4. Expert must not be conduit for hearsay

The last obligation placed on the trial court is that it must ensure that the expert witness is truly testifying as an expert and not merely serving as a conduit through which hearsay is brought before the jury. Assistance to the trier of fact is the basic purpose of expert testimony. To assist the trier of fact the court must ensure that the witness is giving expert opinion and not merely the opinion of an expert. In other words, the expert must bring his own expertise to bear. If the expert merely relates inadmissible hearsay to the fact finder, he is not aiding the fact finder. Essentially, the value the expert brings to the trial process is his ability to apply his expertise to the facts and draw inferences from them....

Notes and Questions

1. Prior to 2000, there was a great deal of confusion about whether and with what restrictions otherwise inadmissible facts or data underlying an expert's opinion could be brought to the jury's attention. In 2000, a third sentence was added to Rule 703 to address this issue. That sentence provides as follows:

> But if the facts or data would otherwise be inadmissible, the proponent of the opinion may disclose them to the jury only if their probative value in helping the jury evaluate the opinion substantially outweighs their prejudicial effect.

Federal Rule of Evidence 703.

Note that the balancing test under Rule 703, unlike Rule 403, is weighted against disclosure to the jury, and is described by the Advisory Committee as creating a "presumption against disclosure." Moreover, even if the balancing test is satisfied, the otherwise inadmissible facts or data may be admitted *only* for the purpose of helping the jury to understand and to scrutinize the expert's reasoning. The jury is to be instructed, under Rule 105, that it is not to use the underlying facts and data as *substantive* evidence, but only to evaluate the reasonableness of the expert's opinion in light of the information that he considered.

Of course, the risk that the jury will be unable to make this distinction is rather high, and the Advisory Committee Note makes clear that the likely effectiveness or ineffectiveness of such an instruction should be taken into consideration in deciding whether to permit the otherwise inadmissible information to be disclosed to the jury.

2. Note that the restrictive balancing test of Rule 703 is applicable only when the *proponent* of the expert seeks to have the underlying facts or data disclosed to the jury. In terms it places no restrictions on the ability of the *opposing* party to bring that information out on cross-examination, and the Advisory Committee Note to Rule 703 makes this explicit. Indeed, it cross references Rule 705, which provides:

> Unless the court orders otherwise, an expert may state an opinion—and give the reasons for it—without first testifying to the underlying facts or data. But the expert may be required to disclose those facts or data on cross-examination.

Rule 705 thus gives opposing counsel the ability to probe the facts and data that form the basis for the expert's opinion in an effort to cast doubt on the opinion. Thus, for example, if the expert indicates that he relied on a particular medical record, the cross-examiner may probe whether the expert took into account certain data in the record unfavorable to the proponent's position.

Yet when an opposing party invokes Rule 705, the jury's consideration of the otherwise inadmissible underlying facts and data are likewise limited to using them to evaluate the expert's opinion. *See United States v. Wright*, 783 F.2d 1091, 1100 (D.C. Cir. 1986). Moreover, there are other consequences:

> Nothing in this Rule restricts the presentation of underlying expert facts or data when offered by an adverse party. *See* Rule 705. Of course, an adversary's attack on an expert's basis will often open the door to a proponent's rebuttal with information that was reasonably relied upon by the expert, *even if that information would not have been discloseable initially under the balancing test provided by this amendment.*

Advisory Committee Note to 2000 Amendment to Rule 703 (emphasis added).

Indeed, the Advisory Committee indicated that the *proponent* can anticipate and bring such facts to the jury's attention:

> Moreover, in some circumstances the proponent might wish to disclose information that is relied upon by the expert in order to "remove the sting" from the opponent's anticipated attack, and thereby prevent the jury from drawing an unfair negative inference. The trial court should take this consideration into account in applying the balancing test provided by this amendment.

3. Although Rule 705 provides that an expert need not disclose the underlying facts and data on direct examination before rendering his opinion, it is subject to the proviso "[u]nless the court orders otherwise." *See University of Rhode Island v. A.W. Chesterton Co.*, 2 F.3d 1200, 1218 (1st Cir. 1993). Moreover, the Rule does not *prevent* an expert from disclosing the underlying facts and data (unless otherwise inadmissible and barred by the Rule 703 balancing test), and there is good reason for the proponent to bring this information out, as the conclusions unsupported by the factual foundation are less likely to carry weight with the jury.

4. In the 2000 Amendment to Rule 702, the Advisory Committee clarified the relationship between Rules 702 and 703:

> There has been some confusion over the relationship between Rules 702 and 703. The amendment makes clear that the sufficiency of the basis of an expert's testimony is to be decided under Rule 702. Rule 702 sets forth the overarching requirement of reliability, and an analysis of the sufficiency of the expert's basis cannot be divorced from the ultimate reliability of the expert's opinion. In contrast, the "reasonable reliance" requirement of Rule 703 is a relatively narrow inquiry. When an expert relies on inadmissible information, Rule 703 requires the trial court to determine whether that information is of a type reasonably relied on by other experts in the field. If so, the expert can rely on the information in reaching an opinion. However, the question whether the expert is relying on a

sufficient basis of information—whether admissible information or not—is governed by the requirements of Rule 702.

Advisory Committee Note to 2000 Amendment to Rule 702.

5. Opinion on the "Ultimate Issue"

As Justice Kennedy's concurring opinion in *United States v. Scheffer* indicated, the common law barred both lay and expert witnesses from testifying to an "ultimate issue" in the case. The common law imposed this rule "to prevent the witness from 'usurping the province of the jury.'"

The Advisory Committee characterized the rationale for the ultimate issue rule as "empty rhetoric," and finding that it deprived the trier of fact from useful information, it enacted Rule 704, which abolished the ultimate issue rule. The Rule was amended by Congress in 1984 to reinstate the rule with respect to expert witness testimony regarding whether a defendant in a criminal case did or did not have a mental state constituting an element of a crime or defense. The motivation for the amendment was as follows:

> The purpose of this amendment is to eliminate the confusing spectacle of competing expert witnesses testifying to directly contradictory conclusions as to the ultimate legal issue to be found by the trier of fact.

S. Rep. No. 98-225, at 230 (1983).

Rule 704 in its present form provides as follows:

(a) **In General—Not Automatically Objectionable.** An opinion is not objectionable just because it embraces an ultimate issue.

(b) **Exception.** In a criminal case, an expert witness must not state an opinion about whether the defendant did or did not have a mental state or condition that constitutes an element of the crime charged or of a defense. Those matters are for the trier of fact alone.

Yet that Rule 704(a) provides that testimony is not barred merely because it embraces the ultimate issue does not mean that such testimony is necessarily admissible. Moreover, the scope of Rule 704(b) is narrower than it appears. The materials that follow explore both of these issues.

Woods v. Lecureux
110 F.3d 1215 (6th Cir. 1997)

MOORE, Circuit Judge.

Plaintiff-Appellant Margaret Woods appeals from the district court's order granting judgment as a matter of law in favor of both defendants in this § 1983 action brought on behalf of her deceased son, Larry M. Billups, who was murdered while incarcerated in the Michigan prison system. Woods contends that the defendants, Michigan prison officials, violated her son's Eighth Amendment rights by failing to prevent his murder....

I. BACKGROUND

Larry Billups was murdered on May 15, 1989, while he was returning to his cell after breakfast at the State Prison of Southern Michigan ("SPSM"), in Jackson, Michigan. The assassins, known members of the Melanic Islamic Palace of the Rising Sun ("the Melanics"), a prison organization, stabbed Billups.... He had been at SPSM for only ten days. Prior to his stay there, he was incarcerated at Kinross Correctional Facility ("KCF"), in Michigan's Upper Peninsula. On April 18, 1989, while still at KCF, Billups was implicated along with several other prisoners in the assault and robbery of his roommate, Morris Barlow. Immediately after that incident, Billups was placed in a segregation unit. Because of the assault, he soon received an "increased custody transfer" to SPSM.

Appellant contends that Billups was murdered as a direct result of his involvement in the attack on Barlow....

Although appellant's complaint originally named as defendants numerous Michigan prison officials, she subsequently voluntarily dismissed all of them except Art Tessmer, the Deputy Warden of Security at KCF, and John Jabe, the Warden at SPSM. The crux of appellant's argument against Tessmer is that he knew of the dangers facing Billups as a result of Billups's participation in the assault on Barlow, but, due to his deliberate indifference, failed to inform the proper authorities at SPSM of these dangers. As for Appellee Jabe, appellant contends that he knew of an unacceptably high risk to prisoners housed in 6-Block, the area in which Billups resided at SPSM, but failed to take the steps to reduce that risk.

The case proceeded to trial. After appellant rested her case, the district court granted both defendants' motions for judgment as a matter of law pursuant to Federal Rule of Civil Procedure 50. The court found that even if Tessmer had known of the dispute between Billups and the Melanics, his failure to act upon that knowledge "might reasonably be characterized as negligent, but certainly not as deliberately indifferent, wanton, or obdurate." In granting Jabe's motion, the court stated that "[t]here is no evidentiary basis for a jury finding deliberate indifference or wanton or obdurate behavior on the part of defendant Jabe." In addition to appealing both of these conclusions, appellant contends that the district court erred in four of its evidentiary rulings. We turn first to the evidentiary issues....

B. Exclusion of "Ultimate Issue" Testimony

Appellant asserts that the district court abused its discretion when it prohibited her expert witness, Dr. Mintzes, from using the term "deliberately indifferent" to describe Tessmer's and Jabe's conduct.... This court recently has stated that "Rule 704 removes the 'general proscription against opinions on 'ultimate issues' and shift[s] the focus to whether the testimony is 'otherwise admissible.'" *United States v. Sheffey*, 57 F.3d 1419, 1425 (6th Cir. 1995).

As the advisory committee notes to Rule 704 indicate, the protections afforded by the other rules of evidence are far from hollow when ultimate issue testimony is being offered:

> The abolition of the ultimate issue rule does not lower the bars so as to admit all opinions. Under Rules 701 and 702, opinions must be helpful to the trier of fact, and Rule 403 provides for exclusion of evidence which wastes time. These provisions afford ample assurances against the admission of opinions which would merely tell the jury what result to reach, somewhat in the manner of the oath-helpers of an earlier day. They also stand ready to exclude opinions phrased in terms of inadequately explored legal criteria. Thus the question, "Did T have capacity to make a will?" would be excluded, while the question, "Did T have sufficient mental capacity to know the nature and extent of his property and the natural objects of his bounty and to formulate a rational scheme of distribution?" would be allowed. McCormick § 12.

FED.R.EVID. 704 Advisory Committee Notes. It is, therefore, apparent that testimony offering nothing more than a legal conclusion—i.e, testimony that does little more than tell the jury what result to reach—is properly excludable under the Rules. It is also appropriate to exclude "ultimate issue" testimony on the ground that it would not be helpful to the trier of fact when "'*the terms used by the witness have a separate, distinct and specialized meaning in the law different from that present in the vernacular.*'" *Sheffey*, 57 F.3d at 1426 (citation omitted) (emphasis in *Sheffey*).

In addition to *Sheffey*'s general pronouncements, two Sixth Circuit cases have confronted the ultimate issue problem as it relates to the term "deliberate indifference." In *Heflin v. Stewart County*, 958 F.2d 709 (6th Cir.), *cert. denied*, 506 U.S. 998 (1992), an expert witness in a § 1983/Eighth Amendment case testified that, in his opinion, the prison officials were "deliberately indifferent" to the medical needs of a pretrial detainee. The court concluded that the district court did not commit "reversible error" by admitting this evidence. Central to the court's conclusion was the fact that the witness "used 'deliberately indifferent' in the way an ordinary layman would to describe such conduct—to state his opinion on the ultimate fact, not to state a legal conclusion." *Id.* In *Berry v. City of Detroit*, 25 F.3d 1342 (6th Cir. 1994), a § 1983/municipal liability case, the plaintiff's expert witness testified that the Detroit Police Department was "gross[ly] negligent" in its training of its officers and that this gross negligence was comparable to "deliberate indifference." The witness then defined deliberate indifference as "[c]onscious knowledge of something and not doing anything about it." Overturning a jury verdict for the plaintiff, this court held that the district court erred by admitting this testimony. We stated that "'deliberate indifference' is a legal term" and that "[i]t is the responsibility of the court, not testifying witnesses, to define legal terms."

Berry and *Heflin* shed light on the difficulty district courts face when determining whether to admit testimony that arguably amounts to a legal conclusion. Although *Heflin* indicates that district courts can exercise some discretion in determining whether the proffered testimony is helpful to the jury, *Berry* teaches that a district court abuses its discretion when it allows a witness to define legal terms, especially terms that carry a considerable amount of legal baggage.

In the present case, the rationale relied on in *Berry* is much more applicable than that in *Heflin*. The following colloquy between Dr. Mintzes and counsel for appellant demonstrates this fact:

Q. Dr. Mintzes, did you form an opinion with respect to the actions or inactions of Mr. Tessmer as they relate to Larry Billups in this matter?

A. Yes, I do [sic].

Q. And could you tell the jury what that opinion is?

A. It was my opinion that, in terms of looking at all the information, that Mr. Tessmer was what I considered, which is a legal term, deliberately indifferent to what was felt to be a known risk of harm to Mr. Billups.

Q. And when you say "deliberately indifferent," what do you mean by that?

A. Well, somebody, when somebody is considered to be deliberate—

THE COURT: I believe that you are asking the witness to testify to a legal conclusion at this point, Mr. Timm.

MR. TIMM: I'll withdraw the question, your Honor.

Testimony such as Dr. Mintzes's, which attempts to tell the jury what result to reach and which runs the risk of interfering with a district court's jury instructions, hardly can be viewed as being helpful to the jury. . . .

[The opinion of Judge Wellford, concurring in part and dissenting in part, is omitted.]

Problem 4-7: Gay Panic Defense

Paul is indicted on charges of murdering Mark. Paul doesn't deny killing Mark, but raises a temporary insanity defense. Paul claims that Mark made a sexual advance, and that Paul, shocked by the advance, went "berserk."

To support his defense, Paul seeks to call Dr. James Lewis, a board-certified psychiatrist, to provide expert witness testimony on "gay panic syndrome." If permitted, Dr. Lewis would testify that gay panic is triggered by a homosexual advance, and that the person — because of his own repressed homosexual feelings — loses control and acts purely instinctively, causing the person to be unable to control the nature of his acts. Dr. Lewis would further testify that he examined Paul, and concluded that he did suffer from gay panic syndrome, and thus was not legally sane when he stabbed Mark.

The prosecution objects to the testimony. How should the court rule?

United States v. Finley
301 F.3d 1000 (9th Cir. 2002)

BRIGHT, Circuit Judge. . . .

Finley owned a law bookstore and ran a bar review course for students of non-accredited law schools. In 1992, Finley began looking for investors to assist him in opening a chain of approximately twenty bookstores across the United States. Finley could not obtain traditional bank financing because of a dispute he had with the IRS over a large tax claim.

In November 1995, a customer mentioned that he had attended an investment seminar in Montana run by Leroy Schweitzer. Inspired by this suggestion, on December 22, 1995, Finley went to Schweitzer's farmhouse in rural Montana to attend the so-called investment seminar. Schweitzer explained that he possessed recorded liens against Norwest Bank of Montana, other banks, and individuals, and that he could draw on these accounts by issuing negotiable instruments.

At the conclusion of the seminar, each attendee received a five-minute audience with Schweitzer to explain the attendee's needs. When he met with Schweitzer, Finley explained his business plan to open a chain of bookstores. Finley also told Schweitzer that he owed the IRS about $180,000 and that he owed a mortgage on his condominium with Great Western Bank.

Schweitzer gave Finley several documents that looked like financial instruments and were entitled, "Comptroller's Warrants" and "Certified Banker's Checks." Schweitzer made one document payable to Finley and the Bank of America for $6,125,000, Finley's estimate of the cost of starting his bookstore chain. Schweitzer made the second document out to Finley and Great Western Bank for $150,000, or about twice the remaining amount Finley owed on his mortgage. The third instrument named the IRS and Finley as payees for $360,000, twice the amount Finley owed in taxes. . . .

[Finley repeatedly attempted to negotiate the instruments, despite being told by various financial institutions as well as agents of the federal government that the instruments were fraudulent. Eventually, Finley was indicted on charges of bank fraud and making false claims against the United States. Finley defended on the ground that he lacked the intent to defraud, the requisite *mens rea* for the charged crimes, and called an expert to testify in support of his defense.]

Dr. Wicks testified that Finley has an atypical belief system. Dr. Wicks explained that most people have an open belief system which is subject to change, but some people have closed belief systems. Closed belief systems are more abnormal because they are fixed and rigid....

Dr. Wicks explained that a delusion is another psychological term for an atypical belief system.... The doctor concluded that Mr. Finley suffered from a delusional disorder from a minimum of 1995 until the present. He elaborated that a person with a delusional disorder can be dissuaded from the delusion "[o]nly with tremendous, tremendous difficulty."

....

Rule 704(b) "limits the expert's testimony by prohibiting him from testifying as to whether the defendant had the mental state or condition that constitutes an element of the crime charged." *Morales*, 108 F.3d at 1035. The "rationale for precluding ultimate opinion testimony applies ... 'to any ultimate mental state of the defendant that is relevant to the legal conclusion sought to be proven.'" *United States v. Campos*, 217 F.3d 707, 711 (9th Cir. 2000) (quoting S. Rep. 98-225 at 231). However, Rule 704(b) allows expert testimony on a defendant's mental state so long as the expert does not draw the ultimate inference or conclusion for the jury. It is, therefore, essential that we distinguish between expert opinions that "necessarily compel" a conclusion about the defendant's *mens rea* and those that do not.

In *Morales*, we concluded that the district court erred in barring expert testimony under Rule 704(b) because the expert's testimony did not compel the conclusion that Morales lacked the *mens rea* of the crime. Morales, charged with willfully making false bookkeeping entries, wanted an accounting expert to testify that her "understanding of accounting principles" was "weak." *Id.* at 1037. We stated:

> Even if the jury believed [the] expert testimony that Morales had a weak grasp of bookkeeping knowledge (and there was evidence to the contrary), the jury would still have had to draw its own inference from that predicate testimony to answer the ultimate factual question—whether Morales willfully made false entries. Morales could have had a weak grasp of bookkeeping principles and still knowingly made false entries.

Id. at 1037.

In *Morales*, we also cited with approval *United States v. Rahm*, in which we reversed the district court's exclusion of a defense expert who was going to testify that Rahm had poor visual perception and consistently overlooked important visual details. In *Rahm*, we drew a distinction between the ultimate issue—whether Rahm knew the bills were counterfeit—and the proffered testimony of the defendant's poor vision, from which the jury could, but was not compelled, to infer that she did not know the bills were counterfeit.

On the other hand, we have applied Rule 704(b) to prohibit certain testimony that does compel a conclusion about *mens rea*. In *Campos*, we upheld a district court's exclusion of a polygraph expert from testifying that the defendant was truthful when she stated she did not know she was transporting marijuana. We determined that the testimony compelled the conclusion that the defendant did not possess the requisite knowledge to commit the crime because polygraph test results offer an implicit opinion about whether the accused is being deceptive about the very matters at issue in the trial.

Dr. Wicks' expert diagnosis that Finley has an atypical belief system falls into the *Morales/Rahm* line of reasoning and can be distinguished from *Campos*. The jury could have accepted the atypical belief diagnosis and still concluded that Finley knowingly defrauded the banks. If credited, Dr. Wicks' testimony established only that Finley's beliefs were rigid and he would distort or disregard information that ran counter to those beliefs. Dr. Wicks did not, and would not be allowed to, testify about Finley's specific beliefs with regard to the financial instruments. The jury was free to conclude that Finley knew the notes were fraudulent, despite the rigidity of his belief system. Just as in *Morales* and *Rahm*, the defense was entitled to present evidence so that the jury could infer from the expert's testimony that the defendant lacked the necessary intent to defraud, but such a conclusion was not necessarily compelled by the diagnosis....

United States v. Hayward
359 F.3d 631 (3d Cir. 2004)

GARTH, Circuit Judge.

Scott Hayward ("Hayward") appeals from the District Court's judgment and sentence. Judgment was entered against Hayward after a jury convicted him of violating 18 U.S.C. §2423(a) (transportation of a minor with intent to engage in criminal sexual activity)....

[Hayward, a cheerleading instructor, was on the road with his students at a cheerleading competition when the conduct at issue, which involved the students, took place.]

The first of [Hayward's] claims is that the District Court improperly allowed expert testimony adduced from behavioral scientist Kenneth Lanning ("Lanning") pertaining to the general profile of an acquaintance molester. The District Court Judge, in response to Hayward's pre-trial motion to bar Lanning's testimony, limited Lanning's testimony to "acquaintance child molesters' pattern of activity," and prohibited Lanning from testifying as to Hayward himself or as to Hayward's intent.

After testifying as to his experience and credentials, Lanning was qualified by the District Court Judge as an expert in the field of behavioral science.[7] Lanning then testified about various types of child molesters, focusing primarily on "acquaintance" child molesters. Lanning described the patterns exhibited by many acquaintance child molesters, including selection of victims from dysfunctional homes, formulation of a customized seduction process, lowering the victim's inhibitions about sex, isolating the victim, and soliciting the victim's cooperation in the victimization process.

Hayward argues that Lanning's testimony violated Rule 704(b) of the Federal Rules of Evidence, which prohibits expert witnesses from testifying with respect to the mental state of a defendant in a criminal case and from stating an opinion or inference as to whether the defendant had the mental state constituting an element of the crime charged.

---

7. Lanning testified that he had been an FBI agent for 30 years, he had been a Supervisory Special Agent in the FBI's Behavioral Sciences Unit for 20 years, he was a founding member of the American Professional Society on the Abuse of Children, he was the author of a monograph entitled "Child Molesters and Behavioral Analysis," he held two masters degrees, and he had taught university courses in behavioral science.

Hayward contends that Lanning's testimony effectively removed the determination of Hayward's intent from the jury, in violation of Rule 704(b).

We have held that under Rule 704(b) "expert testimony is admissible if it merely supports an inference or conclusion that the defendant did or did not have the requisite mens rea, so long as the expert does not draw the ultimate inference or conclusion for the jury and the ultimate inference or conclusion does not necessarily follow from the testimony." *United States v. Bennett*, 161 F.3d 171, 185 (3d Cir. 1998) (quoting *United States v. Morales*, 108 F.3d 1031, 1038 (9th Cir. 1997)) (internal quotations omitted).

Furthermore, in a Seventh Circuit case, in which Lanning qualified as an expert and in which he testified under circumstances similar to those in this case, Lanning's testimony was admitted and upheld against a Rule 704(b) attack identical to Hayward's attack here. See *United States v. Romero*, 189 F.3d 576 (7th Cir. 1999). In *Romero*, Lanning was only permitted to testify to "the methods and techniques employed by preferential child molesters. The prosecution would not ask Lanning to give his opinion about Romero or to comment about his intent or culpability." On redirect examination, however, the

> prosecution posed a series of hypothetical actions to Lanning and asked him if these actions would indicate someone who would act on his sexual fantasies about children ... [T]he hypotheticals described actions taken by Romero that had already been produced in evidence[.]

The Seventh Circuit held that Lanning's responses did not violate Rule 704(b) because "[h]is testimony did not amount to a statement of his belief about what specifically was going through Romero's mind when he met [the victim]."

In this case, Lanning's testimony elucidated the motives and practices of an acquaintance molester. His testimony was admissible under Rule 704(b) because, as in *Romero*, Lanning "never directly opined as to [Hayward's] mental state when he [returned to the hotel room with the cheerleaders]." Rather, Lanning "focused primarily on the modus operandi—on the actions normally taken by child molesters to find and seduce their victims." He drew no conclusion as to Hayward's intent. Thus, his testimony is admissible under Rule 704(b)....

[The opinion of Judge Fuentes, concurring in part and dissenting in part, is omitted.]

Notes and Questions

1. Does Rule 704(a), when coupled with the helpfulness requirement of Rule 702, implicitly draw a line between ultimate questions of law and ultimate questions of fact? Consider the following:

> The committee's [will contest] illustration establishes the starting point for analysis of admissibility by distinguishing between testimony on issues of law and testimony on ultimate facts. While testimony on ultimate facts is authorized under Rule 704, the committee's comments emphasize that testimony on ultimate questions of law is not favored. The basis for this distinction is that testimony on the ultimate factual questions aids the jury in reaching a verdict; testimony which articulates and applies the relevant law, however, circumvents the jury's decision-making function by telling it how to decide the case.

> Following the advisory committee's comments, a number of federal circuits have held that an expert witness may not give an opinion on ultimate issues of law.... The courts in these decisions draw a clear line between permissible testimony

on issues of fact and testimony that articulates the ultimate principles of law governing the deliberations of the jury. These courts have decried the latter kind of testimony as directing a verdict, rather than assisting the jury's understanding and weighing of the evidence.

Specht v. Jensen, 853 F.2d 805, 808 (10th Cir. 1988).

Are you persuaded? Does the *Specht* court mean to say that ultimate issue testimony is *always* permitted for ultimate issues of fact, that it is *never* permitted for ultimate issues of law, or both?

2. Are you persuaded by the fine line that the *Hayward* court draws? Compare the following:

> Dela Cruz argues that the district court erred in excluding certain expert psychological testimony. We have held that Federal Rule of Evidence 704(b) prohibits testimony "from which it necessarily follows, if the testimony is credited, that the defendant did or did not possess the requisite *mens rea*." *United States v. Morales*, 108 F.3d 1031, 1037 (9th Cir. 1997) (en banc). The district court relied on *Morales* in excluding the testimony in question, noting that *Morales* expressed particular concern with expert testimony offered by mental health professionals about a mental state that is an element of the crime. As the district court correctly decided, the fact that Dela Cruz phrased his question in the form of inquiring about the mental state of "a person" and not directly about the mental state of the defendant does not render the question proper.

United States v. Dela Cruz, 358 F.3d 623, 626 (9th Cir. 2004). *But see United States v. Burlingame*, 2006 WL 455989, at *2 (9th Cir. Feb. 24, 2006) ("This court has repeatedly found that expert opinions do not violate 704(b) when they address hypothetical or "typical" situations involving the same evidence as in the case at trial. Biern offered his opinion regarding a "person" and "people involved with scams," but did not address Burlingame's individual mental state. The trial court did not err in admitting the opinion."). *Compare United States v. Are*, 590 F.3d 499, 512–13 (7th Cir. 2009) (holding that Rule 704(b) places only a "'slight' limitation on expert testimony," and that exclusion is not called for "as long as it is made clear, either by the court expressly or in the nature of the examination, that the opinion is based on the expert's knowledge of common criminal practices, and not on some special knowledge of the defendant's mental processes").

6. Court-Appointed Experts

As with most aspects of the adversary system in the United States, it is the individual parties, not the court, who retain and call experts as witnesses. Indeed, it is not uncommon for adversaries to call competing experts who present diametrically opposing opinions on an issue. Many commentators decry this state of affairs and advocate the appointment of "neutral" experts.

Although infrequently invoked, Rule 706 gives trial courts authority to appoint expert witnesses. Rule 706(a) provides that the trial court has discretion to make such an appointment on its own motion or at the request of a party, and that the expert so appointed may be one agreed upon by the parties and/or of the judge's own choosing. Rule 706(d) gives the trial court discretion to disclose to the jury that the expert was appointed by the court. Such an appointment does not prevent the parties from retaining and calling experts of their own choosing, as Rule 706(e) makes clear.

Rule 706(b) provides that the parties have certain rights with respect to court-appointed experts, including the right to be advised of the expert's findings, the right to take the expert's deposition, the right to call the expert to testify, and the right to cross-examine the expert.

Finally, Rule 706(c) addresses the source of compensation for court-appointed experts. In only limited circumstances are public funds available to compensate court-appointed experts; they are available only "in a criminal case or in a civil case involving just compensation under the Fifth Amendment." *See* Fed. R. Evid. 706(c)(1). The purpose of the special provision for Fifth Amendment just compensation cases is to guard against reducing constitutionally guaranteed just compensation by requiring the recipient to pay costs, *see* Advisory Committee Note to Rule 706(c); in all other civil cases, the expert's compensation is paid by "the parties in the proportion and at the time that the court directs— and the compensation is then charged like other costs." *See* Fed. R. Evid. 706(c)(2).

H. Exclusion and Sequestration of Witnesses

United States v. Rhynes

218 F.3d 310 (4th Cir. 2000) (en banc)

KING, Circuit Judge:

Michael Rhynes and several co-defendants were tried before a jury in the Western District of North Carolina on a number of drug-related charges. During the presentation of Rhynes's defense, the district court excluded his sole supporting witness after finding that his lawyer had violated the court's sequestration order. We conclude today that the exclusion of the witness' testimony was improper and constitutes reversible error. The conduct of Rhynes's lawyer did not contravene the district court's sequestration order, and, if it had, the sanction of witness exclusion was unduly severe. Because this error was not harmless, we must vacate Rhynes's conviction and sentence and remand for a new trial....

On September 24, 1996, at the commencement of the trial in Charlotte, North Carolina, a lawyer for one of Rhynes's co-defendants moved for sequestration of the Government's witnesses. In response, the district court entered its sequestration order from the bench.[1] The Government then noted that its "case agent" and a "summary witness" were in the courtroom and intended to "sit[ ] in on the testimony prepared to testify at the end of the trial[.]" The district court granted the Government's request that two of its witnesses be excepted from the sequestration order and another motion that the defense witnesses be sequestered. Thereafter, the lawyer for one of Rhynes's co-defendants sought to have his investigator excepted from the sequestration order, and the court granted the exception "[s]o long as your investigator observes Rule 615 and does not talk to the witnesses about testimony that has just concluded or testimony that has concluded."

. . . .

---

1. The entirety of the court's sequestration order is in the record as follows:
   Well, I do grant the usual sequestration rule and that is that the witnesses shall not discuss one with the other their testimony and particularly that would apply to those witnesses who have completed testimony not to discuss testimony with prospective witnesses, and I direct the Marshal's Service, as much as can be done, to keep those witnesses separate from the— those witnesses who have testified separate and apart from the witnesses who have not yet given testimony who might be in the custody of the marshal.

During the Government's case-in-chief, it presented the testimony of witness D.S. Davis. Davis is a convicted felon and was, at the time of trial, serving a seven-year sentence for participating in a drug conspiracy. Davis testified, *inter alia*, that he first met Alexander in 1990, when he (Davis) asked Alexander to serve as an intermediary in a drug transaction between Davis and Michael Rhynes....

During Rhynes's defense, he testified on his own behalf; then, he called a single witness to corroborate his testimony: Corwin Alexander. Alexander testified on a number of subjects ... before he was asked about the Government's earlier witness, Davis. Alexander explained that, at a meeting between the two, Davis told Alexander that the Government had offered Davis a deal in exchange for information about Rhynes. Alexander then stated, "And he [(Davis)] went off to do his time, and I hear from Tuesday he got up and said —," whereupon the Government objected and requested a bench conference.

At the bench, Mr. Scofield [Rhynes's lawyer] advised the district court that he had discussed Davis's testimony with Alexander: "I specifically told him about that testimony and told him I was going to ask him about that, Your Honor. And I don't think that violates the sequestration order." The district court indicated its belief that the sequestration order had been violated. Mr. Scofield then responded, "I'm sorry then, Your Honor. I've done wrong then because I don't know how else I can prepare him to testify. I told him that that guy told him that he was a drug dealer."

The district court nonetheless granted the Government's motion to strike Alexander's testimony and to exclude him as a witness....

II.

....

B.

It is significant to our consideration of this appeal that the district court invoked "the usual sequestration rule ... that the witnesses shall not discuss one with the other their testimony." This order thus had two parts: (1) the "usual sequestration rule" and (2) that witnesses were not to discuss their testimony with one another ("extending language").

For several reasons, it is apparent that the reference to "the usual sequestration rule" did nothing more than invoke Federal Rule of Evidence 615, the rule relating to sequestration orders. At the outset, the reference to a "rule" in the order was an obvious invocation of Rule 615. The district court's subsequent statements relating to the sequestration order similarly made clear to each of the parties that "the usual sequestration rule" was coextensive and conterminous with Rule 615. First, immediately after entering its order, the court permitted a co-defendant's investigator to remain in the courtroom, but only if the investigator "observes Rule 615." Later, when it initially interrupted Alexander's testimony, the court stated, "It's an absolute breach of the Rule 615"; similarly, when the court decided not to revisit its witness exclusion determination, it noted: "[M]y Rule 615 order was violated as to the testimony of many witnesses." Given these three clear references to Rule 615, we can only conclude that the district court's reference to a "rule" did nothing more than invoke Rule 615.

Because the district court's order involved these two elements, our task here is to first ascertain whether either (1) Rule 615 or (2) the additional admonition that "the witnesses shall not discuss one with the other their testimony" proscribed the conversation Mr. Scofield had with Alexander. We begin with a review of Rule 615 — an analysis that we undertake de novo.

C.

To determine whether Rule 615 proscribes the conduct of Mr. Scofield, we must first consider the language of the Rule itself.... It is clear from the plain and unambiguous language of Rule 615 that lawyers are simply not subject to the Rule. This Rule's plain language relates only to "witnesses," and it serves only to exclude witnesses from the courtroom. Thus, Rule 615 did not prohibit Mr. Scofield from discussing D.S. Davis's testimony with Corwin Alexander.

The district court's bald Rule 615 order was then extended by the statement that "the witnesses shall not discuss one with the other their testimony." Of course, nothing on the face of this extending language addresses the conduct of lawyers in any way. Moreover, the relevant authorities interpreting Rule 615, including court decisions and the leading commentators, agree that sequestration orders prohibiting discussions between witnesses should, and do, permit witnesses to discuss the case with counsel for either party....

In short, neither the bald invocation of Rule 615 nor the extending language relating to discussions between witnesses served to circumscribe the conduct of Mr. Scofield in any way.

D.

The Government has conceded that neither the plain language of the district court's order, nor the provisions of Rule 615, prohibit any conduct by lawyers, and we note that "in all but the most extraordinary circumstance," the inquiry should end here. *Estate of Cowart v. Nicklos Drilling Co.*, 505 U.S. 469, 475 (1992). Nonetheless, the Government asserts that the "purpose and spirit" of the sequestration order were compromised by Mr. Scofield's discussion with Alexander. Specifically, the Government contends that the "truth-seeking" process would be hindered if lawyers were permitted to reveal testimony in the manner exercised by Mr. Scofield. This is basically an argument that Rule 615, the extending language, or the policies underlying sequestration implicitly proscribed Mr. Scofield's conduct; we reject the argument for several reasons.

We have properly recognized the purpose and spirit underlying witness sequestration: it is "designed to discourage and expose fabrication, inaccuracy, and collusion." *Opus 3 Ltd. v. Heritage Park, Inc.*, 91 F.3d 625, 628 (4th Cir. 1996). Put differently, sequestration helps to smoke out lying witnesses: "It is now well recognized that sequestering witnesses 'is (next to cross-examination) one of the greatest engines that the skill of man has ever invented for the detection of liars in a court of justice.'" *Id.* (citing 6 *Wigmore on Evidence* § 1838, at 463).

To the extent that the Government asserts that Mr. Scofield frustrated the purpose and spirit of sequestration, we disagree. The Government asserts that Mr. Scofield's actions undermined the truthfulness of Alexander's testimony, which, in the Government's view, is surely an act that runs afoul of the sequestration order. On the contrary, lawyers are not like witnesses, and there are critical differences between them that are dispositive in this case. Unlike witnesses, lawyers are officers of the court, and, as such, they owe the court a duty of candor, *Model Rules of Professional Conduct* Rule 3.3 (1995) ("Model Rules"). Of paramount importance here, that duty both forbids an attorney from knowingly presenting perjured testimony and permits the attorney to refuse to offer evidence he or she reasonably believes is false. *Id.* Rule 3.3(a)(4), (c). Similarly, an attorney may not "counsel or assist a witness to testify falsely." *Id.* Rule 3.4(b). And, if an attorney believes that a non-client witness is lying on the witness stand about a material issue, he is obliged to "promptly reveal the fraud to the court." *Id.* Rule 3.3, cmt. 4....

Moreover, the purpose and spirit underlying sequestration are not absolute; indeed, we have aptly recognized that even the "powerful policies behind sequestration" must bend to the dictates of the Constitution. *Opus 3 Ltd.*, 91 F.3d at 628.[8] Thus, to the extent that they are implicated in this case, the policies and spirit of sequestration must yield to the constitutional and ethical duties Mr. Scofield sought to effectuate here.[9] That is, in the context of a criminal trial like this one, a defense attorney's duty to his client assumes constitutional stature: "In all criminal prosecutions, the accused shall … have the Assistance of Counsel for his defence." U.S. Const. amend. VI. To all clients, an attorney owes competence. *Model Rules* Rule 1.1. To fulfill this basic duty, the attorney must prepare carefully for the task at hand: "Competent representation requires … thoroughness and preparation reasonably necessary for the representation." *Id.* Rule 1.1(a).

Thorough preparation demands that an attorney interview and prepare witnesses before they testify. No competent lawyer would call a witness without appropriate and thorough pre-trial interviews and discussion. In fact, more than one lawyer has been punished, found ineffective, or even disbarred for incompetent representation that included failure to prepare or interview witnesses.

In this context, Mr. Scofield's actions were necessary in the exercise of his duties, both constitutional and ethical, as a lawyer. First, when the Government called Davis as a witness and began asking him questions about Alexander, Mr. Scofield made clear that he was unaware that Alexander had been implicated as a co-conspirator. Although Davis's subsequent testimony did not implicate Alexander in any specific drug deal, the import of Davis's allegation was clear: Alexander was serving as an intermediary between drug buyers and Rhynes. Faced with an allegation that his prime supporting witness, Alexander, had been assisting, or participating in, a drug conspiracy with Rhynes, Mr. Scofield had ethical (and possibly constitutional) duties to investigate these allegations with Alexander before he put Alexander on the stand. Mr. Scofield was thus compelled to ascertain, if possible: (1) whether Davis's allegations were untrue (or, if true, whether Alexander intended to invoke his Fifth Amendment rights); (2) whether Alexander's denials were credible; and (3) why Davis would make potentially false allegations against Alexander. Put simply, Mr. Scofield needed to fully assess his decision to call Alexander as a witness, and, to fulfill his obligations to his client, Scofield was compelled to discuss Davis's testimony with Alexander.

In response, the Government claims that Mr. Scofield did not violate the sequestration order by merely speaking with Alexander; instead, it was Mr. Scofield's informing Alexander of Davis's testimony that violated the order. Based on this view, the Government as-

---

8. It is important to note that the language of Rule 615 does not require exclusion of all witnesses from the courtroom. While an absolute rule might further promote the truth-seeking policy behind Rule 615, constitutional considerations have required that exceptions be built into the Rule itself. *Opus 3 Ltd.*, 91 F.3d at 628 ("confrontation and due process considerations" drive Rule 615's exceptions). Parties or their representatives, as well as expert witnesses, are authorized by Rule 615 to remain in the courtroom, hear testimony, and subsequently testify. Fed.R.Evid. 615([a])-([c]). In criminal cases these exceptions are applied to allow the prosecution's case agent to remain at counsel table with the prosecutor, hear the other witnesses testify, and nevertheless testify on behalf of the prosecution. In this very case, moreover, the district court's sequestration order specifically exempted the Government's FBI case agent as well as its summary witness.

9. While it is unnecessary for us to reach the issue in this case, we observe that sequestration orders that prevent attorneys from performing their duties as counsel, including discussing trial proceedings with future witnesses, may well violate a criminal defendant's Sixth Amendment rights. The Supreme Court has explicitly forbidden some sequestration orders that prohibit a defendant-witness from conferring with counsel. *Geders v. United States*, 425 U.S. 80, 91 (1976); *accord, United States v. Allen*, 542 F.2d 630, 633 (4th Cir. 1976). And at least one court has extended this reasoning to sequestration orders preventing counsel from discussing prior testimony with non-defendant witnesses.…

serts that counsel had ample room to interview and prepare witnesses without running afoul of the sequestration order. But this conclusion begs the question, "How was counsel to discern the limits of the sequestration order?" Those limits—as declared after the fact by the district court—did not appear on the face of the order, in Rule 615, in controlling precedent, or even in persuasive authorities. In fact, adoption of the Government's position would make it virtually impossible for counsel to know whether they have "ample room" to perform essential tasks without violating an order.[11] This argument thus fails to persuade us.

Further, sequestration is not the only technique utilized to ensure the pursuit of truth at trial. Indeed, if an attorney has inappropriately "coached" a witness, thorough cross-examination of that witness violates no privilege and is entirely appropriate and sufficient to address the issue....

In short, the Government's position requires the implication that by discussing prior trial testimony with Corwin Alexander, Mr. Scofield necessarily coached Alexander or made it likely that Alexander would commit perjury. To the contrary, we must trust and rely on lawyers' abilities to discharge their ethical obligations, including their duty of candor to the court, without being policed by overbroad sequestration orders. Furthermore, we are confident that, if an attorney is lax in his duty of candor, that laxness will normally be exposed—even exploited—by skillful cross-examination.

E.

Undeterred by the weight of contrary authority, the Government asserts that the district court's ruling that its order actually prohibited attorney-witness discussions of testimony is a permissible "interpretation" of the sequestration order. However, it is apparent that the district court was not interpreting its own order; rather, it was interpreting Rule 615. That is, the extending language of the sequestration order does not in any way relate to attorneys, and in each of the post-entry statements relating to the violation of its sequestration order, the district court clearly believed Rule 615—not the extending language in its order—had been violated. In this context, reliance by the Government and my dissenting colleagues on the inherent discretion of a presiding judge is a red herring. We simply do not defer to a district court's legal interpretation of federal rules; those interpretations are reviewed de novo.

Further, the Government cites no authority for the proposition that an unadorned sequestration order, devoid of any reference to lawyers, nevertheless may be interpreted to prohibit lawyers from discussing trial proceedings with prospective witnesses. More importantly, if a district court does not exceed its discretion by interpreting a sequestration order in a manner that: (1) is unsupported by its text; (2) is unsupported by Rule 615; (3) is unprecedented in this circuit; (4) is contrary to the overwhelming weight of persuasive case law and scholarship; and (5) arguably unconstitutionally deprived the defendant of effective assistance of counsel, then the district court's discretion to interpret its orders is effectively limitless. As a practical matter, our adoption of the Government's position would permit trial judges, when faced with any trial activity they dislike, not

---

11. Further, under the Government's argument, it apparently would have no problem if (hypothetically) Mr. Scofield had asked Alexander during trial preparation: "You sold drugs to Davis in August 1997, isn't that true?" On the other hand, the Government would take issue if Mr. Scofield had asked: "Davis testified that you sold drugs to Davis in August 1997. Is that testimony true?" The Government insists that, in such a case, Mr. Scofield would violate the "usual sequestration rule" because his question included the words: "Davis testified." The Government's argument fails because it is simply—and unnecessarily—splitting hairs.

only to order it stopped prospectively, but to *punish* it as if it were a violation of a then-existing order. Such post-hoc exercises of regulatory power are wholly inconsistent with our system of justice.[13] ....

III.

Even if Mr. Scofield had violated a sequestration rule or order, we would still hold, in the context of this case, that the sanction imposed—exclusion of Alexander's testimony—constituted reversible error. "Because exclusion of a defense witness impinges upon the right to present a defense, we are quite hesitant to endorse the use of such an extreme remedy." *United States v. Cropp*, 127 F.3d 354, 363 (4th Cir. 1997). Under these circumstances, we conclude that exclusion of Alexander's testimony in its entirety was unduly severe.

At the outset, sanction analysis must encompass proportionality, and sanctions as extreme as witness exclusion must be proportional to the offense. In this case, when the district court excluded Alexander's testimony, it was aware, through Mr. Scofield's representations, that Alexander had been exposed to Davis's accusation that Alexander was involved in drug deals. However, the district court conducted no examination of Alexander to determine exactly what he had been told; neither did the court attempt to ascertain through Mr. Scofield what he had revealed to Alexander.

More importantly, the proffer of Alexander's testimony covered at least six other Government witnesses and a number of other topics that were crucial to Rhynes's defense. Mr. Scofield specifically represented that, "Your Honor, I do not believe, as I stand here and think about it, that I mentioned anybody else's testimony other than D.S. Davis." Notwithstanding this representation, the district court determined that Alexander's testimony relating to each of the other Government witnesses and other subjects was tainted by the same "coaching" as the testimony relating to D.S. Davis. Significantly, the court apparently made this determination based solely on Mr. Scofield's proffer, but on this record, the court's finding of taint with respect to the other witnesses and other subjects is simply unsubstantiated. The exclusion of Alexander's testimony in its entirety was thus unduly severe and disproportionate to the narrow scope of Mr. Scofield's apparent violation.

We must also reject the Government's contention that, in the circumstances of this case, the sanction was justified and proportional because the "search for truth" was thereby furthered. We agree, for example, that if Alexander had been permitted to testify and his testimony had contradicted Davis's testimony, then one—either Alexander or Davis—was not, in all likelihood, testifying truthfully. However, the adversary system ordinarily can be trusted to separate the liars from the truthful. In this instance, the search for truth would have been better served by permitting the jury to determine who was telling the truth. By contrast, the district court's exclusion of Alexander's testimony left Davis's testimony uncontradicted and may have led the jury to believe, and rely upon, untruthful testimony. Put simply, excluding Corwin Alexander as a witness did nothing to further the search for truth.

Further, the degree of fault or intent encompassed in the violation must be considered in ascertaining the propriety of any given sanction. Given the lack of legal support for the district court's broad interpretation of its order, it is obvious that Mr. Scofield did

---

13. Our decision today does not, in any way, diminish a district court's authority to enter a sequestration order, under appropriate circumstances, that exceeds the scope of Rule 615. If a district court, in its discretion, determines to grant a sequestration order that exceeds the express bounds of Rule 615, the order should at least: (1) be explicit; (2) be of record and timely; and (3) be tailored as narrowly as possible to achieve its purposes without hindering counsel in performance of their duties to clients and the court....

not intend to violate the sequestration order.... An inadvertent misstep by Mr. Scofield was simply insufficient to justify the extreme sanction imposed on Rhynes.

We are also cognizant that although the alleged violation of the sequestration order was effected by Mr. Scofield, the sanction imposed inured to the defendant. There was, of course, no requirement that Rhynes be sanctioned for his lawyer's conduct; indeed, a lawyer may be personally sanctioned for violations of court orders. If, however, a defendant is being sanctioned for his lawyer's conduct, courts should impose the least severe sanction justified under the circumstances. The district court had alternative sanctions at its disposal; we have endorsed at least two others: "sanction of the witness; [and] instructions to the jury that they may consider the violation toward the issue of credibility." *Cropp*, 127 F.3d at 363. Further, there were many other possible corrective measures that could have been taken, including: limiting the scope of the witness' testimony, *see English*, 92 F.3d at 913 (endorsing limitation of witness' testimony following violation of sequestration order); permitting broad cross-examination into the alleged "coaching," *see United States v. Posada-Rios*, 158 F.3d 832, 871–72 (5th Cir. 1998); or any other sanction appropriate under the circumstances. There is no doubt that, under facts like these, the district court could have imposed a less severe sanction.

In short, even had Mr. Scofield's contact with Alexander violated the sequestration order, the district court abused its discretion in imposing the unduly severe sanction of excluding Alexander's testimony in its entirety....

[The separate concurring opinions of Judges Widener, Luttig, and Wilkins, and the dissenting opinion of Chief Judge Wilkinson, are omitted.]

NIEMEYER, Circuit Judge, dissenting....

The sole question raised on this appeal *en banc* is whether the district court's exclusion of Alexander's testimony constituted reversible error. The plurality would hold that Rule 615 does not prohibit counsel for the parties from discussing the testimony of prior witnesses with prospective witnesses because "nothing on the face of [Rule 615] addresses the conduct of lawyers in any way." The plurality would hold further that the demands of attorney preparation, ethics, and constitutional provisions require that the rule permit attorneys to discuss the testimony of prior witnesses with prospective witnesses in preparing them for trial. It adds that if a witness is inappropriately coached, the remedy is through cross-examination, thus eviscerating, in essence, the proscription of Rule 615 as it applies to attorneys.

The government argues on appeal that the "serious and dangerous nature of this argument cannot be overstated. If attorneys are allowed to conduct themselves in a manner that undermines the purpose of court orders, those orders and our function as 'officers of the Court' are rendered meaningless." ...

For the reasons that follow, I heartily agree with the government's position. The plurality's opinion would be without precedent and would all but render Rule 615 a hollow shell, since attorneys try virtually all cases in which a Rule 615 order is imposed. Under the plurality's holding, attorneys could legally undermine sequestration orders simply by acting as "go-betweens," relating to prospective witnesses what has already been testified to by other witnesses....

The mechanism [of sequestering witnesses] is not a creation of Rule 615, but represents the wisdom of the ages. In the book of *Susanna*, in the Apocrypha, Susanna of Biblical times was charged with adultery, for which the penalty was death. Daniel, suspecting complicity between the two prosecutorial witnesses, issued this order: "Separate [the witnesses] far from each other, and I will examine them." Apocrypha, *Susanna*, v. 51 (New Rev. Standard Version). When the process revealed material discrepancies in the witnesses' stories, Susanna was acquitted and the witnesses were beheaded for giving false testimony. Professor Wigmore, characterizing the pedigree and importance of the sequestration rule, states, "There is perhaps no testimonial expedient which, with as long a history, has persisted in this manner without essential change." 6 *Wigmore on Evidence* § 1837, at 457.

While the express directive of Rule 615—that witnesses be "excluded so that they cannot *hear* [other witness'] testimony []"—suggests most immediately the exclusion of witnesses from the courtroom, it has always been understood also to preclude the discussion among witnesses of testimony that has taken place in the courtroom. Common sense commands that if a rule prohibits a witness from "hearing" the testimony of other witnesses, the prohibition is violated if the testimony of a prior witness is repeated and heard in the courthouse corridor or outside on the street....

Even the plurality acknowledges that the sequestration of witnesses under Rule 615 requires that witnesses "not discuss the case among themselves or anyone else...." .... Thus, the common understanding is that the prohibition against "hearing" what other witnesses have stated in the courtroom extends to the learning of testimony outside of the courtroom. We explicitly recognized this in *United States v. McMahon*, 104 F.3d 638 (4th Cir. 1997), where we upheld the contempt conviction of a witness, who was subject to a Rule 615 sequestration order, for reading daily trial transcripts and sending his secretary to the courtroom to find out what was transpiring. The order in *McMahon* was the most simple invocation of Rule 615: "The Government's motion to sequester the Defendant's witnesses will be granted, and the Defendant's witnesses will be excluded from the courtroom." 104 F.3d at 640; *see also Miller v. Universal City Studios, Inc.*, 650 F.2d 1365, 1373 (5th Cir. 1981) (holding that Rule 615 prohibits the reading of trial transcripts); *State v. Steele*, 178 W.Va. 330 (1987) (listening to "mechanical recordings" of courtroom testimony violates sequestration order). As the Fifth Circuit explained in *Miller*, "The opportunity to shape testimony is as great with a witness who reads trial testimony as with one who hears the testimony in open court." 650 F.2d at 1373.

While the plurality does not seem to take issue with the notion that Rule 615 prohibits one witness from speaking with another witness or with anyone else, it would hold that a witness may discuss with an attorney the testimony of another witness....

This observation is remarkable in two respects. First, a rule that prohibits a witness from "hearing" the testimony of other witnesses must include a prohibition against hearing that testimony not only from another witness directly but also through intermediaries. This is a necessary conclusion, as the plurality acknowledges. And second, if Rule 615 precludes a person from acting as an intermediary to relate to one witness the testimony of another, how can we exempt an attorney from the proscription? Just as a discussion among witnesses outside the courtroom would frustrate the rule that one witness cannot hear the testimony of another, a discussion between a witness and an attorney about another witness' testimony frustrates the rule....

Thus, while the plurality seems to endorse an interpretation of Rule 615 that would prohibit witnesses from discussing testimony among themselves or with anyone else, it maintains that the "someone else" does not mean an attorney and that somehow an attorney has a license to violate the proscription and frustrate the rule. Stated otherwise, while two witnesses are prohibited from discussing testimony with each other directly, they may conduct such a discussion through the ears and mouth of an attorney. This conclusion is neither logical nor supported by precedent.

To be sure, the cases and text relied upon by the plurality acknowledge that attorneys may discuss "the case" with witnesses, but this observation does not suggest that the attorneys may, in the face of a sequestration order, relate to a prospective witness the *testimony* that a prior witness has given. The plurality rationalizes its attorney exception on three bases. First, "[t]horough preparation demands that an attorney interview and prepare witnesses before they testify. No competent lawyer would call a witness without appropriate and thorough pre-trial interviews and discussion." But it does not follow from this observation that an attorney cannot fulfill this duty of diligence without violating a sequestration order. The attorney may review facts and arguments with the witness, but the attorney should not be complicit in shaping testimony and matching it with the testimony of other witnesses.

Second, the plurality suggests that the attorney in this case "had ethical (and possibly constitutional) duties to investigate [Davis'] allegations with Alexander before he put Alexander on the stand." Again, however, the attorney could have fulfilled those duties by asking Alexander what he knew of the events about which he was going to testify. But relating to Alexander the testimony of a prior witness allowed Alexander to "hear" the testimony of that prior witness, directly in violation of Rule 615.

Finally, acknowledging that an attorney exception to Rule 615 would permit attorneys to "coach" witnesses, the plurality seeks to provide assurance by identifying other truth-seeking mechanisms: "[I]f an attorney has inappropriately 'coached' a witness, thorough cross-examination of that witness violates no privilege and is entirely appropriate and sufficient to address the issue."

The lofty purpose of Rule 615 deserves greater deference than it would be given if it were allowed to be engulfed by an attorney exception for trial preparation. And the rule is forfeited altogether by arguing that even though the truth-seeking purpose of Rule 615 might be debased by an attorney exception, cross-examination will fill the gap. The rule is given, and we ought to enforce it. And it is totally inconsistent with the "common practice" under the rule to allow an attorney to tell a prospective witness what a prior witness has said on the witness stand. The attorney in this case heard the order from the court, and by telling a prospective witness about the testimony of a prior witness, the attorney directly violated the court's order....

Notes and Questions

1. Does the *Rhynes* plurality miss the point when it declares that an attorney is not a "witness" within the meaning of Rule 615? As Judge Niemeyer points out in dissent, in *United States v. McMahon*, 104 F.3d 638, 640–45 (4th Cir. 1997), the court held that Rule 615 was violated when a witness' secretary sat in court during the testimony of other witnesses, took notes, and obtained copies of daily transcripts and delivered them to her boss. Yet the witness' secretary in *McMahon*, like the lawyer in *Rhynes*, was not a witness, and thus not herself subject to exclusion from court under Rule 615. Is there a sound basis for distinguishing between attorneys and other persons who might act as intermediaries?

2. At common law, the trial court had discretion to decide whether to exclude and sequester witnesses. Rule 615 cabins that discretion in that it gives parties a right to have witnesses excluded upon request, although trial courts retain discretion to issue such or-

ders in the absence of a party request, and also retain the authority to issue orders that are more stringent than what Rule 615 requires. *United States v. Sepulveda*, 15 F.3d 1161, 1176 (1st Cir. 1993). Thus, for example, although Rule 615 has been interpreted as *not* barring witnesses from communicating about the case with one another *before either* of them has testified, *see United States v. Collins*, 340 F.3d 672, 681 (8th Cir. 2003), trial courts retain discretionary authority to bar such communications. *Sepulveda*, 15 F.3d at 1176. Thus, the cases distinguish between what a party is entitled to as of right and what trial courts have the authority to order. The lower courts have split on whether an order under Rule 615, without more, only provides for mere exclusion of witnesses from the courtroom, or whether it also covers sequestration of witnesses (preventing them from communicating with one another outside of the courtroom). *See United States v. Solorio*, 337 F.3d 580, 592 (6th Cir. 2003) (collecting cases).

3. Rule 615(a) provides that a party who is a natural person is not subject to exclusion from the courtroom. The Advisory Committee Note to Rule 615 explains that "[e]xclusion of persons who are parties would raise serious problems of confrontation and due process." For other types of parties, such as corporations and governmental entities, Rule 615(b) provides that "an officer or employee ... designated as the party's representative by its attorney" is not subject to exclusion from the courtroom. With regard to this latter exception, lower courts are split on whether a party can designate multiple representatives. *Compare United States v. Pulley*, 922 F.2d 1283, 1285–86 (6th Cir. 1991) (single representative only), *with United States v. Jackson*, 60 F.3d 128, 134 (2d Cir. 1995) (no specific limit).

4. Rule 615(c) provides that "a person whose presence a party shows to be essential to presenting the party's claim or defense" is not subject to exclusion from the courtroom. This exception is often invoked for expert witnesses, who—pursuant to Rule 703—will sometimes render an opinion based on facts or data presented at trial through the testimony of other witnesses. *See Morvant v. Construction Aggregates Corp.*, 570 F.2d 626, 629 (6th Cir. 1978). Nonetheless, expert witnesses are not automatically exempted, and are likely to be excluded where no showing is made that they need to hear the trial testimony of other witnesses to render their opinion, or where they will also be testifying as fact witnesses. *E.g., Opus 3 Ltd. v. Heritage Park, Inc.*, 91 F.3d 625, 628–29 (4th Cir. 1996).

5. In criminal cases, neither a crime victim nor her family members are viewed as "parties," and thus under Rule 615 they would normally be subject to exclusion if they will be testifying as witnesses. Yet Rule 615(d) excepts from any witness exclusion order "a person authorized by statute to be present," and a number of statutes provide victims and/or their families with a right to attend court proceedings related to the offense. Under 18 U.S.C. § 3771(a)(3), a crime victim has the right not to be excluded from public court proceedings related to the offense, unless the court, after receiving clear and convincing evidence, determines that her testimony would be materially altered if she heard other testimony at that proceeding. If the direct victim of the crime is a minor, deceased, incompetent, or incapacitated, this right is given to the victim's legal guardian, the representative of the victim's estate, family members, or any other persons appointed as suitable by the court. *See* 18 U.S.C. § 3771(e). Moreover, all such persons have an absolute right to remain in the courtroom if they will only be testifying in the sentencing and not the guilt phase of the case. 18 U.S.C. § 3510.

6. Can a party, by designating one of the opposing party's attorneys as a witness, demand under Rule 615 that the attorney-witness be excluded from the courtroom while other witnesses are testifying? *See Milicevic v. Fletcher Jones Imports, Ltd.*, 402 F.3d 912, 916 (9th Cir. 2005) (holding that a party's lawyer falls within Rule 615(c)'s exception for

"a person whose presence a party shows to be essential to presenting the party's claim or defense").

7. Does Rule 615 apply only to testimony given at trial, or does it also apply to testimony given at pre-trial depositions? *See* Fed. R. Civ. P. 30(c)(1) ("The examination and cross-examination of a deponent proceed as they would at trial under the Federal Rules of Evidence, except Rules 103 and 615."); *In re Terra Intern., Inc.*, 134 F.3d 302, 306 (5th Cir. 1998) (holding that, pursuant to Fed. R. Civ. P. 30(c)(1), deposition witnesses are not subject to automatic sequestration, but that the trial court has discretion to exclude particular witnesses where appropriate by issuing a protective order pursuant to Fed. R. Civ. P. 26(c)(5)).

8. Can a trial court exclude a witness from the courtroom even if that witness falls within one of the exceptions set forth in Rule 615? *See United States ex rel. El-Amin v. George Washington University*, 533 F. Supp. 2d 12, 47–48 (D.D.C. 2008) (indicating that the court may have the power to do so under Rules 102 and 611).

Chapter 5

Privileges

A. Introduction

Imagine the following scenario: David is indicted on charges of murdering his business partner, John. David does not deny shooting John, but claims he acted in self-defense. In the course of its investigation of the murder, the government identifies a number of witnesses whose testimony it believes would be helpful in building its case against David. First, it would like to call David's psychologist, whom David met with for several months on a weekly basis prior to the murder, in the hopes that he could testify to any statements David made regarding his dislike of John or his desire to harm him. Second, it would like to call David's wife, who witnessed the altercation between John and David. Third, the government has evidence that David, a member of the Roman Catholic Church, entered a confessional booth in the church shortly after the alleged murder took place, and it seeks to call the priest who took confession to testify to what David said on that night. Fourth, the government would like to call the attorney who is currently representing David to ask him what David said about the incident.

The testimony of these witnesses would without question be extremely relevant to determining David's guilt of the offense charged. David's statements prior to John's death about his dislike for John or his desire to harm John would certainly be relevant to determining whether he was the first aggressor in the altercation. Moreover, any confession of guilt that David made to others after John's death would likewise be quite relevant. And the testimony of an eyewitness to the altercation would be extraordinarily potent evidence on the question whether David acted in self-defense or if he was the first aggressor. Although all of this evidence would prejudice David's case in the sense that it would increase the likelihood of conviction, it would not be unfairly prejudicial in the sense that Rule 403 contemplates, nor is the evidence excludable under any of the categorical rules of exclusion. Nonetheless, David may be able to prevent the government from calling some or all of these witnesses by arguing that his relationships with his psychologist, wife, priest, and attorney are "privileged."

Rules of privilege have some similarities to the categorical rules of exclusion, but also some striking differences. Both types of rules call for the exclusion of evidence based on social policy considerations. However, social policy considerations are only one rationale for the categorical rules of exclusion, which are also grounded in a concern that the evidence is of marginal probative worth and may be given undue weight by jurors. In contrast, rules of privilege, as the above hypothetical demonstrates, very often may result in the exclusion of highly relevant evidence.

The federal rules of evidence, as originally proposed by the Advisory Committee, would have codified a finite set of nine specific privileges, including an attorney-client privilege, a psychotherapist-patient privilege, a spousal privilege, and a privilege for communications to clergy, as well as privileges for trade secrets, state secrets, the identity of government informants, political votes, and a privilege against disclosure of certain reports and returns submitted to government agencies. Under the proposed rules, unless some provision of the Constitution required recognition of a particular privilege (such as the privilege against self-incrimination), federal judges would be without authority to create new privileges or modify those codified in the rules of evidence. Moreover, under the rules as originally proposed by the Advisory Committee, these nine privileges—and only these privileges—would apply in *all* civil and criminal cases heard in federal court, even those actions based on state law.

The reaction to the proposed rules in Congress was severe. Members of Congress expressed concern with the Advisory Committee's omission of certain privileges as well as its inclusion of others. In addition, Congress expressed concern over the proposed rules' disregard of state privilege law in cases in which state law provides the rule of decision, such as diversity cases. Not only did Congress believe the federal interest in superseding state privilege law to be fairly insignificant in such cases, but it was also concerned with the incentives for forum shopping that might occur where federal and state privilege law differed.

Although Congress tinkered with the details of a number of other proposed federal rules of evidence after they were forwarded from the Supreme Court, it scrapped the very detailed proposed rules of privilege in their entirety and replaced them with something altogether different. In their stead, Congress created a single, two-sentence rule—Rule 501—that failed to enumerate *any* specific privileges. Rather, Rule 501's first sentence provides only that "[t]he common law—as interpreted by United States courts in the light of reason and experience—governs a claim of privilege...." Its second sentence provides that "in a civil case, state law governs privilege regarding a claim or defense for which state law supplies the rule of decision." Finally, Congress in a separate statutory provision, currently codified at 28 U.S.C. §2074(b), narrowed the Supreme Court's future rulemaking authority so far as rules of privilege were concerned, providing that "[a]ny ... rule creating, abolishing, or modifying an evidentiary privilege shall have no force or effect unless approved by Act of Congress."

The materials that follow explore the application of Rule 501 in the context of a variety of different claimed privileges. An important goal as you explore these materials is to determine how the federal courts go about determining whether or not particular privileges should be recognized under Rule 501, and if so, what their scope should be. As mentioned above, rules of privilege, like the categorical rules of exclusion, are usually based on furthering some particular social policy. To what extent are the policies justifying the various privileges utilitarian, and to what extent are they based on other considerations? Moreover, to the extent that the privileges are justified on utilitarian grounds, how do the courts go about determining and weighing the offsetting costs and benefits of recognizing and defining particular aspects of privileges under Rule 501?

As you explore these questions, consider, too, whether the courts are adequately equipped to determine these issues by way of case-by-case decision-making, or whether such questions are best determined in a comprehensive manner in a legislative or quasi-legislative setting. In other words, consider the wisdom of Congress replacing the Advisory Committee's detailed rules with a directive to develop privilege law over time on a case-by-case basis based on "reason and experience."

Notes and Questions

1. Rule 501 is given an exalted position relative to the other rules of evidence. For example, while the rules of evidence in general are not applicable in proceedings before a

grand jury, when judges decide preliminary questions under Rule 104(a), and at sentencing, privileges apply in *all* stages of civil and criminal actions. *Compare* Fed. R. Evid. 1101(d), *with* Fed. R. Evid. 1101(c). *See also* Fed. R. Evid. 104(a). Furthermore, evidence is subject to pre-trial discovery in civil proceedings notwithstanding that it is subject to exclusion at trial under a rule of evidence *unless* it is claimed that the evidence is protected by a privilege. *See* Fed. R. Civ. P. 26(b)(1). What justifies the special treatment accorded to privileged evidence?

2. Both the version of Rule 501 proposed by the Advisory Committee and that ultimately adopted by Congress made clear that it was applicable unless, *inter alia*, the United States Constitution or a federal statute provides otherwise. Thus, for example, a claim that evidence is protected by the privilege against self-incrimination is not subject to analysis under Rule 501. The Advisory Committee explained the rationale for excluding such privileges from the rule's scope:

> No attempt is made in these rules to incorporate the constitutional provisions which relate to the admission and exclusion of evidence, whether denominated as privileges or not. The grand design of these provisions does not readily lend itself to codification. The final reference must be the provisions themselves and the decisions construing them. Nor is formulating a rule an appropriate means of settling unresolved constitutional questions.

> Similarly, privileges created by act of Congress are not within the scope of these rules. These privileges do not assume the form of broad principles; they are the product of resolving particular problems in particular terms.

Advisory Committee Note to Proposed Rule 501.

3. Is it not at least somewhat puzzling that Congress would limit the Supreme Court's authority to create or modify privileges by way of rulemaking on the one hand yet substantially expand the power of the federal courts, including the Supreme Court, to do the very same thing by way of common law decision-making? Does not Rule 501 allow the Supreme Court to accomplish by way of granting certiorari in a case raising a question about a privilege the very same thing that 28 U.S.C. § 2074(b) prevents it from doing by way of the rulemaking process?

4. Is the second sentence of Rule 501 required by the *Erie* doctrine? The Advisory Committee thought not, evidently viewing privileges as one of those rules falling within the "uncertain area between substance and procedure ... rationally capable of classification as either." *See* Advisory Committee Note to Proposed Rule 501 (citing *Hanna v. Plumer*, 380 U.S. 460 (1965)). However, an argument could be made that although *Erie* would not prevent Congress from creating such a rule, the Rules Enabling Act would prevent the same result via the rulemaking process. *See* John Hart Ely, *The Irrepressible Myth of Erie*, 87 Harv. L. Rev. 693 (1974).

5. Rule 501 defers to state privilege law only where state law supplies the rule of decision. Often, federal law may incorporate or "borrow" elements of state law to fill in gaps in a federal statute or federal common law cause of action. In such instances, even though reference is made to state law due to its incorporation into the federal cause of action, federal law is supplying the rule of decision in such cases, and thus federal privilege law applies in such cases. *See, e.g., Gannet v. First Nat. State Bank of New Jersey*, 546 F.2d 1072, 1076 (3d Cir. 1976); *Tucker v. United States*, 143 F. Supp. 2d 619, 621–25 (S.D. W. Va. 2001).

6. Even under the version of Rule 501 ultimately adopted by Congress, state privilege law is to some degree undermined to the extent that it provides greater protection than

does federal law, for it is inapplicable in federal question cases. Because people are no less concerned about their confidences being breached in federal litigation than they are in state litigation, doesn't this to some degree chill communications that the states seek to encourage? *See generally* Earl C. Dudley, Jr., *Federalism and Federal Rule of Evidence 501: Privilege and Vertical Choice of Law*, 82 Geo. L.J. 1781 (1994).

7. In diversity cases, Rule 501 provides that state rather than federal privilege law governs. But in cases involving contacts with multiple states, a further question arises: *which* state's privilege law governs? For example, what if the suit is filed in state A (where one of the parties live and where most of the conduct forming the basis for the suit occurred), but the challenged communication took place between attorney and client in state B? While Rule 501 explicitly addresses the vertical (federal vs. state) choice-of-law question, it is silent on the horizontal (state A vs. state B) choice-of-law question. The courts that have addressed this issue have held that the determination of *which* state's privilege law will govern in such a situation is to be determined by the choice-of-law rules of the state in which the federal court sits, *e.g.*, *Abbott Laboratories v. Alpha Therapeutic Corp.*, 200 F.R.D. 401, 404–05 (N.D. Ill. 2001); *Whatley v. Merit Distribution Services*, 191 F.R.D. 655, 659 (S.D. Ala. 2000), a holding that is consistent with the Supreme Court's general approach to choice-of-law questions in diversity cases. *See Klaxon Co. v. Stentor Electric Mfg. Co.*, 313 U.S. 487 (1941). While state choice-of-law rules differ widely, there are two predominant approaches to choice-of-law with regard to evidentiary privileges. Under the classic approach, the forum state's privilege law always governs. *See* Restatement (1st) Conflicts § 597; *Hatfill v. New York Times Co.*, 459 F. Supp. 2d 462, 465–66 (E.D. Va. 2006). Under the modern approach, the court will examine the contacts between the parties, the communication, and the states, but with somewhat of a bias in favor of applying the law of the state whose privilege rules would allow for the admission of the evidence. *See* Restatement (2d) Conflicts § 139; *Bondi v. Grant Thornton Intern.*, 2006 WL 1817313, at *3 (S.D.N.Y. June 30, 2006).

8. Is it clear that Rule 501 as ultimately adopted eliminates all opportunities to take advantage of differences between federal and state privilege law? Consider a plaintiff who has a sexual harassment claim against a co-worker. Consider further that the plaintiff can sue under either a federal statute (Title VII) or an equivalent state statute, or both (although suing under both will not increase the total available damage award). Assume further that a federal psychotherapist-patient privilege exists, but no such privilege exists under state law. If the plaintiff has reason to believe that the co-worker admitted to his psychiatrist that he sexually harassed the plaintiff, and wishes to make use of that evidence, what should she do? If instead the plaintiff made damaging statements to her own psychiatrist (e.g., that she made up or exaggerated the claim), and wishes to prevent the defendant from making use of that evidence, what should she do?

9. Although typically only civil cases can be removed from state to federal court, in a narrow range of circumstances, federal officials subject to criminal charges in state court proceedings may remove the case to federal court. *See* 28 U.S.C. §§ 1442, 1442a. Are such proceedings governed by federal or state rules of privilege?

10. Under the "fruit of the poisonous tree" doctrine, a criminal defendant is entitled not only to have evidence that is obtained from him in violation of the U.S. Constitution suppressed, but also evidence that is derived from the unconstitutionally obtained evidence. *See Wong Sun v. United States*, 371 U.S. 471 (1963). Does a similar doctrine require suppression of evidence derived from evidence obtained in violation of an evidentiary privilege? Should it? *See United States v. Marashi*, 913 F.2d 724, 731 n.11 (9th Cir. 1990) ("Because we have held that the marital communications testimony is admissible, we

need not resolve Marashi's claim that all evidence derived therefrom should be excluded as fruits of the poisonous tree. Suffice it to say that no court has ever applied this theory to *any* evidentiary privilege"); *United States v. Segal*, 313 F. Supp. 2d 774, 780 (N.D. Ill. 2004) ("The attorney-client privilege is an evidentiary privilege, not a constitutional right. The violation of a defendant's attorney-client privilege thus does not require the suppression of derivative evidence.").

B. Attorney-Client Privilege

The oldest and perhaps the most well-known privilege is the attorney-client privilege. Common law decisions applying Rule 501 have come to define the privilege as follows:

> (1) Where legal advice of any kind is sought (2) from a professional legal adviser in his capacity as such, (3) the communications relating to that purpose, (4) made in confidence (5) by the client, (6) are at his insistence permanently protected (7) from disclosure by himself or by the legal adviser, (8) except the protection be waived.

8 Wigmore, Evidence § 2292, at 554 (McNaughton rev. 1961). *See, e.g., Cavallaro v. United States*, 284 F.3d 236, 245 (1st Cir. 2002) (endorsing the Wigmore definition); *United States v. Martin*, 278 F.3d 988, 999 (9th Cir. 2002) (same).

Although this definition seems fairly straightforward, it contains a number of conceptual ambiguities that make it more difficult to apply than appears at first blush. Moreover, even if the definition is satisfied, the courts have identified a number of situations in which the privilege is deemed to be inapplicable. The materials that follow explore each of the elements of the basic definition as well as the various exceptions to the privilege.

Problem 5-1: Drinking & Driving

Tom Trendell, an employee at the University of Washington School of Law, is involved in a hit-and-run accident in which a bicyclist is seriously injured. The next day, Tom goes to the office of Charlie Sherman, a criminal law professor, asks if he can close the door, and then says "I've always considered you a really good friend, and I really need your help. Last night, I had a bit too much to drink, and on the way home from the bar, I ran into a bicyclist and left the scene of the accident." Sherman replies, "Gee, Tom, I'd like to help you but I never actually sat for the bar examination. After all, you don't need to be licensed to practice law in order to teach law, so why would I waste my time taking that silly test? But why don't you go see David Dawning—he works downtown and he has a great track record."

Tom makes an appointment to see Dawning. Later that same afternoon, he arrives in Dawning's office to discuss the case. During their meeting, Dawning asks Tom, "Did you have more than 3 drinks?" Tom nods. "More than 4 drinks?" Tom nods again. This back-and-forth continues until it is established that Tom had 7 drinks, an amount that would put Tom well over the legal blood alcohol content for driving a vehicle. Dawning agrees to take the case, and tells Tom not to speak with anyone else about the case.

Tom is indicted, and the prosecution seeks to call both Sherman and Dawning as witnesses to testify about their conversations with Tom. Tom invokes the attorney-client privilege as to both conversations.

How will the court likely rule on Tom's privilege claims?

Problem 5-2: A Guilty Conscience

Alejandro Moreno, an attorney, is hired by a bank robber with a guilty conscience. The robber has decided to turn over a new leaf, and wants to return his ill-gotten gains to the banks that he robbed. After disclosing all the details of the bank robberies that he committed, the man turns over all the proceeds from the robberies and instructs Moreno to turn the money over to the authorities but not to disclose his identity to them. Moreno contacts the local authorities, tells them that he represents the man who robbed the banks, and arranges to return the money to them. Shortly after he does so, he is issued a subpoena to appear before a grand jury investigating the bank robberies, and when he appears, he is asked to disclose the name of his client. The attorney refuses, claiming that the information is privileged, but the government contends that a client's identity is not considered to be a confidential communication subject to protection by the attorney-client privilege.

How will the court likely rule on Alejandro's privilege claim on behalf of his anonymous client?

In re Grand Jury Subpoenas
906 F.2d 1485 (10th Cir. 1990)

McKAY, Circuit Judge.

This case involves an emergency appeal by several attorneys who were held in contempt and placed in jail because they refused to reveal the source of payment of their fees incurred during their representation of four defendants on drug charges.

I. Facts

Beginning in approximately April of 1989 the grand jury in the Northern District of Oklahoma began investigating James Coltharp and the organization he controlled under a suspicion of connection with illegal drug activity. Mr. Coltharp allegedly employed a "crew" to assist him in his drug efforts. Relators represented four defendants, who were allegedly crew members in the Coltharp organization, on drug charges in the Eastern District of Oklahoma. The grand jury sought fee information from the relators under a suspicion that Mr. Coltharp may have paid the legal fees for his alleged crew members.

On October 5, 1989, the grand jury issued subpoenas to the relators. The relators' clients had been convicted at trial and at least two of the relators had filed appeals for their clients. Each of the relators filed motions to quash the subpoenas which were finally denied on November 21, 1989. The trial court ordered the relators to appear and testify before the grand jury on December 5, 1989.

On December 5, 1989, the relators appeared before the grand jury as the trial court had ordered. However, each relator refused to testify or to provide any of the documents requested in the subpoena. The trial court held each of the relators in contempt for their refusal to comply with the subpoenas and had them immediately incarcerated. Relators filed an emergency Motion to Stay Proceedings in this court. Later that same day we granted the stay and released each of the relators on their own recognizance.

Our issuance of the stay allowed us to hear oral argument on the appeal of this case a few days thereafter.... Relators claim that the fee information sought by the grand jury is subject to the attorney-client privilege....

III. Attorney-Client Privilege

It is well recognized in every circuit, including our own, that the identity of an attorney's client and the source of payment for legal fees are not normally protected by the attorney-client privilege. However, some circuit courts have created exceptions to this general rule for unique circumstances. The three major exceptions are known as the legal advice exception, the last link exception, and the confidential communication exception.

A. *Legal Advice Exception*

Several circuit courts have created an exception to the general rule that client identity and fee information are not protected by the attorney-client privilege where there is a strong probability that disclosure would implicate the client in the very criminal activity for which legal advice was sought. Some of these holdings are now of questionable validity, although they have not been overruled. For example, the Ninth Circuit has more recently interpreted this exception to prohibit disclosure of the source of fees only when disclosure of the identity of the client would be in substance a disclosure of a confidential communication in the professional relationship between the client and the attorney. *See In re Grand Jury Subpoenas*, 803 F.2d 493, 497 (9th Cir. 1986); *In re Osterhoudt*, 722 F.2d 591, 593 (9th Cir. 1983).

We need not decide whether this exception will be adopted in this circuit because it does not apply to this case. In order for the legal advice exception to apply, the person seeking the legal advice must be the client of the attorney involved. In this case, the record before us contains no evidence that relators have made a claim that the person paying their fees was a client of any kind. At a minimum relators must assert that the fee was paid by a client.

Relators must also assert that the client sought legal advice about the very activity for which the fee information is sought. For example, in *Baird v. Koerner*, 279 F.2d 623 (9th Cir. 1960), the Ninth Circuit refused to require an attorney to divulge the identity of his client when that client had consulted him regarding improperly paid taxes, and the attorney had forwarded an anonymous check to the Internal Revenue Service. The IRS sought the name of the client to allow further review of the questionable tax returns. Identifying this client would have implicated the client in the very activity for which the client consulted the attorney—income tax problems. *Id....*

B. *Last Link Exception*

Relators argue in this court, and in the district court, that this circuit should adopt the last link exception which has been adopted in at least two other circuits. The last link exception was largely formulated by the Fifth Circuit in two cases. *See In re Grand Jury Proceedings*, 680 F.2d 1026 (5th Cir. 1982) ("*Pavlick*"), and *In re Grand Jury Proceedings*, 517 F.2d 666 (5th Cir. 1975) ("*Jones*").[1] Partially relying on the *Baird* case, the *Jones* court

---

1. The test has also been adopted by the Eleventh Circuit. *See In re Grand Jury Proceedings*, 689 F.2d 1351 (11th Cir. 1982). However, the Eleventh Circuit has recently interpreted the last link exception to apply only in cases where the disclosure of the client's identity would expose other privileged communications, such as motive or strategy, and when the incriminating nature of privileged communications has created in the client a reasonable expectation that the information would be kept confidential. *In re Grand Jury Proceedings*, 896 F.2d 1267 (11th Cir. 1990). This very recent decision is broadly supportive of the position we adopt on the last link exception.

held that "information, not normally privileged, should also be protected when so much of the substance of the communications is already in the government's possession that additional disclosures would yield substantially probative links in an existing chain of inculpatory events or transactions." This test was further refined in *Pavlick* in which the court stated that it "also recognized [in *Jones*] a limited and narrow exception to the general rule, one that obtains when the disclosure of the client's identity by his attorney would have supplied the last link in an existing chain of incriminating evidence likely to lead to the client's indictment."

Contrary to relators' suggestion in their brief, the last link exception has been explicitly rejected by at least one circuit and implicitly rejected by others. In *In re Grand Jury Investigation*, 723 F.2d 447 (6th Cir. 1983), the Sixth Circuit explicitly rejected the last link exception as formulated by the Fifth Circuit.

> Upon careful consideration this Court concludes that, although language exists in *Baird* to support viability of *Pavlick*'s "last link" exception, the exception is simply not grounded upon the preservation of confidential *communications* and hence not justifiable to support the attorney-client privilege. Although the last link exception may promote concepts of fundamental fairness against self-incrimination, these concepts are not proper considerations to invoke the attorney-client privilege. Rather, the focus of the inquiry is whether disclosure of the identity would adversely implicate the confidentiality of communications. Accordingly, this Court rejects the last link exception as articulated in *Pavlick*.

The last link exception has also been implicitly rejected in the Second, Third, and Ninth Circuits....

Thus, we recognize a split among the circuits over the adoption of the last link exception. This circuit has not spoken directly to this issue....

The last link exception is a very narrow one which is carefully fact based. We need not ultimately decide whether even that narrow exception should apply in this circuit because we are of the view that the facts of this case take it outside the standards of whatever is left of *Jones*, which is the principle precedential base for the exception. Unlike our case, *Jones* involved payment of fees for one client by a person who was also a client of the same attorney. This is an important distinction. There is at least a stronger arguable basis on which to invoke the attorney-client privilege to protect the identity of an actual client than there is to protect the identity of a third person who may implicate the attorney's actual client in some wrongdoing....

We wish to clarify, however, that we do not reject what we consider to be the underlying principle supporting the last link exception. We believe that the Fifth Circuit's articulation of the "last link" exception fails adequately to discipline the thinking of lawyers and courts on this issue. The last link exception ultimately stems from *Baird v. Koerner*, 279 F.2d 623 (9th Cir. 1960), even in the Fifth Circuit. Relying on *Baird*, several circuit courts have backed away from both the legal advice and last link exceptions. These courts have carefully applied the facts and holding of *Baird* to create what is known as the confidential communication exception. The confidential communication exception holds that an exception to the general rule that a client's identity is not privileged exists in the situation where the disclosure of the client's identity would be tantamount to disclosing an otherwise protected confidential communication. We believe that the confidential communication exception represents a more disciplined interpretation of *Baird* than does the Fifth Circuit's last link exception. Thus, we reject the last link exception to the extent it has deviated from the holding of *Baird*.

We agree that a disciplined exception to the attorney client privilege must mirror the facts and analysis of *Baird*. In *Baird* the mere identification of the client would have disclosed the confidential communication from the client that he had committed the crime for which he sought advice. The client in *Baird* sought advice strictly concerning the case then under investigation. We hold that in order to invoke the attorney client privilege under similar facts in this Circuit, the advice sought must have been *Baird*-like. In other words, the advice sought must have concerned the case then under investigation and disclosure of the client's identity would now be, in substance, the disclosure of a confidential communication by the client, such as establishing the identity of the client as the perpetrator of the alleged crime at issue. This case does not involve any claim that the source of the fees was a client who sought advice on any subject. Nor is there any claim that advice was given concerning the case now under investigation. Given these facts, disclosure of the source of the fees would not disclose any confidential communication from client to attorney.

The purpose behind the attorney-client privilege is to preserve *confidential communications* between attorney and client. Information regarding the fee arrangement is not normally part of the professional consultation and therefore it is not privileged even if it would incriminate the client in wrongdoing. In other words, while payment of a fee to an attorney is necessary to obtain legal advice, disclosure of the fee arrangement does not inhibit the normal communications necessary for the attorney to act effectively in representing the client. Absent one of those rare circumstances in which the payment of the fee itself is unlawful or where an actual client paid the fee and sought advice concerning the actual case under investigation as in *Baird*, we hold that fee arrangements are not protected by the attorney-client privilege.

In this case the subpoenas requested seven pieces of information from the relators. The subpoenas asked for the identity of the source of the fees, the amount of the fees, the manner of payment, the date of payment, the name of any others partially responsible for payment of the fee, and whether any part of the fee came from the client or his family. The subpoena also requested all documents relating to the payment or acceptance of the fees, including checks, cashier's checks, deposit slips, receipts, wire transfers, fee contracts, and IRS form 8300's. We hold that none of these requests is protected by the attorney-client privilege and thus must be disclosed, with one exception.

We believe that disclosing the actual fee contracts has the potential for revealing confidential information along with unprotected fee information. Thus, we remand this issue to the district court for its determination of whether, in light of this opinion, the fee contracts contain any confidential communications that are protected by the attorney-client privilege....

Notes and Questions

1. Attorneys play not only the role of legal advisor in life, but also various other roles, such as friend, parent, and child. However, for the attorney-client privilege to apply:

> [T]he attorney must have been engaged or consulted by the client for the purpose of obtaining legal services or advice—services or advice that a lawyer may perform or give in his capacity as a lawyer, not in some other capacity. A communication is not privileged simply because it is made by or to a person who happens to be a lawyer.

Diversified Indus., Inc. v. Meredith, 572 F.2d 596, 602 (8th Cir. 1977). When an attorney is speaking to a friend, co-worker, or family member, he must take care to clarify the role in which he is speaking or listening, for in ambiguous situations, courts tend to hold that an attorney was not consulted in his capacity as a legal advisor and thus that the privilege does not apply. *E.g., United States v. Evans*, 113 F.3d 1457, 1463–64 (7th Cir. 1997); *United States v. Tedder*, 801 F.2d 1437, 1442–43 (4th Cir. 1986).

2. Suppose that a client fails to appear in court on a particular date and he is subsequently indicted for his failure to appear. Does the attorney-client privilege bar his attorney from testifying that he had informed the client of the court date? *See United States v. Gray*, 876 F.2d 1411, 1415 (9th Cir. 1989) (holding that it is not a privileged communication); *United States v. Clemons*, 676 F.2d 124, 125 (5th Cir. Unit B 1982) (same). Is this because the attorney is not acting in his capacity as a legal advisor? If so, in what capacity is he acting? *See United States v. Hall*, 346 F.2d 875, 882 (2d Cir. 1965) (holding that lawyer in that situation is merely serving as a conduit for transmitting a message from the court to the client in his capacity as an officer of the court).

3. Suppose that, in the course of consulting with his attorney, a client states his intent to harm some other person. Does the attorney-client privilege prevent the attorney from testifying to the fact that the client made such threats? *See United States v. Alexander*, 287 F.3d 811, 816 (9th Cir. 2002) (holding that such statements are not covered because they are not being made for the purpose of obtaining legal advice).

4. The party invoking a privilege has the burden of establishing all of its elements. *United States v. BDO Seidman*, 337 F.3d 802, 811 (7th Cir. 2003); *United States v. Martin*, 278 F.3d 988, 999–1000 (2d Cir. 1997). Each element of the privilege must be established by a preponderance of the evidence. *See United States v. Singleton*, 260 F.3d 1295, 1301 (11th Cir. 2001).

5. It is important to distinguish between the attorney-client privilege on the one hand and an attorney's ethical duty of confidentiality on the other, for the latter is generally broader than the former and may thus be applicable even when the former is not:

> The principle of client-lawyer confidentiality is given effect by related bodies of law: the attorney-client privilege, the work product doctrine, and the rule of confidentiality established in professional ethics. The attorney-client privilege and work-product doctrine apply in judicial and other proceedings in which a lawyer may be called as a witness or otherwise required to produce evidence concerning a client. The rule of client-lawyer confidentiality applies in situations other than those where evidence is sought from the lawyer through compulsion of law. The confidentiality rule, for example, applies not only to matters communicated by the client but also to all information relating to the representation, whatever its source.

Model Rule of Professional Responsibility 1.6 cmt. 3.

Although the duty of confidentiality is broader than the attorney-client privilege, the former cannot be invoked in judicial proceedings to avoid disclosure of an attorney-client communication: if the communication falls within an exception to the attorney-client privilege, an attorney must disclose the communication or he will be in contempt of court.

6. Sometimes, two people, such as business partners, may jointly consult an attorney for legal advice. Such communications are privileged in legal disputes with third persons but not in subsequent litigation between the joint clients. Similarly, in cases involving multiple parties, such as criminal cases involving multiple defendants, parties with a common interest and their attorneys may collaborate together, and communications amongst

the parties and their attorneys are protected by the attorney-client privilege. *United States v. Almeida*, 341 F.3d 1318, 1324–25 (11th Cir. 2003); *In re Grand Jury Subpoena*, 274 F.3d 563, 572–73 (1st Cir. 2001). "[H]owever, a party always remains free to disclose his own communications.... Thus, the existence of a joint defense agreement does not increase the number of parties whose consent is needed to waive the attorney-client privilege; it merely prevents disclosure of a communication made in the course of preparing a joint defense by the third party to whom it was made." *In re Grand Jury Subpoena*, 274 F.3d at 572–73. *See also* Proposed Fed. R. Evid. 503(d)(5) ("There is no privilege under this rule ... [a]s to a communication relevant to a matter of common interest between two or more clients if the communication was made by any of them to a lawyer retained or consulted in common, when offered in an action between any of the clients").

7. The privilege applies not only to direct communications between attorney and client but also to communications involving their representatives. *See* Proposed Fed. R. Evid. 503(b). Consider the justification for extending the privilege to communications with intermediaries:

> [I]n contrast to the Tudor times when the privilege was first recognized, the complexities of modern existence prevent attorneys from effectively handling clients' affairs without the help of the others.... "The assistance of these agents being indispensable to his work and the communications of the client being often necessarily committed to them by the attorney or by the client himself, the privilege must include all the persons who act as the attorney's agents."

United States v. Kovel, 296 F.2d 918, 921 (1961) (quoting 8 Wigmore, Evidence § 2301).

8. Who qualifies as a "lawyer" for purposes of the attorney-client privilege? *See* Proposed Fed. R. Evid. 503(a)(2) (defining "lawyer" as "a person authorized, or reasonably believed by the client to be authorized, to practice law in any state or nation"). *See also United States v. Dennis*, 843 F.2d 652, 656–57 (2d Cir. 1988) (holding that initial communications that a person has with a prospective lawyer are privileged even if the client ultimately decides not to retain the lawyer or the lawyer declines to take on the case).

9. The word "communications" includes not only written and spoken statements, but also non-verbal acts intended to convey information to an attorney:

> The privilege extends to nonverbal communicative acts intended to convey information. For example, a client may communicate with a lawyer through facial expressions or other communicative bodily motions or gestures (nodding or shaking the head or holding up a certain number of fingers to indicate number) or acting out a recalled incident. On the other hand, the privilege does not extend to a client act simply because the client performed the act in the lawyer's presence. The privilege applies when the purpose in performing the act is to convey information to the lawyer.

Restatement (Third) of the Law Governing Lawyers § 69 cmt. e (2000).

10. To what extent does the attorney-client privilege protect communications from the *attorney* to the *client*?

> The privilege ... provides a direct protection for confidential communications *from* the *client* to the attorney and a derivative protection for communications *from* the *attorney* to the client, to the extent that the responsive attorney communications reveal the substance of protected client communications.... Some courts have loosely spoken of the privilege as protecting communications *between* the attorney and the client. Those cases, for the most part, however, are

only expressing the factual reality that most responsive attorney communications will indirectly necessitate the application of the privilege....

1 Attorney-Client Privilege in the U.S. § 5:2, at 33–36, 39–40 (2d ed. 2004); *accord United States v. Defazio*, 899 F.2d 626, 635 (7th Cir. 1990); *In re Fischel*, 557 F.2d 209, 211 (9th Cir. 1977).

Upjohn Company v. United States
449 U.S. 383 (1981)

Justice REHNQUIST delivered the opinion of the Court.

We granted certiorari in this case to address important questions concerning the scope of the attorney-client privilege in the corporate context and the applicability of the work-product doctrine in proceedings to enforce tax summonses. With respect to the privilege question the parties and various *amici* have described our task as one of choosing between two "tests" which have gained adherents in the courts of appeals. We are acutely aware, however, that we sit to decide concrete cases and not abstract propositions of law. We decline to lay down a broad rule or series of rules to govern all conceivable future questions in this area, even were we able to do so. We can and do, however, conclude that the attorney-client privilege protects the communications involved in this case from compelled disclosure and that the work-product doctrine does apply in tax summons enforcement proceedings.

I

Petitioner Upjohn Co. manufactures and sells pharmaceuticals here and abroad. In January 1976 independent accountants conducting an audit of one of Upjohn's foreign subsidiaries discovered that the subsidiary made payments to or for the benefit of foreign government officials in order to secure government business. The accountants, so informed petitioner, Mr. Gerard Thomas, Upjohn's Vice President, Secretary, and General Counsel. Thomas is a member of the Michigan and New York Bars, and has been Upjohn's General Counsel for 20 years. He consulted with outside counsel and R. T. Parfet, Jr., Upjohn's Chairman of the Board. It was decided that the company would conduct an internal investigation of what were termed "questionable payments." As part of this investigation the attorneys prepared a letter containing a questionnaire which was sent to "All Foreign General and Area Managers" over the Chairman's signature. The letter began by noting recent disclosures that several American companies made "possibly illegal" payments to foreign government officials and emphasized that the management needed full information concerning any such payments made by Upjohn. The letter indicated that the Chairman had asked Thomas, identified as "the company's General Counsel," "to conduct an investigation for the purpose of determining the nature and magnitude of any payments made by the Upjohn Company or any of its subsidiaries to any employee or official of a foreign government." The questionnaire sought detailed information concerning such payments. Managers were instructed to treat the investigation as "highly confidential" and not to discuss it with anyone other than Upjohn employees who might be helpful in providing the requested information. Responses were to be sent directly to Thomas. Thomas and outside counsel also interviewed the recipients of the questionnaire and some 33 other Upjohn officers or employees as part of the investigation.

On March 26, 1976, the company voluntarily submitted a preliminary report to the Securities and Exchange Commission on Form 8-K disclosing certain questionable payments. A copy of the report was simultaneously submitted to the Internal Revenue Service, which immediately began an investigation to determine the tax consequences of the payments. Special agents conducting the investigation were given lists by Upjohn of all those interviewed and all who had responded to the questionnaire. On November 23, 1976, the Service issued a summons pursuant to 26 U.S.C. §7602 demanding production of:

> "All files relative to the investigation conducted under the supervision of Gerard Thomas to identify payments to employees of foreign governments and any political contributions made by the Upjohn Company or any of its affiliates since January 1, 1971 and to determine whether any funds of the Upjohn Company had been improperly accounted for on the corporate books during the same period.

> "The records should include but not be limited to written questionnaires sent to managers of the Upjohn Company's foreign affiliates, and memorandums or notes of the interviews conducted in the United States and abroad with officers and employees of the Upjohn Company and its subsidiaries."

The company declined to produce the documents specified in the second paragraph on the grounds that they were protected from disclosure by the attorney-client privilege and constituted the work product of attorneys prepared in anticipation of litigation. On August 31, 1977, the United States filed a petition seeking enforcement of the summons under 26 U.S.C. §§7402(b) and 7604(a) in the United States District Court for the Western District of Michigan. That court adopted the recommendation of a Magistrate who concluded that the summons should be enforced. Petitioners appealed to the Court of Appeals for the Sixth Circuit which rejected the Magistrate's finding of a waiver of the attorney-client privilege, but agreed that the privilege did not apply "[t]o the extent that the communications were made by officers and agents not responsible for directing Upjohn's actions in response to legal advice ... for the simple reason that the communications were not the 'client's.'" The court reasoned that accepting petitioners' claim for a broader application of the privilege would encourage upper-echelon management to ignore unpleasant facts and create too broad a "zone of silence." Noting that Upjohn's counsel had interviewed officials such as the Chairman and President, the Court of Appeals remanded to the District Court so that a determination of who was within the "control group" could be made. In a concluding footnote the court stated that the work-product doctrine "is not applicable to administrative summonses issued under 26 U.S.C. §7602."

II

Federal Rule of Evidence 501 provides that [claims of privilege are governed by the common law as interpreted by United States courts in the light of reason and experience]. The attorney-client privilege is the oldest of the privileges for confidential communications known to the common law. 8 J. Wigmore, Evidence §2290 (McNaughton rev. 1961). Its purpose is to encourage full and frank communication between attorneys and their clients and thereby promote broader public interests in the observance of law and administration of justice. The privilege recognizes that sound legal advice or advocacy serves public ends and that such advice or advocacy depends upon the lawyer's being fully informed by the client.... Admittedly complications in the application of the privilege arise when the client is a corporation, which in theory is an artificial creature of the law, and not an individual; but this Court has assumed that the privilege applies when the client is a corporation ... and the Government does not contest the general proposition.

The Court of Appeals, however, considered the application of the privilege in the corporate context to present a "different problem," since the client was an inanimate entity and "only the senior management, guiding and integrating the several operations, ... can be said to possess an identity analogous to the corporation as a whole." The first case to articulate the so-called "control group test" adopted by the court below ... reflected a similar conceptual approach:

> "Keeping in mind that the question is, Is it the corporation which is seeking the lawyer's advice when the asserted privileged communication is made?, the most satisfactory solution, I think, is that if the employee making the communication, of whatever rank he may be, is in a position to control or even to take a substantial part in a decision about any action which the corporation may take upon the advice of the attorney, ... then, in effect, *he is (or personifies) the corporation* when he makes his disclosure to the lawyer and the privilege would apply" (emphasis supplied).

Such a view, we think, overlooks the fact that the privilege exists to protect not only the giving of professional advice to those who can act on it but also the giving of information to the lawyer to enable him to give sound and informed advice.... The first step in the resolution of any legal problem is ascertaining the factual background and sifting through the facts with an eye to the legally relevant....

In the case of the individual client the provider of information and the person who acts on the lawyer's advice are one and the same. In the corporate context, however, it will frequently be employees beyond the control group as defined by the court below — "officers and agents ... responsible for directing [the company's] actions in response to legal advice" — who will possess the information needed by the corporation's lawyers. Middle-level — and indeed lower-level — employees can, by actions within the scope of their employment, embroil the corporation in serious legal difficulties, and it is only natural that these employees would have the relevant information needed by corporate counsel if he is adequately to advise the client with respect to such actual or potential difficulties. This fact was noted in *Diversified Industries, Inc. v. Meredith*, 572 F.2d 596 (CA8 1978) (en banc):

> "In a corporation, it may be necessary to glean information relevant to a legal problem from middle management or non-management personnel as well as from top executives. The attorney dealing with a complex legal problem 'is thus faced with a "Hobson's choice". If he interviews employees not having "the very highest authority", their communications to him will not be privileged. If, on the other hand, he interviews *only* those employees with the "very highest authority", he may find it extremely difficult, if not impossible, to determine what happened.'" *Id.*, at 608–609 (quoting Weinschel, Corporate Employee Interviews and the Attorney-Client Privilege, 12 B.C.Ind. & Com. L.Rev. 873, 876 (1971)).

The control group test adopted by the court below thus frustrates the very purpose of the privilege by discouraging the communication of relevant information by employees of the client to attorneys seeking to render legal advice to the client corporation. The attorney's advice will also frequently be more significant to noncontrol group members than to those who officially sanction the advice, and the control group test makes it more difficult to convey full and frank legal advice to the employees who will put into effect the client corporation's policy....

The narrow scope given the attorney-client privilege by the court below not only makes it difficult for corporate attorneys to formulate sound advice when their client is faced with a specific legal problem but also threatens to limit the valuable efforts of corporate counsel to ensure their client's compliance with the law. In light of the vast and complicated array of regulatory legislation confronting the modern corporation, corporations, unlike most individuals, "constantly go to lawyers to find out how to obey the law," Burnham, The Attorney-Client Privilege in the Corporate Arena, 24 Bus.Law. 901, 913 (1969), particularly since compliance with the law in this area is hardly an instinctive matter....[2] The test adopted by the court below is difficult to apply in practice, though no abstractly formulated and unvarying "test" will necessarily enable courts to decide questions such as this with mathematical precision. But if the purpose of the attorney-client privilege is to be served, the attorney and client must be able to predict with some degree of certainty whether particular discussions will be protected. An uncertain privilege, or one which purports to be certain but results in widely varying applications by the courts, is little better than no privilege at all. The very terms of the test adopted by the court below suggest the unpredictability of its application. The test restricts the availability of the privilege to those officers who play a "substantial role" in deciding and directing a corporation's legal response. Disparate decisions in cases applying this test illustrate its unpredictability....

The communications at issue were made by Upjohn employees[3] to counsel for Upjohn acting as such, at the direction of corporate superiors in order to secure legal advice from counsel.... Information, not available from upper-echelon management, was needed to supply a basis for legal advice concerning compliance with securities and tax laws, foreign laws, currency regulations, duties to shareholders, and potential litigation in each of these areas. The communications concerned matters within the scope of the employees' corporate duties, and the employees themselves were sufficiently aware that they were being questioned in order that the corporation could obtain legal advice. The questionnaire identified Thomas as "the company's General Counsel" and referred in its opening sentence to the possible illegality of payments such as the ones on which information was sought. A statement of policy accompanying the questionnaire clearly indicated the legal implications of the investigation.... This statement was issued to Upjohn employees worldwide, so that even those interviewees not receiving a questionnaire were aware of the legal implications of the interviews. Pursuant to explicit instructions from the Chairman of the Board, the communications were considered "highly confidential" when made, and have been kept confidential by the company. Consistent with the underlying purposes of the attorney-client privilege, these communications must be protected against compelled disclosure.

The Court of Appeals declined to extend the attorney-client privilege beyond the limits of the control group test for fear that doing so would entail severe burdens on discovery and create a broad "zone of silence" over corporate affairs. Application of the attorney-client privilege to communications such as those involved here, however, puts the adversary in no worse position than if the communications had never taken place.

---

2. The Government argues that the risk of civil or criminal liability suffices to ensure that corporations will seek legal advice in the absence of the protection of the privilege. This response ignores the fact that the depth and quality of any investigations, to ensure compliance with the law would suffer, even were they undertaken. The response also proves too much, since it applies to all communications covered by the privilege: an individual trying to comply with the law or faced with a legal problem also has strong incentive to disclose information to his lawyer, yet the common law has recognized the value of the privilege in further facilitating communications.

3. Seven of the eighty-six employees interviewed by counsel had terminated their employment with Upjohn at the time of the interview. Petitioners argue that the privilege should nonetheless apply to communications by these former employees concerning activities during their period of employment. Neither the District Court nor the Court of Appeals had occasion to address this issue, and we decline to decide it without the benefit of treatment below.

The privilege only protects disclosure of communications; it does not protect disclosure of the underlying facts by those who communicated with the attorney:

> "[T]he protection of the privilege extends only to *communications* and not to facts. A fact is one thing and a communication concerning that fact is an entirely different thing. The client cannot be compelled to answer the question, 'What did you say or write to the attorney?' but may not refuse to disclose any relevant fact within his knowledge merely because he incorporated a statement of such fact into his communication to his attorney." *Philadelphia v. Westinghouse Electric Corp.*, 205 F. Supp. 830, 831....

Here the Government was free to question the employees who communicated with Thomas and outside counsel. Upjohn has provided the IRS with a list of such employees, and the IRS has already interviewed some 25 of them. While it would probably be more convenient for the Government to secure the results of petitioner's internal investigation by simply subpoenaing the questionnaires and notes taken by petitioner's attorneys, such considerations of convenience do not overcome the policies served by the attorney-client privilege. As Justice Jackson noted in his concurring opinion in *Hickman v. Taylor*, 329 U.S., at 516: "Discovery was hardly intended to enable a learned profession to perform its functions ... on wits borrowed from the adversary."

Needless to say, we decide only the case before us, and do not undertake to draft a set of rules which should govern challenges to investigatory subpoenas. Any such approach would violate the spirit of Federal Rule of Evidence 501. See S.Rep. No. 93-1277, p. 13 (1974) ("the recognition of a privilege based on a confidential relationship ... should be determined on a case-by-case basis")…. While such a "case-by-case" basis may to some slight extent undermine desirable certainty in the boundaries of the attorney-client privilege, it obeys the spirit of the Rules. At the same time we conclude that the narrow "control group test" sanctioned by the Court of Appeals, in this case cannot, consistent with [the common law, as interpreted by United States courts in the light of reason and experience], Fed. Rule Evid. 501, govern the development of the law in this area.

[The concurring opinion of Chief Justice Burger is omitted.]

Notes and Questions

1. In addition to the "control group" test, lower federal courts, prior to *Upjohn*, had adopted three other approaches to the attorney-client privilege in the corporate context. One approach—alluded to in *Upjohn* as one of the two competing tests that they were asked to choose from—was the so-called "subject matter" test. Under that approach, "an employee of a corporation, though not a member of its control group, is sufficiently identified with the corporation so that his communication to the corporation's attorney is privileged where the employee makes the communication at the direction of his superiors in the corporation and where the subject matter upon which the attorney's advice is sought by the corporation and dealt with in the communication is the performance by the employee of the duties of his employment." *Harper & Row Publishers, Inc. v. Decker*, 423 F.2d 487, 491–492 (7th Cir. 1970), *aff'd by equally divided court*, 400 U.S. 348 (1971). Under another approach, the privilege was extremely broad in the corporate context, covering any communication between a corporation's attorney and *any* of its officers or employees. *See United States v. United Shoe Machinery Corp.*, 89 F. Supp. 357, 359 (D.Mass. 1950). Under yet another approach, the attorney-client privilege was held not to be available to corporations. *See Radiant Burners, Inc. v. American Gas Ass'n*, 207 F. Supp. 771

(N.D. Ill. 1962), *rev'd* 320 F.2d 314 (7th Cir. 1963) (en banc). Are there advantages to the latter two alternatives over both the "control group" and "subject matter" tests? If so, why do you suppose neither of these alternatives gained much traction?

2. Notwithstanding the Supreme Court's decision in *Upjohn*, states remain free to define the scope of the attorney-client privilege in the corporate context differently. The Illinois Supreme Court, for example, in a post-*Upjohn* decision, chose to adopt the control-group test, explaining its rationale as follows:

> The purpose of the attorney-client privilege is to encourage and promote full and frank consultation between a client and legal advisor by removing the fear of compelled disclosure of information.... Under some circumstances, however, the privilege poses an absolute bar to the discovery of relevant and material evidentiary facts, and in the corporate context, given the large number of employees, frequent dealings with lawyers and masses of documents, the "zone of silence grows large.".... That result, in our judgment, is fundamentally incompatible with this State's broad discovery policies looking to the ultimate ascertainment of the truth ... which we continue to find essential to the fair disposition of a lawsuit.... Its potential to insulate so much material from the truth-seeking process convinces us that the privilege ought to be limited for the corporate client to the extent reasonably necessary to achieve its purpose....

Consolidation Coal Co. v. Bucyrus-Erie Co., 432 N.E.2d 250, 256–57 (Ill. 1982) (quoting Simon, *The Attorney-Client Privilege as Applied to Corporations*, 65 Yale L.J. 953, 955 (1956)).

In your view, which court, *Upjohn* or *Consolidation Coal*, struck the correct balance?

3. Notwithstanding the Supreme Court's protestations in *Upjohn* to the contrary, did it in fact adopt a particular test for invoking the federal attorney-client privilege in the corporate context? Can you articulate that test? Is the Court's unwillingness to be more specific inconsistent with its statement in the opinion that "[a]n uncertain privilege, or one which purports to be certain but results in widely varying applications by the courts, is little better than no privilege at all"?

4. One particularly vexing problem with respect to the corporate privilege involves its applicability in shareholder derivative suits brought by a shareholder or group of shareholders. Such suits usually claim that the corporation's officers and directors are not acting in the shareholders' interests. In such a suit, can the corporation's officers and directors, who purport to represent the corporation, invoke the privilege against the shareholders, who also purport to represent the corporation? In such circumstances, courts typically follow an approach first set forth in *Garner v. Wolfinbarger*, 430 F.2d 1093 (5th Cir. 1970):

> Corporate management must manage. It has the duty to do so and requires the tools to do so. Part of the managerial task is to seek legal counsel when desirable, and, obviously, management prefers that it confer with counsel without the risk of having the communications revealed at the instance of one or more dissatisfied stockholders.... But in assessing management assertions of injury to the corporation it must be borne in mind that management does not manage for itself and that the beneficiaries of its action are the stockholders ... it is difficult to rationally defend the assertion of the privilege if all, or substantially all, stockholders desire to inquire into the attorney's communications with corporate representatives who have only nominal ownership interests, or even none at all....

> In summary, we say this. The attorney-client privilege still has viability for the corporate client. The corporation is not barred from asserting it merely because those demanding information enjoy the status of stockholders. But where the

corporation is in suit against its stockholders on charges of acting inimically to stockholder interests, protection of those interests as well as those of the corporation and of the public require that the availability of the privilege be subject to the right of the stockholders to show cause why it should not be invoked in the particular instance....

There are many indicia that may contribute to a decision of presence or absence of good cause, among them the number of shareholders and the percentage of stock they represent; the bona fides of the shareholders; the nature of the shareholders' claim and whether it is obviously colorable; the apparent necessity or desirability of the shareholders having the information and the availability of it from other sources; whether, if the shareholders' claim is of wrongful action by the corporation, it is of action criminal, or illegal but not criminal, or of doubtful legality; whether the communication related to past or to prospective actions; whether the communication is of advice concerning the litigation itself; the extent to which the communication is identified versus the extent to which the shareholders are blindly fishing; the risk of revelation of trade secrets or other information in whose confidentiality the corporation has an interest for independent reasons....

Id. at 1101, 1103–04.

Is such a balancing approach, which has been endorsed by most lower courts, consistent with *Upjohn?*

5. Individual officers, directors, and employees of a corporation, when communicating with the corporation's legal counsel, are speaking with the corporation in their capacity as agents of the corporation and not in their personal capacities. Thus, for example, when control over a corporation passes to a new board of directors, the new board has power to waive the attorney-client privilege as to communications between former board members and the corporation's legal counsel, even over the objection of those former board members. *See CFTC v. Weintraub*, 471 U.S. 343, 349 (1985).

Nonetheless, the presumption that a corporation's legal counsel was speaking to an individual officer, director or employee in his official capacity and not in his personal capacity can be overcome, and thus the individual may be able to claim a personal attorney-client privilege, if he establishes the following:

First, they must show they approached [counsel] for the purpose of seeking legal advice. Second, they must demonstrate that when they approached [counsel] they made it clear that they were seeking legal advice in their individual rather than in their representative capacities. Third, they must demonstrate that the [counsel] saw fit to communicate with them in their individual capacities, knowing that a possible conflict could arise. Fourth, they must prove that their conversations with [counsel] were confidential. And fifth, they must show that the substance of their conversations with [counsel] did not concern matters within the company or the general affairs of the company.

In re Grand Jury Subpoena, 274 F.3d 563, 571 (1st Cir. 2001) (quoting *In re Bevill, Bresler & Schulman Asset Mgmt. Corp.*, 805 F.2d 120, 123 (3d Cir. 1986)).

6. When a government official, such as the President or a Governor, is being investigated on charges of criminal wrongdoing, can he invoke the attorney-client privilege to shield communications that he had with his government legal counsel? *Compare In re: Grand Jury Investigation*, 399 F.3d 527, 534–36 (2d Cir. 2005) (holding that it can be invoked, although leaving open the possibility that the official's successor in office can waive the privilege), *with In re: A Witness Before the Special Grand Jury 2000-2*, 288 F.3d 289, 292–95

(7th Cir. 2002) (holding that it cannot be invoked), *and In re Lindsey*, 158 F.3d 1263, 1272–78 (D.C. Cir. 1998) (same), *and In re Grand Jury Subpoena Duces Tecum*, 112 F.3d 910, 915–21 (8th Cir. 1997) (same). *See also Ross v. City of Memphis*, 423 F.3d 596 (6th Cir. 2005) (not reaching the issue but holding that governmental entities can invoke the privilege in civil proceedings).

What is the rationale for treating this attorney-client relationship differently from the relationship between a client and a private attorney? *See In re: A Witness Before the Special Grand Jury 2000-2*, 288 F.3d at 293 ("government lawyers have a higher, competing duty to act in the public interest.... Their compensation comes not from a client whose interests they are sworn to protect from the power of the state, but from the state itself and the public fisc. It would be both unseemly and a misuse of public assets to permit a public official to use a taxpayer-provided attorney to conceal from the taxpayers themselves otherwise admissible evidence of financial wrongdoing, official misconduct, or abuse of power.").

7. Under the "fiduciary exception" to the attorney-client privilege, when a trustee obtains legal advice to guide the administration of a trust, and not for the trustee's own defense in litigation, the beneficiaries of the trust are entitled to the production of documents related to that advice, on the theory that the legal advice was sought for the beneficiaries' benefit. For a discussion of the fiduciary exception generally as well as in the specific context of the trust relationship between the federal government and Indian tribes, *see United States v. Jicarilla Apache Nation*, 131 S. Ct. 2313 (2011).

Problem 5-3: Monica-Gate

While Bill Clinton was President, a lawsuit was brought against him in federal district court in Arkansas by Paula Jones, claiming that he sexually harassed her when he was governor of Arkansas. During the discovery phase of the lawsuit, Jones' attorneys served a subpoena on one of President Clinton's former interns, Monica Lewinsky. Through her attorney, Francis Carter, Ms. Lewinsky moved to quash the subpoena, and in support of her motion, submitted an affidavit in which she denied having any sexual relationship with President Clinton.

Shortly thereafter, a grand jury already investigating President Clinton on a variety of matters was charged with investigating whether Ms. Lewinsky committed perjury and obstructed justice by making false statements in her affidavit filed in the *Clinton v. Jones* case, violations of 18 U.S.C. §§ 1503, 1623. Her attorney, Francis Carter, was subpoenaed to testify before the grand jury as to his communications with Ms. Lewinsky in connection with the preparation of the affidavit. Carter invoked the attorney-client privilege on behalf of Ms. Lewinsky.

How will the court dispose of Ms. Lewinsky's claim that the communications are protected by the attorney-client privilege?

United States v. Zolin
491 U.S. 554 (1989)

Justice BLACKMUN delivered the opinion of the Court....

I

In the course of its investigation, the IRS sought access to 51 documents that had been filed with the Clerk of the Los Angeles County Superior Court in connection with a case entitled *Church of Scientology of California v. Armstrong*, No. C420 153. The *Armstrong* litigation involved, among other things, a charge by the Church that one of its former members, Gerald Armstrong, had obtained by unlawful means documentary materials relating to Church activities, including two tapes. Some of the documents sought by the IRS had been filed under seal.

The IRS, by its Special Agent Steven Petersell, served a summons upon the Clerk on October 24, 1984, pursuant to 26 U.S.C. §7603, demanding that he produce the 51 documents. The tapes were among those listed. On November 21, IRS agents were permitted to inspect and copy some of the summoned materials, including the tapes.

On November 27, the Church and Mary Sue Hubbard, who had intervened in *Armstrong*, secured a temporary restraining order from the United States District Court for the Central District of California. The order required the IRS to file with the District Court all materials acquired on November 21 and all reproductions and notes related thereto, pending disposition of the intervenors' motion for a preliminary injunction to bar IRS use of these materials. By order dated December 10, the District Court returned to the IRS all materials except the tapes and the IRS' notes reflecting their contents.

On January 18, 1985, the IRS filed in the District Court a petition to enforce its summons. In addition to the tapes, the IRS sought 12 sealed documents the Clerk had refused to produce in response to the IRS summons. The Church and Mary Sue Hubbard intervened to oppose production of the tapes and the sealed documents. Respondents claimed that IRS was not seeking the documents in good faith, and objected on grounds of lack of relevance and attorney-client privilege.

Respondents asserted the privilege as a bar to disclosure of the tapes. The IRS argued, among other things, however, that the tapes fell within the crime-fraud exception to the attorney-client privilege, and urged the District Court to listen to the tapes in the course of making its privilege determination. In addition, the IRS submitted to the court two declarations by Agent Petersell. In the first, Petersell stated his grounds for believing that the tapes were relevant to the investigation. In the second, Petersell offered a description of the tapes' contents, based on information he received during several interviews. Appended to this declaration — over respondents' objection — were partial transcripts of the tapes, which the IRS lawfully had obtained from a confidential source. See March 15, 1985, declaration (filed under seal). In subsequent briefing, the IRS reiterated its request that the District Court listen to the tapes *in camera* before making its privilege ruling.

After oral argument and an evidentiary hearing, the District Court rejected respondents' claim of bad faith. The court ordered production of 5 of the 12 documents....

Turning to the tapes, the District Court ruled that respondents had demonstrated that they contain confidential attorney-client communications, that the privilege had not been waived, and that "[t]he 'fraud-crime' exception to the attorney-client privilege does not apply. The quoted excerpts tend to show or admit past fraud but there is no clear indication that future fraud or crime is being planned." On this basis, the court held that the Clerk "need not produce its copy of the tapes pursuant to the summons." The District Court denied the IRS' motion for reconsideration, rejecting the IRS' renewed request that the court listen to the tapes *in toto*. "While this was at one time discussed with counsel, thereafter Mr. Petersell's declaration was submitted, and no one suggested that this was an inadequate basis on which to determine the attorney-client privilege question."

Respondents appealed to the Court of Appeals for the Ninth Circuit, and the IRS cross-appealed ... the IRS contended that the District Court erred in rejecting the application of the crime-fraud exception to the tapes. In particular, the IRS argued that the District Court incorrectly held that the IRS had abandoned its request for *in camera* review of the tapes, and that the court should have listened to the tapes before ruling that the crime-fraud exception was inapplicable. Respondents contended, in contrast, that the District Court erred in the opposite direction: they argued that it was error for the court to rely on the partial transcripts, because "[i]n this Circuit, a party cannot rely on the communications themselves — whether by listening to the tapes *or reviewing excerpts or transcripts of them* — to bear its burden to invoke the exception but must bear the burden by independent evidence. This is the clear and unambiguous holding of *United States v. Shewfelt*, 455 F.2d 836 (9th Cir.), cert. denied, 406 U.S. 944 (1972)" (emphasis added).

The panel of the Court of Appeals agreed with respondents that, under *Shewfelt*, "the Government's evidence of crime or fraud must come from sources independent of the attorney-client communications recorded on the tapes," thereby implicitly holding that even if the IRS had properly preserved its demand for *in camera* review, the District Court would have been without power to grant it. The Court of Appeals then reviewed "the Government's independent evidence." That review appears to have excluded the partial transcripts, and thus the Court of Appeals implicitly agreed with respondents that it was improper for the District Court to have considered even the partial transcripts. On the basis of its review of the "independent evidence," the Court of Appeals affirmed the District Court's determination that the IRS had failed to establish the applicability of the crime-fraud exception....

III

Questions of privilege that arise in the course of the adjudication of federal rights are [governed by the common law as interpreted by United States courts in the light of reason and experience]. Fed.Rule Evid. 501. We have recognized the attorney-client privilege under federal law, as "the oldest of the privileges for confidential communications known to the common law." *Upjohn Co. v. United States*, 449 U.S. 383, 389 (1981). Although the underlying rationale for the privilege has changed over time ... courts long have viewed its central concern as one "to encourage full and frank communication between attorneys and their clients and thereby promote broader public interests in the observance of law and administration of justice." *Upjohn*, 449 U.S., at 389. That purpose, of course, requires that clients be free to "make full disclosure to their attorneys" of past wrongdoings, *Fisher v. United States*, 425 U.S. 391, 403 (1976), in order that the client may obtain "the aid of persons having knowledge of the law and skilled in its practice," *Hunt v. Blackburn*, 128 U.S. 464, 470 (1888).

The attorney-client privilege is not without its costs. Cf. *Trammel v. United States*, 445 U.S. 40, 50 (1980). "[S]ince the privilege has the effect of withholding relevant information from the factfinder, it applies only where necessary to achieve its purpose." *Fisher*, 425 U.S., at 403. The attorney-client privilege must necessarily protect the confidences of wrongdoers, but the reason for that protection — the centrality of open client and attorney communication to the proper functioning of our adversary system of justice — "ceas[es] to operate at a certain point, namely, where the desired advice refers *not to prior wrongdoing*, but to *future wrongdoing*." 8 Wigmore, § 2298, p. 573 (emphasis in original); see also *Clark v. United States*, 289 U.S. 1, 15 (1933). It is the purpose of the crime-fraud exception to the attorney-client privilege to assure that the "seal of secrecy," *ibid.*, between lawyer and client does not extend to communications "made for the purpose of getting advice for the commission of a fraud" or crime. *O'Rourke v. Darbishire*, [1920] A.C. 581, 604 (P.C.).

The District Court and the Court of Appeals found that the tapes at issue in this case recorded attorney-client communications and that the privilege had not been waived when the tapes were inadvertently given to Armstrong.... These findings are not at issue here. Thus, the remaining obstacle to respondents' successful assertion of the privilege is the Government's contention that the recorded attorney-client communications were made in furtherance of a future crime or fraud.

A variety of questions may arise when a party raises the crime-fraud exception. The parties to this case have not been in complete agreement as to which of these questions are presented here. In an effort to clarify the matter, we observe, first, that we need not decide the quantum of proof necessary ultimately to establish the applicability of the crime-fraud exception.... Rather, we are concerned here with the *type* of evidence that may be used to make that ultimate showing. Within that general area of inquiry, the initial question in this case is whether a district court, at the request of the party opposing the privilege, may review the allegedly privileged communications *in camera* to determine whether the crime-fraud exception applies. If such *in camera* review is permitted, the second question we must consider is whether some threshold evidentiary showing is needed before the district court may undertake the requested review. Finally, if a threshold showing is required, we must consider the type of evidence the opposing party may use to meet it: *i.e.*, in this case, whether the partial transcripts the IRS possessed may be used for that purpose....

A

We consider first the question whether a district court may *ever* honor the request of the party opposing the privilege to conduct an *in camera* review of allegedly privileged communications to determine whether those communications fall within the crime-fraud exception. We conclude that no express provision of the Federal Rules of Evidence bars such use of *in camera* review, and that it would be unwise to prohibit it in all instances as a matter of federal common law.

(1)

At first blush, two provisions of the Federal Rules of Evidence would appear to be relevant. Rule 104(a) provides: ["The court must decide any preliminary question about whether a witness is qualified, *a privilege exists*, or evidence is admissible. In so deciding, the court is not bound by evidence rules, *except those on privilege*."] (emphasis added). Rule 1101(c) provides: ["The rules on privilege apply to all stages of a case or proceeding."] Taken together, these Rules might be read to establish that in a summons-enforcement proceeding, attorney-client communications cannot be considered by the district court in making its crime-fraud ruling: to do otherwise, under this view, would be to make the crime-fraud determination without due regard to the existence of the privilege.

Even those scholars who support this reading of Rule 104(a) acknowledge that it leads to an absurd result.

> "Because the judge must honor claims of privilege made during his preliminary fact determinations, many exceptions to the rules of privilege will become 'dead letters,' since the preliminary facts that give rise to these exceptions can never be proved. For example, an exception to the attorney-client privilege provides that there is no privilege if the communication was made to enable anyone to commit a crime or fraud. There is virtually no way in which the

exception can ever be proved, save by compelling disclosure of the contents of the communication; Rule 104(a) provides that this cannot be done." 21 C. Wright & K. Graham, Federal Practice & Procedure: Evidence § 5055, p. 276 (1977).

We find this Draconian interpretation of Rule 104(a) inconsistent with the Rule's plain language. The Rule does not provide by its terms that all materials as to which a "clai[m] of privilege" is made must be excluded from consideration. In that critical respect, the language of Rule 104(a) is markedly different from the comparable California evidence rule, which provides that "the presiding officer may not require disclosure of information *claimed to be privileged* under this division in order to rule on the claim of privilege." Cal.Evid.Code Ann. § 915(a) (West Supp.1989) (emphasis added). There is no reason to read Rule 104(a) as if its text were identical to that of the California rule.

Nor does it make sense to us to assume, as respondents have throughout this litigation, that once the attorney-client nature of the contested communications is established, those communications must be treated as *presumptively* privileged for evidentiary purposes until the privilege is "defeated" or "stripped away" by proof that the communications took place in the course of planning future crime or fraud....

We see no basis for holding that the tapes in this case must be deemed privileged under Rule 104(a) while the question of crime or fraud remains open....

(2)

Having determined that Rule 104(a) does not prohibit the *in camera* review sought by the IRS, we must address the question as a matter of the federal common law of privileges. See Rule 501. We conclude that a complete prohibition against opponents' use of *in camera* review to establish the applicability of the crime-fraud exception is inconsistent with the policies underlying the privilege.

We begin our analysis by recognizing that disclosure of allegedly privileged materials to the district court for purposes of determining the merits of a claim of privilege does not have the legal effect of terminating the privilege....

Once it is clear that *in camera* review does not destroy the privileged nature of the contested communications, the question of the propriety of that review turns on whether the policies underlying the privilege and its exceptions are better fostered by permitting such review or by prohibiting it. In our view, the costs of imposing an absolute bar to consideration of the communications *in camera* for purpose of establishing the crime-fraud exception are intolerably high.

"No matter how light the burden of proof which confronts the party claiming the exception, there are many blatant abuses of privilege which cannot be substantiated by extrinsic evidence. This is particularly true ... of ... situations in which an alleged illegal proposal is made in the context of a relationship which has an apparent legitimate end." Note, The Future Crime or Tort Exception to Communications Privileges, 77 Harv.L.Rev. 730, 737 (1964). A *per se* rule that the communications in question may never be considered creates, we feel, too great an impediment to the proper functioning of the adversary process....

B

We turn to the question whether *in camera* review at the behest of the party asserting the crime-fraud exception is *always* permissible, or, in contrast, whether the party seeking *in camera* review must make some threshold showing that such review is appropriate. In addressing this question, we attend to the detrimental effect, if any, of *in camera* review on the policies underlying the privilege and on the orderly administration of justice in our courts. We conclude that some such showing must be made.

Our endorsement of the practice of testing proponents' privilege claims through *in camera* review of the allegedly privileged documents has not been without reservation. This Court noted in *United States v. Reynolds*, 345 U.S. 1 (1953), a case which presented a delicate question concerning the disclosure of military secrets, that "examination of the evidence, even by the judge alone, in chambers" might in some cases "jeopardize the security which the privilege is meant to protect." Analogizing to claims of Fifth Amendment privilege, it observed more generally: "Too much judicial inquiry into the claim of privilege would force disclosure of the thing the privilege was meant to protect, while a complete abandonment of judicial control would lead to intolerable abuses."

The Court in *Reynolds* recognized that some compromise must be reached ... it declined to "go so far as to say that the court *may automatically require* a complete disclosure to the judge before the claim of privilege will be accepted *in any case*" (emphasis added). We think that much the same result is in order here.

A blanket rule allowing *in camera* review as a tool for determining the applicability of the crime-fraud exception, as *Reynolds* suggests, would place the policy of protecting open and legitimate disclosure between attorneys and clients at undue risk. There is also reason to be concerned about the possible due process implications of routine use of *in camera* proceedings.... Finally, we cannot ignore the burdens *in camera* review places upon the district courts, which may well be required to evaluate large evidentiary records without open adversarial guidance by the parties.

There is no reason to permit opponents of the privilege to engage in groundless fishing expeditions, with the district courts as their unwitting (and perhaps unwilling) agents. Courts of Appeals have suggested that *in camera* review is available to evaluate claims of crime or fraud only "when justified," *In re John Doe Corp.*, 675 F.2d, at 490, or "[i]n appropriate cases," *In re Sealed Case*, 676 F.2d 793, 815 (1982) (opinion of Wright, J.). Indeed, the Government conceded at oral argument (albeit reluctantly) that a district court would be mistaken if it reviewed documents *in camera* solely because "the government beg[ged it]" to do so, "with no reason to suspect crime or fraud." We agree.

In fashioning a standard for determining when *in camera* review is appropriate, we begin with the observation that "*in camera* inspection ... is a smaller intrusion upon the confidentiality of the attorney-client relationship than is public disclosure." Fried, Too High a Price for Truth: The Exception to the Attorney-Client Privilege for Contemplated Crimes and Frauds, 64 N. C. L. Rev. 443, 467 (1986). We therefore conclude that a lesser evidentiary showing is needed to trigger *in camera* review than is required ultimately to overcome the privilege. The threshold we set, in other words, need not be a stringent one.

We think that the following standard strikes the correct balance. Before engaging in *in camera* review to determine the applicability of the crime-fraud exception, "the judge should require a showing of a factual basis adequate to support a good faith belief by a reasonable person," *Caldwell v. District Court*, 644 P.2d 26, 33 (Colo.1982), that *in camera* review of the materials may reveal evidence to establish the claim that the crime-fraud exception applies.

Once that showing is made, the decision whether to engage in *in camera* review rests in the sound discretion of the district court. The court should make that decision in light of the facts and circumstances of the particular case, including, among other things, the volume of materials the district court has been asked to review, the relative importance to the case of the alleged privileged information, and the likelihood that the evidence produced through *in camera* review, together with other available evidence then before the court, will establish that the crime-fraud exception does apply. The district court is also free to defer its *in camera* review if it concludes that additional evidence in support of the crime-fraud exception may be available that is *not* allegedly privileged, and that production of the additional evidence will not unduly disrupt or delay the proceedings.

C

The question remains as to what kind of evidence a district court may consider in determining whether it has the discretion to undertake an *in camera* review of an allegedly privileged communication at the behest of the party opposing the privilege. Here, the issue is whether the partial transcripts may be used by the IRS in support of its request for *in camera* review of the tapes.

The answer to that question, in the first instance, must be found in Rule 104(a), which establishes that materials that have been determined to be privileged may not be considered in making the preliminary determination of the existence of a privilege. Neither the District Court nor the Court of Appeals made factual findings as to the privileged nature of the partial transcripts, so we cannot determine on this record whether Rule 104(a) would bar their consideration.

Assuming for the moment, however, that no rule of privilege bars the IRS' use of the partial transcripts, we fail to see what purpose would be served by excluding the transcripts from the District Court's consideration. There can be little doubt that partial transcripts, or other evidence directly but incompletely reflecting the content of the contested communications, generally will be strong evidence of the subject matter of the communications themselves. Permitting district courts to consider this type of evidence would aid them substantially in rapidly and reliably determining whether *in camera review* is appropriate.

Respondents suggest only one serious countervailing consideration. In their view, a rule that would allow an opponent of the privilege to rely on such material would encourage litigants to elicit confidential information from disaffected employees or others who have access to the information. We think that deterring the aggressive pursuit of relevant information from third-party sources is not sufficiently central to the policies of the attorney-client privilege to require us to adopt the exclusionary rule urged by respondents. We conclude that the party opposing the privilege may use any nonprivileged evidence in support of its request for *in camera* review, even if its evidence is not "independent" of the contested communications as the Court of Appeals uses that term.[12] ....

Swidler & Berlin v. United States
524 U.S. 399 (1998)

Chief Justice REHNQUIST delivered the opinion of the Court....

This dispute arises out of an investigation conducted by the Office of the Independent Counsel into whether various individuals made false statements, obstructed justice, or

---

12. In addition, we conclude that evidence that is not "independent" of the contents of allegedly privileged communications—like the partial transcripts in this case—may be used not only in the pursuit of *in camera* review, but also may provide the evidentiary basis for the ultimate showing that the crime-fraud exception applies. We see little to distinguish these two uses: in both circumstances, if the evidence has not itself been determined to be privileged, its exclusion does not serve the policies which underlie the attorney-client privilege.

committed other crimes during investigations of the 1993 dismissal of employees from the White House Travel Office. Vincent W. Foster, Jr., was Deputy White House Counsel when the firings occurred. In July 1993, Foster met with petitioner Hamilton, an attorney at petitioner Swidler & Berlin, to seek legal representation concerning possible congressional or other investigations of the firings. During a 2-hour meeting, Hamilton took three pages of handwritten notes. One of the first entries in the notes is the word "Privileged." Nine days later, Foster committed suicide.

In December 1995, a federal grand jury, at the request of the Independent Counsel, issued subpoenas to petitioners Hamilton and Swidler & Berlin for, *inter alia*, Hamilton's handwritten notes of his meeting with Foster. Petitioners filed a motion to quash, arguing that the notes were protected by the attorney-client privilege and by the work-product privilege. The District Court, after examining the notes *in camera*, concluded they were protected from disclosure by both doctrines and denied enforcement of the subpoenas.

The Court of Appeals for the District of Columbia Circuit reversed.... The Court of Appeals thought that the risk of posthumous revelation, when confined to the criminal context, would have little to no chilling effect on client communication, but that the costs of protecting communications after death were high. It therefore concluded that the privilege was not absolute in such circumstances, and that instead, a balancing test should apply. It thus held that there is a posthumous exception to the privilege for communications whose relative importance to particular criminal litigation is substantial....

We granted certiorari ... and we now reverse....

The Independent Counsel argues that the attorney-client privilege should not prevent disclosure of confidential communications where the client has died and the information is relevant to a criminal proceeding....

[C]ases addressing the existence of the privilege after death—most involving the testamentary exception—uniformly presume the privilege survives, even if they do not so hold....

Such testamentary exception cases consistently presume the privilege survives. They view testamentary disclosure of communications as an exception to the privilege: "[T]he general rule with respect to confidential communications ... is that such communications are privileged during the testator's lifetime and, also, after the testator's death unless sought to be disclosed in litigation between the testator's heirs." *Osborn*, 561 F.2d, at 1340. The rationale for such disclosure is that it furthers the client's intent.[2]

Indeed, in *Glover v. Patten*, 165 U.S. 394, 406–408 (1897), this Court, in recognizing the testamentary exception, expressly assumed that the privilege continues after the individual's death. The Court explained that testamentary disclosure was permissible because the privilege, which normally protects the client's interests, could be impliedly waived in order to fulfill the client's testamentary intent.

The great body of this case law supports, either by holding or considered dicta, the position that the privilege does survive in a case such as the present one. Given the language of Rule 501, at the very least the burden is on the Independent Counsel to show that "reason and experience" require a departure from this rule.

The Independent Counsel contends that the testamentary exception supports the posthumous termination of the privilege because in practice most cases have refused to

---

2. About half the States have codified the testamentary exception by providing that a personal representative of the deceased can waive the privilege when heirs or devisees claim through the deceased client (as opposed to parties claiming against the estate, for whom the privilege is not waived)....

apply the privilege posthumously. He further argues that the exception reflects a policy judgment that the interest in settling estates outweighs any posthumous interest in confidentiality. He then reasons by analogy that in criminal proceedings, the interest in determining whether a crime has been committed should trump client confidentiality, particularly since the financial interests of the estate are not at stake.

But the Independent Counsel's interpretation simply does not square with the case law's implicit acceptance of the privilege's survival and with the treatment of testamentary disclosure as an "exception" or an implied "waiver." And the premise of his analogy is incorrect, since cases consistently recognize that the rationale for the testamentary exception is that it furthers the client's intent, see, *e.g.*, *Glover, supra*. There is no reason to suppose as a general matter that grand jury testimony about confidential communications furthers the client's intent. . . .

Despite the scholarly criticism, we think there are weighty reasons that counsel in favor of posthumous application. Knowing that communications will remain confidential even after death encourages the client to communicate fully and frankly with counsel. While the fear of disclosure, and the consequent withholding of information from counsel, may be reduced if disclosure is limited to posthumous disclosure in a criminal context, it seems unreasonable to assume that it vanishes altogether. Clients may be concerned about reputation, civil liability, or possible harm to friends or family. Posthumous disclosure of such communications may be as feared as disclosure during the client's lifetime.

The Independent Counsel suggests, however, that his proposed exception would have little to no effect on the client's willingness to confide in his attorney. He reasons that only clients intending to perjure themselves will be chilled by a rule of disclosure after death, as opposed to truthful clients or those asserting their Fifth Amendment privilege. This is because for the latter group, communications disclosed by the attorney after the client's death purportedly will reveal only information that the client himself would have revealed if alive.

The Independent Counsel assumes, incorrectly we believe, that the privilege is analogous to the Fifth Amendment's protection against self-incrimination. But as suggested above, the privilege serves much broader purposes. Clients consult attorneys for a wide variety of reasons, only one of which involves possible criminal liability. Many attorneys act as counselors on personal and family matters, where, in the course of obtaining the desired advice, confidences about family members or financial problems must be revealed in order to assure sound legal advice. The same is true of owners of small businesses who may regularly consult their attorneys about a variety of problems arising in the course of the business. These confidences may not come close to any sort of admission of criminal wrongdoing, but nonetheless be matters which the client would not wish divulged.

The contention that the attorney is being required to disclose only what the client could have been required to disclose is at odds with the basis for the privilege even during the client's lifetime. In related cases, we have said that the loss of evidence admittedly caused by the privilege is justified in part by the fact that without the privilege, the client may not have made such communications in the first place. See *Jaffee*, 518 U.S., at 12; *Fisher v. United States*, 425 U.S. 391, 403 (1976). This is true of disclosure before and after the client's death. Without assurance of the privilege's posthumous application, the client may very well not have made disclosures to his attorney at all, so the loss of evidence is more apparent than real. In the case at hand, it seems quite plausible that Foster, perhaps already contemplating suicide, may not have sought legal advice from Hamilton if he had not been assured the conversation was privileged.

The Independent Counsel additionally suggests that his proposed exception would have minimal impact if confined to criminal cases, or, as the Court of Appeals suggests, if it is limited to information of substantial importance to a particular criminal case.[3] However, there is no case authority for the proposition that the privilege applies differently in criminal and civil cases, and only one commentator ventures such a suggestion, see Mueller & Kirkpatrick, *supra*, at 380–381. In any event, a client may not know at the time he discloses information to his attorney whether it will later be relevant to a civil or a criminal matter, let alone whether it will be of substantial importance. Balancing *ex post* the importance of the information against client interests, even limited to criminal cases, introduces substantial uncertainty into the privilege's application. For just that reason, we have rejected use of a balancing test in defining the contours of the privilege. See *Upjohn*, 449 U.S., at 393; *Jaffee*, *supra*, at 17–18.

In a similar vein, the Independent Counsel argues that existing exceptions to the privilege, such as the crime-fraud exception and the testamentary exception, make the impact of one more exception marginal. However, these exceptions do not demonstrate that the impact of a posthumous exception would be insignificant, and there is little empirical evidence on this point. The established exceptions are consistent with the purposes of the privilege ... while a posthumous exception in criminal cases appears at odds with the goals of encouraging full and frank communication and of protecting the client's interests. A "no harm in one more exception" rationale could contribute to the general erosion of the privilege, without reference to common-law principles or "reason and experience."

Finally, the Independent Counsel, relying on cases such as *United States v. Nixon*, 418 U.S. 683, 710 (1974), and *Branzburg v. Hayes*, 408 U.S. 665 (1972), urges that privileges be strictly construed because they are inconsistent with the paramount judicial goal of truth seeking. But both *Nixon* and *Branzburg* dealt with the creation of privileges not recognized by the common law, whereas here we deal with one of the oldest recognized privileges in the law. And we are asked, not simply to "construe" the privilege, but to narrow it, contrary to the weight of the existing body of case law.

It has been generally, if not universally, accepted, for well over a century, that the attorney-client privilege survives the death of the client in a case such as this. While the arguments against the survival of the privilege are by no means frivolous, they are based in large part on speculation — thoughtful speculation, but speculation nonetheless — as to whether posthumous termination of the privilege would diminish a client's willingness to confide in an attorney. In an area where empirical information would be useful, it is scant and inconclusive.

Rule 501's direction to look to [the common law as interpreted by United States courts in the light of reason and experience] does not mandate that a rule, once established, should endure for all time. *Funk v. United States*, 290 U.S. 371, 381 (1933). But here the Independent Counsel has simply not made a sufficient showing to overturn the common-law rule embodied in the prevailing caselaw. Interpreted in the light of reason and experience, that body of law requires that the attorney-client privilege prevent disclosure of the notes at issue in this case....

---

3. Petitioners, while opposing wholesale abrogation of the privilege in criminal cases, concede that exceptional circumstances implicating a criminal defendant's constitutional rights might warrant breaching the privilege. We do not, however, need to reach this issue, since such exceptional circumstances clearly are not presented here.

Justice O'Connor, with whom Justice Scalia and Justice Thomas join, dissenting.

Although the attorney-client privilege ordinarily will survive the death of the client, I do not agree with the Court that it inevitably precludes disclosure of a deceased client's communications in criminal proceedings....

As the Court of Appeals observed, the costs of recognizing an absolute posthumous privilege can be inordinately high.... Extreme injustice may occur, for example, where a criminal defendant seeks disclosure of a deceased client's confession to the offense. In my view, the paramount value that our criminal justice system places on protecting an innocent defendant should outweigh a deceased client's interest in preserving confidences. Indeed, even petitioners acknowledge that an exception may be appropriate where the constitutional rights of a criminal defendant are at stake. An exception may likewise be warranted in the face of a compelling law enforcement need for the information. "[O]ur historic commitment to the rule of law ... is nowhere more profoundly manifest than in our view that the twofold aim of criminal justice is that guilt shall not escape or innocence suffer." *Nixon, supra,* at 709; see also *Herrera v. Collins,* 506 U.S. 390, 398 (1993). Given that the complete exclusion of relevant evidence from a criminal trial or investigation may distort the record, mislead the factfinder, and undermine the central truth-seeking function of the courts, I do not believe that the attorney-client privilege should act as an absolute bar to the disclosure of a deceased client's communications. When the privilege is asserted in the criminal context, and a showing is made that the communications at issue contain necessary factual information not otherwise available, courts should be permitted to assess whether interests in fairness and accuracy outweigh the justifications for the privilege.

A number of exceptions to the privilege already qualify its protections, and an attorney "who tells his client that the expected communications are absolutely and forever privileged is oversimplifying a bit." In the situation where the posthumous privilege most frequently arises—a dispute between heirs over the decedent's will—the privilege is widely recognized to give way to the interest in settling the estate. See *Glover v. Patten,* 165 U.S. 394, 406–408 (1897). This testamentary exception, moreover, may be invoked in some cases where the decedent would not have chosen to waive the privilege. For example, "a decedent might want to provide for an illegitimate child but at the same time much prefer that the relationship go undisclosed.".... Nor are other existing exceptions to the privilege—for example, the crime-fraud exception or the exceptions for claims relating to attorney competence or compensation—necessarily consistent with "encouraging full and frank communication" or "protecting the client's interests." Rather, those exceptions reflect the understanding that, in certain circumstances, the privilege "'ceases to operate'" as a safeguard on "the proper functioning of our adversary system." See *United States v. Zolin,* 491 U.S. 554, 562–563 (1989)....

Where the exoneration of an innocent criminal defendant or a compelling law enforcement interest is at stake, the harm of precluding critical evidence that is unavailable by any other means outweighs the potential disincentive to forthright communication. In my view, the cost of silence warrants a narrow exception to the rule that the attorney-client privilege survives the death of the client....

Notes and Questions

1. There are two elements to the crime-fraud exception. First, that the client was engaged in criminal or fraudulent conduct when he sought the advice of counsel, that he

was planning such conduct when he sought the advice of counsel, or that he committed a crime or fraud subsequent to receiving the benefit of counsel's advice. And second, that the assistance sought from the attorney was in furtherance of the criminal or fraudulent activity or was closely related to it. *See In re Grand Jury Investigation (Schroeder)*, 842 F.2d 1223, 1226 (11th Cir. 1987). However, for the crime-fraud exception to apply, the attorney need not have been aware of the client's criminal or fraudulent purpose, and it even applies if the attorney took no steps after the communication to further the crime or fraud. Thus, the crime-fraud exception is applicable in situations in which the attorney unwittingly assists the client as well as those in which the attorney refuses to take steps to further the client's crime or fraud. *See In re Grand Jury Proceedings*, 87 F.3d 377, 380–82 (9th Cir. 1996).

Moreover, because the focus of the crime-fraud exception is on the actions and intent of the client, it is not applicable where an attorney—without his client's encouragement, involvement, or knowledge—engages in unlawful conduct, such as suborning perjury. *See In re Grand Jury Proceedings*, 417 F.3d 18, 23 (1st Cir. 2005) ("the privilege is not lost solely because the client's *lawyer* is corrupt.... The crime-fraud exception requires the *client's* engagement in criminal or fraudulent activity and the *client's* intent with respect to attorney-client communications.").

2. Note that the *Zolin* Court specifically left open the question of "the quantum of proof necessary ultimately to establish the applicability of the crime-fraud exception," a question that the lower courts have struggled with. Consider the following effort to explain that burden:

> As the party seeking to overcome the privilege, the government had the burden of showing that the crime-fraud exception applied.... What was the nature of that burden? Here we encounter some confusion. This court and others have described the required showing in terms of establishing a "prima facie" case.... In terms of the level of proof, is a "prima facie showing" a preponderance of the evidence, clear and convincing evidence, or something else?

> Our opinion in *Sealed Case II* contains this answer: "The government satisfies its burden of proof if it offers evidence that if believed by the trier of fact would establish the elements of an ongoing or imminent crime or fraud." 754 F.2d at 399. We appended a footnote to this statement explaining that although the Second Circuit had framed the test in terms of "probable cause to believe that a crime or fraud had been committed and that the communications were in furtherance thereof" (*see In re John Doe Corp.*, 675 F.3d 482, 491 & n.7 (2d Cir. 1982)), there was "little practical difference" between that standard and the one just quoted from *Sealed Case II*. 754 F.2d at 399 n.3. We confess some difficulty in understanding why the differences between the two formulations were considered slight, but there is no reason to dwell on the matter. It is apparent here that the government failed to make the sort of probable cause showing the Second Circuit would demand, or the showing *Sealed Case II* contemplated.

In re Sealed Case, 107 F.3d 46, 49–50 (D.C. Cir. 1997). Does that clear up the confusion? *Compare United States v. Chen*, 99 F.3d 1495, 1503 (9th Cir. 1996) (defining the quantum of proof as "more than suspicion but less than a preponderance of evidence"). *But see In re Napster, Inc. Copyright Litigation*, 479 F.3d 1078, 1094–96 (9th Cir. 2007) (holding that in civil cases, the party seeking to invoke the crime-fraud exception must establish its elements by a preponderance of the evidence, and distinguishing *Chen* and other grand jury cases in which the lower standard of proof applies), *abrogated on other grounds, Mo-*

hawk Indus., Inc. v. Carpenter, 130 S.Ct. 599 (2009). Why should the quantum of proof necessary to invoke an exception to a privilege be any different from, and indeed lower than, the quantum of proof necessary to establish the elements of the privilege in the first instance? *See Gutter v. E.I. Dupont De Nemours,* 124 F. Supp. 2d 1291, 1307 (S.D. Fla. 2000) (explaining that a party invoking the crime-fraud exception only has the burden of invoking it and producing *some* evidence to support that claim, at which point the burden of *persuasion* shifts to the party invoking the privilege to prove that the crime-fraud exception is inapplicable). Burdens of production and persuasion are discussed in greater detail in Chapter 9.

3. While *Zolin* discussed the examination *in camera* of documents and other tangible evidence of attorney-client communications, the *Zolin* procedure also applies to non-tangible evidence of attorney-client communications, such as the attorney's testimony about what the client said to him. Thus, under the *Zolin* procedure, the attorney may be examined by the trial court judge *in camera* and required to disclose the communication to the judge. *See In re John Doe, Inc.,* 13 F.3d 633, 636–637 (2d Cir. 1994).

4. The *Swidler & Berlin* majority and dissent make note of several recognized exceptions to the attorney-client privilege, including the testamentary exception and the exception for breach of duty by the lawyer or the client. These exceptions were included in Proposed Rule 503, which provided exceptions for "a communication relevant to an issue between parties who claim through the same deceased client," for "a communication relevant to an issue of breach of duty by the lawyer to his client or by the client to his lawyer," or for "a communication relevant to an issue concerning an attested document to which the lawyer is an attesting witness." *See* Proposed Fed. R. Evid. 503(d)(2), (3), (4). With regard to the first of these exceptions, the Advisory Committee reasoned that although the privilege normally survives the client's death, when "the identity of the person who steps into the client's shoes is in issue, as in a will contest, the identity of the person entitled to claim the privilege remains undetermined until the conclusion of the litigation. The choice is thus between allowing both sides or neither to assert the privilege...." Advisory Committee Note to Proposed Fed. R. Evid. 503(d). With regard to the second of these, the Advisory Committee reasoned that "[t]he exception is required by considerations of fairness and policy when questions arise out of dealings between attorney and client," and with regard to the third of these, the Advisory Committee reasoned that "[w]hen the lawyer acts as attesting witness, the approval of the client to his so doing may safely be assumed, and waiver of the privilege as to any relevant lawyer-client communications is a proper result." *Id.*

5. Are you persuaded by the instrumental arguments in favor of the attorney-client privilege? Not everyone has been persuaded by the wisdom of the privilege:

> But if such confidence, when reposed, is permitted to be violated, and if this be known (which, if such be the law, it will be), the consequence will be, that no such confidence will be reposed. Not reposed?—Well: and if it be not, wherein will consist the mischief? The man by the supposition is guilty; if not, by the supposition there is nothing to betray: let the law adviser say every thing he has heard, every thing he can have heard from his client, the client cannot have any thing to fear from it. That it will often happen that in the case supposed no such confidence will be reposed, is natural enough: the first thing the advocate or attorney will say to his client, will be—Remember that, whatever you say to me, I shall be obliged to tell, if asked about it. What, then, will be the consequence? That a guilty person will not in general be able to derive quite so much assis-

tance from his law adviser, in the way of concerting a false defence, as he may do at present.

5 Jeremy Bentham, Rationale of Judicial Evidence 301 (1827).

Problem 5-4: The Misdirected E-Mail

Assume the same facts as in Problem 5-1. After his meeting with Tom, Dawning gets on his computer and types an e-mail message to John Bonning, a legal intern working in his office, that reads "Agreed to take on Tom Trendell as a client today. Client involved in a hit-and-run accident, and indicated that he had seven drinks before getting behind the wheel." The e-mail contained a standard statement prior to the body of the message stating that "THIS MESSAGE CONTAINS CONFIDENTIAL MATERIALS PROTECTED BY THE ATTORNEY-CLIENT PRIVILEGE. IF YOU HAVE RECEIVED THIS MESSAGE IN ERROR, PLEASE DO NOT READ FURTHER AND CONTACT DAVID DAWNING AT 206-555-3343." Dawning accidentally types in the wrong e-mail address, and the message is delivered to Joanne Binnington. Joanne reads the message and — shocked by what she reads — turns a printout of the e-mail over to the police.

In the criminal proceedings against Tom, the prosecution seeks to offer into evidence a copy of the e-mail message, but Dawning seeks to exclude it by invoking the attorney-client privilege. In addition, the prosecution seeks to call Dawning as a witness, over a defense objection, to testify about his conversation with Tom, contending that sending the e-mail message to Binnington waived the attorney-client privilege as to that conversation.

How will the court resolve the privilege claims?

Gray v. Bicknell
86 F.3d 1472 (8th Cir. 1996)

MAGILL, Circuit Judge.

Ralph Gray and Gene Bicknell entered into a series of contracts in connection with the formation of a restaurant joint venture. After the joint venture failed, Gray commenced this diversity action against Bicknell for payment on two promissory notes, breach of contract, and breach of fiduciary duty. Bicknell counterclaimed for breach of contract and contribution on joint obligations.

Gray now appeals from a jury verdict, arguing, in part, that Bicknell waived his attorney-client privilege by inadvertently disclosing two letters written to him by his attorney....

III.

....

C.

In the course of providing discovery documents, Bicknell gave Gray two letters written to Bicknell by his attorney. The letters addressed a wide range of matters relating to the litigation. Both sides agree that absent this disclosure, the letters would have been subject to attorney-client privilege. Gray maintained that Bicknell intended to produce the letters, thereby deliberately and voluntarily waiving his attorney-client privilege with respect to all related documents. Bicknell countered that the litigation involved vast numbers of documents and that, in the course of responding to document requests, paralegals inadvertently included the letters. Bicknell argues that he waived his attorney-client privilege only with respect to those two letters. The district court agreed with Bicknell and held that the disclosure of the letters was inadvertent and that attorney-client privilege continued to protect other, related, documents.

In his motion for a new trial, Gray challenged the district court's ruling on the scope of Bicknell's attorney-client privilege, asserting that his right to a fair trial was materially prejudiced by the district court's denial of his request to review the files and records of Bicknell's attorney. The district court denied the motion. Noting that the Eighth Circuit had yet to define how inadvertent disclosure affects attorney-client privilege, the court followed what it called the "middle of the road" approach which involved an ad hoc balancing of several factors. Order at 5.

On appeal, Gray argues that the district court erred in employing the "middle of the road" approach. We note initially that the district court is in error when it looks to federal common law precedent to assess whether Bicknell inadvertently waived his attorney-client privilege. In diversity actions, state law determines the existence and scope of attorney-client privilege.... Neither the Missouri legislature nor the courts have had occasion to address the degree to which inadvertent disclosure of privileged documents constitutes waiver. Where a state court has yet to decide an issue, we must place ourselves in the position of the state supreme court and determine how that institution would likely resolve the matter.

As noted by this Court in *Pavlik v. Cargill, Inc.*, 9 F.3d 710, 713 (8th Cir. 1993), courts have generally followed one of three distinct approaches to attorney-client privilege waiver based on inadvertent disclosures: (1) the lenient approach, (2) the "middle of the road" approach, which is also called the *Hydraflow* approach, and (3) the strict approach.

Under the lenient approach, attorney-client privilege must be knowingly waived. Here, the determination of inadvertence is the end of the analysis. The attorney-client privilege exists for the benefit of the client and cannot be waived except by an intentional and knowing relinquishment. This Court has reasonably rejected this approach and we believe that the Missouri Supreme Court would do so as well. The lenient test creates little incentive for lawyers to maintain tight control over privileged material. While the lenient test remains true to the core principle of attorney-client privilege, which is that it exists to protect the client and must be waived by the client, it ignores the importance of confidentiality. To be privileged, attorney-client communications must remain confidential, and yet, under this test, the lack of confidentiality becomes meaningless so long as it occurred inadvertently.

The second approach is known as the strict test. Gray urges the Court to adopt such a test and refers to *In re Sealed Case*, 877 F.2d 976 (D.C. Cir. 1989), a case describing the D.C. Circuit's strict test. *In re Sealed Case* creates a strong incentive for careful document management, stating that "[t]he courts will grant no greater protection to those who assert the privilege than their own precautions warrant." *Id.* at 980. Under the strict test, any document produced, either intentionally or otherwise, loses its privileged status with the possible exception of situations where all precautions were taken. Once waiver has occurred, it extends "'to all other communications relating to the same subject matter.'" *Id.* at 981 (quoting *In Re Sealed Case*, 676 F.2d 793, 809 (D.C. Cir. 1982)).

While the strict test has some appeal in that it makes attorneys and clients accountable for their carelessness in handling privileged matters, we believe that Missouri courts would reject it because of its pronounced lack of flexibility and its significant intrusion on the attorney-client relationship. The strict test sacrifices the value of protecting client confidences for the sake of certainty of results. There is an important societal need for people to be able to employ and fully consult with those trained in the law for advice and guidance. The strict test would likely impede the ability of attorneys to fill this need by chilling communications between attorneys and clients. If, when a document stamped "attorney-client privileged" is inadvertently released, it and all related documents lose their privileged status, then clients will have much greater hesitancy to fully inform their attorney.

Finally, there is the middle test, sometimes called the *Hydraflow* test, which served as the basis for the district court's position. *Hydraflow*, 145 F.R.D. at 637. Under the *Hydraflow* test, the court undertakes a five-step analysis of the unintentionally disclosed document to determine the proper range of privilege to extend. These considerations are (1) the reasonableness of the precautions taken to prevent inadvertent disclosure in view of the extent of document production, (2) the number of inadvertent disclosures, (3) the extent of the disclosures, (4) the promptness of measures taken to rectify the disclosure, and (5) whether the overriding interest of justice would be served by relieving the party of its error. If, after completing this analysis, the court determines that waiver occurred, then those documents are no longer privileged. At the court's discretion, the privilege may also be determined to have been waived for related, but-as-yet undisclosed, documents.

We believe that Missouri courts would adopt the middle test. This test strikes the appropriate balance between protecting attorney-client privilege and allowing, in certain situations, the unintended release of privileged documents to waive that privilege. The middle test is best suited to achieving a fair result. It accounts for the errors that inevitably occur in modern, document-intensive litigation, but treats carelessness with privileged material as an indication of waiver. The middle test provides the most thoughtful approach, leaving the trial court broad discretion as to whether waiver occurred and, if so, the scope of that waiver. It requires a detailed court inquiry into the document practices of the party who inadvertently released the document. We therefore conclude that the district court did not abuse its discretion in refusing to grant a new trial....

Federal Rule of Evidence 502

Attorney-Client Privilege and Work Product; Limitations on Waiver

The following provisions apply, in the circumstances set out, to disclosure of a communication or information covered by the attorney-client privilege or work-product protection.

(a) **Disclosure Made in a Federal Proceeding or to a Federal Office or Agency; Scope of a Waiver.** When the disclosure is made in a federal proceeding or to a federal office or agency and waives the attorney-client privilege or work-product protection, the waiver extends to an undisclosed communication or information in a federal or state proceeding only if:

    (1) the waiver is intentional;

    (2) the disclosed and undisclosed communications or information concern the same subject matter; and

    (3) they ought in fairness to be considered together.

(b) **Inadvertent Disclosure.** When made in a federal proceeding or to a federal office or agency, the disclosure does not operate as a waiver in a federal or state proceeding if:

(1) the disclosure is inadvertent;

(2) the holder of the privilege or protection took reasonable steps to prevent disclosure; and

(3) the holder promptly took reasonable steps to rectify the error, including (if applicable) following Federal Rule of Civil Procedure 26(b)(5)(B).

(c) **Disclosure Made in a State Proceeding.** When the disclosure is made in a state proceeding and is not the subject of a state-court order concerning waiver, the disclosure does not operate as a waiver in a federal proceeding if the disclosure:

(1) would not be a waiver under this rule if it had been made in a federal proceeding; or

(2) is not a waiver under the law of the state where the disclosure occurred.

(d) **Controlling Effect of a Court Order.** A federal court may order that the privilege or protection is not waived by disclosure connected with the litigation pending before the court—in which event the disclosure is also not a waiver in any other federal or state proceeding.

(e) **Controlling Effect of a Party Agreement.** An agreement on the effect of disclosure in a federal proceeding is binding only on the parties to the agreement, unless it is incorporated into a court order.

(f) **Controlling Effect of this Rule.** Notwithstanding Rules 101 and 1101, this rule applies to state proceedings and to federal court-annexed and federal court-mandated arbitration proceedings, in the circumstances set out in the rule. And notwithstanding Rule 501, this rule applies even if state law provides the rule of decision.

(g) **Definitions.** In this rule:

(1) "attorney-client privilege" means the protection that applicable law provides for confidential attorney-client communications; and

(2) "work-product protection" means the protection that applicable law provides for tangible material (or its intangible equivalent) prepared in anticipation of litigation or for trial.

Notes and Questions

1. It is well-established that the attorney-client privilege belongs to the client, not the attorney. When an attorney invokes the attorney-client privilege, it is understood that he is doing so on the client's behalf. Similarly, an attorney cannot waive the privilege if the client does not wish to waive the privilege. E.g., *In re von Bulow*, 828 F.2d 94, 100–01 (2d Cir. 1987). Does it not, then, seem strange that under the strict and middle-of-the-road approaches, an attorney can waive the client's privilege through negligence even though he could not do the same thing intentionally? *See Georgetown Manor, Inc. v. Ethan Allen, Inc.*, 753 F. Supp. 936, 937–39 (S.D. Fla. 1991); *Mendenhall v. Barber-Greene Co.*, 531 F. Supp. 951, 954–55 (N.D. Ill. 1982).

2. Which approach to inadvertent waiver does Rule 502 adopt: the lenient approach, the "middle of the road" approach, or the strict approach?

3. The general rule on waiver has historically been that if a waiver of the privilege has occurred with respect to a particular communication between attorney and client, the privilege with respect to all other communications between attorney and client on that

point are likewise deemed waived, commonly referred to as a "subject matter waiver." What is the rationale for such a rule? Consider the following:

> [W]hen [a privilege holder's] conduct touches a certain point of disclosure, fairness requires that his privilege shall cease whether he intended that result or not. He cannot be allowed, after disclosing as much as he pleases, to withhold the remainder. He may elect to withhold or disclose, but after a certain point his election must remain final.

8 Wigmore, Evidence § 2327, at 636 (McNaughton rev. 1961).

Does this same principle apply in the federal courts today? Does it apply where the waiver is inadvertent? Does Rule 502 shed any light on the answers to these questions?

4. Throughout, Rule 502 refers to disclosures that are made *in* a federal or state "proceeding," which arguably means that the rule governs only if the disclosure occurs *after* a suit has commenced. Is that a fair reading of the rule, and if so, what rule governs if a disclosure is made *prior* to the commencement of a suit? *See Eden Isle Marina, Inc. v. United States*, 89 Fed. Cl. 480, 501 n.20, 503 n.21 (Fed. Cl. 2009) (noting the limiting language of Rule 502, but nonetheless choosing to treat such disclosures as if they were disclosed during the pendency of the litigation); *Bickler v. Senior Lifestyle Corp.*, 266 F.R.D. 379, 384 n.4 (D.Ariz. 2010) (looking to federal common law cases predating Rule 502 when the disclosure is made to a *state* agency); *Clarke v. J.P. Morgan Chase & Co.*, 2009 WL 970940, at *5 (S.D.N.Y. Apr. 10, 2009) (noting that the same factors identified in Rule 502 are applied as a matter of federal common law to extrajudicial disclosures). *But see Wi-LAN, Inc. v. LG Electronics, Inc.*, 2011 WL 500072, at *4 (N.D. Cal. Feb. 8, 2011) ("Whatever the basis for presuming otherwise in *Eden Isle Marina*, here [the] disclosure ... undeniably occurred *before*, not in, a 'Federal Proceeding.' The plain language of Rule 502 therefore confirms that the Rule simply does not apply....").

5. Who bears the burden of proving waiver under Rule 502? *See Eden Isle Marina, Inc. v. United States*, 89 Fed. Cl. 480, 503 (Fed. Cl. 2009) (holding that the party invoking the privilege bears the burden of proving that it has *not* been waived); *Amobi v. District of Columbia Dep't of Corrections*, 262 F.R.D. 45, 53 (D.D.C. 2009) (same); *Heriot v. Byrne*, 257 F.R.D. 645, 658 (N.D. Ill. 2009) (same). *See also Callan v. Christian Audigier, Inc.*, 263 F.R.D. 564, 565–566 & n.3 (C.D. Cal. 2009) (noting that Rule 502 does not alter pre-Rule 502 practice placing the burden of proof on the party invoking the privilege). *But see Rhoads Industries, Inc. v. Building Materials Corp. of America*, 254 F.R.D. 216, 223 (E.D. Pa. 2008) (holding that the party seeking to overcome the privilege bears the burden of proof).

6. Where a conflict exists between federal and state privilege law governing waiver of the attorney-client privilege, what principle does Rule 502 adopt for resolving this conflict? As you read the materials in the remainder of this chapter, consider the extent to which this principle is consistent with that employed generally under Rule 501. Which principle is superior for resolving conflicts?

C. Spousal Privileges

Problem 5-5: Love & Loyalty, Federal Style

Gordon Oliver Davis is arrested on charges that he murdered Victor Vance in Yellowstone National Park early in the morning on July 2, 2011. The government initiates criminal proceedings against Davis in federal court, charging him with murder in violation of 18 U.S.C. §1111. In a separate proceeding, Vance's widow files a wrongful death action against Davis in federal court pursuant to 16 U.S.C. §457, which provides the survivors of a deceased person with a federal cause of action for wrongful death where the wrongful or negligent act resulting in death occurs within the boundaries of a national park. Both the government in the criminal case and Vance's widow in the civil case seek to call Mary Ellen Davis, Davis' wife, as a witness. They have cause to believe that Mrs. Davis was awake when her husband returned home on the morning of July 2, 2011, may have seen her husband covered in blood, and may have seen him dispose of the murder weapon. They also believe that at some point, Davis may have said to his wife, when they were alone, that he killed Vance. Both Davis and his wife object on the grounds of privilege.

How will the court dispose of the privilege claims? How, if at all, would your answer differ if Mrs. Davis were willing to testify? If the couple divorced one another at some point after the events in question but prior to the time Mrs. Davis' testimony was sought? If the couple were still legally married at the time Mrs. Davis' testimony was sought, but they were separated? If the couple were not married at the time that the observations and communications took place, but were married at the time of the trial? If Mr. Davis had communicated with Mrs. Davis via an email message that he sent to her using a computer at his workplace? If the couple were never married, but were in a long-term, committed relationship?

Problem 5-6: Love & Loyalty, Minnesota Style

Assume the same facts as in Problem 5-5, except that all the events at issue took place in the State of Minnesota and that the case is being adjudicated in a state court in Minnesota. Minnesota law provides in pertinent part as follows:

> A husband cannot be examined for or against his wife without her consent, nor a wife for or against her husband without his consent, nor can either, during the marriage or afterwards, without the consent of the other, be examined as to any communication made by one to the other during the marriage. This exception does not apply to a civil action or proceeding by one against the other, nor to a criminal action or proceeding for a crime committed by one against the other or against a child of either or against a child under the care of either spouse, nor to a criminal action or proceeding in which one is charged with homicide or an attempt to commit homicide and the date of the marriage of the defendant is subsequent to the date of the offense, nor to an action or proceeding for nonsupport, neglect, dependency, or termination of parental rights.

Minn. Stat. §595.02(1)(a).

How would your answers to the questions posed in Problem 5-5 differ as applied to the facts of this problem?

Problem 5-7: Love & Loyalty, Washington Style

Kevin, a citizen of Washington State, files a lawsuit against ABC Corporation (a New York corporation with its principal place of business in New York and a branch office in Washington State) in federal court, alleging that the latter discriminated against him on the basis of his sex and his sexual orientation. Kevin's claims arise under a Washington State statute as well as Title VII of the Civil Rights Act of 1964, a federal statute.

Under Washington State law, same-sex couples in committed relationships can enter into domestic partnerships, which provide some of the rights and responsibilities of marriage. Moreover, Washington privilege law provides as follows:

> A spouse or domestic partner shall not be examined for or against his or her spouse or domestic partner, without the consent of the spouse or domestic partner; nor can either during marriage or during the domestic partnership or afterward, be without the consent of the other, examined as to any communication made by one to the other during the marriage or the domestic partnership....

Wash. Stat. § 5.60.060(1).

At trial, ABC Corporation seeks to call as a witness Tom, Kevin's domestic partner. They would like to ask Tom to testify about confidential communications that Kevin made to him, but both Tom and Kevin object, claiming that the testimony is privileged under both federal and state law.

What are the best arguments in favor and against a finding that the testimony sought by ABC Corporation is privileged?

Trammel v. United States
445 U.S. 40 (1980)

Mr. Chief Justice BURGER delivered the opinion of the Court.

We granted certiorari to consider whether an accused may invoke the privilege against adverse spousal testimony so as to exclude the voluntary testimony of his wife. This calls for a re-examination of *Hawkins v. United States*, 358 U.S. 74 (1958).

I

On March 10, 1976, petitioner Otis Trammel was indicted with two others, Edwin Lee Roberts and Joseph Freeman, for importing heroin into the United States from Thailand and the Philippine Islands and for conspiracy to import heroin in violation of 21 U.S.C. §§ 952(a), 962(a), and 963. The indictment also named six unindicted co-conspirators, including petitioner's wife Elizabeth Ann Trammel.

According to the indictment, petitioner and his wife flew from the Philippines to California in August 1975, carrying with them a quantity of heroin. Freeman and Roberts assisted them in its distribution. Elizabeth Trammel then traveled to Thailand where she purchased another supply of the drug. On November 3, 1975, with four ounces of heroin on her person, she boarded a plane for the United States. During a routine customs search in Hawaii, she was searched, the heroin was discovered, and she was arrested. After discussions with Drug Enforcement Administration agents, she agreed to cooperate with the Government.

Prior to trial on this indictment, petitioner moved to sever his case from that of Roberts and Freeman. He advised the court that the Government intended to call his wife as an adverse witness and asserted his claim to a privilege to prevent her from testifying against him. At a hearing on the motion, Mrs. Trammel was called as a Government witness under a grant of use immunity. She testified that she and petitioner were married in May 1975 and that they remained married.[1] She explained that her cooperation with the Government was based on assurances that she would be given lenient treatment.[2] She then described, in considerable detail, her role and that of her husband in the heroin distribution conspiracy.

After hearing this testimony, the District Court ruled that Mrs. Trammel could testify in support of the Government's case to any act she observed during the marriage and to any communication "made in the presence of a third person"; however, confidential communications between petitioner and his wife were held to be privileged and inadmissible. The motion to sever was denied.

At trial, Elizabeth Trammel testified within the limits of the court's pretrial ruling; her testimony, as the Government concedes, constituted virtually its entire case against petitioner. He was found guilty on both the substantive and conspiracy charges and sentenced to an indeterminate term of years pursuant to the Federal Youth Corrections Act, 18 U.S.C. § 5010(b).

In the Court of Appeals petitioner's only claim of error was that the admission of the adverse testimony of his wife, over his objection, contravened this Court's teaching in *Hawkins v. United States, supra,* and therefore constituted reversible error. The Court of Appeals rejected this contention. It concluded that *Hawkins* did not prohibit "the voluntary testimony of a spouse who appears as an unindicted co-conspirator under grant of immunity from the Government in return for her testimony."

II

The privilege claimed by petitioner has ancient roots. Writing in 1628, Lord Coke observed that "it hath beene resolved by the Justices that a wife cannot be produced either against or for her husband." 1 E. Coke, A Commentarie upon Littleton 6b (1628). See, generally, 8 J. Wigmore, Evidence § 2227 (McNaughton rev. 1961). This spousal disqualification sprang from two canons of medieval jurisprudence: first, the rule that an accused was not permitted to testify in his own behalf because of his interest in the proceeding; second, the concept that husband and wife were one, and that since the woman had no recognized separate legal existence, the husband was that one. From those two now long-abandoned doctrines, it followed that what was inadmissible from the lips of the defendant-husband was also inadmissible from his wife.

Despite its medieval origins, this rule of spousal disqualification remained intact in most common-law jurisdictions well into the 19th century.... Indeed, it was not until 1933, in *Funk v. United States,* 290 U.S. 371, that this Court abolished the testimonial disqualification in the federal courts, so as to permit the spouse of a defendant to testify in the defendant's behalf. *Funk,* however, left undisturbed the rule that either spouse could prevent the other from giving adverse testimony. The rule thus evolved into one of privilege rather than one of absolute disqualification.

The modern justification for this privilege against adverse spousal testimony is its perceived role in fostering the harmony and sanctity of the marriage relationship. Notwithstanding this benign purpose, the rule was sharply criticized. Professor Wigmore termed

---

1. In response to the question whether divorce was contemplated, Mrs. Trammel testified that her husband had said that "I would go my way and he would go his."

2. The Government represents to the Court that Elizabeth Trammel has not been prosecuted for her role in the conspiracy.

it "the merest anachronism in legal theory and an indefensible obstruction to truth in practice." 8 Wigmore § 2228, at 221. The Committee on Improvements in the Law of Evidence of the American Bar Association called for its abolition. 63 American Bar Association Reports 594–595 (1938). In its place, Wigmore and others suggested a privilege protecting only private marital communications, modeled on the privilege between priest and penitent, attorney and client, and physician and patient. See 8 Wigmore § 2332 *et seq.*[5]

These criticisms influenced the American Law Institute, which, in its 1942 Model Code of Evidence advocated a privilege for marital confidences, but expressly rejected a rule vesting in the defendant the right to exclude all adverse testimony of his spouse. See American Law Institute, Model Code of Evidence, Rule 215 (1942). In 1953 the Uniform Rules of Evidence, drafted by the National Conference of Commissioners on Uniform State Laws, followed a similar course; it limited the privilege to confidential communications and "abolishe[d] the rule, still existing in some states, and largely a sentimental relic, of not requiring one spouse to testify against the other in a criminal action." See Rule 23 (2) and comments. Several state legislatures enacted similarly patterned provisions into law.

In *Hawkins v. United States*, 358 U.S. 74 (1958), this Court considered the continued vitality of the privilege against adverse spousal testimony in the federal courts. There the District Court had permitted petitioner's wife, over his objection, to testify against him. With one questioning concurring opinion, the Court held the wife's testimony inadmissible; it took note of the critical comments that the common-law rule had engendered, but chose not to abandon it. Also rejected was the Government's suggestion that the Court modify the privilege by vesting it in the witness-spouse, with freedom to testify or not independent of the defendant's control. The Court viewed this proposed modification as antithetical to the widespread belief, evidenced in the rules then in effect in a majority of the States and in England, "that the law should not force or encourage testimony which might alienate husband and wife, or further inflame existing domestic differences."

Hawkins, then, left the federal privilege for adverse spousal testimony where it found it, continuing "a rule which bars the testimony of one spouse against the other unless both consent." Id., at 78. Accord, *Wyatt v. United States*, 362 U.S. 525, 528 (1960).[7] However, in so doing, the Court made clear that its decision was not meant to "foreclose whatever changes in the rule may eventually be dictated by 'reason and experience.'" 358 U.S., at 79.

III

A

The Federal Rules of Evidence acknowledge the authority of the federal courts to continue the evolutionary development of testimonial privileges in federal criminal trials

---

5. This Court recognized just such a confidential marital communications privilege in *Wolfle v. United States*, 291 U.S. 7 (1934), and in *Blau v. United States*, 340 U.S. 332 (1951). In neither case, however, did the Court adopt the Wigmore view that the communications privilege be substituted *in place of* the privilege against adverse spousal testimony. The privilege as to confidential marital communications is not at issue in the instant case; accordingly, our holding today does not disturb *Wolfle* and *Blau*.

7. The decision in *Wyatt* recognized an exception to *Hawkins* for cases in which one spouse commits a crime against the other. This exception, placed on the ground of necessity, was a longstanding one at common law. See *Lord Audley's Case*, 123 Eng. Rep. 1140 (1631); 8 Wigmore § 2239. It has been expanded since then to include crimes against the spouse's property, see *Herman v. United States*, 220 F.2d 219, 226 (CA4 1955), and in recent years crimes against children of either spouse, *United States v. Allery*, 526 F.2d 1362 (CA8 1975). Similar exceptions have been found to the confidential marital communications privilege. See 8 Wigmore § 2338.

[governed by the common law as interpreted by United States courts in the light of reason and experience]. Fed.Rule Evid. 501. Cf. *Wolfle v. United States*, 291 U.S. 7, 12 (1934). The general mandate of Rule 501 was substituted by the Congress for a set of privilege rules drafted by the Judicial Conference Advisory Committee on Rules of Evidence and approved by the Judicial Conference of the United States and by this Court. That proposal defined nine specific privileges, including a husband-wife privilege which would have codified the *Hawkins* rule and eliminated the privilege for confidential marital communications. See proposed Fed.Rule Evid. 505. In rejecting the proposed Rules and enacting Rule 501, Congress manifested an affirmative intention not to freeze the law of privilege. Its purpose rather was to "provide the courts with the flexibility to develop rules of privilege on a case-by-case basis," 120 Cong. Rec. 40891 (1974) (statement of Rep. Hungate), and to leave the door open to change. See also S. Rep. No. 93-1277, p. 11 (1974); H. R. Rep. No. 93-650, p. 8 (1973).[8]

Although Rule 501 confirms the authority of the federal courts to reconsider the continued validity of the *Hawkins* rule, the long history of the privilege suggests that it ought not to be casually cast aside. That the privilege is one affecting marriage, home, and family relationships—already subject to much erosion in our day—also counsels caution. At the same time, we cannot escape the reality that the law on occasion adheres to doctrinal concepts long after the reasons which gave them birth have disappeared and after experience suggest the need for change. This was recognized in *Funk* where the Court "decline[d] to enforce ... ancient rule[s] of the common law under conditions as they now exist." For, as Mr. Justice Black admonished in another setting, "[w]hen precedent and precedent alone is all the argument that can be made to support a court-fashioned rule, it is time for the rule's creator to destroy it." *Francis v. Southern Pacific Co.*, 333 U.S. 445, 471 (1948) (dissenting opinion).

B

Since 1958, when *Hawkins* was decided, support for the privilege against adverse spousal testimony has been eroded further. Thirty-one jurisdictions, including Alaska and Hawaii, then allowed an accused a privilege to prevent adverse spousal testimony. The number has now declined to 24.[9] In 1974, the National Conference on Uniform State Laws revised its Uniform Rules of Evidence, but again rejected the *Hawkins* rule in favor of a limited privilege for confidential communications. See Uniform Rules of Evidence, Rule 504. That proposed rule has been enacted in Arkansas, North Dakota, and Oklahoma—each of which in 1958 permitted an accused to exclude adverse spousal testimony. The trend in state

---

8. Petitioner's reliance on 28 U.S.C. § [2074(b)] for the proposition that this Court is without power to reconsider *Hawkins* is ill-founded. That provision limits this Court's *statutory* rulemaking authority by providing that rules "creating, abolishing, or modifying a privilege shall have no force or effect unless ... approved by act of Congress." It was enacted principally to insure that state rules of privilege would apply in diversity jurisdiction cases unless Congress authorized otherwise. In Rule 501 Congress makes clear that § [2074(b)] was not intended to prevent the federal courts from developing testimonial privilege law in federal criminal cases on a case-by-case basis "in [the] light of reason and experience"; indeed Congress encouraged such development.

9. Eight States provide that one spouse is incompetent to testify against the other in a criminal proceeding.... Sixteen States provide a privilege against adverse spousal testimony and vest the privilege in both spouses or in the defendant-spouse alone.... Nine States entitle the witness-spouse alone to assert a privilege against adverse spousal testimony.... The remaining 17 States have abolished the privilege in criminal cases.... In 1901, Congress enacted a rule of evidence for the District of Columbia that made husband and wife "competent but not compellable to testify for or against each other," except as to confidential communications. This provision, which vests the privilege against adverse spousal testimony in the witness-spouse, remains in effect.

law toward divesting the accused of the privilege to bar adverse spousal testimony has special relevance because the laws of marriage and domestic relations are concerns traditionally reserved to the states. Scholarly criticism of the Hawkins rule has also continued unabated.

C

Testimonial exclusionary rules and privileges contravene the fundamental principle that "'the public ... has a right to every man's evidence.'" *United States v. Bryan*, 339 U.S. 323, 331 (1950). As such, they must be strictly construed and accepted "only to the very limited extent that permitting a refusal to testify or excluding relevant evidence has a public good transcending the normally predominant principle of utilizing all rational means for ascertaining truth." *Elkins v. United States*, 364 U.S. 206, 234 (1960) (Frankfurter, J., dissenting). Accord, *United States v. Nixon*, 418 U.S. 683, 709–710 (1974). Here we must decide whether the privilege against adverse spousal testimony promotes sufficiently important interests to outweigh the need for probative evidence in the administration of criminal justice.

It is essential to remember that the *Hawkins* privilege is not needed to protect information privately disclosed between husband and wife in the confidence of the marital relationship—once described by this Court as "the best solace of human existence." *Stein v. Bowman*, 13 Pet., at 223. Those confidences are privileged under the independent rule protecting confidential marital communications. *Blau v. United States*, 340 U.S. 332 (1951); see n. 5, *supra*. The *Hawkins* privilege is invoked, not to exclude private marital communications, but rather to exclude evidence of criminal acts and of communications made in the presence of third persons.

No other testimonial privilege sweeps so broadly. The privileges between priest and penitent, attorney and client, and physician and patient limit protection to private communications. These privileges are rooted in the imperative need for confidence and trust. The priest-penitent privilege recognizes the human need to disclose to a spiritual counselor, in total and absolute confidence, what are believed to be flawed acts or thoughts and to receive priestly consolation and guidance in return. The lawyer-client privilege rests on the need for the advocate and counselor to know all that relates to the client's reasons for seeking representation if the professional mission is to be carried out. Similarly, the physician must know all that a patient can articulate in order to identify and to treat disease; barriers to full disclosure would impair diagnosis and treatment.

The *Hawkins* rule stands in marked contrast to these three privileges. Its protection is not limited to confidential communications; rather it permits an accused to exclude all adverse spousal testimony. As Jeremy Bentham observed more than a century and a half ago, such a privilege goes far beyond making "every man's house his castle," and permits a person to convert his house into "a den of thieves." 5 Rationale of Judicial Evidence 340 (1827). It "secures, to every man, one safe and unquestionable and every ready accomplice for every imaginable crime." *Id.*, at 338.

The ancient foundations for so sweeping a privilege have long since disappeared. Nowhere in the common-law world—indeed in any modern society—is a woman regarded as chattel or demeaned by denial of a separate legal identity and the dignity associated with recognition as a whole human being. Chip by chip, over the years those archaic notions have been cast aside so that "[n]o longer is the female destined solely for the home and the rearing of the family, and only the male for the marketplace and the world of ideas." *Stanton v. Stanton*, 421 U.S. 7, 14–15 (1975).

The contemporary justification for affording an accused such a privilege is also un-persuasive. When one spouse is willing to testify against the other in a criminal proceeding—whatever the motivation—their relationship is almost certainly in disrepair; there is probably little in the way of marital harmony for the privilege to preserve. In these circumstances, a rule of evidence that permits an accused to prevent adverse spousal testimony seems far more likely to frustrate justice than to foster family peace.[12] Indeed, there is reason to believe that vesting the privilege in the accused could actually undermine the marital relationship. For example, in a case such as this the Government is unlikely to offer a wife immunity and lenient treatment if it knows that her husband can prevent her from giving adverse testimony. If the Government is dissuaded from making such an offer, the privilege can have the untoward effect of permitting one spouse to escape justice at the expense of the other. It hardly seems conducive to the preservation of the marital relation to place a wife in jeopardy solely by virtue of her husband's control over her testimony.

IV

Our consideration of the foundations for the privilege and its history satisfy us that "reason and experience" no longer justify so sweeping a rule as that found acceptable by the Court in *Hawkins*. Accordingly, we conclude that the existing rule should be modified so that the witness-spouse alone has a privilege to refuse to testify adversely; the witness may be neither compelled to testify nor foreclosed from testifying. This modification—vesting the privilege in the witness-spouse—furthers the important public interest in marital harmony without unduly burdening legitimate law enforcement needs.

Here, petitioner's spouse chose to testify against him. That she did so after a grant of immunity and assurances of lenient treatment does not render her testimony involuntary....

[The concurring opinion of Justice Stewart is omitted.]

United States v. Singleton
260 F.3d 1295 (11th Cir. 2001)

PER CURIAM:

Donna Singleton (appellant) was indicted on three counts of making false statements to a federally-insured credit union (Title 18 U.S.C. § 1014). The jury convicted her on June 30, 1999 of all three counts.... She contends: (1) that the district court erred by refusing to apply the marital communications privilege to a conversation between the appellant and her then-husband Cedric Singleton (Cedric)....

Facts

The appellant and Cedric began living together in 1992 and were married in January 1995. The marriage was a rocky one involving, during the marriage, allegations of adultery by both partners and physical altercations. Prior to December 1996, appellant filed charges of domestic abuse against Cedric, which resulted in his being jailed. The parties

---

12. It is argued that abolishing the privilege will permit the Government to come between husband and wife, pitting one against the other. That, too, misses the mark. Neither *Hawkins*, nor any other privilege, prevents the Government from enlisting one spouse to give information concerning the other or to aid in the other's apprehension. It is only the spouse's testimony in the courtroom that is prohibited.

separated in December 1996 after another physical altercation involving appellant's boyfriend, Earl Davis. A petition for divorce was filed by appellant in September 1997. The divorce became final in May 1998.

In December 1997, Cedric was visiting his daughter at appellant's residence. While there, he searched for papers related to a prior divorce from another woman, and found documents that indicated that appellant had filed the false loan applications for which she was eventually convicted. In January 1998, he took the documents to the FBI. He agreed with the FBI to wear a recording device and to tape a conversation with appellant. Cedric met the appellant at a restaurant on January 29, 1998. During the taped conversation, appellant made incriminating statements. After the taped conversation, the FBI questioned appellant and obtained her consent to search her residence, where other incriminating evidence was found.

Over the appellant's objection, the taped conversation with Cedric and testimony concerning it were admitted at trial....

Marital Privilege

Appellant's first issue is one of first impression in this circuit. It arises out of the admission into evidence of the conversation taped while the Singletons were married, but separated, and testimony concerning it. There are two recognized types of marital privilege: the marital confidential communications privilege and the spousal testimonial privilege. *Trammel v. United States*, 445 U.S. 40, 50–51 (1980). The marital privilege asserted by the appellant is marital communications privilege....[2] The threshold issue in this case is whether the marital communications privilege applies to communications made while the spouses, although still technically married, are living separate lives with no reasonable expectation of reconciliation (in other words, the couple is "permanently separated"). The appellant, while recognizing that no circuit court has so held, argues that this court, in a case of first impression, should "adopt a bright-line rule that the marital privilege lasts until the marriage formally ends" with a divorce decree. The appellant's justification for this argument is that, "[t]his standard would avoid the intrusive inquiries that were posed to the appellant and her estranged husband in this case." Appellant also argues that such a rule would "create predictability around the duration of the privilege" and would avoid discouraging "communication between couples exploring reconciliation."

The appellant's "bright-line" argument has not been accepted by any circuit court that has considered the availability of the marital communications privilege for a conversation taking place when the spouses are permanently separated....

We agree with the other circuits which have determined that the privilege is not available when the parties are permanently separated; that is, living separately with no reasonable expectation of reconciliation. Our decision is bolstered by the factors generally applicable to privilege assertions, and more particularly, to marital privilege assertions.... The Supreme Court has held that privileges must be narrowly construed because they impede the search for truth. *United States v. Nixon*, 418 U.S. 683, 710 (1974). While the confidentiality of communications during a valid marriage is presumed, there is no reasonable basis for

---

2. Unlike the testimonial privilege, the communications privilege generally survives a terminated marriage. *Pereira v. United States*, 347 U.S. 1, 6 (1954). The unanimous rulings of other circuit courts, however, have held that marital communications made while the parties are legally married but permanently separated are not privileged. The adverse spousal testimonial privilege is sometimes referred to as spousal incompetency. It can be asserted only by the witness-spouse. The marital communication privilege, when available, can be asserted by a defendant to prevent his or her spouse from testifying concerning the communication and to exclude related evidence.

asserting the privilege when the marriage is "moribund." If the spouses are permanently separated at the time of the communication, the reasonableness of the expectation of the spouse who asserts the privilege that the communication will be kept confidential is diminished. There is also less societal interest in protecting the marital relationship of permanently separated spouses, especially when such protection would operate to "severely hamper the truth finding process essential to a criminal trial." *Byrd*, 750 F.2d at 593. The need for a search for truth in judicial proceedings weighs against construing the privilege any more broadly than necessary to achieve its ends. In *Cameron*, the old Fifth Circuit rejected, albeit in a testimonial privilege case, the argument that the privilege should be available in "moribund" marriages. There is no reasonable distinction to be made in the case of a marital communication privilege assertion.

Having determined that the marital communication privilege is not available in cases of permanent separation prior to divorce, we next consider the factors that should be considered by district courts in determining whether there was a permanent separation at the time of the communication. A district court should focus upon the following three objective factors as especially important: (1) Was the couple cohabiting?; (2) if they were not cohabiting, how long had they been living apart?; and (3) had either spouse filed for divorce? A district court may, of course, consider other objective evidence of the parties' intent or lack of intent to reconcile. *See Cameron*, 556 F.2d at 756 (finding permanent separation in testimonial privilege case where there was "a great disparity between the amount of time that the couple cohabited and the time that one of the other chose not to live together," and where one of the spouses already entered into "a more permanent living arrangement with another partner than with his spouse"). A court also may (not must) consider testimony by the spouses themselves regarding their subjective intent, but simply because one or both spouses testifies that the couple intended to stay married and that the communications at issue were thought by them to be protected, the communications need not be deemed privileged where objective factors undermine the credibility of that testimony.

The trial judge conducted a hearing outside the presence of the jury concerning the state of the Singletons' marital relationship at the time of the taped conversation. Once the Government opposed the allowance of the privilege, the burden of proof was on the appellant to prove by a preponderance of the evidence that she and Cedric were not permanently separated at the time of the subject communication. We review a district court's ruling on a claim of evidentiary privilege only for abuse of discretion. Factual findings of a district court are reviewed only for clear error....

The following evidence was presented to the district court: (1) the appellant alleged, in a divorce action complaint filed in September 1997, that Cedric had abandoned her in December 1996; (2) during the marriage Cedric had accused appellant of having affairs with her co-worker(s) and contractor(s) based on documents he found; (3) the appellant, at the time of the taped conversation, was living with Earl Davis, a co-worker; (4) the Singletons had a physical altercation shortly before their December 1996 separation; (5) after December 1996, Cedric lived with appellant's cousin, his own brother, and a former wife named Stephanie; (6) appellant stayed at Cedric's brother's house three or four times while Cedric was there; (7) Cedric spent one night, possibly two nights, at appellant's house after December 1996 (on one of the occasions, her boyfriend showed up; there was an altercation, and Cedric left); (8) in 1997, there was another altercation involving appellant, Earl Davis, and Cedric, in which knives were drawn; (9) the appellant and Cedric continued to trade accusations of infidelity throughout the separation; (10) the spouses had tried marriage counseling around March 1997, and did not thereafter reconcile; (11) the spouses discussed reconciliation in the taped conversation, but appellant also told Cedric that she would shoot him if she had a gun, and several times during the taped conversation, appellant told Cedric that she hated him; (12) appellant also told Cedric, "It's 'cause I hate your ass and this is how I feel about you Cedric. I don't feel nothing nice for you any damn more;" and (13) Cedric testified that, at the time of the taped conversation, reconciliation was unlikely.

We conclude that the district court did not clearly err by finding that the Singletons were permanently separated at the time of the communication and that it did not abuse its discretion in denying the privilege to the appellant....

United States v. Sriram

2001 WL 59055 (N.D. Ill. Jan. 23, 2001)

SCHENKIER, Magistrate J.

The Government has filed this civil action seeking injunctive relief and damages based on its assertion that the defendant, Krishnaswami Sriram ("Dr. Sriram") has submitted numerous false and fraudulent claims for reimbursement for Medicare services. On August 17, 2000, the district judge entered a temporary restraining order that, among other things, froze the following assets: (a) a certificate of deposit in excess of $3 million held in Account Number 700017538 at the Lake Forest Bank & Trust; (b) real estate and improvements located at 611 Hunter Lane in Lake Forest, Illinois; and (c) real estate and improvements located at 715 East Falcon Drive in Arlington Heights, Illinois. The matter presently is before the Court on the Government's request for a preliminary injunction maintaining the freeze on those assets.

This civil action proceeds against the backdrop of a parallel criminal proceeding by the Government against Dr. Sriram, in which an indictment alleges that by his Medicare activities, Dr. Sriram has committed mail fraud in violation of 18 U.S.C. § 1341 and health care fraud in violation of 18 U.S.C. § 1347. In that indictment, the Government also seeks forfeiture of assets, including the three assets described above that are the subject of the preliminary injunction hearing.

Shortly before the preliminary injunction hearing, which commenced on January 16, 2001, the Government indicated its intention to call as a witness Dr. Sriram's wife. The Government indicated that it wished to ask Ms. Sriram questions touching on five different categories: (a) matters relating to her involvement in Sriram's ongoing medical business; (b) her knowledge of sources of family income other than Medicare payments; (c) the source of deposits into the various bank accounts at Lake Forest Bank; (d) the source of payments to pay off the mortgages on the properties in Lake Forest and Arlington Heights; and (e) the source of money used for deposits into Lake Forest Account Number 7000017538. The Government indicated that it had not provided, and would not provide, any assurance that Ms. Sriram's testimony or its fruits would not be used in the criminal proceeding against Dr. Sriram. Nor did the Government disavow the possibility that Ms. Sriram herself might be a target of the criminal investigation.

The defense indicated that Ms. Sriram intended to assert the spousal testimonial privilege. The Government asserted that none of the testimony it seeks from Ms. Sriram would be adverse to Dr. Sriram—although, if so, one might wonder why the Government seeks to offer it. On January 16, 2001, during the taking of evidence at the preliminary injunction hearing, the Court delivered an oral ruling holding that the marital communication privilege applies to this proceeding, and that the propriety of any assertions of that privilege by Ms. Sriram would be considered on a question by question basis. In this opinion, the Court sets forth the reasoning underlying that ruling.

I.

Unlike the marital communications privilege, which confers a privilege upon both spouses against testifying about any confidential communications, the spousal privilege allows the testifying spouse to assert a privilege against providing adverse testimony against the other spouse....

The *Trammel* court recounted the substantial costs exacted by this privilege. Like all privileges, the spousal testimony privilege is at tension with the "fundamental principle that 'the public ... has a right to every man's evidence.'" *Trammel*, 445 U.S. at 50. Moreover, the costs exacted are more extreme than is true with other privileges because the spousal testimonial privilege sweeps more broadly than any other privilege: it is not limited merely to confidential communications, but extends to anything one spouse may have said to another in circumstances where there could be no reasonable expectation of confidentiality. *Id.* at 51. Thus, the privilege seeks "not to exclude private marital communications, but rather to exclude evidence of criminal acts and of communications made in the presence of third persons." *Id....*

II.

.... The cases addressing the privilege typically arise in the context of criminal proceedings. The issue before the Court here is the propriety of a preliminary injunction freezing assets under 18 U.S.C. § 1345. Although that provision is located in the title covering criminal laws, by the express terms of the statute an action brought under Section 1345 is a "civil proceeding." Thus, at the threshold, the Court must confront the question of whether the privilege applies to a civil proceeding.

In *Ryan v. Commissioner*, 568 F.2d 531, 544 (7th Cir. 1977), a case that preceded *Trammel* by three years, the Seventh Circuit discussed but did not decide the question. The Court acknowledged that "an argument can be made that no policy supports the distinction between allowing the privilege against adverse spousal testimony in criminal cases but not in civil cases." However, the Seventh Circuit also noted that a case could be made that the modern rationale for the privilege—the prevention of marital discord—is more weighty in a criminal than a civil matter, "because it encourages the preservation of a marriage that might assist the defendant spouse in his or her rehabilitation efforts." Because independent grounds existed for the Court's decision upholding a tax court refusal to allow assertion of the privilege, the Seventh Circuit found it unnecessary to "fully defend the civil-criminal distinction" and to limit the privilege to instances "where a spouse who is neither a victim nor participant observes evidence of the other spouse's crime."

In *United States v. Yerardi*, 192 F.3d 14, 19 (1st Cir. 1999), the court commented that while some cases assume the privilege may be asserted only in criminal proceedings, "it is hard to find a square holding to this effect." However, the *Yerardi* court suggested that it would draw precisely that distinction in the appropriate case. The court hypothesized that the testifying spouse "could readily be called by the plaintiff in a civil damage action to establish that [the defendant spouse's] negligence had caused a traffic accident in which the plaintiff was injured, and [the testifying spouse] could not ordinarily assert the privilege in such a case even though her testimony might lead to a large damage award against [the defendant spouse]." But in that case, too, the court found it unnecessary to resolve the issue, since there the civil proceeding was "ancillary to a criminal case and seeks to recover a penalty under criminal forfeiture provisions," and in addition, "raises an appreciable risk of contributing to future criminal prosecution of" [ ] the spouse defendant.

This Court doubts that adverse testimony by a spouse ever would be likely to promote a harmonious marital relationship—whether that testimony came in a criminal case, or (as here) a civil case in which the defendant spouse is being pursued for millions of dollars in damages. In that respect, it is difficult to say that the privilege would serve the interest of avoiding marital discord in criminal cases but not in civil cases. However, the Court must balance that interest against the costs of the privilege, which *Trammel* explained are substantial, and the fact that the history of this privilege over the past 70 years shows that the trend has been to restrict rather than expanded [sic] it. Balancing these factors, the Court finds that the spousal testimonial privilege would not apply to adverse testimony given by a spouse in a civil proceeding that is untethered to a criminal proceeding.

However, this is not such an "untethered" civil proceeding. Like *Yerardi*, this case is plainly connected to the pending criminal prosecution. The Government has not represented, and declines to represent, that the fruits of Ms. Sriram's testimony—if adverse to Mr. Sriram—will not be used in the criminal proceeding. In *Yerardi*, the court explained that the Government could overcome the spousal testimonial privilege by making a binding commitment not to use the testimony directly or indirectly in criminal proceedings against the other spouse. And, in *Ryan*, the Seventh Circuit found it significant that the spousal testimony being sought could not be used against the defendant spouse, because the Government had provided a grant of use immunity barring the use of information obtained in any subsequent criminal proceeding....

The Government here has not provided such immunity or assurance, and thus we are faced with a situation similar to that confronted in *Yerardi*. Given the Supreme Court's criticisms of the spousal testimonial privilege in *Trammel*, the day may come when that privilege is abolished altogether. However, the Supreme Court's most recent pronouncement indicates that day has not yet arrived, and on the facts before the Court, we find that the spousal testimonial privilege may be asserted in this case.

That leaves the question of whether the testimony the Government seeks to elicit from Ms. Sriram would be adverse. As the Court has explained above, the reason the privilege applies in this case is because of the potential use of adverse testimony obtained by the Government here in the related criminal case. Thus, the touchstone for whether the testimony sought from Ms. Sriram is "adverse" will not be whether it might assist the government in this civil proceeding, but instead, whether the testimony might be used adversely by the Government in the pending criminal proceeding. Consistent with the prevailing case law, the Court will determine the applicability of the privilege on a question by question basis.

United States v. Etkin

2008 WL 482281 (S.D.N.Y. Feb. 20, 2008)

KENNETH M. KARAS, District Judge.

. . . .

Following a Grand Jury Indictment for extortion in violation of the Hobbs Act, 18 U.S.C. § 1951, Defendant Philip Etkin, former Deputy Sheriff in the Sullivan County Sheriff's Department and investigator in the New York State Police ("NYSP") Task Force, was arrested on September 28, 2007 by Federal Bureau of Investigation ("FBI") agents. At the time of his arrest, Defendant was in a vehicle assigned to him by the NYSP. Among the items seized from the vehicle was a printed email exchange between Defendant and his wife dated March 13, 2007. The email was found in an open portfolio bag that also contained file folders filled with investigative notes and other work materials. The Government provided this email to Defendant's counsel in discovery on October 12, 2007. On October 31, 2007, Defendant's counsel notified the Government by letter of Defendant's objection to the Government's possession and use of the email on the ground that the email was protected by the marital privilege. The Government's refusal to return the email and expressed intention to use the email at trial has prompted the present Motion....

Where marital communications are "made in the presence of a third party, such communications are usually regarded as not privileged because not made in confidence." Though it must be determined on a case-by-case basis, "an employee's expectation of privacy in the content of offices, desks, and files may be reduced by an employer's practices, procedures, and legitimate regulation over the use of the employer's property."

The Government argues that the email did not constitute confidential communication because Defendant sent the email from his work computer, which was owned by the NYSP and which explicitly warned Defendant that his uses of the computer were subject to monitoring by the NYSP. The following flash-screen notice appeared each time Defendant logged onto his work computer:

> For authorized use only. The system and all data are the property of the New York State Police.... Any use of the NYSP computer systems constitutes express consent for the authorized personnel to monitor, intercept, record, read, copy, access and capture such information for use or disclosure without additional prior notice. Users have no legitimate expectation of privacy during any use of this system or in any data on this system. Your access may be logged at any time. By logging into this system, you are agreeing that you have read, and accepted the above terms and conditions.

In order to continue past the notice and complete the log on process, Defendant had to click "OK" or hit the "Enter" key. Defendant would occasionally use a different work computer, which provided the same notice in substance, but had a different final sentence, which read: "If you DO NOT consent to the above do not continue the boot-up process and refrain from further access." Again, in order to continue the log on process, Defendant would have to click "OK" or hit the "Enter" key. According to the Government, Defendant cannot be deemed to have intended for his email exchange with his wife to be confidential because these warnings expressly notified him that it was subject to review by a third person.[5]

Defendant argues that the email exchange between him and his wife was confidential because Defendant did not intend to waive any marital communications privilege by using his work computer. In an effort to further support this argument, Defendant finds it relevant that he was never verbally advised that his use of the computer was subject to monitoring and that the Government failed to offer evidence that the NYSP actually did monitor Defendant's email. Instead, Defendant accuses the Government of attempting to

---

5. The Government relies on three cases, each of which involve marital communications that took place while one of the spouses was incarcerated. In all three cases, the courts held that the marital communications were not confidential because the parties knew that their communications were subject to eavesdropping and monitoring by prison officials and even other inmates. Though not factually on point, the Court is persuaded by the underlying message in these cases: there can no confidential communication where the spouses are on actual or constructive notice that their communications may be overheard, read, or otherwise monitored by third parties.

employ an "after-the-fact justification" for its intrusion into privileged material. Defendant also claims never to have read the computer notices, thereby making them ineffective as a means of rebutting the presumption that the email between Defendant and his wife was confidential.

The Court is persuaded by the rationale underlying ... cases ... dealing with an employee's Fourth Amendment rights in the privacy of a workplace computer. These cases stand for the proposition that employees do not have a reasonable expectation of privacy in the contents of their work computers when their employers communicate to them via a flash-screen warning a policy under which the employer may monitor or inspect the computers at any time.

By virtue of the log-on notices, Defendant is properly charged with knowledge of the fact that any email he sent to his wife from his work computer could be read by a third party. Thus, it is irrelevant that the Government has not established that the NYSP *actually* read Defendant's email. Here, the NYSP notified Defendant every single time he logged onto his computer that he had "no legitimate expectation of privacy" with regard to his uses of the computer and that his log on to the computer constituted consent for NYSP personnel to read or otherwise monitor his use of the computer.... Moreover, Defendant has pointed to no case law establishing that, to be effective, such a notice would have to be verbal or that the Government would have to disprove Defendant's self-serving assertion that he never read the notice, even though, after the screen appeared, Defendant had to affirmatively click "OK" or hit the "Enter" key in order to continue the log on process.

In sum, the issue here is whether the notices that appeared each time Defendant logged onto his work computer sufficiently notified Defendant that any email he sent to his wife from that computer might be read by a third party. The Court finds—without hesitation—that it did. Defendant's claim that he actually did believe that the March 13, 2007 email to his wife would remain confidential therefore is entirely unreasonable. Accordingly, the Court holds that the email communication at issue is not subject to the marital communications privilege because it was not a confidential communication....

Notes and Questions

1. In determining the existence and scope of federal privileges under Rule 501, what weight should be given to developments in state privilege law? The *Trammel* court made note of developments in the adverse spousal testimony privilege in the state courts, and the Supreme Court, citing *Trammel*, has subsequently held that such developments are relevant in deciding whether to retain a federal privilege. *See United States v. Gillock*, 445 U.S. 360, 368 n.8 (1980).

2. Proposed Rule 505(a) would have created an adverse spousal testimony privilege that would have applied only in criminal cases, with the defendant-spouse, not the witness-spouse, holding the privilege. Moreover, no spousal communications privilege would have existed under the proposed rule. *See* Advisory Committee Note to Proposed Rule 505(a). From this, can you make any general conclusion about the role of the proposed rules in determining the scope of federal privileges under Rule 501?

3. There are a number of differences between the two spousal privileges that are attributable to the different policies justifying each of them:

> [T]here are differences in the purposes of the two privileges. The testimonial privilege looks forward with reference to the particular marriage at hand: the privilege is meant to protect against the impact of the testimony on the mar-

riage. The marital communications privilege in a sense, is broader and more abstract: it exists to insure that spouses generally, prior to any involvement in criminal activity or a trial, feel free to communicate their deepest feelings to each other without fear of eventual exposure in a court of law.... There are, therefore, differences in the operation of the privileges. The testimonial privilege, should the witness-spouse assert it, applies to all testimony against a defendant-spouse, including testimony on non-confidential matters and matters which occurred prior to the marriage. The communications privilege, assertable by the defendant himself, applies only to communications made in confidence between the spouses during a valid marriage.... The testimonial privilege, however, may not be asserted after a marriage is terminated, because there is no longer any reason to protect that particular marriage.... By comparison ... "while divorce removes the bar of incompetency, it does not terminate the privilege for confidential marital communications." ... This survival of the communications privilege "is premised on the assumption that confidences will not be sufficiently encouraged unless the spouses are assured that their statements will never be subjected to forced disclosure." ...

United States v. Byrd, 750 F.2d 585, 590–91 (7th Cir. 1984).

4. *Trammel* makes clear that the witness spouse alone is the holder of the adverse spousal testimony privilege. Which spouse is the holder of the marital confidences privilege? *See United States v. Montgomery*, 384 F.3d 1050, 1057–59 (9th Cir. 2004) (collecting cases holding that both spouses hold the privilege, and thus that the communications cannot be revealed unless both of them waive the privilege).

5. As the *Sriram* court indicates, the federal courts have generally assumed that the adverse spousal testimony privilege applies only in criminal cases. In contrast, the spousal communications privilege is generally understood to apply in criminal and civil cases alike. *E.g.*, *United States v. Premises Known As 281 Syossett Woodbury Road*, 862 F. Supp. 847, 852 (E.D.N.Y. 1994). Are there sound reasons to distinguish between the two privileges in this regard? On the applicability of the adverse spousal testimony privilege in civil proceedings, *see* Katherine O. Eldred, *"Every Spouse's Evidence": Availability of the Adverse Spousal Testimonial Privilege in Federal Civil Trials*, 69 U. Chi. L. Rev. 1319 (2002).

6. Does not the logic of the *Singleton* decision suggest that the spousal privileges should apply to couples who are in long-term relationships but are not actually married? Nonetheless, courts that have considered the matter have held that the privilege extends only to those who are legally married:

> The light of present day experience may indicate that more couples are living together without the benefit of marriage, but reason dictates that before the courts extend a marital privilege to benefit a defendant, the defendant must have assumed both the privileges and the responsibilities of a valid marriage....

United States v. Acker, 52 F.3d 509, 515 (4th Cir. 1995). *See also United States v. Rivera*, 527 F.3d 891, 906 n.4 (9th Cir. 2008) (holding privilege inapplicable to unmarried couple that has children together).

What about a couple that wishes to marry but faces a legal impediment to doing so, such as a same-sex couple? *See* Peter Nicolas, *"They Say He's Gay": The Admissibility of Evidence of Sexual Orientation*, 37 Ga. L. Rev. 793, 871–73 (2003); Elizabeth Kimberly (Kyhm) Penfil, *In the Light of Reason and Experience: Should Federal Evidence Law Protect Confidential Communications Between Same-Sex Partners?*, 88 Marq. L. Rev. 815 (2005).

7. The adverse spousal testimony privilege will not apply if the marriage is deemed to be a "sham." *See Lutwak v. United States*, 344 U.S. 604, 614–15 (1953). However, mere suspicious timing of a marriage is insufficient, standing alone, to support a finding that a marriage is a sham. Moreover, a marriage is not necessarily a sham even if a primary motivating factor in its timing was to take advantage of the adverse spousal testimony privilege. Only if the couple entered into the marriage with no intention of thereafter living together as husband and wife will the marriage be deemed a sham. *See In re Grand Jury Proceedings (84-5)*, 777 F.2d 508, 508–09 (9th Cir. 1985); *In re Grand Jury Subpoena of Witness*, 884 F. Supp. 188, 190 (D. Md. 1995).

8. Although the spousal communications privilege applies only to confidential *communications* between spouses (as opposed to conduct of one spouse observed by the other), testimony about the conduct of one's spouse is subject to exclusion under the spousal communications privilege "in the rare instance where the conduct was intended to convey a confidential message from the actor to the observer." *United States v. Estes*, 793 F.2d 465, 467 (2d Cir. 1986); *accord United States v. Bahe*, 128 F.3d 1440, 1443–44 (10th Cir. 1997).

9. Spousal communications are presumed to be confidential, although that presumption may be overcome by proof of facts showing that they were not intended to be private. The presence of a third party negates the presumption of confidentiality. *See Pereira v. United States*, 347 U.S. 1, 6 (1954); *Blau v. United States*, 340 U.S. 332, 333 (1951).

10. As footnote 7 of the *Trammel* opinion indicates, there are exceptions to both of the spousal privileges in cases involving a crime by one spouse against the other or against the children of either spouse. Indeed, some courts have construed the child exception to apply more broadly in any situation in which the victim is "the functional equivalent of a child," such as the situation in which a grandchild is raised by his grandparents. *See United States v. Banks*, 556 F.3d 967, 974–977 (9th Cir. 2009).

In addition, the lower federal courts have created a joint participants exception for communications made between spouses when they are jointly engaged in criminal activity with one another. *See, e.g., United States v. Westmoreland*, 312 F.3d 302, 307 (7th Cir. 2002). While some courts apply it to *both* the adverse spousal and spousal communications privileges, others apply it *only* to the spousal communications privilege. *Compare United States v. Clark*, 712 F.2d 299, 300–02 (7th Cir. 1983) (applying it to both privileges), *with United States v. Ammar*, 714 F.2d 238, 257–58 (3d Cir. 1983) (applying it only to the spousal communications privilege). *See generally United States v. Sims*, 755 F.2d 1239, 1240–43 (6th Cir. 1985) (collecting cases). Do you see the net effect of applying the exception only to the spousal communications privilege?

11. One of the arguments against recognizing testimonial privileges is that the public will be denied valuable evidence, thus undermining the truth-seeking process. Is it entirely clear, particularly in the case of the spousal privileges, that the cost of recognizing the privilege is the loss of valuable testimony? If one spouse is compelled to testify against another, is it clear, or even likely, that she will testify truthfully?

12. Under the laws of some states, spouses are barred from testifying against one another not because of a testimonial privilege, but rather because they are deemed to be incompetent witnesses. In such cases, it is Rule 601, dealing with competency of witnesses, rather than Rule 501, that governs, although the result is the same, since the second sentence of Rule 601, like that of Rule 501, provides for the application of state competency law in cases in which state law provides the rule of decision. *See, e.g., McKenzie v. Harris*, 679 F.2d 8, 11–12 & n.8 (3d Cir. 1982).

D. Psychotherapist Privilege

Jaffee v. Redmond
518 U.S. 1 (1996)

Justice STEVENS delivered the opinion of the Court.

After a traumatic incident in which she shot and killed a man, a police officer received extensive counseling from a licensed clinical social worker. The question we address is whether statements the officer made to her therapist during the counseling sessions are protected from compelled disclosure in a federal civil action brought by the family of the deceased. Stated otherwise, the question is whether it is appropriate for federal courts to recognize a "psychotherapist privilege" under Rule 501 of the Federal Rules of Evidence.

I

Petitioner is the administrator of the estate of Ricky Allen. Respondents are Mary Lu Redmond, a former police officer, and the Village of Hoffman Estates, Illinois, her employer during the time that she served on the police force. Petitioner commenced this action against respondents after Redmond shot and killed Allen while on patrol duty.

On June 27, 1991, Redmond was the first officer to respond to a "fight in progress" call at an apartment complex. As she arrived at the scene, two of Allen's sisters ran toward her squad car, waving their arms and shouting that there had been a stabbing in one of the apartments. Redmond testified at trial that she relayed this information to her dispatcher and requested an ambulance. She then exited her car and walked toward the apartment building. Before Redmond reached the building, several men ran out, one waving a pipe. When the men ignored her order to get on the ground, Redmond drew her service revolver. Two other men then burst out of the building, one, Ricky Allen, chasing the other. According to Redmond, Allen was brandishing a butcher knife and disregarded her repeated commands to drop the weapon. Redmond shot Allen when she believed he was about to stab the man he was chasing. Allen died at the scene. Redmond testified that before other officers arrived to provide support, "people came pouring out of the buildings," and a threatening confrontation between her and the crowd ensued.

Petitioner filed suit in Federal District Court alleging that Redmond had violated Allen's constitutional rights by using excessive force during the encounter at the apartment complex. The complaint sought damages under Rev. Stat. § 1979, 42 U.S.C. § 1983, and the Illinois wrongful-death statute, Ill. Comp. Stat., ch. 740, § 180/1 *et seq.* (1994). At trial, petitioner presented testimony from members of Allen's family that conflicted with Redmond's version of the incident in several important respects. They testified, for example, that Redmond drew her gun before exiting her squad car and that Allen was unarmed when he emerged from the apartment building.

During pretrial discovery petitioner learned that after the shooting Redmond had participated in about 50 counseling sessions with Karen Beyer, a clinical social worker licensed by the State of Illinois and employed at that time by the Village of Hoffman Estates. Petitioner sought access to Beyer's notes concerning the sessions for use in cross-examining Redmond. Respondents vigorously resisted the discovery. They asserted that the contents of the conversations between Beyer and Redmond were protected against involuntary disclosure by a psychotherapist-patient privilege. The district judge rejected this argument. Neither Beyer nor Redmond, however, complied with his order to disclose the contents of Beyer's notes. At depositions and on the witness stand both either refused to answer certain questions or professed an inability to recall details of their conversations.

In his instructions at the end of the trial, the judge advised the jury that the refusal to turn over Beyer's notes had no "legal justification" and that the jury could therefore presume that the contents of the notes would have been unfavorable to respondents. The jury awarded petitioner $45,000 on the federal claim and $500,000 on her state-law claim.

The Court of Appeals for the Seventh Circuit reversed and remanded for a new trial. Addressing the issue for the first time, the court concluded that "reason and experience," the touchstones for acceptance of a privilege under Rule 501 of the Federal Rules of Evidence, compelled recognition of a psychotherapist-patient privilege. "Reason tells us that psychotherapists and patients share a unique relationship, in which the ability to communicate freely without the fear of public disclosure is the key to successful treatment." As to experience, the court observed that all 50 States have adopted some form of the psychotherapist-patient privilege. The court attached particular significance to the fact that Illinois law expressly extends such a privilege to social workers like Karen Beyer. The court also noted that, with one exception, the federal decisions rejecting the privilege were more than five years old and that the "need and demand for counseling services has skyrocketed during the past several years."

The Court of Appeals qualified its recognition of the privilege by stating that it would not apply if, "in the interests of justice, the evidentiary need for the disclosure of the contents of a patient's counseling sessions outweighs that patient's privacy interests." Balancing those conflicting interests, the court observed, on the one hand, that the evidentiary need for the contents of the confidential conversations was diminished in this case because there were numerous eyewitnesses to the shooting, and, on the other hand, that Officer Redmond's privacy interests were substantial. Based on this assessment, the court concluded that the trial court had erred by refusing to afford protection to the confidential communications between Redmond and Beyer.

The United States Courts of Appeals do not uniformly agree that the federal courts should recognize a psychotherapist privilege under Rule 501.... Because of the conflict among the Courts of Appeals and the importance of the question, we granted certiorari....

II

Rule 501 of the Federal Rules of Evidence authorizes federal courts to define new privileges by interpreting "[the] common law [] ... in the light of reason and experience." The authors of the Rule borrowed this phrase from our opinion in *Wolfle v. United States*, 291 U.S. 7, 12 (1934), which in turn referred to the oft-repeated observation that "the common law is not immutable but flexible, and by its own principles adapts itself to varying conditions." ... The Senate Report accompanying the 1975 adoption of the Rules indicates that Rule 501 "should be understood as reflecting the view that the recognition of a privilege based on a confidential relationship ... should be determined on a case-by-case basis." S. Rep. No. 93-1277, p. 13 (1974). The Rule thus did not freeze the law governing the privileges of witnesses in federal trials at a particular point in our history, but rather directed federal courts to "continue the evolutionary development of testimonial privileges." *Trammel v. United States*, 445 U.S. 40, 47 (1980); see also *University of Pennsylvania v. EEOC*, 493 U.S. 182, 189 (1990).

The common-law principles underlying the recognition of testimonial privileges can be stated simply. "'For more than three centuries it has now been recognized as a fundamental maxim that the public ... has a right to every man's evidence. When we come to examine the various claims of exemption, we start with the primary assumption that there is a general duty to give what testimony one is capable of giving, and that any exemptions which may exist are distinctly exceptional, being so many derogations from a positive general rule.'" *United States v. Bryan*, 339 U.S. 323, 331 (1950). Exceptions from the general rule disfavoring testimonial privileges may be justified, however, by a "'public good transcending the normally predominant principle of utilizing all rational means for ascertaining truth.'" *Trammel*, 445 U.S., at 50.

Guided by these principles, the question we address today is whether a privilege protecting confidential communications between a psychotherapist and her patient "promotes sufficiently important interests to outweigh the need for probative evidence...." 445 U.S., at 51. Both "reason and experience" persuade us that it does.

III

Like the spousal and attorney-client privileges, the psychotherapist-patient privilege is "rooted in the imperative need for confidence and trust." *Ibid.* Treatment by a physician for physical ailments can often proceed successfully on the basis of a physical examination, objective information supplied by the patient, and the results of diagnostic tests. Effective psychotherapy, by contrast, depends upon an atmosphere of confidence and trust in which the patient is willing to make a frank and complete disclosure of facts, emotions, memories, and fears. Because of the sensitive nature of the problems for which individuals consult psychotherapists, disclosure of confidential communications made during counseling sessions may cause embarrassment or disgrace. For this reason, the mere possibility of disclosure may impede development of the confidential relationship necessary for successful treatment....

By protecting confidential communications between a psychotherapist and her patient from involuntary disclosure, the proposed privilege thus serves important private interests.

Our cases make clear that an asserted privilege must also "serv[e] public ends." *Upjohn Co. v. United States*, 449 U.S. 383, 389 (1981). Thus, the purpose of the attorney-client privilege is to "encourage full and frank communication between attorneys and their clients and thereby promote broader public interests in the observance of law and administration of justice." *Ibid.* And the spousal privilege, as modified in *Trammel*, is justified because it "furthers the important public interest in marital harmony," 445 U.S., at 53. The psychotherapist privilege serves the public interest by facilitating the provision of appropriate treatment for individuals suffering the effects of a mental or emotional problem. The mental health of our citizenry, no less than its physical health, is a public good of transcendent importance.[10]

In contrast to the significant public and private interests supporting recognition of the privilege, the likely evidentiary benefit that would result from the denial of the privilege is modest. If the privilege were rejected, confidential conversations between psychotherapists and their patients would surely be chilled, particularly when it is obvious that the circumstances that give rise to the need for treatment will probably result in litigation. With-

---

10. This case amply demonstrates the importance of allowing individuals to receive confidential counseling. Police officers engaged in the dangerous and difficult tasks associated with protecting the safety of our communities not only confront the risk of physical harm but also face stressful circumstances that may give rise to anxiety, depression, fear, or anger. The entire community may suffer if police officers are not able to receive effective counseling and treatment after traumatic incidents, either because trained officers leave the profession prematurely or because those in need of treatment remain on the job.

out a privilege, much of the desirable evidence to which litigants such as petitioner seek access—for example, admissions against interest by a party—is unlikely to come into being. This unspoken "evidence" will therefore serve no greater truth-seeking function than if it had been spoken and privileged.

That it is appropriate for the federal courts to recognize a psychotherapist privilege under Rule 501 is confirmed by the fact that all 50 States and the District of Columbia have enacted into law some form of psychotherapist privilege. We have previously observed that the policy decisions of the States bear on the question whether federal courts should recognize a new privilege or amend the coverage of an existing one. See *Trammel*, 445 U.S., at 48–50; *United States v. Gillock*, 445 U.S. 360, 368, n. 8 (1980). Because state legislatures are fully aware of the need to protect the integrity of the factfinding functions of their courts, the existence of a consensus among the States indicates that "reason and experience" support recognition of the privilege. In addition, given the importance of the patient's understanding that her communications with her therapist will not be publicly disclosed, any State's promise of confidentiality would have little value if the patient were aware that the privilege would not be honored in a federal court. Denial of the federal privilege therefore would frustrate the purposes of the state legislation that was enacted to foster these confidential communications.

It is of no consequence that recognition of the privilege in the vast majority of States is the product of legislative action rather than judicial decision. Although common-law rulings may once have been the primary source of new developments in federal privilege law, that is no longer the case. In *Funk v. United States*, 290 U.S. 371 (1933), we recognized that it is appropriate to treat a consistent body of policy determinations by state legislatures as reflecting both "reason" and "experience." That rule is properly respectful of the States and at the same time reflects the fact that once a state legislature has enacted a privilege there is no longer an opportunity for common-law creation of the protection. The history of the psychotherapist privilege illustrates the latter point. In 1972 the members of the Judicial Conference Advisory Committee noted that the common law "had indicated a disposition to recognize a psychotherapist-patient privilege when legislatures began moving into the field." Proposed Rules, 56 F.R.D., at 242. The present unanimous acceptance of the privilege shows that the state lawmakers moved quickly. That the privilege may have developed faster legislatively than it would have in the courts demonstrates only that the States rapidly recognized the wisdom of the rule as the field of psychotherapy developed.[13]

The uniform judgment of the States is reinforced by the fact that a psychotherapist privilege was among the nine specific privileges recommended by the Advisory Committee in its proposed privilege rules. In *United States v. Gillock*, 445 U.S., at 367–368, our holding that Rule 501 did not include a state legislative privilege relied, in part, on the fact that no such privilege was included in the Advisory Committee's draft. The reasoning in *Gillock* thus supports the opposite conclusion in this case. In rejecting the proposed draft that had specifically identified each privilege rule and substituting the present more open-ended Rule 501, the Senate Judiciary Committee explicitly stated that its ac-

---

13. Petitioner acknowledges that all 50 state legislatures favor a psychotherapist privilege. She nevertheless discounts the relevance of the state privilege statutes by pointing to divergence among the States concerning the types of therapy relationships protected and the exceptions recognized. A small number of state statutes, for example, grant the privilege only to psychiatrists and psychologists, while most apply the protection more broadly.... The range of exceptions recognized by the States is similarly varied.... These variations in the scope of the protection are too limited to undermine the force of the States' unanimous judgment that some form of psychotherapist privilege is appropriate.

tion "should not be understood as disapproving any recognition of a psychiatrist-patient ... privileg[e] contained in the [proposed] rules." S. Rep. No. 93-1277, at 13.

Because we agree with the judgment of the state legislatures and the Advisory Committee that a psychotherapist-patient privilege will serve a "public good transcending the normally predominant principle of utilizing all rational means for ascertaining truth," *Trammel,* 445 U.S., at 50, we hold that confidential communications between a licensed psychotherapist and her patients in the course of diagnosis or treatment are protected from compelled disclosure under Rule 501 of the Federal Rules of Evidence.[14]

IV

All agree that a psychotherapist privilege covers confidential communications made to licensed psychiatrists and psychologists. We have no hesitation in concluding in this case that the federal privilege should also extend to confidential communications made to licensed social workers in the course of psychotherapy. The reasons for recognizing a privilege for treatment by psychiatrists and psychologists apply with equal force to treatment by a clinical social worker such as Karen Beyer.[15] Today, social workers provide a significant amount of mental health treatment. See, *e.g.,* U.S. Dept. of Health and Human Services, Center for Mental Health Services, Mental Health, United States, 1994, pp. 85–87, 107–114; Brief for National Association of Social Workers et al. as *Amici Curiae* 5–7 (citing authorities). Their clients often include the poor and those of modest means who could not afford the assistance of a psychiatrist or psychologist, *id.,* at 6–7 (citing authorities), but whose counseling sessions serve the same public goals.[16] Perhaps in recognition of these circumstances, the vast majority of States explicitly extend a testimonial privilege to licensed social workers. We therefore agree with the Court of Appeals that "[d]rawing a distinction between the counseling provided by costly psychotherapists and the counseling provided by more readily accessible social workers serves no discernible public purpose."

---

14. Like other testimonial privileges, the patient may of course waive the protection.

15. If petitioner had filed her complaint in an Illinois state court, respondents' claim of privilege would surely have been upheld, at least with respect to the state wrongful-death action. An Illinois statute provides that conversations between a therapist and her patients are privileged from compelled disclosure in any civil or criminal proceeding. Ill. Comp. Stat., ch. 740, § 110/10 (1994). The term "therapist" is broadly defined to encompass a number of licensed professionals including social workers. Ch. 740, § 110/2. Karen Beyer, having satisfied the strict standards for licensure, qualifies as a clinical social worker in Illinois. 51 F.3d 1346, 1358, n. 19 (CA7 1995).

Indeed, if only a state-law claim had been asserted in federal court, the second sentence in Rule 501 would have extended the privilege to that proceeding. We note that there is disagreement concerning the proper rule in cases such as this in which both federal and state claims are asserted in federal court and relevant evidence would be privileged under state law but not under federal law. See C. Wright & K. Graham, 23 Federal Practice and Procedure § 5434 (1980). Because the parties do not raise this question and our resolution of the case does not depend on it, we express no opinion on the matter.

16. The Judicial Conference Advisory Committee's proposed psychotherapist privilege defined psychotherapists as psychologists and medical doctors who provide mental health services. Proposed Rules, 56 F.R.D., at 240. This limitation in the 1972 recommendation does not counsel against recognition of a privilege for social workers practicing psychotherapy. In the quarter century since the Committee adopted its recommendations, much has changed in the domains of social work and psychotherapy. See generally Brief for National Association of Social Workers et al. as *Amici Curiae* 5–13 (and authorities cited). While only 12 States regulated social workers in 1972, all 50 do today. See American Association of State Social Work Boards, Social Work Laws and Board Regulations: A State Comparison Study 29, 31 (1996). Over the same period, the relative portion of therapeutic services provided by social workers has increased substantially. See U.S. Dept. of Health and Human Services, Center for Mental Health Services, Mental Health, United States, 1994, pp. 85–87, 107–114.

We part company with the Court of Appeals on a separate point. We reject the balancing component of the privilege implemented by that court and a small number of States. Making the promise of confidentiality contingent upon a trial judge's later evaluation of the relative importance of the patient's interest in privacy and the evidentiary need for disclosure would eviscerate the effectiveness of the privilege. As we explained in *Upjohn*, if the purpose of the privilege is to be served, the participants in the confidential conversation "must be able to predict with some degree of certainty whether particular discussions will be protected. An uncertain privilege, or one which purports to be certain but results in widely varying applications by the courts, is little better than no privilege at all."

These considerations are all that is necessary for decision of this case. A rule that authorizes the recognition of new privileges on a case-by-case basis makes it appropriate to define the details of new privileges in a like manner. Because this is the first case in which we have recognized a psychotherapist privilege, it is neither necessary nor feasible to delineate its full contours in a way that would "govern all conceivable future questions in this area." Id., at 386.[19]

V

The conversations between Officer Redmond and Karen Beyer and the notes taken during their counseling sessions are protected from compelled disclosure under Rule 501 of the Federal Rules of Evidence....

Justice SCALIA, with whom THE CHIEF JUSTICE joins as to Part III, dissenting....

I

.... Before proceeding to a legal analysis of the case, I must observe that the Court makes its task deceptively simple by the manner in which it proceeds....

It first frames an overly general question ("Should there be a psychotherapist privilege?") that can be answered in the negative only by excluding from protection office consultations with professional psychiatrists (*i.e.*, doctors) and clinical psychologists. And then, having answered that in the affirmative, it comes to the *only* question that the facts of this case present ("Should there be a social worker-client privilege with regard to psychotherapeutic counseling?") with the answer seemingly a foregone conclusion. At that point, to conclude against the privilege one must subscribe to the difficult proposition, "Yes, there is a psychotherapist privilege, but not if the psychotherapist is a social worker."

Relegating the question actually posed by this case to an afterthought makes the impossible possible in a number of wonderful ways. For example, it enables the Court to treat the Proposed Federal Rules of Evidence developed in 1972 by the Judicial Conference Advisory Committee as strong support for its holding, whereas they in fact counsel clearly and directly against it. The Committee did indeed recommend a "psychotherapist privilege" of sorts; but more precisely, and more relevantly, it recommended a privilege for psychotherapy conducted by "a person authorized to practice medicine" or "a person licensed or certified as a psychologist," Proposed Rule of Evidence 504, 56 F.R.D. 183, 240 (1972), which is to say that *it recommended against the privilege at issue here*. That condemnation is obscured, and even converted into an endorsement, by pushing a "psy-

---

19. Although it would be premature to speculate about most future developments in the federal psychotherapist privilege, we do not doubt that there are situations in which the privilege must give way, for example, if a serious threat of harm to the patient or to others can be averted only by means of a disclosure by the therapist.

chotherapist privilege" into the center ring. The Proposed Rule figures prominently in the Court's explanation of why that privilege deserves recognition, and is ignored in the single page devoted to the sideshow which happens to be the issue presented for decision....

II

To say that the Court devotes the bulk of its opinion to the much easier question of psychotherapist-patient privilege is not to say that its answer to that question is convincing. At bottom, the Court's decision to recognize such a privilege is based on its view that "successful [psychotherapeutic] treatment" serves "important private interests" (namely, those of patients undergoing psychotherapy) as well as the "public good" of "[t]he mental health of our citizenry." I have no quarrel with these premises. Effective psychotherapy undoubtedly is beneficial to individuals with mental problems, and surely serves some larger social interest in maintaining a mentally stable society. But merely mentioning these values does not answer the critical question: Are they of such importance, and is the contribution of psychotherapy to them so distinctive, and is the application of normal evidentiary rules so destructive to psychotherapy, as to justify making our federal courts occasional instruments of injustice? On that central question I find the Court's analysis insufficiently convincing to satisfy the high standard we have set for rules that "are in derogation of the search for truth." *Nixon*, 418 U.S., at 710.

When is it, one must wonder, that *the psychotherapist* came to play such an indispensable role in the maintenance of the citizenry's mental health? For most of history, men and women have worked out their difficulties by talking to, *inter alios*, parents, siblings, best friends, and bartenders—none of whom was awarded a privilege against testifying in court. Ask the average citizen: Would your mental health be more significantly impaired by preventing you from seeing a psychotherapist, or by preventing you from getting advice from your mom? I have little doubt what the answer would be. Yet there is no mother-child privilege.

How likely is it that a person will be deterred from seeking psychological counseling, or from being completely truthful in the course of such counseling, because of fear of later disclosure in litigation? And even more pertinent to today's decision, to what extent will the evidentiary privilege reduce that deterrent? The Court does not try to answer the first of these questions; and it *cannot possibly have any notion* of what the answer is to the second, since that depends entirely upon the scope of the privilege, which the Court amazingly finds it "neither necessary nor feasible to delineate". If, for example, the psychotherapist can give the patient no more assurance than "A court will not be able to make me disclose what you tell me, unless you tell me about a harmful act," I doubt whether there would be much benefit from the privilege at all. That is not a fanciful example, at least with respect to extension of the psychotherapist privilege to social workers. See Del.Code Ann., Tit. 24, § 3913(2) (1987); Idaho Code § 54-3213(2) (1994).

Even where it is certain that absence of the psychotherapist privilege will inhibit disclosure of the information, it is not clear to me that that is an unacceptable state of affairs. Let us assume the very worst in the circumstances of the present case: that to be truthful about what was troubling her, the police officer who sought counseling would have to confess that she shot without reason, and wounded an innocent man. If (again to assume the worst) such an act constituted the crime of negligent wounding under Illinois law, the officer would of course have the absolute right not to admit that she shot without reason in criminal court. But I see no reason why she should be enabled *both* not to admit it in criminal court (as a good citizen should), *and* to get the benefits of psychotherapy by admitting it to a therapist who cannot tell anyone else. And even less reason why she should be enabled to *deny* her guilt in the criminal trial—or in a civil trial for negligence—while yet obtaining the benefits of psychotherapy by confessing guilt to a social worker who cannot testify. It seems to me entirely fair to say that if she wishes the benefits of telling the truth she must also accept the adverse consequences. To be sure, in most cases the statements to the psychotherapist will be only marginally relevant, and one of the purposes of the privilege (though not one relied upon by the Court) may be simply to spare patients needless intrusion upon their privacy, and to spare psychotherapists needless expenditure of their time in deposition and trial. But surely this can be achieved by means short of excluding even evidence that is of the most direct and conclusive effect.

The Court confidently asserts that not much truth-finding capacity would be destroyed by the privilege anyway, since "[w]ithout a privilege, much of the desirable evidence to which litigants such as petitioner seek access ... is unlikely to come into being." If that is so, how come psychotherapy got to be a thriving practice before the "psychotherapist privilege" was invented? Were the patients paying money to lie to their analysts all those years? Of course the evidence-generating effect of the privilege (if any) depends entirely upon its scope, which the Court steadfastly declines to consider. And even if one assumes that scope to be the broadest possible, is it really true that most, or even many, of those who seek psychological counseling have the worry of litigation in the back of their minds? I doubt that, and the Court provides no evidence to support it.

The Court suggests one last policy justification: since psychotherapist privilege statutes exist in all the States, the failure to recognize a privilege in federal courts "would frustrate the purposes of the state legislation that was enacted to foster these confidential communications." This is a novel argument indeed. A sort of inverse pre-emption: The truth-seeking functions of *federal* courts must be adjusted so as not to conflict with the policies *of the States.* This reasoning cannot be squared with *Gillock*, which declined to recognize an evidentiary privilege for Tennessee legislators in federal prosecutions, even though the Tennessee Constitution guaranteed it in state criminal proceedings. *Gillock*, 445 U.S., at 368. Moreover, since, as I shall discuss, state policies regarding the psychotherapist privilege vary considerably from State to State, *no* uniform federal policy can possibly honor most of them. If furtherance of state policies is the name of the game, rules of privilege in federal courts should vary from State to State, *à la Erie R. Co. v. Tompkins*, 304 U.S. 64 (1938).

The Court's failure to put forward a convincing justification of its own could perhaps be excused if it were relying upon the unanimous conclusion of state courts in the reasoned development of their common law. It cannot do that, since *no* State has such a privilege apart from legislation. What it relies upon, instead, is "the fact that all 50 States and the District of Columbia have [1] *enacted into law* [2] *some form* of psychotherapist privilege." Let us consider both the verb and its object: The fact [1] that all 50 States have *enacted* this privilege argues not *for*, but *against*, our adopting the privilege judicially. At best it suggests that the matter has been found not to lend itself to judicial treatment— perhaps because the pros and cons of adopting the privilege, or of giving it one or another shape, are not that clear; or perhaps because the rapidly evolving uses of psychotherapy demand a flexibility that only legislation can provide. At worst it suggests that the privilege commends itself only to decisionmaking bodies in which reason is tempered, so to speak, by political pressure from organized interest groups (such as psychologists and social workers), and decisionmaking bodies that are not overwhelmingly concerned (as courts of law are and should be) with justice.

And the phrase [2] "some form of psychotherapist privilege" covers a multitude of difficulties. The Court concedes that there is "divergence among the States concerning the types of therapy relationships protected and the exceptions recognized." To rest a newly announced federal common-law psychotherapist privilege, assertable from this day forward in all federal courts, upon "the States' *unanimous judgment* that some form of psychotherapist privilege is appropriate," is rather like announcing a new, immediately applicable, federal common law of torts, based upon the States' "unanimous judgment" that *some* form of tort law is appropriate. In the one case as in the other, the state laws vary to such a degree that the parties and lower federal judges confronted by the new "common law" have barely a clue as to what its content might be.

III

Turning from the general question that was not involved in this case to the specific one that is: The Court's conclusion that a social-worker psychotherapeutic privilege deserves recognition is even less persuasive. In approaching this question, the fact that five of the state legislatures that have seen fit to enact "some form" of psychotherapist privilege have elected not to extend *any form* of privilege to social workers ought to give one pause. So should the fact that the Judicial Conference Advisory Committee was similarly discriminating in its conferral of the proposed Rule 504 privilege. The Court, however, has "no hesitation in concluding ... that the federal privilege should also extend" to social workers—and goes on to prove that by polishing off the reasoned analysis with a topic sentence and two sentences of discussion, as follows:

> "The reasons for recognizing a privilege for treatment by psychiatrists and psychologists apply with equal force to treatment by a clinical social worker such as Karen Beyer. Today, social workers provide a significant amount of mental health treatment. Their clients often include the poor and those of modest means who could not afford the assistance of a psychiatrist or psychologist, but whose counseling sessions serve the same public goals."

So much for the rule that privileges are to be narrowly construed.

Of course this brief analysis—like the earlier, more extensive, discussion of the general psychotherapist privilege—contains no explanation of why the psychotherapy provided by social workers is a public good of such transcendent importance as to be purchased at the price of occasional injustice. Moreover, it considers only the respects in which social workers providing therapeutic services are *similar* to licensed psychiatrists and psychologists; not a word about the respects in which they are different. A licensed psychiatrist or psychologist is an expert in psychotherapy—and that may suffice (though I think it not so clear that this Court should make the judgment) to justify the use of extraordinary means to encourage counseling with him, as opposed to counseling with one's rabbi, minister, family, or friends. One must presume that a social worker does *not* bring this greatly heightened degree of skill to bear, which is alone a reason for not encouraging that consultation as generously. Does a social worker bring to bear at least a significantly heightened degree of skill—more than a minister or rabbi, for example? I have no idea, and neither does the Court.... It seems to me quite irresponsible to extend the so-called "psychotherapist privilege" to all licensed social workers, nationwide, without exploring these issues.

Another critical distinction between psychiatrists and psychologists, on the one hand, and social workers, on the other, is that the former professionals, in their consultations with patients, *do nothing but psychotherapy*. Social workers, on the other hand, interview people for a multitude of reasons.... Thus, in applying the "social worker" variant of the "psychotherapist" privilege, it will be necessary to determine whether the information provided to the social worker was provided to him *in his capacity as a psychotherapist*, or in his capacity as an administrator of social welfare, a community organizer, etc. Worse still, if the privilege is to have its desired effect (and is not to mislead the client), it will presumably be necessary for the social caseworker to advise, as the conversation with his welfare client proceeds, which portions are privileged and which are not.

Having concluded its three sentences of reasoned analysis, the Court then invokes, as it did when considering the psychotherapist privilege, the "experience" of the States — once again an experience I consider irrelevant (if not counter-indicative) because it consists entirely of legislation rather than common-law decision. It says that "the vast majority of States explicitly extend a testimonial privilege to licensed social workers." There are two elements of this impressive statistic, however, that the Court does not reveal.

First — and utterly conclusive of the irrelevance of this supposed consensus to the question before us — the majority of the States that accord a privilege to social workers do *not* do so as a subpart of a "psychotherapist" privilege. The privilege applies to *all* confidences imparted to social workers, and not just those provided in the course of psychotherapy....

Second, the Court does not reveal the enormous degree of disagreement among the States as to the scope of the privilege....

Thus, although the Court is technically correct that "the vast majority of States explicitly extend a testimonial privilege to licensed social workers," that uniformity exists only at the most superficial level. No State has adopted the privilege without restriction; the nature of the restrictions varies enormously from jurisdiction to jurisdiction; and 10 States, I reiterate, effectively reject the privilege entirely. It is fair to say that there is scant national consensus even as to the propriety of a social-worker psychotherapist privilege, and none whatever as to its appropriate scope. In other words, the state laws to which the Court appeals for support demonstrate most convincingly that adoption of a social-worker psychotherapist privilege is a job for Congress....

In its consideration of this case, the Court was the beneficiary of no fewer than 14 *amicus* briefs supporting respondents, most of which came from such organizations as the American Psychiatric Association, the American Psychoanalytic Association, the American Association of State Social Work Boards, the Employee Assistance Professionals Association, Inc., the American Counseling Association, and the National Association of Social Workers. Not a single *amicus* brief was filed in support of petitioner. That is no surprise. There is no self-interested organization out there devoted to pursuit of the truth in the federal courts. The expectation is, however, that *this Court* will have that interest prominently — indeed, primarily — in mind. Today we have failed that expectation, and that responsibility. It is no small matter to say that, in some cases, our federal courts will be the tools of injustice rather than unearth the truth where it is available to be found. The common law has identified a few instances where that is tolerable. Perhaps Congress may conclude that it is also tolerable for the purpose of encouraging psychotherapy by social workers. But that conclusion assuredly does not burst upon the mind with such clarity that a judgment in favor of suppressing the truth ought to be pronounced by this honorable Court. I respectfully dissent.

Notes and Questions

1. If a client communicates with a psychotherapist in an effort to further criminal or fraudulent conduct, are such communications privileged? *See In re Grand Jury Proceed-*

ings (Gregory P. Violette), 183 F.3d 71, 77 (1st Cir. 1999) (recognizing a crime-fraud exception to the psychotherapist privilege).

2. Although psychotherapists, like attorneys, have a professional duty of confidentiality, an exception to that duty exists that permits (and sometimes requires) the psychotherapist to warn third persons if the patient indicates an intent to harm such third person during his communications with his psychotherapist. Does a similar exception exist to the federal psychotherapist-client privilege that permits the psychotherapist to testify that the client made such threats in criminal proceedings against the client? Should one exist? The *Jaffee* Court suggested in footnote 19 that such an exception might exist. While one court has identified such an exception, *see United States v. Glass*, 133 F.3d 1356, 1360 (10th Cir. 1998), another court has rejected such an exception, finding that the incremental benefit to society of preventing the client from harming others is outweighed by the risk that such an exception would deter clients from disclosing their violent thoughts to their psychotherapists, making it less likely that they would receive treatment for their violent tendencies:

> [A]nalytically there is little connection between a psychotherapist's state-imposed obligation to report a dangerous patient at the time the patient makes a threat, on the one hand, and the later operation of the federal testimonial privilege, on the other. The [duty to report the threat] is justified on the ground of protection; the societal benefit from disclosing the existence of a dangerous patient out-weighs the private and public cost of the deleterious effect on the psychotherapist-patient relationship. By contrast, ordinarily testimony at a later criminal trial focuses on establishing a past act. There is not necessarily a connection between the goals of protection and proof.

United States v. Chase, 340 F.3d 978, 987 (9th Cir. 2003). *See also United States v. Auster*, 517 F.3d 312, 315–21 & n.5 (5th Cir. 2008) (not specifically recognizing a "dangerous patient" exception to the psychotherapist privilege, but holding that where a patient knows that the psychotherapist is required by law to report threats of violence to the authorities, such communications will be deemed non-confidential and thus outside the scope of the privilege).

3. As the *Jaffee* Court points out in footnote 14, the psychotherapist-patient privilege is subject to waiver. The lower federal courts are heavily split on the sort of litigation conduct that constitutes a waiver of the privilege:

> Those courts taking a broad view of waiver of the psychotherapist-patient privilege have held that when a party makes a claim for emotional distress damages, the privilege has been waived in its entirety. The rationale behind this view is based on fairness considerations.

> Courts adopting a narrow approach to waiver ... conclude that the privilege is waived only when the plaintiff introduces privileged communications in evidence either directly or by calling the particular psychotherapist as a witness.... The plaintiff must use the privileged communication as evidence before the privileged is waived. This approach has been criticized ... because it enables a party who has undergone psychotherapy to offer a selective "history," by limiting the evidence offered at trial to the testimony of a retained, non-treating expert or to only certain treating psychotherapists, thereby preventing discovery of what was told to other treating psychotherapists.

> ... in what has been characterized as a third approach ... the psychotherapist-patient privilege is waived when the plaintiff has taken the affirmative step in

the litigation to place his diagnosis or treatment in issue, by offering evidence of psychiatric treatment or medical expert testimony to establish his claim of emotional harm. However, the mere assertion that the defendant's alleged misconduct caused emotional harm is insufficient to waive the privilege.

Cases have also recognized a fourth "middle approach" which holds that a mere request for damages for ordinary, garden variety claims of mental anguish or emotional distress, as opposed to a cause of action based upon emotional distress, does not place a party's mental condition at issue, and the privilege is not waived. "Garden variety" emotional distress claims are contrasted with complex claims, such that result in a specific psychiatric disorder or prevent a person from working.

Merrill v. Waffle House, Inc., 227 F.R.D. 467, 474–75 (N.D. Tex. 2005).

4. What if a criminal defendant claims that a witness against him has a history of mental illness that is relevant to his credibility as a witness, and seeks to introduce evidence of the witness' mental health history? Does he have a right to introduce such evidence, the psychotherapist-patient privilege notwithstanding? *See United States v. Alperin*, 128 F. Supp. 2d 1251, 1252–54 (N.D. Cal. 2001) (indicating that in such circumstances, the defendant's Sixth Amendment rights may override claims of privilege).

5. What role does state privilege law play in determining the scope of *federal* privilege law? What role do the proposed but rejected federal privilege rules play? Are they merely factors, or do they play a decisive role? How many states must have a privilege (or a particular aspect of a privilege) before a federal court is justified in creating or altering a federal privilege? Is the following a fair summary of the Supreme Court's decisions applying Rule 501?

The Supreme Court has identified several factors that should be considered when assessing a proposed privilege under Rule 501. First, the Court has asked whether there exists a broad consensus in federal and state law in favor of the privilege. Second, the Court has considered whether "Congress has considered the relevant competing concerns but has not provided the privilege itself." Third, the Court has consulted the list of evidentiary privileges recommended by the Advisory Committee of the Judicial Conference in its proposed Federal Rules of Evidence. Finally, "[t]he Supreme Court has instructed that a party seeking judicial recognition of a new evidentiary privilege under Rule 501 demonstrate with a high degree of clarity and certainty that the proposed privilege will effectively advance a public good."

In re Subpoena Issued to Commodity Futures Trading Commission, 370 F. Supp. 2d 201, 208–09 (D.D.C. 2005).

6. Does the logic of *Jaffee* suggest that a federal doctor-patient privilege should be recognized under Rule 501? After all, medical patients frequently discuss sensitive matters with their physicians, and most states recognize such a privilege. Nonetheless, the federal courts that have considered the matter have unanimously held that no such privilege exists. *See, e.g., Patterson v. Caterpillar, Inc.*, 70 F.3d 503, 506–07 (7th Cir. 1995); *United States v. Moore*, 970 F.2d 48, 50 (5th Cir. 1992); *Hancock v. Dodson*, 958 F.2d 1367, 1373 (6th Cir. 1992). Should the lower federal courts reconsider these holdings in light of *Jaffee*? The federal courts have re-affirmed these holdings post-*Jaffee*, without addressing the possible similarities between the two privileges. *E.g., Northwestern Memorial Hosp. v. Ashcroft*, 362 F.3d 923, 926–27 (7th Cir. 2004). Are there sound reasons for distinguishing the two privileges from one another? Does anything in the *Jaffee* opinion suggest how the Supreme Court might address the question whether a federal doctor-patient privilege exists?

7. In footnote 15 of its opinion, the *Jaffee* Court raised but did not decide what a federal court is to do in a case in which a party raises both a federal and state claim, and certain evidence is privileged under state but not federal law (or vice versa). What should a court do in such a situation? Would not a literal application of Rule 501 necessitate applying federal privilege law to the federal claim and state privilege law to the state claim, which could be accomplished by giving the jury an appropriate limiting instruction under Rule 105? Most courts reject this solution, reasoning that "[o]bviously applying two separate disclosure rules with respect to different claims tried to the same jury would be unworkable," *Wm. T. Thompson Co. v. General Nutrition Corp.*, 671 F.2d 100, 104 (3d Cir. 1982), and hold (without any clear rationale) that the federal privilege should control in this situation, *e.g.*, *Hancock v. Hobbs*, 967 F.2d 462, 466–67 (11th Cir. 1992). Are there more desirable alternatives? The Senate Committee's Report on Rule 501 suggested a bias in favor of admissibility in this situation, applying whichever rule would allow for the admission of the challenged evidence. *See* Senate Report No. 93-1277, at 12. Other options would include severing the claims and having them decided by separate juries (an expensive option that courts are unlikely to employ), or dismissing the state-law claim and letting it be adjudicated in a state court before a separate jury, at least where the basis for jurisdiction is the supplemental jurisdiction statute, see 28 U.S.C. § 1367(c)(4). Of course, the final option, which is what the *Jaffee* Court ultimately chose, is to avoid the conflict by creating a federal privilege modeled after state privilege law.

8. Justice Scalia points out that the Supreme Court in *Jaffee* was inundated with amicus briefs from a variety of professional organizations that have an obvious interest in the development of a psychotherapist-patient privilege and effectively lobbied for a particular outcome. Does this, when coupled with the dispute between the majority and the dissent over the benefits and costs of creating such a privilege, suggest that creating privileges is best decided by a representative body such as Congress?

E. Parent-Child Privilege

Problem 5-8: The Bond between Mother and Child

Larry Rose, a sixteen-year-old, is indicted in federal court on charges of possessing with intent to distribute cocaine in violation of a federal statute. The prosecution seeks to call Larry's mother, Diana Rose (with whom he lives), to testify as to conversations she had with him in which he might have mentioned his drug possession and distribution activities. Larry's attorney objects to the government's decision to call Diana, stating that the conversation is privileged.

How will the court likely dispose of the privilege claim? What if Diana is willing to testify? What if Larry were 25 years old, and not still living with Diana? What if instead Diana had been indicted, and the government sought Larry's testimony?

In re Grand Jury
103 F.3d 1140 (3d Cir. 1997)

GARTH, Circuit Judge:

Three appeals presenting the same critical issue are before us.... We scheduled oral argument in all three appeals on the same day inasmuch as they raised the same question— should this court recognize a parent-child privilege? ...

I.

....

Docket Number 95-7354: In the Virgin Islands case, the grand jury sitting in St. Croix subpoenaed the father of the target of the grand jury investigation as a witness. The target of the grand jury proceeding was the son of the subpoenaed witness. The son became the target of a government investigation as a result of "certain transactions that [he] was allegedly involved in." At the time of the alleged transactions, the son was eighteen years old....

The father testified, at a hearing before the district court, that he and his son "ha[d] an excellent relationship, very close, very loving relationship." He further testified that if he were coerced into testifying against his son, "[their] relationship would dramatically change and the closeness that [they] have would end...." The father further explained that the subpoena would impact negatively upon his relationship with his son:

> I will be living under a cloud in which if my son comes to me or talks to me, I've got to be very careful what he says, what I allow him to say. I would have to stop him and say, "you can't talk to me about that. You've got to talk to your attorney." It's no way for anybody to live in this country.

....

Docket Numbers 96-7529 & 96-7530: In the Delaware case, a sixteen year old minor daughter was subpoenaed to testify before the grand jury, as part of an investigation into her father's participation in an alleged interstate kidnapping of a woman who had disappeared. The daughter was scheduled to testify on September 10, 1996. However, on September 9, 1996, a motion to quash subpoena was made by counsel for the daughter and her mother, as well as by separate counsel for the father. . . .

[In each of the cases, the district court overruled the privilege claims.]

. . . .

III.

The central question in these appeals is one of first impression in this court: should we recognize a parent-child testimonial privilege? Appellants argue that recognition is necessary in order to advance important public policy interests such as the protection of strong and trusting parent-child relationships; the preservation of the family; safeguarding of privacy interests and protection from harmful government intrusion; and the promotion of healthy psychological development of children. . . .

Although legal academicians appear to favor adoption of a parent-child testimonial privilege, no federal Court of Appeals and no state supreme court has recognized such a privilege. We too decline to recognize such a privilege. . . .

B. THE STANDARDS PRESCRIBED BY FEDERAL RULE OF EVIDENCE 501 DO NOT SUPPORT THE CREATION OF A PRIVILEGE.

. . . .

It is true that Congress, in enacting Fed.R.Evid. 501, "manifested an affirmative intention not to freeze the law of privilege. Its purpose rather was to 'provide the courts with the flexibility to develop rules of privilege on a case-by-case basis,' and to leave the door open to change." *Trammel v. United States*, 445 U.S. 40, 47 (1980) (quoting 102 Cong. Rec. 40,891 (1974) (statement of Rep. William Hungate)). In doing so, however, we are admonished that privileges are generally disfavored; that "'the public . . . has a right to every man's evidence'"; and that privileges are tolerable "only to the very limited extent that permitting a refusal to testify or excluding relevant evidence has a public good transcending the normally predominant principle of utilizing all rational means for ascertaining truth."

In keeping with these principles, the Supreme Court has rarely expanded common-law testimonial privileges. Following the Supreme Court's teachings, other federal courts, including this court, have likewise declined to exercise their power under Rule 501 expansively. . . .

Neither the appellants nor the dissent has identified any principle of common law, and hence have proved no interpretation of such a principle. Nor has the dissent or the appellants discussed any common-law principle in light of reason and experience. Accordingly, no basis has been demonstrated for this court to adopt a parent-child privilege.

C. CREATING A PARENT-CHILD PRIVILEGE WOULD BE INCONSISTENT WITH THE TEACHINGS OF THE SUPREME COURT AND OF THIS COURT.

1. *Supreme Court*

The Supreme Court's most recent pronouncement in the law of privileges, *Jaffee v. Redmond*, 518 U.S. 1 (1996), which recognized a psychotherapist-patient privilege, supports the conclusion that a privilege should not, and cannot, be created here. In *Jaffee*, the Supreme Court reemphasized that the predominant common-law principle which guides a federal court's determination of whether a privilege applies is the maxim that testimonial privileges are disfavored. . . . An exception to this general rule is justified only when recognition of a privilege would promote a "'public good transcending the normally predominant principle of utilizing all rational means for ascertaining the truth.'"

The *Jaffee* Court emphasized that a court, in determining whether a particular privilege "'promotes sufficiently important interests to outweigh the need for probative evidence,'" must be guided by "reason and experience." Specifically, the *Jaffee* Court instructed that a federal court should look to the "experience" of state courts: "[T]he policy decision of the States bear on the question [of] whether federal courts should recognize a new privilege or amend the coverage of an existing one."

Notably, in recognizing a psychotherapist-patient privilege, the Supreme Court relied on the fact that all fifty states had enacted some form of a psychotherapist privilege. The *Jaffee* Court explained that "it is appropriate to treat a consistent body of policy determinations by state legislatures as reflecting both 'reason' and 'experience.'"

Here, by contrast, only four states have deemed it necessary to protect from disclosure, in any manner, confidential communications between children and their parents. As previously noted, New York state courts have recognized a limited parent-child privilege, and Idaho and Minnesota have enacted limited statutory privileges protecting confidential communications by minors to their parents. In Massachusetts, as we have noted, minor children are statutorily disqualified from testifying against their parents in criminal proceedings. No state within the Third Circuit has adopted a parent-child privilege.

The policy determinations of these four states do not constitute a "consistent body of policy determinations by state[s]" supporting recognition of a parent-child privilege. Indeed, if anything, the fact that the overwhelming majority of states have chosen *not* to create a parent-child privilege supports the opposite conclusion: "reason and experience" dictate that federal courts should refuse to recognize a privilege rejected by the vast majority of jurisdictions.

The *Jaffee* Court also relied on the fact that the psychotherapist-patient privilege was among the nine specific privileges recommended by the Advisory Committee on Rules of Evidence in 1972. Additionally, the *Jaffee* Court noted: "[O]ur holding [*United States v. Gillock*, 445 U.S. 360 (1980)] that Rule 501 did not include a state legislative privilege relied, in part, on the fact that no such privilege was included in the Advisory Committee's draft [of the proposed privilege rules]."

In the instant cases, in contrast to the psychotherapist-patient privilege recognized in *Jaffee*, the parent-child privilege, like the state legislative privilege rejected in *Gillock*, was not among the enumerated privileges submitted by the Advisory Committee. Although this fact, in and of itself, is not dispositive with respect to the question as to whether this court should create a privilege, it strongly suggests that the Advisory Committee, like the majority of state legislatures, did not regard confidential parent-child communications sufficiently important to warrant "privilege" protection.

A federal court should give due consideration, and accord proper weight, to the judgment of the Advisory Committee and of state legislatures on this issue when it evaluates whether it is appropriate to create a new privilege pursuant to Rule 501.

2. *Third Circuit*

.... [T]he parent-child privilege sought to be recognized here is of relatively recent vintage ... and is virtually no more than the product of legal academicians.... Unlike, for example, the attorney-client privilege, which is "the oldest" common-law privilege ... the parent-child privilege lacks historical antecedents.

Furthermore, an analysis of the four Wigmore factors ... does not support the creation of a privilege. Dean Wigmore's four-factor formula requires satisfaction of all four factors in order to establish a privilege:

(1) The communications must originate in a *confidence* that they will not be disclosed.

(2) This element of *confidentiality must be essential* to the full and satisfactory maintenance of the relation between the parties.

(3) The *relation* must be one which in the opinion of the community ought to be sedulously *fostered*.

(4) The *injury* that would inure to the relation by the disclosure of the communications must be *greater than the benefit* thereby gained for the correct disposal of litigation.

In re Grand Jury Investigation, 918 F.2d at 384 (quoting 8 John H. Wigmore, *Evidence* §2285 (J. McNaughton rev. ed. 1961)).

At least two of Wigmore's prerequisite conditions for creation of a federal common-law privilege are not met under the facts of these cases. We refer to the second and fourth elements of the Wigmore test.

First, confidentiality—in the form of a testimonial privilege—is not essential to a successful parent-child relationship, as required by the second factor. A privilege should be recognized only where such a privilege would be indispensable to the survival of the relationship that society deems should be fostered. For instance, because complete candor and full disclosure by the client is absolutely necessary in order for the attorney to function effectively, society recognizes an attorney-client privilege. Without a guarantee of secrecy, clients would be unwilling to reveal damaging information. As a corollary, clients would disclose negative information, which an attorney must know to prove effective representation, only if they were assured that such disclosures are privileged.

In contrast, it is not clear whether children would be more likely to discuss private matters with their parents if a parent-child privilege were recognized than if one were not. It is not likely that children, or even their parents, would typically be aware of the existence or non-existence of a testimonial privilege covering parent-child communications. On the other hand, professionals such as attorneys, doctors and members of the clergy would know of the privilege that attends their respective profession, and their clients, patients or parishioners would also be aware that their confidential conversations are protected from compelled disclosure.[21]

Moreover, even assuming *arguendo* that children and their parents generally are aware of whether or not their communications are protected from disclosure, it is not certain that the existence of a privilege enters into whatever thought processes are performed by children in deciding whether or not to confide in their parents. Indeed, the existence or nonexistence of a parent-child privilege is probably one of the least important considerations in any child's decision as to whether to reveal some indiscretion, legal or illegal, to a parent. Moreover, it is unlikely that any parent would choose to deter a child from revealing a confidence to the parent solely because a federal court has refused to recognize a privilege protecting such communications from disclosure.

Finally, the proposed parent-child privilege fails to satisfy the fourth condition of the Wigmore test. As explained above, any injury to the parent-child relationship resulting from non-recognition of such a privilege would be relatively insignificant. In contrast, the cost of recognizing such a privilege is substantial: the impairment of the truth-seek-

---

21. Notably, the Advisory Committee on the Rules of Evidence reached a similar conclusion with respect to a marital communications privilege....

ing function of the judicial system and the increased likelihood of injustice resulting from the concealment of relevant information....

Moreover, because no clear benefit flows from the recognition of a parent-child privilege, any injury to the parent-child relationship caused by compelled testimony as to confidential communications is necessarily and substantially outweighed by the benefit to society of obtaining all relevant evidence in a criminal case....

An even more compelling reason for rejecting a parent-child privilege stems from the fact that the parent-child relationship differs dramatically from other relationships. This is due to the unique duty owing to the child from the parent. A parent owes the duty to the child to nurture and guide the child. This duty is unusual because it inheres in the relationship and the relationship arises automatically at the child's birth.

If, for example, a fifteen year old unemancipated child informs her parent that she has committed a crime or has been using or distributing narcotics, and this disclosure has been made in confidence while the child is seeking guidance, it is evident to us that, regardless of whether the child consents or not, the parent must have the right to take such action as the parent deems appropriate *in the interest of the child.* That action could be commitment to a drug rehabilitation center or a report of the crime to the juvenile authorities. This is so because, in theory at least, juvenile proceedings are undertaken solely in the interest of the child. We would regard it intolerable in such a situation if the law intruded in the guise of a privilege, and silenced the parent because the child had a privilege to prevent disclosure.

This results in the analysis that any privilege, if recognized, must be dependent upon both the parent and child asserting it. However, in such a case, the privilege would disappear if the parent can waive it. It follows therefore that, if a child is able to communicate openly with a parent and seeks guidance from that parent, the entire basis for the privilege is destroyed if the child is required to recognize that confidence will be maintained only so long as the parent wants the conversation to be confidential. If, however, the parent can waive the privilege unilaterally, the goal of the privilege is destroyed....

It follows then that an effective parent-child privilege requires that the parent's lips be sealed but such a sealing would be inexcusable in the parent-child relationship. No government should have that power....

D. RECOGNITION OF A PARENT-CHILD PRIVILEGE SHOULD BE LEFT TO CONGRESS.

Although we, and our sister courts, obviously have authority to develop and modify the common law of privileges, we should be circumspect about creating new privileges based upon perceived public policy considerations. This is particularly so where there exist policy concerns which the legislative branch is better equipped to evaluate....

The legislature, not the judiciary, is institutionally better equipped to perform the balancing of the competing policy issues required in deciding whether the recognition of a parent-child privilege is in the best interests of society. Congress, through its legislative mechanisms, is also better suited for the task of defining the scope of any prospective privilege. Congress is able to consider, for example, society's moral, sociological, economic, religious and other values without being confined to the evidentiary record in any particular case. Thus, in determining whether a parent-child privilege should obtain, Congress can take into consideration a host of facts and factors which the judiciary may be unable to consider. These considerations are also relevant to determining whether the privilege, if it is to be recognized, should extend to adult children, adopted children or unemancipated minors....

Among additional factors that Congress could consider are other parameters of familial relationships. Does "parent" include step-parent or grand-parent? Does "child" include an adopted child, or a step-child? Should the privilege extend to siblings? Furthermore, if another family member is present at the time of the relevant communication, is the privilege automatically barred or destroyed? ...

Hence, as a court without the ability to consider matters beyond the evidentiary record presented, we should be chary about creating new privileges and ordinarily should defer to the legislature to do so. ... Indeed, the Supreme Court has explained that one basis for its disinclination to recognize new privileges is deference to the legislature:

> We are especially reluctant to recognize a privilege in an area where it appears that Congress has considered the relevant competing concerns but has not provided the privilege itself.

University of Pennsylvania v. EEOC, 493 U.S. at 189.

Congress, too, has recognized the importance of privilege rules insofar as the truth-seeking process is concerned. Congress specifically addressed that subject when it delegated rulemaking authority to the Supreme Court as to rules of procedure and evidence. It did so by identifying and designating the law of privileges as a special area meriting greater legislative oversight. Congress expressly provided that "[a]ny ... rule creating, abolishing, or modifying an evidentiary privilege shall have no force or effect unless approved by Act of Congress." 28 U.S.C. § 2074(b) (1994). In contrast, all other evidentiary rules promulgated by the Supreme Court and transmitted to Congress automatically take effect unless Congress enacts a statute to the contrary. *See* 28 U.S.C. § 2074(a) (1994).

IV.

.... [T]he Virgin Islands privilege which Judge Mansmann would recognize, while characterized as a limited one, would only come into play where a child has made a *confidential communication to a parent in the course of seeking parental advice*. Both of these qualifications—(1) a confidential communication, spoken or written, and (2) arising in the course of seeking parental advice—would have to be determined by a hearing—a mini-trial—which would have the effect of destroying the confidential nature of the communication (since the communication would have to be divulged so that the district court could determine its precise nature). It would also endow the district court with virtually unlimited discretion in granting or denying the privilege (since the dissent provides little guidance to the district court for making such a determination). The exercise of this discretion would undermine the very essence of a privilege that "the participants in the confidential conversation" can predict "with some degree of certainty" that their conversation will be protected. *See Jaffee v. Redmond*, 518 U.S. 1, 18 (1996)....

The entire thrust of the dissent's opinion is that a child should feel confident, in communicating with a parent to seek advice and guidance, that the communication will remain inviolate. However, the dissent, then straddling the fence, also argues that the parent can choose to violate such a confidence and report a confidential communication to others (presumably the authorities) in the interest of parental judgment. *See* Dissenting Opinion at 1160 n. 6. We know of no privilege that can operate in such a two-way fashion and still remain effective....

Finally, we observe that implicit in the various discussions by courts (both federal and state) of the parent-child privilege is the fact that the "strong and trusting parent-child relationships" which the dissent would preserve have existed throughout the years without the concomitant existence of a privilege protecting that relationship....

MANSMANN, Circuit Judge, concurring and dissenting.

I write separately because I am convinced that the testimonial privilege issue raised by the Virgin Islands appeal is substantially different from that presented in the Delaware appeals and should be resolved in favor of the targeted son. The Virgin Islands appeal, which challenges the denial of a motion to quash a grand jury subpoena, requires that we confront an issue of first impression in our circuit: should we make available to a parent and child an evidentiary privilege which could be invoked to prevent compelling that parent to testify regarding confidential communications made to the parent by his child in the course of seeking parental advice and guidance? It appears that this precise question is one of first impression in the federal courts....

II.

....

B.

When a federal court considers extending the scope of a testimonial privilege or recognizing a new privilege, Rule 501 requires that the court engage in a balancing process, weighing the need for confidentiality in a particular communication against the need for relevant evidence in a criminal proceeding. *Trammel*, 445 U.S. at 50. I am convinced that the public good derived from a child's ability to communicate openly with and to seek guidance from his or her parents is of sufficient magnitude to transcend the judicial system's interest in compelled parental testimony.[5]

Recognizing that "our authority is narrow in scope and [to] be exercised only after careful consideration in the face of a strong showing of need for the privilege," *In re Grand Jury Investigation*, 918 F.2d 374, 383 (3d Cir. 1990), I stress that the privilege which I would recognize is a limited one, applying *only* to compelled testimony concerning confidential communications made to a parent by his child in the course of seeking parental advice. Although this case might have been more compelling had the son been a minor at the time of his statements to his father, I would not adopt a bright-line rule applicable only to those who have not reached legal majority. In order to advance the policy interests which the targeted son articulated, I would prefer to leave the particular factors to be considered in determining application of the privilege to development on a case-by-case basis. I expect that these factors would include such variables as age, maturity, whether or not the child resides with the parents, and the precise nature of the communications for which the privilege is claimed. The privilege would apply to situations in which it is invoked by both parent and child; this case does not require that we confront applicability of the privilege where it is invoked by the parent or the child alone.

---

5. In addition to the balancing test laid out in *Trammel*, Dean Wigmore has suggested a four-part test for determining whether or not a particular testimonial privilege should be recognized.... I part company with the majority in the application of this test and am convinced that the factors analyzed under the Rule 501 balancing test are sufficient to satisfy the Wigmore test as well. The first condition of the Wigmore test is satisfied in that the parent-child relationship is one which naturally gives rise to confidential communication. Second, confidentiality underlies the parent child relationship; mutual trust encourages children to consult parents for guidance with the expectation that the parent will, in appropriate circumstances, honor the confidentiality of those statements. Third, the family unit is the building block of our society and the parent-child relationship is at the core of that family unit. Finally, although the majority disputes this point, I am convinced that the damage resulting from compelling a parent to testify against his child, in most if not all cases, outweighs the benefit associated with correct disposal of the litigation.

The goal in recognizing this limited privilege would not be to guarantee confidentiality *per se* but to shield parent-child relationships from the devastating effects likely to be associated with compelled testimony. As one commentator has written:

> [T]o conceive of . . . privileges merely as exclusionary rules, is to start out on the wrong road and, except by happy accident, to reach the wrong destination. They are, or rather by chance of litigation may become, exclusionary rules; but this is incidental and secondary. Primarily they are a right to be let alone, a right to unfettered freedom, in certain narrowly prescribed relationships, from the state's coercive or supervisory powers. . . .

Louisell, *Confidentiality, Conformity, and Confusions: Privileges in Federal Court Today*, 31 Tul. L.Rev. 101, 110–11 (1956). An effective parent-child relationship is one deserving of protection. It rests upon a relationship of mutual trust where the child has the right to expect that the parent will act in accordance with the child's best interest.[6] If the state is permitted to interfere in that relationship by compelling parents to divulge information conveyed to them in confidence by their children, mutual trust, and ultimately the family, are threatened.

While I am aware that the availability of even this limited parent-child privilege may, in some rare circumstances, complicate a criminal fact-finding proceeding, I am convinced that the risk is one well worth bearing. . . . This is especially true where, as here in the Virgin Islands case, the parent is not a co-defendant or a co-witness to a criminal act, and is not alleged to be hiding the instrumentality or the fruits of a criminal act.

I cannot agree with the majority that testimonial privileges must be regarded as automatic impediments to the effectiveness of the judicial system. In limited circumstances these privileges are critical to important policy interests. I am convinced, as was the district court, that "youngsters today are increasingly faced with excruciatingly dangerous and difficult situations" and that "the law ought to do everything possible to encourage children to confide in their parents and turn to [them] in times of trouble." *In re Grand Jury Proceeding*, Misc. No. 95-009, at 9, 10 (D.V.I. June 19, 1995).

C.

The spousal privilege is the only testimonial privilege based on a familial relationship to have received general acceptance in the federal courts. . . . In arguing that we should uphold the father's claim of privilege in this case, I am motivated by many of the same concerns which underlie the spousal privilege.[8]

---

6. While it is true, as the majority says, that few children are likely to be aware of a privilege *per se*, there is, in any event, a certain expectation that this information will not be disclosed.

As the majority points out, there may be circumstances in which a parent, having heard communications from a child, decides that it is in the child's best interest that those communications be divulged. The privilege which I advocate would not interfere with that parental judgment. Presumably, if the parent is indeed acting in the child's best interest, disclosure will not ultimately threaten the family relationship which I seek to protect. Furthermore, if the parent is willing to disclose information which may harm the child, the relationship is already beyond the need for protection.

8. Some commentators have sought to analogize the parent-child privilege to the more widely recognized professional testimonial privileges such as that between attorney and client, priest and penitent, and physician and patient:

> The parent-child relationship is analogous to the privileged professional relationships in many respects. As the professional exercises his skill in the delicate relationship with his client, the parent plays a unique and sensitive role in the life of his "client," the child. In fulfilling this role, the parent must assume many of the same responsibilities as professionals. The parent, for example, often must serve as the child's legal advisor, spiritual counselor,

The policy advanced by the spousal privilege "is the protection of the marital confidences, regarded as so essential to the preservation of the marriage relationship as to outweigh the disadvantages to the administration of justice which the privilege entails." *Wolfle v. United States*, 291 U.S. 7, 14 (1934). Similar concerns are present here:

> Ideally, the child-parent relationship encompasses aspects of the marital relationship—mutual love, affection, and intimacy ... the parent providing emotional guidance and the child relying on him for help and support.... As in the marital ... relation[ship], this optimal child-parent relationship cannot exist without a great deal of communication between the two.... Manifestly, the parent's disclosure of such information to a third party, ... would deter continued communication between child and parent.

Comment, *The Child-Parent Privilege: A Proposal*, 47 Fordham L.Rev. 771, 781 (1979)....

The Court in *Trammel* also recognized that privileges "affecting marriage, home and family relationships," 445 U.S. at 48, are especially worthy of consideration. Within the family structure but beyond the marital partners, I can think of no relationship more fundamental than that between parent and child. Society has an interest in protecting the family structure; the parent-child relationship is amenable to identification and segregation for special treatment.

D.

The parent-child privilege is not a novel or radical concept. "Both ancient Jewish law and Roman law entirely barred family members from testifying against one another based on a desire to promote the solidarity and trust that support the family unit. The Napoleonic Code also prevented the disclosure of confidences between family members." J. Tyson Covey, Note, *Making Form Follow Function: Considerations in Creating and Applying a Statutory Parent-Child Privilege*, 1990 U. Ill. L.Rev. 879, 883. The civil law countries of Western Europe including France, Sweden, and the former West Germany also recognize a privilege covering compelled testimony from family members.

Three states (Idaho, Massachusetts and Minnesota) have adopted some variant of the parent-child privilege by statute, and one state, New York, has judicially recognized the privilege. *In re A & M*, 403 N.Y.S.2d 375 (1978). Furthermore, our review of the caselaw convinces us that although a number of courts have declined to recognize a parent-child privilege in one form or another, the vast majority of those cases, indeed all of the federal cases, are distinguishable, on significant grounds, from the case before us.

Most cases discussing the availability of a parent-child privilege have done so in the context of whether a child should be compelled to testify against a parent. As the court of appeals acknowledged in *In re Grand Jury Proceedings (Starr)*, 647 F.2d 511, 513 n. 4 (5th Cir. 1981), cases involving testimony by a child regarding activities of or communications by a parent are not as compelling as cases "involv[ing] confidential communications from the child to the parent" because the former do not implicate "the desire to avoid discouraging a child from confiding in his parents." ... This distinction separates the Virgin Islands and Delaware appeals.

---

and physical and emotional health expert. The necessity for confidentiality is comparable to that within the professional relationships. Like the attorney, priest, or psychiatrist, parents must establish an atmosphere of trust to facilitate free and open communication. Gregory W. Franklin, Note, *The Judicial Development of the Parent-Child Testimonial Privilege: Too Big for its Britches?* 26 Wm. & Mary L.Rev. 145, 151 (1984).

A second set of cases refusing to recognize a parent-child privilege involve children who were significantly older than the son in this case and did not implicate communications seeking parental advice and guidance.[13] As the Court of Appeals for the Second Circuit has recognized, these cases, too, "present[ ] a weaker claim for recognition of a parent child privilege...." *In re Erato*, 2 F.3d 11, 16 (2d Cir. 1993).

Several cases evaluating a claim of privilege did not have the benefit of the balancing process embodied in Rule 501 of the Federal Rules of Evidence and others did not involve confidential communications made by a child to a parent. Finally, a number of cases rejecting the parent-child privilege involved defendants who sought to bar voluntary testimony offered by their parents. These cases do not present the threat to the family relationship posed in the case before us....

Notes and Questions

1. What weight is to be given to the fact that a particular privilege was not among those in the proposed but rejected rules originally submitted to Congress by the Advisory Committee? After all, those are *rejected* rules! The Supreme Court has suggested that it is relevant:

> Neither the Advisory Committee, the Judicial Conference, nor this Court saw fit, however, to provide the privilege sought by Gillock. Although that fact standing alone would not compel the federal courts to refuse to recognize a privilege omitted from the proposal, it does suggest that the claimed privilege was not thought to be either indelibly ensconced in our common law or an imperative of federalism.

United States v. Gillock, 445 U.S. 360, 367–368 (1980). *See also Williams v. Sprint/United Management Co.*, 2006 WL 266599, at *2 (D. Kan. Feb. 1, 2006) (noting that the proposed rules are a sensible starting point for determining the existence and scope of federal privileges because they restate rather than modify the then-existing common law of privileges, a body of law which was developed under a standard similar to that of Federal Rule 501); *Hopson v. Mayor and City Council of Baltimore*, 232 F.R.D. 228, 240 (D. Md. 2005) (same).

2. The *Grand Jury* majority cites *University of Pennsylvania v. EEOC*, 493 U.S. 182, 189 (1990), for the proposition that the courts should be "reluctant to recognize a privilege in an area where it appears that Congress has considered the relevant competing concerns but has not provided the privilege itself." In that case, the EEOC was investigating a claim of racial and gender discrimination against a university in its tenure process, and sought access to peer review materials of various tenure candidates. The Supreme Court, in rejecting a claim that a confidential peer review privilege should be recognized under Rule 501, pointed to the fact that when Title VII was expanded by Congress to allow for such suits against universities, a concern over the fact that such materials might be subject to disclosure was brought to Congress's attention, but they nonetheless chose to ex-

---

13. While I recognize that the son in this case was 18 and, therefore, under Virgin Island law had reached the "age of majority" at the time of the confidential communication ... I find it significant that the son was living at home when the communications were made. I also find critical the district court's statement that, "It is apparent ... that the confidential communications which ensued were in the nature of a child seeking advice from his father with whom he shared a close and trusting relationship."

pand Title VII without creating a privilege for such documents. *Id.* Does the *Grand Jury* majority point to any comparable evidence with respect to the parent-child privilege?

3. The *Grand Jury* majority cites to 28 U.S.C. § 2074(b) as a reason to exercise caution in recognizing new privileges. Is this consistent with Rule 501? Does that not seem inconsistent with footnote 8 in *Trammel* (citing an earlier version of § 2074(b))?

4. The *Grand Jury* majority states that a parent-child privilege would be intolerable because it would prevent a concerned parent from acting on what her children tell her to seek drug treatment for them or report their crimes to the juvenile authorities. Is not the majority confused about the difference between duties of confidentiality and testimonial privileges?

5. Although no federal court has since recognized a parent-child privilege, one federal appeals court has left open the possibility that such a privilege might be recognized for communications involving minor children. *See United States v. Dunford*, 148 F.3d 385, 390–91 (4th Cir. 1998). Should a distinction be drawn between minor and non-minor children?

6. Recall that Justice Scalia, in his dissent in *Jaffee*, stated that there is no parent-child privilege. What was the basis for his statement? Does it lend support to the *Grand Jury* court's holding? In determining the weight to be given to Justice Scalia's statement, is it relevant that he also believed there not to be a psychotherapist-patient privilege?

7. What justifies treating the marital relationship differently from the parent-child relationship so far as privileges are concerned? Does not recognition of the former compel recognition of the latter? Or are there differences between the two relationships that justify different treatment?

8. During his investigation into former President Bill Clinton, Independent Counsel Kenneth Starr subpoenaed Monica Lewinsky's mother, Marcia Lewis, to testify before a grand jury investigating her daughter. The incident prompted a number of Congressional proposals to create a parent-child testimonial privilege. *See generally* Shonah P. Jefferson, *The Statutory Development of the Parent-Child Privilege: Congress Responds to Kenneth Starr's Tactics*, 16 Ga. St. U. L. Rev. 429 (1999). One such proposal would create both a testimonial and a communications privilege, modeled after the spousal privileges. *See* HR 3433, 109th Cong. (2005).

F. Clergy-Communicant Privilege

Problem 5-9: Forgive Me, Father ...

Defendant, a priest in a diocese of the Roman Catholic Church located within a federal enclave, is under investigation on federal charges of child molestation. The government has reason to believe that the defendant may have told another priest in the church of his acts of child molestation, and subpoenas that priest to testify before a grand jury investigating the charges. But he refuses to testify, asserting a claim that the conversation is privileged.

How will the court dispose of the claim that the conversation is privileged?

In re Grand Jury Investigation
918 F.2d 374 (3d Cir. 1990)

BECKER, Circuit Judge....

I. FACTS AND PROCEDURAL HISTORY

On November 28, 1985, a fire occurred at a house, located in an all-white neighborhood in the Forest Hills section of Pittsburgh, Pennsylvania, that had recently been purchased by a black family. The police and fire departments determined that the fire was the likely result of arson. Within several days of the fire, Mr. and Mrs. George Kampich, Mrs. Kampich's adult son, George Shaw (who is not related legally or by blood to Mr. Kampich), and Patty DiLucente, Shaw's fiancee, sought counseling from the Reverend Ernest Knoche ("Pastor Knoche"), a Lutheran clergyman.[4] All four persons lived in the home next door to the site of the fire. Mr. and Mrs. Kampich are members of Pastor Knoche's church. Although Shaw has occasionally attended services at the church, Shaw and DiLucente are not members. In June of 1989, Shaw and DiLucente were married. In November of 1989, some four years after the counseling session, a grand jury convened by the district court for the Western District of Pennsylvania commenced an investigation of the suspected arson. The grand jury was investigating, in particular, possible violations of 42 U.S.C. § 3631, prohibiting racially motivated housing discrimination, and of 18 U.S.C. § 241, prohibiting conspiracies to violate civil rights.

On November 28, 1989, the government subpoenaed Pastor Knoche to testify before the grand jury about the 1985 counseling session. The government, in support of this subpoena, asserted that it had reason to believe that the Kampiches, Shaw, and DiLucente had planned or participated in the arson and had discussed their involvement with the pastor. In an interview prior to his appearance before the grand jury, Pastor Knoche informed the government that he intended to assert the clergy-communicant privilege and would refuse to answer any questions regarding the counseling session. That day, the government filed a motion in the district court to compel Pastor Knoche to testify before the grand jury.

On November 28th and 29th, the district court held a hearing on the government's motion. In the course of this hearing, the district judge questioned the pastor about the extent of his family and group counseling, the parties involved in the discussion at issue, and the confidentiality of their communications. Pastor Knoche stated that family counseling, in contrast to individual counseling, constituted a typical and important part of his ministry. The Pastor also concurred with the district court's characterization of his ministry as founded upon the Judeo-Christian notion of redemption and forgiveness through counseling and prayer. The Pastor responded, further, that forthrightness and truthfulness on the part of participants, such as Mr. and Mrs. Kampich, Shaw, and DiLucente, are essential to proper counseling and, ultimately, to redemption. He concluded that those whom he spiritually counsels expect that he will keep any communications made to him in strict confidence.

---

4. Pastor Knoche actually had three discussions regarding the November 29, 1985 incident. Only Mr. and Mrs. Kampich were present during the first discussion. The district court held that this first discussion was privileged, and the United States does not challenge that portion of the district court's order on appeal. The government does take issue with the court's denial of its petition to compel Pastor Knoche's testimony concerning the counseling session at which Mr. and Mrs. Kampich, Shaw, and DiLucente all were present. The third discussion, involving Pastor Knoche and the same four individuals, took place in the presence of a police officer. Pastor Knoche does not claim a privilege as to that discussion.

The district court sustained Pastor Knoche's right to assert a clergy-communicant privilege and denied the government's motion to compel his testimony. The district judge, in a colloquy setting forth the basis for his decision, described it as "tough," but concluded that compelling the pastor to testify would break down church-state divisions, infringe upon the right to participate in religious activities, invade a "sacrosanct" area, and, through depriving families of confidential religious counseling, endanger them. This appeal followed.

II. THE EXISTENCE AND CONTOURS OF A CLERGY-COMMUNICANT PRIVILEGE

In federal courts, evidentiary privileges are governed by Rule 501 of the Federal Rules of Evidence. This provision, which was the product of congressional involvement in the rulemaking process, does not contain a specific and exclusive list of privileges recognized in the federal courts. The Rule instead provides the federal courts with flexibility in crafting testimonial privileges....

A. *The Clergy-Communicant Privilege and the History of Rule 501*

The privilege formula adopted by Congress in Rule 501 had its origin in Rule 26 of the Federal Rules of Criminal Procedure. Both the history and the language of Rule 501, therefore, provide us with a mandate to develop evidentiary privileges in accordance with common law principles. This mandate, in turn, requires us to examine federal and state case law and impels us to consult treatises and commentaries on the law of evidence that elucidate the development of the common law. We believe that the proposed rules of evidence adopted by the Supreme Court and submitted to Congress provide us with an appropriate starting point for discerning the existence and scope of the clergy-communicant privilege.

Rule 501 replaced a number of proposed rules concerning evidentiary privileges that were adopted by the Supreme Court following extensive study and analysis by the Advisory Committee responsible for codifying federal rules of evidence. As submitted to Congress, Article V of the proposed rules set out thirteen rules encompassing nine specific privileges, including a privilege for communications to clergymen. Rule 506, delineating the contours of the clergy-communicant privilege, reads as follows:

Communications to Clergymen

(a) *Definitions.* As used in this rule:

(1) A "clergyman" is a minister, priest, rabbi, or other similar functionary of a religious organization, or an individual reasonably believed so to be by the person consulting him.

(2) A communication is "confidential" if made privately and not intended for further disclosure except to other persons present in furtherance of the purpose of the communication.

(b) *General rule of privilege.* A person has a privilege to refuse to disclose and to prevent another from disclosing a confidential communication by the person to a clergyman in his professional character as spiritual adviser.

(c) *Who may claim the privilege.* The privilege may be claimed by the person, by his guardian or conservator, or by his personal representative if he is deceased. The clergyman may claim the privilege on behalf of the person. His authority so to do is presumed in the absence of evidence to the contrary.

The Advisory Committee's note confirms that proposed Rule 506 is expansive in character:

The definition of "confidential" communication is consistent with the use of the term in Rule 503(a)(5) for lawyer-client and in Rule 504(a)(3) for psychotherapist-patient, suitably adapted to communications to clergymen.... *The choice between a privilege narrowly restricted to doctrinally required confessions and a privilege broadly applicable to all confidential communications with a clergyman in his professional character as a spiritual adviser has been exercised in favor of the latter.* Many clergymen now receive training in marriage counseling and the handling of personality problems. Matters of this kind fall readily into the realm of the spirit. The same considerations which underlie the psychotherapist-patient privilege of Rule 504 suggest a broad application of the privilege for communications to clergymen.

The reference in the Advisory Committee's Note to the group counseling practices common to the psychotherapist-patient relationship and the relationship of lawyers to multiple clients indicates that the Supreme Court did not view the privilege as limited solely to confidential relationships between two individuals. Given the requisite showing of confidentiality, proposed Rule 506 would have extended the clergy-communicant privilege to group discussions.

Although Congress chose not to adopt the proposed rules on privileges, it did not disapprove them. The Senate Judiciary Committee's report on Rule 501 states:

> It should be clearly understood that, in approving this general rule as to privileges, the action of Congress should not be understood as disapproving any recognition of ... any ... of the enumerated privileges contained in the Supreme Court rules. Rather, our action should be understood as reflecting the view that the recognition of a privilege based on a confidential relationship and other privileges should be determined on a case-by-case basis.

S.Rep. No. 93-1277, 93rd Cong., 2d Sess. 4, *reprinted* in 1974 U.S.Code Cong. and Admin.News 7051, 7059. We believe that the proposed rules provide a useful reference point and offer guidance in defining the existence and scope of evidentiary privileges in the federal courts. We agree with Judge Weinstein and Professor Berger, who state:

> [I]n many instances, the proposed rules, [used as] [s]tandards, remain a convenient and useful starting point for examining questions of privilege. The [s]tandards are the culmination of three drafts prepared by an Advisory Committee consisting of judges, practicing lawyers and academicians.... Finally, they were adopted by the Supreme Court.... [T]he Advisory Committee in drafting the Standards was for the most part restating the law currently applied in the federal courts.

J. Weinstein & M. Berger, *supra*, at ¶ 501[03].

The history of the proposed Rules of Evidence reflects that the clergy-communicant rule was one of the least controversial of the enumerated privileges, merely defining a long-recognized principle of American law. Although most of the nine privileges set forth in the proposed rules were vigorously attacked in Congress, the privilege covering communications to members of the clergy was not. Indeed, virtually every state has recognized some form of clergy-communicant privilege.[10] The inclusion of the

---

10. .... We note that, although the clergy-communicant privilege is part of the American tradition, it did not exist as part of the English common law.... The climate of hostility in England toward the Roman Catholic Church during the Reformation largely accounts for the nonexistence of the privilege at common law.... There is evidence to suggest, however, that as a matter of judicial discretion judges would often excuse members of the clergy from testifying about confidential communications.

clergy-communicant privilege in the proposed rules, taken together with its uncontroversial nature, strongly suggests that the privilege is, in the words of the Supreme Court "indelibly ensconced" in the American common law. *United States v. Gillock*, 445 U.S. 360, 368 (1980).

B. *Federal Judicial Precedents Recognizing a Clergy-Communicant Privilege*

The first reported federal case recognizing the clergy-communicant privilege through the common law process of decision was decided in 1958, *see Mullen v. United States*, 263 F.2d 275 (D.C. Cir. 1958) (Fahy J., concurring). Judge Fahy's lengthy concurrence in this case traced the history and contours of the clergy-communicant privilege and opined that the admission of a minister's testimony about a conversation, in which the defendant sought spiritual counseling, constituted an additional ground for overturning the jury's verdict against her.

Following *Mullen*, a number of federal courts recognized a common law clergy-communicant privilege....

The Supreme Court, albeit in dicta, subsequently acknowledged the existence of a "priest-penitent" privilege.... The *Trammel* Court, pursuant to Rule 501's mandate to the federal courts to develop common law rules of privilege in a flexible manner, held that the rule precluding the adverse testimony of one spouse against the other, with respect to non-confidential communications, may only be invoked by the witness-spouse. Critiquing an archaic and unduly expansive rule that permitted a defendant to exclude from evidence any adverse spousal testimony, the Court favorably referred to several privileges by analogy, among them, the "priest-penitent" privilege:

> The privileges between priest and penitent, attorney and client, and physician and patient limit protection to private communications. The privileges are rooted in the imperative need for confidence and trust. The priest-penitent privilege recognizes the human need to disclose to a spiritual counselor, in total and absolute confidence, what are believed to be flawed acts or thoughts and to receive priestly consolation and guidance in return.

Id. at 51. *See also United States v. Nixon*, 418 U.S. 683, 709 (1974) ("[G]enerally, an attorney or *a priest* may not be required to disclose what has been revealed in professional confidence" (emphasis added)).

In the wake of the Supreme Court's opinion in *Trammel*, a number of federal district courts and courts of appeal have also acknowledged the clergy-communicant privilege....

Although we have never formally recognized the clergy-communicant privilege, several of our opinions have referred to the privilege in passing. These opinions note that the privilege protecting communications to members of the clergy, like the attorney-client and physician-patient privileges, is grounded in a policy of preventing disclosures that would tend to inhibit the development of confidential relationships that are socially desirable....

C. *The Scope and Contours of the Clergy-Communicant Privilege Adopted*

....

In determining whether a clergy-communicant privilege exists, we weigh Dean Wigmore's four fundamental prerequisites for a privilege against the disclosure of communications:

> (1) The communications must originate in a *confidence* that they will not be disclosed.

(2) This element of *confidentiality must be essential* to the full and satisfactory maintenance of the relation between the parties.

(3) The *relation* must be one which in the opinion of the community ought to be sedulously *fostered*.

(4) The *injury* that would inure to the relation by the disclosure of the communications must be *greater than the benefit* thereby gained for the correct disposal of litigation.

8 *Wigmore* at § 2285.[12] The Advisory Committee Note to proposed Rule 506 adverts to these considerations and concludes that they "seem strongly to favor a privilege for confidential communications to clergymen."

We are, of course, mindful of the broad investigatory powers accorded to the grand jury. We again note, however, that the Rules of Evidence explicitly provide for the application of Rule 501, the more general successor to proposed Rule 506, in grand jury proceedings. *See* Fed.R.Evid. 1101(d)(2). We are satisfied, moreover, that American common law, viewed in the light of reason and experience and the "conditions" properly set forth by Dean Wigmore and by Judge Weinstein, *supra* note 12, compels the recognition of a clergy-communicant privilege. Both state and federal decisions have long recognized the privilege. The Supreme Court Rules Committee also recognized the privilege. That is doubtless because the clergy-communicant relationship is so important, indeed so fundamental to the western tradition, that it must be "sedulously fostered." 8 *Wigmore* at § 2285. Confidence is obviously essential to maintaining the clergy-communicant relationship. Although there are countervailing considerations, we have no doubt that the need for protecting the relationship outweighs them.

We believe that the privilege should apply to protect communications made (1) to a clergyperson[13] (2) in his or her spiritual and professional capacity (3) with a reasonable expectation of confidentiality. As is the case with the attorney-client privilege, the presence of third parties, if essential to and in furtherance of the communication, should not void the privilege. This statement of the contours of the privilege is consistent with the provisions of Rule 506, which, as our study of the federal case law confirms, tracks the

---

12. In analyzing whether this privilege exists under federal common law, we have also considered the balancing process described by Judge Weinstein in *United States v. King*, 73 F.R.D. 103, 105 (E.D.N.Y. 1976). *King* involved the rather different issue of whether a federal court should recognize a state privilege in the context of a prosecution for a federal crime. We find helpful, nonetheless, the factors considered by Judge Weinstein in the following passage from the case:

> [T]he justifiable "principles of the common law" as they relate to matters of developing new privileges — those not firmly embedded in federal law — require the balancing of four factors: first, the federal government's need for the information being sought in enforcing its substantive and procedural policies; second, the importance of the relationship or policy sought to be furthered by the state rule of privilege and the probability that the privilege will advance that relationship or policy; third, in the particular case, the special need for the information sought to be protected; and fourth, in the particular case, the adverse impact on the local policy that would result from non-recognition of the privilege.

13. We believe that Proposed Rule of Evidence 506(a)(1) provides a workable definition of a clergyperson: "A 'clergyman' is a minister, priest, rabbi, or other similar functionary of a religious organization, or an individual reasonably believed so to be by the person consulting him." By endorsing this definition of a clergyperson, we do not intimate that the privilege should be interpreted to comprehend communications to and among members of sects that denominate each and every member as clergy, proclaim that all communications have spiritual significance, or dictate that all communications among members, whether essential to and in furtherance of the purportedly privileged communication or not, shall be confidential.

evolving common law. In addition, we note our agreement with the tenor of the Advisory Committee's Note to proposed Rule 506, which extends the scope of the privilege to encompass not only communications between Roman Catholic priests and their penitents, but also communications between clergy and communicants of other denominations. *See* Proposed Fed. Rule of Evid. 506 advisory committee's note.[14]

Our delineation of the privilege is not comprehensive. We illuminate here and *infra* only those facets and boundaries of the privilege that are implicated in this case. The privilege is a common law rule. The precise scope of the privilege and its additional facets, such as whether a clergyperson should be required to disclose confidential communications when harm to innocent parties is threatened and imminent, are, therefore, most suitably left to case-by-case evolution.[15]

. . . .

Notes and Questions

1. From an instrumental standpoint, is a clergy-communicant privilege necessary to encourage such communications? *See* 1 *McCormick on Evidence* § 762, at 316 (5th ed. 1999) (noting that the strong religious beliefs of penitents will continue to impel them to confess their sins whether or not such communications are privileged).

2. Surprisingly, notwithstanding his strong opposition to most testimonial privileges, Jeremy Bentham actually favored the clergy-communicant privilege:

> I set out with the supposition, that ... the catholic religion was meant to be tolerated. But, with any idea of toleration, a coercion of this nature is altogether inconsistent and incompatible. In the character of penitents, the people would be pressed with the whole weight of the penal branch of law: inhibited from the exercise of this essential and indispensable article of their religions.... To form any comparative estimate of the bad and good effects flowing from this institution, belongs not ... to the design of this work....

5 Jeremy Bentham, Rationale of Judicial Evidence 588–90 (1827).

Are you persuaded by Bentham's effort to distinguish this privilege from other privileges of which he was highly critical, such as the attorney-client and spousal privileges? Is it fair for those who purport to be affiliated with a religious institution to be entitled to a privilege beyond those available to the public at large?

3. The states take a variety of different approaches to the applicability of the clergy-communicant privilege where the communications involve disclosures of child abuse. While

---

14. Indeed, the prospect of restricting the privilege to Roman Catholic penitential communications raises serious first amendment concerns. *See Larsen v. Valente*, 456 U.S. 228, 245–46 (1982) (emphasizing that the establishment clause articulates a "principle of denominational neutrality" and holding that state law "granting a denominational preference" is subject to strict scrutiny).

15. We also need not address at any length the question of who may assert the privilege. The authorities recognizing the privilege would allow it to be asserted, as it was here, by a clergyperson on behalf of a communicant. We need not reach the issue, therefore, of whether Pastor Knoche could assert the privilege on his own behalf.

With respect to the question of which party carries the burden of proof in establishing the privilege's applicability, it is clear, in this Circuit, that a party who asserts a privilege has the burden of proving its existence and applicability.... We note, in addition, that the existence and applicability of a privilege may be undermined by the presumption, rebuttable by the party asserting the privilege, that communications that take place in the presence of third parties are not confidential.

some states treat such communications no differently than any other disclosures, some states except completely such communications from the protection of the clergy-communicant privilege, while others create a duty to disclose the communication to authorities but create no exception to the *testimonial* privilege. *See* Norman Abrams, *Addressing the Tension Between the Clergy-Communicant Privilege and the Duty to Report Child Abuse in State Statutes*, 44 B.C.L. Rev. 1127 (2003); R. Michael Cassidy, *Sharing Sacred Secrets: Is it (Past) Time for a Dangerous Person Exception to the Clergy-Penitent Privilege*, 44 Wm. & Mary L. Rev. 1627 (2003).

4. Can one member of the clergy invoke the clergy-communicant privilege with respect to his communications with another member of the clergy? As with communications from other penitents, the focus is on the capacity in which the communication was made, to wit, whether it was made to the other member of the clergy in his capacity as a spiritual advisor as opposed to his role as a friend or supervisor. *See, e.g., People v. Campobello*, 810 N.E.2d 307, 319–22 (Ill. App. 2 Dist. 2004); *Society of Jesus of New England v. Commonwealth*, 808 N.E.2d 272, 282 n.13 (Mass. 2004).

5. What if a penitent cuts out the middle man, so to speak, and communicates directly to God via "Dear God" entries in her journal; are those entries protected by the clergy-communicant privilege? *See Varner v. Stovall*, 500 F.3d 491, 494–99 (6th Cir. 2007) (upholding the constitutionality of the Michigan clergy-penitent privilege, which protects only communications via clergy and not via journal entries, reasoning that such a restriction is consistent with the "traditional function" of the privilege).

G. Reporter-Source Privilege

In re Grand Jury Subpoena, Judith Miller
397 F.3d 964 (D.C. Cir. 2005)

SENTELLE, Circuit Judge.

An investigative reporter for the New York Times; the White House correspondent for the weekly news magazine Time; and Time, Inc., the publisher of Time, appeal from orders of the District Court for the District of Columbia finding all three appellants in civil contempt for refusing to give evidence in response to grand jury subpoenas served by Special Counsel Patrick J. Fitzgerald. Appellants assert that the information concealed by them, specifically the identity of confidential sources, is protected by a reporter's privilege arising from the First Amendment, or failing that, by federal common law privilege. The District Court held that neither the First Amendment nor the federal common law provides protection for journalists' confidential sources in the context of a grand jury investigation....

I. Background

According to the briefs and record before us, the controversy giving rise to this litigation began with a political and news media controversy over a sixteen-word sentence in the State of the Union Address of President George W. Bush on January 28, 2003. In that address, President Bush stated: "The British government has learned that Saddam Hussein recently sought significant quantities of uranium from Africa." The ensuing public controversy focused not on the British source of the alleged information, but rather on the accuracy of the proposition that Saddam Hussein had sought uranium, a key ingredient in the development of nuclear weaponry, from Africa. Many publications on the subject followed. On July 6, 2003, the New York Times published an op-ed piece by former Ambassador Joseph Wilson, in which he claimed to have been sent to Niger in 2002 by the Central Intelligence Agency ("CIA") in response to inquiries from Vice President Cheney to investigate whether Iraq had been seeking to purchase uranium from Niger. Wilson claimed that he had conducted the requested investigation and reported on his return that there was no credible evidence that any such effort had been made.

On July 14, 2003, columnist Robert Novak published a column in the Chicago Sun-Times in which he asserted ... that "two senior administration officials" told him that Wilson's selection was at the suggestion of Wilson's wife, Valerie Plame, whom Novak described as a CIA "operative on weapons of mass destruction." After Novak's column was published, various media accounts reported that other reporters had been told by government officials that Wilson's wife worked at the CIA monitoring weapons of mass destruction, and that she was involved in her husband's selection for the mission to Niger. One such article, published by Time.com on July 17, 2003, was authored in part by appellant Matthew Cooper....

The Department of Justice undertook an investigation into whether government employees had violated federal law by the unauthorized disclosure of the identity of a CIA agent....

On September 13, 2004, the grand jury issued a further subpoena to Cooper seeking "[a]ny and all documents ... [relating to] conversations between Matthew Cooper and official source(s) prior to July 14, 2003, concerning in any way: former Ambassador Joseph Wilson; the 2002 trip by former Ambassador Wilson to Niger; Valerie Wilson Plame, a/k/a Valerie Wilson, a/k/a Valerie Plame (the wife of former Ambassador Wilson); and/or any affiliation between Valerie Wilson Plame and the CIA." An August 2, 2004 subpoena to Time requested "[a]ll notes, tape recordings, e-mails, or other documents of Matthew Cooper relating to the July 17, 2003 Time.com article entitled 'A War on Wilson?' and the July 21, 2003 Time Magazine article entitled, 'A Question of Trust.'" Cooper and Time again moved to quash the subpoenas, and on October 7, 2004, the District Court denied the motion. The two refused to comply with the subpoenas, and on October 13, 2004, the District Court held that their refusal was without just cause and held both in contempt.

In the meantime, on August 12 and August 14, grand jury subpoenas were issued to Judith Miller, seeking documents and testimony related to conversations between her and a specified government official "occurring from on or about July 6, 2003, to on or about July 13, 2003, ... concerning Valerie Plame Wilson (whether referred to by name or by description as the wife of Ambassador Wilson) or concerning Iraqi efforts to obtain uranium." Miller refused to comply with the subpoenas and moved to quash them. The District Court denied Miller's motion to quash. Thereafter, the court found that Miller had refused to comply without just cause and held her in civil contempt of court also. She also has appealed....

II. Analysis

A. *The First Amendment Claim*

[In this portion of the opinion, the court holds that the First Amendment does not provide a journalist with a right to refuse to reveal the identity of her confidential source in response to a grand jury subpoena, relying on the Supreme Court's decision in *Branzburg v. Hayes*, 408 U.S. 665 (1972).]

B. *The Common Law Privilege*

Appellants argue that even if there is no First Amendment privilege protecting their confidential source information, we should recognize a privilege under federal common law, arguing that regardless of whether a federal common law privilege protecting reporters existed in 1972 when *Branzburg* was decided, in the intervening years much has changed. While appellants argue for an absolute privilege under the common law, they wisely recognize the possibility that a court not recognizing such an absolute privilege might nonetheless find a qualified privilege. They therefore also argue that if there is a qualified privilege, then the government has not overcome that qualified privilege. The Court is not of one mind on the existence of a common law privilege. Judge Sentelle would hold that there is no such common law privilege for reasons set forth in a separate opinion. Judge Tatel would hold that there is such a common law privilege. Judge Henderson believes that we need not, and therefore should not, reach that question. However, all believe that if there is any such privilege, it is not absolute and may be overcome by an appropriate showing. All further believe, for the reasons set forth in the separate opinion of Judge Tatel, that if such a privilege applies here, it has been overcome. Therefore, the common law privilege, even if one exists, does not warrant reversal....

SENTELLE, Circuit Judge, concurring.

As noted in the opinion of the court, I write separately to express my differing basis for affirming the District Court on the common law privilege issue. I would hold that reporters refusing to testify before grand juries as to their "confidential sources" enjoy no common law privilege beyond the protection against harassing grand juries conducting groundless investigations that is available to all other citizens. While I understand, and do not actually disagree with, the conclusion of my colleagues that any such privilege enjoyed by the reporters has been overcome by the showing of the United States, and that we therefore need not determine whether such privilege exists, I find this ordering of issues a bit disturbing. To me, the question of the existence of such privilege *vel non* is logically anterior to the quantum of proof necessary to overcome it....

I base my rejection of the common law privilege theory on foundations of precedent, policy, and separation of powers. As to precedent, I find *Branzburg v. Hayes*, 408 U.S. 665 (1972), to be as dispositive of the question of common law privilege as it is of a First Amendment privilege. While *Branzburg* generally is cited for its constitutional implications, the *Branzburg* Court repeatedly discussed the privilege question in common law terms as well as constitutional. Indeed, the majority opinion by Justice White includes the phrase "common law" no fewer than eight times. More significant than the fact that the Court frequently spoke of the common law is what the Court had to say about it: "at common law, courts consistently refuse to recognize the existence of any privilege authorizing a newsman to refuse to reveal confidential information to a grand jury."

....

Even if appellants are correct that we would have the power to adopt such a privilege in the face of the *Branzburg* precedent, I nonetheless would not accept that invitation. Appellants' argument for our authority to adopt the new privilege begins with the Federal Rules of Evidence. Rule 501, enacted by Congress in the Federal Rules of Evidence in 1975, three years after *Branzburg*, rejected an enumeration of specific federal privileges and provided that privileges in federal criminal cases [shall be governed by the common law as interpreted by United States courts in the light of reason and experience]. Although the rules became effective after *Branzburg*, Rule 501 does not effect any change in the authority of federal courts to adopt evidentiary privileges. Before the enactment of the Federal Rules of Evidence, the authority of the federal courts to adopt common law privileges was governed by case law. The relevant case law provided for precisely the same authority as Congress enacted in the rules. Indeed, the language of the rule is drawn directly from case law governing at the time of *Branzburg*....

Given the venerable origins of the language used in Rule 501, it cannot be said that the courts have more power to adopt privileges today than at the time of *Branzburg*. The power is precisely the same. Thus, the enactment of Rule 501 cannot by itself work any change in the law which should empower us to depart from the Supreme Court's clear precedent in *Branzburg*.

Appellants persist, however, that the state of the common law has changed sufficiently to warrant a new approach. By appellants' count, at the time of the *Branzburg* decision, only seventeen states had enacted what appellants refer to as "shield laws" to protect journalists from forced disclosure of confidential sources or newsgathering materials, while today, thirty-one states (plus the District of Columbia) have such statutes. Nonetheless, I think it remains the prerogative of the Supreme Court rather than inferior federal tribunals to determine whether these changes are sufficient to warrant an overruling of the Court's rejection of such a common law privilege in *Branzburg*.

Furthermore, even if we are authorized to make that decision, reasons of policy and separation of powers counsel against our exercising that authority. While I concede that the adoption of the "shield" by legislation rather than judicial fiat does not prevent the change being considered by the courts in assessing the common law, I find the adoption of the privilege by the legislatures of the states instructive as to how the federal government should proceed, if at all, to adopt the privilege. The statutes differ greatly as to the scope of the privilege, and as to the identity of persons entitled to the protection of the privilege. We have alluded in the majority opinion to the differing decisions of courts as to civil, criminal, and grand jury proceedings. There is also a more fundamental policy question involved in the crafting of such a privilege.

The Supreme Court itself in *Branzburg* noted the difficult and vexing nature of this question, observing that applying such privilege would make it

> necessary to define those categories of newsmen who qualify for the privilege, a questionable procedure in light of the traditional doctrine that liberty of the press is the right of the lonely pamphleteer who uses carbon paper or a mimeograph just as much as of the large metropolitan publisher who utilizes the latest photocomposition methods.

. . . .

Are we then to create a privilege that protects only those reporters employed by Time Magazine, the New York Times, and other media giants, or do we extend that protection as well to the owner of a desktop printer producing a weekly newsletter to inform his neighbors, lodge brothers, co-religionists, or co-conspirators? Perhaps more to the point today, does the privilege also protect the proprietor of a web log: the stereotypical "blogger" sitting in his pajamas at his personal computer posting on the World Wide Web his best product to inform whoever happens to browse his way? If not, why not? How could one draw a distinction consistent with the court's vision of a broadly granted personal right? If so, then would it not be possible for a government official wishing to engage in the sort of unlawful leaking under investigation in the present controversy to call a trusted friend or a political ally, advise him to set up a web log (which I understand takes about three minutes) and then leak to him under a promise of confidentiality the information which the law forbids the official to disclose?

The state legislatures have dealt with this vexing question of entitlement to the privilege in a variety of ways. Some are quite restrictive.... Others are quite inclusive....

The variety of legislative choices among the states only serves to heighten the concern expressed by the majority in *Branzburg*. This concern is reinforced by examination of the *Jaffee* decision, upon which appellants rely. In *Jaffee*, the Supreme Court extended a federal privilege "to confidential communications made to licensed social workers in the course of psychotherapy." There is little definitional problem with the application of this privilege. The court need only ask: Does this "social worker" have a license? If the answer is "yes," then the privilege applies; if it's "no," the privilege does not. If the courts extend the privilege only to a defined group of reporters, are we in danger of creating a "licensed" or "established" press? If we do so, have we run afoul of the breadth of the freedom of the press, that "fundamental personal right" for which the Court in *Branzburg* expressed its concern? Conversely, if we extend that privilege to the easily created blog, or the ill-defined pamphleteer, have we defeated legitimate investigative ends of grand juries in cases like the leak of intelligence involved in the present investigation?

Nor does the identity of the protected persons constitute the only difficult policy decision. *Branzburg* enumerates several concerns. For example, does "the public interest in possible future news about crime from undisclosed, unverified sources ... take precedence over the public interest in pursuing and prosecuting those crimes reported to the press by informants and in thus deterring the commission of such crimes in the future"? Do "agreements to conceal information relevant to the commission of crime avail little to recommend them from the standpoint of public policy"? What are we to do with the historic common law recognition of "a duty to raise the 'hue and cry' and report felonies to the authorities"? Should we be creating immunity from prosecution for "misprision" of a felony—that is, the concealment of a felony?

Should the privilege be absolute or limited? If limited, how limited? Without attempting to catalog, I note that the state statutes provide a variety of answers to that policy question. Therefore, if such a decision requires the resolution of so many difficult policy questions, many of them beyond the normal compass of a single case or controversy such as those with which the courts regularly deal, doesn't that decision smack of legislation more than adjudication? Here, I think the experience of the states is most instructive. The creation of a reporter's privilege, if it is to be done at all, looks more like a legislative than an adjudicative decision. I suggest that the media as a whole, or at least those elements of the media concerned about this privilege, would better address those concerns to the Article I legislative branch for presentment to the Article II executive than to the Article III courts....

KAREN LECRAFT HENDERSON, Circuit Judge, concurring.

I write separately to emphasize that adherence to the principle of judicial restraint—patience in judicial decision-making—would produce a better result in II.B of the majority opinion. Because my colleagues and I agree that any federal common-law reporter's privilege that may exist is not absolute and that the Special Counsel's evidence defeats whatever privilege we may fashion, we need not, and therefore should not, decide anything more today than that the Special Counsel's evidentiary proffer overcomes any hurdle, however high, a federal common-law reporter's privilege may erect....[2] ....

---

2. .... There are ... only three ways of answering the question whether these reporters' confidential source information is protected by a federal common-law privilege: (1) there is no privilege, (2) there is an absolute privilege and (3) there is a qualified privilege. None of us, including the reporters in their brief, would choose door number two, and only one of us heads for door number one. That leaves door number three. But in choosing this route, the critical question is not definitional, as Judge

While I am convinced that we need not, and therefore should not, go further than to conclude, as did the district court, that the Special Counsel's showing decides the case, I feel compelled to comment briefly on my colleagues' opposing conclusions if only to make clear why I think it unwise to advance either of them. I cannot agree with Judge Sentelle's conclusion that the United States Supreme Court has answered the question we now avoid. *Branzburg v. Hayes* addressed only "whether requiring newsmen to appear and testify before state or federal grand juries abridges the freedom of speech and press guaranteed by the *First Amendment*" and "h[e]ld that *it* does not." 408 U.S. 665, 667 (1972) (emphases added). The boundaries of constitutional law and common law do not necessarily coincide, however, and while we are unquestionably bound by *Branzburg's* rejection of a reporter's privilege rooted in the First Amendment, we are not bound by *Branzburg's* commentary on the state of the common law in 1972. Federal Rule of Evidence 501, which came into being nearly three years after *Branzburg*, authorizes federal courts to develop testimonial privileges "in the light of reason and experience," allowing for the often evolving state of the common[ ]law. Judge Sentelle's view also discounts the fact that, even as they rejected a reporter's First Amendment right to withhold testimony from a bona fide grand jury, both the *Branzburg* majority opinion as well as Justice Powell's separate concurrence hint ambiguously at the existence of some special protection for reporters stemming from their significant role in sustaining our republican form of government.

At the same time, I am far less eager a federal common-law pioneer than Judge Tatel as I find less comfort than he in riding *Jaffee v. Redmond*, 518 U.S. 1 (1996), into the testimonial privilege frontier. Just as Rule 501 imposes no "freeze" on the development of the common law, it likewise does not authorize federal courts to mint testimonial privileges for any group — including the "journalistic class," as Judge Sentelle dubs it — that demands one. The Supreme Court has warned that testimonial privileges "are not lightly created nor expansively construed, for they are in derogation of the search for truth." *United States v. Nixon*, 418 U.S. 683, 710 (1974). Accordingly, we should proceed as cautiously as possible "when erecting barriers between us and the truth," *id.*, recognizing that the Legislature remains the more appropriate institution to reconcile the competing interests — prosecuting criminal acts versus constricting the flow of information to the public — that inform any reporter's privilege to withhold relevant information from a bona fide grand jury.

Because *Jaffee* sits rather awkwardly within a jurisprudence marked by a fairly uniform disinclination to announce new privileges or even expand existing ones, and even though it enjoyed the support of an overwhelming majority, I am hesitant to apply its methodology to a case that does not require us to do so. While it would not be the first of its kind, the type of multi-factor balancing test Judge Tatel proposes seems, at least to me, to lack analytical rigor because its application to this case is foreordained. Indeed, I am not convinced that a balancing test that requires more than an evaluation of the essentiality of the information to the prosecution and the exhaustion of available alternative sources thereof is either useful or appropriate. While Judge Tatel makes the centerpiece of his test the balancing of "the public interest in compelling disclosure, measured by the harm the leak caused, against the public interest in newsgathering, measured by the leaked information's value," this court (in the civil context), the United States Department of Justice and the lone district court that has recognized a federal common-law reporter's priv-

---

Tatel sees it, but quantitative: Is the Special Counsel's evidentiary proffer *sufficient* to overcome *any* qualified privilege that may exist? Because we agree that the answer is "yes," there is no need for us to go any further....

ilege in the grand jury context have declined to consider either of these factors in deciding whether to recognize a reporter's exemption from compulsory process. There is a good reason for this: I suspect that balancing "harm" against "news value" may prove unproductive because in most of the projected scenarios—leaks of information involving, for example, military operations, national security, policy choices or political adversaries—the two interests overlap. Furthermore, *Branzburg* warns of the risk inherent in the judicial assessment of the importance of prosecuting particular crimes. And any evaluation of the importance of newsgathering keyed to its perceived "benefit" to the public, seems antithetical to our nation's abiding commitment to the uninhibited trade in ideas. Moreover, to attempt to establish the contours of a reporter's privilege here would tend, unnecessarily, to leave a future panel less maneuverability in a case that might require just that to achieve justice....

For the foregoing reasons, I am convinced that the court would chart the best course by charting the narrowest one and, accordingly, concur only in the judgment with respect to II.B of the majority opinion. In all other respects, I fully concur.

TATEL, Circuit Judge, concurring in the judgment....

II.

.... In 1975—three years after *Branzburg*—Congress enacted Rule 501 of the Federal Rules of Evidence, authorizing federal courts to develop evidentiary privileges in federal question cases according to [the common law as interpreted by United States courts in the light of reason and experience]....

Under Rule 501, that common lawmaking obligation exists whether or not, absent the rule's delegation, Congress would be "the more appropriate institution to reconcile the competing interests ... that inform any reporter's privilege to withhold relevant information from a bona fide grand jury." As the Supreme Court has explained, "Rule 501 was adopted precisely because Congress wished to leave privilege questions to the courts rather than attempt to codify them." *United States v. Weber Aircraft Corp.*, 465 U.S. 792, 803 n. 25 (1984). Thus, subject of course to congressional override, we must assess the arguments for and against the claimed privilege, just as the Supreme Court has done in cases recognizing common law privileges since 1975.

In this case, just as *Jaffee v. Redmond* recognized a common law psychotherapist privilege based on "the uniform judgment of the States," I believe that "reason and experience" dictate a privilege for reporters' confidential sources—albeit a qualified one. Guided by *Jaffee*'s reasoning, I reach this conclusion by considering first whether "reason and experience" justify recognizing a privilege at all, and if so whether the privilege should be qualified or absolute and whether it should cover the communications at issue in this case....

Existence of the Privilege

Under *Jaffee*, the common law analysis starts with the interests that call for recognizing a privilege. If, as the Supreme Court held there, "[t]he mental health of our citizenry is a public good of transcendent importance"—one that trumps the "fundamental maxim that the public has a right to every man's evidence"—then surely press freedom is no less important, given journalism's vital role in our democracy. Indeed, while the *Jaffee* dissenters questioned psychotherapy's "indispensable role in the maintenance of the citizenry's mental health," the First Amendment's express protection for "freedom ... of the press" forecloses any debate about that institution's "important role in the discussion of public affairs," *Mills v. Alabama*, 384 U.S. 214, 219 (1966)....

Like psychotherapists, as well as attorneys and spouses, all of whom enjoy privileges under Rule 501, reporters "depend[ ] upon an atmosphere of confidence and trust," *Jaffee*, 518 U.S. at 10. If litigants and investigators could easily discover journalists' sources, the press's truth-seeking function would be severely impaired. Reporters could reprint government statements, but not ferret out underlying disagreements among officials; they could cover public governmental actions, but would have great difficulty getting potential whistleblowers to talk about government misdeeds; they could report arrest statistics, but not garner first-hand information about the criminal underworld. Such valuable endeavors would be all but impossible, for just as mental patients who fear "embarrassment or disgrace," *id.*, will "surely be chilled" in seeking therapy, *id.* at 12, so will sources who fear identification avoid revealing information that could get them in trouble.

Because of these chilling effects, "[w]ithout a privilege, much of the desirable evidence to which litigants … seek access … is unlikely to come into being." *Id.* Consequently, as with other privileges, "the likely evidentiary benefit that would result from the denial of the privilege is modest." *Id.* At the same time, although suppression of some leaks is surely desirable (a point to which I shall return), the public harm that would flow from undermining all source relationships would be immense.…

It is true, as the special counsel observes, that apart from affidavits and citations to two articles in their reply brief, the reporters present no empirical evidence that denial of the privilege "will have a significant impact on the free flow of information protected by the First Amendment." But the Supreme Court has never required proponents of a privilege to adduce scientific studies demonstrating the privilege's benefits. Rather, as the *Jaffee* dissenters pointed out, the empirical question — "[h]ow likely is it that a person will be deterred from seeking psychological counseling, or from being completely truthful in the course of such counseling, because of fear of later disclosure in litigation?" — was one "[t]he Court [did] not attempt to answer." 518 U.S. at 22–23 (Scalia, J., dissenting). Instead, following the wise precept that common sense need not be "the mere handmaiden of social science data or expert testimonials," *Amatel v. Reno*, 156 F.3d 192, 199 (D.C.Cir.1998), *Jaffee* relied on the traditional common law process: it examined the logical prerequisites of the confidential relationship, taking into account the policy and experience of parallel jurisdictions.

Likewise, in *Trammel v. United States*, while justifying the privilege against adverse spousal testimony in terms of "marital harmony," 445 U.S. at 44–45, 53, the Court allowed waiver by the testifying spouse based not on divorce statistics or psychological studies, but rather on the commonsense supposition that "[w]hen one spouse is willing to testify against the other in a criminal proceeding—whatever the motivation—their relationship is almost certainly in disrepair." And in *Swidler & Berlin v. United States*, 524 U.S. 399 (1998), though finding the "empirical information … scant and inconclusive," the Court held that the attorney-client privilege survives the client's death because "[k]nowing that communications will remain confidential even after death encourages the client to communicate fully and frankly with counsel"—a proposition the Court supported with neither evidence nor even citation. Given these decisions, the equally commonsense proposition that reporters' sources will be more candid when promised confidentiality requires no empirical support.

In any event, the special counsel's confidence that exposing sources will have no effect on newsgathering is unjustified.… As anyone with even a passing interest in news knows, reporters routinely rely on sources speaking on condition of anonymity—a strong indication that leakers demand such protection.…

Turning next, as did *Jaffee*, to the consensus among states, I find support for the privilege at least as strong for journalists as for psychotherapists. Just as in *Jaffee*, where "the fact that all 50 states and the District of Columbia have enacted into law some form of psychotherapist privilege" favored an exercise of federal common lawmaking, so here undisputed evidence that forty-nine states plus the District of Columbia offer at least qualified protection to reporters' sources confirms that "'reason and experience' support recognition of the privilege." Indeed, given these state laws, "[d]enial of the federal privilege ... would frustrate the purposes of the state legislation" by exposing confidences protected under state law to discovery in federal courts.

Making the case for a privilege here even stronger than in *Jaffee*, federal authorities also favor recognizing a privilege for reporters' confidential sources. As noted earlier, we ourselves have limited discovery of reporters' sources in both civil and criminal litigation, as have other federal courts, including some acting on the basis of Rule 501. In addition, the Justice Department guidelines ... establish a federal policy of protecting "news media from forms of compulsory process, whether civil or criminal, which might impair the news gathering function." 28 C.F.R. § 50.10....

Resisting this consensus, the special counsel asserts that *Branzburg* already performed the analysis required by Rule 501, thus "resolv[ing] the common law argument." *Branzburg* did no such thing. As the *Branzburg* majority's very first sentence makes plain, the "issue" in that case was "whether requiring newsmen to appear and testify before state or federal grand juries abridges the freedom of speech and press *guaranteed by the First Amendment*," 408 U.S. at 667 (emphasis added), not whether it abridged the common law.... Indeed, having examined the briefs and lower court opinions, I see no evidence that the parties ever even argued for a separate common law privilege. To be sure, the majority declared that "the great weight of authority is that newsmen are not exempt from the normal duty of appearing before a grand jury and answering questions relevant to a criminal investigation," but that point served only to reinforce the majority's constitutional holding....

Given that the common law issue thus remains open, this court must assess the reporters' claim in light of "reason and experience" today. As *Branzburg* itself observes in describing Congress's powers, privilege rules may require "refashion[ing] ... as experience from time to time may dictate." Bestowing that refashioning power on the federal courts, Rule 501 evidences an "affirmative intention not to freeze the law of privilege," but rather "to leave the door open to change." *Trammel*, 445 U.S. at 47. Consistent with that intent, the Court in *Trammel* modified the privilege against adverse spousal testimony recognized just twenty-two years earlier in *Hawkins v. United States*, 358 U.S. 74 (1958), allowing the testifying spouse to waive the privilege, even though *Hawkins* had held just the opposite. Had the Supreme Court addressed a common law claim in *Branzburg*, lower courts might lack authority to reconsider that case's result notwithstanding the subsequent growth in support for the privilege. Absent such a definitive ruling, however, and despite *Branzburg*'s observation about the "great weight of authority" thirty-three years ago, we must approach the issue with the same open-mindedness demonstrated by *Trammel*.

For much the same reason, the omission of a reporter privilege from the Judicial Conference Advisory Committee's draft rules submitted to Congress in 1972 (and ultimately replaced by Rule 501) need not dictate the outcome here. True, as the special counsel points out, the Supreme Court in *United States v. Gillock*, 445 U.S. 360, 367–68 (1980), declined to recognize a privilege not appearing in the Advisory Committee draft. As that decision acknowledges, however, the draft rules merely reflected what was "thought to be ... indelibly ensconced in our common law" at the time. Accordingly, when the *Jaffee* Court considered whether the psychotherapist privilege extended to social workers, it relied not on the 1972 draft, which covered only licensed psychotherapists, but rather on the reasons for the privilege and the state laws in effect when *Jaffee* was decided. Likewise, here, the dramatic growth in support for the reporter privilege supercedes the Advisory Committee's decades-old choice to omit the privilege from its draft.

Equally inconsequential is the adoption of the reporter privilege in thirty-one states through legislation, rather than judicial action. As the *Jaffee* dissent pointed out, a far greater proportion of states — indeed, every state — established the psychotherapist privilege by statute, yet the majority considered that fact "of no consequence." Nor does it matter that unconventional forms of journalism — freelance writers and internet "bloggers," for example — may raise definitional conundrums down the road. As *Jaffee* makes clear, "[a] rule," such as Rule 501, "that authorizes the recognition of new privileges on a case-by-case basis makes it appropriate to define the details of new privileges in a like manner." After all, "flexibility and capacity for growth and adaptation is the peculiar boast and excellence of the common law." *Hurtado v. California*, 110 U.S. 516, 530 (1884). Here, whereas any meaningful reporter privilege must undoubtedly encompass appellants Cooper and Miller, full-time journalists for *Time* magazine and the *New York Times*, respectively, future opinions can elaborate more refined contours of the privilege — a task shown to be manageable by the experience of the fifty jurisdictions with statutory or common law protections....

Scope of the Privilege

The next step, according to *Jaffee*, is to determine what principles govern the privilege's application in this case. Pointing out that many jurisdictions recognize only qualified protection for reporters, the special counsel argues that the uniform judgment of states must support application of the privilege in the precise context at issue — defiance of grand jury subpoenas — before federal courts may recognize it. That view, however, belonged to the *Jaffee* dissent, not the seven-justice majority. Although the dissenters noted an "enormous degree of disagreement among the States as to the scope of the privilege," particularly as to which professions it covered, the Court extended the privilege to licensed social workers because "[t]he reasons for recognizing a privilege for treatment by psychiatrists and psychologists apply with equal force to treatment by a clinical social worker." Likewise, *Jaffee* rejected a proposed balancing test not because other jurisdictions had done so, but because "[m]aking the promise of confidentiality contingent upon a trial judge's later evaluation of the relative importance of the patient's interest in privacy and the evidentiary need for disclosure would eviscerate the effectiveness of the privilege."

Here, even assuming that some jurisdictions categorically exclude grand jury subpoenas — a proposition for which the special counsel cites no authority — the interests protected by the privilege militate against such a limited approach. Although the public interest in law enforcement may well be at its apex when the government is investigating crime, news stories of paramount First Amendment importance, such as reports about government corruption or wrongdoing, may involve sources who "would surely be chilled" if they thought grand juries could discover their identities from reporters in whom they confide. Furthermore, the special counsel's proposal is quite anomalous, considering that neither the attorney-client, nor the spousal, nor even the psychotherapist privilege gives way to the grand jury's truth-seeking function.

As to the scope of the privilege, however, I agree with the special counsel that protection for source identities cannot be absolute.... Just as attorney-client communications "made for the purpose of getting advice for the commission of a fraud or crime" serve no public interest and receive no privilege, *see United States v. Zolin*, 491 U.S. 554, 563 (1989), neither should courts protect sources whose leaks harm national security while providing minimal benefit to public debate.

Of course, in some cases a leak's value may far exceed its harm, thus calling into question the law enforcement rationale for disrupting reporter-source relationships....

... [M]uch as our civil cases balance "the public interest in protecting the reporter's sources against the private interest in compelling disclosure," so must the reporter privilege account for the varying interests at stake in different source relationships. In other words, to quote the Justice Department subpoena guidelines, "the approach in every case must be to strike the proper balance between the public's interest in the free dissemination of ideas and information and the public's interest in effective law enforcement and the fair administration of justice." 28 C.F.R. §50.10(a).

.... [T]he special counsel urges us to rely on two factors ... first, the requesting party's need for the evidence, and second, that party's exhaustion of alternative sources. While both these considerations are obviously essential to minimizing the burden on news-gathering, they can serve as exclusive measures in the privilege analysis only where there exist means of proof other than compelling the reporter's testimony. When prosecuting crimes other than leaks (murder or embezzlement, say) the government, at least theoretically, can learn what reporters know by replicating their investigative efforts, e.g., speaking to the same witnesses and examining the same documents. Accordingly, if a truly exhaustive investigation has failed to prove a crime that the government reasonably believes has occurred, compelled disclosure of a reporter's source may be justified notwithstanding the attendant burdens on newsgathering. As the special counsel acknowledged at oral argument, however, when the government seeks to punish a leak, a test focused on need and exhaustion will almost always be satisfied, leaving the reporter's source unprotected regardless of the information's importance to the public. The reason for this is obvious: Insofar as the confidential exchange of information leaves neither paper trail nor smoking gun, the great majority of leaks will likely be unprovable without evidence from either leaker or leakee. Of course, in some cases, circumstantial evidence such as telephone records may point towards the source, but for the party with the burden of proof, particularly the government in a criminal case, such evidence will often be inadequate.

In leak cases, then, courts applying the privilege must consider not only the government's need for the information and exhaustion of alternative sources, but also the two competing public interests lying at the heart of the balancing test. Specifically, the court must weigh the public interest in compelling disclosure, measured by the harm the leak caused, against the public interest in newsgathering, measured by the leaked information's value.... Though flexible, these standards (contrary to the special counsel's claim) are hardly unmanageable....

[M]y concurring colleague suggests that my approach pays insufficient deference to Congress. "*Branzburg*," she writes, "warns of the risk inherent in the judicial assessment of the importance of prosecuting particular crimes".... To be sure, insofar as the reporter's testimony is critical in a particular case, privileging the evidence may render that case unprovable. But that risk accompanies any privilege or indeed any rule of evidentiary exclusion. Had Congress believed that judicial decisions excluding evidence interfered with its "legislative judgment" regarding underlying crimes, it would hardly have authorized recognition of common law privileges by enacting Rule 501.

Furthermore, and perhaps even more important, *Branzburg* addressed only a First Amendment privilege claim. In that case, therefore, because Congress cannot overturn constitutionally based decisions, recognizing the asserted privilege would have permanently foreclosed punishment of any crimes dependent on proof subject to the privilege. The qualified privilege I would recognize, however, rests on Rule 501, not the Constitution. If Congress believes that this approach overrides its judgment about what conduct should be criminal, it may simply overturn the privilege and authorize use of the evidence.

Next, the special counsel argues that waivers signed by suspected sources represent an "additional factor" favoring compulsion of the reporters' testimony. As the reporters point out, however, numerous cases (including persuasive district court decisions from this circuit) indicate that only reporters, not sources, may waive the privilege....

As this case law recognizes, a source's waiver is irrelevant to the reasons for the privilege. Because the government could demand waivers — perhaps even before any leak occurs — as a condition of employment, a privilege subject to waiver may, again, amount to no privilege at all, even in those leak cases where protecting the confidential source is most compelling. Moreover, although the attorney-client and psychotherapist privileges are waivable by clients and patients, respectively, that is because those privileges exist to prevent disclosure of sensitive matters related to legal and psychological counseling, a rationale that vanishes when the source authorizes disclosure. In contrast, the reporter privilege safeguards public dissemination of information — the *reporter's* enterprise, not the source's.

Consistent with that purpose, the privilege belongs to the reporter. Not only are journalists best able to judge the imperatives of newsgathering, but while the source's interest is limited to the particular case, the reporter's interest aligns with the public, for journalists must cultivate relationships with other sources who might keep mum if waiving confidentiality at the government's behest could lead to their exposure. Indeed, as compared to counseling-related privileges, the privilege against spousal testimony represents a better analogy. Just as under *Trammel's* waiver theory testifying spouses, regardless of the other spouse's wishes, may judge for themselves whether their testimony will undermine "marital harmony," so should journalists — the experts in newsgathering — base the decision to testify on their own assessment of the consequences, unconstrained by their source's waiver (provided other requirements of the privilege are met).

For their part, appellants insist that a qualified privilege fails to provide the certainty their work requires because sources are unlikely to disclose information without an advance guarantee of secrecy. In particular, they argue that journalists cannot balance a leak's harm against its news value until they know what information the source will reveal, by which time it is too late to prevent disclosure. True enough, but journalists are not the ones who must perform the balancing; sources are. Indeed, the point of the qualified privilege is to create disincentives for the source — disincentives that not only promote the public interest, but may also protect journalists from exploitation by government officials seeking publication of damaging secrets for partisan advantage. Like other recipients of potentially privileged communications — say, attorneys or psychotherapists — the reporter can at most alert the source to the limits of confidentiality, leaving the judgment of what to say to the source. While the resulting deterrent effect may cost the press some leads, little harm will result, for if the disincentives work as they should, the information sources refrain from revealing will lack significant news value in the first place.

In any event, although *Jaffee* said that "[m]aking the promise of confidentiality contingent upon a trial judge's later evaluation ... [will] eviscerate the effectiveness of the privilege," the clash of fundamental interests at stake when the government seeks discovery of a reporter's sources precludes a categorical approach. And ... the "deterrence effect" on beneficial newsgathering will be small if courts make clear that the privilege is "overridden only in rare circumstances."

In short, the question in this case is whether Miller's and Cooper's sources released information more harmful than newsworthy. If so, then the public interest in punishing the wrongdoers—and deterring future leaks—outweighs any burden on newsgathering, and no privilege covers the communication (provided, of course, that the special counsel demonstrates necessity and exhaustion of alternative evidentiary sources).

III.

Applying this standard to the facts of this case ... I have no doubt that the leak at issue was a serious matter. ...

An alleged covert agent, Plame evidently traveled overseas on clandestine missions beginning nearly two decades ago. Her exposure, therefore, not only may have jeopardized any covert activities of her own, but also may have endangered friends and associates from whom she might have gathered information in the past. ...

The leak of Plame's apparent employment, moreover, had marginal news value. To be sure, insofar as Plame's CIA relationship may have helped explain her husband's selection for the Niger trip, that information could bear on her husband's credibility and thus contribute to public debate over the president's "sixteen words." Compared to the damage of undermining covert intelligence-gathering, however, this slight news value cannot, in my view, justify privileging the leaker's identity. ...

In sum, based on an exhaustive investigation, the special counsel has established the need for Miller's and Cooper's testimony. Thus, considering the gravity of the suspected crime and the low value of the leaked information, no privilege bars the subpoenas.

One last point. In concluding that no privilege applies in this case, I have assigned no importance to the fact that neither Cooper nor Miller, perhaps recognizing the irresponsible (and quite possibly illegal) nature of the leaks at issue, revealed Plame's employment, though Cooper wrote about it after Novak's column appeared. Contrary to the reporters' view, this apparent self-restraint spares Miller and Cooper no obligation to testify. Narrowly drawn limitations on the public's right to evidence, testimonial privileges apply "only where necessary to achieve [their] purpose," *Fisher v. United States*, 425 U.S. 391, 403 (1976), and in this case the privilege's purpose is to promote dissemination of useful information. It thus makes no difference how these reporters responded to the information they received, any more than it matters whether an attorney drops a client who seeks criminal advice (communication subject to the crime-fraud exception) or a psychotherapist seeks to dissuade homicidal plans revealed during counseling (information *Jaffee* suggested would not be privileged). In all such cases, because the communication is unworthy of protection, recipients' reactions are irrelevant to whether their testimony may be compelled in an investigation of the source.

Indeed, Cooper's own *Time*.com article illustrates this point. True, his story revealed a suspicious confluence of leaks, contributing to the outcry that led to this investigation. Yet the article had that effect precisely because the leaked information—Plame's covert status—lacked significant news value. In essence, seeking protection for sources whose nefariousness he himself exposed, Cooper asks us to protect criminal leaks so that he can write about the crime. The greater public interest lies in preventing the leak to begin with. Had Cooper based his report on leaks *about* the leaks—say, from a whistleblower who revealed the plot against Wilson—the situation would be different. Because in that case the source would not have revealed the name of a covert agent, but instead revealed the fact that others had done so, the balance of news value and harm would shift in favor of protecting the whistleblower. Yet it appears Cooper relied on the Plame leaks themselves, drawing the inference of sinister motive on his own. Accordingly, his story itself makes the case for punishing the leakers. While requiring Cooper to testify may discourage future leaks, discouraging leaks of this kind is precisely what the public interest requires....

Notes and Questions

1. Of the three concurring opinions filed in *In re: Grand Jury Subpoena, Judith Miller*, which most faithfully applies Rule 501 and the Supreme Court's decisions interpreting that rule? Rule 501 delegates to the federal courts the responsibility of creating new privileges and modifying existing ones. Given that, is Judge Sentelle justified in directing the journalists in the case to air their grievances with the executive and legislative branches? Is Judge Henderson justified in expressing skepticism over the vitality of and hesitation in extending the Supreme Court's 7–2 decision in *Jaffee*? And how well does Judge Tatel's balancing test conform with the Court's rejection of a similar balancing test in *Jaffee* on the ground that "[a]n uncertain privilege, or one which purports to be certain but results in widely varying application by the courts, is little better than no privilege at all"?

2. On April 19, 2005, the D.C. Circuit rejected a petition to rehear *en banc* the panel decision in *In re: Grand Jury Subpoena, Judith Miller. See* 405 F.3d 17 (D.C. Cir. 2005) (en banc). Judge Tatel, one of the judges on the original panel, filed a separate opinion concurring in the denial of rehearing the case *en banc*. In it, he emphasized the narrow scope of the panel's decision:

> Judge Henderson's opinion—which, as the narrowest supporting the result, is the controlling decision of the court—determined neither whether any common law privilege exists nor what standard would govern its application if it did. Hence, future panels of this court remain free to recognize any privilege (or no privilege) consistent with the result in this case, and those panels may, as necessary, clarify the standards governing reporter-source relationships.

Id. at 18 (Tatel, J., concurring). On June 27, 2005, the United States Supreme Court declined to review the decision, *see Miller v. United States*, 545 U.S. 1150 (2005); *Cooper v. United States*, 545 U.S. 1150 (2005). The opinion was re-issued in 2006 with previously redacted material included. *See In re: Grand Jury Subpoena, Judith Miller*, 438 F.3d 1141 (D.C. Cir. 2006) (re-issued opinion); *In re: Grand Jury Subpoena, Judith Miller*, 438 F.3d 1138 (D.C. Cir. 2006) (order re-issuing opinion). *See also In re: Grand Jury Subpoena, Judith Miller*, 493 F.3d 152 (D.C. Cir. 2007) (releasing previously redacted matter).

3. Shortly after the Supreme Court declined to review the decision in *In re: Grand Jury Subpoena, Judith Miller*, parallel bills were introduced in the U.S. House and Senate that would bar any arm of the federal government from compelling a journalist to disclose either the identity of a source or information obtained from a source except under limited circumstances. *See* Free Flow of Information Act of 2005, H.R. 3323, S. 1419, 109th Cong. (July 18, 2005). The bills were re-introduced in amended form in 2007 and again

in 2009. *See* Free Flow of Information Act of 2007, H.R. 2102, S. 1267, 110th Cong. (May 2, 2007); Free Flow of Information Act of 2009, H.R. 985, 111th Cong. (Feb. 11, 2009); Free Flow of Information Act of 2009, S. 448, 111th Cong. (Feb. 13, 2009).

Chapter 6

The "Best Evidence" Rule

A. Introduction

In general, the law of evidence in the United States is a "free market" system in that it does not require parties to introduce the "best" evidence to prove any particular point. Thus, for example, if there were eyewitnesses to an incident who were, respectively, 10, 30, and 80 feet away from the incident, no rule of evidence requires that the parties call the witness who was only 10 feet away, even though he may have been in the best position to see what happened. Or if a defendant is on trial for murder and claims that he acted in self-defense, no rule of evidence prefers eyewitness testimony to forensic evidence, or vice-versa. The philosophy underlying the system is that parties to litigation already have an incentive to offer the "best" or most persuasive evidence possible, namely, their incentive to win the case. And the nature of the adversarial system is such that if one party fails to produce what is viewed as the "superior" evidence, the other party will be sure to bring this to the attention of the trier of fact, or indeed, introduce that evidence himself.

Yet this laissez-faire system is subject to two important exceptions. One of these, the rule against hearsay, is discussed in the next chapter. The other, the focus of this chapter, is the so-called "Best Evidence" Rule, which provides that:

> An original writing, recording, or photograph is required in order to prove its content unless these rules or a federal statute provides otherwise.

Federal Rule of Evidence 1002.

The rule, which at common law was limited to writings only, thus requires production of the original instead of lesser evidence, such as a copy of the same or testimony by a witness as to its content. Recall that in the days before photocopying machines existed, a "copy" usually meant a copy made by hand, in other words, a human being looking at the original and writing or typing its contents onto another piece of paper. The common law thus preferred an original to a copy because of the risks that the content of the copy would intentionally or inadvertently deviate from that of the original. And witness testimony is subject to the same risks as well as the risk that a witness will have insufficient ability accurately to recollect a writing's details. The rule seems all the more sound when one considers that much often rides on the specific wording and even the punctuation of, say, a written contract.

Notwithstanding the simplicity of the language quoted above from Rule 1002, the Best Evidence Rule can actually be quite challenging to apply, and in the end turns out to be a rather narrow rule that is riddled with exceptions. The rule is narrow in that by its terms it applies only when one seeks to "prove [the] content" of a writing, recording, or photograph, and it is subject to a variety of exceptions, codified in Rules 1003 through 1007.

The materials that follow raise and attempt to provide answers to a variety of important questions that arise in applying the Best Evidence Rule. First, what falls within the definition of the phrase "writing, recording, or photograph"? Second, what does it mean to be an "original"? Third, when is one said to be trying to "prove [the] content" of a document? Fourth, what is a "duplicate," and when can it be used in lieu of an original? Fifth, under what circumstances is the proponent of evidence excused from producing an original? Finally, what are the respective roles of judge and jury in applying the rule?

Notes and Questions

1. The Best Evidence Rule actually finds its roots in the Middle Ages, when documents, such as deeds to property and contracts, were viewed as *embodying* the right itself: "[t]o lose one's deed was to lose one's *right*, just as today to lose a money-coin is to lose its purchasing power." 4 Wigmore, Evidence § 1177, at 406–07 (Chadbourn rev. 1972) (emphasis in original). Thus, production of the writing was necessary not so much as a matter of the law of evidence, but rather as a matter of substantive law.

2. At common law, the "Best Evidence" Rule applied only to writings, but Rule 1002 applies to recordings and photographs as well. *See* Advisory Committee Note to Rule 1002. Do the same reasons that justify requiring production of an original of a writing in lieu of secondary evidence of the same also justify requiring production of an original of a recording or a photograph? If so, would those same reasons justify extending the rule to *all* evidence?

B. What Qualifies as a "Writing, Recording, or Photograph"?

Problem 6-1: The Libelous Billboard

While driving down Main Street in his hometown, Bill R. Jones is shocked when he sees a huge billboard that reads, "Bill R. Jones is a thief." Jones learns that the billboard was erected by Lana Smith, and he files a libel suit against her.

At trial, Jones wishes to testify that "I saw a billboard that said 'Bill R. Jones is a thief,'" but Smith's attorney objects on best evidence grounds. Jones' attorney responds that the best evidence rule is inapplicable.

How should the court rule on the objection?

Problem 6-2: The Beer Bottle

Walid is on trial on charges of unlawful possession of alcohol by a minor. At trial, the arresting officer seeks to testify that at the time he arrested Walid, Walid had a brown, glass longneck bottle in his hand with a label that read "Budweiser." Walid's attorney objects on best evidence grounds, but the government responds that the best evidence rule is inapplicable.

How should the court rule on the objection?

United States v. Buchanan
604 F.3d 517 (8th Cir. 2010)

SMITH, Circuit Judge.

. . . .

As part of a narcotics investigation, law enforcement observed [Ronald] Buchanan at two residences — 930 65th Street, Windsor Heights, Iowa ("the 65th Street residence") and 1933 East 33rd Street, Des Moines, Iowa ("the 33rd Street residence") in the fall of 2007. Law enforcement believed that the 65th Street residence was a "stash house" — a place in which drug dealers store money, drugs, and firearms. Law enforcement officials saw Buchanan in three separate vehicles at both addresses — a Chevy Tahoe, a Ford Explorer, and a Chevy Blazer.

Law enforcement executed search warrants for the two residences, the Chevy Blazer, and Buchanan's person on November 2, 2007, at 10 a.m. . . . Buchanan told the officers that he did not live at the 65th Street residence and that it was his girlfriend's home. . . .

Officers discovered drug notes and a set of keys — including one key bearing the number "2010" upon it — on Buchanan's person. . . .

Further investigation determined that the "2010" key matched a large safe under the stairs in the basement of the 65th Street residence. This safe also bore the number "2010" on it and contained within it a manual bearing the same number. The large safe also contained a lease agreement for the 65th Street residence, signed in September 2007, listing Buchanan and Traci Smith, Buchanan's girlfriend, as tenants, a photo of Buchanan, and an Iowa vehicle title for the Chevy Blazer in Buchanan's name. Officers did not seize the safe. . . .

The large safe contained 199.52 grams of cocaine, 176.05 grams of cocaine base, $18,000 in currency, and two digital scales. The quantities of drugs seized were consistent with distribution. The safe also contained other items consistent with distribution — the currency, the digital scales, baggies, red and black rubber bands for bundling currency, and razor blades for shaving larger rocks of crack to smaller rocks for distribution. . . .

Based upon the items seized, law enforcement determined that the 65th Street residence was actually a stash house.

[Buchanan was charged with and convicted of possession of cocaine base and cocaine with the intent to distribute.]

. . . .

According to Buchanan, the district court erroneously permitted law enforcement officers to testify regarding the writings contained within the safe. Buchanan characterizes the government's case as asserting that these writings provided the number of the key that allegedly matched the safe. The government contended the key, purportedly discovered on Buchanan's person, had an inscription matching the key number inscribed in the interior of the safe. The government also alleged that the key matched the safe in which the drugs were discovered. . . .

According to Buchanan, the assertion within the interior of the safe that it was a "2010" model and that the key with the inscription "2010" belonged to the safe is clearly a "writing" or "recording" under Federal Rule of Evidence 1002; therefore, the safe itself — which officers admittedly did not seize — should have been introduced into evidence.

In response, the government asserts that the best evidence rule is inapplicable because the safe was not a "writing" but instead a "chattel."

Federal Rule of Evidence 1002, known as the "best evidence rule," provides that [an original writing, recording, or photograph is required in order to prove its content unless the federal rules of evidence or a federal statute provides otherwise].

The 'Rule' as it exists today, may be stated as follows:

> [I]n proving the terms of a *writing*, where such terms are material, the original writing must be produced, unless it is shown to be unavailable for some reason other than the serious fault of the proponent.

United States v. Duffy, 454 F.2d 809, 811 (5th Cir. 1972) (quoting McCorm[i]ck, Evidence 409 (1954)). The best evidence rule "is applicable only to the proof of the contents of a writing," even though it "is frequently used in general terms." *Id.* The policy-justifications for preferring the original writing include:

> (1) ... precision in presenting to the court the exact words of the writing is of more than average importance, particularly as respects operative or dispositive instruments, such as deeds, wills and contracts, since a slight variation in words may mean a great difference in rights, (2) ... there is a substantial hazard of inaccuracy in the human process of making a copy by handwriting or typewriting, and (3) as respects oral testimony purporting to give from memory the terms of a writing, there is a special risk of error, greater than in the case of attempts at describing other situations generally. In the light of these dangers of mistransmission, accompanying the use of written copies or of recollection, largely avoided through proving the terms by presenting the writing itself, the preference for the original writing is justified.

Id. at 812 (quoting McCorm[i]ck, Evidence 410 (1954)).

In *Duffy*, law enforcement officials testified that the trunk of a stolen car contained two suitcases. According to the witnesses, inside one of the suitcases was a white shirt imprinted with a laundry mark reading "D-U-F." The defendant, charged with transporting a motor vehicle in interstate commerce knowing it to have been stolen, objected to the admission of the testimony about the shirt and requested that the government produce the shirt. The district court overruled the objection and admitted the testimony. On appeal, the defendant argued that such testimony violated the best evidence rule. The Fifth Circuit rejected the defendant's argument, holding:

> The "Rule" is not, by its terms or because of the policies underlying it, applicable to the instant case. The shirt with a laundry mark would not, under ordinary understanding, be considered a writing and would not, therefore, be covered by the "Best Evidence Rule[."] *When the disputed evidence, such as the shirt in this case, is an object bearing a mark or inscription, and is, therefore, a chattel and a writing,* the trial judge has discretion to treat the evidence as a chattel or as a writing. In reaching his decision, the trial judge should consider the policy-consideration behind the "Rule[."] In the instant case, the trial judge was correct in allowing testimony about the shirt without requiring the production of the shirt. Because the writing involved in this case was simple, the inscription "D-U-F[,"] there was little danger that the witness would inaccurately remember the terms of the "writing[."] Also, the terms of the "writing" were by no means central or critical to the case against Duffy. The crime charged was not possession of a certain article, where the failure to pro-

duce the article might prejudice the defense. *The shirt was collateral evidence of the crime. Furthermore, it was only one piece of evidence in a substantial case against Duffy.*

Id. at 812 (emphasis added).

Following *Duffy,* a defendant convicted on various counts related to trafficking in counterfeit watches appealed his conviction, arguing that the district court plainly erred in not requiring the government to produce the actual watches sold as the best evidence that he had trafficked in counterfeit goods. *United States v. Yamin,* 868 F.2d 130, 132 (5th Cir. 1989). The court rejected the defendant's argument, explaining:

> This novel argument appears plausible because it is, at least in part, the writing on the watch that makes it a counterfeit. Thus it may be argued that it is the content of that writing that must be proved. The purpose of the best evidence rule, however, is to prevent inaccuracy and fraud when attempting to prove the contents of a writing. Neither of those purposes was violated here. The viewing of a simple and recognized trademark is not likely to be inaccurately remembered. While the mark is in writing, it is more like a picture or a symbol than a written document. In addition, an object bearing a mark is both a chattel and a writing, and the trial judge has discretion to treat it as a chattel, to which the best evidence rule does not apply.

Id. at 134.

Here, the district court appropriately treated the safe as chattel. The policy considerations behind the best evidence rule, as in *Duffy* and *Yamin,* are not implicated. The writing — "2010" — was simple, meaning that little danger existed that the witness would inaccurately remember the terms of the "writing" on the safe. And, as the district court noted, the likelihood of fraud was small because the government also admitted into evidence the safe's instructional manual, which was found inside the safe and also bore the number "2010."

Moreover, as the district court explained, "the testimony regarding the inscription on the safe was only a small part of the substantial evidence presented against Buchanan." The numeric inscription was not "critical" to the case against Buchanan; instead, the safe was merely collateral evidence of the crime. . . .

Seiler v. Lucasfilm, Ltd.
808 F.2d 1316 (9th Cir. 1986)

FARRIS, Circuit Judge. . . .

Seiler contends that he created and published in 1976 and 1977 science fiction creatures called Garthian Striders. In 1980, George Lucas released The Empire Strikes Back, a motion picture that contains a battle sequence depicting giant machines called Imperial Walkers. In 1981 Seiler obtained a copyright on his Striders, depositing with the Copyright Office "reconstructions" of the originals as they had appeared in 1976 and 1977.

Seiler contends that Lucas' Walkers were copied from Seiler's Striders which were allegedly published in 1976 and 1977. Lucas responds that Seiler did not obtain his copyright until one year after the release of The Empire Strikes Back and that Seiler can produce no documents that antedate The Empire Strikes Back.

[At trial, Seiler proposed to introduce into evidence his "reconstructions," but the trial court held that their admission was barred by the Best Evidence Rule]. . . .

The best evidence rule embodied in Rules 1001–1008 represented a codification of longstanding common law doctrine. Dating back to 1700, the rule requires not, as its common name implies, the best evidence in every case but rather the production of an original document instead of a copy. Many commentators refer to the rule not as the best evidence rule but as the original document rule....

Writings and recordings are defined in Rule 1001[(a)] as "letters, words, [] numbers, or their equivalent[] set down [in any form]."

The Advisory Committee Note supplies the following gloss:

> Traditionally the rule requiring the original centered upon accumulations of data and expressions affecting legal relations set forth in words and figures. This meant that the rule was one essentially related to writings. Present day techniques have expanded methods of storing data, yet the essential form which the information ultimately assumes for usable purposes is words and figures. Hence the considerations underlying the rule dictate its expansion to include computers, photographic systems, and other modern developments.

Some treatises, whose approach seems more historical than rigorously analytic, opine without support from any cases that the rule is limited to words and figures.

We hold that Seiler's drawings were "writings" within the meaning of Rule 1001([a]); they consist not of "letters, words, [or] numbers" but of "their equivalent." To hold otherwise would frustrate the policies underlying the rule and introduce undesirable inconsistencies into the application of the rule.

In the days before liberal rules of discovery and modern techniques of electronic copying, the rule guarded against incomplete or fraudulent proof. By requiring the possessor of the original to produce it, the rule prevented the introduction of altered copies and the withholding of originals. The purpose of the rule was thus long thought to be one of fraud prevention, but Wigmore pointed out that the rule operated even in cases where fraud was not at issue, such as where secondary evidence is not admitted even though its proponent acts in utmost good faith. Wigmore also noted that if prevention of fraud were the foundation of the rule, it should apply to objects as well as writings, which it does not.

The modern justification for the rule has expanded from prevention of fraud to a recognition that writings occupy a central position in the law. When the contents of a writing are at issue, oral testimony as to the terms of the writing is subject to a greater risk of error than oral testimony as to events or other situations. The human memory is not often capable of reciting the precise terms of a writing, and when the terms are in dispute only the writing itself, or a true copy, provides reliable evidence. To summarize then, we observe that the importance of the precise terms of writings in the world of legal relations, the fallibility of the human memory as reliable evidence of the terms, and the hazards of inaccurate or incomplete duplication are the concerns addressed by the best evidence rule.

Viewing the dispute in the context of the concerns underlying the best evidence rule, we conclude that the rule applies....

The facts of this case implicate the very concerns that justify the best evidence rule. Seiler alleges infringement by The Empire Strikes Back, but he can produce no documentary evidence of any originals existing before the release of the movie. His secondary evidence does not consist of true copies or exact duplicates but of "reconstructions" made after The Empire Strikes Back. In short, Seiler claims that the movie infringed his originals, yet he has no proof of those originals.

The dangers of fraud in this situation are clear. The rule would ensure that proof of the infringement claim consists of the works alleged to be infringed. Otherwise, "reconstructions" which might have no resemblance to the purported original would suffice as proof for infringement of the original....

Seiler argues that the best evidence rule does not apply to his work, in that it is artwork rather than "writings, recordings, or photographs." He contends that the rule both historically and currently embraces only words or numbers. Neither party has referred us to cases which discuss the applicability of the rule to drawings.

To recognize Seiler's works as writings does not, as Seiler argues, run counter to the rule's preoccupation with the centrality of the written word in the world of legal relations. Just as a contract objectively manifests the subjective intent of the makers, so Seiler's drawings are objective manifestations of the creative mind. The copyright laws give legal protection to the objective manifestations of an artist's ideas, just as the law of contract protects through its multifarious principles the meeting of minds evidenced in the contract. Comparing Seiler's drawings with Lucas' drawings is no different in principle than evaluating a contract and the intent behind it. Seiler's "reconstructions" are "writings" that affect legal relations; their copyrightability attests to that.

A creative literary work, which is artwork, and a photograph whose contents are sought to be proved, as in copyright, defamation, or invasion of privacy, are both covered by the best evidence rule. We would be inconsistent to apply the rule to artwork which is literary or photographic but not to artwork of other forms. Furthermore, blueprints, engineering drawings, architectural designs may all lack words or numbers yet still be capable of copyright and susceptible to fraudulent alteration. In short, Seiler's argument would have us restrict the definitions of Rule 1001([a]) to "words" and "numbers" but ignore "or their equivalent." We will not do so in the circumstances of this case.

Our holding is also supported by the policy served by the best evidence rule in protecting against faulty memory. Seiler's reconstructions were made four to seven years after the alleged originals; his memory as to specifications and dimensions may have dimmed significantly. Furthermore, reconstructions made after the release of the Empire Strikes Back may be tainted, even if unintentionally, by exposure to the movie. Our holding guards against these problems....

Notes and Questions

1. The *Duffy* case—relied upon by the *Buchanan* court in interpreting the scope of the best evidence rule—predates the Federal Rules of Evidence. Is *Duffy*'s holding consistent with the broad definition of writing as subsequently codified in Rule 1001(a)?

2. Is it sound to distinguish between a typical document on the one hand and an inscribed object on the other? Although Wigmore wrote that the question whether to treat an inscribed object as a writing or not should be left to the trial court's discretion, he noted the challenges of drawing lines between documents and inscribed chattels:

> It is impracticable to base any distinction upon the *material* bearing the inscription; for a notice board or a tombstone may deserve the application of the rule as well as a sheet of notepaper. Nor is it practicable to distinguish according to the *number of words*; for each number is but one higher than the preceding....

4 Wigmore, Evidence § 1182, at 421 (Chadbourn rev. 1972) (emphasis in original).

3. Should the practical difficulty or impossibility of bringing something into court be a factor in determining whether it should be deemed a writing or chattel? Consider the following:

> If the production of the thing on which the inscription is found is indispensable, it would be impossible to proceed in many cases. If a sign were painted on a house, it would hardly be contended that the house would have to be produced, nor can it be said that the law converts the court-room into a receptacle for wagons, boxes, tombstones, and the like, on which one's name may be written.

Kansas Pac. Ry. Co. v. Miller, 2 Colo. 442, 462 (1874). *See also* McCormick, Evidence § 199 (1954) (indicating that difficulty of production is a relevant consideration).

4. Would the various factors discussed by the *Buchanan* court in deciding whether or not to apply the best evidence rule to an inscribed chattel apply with equal force to typical documents? Are those factors codified in the best evidence rule? Should they be?

5. Is the definition of "writing" broad enough to cover words that appear on a computer screen? *See* Advisory Committee Note to Rule 1001(a) and (b).

C. What Qualifies as an Original?

Problem 6-3: Dangerous

Shortly after Michael Jackson released the song "Dangerous," Crystal Cartier brought a copyright infringement suit against him. Ms. Cartier's suit alleged that she recorded a song called "Dangerous" directly onto a master tape, made copies of the master tape, and sent those copies as demo tapes to various performers, including Jackson.

Ms. Cartier seeks to offer the master tape into evidence, but Mr. Jackson's attorney asserts that the best evidence rule requires that the original be offered into evidence and that the master tape is not the original.

How should the court rule on the objection?

Problem 6-4: The Threatening E-mail Revisited

Assume the same facts as in Problem 2-6. The government offers into evidence a printout of the e-mail message sent from David to Lisa. David's attorney objects, contending that the best evidence rule requires that the original be offered into evidence and that the printout of the e-mail message is not the original.

How should the court rule on the objection?

United States v. Rangel
585 F.2d 344 (8th Cir. 1978)

PER CURIAM.

Tiburcio A. Rangel appeals his conviction of knowingly and fraudulently demanding that a debt due from the United States be paid by virtue of a false instrument, in violation of 18 U.S.C. § 1003. We affirm the judgment of conviction.

Rangel, an employee of the United States Environmental Protection Agency, submitted three vouchers to the E.P.A. requesting reimbursement for lodging costs incurred in conjunction with three business trips. To each voucher he allegedly attached a photocopy of a duplicate, or a customers' copy of a Master Charge sales slip, as documentation for lodging expenses incurred. Photocopies of these Master Charge customer receipts submitted by Rangel were introduced into evidence with the vouchers, as were the corresponding duplicate merchant copies, which had been retained by the hotelkeepers. In each instance the photocopies submitted by Rangel showed greater lodging expenses than did the duplicate merchant copies. The invoice number on the merchant copies matched the number of the photocopied customer copies Rangel submitted to the E.P.A. The total amount Rangel received in excess of his actual lodging was approximately $53.59.

On appeal Rangel's main contention focuses on the admission of the travel authorization forms, travel vouchers and photocopied Master Charge receipts submitted to the E.P.A. Rangel contends the admission of these exhibits into evidence violated the best evidence rule....

Rangel challenges the admissibility of the customer photocopies because they are not the "original" altered receipts and therefore did not constitute the "best evidence." We disagree. The government had to prove the contents of the photocopy of the altered receipt since the photocopy, not the altered receipt, was identified as the document Rangel had submitted to support his demand for payment. Thus the photocopies were admitted as originals....

Rangel's challenge to the merchant copies is also based on the best evidence rule.... The merchants' copies were described by the district court as carbon copies of Master Charge sales slips, and as such were properly admitted as originals under Fed.R.Evid. 1001([d])....

Notes and Questions

1. It appears from *Rangel* that the "original" of a document does not necessarily mean "first." What, then, is the definition of "original" for purposes of the best evidence rule? *See Martinez v. Abbott Laboratories*, 356 F. Supp. 2d 898, 904 n.3 (N.D. Ill. 2005) ("the decision-maker relied solely on the two-page copy, not the original work order.... Here the copy is, itself, the original for purposes of [the Best Evidence Rule]").

2. The best evidence rule seems to contemplate that there can be multiple originals of a document. Rule 1001(d) defines the original of a writing or recording as "the writing or recording itself or any counterpart intended to have the same effect by the person who executed or issued it." The Advisory Committee Note to Rule 1001(d) explains that "[a] carbon copy of a contract executed in duplicate becomes an original, as does a sales ticket carbon copy given to a customer." *See Greater Kansas City Laborers Pension Fund v. Thummel*, 738 F.2d 926, 928 (8th Cir. 1984) (holding all carbon copies of a contract executed in quadruplicate are originals).

3. How is it in *Rangel* that the photocopy of the altered customer copies of the charge slips and the unaltered merchant copies of the charge slips are both originals in this case? Does it depend on the purposes for which each of the sets of documents are being offered?

4. Is the "original" of a photograph a negative? *See* Fed. R. Evid. 1001(d) ("An 'original' of a photograph includes the negative or a print from it."); Advisory Committee Note to Fed. R. Evid. 1001(d) ("While strictly speaking the original of a photograph might be thought to be only the negative, practicality and common usage require that

any print from the negative be regarded as an original."). Note that a photograph still must be authenticated in accordance with Rule 901, typically under Rule 901(b)(1) (testimony of a witness with knowledge) or Rule 901(b)(9) (evidence about a process or system).

5. Is the "original" of data that appears on a computer screen, such as an e-mail or a chat room conversation, the computer itself? In other words, must the entire computer be brought in to display the e-mail or chat room conversation? Must an electronic copy of it be introduced into evidence? *See* Fed. R. Evid. 1001(d) ("For electronically stored information, 'original' means any printout—or other output readable by sight—if it accurately reflects the information."); Advisory Committee Note to Fed. R. Evid. 1001(d) ("[P]racticality and usage confer the status of original upon any computer printout."). Such printouts must be authenticated in accordance with Rule 901, typically under Rule 901(b)(9) (process or system).

6. Notwithstanding Rule 1001(d)'s definition, whether data on a computer is an "original" or not may depend on the manner in which the information made its way into the computer and the purpose for which it is being offered. Consider, for example, a mail-order business. If an order form were to be received in the mail from a customer, and an employee manually wrote down the details into a ledger, surely what was written down in the ledger would not be an "original," but merely a copy, and a hand-copy at that. Why should the result be any different if the information were entered into a computer? To be sure, a printout from a computer is an original of what is on the computer, but what is on the computer may be merely a copy of something else, and Rule 1001(d) surely does not convert a printout of the same into an original when what is on the computer would not be.

D. What Constitutes Proving Contents of a Writing, Recording, or Photograph?

Problem 6-5: The Libelous Billboard Revisited

Assume the same facts as in Problem 6-1. Assume further that the court holds that a billboard is a "writing" for purposes of the best evidence rule.

Does the best evidence rule bar Jones' testimony?

Problem 6-6: A Picture Is Worth a Thousand Words Revisited

Assume the same facts as in Problem 2-3. The prosecution seeks to call two people as witnesses. First, they seek to call Tom, a First National customer who was present during the robbery and would testify that he saw Michael enter the bank and point a gun at a teller. Second, they seek to call William, an employee of Federal Savings & Loan. William is responsible for maintaining the bank's cameras, and would testify to what he saw Michael doing on the tape.

The defense objects on the ground that the testimony of both Tom and William is barred by the best evidence rule.

How should the court rule on the objection?

Problem 6-7: The Alibi

David is on trial on charges of murder. David denies the charge and presents an alibi, contending that at the time of the alleged murder, he was at the Platinum Gym. His close friend, Tom, testifies that he was with David at the gym during the period in question.

The prosecution calls as a witness Marie, an employee at Platinum Gym. If permitted, Marie would testify that each member's identification card is swiped in a card reader upon entering the gym, which in turn records the member's name and the time of their visit on the gym's computer. Marie would further testify that she examined the computer file for the date in question, and that it did not show that David entered the gym on that date. David's attorney objects to the testimony on best evidence grounds.

How should the court rule on the objection?

United States v. Gonzales-Benitez
537 F.2d 1051 (9th Cir. 1976)

KENNEDY, Circuit Judge:

Aida Gonzales-Benitez and Ambrosio Hernandez-Coronel were convicted for importing and distributing heroin in violation of 21 U.S.C. §§ 952(a), 960(a) (1), 841(a)(1)....

Ana Maria Gutierrez, a paid informer who had worked on prior occasions with the Drug Enforcement Administration, initiated a series of telephone conversations with appellant Gonzales, who was staying in Culiacan, Mexico. Gonzales indicated she could obtain good quality heroin for the informant. Gonzales asked if Gutierrez would distribute the narcotic to reliable persons, and Gutierrez responded that her buyers could be trusted. In June Mrs. Gutierrez and her daughter traveled to Culiacan, where they spent all day with Gonzales and also met with appellant Hernandez. Together they discussed delivery and transportation of heroin in further detail. Gonzales offered to sell 16 ounces to Gutierrez and allow Hernandez to travel to the border with Gutierrez for protection, but the informer refused to make a purchase at that time.

There followed other telephone conversations and another meeting in which Mrs. Gutierrez introduced Gonzales to a purported buyer, Hector Berrellez. Berrellez was an agent for the Drug Enforcement Administration.

Thereafter a sale was arranged. It was agreed that Berrellez would take delivery of the drugs within the United States. On the day of the border crossing Mrs. Gutierrez and her daughter met with Gonzales and Hernandez in a hotel room in Nogales, Mexico. Appellants produced 13 ounces of heroin and Hernandez stated he would bring two additional kilograms of heroin the next day. He demonstrated certain belts with pouches which he used to transport heroin on his person.

The heroin was then secreted in Mrs. Gutierrez' purse. Gonzales left and walked across the border by herself, while the other three drove through the border checkpoint with the heroin. The crossing was accomplished in Mrs. Gutierrez' car. Hernandez was in the front seat. He had removed the heroin from the purse and placed it in a grocery bag which he held on his lap. He placed cheese in the bag to mask any heroin smell.

The three met Gonzales on the Arizona side and together they drove to the motel to meet Berrellez, the ostensible buyer. After Berrellez took possession of the heroin, a signal was given and appellants were arrested....

Appellants contend the trial court erred in permitting testimony that related their conversations with the informers during a certain meeting in a motel room in Arizona. They claim that since the conversations were recorded on tapes, the tapes themselves, and not testimony of one of the participants, were the "best evidence" of the conversations. We are puzzled that this argument should be advanced so seriously and would not consider it if attorneys for both appellants had not argued the point so strenuously both in their briefs and in the court below. Certainly the trial court was correct in dismissing the objection out of hand.

The appellants simply misconstrue the purpose and effect of the best evidence rule. The rule does not set up an order of preferred admissibility, which must be followed to prove any fact. It is, rather, a rule applicable only when one seeks to prove the contents of documents or recordings. Fed.R.Evid. 1002. Thus, if the ultimate inquiry had been to discover what sounds were embodied on the tapes in question, the tapes themselves would have been the "best evidence."

However, the content of the tapes was not in itself a factual issue relevant to the case. The inquiry concerned the content of the conversations. The tape recordings, if intelligible, would have been admissible as evidence of those conversations. But testimony by the participants was equally admissible and was sufficient to establish what was said....

United States v. Bennett
363 F.3d 947 (9th Cir. 2004)

FISHER, Circuit Judge:

This case arises from the boarding and search of defendant-appellant Vincent Franklin Bennett's boat by members of a joint task force targeting smuggling activity from Mexico into Southern California. Coronado Police Officer Keith James initially spotted Bennett's boat near the U.S.-Mexico border on January 27, 2000, as the boat traveled north along the California coastline. Officer Sandy Joseph Sena, another task force member, boarded Bennett's boat at the entrance to San Diego Bay and eventually directed Bennett to dock his boat.

After the docking, members of the task force made multiple efforts over many hours to find drugs on Bennett's boat. When drilling three or four holes in the boat proved unproductive, they stored the boat overnight, hauled it to a Coast Guard facility the next day and x-rayed it. The x-ray revealed what turned out to be 1,541.5 pounds of marijuana.

Bennett was convicted on one count of importation of marijuana under 21 U.S.C. §§ 952 and 960, and one count of possession with intent to distribute marijuana under 21 U.S.C. § 841(a)(1).... Bennett appeals ... evidentiary rulings ... that occurred during trial....

Illegal importation occurs when a defendant imports a controlled substance into the United States from "any place outside thereof." 21 U.S.C. § 952(a); *see United States v. Cabaccang*, 332 F.3d 622, 625–32 (9th Cir. 2003) (en banc).

Here, although Bennett's boat was heading north (away from Mexico) when officers first spotted it, the boat was in U.S. waters at the time. Thus, the government on appeal relies chiefly on three other items of evidence that Bennett imported drugs from outside the United States. First, U.S. Customs Officer Malcolm McCloud Chandler testified that he discovered a global positioning system ("GPS") while searching Bennett's boat and that the GPS revealed that Bennett's boat had traveled from Mexican waters to San Diego Bay....

Bennett's most serious challenge to the evidence supporting his importation conviction relates to Chandler's testimony about the global positioning system he discovered during his search of Bennett's boat. A GPS device uses global positioning satellites to track and record the location of the device and, therefore, the location of any object to which it is attached. The GPS came with a "backtrack" feature that graphed the boat's journey that day. Chandler testified that the backtrack feature mapped Bennett's journey from Mexican territorial waters off the coast of Rosarito, Mexico, to the Coronado Islands and then north to San Diego Bay.... Chandler acknowledged on cross-examination that he had not taken possession of the GPS device itself or obtained any record of the data contained therein....

The best evidence rule provides that the original of a "writing, recording, or photograph" is required to prove the contents thereof. Fed.R.Evid. 1002.... An original is the writing or recording itself, a negative or print of a photograph or, [for electronically stored information, any printout or other output readable by sight if it accurately reflects the information.] Fed.R.Evid. 1001([d]).

Where the rule applies, the proponent must produce the original (or a duplicate, *see* Fed.R.Evid. 1003) or explain its absence. Fed.R.Evid. 1002, 1004. The rule's application turns on "whether contents are sought to be proved." Fed.R.Evid. 1002 Advisory Committee's note. "[A]n event may be proved by nondocumentary evidence, even though a written record of it was made." *Id.* Accordingly, the rule is inapplicable when a witness merely identifies a photograph or videotape "as a correct representation of events which he saw or of a scene with which he is familiar." *Id.*; *see also United States v. Workinger*, 90 F.3d 1409, 1415 (9th Cir. 1996) ("[A] tape recording cannot be said to be the best evidence of a conversation when a party seeks to call a participant in or observer of the conversation to testify to it. In that instance, the best evidence rule has no application at all."). However, the rule does apply when a witness seeks to testify about the contents of a writing, recording or photograph without producing the physical item itself—particularly when the witness was not privy to the events those contents describe. *See* Fed.R.Evid. 1002 Advisory Committee's note.

That is the nature of Chandler's GPS testimony here and why his testimony violated the best evidence rule. First, the GPS display Chandler saw was a writing or recording because, according to Chandler, he saw a graphical representation of data that the GPS had compiled about the path of Bennett's boat. *See* Fed.R.Evid. 1001[(a), (b)]. Second, Chandler never actually observed Bennett's boat travel the path depicted by the GPS. Thus, Chandler's testimony concerned the "content" of the GPS, which, in turn, was evidence of Bennett's travels. Fed.R.Evid. 1002. At oral argument, the government admitted that the GPS testimony was offered solely to show that Bennett had come from Mexico. Proffering testimony about Bennett's border-crossing instead of introducing the GPS data, therefore, was analogous to proffering testimony describing security camera footage of an event to prove the facts of the event instead of introducing the footage itself.

This is precisely the kind of situation in which the best evidence rule applies.... Yet the government did not produce the GPS itself—or a printout or other representation of such data, *see* Fed.R.Evid. 1001([d])—which would have been the best evidence of the data showing Bennett's travels. Instead, the government offered only Chandler's GPS-based testimony about an event—namely, a border-crossing—that he never actually saw....

We therefore hold that Chandler's GPS-based testimony was inadmissible under the best evidence rule....

United States v. Diaz-Lopez
625 F.3d 1198 (9th Cir. 2010)

GOULD, Circuit Judge:

....

Diaz was born in and is a citizen of Mexico. On February 13, 2009, a Border Patrol agent found and arrested Diaz on a road in California, north of the United States-Mexico border. The government charged Diaz under 8 U.S.C. § 1326(a) with being a removed alien found in the United States without permission. At a bench trial, the government introduced testimony from a Border Patrol agent stating that he had performed a search of the Computer Linked Application Information Management System ("CLAIMS") database using Diaz's name, alien number, and date of birth, and had found no record of Diaz having filed a Form I-212, which is the required application for permission to reapply for admission to the United States after having been previously removed.

The district court found Diaz guilty and sentenced him to twenty-one months in prison and three years of supervised release. This appeal followed....

Diaz ... argues that the agent's testimony regarding the results of the CLAIMS database search violated Federal Rule of Evidence 1002, which codifies a principle long referred to at common law as the "best evidence rule." Diaz's assertion challenging the testimony under the best evidence rule presents a question of first impression in our circuit. We must decide if testimony that a search of a computer database revealed no record of a matter violates the best evidence rule when it is offered without the production of an "original" printout showing the search results. We hold that it does not.

As we previously have observed, the best evidence rule "requires not, as its common name implies, the best evidence in every case but rather the production of an original document instead of a copy." *Seiler v. Lucasfilm, Ltd.*, 808 F.2d 1316, 1318 (9th Cir. 1986). Federal Rule of Evidence 1002, on its face, is simple and clear in its statement.... But despite its simple name and concise definition, experience has shown that application of this principle, as with other difficult questions of the law of evidence, may not "safely be handled in slap-dash fashion." John MacArthur Maguire, *Evidence: Common Sense and Common Law,* at v (1947).

The scope, application, and relevance of the best evidence doctrine have been debated by treatise-writers for centuries. Professor Thayer thought it would "help to clear the subject, and keep our heads clear, if we drop the name and the notion of any specific rule of the Best Evidence." James Bradley Thayer, *A Preliminary Treatise on Evidence at the Common Law* 507 (Boston, Little, Brown, and Co. 1898). A century later, however, the name is still with us. Although the best evidence doctrine in the federal courts has since been refined to encompass only the requirement for originals set out in the Federal Rules of Evidence (and in no way involves comparing evidence to determine which is "the best"), it has also been enlarged to include not just writings, but also recordings and photographs. The modern doctrine appears to be a rule of evolving scope (applying to ever-increasing varieties of media) with less-frequent application (owing to the easy availability of exact duplicates, modern discovery procedures, and exceptions to the federal version of the best evidence rule).

The animating purpose of the best evidence rule has been persuasively summarized as follows:

> [P]resenting to a court the exact words of a writing is of more than average importance, particularly in the case of operative or dispositive instruments such as deeds, wills or contracts, where a slight variation of words may mean a great difference in rights. In addition, it is to be considered (1) that there has been substantial hazard of inaccuracy in some of the commonly utilized methods of making copies of writings, and (2) oral testimony purporting to give the terms of a writing from memory is probably subject to a greater risk of error than oral testimony concerning other situations generally. The danger of mistransmitting critical facts which accompanies the use of written copies or recollection, but which is largely avoided when an original writing is presented to prove its terms, justifies preference for original documents.

2 George E. Dix et al., *McCormick on Evidence* § 232 (Kenneth S. Broun, ed., 6th ed. 2009). Professor Wigmore offered a similar explanation of the "fundamental notion" of the best evidence rule:

> [I]n writings the smallest variation in words may be of importance.... Thus the rule applies only to the *terms of the document,* and not to any *other facts about the document.* In other words, the rule ... does not apply to exclude testimony which concerns the document without aiming to establish its terms....

4 John Henry Wigmore, *Evidence in Trials at Common Law,* § 1242 at 574 (James H. Chadbourn rev. 1972).

We turn now to the issue presented by Diaz on this appeal. Diaz contends that, under Federal Rule of Evidence 1002, the government was required to produce an "original" to show that the CLAIMS database did not contain any record of Diaz having filed an I-212. When records or data are stored [electronically, any printout or other output readable by sight that accurately reflects the information qualifies as an "original."] Fed.R.Evid. 1001[(d)]. Diaz argues that the government should have introduced a printout of the search results from the CLAIMS database rather than testimony from the agent performing the search.

Diaz is correct that the CLAIMS database falls within the scope of the best evidence rule.... The next question is whether the evidence was introduced [to prove the content of a writing, recording, or photograph.] Fed.R.Evid. 1002. We conclude that it was not. The agent's testimony that he searched the database and found no record of Diaz having filed an I-212 is similar to testimony "that an event did *not* occur because relevant records contain no mention of it. This negative type of testimony is usually held not to constitute proof of contents and thus not to require production of records." Dix et al., *supra,* at § 234. Indeed, the advisory committee's note to Rule 1002 states that the best evidence rule does not apply to "testimony that books or records have been examined and found not to contain any reference to a designated matter." Fed.R.Evid. 1002, advisory committee's note.

Diaz concedes that if no record were found pursuant to an agent's physical search of an A-file, testimony to that effect would be admissible under Federal Rule of Evidence 1002. However, Diaz asserts that, although the Rule applies to computer databases, the advisory committee note's limitation on the Rule applies only to searches of "physical" records.

We decline to adopt such a position. First, we do not see any meaningful difference between a search of a physical file and a search of a database. Databases contain "physical" records, too, even if those records are not printed on paper. Second, the best evidence rule, like us, now survives in the twenty-first century. It is common sense, and not mere symmetry, to say that because the rule applies to computer databases, the rule's limitations must also apply to such databases. It is reasonable to apply the best evidence rule to new circumstances as technology evolves, but when the rule is extended, courts will necessarily be required to decide if the limits on the rule extend as well. When, by virtue of new technology, the best evidence rule can be applied to testimony about databases, the traditional limits on the rule should be properly extended as well.

Our decision here does not conflict with our holding in *United States v. Bennett*, 363 F.3d 947 (9th Cir.2004). There, we held that testimony about data retrieved from a boat's global positioning system ("GPS") was barred by the best evidence rule because the testimony had been introduced to prove the "content" of the GPS, which, in turn, was evidence that the defendant had come from Mexico. But *Bennett* concerned testimony about the *contents* of the GPS data, not testimony about the *absence* of data. In that case, we concluded that "the GPS itself—or a printout or other representation of such data—... would have been the best evidence of the data showing [the defendant's] travels." We reached that decision because the testimony about the GPS data was introduced to prove its content (i.e., the location and travels of a boat). In Diaz's case, the government did not introduce testimony to prove the content of a writing; rather, the government introduced testimony to prove that a particular record was *not* part of the contents of a database. Moreover, the testimony about the search of the database was not testimony in which "the smallest variation in words may be of importance." Wigmore, *supra*.

It might be contended that, while the "smallest variation in words" is not of importance in the case of testimony regarding the negative results of a database search, such variations may well be significant if the testimony is offered to prove what particular search terms were used to search a database. However, even if Diaz had raised this argument, it would not aid his case. Any dispute about the particular search terms used by the agent for searching the CLAIMS database is not a dispute about the contents of the database, or about the contents of any records in the database, but rather a dispute about the specific actions performed by the agent. As a result, the best evidence rule would not apply because it applies only to writings, recordings, and photographs (as defined by Federal Rule of Evidence 1001), and not to actions. Moreover, even if the search terms used to search the database were genuinely in dispute, Diaz was free to cross-examine the agent who performed the search. Any doubts that might be raised by Diaz regarding the completeness of the search or the search terms used are a proper subject for a reasonable cross-examination, and go to the weight accorded to the testimony, not its admissibility under the best evidence rule....

Notes and Questions

1. There are two different circumstances in which one is said to be seeking to prove the contents of a writing, and thus two circumstances in which the best evidence rule requires production of the original. First, when proof of the content of a writing, recording, or photograph is an element of the underlying substantive offense (the "legal aspect" of the best evidence rule). And second, when practical circumstances make it necessary to prove the content of a writing, recording, or photograph (the "practical aspect" of the best evidence rule).

Libel suits are examples of the legal aspect of the best evidence rule in action: the underlying substantive law requires that the plaintiff be defamed in writing, and thus an element of the underlying offense requires proving that a writing was published by the defendant that contains defamatory matter about the plaintiff.

The *Bennett* case is an example of the practical aspect of the best evidence rule in action: nothing in the underlying substantive law requires proof of crossing the border by way of GPS technology. Yet because the GPS reading is the government's only evidence that the defendant crossed the border, it must prove that point by use of the GPS reading, which implicates the best evidence rule. *See generally Lorraine v. Markel American Ins. Co.*, 241 F.R.D. 534, 578–79 (D. Md. 2007) ("Whether the content is at issue is determined on a case-by-case basis. For example, proof that someone is married may be made by the testimony of a witness to the ceremony. The marriage license is not required. However, the rule applies if the only proof of the marriage is by the record itself. Similarly, someone who heard a politician give a speech may testify to what was said without the video recording of the speech, because the content of the recording is not at issue. In contrast, if the only way to prove the content of the speech is by the video, because there are no witnesses available to testify, the rule would apply to the video recording.").

2. In *United States v. Donato-Morales*, 382 F.3d 42 (1st Cir. 2004), the defendant was on trial for larceny from the United States for shoplifting a videocassette recorder from a store located on an Army base. The government claimed that the defendant removed a more expensive "746" model from its box and put it in a box for the less expensive "445" model. A conviction under the statute at issue requires proof that the defendant intended to steal a "thing of value," necessitating that the government prove that the price of the "746" model was more expensive than that of the "445" model. While the box for the "445" model had a price tag on it (and was admitted into evidence), the box for the "746" model did not, and so the government offered the testimony of a guard who determined the price of the "746" by using a price scanner. The court rejected a best evidence rule challenge to the guard's testimony:

> Donato argues that the government violated the best evidence rule, Fed.R.Evid. 1002, by relying on the security officer's testimony of the price rather than a written printout from the scanner that the officer used to determine the price. The district court correctly rejected this objection at trial. The best evidence rule applies only to evidence submitted to prove the content of writings, recordings, or photographs. The officer's testimony was not offered to prove the content of the scanner display, but rather the price of the VCR.

Id. at 45 n.2. Is the *Donato-Morales* court's holding correct? Can it be reconciled with *Bennett*?

3. Recall from Chapter 4 that Rule 703 permits experts to base their opinions on items not admitted into evidence, such as medical records and x-rays. The Advisory Committee Note to Rule 1002 makes clear that the best evidence rule is subject to Rule 703: "It should be noted, however, that Rule 703 allows an expert to give an opinion based on matters not in evidence, and the present rule must be read as being limited accordingly in its application."

4. Sometimes, juries are permitted to view transcripts of tape recordings that they listen to in court. Is that consistent with the best evidence rule? Consider the following:

> When an audio recording is in English, the common practice is to play the recording, make a transcript available, mark the transcript as an exhibit, and use it as an aid. Our court, and many others, have approved such use of transcripts as

aids to the jury, provided the court makes clear to the jury that the tape rather than the transcript constitutes the best evidence....

Parties frequently ... use the transcripts only as aids and fail to admit them in evidence. The usual reason given for not introducing transcripts in evidence is that the wiretap tapes themselves are the best evidence of the conversation, not the transcripts.

The best evidence rule requires that the tape recordings themselves must be furnished, absent agreement to the contrary, but does not require that English translations of those tapes be excluded from evidence. Non-English recordings present unique problems.... Accordingly, almost 20 years ago, this court approved the introduction in evidence of English transcripts for wiretaps of Spanish conversations, provided the reliability issues were worked out.... This practice of admitting reliable English transcripts in evidence is entirely consistent with the best evidence rule. The rationale behind the best evidence rule—that "the [recording itself] is a more reliable, complete and accurate source of information as to its contents and meaning than anyone's description" of it—is not undercut when the original recording is played to the jury and the undisputedly accurate English transcript is admitted in evidence.

United States v. Morales-Madera, 352 F.3d 1, 7–9 (1st Cir. 2003).

E. Duplicates

Recall that earlier in the chapter, the best evidence rule was described as a doctrine "riddled with exceptions." Perhaps among the more significant of these exceptions is Rule 1003, which provides:

A duplicate is admissible to the same extent as the original unless a genuine question is raised about the original's authenticity or the circumstances make it unfair to admit the duplicate.

Lest you believe that Rule 1003 completely undercuts the best evidence rule, keep in mind that the definition of "duplicate" is not the same as the definition of "copy." Recall that a "copy" historically included copies made by hand. The definition of "duplicate" is much narrower:

A "duplicate" means a counterpart produced by a mechanical, photographic, chemical, electronic, or other equivalent process or technique that accurately reproduces the original.

Federal Rule of Evidence 1001(e).

The rule thus contemplates techniques of duplication that eliminate the possibility of error, such as reproducing a document on a photocopier. But "[c]opies subsequently produced manually, whether handwritten or typed, are not within the definition." Advisory Committee Note to Rule 1001(e). Similarly, a transcript of a recording would not fall within the definition of "duplicate."

Yet, while the risk of *inadvertent* error in copying is virtually eliminated if one uses, say, a photocopier, the risk of *intentional* alterations remain. Moreover, there might be other reasons why a duplicate, even if produced by mechanical means, would be an inadequate substitute for the original. Accordingly, the general principle of admissibility in Rule 1003 is subject to exceptions when questions are raised about the authenticity of the original or circumstances would make it unfair to admit the duplicate in lieu of the original.

United States v. Haddock
956 F.2d 1534 (10th Cir. 1992)

TACHA, Circuit Judge.

Defendant-appellant Kenneth E. Haddock appeals a jury verdict convicting him on two counts of misapplication of bank funds in violation of 18 U.S.C. § 656, six counts of bank fraud in violation of 18 U.S.C. § 1344, one count of false statement to a federally insured bank under 18 U.S.C. § 1014, and one count of making false statements to the Federal Deposit Insurance Corporation (FDIC) under 18 U.S.C. § 1007....

At trial and outside the jury's presence, counsel for Haddock proffered photocopies of six documents as evidence supporting Haddock's defense. The district court denied admission of these photocopies into evidence on the basis that "they did not have enough indication of reliability at this time that the court felt that [it] could allow them under the Rules of Evidence." In a memorandum reexamining that order, the court concluded that "the government had raised a genuine issue as to the authenticity of the originals." Defendant contends that these documents were admissible under the Federal Rules of Evidence....

Under Rule 1001[(e)] of the Federal Rules of Evidence, photocopies are considered duplicates. Rule 1003 provides that "[a] duplicate is admissible to the same extent as [the] original unless [] a genuine question is raised [about] the [original's] authenticity [] or [] the circumstances [make it] unfair to admit the duplicate []." Fed.R.Evid. 1003. Rule 1003 is part of a broadened set of evidentiary rules that reflect the fact that, due to modern and accurate reproduction techniques, duplicates and originals should normally be treated interchangeably. However, despite our age of technology, a trial court must still be wary of admitting duplicates "where the circumstances surrounding the execution of the writing present a substantial possibility of fraud." 5 Jack B. Weinstein & Margaret A. Berger, *Weinstein's Evidence* ¶ 1003[02], at 1003–9 (1991).

With regard to each of these photocopies, evidence presented at trial indicates that only Haddock could recall ever seeing either the original or a copy of these documents. Except for Haddock, no one — including in some cases persons who allegedly typed the document and persons to whom the original allegedly was sent — was familiar with the contents of the photocopies. In addition, witnesses testified that several of the documents bore markings and included statements that did not comport with similar documents prepared in the ordinary course of business at the Bank of White City and at the Bank of Herington. Under these circumstances, we hold that the district court did not abuse its discretion by excluding these photocopied documents from evidence....

Notes and Questions

1. When might it be "unfair" to admit photocopies in lieu of an original? Although the cases are few and far between, they appear to apply this proviso when the photocopies are incomplete or illegible. *E.g., Amoco Production Co. v. United States*, 619 F.2d 1383, 1391 (10th Cir. 1980). The proviso is also applied by courts in situations in which only the original would display features that might allow the party against whom the evidence is offered to prove his lack of culpability. *See United States v. Burston*, 608 F. Supp. 2d

828, 830–32 (E.D. Mich. 2008) (a case in which accused is alleged to have endorsed check; inability to conduct handwriting analysis on endorsement signature on duplicate makes the duplicate inadmissible in lieu of the original).

2. Is a challenge to the authenticity of the *duplicate* (as opposed to the authenticity of the *original*) a basis for denying admission of a duplicate under Rule 1003? *See* 31 Charles Alan Wright & Victor James Gold, Federal Practice and Procedure: Evidence § 8004 (2000) (noting that a challenge to the authenticity of the duplicate is a separate issue not covered by Rule 1003 but is instead covered by Rule 901, and thus that where the challenge is to the authenticity of the duplicate, the trial court should not exclude it unless no reasonable jury could conclude that it was authentic).

3. Reconsider the facts of Problem 6-1 and 6-5. Assuming that a billboard is deemed to be a writing, does Rule 1003 provide a practical way of complying with the best evidence rule?

4. Is a duplicate of a duplicate admissible under Rule 1003? *See United States v. Carroll*, 860 F.2d 500, 507 (1st Cir. 1988) (holding that it is).

5. Is a digitally enhanced copy of a videotape in which the brightness or contrast is adjusted or in which selected images are enlarged, or a digitally enhanced copy of an audiotape in which the volume is increased, a "duplicate" as defined in Rule 1001(e)? *See United States v. Seifert*, 351 F. Supp. 2d 926, 926–29 (D.Minn. 2005) (holding that they are); *United States v. Johnson*, 362 F. Supp. 2d 1043, 1067 (N.D. Iowa 2005) (holding the same for an audiotape).

F. Production of Original Excused

Problem 6-8: The Chat Room Revisited

Assume the same facts as in Problem 2-7. Assume further that when the instant message appeared on his computer, Steve did not print out a copy of it, and his computer automatically deleted any electronic copy of the message when he closed the instant message window. The government objects to the admission of Steve's testimony, contending that it violates the best evidence rule.

How should the court rule on the objection?

United States v. Marcantoni
590 F.2d 1324 (5th Cir. 1979)

TJOFLAT, Circuit Judge:

Charlie and Helen Suzanne Tune Marcantoni, husband and wife, were convicted in two counts of armed bank robbery and assault with a dangerous weapon during the commission thereof in violation of 18 U.S.C. §§ 2, 2113(a), (d) (1976). In this appeal, the Marcantonis contend that ... reversible error occurred in the court's admission of some damaging evidence tending to show that a part of the "bait money" taken during the robbery was in their possession three days later. We find no merit in this latter contention. ...

On Friday, August 6, 1976, at approximately 9:10 a. m., a white male, standing 5'9"–5'10", weighing 170–180 pounds, and wearing a motorcycle helmet with tinted brown sun visor, entered the Tampa Federal Savings & Loan Association (the Bank), Tampa, Florida, and went to the only teller window open at that time. The teller, Tina Brown, looked up into the barrel of a shotgun, screamed and ducked to the floor. The head teller, Debra Beckerink, realizing the situation, walked to Ms. Brown's window and began pulling bills of small denominations out of the money drawer and placing them in a bag. The gunman nervously commanded Beckerink to "give [him] the big bills." Record, vol. 3, at 10. She complied, supplying him in the process with $3,791.00, including ten $10 bills of bait money.[2] The gunman then ran out of the Bank, firing a shot at the sidewalk as he left, and jumped into the back seat of a waiting getaway car being driven by a white, blond-haired female....

[An investigation ensued, that eventually led the police to the Marcantonis.]

The following Monday morning, August 9, 1976, Charlie Marcantoni consented to and assisted in a search of his Rogers Avenue residence by the Tampa police. During the search, Detective Edward Brodesser examined several hundred dollars in currency and recorded the serial numbers from the faces of the $10 bills he found, but he did not seize the bills. Later in the day separate lineups were conducted with respect to each of the Marcantonis, and they were identified as the gunman and driver involved in the robbery.

On August 13, 1976, Detective Brodesser returned to the Marcantoni residence on Rogers Avenue with a search warrant authorizing the seizure of any of the bait money that might be there. Following his August 9 search of the residence Brodesser had learned that the serial numbers he had recorded from two of the $10 bills he had uncovered during the search matched the serial numbers of two $10 bills on the Bank's list of the bait money taken in the robbery. Brodesser was unable to find these bills on August 13, however, when he returned with the search warrant. Six days later the Marcantonis were indicted.

At the trial, the Government proved its case mainly through the testimony of three Bank tellers who witnessed the robbery, two bystanders who witnessed the getaway, and Detective Brodesser and an expert from the U.S. Bureau of Printing and Engraving who, together, established that two of the $10 bills seen by Brodesser during his initial search of the Marcantoni residence were part of the bait money....

The Marcantonis'... objection to the reception of Brodesser's testimony is that [the best evidence rule] required the Government to introduce the two bills in evidence. Brodesser's testimony, they argue, was secondary evidence of the contents of the bills and not admissible because the Government failed to establish any of the conditions to the admissibility of secondary evidence specified by Fed.R.Evid. 1004* ....

---

2. Bait money was kept in each teller's money drawer. When the bait money in question was removed, a silent alarm to the Tampa Police Department activated. The denominations, serial numbers, series years, and the bank of issue of each bait money bill had been recorded by the Bank.

* Editor's Note: Rule 1004 provides as follows:
  An original is not required and other evidence of the content of a writing, recording, or photograph is admissible if:
  (a)   all the originals are lost or destroyed, and not by the proponent acting in bad faith;
  (b)   an original cannot be obtained by any available judicial process;
  (c)   the party against whom the original would be offered had control of the original; was at that time put on notice, by pleadings or otherwise, that the original would be a subject of proof at the trial or hearing; and fails to produce it at the trial or hearing; or
  (d)   the writing, recording, or photograph is not closely related to a controlling issue.

The Government made no formal attempt to qualify Brodesser's recital of the incriminating serial numbers as secondary evidence admissible under the rule. First, as the Government concedes, it did not undertake to show that the two bills were lost or destroyed. Second, it was not established that the Marcantonis were served notice that the contents of the bills would be a subject of proof at trial, and no process was directed to them to produce the bills in court. Finally, the Government did not, and in our opinion could not, contend that the evidence was "not closely related to a controlling issue."

There was little if anything in the argument of counsel that even addressed the qualifications of rule 1004 or, much less, whether they had been met in this instance. In overruling the Marcantonis' objection, the trial judge, quite understandably we think, gave no reasons for his decision....

[W]e must assume that the court was satisfied that at least one of those conditions had been established. It should have been obvious after Detective Brodesser's return to the Marcantoni residence with a search warrant failed to produce the two $10 bills in question that the bills would not be available to the prosecution for trial. We have no difficulty in concluding that, under the circumstances of this case, the trial judge would have been authorized to find, under section ([a]) of the rule, that the two bills were "lost or [] destroyed." Surely, the Marcantonis could not have contended that the unavailability of the bills was the product of Government "bad faith." The trial judge could also have found, under section ([b]) of the rule, that [an original could not be obtained by any available judicial process.] Even assuming that the Marcantonis were amenable to a subpoena directing the production of the bills at trial,[5] we think it unrealistic to expect that they would have readily produced the two instruments that would have made the Government's case against them complete. In short, the Government was not required to go through the motion of having a subpoena issued, served and returned unexecuted in order to establish, under section ([b]), that the bills were unobtainable.

As for section ([c]) of the rule, a legitimate argument can be made on this record that the Marcantonis were "put on notice" that the serial numbers of the two $10 bills "would be a subject of proof" at the trial, and that, having not produced them at trial, the Marcantonis could not object to the use of Brodesser's notes. In sum, although the trial judge, in overruling the Marcantonis' best evidence objection, should have announced the predicate to admissibility he found to have been established under rule 1004, his decision to receive the evidence was correct....

State v. Espiritu

176 P.3d 885 (Haw. 2008)

Opinion of the court by ACOBA, J.

[In this case, Christopher K. Espiritu (Petitioner) seeks review of his conviction for attempted murder and related counts in connection with an incident in which he shot a woman with whom he previously had a relationship (Complainant).]

After the shooting, Detective Viela interviewed the Complainant. During the interview, the Complainant showed Detective Viela four text messages that she saved on her

---

5. We think it fairly debatable whether the Marcantonis could have been compelled, in the face of the fifth amendment privilege against self-incrimination, to produce the two $10 bills for use by the prosecution at trial. *See generally Bellis v. United States*, 417 U.S. 85 (1974); *United States v. Hankins*, 565 F.2d 1344 (5th Cir. 1978).

cell phone and alleged that Petitioner sent these messages to her between November 29, 2002, and December 4, 2002. Petitioner's defense counsel objected to the Complainant testifying about the contents of the text messages....

C.

1.

Petitioner also argues that the court committed error in allowing the Complainant to testify "because her testimony neither constituted the original nor a duplicate of the text message" as required by HRE Rule 1002 (1993). Petitioner contends that the original text messages for purposes of HRE Rule 1002 "would have consisted of the cell phone itself with the saved messages or a printout of the messages." Respondent counters that (1) HRE 1002 is inapplicable in this case because a text message does not qualify as a writing, recording, or photograph; (2) there was no evidence that it was possible to obtain a printout of the messages; (3) that no photographs were taken of the messages does not preclude the admission of the Complainant's testimony about the messages; (4) even if HRE Rule 1002 is applicable here, HRE Rule 1004 (1993) allows the admission of other evidence in place of the original where the original is lost or destroyed....

HRE Rule 1002 provides that "[t]o prove the content of a writing, recording, or photograph, the original writing, recording, or photograph is required, except as otherwise provided in these rules or by statute."[6] A writing or recording is defined in HRE 1001 (1993) as "consist[ing] of letters, words, sounds, or numbers, or their equivalent, set down by handwriting, typewriting, printing, photostating, photographing, magnetic impulse, mechanical or electronic recording, or other form of data compilation." This definition is identical to FRE Rule 1001.

Contrary to Respondent's assertion, a text message is a writing because it consists of letters, words, or numbers set down by mechanical or electronic recording, or other form of data compilation. Although neither party makes this assertion, text messages received on cell phones appear akin to messages received on computers and email for purposes of HRE Rule 1002. Thus, HRE Rule 1002 which requires an original in order to prove the content of a writing is applicable unless an exception under the HRE or a statute provides otherwise.

2.

Although HRE Rule 1002 would ordinarily preclude the admission of testimony about the text messages because such testimony is not an original, the testimony here is admissible because HRE Rule 1004 applies to the text messages such that other evidence may be admitted to prove the content of the text messages. HRE Rule 1004 provides an exception to the original writings requirement of HRE Rule 1002 inasmuch as HRE Rule 1004 provides that:

> The original or a duplicate is not required, and other evidence of the contents of a writing, recording, or photograph is admissible if:
>
> (1) *Originals lost or destroyed.* All originals are lost or have been destroyed, unless the proponent lost or destroyed them in bad faith[.] (emphasis added).

---

6. HRE Rule 1002 is identical to Federal Rules of Evidence (FRE) Rule 1002 except that the word "statute" in HRE Rule 1002 is substituted for the phrase "Act of Congress" found in FRE Rule 1002. [Editor's Note: The current version of Federal Rules 1001, 1002, and 1004 differ from their Hawaii counterparts in terms but not in substance as a result of the 2011 restyling of the Federal Rules of Evidence.]

This Rule is identical to FRE Rule 1004 except that HRE Rule 1004 eliminates the need for a duplicate as well if the aforementioned condition is met.

The Complainant no longer had the actual text messages because the Complainant no longer had the cell phone or the cell phone service from Verizon through which she received the messages. No other original version of the text messages appear to have existed because there is no indication from the record that the text messages were ever printed out, nor is it clear that it was possible for the messages to be printed from the phone. Thus, for purposes of HRE Rule 1004, the original text messages were "lost or destroyed."

Petitioner argues that "the original writing was lost or destroyed due to the bad faith of the State of Hawai'i." However, there is no evidence that Respondent exercised bad faith that led to the loss of the cell phone, which Petitioner contends was the "original" for purposes of HRE Rule 1002. Bad faith cannot reasonably be inferred because the Complainant failed to preserve text messages for over two years on a cell phone for which she discontinued service. Similarly, bad faith cannot be inferred because the text messages were not printed out when there is no indication that such a printout was even possible.

Indeed, courts agree that HRE Rule 1004(1) is "particularly suited" to electronic evidence "[g]iven the myriad ways that electronic records may be deleted, lost as a result of system malfunctions, purged as a result of routine electronic records management software (such as the automatic deletion of e-mail after a set time period) or otherwise unavailable...." *Lorraine v. Markel Am. Ins. Co.*, 241 F.R.D. 534, 580 (D. Md. 2007).

Petitioner argues that Respondent "should not be excused from producing the original or a duplicate of the text messages, which are otherwise inadmissible under the best evidence rule," because Respondent "has not shown that it would have been impossible or even difficult to download, photograph, or print out the data from [the Complainant's] cell phone." In support of this argument, Petitioner cites *United States v. Bennett*, 363 F.3d 947, 953–54 (9th Cir. 2004), wherein the Court of Appeals for the Ninth Circuit held that in accordance with the best evidence rule, the court could not admit secondary evidence pertaining to a global positioning system (GPS) reading as the government failed to show that it would have been difficult or impossible to download or print out the GPS data. That case is distinguishable in that there was no evidence that the GPS data had been lost or destroyed. Rather, the witness testifying about the data stated that he was not the GPS custodian and it was not necessary to videotape or photograph the GPS contents.

In contrast, here, it appears that the cell phone containing the text messages is unavailable. The Complainant testified that she changed cell phone service providers since the time of the accident. Furthermore, Petitioner concedes that "the original cell phone is no longer available and there is no indication that any photographs exist of the text messages" therefore, "neither the original nor any duplicates exist."

.... The plain language of HRE Rule 1004 states that an original or duplicate is not required to prove the contents of a writing or recording so long as the originals are lost or destroyed and such loss or destruction was not due to the bad faith of the proponent of the evidence. There is no requirement that the proponent must show that it was impossible or difficult to download or print out the writing at the time that it existed....

Notes and Questions

1. Note that once any of the exceptions to Rule 1004 are satisfied, a party is free to use *any* method it wishes to prove the contents of the writing, recording, or photograph:

The rule recognizes no "degrees" of secondary evidence. While strict logic might call for extending the principle of preference beyond simply preferring the original, the formulation of a hierarchy of preferences and a procedure for making it effective is believed to involve unwarranted complexities. Most, if not all, that would be accomplished by an extended scheme of preferences will, in any event, be achieved through the normal motivation of a party to present the most convincing evidence possible and the arguments and procedures available to his opponent if he does not.

Advisory Committee Note to Rule 1004.

This means, does it not, that even though Rule 1003 *permits* a party to use a duplicate in lieu of an original, if the original is destroyed or otherwise unavailable, a party is free to prove the contents of that original by way of testimony as to its contents, *even if a duplicate exists*? *See United States v. Standing Soldier*, 538 F.2d 196, 203 n.8 (8th Cir. 1976) (so holding). If this is so, does the textual difference between Federal Rule 1004 and its Hawaii counterpart have the significance that the *Espiritu* court attributes to it?

2. Absent affirmative evidence of a document's destruction, parties typically prove that an item has been lost or destroyed by producing evidence that a diligent search has failed to turn up an original. *E.g., United States v. McGaughey*, 977 F.2d 1067, 1071 (7th Cir. 1992).

3. That the proponent is responsible for the destruction or loss of the original does not necessarily imply "bad faith." For example, "bad faith" will not be found where the document was destroyed as part of a routine policy of destroying outdated documents or simply due to negligence. *E.g., Estate of Gryder v. Commissioner*, 705 F.2d 336, 338 (8th Cir. 1983).

Moreover, because the focus is on the *proponent's* bad faith, loss or destruction of the originals by a third party, even if done in bad faith, will not prevent a party from invoking Rule 1004(a). *See United States v. Zapata*, 356 F. Supp. 2d 323, 331 (S.D.N.Y. 2005) ("the originals in this case were not destroyed in bad faith; rather, they were destroyed without the involvement of the Government as part of an internal records retention policy at Western Union").

4. In *Seiler*, would it not have been possible for Seiler to invoke Rule 1004(a) to get his "reconstructions" into evidence? *See Seiler v. Lucasfilm, Ltd.*, 808 F.2d 1316, 1320 (1986) (upholding trial court's refusal to admit the reconstructions under Rule 1004(a) based on a finding of bad faith loss or destruction).

5. Rule 1004(c) excuses a party from producing an original that is under the control of the party against whom it is offered, provided the party is put on notice that its contents would be a subject of proof at the proceeding. Could Ms. Cartier have invoked this rule in Problem 6-3 to get the master tape admitted into evidence?

6. Rule 1004(d) provides, in effect, that the trial court can dispense with the requirements of the best evidence rule for so-called "collateral" matters, or matters that are "not closely related to a controlling issue." The Advisory Committee explains that "[w]hile difficult to define with precision, situations arise in which no good purpose is served by production of the original." Could one explain the result in *Buchanan* on such grounds?

7. The Louisiana counterpart to Federal Rule 1004 contains an additional exception, providing as follows:

The original is not required, and other evidence of the contents of a writing, recording, or photograph is admissible if:

....

(5) **Impracticality of producing original.** The original, because of its location, permanent fixture, or otherwise, cannot as a practical matter be produced in court; or the cost or other consideration to be incurred in securing the original is prohibitive and it appears that a copy will serve the evidentiary purpose.

La. Code Evid. Art. 1004.

Is the inclusion of this provision superior to the approach embraced in *Buchanan* for dealing with inscribed chattels?

8. Note that if one of Rule 1003's exceptions are applicable, that means only that you cannot introduce the duplicate in lieu of the original *in the absence of an excuse for non-production of the original.* If production of the original is excused under Rule 1004, a duplicate is one sort of "other evidence" contemplated by Rule 1004.

9. Rule 1005 provides a special modification to the best evidence rule for a public record, defined to include both an "official record" as well as "a document that was recorded or filed in a public office as authorized by law." The first of these refers to documents produced by government officials, while the latter involves documents produced by private persons but recorded or filed with the government, such as deeds and mortgages.

Rule 1005 treats such documents differently than Rules 1002–1004 treat other documents. It is more permissive in that it automatically allows resort to a certified or compared copy of a public record in lieu of an original without either of the exceptions that apply for duplicates under Rule 1003. Yet unlike Rule 1004, it does recognize degrees of secondary evidence, providing that resort to other methods of proof is permitted only if a certified or compared copy cannot be obtained with "reasonable diligence." The Advisory Committee explains that "[r]ecognition of degrees of secondary evidence in this situation is an appropriate *quid pro quo* for not applying the requirement of producing the original." Advisory Committee Note to Rule 1005.

The rationale for the differential treatment of public records is a concern with the disruption and inconvenience to public and the government of removing the original public records. *Id.*

Note that a "copy" as used in this context differs from a "duplicate" as used in Rule 1003. A "copy" under Rule 1005 need not be reproduced by mechanical means (indeed it can be a hand-written copy), and it must be certified as provided in Rule 902, or supported by the testimony of a witness who has compared it with the original.

10. Suppose that in Problem 6-1, Smith concedes—either at trial or in a pleading—that she erected the billboard, but raises truth as a defense. If the court holds that a billboard is a "writing" for purposes of the best evidence rule, would Smith's defense provide Jones with a means of circumventing the best evidence rule?

Rule 1007 creates an exception to the best evidence rule that allows evidence of certain admissions of the party against whom the evidence is offered to be used to prove the contents of a document, providing as follows:

> The proponent may prove the content of a writing, recording, or photograph by the testimony, deposition, or written statement of the party against whom the evidence is offered. The proponent need not account for the original.

Note that it is only written statements by the opposing party and oral testimony by an opposing party that can be used; the rule does not allow the use of *oral* admissions (such as verbal statements made other than when testifying). While the rationale for the overall rule is that a party can ill complain that his own words were inaccurate or untrue, it is too easy for a party to falsely allege that an opposing party made an oral admission, which — unlike a written admission or one made while testifying — cannot be readily verified.

"Because Rule 1007 so seldom is used or discussed in cases, most lawyers are unaware of it. However, given the frequency with which deponents are asked questions about the content of writings, recordings and photographs, it is prudent to remember that if the deponent is a person whose testimony would qualify as an admission under any of the five varieties recognized by Rule 801(d)(2), then the deposition testimony may be admitted to prove the contents of the writings, recordings and photographs described. The same is true for written responses to Fed.R.Civ.P. 33 [Interrogatories] and 36 [Requests for Admission] discovery that ask for a description of the contents of a writing, recording or photograph." *Lorraine v. Markel American Ins. Co.*, 241 F.R.D. 534, 582 (D. Md. 2007).

G. Summaries

United States v. Bray
139 F.3d 1104 (6th Cir. 1998)

RYAN, Circuit Judge....

James Bray and his eventual codefendant Robert Owczarzak worked together as postal employees in Bay City, Michigan for over 20 years and, over the course of time, became close friends....

Both Bray and Owczarzak were transferred in 1989 to a Bay City postal substation, where they were the sole full-time employees. They worked as window clerks, selling stamps and other items. At some point in late 1989, Owczarzak began embezzling, taking money from the cash he received for the sale of postage stamps. His scheme was doomed to fail, however, because the accounts of window clerks are audited by supervisors at least once every 120 days. Postal clerks keep track of all their daily transactions on forms known as 1412 forms; during an audit, a supervisor counts a clerk's stock of stamps plus his cash on hand — referred to as the clerk's "accountability" — and then compares the 1412 forms with stamp-requisition forms to determine whether the money taken in by the clerk corresponds with the number of stamps sold. On one occasion, in order to conceal his embezzlement before a scheduled audit, Owczarzak asked Bray to lend him some of Bray's stamp stock, so that his accountability would accord with the written records.

Apparently, Bray decided that Owczarzak's newest scheme sounded like a good idea. Therefore, he too began embezzling, and he and Owczarzak began trading stamp stock back and forth at the time of the periodic audits. By January 1995, the two together had embezzled approximately $52,000, approximately 40% of which was attributable to Bray. It was at this time that Bray's accounts were subjected to a surprise audit. Although he managed to importune a part-time clerk to give him some stamps temporarily, he borrowed too much and the resulting $800 overage triggered an investigation. When, subsequently,

Owczarzak asked to borrow some of Bray's stamps in order to cover an upcoming audit of his own, Bray refused; Owczarzak then confessed the entire scheme to postal authorities, implicating Bray....

At Bray's trial, the government offered in evidence, and the district court admitted, four exhibits—112, 113, 114, and 115. All four were charts prepared by Postal Inspector William Pollard, based on information he derived from forms 1412, and all four contained analysis of the records relating to the reported sales of stamps compared to the stamps ordered. The first two charts, exhibits 112 and 113, summarized the information relating to Bray and Owczarzak's activities in 1993 and 1994, compiling it on a quarterly basis; the second two charts, exhibits 114 and 115, summarized the same data for the employees who replaced Bray and Owczarzak, but because the data spanned only a four-month period, the charts compiled the data only on a monthly basis. The charts for Bray and Owczarzak reflected a consistent pattern of sales but increased stamp orders over time; the charts for the replacement employees showed basically identical levels of sales and stamp orders. According to Pollard, the contrast in these patterns supported the government's allegation of embezzlement, as it indicated that the conspirators needed to make increasingly large stamp orders in order to make their figures balance at audit time.

[The defendant objected to the admission of the exhibits, arguing that the government was obligated to introduce into evidence the disaggregate data summarized in the charts, and that the jury should be instructed that the charts themselves are not evidence.]

Bray now argues that the district court committed reversible error by admitting the government's summary exhibits without admitting the underlying documents and without giving a limiting instruction....

The text of [Rule 1006]* and the cases construing it make clear that there are several preconditions to admitting a 1006 summary chart. First, the documents (or recordings or photographs) must be so "voluminous" that they "cannot [be] conveniently [] examined in court" by the trier of fact. That is, the documents must be sufficiently numerous as to make comprehension "difficult and ... inconvenient." *United States v. Seelig*, 622 F.2d 207, 214 (6th Cir. 1980); *see Martin v. Funtime, Inc.*, 963 F.2d 110, 115 (6th Cir. 1992). On the other hand, it is not necessary that the documents be so voluminous as to be "literally impossible to examine." *United States v. Scales*, 594 F.2d 558, 562 (6th Cir. 1979).

Second, the proponent of the summary must also have made the documents "available for examination or copying, or both, by other parties at [a] reasonable time and place." Fed.R.Evid. 1006; *see Scales*, 594 F.2d at 562.

> The purpose of this requirement is to provide the opposing party who desires to attack the authenticity or accuracy of a chart, summary, or calculation, with an opportunity to prepare for cross-examination, or to offer exhibits of its own as rebuttal evidence, which would serve to counteract the impression made on the jury by the proponent's witness.

6 Weinstein's Federal Evidence § 1006.06[1], p. 1006–14 (Joseph M. McLaughlin ed., 2d ed. 1997).

---

* Editor's Note: Rule 1006 provides as follows:
  The proponent may use a summary, chart, or calculation to prove the content of voluminous writings, recordings, or photographs that cannot be conveniently examined in court. The proponent must make the originals or duplicates available for examination or copying, or both, by other parties at a reasonable time and place. And the court may order the proponent to produce them in court.

Third, and relatedly, "'[c]ommentators and other courts have agreed that Rule 1006 requires that the proponent of the summary establish that the underlying documents are admissible in evidence.'" *Martin*, 963 F.2d at 116 (quoting *United States v. Johnson*, 594 F.2d 1253, 1256 (9th Cir. 1979)). Thus, if the underlying documents are hearsay and not admissible under any exception, a chart or other summary based on those documents is likewise inadmissible. *See generally* Fed.R.Evid. 801–805. The same principle would render inadmissible a summary based on documents that are inadmissible for any other reason, such as irrelevancy, unfair prejudice, or lack of authenticity. *See generally* Fed.R.Evid. 401–403, 901(a). But given Rule 1006's provision that the underlying documents need not themselves be in evidence, however, it is plain that a summary admitted under Rule 1006 is itself the evidence that the trier of fact should consider.

Fourth, reasonably enough, a summary document "must be accurate and nonprejudicial." *Gomez v. Great Lakes Steel Div., Nat'l Steel Corp.*, 803 F.2d 250, 257 (6th Cir. 1986). This means first that the information on the document summarizes the information contained in the underlying documents accurately, correctly, and in a nonmisleading manner. Nothing should be lost in the translation. It also means, with respect to summaries admitted in lieu of the underlying documents, that the information on the summary is not embellished by or annotated with the conclusions of or inferences drawn by the proponent, whether in the form of labels, captions, highlighting techniques, or otherwise. Once a Rule 1006 summary is admitted, it may go to the jury room, like any other exhibit. Thus, a summary containing elements of argumentation could very well be the functional equivalent of a mini-summation by the chart's proponent every time the jurors look at it during their deliberations, particularly when the jurors cannot also review the underlying documents.

Fifth and finally, a summary document must be "'properly introduced before it may be admitted into evidence.'" *Martin*, 963 F.2d at 115–16 (quoting *Scales*, 594 F.2d at 563). In order to lay a proper foundation for a summary, the proponent should present the testimony of the witness who supervised its preparation.

Bray does not challenge the voluminousness of the underlying documents, that is, the forms 1412. Since the scheme continued over a two-year period, and since the forms were completed on a daily basis, we estimate that there would be more than 500 forms for each of Bray and Owczarzak. In addition, there would be about 100 forms for each of the two replacement employees. Given this volume, it seems to us that the forms 1412 could not have been "conveniently [] examined in court," Fed.R.Evid. 1006, by the jury. However, because the issue is not before us, we simply assume but do not decide that the forms 1412 were sufficiently numerous to satisfy Rule 1006....

Because the summaries were admitted under Rule 1006, the district court did not err by failing to require that the underlying documents be in evidence.

Since Rule 1006 authorizes the admission in evidence of the summary itself, it is generally inappropriate to give a *limiting* instruction for a Rule 1006 summary. This is a point, however, on which in the past this court has been less than clear....

The problem hinges on the distinction between Rule 1006 summaries and summaries used as "pedagogical devices," which are more properly considered under Rule 611(a). The distinction was clearly explained in *Gomez*:

> Contents of charts or summaries admitted as evidence under Rule 1006 must fairly represent and be taken from underlying documentary proof which is too voluminous for convenient in-court examination, and they must be accurate and nonprejudicial. Such summaries or charts admitted *as evidence* under Rule

1006 are to be distinguished from summaries or charts used as pedagogical devices which organize or aid the jury's examination of testimony or documents
which are themselves admitted into evidence. Such pedagogical devices "are more
akin to argument than evidence.... Quite often they are used on summation."
Generally, such a summary is, and should be, accompanied by a limiting instruction which informs the jury of the summary's purpose and that it does not
itself constitute evidence.

Gomez, 803 F.2d at 257–58. In other words, summary exhibits that are used as pedagogical devices do not, "strictly speaking, ... fall within the purview of Rule 1006." *United States
v. Paulino*, 935 F.2d 739, 753 (6th Cir. 1991).

We understand the term "pedagogical device" to mean an illustrative aid such as information presented on a chalkboard, flip chart, or drawing, and the like, that (1) is used
to summarize or illustrate evidence, such as documents, recordings, or trial testimony, that
has been admitted in evidence; (2) is itself not admitted into evidence; and (3) may reflect to some extent, through captions or other organizational devices or descriptions,
the inferences and conclusions drawn from the underlying evidence by the summary's
proponent. This type of exhibit is "'more akin to argument than evidence' since [it] organize[s] the jury's examination of testimony and documents already admitted in evidence." *Id.* Trial courts have discretionary authority to permit counsel to employ such
pedagogical-device "summaries" to clarify and simplify complex testimony or other information and evidence or to assist counsel in the presentation of argument to the court
or jury. This court has held that Fed.R.Evid. 611(a) provides an additional basis for the
use of such illustrative aids, as an aspect of the court's authority concerning the "mode ...
of interrogating witnesses and presenting evidence." *Paulino*, 935 F.2d at 753 n. 7....

We note in passing that in appropriate circumstances not only may such pedagogical-
device summaries be used as illustrative aids in the presentation of the evidence, but they
may also be admitted into evidence even though not within the specific scope of Rule
1006. Such circumstances might be instances in which such pedagogical device is so accurate and reliable a summary illustration or extrapolation of testimonial or other evidence in the case as to reliably assist the factfinder in understanding the evidence, although
not within the specific requirements of Rule 1006.

To recapitulate, there are three kinds of summaries:

(1) **Primary-evidence summaries**, such as those at issue here, which summarize "voluminous writings, recordings, or photographs" that, because they are so voluminous,
"cannot [be] conveniently [] examined in court." Fed.R.Evid. 1006. In this instance, the
summary, and not the underlying documents, is the evidence to be considered by the
factfinder.

(2) **Pedagogical-device summaries** or illustrations, such as chalkboard drawings, graphs,
calculations, or listings of data taken from the testimony of witnesses or documents in evidence, which are intended to summarize, clarify, or simplify testimonial or other evidence that has been admitted in the case, but which are not themselves admitted, instead
being used only as an aid to the presentation and understanding of the evidence. For
these the jury should be instructed that the summaries are not evidence and were used
only as an illustrative aid.

(3) **Secondary-evidence summaries** that are a combination of (1) and (2), in that they
are not prepared entirely in compliance with Rule 1006 and yet are more than mere pedagogical devices designed to simplify and clarify other evidence in the case. These secondary-evidence summaries are admitted in evidence not in lieu of the evidence they

summarize but *in addition thereto*, because in the judgment of the trial court such summaries so accurately and reliably summarize complex or difficult evidence that is received in the case as to materially assist the jurors in better understanding the evidence. In the *unusual* instance in which this third form of secondary evidence summary is admitted, the jury should be instructed that the summary is not independent evidence of its subject matter, and is only as valid and reliable as the underlying evidence it summarizes. *See United States v. Citron*, 783 F.2d 307, 317 n. 10 (2d Cir. 1986).

Since, in this case, it is clear that the summaries at issue are within the first of the three categories we have described, and were admitted under Rule 1006, the district court's refusal to give a limiting instruction in its final instructions to the jury was proper....

H. Role of Judge and Jury

Recall from Chapter 1 that Rules 104(a) and 104(b) carefully define the judge's role in deciding whether to admit or exclude evidence so as to ensure that in deciding preliminary questions concerning the admissibility of evidence, the judge does not undercut the right to trial by jury. Rule 1008 plays a similar role with respect to the operation of the best evidence rule.

The first sentence of Rule 1008 provides:

> Ordinarily, the court determines whether the proponent has fulfilled the factual conditions for admitting other evidence of the content of a writing, recording, or photograph under Rule 1004 or 1005.

The Advisory Committee Note to Rule 1008 explains the first sentence as follows:

> Most preliminary questions of fact in connection with applying the rule preferring the original as evidence of contents are for the judge, under the general principles announced in Rule 104. Thus, the question whether the loss of the originals has been established, or of the fulfillment of other conditions specified in Rule 1004 is for the judge.

Accordingly, it is the judge who decides such preliminary questions of fact as whether the originals have been lost or destroyed, and if so, whether it was in bad faith, under Rule 1004(a), or whether the originals are not obtainable under Rule 1004(b). Similarly, a judge would decide whether "reasonable diligence" has been exercised under Rule 1005.

However, the second sentence of Rule 1008 limits the role of the judge for certain questions that arise involving the application of the best evidence rule:

> But in a jury trial, the jury determines—in accordance with Rule 104(b)—any issue about whether:
>
> (a) an asserted writing, recording, or photograph ever existed;
>
> (b) another one produced at the trial or hearing is the original; or
>
> (c) other evidence of content accurately reflects the content.

The Advisory Committee Note to Rule 1008 explains the second sentence as follows:

> However, questions may arise which go beyond the mere administration of the rule preferring the original and into the merits of the controversy. For example, plaintiff offers secondary evidence of the contents of an alleged contract, after

first introducing evidence of loss of the original, and defendant counters with evidence that no such contract was ever executed. If the judge decides that the contract was never executed and excludes the secondary evidence, the case is at an end without ever going to the jury on a central issue. The latter portion of the instant rule is designed to insure treatment of these situations as raising jury questions. The decision is not one for uncontrolled discretion of the jury but is subject to the control exercised generally by the judge over jury determinations.

Consider a typical breach of contract suit. Rule 1008(a) refers to the situation in which the plaintiff seeks to invoke Rule 1004, claiming, say, that the original of the contract has been lost, and the defendant counters that there was nothing to lose because no such contract ever existed. Rule 1008(a) instructs that the court is to decide only whether there is sufficient evidence that the trier of fact reasonably could find that such a contract existed. Having done so, the court is then to decide only whether, given that a reasonable jury could find that the contract existed, the plaintiff has satisfied the court that all such originals are lost or destroyed.

Once the court has decided to permit the introduction of secondary evidence under Rule 1004, Rule 1008(c) makes clear that it is up to the jury to evaluate the secondary evidence offered. Thus, if the court holds that secondary evidence of contents is permitted because the original is lost or destroyed, and the parties each testify to their own version of the contents of the original, it is for the jury to decide whom to believe.

Finally, Rule 1008(b) refers to the situation in which both parties introduce what they purport to be originals of the contract. So long as a reasonable jury could believe each one to be the authentic original, the question is one for the jury to decide, and both are to be admitted.

Notes and Questions

1. Do you see why the second sentence of Rule 1008 is necessary to maintain the respective roles of judge and jury in deciding questions of authentication under Rule 901?

2. Are you persuaded that a judge can perform the mental gymnastics necessary to apply Rule 1008(a)? After all, if the judge doesn't believe that the original ever existed, how likely is she to be persuaded that it was lost or destroyed?

3. Who decides whether a genuine question has been raised as to the authenticity of the original under Rule 1003? Is there a tension between Rules 1003 and 1008(c)? If a genuine question has been raised as to the authenticity of the original within the meaning of Rule 1003, but the original is deemed lost, destroyed, or unavailable under Rule 1004, is a duplicate admissible? See *Pro Bono Investments, Inc. v. Gerry*, 2005 WL 2429777, at *5 (S.D.N.Y. Sept. 30, 2005) (holding that a duplicate is not admissible under Rule 1003 when a genuine question has been raised as to authenticity of the original, and that its admissibility turns on the judge finding that the prerequisites for excusing production of the original under Rule 1004 are satisfied *and* finding that "evidence has been introduced sufficient to support a *finding by a reasonable juror* that the secondary evidence accurately reflects the original") (emphasis added).

Chapter 7

The Rule against Hearsay

A. Introduction

Assume that the police have been called to intervene in a fight taking place between Bob and Tom. After breaking up the fight, the police question Wanda, who was present when the fight broke out. When asked who started the fight, Wanda pointed her finger at Bob. She also later said to an officer that "Bob struck the first blow," and subsequent to that, she wrote out and signed a statement to the same effect.

Bob is eventually indicted on charges of assault. Pretty clearly, Wanda, as an eyewitness to the altercation, could be called as a witness and asked to testify to what she saw. But what if she does not appear as a witness, either because the prosecution chooses not to call her or because she has died or simply cannot be found. Can the prosecution call the police officer to the stand and ask him to testify to the fact that when asked who started the fight, Wanda pointed at Bob? That she later told him that "Bob struck the first blow"? Alternatively, or in addition, can the prosecution offer Wanda's signed statement into evidence?

Here, the prosecution's proffered evidence runs up against the rule against hearsay. That rule, codified in Rule 802, provides that "[h]earsay is not admissible" unless a rule of evidence or other federal rule or statute "provides otherwise." Of course, that means very little without a definition of the word "hearsay." That definition is set forth in Rule 801(c):

"Hearsay" means a statement that:

(1) the declarant does not make while testifying at the current trial or hearing; and

(2) a party offers in evidence to prove the truth of the matter asserted in the statement.

The word "declarant" is defined in Rule 801(b) as the "person who made the statement," while the word "statement" is defined in Rule 801(a) as:

a person's oral assertion, written assertion, or nonverbal conduct, if the person intended it as an assertion.

Accordingly, combining Rule 802 with the definitions set forth in Rule 801, you get the following rule:

A person's oral, written, or nonverbal assertion, other than one made while testifying at the current trial or proceeding, offered in evidence to prove the truth of the matter asserted in the statement, is not admissible unless a rule of evidence or other federal rule or statute provides otherwise.

Setting aside momentarily what it means to be offered in evidence "to prove the truth of the matter asserted in the statement" and the "provides otherwise" caveat, it would appear that all three pieces of evidence offered by the prosecution are potentially subject to exclusion under the rule against hearsay. So long as something qualifies as an "assertion" (more on that shortly too), the definition of "statement" makes clear that it matters not whether that assertion is made orally, in writing, or using nonverbal conduct, such as pointing or nodding.

What is the justification for excluding hearsay? In other words, why do the rules of evidence require that Wanda be called to the stand to testify that she saw Bob strike the first blow, instead of admitting into evidence the officer's testimony that she pointed to Bob or told him that or her written statement to that effect?

Hearsay evidence is thought to contain four weaknesses, and thus four risks are thought to be associated with its use: faulty perception, faulty memory, faulty communication, and insincerity.

The first weakness of hearsay evidence is that the declarant may have misperceived the event in question. Perhaps the declarant has less than perfect hearing or vision, or her location relative to the event that she perceived was such that her view was partially obstructed, or she did not watch the event without interruption. For example, it is possible that Wanda had turned her head just before the fight started and didn't see that Tom in fact struck the first blow.

The second weakness of hearsay evidence is that, even if the declarant accurately perceived the events in question at the time they occurred, her memory of those events when she later describes them may not be fully accurate.

The third weakness of hearsay evidence is that, even if the declarant accurately perceived the events in question at the time they occurred and accurately recalls them, it is possible that in communicating those events to another person, she might misspeak or be misunderstood. Thus, for example, Wanda might have said "Bob" even though she meant to say "Tom." Or perhaps she said "Tom," but because it sounds somewhat like "Bob," the police officer thought she said "Bob." Or perhaps Tom and Bob were standing relatively close to one another, and she was in fact pointing at Tom even though the officer thought that she was pointing at Bob.

The fourth weakness of hearsay evidence is that the declarant may have perceived and recalled the events accurately, and is communicating clearly and being understood, but she is not telling the truth. For example, perhaps Tom and Wanda are good friends, or Wanda has no relationship with Tom but really dislikes Bob. Wanda thus may have lied in her communications with the police officer to protect Tom or to "get" Bob.

Of course, all of these risks are present, are they not, even if Wanda appears as a witness and testifies that she saw Bob strike the first blow? It is still possible that she misperceived the event, that she is not recalling the event correctly, that she is not communicating what happened to the jury accurately, or that she is intentionally misleading the jury. However, the difference is that these risks are minimized if Wanda appears as a witness at trial due to a variety of safeguards that are an integral part of the trial process.

First, Wanda is subject to cross-examination by Bob's attorney when she testifies at trial. He can explore weaknesses in Wanda's ability to accurately perceive the events in question by asking her whether she was wearing her glasses at the time, how far she was from the fight, whether her view was obstructed, and whether she was watching the two continuously. He can clarify her answers to ensure that they accurately reflect what she meant to say and that they were correctly understood. He can explore any weaknesses in the sincerity of her testimony by asking her about her personal feelings toward Bob and Tom.

Second, Wanda is under oath when she testifies at trial. Although not everybody testifies truthfully when under oath, most people, while willing to color the truth or blatantly lie when speaking in an informal setting, are unlikely to do so when they are under oath and subject to penalty of perjury.

Finally, when Wanda testifies at trial, her demeanor can be observed directly by the trier of fact, who can judge her credibility and in turn decide how much weight to give to her testimony.

The materials that follow examine three critical aspects to the rule against hearsay, namely, who qualifies as a "declarant," what it means to be offered in evidence "to prove the truth of the matter asserted," and what qualifies as an "assertion." The remainder of the chapter examines various exceptions to the rule against hearsay, and concludes with materials that examine the relationship between the hearsay doctrine and the Confrontation Clause of the U.S. Constitution.

Notes and Questions

1. The definition of hearsay excludes all statements except those made "while testifying at *the current trial or hearing*." Fed. R. Evid. 801(c)(1) (emphasis added). The use of the phrase "the current trial or hearing" and not "a trial or hearing" is critical: statements made in *other* court proceedings, even prior trials of the same case, *are* hearsay subject to exclusion unless they fit within an exception to the rule.

2. The hearsay problem does not disappear simply because a declarant gets on the stand and repeats his or her own prior out-of-court statements. Thus, while in the example set forth in the text, Wanda could appear and testify that she saw Bob strike the first blow, the hearsay rule would bar her from testifying that "I told the officer that I saw Bob strike the first blow," or testifying that "I pointed to Bob when asked by the officer who struck the first blow," or testifying that "I wrote out a statement in which I indicated that Bob struck the first blow."

3. Chapter 4 addressed the complex meaning of Rule 602's personal knowledge requirement where hearsay evidence falling within an exception to the hearsay rule is involved. In addition, the rule against hearsay and Rule 602

> intersect if a witness satisfies Rule 602's personal knowledge requirement by relying on the truth of an out-of-court statement. "If the testimony of the witness purports to repeat an out-of-court statement, hearsay is the proper objection. If the testimony on its face purports to be based on direct perception of the facts described but is actually based on an out-of-court statement about those facts, the objection should be lack of personal knowledge."

United States v. Davis, 596 F.3d 852, 856 (D.C. Cir. 2010).

B. Who Qualifies as a "Declarant"?

Problem 7-1: "She Barked"

On the afternoon of January 15, 2012, police officer Debbie Perkins was dispatched to the corner of Fifth & Main Streets in response to a 911 call indicating that gunshots were heard. When she arrived at the scene, she found Valerie Albertson, dead of an apparent gunshot wound. Beside her body, Perkins found a black baseball cap.

Perkins radioed in for assistance, and shortly thereafter, Officer David French of the K-9 unit arrived with his bloodhound, Sophie. Perkins recognized Sophie as the department's trailing dog, a type of dog that is trained to lead officers to a person by smelling an article left behind by that person.

Sophie then sniffed the baseball cap, and started running, with French in tow. As Sophie approached a man later identified as Robert Barrone, she alerted by barking. Barrone was arrested and taken to police headquarters.

Barrone is indicted on charges of murder. The prosecution seeks to have French, an expert on trailing dogs, testify as to Sophie's training and to the fact that she led him to Barrone. Barrone's attorney objects, contending that French's testimony that Sophie barked when she approached Barrone is hearsay.

Is the challenged testimony hearsay?

Terrell v. State
239 A.2d 128 (Md. 1968)

THOMPSON, Judge:

. . . .

On September 20, 1966, at approximately 10:15 P.M. three Negro males, two of whom displayed revolvers, held up the desk clerk at the Park Silver Motel.... Inspector Howes of the Montgomery County Police Department was the first officer who responded to the clerk's call. He testified that upon his arrival he observed a trail of coins leading from the front of the motel to a nearby alley. He stayed at the entrance to the alley to protect the scene until Fred Helton, an officer of the K-9 Corps with his dog, "Rocky," a German Shepherd K-9 dog, arrived at the scene. Officer Helton started the dog on a track at the entrance to the alley. The dog led the officer up the alley and turned right into another alley leading out of Eastern Avenue.... Three people were in the automobile; one of whom was Joel Terrell, Jr., the appellant.... the three suspects were ordered out of the car and placed in separate police vehicles; within a few minutes the motel clerk was brought to the scene and identified the three persons as the ones who had robbed him....

Terence P. Cahill was qualified as an expert in the training of dogs for use by law enforcement agencies.... He testified that he trained this particular German Shepherd dog and Officer Helton daily for a period of fifteen weeks and once a week for many weeks thereafter; he further testified that the dog was reliable in the tracking of human beings and had been given an excellent rating in his fifteen week training course. Officer Helton also testified that the dog had been trained in tracking and had shown ability to follow a trail.

I

The first question presented is whether or not the evidence of tracking by the German Shepherd police dog was properly admitted into evidence....

Today, twenty-five jurisdictions in the United States have decided cases involving tracking by dogs. Nineteen have followed the majority thinking while six may be classified as minority orientated.... The minority cases have stressed six objections to the use of such evidence....

A third criticism is "that the life and liberty of a free citizen ought not to be put in jeopardy on the testimony of dogs", 94 A.L.R. 413, 416, 418 (1935). This idea was stressed in State v. Storm, 125 Mont. 346 (1952). However, it is not the dog but the handler who reports on the dog's behavior, training, and ability. This leads to three other minority views, i. e. The dog cannot be cross-examined, his trainer's testimony is hearsay and the accused is not confronted by his accusor, the dog.

Who is the proper person to question? The minority states that it is the dog while the majority states that it is the trainer.... the dog's actions are predictable if he has been properly trained and the trail has been adequately followed. The trainer should be questioned to see if the dog was properly trained and the trail followed correctly—for if this has been done, the dog's thoughts, mannerism and such need not be looked into and if this foundation is not laid, then the evidence is excluded. It is the trainer who controls the dog, therefore, he should be the one to be examined and cross-examined. Therefore, "the accused does have an opportunity to confront and cross-examine these witnesses who give evidence." 33 Yale L.Rev. 216 (1923). The trainer stays with the dogs so he testifies as to his own observations. This would not be hearsay.... The Montana Supreme Court in State v. Storm held that such evidence was a conclusion and therefore hearsay. It should be noted that in many trials, human evidence of the performance of a machine such as radar or a breathilizer are admitted.

> "It is the human testimony that makes the trailing done by the animal competent; and its actions are described by human testimony as it would describe the operations of a piece of intricate machinery." State v. Dickerson, 77 Ohio St. 34 (1907).

....

United States v. Washington
498 F.3d 225 (4th Cir. 2007)

NIEMEYER, Circuit Judge:

Dwonne Washington was convicted of driving on the Baltimore-Washington Parkway, in the territorial jurisdiction of the United States in Prince George's County, Maryland, while under the influence of alcohol or drugs, in violation of 36 C.F.R. §4.23(a)(1), and of unsafe operation of a vehicle, in violation of 36 C.F.R. §4.22.

At trial, the government offered, over Washington's objection, the expert testimony of Dr. Barry Levine, the Director of the Forensic Toxicology Laboratory of the Armed Forces Institute of Pathology, to prove that a blood sample, taken from Washington the night of his arrest and tested at Dr. Levine's lab, contained phencyclidine ("PCP") and alcohol and that Washington's conduct and unsafe driving during the night of his arrest were attributable to the presence of PCP and alcohol in Washington's blood. In Washington's view, the raw data generated by the forensic lab's diagnostic machines and relied on by Dr. Levine to give his testimony amounted to testimonial hearsay statements of the lab technicians who operated the machines....

Without deciding whether Dr. Levine's testimony actually introduced into evidence the raw data on which he relied to give his testimony, we nonetheless conclude that the data on which Dr. Levine relied (1) did not constitute the statements of the lab technicians; (2) were not hearsay statements....

II

....

In the case before us, the "statements" in question are alleged to be the assertions that Washington's blood sample contained PCP and alcohol. But those statements were never made by the technicians who tested the blood. The most the technicians could have said was that the *printed data* from their chromatograph machines showed that the blood contained PCP and alcohol. The machine printout is the only source of the statement, and no *person* viewed a blood sample and concluded that it contained PCP and alcohol....

Thus, we reject the characterization of the raw data generated by the lab's machines as statements *of the lab technicians* who operated the machines. The raw data generated by the diagnostic machines are the "statements" *of the machines* themselves, not their operators....

Obviously, the lab technicians made no statements of any kind, and they did not say or write the information generated by the machines. The machines generated data by manipulating blood through a common scientific and technological process. The lab technicians' role was simply to operate the machines. The "statement" that Washington's blood contained PCP and alcohol is a conclusion drawn only from the machines' data, and its source was independent of human observation or reporting. Only the machine, through its diagnostic and technical process, could provide facts about the chemical composition of Washington's blood. Accordingly, the raw data generated by the machines were not the statements of technicians.

....

[After quoting the definition of declarant, which Rule 801(b) defines as "the *person* who made the statement," the court proceeds to hold as follows:]

Only a *person* may be a declarant and make a statement. Accordingly, "nothing 'said' by a machine ... is hear-say." 4 Mueller & Kirkpatrick, *Federal Evidence*, § 380, at 65 (2d ed. 1994). *See United States v. Hamilton*, 413 F.3d 1138, 1142–43 (10th Cir. 2005) (concluding that the computer-generated header information accompanying pornographic images retrieved from the Internet was not a hearsay statement because there was no "person" acting as a declarant); *United States v. Khorozian*, 333 F.3d 498, 506 (3d Cir. 2003) (concluding that an automatically generated time stamp on a fax was not a hearsay statement because it was not uttered by a person); *People v. Holowko*, 486 N.E.2d 877, 878–79 (1985) (concluding "that the printout of results of computerized telephone tracing equipment is not hearsay evidence" but rather "a self-generated record of its operations").

....

Any concerns about the reliability of such machine-generated information is addressed through the process of authentication not by hearsay or Confrontation Clause analysis. When information provided by machines is mainly a product of "mechanical measurement or manipulation of data by well-accepted scientific or mathematical techniques," 4 Mueller & Kirkpatrick, *supra* § 380, at 65, reliability concerns are addressed by requiring the proponent to show that the machine and its functions are reliable, that it was correctly adjusted or calibrated, and that the data (in this case, the blood) put into the machine was accurate (i.e., that the blood put into the machine was the defendant's). In other words, a foundation must be established for the information through authentication, which Federal Rule of Evidence 901(b)(9) allows such proof to be authenticated by evidence [describing a process or system and showing that it produces an accurate result]. But none of these concerns were issues below, nor are they issues in this appeal.[3]

. . . .

MICHAEL, Circuit Judge, dissenting:

. . . .

In only one circumstance is a computer-generated assertion not considered the statement of a person: when the assertion is produced without any human assistance or input. In *United States v. Hamilton*, 413 F.3d 1138 (10th Cir. 2005), one of two federal cases relied on by the majority, the Tenth Circuit concluded that the computer-generated header information that accompanied a pornographic image on the internet was not a hearsay statement. "Of primary importance to this ruling," however, "[wa]s the uncontroverted fact that the header information was automatically generated by the computer ... *without the assistance or input of a person.*" *Id.* at 1142 (emphasis added). Similarly, in *United States v. Khorozian*, 333 F.3d 498 (3d Cir. 2003), the other federal case cited by the majority, the Third Circuit determined that the transmission information on a faxed document was not a hearsay statement because it was automatically generated by the fax machine.

Unlike the header information on a web page or fax, computerized laboratory equipment cannot detect, measure, and record toxin levels in blood samples without the assistance or input of a trained laboratory technician.... A technician conducting a blood toxicology test must follow a "step-by-step procedure." He must, among other things, calibrate the testing instrument; withdraw the appropriate portion of blood from the larger sample; insert, without contamination, the smaller test sample into the instrument; initiate the test; and monitor the instrument while the test is in progress. Finally, as the record in this case reveals, the technician reviews and annotates the results and signs the report. In light of the significant role that the technician plays in conducting the test and generating accurate results, the results cannot be attributed solely to the machine....

Notes and Questions

1. What distinguishes humans from machines and animals such that the drafters of the hearsay rule opted to encompass only statements made by the former within its scope? Which of the hearsay risks is of particular concern where humans are involved?

2. Would evidence that a particular phone number was displayed on a cellular telephone when an incoming call was received be hearsay if offered to prove that a call was

---

3. The dissenting opinion universally mixes authentication issues with its argument about "statements" from the machine that the blood contains PCP and alcohol. Obviously, if the defendant wished to question the manner in which the technicians set up the machines, he would be entitled to subpoena into court and cross-examine the technicians. But once the machine was properly calibrated and the blood properly inserted, it was the machine, not the technicians, which concluded that the blood contained PCP and alcohol. The technicians never make that determination and accordingly could not be cross-examined on the veracity of that "statement."

made from that particular number? *See People v. Buckner*, 228 P.3d 245, 249–50 (Colo. 2009) (holding that such machine-generated information does not involve a "declarant"); *Tatum v. Commonwealth*, 440 S.E.2d 133, 135–36 (Va. 1994) (same).

3. When considering the admissibility of computer records, it is important to distinguish between records that are computer-*generated* and those that are merely computer-*stored*:

> Computer-generated records create unique problems in the context of the rule against hearsay. Some courts have distinguished among types of computer records ... by classifying them as computer generated or computer stored — computer-generated records being records generated solely by the electrical or mechanical operation of a computer, and computer-stored records being generated by humans and containing statements implicating the hearsay rule. At least one publication has suggested that some computer or electronic records might constitute a hybrid, containing both computer-stored records and "human statements," as well as computer-generated data.

> The classification of the records as computer-generated or computer-stored bears directly on the question whether the admission of the records would violate the rule against hearsay. Because computer-generated records, by definition, do not contain a statement from a person, they do not necessarily implicate hearsay concerns. Instead, the reliability concern with respect to computer-generated records stems from authentication of the generative process that created the records. As for records that constitute a hybrid of both processes, both hearsay and authentication issues may be present.

Commonwealth v. Thissell, 928 N.E.2d 932, 937 n.13 (Mass. 2010).

4. Does it make sense to distinguish between things that are generated by persons and those that are generated by machines? After all, aren't machines created by, and thus an extension of, humans? *See United States v. Lamons*, 532 F.3d 1251, 1263 n.23 (11th Cir. 2008) ("To be sure, there can be no statements which are wholly machine-generated in the strictest sense; all machines were designed and built by humans. But certain statements involve so little intervention by humans in their generation as to leave no doubt that they are wholly machine-generated for all practical purposes.").

5. In a report to Parliament, The Law Commission of the United Kingdom identified the challenges associated with statements produced by machines and proposed a solution:

> There is an additional difficulty where it is sought to adduce a statement generated by a machine. Usually the statement will be included in a document produced by the machine, such as a computer printout; but it could equally be a reading on a gauge, or even the mechanical equivalent of an oral statement.

> The present law draws a distinction according to whether the statement consists of, or is based upon, only what the machine itself has observed; or whether it incorporates, or is based upon, information supplied by a human being.

> **Statements not based on human input**

> The hearsay rule does not apply to tapes, films or photographs which record a disputed incident actually taking place, or to documents produced by machines which automatically record an event or circumstance (such as the making of a telephone call from a particular number, or the level of alcohol in a person's breath). In such a case the court is not being asked to accept the truth of an assertion made by any person. The evidence is not hearsay but real evidence.

Our draft Bill preserves this rule by confining the word "statement" to a representation *made by a person*. The conclusions printed out (or "spoken") by a machine are not a statement for the purposes of the Bill, and therefore the hearsay rule does not apply to them.

Statements based on human input

By contrast, the present law does sometimes exclude evidence of a statement generated by a machine, where the statement is based on information fed into the machine by a human being. In such a case, it seems, the statement by the machine is admissible *only* if the facts on which it is based are themselves proved....

We believe that this distinction is well-founded and should clearly be preserved.... The question is, on what basis should such evidence be excluded? One view is that it is hearsay, because it is tantamount to a statement made by the person who fed the data into the machine. An alternative view is that the statement by the machine, properly understood, is conditional on the accuracy of the data on which it is based; and that, if those data are not proved to have been accurate, the statement therefore has no probative value at all. The question of hearsay does not arise, because the statement is simply irrelevant.

We believe that the latter view is closer to the truth, and that it is therefore unnecessary to complicate our hearsay rule by extending it to statements made by machines on the basis of human input. On the other hand we do not think it would be safe to assume that everyone will share this view. We must anticipate the argument that, if such statements are inadmissible at present, that is because they are hearsay; that, under our recommendations, they would no longer be hearsay, because our formulation of the rule would apply only to representations made by people; and that they would therefore cease to be inadmissible.

We have therefore concluded that a separate provision is necessary, independent of the hearsay rule. **We recommend that, where a representation of any fact is made otherwise than by a person, but depends for its accuracy on information supplied by a person, it should not be admissible as evidence of the fact unless it is proved that the information was accurate.**

The Law Commission, Report No. 245, *Evidence in Criminal Proceedings: Hearsay and Related Topics*, ¶¶ 7.42–7.50 (1997).

When Parliament codified the hearsay rule in 2003, it followed The Law Commission's recommendation of defining "statement" for purposes of the hearsay rule as "any representation of fact or opinion made by a *person*...." *Criminal Justice Act* 2003, c. 44, § 115(2) (emphasis added). It further provided, in accordance with The Law Commission's recommendation, that:

(1) Where a representation of any fact—

> (a) is made otherwise than by a person, but
>
> (b) depends for its accuracy on information supplied (directly or indirectly) by a person,
>
> the representation is not admissible in criminal proceedings as evidence of the fact unless it is proved that the information was accurate.

....

Criminal Justice Act 2003, c. 44, § 129.

Are you persuaded by The Law Commission's proposal to remove from the scope of the hearsay rule statements produced by machines—even those based on human input—and to instead exclude them by means of a separate provision? Is it in fact less complicated than the pre-existing common law The Law Commission sought to displace, or is it unnecessarily formalistic?

C. What Does It Mean to Be Offered to Prove the Truth of the Matter Asserted?

As the definition of hearsay set forth in Rule 801(c) makes clear, a statement is hearsay only if it is "offer[ed] in evidence to prove the truth of the matter asserted in the statement." By contrast,

> If the significance of an offered statement lies solely in the fact that it was made, no issue is raised as to the truth of anything asserted, and the statement is not hearsay.

Advisory Committee Note to Rule 801(c).

The materials that follow explore the distinction between those statements that are offered "to prove the truth of the matter asserted in the statement" and those in which a statement's significance lies solely in the fact that it was made.

Problem 7-2: Blowing Hot and Cold

Recall the facts of the introductory hypothetical in this chapter, in which Wanda witnessed a fight between Bob and Tom, and informed the police that Bob struck the first blow. Assume that Wanda does appear as a witness, but to the prosecution's surprise, she testifies that "Tom struck the first blow."

The prosecution seeks to call the police officer as a witness to testify to what Wanda had previously said to him, but Bob's attorney raises a hearsay objection.

Is the challenged testimony necessarily hearsay?

Goodman v. Pennsylvania Turnpike Comm'n
293 F.3d 655 (3d Cir. 2002)

AMBRO, Circuit Judge....

Goodman began his career with the (Pennsylvania Turnpike) Commission in 1976 as an Equipment Operator in the maintenance department. After fifteen months, Goodman moved into fare collections and received training as a Toll Collector before becoming an Assistant District Manager. In that capacity, Goodman reported to Frank Flaherty, the District Manager. In December of 1994, Flaherty retired, leaving a vacancy in his position as District V Manager for Fare Collections. On December 23, 1994, the Commission named Goodman Acting District Manager and posted the promotion opportunity.

The Commission follows specific policies governing the promotion process outlined in Policy Letter 65, Policy and Procedure for Promoting Employees. Policy Letter 65 was adopted in 1992, after consultation with outside legal counsel, to improve the efficiency and fairness of promotion decisions, and to comply with the United States Supreme Court's decision in *Rutan v. Republican Party of Illinois*, 497 U.S. 62 (1990), which held that public employers could be held liable under 42 U.S.C. § 1983 and the First Amendment for discriminating against certain employees because of their political affiliation....

The Commission's governing body comprises four Turnpike Commissioners who are appointed by the Governor and confirmed by a two-thirds majority of the State Senate. The Secretary of Transportation sits as a fifth member with the Commissioners. During the promotion process for the District V Manager for Fare Collections position, the Commissioners were Robert A. Brady, James J. Dodaro, Robert A. Gleason, Jr., James F. Malone, and Secretary of Transportation Bradley Mallory. From 1985 until the time of trial, the Commissioners were balanced in terms of political affiliation, two Democrats and two Republicans. The Secretary of Transportation, however, tipped the scale in the direction of the political party of the Governor. The Personnel Committee, at the relevant time, consisted of Executive Director John Durbin, Associate Executive Director Deborah Everly, Risk Manager Dennis Genevie, Assistant Executive Director Melvin Shelton, and Assistant Executive Director Michael Kennedy. Each Commissioner is represented by one member of the Personnel Committee, thus maintaining the same split in political affiliation among the Personnel Committee as among the Commissioners....

The Commission posted the District V Manager position.... Goodman, along with seven other candidates (including Lee Becker), was interviewed by Samuel Sadler, Deputy Executive Director for Fare Collections, and two other district managers in the Fare Collections Department. This interview committee recommended Goodman, Becker, and Andre Coleman to the Personnel Committee. These candidates obtained the three top scores on the interviews....

At its meeting in February 1996 ... after much discussion, the Personnel Committee voted on the candidate each member thought was the best. Genevie and Shelton voted for Goodman, while Durbin, Everly, and Kennedy voted for Becker. This vote was split along party lines: the two Democrats voted for Goodman and the three Republicans voted for Becker. Becker is a registered Republican and was the Ward Committeeman for East Penn Township. The Personnel Committee ultimately recommended Becker for the promotion and the Commissioners approved him on February 20, 1996.

Goodman then initiated suit in the Eastern District of Pennsylvania, relying on *Rutan*. He alleges that he was not promoted because he and his family members were registered, active Democrats, and because Becker was a registered Republican affiliated with, and supported by, State Senator James Rhoades. Goodman sued the Commission....

A jury trial began on November 15, 1999, before Magistrate Judge Rapoport, with Goodman offering testimony and exhibits.... His arguments focused on the political rivalry between the Goodman family and Republican State Senator Rhoades. Goodman claims that political support from Senator Rhoades and his aide, Clyde "Champ" Holman, on behalf of Becker resulted in Becker being promoted instead of Goodman....

[A]t trial Becker testified that he heard about his promotion from his boss, Sadler. He specifically stated that he did not hear of the promotion from Holman, and specifically denied ever telling Goodman that he heard about the promotion from Holman. Holman also denied any such conversation occurred.

Goodman's counsel recalled him in an effort to impeach Becker's statement. Over the Commission's objection, Goodman testified that Becker had told him that he, Becker, had learned about his promotion from Holman. Goodman also introduced, over objection, similar testimony from his father, Cornelius Goodman, that Holman told him that Senator Rhoades was responsible for Becker's promotion. Goodman's attorney stated multiple times that he was introducing these statements to impeach Becker's and Holman's contrary testimony under Rule 607 of the Federal Rules of Evidence. . . .

On appeal, the Commission argues that the Magistrate Judge erroneously admitted . . . the testimony of Goodman and his father relating to statements that Becker allegedly made to Goodman and that Champ Holman (Senator Rhoades' aide) allegedly made to Goodman's father. . . .

The Magistrate Judge admitted Goodman's testimony that Becker told him that "Champ [Holman] called me last night and told me that I got the job." This testimony followed Becker's taking the stand and denying that he learned of the promotion from Holman. The Magistrate Judge also admitted testimony by Cornelius Goodman, Goodman's father, that Holman twice told him that Senator Rhoades was "to blame" for Becker's promotion over Goodman. This testimony similarly came after Holman testified that he did not make those statements. The Commission argues that both statements were inadmissible hearsay offered for the truth of the matter asserted. On the other hand, Goodman argues that the statements were not hearsay. . . .

We conclude that under the circumstances these statements should not be deemed hearsay. . . . In this case, Goodman's counsel noted explicitly at trial that the statements of Goodman and his father were introduced to impeach the testimony of Becker and Holman. It made sense for Goodman to introduce the statements for this purpose. Regardless whether Holman actually told Becker about his promotion, and regardless whether Senator Rhoades was in fact "to blame" for the promotion, witnesses who make such statements and later deny them tend to lack credibility, and may be impeached on that ground. Thus, the statements are direct evidence by which the jury could assess Becker's and Holman's truthfulness. In this case they were not introduced "to prove the truth of the matter asserted" and therefore lack the defining characteristic of hearsay under the Federal Rules. . . .

Problem 7-3: The Elm Street Garage

David is walking on the sidewalk along Elm Street when he is struck by a car exiting the Elm Street Garage, a privately owned underground parking facility.

David's attorney files a negligence action against the owner of the Elm Street Garage. Under the governing law, a property owner's awareness of the existence of a dangerous condition on his property bears on his liability for negligence. David's attorney wishes to call as a witness Theresa, who if permitted, would testify that three weeks before the incident involving David, she was walking past the exit of the Elm Street Garage and was nearly hit by a car that was emerging from the garage. She would further testify as follows:

> "A few days after that car almost ran me over, I went to the manager's office and said to him, 'I was almost hit by a car exiting your garage the other day.'"

The attorney for the owner of the Elm Street Garage raises a hearsay objection.

Is the challenged testimony necessarily hearsay?

United States v. Hanson
994 F.2d 403 (7th Cir. 1993)

KANNE, Circuit Judge....

I.

Keyte Hanson was an officer of Northwestern Mutual Life Insurance Company ("NML") and manager of its Education and Field Training Division ("EFTD"). Via the EFTD, NML ran a program which offered motivational books and tapes to its insurance agents. At the program's inception, an outside vendor purchased, packaged and shipped all the books and tapes ordered by NML agents. In the 1970s, the original outside vendor terminated its services, and an organization named Achievement Wise Associates ("AWA") took over the purchasing, shipping and handling needs of the NML program.

During 1985, 1986 and 1987, AWA netted at least $52,000 by performing these services for NML. Apparently no one reported this income to the Internal Revenue Service ("IRS"). This case revolves around the question of who was responsible for reporting AWA's income. The government believed that Keyte Hanson and his wife, Diane, were responsible for reporting AWA's income and a federal grand jury agreed. On April 2, 1991, the Hansons were indicted for willfully failing to report AWA's income on their 1985, 1986 and 1987 tax returns.

At trial, the Hansons admitted that they had not reported AWA income, but claimed that they did not believe that it was their income to report. According to the Hansons, AWA was formed and operated by their six children to provide them with part-time jobs and money for college. The Hansons maintained that AWA's income was either paid to the children in cash or saved and subsequently used for their college educations.

The government presented quite a different picture. According to the prosecutor, Diane and Keyte formed AWA, played active roles in the business and deliberately concealed their involvement from NML....

II.

In order to convict the Hansons, the government had to prove that they violated 26 U.S.C. § 7206(1), which penalizes any person who

> [w]illfully makes and subscribes any return, statement, or other document, which contains or is verified by a written declaration that it is made under the penalties of perjury, and which he does not believe to be true and correct as to every material matter....

At trial, it was undisputed that the Hansons had not reported AWA income when they should have done so; thus, the only issue was whether the Hansons knew that they should have reported the income when they omitted it. To prove that the Hansons had the requisite guilty states of mind, the government stressed two main facts: Mr. Hanson's activities designed to conceal his family's connection to AWA from his employer, and Keyte and Diane Hanson's use of AWA funds for their personal purposes.

Apparently Mr. Hanson had an explanation for one of his concealment activities. During direct examination, Mr. Hanson was asked why he did not reveal his family's ownership of AWA on NML's conflict disclosure form. In answering, Mr. Hanson started to describe a conversation he had with Bob Templin, a NML vice president, concerning the proper completion of the form. Mr. Hanson stated that he told Mr. Templin that "my children were providing a service to Northwestern Mutual, it was not a big deal." When Mr. Hanson attempted to relate Mr. Templin's response, the court sustained a hearsay objection by the government.

During a side bar, Mr. Hanson's counsel made the following proffer:

> If Mr. Hanson had been allowed to continue to testify, he would have said that his superior had told him that he was not required to report on the conflict of interest form the circumstances that he had just related to the superior which he did testify about.... Hearsay is defined at Rule 801(c) as an out of court statement offered in evidence to prove the truth of the matter asserted.... [T]he evidence was not being offered for the truth but rather for the effect it had upon the state of mind of Mr. Hanson.

Further, counsel suggested that the court give a cautionary instruction. The court disagreed, concluding that the evidence was being offered for the truth of the matter. The Hansons maintain that the district court's decision was an error....

Hearsay is an out of court statement offered for the truth of the matter asserted. Fed.R.Evid. 801(c). In this case, the Hansons sought to introduce Mr. Templin's out of court statement that Mr. Hanson did not have to disclose his family's connections with AWA on the NML conflict form. However, by introducing such evidence, the Hansons were not trying to prove that Mr. Hanson, in fact, was required to make a disclosure. Rather, the Hansons sought to use Mr. Templin's statement to show the effect it had on Mr. Hanson.

An out of court statement that is offered to show its effect on the hearer's state of mind is not hearsay. In *Harris*, the defendant had received more than a half a million dollars from a male paramour. She considered the money a nontaxable gift; the government disagreed and charged her with willfully failing to file income tax returns. At trial, the defendant proffered three letters from her lover in which he wrote that he loved her and loved giving her gifts. We concluded that the district court erred in excluding the letters as hearsay, stating:

> But the letters were not hearsay for the purpose of showing what Harris believed, because her belief does not depend on the actual truth of the matters asserted in the letters. Even if [her lover] were lying, the letters could have caused Harris to believe in good faith that the things he gave her were intended as gifts.... This good faith belief, in turn, would preclude any finding of willfulness on her part.

The principle in the instant case is identical. It does not matter whether Mr. Templin was telling Mr. Hanson the truth when he told him he did not have to disclose his connections to AWA to NML. What matters is whether such a conversation caused Mr. Hanson to have a good faith belief that he did not have to disclose, which would allow him to at least partially rebut the government's argument that he was concealing information about AWA from NML. Because the Hansons offered Mr. Templin's statement only to demonstrate its effect on Mr. Hanson's state of mind, we conclude that the proffered testimony was not hearsay and the district court erred in excluding it....

Problem 7-4: The Slanderous Statement

Lisa, an art dealer, finds out that Debbie has been telling people that Lisa knowingly sells forged artwork. Outraged, Lisa brings a lawsuit against Debbie for slander.

At trial, Lisa calls as witnesses a number of people who, if permitted, would testify that Debbie told them that Lisa knowingly sells forged artwork. Debbie's attorney raises a hearsay objection.

Is the challenged testimony necessarily hearsay?

Problem 7-5: I'm Alive!

George and Mary, who were married to one another, are both killed in a car accident. George's will provided that if Mary survived him, his entire estate would go to her; otherwise the entire estate would go to his brother, John. Mary's will provided that if George survived her, her entire estate would go to him; otherwise, the entire estate would go to her sister, Ellen. Thus, depending on whether George or Mary died first, either Ellen or John would end up inheriting the entirety of both of their estates.

In consolidated probate proceedings, Ellen seeks to call Donna, an eyewitness to the accident. Donna would testify that as she approached the car, she heard a female voice cry out, "Help me, I'm alive," and that she heard nothing else after that. John raises a hearsay objection.

Is the challenged testimony necessarily hearsay?

United States v. Montana
199 F.3d 947 (7th Cir. 1999)

POSNER, Chief Judge.

The defendant was convicted of bank robbery and related offenses and given a very long sentence—almost 30 years. James Dodd committed the actual robbery; Montana drove the getaway car. Dodd pleaded guilty, and testified at Montana's trial, as Montana's witness, that Montana had not known that Dodd was planning to rob the bank. Shortly before the end of the trial, Dodd gave Montana's lawyer a note for Montana's mother, who after she read it told the lawyer that the note demanded money in exchange for Dodd's having testified favorably to Montana. The following morning, a deputy U.S. marshal heard Dodd tell Montana to tell Montana's father that "it's going to be $10,000" for the favorable testimony. The district judge allowed the marshal to testify to what he had heard....

The government argues that it was admissible as a "verbal act," thus echoing the linguist's distinction between performative and illocutionary utterances. The latter narrate, describe, or otherwise convey information, and so are judged by their truth value (information is useful only if true—indeed is *information* only if it is true); the former—illustrated by a promise, offer, or demand—commit the speaker to a course of action. Performative utterances are not within the scope of the hearsay rule, because they do not make any truth claims. Had the marshal overheard Dodd tell Montana, "your father has promised me $10,000," Dodd's overheard statement would have been hearsay, because its value as evidence would have depended on its being truthful, that is, on such a promise having actually been made. But what in fact was overheard was merely a demand—in effect, "give me $10,000"—and so the only issue of credibility was whether the marshal was reporting the demand correctly, and *his* testimony was not hearsay....

Notes and Questions

1. In cases in which a property owner's awareness of the existence of a dangerous condition on his property bears on his liability for negligence (such as in Problem 7-3), why isn't testimony that someone mentioned the allegedly dangerous condition to the owner hearsay? After all, to succeed on the claim of negligence, the plaintiff has to prove that a

dangerous condition existed, and doesn't such testimony, if accepted by the trier of fact as true, do just that, making it hearsay? Consider the following explanation:

> Virtually all claims where notice is required will involve an overlap between the content of the notice and the ultimate fact to be proved. Notice does not depend on the truth of the facts stated but does depend on the content of the facts stated. Of course, to recover, plaintiff must ultimately prove the truth of the content of the notice statement. But, whether true or not, the [notice statement] arguably alerted defendant to a potential problem, an issue separate from the truth of the statements in the [notice statement]. Independent evidence is required to prove the truth of the existence of the dangerous condition.... For example, the content of a store customer's report of a slippery floor may be admissible as notice of a potential problem but the statement's assertion that the floor was slippery may not be considered for its truth that the floor was slippery.

James A. Adams & Joseph P. Weeg, 7 Ia. Prac., Evidence § 5.801:4 (2008 ed.)

2. In a case that preceded *Montana*, the Seventh Circuit illustrated the verbal acts doctrine with this colorful example:

> The other characterization of the demand is as a verbal act, what philosophers of language call a performative utterance, to which truth is irrelevant. When the groom in a marriage ceremony says "I do," he is not making a statement that may be true or false; he is performing an act (inessentially verbal — it could be a handshake instead) that has legal consequences; and anyone who heard his words could testify that he uttered them, without running afoul of the hearsay rule.

Twin City Fire Ins. Co. v. Country Mut. Ins. Co., 23 F.3d 1175, 1182 (7th Cir. 1994).

3. Examples of statements that have independent legal significance in that they give rise to legal consequences merely because they are said include those associated with forming a contract (offer and acceptance), defamatory statements, threatening statements, and statements offering a bribe. *See, e.g., Noviello v. City of Boston*, 398 F.3d 76, 84–85 (1st Cir. 2005) ("The insults and taunting that the plaintiff recounts do not create hearsay problems; those statements are not offered for their truth, but, rather, to show that the words were spoken (and thus contributed to the hostile work environment).").

4. In Problem 7-5, does the statement's significance lie in its assertive aspect or its performative aspect? What if the female voice had instead cried out, "I'm dead," or "I'm hungry"? What if the female voice had cried out, "My husband's dead"?

5. For an arrest (and a warrantless search incident to such arrest) to be constitutionally valid, law enforcement officers are required to have probable cause to believe that a person has committed or is committing a crime. At an evidentiary suppression hearing in which the validity of the arrest and search is at issue, can an officer claiming that his search was supported by probable cause testify to statements that other people made to him that suggested that the arrestee committed a crime? *See United States v. Dorsey*, 418 F.3d 1038, 1044 (9th Cir. 2005) ("Potter's statement 'was not received or considered for the truth of the matter as to whether Dorsey had in fact trespassed since that ultimate issue would be decided by a different forum.' Potter's statement was offered to demonstrate that the officers were reasonable in believing that a crime had occurred; in that context, the statement was not hearsay because it was not offered for the truth of the matter asserted.").

6. Suppose that the accused in a criminal case is charged with, *inter alia*, perjuring himself at a prior proceeding. Is testimony that the accused made those false statements

at a prior proceeding hearsay? *See Anderson v. United States*, 417 U.S. 211, 219–20 (1974) ("The [prior] testimony ... was not admitted into evidence ... to prove the truth of anything asserted therein. Quite the contrary, the point of the prosecutor's introducing those statements was simply to prove that the statements were made so as to establish a foundation for later showing, through other admissible evidence, that they were false.").

Problem 7-6: I'm the President

Shortly before he died, Tom drafted a will in which he left his entire estate to a religious organization. His children challenged the will, claiming that Tom lacked testamentary capacity at the time he drafted the will. At trial, his children wished to testify that, on several occasions shortly before he drafted the will, Tom would introduce himself to people as the President of the United States. The religious organization objects on hearsay grounds.

Is the challenged testimony necessarily hearsay?

United States v. Parry
649 F.2d 292 (5th Cir. Unit B 1981)

LEWIS R. MORGAN, Circuit Judge.

The question in this case is whether the district court erred in excluding certain testimony by the appellant's mother as inadmissible hearsay. We conclude that the evidence should have been admitted and therefore reverse appellant's convictions and remand for a new trial.

Scott Parry was tried before a jury and convicted in consolidated cases of conspiring to distribute phencyclidine hydrochloride (PCP) and of possessing with intent to distribute PCP and dl-methamphetamine hydrochloride. At trial the government presented its case primarily through the testimony of two undercover agents with the Drug Enforcement Administration, Robert Starratt and Douglas Driver. Essentially, these agents testified that Parry had acted as a middleman or intermediary in arranging three separate drug transactions between the agents and certain individuals who had drugs for sale.

In his defense to these charges, Parry did not deny that he had participated in the drug transactions described by the DEA agents but argued that, during each of these transactions, he had proceeded upon the good faith belief that he was working *for* the agents, assisting them in locating drug dealers. As proof of the purity of his intentions, Parry testified that he had learned that Starratt was an undercover agent several days before he had met the agent or engaged in any of the activities alleged in the indictment. Although Parry conceded that he never entered into any formal agreement to cooperate with the agents, he argued that, at least from his perspective, there was an implied understanding that he would lead the agents to drug sources.

In support of his position that he had known from the outset of the agents' identities, Parry related a conversation he had had with his mother shortly after he met Agent Starratt in October 1974 and well in advance of his arrest in January 1975. Parry testified that, in response to his mother's inquiry, he had stated that the person who had frequently telephoned her home asking to speak to Parry was a narcotics agent with whom he was then working. In an effort to corroborate his story, Parry called his mother as a witness. Outside the presence of the jury his mother testified that

> Scott received several phone calls and I would tell Scott that Bob called and I questioned Scott on who he was because I thought at first it was a painting job

and Scott had said—told me that his name was Bob Starratt, he was working with him, he was a narcotics agent, he was working with and not to worry.

Although the government voiced no objection to the proffered testimony, the court ruled that Parry's mother could not testify to "any conversations that she had with her son or that her son had with her." Parry's objection that his mother's testimony was not hearsay and therefore should not be excluded was overruled by the district court.

It is our judgment that the court erred in excluding the proffered testimony. First, we find that Parry's out-of-court statement to his mother is simply outside the scope of the hearsay prohibition.... The reasons for excluding hearsay are clear: when an out-of-court statement is offered as a testimonial assertion of the truth of the matter stated, we are vitally interested in the credibility of the out-of-court declarant. Because a statement made out of court is not exposed to the normal credibility safeguards of oath, presence at trial, and cross-examination, the jury has no basis for evaluating the declarant's trustworthiness and thus his statement is considered unreliable. Implicit in both the definition and justification for the rule, however, is the recognition that whenever an out-of-court statement is offered for some purpose other than to prove the truth of the matter asserted, the value of the statement does not rest upon the declarant's credibility and, therefore, is not subject to attack as hearsay.

Parry contends, and we agree, that in this case the excluded testimony was not offered to evidence the truth of the matter asserted in the out-of-court statement. Parry's mother sought to testify that her son had stated that the person who had been telephoning her home was a narcotics agent and that he, Parry, was working with the agent. As Parry explained to the district court, this statement was not offered to prove that the caller was a narcotics agent or that Parry was working with the agent, but to establish that Parry had knowledge of the agent's identity when he spoke. In other words, Parry offered the statement as the basis for a circumstantial inference by the jury that, if this statement was in fact made—a question which the in-court witness could testify to while under oath, before the jury, and subject to cross-examination—then Parry probably knew of the agent's identity. Using an out-of-court utterance as circumstantial evidence of the declarant's knowledge of the existence of some fact, rather than as testimonial evidence of the truth of the matter asserted, does not offend the hearsay rule....

Problem 7-7: The Bumper Sticker

Randy Jones is on trial on charges that he hit a pedestrian with his car and fled the scene. The prosecution seeks to offer testimony during its case-in-chief by Wilma, a witness to the accident, that the car that struck the pedestrian was a silver 1993 Toyota Tercel with a missing taillight and a bumper sticker that read, "Property of Randy Jones," as well as testimony by Randy's neighbor, Doug, that Randy owns a silver 1993 Toyota Tercel with a missing taillight and a bumper sticker that reads, "Property of Randy Jones." Randy's attorney raises a hearsay objection.

Is the challenged testimony necessarily hearsay?

United States v. Snow

517 F.2d 441 (7th Cir. 1975)

SNEED, Circuit Judge:

Bill Snow was convicted by a jury for having knowingly possessed an unregistered firearm, in violation of 26 U.S.C. § 5861(d) and § 5871. To support its contention that the weapon was knowingly possessed by Bill Snow, the government, after establishing what the trial court regarded as a proper foundation, was permitted to introduce into evidence the brief case in which the gun was found. Affixed to the brief case was a red tape with the lettering "Tri. Tron. Electronics" and "Bill Snow"....

[T]he evidence tended to show that the case with the affixed red tape was found on premises frequently visited by the defendant by police officers properly on such premises, that at that time the unregistered firearm, an automatic weapon, was found within the case, that a latent fingerprint of the defendant was found on the weapon, that the weapon and the case with the affixed tape remained within the custody of the authorities from the time of its discovery to the trial, and that the defendant, prior to the discovery of the case by the police, had been seen with a case which had a name tape affixed thereto on the premises at which the case was found....

The appellant insists that the tape is inadmissible hearsay. His argument is relatively simple. He asserts that the tape is a statement made out of court offered as an assertion to show the truth of the matter asserted therein, the probative value of which rests upon the credibility of the out-of-court asserter. The assertion, of course, is "This case belongs to Bill Snow," a reasonable interpretation of the lettering appearing on the tape.

We reject this view. In doing so, we are required to examine some fundamental principles of the law of evidence. Wigmore classifies evidentiary facts in the following manner:

> There are two possible modes of proceeding for the purpose of producing persuasion on the part of the tribunal as to the Proposition at issue.
>
> The first is by the presentation of the *thing itself* as to which persuasion is desired.
>
> The second is the presentation of some *independent fact* by inference from which the persuasion is to be produced. Instances of the first are the production of a blood-stained knife; the exhibition of an injured limb; the viewing of premises by the jury; the production of a document.
>
> The second falls further into two classes, according as the basis of inference is (a) the *assertion of a human being* as to the existence of the thing in issue, or (b) *any other fact*; the one is termed Testimonial or Direct Evidence, the other Circumstantial or Indirect Evidence.

1 Wigmore on Evidence, §24 (3rd ed. 1940) (emphasis supplied). The case with the affixed tape without question falls within the second possible mode of proceeding set forth above. The appellant's position when placed within the framework of this analysis is that the tape is "an assertion of a human being as to the existence of the thing in issue." The position of the United States and the trial judge, on the other hand, is that the tape, like the case to which it is affixed, is "Circumstantial or Indirect Evidence." We adhere to this view.

Continuing with Wigmore's analytics, the hearsay rule "signifies *a rule rejecting assertions, offered testimonially, which have not been in some way subjected to the test of cross-examination.*" 5 Wigmore §1362 (Chadbourn rev. 1974). To exclude the name tape as hearsay, therefore, it would be necessary to find that the tape is a testimonial assertion of the proscribed sort which is not admissible under any exception to the hearsay rule.

It is clear that under Wigmore's classification scheme the name tape constitutes an evidentiary fact, other than an assertion "from which the truth of the matter asserted is desired to be inferred," 1 Wigmore, §25 (3rd ed. 1940), which he describes as a "mechanical trace" designed to show that at some previous time a certain act was or was not done. 1 Wigmore §148 (3rd ed. 1940). A "mechanical trace," thus, is a type of circumstantial evidence. Examples offered by Wigmore of "mechanical traces" are, *inter alia*, the presence upon the person or premises of articles, fragments, stains, tools, brands on animals and timber, tags, signs, license plates, fingerprints, foot marks, and documents. 1 Wigmore §§ 148–157 (3rd ed. 1940)....

Notes and Questions

1. Toward the beginning of its decision, the *Snow* court writes that "the defendant, prior to the discovery of the case by the police, had been seen with a case which had a name tape affixed thereto." Is this fact relevant to the *Snow* court's rationale for admissibility? Is it decisive?

2. In *Snow*, another piece of evidence offered by the government was "a latent fingerprint of the defendant ... found on the weapon." The defendant, while objecting to the admission of the name tape on hearsay grounds, raised no such objection with respect to the fingerprint. In what way is a fingerprint (or a trace of DNA) similar to the tape? In what way is it different?

3. In *United States v. Potwin*, 136 Fed. Appx. 609, 611 (5th Cir. 2005), Henry David Potwin was on trial on charges of possession of heroin by an inmate in a federal prison. At trial, Potwin claimed that the drugs were planted on him by another inmate with whom he was not on good terms, J.J. Cantu. At trial, Potwin sought to have a police officer testify that he heard Cantu call Potwin a rat, but the trial court sustained a hearsay objection to the testimony. On review, the appeals court reversed, noting that "Officer Manuel's testimony that Cantu called Potwin a rat was not offered to prove the content of Cantu's out-of-court statement, i.e., that Potwin was, in fact, a rat." What is the non-hearsay purpose for which Officer Manuel's testimony was relevant?

D. What Is an "Assertion"?

Problem 7-8: Nobody Else Complained

Shortly after eating at a restaurant, Lisa became extremely ill. She went to her doctor, who after performing tests informed her that she tested positive for staphylococcus. Believing that her exposure resulted from improper health precautions at the restaurant, Lisa brought suit against its owner.

In its defense, the restaurant's owner called the manager as a witness, who if permitted would testify that "No other customers who ate at the restaurant during the week that Lisa ate there ever complained that they got sick." Lisa's attorney raises a hearsay objection.

Is the challenged testimony hearsay?

Problem 7-9: Say Something If It Hurts ...

While riding her bicycle, Susan is struck by a car backing out of a driveway driven by Louis. Susan brings a negligence suit against Louis in federal court, invoking that court's diversity jurisdiction. In her case-in-chief, Susan testifies that as a result of the accident, she sustained injuries to both her arms and her right leg. During cross-examination of Susan, Louis's attorney asks Susan, "Isn't it true that the injuries to your arms were caused by an accident two months earlier with Jim?"

Susan's attorney seeks to call Ellen as a witness. If permitted, Ellen, a friend of Susan's, would testify that she witnessed the accident Susan had with Jim, called for an ambulance, rushed to Susan's side, and said to Susan, "While we are waiting for the medics to arrive, I am going to put pressure up and down each of your arms and legs; say something when I touch a spot that hurts." Ellen would further testify that Susan agreed, and that although Susan spoke up several times when she pressed on spots along her left leg, she did not say anything when she pressed on spots along her arms or her right leg. Louis's attorney raises a hearsay objection with respect to Ellen's testimony that Susan "did not say anything when she pressed on spots along her arms."

Is the challenged testimony hearsay?

Wilson v. Clancy
747 F. Supp. 1154 (D.Md. 1990)

SMALKIN, District Judge.

This is a diversity case, in which the plaintiff, a disappointed testamentary beneficiary, brings a third-party malpractice suit against the attorney who drafted the 1987 Last Will and Testament of Dr. Thomas A. Hurney. The matter is before the Court on a summary judgment motion....

The defendant was a longtime family friend and attorney for Dr. Hurney, the testator. In 1968, the defendant prepared wills for Dr. and Mrs. Hurney, under which, at the death of the last of them, their property would be divided among their relatives in such a fashion that the plaintiff would, in effect, receive a one-eighth share. By 1987, the Hurneys' physical conditions had deteriorated to the extent that Mrs. Hurney was in a nursing home and Dr. Hurney, although not institutionalized, required home health care. The parties agree that Dr. Hurney engaged Mr. Clancy in 1987 to draft a new will (the 1987 will) for him (the plaintiff does not allege that Mr. Clancy was ever engaged to draft a new will for Mrs. Hurney), whereby trusts were created to take care of Mrs. Hurney following the death of Dr. Hurney and to take care of another aged relative of Dr. Hurney (his sister) until her death, should Mrs. Hurney have predeceased him. Under this new will, after the deaths of these two people, the trusts were to terminate and the residue was to be split in half between plaintiff and another relative of Dr. (but not Mrs.) Hurney. The trusts were to be funded with all of Dr. Hurney's property.

Dr. Hurney predeceased Mrs. Hurney, owning essentially no property in his own name at the time of his death, the couple's valuable assets being then held by them jointly with right of survivorship, as they had been when the 1987 will was drafted. Meanwhile, it will be remembered, Mrs. Hurney's Last Will and Testament at her death was her 1968 will, giving plaintiff a one-eighth share, not a one-half share, in her estate.

As can readily be seen, had Dr. Hurney held sole title to all the couple's valuable property at his death, Mrs. Hurney's 1968 will would have been *de facto* defunct, and plaintiff would have taken half the Hurneys' property under the Doctor's 1987 will. Unfortunately for plaintiff, as noted above, all the couple's property (except Dr. Hurney's Rolex wristwatch and a $6000 car) was held by the couple at the time of Dr. Hurney's death in a joint tenancy with the right of survivorship. Accordingly, it passed directly to Mrs. Hurney outside the Doctor's 1987 will, and, upon Mrs. Hurney's death, it passed under Mrs. Hurney's 1968 will, the net result being that plaintiff wound up with about $220,000 less than she would have, had Dr. Hurney held the couple's valuable property in his sole name at the time of his death....

[T]here could be malpractice only if defendant did not realize, or advise his client of, the need to change the titling of the couple's substantial property to Dr. Hurney's sole name to bring it within his testamentary estate.

The defendant has testified on deposition that he realized that the jointly held property of the Hurney couple could not pass to the named residual beneficiaries under the Doctor's 1987 will, and that, accordingly, he advised Dr. Hurney repeatedly that, in order for the 1987 will to be effective in accordance with Dr. Hurney's wishes, Dr. Hurney would have to see to it that the couple's property was transferred from joint ownership to Dr. Hurney's sole ownership....

The defendant, having produced evidence that he fulfilled his duty to advise Dr. Hurney to change the ownership form of the couple's property in order to effectuate the 1987 will's intent, is entitled to summary judgment unless the plaintiff can come up with some evidence to generate a triable dispute on this sole dispositive fact....

In an attempt to stave off summary judgment, plaintiff ... has found a previously undiscovered witness, a Ms. Bouman, who had done Dr. Hurney's bookkeeping and tax work in the several years before his death. Her affidavit ... proffers testimony to the effect that neither Mr. Clancy nor Dr. Hurney ever mentioned to her that Dr. Hurney would need to change the titling of his assets in order to make the 1987 will effective. Plaintiff argues that, from this evidence, she is entitled to the inference that such advice was never given Dr. Hurney by Mr. Clancy....

At common law, there was substantial authority that the silence of an individual or group of individuals is hearsay, as an "implied assertion." *See* cases collected and discussed in Professor Morgan's famous article, "Hearsay Dangers and the Application of the Hearsay Concept," 62 Harv.L.Rev. 177, 213 (1948). It appears to be the intent of the limitation of the hearsay definition under Fed.R.Evid. 801(a)[] to non-verbal conduct "intended [by the declarant] as an assertion" to do away with the notion that "implied assertions" are within the hearsay prohibition. *See McCormick on Evidence* § 250 at 743 (1984). *See also* 4 J. Weinstein and M. Berger, *Weinstein's Evidence* ¶ 801(a)[01] at p. 801-61 (1990). Although there appears not to be any significant case law on this topic since the adoption of the Federal Rules of Evidence, and although a case might still be made for treating silence as hearsay, the Court is of the opinion that, as the cited authorities agree, silence, at least where there is no showing of intentional silence on a particular occasion intended as an assertion when the silence was kept, is no longer within the hearsay realm....

Problem 7-10: Did You Know?

Tom, a second-year law student, is studying in the law school library. He walks away from his desk momentarily, leaving behind his textbooks and his laptop. When he returns, the laptop is gone. His friend, Jennifer, says to him, "Hey, did you know that Larry took your laptop?"

Tom subsequently brings a suit against Larry for conversion, and at trial, Tom wishes to testify to what Jennifer said to him when he returned to his desk. Larry objects that the testimony is hearsay.

Is the challenged testimony hearsay?

United States v. Wright
343 F.3d 849 (6th Cir. 2003)

COLE, Circuit Judge.

Defendant Appellant Ward Wesley Wright appeals his jury conviction and sentence for the use of interstate commerce facilities in the commission of murder for hire, interstate travel in aid of a crime of violence, and conspiracy to possess with intent to distribute and to distribute cocaine....

Brian Chase, Raymond Kelsey, and William Arbelaez met while serving time in a Minnesota prison. After all three had been released in 1992, Chase met Wright while they were both bouncers at a bar in Michigan. Wright was a member of the Avengers Motorcycle Club (the "Avengers") and was involved with cocaine distribution through the club. Arbelaez, a Colombian national who trafficked cocaine, began supplying cocaine to Chase from Colombia, and Chase in turn began selling cocaine to Wright....

In 1993, Arbelaez began supplying cocaine to Chase from Colombia and Kelsey became the pilot of the operation. In February, Kelsey flew to Los Angeles to retrieve a fifty-kilogram shipment of cocaine and then flew to Detroit to deliver it to Chase. Chase sold part of the shipment to David "Slap" Moore, a member of the Avengers, who would eventually become Chase's primary distributor....

Moore introduced Chase to his main customer in Detroit, and Chase supplied cocaine directly to that customer. Moore wanted a commission from Chase for the sales to his customer, but Chase refused. Moore told Chase that he "knew how to take care of business," and Chase believed that this was a threat and that Moore intended to kill him. Chase then discussed the "Moore problem" with Wright and told Wright that he was willing to give Moore $40,000 to end the dispute. Chase offered Wright $10,000 to broker the deal with Moore, but Wright was unable to arrange a deal. Wright then suggested, "Why don't you just give me the money and I'll kill Mr. Moore." A few days later, Wright told Chase that Moore had given another Avenger a gun and $10,000 for a contract murder and that Chase was the target. Chase and Kelsey then decided to kill Moore to end the dispute and the perceived threat.

In July 1993, William Anderson Burke, a past national president of the Avengers, was involved in a motorcycle accident in Columbus, Ohio. Moore, as an officer in the Avengers, traveled to Columbus to await Burke's release from the hospital. Chase and Wright decided that Wright could kill Moore while he was in Columbus, and Wright agreed to accept $50,000 to commit the murder. Wright's girlfriend, and later wife, Brenda Schneider, called Moore's wife to determine what hotel Moore was staying at in Columbus.

On July 29, 1993, Wright obtained a .22-caliber pistol and a car that had been purchased by Chase and Kelsey, and drove to Columbus. Wright found Moore's hotel room in the early hours of July 30, and asked Moore if he could stay the night. After Moore let him in and went back to sleep, Wright shot Moore in the head twice....

Wright argues that the district court erred in admitting a hearsay statement made by Leah Moore, the wife of Moore. The testimony was elicited to show that Wright learned the whereabouts of Moore by having his girlfriend call Leah. Leah testified that she had a conversation with Brenda, then-girlfriend of the Defendant, on the day of Moore's murder. She also testified that she heard Brenda relay the information regarding Moore's whereabouts to Wright. Defense counsel objected, but the district court overruled the objection. Leah's testimony was as follows:

A. Brenda called me.

Q. Brenda who?

A. [Wright's] girlfriend.

Q. Did you recognize her voice?

A. Yes.

Q. Was there anyone else in the area of the phone that you could hear?

A. [Wright] was in the background.

Q. What did Brenda say?

Mr. Amberg: Hearsay. Objection.

[Prosecutor]: Your Honor, I believe again, the answer is going to be a question.
A question is not hearsay.

THE COURT: Go ahead.

THE WITNESS: She asked me where my husband was.

The Government argues that Leah's testimony about Brenda's question was not hearsay because "a question is by definition not hearsay."

.... While this Court has not specifically addressed the issue presented by Wright, a question is typically not hearsay because it does not assert the truth or falsity of a fact. A question merely seeks answers and usually has no factual content....

In this case, Brenda's question to Leah can be summarized as "Where is your husband?" In making that statement, Brenda is not asserting anything. She is only attempting to extract information from Leah. This inquiry from Brenda is not being used to prove the truth of the matter asserted and therefore, as the Government argues, it is not hearsay....

Notes and Questions

1. On the question whether evidence of the absence of complaints should be deemed hearsay, *see Cain v. George*, 411 F.2d 572, 573 (5th Cir. 1969); *Silver v. New York Cent. R. Co.*, 105 N.E.2d 923, 926–27 (Mass. 1952). On the question whether silence can be deemed hearsay, *see Brooks v. Price*, 121 Fed. Appx. 961, 967 (3d Cir. 2005) ("Silence or failure to act can be a statement under the rule so long as it was intended by the person as an assertion.").

2. For an example of a case finding a statement in the form of a question to be an assertion and thus hearsay, *see United States v. Summers*, 414 F.3d 1287, 1300 (10th Cir. 2005) (holding that statement by co-defendant to police upon arrest in which he remarked "How did you guys find us so fast?" was hearsay, reasoning that "It begs credulity to assume that in positing the question Mohammed was exclusively interested in modern methods of law enforcement, including surveillance, communication, and coordination. Rather, fairly construed the statement intimated both guilt and wonderment at the ability of the police to apprehend the perpetrators of the crime so quickly.")

Problem 7-11: "He Barked"

Assume the same facts as in Problem 7-1, except that (1) when Perkins arrived at the scene of the crime, she found a driver's license with the name "Robert Barrone" on it next to the black baseball cap; and (2) when French arrived, he was accompanied not by Sophie but instead by one William Smith.

French introduced Smith to Perkins as the department's new trailing person, an individual with an acute sense of smell akin to a bloodhound who, like a trailing dog, can lead officers to a person by smelling an article left behind by that person.

Smith got down on his hands and knees, sniffed the baseball cap, and started running, with French in tow. As Smith approached a man later identified as Robert Barrone, he alerted by barking. Barrone was arrested and taken to police headquarters.

At trial, the prosecution seeks to have French, an expert on trailing people, testify as to Smith's training and to the fact that he led him to Barrone. The prosecution also seeks to offer into evidence the driver's license, as well as Perkins' testimony that she found it next to Albertson's body. Barrone's attorney objects, contending that French's testimony that Smith barked when he approached Barrone is hearsay, as is the driver's license.

Is the challenged testimony hearsay?

Problem 7-12: Under a Watchful Eye

Pursuant to a warrant, law enforcement officials inspected a large crate that arrived in Los Angeles via ship and discovered that it contained approximately 60 pounds of marijuana. The crate was re-sealed and the officers waited for it to be picked up. Mark, a teenage boy, arrived in a van to pick up the package, at which time Mark was intercepted by the officers. Mark said that he was picking up the box at someone else's request, and agreed to cooperate with the police by letting them accompany him as he delivered the package.

Mark subsequently dialed a phone number, dialed some sort of code, and hung up. He then drove with the package to an alley, and waited there. Soon, a man later determined to be William Jones opened the back door of the van, but upon seeing the officers, fled.

William was later apprehended and indicted on charges of possession of marijuana with the intent to distribute the same. By the time of his trial, however, Mark had disappeared and thus could not be called as a witness. The officers who apprehended Mark sought to testify about the events following their conversation with Mark, but William's attorney raised a hearsay objection.

Is the challenged testimony hearsay?

Miller v. Dillard's, Inc.
166 F. Supp. 2d 1326 (D. Kan. 2001)

CROW, Senior District Judge.

This diversity jurisdiction case comes before the court on defendant Dillard's Inc.'s motion for summary judgment. The sole claim brought by the two plaintiffs, Stacey Ann Miller and Brently Ian Dorsey, is a state law tort claim for negligent supervision. Plaintiff's claim arises from their detention, inquiry and search as purported shoplifting suspects by a person plaintiffs believe was employed by Dillard's....

For purposes of this motion, the court considers the following facts, stated in the light most favorable to the plaintiffs, to be uncontroverted....

6. Plaintiffs exited the mall through the Dillard's doors and walked diagonally across the parking lot to Miller's vehicle. When plaintiffs arrived at their car, they were confronted by an individual who identified himself as a law enforcement officer working security for Dillard's. Plaintiffs neither saw the security guard inside Dillard's nor saw him walk out of Dillard's. The security guard was not wearing a uniform but was in plain clothes. Plaintiffs do not recall whether the security guard said he worked for the Topeka Police Department or the Kansas Highway Patrol.

7. After displaying what appeared to be a law enforcement badge, the security guard said they could not find the green and white swimsuit and asked Miller and Dorsey what they had done with it. Plaintiffs tried to explain that the swimsuit had been returned to the rack in the store, but the security guard proceeded to put their belongings on the hood of the car and to search their purchases. The security guard then asked Miller to open her purse so that he could view its contents, and she complied. The security guard then asked Miller to lift her blouse so that he could see if she had forgotten to take off the green and white swimsuit. Miller complied, lifting her blouse to just below her brassiere for a few seconds.

8. Plaintiffs found the manner of the security guard to be very "gruff" and his words to be "very accusing." He offered no apology upon finding no stolen items. Plaintiff Dorsey believes that the incident in the parking lot occurred because plaintiffs were an interracial couple, as Miller had shopped at Dillard's before without incident when unaccompanied by Dorsey.

9. The encounter in the parking lot lasted approximately ten minutes. When it concluded, Miller saw the security guard walk into the Dillard's store. Plaintiffs admit that the man could have been just somebody in the parking lot. Neither plaintiff knows the identity of the security guard nor have they seen him since the encounter.

10. Dillard's hires off-duty law enforcement officers from the Topeka Police Department and the Kansas Highway Patrol to work as security guards....

13. Dillard's may or may not have required its security guards to wear uniforms on the date of the incident in the parking lot. At some unspecified point in time, Dillard's established a new policy that its guards would wear uniforms instead of plain clothes....

Plaintiffs first attempt to establish a duty flowing from Dillard's by showing that the security guard was an employee of Dillard's. To prove this point, plaintiffs rely upon statements made and questions asked by the security guard. Defendant counters that the statement of the person to the effect that he was a security guard working for Dillard's is inadmissible hearsay....

The definition of a "statement" for hearsay purposes expressly includes [nonverbal conduct, if the person intended it as an assertion]. Fed.R.Evid. 801(a), (c). The security guard's non-verbal act of showing the plaintiffs his badge was clearly the equivalent of words, assertive in nature, and to be regarded as a statement. Showing the badge was just another way of asserting that he was regularly employed as a law enforcement officer. His showing of the badge evidenced the truth of the fact he asserted verbally contemporaneously therewith, *i.e.*, that he was a law enforcement officer. As such, his act of showing a badge constitutes hearsay, and is inadmissible....

United States v. Zenni

492 F. Supp. 464 (E.D. Ky. 1980)

BERTELSMAN, District Judge.

This prosecution for illegal bookmaking activities presents a classic problem in the law of evidence, namely, whether implied assertions are hearsay. The problem was a controversial one at common law, the discussion of which has filled many pages in the treatises and learned journals.[2] Although the answer to the problem is clear under the Federal Rules of Evidence, there has been little judicial treatment of the matter, and many members of the bar are unfamiliar with the marked departure from the common law the Federal Rules have effected on this issue.

FACTS

The relevant facts are simply stated. While conducting a search of the premises of the defendant, Ruby Humphrey, pursuant to a lawful search warrant which authorized a search for evidence of bookmaking activity, government agents answered the telephone several times. The unknown callers stated directions for the placing of bets on various sporting events. The government proposes to introduce this evidence to show that the callers believed that the premises were used in betting operations. The existence of such belief tends to prove that they were so used. The defendants object on the ground of hearsay.

COMMON LAW BACKGROUND

At common law, the hearsay rule applied "only to evidence of out-of-court statements offered for the purpose of proving that the facts are as asserted in the statement."

On the other hand, not [every] out-of-court expression is common law hearsay. For instance, an utterance offered to show the publication of a slander, or that a person was given notice of a fact, or orally entered into a contract, is not hearsay.

In the instant case, the utterances of the absent declarants are not offered for the truth of the words,[7] and the mere fact that the words were uttered has no relevance of itself.[8] Rather they are offered to show the declarants' belief in a fact sought to be proved. At common law this situation occupied a controversial no-man's land. It was argued on the one hand that the out-of-court utterance was not hearsay, because the evidence was not offered for any truth stated in it, but for the truth of some other proposition inferred from it. On the other hand, it was also argued that the reasons for excluding hearsay applied, in that the evidence was being offered to show declarant's belief in the implied proposition, and he was not available to be cross-examined. Thus, the latter argument was that there existed strong policy reasons for ruling that such utterances were hearsay.

---

2. *See e.g., McCormick on Evidence* § 250 (2d Ed. 1972); Morgan, *Basic Problems of Evidence* (1976); *Weinstein's Evidence* ¶ 801. Falknor, *The "Hear-Say" Rule as a "See-Do" Rule: Evidence of Conduct*, 33 Rocky Mt.L.Rev. 133 (1961) contains a particularly penetrating and succinct analysis. (*See also* authorities in note 15, *infra*.)

7. That is, the utterance, "Put $2 to win on Paul Revere in the third at Pimlico," is a direction and not an assertion of any kind, and therefore can be neither true nor false.

8. *Cf. United States v. McLennan*, 563 F.2d 943 (9th Cir. 1977), in a criminal case, the defense was advice of counsel. Statements made by counsel to the defendant were not hearsay, because it was relevant what the advice was. Of a similar nature would be a policeman's statement, "Go through the stop sign," if it were illegal to go through it unless directed by an officer. Other examples of expression admissible as non-hearsay, because they are verbal acts, relevant merely because they occurred, are "I agree" offered to show a contract was made; or "He took a bribe," offered to show a slander was published.

The classic case, which is discussed in virtually every textbook on evidence, is *Wright v. Tatham*, 7 Adolph. & E. 313, 386 (Exch. Ch. 1837), and 5 Cl. & F. 670, 739 (H.L. 1838). Described as a "celebrated and hard-fought cause," *Wright v. Tatham* was a will contest, in which the will was sought to be set aside on the grounds of the incompetency of the testator at the time of its execution. The proponents of the will offered to introduce into evidence letters to the testator from certain absent individuals on various business and social matters. The purpose of the offer was to show that the writers of the letters believed the testator was able to make intelligent decisions concerning such matters, and thus was competent.

One of the illustrations advanced in the judicial opinions in *Wright v. Tatham* is perhaps even more famous than the case itself. This is Baron Parke's famous sea captain example. Is it hearsay to offer as proof of the seaworthiness of a vessel that its captain, after thoroughly inspecting it, embarked on an ocean voyage upon it with his family?

The court in *Wright v. Tatham* held that implied assertions[11] of this kind were hearsay. The rationale, as stated by Baron Parke, was as follows:

> "The conclusion at which I have arrived is, that proof of a particular fact which is not of itself a matter in issue, but which is relevant only as implying a statement or opinion of a third person on the matter in issue, is inadmissible in all cases where such a statement or opinion not on oath would be of itself inadmissible; and, therefore, in this case the letters which are offered only to prove the competence of the testator, that is the truth of the implied statements therein contained, were properly rejected, as the mere statement or opinion of the writer would certainly have been inadmissible."

This was the prevailing common law view, where the hearsay issue was recognized. But frequently, it was not recognized. Thus, two federal appellate cases involving facts virtually identical to those in the case at bar did not even discuss the hearsay issue, although the evidence admitted in them would have been objectionable hearsay under the common law view.

THE FEDERAL RULES OF EVIDENCE

The common law rule that implied assertions were subject to hearsay treatment was criticized by respected commentators for several reasons....

In a frequently cited article the following analysis appears:

> "But ought the hearsay rule be deemed applicable to evidence of conduct? As Mc-Cormick has observed, the problem 'has only once received any adequate discussion in any decided case,' *i.e.*, in *Wright v. Tatham*, already referred to. And even in that case the court did not pursue its inquiry beyond the point of concluding that evidence of an 'implied' assertion must necessarily be excluded wherever evidence of an 'express' assertion would be inadmissible. But as has been pointed out more than once (although I find no *judicial* recognition of the difference), the 'implied' assertion is, from the hearsay standpoint, not nearly as vulnerable as an express assertion of the fact which the evidence is offered to establish.

> "This is on the assumption that the conduct was 'nonassertive;' that the passers-by had their umbrellas up for the sake of keeping dry, not for the purpose of

---

11. The problem is the same whether the relevant assertion is implied from verbal expression, such as that of the betters in the instant case or the letter writers in *Wright*, or from conduct, as in the sea captain example.

telling anyone it was raining; that the truck driver started up for the sake of resuming his journey, not for the purpose of telling anyone that the light had changed; that the vicar wrote the letter to the testator for the purpose of settling the dispute with the latter, rather than with any idea of expressing his opinion of the testator's sanity. And in the typical 'conduct as hearsay' case this assumption will be quite justifiable.

"On this assumption, it is clear that evidence of conduct must be taken as freed from at least one of the hearsay dangers, *i.e.*, mendacity. A man does not lie to himself. Put otherwise, if in doing what he does a man has no intention of asserting the existence or non-existence of a fact, it would appear that the trustworthiness of evidence of this conduct is the same whether he is an egregious liar or a paragon of veracity. Accordingly, the lack of opportunity for cross-examination in relation to his veracity or lack of it, would seem to be of no substantial importance. Accordingly, the usual judicial disposition to equate the 'implied' to the 'express' assertion is very questionable."[16]

The drafters of the Federal Rules agreed with the criticisms of the common law rule that implied assertions should be treated as hearsay and expressly abolished it. They did this by providing that no oral or written expression was to be considered as hearsay, unless it was an "assertion" concerning the matter sought to be proved and that no nonverbal conduct should be considered as hearsay, unless it was intended to be an "assertion" concerning said matter.[18] ....

"Assertion" is not defined in the rules, but has the connotation of a forceful or positive declaration.

The Advisory Committee note concerning this problem states:

"The definition of 'statement' assumes importance because the term is used in the definition of hearsay in subdivision (c). *The effect of the definition of 'statement' is to exclude from the operation of the hearsay rule all evidence of conduct, verbal or nonverbal, not intended as an assertion. The key to the definition is that nothing is an assertion unless intended to be one.*

"It can scarcely be doubted that an assertion made in words is intended by the declarant to be an assertion. Hence verbal assertions readily fall into the category of 'statement.' Whether nonverbal conduct should be regarded as a statement for purposes of defining hearsay requires further consideration. Some nonverbal conduct, such as the act of pointing to identify a suspect in a lineup, is clearly the equivalent of words, assertive in nature, and to be regarded as a statement. Other nonverbal conduct, however, may be offered as evidence that the person acted as he did because of his belief in the existence of the condition sought to

---

16. Falknor, *supra* note 2, at 136. The context makes clear that the author would apply the same analysis "where the conduct, although 'verbal,' is relevant, not as tending to prove the truth of what was said, but circumstantially, that is, as manifesting a belief in the existence of the fact the evidence is offered to prove." *Id.* at 134.

18. *See* the sea captain illustration discussed, *supra*. In an unpublished ruling this court recently held admissible as non-hearsay the fact that a U.S. mining inspector ate his lunch in an area in a coal mine now alleged to have been unsafe, and that other inspectors who observed operations prior to a disastrous explosion issued no citations, when it would have been their duty to do so, if there had been safety violations. These non-assertive acts would have been hearsay under the rule of *Wright v. Tatham* but are not hearsay under Rule 801 of the Federal Rules of Evidence, because the inspectors did not intend to make assertions under the circumstances. *Boggs v. Blue Diamond Coal Company* (E.D.Ky. No. 77-69, Pikeville Division).

be proved, from which belief the existence of the condition may be inferred. This sequence is, arguably, in effect an assertion of the existence of the condition and hence properly includable within the hearsay concept. *See* Morgan, "Hearsay Dangers and the Application of the Hearsay Concept," 62 Harv.L.Rev. 177, 214, 217 (1948), and the elaboration in Finman, "Implied Assertions as Hearsay: Some Criticisms of the Uniform Rules of Evidence," 14 Stan.L.Rev. 682 (1962). Admittedly evidence of this character is untested with respect to the perception, memory, and narration (or their equivalents) of the actor, *but the Advisory Committee is of the view that these dangers are minimal in the absence of an intent to assert and do not justify the loss of the evidence on hearsay grounds.* No class of evidence is free of the possibility of fabrication, but the likelihood is less with nonverbal than with assertive verbal conduct. The situations giving rise to the nonverbal conduct are such as virtually to eliminate questions of sincerity. Motivation, the nature of the conduct, and the presence or absence of reliance will bear heavily upon the weight to be given the evidence. Falknor, "The 'Hear-Say' Rule as a 'See-Do' Rule: Evidence of Conduct," 33 Rocky Mt.L.Rev. 133 (1961). *Similar considerations govern nonassertive verbal conduct and verbal conduct which is assertive but offered as a basis for inferring something other than the matter asserted,* also excluded from the definition of hearsay by the language of subdivision (c)" (emphasis added).

This court, therefore, holds that, "Subdivision (a)[] of Rule 801 removes implied assertions from the definition of statement and consequently from the operation of the hearsay rule."

Applying the principles discussed above to the case at bar, this court holds that the utterances of the betters telephoning in their bets were nonassertive verbal conduct, offered as relevant for an implied assertion to be inferred from them, namely that bets could be placed at the premises being telephoned. The language is not an assertion on its face, and it is obvious these persons did not intend to make an assertion about the fact sought to be proved or anything else.[21]

As an implied assertion, the proffered evidence is expressly excluded from the operation of the hearsay rule by Rule 801 of the Federal Rules of Evidence, and the objection thereto must be overruled. An order to that effect has previously been entered.

United States v. Reynolds
715 F.2d 99 (3d Cir. 1983)

A. LEON HIGGINBOTHAM, Jr., Circuit Judge:

William Parran, defendant/appellant, and a co-defendant, Curtis Reynolds, were indicted by a federal Grand Jury in the Western District of Pennsylvania. Count One of the

---

21. A somewhat different type of analysis would be required by words non-assertive in form, but which under the circumstances might be intended as an assertion. For example, an inspector at an airport security station might run a metal detector over a passenger and say "go on through." In the absence of the inspector, would testimony of this event be objectionable hearsay, if offered for the proposition that the passenger did not have a gun on him at that time? Although Rule 801(a) does not seem to require a preliminary determination by the trial court whether verbal conduct is intended as an assertion, it is submitted that such a determination would be required in the example given. If an assertion were intended the evidence would be excluded. If not, it would be admissible. This result is implicit in the policy of the drafters of the Federal Rules of Evidence that the touchstone for hearsay is the intention to make an assertion.

three-count indictment charged that Parran and Reynolds, in violation of 18 U.S.C. § 371, conspired with each other to violate 18 U.S.C. § 1708 by possessing a Pennsylvania unemployment compensation check, knowing that the check had been stolen. It also charged that Parran and Reynolds conspired to violate 42 U.S.C. § 408(g) by using the social security number of the payee of the check, Stanford D. David, in an effort to cash the check. Counts Two and Three charged Parran and Reynolds with the substantive offenses alleged as the objects of the conspiracy in Count One....

Parran appeals these convictions, relying on several grounds.... We are persuaded by Parran on one issue, that the district court erred in admitting into evidence the testimony from a postal inspector as to the statement Reynolds allegedly made after his arrest. In that statement Reynolds allegedly said in the presence of the postal inspector and Parran, "I didn't tell them anything about you." Because we believe that, in the context of this case, co-defendant Reynolds' statement was prejudicial hearsay evidence, its admission in this joint trial for the purpose of proving Parran's conspiratorial endeavor, as well as the substantive offenses charged, constitutes reversible error....

II.

....

Out-of-court statements are not always hearsay. Thus, the Federal Rules of Evidence explain that "[i]f the significance of an offered statement lies solely in the fact that it was made, no issue is raised as to the truth of anything asserted, and the statement is not hearsay." Fed.R.Evid. 801(c) advisory committee note....

Assume, for example, that the very fact in controversy was whether there was speech. The witness' testimony as to "the fact of [Reynolds' statement, "I didn't tell them anything about you"] rather than the content of the statement permits the inference [that there was speech] and that testimony involves no problem of the statement's ambiguity, or of sincerity, memory, or perception" of the declarant. The reason is that it is the witness' personal experience that is the focus of the inquiry. Similarly, testimony recounting the above statement would qualify as non-hearsay if offered on the issue as to whether the declarant was capable of speaking English. Whether the content of the declarant's statement is true is irrelevant to the statement's probative value in the two examples above because it is offered for the fact that it was said. The statement clearly would be non-hearsay.

III.

In the case before us the government argues that Reynolds' statement implicating Parran was not offered for the truth of the matter asserted. The government suggests that the statement, irrespective of its truth, is probative of defendant's guilt. The government, however, views what Reynolds asserted in a very narrow manner. Indeed, it suggests that the only assertion contained in Reynolds' statement is its express assertion that Reynolds had not said anything to the arresting officers about Parran. Because the government did not offer Reynolds' statement into evidence to prove he had not said anything about Parran, at the time of Reynolds' arrest, the government concludes that the statement cannot possibly be hearsay.

This argument ignores what legal commentators have expressly recognized and what the courts have implicitly recognized. That is, statements containing express assertions may also contain implied assertions qualifying as hearsay and susceptible to hearsay objections. This situation arises when the matter which the declarant intends to assert is different from the matter to be proved, but the matter asserted, if true, is circumstantial evidence of the matter to be proved. In this situation too, the statement is subject to a hearsay objection.

D. Louisell & C. Mueller, Federal Evidence 94 n. 84 (1980).

In the instant case the government seeks to use Reynolds' statement, "I didn't tell them anything about you," as circumstantial evidence "for the purpose of establishing the existence of a conspiracy between the two defendants, as well as their joint participation in the substantive offenses charged in Counts Two and Three of the indictment." The government argues that "[t]he significance of the statement was that it was made."

Reynolds' statement is, however, ambiguous and susceptible to different interpretations. As the government uses it, the statement's probative value depends on the truth of an assumed fact it implies. Unless the trier assumes that the statement implies that Reynolds did not tell the postal inspectors that Parran was involved in the conspiracy to defraud, even though Parran was in fact involved, the statement carries no probative weight for the government's case. For if the trier assumes that the statement implied that Reynolds did not tell the postal inspectors that Parran was involved because there was nothing to tell, the statement has no relevance to the government's case. Its only relevance to the government's case is tied to an assumed fact of petitioner's guilt that the government argues the utterance proves. Thus, depending on the interpretation given the content of Reynolds' statement, it is either probative or not. Consequently, we believe that, as the government uses it, the statement's relevance goes well beyond the fact that it was uttered. It is not merely intended to prove that Reynolds could speak, or that he could speak in English, or even that he directed a statement toward Parran. Instead, the government offers it to prove the truth of the assumed fact of defendant's guilt implied by its content.

The legal commentators referred to above would regard Reynolds' statement as inadmissible hearsay.... Reynolds' statement in this case was not offered for the purpose of proving its express meaning—that Reynolds did not say anything about Parran. Rather it was offered for the implied assertion that Parran was involved in the crimes for which the two were charged and tried. Therefore, we hold that the statement here ... constitutes hearsay because it was introduced to prove its implied assertion of Parran's guilt....

Mosley v. State
141 S.W.3d 816 (Tex. 2004)

Opinion by Justice ROSS.

Walter Mosley, Jr., was found guilty by a jury of aggravated sexual assault on his three-year-old step-granddaughter.[1] The jury assessed his punishment at twenty-six years' imprisonment....

In this case, Christy McCoy, Jane's mother, testified as the outcry witness. She testified that Mosley is married to her mother and that Jane spent a lot of time at their house....

Mosley contends McCoy's testimony concerning a statement attributed to her mother was hearsay and should have been excluded. The testimony came during the following exchange:

Q Okay. After you took [Jane] to the bedroom, looked at her, saw that her private area was a little bit red, what did you do?

---

1. We refer to the step-granddaughter by the pseudonym Jane Doe, which was used in the indictment.

A I called my mother. I called my mother and told her what [Jane] had just told me and my mom was like—.

[Defense Counsel]: Your Honor, I would object to any testimony—.

THE COURT: I'm going to sustain.

[Defense Counsel]: That'd be hearsay.

[Prosecutor]: Your Honor, if I could, we're not offering it for the truth of the matter, sir. It was to show the state of mind.

[Defense Counsel]: We still object, Your Honor. That's—that has no indication of state of mind.

. . . .

[Prosecutor]: The evidence is going to be that she called to tell her mother what [Jane] told her and her response was, Well, I can't watch them all the time, which suggests that she knew they were alone together and she knew what was happening. It's not being offered for the truth of the matter, sir.

[Defense Counsel]: Judge, our client's wife's state of mind has nothing to do with this.

THE COURT: Well, no, it's not a state of mind.

[Prosecutor]: It's not hearsay. I'm not offering it for the truth of the matter asserted.

. . . .

THE COURT: I'm going to overrule the objection.

. . . .

Q . . . . So you called your mother and you told her what [Jane] just said to you. What was her response?

A Well, I can't watch them all the time.

Q Those were her exact words?

A Those are exact words.

. . . .

Hearsay is defined by the Rules of Evidence as a statement, other than one made by the declarant while testifying at the trial, offered into evidence to prove the truth of the matter asserted. TEX.R. EVID. 801(d). "Matter asserted" includes any matter explicitly asserted, and any matter implied by a statement, if the probative value of the statement as offered flows from the declarant's belief as to the matter. TEX.R. EVID. 801(c). The State contends the statement, "Well, I can't watch them all the time," was not offered for the truth of the declarant's ability to watch Mosley and Jane all the time, and was, therefore, not hearsay. The State would be correct if we were applying federal rules. See *United States v. Ybarra*, 70 F.3d 362, 366 n. 1 (5th Cir. 1995) (finding testimony that declarant said Ybarra would not come home as long as police were there was offered to prove Ybarra lived at house; therefore, statement was not offered to prove truth of matter asserted and, by definition, was not hearsay).

The Rules of Evidence on hearsay are much broader than the federal rules. Relevant to this case is the absence of a definition for "matter asserted" in the federal rules. In Texas, "truth of the matter asserted" includes any matter explicitly asserted, but also includes within hearsay any matter implied by a statement, if the probative value of the statement as offered flows from the declarant's belief as to the matter. *See* TEX.R. EVID. 801(c). Therefore, the implication of the out-of-court statement is a "matter asserted" and is inadmissible hearsay if the statement is offered for the implication....

We hold that McCoy's testimony concerning her mother's statement was hearsay. Rule of Evidence 801(c) treats the implication of the out-of-court statement as a "matter asserted" and hearsay if offered for the implication. As illustrated by the State during trial, the statement was offered for the implication that McCoy's mother knew Mosley and Jane were alone together and that she knew Jane was being sexually assaulted. This is an implied "matter asserted" under the Rules of Evidence and was, therefore, hearsay. The trial court erred in overruling Mosley's objection....

United States v. Snow
517 F.2d 441 (7th Cir. 1975)

SNEED, Circuit Judge:

[In an earlier portion of the opinion, excerpted above, the court held that the hearsay rule did not bar admission of a piece of tape — with the defendant's name on it — affixed to a briefcase containing an unregistered firearm. The court's rationale in the earlier portion of the opinion was that the tape was a "mechanical trace," or identifying mark, and was thus relevant for some reason other than to prove the truth of the matter asserted. The court then proceeded to set forth a second reason why the hearsay rule did not prevent the tape from being admitted into evidence.]

The firmness with which we are able to assert that under Wigmore's analysis the name tape before us is circumstantial evidence is strengthened when the cases are reviewed which he collected to illustrate that tags, signs, etc. are "mechanical traces." These cases include instances in which the uniform of the driver of a vehicle was admissible to prove the identity of his employer, or the name on a wagon or truck to prove ownership of the vehicle, the name on a dog collar to prove ownership of dog, the wearing of a uniform to prove employment by the persons whose name appears on the uniform, and lettering on a locomotive to prove its ownership.

Perhaps the most compelling evidence of Wigmore's view is his comment on *People v. Hill*, 198 N.Y. 64 (1910). An issue in *Hill* was the admissibility of a bunch of keys with a name tag bearing the defendant's name found near the place where the homicide occurred for which the defendant was being tried. The New York Court of Appeals expressed some doubt about the admissibility of the keys and tag although the court did not indicate that its doubt rested in any way upon the assumed hearsay character of the tag. Wigmore, in a note, observed:

> ... [T]his case shows how different a man the judge is when reasoning about his own affairs at home and reasoning in the judicial straitjacket; suppose he had forbidden a certain young man to court his daughter and then one morning found on the parlor floor by the sofa a bunch of keys with the tabooed young man's name; would he hold that there was some doubt whether the evidence was properly admitted?

The present antiquarian flavor of the example Wigmore chose to demonstrate his belief that the name tag was admissible should not detract from the force of his observation. The rules of evidence since Wigmore's time have changed much less than the practices of courtship.

Treating the name tape as circumstantial evidence, whether viewed as part of the case or separate and apart from the case, permits its admissibility to be governed initially by the standard of relevancy. To meet this standard it is only necessary to show that the name tape renders the inference that the appellant owned the case more probable than it would be without the name tape. Our review of the trial transcript convinces us that the careful foundation built by the prosecution at the insistence of the trial judge enabled the name tape to meet this test.

We are aware, as was the trial court, that the inference sought to be drawn by the prosecution from the name tape might be false. Someone other than the defendant may have placed his name on a case that never belonged to him and into which they placed the automatic weapon. Wigmore teaches, however, that all circumstantial evidence is subject to being explained away. 1 Wigmore, § 148 (3rd ed. 1940). Once the standard of relevancy is met, the existence of the possibility of explaining it away can not be employed to deny admission. The party seeking to avoid the inference for which the evidence is offered must attempt the explanation and it is for the fact finder to determine whether he succeeds. In this case the jury found the appellant's explanation unconvincing. There exists no reason to overturn their conclusion.

The soundness of our view that evidence such as the name tag here before us is not hearsay very likely would be beyond question had the words appearing on the tape been stamped on the case. The distinction between a named stamped and printed on an affixed tape, however, goes only to the probative force of an offered explanation. The circumstantial character of the evidence before us is underscored, moreover, when it is pointed out that had clothing or other articles bearing Bill Snow's name been found in the case their admissibility very likely would not have been disputed....

United States v. Serrano

434 F.3d 1003 (7th Cir. 2006)

TERENCE T. EVANS, Circuit Judge.

Roberto Serrano, also known as Eddie Roncone, was tried and convicted for aiding and abetting distribution of cocaine in violation of 21 U.S.C. § 841(a)(1) and 18 U.S.C. § 2. In this appeal he challenges certain evidence introduced at his trial....

In February 2003, Fort Wayne, Indiana, undercover police officer Steven Espinoza purchased a quarter-ounce of cocaine from one Jose Hernandez at a residence, 4506 Spatz Avenue in Fort Wayne. The officer subsequently arranged to make a larger buy of one and a half kilograms for some $33,000.

On April 4, 2003, Espinoza and another undercover officer met Hernandez at a prearranged location, then proceeded to the 4506 Spatz Avenue residence. There were four other people in the house, one of whom was Serrano. Once inside, Hernandez placed a one-kilo brick of cocaine on the dining room table. Espinoza asked for the rest of it. According to Espinoza's testimony at trial, at that point Serrano got up from a couch in the adjoining room and appeared in the dining room doorway. Hernandez asked Serrano in Spanish where the other half-kilo was. Serrano twice pointed to a cabinet and said the cocaine was "in the corner." Hernandez then retrieved another half-kilo from inside the cabinet and handed it to Espinoza.

After the deal was complete, other officers entered, detained the suspects, and procured a search warrant. In Serrano's wallet officers found an Indiana driver's license with Serrano's picture, the name Eddie Roncone, and the address 4506 Spatz Avenue. They also found a state-issued ID card with Serrano's picture, the name Eddie Roncone, and an address of 3317 Evans Street in Fort Wayne. In a search of the house, police found two handguns, a large bag of marijuana, scales, and materials used to package and wrap cocaine; in the basement they found a cocaine press and chemicals used for cutting the drug.

After being taken to the police station and waiving his right to counsel, Serrano told the officer who interviewed him that he lived at the Spatz Avenue address but had never been into the basement. Later, at his trial, Serrano testified that he had "previously lived at Spatz," but that at the time of the bust he was living at 547 East Pettit.

At trial, in addition to Serrano's driver's license, state ID, and other exhibits, the government introduced automobile insurance cards, insurance declarations, and related correspondence, all bearing the name Eddie Roncone and the address 4506 Spatz Avenue. Five of these documents were found inside the house during the search; the other three came out of the trash which officers had pulled from the alley behind the house in the days before the April 4 drug buy and arrest.

Serrano's attorney objected on the grounds that the documents were hearsay, but the judge (The Honorable Theresa L. Springmann) allowed the jury to see them. Serrano now appeals that ruling....

Hearsay is a statement, other than one made by the declarant while testifying, that is "offer[ed] in evidence to prove the truth of the matter asserted." Fed.R.Evid. 801(c). Because the insurance documents carry a name and address, Serrano contends they were offered for their "assertion" that "Eddie Roncone" lived at 4506 Spatz Avenue. Since no one from the insurance company testified at trial, and since the documents apparently are not covered by any exception to the hearsay bar, Serrano concludes they were inadmissible.

Serrano was convicted under the aiding and abetting statute, 18 U.S.C. § 2. The crime of aiding and abetting requires knowledge of the illegal activity that is being aided and abetted, a desire to help it succeed, and some act of helping. Serrano doesn't deny he was present at the drug transaction or that he helped it along by indicating where some of the cocaine was kept. But he maintains that unless the government showed he was more than a visitor to the Spatz Avenue address, the jury could not have found that he had knowledge of and intent to participate in the drug enterprise being conducted there. "The residency issue was essentially," he says, his "only defense."

Many courts, including ours, have held that merchandise receipts, utility bills, and similar documents are not hearsay when they are offered as circumstantial evidence to link a defendant to a particular place, to other defendants, or to an illegal item.

In such cases, the documents are not introduced for the truth of the matters they assert — for example, that the defendant rented a car, bought a television, or used 500 kilowatt hours of electricity. Rather, the documents are "introduced for the inferences that may be drawn circumstantially from [their] existence or from where [they are] found, regardless of whether the assertions contained therein are true or not." *McIntyre*, 997 F.2d at 702 n.16. *See also* Fed. R. Evid. 801 Advisory Committee Notes to 1972 Proposed Rules (noting that the rule excludes from the definition of hearsay "verbal conduct which is assertive but offered as a basis for inferring something other than the matter asserted").

Applying this reasoning to our case, the insurance documents were probative of a connection between Serrano and the house where he was observed assisting the commission of a cocaine-trafficking crime. The government's case did not depend on proving that on

April 4, 2003, Serrano was legally domiciled at 4506 Spatz Avenue, as opposed to the address on his state ID, or the address he gave at trial. Rather, the government had to show that Serrano was more than someone who had just stopped by to borrow a lawnmower, then unwittingly found himself helping to facilitate a drug sale. Serrano does not maintain that the police planted evidence or that someone else's refuse was intermingled with the garbage behind 4506 Spatz Avenue. Thus, the insurance documents were admissible for the inference that could be drawn from where they were found. When someone's important personal papers turn up inside a house or in the trash right outside, it is reasonable to believe, in the absence of some believable alternative explanation, that their owner is affiliated in some way with the premises.

Because they contained written information about his name and address, Serrano argues that the insurance documents "could have come from anywhere and still served the government's purpose." But that's not so. Imagine that, rather than searching the house or its trash, the police had instead combed through the city landfill, found the same documents, and sought to use them to show that Roncone/Serrano lived at or was somehow connected to 4506 Spatz Avenue. That *would* be hearsay; the documents would lose their inferential value because they weren't found anywhere near the scene of a crime.

Finally, Serrano asserts that had the insurance documents "contained nothing more than the identifying name they would have been admissible." But the fact they also contained an address, he believes, gave them "evidentiary significance totally independent of their physical location," and meant that "the jury would take with it when it retired to deliberate eight documents bolstering the government's case and attacking Mr. Serrano's only defense." We don't agree that the fact the documents bore an address made them hearsay. Judge Springmann allowed them with the understanding the government was using them only to show Serrano was "connected" to the house. Had Serrano's trial counsel wanted the judge to lecture the jury about the fine points of hearsay, he could have asked for a limiting instruction on the evidence, but he did not.

It should also be noted that it was Serrano's trial counsel, not the government, who drew attention to the documents during closing arguments, in the course of trying to explain why his client maintained multiple addresses. Indeed, Serrano's trial counsel earlier had introduced utility bills in an attempt to show that Serrano really lived at 547 East Pettit. In contrast to the circumstantial value of the insurance documents, trying to use the utility bills in this way clearly *was* hearsay....

Notes and Questions

1. Which opinion, *Zenni* or *Reynolds*, is more consistent with the intent expressed by the drafters of Rule 801? Assuming that it is *Zenni* (which states the majority view), is the federal approach superior or inferior to the Texas approach as set forth in *Mosley*? Which approach is most consistent with the policies that underlie the hearsay rule?

2. In *United States v. Lopez-Moreno*, 420 F.3d 420 (5th Cir. 2005), the defendant was on trial on charges of transporting an undocumented alien in his van. An element of the crime is that the person the defendant was transporting was in the United States illegally. To prove this element of the offense, the government, over a hearsay objection, offered into evidence a copy of a Mexican voter identification card that one of the passengers had on him at the time that the van was stopped by authorities. The court held that "[t]he photocopy of the voter identification card cannot be characterized as hearsay because it is not, and does not contain, an assertion, or nonverbal conduct intended to be an asser-

tion, offered to prove the truth of the matter asserted." *Id.* at 436. Is the holding correct, and if so, why?

3. In *United States v. Hensel*, 699 F.2d 18 (1st Cir. 1983), part of the government's case involved connecting the defendant to a particular place:

> Hensel claims that the trial court erred in admitting into evidence a glass found at the Turkey Cove property. The glass had on it the word "Dink," Hensel's nickname, and tended to tie Hensel to those at Turkey Cove. As admitted to show this relation, Hensel states, the glass was hearsay....
>
> The fact that the word "Dink" appears on the glass does not itself make the glass hearsay evidence, for no assertion intended by the act of putting the word on the glass was relevant to the chain of inferences the government wished the jury to draw. The jury was not asked to infer anything about the person who put the name on the glass, who for all we know or care works in a factory that turns out "name" glasses by the score. Rather, the jury was asked to infer that Dink Hensel was likely to have possessed a glass with the name "Dink" on it and that he, or someone he knew, placed it in the house at Turkey Cove. The first of these inferences is merely circumstantial. There is no obvious way it depends upon the statement or state of mind of any out-of-court declarant.
>
> The second of these inferences could involve hearsay only if one accepts a highly complex line of argument: Hensel might claim that he would like to cross-examine the "unknown" person who brought the glass to Turkey Cove on the ground that this out-of-court person's state of mind is relevant to the validity of the second inference. In order to invoke the hearsay rule, Hensel would have to argue that this individual's "nonverbal conduct" in placing the glass in the house was "intended [by him] as an assertion," Fed.R.Evid. 801(a)(2), that "Hensel was here." Even were one to make the heroic assumption that this was Hensel's argument, it fails. It fails because Hensel did not preliminarily show the district judge that placing the glass in the house was intended as an "assertion" (*e.g.*, that it was designed to "frame" Hensel). Yet, the Federal Rules of Evidence "place the burden [of proving such an assertive intent] upon the party claiming that the intention existed." Fed.R.Evid. 801 Advisory Committee note (a). Hence, the glass was not shown to be hearsay and it was properly admitted.

Id. at 31.

4. In the second part of the *Snow* opinion, the court writes that using "the name on a wagon or truck to prove ownership of the vehicle" is not a hearsay use of the evidence. How is that so? When a company puts its name on the side of its vehicle, what, exactly, is it asserting? What was asserted on the tape in *Snow*? On the glass in *Hensel*?

5. The presumption under the federal rules of evidence is that conduct is *not* intended to be assertive:

> When evidence of conduct is offered on the theory that it is not a statement, and hence not hearsay, a preliminary determination will be required to determine whether an assertion is intended. The rule is so worded as to place the burden upon the party claiming that the intention existed; ambiguous and doubtful cases will be resolved against him and in favor of admissibility.

Advisory Committee Note to Rule 801(a).

Of what relevance is that to the holdings in *Snow, Hensel,* and *Zenni?*

6. If one accepts the second part of the *Snow* opinion, is there much left to the hearsay rule? Are there ways in which one can distinguish cases such as *Snow* on the one hand from *Hensel* and *Serrano* on the other? For criticism of the *Snow* opinion, *see* Michael Fenner, *Law Professor Reveals Shocking Truth About Hearsay,* 62 UMKC L. Rev. 1, 16 & n. 79 (1993).

7. An element of numerous federal offenses is that there is movement of prohibited items, such as guns or child pornography, in interstate or foreign commerce. Under *Snow,* could the government offer into evidence the inscription on a product indicating that it was made in a particular state or country to prove its movement in interstate commerce? *See United States v. Alvarez,* 972 F.2d 1000, 1004 (9th Cir. 1992) (so holding), *overruled on other grounds, Kawashima v. Mukasi,* 530 F.3d 1111, 1116 (9th Cir. 2008). *Accord United States v. Brown,* 2009 WL 2090193, at *10–*11 (S.D. Ind. July 13, 2009).

———————

As the cases in this section of Chapter 7 demonstrate, since the codification of the federal rules of evidence, courts have struggled with the concept of an "intention to assert" embodied in the definition of hearsay. Armed with the benefit of over three decades of judicial experience with the existing definition of hearsay, should policymakers in the United States reconsider and perhaps adjust the definition of hearsay to address the grey areas represented by these cases?

Although there has been no serious effort to review and revise the definition of hearsay in the United States, policymakers in the United Kingdom—armed with analogous judicial experience using the common law definition of hearsay—more recently conducted an exhaustive review and revision of the definition of hearsay. What follows is an excerpt from a 1997 report by the Law Commission of the United Kingdom on the subject, followed by the text of the 2003 Act of Parliament enacting the recommended definition into law.

After reading the report and the 2003 Act, apply the United Kingdom's definition of hearsay to the cases in this section. Does the United Kingdom's definition provide a more clear-cut answer to the hearsay issues raised in the cases than does the definition set forth in Rule 801? Which definition is more likely across the run of cases to produce answers that are consistent with the policies underlying the rule against hearsay?

The Law Commission of the United Kingdom, Report No. 245

Evidence in Criminal Proceedings: Hearsay and Related Topics,
¶¶ 7.2–7.40 (1997)

There are two basic ways of proving a fact in issue. First, it may be proved by proving some other fact which renders it more likely to be true; the other fact is directly probative of the fact to be proved. Second, it may be proved by means of a person's *assertion* that it is true. The hearsay rule applies only to the latter form of proof....

Often it will be clear whether a person's words or conduct are adduced as proof of a fact on the basis that they are directly probative of it ... or on the basis that they amount to an assertion of it. But it is sometimes debatable which of these is the case.

Borderline Cases

"Implied assertions"

In *Wright v. Doe d Tatham,* for example, the issue was whether letters written to a man in which the writers appeared to assume the sanity of the recipient could be evidence of his sanity. Parke B held that the letters were hearsay because they were not directly probative of the fact to be proved, but only an assertion of it. He explained his decision with a now notorious illustration of a sea-captain who boards a ship, from which fact a court might be tempted to infer that the ship was sea-worthy. Parke B said the hearsay rule would apply to such conduct, and evidence of it would be inadmissible.

Parke B's approach was approved by a bare majority of the House of Lords in *Kearley*. The issue was whether, on a charge of possessing drugs with intent to supply, a prosecutor could rely on evidence by the police that they had been to the home of the defendant when he was not there, and had there received telephone and personal calls from people (who were not called as witnesses) asking about drugs that the defendant had for sale. It was held that the hearsay rule applies where it is sought to draw an inference of fact from words or conduct which are intended to be assertive of some other fact, or are not intended to be assertive at all....

Evidence of the kind that was excluded in *Wright* and *Kearley* is usually referred to as an *implied assertion*....

[T]he word "implied" here is used in an unusual sense. Normally it refers to a statement which is not expressly spoken or written but is intended to be understood from what is said or done. But where there *is* an assertion of the fact to be proved, it is immaterial whether that assertion is express or (in the ordinary sense) implied. An assertion of a fact is no less of an assertion because it is implicit in an express assertion of a different fact, or because it takes the form of non-verbal conduct such as a gesture. An assertion can therefore be implied (in the ordinary sense) without being what is described in the context of hearsay as an "implied assertion".

.... We agree that all assertions should be caught by the rule if they are adduced as evidence of the fact asserted, irrespective of whether they are express or implied. But this is not the issue, and it is only the use of the expression "implied assertions" that suggests it is. The question is whether, in a case such as *Wright* or *Kearley*, there is an assertion at all.

Negative assertions

Closely connected to the problem of "implied assertions" is that of *negative* assertions. For the purposes of the hearsay rule it is obviously immaterial whether the fact to be proved is positive or negative, provided that an assertion of the fact is adduced as evidence of its truth. The difficulty arises where it is debatable whether the evidence of a negative fact is an assertion of it, or a fact suggesting in some other way that it is true.

Suppose, for example, that the fact to be proved is the fact that a particular event did not occur. The fact-finders may be invited to reason that, if it had occurred, its occurrence would have been recorded; and that, since its occurrence was not recorded, it did not occur. But is the non-recording of the event an *assertion* that it did not occur, or is it directly probative? In *Shone* the evidence of a stock clerk and a sales manager that workers would have made entries on record cards if certain items had been lawfully disposed of, that there were no such entries, and that those items must therefore have been stolen, was held not to be hearsay but direct evidence of that fact. It seems that, if an inference is drawn from what a document says, the document is hearsay; but if an inference is drawn from what it does *not* say (or from the fact that no document exists), that is direct evidence....

Identification evidence

Yet another difficult case is that in which it is sought to adduce an utterance or writing as evidence of identification. The person identified may be the very person who is alleged to have spoken or written the words relied upon, or some other person. In either case it may be doubtful whether the words in question are an assertion of that person's identity, or are directly probative of it.

In *Rice* the Crown adduced a used airline ticket to Manchester, bearing the names "Rice and Moore", in support of the evidence of a co-defendant named Hoather that he had flown to Manchester with Rice at about the time of the flight to which the ticket related, and that Rice had booked their ticket. The Court of Appeal doubted that the ticket could be admissible as evidence that the *booking* had been made by a person called Rice: for that purpose it was hearsay. But it was held to be permissible for the jury to infer that the ticket had been *used* by someone called Rice, because of

> The balance of probability recognised by common sense and common knowledge that an air ticket which has been used on a flight and which has a name upon it has more likely than not been used by a man of that name ...

The distinction between these two uses of the ticket seems artificial: it was no more likely that the ticket had been *used* by someone called Rice than that it had been *issued* to someone of that name. In our view it would have been better to treat the ticket as direct evidence, and admissible, on the latter issue as well as the former.

Rice was considered, and a similar conclusion reached, in *Lydon*. A gun, allegedly used in a robbery, had been found by the side off a road which would have been used by the getaway car. Nearby were found two rolled-up pieces of paper bearing the words "Sean rules." The appellant's first name was Sean. It was held that this was not hearsay but direct evidence.

> The inference that the jury could draw from the words written on the piece of paper is that the paper had been in the possession of someone who wished to write "Sean rules", and that person would presumably either be named Sean himself or at least be associated with such a person, and thus it creates an inferential link with the appellant.

It would have made no difference to the evidence's admissibility, but only to its weight, if the pieces of paper had borne the appellant's name in full. They were not so much an *assertion* by the writer (that his name was Sean) as something that a person *not* named Sean (and not associated with such a person) would be unlikely to write.

Our provisional proposal: intention to assert

These borderline cases are not precisely analogous to one another. But they appear to have at least one feature in common, and one which is absent in the case of statements to which the hearsay rule *clearly* applies. This common feature is the fact that, while the words or conduct relied upon *may in fact* cause others to draw certain inferences, it is not the *intention* of the person whose words or conduct are in question that they should have that effect....

We therefore take the view that a person's words or conduct should not be regarded as asserting a fact, and therefore should not be caught by the hearsay rule if adduced as evidence of that fact, unless that person *intends* to assert that fact....

Modification of the provisional proposal

....

What is an intention to assert?

ASSERTING A FACT AND CAUSING ANOTHER TO BELIEVE IT

As more than one respondent pointed out, the idea of an "intention to assert" is ambiguous. The crucial question, we have argued, is whether the person whose words or conduct are in question intended to convey the impression that the fact which it is now sought to infer from those words or that conduct was true. Only if that person did not intend to convey that impression can it safely be assumed that he or she was not deliberately seeking to mislead. It follows that what is crucial is not the way in which that person happened to express himself or herself, but the impression that his or her words or conduct were intended to convey.

Thus evidence that a caller said "Can I have my usual stuff?" would be admissible to prove that the accused did habitually supply unlawful drugs; but this is not because the caller's *words* do not amount to an assertion. It is because the caller's intention is not to give anyone the impression that the person addressed is a drug-dealer, but simply to request drugs. The caller intends the words to be heard only by a person whom the caller believes to be a drug-dealer: obviously the caller has no wish to convince that person, or anyone else, that that person *is* a drug-dealer.

From this point of view it makes no difference that the caller says "The stuff you sold me last week was bad". The inference to be drawn from these words is essentially the same as in the case of the words "Can I have my usual stuff?" — namely that the person whom the caller intends to address is in the habit of supplying drugs to the caller. On its face, admittedly, this is an express assertion that the person addressed sold drugs to the caller last week; and, since the caller obviously intends to say exactly what he or she does say, in one sense the caller intends to assert that fact. But it is not the caller's intention to cause the person addressed to infer that that fact is true, since he or she already knows it. In *that* sense there is no intention to assert.

The point may be further illustrated by reference to *Teper*. The defendant was charged with arson of his own shop. A woman had been heard to shout to a passing motorist "Your place burning and you going away from the fire". If the woman's intention were to draw the attention of bystanders to the fact that Teper was leaving the scene, her words would be hearsay, since she might have been trying to mislead the bystanders. If, however, she was intending *only* to indicate to the motorist that she knew he was Teper, she could not be seeking to *mislead* anyone about who he was. If he was Teper, he knew he was; and if he was not, she could not hope to convince him that he was. She might still be *asserting* that he was Teper, but she would not be intending to *persuade* anyone of this....

This reasoning suggests that the crucial question should be, not whether the maker of the statement appears to have intended to *assert* the fact which the statement is adduced to prove, but whether he or she appears to have intended to *cause another person to believe* that fact.

CAUSING A PERSON TO ACT ON THE BASIS THAT A FACT IS TRUE

However, we think it would be going too far to say that a statement should *never* fall within the hearsay rule unless it appears to have been intended to cause another to believe the fact stated. We have argued that a statement should be regarded as hearsay if it seems possible that it may have been deliberately fabricated; and there may be cases where a statement is deliberately fabricated although it is not intended that another person should believe it to be true. This may be so if it is intended that another person, while not necessarily *believing* the fact stated, should *act on the basis that it is true*.

Suppose, for example, that A's job involves reimbursing his colleagues for their travelling expenses. It is sought to prove that his colleague B travelled to Glasgow on a particular date, by adducing her claim form in which she stated that she had done so. We believe that that evidence should fall within the hearsay rule, because the claim might be fabricated. But if it were necessary, in order to bring a statement within the hearsay rule, to show that it was made with the intention of causing a person to *believe* it, it might be argued that B's claim is made with no such intention. It may be that, when a claim is submitted to A, all he is required to do is to check that it complies with the rules laid down for such claims; and if it does, he automatically pays it. If B tells him she has been to Glasgow on business, he will pay for that journey. He will not consider whether he *believes* that B has been to Glasgow, and it is probably of no concern to B whether he believes it or not. But she does intend that he should act on the basis that it is true; and we believe that this should be sufficient to bring her statement within the hearsay rule.

CAUSING A MACHINE TO OPERATE

Similarly, we believe that a statement should fall within the hearsay rule in any case where it is made with the intention that some action should be taken on the basis that the fact stated is true—even if the taking of that action involves no human intervention, but only the operation of a machine. Suppose, for example, that the processing of B's expenses claim is carried out not by A but by a computer system, which has been programmed to print a cheque for the appropriate amount if the information provided by the claimant appears to meet the specified criteria. Clearly the risk of fabrication is just as great as if the information were given to a human, and it would be arbitrary to apply different rules to the two cases....

Criminal Justice Act 2003
c. 44, § 115 United Kingdom

....

(3) A matter stated is one to which this Chapter applies if (and only if) the purpose, or one of the purposes, of the person making the statement appears to the court to have been—

(a) to cause another person to believe the matter, or

(b) to cause another person to act or a machine to operate on the basis that the matter is as stated.

....

E. Statements That Are "Not Hearsay"

The materials that you have examined thus far have explored statements that are not subject to exclusion under the hearsay rule because they fall outside the definition set forth in Rule 801(c), either because they are not a "statement" as that phrase is defined in Rule 801(a), or because they are not offered "to prove the truth of the matter asserted in the statement" under Rule 801(c)(2).

However, even though something falls within the literal definition of hearsay set forth in Rule 801(c), it may nonetheless be deemed "not hearsay." Rule 801(d) takes two categories of statements—prior statements by a witness (Rule 801(d)(1)) and statements of an opposing party (Rule 801(d)(2))—which in turn are divided, respectively, into three and five subcategories, and declares them to be "not hearsay," even though they are "statements" within the meaning of Rule 801(a) and even though they are offered "to prove the truth of the matter asserted."

The materials that follow explore in detail each of the sub-categories of Rules 801(d)(1) and 801(d)(2).

1. Prior Statements by a Witness

Rule 801(d)(1) defines as "not hearsay" three types of prior statements by a witness:

(d) **Statements That Are Not Hearsay.** A statement that meets the following conditions is not hearsay:

  (1) *A Declarant-Witness's Prior Statement.* The declarant testifies and is subject to cross-examination about a prior statement, and the statement:

    (A) is inconsistent with the declarant's testimony and was given under penalty of perjury at a trial, hearing, or other proceeding or in a deposition;

    (B) is consistent with the declarant's testimony and is offered to rebut an express or implied charge that the declarant recently fabricated it or acted from a recent improper influence or motive in so testifying; or

    (C) identifies a person as someone the declarant perceived earlier.

A common requirement for invoking each of the three subcategories of Rule 801(d)(1) is that the "declarant testifies and is subject to cross-examination about a prior statement." In other ways, however, the provisions differ substantially from one another. Rule 801(d)(1)(A) paves the way for admitting the declarant's "inconsistent" statements — not merely to impeach the witness' credibility but also as substantive proof of the matters contained within those statements — but only if they were made in certain types of proceedings. Rule 801(d)(1)(B) provides for the admission of a declarant's prior "consistent" statements without regard to the setting in which those prior statements were made, but only when offered "to rebut an express or implied charge that the declarant recently fabricated it or acted from a recent improper influence or motive in so testifying." Finally, Rule 801(d)(1)(C) provides for the admission of a declarant's prior statement identifying a person after "perceive[ing]" that person, without regard to the setting in which the prior identification took place and without regard to whether the statement is consistent or inconsistent with the declarant's testimony at trial.

The materials that follow explore the separate and common requirements of each of the subcategories of Rule 801(d)(1), as well as the rationales for those requirements.

Problem 7-13: Blowing Hot and Cold Revisited

Recall the facts of the introductory hypothetical in this chapter, in which Wanda witnessed a fight between Bob and Tom. In which of the following scenarios could the prosecution overcome a hearsay objection through resort to Rule 801(d)(1)(A)?

1. At trial, the prosecution calls Wanda as a witness who, to its surprise, testifies that "Tom struck the first blow." In response, the prosecution seeks to call a police officer who interviewed Wanda right after the fight took place, who if permitted would testify that Wanda said to him "Bob struck the first blow."

2. At trial, the prosecution calls Wanda as a witness who, to its surprise, testifies that "Tom struck the first blow." In response, the prosecution seeks to call

a member of the prosecutor's office who was present during Wanda's testimony before the grand jury, who if permitted would testify that Wanda testified that "Bob struck the first blow."

3. At trial, the prosecution calls Wanda as a witness who, to its surprise, testifies that she cannot remember what happened. In response, the prosecution seeks to call a member of the prosecutor's office who was present during Wanda's testimony before the grand jury, who if permitted would testify that Wanda testified that "Bob struck the first blow."

4. How, if at all, would your answer differ if you were instead applying the Montana version of Rule 801(d)(1)(A), excerpted below?

United States v. Dietrich
854 F.2d 1056 (7th Cir. 1988)

FLAUM, Circuit Judge.

John Dietrich was convicted of conspiring to sell counterfeit notes in violation of 18 U.S.C. § 371 and selling counterfeit notes in violation of 18 U.S.C. § 473....

Dietrich's second contention on appeal is that the district court erred when it admitted a prior inconsistent statement of one of the government's witnesses as substantive evidence. On October 11, 1985, Angel Thomas gave a written sworn statement to two Secret Service Agents. In her statement, Thomas indicated that she and her common-law husband, Charles Peek, had met with Dietrich and his wife. During the meeting Dietrich supposedly showed Thomas and Peek a number of counterfeit $100 federal reserve notes and assured them that the bills were easy to pass. According to Thomas' statement, Dietrich wanted Peek and Thomas to get rid of $10,000 worth of counterfeit currency. Thomas further stated that neither she nor Peek took any of the counterfeit money, and that she never saw Dietrich after their meeting.

At trial Thomas testified that she did not know John Dietrich. When the Assistant United States Attorney pointed to Dietrich in the courtroom, Thomas testified that she had never seen him before. As a result, the government sought to question Thomas on her prior inconsistent statement. In response to this line of questioning, Thomas admitted making the statement. She testified, however, that she had lied during the interview to help Peek, who was then awaiting trial on separate counterfeiting charges. Thomas further testified that the agents who took the statement pressured her into giving it by threatening to arrest her on charges of passing counterfeit currency unless she told them about Dietrich. According to Thomas, she made up the story about Dietrich to avoid arrest and to help her husband....

[T]he government claims that the statement was properly admitted under Federal Rule of Evidence 801(d)(1)(A).... If a prior inconsistent statement meets the requirements of Rule 801(d)(1)(A) it may be admitted as substantive evidence to establish the truth of the matter asserted. A prior inconsistent statement that does not meet one of the criteria of Rule 801(d)(1)(A), however, may be used only for the purpose of impeaching the witness. Fed.R.Evid. 801(d)(1)(A) (advisory committee notes).

Dietrich admits that Thomas' statement was inconsistent with her testimony at trial, and that the prior statement was given under oath subject to the penalties of perjury. Both parties admit that Thomas' interview with the Secret Service Agents did not occur during a trial, hearing, or deposition. Thus, the statement was properly admitted only if the interview constituted an "other proceeding" for purposes of Rule 801(d)(1)(A). We conclude that it did not.

The term "other proceeding" is not unlimited. A typical police station interrogation, for example, is not an "other proceeding" within the meaning of the Rule. *See, e.g., United States v. Day*, 789 F.2d 1217, 1222 (6th Cir. 1986) (collecting cases). "'The Rule seems to contemplate situations in which an official verbatim record is routinely kept, whether stenographically or by electronic means, under legal authority.'" *United States v. Livingston*, 661 F.2d 239, 240 (D.C. Cir. 1981) (quoting 4 D. Louisell & C. Mueller, *Federal Evidence* § 419 at 171 (1980)).

The term "other proceeding" includes grand jury proceedings, even though the declarant is not subject to cross-examination during the grand jury proceeding. Fed.R.Evid. 801(d)(1)(A) (conference committee notes). An immigration proceeding also has been held to constitute an "other proceeding" under Rule 801(d)(1)(A). *United States v. Castro-Ayon*, 537 F.2d 1055 (9th Cir.), *cert. denied*, 429 U.S. 983 (1976). The *Castro-Ayon* court concluded that the immigration proceeding was acceptable for purposes of the Rule because it contained many of the same procedural protections as a grand jury proceeding. For instance, both proceedings are "investigatory, ex parte, inquisitive, sworn, basically prosecutorial, held before an officer other than the arresting officer, recorded, and held in circumstances of some legal formality." In fact, as the court noted, a witness in an immigration proceeding is actually afforded more procedural protections than is a grand jury witness.

In contrast, Thomas gave her prior inconsistent statement during an interview with two Secret Service Agents in her home. When the agents arrived, they searched Thomas' home and car with her consent. They informed her that Charles Peek had been arrested, and according to Thomas they indicated that she might also be arrested for passing a counterfeit $100 bill unless she cooperated with them. Thomas then agreed to talk to the agents. No one was present during the interview except Thomas and the two agents, and the interview was not recorded. Thomas simply spoke to the agents who then wrote down what she had told them, and she signed the written statement verifying its truth. *See Livingston*, 661 F.2d at 240 (witness' prior statement to postal inspector inadmissible under Rule 801(d)(1)(A) for failure to satisfy "other proceeding" requirement where inspector went to witness' house, asked her questions, took notes, wrote a statement based on her answers, and witness signed statement attesting to its accuracy).

Thomas' statement was given to the same agents who had the authority to arrest her, the interview was not prosecutorial, it was not recorded, and there were no indicia of legal formality. The circumstances surrounding Thomas' statement did not differ significantly from a typical police station interrogation. Thomas' interview therefore does not qualify as an "other proceeding" pursuant to Rule 801(d)(1)(A), and the admission of her statement was erroneous.[5] ....

---

5. While this statement should not have been admitted as substantive evidence, it could have been properly used to impeach Thomas. Some commentators have questioned the ability of jurors to distinguish between the use of evidence for impeachment purposes and its substantive value. *See, e.g.,* 4 J. Weinstein and M. Berger, *Weinstein's Evidence* ¶ 801(d)(1)(A)[01]. The distinction is important, however, for the continued vitality of the Rules as drafted. *Livingston*, 661 F.2d at 243. *See also United States v. Ragghianti*, 560 F.2d 1376, 1381 (9th Cir. 1977) ("There is a crucial distinction between the use of a prior inconsistent statement of a witness only to impeach the credibility of the witness and its use to prove as a fact what is contained in the statement.").

Montana Rule of Evidence 801

Definitions

The following definitions apply under this article:

....

(d) Statements which are not hearsay. A statement is not hearsay if:

(1) Prior statement by witness. The declarant testifies at the trial or hearing and is subject to cross-examination concerning the statement, and the statement is (A) inconsistent with the declarant's testimony....

COMMISSION COMMENTS

....

Clause 801(d)(1)(A) is not the same as the Federal Rule.... The clause deletes the oath requirement as unnecessary and harmful to the usefulness of the rule. The Commission believes that prior inconsistent statements should be admissible as substantive evidence. Although the rule does not specifically call for this result, the Advisory Committee Note to Federal Rule 801(d)(1)(A) states: "Prior inconsistent statements traditionally have been admissible to impeach but not as substantive evidence. Under the rule, they are substantive evidence". An argument in favor of this position, in addition to the consideration that the hearsay rule should not apply, is that the jury may consider this type of statement (when introduced for impeachment purposes) as substantive evidence because of a failure to regard the typical cautionary instruction. It can also be noted that this statement is always made closer in time to the event, free from any influences, and therefore has an assurance of trustworthiness like many hearsay exceptions....

Problem 7-14: The Improper Motive

William is on trial on charges of bank fraud related to activities that took place between 2002 and 2011. The FBI had been investigating the activities since 2009, and began questioning William and a variety of people who worked with William, including Tom. In 2011, both William and Tom were indicted, but before the case went to trial, Tom entered into a plea agreement with the government. Tom is called as a witness on the government's behalf, and on cross-examination, William's attorney asks Tom "Isn't it true that you have entered into a plea agreement with the government?" and "Isn't it true that the government will recommend a sentence for you to the court after you testify in this case?" Tom answers both questions in the affirmative.

The government's attorney then seeks to call the FBI agents who interviewed Tom in 2009 and have them testify to what he said at the time (which corroborated what Tom had testified to on the stand), but William's attorney raises a hearsay objection.

How should the government respond to the objection, and how will the court likely rule?

Tome v. United States

513 U.S. 150 (1995)

Justice KENNEDY delivered the opinion of the Court, except as to Part II-B.

Various Federal Courts of Appeals are divided over the evidence question presented by this case.... The question is whether out-of-court consistent statements made after the alleged fabrication, or after the alleged improper influence or motive arose, are admissible under [Rule 801(d)(1)(B)]....

II

The prevailing common-law rule for more than a century before adoption of the Federal Rules of Evidence was that a prior consistent statement introduced to rebut a charge of recent fabrication or improper influence or motive was admissible if the statement had been made before the alleged fabrication, influence, or motive came into being, but it was inadmissible if made afterwards. As Justice Story explained: "[W]here the testimony is assailed as a fabrication of a recent date, ... in order to repel such imputation, proof of the *antecedent* declaration of the party may be admitted." *Ellicott v. Pearl*, 10 Pet. 412, 439 (1836) (emphasis added).

McCormick and Wigmore stated the rule in a more categorical manner: "[T]he applicable principle is that the prior consistent statement has no relevancy to refute the charge unless the consistent statement was made before the source of the bias, interest, influence or incapacity originated." E. Cleary, McCormick on Evidence § 49, p. 105 (2d ed. 1972) (hereafter McCormick). See also 4 J. Wigmore, Evidence § 1128, p. 268 (J. Chadbourn rev. 1972) (hereafter Wigmore) ("A consistent statement, at a *time prior* to the existence of a fact said to indicate bias ... will effectively explain away the force of the impeaching evidence" (emphasis in original)). The question is whether Rule 801(d)(1)(B) embodies this temporal requirement. We hold that it does.

A

....

Rule 801 defines prior consistent statements as nonhearsay only if they are offered to rebut a charge of "recent fabrication or improper influence or motive." Fed.Rule Evid. 801(d)(1)(B).* Noting the "troublesome" logic of treating a witness' prior consistent statements as hearsay at all (because the declarant is present in court and subject to cross-examination), the Advisory Committee decided to treat those consistent statements, once the preconditions of the Rule were satisfied, as nonhearsay and admissible as substantive evidence, not just to rebut an attack on the witness' credibility. See Advisory Committee's Notes on Fed.Rule Evid. 801(d)(1). A consistent statement meeting the requirements of the Rule is thus placed in the same category as a declarant's inconsistent statement made under oath in another proceeding, or prior identification testimony, or admissions by a party opponent. See Fed.Rule Evid. 801.

The Rules do not accord this weighty, nonhearsay status to all prior consistent statements. To the contrary, admissibility under the Rules is confined to those statements offered to rebut a charge of "recent fabrication or improper influence or motive," the same phrase used by the Advisory Committee in its description of the "traditiona[l]" common law of evidence, which was the background against which the Rules were drafted. Prior

---

* Editor's Note: The quoted phrase in Rule 801(d)(1)(B) was restyled in 2011 to read "that the declarant recently fabricated it or acted from a recent improper influence or motive in so testifying."

consistent statements may not be admitted to counter all forms of impeachment or to bolster the witness merely because she has been discredited. In the present context, the question is whether A.T.'s out-of-court statements rebutted the alleged link between her desire to be with her mother and her testimony, not whether they suggested that A.T.'s in-court testimony was true. The Rule speaks of a party rebutting an alleged motive, not bolstering the veracity of the story told.

This limitation is instructive, not only to establish the preconditions of admissibility but also to reinforce the significance of the requirement that the consistent statements must have been made before the alleged influence, or motive to fabricate, arose. That is to say, the forms of impeachment within the Rule's coverage are the ones in which the temporal requirement makes the most sense. Impeachment by charging that the testimony is a recent fabrication or results from an improper influence or motive is, as a general matter, capable of direct and forceful refutation through introduction of out-of-court consistent statements that predate the alleged fabrication, influence, or motive. A consistent statement that predates the motive is a square rebuttal of the charge that the testimony was contrived as a consequence of that motive. By contrast, prior consistent statements carry little rebuttal force when most other types of impeachment are involved. McCormick § 49, p. 105 ("When the attack takes the form of impeachment of character, by showing misconduct, convictions or bad reputation, it is generally agreed that there is no color for sustaining by consistent statements. The defense does not meet the assault"); see also 4 Wigmore § 1131, p. 293 ("The broad rule obtains in a few courts that consistent statements may be admitted *after* impeachment of any sort — in particular after any impeachment by *cross-examination*. But there is no reason for such a loose rule").

There may arise instances when out-of-court statements that postdate the alleged fabrication have some probative force in rebutting a charge of fabrication or improper influence or motive, but those statements refute the charged fabrication in a less direct and forceful way. Evidence that a witness made consistent statements after the alleged motive to fabricate arose may suggest in some degree that the in-court testimony is truthful, and thus suggest in some degree that that testimony did not result from some improper influence; but if the drafters of Rule 801(d)(1)(B) intended to countenance rebuttal along that indirect inferential chain, the purpose of confining the types of impeachment that open the door to rebuttal by introducing consistent statements becomes unclear. If consistent statements are admissible without reference to the timeframe we find imbedded in the Rule, there appears no sound reason not to admit consistent statements to rebut other forms of impeachment as well. Whatever objections can be leveled against limiting the Rule to this designated form of impeachment and confining the rebuttal to those statements made before the fabrication or improper influence or motive arose, it is clear to us that the drafters of Rule 801(d)(1)(B) were relying upon the common-law temporal requirement.

The underlying theory of the Government's position is that an out-of-court consistent statement, whenever it was made, tends to bolster the testimony of a witness and so tends also to rebut an express or implied charge that the testimony has been the product of an improper influence. Congress could have adopted that rule with ease, providing, for instance, that "a witness' prior consistent statements are admissible whenever relevant to assess the witness' truthfulness or accuracy." The theory would be that, in a broad sense, any prior statement by a witness concerning the disputed issues at trial would have some relevance in assessing the accuracy or truthfulness of the witness' in-court testimony on the same subject. The narrow Rule enacted by Congress, however, cannot be understood to incorporate the Government's theory.

Our analysis is strengthened by the observation that the somewhat peculiar language of the Rule bears close similarity to the language used in many of the common-law cases that describe the premotive requirement. "Rule 801(d)(1)(B) employs the precise language — 'rebut[ting] … charge[s] … of recent fabrication or improper influence or motive' — consistently used in the panoply of pre-1975 decisions." Ohlbaum, The Hobgoblin of the Federal Rules of Evidence: An Analysis of Rule 801(d)(1)(B), Prior Consistent Statements and a New Proposal, 1987 B. Y. U. L. Rev. 231, 245. See, *e.g., Ellicott v. Pearl,* 10 Pet. at 439.

The language of the Rule, in its concentration on rebutting charges of recent fabrication or improper influence or motive to the exclusion of other forms of impeachment, as well as in its use of wording that follows the language of the common-law cases, suggests that it was intended to carry over the common-law premotive rule.

B

Our conclusion that Rule 801(d)(1)(B) embodies the common-law premotive requirement is confirmed by an examination of the Advisory Committee's Notes to the Federal Rules of Evidence. We have relied on those well-considered Notes as a useful guide in ascertaining the meaning of the Rules. See, *e.g., Huddleston* v. *United States,* 485 U.S. 681, 688 (1988); *United States* v. *Owens,* 484 U.S. 554, 562 (1988). Where, as with Rule 801(d)(1)(B), "Congress did not amend the Advisory Committee's draft in any way … the Committee's commentary is particularly relevant in determining the meaning of the document Congress enacted." *Beech Aircraft Corp.* v. *Rainey,* 488 U.S. 153, 165–166, n. 9 (1988). The Notes are also a respected source of scholarly commentary. Professor Cleary was a distinguished commentator on the law of evidence, and he and members of the Committee consulted and considered the views, criticisms, and suggestions of the academic community in preparing the Notes.

The Notes disclose a purpose to adhere to the common law in the application of evidentiary principles, absent express provisions to the contrary. Where the Rules did depart from their common-law antecedents, in general the Committee said so.… The Notes give no indication, however, that Rule 801(d)(1)(B) abandoned the premotive requirement. The entire discussion of Rule 801(d)(1)(B) is limited to the following comment:

> "Prior consistent statements traditionally have been admissible to rebut charges of recent fabrication or improper influence or motive but not as substantive evidence. Under the rule they are substantive evidence. The prior statement is consistent with the testimony given on the stand, and, if the opposite party wishes to open the door for its admission in evidence, no sound reason is apparent why it should not be received generally."

Notes on Rule 801(d)(1)(B).

Throughout their discussion of the Rules, the Advisory Committee's Notes rely on Wigmore and McCormick as authority for the common-law approach. In light of the categorical manner in which those authors state the premotive requirement, it is difficult to imagine that the drafters, who noted the new substantive use of prior consistent statements, would have remained silent if they intended to modify the premotive requirement.… [W]e do not think the drafters of the Rule intended to scuttle the whole premotive requirement and rationale without so much as a whisper of explanation.…

Our conclusion is bolstered by the Advisory Committee's stated "unwillingness to countenance the general use of prior prepared statements as substantive evidence." See Notes on Rule 801(d)(1). Rule 801(d)[(1)], which "enumerates three situations in which the statement is excepted from the category of hearsay," *ibid.*, was expressly contrasted by the Committee with Uniform Rule of Evidence 63(1) (1953), "which allows *any* out-of-court statement of a declarant who is present at the trial and available for cross-examination." Notes on Rule 801(d)(1) (emphasis added). When a witness presents important testimony damaging to a party, the party will often counter with at least an implicit charge that the witness has been under some influence or motive to fabricate. If Rule 801 were read so that the charge opened the floodgates to any prior consistent statement that satisfied Rule 403, as the Tenth Circuit concluded, the distinction between rejected Uniform Rule 63(1) and Rule 801(d)(1)(B) would all but disappear....

The position taken by the Rules reflects a compromise between the views expressed by the "bulk of the case law ... against allowing prior statements of witnesses to be used generally as substantive evidence" and the views of the majority of "writers ... [who] ha[d] taken the opposite position." *Ibid.* That compromise was one that the Committee candidly admitted was a "judgment ... more of experience than of logic." *Ibid.*....

D

. . . .

We are aware that in some cases it may be difficult to ascertain when a particular fabrication, influence, or motive arose. Yet, as the Government concedes, a majority of common-law courts were performing this task for well over a century, and the Government has presented us with no evidence that those courts, or the judicial circuits that adhere to the rule today, have been unable to make the determination....

[The concurring opinion of Justice Scalia and the dissenting opinion of Justice Breyer are omitted.]

Problem 7-15: "Everyone Barked"

Assume the same facts as in Problems 7-1 and 7-11, except that when Perkins arrived at the scene of the crime, she also found a woman crying nearby, one Wanda Brown, who told her that she witnessed the shooting.

Assume further that after Barrone was arrested and taken to police headquarters, Brown identified him to Perkins as the person who shot Albertson.

The prosecution is unable to procure Brown's attendance at trial. However, at trial, it seeks to offer into evidence Perkins's testimony that Brown identified Barrone as the shooter. Barrone's attorney objects, contending that the testimony is hearsay.

How should the prosecution respond to the objection, and how will the court likely rule?

Problem 7-16: The Purloined Stamp Collection

On the evening of April 5, 2011, Arthur Reed opened the door of his apartment and began to walk in. As he entered, he was shoved into the apartment by a man wearing a mask and holding a gun, who said to Arthur, "I won't hurt you if you do as I say. All I want is that rare stamp collection of yours." Arthur complied with the masked man's instructions, and the man quickly left, leaving Arthur unharmed.

Arthur called the police to report the crime. Shortly thereafter, Officer Joan Smith arrived at the scene of the crime to take a report from Arthur. Arthur told

Smith exactly what the masked man said, and then told her, "As soon as he spoke, I knew it was Pete Rivers. He and I have known each other for some time, and he has a very distinctive voice."

Rivers is eventually indicted on charges of armed robbery. The prosecution calls Arthur as a witness, but to its surprise, he claims an inability to remember anything about the incident.

The prosecution seeks to call Smith as a witness to testify about what Arthur said to her, but Rivers's attorney raises a hearsay objection.

How should the prosecution respond to the objection, and how will the court likely rule?

United States v. Owens
484 U.S. 554 (1988)

Justice SCALIA delivered the opinion of the Court.

This case requires us to determine whether either the Confrontation Clause of the Sixth Amendment or Rule 802 of the Federal Rules of Evidence bars testimony concerning a prior, out-of-court identification when the identifying witness is unable, because of memory loss, to explain the basis for the identification.

I

On April 12, 1982, John Foster, a correctional counselor at the federal prison in Lompoc, California, was attacked and brutally beaten with a metal pipe. His skull was fractured, and he remained hospitalized for almost a month. As a result of his injuries, Foster's memory was severely impaired. When Thomas Mansfield, an FBI agent investigating the assault, first attempted to interview Foster, on April 19, he found Foster lethargic and unable to remember his attacker's name. On May 5, Mansfield again spoke to Foster, who was much improved and able to describe the attack. Foster named respondent as his attacker and identified respondent from an array of photographs.

Respondent was tried in Federal District Court for assault with intent to commit murder under 18 U.S.C. § 113(a). At trial, Foster recounted his activities just before the attack, and described feeling the blows to his head and seeing blood on the floor. He testified that he clearly remembered identifying respondent as his assailant during his May 5th interview with Mansfield. On cross-examination, he admitted that he could not remember seeing his assailant. He also admitted that, although there was evidence that he had received numerous visitors in the hospital, he was unable to remember any of them except Mansfield, and could not remember whether any of these visitors had suggested that respondent was the assailant. Defense counsel unsuccessfully sought to refresh his recollection with hospital records, including one indicating that Foster had attributed the assault to someone other than respondent. Respondent was convicted and sentenced to 20 years' imprisonment to be served consecutively to a previous sentence.

On appeal, the United States Court of Appeals for the Ninth Circuit considered challenges based on the Confrontation Clause and Rule 802 of the Federal Rules of Evidence.[1]

---

1. This case has been argued, both here and below, as though Federal Rule of Evidence 801(d)(1)(C) were the basis of the challenge. That is substantially but not technically correct. If respondent's arguments are accepted, it is Rule 802 that would render the out-of-court statement inadmissible as hearsay; but as explained in Part III, it is ultimately Rule 801(d)(1)(C) that determines whether Rule 802 is applicable.

By divided vote it upheld both challenges (though finding the Rule 802 violation harmless error), and reversed the judgment of the District Court. 789 F.2d 750 (1986). We granted certiorari, to resolve the conflict with other Circuits on the significance of a hearsay declarant's memory loss both with respect to the Confrontation Clause, and with respect to Rule 802.

II

[In this Part of the opinion, the Court holds that admission of the evidence did not violate the defendant's Confrontation Clause rights, an issue taken up in the last section of this chapter.]

III

Respondent urges as an alternative basis for affirmance a violation of Federal Rule of Evidence 802, which generally excludes hearsay. Rule 801(d)(1)(C) defines as not hearsay a prior statement [identifying a person as someone the declarant perceived earlier,] if the declarant "testifies at the trial or hearing and is subject to cross-examination concerning the statement."* The Court of Appeals found that Foster's identification statement did not come within this exclusion because his memory loss prevented his being "subject to cross-examination concerning the statement."

....

It seems to us that the more natural reading of "subject to cross-examination concerning the statement" includes what was available here. Ordinarily a witness is regarded as "subject to cross-examination" when he is placed on the stand, under oath, and responds willingly to questions. Just as with the constitutional prohibition, limitations on the scope of examination by the trial court or assertions of privilege by the witness may undermine the process to such a degree that meaningful cross-examination within the intent of the Rule no longer exists. But that effect is not produced by the witness' assertion of memory loss — which, as discussed earlier, is often the very result sought to be produced by cross-examination, and can be effective in destroying the force of the prior statement. Rule 801(d)(1)(C), which specifies that the cross-examination need only "concer[n] the statement," does not on its face require more.

This reading seems even more compelling when the Rule is compared with Rule 804(a)(3), which defines "[u]navailab[ility] as a witness" to include situations in which a declarant "testifies to a lack of memory of the subject matter of the declarant's statement."** Congress plainly was aware of the recurrent evidentiary problem at issue here — witness forgetfulness of an underlying event — but chose not to make it an exception to Rule 801(d)(1)(C).

The reasons for that choice are apparent from the Advisory Committee's Notes on Rule 801 and its legislative history. The premise for Rule 801(d)(1)(C) was that, given adequate safeguards against suggestiveness, out-of-court identifications were generally preferable to courtroom identifications. Advisory Committee's Notes on Rule 801. Thus, despite the traditional view that such statements were hearsay, the Advisory Committee believed that their use was to be fostered rather than discouraged. Similarly, the House Report on the Rule noted that since, "[a]s time goes by, a witness' memory will fade and his iden-

---

* Editor's Note: The quoted phrase in Rule 801(d)(1) was restyled in 2011 to read: "testifies and is subject to cross-examination about a prior statement."

** Editor's Note: The quoted phrase in Rule 804(a)(3) was restyled in 2011 to read: "testifies to not remembering the subject matter."

tification will become less reliable," minimizing the barriers to admission of more contemporaneous identification is fairer to defendants and prevents "cases falling through because the witness can no longer recall the identity of the person he saw commit the crime." H. R. Rep. No. 94-355, p. 3 (1975). See also S. Rep. No. 94-199, p. 2 (1975). To judge from the House and Senate Reports, Rule 801(d)(1)(C) was in part directed to the very problem here at issue: a memory loss that makes it impossible for the witness to provide an in-court identification or testify about details of the events underlying an earlier identification.

Respondent argues that this reading is impermissible because it creates an internal inconsistency in the Rules, since the forgetful witness who is deemed "subject to cross-examination" under 801(d)(1)(C) is simultaneously deemed "unavailable" under 804(a)(3). This is the position espoused by a prominent commentary on the Rules, see 4 J. Weinstein & M. Berger, Weinstein's Evidence 801-120 to 801-121, 801-178 (1987). It seems to us, however, that this is not a substantive inconsistency, but only a semantic oddity resulting from the fact that Rule 804(a) has for convenience of reference in Rule 804(b) chosen to describe the circumstances necessary in order to admit certain categories of hearsay testimony under the rubric "Unavailab[ility] as a witness." These circumstances include not only absence from the hearing, but also claims of privilege, refusals to obey a court's order to testify, and inability to testify based on physical or mental illness or memory loss. Had the rubric instead been "unavailability as a witness, memory loss, and other special circumstances" there would be no apparent inconsistency with Rule 801, which is a definition section excluding certain statements entirely from the category of "hearsay." The semantic inconsistency exists not only with respect to Rule 801(d)(1)(C), but also with respect to the other subparagraphs of Rule 801(d)(1). It would seem strange, for example, to assert that a witness can avoid introduction of testimony from a prior proceeding that is inconsistent with his trial testimony, see Rule 801(d)(1)(A), by simply asserting lack of memory of the facts to which the prior testimony related. But that situation, like this one, presents the verbal curiosity that the witness is "subject to cross-examination" under Rule 801 while at the same time "unavailable" under Rule 804(a)(3). Quite obviously, the two characterizations are made for two entirely different purposes and there is no requirement or expectation that they should coincide....

[The dissenting opinion of Justice Brennan is omitted.]

State v. Canady
911 P.2d 104 (Haw. 1996)

ACOBA, Judge.

[Steven Canady was convicted of physically abusing a family or household member. At trial, the Complainant claimed that she could not recall who or what caused her injuries, nor could she remember whether she had a conversation with a police officer regarding the incident. The police officer's testimony about what the complainant had said was admitted into evidence at trial, and on appeal the State contended that it was admissible as a prior inconsistent statement under Hawaii's version of Rule 801(d)(1)(A)].

In *United States v. Owens*, the United States Supreme Court considered the application of FRE Rule 801(d)(1)(C).... The Court reasoned that, under a "natural reading" of the phrase "'subject to cross-examination concerning the statement'" in FRE Rule 801(d)(1), all that is required is that the witness "is placed on the stand, under oath, and responds willingly to questions[,]" even if the witness was unable to testify about any of the events set forth in the prior statement. Under its reading, the Court found that FRE Rule 801(d)(1)(C)'s language "does not[,] on its face[,] require more."

In support of its holding, the *Owens* Court compared the language of FRE Rule 801(d)(1) to FRE Rule 804(a)(3) which defined an unavailable witness as a person who "'testifies to a *lack of memory of the subject matter* of the declarant's statement.'" The Court focused on the difference between the words "subject to cross-examination concerning the statement" in FRE Rule 801(d)(1) and "lack of memory of the subject matter of the defendant's statement" in FRE Rule 804(a)(3). This difference was seen as indicating that "Congress plainly was aware of the recurrent evidentiary problem at issue ... — witness forgetfulness of an underlying event — but chose not to make [witness forgetfulness] an exception to [the admissibility of an out-of-court identification under] [FRE] Rule 801(d)(1)(C)."

Our parallel rule, HRE Rule 802.1(1), in contrast to FRE Rule 801(d)(1), requires that the "declarant [be] subject to cross-examination concerning *the subject matter* of the declarant's statement[.]" The scope of this requirement has not yet been addressed in this jurisdiction. We are not aware of any other jurisdiction which has a similarly worded rule....

Unlike the contrasting language of FRE Rules 801(d)(1)(C) and 804(a)(3) that the *Owens* Court relied on, the "inconsistent statement" provision of HRE Rule 802.1(1) and the "lack of memory" provision of HRE Rule 804(a)(3) are not significantly distinguishable. HRE Rule 804(a)(3) employs the same "subject matter" language as HRE Rule 802.1(1), stating that a witness is unavailable if the witness "[t]estifies to a lack of memory of *the subject matter* of the declarant's statement[.]"

Although the commentary to HRE Rule 802.1 is not evidence of legislative intent, it is "an aid in understanding" the rule. The commentary to HRE Rule 802.1 explains that under the common law, prior inconsistent statements were considered hearsay and could only be used to impeach a witness. Commentary to HRE Rule 802.1 (1993). The FRE modified the common-law rule and allowed prior inconsistent statements to be used as substantive proof of the matters asserted in the statement, if the statement was "'given under oath subject to the penalty of perjury at a trial, hearing, or other proceeding, or in a deposition[.]'" *Id.* (quoting FRE Rule 801(d)(1)(A)).* HRE Rule 802.1 adopted this federal exception to the common law, and went further by adding two more exceptions to the hearsay objection for signed or adopted statements and recorded statements. *Id.* These exceptions were justified if the statements' trustworthiness was assured on two grounds: (1) the statements could "fairly be attributed" to the witness; and (2) the witnesses themselves were "subject to cross examination concerning the subject matter of the statement." *Id.*

> The situation envisioned is one where the witness has testified about an event and his [or her] prior written statement also describes that event but is inconsistent with his [or her] [present] testimony. Since the witness can be cross-examined about the event and the statement, the trier of fact is free to credit his [or her] present testimony or his [or her] prior statement in determining where the truth lies.

Id. Consequently, the rule was intended to exclude the prior statements of a witness who could no longer remember the underlying events described in the statement. *See id.* Absent the opportunity to cross-examine a witness about the material events described in a prior statement, the statement would lack one of the twin guarantees of trustworthiness supporting its admissibility as *substantive* evidence of the matters asserted in the statement.

---

* Editor's Note: The quoted phrase in Rule 801(d)(1)(A) was restyled in 2011 to read: "given under penalty of perjury at a trial, hearing, or other proceeding or in a deposition."

Hence, unlike FRE Rule 801(d)(1), HRE Rule 802.1(1) requires more of the witness than just that he or she be "placed on the stand, under oath and respond[ ] willingly to questions." *Owens*, 484 U.S. at 561. We hold that HRE Rule 802.1(1) requires, as a guarantee of the trustworthiness of a prior inconsistent statement, that the witness be subject to cross-examination about the subject matter of the prior statement, that is, that the witness be capable of testifying substantively about the event, allowing the trier of fact to meaningfully compare the prior version of the event with the version recounted at trial before the statement would be admissible as substantive evidence of the matters stated therein.

Here, the subject matter of the Statement referred to the identity of Complainant's assailant and how Complainant sustained her injuries. At trial, Complainant testified that she could not recall the events that she allegedly described in the Statement. She was, therefore, not able to testify about the substantive events reported in the Statement. Because the witness could not be "cross-examined about the event[s,]" the trier of fact was not "free to credit the present testimony or the prior statement" to determine "where the truth [lay]." Accordingly, under the present state of the record, the Statement was not admissible under HRE Rule 802.1(1) because Complainant could not be "subject[ed] to cross examination concerning the subject matter of the statement" as "envisioned" under the Rule....

Notes and Questions

1. As originally proposed by the Advisory Committee, Rule 801(d)(1)(A) would have permitted *any* prior statement that was inconsistent with the declarant's testimony at trial to be admitted as substantive proof of the matter asserted in that prior statement, without regard to whether the statement was made in a formal setting. *See* Advisory Committee Note to Rule 801(d)(1)(A). Thus, under the Advisory Committee's original proposal, there would be no distinction between the impeaching use and the substantive use of prior inconsistent statements. In support of its proposal, the Advisory Committee cited the commentary to an analogous provision of California's evidence code:

> "Section 1235 admits inconsistent statements of witnesses because the dangers against which the hearsay rule is designed to protect are largely nonexistent. The declarant is in court and may be examined and cross-examined in regard to his statements and their subject matter. In many cases, the inconsistent statement is more likely to be true than the testimony of the witness at the trial because it was made nearer in time to the matter to which it relates and is less likely to be influenced by the controversy that gave rise to the litigation. The trier of fact has the declarant before it and can observe his demeanor and the nature of his testimony as he denies or tries to explain away the inconsistency. Hence, it is in as good a position to determine the truth or falsity of the prior statement as it is to determine the truth or falsity of the inconsistent testimony given in court. Moreover, Section 1235 will provide a party with desirable protection against the 'turncoat' witness who changes his story on the stand and deprives the party calling him of evidence essential to his case."

Advisory Committee Note to Rule 801(d)(1)(A).

The House Judiciary Committee balked, expressing concern over the reliability of such evidence, and amended the provision so as to limit the substantive use of prior inconsistent statements to those made in certain formal settings:

> The Rule as amended draws a distinction between types of prior inconsistent statements ... and allows only those made while the declarant was subject to

cross-examination at a trial or hearing or in a deposition, to be admissible for their truth. The rationale for the Committee's decision is that (1) unlike in most other situations involving unsworn or oral statements, there can be no dispute as to whether the prior statement was made; and (2) the context of a formal proceeding, an oath, and the opportunity for cross-examination provide firm additional assurances of the reliability of the prior statement.

Report of House Committee on the Judiciary, House Report No. 93-650.

The Senate Judiciary Committee expressed concern with the House amendment to Rule 801(d)(1)(A), indicating that the requirement that the prior statement must have been subject to cross-examination would "preclud[e] even the use of grand jury statements," because criminal defendants lack the right to appear and examine grand jury witnesses, and reinstated the Rule as originally proposed. *See* Report of Senate Committee on the Judiciary, Senate Report No. 93-1277.

Eventually, Congress settled on the language now set forth in Rule 801(d)(1)(A), with the language of the House amendment tweaked to ensure that grand jury testimony *would* be admissible under Rule 801(d)(1)(A):

> [T]he rule now requires that the prior inconsistent statement be given under oath subject to the penalty of perjury at a trial, hearing, or other proceeding, or in a deposition. The rule as adopted covers statements before a grand jury.

Report of the House-Senate Conference Committee, House Report No. 93-1597.

2. The phrase "inconsistent" as used in Rule 801(d)(1)(A) is broadly construed. In other words, it is not limited to "pure" instances of inconsistency, such as when the declarant testifies that "the car went through the red light," and his prior statement was that "the car *did not* go through the red light":

> As long as people speak in nonmathematical languages such as English, however, it will be difficult to determine precisely whether two statements are inconsistent. But we do not read the word "inconsistent" in Rule 801(d)(1)(A) to include only statements diametrically opposed or logically incompatible. Inconsistency "may be found in evasive answers, ... silence, or changes in positions." In addition, a purported change in memory can produce "inconsistent" answers. Particularly in a case of manifest reluctance to testify, "if a witness has testified to [certain] facts before a grand jury and forgets ... them at trial, his grand jury testimony ... falls squarely within Rule 801(d)(1)(A)."

United States v. Williams, 737 F.2d 594, 608 (7th Cir. 1984).

For similar reasons, a statement "need not be identical in every detail to the declarant's ... testimony at trial" to be deemed "consistent" for purposes of Rule 801(d)(1)(B). *United States v. Vest*, 842 F.2d 1319, 1329 (1st Cir. 1988).

3. If the requirements of Rule 801(d)(1) are satisfied, *anyone* who heard the prior statement can testify as to the content of that statement. In other words, there is no requirement that the declarant herself testify as to the content of the prior statement, only that she be "subject to cross-examination" concerning it. *See United States v. Montague*, 958 F.2d 1094, 1099 (D.C. Cir. 1992) (collecting cases). Moreover, it is not necessary that the prior statement be disclosed to the declarant before another witness is called to testify as to the content of that prior statement. So long as the declarant is available to be recalled as a witness to be cross-examined concerning the statement, the "subject to cross-examination" requirement is satisfied. *See United States v. Green*, 258 F.3d 683, 690–92 (7th Cir. 2001).

4. To satisfy Rule 801(d)(1)(B)'s pre-motive requirement, it is only necessary that the prior consistent statement was made before the *specific* motive alleged by the attacking party arose. In other words, that there may have been other improper motives at the time does not prevent the use of Rule 801(d)(1)(B) to use the statement to rebut the motive specifically charged by the attacking party. *United States v. Wilson*, 355 F.3d 358, 361–62 (5th Cir. 2003). Moreover, the improper motive that Rule 801(d)(1)(B) is concerned with is that of the *declarant*. Thus, where a third party has some motive to improperly influence the declarant, the pertinent date for purposes of Rule 801(d)(1)(B) is the date on which the third party brings that influence to bear on the declarant, *not* the date when the third party develops a motive to improperly influence the declarant. *See United States v. Bordeaux*, 400 F.3d 548, 557 (8th Cir. 2005).

5. A statement is admissible under Rule 801(d)(1)(B) only if it is offered to "rebut an express or implied charge that the declarant recently fabricated it or acted from a recent improper influence or motive in so testifying." How does a court determine whether such a charge has been made? *See United States v. Frazier*, 469 F.3d 85, 88–89 & n.2 (3d Cir. 2006) (holding that the trial court must make an objective determination whether the impeaching counsel's trial tactics could reasonably be taken by a jury to suggest that the witness consciously altered his testimony, taking into account not only counsel's actual words but also the tone of his voice, gestures, and other nuances).

6. Chapter 10 considers the use of prior inconsistent and prior consistent statements for non-substantive purposes, namely, for purposes of impeachment and rehabilitation of witnesses. Whether evidence that fails to satisfy the narrow requirements of Rule 801(d)(1)(B) can nonetheless be used to rehabilitate a witness' credibility is taken up in that chapter.

7. Is the phrase "identifies a person as someone the declarant perceived earlier" limited to statements identifying a *specific* person, or do statements regarding the characteristics of the person identified, such as hair color, eye color, height, and the like, fit within the exception? *See United States v. Brink*, 39 F.3d 419, 425–26 (3d Cir. 1994) (admitting under Rule 801(d)(1)(C) prior statement by declarant in which she described the color of the perpetrator's eyes).

8. While Rule 801(d)(1)(C) is most often used to inculpate a defendant, such as producing evidence of the declarant's prior statement identifying the defendant as the perpetrator of the crime after the declarant changes his story or claims that his memory has failed, the rule is not limited to such uses. It can be used to exculpate a defendant, such as by introducing a prior statement of identification by the declarant that differs from the declarant's testimony at trial. *See, e.g., United States v. Brink*, 39 F.3d 419, 425–26 (3d Cir. 1994) (declarant testified that she did not remember perpetrator's eye color; defendant, whose eyes are light-colored, can introduce prior statement by declarant in which she identified the perpetrator as having dark eyes).

2. Statements of an Opposing Party

Rule 801(d)(2) defines as "not hearsay" five different categories of statements made by a party or by certain people associated with a party when offered into evidence *against* that party:

    (d) **Statements That Are Not Hearsay.** A statement that meets the following conditions is not hearsay:

(2) *An Opposing Party's Statement.* The statement is offered against an opposing party and:

(A) was made by the party in an individual or representative capacity;

(B) is one the party manifested that it adopted or believed to be true;

(C) was made by a person whom the party authorized to make a statement on the subject;

(D) was made by the party's agent or employee on a matter within the scope of that relationship and while it existed; or

(E) was made by the party's coconspirator during and in furtherance of the conspiracy.

The statement must be considered but does not by itself establish the declarant's authority under (C); the existence or scope of the relationship under (D); or the existence of the conspiracy or participation in it under (E).

The materials that follow explore a variety of questions that arise in applying this set of provisions, and in particular, the foundation that must be laid in order to invoke them.

a. Individual Statements

Problem 7-17: Anything You Say Can and Will Be Used against You . . .

Leon is on trial on charges of sexually assaulting Lucinda, who died just before the trial began. At trial, the government seeks to offer into evidence testimony by Reggie that he heard Leon say that he forced Lucinda to have sex with him against her will, contending that it is admissible under Rule 801(d)(2)(A). Leon, through his attorney, denies that he ever made such a statement and objects to the admission of Reggie's testimony.

Later in the trial, Leon seeks to offer into evidence testimony by Rhonda that Lucinda said to her, "I willingly had sex with Leon," contending that it is admissible under Rule 801(d)(2)(A).

How should the court rule on the admissibility of Reggie's testimony? In making this determination, of what significance is it that Leon denies having made the statement? How should the court rule on the admissibility of Rhonda's testimony?

United States v. Reed
227 F.3d 763 (7th Cir. 2000)

WILLIAMS, Circuit Judge.

Defendant Dwayne Reed was charged with bank robbery under 18 U.S.C. § 2113(a). During his first trial, Reed testified. . . . That trial ended with a hung jury, and the district judge declared a mistrial. Six months later, Reed was retried and the jury returned a guilty verdict. At the second trial. . . . Reed . . . decided not to testify a second time. The district judge . . . admitted Reed's entire testimony from the first trial as an admission by a party opponent under Federal Rule of Evidence 801(d)(2)(A). After the jury's guilty verdict, the district judge sentenced Reed to 240 months in prison.

Reed now appeals, arguing that the district court ... wrongly admitted Reed's entire testimony under Rule 801(d)(2)(A)....

Reed's prior testimony was admitted as an admission of a party opponent under Federal Rule of Evidence 801(d)(2)(A), which provides that a statement is not hearsay and may be admitted when the statement in question is offered against a party and is the party's own statement. Reed now makes two general arguments: (1) each of the statements that the government sought to include were not against his interest and (2) the district judge erred when he failed to require redaction of Reed's testimony, so that only the statements against Reed's interest remained....

Reed's ... argument fails because, contrary to Reed's assertion, statements admitted under Rule 801(d)(2)(A) need not be inculpatory. *See United States v. McGee*, 189 F.3d 626, 631–32 (7th Cir. 1999). While Reed acknowledges that admissions need not be inculpatory, he argues that to be admissible under Rule 801(d)(2)(A), an admission must be contrary to the trial position of the party. This is not the law and Reed has not persuaded us that it should be. Rule 801(d)(2)(A) merely renders a statement nonhearsay if it was made by the party against whom it is offered. As we stated in *McGee*, the statements need neither be incriminating, inculpatory, against interest, nor otherwise inherently damaging to the declarant's case. Rule 801(d)(2)(A) simply admits those statements made by one party, but offered as evidence by the opposing party. Therefore, the mere fact that the admitted testimony consisted of statements made by Reed, but offered by the government in its prosecution of him, makes Reed's testimony admissible under Rule 801(d)(2)(A)....

Pau v. Yosemite Park and Curry Co.
1994 WL 609421 (9th Cir. Nov. 3, 1994)

MEMORANDUM

This case involves a fatal bicycle accident in Yosemite National Park. A jury found Yosemite Park and Curry Company ("Curry Company") not liable for the death of Eleanor Wai-Ching So. The family and estate of the decedent (collectively the "Paus") appeal the denial of summary judgment and several evidentiary rulings by the trial judge....

The Paus contend that the district court abused its discretion by allowing Ranger Bryant to testify regarding Mr. Pau's statement as to the cause of the crash. Reading from his investigative report of the accident, Bryant testified: "It is the opinion of Mr. Pau, that due to the speed, Mrs. Pau did not remember to use the foot brake." At trial, the Paus' attorney objected to the testimony on the ground that it was "pure hearsay" and "pure speculation," and that the potential for unfair prejudice substantially outweighed the probative value of the statement. The district court allowed the statement to be admitted as an admission of a party opponent. *See* Fed.R.Evid. 801(d)(2)(A).

The statement is not hearsay under rule 801(d)(2)(A). The statement was made by Mr. Pau, a party to the action, and was offered by Curry Company against him at trial. Mr. Pau's counsel repeatedly objected that the statement was "pure speculation" on Mr. Pau's part. Whether Mr. Pau was speculating when he made the statement is irrelevant to the statement's admissibility. Admissions of a party opponent need not be based upon personal knowledge and are not subject to rule 701. See 4 Jack B. Weinstein et al., *Weinstein's Evidence* § 801(d)(2)(A)[01] (1994); Fed.R.Evid. 801(d)(2)(A) advisory committee's note (admissions are free "from the restrictive influences of the opinion rule and the rule requiring first hand knowledge")....

Notes and Questions

1. A party cannot invoke Rule 801(d)(2)(A) to bring his *own* prior statements into evidence. As the plain text of Rule 801(d)(2)(A) makes clear, it applies only when offered *against* the party who made the statement. *See United States v. Marin*, 669 F.2d 73, 84 (2d Cir. 1982).

2. What justifies the generous rules of admissibility for admissions of an opposing party? Consider the following explanation:

> Trustworthiness is not a separate requirement for admission under Rule 801(d)(2)(A). The admissibility of statements of a party-opponent is grounded not in the presumed trustworthiness of the statements, but on "a kind of estoppel or waiver theory, that a party should be entitled to rely on his opponent's statements." *United States v. DiDomenico*, 78 F.3d 294, 303 (7th Cir. 1996). As noted in the advisory committee notes to Rule 801(d)(2)(A), admissions by a party-opponent are excluded from the category of hearsay "on the theory that their admissibility in evidence is the result of the adversary system rather than satisfaction of the conditions of the hearsay rule." Evid. 801 advisory committee's note.
>
>> No guarantee of trustworthiness is required in the case of an admission. The freedom which admissions have enjoyed from technical demands of searching for an assurance of tru[st]worthiness in some against-interest circumstance, and from the restrictive influences of the opinion rule and the rule requiring firsthand knowledge, when taken with the apparently prevalent satisfaction with the results, calls for generous treatment of this avenue to admissibility.

Jewell v. CSX Transportation, Inc., 135 F.3d 361, 365–66 (6th Cir. 1998) (quoting Advisory Committee Note to Rule 801(d)(2)).

3. What if the party whose statement is being offered against him claims that he never made the statement? What role does the judge play in determining whether the alleged statement was made? Is this a Rule 104(a) determination in that the judge must be persuaded that the statement was made, or is it a question of conditional relevancy for which the judge plays only a screening role under Rule 104(b)? *See Jones v. National Am. Univ.*, 608 F.3d 1039, 1045 (8th Cir. 2010) (treating it as a question of conditional relevancy under Rule 104(b)); *United States v. Harvey*, 117 F.3d 1044, 1050 (7th Cir. 1997) (noting but not deciding the issue). *See also* Michael H. Graham, 3 Handbook of Fed. Evid. §801.1, at n.1 (5th ed. 2004) ("[I]f a statement is being offered as an admission of a party-opponent, Rule 801(d)(2)(A), whether the party-opponent actually made the alleged statement, e.g., 'I didn't see the stop sign', is a matter of conditional relevancy.... To the extent *United States v. Harvey* suggests that there is confusion or conflict as to the foregoing, it is incorrect and should not be followed.")

4. Suppose that two individuals, A and B, are co-defendants in a criminal trial on charges of robbery. The prosecution wishes to offer into evidence A's statement after the robbery that "B and I robbed the bank." Although hearsay, the statement would be an admission of a party-opponent, and thus admissible when offered against A. But unless it fit some exception to the hearsay rule as against B, it would be hearsay when offered against B. Normally, Rule 105 provides for the giving of a limiting instruction when evidence is admissible as to one party but not as to another. But the Supreme Court, in *Bruton v. United States*, 391 U.S. 123 (1968), held that, unless A testifies at the trial (and is subject to cross-examination by B), it is a violation of the Confrontation Clause to admit in their joint trial A's confession that implicates B, and that a limiting instruction

cannot cure the problem. However, because *Bruton* is grounded in the Confrontation Clause, it does not apply in other situations involving multiple parties, such as a civil action in which an admission by one of multiple party-opponents is admissible against that party-opponent under Rule 801(d)(2)(A), but not against the other party-opponents. Nonetheless, exclusion may be called for under Rule 403.

5. If an action is brought on behalf of a decedent by his estate, are statements that were made by the deceased considered admissions of a party-opponent under Rule 801(d)(2)(A)? *Compare Estate of Shafer v. C.I.R.*, 749 F.2d 1216, 1220 (6th Cir. 1984) ("Since Arthur, through his estate, is a party to this action, his statements are a 'classic example of an admission'"), *with In re Cornfield*, 365 F. Supp. 2d 271, 277 (E.D.N.Y. 2004) ("Rule 801(d)(2)(A) altered the common law rule by providing only for the admission of statements made by a party to the action. Privity-based admissions were abolished.").

6. In criminal cases, it is clear that the accused is a party and thus that his statements can be offered against him under Rule 801(d)(2)(A), as illustrated in the *Reed* case. Are statements made by the victim in a criminal case likewise admissible under Rule 801(d)(2)(A) when offered into evidence by the accused? *See Willover v. State*, 70 S.W.3d 841, 847 n.10 (Tex. 2002) (collecting cases holding that the victim in a criminal case is *not* a party-opponent within the meaning of Rule 801(d)(2)).

b. Adoptive Statements

United States v. Ward
377 F.3d 671 (7th Cir. 2004)

FLAUM, Chief Judge.

On October 26, 2001, Gregory and Aishauna Ward, a recently married couple, robbed the bank where Ms. Ward was employed. They were subsequently tried and convicted for conspiring to rob a bank, using force, violence, or intimidation to rob a bank, and using a firearm during the commission of a crime of violence. Gregory Ward now appeals his conviction, and Aishauna Ward appeals her conviction and sentence....

I. BACKGROUND

At approximately 7:00 a.m. on October 26, 2001, Aishauna Ward arrived for work.... Ms. Ward was not originally scheduled to work the morning shift, but she had instead volunteered to replace a sick colleague. Her only co-worker that morning was Shantel James.

While James was sitting inside the bank's glass enclosed office and preparing for the start of business, she noticed Ms. Ward speaking to a man near the teller line. A few minutes later Ms. Ward came into the office with the man, who was then wearing a bandana over his face and a black leather coat with the hood over his head. The man pointed a gun at James and demanded that Ms. Ward fill a bag with money.

Ms. Ward complied with the robber's directions. The robber allowed her to walk unescorted through an opaque door and down a hallway to the bank's vault. Once she reached the vault, Ms. Ward filled the bag with $209,000 and then returned to where the robber was located....

The robber forced James outside of the Jewel store and approximately four store lengths' down the street when he then instructed her to walk slowly back to the bank while he drove away....

Six days later, Ms. Ward and her husband Gregory were arrested for the robbery of the TCF Bank branch....

Mr. and Ms. Ward subsequently were charged with conspiring to rob a bank and using a firearm during the commission of a crime of violence. After Mr. Ward was released on bond, he called his sister on December 3, 2001. Mr. Ward asked his sister if he could retrieve a bag he had given her to hold following the robbery. Mr. Ward's sister informed him that the bag, which initially contained $50,000 in cash, was being safeguarded by family friend Kimberly Gardner and her boyfriend Michael Bryant.

A few hours later, Mr. Ward and his sister drove to Gardner's apartment to retrieve the bag. Suspiciously, the bag could not be located, which caused Mr. Ward to become upset. Mr. Ward, his sister, and Gardner and Bryant all stood around the kitchen and bathroom area of Gardner's apartment, and Mr. Ward's sister then said, "I don't believe he's getting ready to go to jail for 10 years for something he doesn't even have" and that the money was "the money they got when they robbed the bank." Mr. Ward did not respond, but a few minutes later stated that "something got to give or else I'm gon' catch a murder before I go back to jail." Mr. Ward and his sister then left the apartment, and on the way home, he said, "she's not going to believe [that I don't] have the money."

The next day, Gardner and Bryant turned Mr. Ward's missing bag over to the FBI. By this point there was only $23,000 left in the bag, some of which was sequentially numbered $20 bills. Gardner agreed to testify regarding the previous day's events and in turn the government agreed not to prosecute her for spending bank robbery proceeds. With the help of Gardner's testimony, both Gregory and Aishauna Ward were convicted of all of the charges against them after a three-day jury trial. They now appeal.

II. Discussion

Gregory and Aishauna Ward begin by challenging the admission of Gardner's testimony regarding the events of December 3, 2001. Specifically, they contend that Gardner should not have been allowed to testify that after Mr. Ward's sister said, "that's the money they got when they robbed the bank," Mr. Ward remained silent. Ms. Ward argues separately that even if this testimony was allowed against Mr. Ward, it should not have been used against her.

We begin by determining whether this evidence was admissible against Mr. Ward. Although Mr. Ward argues that his sister's statement was hearsay and thus should have been excluded, the district court found that Mr. Ward's silence in the face of his sister's assertion that he had robbed a bank was an adoptive admission. Under Federal Rule of Evidence 801(d)(2)(B), a statement is not hearsay if it is offered against a party and is [one the party manifested that it adopted or believed to be true]. It is not necessary for one to use any specific language to adopt another's statement. Rather, a statement may be adopted as long as the statement was made in the defendant's presence, the defendant understood the statement, and the defendant has the opportunity to deny the statement but did not do so. We review the district court's determination that Mr. Ward's silence was an adoptive admission for an abuse of discretion.

Mr. Ward argues that the district court did abuse its discretion because there was no evidence that he heard or understood his sister's statement. He begins by distinguishing his case from *United States v. Andrus*, 775 F.2d 825, 839 (7th Cir. 1985), in which the defendant was found to have adopted another's statement partly because both were seated at the same table during the relevant discussion. From *Andrus*, Mr. Ward concludes that the government must prove that both the speaker and listener were in a confined space in order to establish that they could hear and understand each other. However, we decline to adopt such a narrow interpretation of the adoptive admission rule. While proof of proximity may be helpful to show that one heard and understood another, it is not determinative. A defendant may also demonstrate his cognizance of a conversation by his statements and conduct during or after the conversation.

In this case, Mr. Ward's location as well as his verbal responses show that he heard and understood the conversation taking place around him. While there was no testimony to establish the exact place each person was standing during the conversation, the witnesses did testify that Mr. Ward, his sister, and Gardner and Bryant were all in the kitchen and bathroom area of Gardner's basement apartment. Mr. Ward argues that the size of the kitchen and bathroom area was never specified, but the evidence did show that all four parties were together and having a heated discussion about Mr. Ward's $50,000. This, obviously, is a conversation in which Mr. Ward had a great interest. He was angry that the money was missing, and at various points in the conversation told Gardner that he trusted her because he knew her, but that he did not know Bryant. Mr. Ward's sister was also angry and stated that she could not believe her brother was going to jail for something he no longer had. A few moments later, Mr. Ward threatened Gardner and Bryant that if something did not change, he was going to "catch a murder" before he went to jail. This give and take between Mr. Ward and his sister, as well as Mr. Ward and the other parties to the conversation, indicates that each could hear and understand the other.

Thus, the district court did not abuse its discretion by admitting evidence that Mr. Ward remained silent when his sister said, "that's the money they got when they robbed the bank." This statement was made during the conversation discussed above, in which Mr. Ward was an active participant. Moreover, Mr. Ward's silence qualifies as an admission because his sister's accusation is the type of statement that a party normally would respond to if innocent. *See* Fed.R.Evid. 801(d)(2)(B) Advisory Note to Subdivision d (stating that "[w]hen silence is relied upon, the theory is that the person would, under the circumstances, protest the statement made in his presence, if untrue"). For these reasons, the statement was properly admitted against Mr. Ward....

United States v. Paulino
13 F.3d 20 (1st Cir. 1994)

SELYA, Circuit Judge....

This case finds its genesis in an undercover investigation of narcotics trafficking conducted by the Providence, Rhode Island police department. The investigation focused on an apartment building at 70 Peace Street. In due course, the police began paying special attention to apartment 706. On several occasions in late May and early June of 1992, they observed appellant [Temistocles Paulino] in and around the apartment.

After intensive surveillance, an informant, acting under police auspices, entered apartment 706 during early June and made a controlled purchase of cocaine from the principal suspect, Moreno, inside the apartment. While the transaction was in progress detectives observed Paulino peering from a window. The officers subsequently obtained a search warrant and executed it on June 11, 1992. They discovered appellant in the kitchen....

Although the tiny apartment contained little more than a kitchen, bathroom, and bedroom, it nevertheless disclosed bountiful evidence of drug trafficking activities. Detectives found an assortment of drugs in the bedroom....

From atop the coffee table, the police confiscated a collection of drug paraphernalia.... On a chair next to the table, under a shirt, within easy reaching distance of the drugs, officers spotted a loaded revolver. On appellant's person, officers found a key to the apartment's front door. No other key to the apartment was located....

[Paulino was arrested, indicted, and convicted of various narcotics charges.]

Appellant's most touted assignment of error relates to a so-called "customer's receipt" for a Postal Service money order discovered on a kitchen shelf. The receipt bore appellant's name (although his given name, "Temistocles," was spelled with two surplus letters, *viz*, "Temistomecles"), listed his address as "70 Peace $ 706 Prov. RI 02907," and purported to corroborate payment to "Tower Management" in an amount of $280. In the "used for" space, someone had written "May rent."

At trial, the prosecution offered the receipt to prove the truth of the matter asserted therein: that appellant had paid the apartment rent for May 1992—a period when the apartment was used as a drug distribution outlet....

In overruling appellant's hearsay objection, the district court did not specifically identify a hearsay exclusion or exception that removed the barrier to introduction of the evidence....

In the present situation, we believe the receipt can be classified as an adoptive admission, and, therefore, that it eludes the hearsay bar.... In applying this doctrine, courts frequently have construed possession of a written statement as an adoption of what its contents reveal. *See, e.g., United States v. Ospina*, 739 F.2d 448, 451 (9th Cir.) (involving a receipt for a hotel room), *cert. denied*, 469 U.S. 887 (1984) *and* 471 U.S. 1126 (1985); *United States v. Marino*, 658 F.2d 1120, 1124–25 (6th Cir. 1981) (involving possession of airline tickets).

We think that the correct approach, exemplified by *Ospina*, is that "possession plus" can evidence adoption. Put another way, so long as the surrounding circumstances tie the possessor and the document together in some meaningful way, the possessor may be found to have adopted the writing and embraced its contents. Over and above possession, the tie is very strong here: appellant held the only known key to the apartment; he had frequented the premises; the saved document bore his name; and he was, at the very least, privy to the criminal enterprise. Consequently, the record is sufficient to permit a finding that appellant possessed and adopted [] the receipt....

Notes and Questions

1. The excerpt from *Ward* explains why the statement by Gregory Ward's sister is admissible against Gregory. Does the same rationale justify admitting the statement against Aishauna Ward? If not, does she have an additional ground on appeal not available to Gregory?

2. As with all other rules of evidence, Rule 801(d)(2)(B) is trumped by constitutional doctrines that would dictate a contrary result. Thus, for example, it is unconstitutional to introduce evidence that a criminal defendant remained silent after he was given a *Miranda* warning advising him of his right to remain silent. *See Doyle v. Ohio*, 426 U.S. 610 (1976); Advisory Committee Note to Rule 801(d)(2)(B).

3. Just as with individual admissions under Rule 801(d)(2)(A), personal knowledge of the statement adopted is not required under Rule 801(d)(2)(B):

> While knowledge of contents would ordinarily be essential, this is not inevitably so: "X is a reliable person and knows what he is talking about."

Advisory Committee Note to Rule 801(d)(2)(B). *See also Pillsbury Co. v. Cleaver-Brooks Div. of Aqua-Chem, Inc.*, 646 F.2d 1216, 1218 (8th Cir. 1981) ("personal knowledge is not a prerequisite for the adoption of another's statement pursuant to Rule 801(d)(2)(B)").

4. Can you adopt the contents of an e-mail message by forwarding it to someone else? *See Sea-Land Service, Inc. v. Lozen International, LLC*, 285 F.3d 808, 821 (9th Cir. 2002) (so holding where line added by person forwarding message implicitly adopted the contents of the forwarded e-mail by using the phrase, "Yikes, Pls note the rail screwed us up …").

5. Are you persuaded that the defendant in *Paulino* adopted the contents of the rent receipt? The *Marino* case, on which both *Paulino* and *Ospina* rely, reasoned that "[j]ust as silence in the face of an accusation may constitute an admission to its truth, possession of a written statement becomes an adoption of its contents." *United States v. Marino*, 658 F.2d 1120, 1125 (6th Cir. 1981). Do you agree?

6. What role does the judge play in determining whether a party adopted a statement? Is this a Rule 104(a) determination in that the judge must be persuaded that the statement was made, or is it a question of conditional relevancy for which the judge plays only a screening role under Rule 104(b)? *Compare United States v. Sears*, 663 F.2d 896, 904 (9th Cir. 1981) ("The court's judgment, however, is only a preliminary or threshold determination. The jury is primarily responsible for deciding whether, in light of all the surrounding facts and circumstances, the defendant actually heard, understood, and acquiesced in the statement."), *with Weston-Smith v. Cooley Dickinson Hospital*, 282 F.3d 60, 67 (1st Cir. 2002) ("trial judge plays a screening role"), *and United States v. Harrison*, 296 F.3d 994, 1001 (10th Cir. 2002) (treating it as a Rule 104(a) issue for the judge to decide). Is it possible that the answer is mixed, for example, that the trial court decides whether, under the circumstances, the person would have remained silent, but leaves it to the jury to decide whether the statement was made and whether the defendant in fact remained silent? *See* McCormick, Evidence §§ 261–262 (1992) (contending that the trial court should decide whether under the circumstances an innocent person would have responded); *see also* Advisory Committee Note to Rule 801(d)(2)(B) ("When silence is relied upon, the theory is that the person would, under the circumstances, protest the statement made in his presence, if untrue. The decision in each case calls for an evaluation in terms of probable human behavior.").

c. Statements of Agents and Employees

Problem 7-18: The Slip-and-Fall

Kevin is seriously injured when he slips and falls on the sidewalk in front of Treetop Apartments, an apartment complex. His friend Tanya, who lives across the street from Treetop Apartments and who was walking with him when he fell, took him back to her apartment and called an ambulance for him. After Kevin was taken to the hospital, Tanya looked up Treetop Apartments in the telephone book and dialed the listed number. When the person on the other end answered "Treetop Apartments," Tanya told her about the icy condition on the sidewalk and asked her to send someone down to salt and shovel the sidewalk.

About 20 minutes later, a man showed up in front of Treetop Apartments with a shovel and a bucket of salt. His shirt had a logo on it that read "Treetop Apartments," as did his vehicle. Tanya went across the street to speak with him about the sidewalk. The man said to Tanya, "I've been doing grounds maintenance for Treetop for 10 years, and we've constantly had problems with keeping this sidewalk free of ice. Our gutters discharge onto the sidewalk, and although we have known about the problem for some time, we have not been able to cover the costs of re-directing the gutters or paying someone on our maintenance staff to regularly remove ice from the sidewalk."

Kevin brings a negligence suit against Treetop Apartments. To support his claim of negligence, Kevin's attorney seeks to call Tanya to testify to what the man who showed up at the apartment building said to her. The attorney for Treetop Apartments raises a hearsay objection.

How should Kevin's attorney respond, and how will the court likely rule?

Mahlandt v. Wild Canid Survival & Research Center, Inc.

588 F.2d 626 (8th Cir. 1978)

VAN SICKLE, District Judge.

This is a civil action for damages arising out of an alleged attack by a wolf on a child. The sole issues on appeal are as to the correctness of three rulings which excluded conclusionary statements against interest. Two of them were made by a defendant, who was also an employee of the corporate defendant; and the third was in the form of a statement appearing in the records of a board meeting of the corporate defendant.

On March 23, 1973, Daniel Mahlandt, then 3 years, 10 months, and 8 days old, was sent by his mother to a neighbor's home on an adjoining street to get his older brother, Donald. Daniel's mother watched him cross the street, and then turned into the house to get her car keys. Daniel's path took him along a walkway adjacent to the Poos' residence. Next to the walkway was a five foot chain link fence to which Sophie had been chained with a six foot chain. In other words, Sophie was free to move in a half circle having a six foot radius on the side of the fence opposite from Daniel.

Sophie was a bitch wolf, 11 months and 28 days old, who had been born at the St. Louis Zoo, and kept there until she reached 6 months of age, at which time she was given to the Wild Canid Survival and Research Center, Inc. It was the policy of the Zoo to remove wolves from the Children's Zoo after they reached the age of 5 or 6 months. Sophie was supposed to be kept at the Tyson Research Center, but Kenneth Poos, as Director of Education for the Wild Canid Survival and Research Center, Inc., had been keeping her at his home because he was taking Sophie to schools and institutions where he showed films and gave programs with respect to the nature of wolves. Sophie was known as a very gentle wolf who had proved herself to be good natured and stable during her contacts with thousands of children, while she was in the St. Louis Children's Zoo.

Sophie was chained because the evening before she had jumped the fence and attacked a beagle who was running along the fence and yapping at her.

A neighbor who was ill in bed in the second floor of his home heard a child's screams and went to his window, where he saw a boy lying on his back within the enclosure, with a wolf straddling him. The wolf's face was near Daniel's face, but the distance was so great that he could not see what the wolf was doing, and did not see any biting. Within about 15 seconds the neighbor saw Clarke Poos, about seventeen, run around the house, get the wolf off of the boy, and disappear with the child in his arms to the back of the house. Clarke took the boy in and laid him on the kitchen floor.

Clarke had been returning from his friend's home immediately west when he heard a child's cries and ran around to the enclosure. He found Daniel lying within the enclosure, about three feet from the fence, and Sophie standing back from the boy the length of her chain, and wailing. An expert in the behavior of wolves stated that when a wolf licks a child's face that it is a sign of care, and not a sign of attack; that a wolf's wail is a sign of compassion, and an effort to get attention, not a sign of attack. No witness saw or knew how Daniel was injured. Clarke and his sister ran over to get Daniel's mother. She says that Clarke told her, "a wolf got Danny and he is dying." Clarke denies that statement.

The defendant, Mr. Poos, arrived home while Daniel and his mother were in the kitchen. After Daniel was taken in an ambulance, Mr. Poos talked to everyone present, including a neighbor who came in. Within an hour after he arrived home, Mr. Poos went to Washington University to inform Owen Sexton, President of Wild Canid Survival and Research Center, Inc., of the incident. Mr. Sexton was not in his office so Mr. Poos left the following note on his door:

> Owen, would call me at home, 727-5080? Sophie bit a child that came in our back yard. All has been taken care of. I need to convey what happened to you.

Denial of admission of this note is one of the issues on appeal.

Later that day, Mr. Poos found Mr. Sexton at the Tyson Research Center and told him what had happened. Denial of plaintiff's offer to prove that Mr. Poos told Mr. Sexton that, "Sophie had bit a child that day," is the second issue on appeal.

A meeting of the Directors of the Wild Canid Survival and Research Center, Inc., was held on April 4, 1973. Mr. Poos was not present at that meeting. The minutes of that meeting reflect that there was a "great deal of discussion ... about the legal aspects of the incident of Sophie biting the child." Plaintiff offered an abstract of the minutes containing that reference. Denial of the offer of that abstract is the third issue on appeal.

Daniel had lacerations of the face, left thigh, left calf, and right thigh, and abrasions and bruises of the abdomen and chest. Mr. Mahlandt was permitted to state that Daniel had indicated that he had gone under the fence. Mr. Mahlandt and Mr. Poos, about a month after the incident, examined the fence to determine what caused Daniel's lacerations. Mr. Mahlandt felt that they did not look like animal bites. The parallel scars on Daniel's thigh appeared to match the configuration of the barbs or tines on the fence. The expert as to the behavior of wolves opined that the lacerations were not wolf bites or wounds caused by wolf claws. Wolves have powerful jaws and a wolf bite will result in massive crushing or severing of a limb. He stated that if Sophie had bitten Daniel there would have been clear apposition of teeth and massive crushing of Daniel's hands and arms which were not injured. Also, if Sophie had pulled Daniel under the fence, tooth marks on the foot or leg would have been present, although Sophie possessed enough strength to pull the boy under the fence.

The jury brought in a verdict for the defense.

The trial judge's rationale for excluding the note, the statement, and the corporate minutes, was the same in each case. He reasoned that Mr. Poos did not have any personal knowledge of the facts, and accordingly, the first two admissions were based on hearsay; and the third admission contained in the minutes of the board meeting was subject to the same objection of hearsay, and unreliability because of lack of personal knowledge.

The Federal Rules of Evidence became effective in July 1975 (180 days after passage of the Act). Thus, at this time, there is very little case law to rely upon for resolution of the problems of interpretation.

The relevant rule here is [Rule 801(d)(2)(A)-(D)]....

So the statement in the note pinned on the door is not hearsay, and is admissible against Mr. Poos. It was his own statement, and as such was clearly different from the reported statement of another. Example, "I was told that...." It was also a statement of which he had manifested his adoption or belief in its truth. And the same observations may be made of the statement made later in the day to Mr. Sexton that, "Sophie had bit a child...."

Are these statements admissible against Wild Canid Survival and Research Center, Inc.? They were made by Mr. Poos when he was an agent or servant of the Wild Canid Survival and Research Center, Inc., and they concerned a matter within the scope of his agency, or employment, i.e., his custody of Sophie, and were made during the existence of that relationship.

Defendant argues that Rule 801(d)(2) does not provide for the admission of "in house" statements; that is, it allows only admissions made to third parties.

The notes of the Advisory Committee on the Proposed Rules discuss the problem of "in house" admissions with reference to Rule 801(d)(2)(C) situations. This is not a (C) situation because Mr. Poos was not authorized or directed to make a statement on the matter by anyone. But the rationale developed in that comment does apply to this (D) situation. Mr. Poos had actual physical custody of Sophie. His conclusions, his opinions, were obviously accepted as a basis for action by his principal. As the Advisory Committee points out in its note on (C) situations:

> ... communication to an outsider has not generally been thought to be an essential characteristic of an admission. Thus a party's books or records are usable against him, without regard to any intent to disclose to third persons. V Wigmore on Evidence § 1557.

Weinstein's discussion of Rule 801(d)(2)(D) (Weinstein's Evidence § 801(d)(2)(D)(01), p. 801-137), states that:

> Rule 801(d)(2)(D) adopts the approach ... which, as a general proposition, makes statement made by agents within the scope of their employment admissible.... Once agency, and the making of the statement while the relationship continues, are established, the statement is exempt from the hearsay rule so long as it relates to a matter within the scope of the agency.

After reciting a lengthy quotation which justifies the rule as necessary, and suggests that such admissions are trustworthy and reliable, Weinstein states categorically that although an express requirement of personal knowledge on the part of the declarant of the facts underlying his statement is not written into the rule, it should be. He feels that is mandated by Rules 805 and 403....

[W]hile both Rule 805 and Rule 403 provide additional bases for excluding otherwise acceptable evidence, neither rule mandates the introduction into Rule 801(d)(2)(D) of an implied requirement that the declarant have personal knowledge of the facts underlying his statement. So we conclude that the two statements made by Mr. Poos were admissible against Wild Canid Survival and Research Center, Inc.

As to the entry in the records of a corporate meeting, the directors as primary officers of the corporation had the authority to include their conclusions in the record of the meeting. So the evidence would fall within 801(d)(2)(C) as to Wild Canid Survival and Research Center, Inc., and be admissible. The "in house" aspect of this admission has already been discussed, Rule 801(d)(2)(D), *supra*.

But there was no servant, or agency, relationship which justified admitting the evidence of the board minutes as against Mr. Poos.

None of the conditions of 801(d)(2) cover the claim that minutes of a corporate board meeting can be used against a non-attending, non-participating employee of that corporation. The evidence was not admissible as against Mr. Poos.

There is left only the question of whether the trial court's rulings which excluded all three items of evidence are justified under Rule 403. He clearly found that the evidence was not reliable, pointing out that none of the statements were based on the personal knowledge of the declarant.

Again, that problem was faced by the Advisory Committee on Proposed Rules. In its discussion of 801(d)(2) exceptions to the hearsay rule, the Committee said:

> The freedom which admissions have enjoyed from technical demands of searching for an assurance of trustworthiness in some against-interest circumstances, and from the restrictive influences of the opinion rule and the rule requiring first hand knowledge, when taken with the apparently prevalent satisfaction with the results, calls for generous treatment of this avenue to admissibility.

So here, remembering that relevant evidence is usually prejudicial to the cause of the side against which it is presented, and that the prejudice which concerns us is unreasonable prejudice; and applying the spirit of Rule 801(d)(2), we hold that Rule 403 does not warrant the exclusion of the evidence of Mr. Poos' statements as against himself or Wild Canid Survival and Research Center, Inc.

But the limited admissibility of the corporate minutes, coupled with the repetitive nature of the evidence and the low probative value of the minute record, all justify supporting the judgment of the trial court under Rule 403....

Notes and Questions

1. At common law, admissions by an agent could be admitted into evidence against the principal only for agents who were authorized to speak on the principal's behalf. For some types of agents, such as attorneys, speaking authority is assumed, but for most, it must be expressly conferred. Rule 801(d)(2)(C) reflects the narrow scope of the vicarious admissions doctrine at common law, albeit expanded, as the discussion in *Mahlandt* indicates, to cover statements made internally. Under the common law rule, a statement made by an agent regarding a matter that related to his duties for his principal generally could not be admitted against the employer, as employees typically lacked authority to *speak* on the principal's behalf. For example, under the common law rule, if the driver of a company's delivery truck were to get into an accident with another individual, and that individual sued the company on a theory of *respondeat superior*, nothing that the driver of the truck said at the scene of the accident—even though it related to his employment—could be admitted into evidence as a vicarious admission against the company, because he lacked authority to speak on the company's behalf.

Before the federal rules of evidence were adopted, courts started to stray from the confines of the common law rule:

> To say, in these circumstances, that the owner of a motor truck may constitute a person his agent for the purpose of the operation of such truck over public streets and highways, and to say at the same time that such operator is no longer

the agent of such owner when an accident occurs, for the purpose of truthfully relating the facts concerning the occurrence to an investigating police officer on the scene shortly thereafter, seems to me to erect an untenable fiction, neither contemplated by the parties nor sanctioned by public policy.

Martin v. Savage Truck Line, 121 F. Supp. 417, 419 (D.D.C. 1954).

Rule 801(d)(2)(D) dramatically expanded the scope of the vicarious admissions doctrine. The Advisory Committee explained its rationale as follows:

> The tradition has been to test the admissibility of statements by agents, as admissions, by applying the usual test of agency. Was the admission made by the agent acting in the scope of his employment? Since few principals employ agents for the purpose of making damaging statements, the usual result was exclusion of the statement. Dissatisfaction with this loss of valuable and helpful evidence has been increasing. A substantial trend favors admitting statements related to a matter within the scope of the agency or employment.

Advisory Committee Note to Rule 801(d)(2)(D).

2. The determination whether someone qualifies as a person's "agent or employee," as well as the question whether something falls "within the scope of that relationship," is governed by federal common law principles of agency law. *Gomez v. Rivera Rodriguez*, 344 F.3d 103, 116 (1st Cir. 2003); *Lippay v. Christos*, 996 F.2d 1490, 1497 (3d Cir. 1993); *Boren v. Sable*, 887 F.2d 1032, 1038 (10th Cir. 1989).

3. In employment discrimination cases, for something to be deemed within the scope of a declarant's employment for purposes of Rule 801(d)(2)(D), federal case law holds that the declarant must be involved in the decisionmaking process affecting the employment action at issue. *See Talavera v. Shah*, 638 F.3d 303, 309 (D.C. Cir. 2011); *Young v. James Green Management, Inc.*, 327 F.3d 616, 622 n.2 (7th Cir. 2003); *United States v. Rioux*, 97 F.3d 648, 661 (2d Cir. 1996).

4. A statement can be admitted under Rule 801(d)(2)(D) only if made at a time when the agency or employment relationship existed. Thus, a statement made by a former employee or agent is not admissible against her principal. *E.g., Young v. James Green Management, Inc.*, 327 F.3d 616, 622–23 (7th Cir. 2003). Do you see why this is a logical limitation on the doctrine?

5. When a principal is sued on a theory of *respondeat superior*, and the plaintiff seeks to introduce the statements of the principal's agent under Rule 801(d)(2)(D), is there not an overlap between the task of determining whether the statements are admissible and the ultimate determination of liability? What is the judge's role in determining whether a statement satisfies the requirements of Rule 801(d)(2)(D)? *See Riley v. K Mart Corp.*, 864 F.2d 1049, 1055 n.8 (3d Cir. 1988) (Rule 104(a) issue for the judge to decide). Can the judge's rulings on the admissibility of statements under Rule 801(d)(2)(D) have a subtle impact on the outcome of the case, depending on the judge's view of the merits?

6. Is a government agent an "agent" for purposes of Rule 801(d)(2)(D), such that his statements can be offered against the government in a criminal prosecution brought by the government? *Compare United States v. Yildiz*, 355 F.3d 80, 82 (2d Cir. 2004) (holding that common law rule that statements of government agents are not admissions of the sovereign is incorporated into Rule 801(d)(2)(D)), *with United States v. Branham*, 97 F.3d 835, 850–51 (6th Cir. 1996) (statements by government agents can be admitted as admissions against the government in criminal cases).

7. Do the statements of an independent contractor qualify as statements of a party's agent under Rule 801(d)(2)(D)? *Compare Dora Homes, Inc. v. Epperson*, 344 F. Supp. 2d 875, 885 (E.D.N.Y. 2004) (stating in blanket terms that they do not), *with United States v. Bonds*, 608 F.3d 495, 505 (9th Cir. 2010) (holding that while an independent contractor is not ordinarily an agent under Rule 801(d)(2)(D), a finding that a declarant is an independent contractor does not foreclose the possibility that they are an agent for some purposes) *and Condus v. Howard Sav. Bank*, 986 F. Supp. 914, 915–17 (D.N.J. 1997) (distinguishing between "agent independent contractors" and "non-agent independent contractors").

d. Statements by Coconspirators

Problem 7-19: The Drug Cartel

Marie, Tom, and Robert are indicted and jointly tried on charges of possession and distribution of marijuana and conspiracy to do the same. At trial, the government seeks to offer into evidence the following pieces of evidence:

1. Testimony by Paula as to the following statement made by Marie to Paula: "Why don't you get involved in our business? Tom, Robert, and I are each netting about $20,000 per week selling weed, and the sky is really the limit." As it turns out, Paula is an undercover government informant.

2. Testimony by William that when Tom was out at a bar with him and with their other friend Charles, Charles asked Tom, "How is it that you have so much money all of a sudden? Are you and those friends of yours, Marie and Robert, selling drugs?" and Tom just smiled and said nothing.

3. Testimony by Donna, a drug enforcement officer who arrested Robert after
    he made a controlled sale of drugs to her, that Robert said to her, "Look,
    I'm just a cog in all of this; Marie is the mastermind."

*All three parties raise hearsay objections. How should the government respond,
and how will the court likely rule?*

Bourjaily v. United States
483 U.S. 171 (1987)

Chief Justice REHNQUIST delivered the opinion of the Court.

.... We granted certiorari to answer three questions regarding the admission of statements under Rule 801(d)(2)(E): (1) whether the court must determine by independent
evidence that the conspiracy existed and that the defendant and the declarant were members of this conspiracy; (2) the quantum of proof on which such determinations must be
based; and (3) whether a court must in each case examine the circumstances of such a statement to determine its reliability.

In May 1984, Clarence Greathouse, an informant working for the Federal Bureau of
Investigation (FBI), arranged to sell a kilogram of cocaine to Angelo Lonardo. Lonardo
agreed that he would find individuals to distribute the drug. When the sale became imminent, Lonardo stated in a tape-recorded telephone conversation that he had a "gentle-
man friend" who had some questions to ask about the cocaine. In a subsequent telephone
call, Greathouse spoke to the "friend" about the quality of the drug and the price. Greathouse
then spoke again with Lonardo, and the two arranged the details of the purchase. They
agreed that the sale would take place in a designated hotel parking lot, and Lonardo would
transfer the drug from Greathouse's car to the "friend," who would be waiting in the parking lot in his own car. Greathouse proceeded with the transaction as planned, and FBI agents
arrested Lonardo and petitioner immediately after Lonardo placed a kilogram of cocaine
into petitioner's car in the hotel parking lot. In petitioner's car, the agents found over
$20,000 in cash.

Petitioner was charged with conspiring to distribute cocaine, in violation of 21 U.S.C.
§ 846, and possession of cocaine with intent to distribute, a violation of 21 U.S.C.
§ 841(a)(1). The Government introduced, over petitioner's objection, Angelo Lonardo's
telephone statements regarding the participation of the "friend" in the transaction. The
District Court found that, considering the events in the parking lot and Lonardo's statements over the telephone, the Government had established by a preponderance of the
evidence that a conspiracy involving Lonardo and petitioner existed, and that Lonardo's
statements over the telephone had been made in the course of and in furtherance of the
conspiracy. Accordingly, the trial court held that Lonardo's out-of-court statements satisfied Rule 801(d)(2)(E) and were not hearsay.... The United States Court of Appeals for
the Sixth Circuit affirmed....

Before admitting a co-conspirator's statement over an objection that it does not qualify under Rule 801(d)(2)(E), a court must be satisfied that the statement actually falls
within the definition of the Rule. There must be evidence that there was a conspiracy involving the declarant and the nonoffering party, and that the statement was made "during [] and in furtherance of the conspiracy." Federal Rule of Evidence 104(a) provides
[that the court decides preliminary questions about whether evidence is admissible]. Petitioner and the Government agree that the existence of a conspiracy and petitioner's involvement in it are preliminary questions of fact that, under Rule 104, must be resolved

by the court. The Federal Rules, however, nowhere define the standard of proof the court must observe in resolving these questions.

We are therefore guided by our prior decisions regarding admissibility determinations that hinge on preliminary factual questions. We have traditionally required that these matters be established by a preponderance of proof. Evidence is placed before the jury when it satisfies the technical requirements of the evidentiary Rules, which embody certain legal and policy determinations. The inquiry made by a court concerned with these matters is not whether the proponent of the evidence wins or loses his case on the merits, but whether the evidentiary Rules have been satisfied. Thus, the evidentiary standard is unrelated to the burden of proof on the substantive issues, be it a criminal case or a civil case. The preponderance standard ensures that before admitting evidence, the court will have found it more likely than not that the technical issues and policy concerns addressed by the Federal Rules of Evidence have been afforded due consideration.... We think that our previous decisions in this area resolve the matter. Therefore, we hold that when the preliminary facts relevant to Rule 801(d)(2)(E) are disputed, the offering party must prove them by a preponderance of the evidence.[1]

Even though petitioner agrees that the courts below applied the proper standard of proof with regard to the preliminary facts relevant to Rule 801(d)(2)(E), he nevertheless challenges the admission of Lonardo's statements. Petitioner argues that in determining whether a conspiracy exists and whether the defendant was a member of it, the court must look only to independent evidence—that is, evidence other than the statements sought to be admitted. Petitioner relies on *Glasser* v. *United States*, 315 U.S. 60 (1942), in which this Court first mentioned the so-called "bootstrapping rule." The relevant issue in *Glasser* was whether Glasser's counsel, who also represented another defendant, faced such a conflict of interest that Glasser received ineffective assistance. Glasser contended that conflicting loyalties led his lawyer not to object to statements made by one of Glasser's co-conspirators. The Government argued that any objection would have been fruitless because the statements were admissible. The Court rejected this proposition:

> "[S]uch declarations are admissible over the objection of an alleged co-conspirator, who was not present when they were made, only if there is proof *aliunde* that he is connected with the conspiracy.... Otherwise, hearsay would lift itself by its own bootstraps to the level of competent evidence."

The Court revisited the bootstrapping rule in *United States* v. *Nixon*, 418 U.S. 683 (1974), where again, in passing, the Court stated: "Declarations by one defendant may also be admissible against other defendants upon a sufficient showing, *by independent evidence*, of a conspiracy among one or more other defendants and the declarant and if the declarations at issue were in furtherance of that conspiracy." Read in the light most favorable to petitioner, *Glasser* could mean that a court should not consider hearsay statements at all in determining preliminary facts under Rule 801(d)(2)(E). Petitioner, of course, adopts this view of the bootstrapping rule. *Glasser*, however, could also mean that a court must have *some* proof *aliunde*, but may look at the hearsay statements themselves in light of this independent evidence to determine whether a conspiracy has been

---

1. We intimate no view on the proper standard of proof for questions falling under Federal Rule of Evidence 104(b) (conditional relevancy). We also decline to address the circumstances in which the burden of coming forward to show that the proffered evidence is inadmissible is appropriately placed on the nonoffering party. Finally, we do not express an opinion on the proper order of proof that trial courts should follow in concluding that the preponderance standard has been satisfied in an ongoing trial.

shown by a preponderance of the evidence. The Courts of Appeals have widely adopted the former view and held that in determining the preliminary facts relevant to co-conspirators' out-of-court statements, a court may not look at the hearsay statements themselves for their evidentiary value.

Both *Glasser* and *Nixon*, however, were decided before Congress enacted the Federal Rules of Evidence in 1975. These Rules now govern the treatment of evidentiary questions in federal courts. [The Court quotes the portion of Rule 104(a) that provides that the court is not bound by the rules of evidence (except those on privilege) when deciding preliminary questions concerning the admissibility of evidence.] The question thus presented is whether any aspect of *Glasser*'s bootstrapping rule remains viable after the enactment of the Federal Rules of Evidence.

Petitioner concedes that Rule 104, on its face, appears to allow the court to make the preliminary factual determinations relevant to Rule 801(d)(2)(E) by considering any evidence it wishes, unhindered by considerations of admissibility. That would seem to many to be the end of the matter. Congress has decided that courts may consider hearsay in making these factual determinations. Out-of-court statements made by anyone, including putative co-conspirators, are often hearsay. Even if they are, they may be considered, *Glasser* and the bootstrapping rule notwithstanding. But petitioner nevertheless argues that the bootstrapping rule, as most Courts of Appeals have construed it, survived this apparently unequivocal change in the law unscathed and that Rule 104, as applied to the admission of co-conspirator's statements, does not mean what it says. We disagree.

Petitioner claims that Congress evidenced no intent to disturb the bootstrapping rule, which was embedded in the previous approach, and we should not find that Congress altered the rule without affirmative evidence so indicating. It would be extraordinary to require legislative history to *confirm* the plain meaning of Rule 104. The Rule on its face allows the trial judge to consider any evidence whatsoever, bound only by the rules of privilege. We think that the Rule is sufficiently clear that to the extent that it is inconsistent with petitioner's interpretation of *Glasser* and *Nixon*, the Rule prevails.[2]

Nor do we agree with petitioner that this construction of Rule 104(a) will allow courts to admit hearsay statements without any credible proof of the conspiracy, thus fundamentally changing the nature of the co-conspirator exception. Petitioner starts with the proposition that co-conspirators' out-of-court statements are deemed unreliable and are inadmissible, at least until a conspiracy is shown. Since these statements are unreliable, petitioner contends that they should not form any part of the basis for establishing a conspiracy, the very antecedent that renders them admissible.

Petitioner's theory ignores two simple facts of evidentiary life. First, out-of-court statements are only *presumed* unreliable. The presumption may be rebutted by appropriate proof. Second, individual pieces of evidence, insufficient in themselves to prove a point, may in cumulation prove it. The sum of an evidentiary presentation may well be greater than its constituent parts. Taken together, these two propositions demonstrate that a piece of evidence, unreliable in isolation, may become quite probative when corroborated by

---

2. The Advisory Committee Notes show that the Rule was not adopted in a fit of absentmindedness. The Note to Rule 104 specifically addresses the process by which a federal court should make the factual determinations requisite to a finding of admissibility.... "An item, offered and objected to, *may itself be considered in ruling on admissibility*, though not yet admitted in evidence." We think this language makes plain the drafters' intent to abolish any kind of bootstrapping rule. Silence is at best ambiguous, and we decline the invitation to rely on speculation to import ambiguity into what is otherwise a clear rule.

other evidence. A *per se* rule barring consideration of these hearsay statements during preliminary factfinding is not therefore required. Even if out-of-court declarations by co-conspirators are presumptively unreliable, trial courts must be permitted to evaluate these statements for their evidentiary worth as revealed by the particular circumstances of the case. Courts often act as factfinders, and there is no reason to believe that courts are any less able to properly recognize the probative value of evidence in this particular area. The party opposing admission has an adequate incentive to point out the shortcomings in such evidence before the trial court finds the preliminary facts. If the opposing party is unsuccessful in keeping the evidence from the factfinder, he still has the opportunity to attack the probative value of the evidence as it relates to the substantive issue in the case.

We think that there is little doubt that a co-conspirator's statements could themselves be probative of the existence of a conspiracy and the participation of both the defendant and the declarant in the conspiracy. Petitioner's case presents a paradigm. The out-of-court statements of Lonardo indicated that Lonardo was involved in a conspiracy with a "friend." The statements indicated that the friend had agreed with Lonardo to buy a kilogram of cocaine and to distribute it. The statements also revealed that the friend would be at the hotel parking lot, in his car, and would accept the cocaine from Greathouse's car after Greathouse gave Lonardo the keys. Each one of Lonardo's statements may itself be unreliable, but taken as a whole, the entire conversation between Lonardo and Greathouse was corroborated by independent evidence. The friend, who turned out to be petitioner, showed up at the prearranged spot at the prearranged time. He picked up the cocaine, and a significant sum of money was found in his car. On these facts, the trial court concluded, in our view correctly, that the Government had established the existence of a conspiracy and petitioner's participation in it.

We need not decide in this case whether the courts below could have relied solely upon Lonardo's hearsay statements to determine that a conspiracy had been established by a preponderance of the evidence. To the extent that *Glasser* meant that courts could not look to the hearsay statements themselves for any purpose, it has clearly been superseded by Rule 104(a). It is sufficient for today to hold that a court, in making a preliminary factual determination under Rule 801(d)(2)(E), may examine the hearsay statements sought to be admitted....

[The concurring opinion of Justice Stevens and the dissenting opinion of Justice Blackmun are omitted.]

Romani v. State
542 So.2d 984 (Fla. 1989)

MCDONALD, Justice.

....

Dr. Olga Romani was charged with and convicted of conspiracy to commit first-degree murder and the first-degree murder of Dr. Gerado DeMola.... The facts pertinent at this time are that the conspiracy involved at least nine people ... The trial court denied defense counsel's motions to exclude the coconspirators' hearsay statements, holding that sufficient evidence had been produced to demonstrate a conspiracy.

The district court held that the trial judge could consider the coconspirator hearsay statements in determining the out-of-court declarant's participation in the conspiracy. The court made this determination based upon *Bourjaily v. United States*, 483 U.S. 171

(1987), which held that a court, in making preliminary factual determinations, may examine the hearsay statements sought to be admitted. In *Bourjaily* the Supreme Court explained that out-of-court statements are only presumed unreliable and that the presumption may be rebutted. "[A] piece of evidence, unreliable in isolation, may become quite probative when corroborated by other evidence." Moreover, Federal Rule of Evidence 104(a) provides that in determining preliminary questions concerning admissibility, the court [is not bound by the rules of evidence, except those on privilege].

We decline to adopt the federal approach laid out in *Bourjaily* and approved by the district court in *Romani*. There is no counterpart to rule 104(a) in the Florida Evidence Code. To the contrary, the Florida Code provides for a jury instruction that each member's participation in the conspiracy must be proved by independent evidence. §90.803(18)(e). In accordance with the statute and prior Florida case law, we have required that a court rely upon independent evidence to prove a conspiracy, and each member's participation in it, before admitting coconspirator hearsay statements. We are apprehensive that adopting the *Bourjaily* rule would frequently lead to the admission of statements which are not reliable. Our present rule of disallowing the statement itself in determining its admissibility helps assure that a defendant is convicted only on credible evidence....

Notes and Questions

1. In 1997, the Advisory Committee amended Rule 801(d)(2) to add an additional sentence at the end of it that, in its present form, reads as follows:

> The statement must be considered but does not by itself establish the declarant's authority under (C); the existence or scope of the relationship under (D); or the existence of the conspiracy or participation in it under (E).

The Advisory Committee explained the reasons for the amendment as follows:

> Rule 801(d)(2) has been amended in order to respond to three issues raised by *Bourjaily v. United States*, 483 U.S. 171 (1987). First, the amendment codifies the holding in *Bourjaily* by stating expressly that a court shall consider the contents of a coconspirator's statement in determining "the existence of the conspiracy and the participation therein of the declarant and the party against whom the statement is offered." According to *Bourjaily*, Rule 104(a) requires these preliminary questions to be established by a preponderance of the evidence.
>
> Second, the amendment resolves an issue on which the Court had reserved decision. It provides that the contents of the declarant's statement do not alone suffice to establish a conspiracy in which the declarant and the defendant participated. The court must consider in addition the circumstances surrounding the statement, such as the identity of the speaker, the context in which the statement was made, or evidence corroborating the contents of the statement in making its determination as to each preliminary question....
>
> Third, the amendment extends the reasoning of *Bourjaily* to statements offered under subdivisions (C) and (D) of Rule 801(d)(2)....

Advisory Committee Note to 1997 Amendment to Rule 801(d)(2).

2. To invoke Rule 801(d)(2)(E), it is not necessary that the defendant be *charged* with conspiracy; it is only necessary that there is sufficient evidence that the trial court can find by a preponderance of the evidence, under Rule 104(a), that there existed a conspiracy of which the declarant and the defendant were members. *E.g., United States v.*

Rea, 621 F.3d 595, 604 (7th Cir. 2010); *United States v. Candelaria-Silva*, 162 F.3d 698, 706 (1st Cir. 1998). Indeed, even if conspiracy is charged alongside other substantive charges, the fact that there is insufficient evidence to sustain a conviction on the conspiracy charge does not necessarily undermine the admissibility of evidence under Rule 801(d)(2)(E) that was used to support the other substantive charges. *E.g., United States v. Desena*, 260 F.3d 150, 158 (2d Cir. 2001). Do you see why this is so?

Moreover, because a *charge* of conspiracy is not an essential prerequisite for invoking Rule 801(d)(2)(E), it can be invoked not only in criminal cases but also in civil cases. *Paul F. Newton & Co. v. Texas Commerce Bank*, 630 F.2d 1111, 1121 (5th Cir. 1980).

3. Under Rule 801(d)(2)(E), statements made by those who earlier joined the conspiracy can be admitted against those who later joined the conspiracy:

> [A] conspiracy is like a train. When a party knowingly steps aboard, he is part of the crew, and assumes conspirator's responsibility for the existing freight— or conduct—regardless of whether he is aware of just what it is composed.

United States v. Baines, 812 F.2d 41, 42 (1st Cir. 1987). *Accord United States v. Farhane*, 634 F.3d 127, 161 n.35 (2d Cir. 2011).

4. Although a conspiracy charge is not a necessary prerequisite to invoking Rule 801(d)(2)(E), often conspiracy will be charged. In these instances, there will be some degree of overlap between the role of the judge in determining the admissibility of evidence under Rule 801(d)(2)(E) and the jury's role, because both will be deciding whether a conspiracy existed, although the judge need only be persuaded by a preponderance of the evidence while the jury must be persuaded beyond a reasonable doubt. When a trial judge admits evidence under Rule 801(d)(2)(E), based on a finding that a conspiracy existed, she must be careful not to prejudice the jury by exposing it to her finding:

> In the present case, having in mind his duty to decide these preliminary questions of admissibility, the trial judge told the jury shortly after the start of trial, "we'll get to the point eventually where I will be telling you if the government proves a conspiracy."
>
> ...
>
> [T]here is every need for the judge not to couch his rulings in terms that may unduly influence the jury. Thus, where ... the preconditions to admissibility include elements of the offenses with which the defendants are charged, disclosure to the jury that the government has established those elements to the satisfaction of the judge is especially inappropriate. When the government has persuaded the judge that the prerequisites for admission of coconspirator statements have been established, the judge should make his ... findings outside the presence of the jury, and the jury should not be told what facts the judge believes have been established.

United States v. Tracy, 12 F.3d 1186, 1199–1200 (2d Cir. 1993).

5. In those cases in which a conspiracy *is* charged, the evidence that will be offered as substantive evidence in support of the conspiracy charge is also relevant to establishing the prerequisites for admitting that very same evidence under Rule 801(d)(2)(E). This raises the question of "which comes first, the chicken or the egg?" Note that the Supreme Court left this question open in footnote 1 of its opinion in *Bourjaily*, and the issue was not addressed by the 1997 Amendment to Rule 801(d)(2)(E). Although some circuits express clear preferences, many leave the decision to the discretion of the trial court:

> In *Santiago*, we reaffirmed that the evidence as to these elements can be submitted to the court by way of proffer before trial, and the court can admit the state-

ment(s) subject to its later determination that, based on all of the evidence admitted at trial, the Government has proved by a preponderance of that evidence all three requisite foundational elements. We also have approved other procedures a district court can employ in making the preliminary admissibility determination ... including the following: the court can rule on each statement as it is elicited based on the evidence the Government has adduced to that point; the court can, even in the absence of a pretrial proffer, conditionally admit the body of coconspirator's statements subject to the Government's eventual proof of the foundational elements (the penalty for not so proving being a possible mistrial); or the court can hold a "full blown" preliminary hearing to consider all evidence concerning the statements. *United States v. Andrus*, 775 F.2d 825, 836–37 (7th Cir. 1985) (we discouraged the latter as inefficient and potentially duplicative).

United States v. Cox, 923 F.2d 519, 526 (7th Cir. 1991).

The following represents (or perhaps exceeds) the outer limits on trial court deference in this regard:

The finding, clearly necessary for admission of hearsay statements of the detectives made during the extortion conspiracy, was rendered by the trial judge *after* the jury verdict.... This delay, says Murphy, was error and should invalidate the finding (and evidence admitted pursuant to it) because this court's precedent allegedly requires the finding before the case goes to the jury.

Well, yes and no. The case law in this circuit anticipates that the finding will be made after all of the evidence is in but before the case goes to the jury. The case law explicitly provides that the *Petrozziello* finding should be based on *all* of the evidence, which explains why the judge must wait until all parties have presented their cases. And, of course, trial counsel normally need to know, before they sum up and argue about the evidence to the jury, whether the evidence to be considered by the jury in its deliberations will include hearsay statements provisionally admitted (in the expectation that "all" of the evidence may lead to an affirmative *Petrozziello* finding)....

An explicit *Petrozziello* finding, before the case goes to the jury, is surely the better practice (absent very unusual circumstances).... Of course, the district court would have faced some difficulty if its post-verdict review of the record had persuaded it to come out the other way on its formal *Petrozziello* finding, but that interesting problem did not arise.

United States v. Murphy, 193 F.3d 1, 7–8 (1st Cir. 1999).

6. Is Rule 801(d)(2)(E) a natural and reasonable extension of Rule 801(d)(2)(D)? Consider the following:

[T]he principle that allows the admission of conspirator X to be treated as the admission of defendant conspirator Y, usable against Y as the admission of a party provided that the statement is made in furtherance of the conspiracy, disquiets those who believe that the concept of conspiracy gives prosecutors too much power. The rationalization for the principle is that conspirators are each others' agents (and therefore principals), and the principal is bound by the agent's words and deeds, provided they are within the scope of the agency, so that an admission by one is an admission by all and can be used against all as "their" admission.

This translation of commercial principles of agency into the law of evidence is one of the less impressive examples of what Coke called the "artificial reason" of the law. The concern behind the hearsay principle is with the reliability of evidence rather than with the facilitation of enterprise—and anyway the law of conspiracy is designed to discourage rather than to facilitate enterprise. Because a statement to be admissible as the statement of a party need not have been against interest when made (or at any time for that matter), the admissibility of such a statement cannot convincingly be grounded in the presumed trustworthiness of a statement that is against the utterer's self-interest to give. The standard justification of its admissibility is a kind of estoppel or waiver theory, that a party should be entitled to rely on his opponent's statements. It has, it seems to us, rather little force as applied to the admissibility of a coconspirator's statement. About all that can be said in favor of the rule is that since the statements of agents of legitimate enterprises are imputed to the enterprise through the operation of the law of agency on the party-admission rule, illegitimate enterprises, such as criminal conspiracies, should not receive more favorable treatment.

United States v. DiDomenico, 78 F.3d 294, 303 (7th Cir. 1996).

Note that Rule 801(d)(2)(D) is actually broader than Rule 801(d)(2)(E), as it does not require that the statement be made "in furtherance of" the principal's enterprise. The Advisory Committee explained the rationale for so limiting Rule 801(d)(2)(E):

The limitation upon the admissibility of statements of co-conspirators to those made "during the course and in furtherance of the conspiracy" is in the accepted pattern. While the broadened view of agency taken in item (iv) might suggest wider admissibility of statements of co-conspirators, the agency theory of conspiracy is at best a fiction and ought not to serve as a basis for admissibility beyond that already established.

Advisory Committee Note to Rule 801(d)(2)(E).

7. How does one distinguish those statements that are "in furtherance of" a conspiracy from those that are not? Consider the following:

Statements which further the conspiracy must be distinguished from mere idle chatter, narrative declarations, and superfluous casual remarks which do not further the conspiracy. Statements made in furtherance of a conspiracy can take a variety of forms. Some examples include comments designed to assist in recruiting potential members, to inform other members about the progress of the conspiracy, to control damage to or detection of the conspiracy, to hide the criminal objectives of the conspiracy, or to instill confidence and prevent the desertion of other members. Courts assess a statement's ability to advance the conspiracy in the context in which the statement was made. "The statement need not have been made exclusively, or even primarily, to further the conspiracy." Rather, the record need only contain some reasonable basis for concluding that the statement in question furthered the conspiracy in some respect.

United States v. Johnson, 200 F.3d 529, 533 (7th Cir. 2000).

8. Rule 801(d)(2)(E)'s "in furtherance of" requirement is satisfied so long as the statement was made with the apparent *intent* to promote the objectives of the conspiracy. In other words, that the statement in fact turns out not to advance the conspiracy's objectives—such as when the statement is made to someone who turns out to be an undercover informant or government investigator—is *irrelevant* for purposes of determining a statement's admissibility under Rule 801(d)(2)(E). *See, e.g., United States v. Clark*, 18 F.3d 1337, 1342 (6th Cir. 1994). However, as a matter of law, a "conspiracy" cannot exist

solely between one individual and a government agent, and thus statements made to a government agent can only be admitted into evidence under Rule 801(d)(2)(E) if there are at least two individuals other than the government agent involved in the conspiracy. *See United States v. Castellini*, 392 F.3d 35, 51 n.11 (1st Cir. 2004).

9. Can Rules 801(d)(2)(B) and 801(d)(2)(E) be used in tandem with one another to admit statements adopted by one member of the conspiracy against other members of the conspiracy? Is the language of Rule 801(d)(2)(E) broad enough to encompass statements *adopted* by other members of the conspiracy? *See United States v. Molina*, 1989 WL 85011, at *2 (N.D. Ill. July 20, 1989) (rejecting "'tag team' operation" of Rules 801(d)(2)(B) and 801(d)(2)(E)).

10. Statements by members of a conspiracy are often offered under Rule 801(d)(2)(E) to prove the truth of the matter asserted. Sometimes, however, they are not offered to prove the truth of the matter asserted, and thus there is no need to resort to Rule 801(d)(2)(E):

> Statements by coconspirators are commonly introduced at trial simply because the statements themselves are part of the plotting to commit a crime. The coconspirator is not asserting the truth of a historical event. Rather, he is directing the conduct of a fellow conspirator or agreeing to follow directions. Even statements about historical events—such as an assertion that the targeted victim had shot a member of the gang plotting revenge—typically are not offered for their truth; whether the target actually committed the alleged offense is irrelevant to the guilt of the plotters.

United States v. Faulkner, 439 F.3d 1221, 1226 (10th Cir. 2006).

F. Unrestricted Hearsay Exceptions

Rule 803 sets forth a list of 23 so-called "unrestricted" exceptions to the hearsay rule. They are so named because they can, as a general rule, be invoked without regard to whether or not the declarant is available to testify as a witness. Thus, for example, these exceptions can be invoked, allowing a witness to testify to what the declarant said, even though the declarant is alive and able to be called as a witness, although the proponent has opted not to call him. The rationale for permitting the use of these exceptions even if the declarant is available to testify as a witness is that hearsay statements falling within these exceptions "possess circumstantial guarantees of trustworthiness sufficient to justify nonproduction of the declarant in person at the trial even though he may be available." Advisory Committee Note to Rule 803.

The following materials explore each of these 23 unrestricted exceptions, with an emphasis on those that are encountered with greater frequency.

1. Present Sense Impressions and Excited Utterances

Problem 7-20: The Instant Message

Robert Fox is on trial on charges of murdering his girlfriend, Deborah Riley. The murder is alleged to have taken place on January 5, 2012, at 11:30 p.m. As proof that Fox was with Riley at the time of the murder, the prosecution seeks to offer testimony by David Smith. Smith would testify that he and Riley were chatting with one another in an online "chat room" operated by Compu-Surf. According to Smith, at around the time of the alleged murder, he received an instant message from Riley that read, "David, I'll have to talk to you a little bit later. Robert just walked into the room." Fox's attorney objects on hearsay grounds.

How should the prosecution respond to the objection? How will the court likely rule?

Problem 7-21: The Cottage Cheese

While shopping at the Piggy-Wiggy Market, Marie slips and falls on what she later discovers is cottage cheese. Upon falling, Marie hears another customer yell, "Oh my God! Are you OK? I told them to clean that up two hours ago!" Marie is eventually taken to a hospital, where she is treated for a broken wrist.

Marie brings suit against the Piggy-Wiggy Market for negligence. She has not been able to locate the unidentified customer who made the statement, but she and several other witnesses are prepared to testify to what that person said, contending that it is relevant to show that the defendant had notice of the dangerous condition. The defendant objects, contending that the proffered testimony is "double hearsay."

How should Marie's attorney respond to the objection? How will the court likely rule? What if instead the unidentified customer said "two minutes ago"?

Problem 7-22: The Crushed Collection

Two vehicles, a red Saturn driven by Janet and a UPS delivery truck driven by Don, collide with one another at the intersection of Fifth and Main. Janet and her passenger, Francine, get out of their car, and as they approach the truck they are met partway by Don. As they approach one another, Francine cries out, "My God! I told her weeks ago that the brakes were shot and needed to be repaired!" Don very calmly responds, "Funny, about two weeks ago, I told my boss that the brakes on this truck needed to be replaced." While none of them are physically injured, Janet had in the trunk of her car several valuable figurines from her Royal Doulton figurine collection, all of which were damaged in the crash.

Janet brings a diversity action against Don and UPS in federal district court. Don and UPS counterclaim against Janet and raise a contributory negligence defense.

At trial, Janet wishes to testify as to what Don said, while Don and UPS wish to have Don testify as to what Francine said. Each side objects to the evidence proffered by the other side, contending that it is "double hearsay."

How should the parties respond to one another's objections? If the testimony is not admissible under Rules 803(1) or 803(2), is it admissible under any of the other exceptions to the hearsay rule that you have studied thus far?

United States v. Mejia-Velez

855 F. Supp. 607 (E.D.N.Y. 1994)

KORMAN, District Judge.

Wilson Alejandro Mejia-Velez ("Velez") was convicted after a jury trial of murdering, for money, Manuel de Dios Unanue ("de Dios")....

The jury ... heard testimony from two eyewitnesses who claimed that they saw de Dios's killer. While they were not able to identify the defendant as the shooter, the descriptions they gave were consistent with the physical appearance of the defendant. The first, John Martin Gajewski ("Gajewski"), testified that as he was walking down 83rd Street, approaching the Meson Asturias, he saw a man cross his path, withdraw a gun, and enter the vestibule of the restaurant with his arm raised. Gajewski heard two shots from inside the restaurant as he saw the man stand with his arm raised in the vestibule. Gajewski then saw the man run out of the restaurant and across the street. After witnessing this incident, Gajewski testified that he proceeded to the first telephone he could find, and "within three or four minutes," placed a call to "911." In this call, Gajewski described the man with the gun as follows: "very, very thin.... I think white ... about five ten, wearing sneakers, a gray sweatshirt with the hood up, and white dungaree-type tight pants." Sixteen minutes later, Gajewski called 911 once again, and gave the same description.

The second eyewitness was Jose Maria Aguera ("Aguera"), the owner of the Meson Asturias, who was working behind the bar at the moment de Dios was shot. Aguera testified that as de Dios sat at the bar, a man entered the restaurant, approached and then shot de Dios from behind. At trial, Aguera described the shooter as a man in his twenties, clean shaven and without a moustache, with skin of "a light color" and wearing a gray-hooded shirt. Immediately after the shooting, Aguera likewise placed a call to 911, describing the assailant as a male Hispanic, wearing a "white and gray" shirt....

At trial, the jury heard testimony from two witnesses, John Gajewski and Jose Aguera, who were both at the scene of the shooting and who, moments thereafter, placed telephone calls to "911." The United States Attorney was also permitted, over objection, to introduce audio-taped recordings of the emergency telephone calls. The recordings were admitted as "present sense impressions" pursuant to Fed.R.Evid. 803(1), and as "excited utterances" pursuant to Fed.R.Evid. 803(2).

Rule 803(1) of the Federal Rules of Evidence provides an exception to the general rule against hearsay for any statement "describing or explaining an event or condition[,] made while [or immediately after] the declarant [] perceiv[ed it]." The theory behind this exception is essentially twofold. First, the immediacy requirement reduces the opportunity for reflection, and thus minimizes the likelihood of deception or fabrication on the part of the declarant. Secondly, immediacy also greatly reduces the likelihood that the declarant will have inaccurately remembered the event in question.

By its own terms, application of Rule 803(1) has three distinct requirements: i) the statement must describe or explain the event perceived; ii) the declarant must have in fact perceived the event described; and iii) the description must be "substantially contemporaneous" with the event in question. In the instant case, these requirements are amply satisfied by the 911 telephone recordings.

The statements made on these recordings clearly describe the events perceived by the telephone callers. Gajewski and Aguera each describe the fact that there had been a shooting. Both men give the location and a description of the assailant. Moreover, it is certain that both callers witnessed the events that they describe. There was simply no reason for them to telephone 911, other than to report the shooting. Finally, the telephone calls were "substantially contemporaneous" with the shooting, within the meaning of Rule 803(1). The Advisory Committee Notes to the rule expressly recognize that "in many, if not most, instances precise contemporaneity is not possible, and hence a slight lapse is allowable" between the event perceived and the declarant's statement. Fed.R.Evid. 803(1) Advisory Committee Note. Courts applying Rule 803(1) have noted that "[t]here is no *per se* rule indicating what time interval is too long."

In the instant case, Aguera's phone call was placed immediately after the murder, from the very room where the shooting took place. In fact, the call was made so hastily that, due to the confusion following the shooting, in the middle of the conversation Aguera had to pick up the receiver in an adjacent room so that he could hear the operator more clearly. The first call made by Gajewski was received by the 911 dispatcher just two minutes after the end of Aguera's call. Gajewski testified that immediately following the shooting, he signaled to the patrons inside the restaurant that he would call for help and then sought the first available telephone. Because there was just a "slight lapse" between the shooting and the placing of these two phone calls, both of these calls meet the "contemporaneity" requirement of Rule 803(1).

The second call placed by Gajewski was admittedly 16 minutes after the completion of his first call. This call, however, was also made without any motivation for fabrication on Gajewski's part. Indeed, his recitation of the event was consistent with his first call and with the other testimony in the case. Under these circumstances, the interlude between the shooting and Gajewski's second call falls sufficiently within the time period permitted by Rule 803(1). *See Blakey*, 607 F.2d at 785–86 (applying rule where interval was potentially 23 minutes); *United States v. Obayagbona*, 627 F. Supp. 329 (E.D.N.Y.1985) (Weinstein, J.) (applying rule where interval was 14 minutes and 25 seconds); *cf. Hilyer v. Howat Concrete Co., Inc.*, 578 F.2d 422, 426 n. 7 (D.C. Cir. 1978) (statement made between 15 and 45 minutes after event inadmissible under exception). The requirements of Rule 803(1) were therefore satisfied by each of the three telephone recordings in this case.

Moreover, even if the calls were not significantly contemporaneous to meet the present sense exception to the hearsay rule, they were admissible as "excited utterances." *See* Fed.R.Evid. Rule 803(2). Pursuant to Rule 803(2), ex[c]ited utterances are defined as those statements "relating to a startling event or condition[,] made while the declarant was under the stress of excitement [that it] caused []."

As the Advisory Committee Notes indicate, the present sense impression exception and the excited utterance exception "overlap, though based on somewhat different theories." Fed.R.Evid. 803 Advisory Committee Note. The theory behind the excited utterance exception is that "circumstances may produce a condition of excitement which temporarily stills the capacity of reflection and produces utterances free of conscious fabrication." *Id.* The two conditions for the application of this exception are that there has been a startling event and that the offered statements were made during the period of excitement, and in reaction to that event.

It is clear that the recordings in the instant case satisfy both requirements of the excited utterance exception. A shooting, even in this day and age, is a startling event. Moreover, the sheer panic in the voices of Gajewski and Aguera, heard on the recordings, is proof that the calls were made while the declarants remained under the excitement of the situation. *See Obayagbona*, 627 F. Supp. at 338 (court's "[d]etermination of excitement [was] facilitated by [a] recording")....

Miller v. Keating

754 F.2d 507 (3d Cir. 1984)

STERN, District Judge:

The district court admitted into evidence a statement, made by an unidentified declarant at the scene of an automobile accident, amounting to an accusation that the accident was the fault of plaintiff Carol Miller....

On January 18, 1982, Carol Miller was driving her white Ford LTD east on U.S. Route 22, a limited access highway, near Easton, Pennsylvania. She carried a passenger named Annette Vay. It is undisputed that Miller and Vay were traveling behind a UPS truck and that both vehicles switched into the lefthand lane to avoid a stalled vehicle in the righthand lane near the 25th Street exit ramp. It is also undisputed that, soon thereafter, the Miller car was struck from behind by defendant Texaco's tractor-trailer driven by co-defendant Lawrence Keating. The force of the collision propelled the Miller car first into the side of a car stopped in the righthand lane and then into the rear of the UPS truck. Mrs. Miller sustained serious injuries in the collision. The driver of the car stopped in the righthand lane was Kenneth Parris. His wife, Elfriede Parris, was a passenger.

One dispute at trial was over the amount of time that elapsed between the moment when Mrs. Miller pulled into the lefthand lane and the moment when her car was struck from the rear. Another conflict focused on whether the Miller car was stopped behind the UPS truck or was still moving when it was hit by the Texaco tractor-trailer....

It is the testimony of the Parrises about an incident occurring after the accident that gives rise to this appeal. After being hit in the left side, Mr. Parris pulled his car over. He testified that he left his car, comforted one of the victims in the Miller car, then walked to the rear of the Miller car where his wife was writing down the license plate number of the Miller car. At that point, a man approached and said, "the bastard tried to cut in." In somewhat inconsistent testimony, Mrs. Parris stated that she and her husband "were running towards the car, and I heard this person that was driving—running towards us— ... [a]nd said the s.o.b. or some words like that, tried to cut in." Mr. Parris could not identify the declarant beyond saying that he was a white male. Mrs. Parris could do no better. There is no indication in the record why she thought the declarant was a driver or which vehicle he drove. Mr. Parris testified that he did not know what vehicle the declarant was driving.

Over objections, the trial judge allowed the Parrises to relate their versions of the declaration to the jury....

As the trial judge ... recognized, the excited utterance exception of Fed.R.Evid. 803(2) provides the most likely basis for admitting the statement. The question before us, therefore, is whether that statement by the unknown declarant should have been admitted under Fed.R.Evid. 803(2)....

We do not conclude ... that statements by unidentified declarants are ipso facto inadmissible under Fed.R.Evid. 803(2). Such statements are admissible if they otherwise meet the criteria of 803(2). But unlike unavailability, which is immaterial to admission under Rule 803, the unidentifiability of the declarant is germane to the admissibility determination. A party seeking to introduce such a statement carries a burden heavier than where the declarant is identified to demonstrate the statement's circumstantial trustworthiness.

At minimum, when the declarant of an excited utterance is unidentified, it becomes more difficult to satisfy the established case law requirements for admission of a statement under Fed.R.Evid. 803(2). Wigmore defines these requirements as: (1) a startling occasion, (2) a statement relating to the circumstances of the startling occasion, (3) a declarant who appears to have had opportunity to observe personally the events, and (4) a statement made before there has been time to reflect and fabricate. 6 J. Wigmore, *Evidence* §§ 1750–51 (J. Chadbourn rev. 1976). There is no doubt that the present case presents a startling occasion and little doubt that the declarant's statement relates to the circumstances of the occurrence. Partly because the declarant is unidentified, however, problems arise with the last two requirements: personal knowledge and spontaneity.

The first of these expresses the familiar principle that a witness may not testify about a subject without personal knowledge. Fed.R.Evid. 602. This rule applies with equal force to hearsay statements. To be admissible, the declarant of an excited utterance must personally observe the startling event. The burden of establishing perception rests with the proponent of the evidence. As in all questions of admissibility, the resolution of any dispute of fact necessary to the question is confided to the trial judge to be decided by a preponderance of the evidence. And while the trial judge is not confined to legally admissible evidence in making the determination, Fed.R.Evid. 104(a), still he must make the findings necessary to support admissibility.

Direct proof of perception, or proof that forecloses all speculation is not required. On the other hand, circumstantial evidence of the declarant's personal perception must not be so scanty as to forfeit the "guarantees of trustworthiness" which form the hallmark of all exceptions to the hearsay rule. Fed.R.Evid. 803 advisory committee note. When there is no evidence of personal perception, apart from the declaration itself, courts have hesitated to allow the excited utterance to stand alone as evidence of the declarant's opportunity to observe. In some cases, however, the substance of the statement itself does contain words revealing perception. A statement such as, "I saw that blue truck run down the lady on the corner," might stand alone to show perception if the trial judge finds, from the particular circumstances, that he is satisfied by a preponderance that the declarant spoke from personal perception. . . .

In the present case, however, the record is empty of any circumstances from which the trial court could have inferred, by a preponderance, that the declarant saw Miller "cut in." The disputed declaration itself does not proclaim it. Indeed, the district judge acknowledged as much in his opinion denying plaintiffs' motion for a new trial. Nevertheless, he drew an inference of perception, reasoning that "the declarant would have made the declaration only if he was in a position to observe the collision." Yet the statements reported by the Parrises — "the bastard tried to cut in" and "the s.o.b., or some words like that, tried to cut in" — alone, do not show more likely than not that the declarant saw the event. The declarant might have been drawing a conclusion on the basis of what he saw as he approached the scene of the accident. He might have been hypothesizing or repeating what someone else had said. It is even possible that the declarant was talking about some other driver who had just cut in front of him. It is far from unlikely that the declarant was a participant in the accident, for the Parrises could never identify or exclude anyone as the speaker. And the tenor of the declaration, i.e., "the bastard tried to cut in," suggests at least the possibility that the declarant was a participant with a natural degree of bias. The self-serving exclamation by a participant in an auto accident "it was the other guy's fault," is hardly likely to qualify as trustworthy.

The circumstances external to the statement itself not only fail to demonstrate that the declarant was in a position to have seen what happened, they also fail to show that the declarant was excited when he spoke. No one so testified, and the trial judge made no finding of excitement. Thus, this last prong of the test for admissibility is also unsatisfied.

The assumption underlying the hearsay exception of Rule 803(2) is that a person under the sway of excitement temporarily loses the capacity of reflection and thus produces statements free of fabrication. Since lack of capacity to fabricate is the justification for excited utterances, courts have recognized that the length of time separating the event from the statement may be considerably longer than for statements qualifying under the present sense impression exception of Rule 803(1), which is based on the lack of time to fabricate....

Miller v. Crown Amusements, Inc.

821 F. Supp. 703 (S.D. Ga. 1993)

EDENFIELD, Chief Judge.

The Plaintiff moves the Court to render a pretrial determination of the admissibility of a 911 phone call made by an unidentified person shortly after an accident occurred. For reasons stated below, the Court finds that this evidence falls within the present sense exception to the hearsay rule, and, therefore, finds that this evidence is **ADMISSIBLE.**

FACTS

On October 14, 1990, the Plaintiff, David Miller, and his sister-in-law, Linda Carper, were travelling south on Interstate-95 ("I-95"), near Pooler, Georgia, when they observed a pick-up truck on the side of the highway. Upon stopping to render assistance, Miller and Carper discovered that the driver of the truck, Charles Shideler, needed a spare part, which Miller had at his residence. Miller and Carper drove to Miller's house to obtain the part and returned. Miller and Shideler then began work on the left rear wheel of Shideler's truck, while Carper stood at the front of the truck. While the men were repairing the wheel, a trailer truck drove by, striking Shideler, and possibly Miller. Miller suffered various injuries, including a broken leg; Shideler was killed. The truck did not stop; in addition, Carper did not observe the accident.

After asking Miller and Shideler whether they were injured, Carper, a Pooler resident, immediately drove south on I-95; exited at the Savannah exit on I-16; exited I-16 at the I-95 North exit; and travelled I-95 North to Georgia Highway 80 to the Gate Exxon station in Pooler, where she called 911. According to Chatham County Police records, Carper's call was made at 12:11:43 P.M. Driving at speeds not exceeding 60 miles per hour, the approximate time to travel Carper's route, 4.5 miles, is 6 and a half minutes.

Chatham County Police received another 911 call, from an unidentified caller at a pay phone at Mac's Oasis Chevron, located at I-95 and Georgia 204, at 12:13:53 P.M. Calls to 911 are automatically recorded, and the following is a transcription of the entire dialogue.

DISPATCHER: How can I help you?

CALLER (FEMALE): Good afternoon, I'm on Highway 95 South and I was in quite a bit of heavy traffic, when we noticed a truck which was pulling a trailer, but I couldn't get a license number because of the trailer and the heavy traffic, but it said "Crown Amusements" on the side of the truck and as he went by a broken down truck, two vehicles were broken down by the side of the road and the young man was kneeling beside it and one was underneath. And as he went by he sideswiped and hit one of the young men. He made no attempt to stop. This was in the area of mile marker 99 or 98, perhaps between the two. Ah, this is my first opportunity to reach a phone.

DISPATCHER: Okay, there is — he sideswiped a person or vehicle?

CALLER: There are two vehicles there now.

DISPATCHER: Yes, ma'am, I've got that. I need to know whether he hit the vehicle or a person.

CALLER: The person.

CALLER: O.K., now I don't know if they will call through or not, but that's all I can tell you about the truck that did it. It said "Crown Amusement."

DISPATCHER: O.K.

CALLER: Have you got everything?

DISPATCHER: Yes, ma'am.

CALLER: Alright, thank you.

DISPATCHER: Alright, you're welcome.

The distance from the incident to where this second call was placed is 6.3 miles, which would require approximately 8 minutes, 45 seconds to travel, driving at speeds not exceeding 60 miles per hour. In addition, there are no observable businesses, stores, houses, or pay phones on I-95 south between the incident location and Georgia 204 and I-95.

DISCUSSION

The Defendant argues that the recording of the 911 call made by the unidentified caller is inadmissible hearsay. The Plaintiff, however, asserts it is admissible as a present sense impression under Rule 803(1) of the Federal Rules of Evidence....

.... the Court must find by a preponderance of the evidence that the declarant observed the incident. Fed.R.Evid. 803(1). *See also Miller v. Keating*, 754 F.2d 507, 511 (3d Cir. 1985). When a declarant is an unidentified bystander, a court should be hesitant to uphold the statement of the declarant as sufficient to demonstrate that the declarant actually perceived the incident. Fed.R.Evid. 803(1), Advisory Committee's Note. However, "direct proof of perception, or proof that forecloses all speculation is not required." *Miller*, 754 F.2d at 511. Indeed, in *Miller*, the Third Circuit Court of Appeals observed that a statement such as "I saw that ... truck run down the lady...." may stand alone to show perception, if the trial judge finds, from the particular circumstances, that he is satisfied by a preponderance of the evidence that the declarant spoke from personal perception.

Because the declarant who made this call is unidentified and is unavailable to testify, this issue presents a difficult matter to the Court. After careful consideration, however, the Court finds by a preponderance of the evidence that the declarant observed the accident. The caller specifically stated, "[W]e *noticed* [the truck sideswipe a person]," thus indicating actual perception of the accident. Furthermore, the timing of the declarant's call, which was received approximately 2 minutes after the call placed by Carper, who was at the scene of the accident, strongly suggests that the declarant observed the accident. This 2 minute interval is consistent with the differences in distances and in driving times to each calling location.

Furthermore, the caller's statements indicate that she was travelling south on I-95 and exited at Highway 204. The caller said, "[T]his is my first opportunity to reach a phone," which would be accurate if she travelled on I-95 to Highway 204, as there are no phones along I-95 and no buildings until the Interstate intersects Highway 204. In addition, the caller's incorrect identification of the mile marker[2] is consistent with her having traveled

---

2. The caller stated that the accident took place "in the area of mile marker 99 or 98." In actuality, the accident occurred within 100 yards south of marker 100.

this route. There is no mile marker 99 because of the I-16 and I-95 interchange, and the next posted mile marker reads 98. The caller would have had no reason to have been looking for mile markers until being startled by the incident. The Court also observes that, in this situation, due to tape recording, there is no uncertainty as to the content of the declarant's statement, which serves to heighten the reliability of the evidence. Accordingly, the Court finds by a preponderance of the evidence that the caller actually perceived the event. . . .

Colorado Rule of Evidence 803
Hearsay Exceptions; Availability of Declarant Immaterial

The following are not excluded by the hearsay rule, even though the declarant is available as a witness:

(1) **Spontaneous Present Sense Impression.** A spontaneous statement describing or explaining an event or condition made while the declarant was perceiving the event or condition.

Committee Comment

The change reflected above was based on the fact that neither immediacy nor spontaneity would be guaranteed by the Federal rule. Colorado case law requires that a present sense impression be instinctive and spontaneous in order to be admissible. *See Denver City Tramway Co. v. Brumley*, 51 Colo. 251, 116 P. 1051 (1911). It was felt that the requirements set forth in that opinion constitute a greater guarantee of trustworthiness than the Federal rule, *i.e.*, spontaneity is the most important factor governing trustworthiness. This is especially true when there is no provision that the declarant be unavailable as a witness.

. . . .

Notes and Questions

1. The Advisory Committee Note to Rules 803(1) and (2) explains that the most significant difference between the two exceptions is "the time lapse allowable between event and statement." Only Rule 803(1) has a time limit, which the Advisory Committee describes as one of "substantial contemporaneity," recognizing that "in many, if not most, instances precise contemporaneity is not possible, and hence a slight lapse is allowable." Are you persuaded that delays of up to 23 minutes, as indicated in the case law, are consistent with this limitation? Is such a period sufficiently short to "negate the likelihood of deliberate or conscious misrepresentation," the theory that the Advisory Committee invokes to justify the exception? *See Lust v. Sealy, Inc.*, 383 F.3d 580, 588 (7th Cir. 2004) ("As with much of the folk psychology of evidence, it is difficult to take this rationale entirely seriously, since people are entirely capable of spontaneous lies in emotional circumstances. 'Old and new studies agree that less than one second is required to fabricate a lie.'") How did the drafters of Colorado Rule 803(1) address this issue? *See People v. Czemerynski*, 786 P.2d 1100, 1107 (Colo. 1990) ("C.R.E. 803(1) is more restrictive than the relevant Federal Rule of Evidence 803(1) which treats as a present sense impression a description made immediately after perception. The federal rule differs in that it does not include the contemporaneous requirement of the Colorado rule."). Is the Colorado approach superior in this regard, or does it go too far in the opposite direction?

2. A second difference between Rules 803(1) and (2) is that the latter requires a "startling" event or condition, while under the former, the event or condition need not be startling. As you can see from the cases excerpted above, the judge appears to use his or her common sense in determining whether or not something is "startling" or not.

3. A third difference between Rules 803(1) and (2) is the mental state of the declarant. No special mental state is required for the former, but for the latter, the declarant must be "under the stress of excitement" caused by the event or condition when the statement is made. The Advisory Committee Note indicates that "there are no pat answers" as to how long the period of excitement lasts, and that "the character of the transaction or event will largely determine the significance of the time factor." Courts consider a variety of factors in making the subjective determination whether the declarant was excited when the statement was made:

> Although the lapse of time between the startling event and the declarant's statement is relevant to whether the declarant made the statement while under the stress of excitement, the temporal gap between the event and the utterance is not itself dispositive. Other relevant factors include: the characteristics of the event; the subject matter of the statement; whether the statement was made in response to an inquiry; and the declarant's age, motive to lie and physical and mental condition. If the trial court has access to a recording of the declarant's statement, it may also consider the declarant's "tone and tenor of voice" in determining whether the declarant made that statement while under the stress of excitement.

United States v. Alexander, 331 F.3d 116, 122–23 (D.C. Cir. 2003). Nonetheless, many courts do treat the length of time between the event and the statement as a critical factor in determining whether or not the statement qualifies as an excited utterance. *See, e.g., United States v. Davis*, 577 F.3d 660, 669 (6th Cir. 2009) (requiring that "the statement must be made before there is time to contrive or misrepresent"); *United States v. Taveras*, 380 F.3d 532, 537 (1st Cir. 2004) ("The time lapse in most excited utterance cases is usually a few seconds or a few minutes. In extreme circumstances, we have even accepted a delay of a few hours.").

4. A final difference between Rules 803(1) and (2) is the scope of the content of the statements admissible under each of the exceptions:

> Permissible *subject matter* of the statement is limited under Exception (1) to description or explanation of the event or condition, the assumption being that spontaneity, in the absence of a startling event, may extend no farther. In Exception (2), however, the statement need only "relate" to the startling event or condition, thus affording a broader scope of subject matter coverage. 6 Wigmore §§ 1750, 1754. See Sanitary Grocery Co. v. Snead, 90 F.2d 374 (1937), slip-and-fall case sustaining admissibility of clerk's statement. "That has been on the floor for a couple of hours," and Murphy Auto Parts Co., Inc. v. Ball, 249 F.2d 508 (1957), upholding admission, on issue of driver's agency, of his statement that he had to call on a customer and was in a hurry to get home.

Advisory Committee Note to Rules 803(1) and (2).

5. Note that exceptions such as Rules 803(1) and (2) impose no requirement of corroboration that the events described in the statement occurred:

> [C]ourts sometimes focus on the corroboration or the lack thereof in admitting or excluding present sense impressions, but the truth is that the rule does not condition admissibility on the availability of corroboration. The lack of another witness who could independently verify Lewellen's observations ... bore upon the weight owed to this evidence but did not bar its admission.

United States v. Ruiz, 249 F.3d 643, 647 (7th Cir. 2001). *See also* Advisory Committee Note to Rules 803(1) and (2) ("Whether *proof of the startling event* may be made by the statement itself is largely an academic question, since in most cases there is present at least circumstantial evidence that something of a startling nature must have occurred.... Nevertheless, on occasion the only evidence may be the content of the statement itself, and rulings that it may be sufficient are described as 'increasing'....").

6. Rule 803(1) creates an exception for statements describing events or conditions that are *perceived* by the declarant. Does this language encompass only events or conditions that are perceived by *sight*, or does it also cover those that are perceived through other means? *See Solomon v. Waffle House, Inc.*, 365 F. Supp. 2d 1312, 1319 (N.D. Ga. 2004) (admitting under Rule 803(1) statement by restaurant patron upon putting food into her mouth that it did not taste good).

7. To successfully invoke Rule 803(1), the Seventh Circuit requires a finding that the statement was made "without calculated narration." *See, e.g., Cody v. Harris*, 409 F.3d 853, 860 (7th Cir. 2005). What is the basis for grafting such a requirement onto Rule 803(1)? *See United States v. Woods*, 301 F.3d 556, 562 (7th Cir. 2002) ("The calculated narration consideration is based on the rule's requirement that the statement be 'made *while* the declarant was perceiving the event.' The exception is based on the theory that it is less likely for a declarant to 'deliberate or conscious[ly] misrepresent' the event if there is 'substantial contemporaneity' between the statement and the event. A declarant who deliberates about what to say or provides statements for a particular reason creates the possibility that the statements are not contemporaneous, and, more likely, are calculated interpretations of events rather than near simultaneous perceptions.")

8. For an example of a case admitting an e-mail message under Rule 803(1), *see United States v. Ferber*, 966 F. Supp. 90, 99 (D. Mass. 1997); *see also New York v. Microsoft Corp.*, 2002 WL 649951, at *2 (D.D.C. Apr. 12, 2002) (not admitting e-mail but recognizing that under correct circumstances it could qualify under Rule 803(1)).

9. In *Mejia-Velez*, was it even necessary to invoke Rules 803(1) and 803(2)? Asked somewhat differently, suppose that the statements by the two eyewitnesses did not fit the requirements of either Rule 803(1) or 803(2). Given that the two eyewitnesses appeared at trial, did the prosecution have any other rules at its disposal?

10. Why, in the *Crown Amusements* case, was no objection raised to the fact that the anonymous caller said that the truck that left the scene had the phrase "Crown Amusements" on its side? In other words, why wasn't an objection made that this constituted "double hearsay"? In what ways are this statement and the statements in Problems 7-21 and 7-22 similar?

11. Why, in the *Crown Amusements* case, do you suppose that Rule 803(1) was invoked instead of 803(2), thus necessitating an explanation of why the time between the incident and the event was not too long to qualify under Rule 803(1)?

2. Statements Made for Medical Diagnosis or Treatment

Problem 7-23: The Hit & Run Accident

Penelope is walking down the street when she is struck by a car driven by David, who drives off. William, who hears the crash, immediately runs out of his house and goes up to Penelope, who says to him "David just ran me over with his car!" William drives Penelope to the hospital, where she is checked in and admitted overnight for testing. When she wakes up the next morning, she sees that she has a roommate, Lisa. Lisa asks her why she ended up in the hospital, and Penelope says to her, "I was run over yesterday by this guy I know named David." Later, Penelope repeats this statement to John, a physician at the hospital, who drops in to see her.

Shortly after John leaves, Penelope starts to experience severe discomfort, and Lisa calls for help. Medical personnel arrive and try to help Penelope, but she dies. An autopsy later reveals that she died of internal bleeding that was likely the result of the car accident.

Penelope's survivors bring a suit against David for wrongful death. To prove that David was responsible for causing her injuries, the plaintiffs seek to call William, Lisa, and John as witnesses to testify to what Penelope told them. David's attorney raises hearsay objections to the testimony of all three witnesses.

How should the plaintiffs' attorney respond to the objections, and how will the court likely rule?

United States v. Renville
779 F.2d 430 (8th Cir. 1985)

JOHN R. GIBSON, Circuit Judge.

Harvey Renville was convicted by a jury of two counts of sexual abuse of his eleven year old stepdaughter under 18 U.S.C. §§ 13, 1152 (1982).... Renville [contends that] ... the district court erred in permitting a physician to testify to statements of the victim during an examination identifying Renville as her abuser, under Federal Rule of Evidence 803(4)* ....

Renville, an Indian, resided with his family on the Sisseton Indian Reservation in South Dakota. At the time of the offense, Renville was employed as a tribal police officer. In March 1982, a detention hearing was held in South Dakota concerning the victim's half-brother, Joe. At the hearing, Joe testified that the victim had admitted to him that she had been sexually abused by Renville. These allegations eventually were referred to Roberts County Deputy Sheriff Holly Butrum, who interviewed the victim to determine whether, as an emergency measure, she should be removed from her home....

A few weeks later, while in the care of foster parents, the victim was examined by Dr. Clark Likness, a physician specializing in family practice medicine. Dr. Likness testified at trial, again over Renville's objection, that during the examination the victim recounted acts of anal intercourse and cunnilingus performed by Renville.

At trial, the victim recanted her earlier accusations against Renville, and denied having told anyone except Deputy Sheriff Butrum that he was the individual who had abused her. The jury found Renville guilty on both counts. He was sentenced to two concurrent fifteen year terms....

---

* Editor's Note: Rule 803(4) creates an exception to the hearsay rule for:
  A statement that:
  (A) is made for—and is reasonably pertinent to—medical diagnosis or treatment; and
  (B) describes medical history; past or present symptoms or sensations; their inception; or their general cause.

[T]he defendant argues that the hearsay exception found in Federal Rule of Evidence 803(4) does not encompass statements of fault or identity made to medical personnel.... The crucial question under the rule is whether the out-of-court statement of the declarant was "reasonably pertinent" to diagnosis or treatment. In *United States v. Iron Shell*, 633 F.2d 77 (8th Cir. 1980), this court set forth a two-part test for the admissibility of hearsay statements under rule 803(4): first, the declarant's motive in making the statement must be consistent with the purposes of promoting treatment; and second, the content of the statement must be such as is reasonably relied on by a physician in treatment or diagnosis. The test reflects the twin policy justifications advanced to support the rule. First, it is assumed that a patient has a strong motive to speak truthfully and accurately because the treatment or diagnosis will depend in part upon the information conveyed. The declarant's motive thus provides a sufficient guarantee of trustworthiness to permit an exception to the hearsay rule. Second, we have recognized that "a fact reliable enough to serve as the basis for a diagnosis is also reliable enough to escape hearsay proscription."

The court in *Iron Shell* recognized, however, that a declarant's statements relating the identity of the individual allegedly responsible for his injuries or condition "would seldom, if ever," be reasonably pertinent to treatment or diagnosis. The court relied in part on the advisory committee notes to rule 803(4), which conclude that statements of fault ordinarily are not admissible under the rule. The notes suggest, as an example, that "a patient's statement that he was struck by an automobile would qualify, but not his statement that the car was driven through a red light." *See also United States v. Narciso*, 446 F. Supp. 252, 289 (E.D.Mich.1977) (statement by a patient he was shot would be admissible but not a statement he was shot by a white man). Statements of fault generally meet neither criterion for admission set forth in *Iron Shell*. Statements of identity seldom are made to promote effective treatment; the patient has no sincere desire to frankly account for fault because it is generally irrelevant to an anticipated course of treatment. Additionally, physicians rarely have any reason to rely on statements of identity in treating or diagnosing a patient. These statements are simply irrelevant in the calculus in devising a program of effective treatment.

The court in *Iron Shell* and the Advisory Committee used words of generality, however, not exclusion. *Iron Shell*, 633 F.2d at 84 (statements of fault "would seldom" be pertinent); Fed.R.Evid. 803(4) advisory committee notes (statements of fault "not ordinarily admissible"). We believe that a statement by a child abuse victim that the abuser is a member of the victim's immediate household presents a sufficiently different case from that envisaged by the drafters of rule 803(4) that it should not fall under the general rule. Statements by a child abuse victim to a physician during an examination that the abuser is a member of the victim's immediate household *are* reasonably pertinent to treatment.

Statements of this kind differ from the statements of fault identified by the Rules Advisory Committee and properly excluded under our past decisions in a crucial way: they are reasonably relied on by a physician in treatment or diagnosis. First, child abuse involves more than physical injury; the physician must be attentive to treating the emotional and psychological injuries which accompany this crime. The exact nature and extent of the psychological problems which ensue from child abuse often depend on the identity of the abuser. The general rule banning statements of fault is premised on the assumption that the injury is purely somatic. This is evident from the examples put forth by the courts and commentators discussing the rule. In each example, the medical treatment contemplated was restricted to the physical injuries of the victim; there is no psychological component of treatment which could relate to the identity of the individual at fault. Furthermore, in each example the statement of fault is not relevant to prevention of recurrence of the injury. Sexual abuse of children at home presents a wholly different situation.

Second, physicians have an obligation, imposed by state law, to prevent an abused child from being returned to an environment in which he or she cannot be adequately protected from recurrent abuse. This obligation is most immediate where the abuser is a member of the victim's household, as in the present case. Information that the abuser is a member of the household is therefore "reasonably pertinent" to a course of treatment which includes removing the child from the home.

The defendant contends that our decision in *Iron Shell* holds to the contrary. In *Iron Shell*, this court held that rule 803(4) did not bar the testimony of a physician reciting statements by a nine year old child abuse victim where the child's statements were related to her physical condition and a detailed chronology of the sexual assault, but did not touch on the identity of the assaulting individual. The defendant here seizes on language in the opinion, discussed above, that statements by the victim of "who assaulted her * * *, would seldom, if ever," be admissible. However, the court in *Iron Shell* considered only the admissibility of a child abuse victim's statements relating the course of events and the conduct of the assailant during the attack; the court did not purport to decide whether statements of fault by child abuse victims are admissible under rule 803(4). Moreover, the defendant in *Iron Shell* was not a member of the victim's household, and statements relating to identity therefore were not reasonably pertinent to the physician's obligation to insure that the child be removed from an environment in which she was vulnerable to recurring abuse.

We therefore believe that statements of identity to a physician by a child sexually abused by a family member are of a type physicians reasonably rely on in composing a diagnosis and course of treatment. Admission of these statements, therefore, is fully consistent with the rationale underlying the second component of the *Iron Shell* test.

Statements of identity in this unique context also meet the first part of the *Iron Shell* test, which focuses on the declarant's motivation for giving the information. As we discussed above, this component reflects the premise underlying the rule that the patient's selfish interest in receiving proper treatment guarantees the trustworthiness of the statements. Statements of fault traditionally have failed to meet this criterion. Ordinarily, when an individual identifies the person responsible for his injuries or condition, he does so without reasonable expectation that the information will facilitate treatment.

However, this conclusion rests on the obvious assumption that the declarant is responding under the impression that he is being asked to make an accusation that is not relevant to the physician's diagnosis or treatment. This assumption does not hold where the physician makes clear to the victim that the inquiry into the identity of the abuser is important to diagnosis and treatment, and the victim manifests such an understanding. In such circumstances, the victim's motivation to speak truthfully is the same as that which insures reliability when he recounts the chronology of events or details symptoms of somatic distress.

We believe these circumstances are present in this case. Before questioning the child, Dr. Likness explained to her that the examination and his prospective questions were necessary to obtain information to treat her and help her overcome any physical and emotional problems which may have been caused by the recurrent abuse. Nothing in the record indicates that the child's motive in making these statements was other than as a patient responding to a physician questioning for prospective treatment.

Therefore, we conclude that in the circumstances of this case, there were sufficient indicia of the declarant's proper motivation to ensure the trustworthiness of her statements to the testifying physician. Since the statements are trustworthy, and the type on which physicians reasonably rely in treatment or diagnosis, they meet the criteria for admission set forth in *Iron Shell*....

State v. Lawrence
752 So.2d 934 (La. 1999)

MURRAY, Judge.

Michael A. Lawrence appeals his convictions for forcible rape and aggravated crime against nature, as well as his sentences as a second felony offender on both counts....

On the evening of April 13, 1993, twelve-year-old D.M. told her mother, Vita, and then her stepfather, Henry, that Uncle Michael had sexually abused her on several occasions within the past six months. Vita called D.M.'s pediatrician, Dr. Janet D. Barnes, who agreed to see them the next day....

The next morning, Vita took D.M. to make a police report. Detective Cathey Carter of the New Orleans Police Department's Rape and Child Abuse Division spoke with D.M. alone, then interviewed each of the child's parents. She immediately arranged for D.M. to be examined by Dr. Katheryne A. Coffman, Director of the Sexual Abuse Clinic at Children's Hospital, the next week....

After their meetings with Det. Carter, D.M. and her parents went to see Dr. Barnes, who had last treated the child in May 1992 for nervous stomach. Dr. Barnes spoke with each of them alone, beginning with Vita, then D.M., and ending with Henry, summarizing their accounts as she went along. She then performed a limited pelvic exam, cut short by D.M.'s discomfort, and took some tissue samples for lab testing....

Although D.M. had been scheduled to see Dr. Coffman the week of April 19th, a confrontation with a family member resulted in the postponement of that visit until April 30, 1993. Dr. Coffman spoke with D.M., then with her mother, then did a complete physical, including a pelvic exam, tissue swabs from the vagina and throat, and blood and urine samples. After completion of the examination, Dr. Coffman obtained permission to send a copy of her report to Det. Carter and D.M.'s counselor, but made no treatment recommendations....

Mr. Lawrence next asserts that neither Dr. Barnes nor Dr. Coffman should have been allowed to detail what D.M. told them because none of the requirements for an exception to the hearsay rule were met....

Article 803(4) of the Code of Evidence provides that even though a declarant is available for trial, the hearsay rule will not exclude testimony concerning out-of-court statements that are:

> Statements made for purposes of medical treatment and medical diagnosis in connection with treatment and describing medical history, or past or present symptoms, pain, or sensations, or the inception or general character of the cause or external source thereof insofar as reasonably pertinent to treatment or diagnosis in connection with treatment.

The comments under this statute specify that it "follows Federal Rule of Evidence 803(4) but.... excludes from its coverage statements made solely for the purpose of diagnosis."

This court considered the scope of this hearsay exception under circumstances similar to those here in *State v. Coleman*. After reviewing the jurisprudence under this Article, as well as cases arising prior to the adoption of the Code of Evidence, it was held that the extent to which a physician's hearsay testimony is admissible under this exception must be determined by the *purpose* of the examination at issue. The *Coleman* court concluded that, under the facts presented there, the doctor should not have been permitted to testify as to the events described by the victim and her mother because:

> Although a subsidiary purpose of Dr. Coffman's evaluation was to identify and treat any sexually transmitted diseases or other physical harm that may have resulted from rape, the principal reason for the examination was forensic. [The victim] was referred to Dr. Coffman by the District Attorney eighteen months after the rape was alleged to have occurred.... The report of the examination was provided only to the District Attorney. [The victim] received no treatment as a result of [this] evaluation.

....

In this case, Det. Carter testified that she referred D.M. to Dr. Coffman for an examination as part of her usual procedure because "[w]hen there's a case like that where there's maybe some type of trauma from a penetration ... we contact the doctor." Similarly, the prosecutor acknowledged during the *in camera* proceedings that the primary purpose for the referral was to determine if sexual abuse had occurred "along with" treating the child, if necessary. Dr. Coffman's report, admitted into evidence as exhibit S-1, reflects that the patient had been referred by the police "for evaluation of alleged sexual abuse;" that consent was obtained to send the report to Det. Carter and D.M.'s therapist, but not Dr. Barnes; and that lab tests were performed but no further treatment or follow-up was expected. In fact, Dr. Coffman acknowledged that D.M. and her mother said that Dr. Barnes had already obtained cultures for testing at the exam two weeks earlier.

The evidence thus establishes that although Dr. Coffman testified that an accurate and detailed history was generally necessary to treat victims of sexual abuse, this was not the primary purpose of her examination in this case. Instead, as in *Coleman*, the history was taken in conjunction with an attempt to determine if scientific evidence existed to confirm the child's allegations. Because Article 803(4) permits the admission only of hearsay statements necessary for medical treatment, or for a diagnosis in connection with treatment, Dr. Coffman's testimony regarding D.M.'s account of the events at issue was erroneously admitted at trial.

In contrast, the evidence regarding Dr. Barnes' examination compels the conclusion that her testimony as to D.M.'s out-of-court statements was properly admitted under Article 803(4). Vita contacted Dr. Barnes immediately for professional advice in helping her daughter, and the child was examined the next day to determine whether any physical injury or disease had resulted from the assaults. Although the doctor did not testify in detail about the tests and treatment she ordered, D.M.'s medical records were admitted into evidence. These records establish that the child was tested for HIV and other sexually transmitted diseases, and that Vita was notified of the results three days later. Additionally, the records demonstrate that as a result of Dr. Barnes' interview and examination, she referred D.M. to a therapist for psychological counseling. Therefore, D.M.'s statements to Dr. Barnes regarding the assaults by Mr. Lawrence were made for purposes of medical treatment and were thus properly admitted under the hearsay exception of Article 803(4)....

Notes and Questions

1. The assurance of reliability of statements made for purposes of medical treatment rests on the assumption that the patient has a strong motivation to be truthful, because

effective treatment depends on accurate information. *See United States v. Tome*, 61 F.3d 1446, 1449 (10th Cir. 1995); Advisory Committee Note to Rule 803(4).

2. *Renville's* holding has been adopted by a number of other circuits. *E.g., United States v. George*, 960 F.2d 97, 99–100 (9th Cir. 1992); *Morgan v. Foretich*, 846 F.2d 941, 949 (4th Cir. 1988). In addition, the Tenth Circuit has extended it to cover spousal abuse. *See United States v. Joe*, 8 F.3d 1488, 1494–95 (10th Cir. 1993).

3. Subsequent to *Renville*, the Eighth Circuit has stressed that even in the case of a child who is being sexually abused by someone residing in their house, statements by the child to a physician identifying the perpetrator are admissible under Rule 803(4) only if the physician makes clear the importance of the information to diagnosis and treatment:

> [W]e have upheld the admission of hearsay statements identifying the abuser to a physician "where the physician makes clear to the victim that the inquiry into the identity of the abuser is important to diagnosis and treatment, and the victim manifests such an understanding." *United States v. Renville*, 779 F.2d 430, 438 (8th Cir. 1985). But in this case, the government's evidence regarding V.G.'s identity statement to Dr. Jones does not satisfy this rigorous standard.... Dr. Jones did not explain to V.G. that identifying her abuser was pertinent to her diagnosis and treatment....

> Rule 803(4) is premised on the patient's selfish motive in receiving proper medical treatment; therefore, the proponent must establish that the declarant's frame of mind when making the hearsay declaration "was that of a patient seeking medical treatment."

United States v. Gabe, 237 F.3d 954, 958 (8th Cir. 2001) (quoting *Olesen v. Class*, 164 F.3d 1096, 1098 (8th Cir. 1999)). *But see Danaipour v. McLarey*, 386 F.3d 289, 297 n.1 (1st Cir. 2004) ("We reject the notion, adopted by at least one circuit, that identifications by children who are abuse victims to doctors are only admissible 'where the physician makes clear to the victim that the inquiry into the identity of the abuser is important to diagnosis and treatment, and the victim manifests such an understanding.' There are many ways in which a party wishing to enter into evidence a statement under Rule 803(4) can demonstrate that the statement was made for the purpose of diagnosis or treatment; a per se rule requiring a doctor to explain to the victim why a statement naming an abuser is important to diagnosis and treatment is unnecessarily inflexible.").

4. Note that the statement need not be made to a physician to fall within Rule 803(4), for it requires only that the statement be "made for ... medical diagnosis or treatment," and thus covers statements made to those who serve as intermediaries between the patient and the physician. *See* Advisory Committee Note to Rule 803(4) ("Under the exception the statement need not have been made to a physician. Statements to hospital attendants, ambulance drivers, or even members of the family might be included."). *Accord Mendez v. United States*, 732 F. Supp. 414, 423 (S.D.N.Y. 1990). However, the exception is one-sided, in that its language only covers statements made *from* the patient (directly or via intermediaries) *to* the physician, not the other way around. *See Field v. Trigg County Hosp., Inc.*, 386 F.3d 729, 735–36 (6th Cir. 2004); *Bombard v. Fort Wayne Newspapers, Inc.*, 92 F.3d 560, 564 (7th Cir. 1996).

5. The exception has been interpreted to cover statements made to psychiatrists, psychologists, and social workers when made for the purpose of obtaining mental health diagnosis or treatment. *E.g, United States v. Kappell*, 418 F.3d 550, 556 (6th Cir. 2005); *Morgan v. Foretich*, 846 F.2d 941, 949–50 (4th Cir. 1988).

6. Note that Rule 803(4) covers not only statements made for treatment, but also those made for *diagnosis*. This would include, for example, statements made by an injured plaintiff to a doctor that he has retained as an expert to testify in a suit against the individual responsible for his injuries. This represents a significant departure from the common law exception, which was limited to statements made for purposes of treatment. The Advisory Committee explained the expansion as follows:

> Conventional doctrine has excluded from the hearsay exception, as not within its guarantee of truthfulness, statements to a physician consulted only for the purpose of enabling him to testify. While these statements were not admissible as substantive evidence, the expert was allowed to state the basis of his opinion, including statements of this kind. The distinction thus called for was one most unlikely to be made by juries. The rule accordingly rejects the limitation. This position is consistent with the provision of Rule 703 that the facts on which expert testimony is based need not be admissible in evidence if of a kind ordinarily relied upon by experts in the field.

Advisory Committee Note to Rule 803(4).

Is the admission of such statements consistent with the rationale underlying the exception? Does Article 803(4) of the Louisiana Code of Evidence represent a sounder approach?

3. Then-Existing Mental, Emotional, or Physical Condition

Codified in Rule 803(3) is a potentially sweeping exception to the hearsay rule, which provides an exception for:

> A statement of the declarant's then-existing state of mind (such as motive, intent, or plan) or emotional, sensory, or physical condition (such as mental feeling, pain, or bodily health), but not including a statement of memory or belief to prove the fact remembered or believed unless it relates to the validity or terms of the declarant's will.

The potentially unlimited reach of this exception is cabined by two provisions. The first of these is the limitation to statements about the declarant's "then-existing" mental, emotional, or physical condition. In other words, the exception covers a statement by a declarant referring to physical pain or feelings that the person is experiencing when making the statement, such as "My ankle hurts," or "I feel sad," but not statements by a declarant in which he describes past physical pain or feelings, such as "My ankle hurt last week," or "I felt sad the other day." The second provision cabining the scope of Rule 803(3) is the clause excluding from its coverage "a statement of memory or belief to prove the fact remembered or believed."

The following materials explore the scope of Rule 803(3), including the effect of these limiting provisions.

Problem 7-24: The Reverberating Clang

On February 1, 2012, Donald Jones is indicted on charges of murder for stabbing his wife, Veronica Jones, to death. The prosecution's theory is that Donald killed Veronica on the evening of December 15, 2011, when Veronica told Donald that she was planning to leave him.

During its case-in-chief, the prosecution calls Anita, a close friend of Veronica, to the stand. Anita would testify that on the morning of December 15, 2011, Veronica stopped by Anita's house and told Anita:

> "I'm going to tell him tonight that I'm divorcing him. I sure am scared to tell him, though. The last time I threatened to leave, he went 'nutso' on me and beat me up real bad."

Donald's attorney raises a hearsay objection. Assume that there is a great deal of other evidence showing that Donald and Veronica were together alone on the evening of December 15, 2011.

How should the prosecution respond to the hearsay objection, and how will the court likely rule?

Problem 7-25: The Last Meeting

Benjamin is on trial on charges of murdering Thomas. At his trial, the prosecution seeks to call Tanya, a close friend of Thomas, who if permitted would testify that on the day of the alleged murder, Thomas said to her, "I am meeting Benjamin tonight to discuss my dating his ex-girlfriend." Benjamin's attorney raises a hearsay objection. Assume that there is no other evidence showing that Thomas and Benjamin met that night.

How should the prosecution respond, and how will the court likely rule?

Mutual Life Ins. Co. of New York v. Hillmon
145 U.S. 285 (1892)

On July 13, 1880, Sallie E. Hillmon, a citizen of Kansas, brought an action against the Mutual Life Insurance Company, a corporation of New York, on a policy of insurance, dated December 10, 1878, on the life of her husband, John W. Hillmon, in the sum of $10,000, payable to her within sixty days after notice and proof of his death. On the same day the plaintiff brought two other actions, the one against the New York Life Insurance Company, a corporation of New York, on two similar policies of life insurance, dated, respectively, November 30, 1878, and December 10, 1878, for the sum of $5000 each; and the other against the Connecticut Mutual Life Insurance Company, a corporation of Connecticut, on a similar policy, dated March 4, 1879, for the sum of $5000.

In each case the declaration alleged that Hillmon died on March 17, 1879, during the continuance of the policy, but that the defendant, though duly notified of the fact, had refused to pay the amount of the policy, or any part thereof; and the answer denied the death of Hillmon, and alleged that he, together with John H. Brown and divers other persons, on or before November 30, 1878, conspiring to defraud the defendant, procured the issue of all the policies, and afterwards, in March and April, 1879, falsely pretended and represented that Hillmon was dead, and that a dead body which they had procured was his, whereas in reality he was alive and in hiding....

At the trial plaintiff introduced evidence tending to show that on or about March 5, 1879, Hillmon and Brown left Wichita, in the State of Kansas, and traveled together through southern Kansas in search of a site for a cattle ranch; that on the night of March

18, while they were in camp at a place called Crooked Creek, Hillmon was killed by the accidental discharge of a gun; that Brown at once notified persons living in the neighborhood; and that the body was thereupon taken to a neighboring town, where, after an inquest, it was buried. The defendants introduced evidence tending to show that the body found in the camp at Crooked Creek on the night of March 18 was not the body of Hillmon, but was the body of one Frederick Adolph Walters. Upon the question whose body this was, there was much conflicting evidence, including photographs and descriptions of the corpse, and of the marks and scars upon it, and testimony to its likeness to Hillmon and to Walters.

The defendants introduced testimony that Walters left his home at Fort Madison, in the State of Iowa, in March, 1878, and was afterwards in Kansas in 1878, and in January and February, 1879; that during that time his family frequently received letters from him, the last of which was written from Wichita; and that he had not been heard from since March, 1879. The defendants also offered the following evidence:

[The Court here describes letters written by Walters to his sister and his fiancée in which he indicated that he was travelling in a westbound direction with Hillmon].

. . . .

Mr. Justice GRAY, after stating the case as above, delivered the opinion of the court. . . .

The matter chiefly contested at the trial was the death of John W. Hillmon, the insured; and that depended upon the question whether the body found at Crooked Creek on the night of March 18, 1879, was his body or the body of one Walters. . . .

The evidence that Walters was at Wichita on or before March 5, and had not been heard from since, together with the evidence to identify as his the body found at Crooked Creek on March 18, tended to show that he went from Wichita to Crooked Creek between those dates. Evidence that just before March 5 he had the intention of leaving Wichita with Hillmon would tend to corroborate the evidence already admitted, and to show that he went from Wichita to Crooked Creek with Hillmon. Letters from him to his family and his betrothed were the natural, if not the only attainable, evidence of his intention. . . .

A man's state of mind or feeling can only be manifested to others by countenance, attitude or gesture, or by sounds or words, spoken or written. The nature of the fact to be proved is the same, and evidence of its proper tokens is equally competent to prove it, whether expressed by aspect or conduct, by voice or pen. When the intention to be proved is important only as qualifying an act, its connection with that act must be shown, in order to warrant the admission of declarations of the intention. But whenever the intention is of itself a distinct and material fact in a chain of circumstances, it may be proved by contemporaneous oral or written declarations of the party.

The existence of a particular intention in a certain person at a certain time being a material fact to be proved, evidence that he expressed that intention at that time is as direct evidence of the fact as his own testimony that he then had that intention would be. After his death these can hardly be any other way of proving it; and while he is still alive, his own memory of his state of mind at a former time is no more likely to be clear and true than a bystander's recollection of what he then said, and is less trustworthy than letters written by him at the very time and under circumstances precluding a suspicion of misrepresentation.

The letters in question were competent, not as narratives of facts communicated to the writer by others, nor yet as proof that he actually went away from Wichita, but as evidence that, shortly before the time when other evidence tended to show that he went away, he had the intention of going, and of going with Hillmon, which made it more probable both that he did go and that he went with Hillmon than if there had been no proof of such intention. In view of the mass of conflicting testimony introduced upon the question whether it was the body of Walters that was found in Hillmon's camp, this evidence might properly influence the jury in determining that question.

The rule applicable to this case has been thus stated by this court: "Wherever the bodily or mental feelings of an individual are material to be proved, the usual expressions of such feelings are original and competent evidence. Those expressions are the natural reflexes of what it might be impossible to show by other testimony"....

Upon an indictment of one Hunter for the murder of one Armstrong at Camden, the Court of Errors and Appeals of New Jersey unanimously held that Armstrong's oral declarations to his son at Philadelphia, on the afternoon before the night of the murder, as well as a letter written by him at the same time and place to his wife, each stating that he was going with Hunter to Camden on business, were rightly admitted in evidence. Chief Justice Beasley said: "In the ordinary course of things, it was the usual information that a man about leaving home would communicate, for the convenience of his family, the information of his friends, or the regulation of his business. At the time it was given, such declarations could, in the nature of things, mean harm to no one; he who uttered them was bent on no expedition of mischief or wrong, and the attitude of affairs at the time entirely explodes the idea that such utterances were intended to serve any purpose but that for which they were obviously designed. If it be said that such notice of an intention of leaving home could have been given without introducing in it the name of Mr. Hunter, the obvious answer to the suggestion, I think, is that a reference to the companion who is to accompany the person leaving is as natural a part of the transaction as is any other incident or quality of it. If it is legitimate to show by a man's own declarations that he left his home to be gone a week, or for a certain destination, which seems incontestable, why may it not be proved in the same way that a designated person was to bear him company? At the time the words were uttered or written, they imported no wrongdoing to any one, and the reference to the companion who was to go with him was nothing more, as matters then stood, than an indication of an additional circumstance of his going. If it was in the ordinary train of events for this man to leave word or to state where he was going, it seems to me it was equally so for him to say with whom he was going." *Hunter v. State*, 11 Vroom (40 N. J. Law), 495, 534, 536, 538.

Upon principle and authority, therefore, we are of opinion that the two letters were competent evidence of the intention of Walters at the time of writing them, which was a material fact bearing upon the question in controversy; and that for the exclusion of these letters ... the verdicts must be set aside, and a new trial had....

Shepard v. United States
290 U.S. 96 (1933)

Mr. Justice CARDOZO delivered the opinion of the Court.

The petitioner, Charles A. Shepard, a major in the medical corps of the United States army, has been convicted of the murder of his wife, Zenana Shepard, at Fort Riley, Kansas, a United States military reservation....

The crime is charged to have been committed by poisoning the victim with bichloride of mercury. The defendant was in love with another woman, and wished to make her his wife. There is circumstantial evidence to sustain a finding by the jury that to win himself his freedom he turned to poison and murder. Even so, guilt was contested and conflicting inferences are possible. The defendant asks us to hold that by the acceptance of incompetent evidence the scales were weighted to his prejudice and in the end to his undoing.

The evidence complained of was offered by the government in rebuttal when the trial was nearly over. On May 22, 1929, there was a conversation in the absence of the defendant between Mrs. Shepard, then ill in bed, and Clara Brown, her nurse. The patient asked the nurse to go to the closet in the defendant's room and bring a bottle of whisky that would be found upon a shelf. When the bottle was produced, she said that this was the liquor she had taken just before collapsing. She asked whether enough was left to make a test for the presence of poison, insisting that the smell and taste were strange. And then she added the words, "Dr. Shepard has poisoned me."

. . . .

She said, "Dr. Shepard has poisoned me." The admission of this declaration, if erroneous, was more than unsubstantial error. As to that the parties are agreed. The voice of the dead wife was heard in accusation of her husband, and the accusation was accepted as evidence of guilt. If the evidence was incompetent, the verdict may not stand. . . .

Witnesses for the defendant had testified to declarations by Mrs. Shepard which suggested a mind bent upon suicide, or at any rate were thought by the defendant to carry that suggestion. More than once before her illness she had stated in the hearing of these witnesses that she had no wish to live, and had nothing to live for, and on one occasion she added that she expected some day to make an end to her life. This testimony opened the door, so it is argued, to declarations in rebuttal that she had been poisoned by her husband. They were admissible, in that view, not as evidence of the truth of what was said, but as betokening a state of mind inconsistent with the presence of suicidal intent. . . .

The defendant had tried to show by Mrs. Shepard's declarations to her friends that she had exhibited a weariness of life and a readiness to end it, the testimony giving plausibility to the hypothesis of suicide. By the proof of these declarations evincing an unhappy state of mind the defendant opened the door to the offer by the Government of declarations evincing a different state of mind, declarations consistent with the persistence of a will to live. The defendant would have no grievance if the testimony in rebuttal had been narrowed to that point. What the Government put in evidence, however, was something very different. It did not use the declarations by Mrs. Shepard to prove her present thoughts and feelings, or even her thoughts and feelings in times past. It used the declarations as proof of an act committed by some one else, as evidence that she was dying of poison given by her husband. This fact, if fact it was, the Government was free to prove, but not by hearsay declarations. It will not do to say that the jury might accept the declarations for any light that they cast upon the existence of a vital urge, and reject them to the extent that they charged the death to some one else. Discrimination so subtle is a feat beyond the compass of ordinary minds. The reverberating clang of those accusatory words would drown all weaker sounds. It is for ordinary minds, and not for psychoanalysts, that our rules of evidence are framed. They have their source very often in considerations of administrative convenience, of practical expediency, and not in rules of logic. When the risk of confusion is so great as to upset the balance of advantage, the evidence goes out.

These precepts of caution are a guide to judgment here. There are times when a state of mind, if relevant, may be proved by contemporaneous declarations of feeling or intent. *Mutual Life Ins. Co.* v. *Hillmon*, 145 U.S. 285, 295. Thus, in proceedings for the probate of a will, where the issue is undue influence, the declarations of a testator are competent to prove his feelings for his relatives, but are incompetent as evidence of his conduct or of theirs. In suits for the alienation of affections, letters passing between the spouses are admissible in aid of a like purpose. In damage suits for personal injuries, declarations by the patient to bystanders or physicians are evidence of sufferings or symptoms, but are not received to prove the acts, the external circumstances, through which the injuries came about. Even statements of past sufferings or symptoms are generally excluded, though an exception is at times allowed when they are made to a physician. So also in suits upon insurance policies, declarations by an insured that he intends to go upon a journey with another, may be evidence of a state of mind lending probability to the conclusion that the purpose was fulfilled. *Mutual Life Ins. Co.* v. *Hillmon, supra.* The ruling in that case marks the high water line beyond which courts have been unwilling to go. It has developed a substantial body of criticism and commentary. Declarations of intention, casting light upon the future, have been sharply distinguished from declarations of memory, pointing backwards to the past. There would be an end, or nearly that, to the rule against hearsay if the distinction were ignored.

The testimony now questioned faced backward and not forward. This at least it did in its most obvious implications. What is even more important, it spoke to a past act, and, more than that, to an act by some one not the speaker. Other tendency, if it had any, was a filament too fine to be disentangled by a jury....

United States v. Houlihan

871 F. Supp. 1495 (D. Mass. 1994)

YOUNG, District Judge.

I. BACKGROUND

In the early morning hours of Monday, March 2, 1992, James Boyden Jr. was found dead in the vicinity of Spice Street, Charlestown. He had been shot in the back of the head.

On the eve of trial involving federal charges arising out of this and other murders, attempted murders, and allegedly related misconduct, the government moved *in limine* for an Order permitting it to offer, through percipient witnesses, hearsay statements made by James Boyden Jr....

On the evening before he was found dead, James Boyden Jr. was hanging out in his sister's Charlestown apartment drinking beer, departing at about 8:00 PM. As he was leaving, he allegedly told his sister that he was going out "to meet Billy Herd." William "Billy" Herd ("Herd") is a co-defendant in this case....

The government [sought] to admit the statement of James Boyden Jr. to his sister that he intended to meet Herd as relevant circumstantial evidence that it was Herd who killed him later that evening. The government argued that this statement is admissible because it constitutes a statement of a then existing mental or emotional condition under Federal Rule of Evidence 803(3) ("Rule 803(3)"). Over objection, the Court admitted the statement and Marie Boyden Connors was allowed so to testify. This memorandum explains the Court's reasoning.

II. ANALYSIS

This case presents an issue of first impression in the First Circuit, namely, whether the out-of-court statement of a victim-declarant of an intention to meet with a defendant on the evening of the victim's murder can be admitted at trial as circumstantial evidence of the meeting.... although the statement of James Boyden Jr. that he was going to meet Herd would clearly be admissible, if relevant, as a statement of James Boyden Jr.'s **own** intention, it is unclear whether it can be admitted against others—the defendants here— as evidence that the meeting **actually** took place.

A. The Common Law Prior to Rule 803(3)

Prior to the adoption of the Federal Rules of Evidence, the Supreme Court addressed this issue in the famous case of *Mutual Life Insurance Co. of New York v. Hillmon*, 145 U.S. 285 (1892). In *Hillmon*, an insurance company sought to introduce out-of-court statements by a declarant, Walters, that he intended to travel with the insured, Hillmon. The hearsay statement was used as the principal proof that Hillmon had actually traveled with Walters. In holding this statement admissible, the Supreme Court cited with approval *Hunter v. State*, 11 Vroom (40 N.J.L.) 495, 534, 536–38 (1878), a criminal case which involved facts similar to the case at issue here. In *Hunter*, the Court of Errors and Appeals (now the Supreme Court) of New Jersey held that a victim-declarant's out-of-court statements to his wife and son, just prior to his murder, that he was planning to meet with the defendant were admissible to prove the defendant's subsequent conduct. *See Hillmon*, 145 U.S. at 299 (paraphrasing the *Hunter* case). The rationale of the New Jersey court was explicitly adopted by the Supreme Court in *Hillmon*. *Id.* Thus, under *Hillmon*, out-of-court statements of a declarant are admissible to prove the subsequent conduct of others.

The analysis, however, does not end here. In 1973, Congress codified *Hillmon* in Federal Rule of Evidence 803(3). The question for this Court, then, is whether in enacting Rule 803(3) Congress codified in full the reasoning of *Hillmon*, or whether it sought to limit the case's application.

B. Rule 803(3) and its Legislative History

Rule 803(3) states that a declarant's out-of-court statement of intent is admissible at trial as an exception to the rule against hearsay. The text of the rule is silent as to whether such statements are admissible against third parties.

Unfortunately, the legislative history of Rule 803(3) only serves to obfuscate the analysis. While the Advisory Committee's Note to Rule 803(3) states that "the rule of *Mutual Life Insurance Co. v. Hillmon*, allowing evidence of intention as tending to prove the doing of the act intended, is, of course, left undisturbed," the Report of the House Judiciary Committee states that "the committee intends that the rule be construed to limit the doctrine of *Mutual Life Insurance Co. v. Hillmon*, so as to render statements of intent by a declarant admissible only to prove his future conduct, not the future conduct of another person." The Senate Report and the Conference Report are silent on this point.[2]

C. Circuit Split

Courts that have had the opportunity to consider the application of Rule 803(3) are divided.

1. Second & Fourth Circuit Approach—Requirement of Corroborating Evidence—Some courts have held that a declarant's statement of intent may be admitted against a non-declarant only when there is independent evidence connecting the declarant's statement

---

2. This silence is revealing as it indicates that only one chamber of Congress (indeed, only one committee of that chamber) approved the limitation of the *Hillmon* doctrine urged by the defense.

with the non-declarant's conduct. *See United States v. Jenkins*, 579 F.2d 840, 842–43 (4th Cir.), *cert. denied*, 439 U.S. 967 (1978) (declarant's statement of intent is not admissible to prove subsequent conduct of third party, but is admissible to prove **why** third party acted as he did where there exists independent evidence that third party did in fact engage in the alleged conduct).

Similarly, the Second Circuit has held that "declarations of intentions or future plans are admissible against a nondeclarant when they are linked with independent evidence that corroborates the declaration." *United States v. Nersesian*, 824 F.2d 1294, 1325 (2d Cir.), *cert. denied*, 484 U.S. 958 (1987).…

2. Ninth Circuit Approach—No Corroborating Evidence Necessary—To the contrary, the Ninth Circuit has held that statements of a declarant's intent are admissible under Rule 803(3) to prove subsequent conduct of a person other than the declarant without corroborating evidence. *See United States v. Pheaster*, 544 F.2d 353, 374–80 (9th Cir. 1976) (in kidnapping prosecution, trial court did not err in admitting testimony of a friend of the victim that shortly before the victim disappeared he told his friend that he was going to meet a person with the same name as the defendant). In holding statements of intent admissible against third parties, the *Pheaster* court recognized that such testimony could be unreliable, but rejected this as grounds for its exclusion. The Ninth Circuit explained that

> [t]he inference from a statement of present intention that the act intended was in fact performed is nothing more than an inference.… The possible unreliability of the inference to be drawn from the present intention [of the declarant] is a matter going to the weight of the evidence which might be argued to the trier of fact, but it should not be a ground for completely excluding the admittedly relevant evidence.

The court also acknowledged the "theoretical awkwardness" of applying a state of mind exception to prove conduct, but dismissed this objection because of the impressive array of authority favoring such application.

After disposing of these arguments, the Ninth Circuit considered both the California counterpart to Rule 803(3) and the newly enacted Federal Rules of Evidence (which were not in force at the time of the trial below). The Ninth Circuit concluded that the *Hillmon* doctrine (allowing use of such testimony) remains undisturbed (1) because the text of the statute does not explicitly prohibit the use of declarant's statements of intent to prove the conduct of third persons, and (2) because of the contradictory nature of the legislative history of the rule.

III. GROUND OF DECISION

As the Federal Rules of Evidence were enacted by Congress, this Court must interpret them as it would any statutory mandate. In examining Rule 803(3) as a statute, we begin with the text. The language of Rule 803(3) clearly says that statements of intent are admissible. Thus, because it does not **by its terms** limit the class of persons against whom such statements of intent may be admitted, this Court rules that Rule 803(3) codifies *Hillmon* as written and does not disturb its conclusion or its reasoning.

The Court's holding is supported by examining Rule 803(3) in the context of the rest of the Federal Rules of Evidence. The Rules are replete with examples of Congress' familiarity with the concept of limited admissibility. *Compare* Fed.R.Evid. 803(3) *with* Fed.R.Evid. 404(a) (limiting circumstances in which character evidence may be admitted); Fed.R.Evid. 404(b) (limiting purposes for which evidence of other crimes, wrongs, or

acts may be admitted); Fed.R.Evid. 407 (limiting purposes for which subsequent remedial measures may be admitted); Fed.R.Evid. 408 (limiting purposes for which compromises and offers to compromise may be admitted); and Fed.R.Evid. 411 (limiting purposes
for which evidence of liability insurance may be admitted). Thus, had Congress intended
to limit the admissibility of such statements, it presumably would have done so. This
Court will not venture to graft a limitation where none exists.

As Rule 803(3) is unambiguous,[4] this Court is unpersuaded by appeals to legislative history. *See Cabral v. INS,* 15 F.3d 193, 194 (1st Cir. 1994) ("We look to the legislative history only if 'the literal words of the statute create ambiguity or lead to an unreasonable
interpretation'"); *United States v. Charles George Trucking Co.,* 823 F.2d 685, 688 (1st Cir.
1987) (if the language of the statute is reasonably definite, it must be regarded as conclusive,
and legislative history should not be consulted). Even if the Court were properly to engage in an examination of Rule 803(3)'s legislative history, the conflicting nature of that
evidence, **see supra**, would nevertheless lead us right back to the text. *See Citizens to Preserve Overton Park, Inc. v. Volpe,* 401 U.S. 402, 412 n. 29 (1971) (where the legislative history is ambiguous the Court must consider only the statute itself to discern legislative
intent). Therefore, such an inquiry is unnecessary.

Likewise, this Court is not persuaded by the decisions of the Fourth and Second Circuits requiring independent evidence before such testimony can be admitted. Indeed,
this requirement is without foundation in either the text or the legislative history of Rule
803(3). Thus, while the approach adopted by the Second and Fourth Circuits may seem
practical and fair, it is really little more than judicial policymaking.

This Court finds the decisions of the Ninth Circuit, with their emphasis on text and
Supreme Court precedent, more persuasive.

Thus, James Boyden Jr.'s statement that he was going out "to meet Billy Herd" is admissible against Herd under Fed.R.Evid. 803(3). Although it is true that James Boyden Jr.'s
statement of intent is only circumstantial evidence that he actually met Herd, this statement will be allowed to function as part of the larger array of evidence before the jury so
that they may decide for themselves what weight — if any — to give Ms. Connors' testimony....

Notes and Questions

1. Rules 803(3) and 803(4) are both similar in that both exceptions cover statements
by a declarant regarding his physical pain, suffering, or medical condition, but differ in
ways that make the two exceptions simultaneously broader and narrower than one another.
First, while Rule 803(4) covers such statements only when made for the purpose of obtaining medical diagnosis and treatment, Rule 803(3) covers such statements without regard to the purpose for which the statements were made. Second, while Rule 803(4) covers
statements that reference present *or* past pain, suffering, or medical conditions, Rule
803(3) covers only statements referencing *present* pain, suffering, or medical conditions.

---

4. One might argue that Rule 803(3) is ambiguous because on its face it provides no guidance as
to whether it includes statements implicating the conduct of third parties. This, however, is a misunderstanding of the "plain meaning rule." Under this canon of construction, legislative history may
only be consulted when the **meaning of the words** is in dispute; questions regarding the **application**
of a statute to the facts of a particular case do not render a statute ambiguous. Thus, despite ambiguity in the application of Rule 803(3), the text of the rule is in fact plain and the use of legislative
history is therefore unwarranted.

Finally, while Rule 803(4) covers not only statements describing pain, suffering, or medical condition, but also statements as to what *caused* the pain (to the extent necessary for medical diagnosis and treatment), Rule 803(3) covers only the statements referencing the present pain, suffering, or medical condition, not statements regarding the cause of the injury.

2. It is important to distinguish between the use of a statement as circumstantial evidence of a person's state of mind, and use of a statement as direct evidence of one's state of mind. The former use is not hearsay, while the latter, although hearsay, falls within the exception set forth in Rule 803(3):

> In showing the declarant's state of mind the statements may either consist of direct or circumstantial evidence. Thus the statement "X is no good" circumstantially indicates the declarant's state of mind toward X and, where that mental state is a material issue in the case, such statement would be admissible with a limiting instruction. Technically it is not even hearsay since it is not being admitted for the truth of the matter alleged. We do not care whether X is in fact "no good" but only whether the declarant disliked him. However direct statements are also admitted. Thus the statement "I hate X" is direct evidence of the declarant's state of mind and, since it is being introduced for the truth of the matter alleged, must be within some exception to the hearsay rule in order to be admissible.

United States v. Brown, 490 F.2d 758, 762–63 (D.C. Cir. 1974). *See also Smith v. Duncan*, 411 F.3d 340, 346 n.4 (2d Cir. 2005) ("Offering evidence under the state of mind *exception* to the hearsay rule is different than offering it for a non-hearsay purpose—here, to show declarant's state of mind. The *exception* to the hearsay rule is invoked when the statement is offered for the truth of the matter asserted *and* shows the declarant's state of mind (e.g., 'I hate X.'). In contrast, 'the mere utterance of a statement, without regard to its truth, may indicate circumstantially the state of mind ... of the declarant' and is *not* hearsay (e.g. 'I am Napoleon.').").

3. Although Rule 801(d)(2)(A) is available to admit statements regarding the physical, mental, or emotional condition of an opposing party, it cannot be used by a party to introduce his own statements, nor can it be used to introduce the statements of a victim in a criminal case, who is not viewed as a party for purposes of Rule 801(d)(2)(A). Accordingly, Rule 803(3) is useful to a criminal defendant who seeks to introduce evidence of his own prior statements to show good faith, duress, or other states of mind relevant to his defense, or to introduce statements of a victim or another person not party to the action whose state of mind is somehow relevant in the case.

4. Do you see why, absent the proviso excluding "a statement of memory or belief to prove the fact remembered or believed," the language of Rule 803(3) would necessarily encompass statements of fact such as "Dr. Shepard has poisoned me"? Implicitly, are not all such statements preceded by the words "I think," "I believe," or "I remember," and are not thoughts, beliefs, and memories properly characterized as "state[s] of mind"?

5. Is it always clear whether a declarant is speaking of his then-existing or prior state of mind? In *United States v. Naiden*, 424 F.3d 718 (8th Cir. 2005), the adult defendant was tried and convicted on charges of enticing a child over the Internet to engage in unlawful sexual activity with him. The defendant claimed that he did not intend to have sex with a minor, and sought unsuccessfully at trial to offer the testimony of his friend, who would testify that the day after the defendant met the child, he told his friend that he met someone online who said that she was fourteen, but that he did not believe that she really was fourteen. The majority concluded that the testimony was inadmissible under

Rule 803(3), concluding that it was a "[d]eclaration[] about 'a past attitude or state of mind,'" *id.* at 722–23, but the concurrence disagreed, concluding that the defendant's "use of present tense in stating 'I do not believe it' shows the statement manifested [his] belief at the time of his discussion with [his friend]." *Id.* at 724 (Bye, J., concurring). The majority opinion expressed concern that the defendant's statement to his friend was made "after he had ample opportunity to reflect on the situation" and thus was likely an effort to make a "deliberate misrepresentation of a former state of mind," but the concurrence believed that instead "the jury should consider evidence of the self-serving nature of the statement in determining how much weight to give it." *Compare Naiden,* 424 F.3d at 722–23, *with id.* at 725 (Bye, J., concurring). Which opinion is more persuasive?

6. The scope of Rule 803(3) is substantially narrowed by the proviso excluding "a statement of memory or belief to prove the fact remembered or believed," allowing only for the admission of statements relating to the declarant's then-existing physical, mental, or emotional condition, *not* the reasons for that condition. For example, in *United States v. Cohen,* 631 F.2d 1223 (5th Cir. 1980), Cohen was on trial for various federal offenses. Cohen did not deny that he committed the offenses, but claimed that he was under duress due to threats made by his co-conspirator, one Galkin. To support his defense, he sought to admit under Rule 803(3) testimony by witnesses that, at the time the threats were allegedly made, Cohen said to them, "I'm scared because Galkin threatened me":

> Appellant seeks to stretch the limited scope of admissibility under F.R.E. 803(3). That rule by its own terms excepts from the ban on hearsay such statements as might have been made by Cohen of his then existing state of mind or emotion, but expressly excludes from the operation of the rule a statement of belief to prove the fact believed. The rule thus permitted the witnesses to relate any out-of-court statements Cohen had made to them to the effect that he was scared, anxious, sad, or in any other state reflecting his then existing mental or emotional condition. And this for the purpose of proving the truth of the matter asserted in the statement—that Cohen actually was afraid or distraught—because the preamble to F.R.E. 803 provides that such testimony "[is] not excluded by the [rule against] hearsay." But the state-of-mind exception does not permit the witness to relate any of the declarant's statements as to why he held the particular state of mind, or what he might have believed that would have induced the state of mind. If the reservation in the text of the rule is to have any effect, it must be understood to narrowly limit those admissible statements to declarations of condition—"I'm scared"—and not belief—"I'm scared because Galkin threatened me." Cohen's witnesses were permitted to relate any direct statements he had made concerning his state of mind but were prevented only from testifying as to his statements of belief—that he believed that Galkin was threatening him.

Id. at 1225. *Accord United States v. Joe,* 8 F.3d 1488, 1492–93 (10th Cir. 1993) (witness could testify that murder victim expressed fear of her husband under 803(3), but could not testify as to the victim's stated basis for that fear).

7. The *Shepard* Court declares that "[t]here would be an end, or nearly that, to the rule against hearsay" if statements of memory could be admitted to prove the fact remembered. Why would there be an end to the hearsay rule absent this limitation on Rule 803(3)?

8. *United States v. Pheaster,* 544 F.2d 353 (9th Cir. 1976), discussed in the *Houlihan* case, although interpreting Rule 803(3) to fully encompass *Hillmon,* noted the theoretical problems with it:

A much more significant and troubling objection is based on the inconsistency of such an inference with the state of mind exception. This problem is more easily perceived when one divides what is really a compound statement into its component parts. In the instant case, the statement by Larry Adell, "I am going to meet Angelo in the parking lot to get a pound of grass", is really two statements. The first is the obvious statement of Larry's intention. The second is an implicit statement of Angelo's intention. Surely, if the meeting is to take place in a location which Angelo does not habitually frequent, one must assume that Angelo intended to meet Larry there if one is to make the inference that Angelo was in the parking lot and the meeting occurred. The important point is that the second, implicit statement has nothing to do with Larry's state of mind. For example, if Larry's friends had testified that Larry had said, "Angelo is going to be in the parking lot of Sambo's North tonight with a pound of grass", no state of mind exception or any other exception to the hearsay rule would be available. Yet, this is in effect at least half of what the testimony did attribute to Larry.

Pheaster, 544 F.2d at 376–77.

9. Not only do statements such as those at issue in *Hillmon* implicitly involve a statement about the future intent of another person, but also implicit in such statements are backward-pointing statements of the sort held by *Shepard* to be impermissible. After all, implicit in the statement "I am going to meet Angelo in the parking lot" is the fact that the speaker has previously had some sort of discussion with Angelo in the past regarding such a meeting. Is the answer to these concerns that the implicit assertions contained within these statements, while perhaps hearsay under *Wright v. Tatham*, would not be hearsay under the federal rules of evidence?

10. Florida's version of Federal Rule 803(3) provides in pertinent part as follows: "The provision of § 90.802 to the contrary notwithstanding, the following are not inadmissible as evidence, even though the declarant is available as a witness.... A statement of the declarant's then-existing state of mind, emotion, or physical sensation, including a statement of intent, plan, motive, design, mental feeling, pain, or bodily health, when such evidence is offered to.... Prove or explain acts of subsequent conduct of the declarant...." Florida Evidence Code § 90.803(3). Does the Florida rule do a better job of answering the question raised in *Houlihan* and *Pheaster*?

11. Note that while Rule 803(3) generally excludes statements of memory or belief to prove the fact remembered or believed, an exception is made when the statement "relates to the validity or terms of the declarant's will." The Advisory Committee explains that this proviso rests on "practical grounds of necessity and expediency rather than logic," Advisory Committee Note to Rule 803(3), the necessity being that the declarant is dead and thus cannot testify to those issues. But why is the necessity any greater in such cases than in any other case in which the declarant has died?

4. Recorded Recollection

Problem 7-26: The License Plate

David is walking down the street, talking on his cellular telephone with Nancy when he sees a car skid, run into a pedestrian, and drive off. David reads the license plate number to Nancy over the phone. About an hour later, Nancy jots the license plate number down on a piece of paper.

The driver is eventually arrested and indicted. David testifies at the trial, but when asked, he is unable to remember the license plate number of the car that he saw. The prosecution seeks to offer into evidence the piece of paper on which Nancy jotted down the license plate number, but the defense objects, contending that it is "triple hearsay."

How should the court rule on the objection? What are the various ways in which the prosecution can make use of the slip of paper? Suppose that David does not appear as a witness at trial, but Nancy does. Would Nancy's testimony about what David said to her be admissible?

United States v. Hernandez
333 F.3d 1168 (10th Cir. 2003)

EBEL, Circuit Judge.

On March 26, 2001, a jury convicted Lazaro Alexander Hernandez ("Defendant") on one count of possession of a firearm by a prohibited person.... On appeal to this Court, Defendant argues that ... the district court erred when, pursuant to the recorded recollection exception to the hearsay rule, it admitted hearsay testimony linking Defendant to the gun that he was convicted of possessing....

On July 3, 1999, Defendant attended his nephew **Alex's** birthday party at the Cheyenne, Wyoming home of his sister **Connie Hernandez**. Also attending the party was **Shane Crofts**, an Army officer who was Connie Hernandez's boyfriend and the father of Alex. Shane lived in Brighton, Colorado. During the party, Defendant asked Shane if he could smoke a cigarette in Shane's car. Shane agreed and gave Defendant his car keys, which Defendant returned when he was finished. Later that day, Shane noticed that his garage door opener, which he usually kept in his car, was missing. The opener was found a few days later in Connie's side yard in a place that had previously been searched.

When Shane returned to his house in Brighton, Colorado the next morning, he discovered that all of his firearms, as well as other items, had been stolen from the top shelf of his bedroom closet. One of the stolen firearms was a Beretta 9 millimeter semiautomatic pistol that Shane's father, **Christopher ("Kip") Crofts**, had given to him....

About a month later, Defendant asked two friends, **Kirk and Tracy Allen**, to store a gun for him at their house....

At one point during that summer, Tracy Allen mentioned to Defendant's sister Renee Hernandez that Defendant was storing a gun at their house. Renee Hernandez asked her for the gun's serial number, but Tracy Allen initially refused to give it to her. Instead, Tracy Allen called another friend, **Jacqueline Grant**, and recited the serial number to her so that Jacqueline Grant could record it. When Renee Hernandez called Tracy Allen back several days later to ask again for the serial number, Defendant had already taken back the gun, so Tracy Allen called Jacqueline Grant for the serial number. After Jacqueline Grant told Tracy Allen the number, Tracy Allen called Renee Hernandez and recited the number to her over the phone. Renee Hernandez then wrote the number down.

Shortly before Christmas 1999, a friend of Defendant came to Renee Hernandez's house and dropped off a black duffel bag. Inside the duffel bag were the Beretta 9 millimeter firearm and some of Defendant's personal possessions. The duffel bag and Defendant's personal possessions contained therein were positively identified as Defendant's by his former live-in girlfriend, **Elizabeth Fanning**. Renee Hernandez gave the duffel bag and its contents, including the gun, to Shane Crofts, who then turned them over to federal authorities.

On July 20, 2000, Defendant was indicted in the United States District Court for the District of Wyoming on a single count of possession of a firearm (the Beretta) by a prohibited person....

Defendant argues that the district court improperly admitted hearsay testimony about the serial number of the gun he was charged with possessing. Specifically, he claims that the exhibits read into the record containing the serial number of the gun did not satisfy the requirements of the recorded recollection exception to the hearsay rule because they were not "made" by a single witness or "adopted" by a single witness. *See* Fed.R.Evid. 803(5). The serial number evidence was important because it was recorded from the gun Defendant asked Tracy Allen to store for him, thereby providing direct evidence that Defendant possessed the gun at issue. We conclude that the district court did not abuse its discretion and that the evidence was properly admitted under Rule 803(5).

At trial, Tracy Allen was asked if she could remember the serial number of the gun that she said Defendant stored at her home. She said that she could not. She did, however, testify that she had accurately recited the serial number to two people — Jacqueline Grant and Renee Hernandez — who themselves testified that they accurately wrote down the serial number. The chain of events was as follows: Renee Hernandez heard that Defendant was keeping a gun at Tracy Allen's house. Renee Hernandez then called Tracy Allen to ask for the serial number of the gun. Tracy Allen refused to give it to her. After that conversation, Tracy Allen called Jacqueline Grant and asked her to write down the serial number, which Tracy Allen read off the gun, which was in front of her. Jacqueline Grant wrote down the number. Renee later called Tracy Allen a second time, again asking her for the serial number. At that point, Tracy Allen agreed to give it to her. But by this time, the gun was no longer at Tracy Allen's home, so she did not have the serial number in her possession. Therefore, Tracy Allen called Jacqueline Grant and asked Grant to recite the serial number back to her. Jacqueline Grant agreed and read the number to Tracy Allen. Tracy Allen then called back Renee Hernandez and recited the serial number to her. Renee Hernandez wrote down the serial number as Tracy Allen was saying it. At no time after these phone conversations did Tracy Allen examine the writings made by Jacqueline Grant and Renee Hernandez.

Tracy Allen, Jacqueline Grant, and Renee Hernandez all testified at trial that they performed their roles accurately. Tracy Allen testified that she accurately read the serial number from the gun to Jacqueline Grant, and that she later recited it accurately to Renee Hernandez. Jacqueline Grant testified that she accurately wrote down the serial number when Tracy Allen recited it to her, and that she accurately read the serial number back to Tracy Allen pursuant to Allen's subsequent request. Renee Hernandez testified that she accurately wrote down the serial number when Tracy Allen recited it to her. The notes made by Jacqueline Grant and Renee Hernandez were read into the record but not themselves introduced as evidence....

Rule 803(5) is the exception to the hearsay rule for recorded recollections. [The court proceeds to cite the language of the rule, focusing its attention on the phrase "made or adopted by the witness when the matter was fresh in the witness's memory" found in Rule 803(5)(B)].

The most logical reading of the phrase "by the witness" is that that phrase modifies both of the preceding verbs "made" and "adopted." As explained in one leading treatise:

A somewhat different type of cooperative report is involved when one person orally reports facts to another person, who writes them down. A store clerk or timekeeper, for example, may report information to a bookkeeper. In this situation, courts have held the written statement admissible if the person reporting the facts testifies to the correctness of the oral report (although at the time of the testimony, the detailed facts cannot be remembered) and the recorder of that statement testifies to faithfully transcribing the oral report. While subject to some ambiguity because of inartful drafting by Congress, the Federal Rule continues to permit admission of such multi-party statements.

2 *McCormick On Evidence* § 283, at 247 (John W. Strong ed., 5th ed.1999). The authors of the *McCormick* treatise base their reading of the rule in part on the Senate committee report commenting on a change to the rule:

> The committee does not view the House amendment [adding the words "or adopted by the witness"] as precluding admissibility in situations in which multiple participants were involved.

> When the verifying witness has not prepared the report, but merely examined it and found it accurate, he has adopted the report, and it is therefore admissible. *The rule should also be interpreted to cover other situations involving multiple participants, e.g., ... information being passed along a chain of persons....*

The issue of the admissibility of recorded recollections constructed by more than one person has not appeared with frequency in the case law. Nevertheless, at least two circuits have suggested that a past recollection is admissible where it is the product of an oral report of facts by one witness to another who writes them down. *See United States v. Schoenborn*, 4 F.3d 1424, 1427–28 (7th Cir. 1993); *United States v. Booz*, 451 F.2d 719, 725 (3d Cir. 1971) (analyzing the common-law version of 803(5) prior to the adoption of the Federal Rules of Evidence). Prominent treatises also endorse this reading of Rule 803(5)....

These readings are consistent with the purpose of the hearsay rule and the reasons why there are exceptions to that rule. The purpose of the hearsay rule is to preclude a class of evidence considered to be generally less reliable than in-person testimony of events observed by the testifying witness. The exceptions to the general rule excluding hearsay "recognize numerous [instances] where circumstantial guarantees of trustworthiness justify" acceptance of a hearsay statement as evidence of the truth of the matter asserted. Recollections recorded through the efforts of more than one person under Rule 803(5) possess such circumstantial guarantees of trustworthiness. Such recollections have sufficient indicia of accuracy to be admitted in evidence when the parties who jointly constructed the record testify that, on the one hand, the facts contained in the record were observed and reported accurately, and on the other hand, that the report was accurately transcribed.

We hold that a recorded recollection compiled through the efforts of more than one witness is admissible under Rule 803(5), where, as here, each participant in the chain testifies at trial as to the accuracy of his or her piece of the chain. Therefore, the district court properly admitted the serial number records of Jacqueline Grant and Renee Hernandez. Jacqueline Grant's statement is admissible because Tracy Allen testified that she accurately read the serial number off the gun to Jacqueline Grant, and Jacqueline Grant testified that she accurately recorded it. The serial number that Renee Hernandez recorded is also admissible, although in the case of her record there is an extra link in the chain between the observation of the number by Tracy Allen and Renee Hernandez's recording of it: Tracy Allen read the number to Jacqueline Grant, Jacqueline Grant read the number back to Tracy Allen (who at that point no longer had the gun), and Tracy Allen recited the number to Renee Hernandez. But again, each witness testified that the transfer and recording of the information at each step of the chain occurred accurately. That testimony constitutes sufficient indicia of reliability to bring the recorded serial number within the ambit of Rule 803(5)....

Colorado Rule of Evidence 803

Hearsay Exceptions; Availability of Declarant Immaterial

The following are not excluded by the hearsay rule, even though the declarant is available as a witness:

....

(5) Recorded Recollection. A past recollection recorded when it appears that the witness once had knowledge concerning the matter and: (A) can identify the memorandum or record, (B) adequately recalls the making of it at or near the time of the event, either as recorded by the witness or by another, and (C) can testify to its accuracy. The memorandum or record may be read into evidence but may not itself be received unless offered by an adverse party.

Committee Comment

The change reflected above was made because the Federal rule is more restrictive than the Colorado rule, which does not require absence of a present recollection to be expressly shown as a preliminary to use of recorded recollection.

....

Delaware Rule of Evidence 803

Hearsay Exceptions; Availability of Declarant Immaterial

The following are not excluded by the hearsay rule, even though the declarant is available as a witness:

....

(5) Recorded Recollection. A memorandum or record concerning a matter about which a witness once had knowledge but now has insufficient recollection to enable him to testify fully and accurately, shown to have been made or adopted by the witness when the matter was fresh in his memory and to reflect that knowledge correctly. If admitted, the memorandum or record may be read into evidence or may be received as an exhibit in the court's discretion.

....

COMMENT

....

D.R.E. 803(5) tracks F.R.E. 803(5) except that the last sentence was revised in 1980. The revision was made to enable the court to decide whether recorded recollection once admitted as evidence may be received as an exhibit or merely read. It is intended by this change to permit, in the court's discretion, the admission of a recorded recollection as an exhibit regardless of who offered it. The court should weigh whether the admission as an exhibit would unduly influence the jury....

Notes and Questions

1. It is important to distinguish the exception for a recorded recollection from the use of a writing or something else to revive a witness' memory so that she can testify from *present* memory. First, while *anything* can be used to refresh a witness' memory, only writings, and specifically, only those writings that meet certain foundational requirements, can be offered under Rule 803(5). Second, a witness who is using a writing to refresh his memory cannot read from the writing while testifying, because he is supposed to be testifying from *present* memory. In contrast, under Rule 803(5), the writing *must* be read into evidence, because it is the contents of the writing, and not the witness' memory, that is being offered into evidence. Finally, the writing or other aid used to refresh a witness' memory is *not* evidence (and thus not subject to the hearsay rule), while a writing offered under Rule 803(5) *is* evidence. The distinction was examined in Chapter 4, in *United States v. Riccardi*, 174 F.2d 883 (3d Cir. 1949).

2. Note that the requirement that the writing was made or adopted when the matter was "fresh" in the declarant's memory is not interpreted to impose a specific time limit:

> Contemporaneousness is not required in determining whether an event was sufficiently fresh to satisfy FRE 803(5). *See United States v. Patterson*, 678 F.2d 774, 779 (9th Cir. 1982). In fact, the Advisory Committee's notes to FRE 803(5) state that "[n]o attempt is made in the exception to spell out the method of establishing the initial knowledge or the contemporaneity and accuracy of the record, leaving them to be dealt with as the circumstances of the particular case might indicate." Some courts have found periods from ten months to three years to be "fresh," while others have ruled that alcohol or drugs might undermine the freshness of a record made only a few days after the event. *See Patterson*, 678 F.2d at 779 (holding a delay of ten months satisfied the freshness requirement); *United States v. Senak*, 527 F.2d 129 (7th Cir. 1975) (holding a three-year delay satisfied the rule).

United States v. Smith, 197 F.3d 225, 231 (6th Cir. 1999).

In determining whether a recorded recollection was made when the witness' memory was "fresh," courts sometimes look to the face of the writing itself: the more specific and detailed it is, the more likely it is that it was made when the matter was fresh in the witness' memory. *See United States v. Patterson*, 678 F.2d 774, 779 & n.4 (9th Cir. 1982) (citing *United States v. Senak*, 527 F.2d 129, 141 (7th Cir. 1975)).

3. According to the Advisory Committee, there are no concerns with the reliability of such evidence: "The guarantee of trustworthiness is found in the reliability inherent in a record made while events were still fresh in mind and accurately reflecting them." Advisory Committee Note to Rule 803(5). If so, why is a prerequisite to the exception a showing that the declarant's memory of the information memorialized is impaired? The Advisory Committee explains:

> The principal controversy attending the exception has centered, not upon the propriety of the exception itself, but upon the question whether a preliminary requirement of impaired memory on the part of the witness should be imposed. The authorities are divided. If regard be had only to the accuracy of the evi-

dence, admittedly impairment of the memory of the witness adds nothing to it and should not be required. Nevertheless, the absence of the requirement, it is believed, would encourage the use of statements carefully prepared for purposes of litigation under the supervision of attorneys, investigators, or claim adjusters. Hence the example includes a requirement that the witness not have "sufficient recollection to enable him to testify fully and accurately."

4. What is the rationale for the proviso at the end of Rule 803(5) that "the record may be read into evidence but may be received as an exhibit only if offered by an adverse party"? *See Tracinda Corp. v. DaimlerChrysler AG*, 362 F. Supp. 2d 487, 497 (D. Del. 2005) ("the rationale behind the rule's requirement that the article be read into evidence rather than admitted as an exhibit is to prevent the trier of fact from being overly impressed by the writing"). Is such a categorical rule necessary, or does the discretionary approach taken in Delaware's version of the rule make more sense?

5. Does Rule 803(5) encompass those recollections that are *audio*-recorded by a declarant? In such a case, how is the audio-recorded recollection *read* into evidence consistent with the proviso at the end of Rule 803(5)? *See United States v. Sollars*, 979 F.2d 1294, 1298 (8th Cir. 1992) (interpreting Rule 803(5) as encompassing audio-recorded recollections, and permitting the recording to be *played* to the jury).

6. Note that unlike every other exception set forth in Rule 803, the exception for recorded recollections applies only if a showing is first made that better evidence—namely the author testifying based on present memory—is not available. The Advisory Committee explained its decision to place it in Rule 803 as follows:

> Locating the exception at this place in the scheme of the rules is a matter of choice. There were two other possibilities. The first was to regard the statement as one of the group of prior statements of a testifying witness which are excluded entirely from the category of hearsay by Rule 801(d)(1). That category, however, requires that declarant be "subject to cross-examination," as to which the impaired memory aspect of the exception raises doubts. The other possibility was to include the exception among those covered by Rule 804. Since unavailability is required by that rule and lack of memory is listed as a species of unavailability by the definition of the term in Rule 804(a)(3), that treatment at first impression would seem appropriate. The fact is, however, that the unavailability requirement of the exception is of a limited and peculiar nature. Accordingly, the exception is located at this point rather than in the context of a rule where unavailability is conceived of more broadly.

Advisory Committee Note to Rule 803(5).

7. If a writing was made immediately after the event in question, it may be possible to admit the writing under Rule 803(1), the exception for present sense impressions, which differs in several important ways from Rule 803(5). First, while a writing offered under Rule 803(1) must have been made *while perceiving or immediately thereafter* (no more than a few minutes later), one offered under Rule 803(5) need only have been made when *fresh* in the declarant's mind (can be days or months later). Second, the declarant need *not* be called as a witness under Rule 803(1), but *must* be called to the stand under Rule 803(5). Third, a writing can be admitted under Rule 803(1) even if the declarant has full memory of incident. By contrast, a writing can be admitted under Rule 803(5) only if the declarant testifies to a loss of memory concerning the incident. Finally, a writing offered under Rule 803(1) can be received into evidence as an exhibit, while one offered under Rule 803(5) can only be read into evidence.

5. Records of a Regularly Conducted Activity

In the course of conducting their affairs, businesses are constantly generating memos, reports, and other documents that relate to those affairs. Although such documents are generated for the purpose of operating the business, on occasion such documents become relevant in subsequent litigation.

Yet even when such a document consists of the first-hand observations of the person who generated the document, it is, like any other document, hearsay. And the problem is even more complex with documents generated by businesses and other organizations. Typically, such documents are the end result of a complex web of communications amongst employees of the organization. The person who generates the document sometimes has no personal knowledge of *any* of the matters described in the document, and may simply be recording information given to her by other employees, who in turn are simply passing on communications from other employees. Thus, such documents typically contain multiple layers of hearsay. Accordingly, absent some exception to the hearsay rule for such documents, the hearsay rule would require that, instead of admitting the document into evidence, the proponent of the evidence call as witnesses all of the employees who have first-hand knowledge of the matters described in the document.

Consider, for example, a report of the gross monthly sales of a grocery store chain. Such a report typically consists of amounts entered into cash registers by individual cashiers who are engaged in transactions with customers, which are totaled by managerial personnel in the store who, along with managerial personnel in other stores, forward that information to headquarters, where the totals as reported from each store are summed and used to generate the sales report. Who are the people with personal knowledge of the information that makes up the sales report? Not the staff at headquarters, nor even the individual store managers. Rather, it is the hundreds, perhaps thousands, of cashiers in each store who participated in the transactions. Thus, to the extent that the gross monthly sales of that grocery store chain are relevant in subsequent litigation, a strict application of the hearsay rule would require that each of the cashiers be called to testify about the gross amount of their transactions that month. Even assuming that the cashiers could recollect those amounts, the process of calling each of them as witnesses would grind the already slow process of litigation to a near stand-still.

Fortunately for the proponents of such evidence, there is an alternative. Rule 803(6) creates an exception to the hearsay rule for:

A record of an act, event, condition, opinion, or diagnosis if:

(A) the record was made at or near the time by — or from information transmitted by — someone with knowledge;

(B) the record was kept in the course of a regularly conducted activity of a business, organization, occupation, or calling, whether or not for profit;

(C) making the record was a regular practice of that activity;

(D) all these conditions are shown by the testimony of the custodian or another qualified witness, or by a certification that complies with Rule 902(11) or (12) or with a statute permitting certification; and

(E) neither the source of information nor the method or circumstances of preparation indicate a lack of trustworthiness.

The Advisory Committee Note to Rule 803(6) justifies the exception partially on the grounds of necessity, describing as "burdensome and crippling" a rule that would require producing every person who participated in the gathering, transmitting, and recording of the information contained in such documents. It goes on to justify the exception on the grounds of reliability:

> The element of unusual reliability of business records is said variously to be supplied by systematic checking, by regularity and continuity which produce habits of precision, by actual experience of business in relying upon them, or by a duty to make an accurate record as part of a continuing job or occupation.

Advisory Committee Note to Rule 803(6).

Although typically referred to as the "business" records exception to the hearsay rule, Rule 803(6)(B) makes clear that it covers all sorts of entities, including "a business, organization, occupation, or calling, whether or not for profit." While this broad definition thus encompasses records produced by sole proprietorships, non-profit organizations such as churches, and even unlawful businesses (such as those engaged in prostitution or the sale of illegal drugs), it does not encompass records of a purely personal nature, such as personal diaries or personal financial records.

The exception applies only to a record that is made "at or near the time" of the events that are the subject of the record, and only if it is the "regular practice" of the business to generate such records. Furthermore, while the person who generated the record need not have personal knowledge of the matters contained therein, the requirement that the record be made "by—or from information transmitted by—someone with knowledge," means that it must be based on the personal knowledge of *someone* along the chain of communications.

Yet, are there any restrictions on who that "someone" can be? Moreover, what is the effect of the trustworthiness proviso in Rule 803(6)(E)? The following materials explore these and other questions that arise in applying Rule 803(6).

United States v. Vigneau
187 F.3d 70 (1st Cir. 1999)

BOUDIN, Circuit Judge....

From around February 1995 to at least the end of that year, Patrick Vigneau and Richard Crandall conducted a venture to acquire marijuana and steroids in the Southwest and resell them in the Northeastern United States. Crandall obtained the marijuana and steroids from suppliers in El Paso, Texas, and in Mexico, and sent the drugs to Patrick Vigneau in Rhode Island and southeastern Massachusetts. Patrick Vigneau, who distributed the drugs to retail dealers, used others to assist him, including his brother Mark Vigneau and one Joseph Rinaldi.

Some of the proceeds from these Northeastern sales had to be sent to Crandall in Texas so that he could pay suppliers and share in the profits. Patrick Vigneau transmitted funds to Crandall primarily through Western Union money orders. The money orders were sent by Patrick Vigneau or others, sometimes in the sender's true name but often using false or borrowed names. Timothy Owens, who assisted Crandall in acquiring drugs, frequently picked up the checks from Western Union, cashed them, and gave the money to Crandall....

The jury convicted Patrick Vigneau of participating in a continuing criminal enterprise, 21 U.S.C. § 848; possession of marijuana and attempted possession of marijuana (both with intent to distribute) and conspiracy to distribute marijuana, *id.* §§ 841, 846; and 21 counts of money laundering on specific occasions and conspiracy to launder money, 18 U.S.C. § 1956. Patrick Vigneau was later sentenced to 365 months in prison. He now appeals, challenging his conviction but not his sentence.

On this appeal, Patrick Vigneau's strongest claim is that the district court erred in allowing the government to introduce, without redaction and for all purposes, Western Union "To Send Money" forms, primarily in support of the money laundering charges. These forms, as a Western Union custodian testified, are handed by the sender of money to a Western Union agent after the sender completes the left side of the form by writing (1) the sender's name, address and telephone number; (2) the amount of the transfer; and (3) the intended recipient's name and location. The Western Union clerk then fills in the right side of the form with the clerk's signature, date, amount of the transfer and fee, and a computer-generated control number; but at least in 1995, Western Union clerks did not require independent proof of the sender's identity.

Western Union uses the control number affixed by the clerk to correlate the information on the "To Send Money" form with the corresponding "Received Money" form and with the canceled check issued by Western Union to pay the recipient. The original forms are usually discarded after six months, but the information provided by the sender, as well as the information from all records associated with the money transfer, are recorded in a computer database. In this case, for some transfers the government had the forms completed by the sender, but for most it had only the computer records.

The government introduced over 70 records of Western Union money transfers. Patrick Vigneau's name, address and phone number appeared as that of the sender on 21 of the "To Send Money" forms (11 other names, including fictional names and those of Mark Vigneau and of other defendants, appeared as those of the senders on the other forms), and those 21 forms corresponded to the 21 specific counts of money laundering on which Patrick Vigneau was ultimately convicted by the jury. Patrick Vigneau's most plausible objection, which was presented in the district court and is renewed on appeal, is that his name, address and telephone number on the "To Send Money" forms were inadmissible hearsay used to identify Patrick Vigneau as the sender.

Hearsay, loosely speaking, is an out-of-court statement offered in evidence to prove the truth of the matter asserted. Fed.R.Evid. 801(c). Whoever wrote the name "Patrick Vigneau" on the "To Send Money" forms was stating in substance: "I am Patrick Vigneau and this is my address and telephone number." Of course, if there were independent evidence that the writer was Patrick Vigneau, the statements would constitute party-opponent admissions and would fall within an exception to the rule against hearsay, Fed.R.Evid. 801(d)(2) (the rule says admissions are "not hearsay," but that is an academic refinement). However, the government cannot use the forms themselves as bootstrap-proof that Patrick Vigneau made the admission.

Instead, the government argues that the "To Send Money" forms and the computerized information reflecting those forms and the correlated material were admissible under the business records exception. Fed.R.Evid. 803(6).... The district judge ... admitted the "To Send Money" forms (or equivalent computer records) without redaction and for all purposes....

The district judge was correct that the "To Send Money" forms literally comply with the business records exception because each form is a business record, and in this case, the computer records appeared to be a trustworthy account of what was recorded on the original "To Send Money" forms. The difficulty is that despite its language, the business records exception does not embrace statements contained within a business record that were made by one who is *not* a part of the business if the embraced statements are offered for their truth. The classic case is *Johnson v. Lutz*, 253 N.Y. 124 (N.Y.1930), which excluded an unredacted police report incorporating the statement of a bystander (even though the police officer recorded it in the regular course of business) because the informant was not part of that business. The Advisory Committee Notes to Rule 803(6) cite *Johnson v. Lutz* and make clear that the rule is intended to incorporate its holding.

Johnson v. Lutz is not a technical formality but follows directly from the very rationale for the business records exception. When a clerk records the receipt of an order over the telephone, the regularity of the procedure, coupled with business incentives to keep accurate records, provide reasonable assurance that the record thus made reflects the clerk's original entry. Thus the business record, although an out-of-court statement and therefore hearsay, is admitted without calling the clerk to prove that the clerk received an order.

But no such safeguards of regularity or business checks automatically assure the *truth* of a statement *to* the business by a stranger to it, such as that made by the bystander to the police officer or that made by the money sender who gave the form containing his name, address, and telephone number to Western Union. Accordingly, the *Johnson v. Lutz* gloss excludes this "outsider" information, where offered for its truth, unless some other hearsay exception applies to the outsider's own statement. This gloss on the business records exception, which the Federal Rules elsewhere call the "hearsay within hearsay" problem, Fed.R.Evid. 805, is well-settled in this circuit. Other circuits are in accord.

Of course, "hearsay within hearsay" is often trustworthy but hearsay is not automatically admissible merely because it is trustworthy....

Nor does the reference to "trustworthiness" in the business records rule comprise an independent hearsay exception. Fed.R.Evid. 803(6). That reference was not designed to limit *Johnson v. Lutz* to untrustworthy statements — after all, the statement to the police officer was probably trustworthy — but rather to exclude records that would normally satisfy the business records exception (*e.g.*, the clerk's computerized record of calls received) where *inter alia* the opponent shows that the business record or system itself was not reliable (*e.g.*, the computer was defective).

Of course, in some situations, the statement by the "outsider" reflected in the business record may be admissible not for its truth but for some other purpose,[5] but the disputed "To Send Money" forms here were admitted by the district court for all purposes, including as proof of the sender's identity....

No doubt, the "To Send Money" forms were relevant to the government's case regardless of whether Patrick Vigneau (or any other named sender) was the person who made an individual transfer: they showed transfers of money from Rhode Island directed to Crandall and others that tended to support the general description of the drug and money laundering activities described by the government's witnesses. Thus, the forms could have been offered in redacted form, omitting the information identifying Patrick Vigneau as the sender of 21 of the forms. But that is not what happened.

---

5. See *United States v. Franks*, 939 F.2d 600, 601–02 (8th Cir. 1991) (Federal Express receipts admissible to show that someone received package who signed specific name); *United States v. Lieberman*, 637 F.2d 95, 101 (2d Cir. 1980) (hotel registry card admissible to show that someone checked in using specific name).

Some cases have admitted under the business records exception "outsider" statements contained in business records, like the sender's name on the Western Union form, where there is evidence that the business itself used a procedure for *verifying* identity (*e.g.*, by requiring a credit card or driver's license). Probably the best analytical defense of this gloss is that in such a case, the verification procedure is circumstantial evidence of identity that goes beyond the mere bootstrap use of the name to establish identity. While this gloss may well represent a reasonable accommodation of conflicting values, verification was not Western Union's practice at the time....

We thus conclude ... that the sender name, address and telephone number on the forms should not have been admitted for their truth....

Ebenhoech v. Koppers Industries, Inc.
239 F. Supp. 2d 455 (D.N.J. 2002)

SIMANDLE, District Judge....

On November 2, 1998, plaintiff Albert Ebenhoech, as chief chemical operator at Solutia, Inc., slipped and fell about fifteen feet off the side of a tank car and severely injured his left leg. Plaintiff alleges that defendant Koppers Industries should be liable under a negligence or products liability theory for spilling a hazardous chemical called phthalic anhydride ["PAA"] on the rail car and for not cleaning it off prior to shipping the car to Solutia....

In this motion, plaintiffs seek to exclude an unusual incident report created by plaintiff's employer after the accident....

The report is relevant evidence of the accident's occurrence and cause. It describes the chronology of the incident and determines that its primary cause was the "at-risk behavior of working at an elevated location without fall protection." The report includes observations that form the basis for the conclusion, such as plaintiff's lack of personal fall protection, Solutia's improper facilities for cleaning PAA, and the soda ash solution's "extremely" slippery nature when used on smooth tank cars....

However, while the report is relevant, this Court finds that it is not admissible. Defendant admits that it is hearsay, but argues that the regularly conducted activity exception ... to the hearsay rule allow[s] the admission of the report....

Plaintiffs argue that the reports should be excluded because they were not made in the regular course of business. In support of their argument, they cite *Palmer v. Hoffman*, 318 U.S. 109 (1943) in which the Supreme Court upheld the exclusion of an employee's report about an accident. The Court held that:

> it is manifest that in this case those reports are not for the systematic conduct of the enterprise as a railroad business. Unlike payrolls, accounts receivable, accounts payable, bills of lading and the like, these reports are calculated for use essentially in the court, not in the business. Their primary utility is in litigating, not in railroading.

The business records exception was not intended to "make admissible all evidence, no matter how incompetent or irrelevant, merely by virtue of the fact that it appeared in a business record." Instead, it was meant to "admit into evidence entries of a purely clerical or routine nature not dependent upon speculation, conjecture or opinion." Courts have therefore found that the exception applies to business records which are reliable and trustworthy because the employee was motivated to be accurate because the business depends on accuracy of the record to conduct its affairs, and created the record in a habitual manner.

In *Palmer*, the Supreme Court found that the incident report was not trustworthy and was not admissible because (1) the business had motivation to skew the record because it was prepared in anticipation of litigation, and (2) the record was not routinely created, but was only created because of an unusual accident. The Third Circuit has cited *Palmer* for the proposition that the motivation of the report's writer is key to deciding whether the report is admissible under Rule 803(6). *Casoni*, 950 F.2d at 911, n. 10; *see also Sinkovich*, 232 F.3d at 205 (excluding report when "primary motive" for its creation was litigation).

Here, the report is not admissible as a record of a regularly conducted business because (1) it was prepared with the knowledge that the event could lead to litigation and (2) it was not routinely created. The report indicates the possibility of litigation by titling the document "recordable injury," by classifying the incident as "OSHA Recordable/Days Away Case," and by investigating the cause of an accident that left an employee with a "seriously" injured left ankle. The report also shows that the incident was not common, leading to the conclusion that the report was not routinely created. The report's title alone indicates that the report was made to document an "unusual incident." The report also indicates that the chief operator on site stated that "he had performed this cleaning task several times in the past without incident, although this was the first time that the operation required work outside of the platformed dome area." Additionally, the report includes an analysis of the consequences of behavior like plaintiff's and finds that the certain consequences of "working outside of the guarded area on top of a phthalic anhydride rail car without fall protection" are "job completed," "save time," and "meet deadline." The uncertain consequences include "nothing bad happens" and "injury or death." This Court finds that a report created after an "unusual incident" that occurred during the "first time that the operation required work outside the platformed dome area" and led to the "uncertain consequence" of "injury" is not a report made in the regular course of business....

United States v. Gentry
925 F.2d 186 (7th Cir. 1991)

EASTERBROOK, Circuit Judge.

In the wake of a few maniacs who poisoned foods and medicines, causing not only deaths but also great expense as firms recalled their products, there followed extortion: people threatened to announce that they had poisoned a particular firm's products unless the manufacturer bought them off. To deal with the plague, Congress enacted 18 U.S.C. § 1365(c)(1), which makes it a felony to communicate a false report of food tampering.

Kevin Mark Gentry is no extortionist, but he made a false report of food tampering. On May 2, 1989, he told fellow employees—plus the security force of the mall where he worked—that he had bit into a pin when he ate M & M candy bought from a vending machine. One of Gentry's fellow employees found some metal embedded in the candy. Sheriff's deputies who investigated the report found Gentry's claim hard to believe and asked him to take a polygraph test. Gentry did; the examiner concluded that he was lying; after the examiner switched off the machine, Gentry confessed that he had put the pin in the candy and made the report to get attention. He was prosecuted for violating § 1365(c)(1) and received a sentence of 12 months' imprisonment....

Gentry ... objects to testimony from an employee of the manufacturer that there were no other reports of pins in M & M candy. The testimony was relevant; it implies that the pin came from Gentry rather than the factory (or a tamperer other than Gentry). And Fed.R.Evid. 803(7) allows this use of business records to show the nonoccurrence of an event....

Notes and Questions

1. As the *Vigneau* case indicates, the Advisory Committee indicated that Rule 803(6) applies only when someone who works within the organization has personal knowledge of the matter contained in the record:

> Sources of information presented no substantial problem with ordinary business records. All participants, including the observer or participant furnishing the information to be recorded, were acting routinely, under a duty of accuracy, with employer reliance on the result, or in short "in the regular course of business." If, however, the supplier of the information does not act in the regular course, an essential link is broken; the assurance of accuracy does not extend to the information itself, and the fact that it may be recorded with scrupulous accuracy is of no avail. An illustration is the police report incorporating information obtained from a bystander: the officer qualifies as acting in the regular course but the informant does not. The leading case, Johnson v. Lutz, 253 N.Y. 124 (1930), held that a report thus prepared was inadmissible. Most of the authorities have agreed with the decision.... The rule follows this lead in requiring an informant with knowledge acting in the course of the regularly conducted activity.

Advisory Committee Note to Rule 803(6).

What part of the text of Rule 803(6) codifies this "in the course" requirement?

2. As the *Vigneau* court explains, even if a business record contains information from an outsider, and is thus "hearsay within hearsay," it may nonetheless be admissible. Rule 805 provides that "[h]earsay within hearsay is not excluded by the rule against hearsay if each part of the combined statements conforms with an exception to the rule." The Advisory Committee gives examples of hearsay within hearsay that are nonetheless admissible because each layer of the statement falls within an exception to the hearsay rule:

> Thus a hospital record might contain an entry of the patient's age based on information furnished by his wife. The hospital record would qualify as a regular entry except that the person who furnished the information was not acting in the routine of the business. However, her statement independently qualifies as a statement of pedigree (if she is unavailable) or as a statement made for purposes of diagnosis or treatment, and hence each link in the chain falls under sufficient assurances. Or, further to illustrate, a dying declaration may incorporate a declaration against interest by another declarant.

Advisory Committee Note to Rule 805.

The word "exception" as used in Rule 805 includes not only those statements formally called "exceptions" in Rules 803, 804, and 807, but also those statements which are defined as "not hearsay" in Rule 801(d). Moreover, as the *Vigneau* case indicates, if the statement from the outsider is relevant for a non-hearsay purpose, it can be admitted for that limited purpose.

3. Rule 803(11), in one narrow circumstance, effectively eliminates the "in the course" requirement when invoked in conjunction with Rule 803(6). It creates an exception to the hearsay rule for:

> A statement of birth, legitimacy, ancestry, marriage, divorce, death, relationship by blood or marriage, or similar facts of personal or family history, contained in a regularly kept record of a religious organization.

Federal Rule of Evidence 803(11).

The Advisory Committee explains the interaction between the two rules and the rationale for Rule 803(11):

> Records of activities of religious organizations are currently recognized as admissible at least to the extent of the business records exception to the hearsay rule, and Exception (6) would be applicable. However, both the business record doctrine and Exception (6) require that the person furnishing the information be one in the business or activity. The result is such decisions as Daily v. Grand Lodge, 311 Ill. 184 (1924), holding a church record admissible to prove fact, date, and place of baptism, but not age of child except that he had at least been born at the time. In view of the unlikelihood that false information would be furnished on occasions of this kind, the rule contains no requirement that the informant be in the course of the activity.

Advisory Committee Note to Rule 803(11). Are you persuaded by the Advisory Committee's rationale? *Compare* Tennessee R. Evid. 803(11) Advisory Commission Comment ("The Commission did not believe records of religious organizations were uniformly reliable enough to satisfy hearsay exception requirements.").

4. The *Vigneau* court suggests that the outcome might have differed had an employee of the business verified the identity of the sender, for example, by having them show identification. Why would the use of such a procedure alter the admissibility of the evidence? *See generally United States v. Reyes*, 157 F.3d 949, 952 (2d Cir. 1998) ("the rule is that the individual with the business duty and the hearsay declarant should be the same person, but this and other circuits have recognized an exception to the general rule: The person making the record need not have a duty to report so long as someone has a duty to verify the information reported.")

5. The Advisory Committee discussed the relationship between the *Palmer* case and Rule 803(6) at length:

> Problems of the motivation of the informant have been a source of difficulty and disagreement. In Palmer v. Hoffman, 318 U.S. 109 (1943), exclusion of an accident report made by the since deceased engineer, offered by defendant railroad trustees in a grade crossing collision case, was upheld. The report was not "in the regular course of business," not a record of the systematic conduct of the business as a business, said the Court. The report was prepared for use in litigating, not railroading. While the opinion mentions the motivation of the engineer only obliquely, the emphasis on records of routine operations is significant only by virtue of impact on motivation to be accurate. Absence of routineness raises lack of motivation to be accurate. The opinion of the Court of Appeals had gone beyond mere lack of motive to be accurate: the engineer's statement was "dripping with motivations to misrepresent." Hoffman v. Palmer, 129 F.2d 976, 991 (2d Cir. 1942). The direct introduction of motivation is a disturbing factor, since absence of motive to misrepresent has not traditionally been a requirement

of the rule; that records might be self-serving has not been a ground for exclusion. As Judge Clark said in his dissent, "I submit that there is hardly a grocer's account book which could not be excluded on that basis." 129 F.2d at 1002. A physician's evaluation report of a personal injury litigant would appear to be in the routine of his business. If the report is offered by the party at whose instance it was made, however, it has been held inadmissible, otherwise if offered by the opposite party.

The decisions hinge on motivation and which party is entitled to be concerned about it. Professor McCormick believed that the doctor's report or the accident report were sufficiently routine to justify admissibility. McCormick § 287, p. 604. Yet hesitation must be experienced in admitting everything which is observed and recorded in the course of a regularly conducted activity.... Some decisions have been satisfied as to motivation of an accident report if made pursuant to statutory duty, since the report was oriented in a direction other than the litigation which ensued. The formulation of specific terms which would assure satisfactory results in all cases is not possible. Consequently the rule proceeds from the base that records made in the course of a regularly conducted activity will be taken as admissible but subject to authority to exclude if "the sources of information or other circumstances indicate lack of trustworthiness."

Advisory Committee Note to Rule 803(6). Which aspects of *Palmer* are codified by Rule 803(6)?

6. While a party seeking to invoke Rule 803(6) has the burden of establishing that the evidence satisfies the elements of the exception, it is the party who opposes the admission of evidence under Rule 803(6) who has the burden of invoking the trustworthiness proviso and persuading the court that the record is not trustworthy. *E.g., Shelton v. Consumer Products Safety Com'n,* 277 F.3d 998, 1010 (8th Cir. 2002).

7. Traditionally, a party seeking to invoke Rule 803(6) has been required to call to the stand "the custodian or another qualified witness" to establish the elements of the exception. The standard for qualifying as a witness is a liberal one: the witness need only be familiar with the company's recordkeeping practices in general, and need not be in control of or have individual knowledge about the preparation of the particular records being offered into evidence. *E.g., United States v. Jenkins,* 345 F.3d 928, 935 (6th Cir. 2003). Indeed, so long as the person has the requisite familiarity, he need not even be an employee of the organization. *E.g., United States v. Hathaway,* 798 F.2d 902, 906–07 (6th Cir. 1986).

Under an amendment to Rule 803(6) that took effect in 2000, it is no longer necessary that such a witness personally appear and testify. Instead, she can submit a certification in conformance with Rules 902(11) or 902(12). Such a certification has the effect of providing the necessary foundation both to authenticate the records and to invoke Rule 803(6). Parties intending to use certifications in lieu of live testimony are required to satisfy notice requirements to the opposing parties in accordance with Rules 902(11) and 902(12).

8. How long after the events in question occur can a record be made and still be admissible under Rule 803(6)? The rule states only that it be made "at or near the time" of the event—what does that mean? *See United States v. Strother,* 49 F.3d 869, 876 (2d Cir. 1995) (six months is too long); *Wheeler v. Sims,* 951 F.2d 796, 804 (7th Cir. 1992) (eleven days is not too long); *United States v. Lemire,* 720 F.2d 1327, 1350 (D.C. Cir. 1983) (one year and ten months is too long); *United States v. Williams,* 661 F.2d 528, 531 (5th Cir.

1981) (three years is too long); *Lamar v. Experian Information Systems,* 408 F. Supp. 2d 591, 596 (N.D. Ill. 2006) (five months is too long).

9. Rule 803(7), cited in *Gentry,* provides an exception to the hearsay rule for:

Evidence that a matter is not included in a record described in paragraph (6) if:

(A) the evidence is admitted to prove that the matter did not occur or exist;

(B) a record was regularly kept for a matter of that kind; and

(C) neither the possible source of the information nor other circumstances indicate a lack of trustworthiness.

Is Rule 803(7) necessary? Isn't the evidence covered by Rule 803(7) akin to silence, in the sense of non-complaint, which is not hearsay within the meaning of Rule 801(c)? The Advisory Committee, while doubting the need for Rule 803(7), included it to alleviate any doubts as to the admissibility of such evidence:

Failure of a record to mention a matter which would ordinarily be mentioned is satisfactory evidence of its nonexistence. While probably not hearsay as defined in Rule 801, supra, decisions may be found which class the evidence not only as hearsay but also as not within any exception. In order to set the question at rest in favor of admissibility, it is specifically treated here.

Advisory Committee Note to Rule 803(7). *Compare* Tennessee R. Evid. 803(7) Advisory Commission Comment ("It is doubtful that the absence of a business entry poses a hearsay problem. Consequently, although F.R.Evid. 803(7) contains a purported exception, the Commission found no need for an exception.").

6. Public Records

Like private businesses, public entities are constantly generating memos, reports, and other documents that relate to their affairs. And like business records, public records, while generated primarily for conducting the public's business, on occasion become relevant in subsequent litigation.

To facilitate the admission of such documents, Rule 803(8) provides an exception to the hearsay rule for:

A record or statement of a public office if:

(A) it sets out:

(i) the office's activities;

(ii) a matter observed while under a legal duty to report, but not including, in a criminal case, a matter observed by law-enforcement personnel; or

(iii) in a civil case or against the government in a criminal case, factual findings from a legally authorized investigation; and

(B) neither the source of information nor other circumstances indicate a lack of trustworthiness.

Note that unlike Rule 803(6), Rule 803(8) does not require that a foundation witness be called. This is consistent with the special status given to public records under the rules governing authentication and the best evidence rule. *See* Fed. R. Evid. 902, 1005.

Moreover, Rule 803(8) differs from Rule 803(6) in that it divides public records into three different categories, and limits the admissibility of particular public records under certain circumstances. The materials that follow explore the application of the various provisions of Rule 803(8) and the justification for the limitations contained therein.

Problem 7-27: The Police Report

James Wallingford and Robert Mills, police officers patrolling together, notice a car drive by with a partially obstructed license plate (a violation of state law), and pull the car over. While speaking with the driver, Tom Braun, they see that the passenger, Kate Kline, has an open purse at her feet with what appears to be a gun in it. They force the two out of the car and question them separately.

Under questioning, Kate says to Wallingford that Tom shoved the gun into her purse when he heard the police car's siren. After further investigation, Tom—who has a prior criminal record—is indicted in federal court on charges of being a felon in possession of a firearm, a violation of 18 U.S.C. §922(g)(1).

The prosecution does not call Kate or Officer Wallingford as witnesses. Instead, it seeks to offer into evidence a copy of a police report written out by Officer Wallingford in which he has memorialized both his observations at the scene of the arrest as well as what Kate said to him. Tom's attorney raises a hearsay objection. The prosecution responds that it is admissible under Rules 803(6) and 803(8).

How should the court dispose of the objection? If Officer Wallingford appears on the stand and testifies that he cannot remember what happened, could the report be read to the jury under Rule 803(5)? If Tom wanted to offer the police report into evidence, could he?

Problem 7-28: Cocaine and Cartography

Richard Turpin is on trial, charged with several counts of selling cocaine in a drug-free zone. An essential element of the offense is that the drugs are sold within 1000 feet of a public school.

At trial, the prosecution calls several witnesses who testify that Turpin sold them cocaine at various locations within the City of Danger Bay. Specifically, the witnesses testify that Turpin sold them cocaine at the intersections of North Royal Avenue and Doulton Street West, Zanoo Street West and North Moosh Avenue, and Kangaroo Court West and North Stockholm Avenue.

To prove that these locations fall within 1000 feet of a public school, the government seeks to offer into evidence a map created by Mr. O.K. Cole, who is employed in the Geographic Information Systems (GIS) Division of the City of Danger Bay. The map—which is reproduced below—depicts Sairey Gamp Elementary School and the surrounding area. Drawn onto the map is a circle marking the area within 1000 feet of Sairey Gamp Elementary School, a public school in the City of Danger Bay.

Turpin's attorney objects to the introduction of the map into evidence, contending that it is hearsay and possibly double hearsay.

How should the prosecution respond to the objection? How will the court likely dispose of the objection?

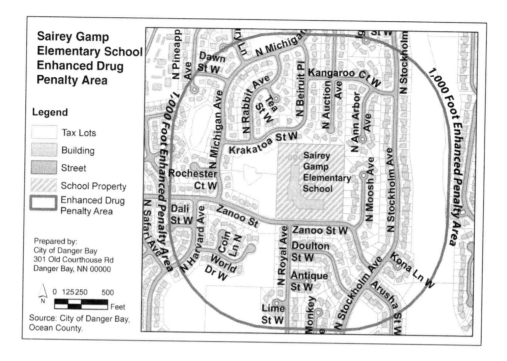

Problem 7-29: *The Unregistered Firearm*

Paul is on trial on charges of violating a federal statute that makes it a crime to possess certain types of firearms that have not been registered with a national firearms registry maintained by the U.S. Bureau of Alcohol, Tobacco, and Firearms ("ATF").

At trial, as proof that the firearm was not registered, the prosecution offers into evidence a written statement, signed by Tom Rogers, an employee of the ATF. The statement, certified in accordance with the requirements of Rule 902, states that Tom did a diligent search of the ATF's records but found no evidence that Paul had registered his firearm. Paul's attorney raises a hearsay objection to the admission of the statement.

How should the prosecution respond to the objection? How will the court likely dispose of the objection?

United States v. Oates

560 F.2d 45 (2d Cir. 1977)

WATERMAN, Circuit Judge:

This is an appeal from a judgment of the United States District Court for the Eastern District of New York convicting appellant [Oates], following a six-day jury trial, of possession of heroin with intent to distribute, and of conspiracy to commit that substantive offense....

Appellant ... claims that the trial court committed error by admitting into evidence at trial two documentary exhibits purporting to be the official report and accompanying worksheet of the United States Customs Service chemist who analyzed the white powdery substance seized from [Oates' co-defendant] Isaac Daniels. The documents, the crucial nature of which is beyond cavil, concluded that the powder examined was heroin. Appellant contends, first of all, that under the new Federal Rules of Evidence (hereinafter "FRE") the documents should have been excluded as hearsay and, alternatively, that, even if they were not inadmissible on that basis, their exclusion was nonetheless required because their admission into evidence over appellant's objection would have violated and did violate appellant's right under the Sixth Amendment to the United States Constitution to confront the witnesses against him....

At trial the government had planned upon calling as one of its final witnesses a Mr. Milton Weinberg, a retired United States Customs Service chemist who allegedly had analyzed the white powder seized from Isaac Daniels....

Before the onset of Weinberg's bronchial condition, the prosecutor had planned to call Weinberg for the purpose of eliciting from him testimony that Weinberg had analyzed the powder seized from Daniels and found it to be heroin. When Weinberg became "unavailable," the government decided to call another Customs chemist, Shirley Harrington, who, although she did not know Weinberg personally, was able to testify concerning the regular practices and procedures used by Customs Service chemists in analyzing unknown substances. Through Mrs. Harrington the government was successful in introducing Exhibits 13 and 12 which purported to be, respectively, the handwritten worksheet used by the chemist analyzing the substance seized from Daniels and the official typewritten report of the chemical analysis. The report summarizes salient features of the worksheet. Mrs. Harrington claimed to be able to ascertain from the face of the worksheet the various steps taken by Weinberg to determine whether the unknown substance was, as suspected, heroin. When the defense voiced vigorous objection to the attempt to introduce the documents through Mrs. Harrington, the government relied upon three different hearsay exceptions contained in the new Federal Rules of Evidence to support its position that the documents were admissible. While principal reliance was placed on the modified "business records" exception found in FRE 803(6), the evidence was also claimed to be admissible under FRE 803(8) as a "public record" or under FRE [807]. The defense was primarily concerned that the defendant was being denied his Sixth Amendment right to confront his accusers, in this case, the missing chemist Weinberg....

The remarks [of the Advisory Committee] evince a clear intention to draft the rules in such a way as to eliminate, if possible, any tension between the hearsay rule as embodied in Article VIII of the Federal Rules of Evidence and the confrontation clause.

These efforts to avert the possibility of conflict between the hearsay exceptions and the confrontation clause find their most emphatic expression in FRE 803(8) and it is to that provision that we now turn. On this appeal the government and the appellant are in complete disagreement over the materiality of FRE 803(8) to the issue of whether the chemist's report and worksheet were excludable as hearsay. Although at trial the government placed some reliance on FRE 803(8), the so-called "public records and reports" exception to exclusion, in its brief in this court it completely ignores the provision, apparently abandoning any reliance on it for reasons we shall discuss below. Instead, it urges us to find that the challenged evidence falls easily within the scope of what has traditionally been labeled the "business records exception" to the hearsay exclusionary rule, the codification of which in the Federal Rules of Evidence is found in FRE 803(6). Appellant, on the other hand, vigorously asserts that the issue of whether the chemist's report and worksheet were fatal hearsay can be correctly evaluated only by a careful study of the precise wording of FRE 803(8) and the legislative intent underlying the enactment of that rule.

While the problem presented is not susceptible of any facile solution, we believe that, on balance, appellant's emphasis on the importance of FRE 803(8) is well-founded. It would certainly seem to be the exception which would logically come to mind if a question arose as to the admissibility of reports of the kind we are considering in this case. Moreover, although as a general rule there is no question that hearsay evidence failing to meet the requirements of one exception may nonetheless satisfy the standards of another exception, *see, e. g., United States v. Smith*, 521 F.2d 957, 964 (D.C. Cir. 1975), and there thus might be no need to examine FRE 803(8) at all, we agree with appellant that both the language of Rule 803(8) and the congressional intent, as gleaned from the explicit language of the rule and from independent sources, which impelled that language have impact that extends beyond the immediate confines of exception (8) itself. We therefore regard FRE 803(8) as the proper starting point for our evidentiary analysis.

That the chemist's report and worksheet could not satisfy the requirements of the "public records and reports" exception seems evident merely from examining, on its face, the language of FRE 803(8)....

It is manifest from the face of item [(A)(iii)] that "factual findings resulting from an investigation made pursuant to authority granted by law"* are not shielded from the exclusionary effect of the hearsay rule by "the public records exception" if the government seeks to have those "factual findings" admitted *against* the accused in a criminal case. It seems indisputable to us that the chemist's official report and worksheet in the case at bar can be characterized as reports of "factual findings resulting from an investigation made pursuant to authority granted by law." The "factual finding" in each instance, the conclusion of the chemist that the substance analyzed was heroin, obviously is the product of an "investigation," supposedly involving on the part of the chemist employment of various techniques of scientific analysis. Furthermore, in view of its reliance on the chemist's report at trial and its representation to the district court that "chemical analys[e]s of unidentified substances are indeed a regularly conducted activity of the Customs laboratory of Customs chemists," the government here is surely in no position to dispute the fact that the analyses regularly performed by United States Customs Service chemists on substances lawfully seized by Customs officers are performed pursuant to authority granted by law.

Though with less confidence, we believe that the chemist's documents might also fail to achieve status as public records under FRE 803(8)[(A)(ii)] ... the reports in this case conceivably could also be susceptible of the characterization that they are "reports ... setting forth ... [] matters observed pursuant to duty imposed by law as to which matters there was a duty to report."** If this characterization is justified, the difficult question would be whether the chemists making the observations could be regarded as "[] law[-] enforcement personnel." We think this phraseology must be read broadly enough to make its prohibitions against the use of government-generated reports in criminal cases coterminous with the analogous prohibitions contained in FRE 803(8)[(A)(iii)]. We would thus construe "[] law enforcement personnel" to include, at the least, any officer or employee of a governmental agency which has law enforcement responsibilities....

Our conclusion that the chemist's report and worksheet do not satisfy the standards of FRE 803(8) comports perfectly with what we discern to be clear legislative intent not

---

* Editor's Note: This phrase was restyled in 2011 to read "factual findings from a legally authorized investigation."

** Editor's Note: This phrase was restyled in 2011 to read "a matter observed while under a legal duty to report."

only to exclude such documents from the scope of FRE 803(8) but from the scope of FRE 803(6) as well. The reason why such a restrictive approach was adopted can be established by referring to the Advisory Committee's Notes and by examining the way in which Congress revised the draft legislation proposed by the Advisory Committee and which the Supreme Court submitted to Congress. As already explained, an overriding concern of the Advisory Committee was that the rules be formulated so as to avoid impinging upon a criminal defendant's right to confront the witnesses against him. The Advisory Committee, in unequivocal language, offers the specter of collision with the confrontation clause as the explanation for the presence of FRE 803(8)[(A)(iii)] in its proposed (and, since FRE 803(8)[(A)(iii)] was unaltered during the legislative process, final) form:

> In one respect, however, the rule with respect to evaluative reports under [FRE 803(8)(A)(iii)] is very specific: they are admissible only in civil cases and against the government in criminal cases in view of the *almost certain collision with confrontation rights which would result from their use against an accused in a criminal case.*

Advisory Committee's Notes, Note to Paragraph (8) of Rule 803. This preoccupation with preserving the confrontation rights of criminal defendants was shared by a Congress which established enhanced protection for those rights by substantially amending the proposed language of FRE 803(8)[(A)(ii)]. An amendment offered by Representative David Dennis added important qualifying language to item [(A)(ii)] which before the amendment deemed as "public records" under FRE 803(8) "matters observed pursuant to duty imposed by law as to which matters there was a duty to report." The amendment qualified the foregoing language by adding "excluding, however, in criminal cases matters observed by police officers and other law enforcement personnel."* In the debate that followed the offer of this amendment, the accused's right to confront the witnesses against him was advanced as the impetus for the proposal....

[The court cites floor statements by several members of Congress that appeared to reflect an understanding that the provisos in Rules 803(8)(A)(ii) and 803(8)(A)(iii) would absolutely bar the use of such evidence in the circumstances delineated in those exceptions.]

We thus think it manifest that it was the clear intention of Congress to make evaluative and law enforcement reports absolutely inadmissible against defendants in criminal cases. Just as importantly, it must have been the unquestionable belief of Congress that the language of FRE 803(8)[(A)(ii)] and [(A)(iii)] accomplished that very result.

Despite what we perceive to be clear congressional intent that reports not qualifying under FRE 803(8)[(A)(ii)] or [(A)(iii)] should, and would, be inadmissible against defendants in criminal cases, the government completely ignores those provisions ... and argues instead that the chemist's report and worksheet in the case at bar fall clearly within the literal terms of the modified business records exception to the hearsay rule contained in FRE 803(6)....

[T]he government's argument that the documents in this case satisfy the requirements of the modified "business records" exception is not altogether unappealing if it is assessed strictly on the basis of the literal language of FRE 803(6) and without reference to either the legislative history or the language of FRE 803(8)[(A)(ii)] and [(A)(iii)]. For instance, it is true that, traditionally, a proponent's inability to satisfy the requirements of one

---

* Editor's Note: This phrase was restyled in 2011 to read "but not including, in a criminal case, a matter observed by law-enforcement personnel."

hearsay exception does not deny him the opportunity to attempt to meet the standards of another. Secondly, it is clear from the explicit inclusion of the words "opinion[]" and "diagnos[i]s" in FRE 803(6) that, in one sense anyway, Congress intended to expand, or at least ratify, the view of prior court cases that had expanded the concept of what constitutes a "business record." The Advisory Committee's Notes confirm this. Advisory Committee's Notes, Note to Paragraph (6) of Rule 803. It is reasonable to assume that a laboratory analysis may well be an "opinion." Thirdly, the testimony of Mrs. Harrington, a "qualified witness," established that it was a regular practice of the Customs laboratory to make written reports of their analyses and that these particular written reports were made in the regular course of the laboratory's activities....

For purposes of our present analysis, we thus consider the situation to be that the chemist's documents might appear to be within the literal language of FRE 803(6) although there is clear congressional intent that such documents be deemed inadmissible against a defendant in a criminal case. This would not be the first time that a court has encountered a situation pitting some literal language of a statute against a legislative intent that flies in the face of that literal language. Our function as an interpretive body is, of course, to construe legislative enactments in such a way that the intent of the legislature is carried out. In recognition of this responsibility numerous courts have either applied, or at least recognized, the principle that, despite the existence of literal language that might dictate a contrary result, a court should interpret a statute in such a way as to effectuate clear legislative intent....

In light of this paramount importance of legislative intent, we shall now attempt to ascertain the legislative intent underlying FRE 803(6) ... [O]ur task is considerably facilitated by the presence of both explicit explanations of the *meaning* of relevant provisions of the Federal Rules of Evidence, and an abundant supply of information relating to one important *purpose* in drafting those provisions as they were drafted.

As already mentioned, Representative William Hungate, in presenting the report of the Committee of Conference to the House of Representatives, left no doubt that it was the belief of the Committee of Conference that under the new Federal Rules of Evidence the effect of FRE 803(8)[(A)(ii)] and [(A)(iii)] was to render law enforcement reports and evaluative reports inadmissible against defendants in criminal cases. It is thus clear that the only way to construe FRE 803(6) so that it is reconcilable with this intended effect is to interpret FRE 803(6) and the other hearsay exceptions in such a way that police and evaluative reports not satisfying the standards of FRE 803(8)[(A)(ii)] and [(A)(iii)] may not qualify for admission under FRE 803(6) or any of the other exceptions to the hearsay rule. That Congress must have understood that all the hearsay exceptions would be construed in light of the carefully drafted proscriptions of FRE 803(8) is also demonstrated, as discussed earlier in this opinion, by Representative Dennis' categorical remarks to that effect.

Even if the remarks of Representatives Hungate and Dennis were not as clear as they are, we could still reach the same conclusion that, in view of the articulated purpose behind the narrow drafting of FRE 803 in general and FRE 803(8) in particular, FRE 803(6) must be read in conjunction with FRE 803(8)[(A)(ii)] and [(A)(iii)]. Specifically, the pervasive fear of the draftsmen and of Congress that interference with an accused's right to confrontation would occur was the reason why in criminal cases evaluative reports of government agencies and law enforcement reports were expressly denied the benefit to which they might otherwise be entitled under FRE 803(8). It follows that this explanation of the reason for the special treatment of evaluative and law enforcement reports under FRE 803(8) applies with equal force to the treatment of such reports under *any* of the other exceptions to the hearsay rule. The prosecution's utilization of any hearsay exception to achieve admission of evaluative and law enforcement reports would serve to deprive the accused of the opportunity to confront his accusers as effectively as would reliance on a "public records" exception. Thus, there being no apparent reason why Congress would tolerate the admission of evaluative and law enforcement reports by use of some other exception to the hearsay rule (for example, the "business records" exception of FRE 803(6) or the "open-ended" exception[] of FRE [807]), it simply makes no sense to surmise that Congress ever intended that these records could be admissible against a defendant in a criminal case under *any* of the Federal Rules of Evidence's exceptions to the hearsay rule. As noted, the accuracy of this reasoning is borne out dramatically by the remarks of Representative Dennis in response to fears expressed by Representative Holtzman that police reports clearly inadmissible under FRE 803(8) might be able to qualify under FRE [807].

We are not the first court to indulge in a less than literal construction of a hearsay exception so as to effectuate congressional intent. An issue addressed by the D.C. Circuit in *United States v. Smith, supra,* 521 F.2d at 968–69 n.24, was whether the police reports of FRE 803(8)[(A)(ii)] are admissible *against* the government. While conceding that "[o]n its face, 803(8)[(A)(ii)] appears to [say that they are not, the court was] convinced, however, that 803(8)[(A)(ii)] should be read, in accordance with the obvious intent of Congress and in harmony with 803(8) [(A)(iii)] to authorize the admission of the reports of police officers and other law enforcement personnel at the request of the defendant in a criminal case." The "obvious intent of Congress" in enacting FRE 803(8)[(A)(ii)] was found to be that "use of reports against defendants would be unfair." "Since there [was] no apparent reason to allow defendants to use the reports admitted by 803(8)[(A)(iii)] but not those governed by 803(8)[(A)(ii)] [, the court concluded] that a police report ... is an exception to the new hearsay rules when introduced at the request of the defense."... As have we, the court in *Smith* liberally construed the new hearsay rules and, in fact, carved out an implied exception to the explicit language of the rules. In so doing, *Smith* was attempting to harmonize two provisions which, if read literally, might produce a result clearly at odds with the legislative intent. Our approach in the case at bar closely parallels that taken by the D.C. Circuit in *Smith.*

While reading an implied exception into FRE 803(6) is, to be sure, a less than literal way of construing that provision, the rules of statutory construction discussed earlier in this opinion certainly warrant such treatment when the legislative intent is as clear as it is here.... An examination of this information convinces us that when there is tension between the confrontation clause of the Sixth Amendment to the United States Constitution and the literal language of the various hearsay exceptions it was the congressional intent that a less literal reading of the rules would be justified....

If we were to construe FRE 803(6) in an overly literal fashion and find that the chemist's report and worksheet constituted "business records" under that rule, the collision which the Congress so assiduously tried to "avoid inviting" would be that much nearer to occurring, for, under the circumstances of the case at bar, there exist legitimate doubts regarding the constitutionality of the introduction of these documents....

Notes and Questions

1. Suppose that in *Oates*, Milton Weinberg, the chemist who authored the reports, *did* appear on the stand and was subject to cross-examination. In that instance, could the reports have been admitted under Rule 803(6)? Could they have been admitted under Rule 803(5) if he appeared and testified that he could not remember what he wrote? Consider the following:

Assuming for the moment King's assertion that the SSA forms fall within the Rule 803(8)[(A)(iii)] exclusion, we disagree that their admittance as business records under Rule 803(6) is precluded. Our reading of the legislative history indicates that the exclusions arose from a congressional concern that police and other investigative reports would be admitted in lieu of requiring actual testimony by the police officer or investigator. Underlying this concern is recognition of the relative unreliability of such reports compared to direct testimony of the authoring officer or investigator. Where the author does not testify, congressional intent would be thwarted if the reports were admitted under another hearsay exception. Consistent with this reading of congressional intent, we held in *United States v. Sawyer*, 607 F.2d 1190 (7th Cir. 1979), that the recorded recollections of a law enforcement officer who testified at trial were admissible under Rule 803(5) notwithstanding their inadmissibility under Rule 803(8)[(A)(ii)]. The accompanying testimony of the author minimizes the danger of unreliability by giving the trier of fact the opportunity to weigh his credibility and consider the circumstances surrounding preparation of the report. *Sawyer* controls King's argument on this issue; we hold accordingly that because the claims representatives who filled out the admitted forms testified at trial, the arguable applicability of the Rule 803(8)[(A)(iii)] exclusion does not preclude admissibility under another exception to the hearsay rule.

United States v. King, 613 F.2d 670, 673 (7th Cir. 1980). *Accord United States v. Sokolow*, 91 F.3d 396, 404–05 (3d Cir. 1996) (collecting cases).

2. Just as Rule 803(7) creates an exception for evidence of the non-existence of a business record, so Rule 803(10) creates an exception for evidence of the non-existence of a public record:

Testimony—or a certification under Rule 902—that a diligent search failed to disclose a public record or statement if the testimony or certification is admitted to prove that:

(A) the record or statement does not exist; or

(B) a matter did not occur or exist, if a public office regularly kept a record or statement for a matter of that kind.

Note that there are no provisos equivalent to those set forth in Rules 803(8)(A)(ii) and 803(8)(A)(iii). Would the concerns regarding the Confrontation Clause raised in *Oates* compel that such limits to be read into Rule 803(10)? Historically, courts have rejected such arguments. *E.g., United States v. Yakobov*, 712 F.2d 20, 26–27 (2d Cir. 1983). However, recent U.S. Supreme Court cases—examined later in the chapter—have raised concerns that Rule 803(10)'s certification provision may be unconstitutional when invoked against the accused in a criminal case. Accordingly, a pending, proposed amendment to Rule 803(10) would require a prosecutor seeking to offer a certification under Rule 803(10) to provide advance notice to the accused, and would allow it to be admitted only if the accused failed to object.

3. Just as with Rule 803(6), it is important when applying Rule 803(8) to be on the watch for statements of outsiders contained within a public record. Such statements are hearsay within hearsay, and are thus admissible only if they, too, fall within an exception to the hearsay rule. *E.g., United States v. Mackey*, 117 F.3d 24, 28–29 (1st Cir. 1997).

4. Recall that when an expert testifies and renders an opinion, he is permitted to base his opinion on inadmissible hearsay. *See* Fed. R. Evid. 703. Can "factual findings" that are based in part on inadmissible hearsay nonetheless be admitted under Rule 803(8)? While there is no *per se* bar on opinions based on such statements, to the extent that they

are based solely or primarily on the hearsay statements of interested persons, they are subject to exclusion under the trustworthiness proviso. *E.g., Faries v. Atlas Truck Body Mfg. Co.*, 797 F.2d 619, 623–24 (8th Cir. 1986).

5. Are you persuaded by the *Oates* court's interpretation of the phrase "law-enforcement personnel" in Rule 803(8)(A)(ii)? *Compare United States v. Rosa,* 11 F.3d 315, 332 (2d Cir. 1993) (holding that medical examiner does not fall within the scope of that phrase). What if the report was produced by a private laboratory at the request of law enforcement personnel? *See United States v. Blackburn*, 992 F.2d 666, 672 (7th Cir. 1993) ("[W]e think a private company that conducts tests independently with its own equipment and prepares reports by itself based on those tests, even if at the instance of a governmental agency, is not part of the prosecution team.").

6. As indicated in *Oates*, the D.C. Circuit, in *United States v. Smith*, held that Rule 803(8)(A)(ii)'s law enforcement exception applied only to documents offered by the prosecution, not to those offered by the defense. Are you persuaded by the *Smith* court's rationale for so interpreting that provision? *Compare United States v. Insaulgarat*, 378 F.3d 456, 465–66 (5th Cir. 2004) (noting that substantial authority supports the *Smith* position but following its prior precedent holding that "[t]he plain language of the rule does not distinguish between a defendant's and a prosecutor's use of a police report"); Alabama R. Evid. 803(8) ("Records, reports, statements, or data compilations, in any form, of public offices or agencies, setting forth ... (B) matters observed pursuant to duty imposed by law as to which matters there was a duty to report, excluding, however, *when offered against the defendant* in criminal cases, matters observed by police officers and other law enforcement personnel....") (emphasis added).

7. Does the "law-enforcement personnel" proviso in Rule 803(8)(A)(ii) require the exclusion of *all* records generated by law enforcement personnel? *See United States v. Lopez-Moreno*, 420 F.3d 420, 437 (5th Cir. 2005) ("the law enforcement exception ... was directed at observations by law enforcement officers at the scene of a crime or in the course of investigating a crime and did not apply to 'recording routine, objective observations, made as part of the everyday function of the preparing official or agency'"). *Accord United States v. Edelmann*, 458 F.3d 791, 813 (8th Cir. 2006). What basis is there for making such an exception to the proviso? Consider the following:

> Drawing a line at routine, non-adversarial documents would best comport with the purpose for which Congress originally approved the exception. The Rule's enactment history indicates that "the reason for this exclusion is that observations by police officers at the scene of the crime or the apprehension of the defendant are not as reliable as observations by public officials in other cases because of the adversarial nature of the confrontation between the police and the defendant in criminal cases." Congress was generally "concerned about prosecutors attempting to prove their cases in chief simply by putting into evidence police officers' reports of their contemporaneous observations of crime."
>
> Recognizing this intent, those circuits to have considered the issue have all found that the limitation in Rule 803(8)[(A)(ii)] does not exclude routine observations that are inherently non-adversarial.

United States v. Dowdell, 595 F.3d 50, 70–71 (1st Cir. 2010).

8. Note that Rule 803(8)(A)(iii)'s hearsay exception for records setting out "factual findings from a legally authorized investigation" encompasses not merely the "facts" detailed in such records, but also conclusions and opinions contained in such reports. *See Beech Aircraft Corp. v. Rainey*, 488 U.S. 153 (1988).

9. What sort of circumstances might indicate a lack of trustworthiness under Rule 803(8)(B)? *See United States v. Spano*, 421 F.3d 599, 604 (7th Cir. 2005) ("The provision is tailor-made for a case in which the records are controlled by the defendants themselves rather than by clerks assumed to be disinterested.").

10. Can material posted on a government entity's website be offered into evidence under Rule 803(8)? *See Allen v. Saif Corp.*, 2005 WL 708402, at *3 (D. Or. Mar. 29, 2005) (holding that it can); *EEOC v. E.I. Du Pont de Nemours & Co.*, 2004 WL 2347559, at *1–*2 (E.D. La. Oct. 18, 2004) (holding that a printout from a government entity's website falls within the hearsay exception set forth in Rule 803(8) and that it is self-authenticating under Rule 902(5)).

11. Note that Rule 803(8) applies only to documents *generated* by a public agency. In other words, the mere fact that a document is *filed* with a public agency does not make that document a public document. However, several other exceptions to the hearsay rule provide, in limited instances, for the admission of documents that are created by private individuals and reported to a public agency.

First, Rule 803(9) provides an exception for "[a] record of a birth, death, or marriage, if reported to a public office in accordance with a legal duty." Second, Rule 803(14) provides an exception for

> The record of a document that purports to establish or affect an interest in property if:
>
> (A) the record is admitted to prove the content of the original recorded document, along with its signing and its delivery by each person who purports to have signed it;
>
> (B) the record is kept in a public office; and
>
> (C) a statute authorizes recording documents of that kind in that office.

12. While a marriage certificate issued by a public official would be admissible under Rule 803(8), a marriage certificate issued by a private individual, such as a member of the clergy, who is authorized by law to perform marriages, would not be admissible under that rule. However, such certificates are admissible under Rule 803(12), which provides an exception for

> A statement of fact contained in a certificate:
>
> (A) made by a person who is authorized by a religious organization or by law to perform the act certified;
>
> (B) attesting that the person performed a marriage or similar ceremony or administered a sacrament; and
>
> (C) purporting to have been issued at the time of the act or within a reasonable time after it.

7. Prior Court Judgments

Problem 7-30: Don't Judge Me!

In each of the following scenarios in which a prior court judgment is offered into evidence, determine whether and how the proponent of the evidence could overcome a hearsay objection:

(1) In a prosecution under a statute that makes it a criminal offense for a person convicted of any crime to possess a firearm, evidence that the defendant had, before being found in possession of the firearm, been previously convicted for a crime punishable by a maximum of six months in prison, offered by the prosecution to prove the prior conviction element of the charged offense.

(2) In a civil action against the defendant for the wrongful death of a person, evidence that he had previously been convicted of manslaughter of that person, an offense punishable by a maximum of ten years in prison, offered by the plaintiff to prove that the defendant caused the person's death.

(3) In a civil action against the defendant for the wrongful death of a person, evidence that he had previously been acquitted of manslaughter of that person, an offense punishable by a maximum of ten years in prison, offered by the defendant to prove that he did not cause the person's death.

Sometimes, a prior court judgment may have a preclusive effect in subsequent litigation under the doctrines of claim and issue preclusion. However, assuming that a prior judgment has no such effect, can evidence of the judgment nonetheless be offered as proof of any facts essential to sustain the judgment? In other words, even if a prior judgment lacks preclusive effect, does it have evidentiary effect, in the sense that it can be introduced and given whatever weight the trier of fact deems appropriate?

Absent an exception to the hearsay rule, evidence of a prior court judgment offered in subsequent litigation, when offered into evidence to prove the truth of the matter asserted therein, would be excluded as hearsay: "[I]n effect [prior judgments] simply quote the assertion of 12 jurors (who did not themselves perceive the acts charged) that the person did or didn't do the acts." *United States v. Bailey*, 319 F.3d 514, 518 (D.C. Cir. 2003).

Two exceptions to the hearsay rule address the use of evidence of prior judgments to prove the truth of the matter asserted therein. First, Rule 803(22) creates an exception for

Evidence of a final judgment of conviction if:

(A) the judgment was entered after a trial or guilty plea, but not a nolo contendere plea;

(B) the conviction was for a crime punishable by death or by imprisonment for more than a year;

(C) the evidence is admitted to prove any fact essential to the judgment; and

(D) when offered by the prosecutor in a criminal case for a purpose other than impeachment, the judgment was against the defendant.

The pendency of an appeal may be shown but does not affect admissibility.

Second, Rule 803(23) creates an exception for

A judgment that is admitted to prove a matter of personal, family, or general history, or boundaries, if the matter:

(A) was essential to the judgment; and

(B) could be proved by evidence of reputation.

Together, these two exceptions permit most uses of evidence of a prior criminal judgment involving a serious offense to prove the truth of the matter asserted therein and very limited use of evidence of prior civil judgments to prove the truth of the matter asserted therein. Courts have rejected efforts to circumvent the narrow scope of these exceptions via Rule 803(8)(A)(iii):

> Rule 803(8) was not intended to allow the admission of findings of fact by courts. Rule 803(8) is limited to investigations: "A judge in a civil trial is not an investigator, rather a judge." *Nipper v. Snipes*, 7 F.3d 415, 417 (4th Cir. 1993). The advisory committee notes to Rule 803(8) also indicate that the intent of the rule's drafters was to allow for the admission of investigations by officials in the executive branch; there is no indication in those notes that the committee intended this exception to include findings of fact by judges. *Id.*; *see also Jones*, 29 F.3d at 1554. In addition, the Federal Rules of Evidence specifically allow for the admission of certain kinds of judgments or their underlying facts as evidence, *see* Fed.R.Evid. 803(22) (previous conviction); R. 803(23) (personal, family, or general history and boundaries), which dissuades us from concluding that Rule 803(8) provides a blanket ground for the admission of prior judgments. A contrary conclusion by us would effectively eliminate the narrow nature of these hearsay exceptions and render them redundant.

Herrick v. Garvey, 298 F.3d 1184, 1192 (10th Cir. 2002).

However, Rule 803(8)(A)(iii) does encompass findings by executive branch officials who act in quasi-judicial roles, such as administrative law judges. *See, e.g.*, *Zeus Enterprises, Inc. v. Alphin Aircraft, Inc.*, 190 F.3d 238, 242 (4th Cir. 1999) ("Because *Nipper* is limited to excluding the findings of judges in the judicial branch, it does not require us to exclude the decision of an ALJ who is an officer in the executive branch"); *United States v. Nelson*, 365 F. Supp. 2d 381, 388 (S.D.N.Y. 2005) ("[T]he findings of a judge employed in the *executive* branch of government, as distinguished from the *judicial* branch, are encompassed by [the public records] exception to the hearsay rule.").

In addition, courts have rejected efforts to admit criminal judgments of *acquittal* in subsequent litigation:

> It is well established, however, that evidence of prior acquittals is generally inadmissible.... "A judgment of acquittal is relevant to the legal question of whether the prosecution is barred by the constitutional doctrine of double jeopardy or of collateral estoppel. But once it is determined that these pleas in bar have been rejected, a judgment of acquittal is not usually admissible to rebut inferences that may be drawn from the evidence that was admitted." *United States v. Viserto*, 596 F.2d 531, 537 (2d Cir. 1979). "[A]lso a judgment of acquittal is hearsay. The Federal Rules of Evidence except from the operation of the hearsay rule only judgments of conviction, Rule 803(22), not judgments of acquittal." *Id.* Judgments of acquittal, however, are still inadmissible in large part because they may not present a determination of innocence, but rather only a decision that the prosecution has not met its burden of proof beyond a reasonable doubt. Finally, even if the judgments of acquittal were admissible, exclusion under Fed.R.Evid. 403 would be justified — and highly recommended — because the danger of jury confusion would greatly outweigh the evidence's limited probative value.

United States v. Gricco, 277 F.3d 339, 352–53 (3d Cir. 2002).

Keep in mind that resort to a hearsay exception is necessary only when evidence of the prior judgment is offered to prove the *truth* of the matter asserted therein. In other words, it is only when evidence of a prior judgment is offered to prove the truth of the assertion by the trier of fact in those proceedings (such as, for example, the assertion by the trier of fact contained in a judgment of conviction in a murder case that the defendant caused the victim's death) that a hearsay use is being made of the prior judgment and thus that resort to a hearsay exception is necessary. Sometimes, however, the mere *fact* of a prior judgment of conviction or liability, rather than the conduct underlying the prior judgment, is relevant. In such a situation, the assertion of guilt or liability by the trier of fact in the earlier proceeding is relevant merely because it was *made*, and is thus not hearsay when offered for that purpose. *See, e.g., United States v. Adedoyin*, 369 F.3d 337, 344–345 (3d Cir. 2004) (holding, in a prosecution for improper entry into the United States by an alien, that evidence of the defendant's prior conviction was not hearsay because it "was not introduced for the purpose of establishing any of the facts related to the underlying conviction. It was admitted to prove the fact of the conviction itself.") *See also United States v. Boulware*, 384 F.3d 794, 806 (9th Cir. 2004) ("A prior judgment is therefore hearsay to the extent that it is offered to prove the truth of the matters asserted in the judgment. A prior judgment is not hearsay, however, to the extent that it is offered as legally operative verbal conduct that determined the rights and duties of the parties.").

8. Reputation and Personal or Family History

Problem 7-31: They Say It's Your Birthday . . .

David is indicted on charges of violating his state's statutory rape law. The statute provides that a person is guilty of statutory rape if he or she is over eighteen years of age and he or she engages in sexual intercourse with a person under sixteen years of age. According to the indictment, at the time of the events in question, David was twenty years old and the alleged victim, Rebecca, was fourteen years old.

At trial, to prove the respective ages of David and Rebecca, the prosecution seeks to offer into evidence, over hearsay objections by the defense, the following:

(1) Testimony by Rebecca as to her date of birth.

(2) Testimony by Wanda that she met Rebecca's mother, Donna, at a school function once, and that Donna told her Rebecca's date of birth. Wanda would testify to what Donna said.

(3) Records from the church that Rebecca and her family belong to, indicating Rebecca's date of birth. The records were created by church officials, but the information contained within them was obtained from self-reporting by members of the church as to the birth of their children.

(4) A family tree from Rebecca's house that indicates Rebecca's date of birth.

(5) A certified copy of a record from the office of vital statistics of the county in which David was born, indicating his date of birth. While the information is recorded in the record by county officials, the data is provided by hospitals in the county that are required under state law to report births to the county.

How should the prosecution respond to the hearsay objections? How should the court dispose of the objections?

Blackburn v. United Parcel Service, Inc.
179 F.3d 81 (3d Cir. 1999)

BECKER, Chief Judge.

[Blackburn, an employee of United Parcel Service, brought a diversity action in federal court under New Jersey's "whistleblower" statute (CEPA), claiming that he was fired after bringing possible antitrust violations to the attention of his superiors. The trial court granted summary judgment in favor of the defendant. Under the statute, once a plaintiff makes out a prima facie case of retaliatory discharge, the burden of production shifts to the defendant to articulate a legitimate reason for the discharge. If the employer does so, the employee then has the burden of persuading the trier of fact that the employer's proffered legitimate reason is merely a pretext, and that retaliation was the true basis for the discharge.]

B. *UPS's Stated Reason for the Discharge*

UPS's stated reason for firing Blackburn was his violation of the company's anti-nepotism, favoritism, integrity, and accountability policies, which it placed in the record. UPS adduced evidence that Blackburn failed to divulge that Shepard was his relative, and that he recommended her for positions within UPS without disclosing to the relevant decisionmakers that she was his sister-in-law. UPS also offered evidence that it has consistently enforced its antinepotism policy, which supports its proffer that Blackburn's violation of this policy was the actual reason he was discharged.... Therefore, UPS has met its burden of production at the second step of the burden-shifting analysis. It is thus incumbent upon Blackburn to offer sufficient admissible evidence that this justification is pretextual and that the real reason that he was fired was for complaining about UPS's possible antitrust violations to survive UPS's motion for summary judgment....

C. *Pretext*

1. Blackburn's Evidence

In order to meet his burden, Blackburn must point to admissible evidence in the record "showing that there is a genuine issue for trial." Fed.R.Civ.P. 56(e)....

Blackburn's stronger argument for pretext — and one that would be sufficient to preclude summary judgment, if supported by adequate admissible evidence — is that UPS did not consistently enforce its anti-nepotism policy, which, according to UPS, was the primary basis for his discharge. If Blackburn has presented admissible evidence that would raise a fact question whether UPS enforced its antinepotism policy, it would be for a jury to decide whether UPS's proffered reason for firing him was pretextual. Given our assumption that Blackburn has presented sufficient evidence to meet his prima facie burden under CEPA, we would have to reverse summary judgment in UPS's favor if a fact issue regarding pretext existed.

In support of his pretext argument, Blackburn provides numerous examples of UPS employees who were related to other employees yet allegedly were not disciplined or terminated for this apparent violation of the anti-nepotism policy. His examples include brothers-in-law, siblings, spouses, uncles and nephews, fathers and sons, and intimate relationships between employees who were dating or living together. UPS responds with evidence that, within the last five years, twenty-nine people at Mahwah left UPS in accordance with the anti-nepotism policy, and that no exceptions currently exist there....

Blackburn has no personal knowledge of any of the alleged relationships listed above. Rather, he testified in his deposition that he was told of these relationships by other persons. The alleged relationships are offered for their own truth. Therefore, Blackburn's information is based on hearsay, and in some cases on multiple hearsay, so that it must fall within an exception to the rule against hearsay to be admissible....

4. Rule 803(19): Reputation Concerning Personal or Family History

As all of Blackburn's evidence that we are considering here involves "personal or family history," the hearsay exception in Rule 803(19)* would appear to be a particularly appropriate basis for finding the evidence admissible....

a. Background Principles

The matters of personal and family history that are within the ambit of Rule 803(19) are often difficult to prove through personal knowledge. For example, if a witness has not been present at someone's wedding, or has not personally seen that person's valid marriage license and executed marriage certificate, he or she presumably could only testify regarding the marriage on the basis of hearsay. However, "[m]arriage is universally conceded to be a proper subject of proof by evidence of reputation in the community." Fed.R.Evid. 803(19) advisory committee's note. This is no doubt because a well-grounded belief that two persons are married—by those who know them, have attended their family functions, and have regarded them as a married couple—is sufficiently reliable evidence to prove the fact of the marriage. Other matters of personal and family history also "seem to be susceptible to being the subject of well founded repute." *Id.* That two community members are brothers or that a member of the community is another member's father are likely to be matters that have been discussed within the community and that have become well-established "facts" if no reason has been presented to doubt their truth. Therefore, reputations regarding relationships and other personal and family matters within a well-defined community are considered to have the circumstantial guarantee of trustworthiness that justifies a hearsay exception.

In applying the Rule 803(19) exception to Blackburn's evidence of relatives working at UPS, we must answer at least two questions. First, does a person's place of work come within the Rule's coverage? And second, what foundation is required for testimony to be admitted under Rule 803(19)? In other words, is Blackburn's evidence sufficiently based on actual "reputation," or is it based on some other, less reliable foundation such as rumor or speculation?

b. Relevant Community for Reputation

On the first question, we believe that Rule 803(19), in referring to "reputation ... among a person's associates[] or in the community," encompasses one's reputation at a place of work. The advisory committee certainly foresaw this application of the exception in Rule 803(19): "The 'world' in which the reputation may exist ... has proved capable of expanding with changing times from the single uncomplicated neighborhood, in which all activities take place, to the multiple and unrelated worlds of work, religious affiliation, and social activity, in each of which a reputation may be generated." Fed.R.Evid. 803(19) advisory committee's note. In the context of reputation evidence of a person's character, "courts have readily extended the concept of community to include the community in

---

* Editor's Note: Rule 803(19) provides an exception to the hearsay rule for "[a] reputation among a person's family by blood, adoption, or marriage—or among a person's associates or in the community—concerning the person's birth, adoption, legitimacy, ancestry, marriage, divorce, death, relationship by blood, adoption, or marriage, or similar facts of personal or family history."

which one works, as well as where one lives." *United States v. Oliver*, 492 F.2d 943, 946 (8th Cir. 1974).[12]

Both before and since enactment of the Federal Rules, commentators have made the same point. *See* 5 *Wigmore on Evidence* § 1616, at 591 (James H. Chadbourn rev. 1974) ("The traditional requirement about 'neighborhood' reputation was appropriate to the conditions of the time; but it should not be taken as imposing arbitrary limitations not appropriate in other times."); 5 *Weinstein's Federal Evidence* § 803.24[2] (Joseph M. McLaughlin ed., 2d ed. 1999) ("Allowing such proof [under Rule 803(19)] to come from 'associates' reflects the fact that nowadays a person's reputation may no longer exclusively be found in the place where the person lives, but frequently can only be ascertained from coparticipants in the varied activities that make up a modern person's world.").

c. Trustworthiness of Reputation Evidence Concerning Family History; Foundational Requirements

As for the basis of the reputation evidence regarding relationships within a workplace, we find little guidance in the sparse case law surrounding Rule 803(19).[13] We believe, however, that the principle behind admitting such evidence despite its hearsay origin — i.e., "that general reputation about facts of interest to the community is probably trustworthy," Saltzburg et al., *supra*, at 1699 — requires that a proponent of Rule 803(19) evidence establish that the reputation testimony arises from sufficient inquiry and discussion among persons with personal knowledge of the matter to constitute a trustworthy "reputation." Rumors and speculation are clearly insufficient in this regard. Testimony by a declarant that he heard, from some unknown source, that two people were related in some way would be inadmissible under Rule 803(19). Rather, what is required is the laying of a foundation of knowledge grounded in inquiry, discussion, interactions, or familiarity "among a person's associates[] or in the community" in which he works.

We find support for our reading of the Rule in a number of places. In discussing the rationale behind the Rule, Weinstein notes that "it is likely that these matters have been sufficiently inquired about and discussed with persons having personal knowledge so that a trustworthy consensus has been reached." *Weinstein's Federal Evidence*, *supra*, § 803.24[1]. Weinstein continues:

> Before a witness can testify to reputation, the witness must be qualified by showing membership in a group that could have been familiar with the personal or family history of the person in question, namely, family, associates or community.... The judge should consider ... not only the foundation that has been laid for the reception of this reputation evidence, but also such factors as the sig-

---

12. We of course do not decide here whether a witness could testify regarding someone's reputation for good (or bad) character within a work community as this issue is not before us.

13. This court has cited Rule 803(19) in holding that a witness' testimony regarding her own age "can be considered reputation concerning personal or family history, for which an exception has been made to the hearsay rule under the Federal Rules of Evidence." *Government of V.I. v. Joseph*, 765 F.2d 394, 397 n. 5 (3d Cir. 1985). A district court within our circuit has held that family members' statements that a particular person lived with the plaintiff, supported her financially, and held her out as his child, were admissible under Rule 803(19) in a proceeding to determine if the plaintiff was the person's child. *See McBride v. Heckler*, 619 F. Supp. 1554, 1561–62 (D.N.J.1985). More recently, the Second Circuit invoked the Rule to find that testimony by a criminal defendant's father regarding his belief as to where the defendant was born was admissible. *See United States v. Jean-Baptiste*, 166 F.3d 102, 110 (2d Cir. 1999).

nificance and nature of the fact towards which the proof is directed, the availability of other evidence, and the nature of the litigation.

Id. § 803.24[3]. In discussing the similar hearsay exception in Rule 803(20), for reputation concerning boundaries or general history, Saltzburg explains:

> [I]t is considered unlikely that a falsehood could become generally accepted as truth in the community, where the matter is of importance to the community.... [T]he testimony must report a general consensus in the community, an assertion of the group as opposed to one or a few of its constituents. The fact that the information has been considered by and was subject to the general scrutiny of the community is an essential guarantee of reliability for the exception.

Saltzburg et al., *supra*, at 1699. As these comments indicate, when a matter has been sufficiently discussed within a well-defined community so that its truth has obtained "circumstantial guarantees of trustworthiness," Fed.R.Evid. 807, it is properly the subject of reputation testimony.

We find further support for our interpretation of the requirements of Rule 803(19) in the more extensive discussion of the required foundation for testimony regarding character reputation. *See* Fed.R.Evid. 404(a), 405(a), 803(21). We acknowledge that reputation about someone's character and reputation of family relationships are, in many ways, very different concepts. The first might be thought of as a collective community opinion, while the second involves a factual issue. Both, however, require a foundation that is trustworthy and a well-defined "community" that is capable of, in a figurative sense, forming an opinion or discerning a fact. *Cf. Webster's Third New International Dictionary* 1929 (1966) (defining reputation as "a particular character in popular estimation or ascription"). We therefore find persuasive those authorities that have discussed the foundation that must be laid before a witness may testify about the community's opinion of someone.

The leading case in this area predates the Federal Rules of Evidence, but is helpful nonetheless. In *Michelson v. United States*, 335 U.S. 469 (1948), the Supreme Court discussed character evidence in the context of a criminal trial. It noted that a witness who testifies about a defendant's character is "allowed to summarize what he has heard in the community, although much of it may have been said by persons less qualified to judge than himself." *Id.* at 477. The Court limited this rule, however: "[T]he witness must qualify to give an opinion by showing such acquaintance with the defendant, the community in which he has lived and the circles in which he has moved, as to speak with authority of the terms in which generally he is regarded." *Id.* at 478.

In a pre-Federal Rules case applying the hearsay exception we are considering here (for reputation of family matters), the Ninth Circuit reiterated the Supreme Court's point in *Michelson*:

> It is not every statement or tradition in the family that can be admitted in evidence. The tradition must be from persons having such a connection with the party to whom it relates, that it is natural and likely, from their domestic habits and connections, that they are speaking the truth, and that they could not be mistaken.

Young Ah Chor v. Dulles, 270 F.2d 338, 344 (9th Cir. 1959). In *Whiting v. United States*, 296 F.2d 512 (1st Cir. 1961), government witnesses had testified at a criminal trial regarding the defendant's reputation on the basis of hearsay of unknown origin. The court of appeals vacated the conviction, finding the testimony to be inadmissible, as "there must be some demonstrable basis evincing the competence of the witness to give his opinion" about the defendant's character. *Id.* at 517. While we have held that a witness need not know the defendant personally in order to testify about his character, we have found it sufficient if the witness "knew of [him] and his reputation among the community and the persons making up at least one of the circles which [he] frequented." *United States v. Neff,* 475 F.2d 861, 863 (3d Cir. 1973).

From these cases, we discern a clear principle: A witness who wishes to testify about someone's reputation within a community must demonstrate that he or she knows of the person and is truly familiar with the "community" in which the reputation has been formed, and that the basis of the reputation is one that is likely to be reliable. Where the alleged reputation is based on nothing more than rumors of unknown origins, or a single instance of "someone told me so," a proper foundation has not been laid for admitting such evidence under Rule 803(19).[14]

d. Applying Rule 803(19) to Blackburn's Evidence

We must now determine whether any of Blackburn's evidence involving allegedly related persons working at UPS is likely to be admissible under the exception in Rule 803(19). We note preliminarily that our determination that a workplace may constitute a "community" under Rule 803(19) is limited by the requirement that a proponent of such evidence establish a reliable foundation for admitting this hearsay testimony. In other words, allegations regarding relationships at far-flung facilities of a large employer such as UPS almost certainly cannot be admissible as reputation evidence within a community or among one's associates.[15] Blackburn has not, in many cases, identified the UPS facility at which allegedly related persons were working. In order to meet his burden of establishing a reliable basis for the alleged reputations he invokes, he would need to identify the "community" in which those reputations exist.[16] Because we find that, even without this identification of the appropriate community, most of Blackburn's evidence would be inadmissible—and because, at all events, we conclude that his relevant, possibly admissible evidence is insufficient for him to survive summary judgment—we do not dwell on the shortcomings in his evidence regarding the work location of most of the allegedly related persons he offers.

Blackburn testified that "[i]t was known by myself, certainly, and numerous other people, I presume, that Bill and Art [Weyrauch] were brothers. I believe that it was a regular topic of discussion." Although the requirements we have set forth above regarding admission of such reputation evidence may not be met by Blackburn's testimony, we will assume that upon further development of the background to his allegations, this testimony might be admissible at trial, and we therefore consider it below in our analysis of whether summary judgment for UPS was properly granted.

As for Don McKenny and Vern Cormie, Blackburn could not state how they were related, and admitted that the basis of his information that they were related was "some-

---

14. Of course, if each hearsay link in the communication chain falls under some exception, the evidence may be admissible. *See* Fed.R.Evid. 805. For example, if witness *A* knows nothing of an individual's reputation, but declarant *B*, who is qualified under Rule 803(19) to testify thereto, informs *A* of the individual's relationship, and the statement from *B* to *A* falls under some hearsay exception, *A*'s testimony about the individual's relationship would be admissible.

15. UPS currently has 326,800 employees worldwide, and 291,500 in the United States alone, at more than 1700 facilities.

16. We do note that most of Blackburn's examples appear to concern UPS employees at facilities in Northern New Jersey, which might constitute an adequate community for Rule 803(19) purposes, assuming that they are somehow linked to each other.

thing that I was told by someone I worked with at UPS sometime before I left the company." This clearly fails to meet the standards we have outlined for reputation evidence under Rule 803(19). Not only does it appear that Blackburn does not know McKenny and Cormie (i.e., he could not identify their alleged relationship), but the source of his information — "something that I was told by someone" — cannot even be identified, let alone measured for its trustworthiness.

The same is true of the alleged relationships between Joe Rossano, Jack Davies, and Joe Reynolds (relationship unknown, and information based on "something that someone told [Blackburn]"); between Lorrain Curley and Dan Grace (source of information unknown); between Karen Montemarano and an unknown driver; between Kathleen Jewell and an unnamed relative ("I just remember that she had a relative of some type working there"); and between Howard Kaufman and "Mindy" ("it was my understanding" that they were related). Each of these cases fails to meet the standard we have established for admitting hearsay evidence under the exception for reputation concerning family matters. In each case, Blackburn does not appear to be familiar with the persons named, fails to identify the community involved, and does not establish any basis, let alone a reliable one, for the information that he is offering. In other words, he has failed demonstrably to identify a reputation concerning family relationships that would bring this testimony within the exception in Rule 803(19)....

Moore v. Goode
375 S.E.2d 549 (W. Va. 1988)

MILLER, Justice:

....

Custer Waldo Morris, a widower without issue, died on September 13, 1981.... His last will and testament gave all his property, real and personal, in equal shares, to his surviving brothers and sisters. On September 14, 1981, Avis S. Moore, the executrix of the will and the County Clerk of Clay County, listed as the beneficiaries Harry Morris, Goldie I. Douglas, Merle Rogers, Hallie Talley, and Ruie Robertson. They are the surviving brother and sisters of Mr. Morris, born to Isaac N. Morris in lawful wedlock.

Approximately one year later, Sarah Goode claimed to be a half-blood sister of the decedent and entitled to share in his estate. She alleged that she had been born out of wedlock to the late Isaac N. Morris, the father of Custer Waldo Morris. Ms. Moore, as executrix, instituted this action for a determination of the beneficiaries under the will.... Depositions were taken and various documents produced by the parties....

Sarah Goode's testimony was essentially that both her mother and her grandmother, Sarah Fitzwater, who was deceased, had informed her when she was a young girl that Isaac N. Morris was her father. She also testified that her original attorney, Mr. Douglas, who was distantly related to the Morris family, had indicated that her father was Isaac N. Morris. She also spoke of a visit with one of the beneficiaries of the will, Harry Morris, after the suit had been filed. He gave her a photograph of Isaac N. Morris and said that he was her father.

The court ruled that Sarah Goode's testimony concerning the remarks of her mother and grandmother were inadmissible as hearsay. The court did not consider her testimony about Mr. Douglas and the statements of Harry Morris as to her paternity.

This testimony related to family history, which is one of the exceptions at common law to the hearsay rule. This exception is based on a recognition that it is often impossible to establish by independent means the facts of family relationships where several generations are involved and the members are dead or scattered in other jurisdictions. At common law, family history or pedigree could be proved in one of two ways: by general reputation evidence or by specific extrajudicial statements from family members who were unavailable at trial. Where specific statements are sought to be introduced, several restrictions had to be met, i.e., the declaration had to be made by family members, the declarant had to be unavailable, the statements had to have been made prior to the litigation in which it is offered (ante litem motam), and there had to be no apparent motive for the declarant to misrepresent the facts.

We have in general followed the common law distinction between general reputation of family history and specific statement testimony....

In the Rules of Evidence, the family history exception by reputation testimony is found in Rule 803(19). Rule 804(b)(4) relates to specific statements concerning a person's family relationship and has altered the common law rule to some degree. This section still retains the initial qualification that the declarant be unavailable as a witness. It does not require that the statements be made in advance of the litigation. The rule specifically provides that the declarant need not have "means of acquiring personal knowledge of the matter stated." It is not necessary that the declarant be family related if "so intimately associated with the other's family as to be likely to have accurate information concerning the matter declared." Rule 804(b)(4)....

As earlier pointed out, Sarah Goode's testimony involved specific statements made by family members. We believe the court erred in rejecting her testimony as to her grandmother's statement. Her grandmother was dead at the time of trial, and the statement came within Rule 804(b)(4), upon the showing of unavailability. For the same reason, however, the specific statements of Sarah Goode's mother, Mr. Douglas, and Mr. Morris were inadmissible simply because these individuals were all available....

Notes and Questions

1. Rule 803(19) is important not only because it permits a witness to testify about some *other* person's reputed personal or family history, but also because it paves the way for a person to testify about his *own* personal or family history. Think about it: a person almost certainly lacks personal knowledge of his own date and place of birth, who his parents and siblings are, what his name is, and other facts of personal or family history. Accordingly, a person can overcome a hearsay objection to testifying to such facts by invoking Rule 803(19). *E.g., Government of Virgin Islands v. Joseph*, 765 F.2d 394, 397 n.5 (3d Cir. 1985).

2. Rule 804(b)(4) creates an exception to the hearsay rule for

A statement about:

(A) the declarant's own birth, adoption, legitimacy, ancestry, marriage, divorce, relationship by blood, adoption, or marriage, or similar facts of personal or family history, even though the declarant had no way of acquiring personal knowledge about that fact; or

(B) another person concerning any of these facts, as well as death, if the declarant was related to the person by blood, adoption, or marriage or was so intimately associated with the person's family that the declarant's information is likely to be accurate.

As indicated in *Moore*, this exception can be invoked only if the declarant is "unavailable," a concept explored in more detail later in the chapter. It differs from Rule 803(19) in that it suffices to invoke this exception that the declarant made a statement regarding his own personal or family history or that of someone to whom the declarant is related "by blood, adoption, or marriage" or with whose family the declarant is "intimately associated." Rule 804(b)(4) thus excuses two layers of hearsay: the external layer, namely the statement by a declarant about his own personal or family history or that of someone with whom he is related or associated, and the internal layer, namely the fact that the declarant obtained that information from other sources.

3. Another exception to the hearsay rule for personal or family history is set forth in Rule 803(13), which creates an exception to the hearsay rule for

> A statement of fact about personal or family history contained in a family record, such as a Bible, genealogy, chart, engraving on a ring, inscription on a portrait, or engraving on an urn or burial marker.

Unlike Rule 804(b)(4), no showing that the person who made the statement is unavailable is required. What is the justification for this exception?

4. Should there be a hearsay exception for statements of personal or family history contained in *tattoos*? *See* Wash. R. Evid. 803(a)(13) (including such statements in the hearsay exception for family records!); Judicial Council Comment to Wash. R. Evid. 803(a)(13) ("The drafters felt that tattoos often reflect personal or family history and are apt to be as trustworthy as the other items listed in the rule.").

5. For a case with fascinating facts that surveys and applies the various exceptions to the hearsay rule that can be invoked to introduce evidence proving that two people were married to one another, see *McMorrow v. Schweiker*, 561 F. Supp. 584 (D.N.J. 1982) (reviewing denial of a claim for widow's insurance benefits under the Social Security Act, based on the absence of proof that the decedent and the claimant were married to one another, in a case in which the official records of the marriage and the couple's own copy of their marriage certificate were burned in separate fires, and in which most witnesses to the marriage, including the officiating minister, had died).

6. Do Rule 803(19) and other hearsay exceptions that encompass statements of "personal or family history" encompass evidence of non-marital relationships? *See United States v. Brodie*, 326 F. Supp. 2d 83, 97 (D.D.C. 2004) (raising but not deciding whether Rule 803(19) can be invoked to introduce evidence about dating relationships or friendships); Peter Nicolas, *"They Say He's Gay": The Admissibility of Evidence of Sexual Orientation*, 37 Ga. L. Rev. 793 (2003) (arguing that the phrase "personal or family history" is broad enough to encompass evidence of non-marital same-sex relationships).

7. Historically, the common law antecedent to Rule 803(19) was invoked to introduce evidence of reputation as to a person's race when the ability to exercise certain rights (such as the right to vote) depended on one's race. *See* 5 Wigmore, Evidence § 1605, at 574–75 (Chadbourn rev. 1974). For a modern case applying Rule 803(19) to introduce evidence that a person is a member of a racial minority, see *Annett v. University of Kansas*, 82 F. Supp. 2d 1230, 1242–1243 (D. Kan. 2000) (holding admissible under Rule 803(19) plaintiff's testimony about his Native American ancestry in a Title VII case as proof that he is a member of a class entitled to protection under that provision).

8. Rule 803(20), discussed in *Blackburn*, creates an exception to the hearsay rule for

A reputation in a community—arising before the controversy—concerning boundaries of land in the community or customs that affect the land, or concerning general historical events important to that community, state, or nation.

At common law, such evidence was admissible only if it involved an "ancient" matter, meaning one for which no living witnesses were available. *See* 5 Wigmore, Evidence §§ 1582, 1597, at 545, 561 (Chadbourn rev. 1974). Yet Rule 803(20) eliminates this requirement, providing only that in the case of reputation regarding land customs and boundaries that it "antedate the controversy." Advisory Committee Note to Rule 803(20).

9. Rule 803(21), discussed in *Blackburn*, which creates an exception to the hearsay rule for "[a] reputation among a person's associates or in the community concerning the person's character," disposes only of the hearsay objection to the use of such evidence. Whether such evidence is ultimately admissible is dependent upon the restrictions set forth in Rules 404 and 405.

10. Can Rule 803(21) be invoked to offer evidence about the reputation of an entity, such as a place of business? *See Dick v. Phone Directories Co.*, 397 F.3d 1256, 1266 n.5 (10th Cir. 2005) (holding that the exception is in terms limited to reputation evidence of a *person*'s character).

Our angels are well-acquainted with you, your community, and the circles in which you moved.

stus.com

9. Learned Treatises and Other Documents

Problem 7-32: The Crushed Collection Revisited

Assume the same facts as in Problem 7-22. At trial, Janet offers into evidence several of her damaged Royal Doulton figurines, which include *Darling* (HN 1), *Granny Owl* (HN 187), and *Freddie Bunnykin* (D6024). To prove the value of the damaged figurines, she seeks to offer into evidence copies of three price guides issued by *The Charlton Press* entitled *Royal Doulton Figurines, Royal Doulton Animals,* and *Royal Doulton Collectibles* that list the value of the figurines as $3,500, $4,000, and $3,500, respectively. Don and UPS object to the admission of the price guides, contending that they are hearsay.

How should Janet respond to the objection, what should Don and UPS argue in response, and how will the court likely rule?

Costantino v. David M. Herzog, M.D., P.C.

203 F.3d 164 (2d Cir. 2000)

McLAUGHLIN, Circuit Judge:

Dr. David Herzog was the obstetrician who delivered Amanda Costantino. During the delivery, Amanda's shoulder got trapped behind her mother's pubic bone, a condition known as "shoulder dystocia." While attempting to remedy the condition, Dr. Herzog performed: (1) the McRoberts maneuver: pulling Mrs. Costantino's legs toward her head and applying pressure to the area above her pubic bone; (2) the Woods corkscrew: reaching into the womb and rotating baby Amanda to release her trapped shoulder; and (3) the Posterior Arm Sweep: delivering Amanda's free posterior arm to create more space. Ultimately, Dr. Herzog delivered Amanda, but she was born with "Erb's Palsy," an impairment to the nerves running to the arm.

The Costantinos filed a diversity action against Dr. Herzog ... alleging that by pulling and rotating Amanda's head during the delivery, he had caused her Erb's Palsy. They claimed that Dr. Herzog had deviated from accepted standards of obstetrical practice, and had therefore committed malpractice under governing New York law....

The defense ... sought to justify Dr. Herzog's management of Amanda's delivery by introducing a 15-minute videotape from ACOG's* audiovisual library, entitled "Shoulder Dystocia." The tape was, according to the defense, "put out by [ACOG] to educate physicians" and portrayed the various techniques recommended to remedy shoulder dystocia.

Both the parties and Judge Gleeson recognized that the ACOG video was hearsay under Federal Rule of Evidence 801. The defense nevertheless sought to introduce it pursuant to the "learned treatise" exception to the hearsay rule set forth in Rule 803(18).** Plaintiffs objected, arguing that Rule 803(18) enumerates only "[] treatise[s], periodical[s], or pamphlet[s]" as learned treatises, and therefore could not encompass videotapes. Plaintiffs also argued that no foundation had been laid for the video.

After an *in camera* review of the videotape, Judge Gleeson ruled it admissible. With respect to whether a video could qualify as a learned treatise under Rule 803(18), Judge Gleeson reasoned: "I think ... focusing on the distinction between ... something in the form of a periodical or a book, as opposed [to] a videotape is just overly artificial."

---

* Editor's Note: "ACOG" refers to the American College of Obstetricians and Gynecologists.
** Editor's Note: Rule 803(18) creates an exception to the hearsay rule for:
A statement contained in a treatise, periodical, or pamphlet if:
(A) the statement is called to the attention of an expert witness on cross-examination or relied on by the expert on direct examination; and
(B) the publication is established as a reliable authority by the expert's admission or testimony, by another expert's testimony, or by judicial notice.
If admitted, the statement may be read into evidence but not received as an exhibit.

As to the foundation, Judge Gleeson found, based on his *in camera* review, that the ACOG video "was a dissemination to the doctors in the relevant medical community of how they should go about dealing with this problem [of shoulder dystocia]." He also found that it had been "well established" through trial testimony that ACOG was "the source of authoritative information regarding the practices to be used by obstetricians in these circumstances." Included in the trial testimony regarding ACOG and the videotape, were Dr. Nathanson's concessions that he had: (1) viewed the videotape at a staff conference some years ago; and (2) testified in a prior action that he generally accepted "the standards promulgated by ACOG" within the field of obstetrics as "authoritative."

The ACOG video was played twice during trial. It was played in its entirety during the cross-examination of plaintiffs' expert, Dr. Nathanson, and portions were replayed during the direct examination of defendants' own expert Dr. James Howard....

In addition to the ACOG video, the defense introduced as learned treatises, over objection, two articles published in the *American Journal of Obstetrics and Gynecology*. The first was entitled, *Shoulder Dystocia, an Analysis of Risks and Obstetrical Maneuvers*, and was written by Dr. James Nocon of the University of Indiana Medical School. Before this article was read to Dr. Herzog on cross-examination, he testified on voir dire that he: (1) did not know of the article's author, Dr. Nocon; and (2) had not read the specific article until "two minutes" before beginning his testimony about it.

Later, during cross-examination of plaintiffs' expert, Dr. Nathanson, defense counsel sought to introduce a different article written by Robert Gherman, an obstetrics professor at the University of Southern California and also published in the *American Journal of Obstetrics and Gynecology*. Though Dr. Nathanson refused to concede the authoritativeness of that journal (based on his apparent belief that "no journal is authoritative"), Judge Gleeson allowed the defense to read [a] statement from Dr. Gherman's article....

Defense counsel also read a different portion of the same article to defendant's expert, Dr. Howard, during direct examination. Dr. Howard did not testify that he relied on the article in any way.

After trial, the jury found for Dr. Herzog on the issue of liability. The Costantinos now appeal, arguing that Judge Gleeson erred in admitting: (1) the ACOG video; and (2) the two articles from the *American Journal of Obstetrics and Gynecology*....

The primary question presented is whether videotapes can be admitted as learned treatises pursuant to Rule 803(18). We are the first federal Court of Appeals to address this question, though various state courts have considered it under their cognate learned treatise exceptions, and have forged no consensus....

The rationale for this exception is self-evident: so long as the authority of a treatise has been sufficiently established, the factfinder should have the benefit of expert learning on a subject, even though it is hearsay.

Emphasizing plain language, the Costantinos argue that videos cannot fall within the scope of Rule 803(18) because unlike "[] treatise[s], periodical[s], or pamphlet[s]," they are not specifically listed in the Rule....

[W]e agree with Judge Gleeson that it is just "overly artificial" to say that information that is sufficiently trustworthy to overcome the hearsay bar when presented in a printed learned treatise loses the badge of trustworthiness when presented in a videotape. We see no reason to deprive a jury of authoritative learning simply because it is presented in a visual, rather than printed, format. In this age of visual communication a videotape may often be the most helpful way to illuminate the truth in the spirit of Rule 102.*

In sum, we agree with the Texas Court of Appeals that "[v]ideotapes are nothing more than a contemporary variant of a published treatise, periodical or pamphlet." *Loven v. State*, 831 S.W.2d 387, 397 (Tex.Ct.App.1992). Accordingly, we hold that videotapes may be considered learned treatises under Rule 803(18)....

The Costantinos argue that even assuming that the ACOG video may be a learned treatise, Judge Gleeson erred in admitting it without a proper foundation. We disagree.

Rule 803(18) explicitly requires trial judges to act as gatekeepers, ensuring that any treatise admitted is "authoritative." *Schneider v. Revici*, 817 F.2d 987, 991 (2d Cir. 1987). Thus, trial judges must first determine that the proffered treatise is "trustworth[y] ... as viewed by professionals in [the relevant] field." *Id.*; *see* Fed.R.Evid. 803(18) Advisory Committee Note. In making this evaluation, trial judges need not be draconian. "Since the object of [Rule 803(18)] is to make valuable information available to the trier of fact, trial judges should not insist on a quantum of proof ... that the proponent cannot meet." *See Weinstein's Federal Evidence* § 803.23[4] (2d ed.1997)....

The Costantinos invite us to apply the reasoning of *Meschino v. North American Drager, Inc.*, 841 F.2d 429 (1st Cir. 1988). There, the First Circuit ruled that it was not enough that the trade magazine in which an article appeared was reputable; the author of the particular article must also ... be shown to be an authority before the article could be used as a learned treatise pursuant to Rule 803(18). The Court reasoned that "[i]n these days of quantified research, and pressure to publish, an article does not reach the dignity of a 'reliable authority' merely because some editor, even a most reputable one, sees fit to circulate it."

The Costantinos argue that *Meschino* requires reversal because Judge Gleeson's sole basis for accepting the video as authoritative was its sponsorship by ACOG. They claim that no testimony was offered that the video itself had received acceptance in the medical profession, or that its narrator, Dr. Young, was considered an authority in the field. And these omissions were particularly devastating, the Costantinos maintain, because as the *Simmons* court noted, it is unclear that the "careful, professional criticism" which ensures the reliability of printed treatises, also attends the production and dissemination of videotapes. 551 N.E.2d at 543.

These arguments are unavailing. Even assuming that the potential authoritativeness of videotapes is somehow more suspect than that of materials like "pamphlet[s]" explicitly listed by the Rule, we cannot fault the district court's performance as a gatekeeper in this case.

We, of course, agree with the *Meschino* court that the contents of a periodical cannot be automatically qualified "wholesale" under Rule 803(18) merely by showing that the periodical itself is highly regarded. We do not, however, read *Meschino* to say that the reputation of the periodical containing the proffered article is irrelevant to the authoritativeness inquiry. Publication practices vary widely, and an article's publication by an esteemed periodical which subjects its contents to close scrutiny and peer review, obviously reflects well on the authority of the article itself. Indeed, because the authoritativeness inquiry is governed by a "liberal" standard, good sense would seem to compel

---

* Editor's Note: Rule 102 provides as follows: "These rules should be construed so as to administer every proceeding fairly, eliminate unjustifiable expense and delay, and promote the development of evidence law, to the end of ascertaining the truth and securing a just determination."

recognizing some periodicals—provided there is a basis for doing so—as sufficiently esteemed to justify a presumption in favor of admitting the articles accepted for publication therein.

Turning to the instant case, there is no small irony in plaintiffs' complaint that ACOG sponsorship was insufficient to establish the video as an authority. After all, while plaintiffs' own expert Dr. Nathanson refused to concede the authoritativeness of the video itself, he nevertheless: (1) touted himself as a member of ACOG; (2) praised ACOG as an organization that "publishes a great deal of material which serve[s] to contribute to setting a standard of care for obstetricians and gynecologists;" and (3) testified in a prior action that he generally accepted "the standards promulgated by ACOG" within the field of obstetrics as "authoritative." Moreover, Dr. Nathanson relied in part on ACOG publications in reaching his opinion that Dr. Herzog had committed malpractice.

In any event, other factors—quite apart from ACOG's status as a reputable organization—established the authoritativeness of the video. In particular, Dr. Nathanson recalled seeing a version of the ACOG video at a staff conference, "inferentially conced[ing]" that it was exactly what the defense said it was: a training resource for the continuing medical education of obstetricians and gynecologists. And the video's use as a training resource—"written primarily and impartially for professionals, subject to scrutiny and exposure for inaccuracy, with the reputation [of its producers and sponsors] at stake"—is clearly an important index of its authoritativeness under Rule 803(18). Fed.R.Evid. 803(18) Advisory Committee Note.

Moreover, Judge Gleeson himself took the additional precaution of reviewing the ACOG video *in camera*. Through that review, Judge Gleeson knew that the tape's narrator, Dr. Young, was a physician at Dartmouth College's Hitchcock Medical Center, and that the video itself had won an ACOG award, credentials which compared favorably with those of any expert who testified at trial. And after the same review, Judge Gleeson found that the video was what the defense represented it to be: a training resource—with recommendations culled from the "available literature"—used to show doctors "how they should go about dealing with this problem [of shoulder dystocia]." Having viewed the videotape ourselves, and having observed its clinical format, as well as its calm and instructional tone, we cannot say this finding amounts to "manifest error."

In sum, we conclude that Judge Gleeson's determination that the ACOG video was sufficiently authoritative to deserve admission rested on an appropriate foundation. This was not a case in which there was "no basis" for finding the proffered treatise trustworthy. And while some of the indicia of the video's reliability came to light through Judge Gleeson's independent *in camera* review, rather than through testimony, the authoritativeness inquiry is a freewheeling one and may be conducted by "any means." Fed.R.Evid. 803(18) Advisory Committee Note; *see also Weinstein's Federal Evidence* § 803.23[4] (2d ed.1997) ("trial judge[s] should be liberal in allowing other proof of . . . authoritativeness, so long as it indicates that the [treatise] is recognized by the medical profession")....

The Costantinos final argument is that the admission of the two articles from the *American Journal of Obstetrics and Gynecology* also requires reversal. Once again, plaintiffs argue lack of proper foundation. First, they complain that because Dr. Herzog testified that he had not seen Dr. James Nocon's article until shortly before testifying about it, he could not have "relied" upon that article as required by Rule 803(18). Second, they protest that there was no testimony establishing the authoritativeness of either Dr. Nocon's article, or the second article written by obstetrics professor Robert Gherman of the University of Southern California.

We will not tarry long on these arguments. It is not essential that a testifying expert rely on a learned treatise on direct examination. If he did not, a sufficient foundation is laid if the treatise is "called to the attention of [the] expert [on]cross[-]examination." Fed.R.Evid. 803(18). The essential notion is that the jury enjoys "explanation, context and perspective" on the treatise's contents. Mueller & Kirkpatrick, *Evidence* § 8.52, 998. That is exactly what happened on defense counsel's cross-examination of Dr. Herzog.

As to authoritativeness, Dr. Herzog testified that the *American Journal of Obstetrics and Gynecology* is "probably the most reputable journal in our field and if it's accepted for publication, then we know it's quality information being presented." Plaintiffs' own expert, Dr. Nathanson, backed Dr. Herzog on this point, testifying that articles are published in the *American Journal of Obstetrics and Gynecology* only after "other obstetricians and gynecologists ... review them for accuracy and believability." The district court was properly satisfied with this foundation....

Colorado Rule of Evidence 803
Hearsay Exceptions; Availability of Declarant Immaterial

The following are not excluded by the hearsay rule, even though the declarant is available as a witness....

(18) Learned Treatises. To the extent called to the attention of an expert witness upon cross-examination or relied upon by him in direct examination, statements contained in published treatises, periodicals, or pamphlets on a subject of history, medicine or other science or art, established as a reliable authority by the testimony or admission of the witness or by other expert testimony or by judicial notice. If admitted, the statements may be read into evidence and may be received as exhibits, as the court permits.

Committee Comment

Unlike the Federal Rule, the Colorado Rule allows the learned treaties to be admitted as exhibits in the discretion of the court....

Michigan Rule of Evidence 707
Use of Learned Treatises for Impeachment

To the extent called to the attention of an expert witness upon cross-examination, statements contained in published treatises, periodicals, or pamphlets on a subject of history, medicine, or other science or art, established as a reliable authority by the testimony or admission of the witness or by other expert testimony or by judicial notice, are admissible for impeachment purposes only. If admitted, the statements may be read into evidence but may not be received as exhibits.

State v. Shaw
86 P.3d 823 (Wash. 2004)

BECKER, C.J.:

....

Someone stole Daryl Ayers' 1987 Honda Accord in June 2001. Police located the car and saw Shaw get into it and try to start it with a screwdriver. Shaw was arrested; the car was returned.

The State charged Shaw with first degree possession of stolen property. At trial before a jury, the investigating detective testified that he used the Kelley Blue Book internet site to research the Accord's value. He explained what information the site requires to value a car. After entry of this information, the site provides two different values for the car in question—the retail value and the private party value. The private party value is the lower of the two numbers, reflecting what one would expect to pay in a private rather than a dealer sale.

Overruling a defense hearsay objection, the trial court allowed the detective to testify that the private party value for the Accord was $2,520. The court also admitted the computer generated report as an exhibit....

The jury convicted Shaw of first degree possession of stolen property. He appeals, and contends it was error to admit the Blue Book evidence. He asks this court to reverse that conviction and remand for sentencing on the lesser included offense of second degree possession of stolen property....

A person is guilty of first degree possession of stolen property if he or she possesses stolen property valued at more than $1,500. If the value is in the range of $250 to $1,500, the crime is second degree possession of stolen property....

The only evidence that the Accord had value in excess of $1,500 was the detective's testimony about value obtained from the Kelley Blue Book website. The detective testified that he uses the Blue Book cite to follow-up his investigation of stolen cars, in order to estimate the value of the stolen car. He itemized the information the system requires to estimate a car's value: odometer reading, general condition of car, options, year, make, and model. He also testified that to his knowledge, Kelley Blue Book

> is the most definitive and most widely used estimate of car values. When you buy a used car and apply for a loan banks generally use Kelley Blue Book value to establish the amount of loan, interest rate and that type of thing.

> Based on the history of the Kelley Blue Book and the amount of information available, the amount of information they require to make the estimate of the value, I believe is the most accurate.

The State contends the Blue Book value was properly admitted under ER 803(a)(17):

> **Specific exceptions.** The following are not excluded by the hearsay rule, even though the declarant is available as a witness:
>
> ...
>
> (17) *Market Reports, Commercial Publications.* Market quotations, tabulations, lists, directories, or other published compilations, generally used and relied upon by the public or by persons in particular occupations.

Other jurisdictions have held that recognized used car price guides fit within this exception to the hearsay rule. Shaw argues that a contrary conclusion is dictated in Washington by *State v. Rainwater*, 876 P.2d 979 (1994). *Rainwater* is a decision affirming the admission, as business records, of price tags from stolen clothes to prove their value. The court stated, "The rule we adopt today will not apply to new and used automobiles or to other merchandise for which the 'sticker price' is merely a clue to the probable range for reasonable negotiations." And price tags "constitute substantial evidence of market value *only so long as* the case involves a retail store that is commonly known to sell its goods for a non negotiable price as shown on the tag."

Relying on these statements, Shaw argues the Blue Book, like a sticker price, is not a reliable indicator of value. But the Kelley Blue Book is not a sticker price or a price tag placed on a car to market it. As the foundation laid by the detective's testimony showed, it is a publication used to determine what a person might expect to pay when buying a used car, or to receive when selling one....

Notes and Questions

1. Note that Rule 803(18)(B) provides three ways in which treatises and similar materials can be shown to be reliable authorities. First, a party seeking to offer such a treatise into evidence can get the expert that the party is examining or cross-examining to admit to the treatise's reliability. Second, a party may have another expert testify to the reliability of the treatise. Finally, a party can ask the trial court to take judicial notice of the reliability of the treatise. These latter two options were included to "avoid[] the possibility that the expert may at the outset block cross-examination by refusing to concede reliance or authoritativeness." Advisory Committee Note to Rule 803(18).

2. Rule 803(18) is justified both on the grounds of necessity and trustworthiness. Such evidence is thought to be necessary because it is impossible (or nearly so) for a party to produce as live witnesses the preeminent experts in the field, and prohibiting the works of such experts deprives the trier of fact of useful information. Moreover, such evidence is reliable because such authors have an incentive to be careful in what they write so as to avoid being exposed for inaccuracy and having their professional reputations harmed as a result. *See* 6 Wigmore, Evidence §§ 1691, 1692, at 5–7 (Chadbourn rev. 1976).

3. A number of the requirements of Rule 803(18) are designed to avoid the risk that jurors will misunderstand or misuse such evidence:

> The rule avoids the danger of misunderstanding and misapplication by limiting the use of treatises as substantive evidence to situations in which an expert is on the stand and available to explain and assist in the application of the treatise if desired. The limitation upon receiving the publication itself physically in evidence, contained in the last sentence, is designed to further this policy.

Advisory Committee Note to Rule 803(18). Compare the approach taken by Federal Rule 803(18) with that of its Colorado and Michigan counterparts. Which of the three does the best job of balancing the benefits and dangers of permitting evidentiary use of treatises and similar materials?

4. Somewhat related to Rule 803(18) is Rule 803(17), which provides an exception for

> Market quotations, lists, directories, or other compilations that are generally relied on by the public or by persons in particular occupations.

Such materials are thought to be trustworthy as a result of "general reliance by the public or by a particular segment of it, and the motivation of the compiler to foster reliance by being accurate." Advisory Committee Note to Rule 803(17). The exception, which includes such materials as telephone books and stock market reports in newspapers, is viewed as necessary given that it would be virtually impossible to call as live witnesses all of the people with first-hand knowledge who provided the information on which such materials are based.

5. Rule 803(16) provides an exception for "[a] statement in a document that is at least 20 years old and whose authenticity is established." The exception is thought to be necessary because the passage of time reduces or eliminates the number of witnesses with first-hand knowledge, and even if such witnesses remain, the value of their testimony is

in any event likely diminished by faded memory. And evidence admitted via this exception is thought to be reliable because "age affords assurance that the writing antedates the present controversy." Advisory Committee Note to Rule 803(16).

This exception is discussed in greater detail in connection with Rule 901(b)(8), which provides the means of authenticating ancient documents. *See supra* Chapter 2.

6. If a document qualifies as an ancient document under Rule 803(16), does that pave the way for admitting not only the first-hand observations of the author of the document, but also for hearsay statements of other people that are recorded in the document by the author? *See Hicks v. Charles Pfizer & Co.*, 466 F. Supp. 2d 799, 806–07 (E.D. Tex. 2005) (noting a split on the issue but concluding that the exception "permits the introduction of statements only where the declarant is the author of the document," and that "other hearsay exceptions must be used to render each individual layer of hearsay admissible"). The *Hicks* court reasoned that "Rule 805 would be superfluous if the explicit hearsay exceptions excused double hearsay." *Id.*

7. Rule 803(15) provides an exception for

> A statement contained in a document that purports to establish or affect an interest in property if the matter stated was relevant to the document's purpose — unless later dealings with the property are inconsistent with the truth of the statement or the purport of the document.

The exception is justified primarily by the reliability of evidence that falls within the scope of the exception:

> The circumstances under which dispositive documents are executed and the requirement that the recital be germane to the purpose of the document are believed to be adequate guarantees of trustworthiness, particularly in view of the nonapplicability of the rule if dealings with the property have been inconsistent with the document. The age of the document is of no significance, though in practical application the document will most often be an ancient one.

Advisory Committee Note to Rule 803(15).

Although traditionally applied to deeds of real property, the exception has been applied to documents affecting interests in personal property as well. *E.g., United States v. Weinstock*, 863 F. Supp. 1529, 1532–35 (D. Utah 1994). Indeed, one recent decision holds that statements contained in a prior court judgment fall within the scope of Rule 803(15) to the extent that the judgment established or affected an interest in property. *See United States v. Boulware*, 384 F.3d 794, 807 (9th Cir. 2004) ("Although the [advisory committee] note uses the example of a deed, a judgment that establishes the ownership of disputed items of property is no less of a dispositive document, and the judgment's recital of facts is no less exempt from the hearsay rule."). Is that consistent with the treatment of judgments when offered under Rule 803(8)?

G. Restricted Hearsay Exceptions

Save for the hybrid case of Rule 803(5), all of the exceptions to the hearsay rule set forth in Rule 803 are "unrestricted," meaning that statements falling within the scope of such exceptions bear sufficient indicia of reliability that they can be admitted without regard to whether the person who made the statement is able and willing to testify in court. For example, if a statement satisfies the requirements of the exception for excited utterances, a party is free to call a witness who heard the statement to testify to what the declarant said instead of calling the declarant himself to testify as a witness, even though the declarant is alive and willing to testify if called as a witness by the party.

Rule 804 contains a series of so-called "restricted" hearsay exceptions, exceptions that can be invoked only if the proponent first makes a showing that the declarant is "unavailable as a witness." The Advisory Committee explains the reason for the distinction between the two sets of exceptions as follows:

> Rule 803 is based upon the assumption that a hearsay statement falling within one of its exceptions possesses qualities which justify the conclusion that whether the declarant is available or unavailable is not a relevant factor in determining admissibility. The instant rule proceeds upon a different theory: hearsay which admittedly is not equal in quality to testimony of the declarant on the stand may nevertheless be admitted if the declarant is unavailable and if his statement meets a specified standard. The rule expresses preferences: testimony given on the stand in person is preferred over hearsay, and hearsay, if of the specified quality, is preferred over complete loss of the evidence of the declarant.

Advisory Committee Note to Rule 804(b).

Rule 804(a) defines the circumstances under which a declarant is deemed to be unavailable as a witness:

> A declarant is considered to be unavailable as a witness if the declarant:
>
> (1) is exempted from testifying about the subject matter of the declarant's statement because the court rules that a privilege applies;
>
> (2) refuses to testify about the subject matter despite a court order to do so;
>
> (3) testifies to not remembering the subject matter;
>
> (4) cannot be present or testify at the trial or hearing because of death or a then-existing infirmity, physical illness, or mental illness; or
>
> (5) is absent from the trial or hearing and the statement's proponent has not been able, by process or other reasonable means, to procure:
>
>   (A) the declarant's attendance, in the case of a hearsay exception under Rule 804(b)(1) or (6); or
>
>   (B) the declarant's attendance or testimony, in the case of a hearsay exception under Rule 804(b)(2), (3), or (4).
>
> But this subdivision (a) does not apply if the statement's proponent procured or wrongfully caused the declarant's unavailability as a witness in order to prevent the declarant from attending or testifying.

The next section takes a closer look at the unavailability requirement, while the sections that follow it explore the individual exceptions that can be invoked once a showing of unavailability has been made.

1. Unavailability

United States v. Williams
927 F.2d 95 (2d Cir. 1991)

VAN GRAAFEILAND, Circuit Judge:

Following a ten-week jury trial before Judge Griesa in the Southern District of New York, the above-named defendants-appellants were convicted of conspiring to violate the narcotics laws....

Four of the original defendants charged with drug conspiracy pleaded guilty.... All four were serving their sentences when the second trial took place.

These four men were linked to the charged narcotics conspiracy by considerable proof at trial and were mentioned frequently during the trial as participants in drug transactions. However, when the prosecutor contacted the attorneys for the four men to inquire about their clients' willingness to testify, he was informed that each of the clients would invoke his Fifth Amendment privilege if called as a witness. The Government then sought permission from the district court to use the prisoners' guilty plea allocutions as statements against interest pursuant to Fed.R.Evid. 804(b)(3). The district court accepted the prosecutor's representations as reliable and, after redacting all references to the named defendants, admitted the redacted allocutions....

Although the record is clear that Judge Griesa found the pleading defendants to be unavailable, appellants contend that Judge Griesa could not properly have made this ruling without these defendants having appeared before him to claim the privilege. Although in the ordinary case this would have been the preferred practice, personal appearance and claim of privilege were not the *sine qua non* of its grant in the instant case. In this respect, subdivisions (a)(1) and (a)(2) of Rule 804 must be distinguished. Subdivision (a)(2) identifies as "unavailable" a witness who persists in refusing to testify despite an order of the court to do so. This obviously contemplates presence of the witness in court. Subdivision (a)(1), on the other hand, identifies as "unavailable" a witness who is exempted by a court ruling on the ground of privilege. Such a ruling can be made, as in the instant case, with or without the witness being haled into court.

Appellants have suggested no reason why Judge Griesa should not have believed the representations of the attorneys for the incarcerated defendants concerning their clients' intentions to rely on their Fifth Amendment privileges. The law does not require the doing of a futile act. We conclude that both the prosecution and Judge Griesa acted reasonably and in good faith and that Judge Griesa's finding of unavailability based on his ruling concerning testimonial privilege has ample support in the record....

United States v. Carson
1987 WL 37646 (4th Cir. 1987)

PER CURIAM:

Gregory Carson was convicted of assault resulting in serious bodily injury after a stabbing incident at Lorton Reformatory, where Carson was an inmate. At trial, the victim of the stabbing professed himself unable to remember any details of the incident, even though he was permitted to refresh his memory by looking through the transcript of his grand jury testimony about the stabbing. The trial judge declared the victim unavailable as a witness and allowed his grand jury testimony to be read to the jury....

The first issue raised here is whether Edwards' alleged inability to remember what happened rendered him an unavailable witness under Rule 804 of the Federal Rules of Evidence. Carson contends that Edwards' statement on the witness stand that he could not recall the day of the stabbing or what had happened to him that day was an insufficient basis for the trial court's decision to declare him unavailable. Carson argues that the government should have given notice to defense counsel of Edwards' loss of memory and submitted medical records from the prison. In the alternative, recognizing that the failure to recall may have stemmed from a simple fear of retaliation, Carson insists that a hearing should have been held outside the presence of the jury and Edwards should there have been pressured to testify before the trial court could properly declare him unavailable. Carson cites *United States v. Garner*, 574 F.2d 1141 (4th Cir.), *cert. denied*, 439 U.S. 936 (1978), *United States v. West*, 574 F.2d 1131 (4th Cir. 1978), and *United States v. Murphy*, 696 F.2d 282 (4th Cir. 1982), in support of his arguments. His reliance on these cases is misplaced.

First, in *West*, the witness had been killed. There was no question that he was unavailable and the government was able to give prior notice of the fact to the defendant.

In *Garner* and in *Murphy*, the witness was unavailable because he simply refused to testify. In that circumstance, the court is required to use its best efforts to persuade the witness to testify before making a finding that he is unavailable under Rule 804(a)(2). Here however, the witness claimed that he could not remember the event he was to testify about. In such a case, whether the claim is true or false, whether it is based on a physical condition or on fear, Rule 804(a)(3) requires no more than that the witness testify to a lack of memory, as Edwards did, in order to be found unavailable. Therefore, the district court did not err in declaring Edwards an unavailable witness....

United States v. McGuire
307 F.3d 1192 (9th Cir. 2002)

GOULD, Circuit Judge....

McGuire and Petersen were members of a group called the "Montana Freemen," which was hostile to the United States government.... The district court that convicted the Freemen described the group's activities as "an unusually large and complex criminal scheme" involving hundreds of persons and millions of dollars in losses.

McGuire participated in the fraud by using Freemen financial instruments to purchase various goods and services. Twenty-two fraudulent checks were made out to him, including several presented for payment of debts and used to buy merchandise from L.L. Bean. McGuire also was convicted of robbery for taking sound recording equipment from a three-person ABC news television crew that had come to Justus Township to interview the Freemen. Petersen participated in the fraud by attempting to deposit unfunded Freemen checks....

A first trial resulted in a hung jury. Before retrial, the doctor for one of the ABC news crew robbery victims wrote to the court to say that the victim would be unable to travel to Montana for the trial and would be unable to testify by video because of her pregnancy. Over McGuire's objection, the district court allowed the victim's videotaped testimony from the first trial to be admitted. A jury convicted McGuire of bank fraud, robbery, and four firearms violations, and he was sentenced to 180 months imprisonment. Petersen was convicted on two counts of bank fraud and one count of mail fraud. She was sentenced to time served and five years of supervised release....

The Federal Rules of Evidence prohibit the admission of hearsay statements except under certain specified circumstances. Fed.R.Evid. 802. One of those circumstances is the "former testimony" hearsay exception of Rule 804(b)(1).... The 804(b)(1) exception to the hearsay rule does not apply, however, unless the witness is "unavailable" under Rule 804(a).

McGuire challenges the district court's decision to permit the introduction of former testimony by ABC news producer Alison Sesnon, a victim of McGuire's robbery. McGuire argues the court erred in finding that the witness' pregnancy, as described by her doctor, made her "unavailable" within the meaning of Rule 804(a). We review for an abuse of discretion.

Under Rule 804(a)(4), a witness is unavailable if she [cannot be present or testify at the trial or hearing because of death or a then-existing infirmity, physical illness, or mental illness]. In determining whether a witness is unavailable under this rule, courts have considered factors such as the nature of the infirmity, the expected time of recovery, the reliability of the evidence concerning the infirmity, and other special circumstances.

It was not inappropriate for the district court to have credited Sesnon's doctor's written opinion that Sesnon's pregnancy (she was twenty-eight weeks pregnant) made her unable to undergo the stresses of testimony. There is nothing wrong with a district court's relying on a physician's statement when assessing availability. A pregnancy in its seventh month poses special risks for a mother and her unborn child that may be exacerbated by the stress of trial. These risks in late pregnancy, when attested to by a physician, are an "infirmity" within the meaning of the Rule. In addition, had Sesnon carried her child to term before testifying, she would have been pregnant—and presumably unable to testify—for at least another eight weeks. In the past, we have deemed a witness "unavailable" when medical necessity rendered the witness unable to testify for a far shorter, one- to two-week period. And there is no reason to doubt the reliability of the evidence concerning her infirmity. Finally, the trial in this case involved scores of witnesses (many of whom were required to travel long distances to the trial), ten defense attorneys, and a judge from another judicial district sitting by designation. The district judge's decision to adhere to the trial date to accommodate so many competing schedules was not improper. The district court was well within its discretion in determining that Sesnon was unavailable under Rule 804(a)(4)....

United States v. Kehm

799 F.2d 354 (7th Cir. 1986)

EASTERBROOK, Circuit Judge.

Ronald Markowski organized a smuggling ring to import drugs from South America via the Bahamas. Forty-one participants were indicted in Indiana. Most of the cases have been concluded. Today we deal with two of the participants in Markowski's organization, Charles Kehm and Steven Greenberg.... In separate trials, Kehm and Greenberg were convicted of conspiring to import and distribute marijuana and cocaine....

Nigel Bowe, an attorney and citizen of the Bahamas, may have been one of the conspirators. In the Bahamas he has remained. The prosecutor left Bowe out of the indictment because at the time he thought there was no extradition treaty with the Bahamas, making an effort to prosecute Bowe futile. Greenberg wanted Bowe's testimony, believing it would be helpful. But preliminary discussions with Bowe were fruitless; he refused to come to the United States voluntarily, and the extradition treaty with the Bahamas is limited to extradition for trial or punishment. Greenberg therefore moved for leave to take Bowe's deposition in the Bahamas....

The district court was not satisfied by the parties' joint representations that Bowe would be unavailable at trial. Recognizing how unusual a criminal deposition is, the court insisted that an affidavit of unavailability be obtained. Bowe supplied the affidavit.... The judge took Bowe at his word and authorized the taking of a deposition in the Bahamas. The deposition was taken, with Greenberg present, by an attorney for Greenberg and one of the prosecutors.

Things did not turn out as Greenberg wished. He did not offer the deposition for use at the trial; the prosecutor did. Greenberg then executed a smart about-face and argued that Bowe was available for trial after all, making the deposition inadmissible under Fed.R.Evid. 804. The judge, choosing to believe Bowe's affidavit and his statements at the deposition that he would not go to the United States, allowed the deposition into evidence. After trial Greenberg procured a new affidavit, in which Bowe stated: "I was never unavailable to the government as a witness." The price for this "availability" presumably was immunity from prosecution, though the affidavit does not make this explicit. At all events, the district court ultimately denied Greenberg's motion for a new trial, holding that Bowe's first affidavit was honest and his second affidavit a fib.

....

Rule 804(a)(5) states that a person is unavailable if [they are absent from the hearing and the proponent of the person's statement has been unable to procure his attendance by process or other reasonable means]. The prosecutor did not try to issue compulsory process to Bowe; indeed the prosecutor did not try *any* means, "reasonable" or otherwise, to secure Bowe's attendance at trial. Greenberg insists that the prosecutor's inaction precludes a finding of unavailability. The prosecutor replies that a request would have been futile, to which Greenberg responds that the United States could have extradited Bowe as an "unindicted co-conspirator" or in a pinch could have indicted Bowe and extradited him as a fugitive from justice.

Futility excuses a request. Neither Rule 804(a)(5) nor the constitution requires the prosecutor to butt his head against a wall just to see how much it hurts. But futility is a matter of degree. Maybe the prosecutor could have prevailed on the President to negotiate a new treaty. There is almost always some avenue to be pursued, albeit with minuscule chance of success. So the question is not one of absolutes, it is one of degrees, and a favorable outcome need not be certain to make it necessary to act. The advisory committee's note to Rule 804(a)(5) refers to *Barber v. Page*, 390 U.S. 719 (1968), as the standard for the reasonableness of efforts to obtain non-resident witnesses, and *Barber* holds that a prosecutor may not omit making a request just because the answer is not a sure thing.

The declarant in *Barber* was in federal prison in Texas; a state prosecutor in Oklahoma did not request the federal government to make him available for trial, stating that the federal government had discretion not to comply with such a request. Although the federal government would have had discretion to say no, it was the "policy" of federal officials to "permit federal prisoners to testify in state court criminal proceedings pursuant to writs of habeas corpus *ad testificandum* issued out of state courts." The policy was not invariant, but "'the possibility of a refusal is not the equivalent of asking and receiving a rebuff.' In short, a witness is not 'unavailable'... unless the prosecutorial authorities have made a good-faith effort to obtain his presence at trial. The State made no such effort here, and, so far as the record reveals, the sole reason why [the declarant] was not present to testify in person was because the State did not attempt to seek his presence." *Barber* dealt with a declarant in the United States, but there is no reason why the principle stops at the border.

The favorable response need not be certain; *Barber* establishes this. Need it be more likely than not that the response would be favorable? Is a 10% chance of a favorable outcome enough to require the prosecutor to try? Both the constitution and Rule 804 strongly favor live testimony, and it is always easy to ask politely. Because the cost of the request is low and the benefit of a favorable response high, it is necessary to ask even when the answer is likely to be no. Nothing ventured nothing gained. Here, however, the probability of a favorable response under current law was low, and the probability that Bowe would testify at all if haled into this country was low as well; the combined probability was close to zero. Even a small expenditure of time by prosecutor and Department of State is unnecessary when the joint probability is so low.

First things first. The chance Bowe could have been brought to the United States as a witness was vanishingly small. The only treaty in question, which covers extradition, does not authorize compulsory process to produce witnesses. A polite request to turn Bowe over would have been an insult to Bahamian officials. No civilized country will turn over one of its nationals to a foreign power, against the person's will, in the absence of a treaty. The State Department was unlikely to request the Bahamas to send a team of goons to Bowe's house to spirit him out of the country in the dead of night. Nothing short of a new treaty could have produced Bowe's involuntary appearance in the United States as a witness. The existing treaty with the Bahamas allows extradition only of a person who has been "accused or convicted" of one of the listed offenses. Article 9 of the treaty says that there shall be extradition "only if the evidence be found sufficient" to justify a trial. The treaty does not refer to "unindicted co-conspirators", let alone to co-conspirators who are unnamed. The only way the United States could have secured Bowe's presence under the treaty, then, would have been to have indicted him and convinced authorities in the Bahamas that the evidence was sufficient.

Suppose that had been done. Would Bowe then have been available to be a witness at trial? This is most unlikely, because Bowe would have possessed a privilege not to incriminate himself. A testimonial privilege is an independent ground of "unavailability." Fed.R.Evid. 804(a)(1). The government could have overridden the privilege by granting Bowe testimonial immunity, but the government need not grant immunity to produce testimony. Testimonial immunity is the only one at issue. Transactional immunity would have made Bowe a voluble witness but would have spoiled the ground of his extradition from the Bahamas. When Bowe said that he had never been unavailable as a witness for the government, he must have meant a witness with transactional immunity; Bowe was quite unwilling to expose himself to criminal prosecution. So Bowe's condition for testimony was out of the question, a less sweeping immunity was unnecessary, and without either kind of immunity Bowe would have been "unavailable" whether physically in the United States or the Bahamas.

So a request in this case was exceptionally unlikely to make Bowe available as a witness. Rule 804 does not require pointless gestures. Once Bowe swore that he would neither appear nor testify voluntarily, the prosecutor was stymied. Greenberg therefore was right when he requested permission to take the deposition: Bowe is "unavailable" as a witness, and the deposition was admissible at trial....

United States v. Peterson

100 F.3d 7 (2d Cir. 1996)

KEARSE, Circuit Judge:

Defendant Shawn Peterson appeals from a judgment ... convicting him, as a convicted felon, of possessing a firearm....

At approximately 12:50 a.m., New York City Police Officers Michael Saladino and Ischaler Grant were patrolling a high-crime area of Brooklyn in which police had made numerous arrests for weapons and narcotics offenses.... They observed three men, including Peterson, who had been standing on the sidewalk; when the men noticed the officers, they ducked behind a parked vehicle. Suspicions aroused, the officers parked and exited their car.... The officers ... produced their identification and asked the men their names, addresses, and reasons for being at that location.

Peterson, who wore a noticeably bulging knapsack on his back, gave his name; as to his address, he at first stuttered Georgia but then changed his answer to Hempstead (a New York town). He appeared nervous, agitated, and evasive. He told the officers that he had come to visit a friend; when asked the friend's name, he did not answer.... When Peterson was asked what was in the knapsack, he responded, "what knapsack?" After Saladino pointed out the obvious, Peterson responded that there was nothing in the knapsack. When Saladino stated that he could clearly see that there was something in the knapsack, Peterson stated, "it's not my knapsack." Saladino then asked whether he could examine it, and Peterson removed the bag and handed it to Saladino. Inside the knapsack, Saladino found two .25 caliber semi-automatic handguns and several rounds of ammunition.

Peterson was arrested and taken to the police station. After being advised of his *Miranda* rights, he told the police that he had been given the knapsack by Anthony Woods, one of the men on the scene who had departed. Peterson admitted that he had given Saladino permission to search the bag.

In October 1994, Peterson was indicted by a New York State grand jury for firearm possession. In February 1995, on the basis that he had been convicted of a felony in New York State in 1988, Peterson was indicted by a federal grand jury for possession of firearms by a felon....

Peterson did not testify, but he sought to introduce testimony he had given to the state grand jury that had indicted him based on the same conduct. Before the state grand jury, Peterson had testified to the effect that the knapsack did not belong to him and that he had been asked by Woods to hold it "for a second" just as the police officers arrived on the scene. The trial court ruled that the testimony was not admissible against the government....

In the state grand jury proceeding, Peterson testified that he had been asked by Woods to hold the knapsack "for a second" just as the police officers arrived on the scene. At trial in the present case, Peterson declined to testify, invoking his Fifth Amendment privilege against self-incrimination, but attempted unsuccessfully to introduce his state grand-jury testimony. He contends that the trial court erred in ruling that the testimony was not admissible under Fed.R.Evid. 804(b)(1). We disagree for several reasons....

[T]he "true spirit" of Rule 804(b)(1), inaptly invoked here by Peterson, would properly have led the district court to reject Peterson's proffer on the ground that his invocation of his Fifth Amendment privilege against self-incrimination did not make him "unavailable" within the meaning of Rule 804. In general, a person who properly invokes his Fifth Amendment privilege, leaving others powerless to compel his testimony, is considered to be unavailable to others for purposes of Rule 804. However, the Rule expressly provides that [a declarant is not unavailable as a witness if the statement's proponent procured or wrongfully caused the declarant's unavailability as a witness in order to prevent the declarant from attending or testifying]. Fed.R.Evid. 804(a). When the defendant invokes his Fifth Amendment privilege, he has made himself unavailable to any other party, but he is not unavailable to himself.

At least one other circuit has ruled that a defendant who exercises his privilege not to testify at a second trial of his case is not entitled to introduce the testimony he gave at the first trial:

> The sponsor of a declarant's former testimony may not create the condition of unavailability and then benefit therefrom. The rule [the defendant] relies upon was designed to ensure one access to testimony where, by the actions of the opponent, or at least through no fault of the testimony's proponent, a desired witness becomes unavailable. In the instant case, [the defendant] created his own unavailability by invoking his fifth amendment privilege against self-incrimination.

United States v. Kimball, 15 F.3d 54, 55–56 (5th Cir.), *cert. denied*, 513 U.S. 999 (1994). It would have been well within the discretion of the district court in the present case to exclude Peterson's prior grand jury testimony on the ground that he did not, by exercising his Fifth Amendment right not to testify, become unavailable within the meaning of Rule 804....

Notes and Questions

1. Rule 804(a)(2) applies only if a witness "refuses to testify about the subject matter despite a court order to do so." This exception is thus applicable only if the witness has appeared in court, has been ordered by the court to testify (usually under threat of contempt), and yet nonetheless refuses to testify. *See United States v. Zappola*, 646 F.2d 48, 54 (2d Cir. 1981).

2. The *Carson* court is correct not to concern itself over whether the claim of failed memory under Rule 804(a)(3) is real or feigned, isn't it? Although the House Committee on the Judiciary expressed its understanding that the trial judge would be free to disbelieve the declarant's testimony as to his claimed lack of memory, *see* Report of House Committee on the Judiciary, House Report No. 93-650, as a practical matter, what would be the result? *See United States v. Miller*, 852 F.2d 569 (6th Cir. 1988) (describing authentic claims of memory loss as falling within the scope of Rule 804(a)(3) and feigned claims of memory loss as falling within the scope of Rule 804(a)(2)).

3. The *McGuire* court is correct to hold that a temporary disability is sufficient to invoke Rule 804(a)(4), isn't it? After all, Rule 804(a)(4) requires only that there be a "then-existing" physical or mental illness or infirmity.

4. When a party relies on Rule 804(a)(5) as the basis for unavailability, that provision requires that he attempt to obtain the witness' deposition before resorting to the hearsay exceptions for dying declarations (804(b)(2)), statements against interest (804(b)(3)), and statements of personal or family history (804(b)(4)). *See* Report of House Committee on the Judiciary, House Report No. 93-650 ("The amendment is designed primarily to require that an attempt be made to depose a witness (as well as to seek his attendance)

as a precondition to the witness being deemed unavailable.") This requirement is dispensed with when the exceptions for former testimony (804(b)(1)) and for forfeiture by wrongdoing (804(b)(6)) are invoked. Do you see why?

5. Rule 804(a)'s final sentence makes clear that a party cannot rely on a declarant's unavailability to invoke an exception to the hearsay rule set forth in Rule 804(b) if the party "procured or wrongfully caused the declarant's unavailability as a witness in order to prevent the declarant from attending or testifying." That provision pretty clearly applies if a party threatens the declarant with harm to prevent him from testifying. *E.g., United States v. Pizarro*, 756 F.2d 579, 583 (7th Cir. 1985). But as *Kehm* implies, and other cases hold, the government's refusal to grant a witness immunity does not constitute procurement or wrongdoing on the government's part. *E.g., United States v. Lang*, 589 F.2d 92, 95–96 (2d Cir. 1978).

6. The determination whether a witness is "unavailable" within the meaning of Rule 804(a) is a question for the judge alone to decide under Rule 104(a). *See Williams v. United Dairy Farmers*, 188 F.R.D. 266, 271–272 (S.D. Ohio 1999).

2. Former Testimony

Rule 804(b)(1) provides an exception to the hearsay rule, if the declarant is unavailable as a witness, for

> Testimony that:
>
> **(A)** was given as a witness at a trial, hearing, or lawful deposition, whether given during the current proceeding or a different one; and
>
> **(B)** is now offered against a party who had—or, in a civil case, whose predecessor in interest had—an opportunity and similar motive to develop it by direct, cross-, or redirect examination.

In some sense, it is hard to understand why this exception, unlike the exceptions in Rule 803, requires a showing of unavailability. After all, evidence admitted under this exception much more closely resembles the sort of evidence that the hearsay rule is designed to encourage, namely, direct testimony before the trier of fact:

> Former testimony does not rely upon some set of circumstances to substitute for oath and cross-examination, since both oath and opportunity to cross-examine were present in fact. The only missing one of the ideal conditions for the giving of testimony is the presence of trier and opponent ("demeanor evidence"). This is lacking with all hearsay exceptions. Hence it may be argued that former testimony is the strongest hearsay and should be included under Rule 803. However, opportunity to observe demeanor is what in a large measure confers depth and meaning upon oath and cross-examination. Thus in cases under Rule 803 demeanor lacks the significance which it possesses with respect to testimony.

Advisory Committee Note to Rule 804(b)(1).

Three critical questions arise in applying Rule 804(b)(1). First, when does a party have an "opportunity" to develop testimony? Second, when does a party have a "similar motive" to do so? Finally, what is the scope of the phrase "predecessor in interest"? The following materials explore these questions.

Problem 7-33: The Absent-Minded Witness

Donald is indicted on charges of conspiracy to commit wire fraud. The prosecution calls Lisa to testify to the details of Donald's participation in the wire fraud scheme. On the stand, Lisa claims that she cannot remember the details, although the prosecution attempts to refresh her memory. The prosecution then seeks to introduce Lisa's testimony before the grand jury, where she set forth the details of the scheme. Donald objects on hearsay grounds.

How should the prosecution respond, and how will the court likely rule? What if Lisa's prior testimony had been given in a preliminary hearing? Suppose instead that Lisa's testimony before the grand jury was favorable toward Donald: can Donald bring the statement in under the "former testimony" exception? If Donald had testified before the grand jury, but at trial invoked his privilege against self-incrimination, could the government offer the statement into evidence?

Problem 7-34: The Maple Syrup

Paula slips and falls in a supermarket and brings suit against its owner alleging that she slipped on maple syrup that was on the floor. Wendy, who witnessed the fall, testifies at trial that she discovered Paula on the floor and noticed that there was maple syrup on the bottom of her shoes. But a mistrial is declared because the jury deadlocks.

At retrial, Paula introduces evidence that Wendy has died, and she offers into evidence a transcript of Wendy's testimony in the first trial. The owner of the supermarket raises a hearsay objection.

How should Paula's attorney respond, and how will the court likely rule?

Problem 7-35: The Car Accident

Walter witnesses an accident in which David's car crashes into Pam's car. Pam brings suit against David, and Walter testifies on Pam's behalf. George, a passenger in Pam's car, brings his own, subsequent suit against David. By that time, Walter has died, and George offers into evidence a transcript of Walter's testimony at Pam's trial. David raises a hearsay objection.

How should George's attorney respond, and how will the court likely rule?

Problem 7-36: Arson

Pete is on trial on charges of committing arson. Wallace, an eyewitness, testifies on behalf of the prosecution. Subsequently, Pete sues his insurance company to recover for losses sustained in the fire. By this time, Wallace has died. The insurance company offers evidence of Wallace's death and a transcript of his testimony in the arson prosecution. Pete raises a hearsay objection.

How should the insurance company respond, and how will the court likely rule? Suppose instead that Pete had sued the insurance company first, and Wallace testified in that suit as a witness for the insurance company. Wallace died shortly thereafter, and the government later brought criminal charges against Pete for committing arson. Could the prosecution introduce into evidence a transcript of Wallace's testimony in the civil case?

United States v. DiNapoli

8 F.3d 909 (2d Cir. 1993) (en banc)

JON O. NEWMAN, Chief Judge:

On this criminal appeal, which is before our Court on remand from the Supreme Court, we have given in banc consideration to a fairly narrow issue of evidence that has potentially broad implications for the administration of criminal justice. The issue concerns Rule 804(b)(1) of the Federal Rules of Evidence.... Our precise issue is whether the prosecution had a "similar motive to develop" the testimony of two grand jury witnesses compared to its motive at a subsequent criminal trial at which the witnesses were unavailable....

Briefly, the case concerns conspiracy and substantive charges under the Racketeer Influenced and Corrupt Organizations Act ("RICO") against several defendants accused of participating in a bid-rigging scheme in the concrete construction industry in Manhattan. The trial evidence indicated the existence of a "Club" of six concrete construction companies that during 1980–1985 rigged the bids for concrete superstructure work on nearly every high-rise construction project in Manhattan involving more than $2 million of concrete work. Organized crime figures, notably members of the Genovese Family, orchestrated the scheme and enforced adherence to the bid allocations.

The grand jury investigating the matter returned its first indictment on March 20, 1986. That indictment alleged the essential aspects of the criminal activity and named all of the appellants as defendants. The grand jury continued its investigation in an effort to identify additional participants and additional construction projects that might have been victimized by the bid-rigging scheme. In this subsequent phase of the inquiry, the grand jury called Frederick DeMatteis and Pasquale Bruno as witnesses. They had been principals in Cedar Park Concrete Construction Corporation ("Cedar Park"), a company that other grand jury witnesses had testified had been briefly involved in the scheme. DeMatteis and Bruno, both testifying under grants of immunity, denied awareness of a bid-rigging scheme.

DeMatteis testified in the grand jury on three occasions in 1986—June 3, June 12, and June 19. His first two appearances primarily concerned background questioning about the construction industry and Cedar Park. At his third appearance, the prosecutor pointedly asked whether DeMatteis had been instructed not to bid on the Javits Convention Center project and whether he was aware of an arrangement whereby the successful bidder paid two percent of the bid price to organized crime figures. DeMatteis denied both the instruction not to bid and awareness of the two percent arrangement. The prosecutor, obviously skeptical of the denials, pressed DeMatteis with a few questions in the nature of cross-examination. However, in order not to reveal the identity of then undisclosed cooperating witnesses or the existence of then undisclosed wiretapped conversations that refuted DeMatteis's denials, the prosecutor refrained from confronting him with the substance of such evidence. Instead, the prosecutor called to DeMatteis's attention the substance of only the one relevant wiretapped conversation that had already become public—a tape played at a prior trial.

Bruno testified at the grand jury on September 11, 1986. Much of the questioning concerned the operations of Cedar Park. Like DeMatteis, Bruno was asked about and denied knowledge of the "Club" and the two percent arrangement for successful bidders. And, like DeMatteis, he was briefly cross-examined and confronted with the contents of the publicly disclosed tape from the *Persico* trial but not with any of the information from undisclosed witnesses or wiretaps. After his denials and after giving an answer that sharply conflicted with an answer given by DeMatteis, Bruno was briefly excused from the grand jury room. Upon his return, after the prosecutor had consulted with the grand jury, he was told by the prosecutor of the grand jury's "strong concern" that his testimony had "not been truthful." Four days later, Bruno's lawyer wrote the prosecutor stating that many of Bruno's answers had been inaccurate. The lawyer suggested that the prosecutor should resubmit his questions to Bruno in writing and that Bruno would respond by affidavit. The prosecutor declined the suggestion.

A thirteen-month trial ... ended on May 4, 1988, with the convictions of nine defendants.... During the trial, the defendants endeavored to call DeMatteis and Bruno as witnesses. Both invoked the privilege against self-incrimination. The defendants then offered the testimony DeMatteis and Bruno had given to the grand jury. After examining sealed affidavits presented by the prosecution, the District Court (Mary Johnson Lowe, Judge) refused to admit the grand jury testimony as prior testimony under Rule 804(b)(1). Judge Lowe appears not to have made specific findings with respect to the grand jury testimony. Instead, she ruled generally that the "motive of a prosecutor ... in the investigatory stages of a case is far different from the motive of a prosecutor in conducting the trial" and hence the "similar motive" requirement of Rule 804(b)(1) was not satisfied....

Our initial task is to determine how similarity of motive at two proceedings will be determined for purposes of Rule 804(b)(1). In resolving this matter, we do not accept the position, apparently urged by the appellants, that the test of similar motive is simply whether at the two proceedings the questioner takes the same side of the same issue. The test must turn not only on whether the questioner is on the same side of the same issue at both proceedings, but also on whether the questioner had a substantially similar interest in asserting that side of the issue. If a fact is critical to a cause of action at a second proceeding but the same fact was only peripherally related to a different cause of action at a first proceeding, no one would claim that the questioner had a similar motive at both proceedings to show that the fact had been established (or disproved). This is the same principle that holds collateral estoppel inapplicable when a small amount is at stake in a first proceeding and a large amount is at stake in a second proceeding, even though a party took the same side of the same issue at both proceedings. This suggests that the questioner must not only be on the same side of the same issue at both proceedings but must also have a substantially similar degree of interest in prevailing on that issue.

Whether the degree of interest in prevailing on an issue is substantially similar at two proceedings will sometimes be affected by the nature of the proceedings. Where both proceedings are trials and the same matter is seriously disputed at both trials, it will normally be the case that the side opposing the version of a witness at the first trial had a motive to develop that witness' testimony similar to the motive at the second trial. The opponent, whether shouldering a burden of proof or only resisting the adversary's effort to sustain its burden of proof, usually cannot tell how much weight the witness' version will have with the fact-finder in the total mix of all the evidence. Lacking such knowledge, the opponent at the first trial normally has a motive to dispute the version so long as it can be said that disbelief of the witness' version is of some significance to the opponent's side of the case; the motive at the second trial is normally similar.

The situation is not necessarily the same where the two proceedings are different in significant respects, such as their purposes or the applicable burden of proof. The grand jury context, with which we are concerned in this case, well illustrates the point. If a prosecutor is using the grand jury to investigate possible crimes and identify possible criminals, it may be quite unrealistic to characterize the prosecutor as the "opponent" of a witness' version.[4] At a preliminary stage of an investigation, the prosecutor is not trying to prove any side of any issue, but only to develop the facts to determine if an indictment is warranted. Even if the prosecutor displays some skepticism about particular testimony (not an uncommon response from any questioner interested in eliciting the truth), that does not mean the prosecutor has a motive to show the falsity of the testimony, similar to the motive that would exist at trial if an indictment is returned and the witness' testimony is presented by a defendant to rebut the prosecutor's evidence of guilt.

Even in cases like the pending one, where the grand jury proceeding has progressed far beyond the stage of a general inquiry, the motive to develop grand jury testimony that disputes a position already taken by the prosecutor is not necessarily the same as the motive the prosecutor would have if that same testimony was presented at trial. Once the prosecutor has decided to seek an indictment against identified suspects, that prosecutor may fairly be characterized as "opposed" to any testimony that tends to exonerate one of the suspects. But, because of the low burden of proof at the grand jury stage, even the prosecutor's status as an "opponent" of the testimony does not necessarily create a motive to challenge the testimony that is *similar* to the motive at trial. At the grand jury, the prosecutor need establish only probable cause to believe the suspect is guilty. By the time the exonerating testimony is given, such probable cause may already have been established to such an extent that there is no realistic likelihood that the grand jury will fail to indict. That circumstance alone will sometimes leave the prosecutor with slight if any motive to develop the exonerating testimony in order to persuade the grand jurors of its falsity.

Moreover, the grand jury context will sometimes present additional circumstances that render the prosecutor's motive to challenge the exonerating testimony markedly dissimilar to what the prosecutor's motive would be at trial. Frequently the grand jury inquiry will be conducted at a time when an investigation is ongoing. In such circumstances, there is an important public interest in not disclosing prematurely the existence of surveillance techniques such as wiretaps or undercover operations, or the identity of cooperating witnesses. The results of such techniques and the statements of such witnesses might be powerful ammunition to challenge the grand jury witness' exonerating testimony. By the time of trial, however, the public interest in not disclosing such ammunition will normally have dissipated, and the prosecutor will have a strong motive to confront the witness with all available contradictory evidence.

In recognizing these factors that distinguish the grand jury context from the trial context, we do not accept the position, urged by the Government..., that a prosecutor "generally will not have the same motive to develop testimony in grand jury proceedings as he does at trial.".... Our point is simply that the inquiry as to similar motive must be fact

---

4. In recommending Rule 804(b)(1), the Advisory Committee discussed the offeror of testimony at the prior proceeding in terms primarily applicable to trials and did not discuss at all the situation where the prior proceeding was a grand jury. Recognizing the difficulty of fashioning the proper approach where testimony is offered at a subsequent proceeding against a party who had offered the testimony at a prior proceeding, the Committee suggested recognizing "direct and redirect examination of *one's own witness*" as the equivalent of cross-examining an opponent's witness." Fed.R.Evid. 804 advisory committee's note (emphasis added). It will not always be accurate to characterize every grand jury witness as the prosecutor's "own" witness.

specific, and the grand jury context will sometimes, but not invariably, present circumstances that demonstrate the prosecutor's lack of a similar motive....

Nor are we persuaded by the Government's contention that the absence of similar motive is conclusively demonstrated by the availability at the grand jury of some cross-examination opportunities that were forgone. In virtually all subsequent proceedings, examiners will be able to suggest lines of questioning that were not pursued at a prior proceeding. In almost every criminal case, for example, the Government could probably point to some aspect of cross-examination of an exonerating witness that could have been employed at a prior trial and surely at a prior grand jury proceeding. Though the availability of substantial ways of challenging testimony that were not pursued by an examiner is pertinent to the "similar motive" inquiry, especially when such techniques appear far more promising compared to the cross-examination undertaken, the unused methods are only one factor to be considered.

The proper approach, therefore, in assessing similarity of motive under Rule 804(b)(1) must consider whether the party resisting the offered testimony at a pending proceeding had at a prior proceeding an interest of substantially similar intensity to prove (or disprove) the same side of a substantially similar issue. The nature of the two proceedings—both what is at stake and the applicable burden of proof—and, to a lesser extent, the cross-examination at the prior proceeding—both what was undertaken and what was available but forgone—will be relevant though not conclusive on the ultimate issue of similarity of motive.

Having identified the proper approach to the determination of whether a similar motive existed, we might ordinarily remand to the District Court to apply the governing principles to the precise facts of this case. We decline to do so, however, both to avoid further delay in this already long-delayed matter and because this is the unusual case in which it can be shown beyond reasonable dispute that the prosecutor had no interest at the grand jury in proving the falsity of the witnesses' assertion that the "Club" did not exist. Two circumstances independently suffice. First, the defendants had already been indicted, and, as appellants' counsel conceded at argument, there existed no putative defendant as to whom probable cause was in issue. At most the Government had an interest in investigating further to see *whether* there might be additional defendants or additional projects within the criminal activity of the existing defendants. As to these matters, the prosecutor had no interest in showing that the denial of the Club's existence was false. The grand jury had already been persuaded, at least by the low standard of probable cause, to believe that the Club existed and that the defendants had participated in it to commit crimes. It is fanciful to think that the prosecutor would have had any substantial interest in showing the falsity of the witnesses' denial of the Club's existence just to persuade the grand jury to add one more project to the indictment.

Second, the grand jurors had indicated to the prosecutor that they did not believe the denial. The record is clear on this point. After a consultation with the grand jury, the prosecutor told Bruno, in the grand jurors' presence, that there was "strong concern on the part of the grand jury" that his testimony had "not been truthful." A prosecutor has no interest in showing the falsity of testimony that a grand jury already disbelieves.

These two circumstances dispel similarity of motive, and the absence of similar motive is not rebutted by the limited cross-examination undertaken by the prosecutor at the grand jury. A prosecutor may have varied motives for asking a few challenging questions of a grand jury witness who the prosecutor thinks is lying. The prosecutor might want to afford the witness a chance to embellish the lie, thereby strengthening the case for a subsequent perjury prosecution. Or the prosecutor might want to provoke the witness into volunteering some critical new fact in the heat of an emphatic protestation of innocence. In this case, the cross-examination that occurred does not significantly show similarity of motive. Moreover, the strong inference of dissimilarity from the two factors already discussed is powerfully reenforced by the prosecutor's careful limitation of questioning to matters already publicly disclosed, the lack of questioning on the basis of undisclosed wiretaps and reports of cooperating witnesses, and the lack of any follow-up in response to Bruno's generous offer to correct inaccuracies in his testimony.

Since the grand jury as fact-finder had already resolved the issue of the Club's existence in the prosecutor's favor and had announced disbelief of the witnesses' contrary statements, dissimilarity of motive is beyond dispute. The District Court's exclusion of the witnesses' grand jury testimony was therefore entirely correct....

GEORGE C. PRATT, Circuit Judge, (joined by MINER and ALTIMARI, Circuit Judges), dissenting....

The in banc majority ... now concludes, as a matter of law, that the prosecutor's motive was not "similar". In doing so, it applies a gloss to the language of the rule that would find a similar motive only when the party against whom the testimony is offered had "an interest of substantially similar intensity to prove (or disprove) the same side of a substantially similar issue". As a practical matter, the gloss effectively rewrites the rule from "similar motive" to "same motive".

Not only is the majority's test more stringent than the rule itself, it could also prove to be extremely difficult to administer, for on its face this test would require the district judge to compare the "intensity of interest" that the prosecutor possessed before the grand jury with his "intensity of interest" at the trial. Careful examination of those two states of the prosecutor's mind would require a district judge to conduct an evidentiary hearing not only into what information was available to the prosecutor at the two different times, but also into what he was thinking about that information at both of those times.

The majority sidesteps the problem in this case, however, by accepting at face value the prosecutor's *post hoc*, self-serving, un-crossexamined statements as to his own motives, and concluding, as a matter of law, that his motives at the two proceedings were not "similar". At the very least, this issue of fact should be decided in the first instance by a district judge, not an in banc appellate court....

[The dissenting opinion of Judge Miner is omitted.]

Problem 7-37: The Antitrust Action

The federal government brings a civil antitrust action against Microsoft. Wanda testifies in that proceeding on Microsoft's behalf, and is subject to cross-examination by government lawyers. Subsequently, a private antitrust action is brought against Microsoft by Oracle. Microsoft offers evidence that Wanda has died, and seeks to introduce the transcript of her former testimony into evidence. Oracle raises a hearsay objection.

How should Microsoft respond, and how will the court likely rule?

Lloyd v. American Export Lines, Inc.
580 F.2d 1179 (3d Cir. 1978)

ALDISERT, Circuit Judge....

This lawsuit emanates from a violent altercation between Alvarez and a fellow crew member, electrician Frank Lloyd, that occurred on September 7, 1974, when their ship, the SS EXPORT COMMERCE, was in the port of Yokohama, Japan. Lloyd filed an action against Export in the district court, alleging negligence under the Jones Act, and unseaworthiness under general maritime law, seeking redress for the injuries sustained in the fight. Export joined Alvarez as a third-party defendant and Alvarez, in turn, counterclaimed against Export, alleging, as did Lloyd, negligence and unseaworthiness. Lloyd did not proceed in his case as plaintiff, failing to appear on seven occasions for a pretrial deposition, and failing to appear when the case was called for trial on November 18, 1976. Accordingly, his complaint was dismissed by the district court for failure to prosecute, and thereafter trial was had on Alvarez' counterclaim. The jury found that although Export had not breached its warranty of seaworthiness, it was nevertheless negligent, and its negligence contributed to Alvarez' injuries. The jury returned a verdict in favor of Alvarez against Export in the amount of $95,000.

It was Alvarez' theory that Export negligently failed to use reasonable precautions to safeguard him from Lloyd after Export had knowledge of Lloyd's dangerous propensities....

The jury was not permitted to hear any version of the fight other than that of Alvarez; it was denied the opportunity of hearing the account rendered by Lloyd, who was the other participant in the affray and its only other eyewitness. It is the refusal of the district court to admit a public record of a prior proceeding and excerpts of Lloyd's testimony therein that constitutes the major thrust of Export's appeal. Export contends that this evidence was admissible in the form of transcripts and a final report from a Coast Guard hearing conducted intermittently from January 20, 1975 through January 6, 1976, the purpose of which was to determine whether Lloyd's merchant mariner's document should have been suspended or revoked on the basis of charges of misconduct brought against him for the fight with Alvarez. At that hearing, both Lloyd and Alvarez were represented by counsel and testified under oath....

We turn now to the more difficult question: did Alvarez or a "predecessor in interest" have the "opportunity and similar motive to develop [the testimony] by direct, cross[-,] or redirect examination" as required by Rule 804(b)(1)? In rejecting the proffered evidence, the district court took a strict view of the new rule, one that we do not share.

We note at the outset that inasmuch as Congress did not define "predecessor in interest", that interpretive task is left to the courts. We find no definitive guidance in the reports accompanying language changes made as the Rules were considered, in turn, by the Supreme Court and the houses of Congress. As originally submitted by the Supreme Court, Rule 804(b)(1) would have allowed prior testimony of an unavailable witness to be received in evidence if the party against whom it was offered, or a person with "motive and interest similar", had an opportunity to examine the witness. The House of Representatives adopted the present language, the Committee on the Judiciary offering this rationale:

> Rule 804(b)(1) as submitted by the Court allowed prior testimony of an unavailable witness to be admissible if the party against whom it is offered or a person "with motive and interest similar" to his had an opportunity to examine the witness. The Committee considered that it is generally unfair to impose upon the party against whom the hearsay evidence is being offered responsibility for the manner in which the witness was previously handled by another party. The sole exception to this, in the Committee's view, is when a party's predecessor in interest in a civil action or proceeding had an opportunity and similar motive to

examine the witness. The Committee amended the Rule to reflect these policy determinations.[5]

The Senate Committee on the Judiciary viewed the import of this change as follows:

> Former testimony.—Rule 804(b)(1) as submitted by the Court allowed prior testimony of an unavailable witness to be admissible if the party against whom it is offered or a person "with motive and interest similar" to his had an opportunity to examine the witness.
>
> The House amended the rule to apply only to a party's predecessor in interest. Although the committee recognizes considerable merit to the rule submitted by the Supreme Court, a position which has been advocated by many scholars and judges, we have concluded that the difference between the two versions is not great and we accept the House amendment.

We, too, fail to see a compelling difference between the two approaches....

Although Congress did not furnish us with a definition of "predecessor in interest," our analysis of the concept of interests satisfies us that there was a sufficient community of interest shared by the Coast Guard in its hearing and Alvarez in the subsequent civil trial to satisfy Rule 804(b)(1). Roscoe Pound has taught us that interests in law are "the claims or demands or desires which human beings, either individually or in groups or associations or relations, seek to satisfy...." The interest implicated here was a claim or desire or demand which Alvarez as an individual, and the Coast Guard as a representative of a larger group, sought to satisfy, and which has been recognized as socially valid by authoritative decision-makers in our society.

Individual interests, like those of Alvarez, are involved immediately in the individual life, in the Pound formulation, and asserted in title of that life. Public interests, like those of the Coast Guard, are involved in the life of a politically organized society, here the United States, and asserted in title of that entity. Thus, Alvarez sought to vindicate his individual interest in recovering for his injuries; the Coast Guard sought to vindicate the public interest in safe and unimpeded merchant marine service. Irrespective of whether the interests be considered from the individual or public viewpoints, however, the nucleus of operative facts was the same—the conduct of Frank Lloyd and Roland Alvarez aboard the SS EXPORT COMMERCE. And although the results sought in the two proceedings differed—the Coast Guard contemplated sanctions involving Lloyd's mariner's license, while Alvarez sought private substituted redress, *i.e.*, monetary damages—the basic interest advanced by both was that of determining culpability and, if appropriate, exacting a penalty for the same condemned behavior thought to have occurred.[12] The Coast Guard investigating officer not only preferred charges against Lloyd but functioned as a prosecutor at the subsequent proceeding as well. Thus, he attempted to establish at the Coast Guard hearing what Alvarez attempted to establish at the later trial: Lloyd's intoxication, his role as the aggressor, and his prior hostility toward Alvarez. Dean Pound

---

5. We do not accept the view that this change in wording signaled a return to the common law approach to former testimony, requiring privity or a common property interest between the parties.

12. In this regard, McCormick takes the position that "insistence upon precise identity of issues, which might have some appropriateness if the question were one of res judicata or estoppel by judgment, are out of place with respect to former testimony where the question is not of binding anyone, but merely of the salvaging, for what it may be worth, of the testimony of a witness not now available in person.... It follows that neither the form of the proceeding, the theory of the case, nor the nature of the relief sought needs be the same." McCormick, Handbook of the Law of Evidence § 257 at 261 (2d ed. 1972).

50

recognized that there can be such a community of individual and public interests as this: "It must be borne in mind that often we have here different ways of looking at the same claims or same type of claims as they are asserted in different titles."

Moreover, although our precise task is to decide whether the Coast Guard investigating officer was Alvarez' predecessor in interest, it is equally important to respect always the fundamentals that underlie the hearsay rule, and the reasons for the exceptions thereto. Any fact-finding process is ultimately a search for truth and justice, and legal precepts that govern the reception of evidence must always be interpreted in light of this. Whether it be fashioned by rules of decision in cases or controversies, or promulgated by the Supreme Court with the approval of Congress, or designed and adopted by Congress, every rule of evidence is a means to an end, not an end in itself. We strive to avoid interpretations that are wooden or mechanical, like obsolete common law pleadings, and to favor those that facilitate the presentation of a complete picture to the fact-finder. With this approach in mind, we are satisfied that there existed, in the language of Rule 804(b)(1), sufficient "opportunity and similar motive [for the Coast Guard investigating officer] to develop [Lloyd's] [testimony]" at the former hearing to justify its admission against Alvarez at the later trial.

While we do not endorse an extravagant interpretation of who or what constitutes a "predecessor in interest," we prefer one that is realistically generous over one that is formalistically grudging. We believe that what has been described as "the practical and expedient view" expresses the congressional intention: "if it appears that in the former suit a party having a like motive to cross-examine about the same matters as the present party would have, was accorded an adequate opportunity for such examination, the testimony may be received against the present party." Under these circumstances, the previous party having like motive to develop the testimony about the same material facts is, in the final analysis, a predecessor in interest to the present party....

STERN, District Judge, concurring.

I join in the majority opinion, except insofar as it construes the "predecessor in interest" language of Rule 804(b)(1). The majority here holds that because the Coast Guard investigating officer shared a community of interest with Alvarez he was Alvarez's predecessor in interest. I believe that this analysis is contrary to the Rule's clear language and is foreclosed by its legislative history....

It is true that Congress nowhere defined "predecessor in interest," but it seems clear that this phrase, a term of art, was used in its narrow, substantive law sense. Although the commentators have expressed disapproval of this traditional and restrictive rule, they recognize that a "predecessor in interest" is defined in terms of a privity relationship.

> "'The term "privity" denotes mutual or successive relationships to the same rights of property, and privies are distributed into several classes, according to the manner of this relationship. Thus, there are privies in estate, as donor and donee, lessor and lessee, and joint tenants; privies in blood, as heir and ancestor, and co-parceners; privies in representation, as executor and testator, administrator and intestate; privies in law, where the law, without privity of blood or estate casts the land upon another, as by escheat.'"

Metropolitan St. Ry. v. Gumby, 99 F. 192 (2nd Cir. 1900), *quoted in* 11 Moore's Federal Practice § 804.04[2], at VIII-265. *See also* 4 J. Weinstein & M. Berger, Weinstein's Evidence, at 804–65.

The majority rejects the view that the Rule's wording signals a return to the common law approach requiring privity or a common property interest between the parties, and finds it sufficient that the Coast Guard investigator shared a community of interest with Alvarez. But community of interest seems to mean only that the investigating officer sought to establish the same facts as Alvarez attempted to prove in the instant suit. Used in this sense, community of interest means nothing more than similarity of interest or similarity of motive. But similar motive is a separate prerequisite to admissibility under 804(b)(1) and thus the majority's analysis which reads "predecessor in interest" to mean nothing more than person with "similar motive" eliminates the predecessor in interest requirement entirely.

Moreover, while I appreciate the fact that the Coast Guard investigator sought to establish Lloyd's wrongdoing and that Alvarez sought to do the same, I do not believe that this establishes the kind of "common motive" sufficient to satisfy 804(b)(1).

A prosecutor or an investigating officer represents no ordinary party. He shoulders a peculiar kind of duty, even to his very adversary, a duty which is foreign to the adversarial process among ordinary litigants. The prosecutor, it is true, must seek to vindicate the rights of the alleged victim, but his interests go far beyond that. His interest in a prosecution is not that he shall win a case, but that justice shall be done.

The interests of an attorney representing the government surely overlap with those of the private litigant, but they do not coincide. The investigating officer was under no duty to advance every arguable issue against Lloyd in the vindication of Alvarez's interests, as Alvarez's own counsel would have been. He simply did not represent Alvarez.

Thus, even if I could agree that Congress intended to relax the common law requirement of actual privity between the parties before prior testimony could be admitted, I cannot endorse a rule which would automatically render admissible against a party evidence which was elicited in a different proceeding by an unrelated person merely because both shared an interest in establishing the same facts. The majority's holding makes admissible against Alvarez the testimony of all witnesses who appeared at the Coast Guard hearing—not just Lloyd—and this without any showing of necessity by the proponent of such evidence. Indeed, under the majority view, all kinds of testimony adduced at all kinds of administrative hearings—hearings before the Civil Aeronautics Board on airplane disasters; hearings before the Federal Communications Commission on misuse of broadcast licenses; hearings before the Securities and Exchange Commission on securities fraud, just by way of example—would be admissible in subsequent civil suits, albeit that the parties were entirely different. With all due respect, I think this goes too far. The net result would be charging the party against whom the hearsay evidence is being offered with all flaws in the manner in which the witness was previously handled by another, and all flaws in another's choice of witnesses, the very result characterized by the House Judiciary Committee as "generally unfair."

....

Notes and Questions

1. There is a major distinction, so far as Rule 804(b)(1) is concerned, between offering grand jury testimony and preliminary hearing testimony against a criminal defendant. Quite apart from the question whether the defendant had a "similar motive" to develop the witness' testimony in the prior proceeding is the question whether the defendant had the *opportunity* to do so. While defendants have the ability to examine witnesses called by the government in preliminary hearings, they have no right to examine witnesses who are called before a grand jury. Accordingly, while testimony at a defen-

dant's preliminary hearing can be offered against him under Rule 804(b)(1), testimony before the grand jury that indicted him cannot. *Compare United States v. Avants*, 367 F.3d 433, 444 (5th Cir. 2004) (preliminary hearing), *with United States v. Clarke*, 2 F.3d 81, 83 (4th Cir. 1993) (grand jury).

2. Suppose that the government indicts two individuals, A and B, on charges of conspiring with one another to commit certain crimes, and that A enters a guilty plea while B enters a not guilty plea and forces his case to trial. To the extent that A is unavailable as a witness at B's trial and makes statements during his plea allocution that exculpate B, can B offer A's plea allocution into evidence under Rule 804(b)(1)? *See United States v. Jackson*, 335 F.3d 170, 176–78 (2d Cir. 2003) (holding that he cannot, reasoning that in a plea proceeding, the government lacks the opportunity to cross-examine the person entering the plea, and that the government lacks a similar motive because the only purpose of a plea allocution is to ensure that there is an adequate factual basis for the plea).

3. For criticism of the Second Circuit's approach in *DiNapoli, see United States v. McFall*, 558 F.3d 951, 962–63 (9th Cir. 2009) (holding that, by focusing on the *intensity* of the motivation, "the Second Circuit required comparison of motives at a fine-grained level of particularity" that is inconsistent with the rule's plain text, which requires only a "similar" not an "identical" motive, and preferring instead an approach endorsed by the D.C. Circuit that compares "motives at a high level of generality," under which no distinction would be made between the government's motive before the grand jury and at trial since, in both instances, the evidence would be directed at the same issue, to wit, the accused's guilt or innocence of the crime charged).

4. It is important to consider both Rule 804(b)(1) (former testimony) and Rule 801(d)(1)(A) (prior inconsistent statement) in tandem, as it is often the case that a statement that just fails to fit one will fit the other. Interestingly enough, a witness who appears on the stand and testifies to a lack of memory concerning a prior statement "is 'subject to cross-examination' under Rule 801 while at the same time 'unavailable' under Rule 804(a)(3)." *United States v. Owens*, 484 U.S. 554, 563–64 (1988). And while grand jury testimony is never admissible against a defendant under Rule 804(b)(1), it may be admissible when offered against a defendant under Rule 801(d)(1)(A), as the phrase "proceeding" in the latter rule encompasses grand jury proceedings.

5. Rule 804(b)(1) addresses the hearsay problem that arises when a person who was present when former testimony was given seeks to testify as to what he heard an unavailable declarant testify to at a former proceeding. Yet to the extent that one seeks to introduce an unavailable declarant's former testimony by offering a *transcript* of those proceedings into evidence, don't you actually have not just a hearsay problem but rather a hearsay-within-hearsay problem? Consider the following:

> Although the former testimony of a witness can ... be proven by the testimony of someone who heard it first-hand at the earlier proceeding, it is more typically the case that it will be proven by means of a *transcript* of the witness's testimony. In such an instance, one has hearsay-within-hearsay, with the inner layer being the witness's testimony in the earlier proceedings and the outer layer being the court reporter's written assertion as to what the witness said. ... The transcript asserts (in writing) that the witness (orally) asserted that he saw the accused shoot the victim. Its relevancy turns on the veracity of both the unavailable witness *and* the court reporter, for the prosecution is almost certainly offering it to prove the truth of what they collectively assert, to wit, that the accused shot the victim. ...

Few courts and commentators have taken note of the outer (transcript) layer of hearsay, but those that have addressed it have identified two hearsay exceptions that pave the way to admitting the testimony. First, if the court reporter appears at trial but cannot recall what the witness testified to, the transcript can be admitted under Federal Rule of Evidence 803(5) or its state law equivalent, the hearsay exception for a past recollection recorded. Alternatively, it can be admitted under Federal Rule of Evidence 803(8), the hearsay exception for public records. Furthermore, some jurisdictions have created specially tailored statutes to overcome the hearsay problem raised by the transcript....

Peter Nicolas, *But What if the Court Reporter is Lying? The Right to Confront Hidden Declarants Found in Transcripts of Former Testimony*, 2010 B.Y.U. L. Rev. 1149, 1158–61 (2010).

6. Assume that in Problem 7-35, Walter had instead testified on David's behalf. Under the logic of *Lloyd*, if Walter is unavailable to testify in George's subsequent suit against David, shouldn't David be able to offer Walter's testimony against George under Rule 804(b)(1) on the theory that Pam was George's "predecessor in interest"? If not, in what way is *Lloyd* distinguishable?

7. Isn't the *Lloyd* court's interpretation of "predecessor in interest" consistent with the approach of Rules 803(22) and 803(23), which permit the admission of certain prior judgments? After all, Rules 803(22) and 803(23) are permitting prior judgments to be given evidentiary effect even when they lack preclusive effect, so shouldn't Rule 804(b)(1) likewise be decoupled from preclusion doctrine?

3. Dying Declarations

Problem 7-38: The Last Breath

After receiving a 911 telephone call indicating that a gunshot was heard near the corner of Fifth and Main, officers Lisa Carr and Tom Parker drive to that location, where they discover John Allen and Marie Carlson lying on the sidewalk in a pool of blood, each with several gunshot wounds. Marie is dead, but John is still alive. John motions the officers close to him and struggles to say:

> "It ... won't ... be ... long ... before ... I ... join ... Marie ... Patrick ... Miller ... did ... this ... to ... us ... Patrick ... also ... is ... the ... one ... who ... robbed ... First ... National ... Bank ... last ... month."

Shortly thereafter, John dies. Patrick Miller is eventually indicted in federal court on charges of murdering both John and Marie, and separately indicted in federal court on charges of robbing the First National Bank. The government, over a hearsay objection, seeks to offer in both proceedings testimony by officers Carr and Parker as to what John said to them before he died.

How should the court rule on the hearsay objection? How, if at all, would the answer differ if John survived and Patrick was charged with attempted murder with respect to John? Would the evidence be admissible in a civil action for wrongful death brought by Marie and John's survivors? How, if at all, would your answers differ if the cases were instead being litigated in state courts in Connecticut, Pennsylvania, or Utah?

Shepard v. United States

290 U.S. 96 (1933)

Mr. Justice Cardozo delivered the opinion of the Court.

The petitioner, Charles A. Shepard, a major in the medical corps of the United States Army, has been convicted of the murder of his wife, Zenana Shepard, at Fort Riley, Kansas, a United States military reservation.... The crime is charged to have been committed by poisoning the victim with bichloride of mercury....

The evidence complained of was offered by the Government in rebuttal when the trial was nearly over. On May 22, 1929, there was a conversation in the absence of the defendant between Mrs. Shepard, then ill in bed, and Clara Brown, her nurse. The patient asked the nurse to go to the closet in the defendant's room and bring a bottle of whisky that would be found upon a shelf. When the bottle was produced, she said that this was the liquor she had taken just before collapsing. She asked whether enough was left to make a test for the presence of poison, insisting that the smell and taste were strange. And then she added the words "Dr. Shepard has poisoned me."

....

1. Upon the hearing in this court the Government finds its main prop in the position that what was said by Mrs. Shepard was admissible as a dying declaration. This is manifestly the theory upon which it was offered and received. The prop, however, is a broken reed. To make out a dying declaration the declarant must have spoken without hope of recovery and in the shadow of impending death. The record furnishes no proof of that indispensable condition....

We have said that the declarant was not shown to have spoken without hope of recovery and in the shadow of impending death. Her illness began on May 20. She was found in a state of collapse, delirious, in pain, the pupils of her eyes dilated, and the retina suffused with blood. The conversation with the nurse occurred two days later. At that time her mind had cleared up, and her speech was rational and orderly. There was as yet no thought by any of her physicians that she was dangerously ill, still less that her case was hopeless. To all seeming she had greatly improved, and was moving forward to recovery. There had been no diagnosis of poison as the cause of her distress. Not till about a week afterwards was there a relapse, accompanied by an infection of the mouth, renewed congestion of the eyes, and later hemorrhages of the bowels. Death followed on June 15.

Nothing in the condition of the patient on May 22 gives fair support to the conclusion that hope had then been lost. She may have thought she was going to die and have said so to her nurse, but this was consistent with hope, which could not have been put aside without more to quench it. Indeed, a fortnight later, she said to one of her physicians, though her condition was then grave, "You will get me well, won't you?" Fear or even belief that illness will end in death will not avail of itself to make a dying declaration. There must be "a settled hopeless expectation" (Willes, J. in Reg. v. Peel, 2 F. & F. 21, 22) that death is near at hand, and what is said must have been spoken in the hush of its impending presence. Despair of recovery may indeed be gathered from the circumstances if the facts support the inference. There is no unyielding ritual of words to be spoken by the dying. Despair may even be gathered though the period of survival outruns the bounds of expectation. What is decisive is the state of mind. Even so, the state of mind must be exhibited in the evidence, and not left to conjecture. The patient must have spoken with the consciousness of a swift and certain doom.

What was said by this patient was not spoken in that mood. There was no warning to her in the circumstances that her words would be repeated and accepted as those of a dying wife, charging murder to her husband, and charging it deliberately and solemnly as a fact within her knowledge. To the focus of that responsibility her mind was never brought. She spoke as one ill, giving voice to the beliefs and perhaps the conjectures of the moment. The liquor was to be tested, to see whether her beliefs were sound. She did not speak as one dying, announcing to the survivors a definitive conviction, a legacy of knowledge on which the world might act when she had gone.

The petitioner insists that the form of the declaration exhibits other defects that call for its exclusion, apart from the objection that death was not imminent and that hope was still alive. Homicide may not be imputed to a defendant on the basis of mere suspicions, though they are the suspicions of the dying. To let the declaration in, the inference must be permissible that there was knowledge or the opportunity for knowledge as to the acts that are declared. The argument is pressed upon us that knowledge and opportunity are excluded when the declaration in question is read in the setting of the circumstances. . . . The form is not decisive, though it be that of a conclusion, a statement of the result with the antecedent steps omitted. "He murdered me," does not cease to be competent as a dying declaration because in the statement of the act there is also an appraisal of the crime. One does not hold the dying to the observance of all the niceties of speech to which conformity is exacted from a witness on the stand. What is decisive is something deeper and more fundamental than any difference of form. The declaration is kept out if the setting of the occasion satisfies the judge, or in reason ought to satisfy him, that the speaker is giving expression to suspicion or conjecture, and not to known facts. The difficulty is not so much in respect of the governing principle as in its application to varying and equivocal conditions. In this case, the ruling that there was a failure to make out the imminence of death and the abandonment of hope relieves us of the duty of determining whether it is a legitimate inference that there was the opportunity for knowledge. We leave that question open. . . .

United States v. Angleton
269 F. Supp. 2d 878 (S.D. Tex. 2003)

ROSENTHAL, District Judge. . . .

[Defendant Robert Angleton is on trial for commissioning the murder of his wife, Doris Angleton. Robert Angleton seeks to offer into evidence five handwritten notes ("jail notes") that his brother, Roger Angleton, wrote in prison prior to committing suicide in which he indicated that he, not his brother, was responsible for the murders. Robert Angleton seeks to have the letters admitted pursuant to Federal Rule of Evidence 804(b)(2), which provides an exception to the hearsay rule for, "[i]n a prosecution for homicide or in a civil case, a statement that the declarant, while believing the declarant's death to be imminent, made about its cause or circumstances."]

"The dying declaration exception to the rule against admission [is] based on the belief that persons making such statements are unlikely to lie." *Idaho v. Wright*, 497 U.S. 805, 820 (1990). "The sense of impending death is presumed to remove all temptation to falsehood, and to enforce as strict an adherence to the truth as would the obligation of oath." *Id.* (quoting *Mattox v. United States*, 146 U.S. 140, 152 (1892)).

Although the dying declaration is a "firmly rooted" exception to the hearsay rule, it has long been recognized as among the less reliable forms of hearsay. In addition to the risks of distorted or misunderstood communications that impending death may present, "experience suggests that the desire for revenge or self-exoneration or to protect ones loved ones may continue until the moment of death."

Dying declarations are admissible only in homicide prosecutions and civil cases. To satisfy the dying declaration exception to the hearsay rule, the statement must be made at a time when the declarant believes death is imminent. "To make out a dying declaration, the declarant must have spoken without hope of recovery and in the shadow of impending death." *Shepard v. United States*, 290 U.S. 96, 99 (1933). "Fear or even belief that illness will end in death will not avail of itself to make a dying declaration. There must be a settled hopeless expectation that death is near at hand, and what is said must be spoken in the hush of its impending presence." *Id.* at 100. "The state of mind must be exhibited in the evidence, and not left to conjecture. The patient must have spoken with the consciousness of a swift and certain doom." *Id.* Not every statement made under such conditions is admissible. Only statements directly relating to the "cause or circumstances" of the declarant's death are admissible.

A court may look at the facts and circumstances surrounding the out-of-court statement to determine whether the declarant made the statements in the belief that death was imminent. *Webb v. Lane*, 922 F.2d 390, 395 (7th Cir. 1991). Evidence bearing on the timing issue may include "the nature and extent of the wounds ... inflicted being obviously such that [the declarant] must have felt or known he could not survive." *Id.* (quoting *Mattox*, 146 U.S. at 152). "The length of time elapsing between the making of the declaration and the death is to be considered, although ... it is the impression of almost immediate dissolution, and not the rapid succession of death, that renders the testimony admissible." *Mattox*, 146 U.S. at 151. "The evidence must be received with the utmost caution, and, if the circumstances do not satisfactorily disclose that the awful and solemn situation in which he is placed is realized by the dying man because of the hope of recovery, [the declaration] ought to be rejected." *Id.* at 152.

The statement must also directly relate to the cause or circumstances of the declarant's death in order to be admissible. FED. R. EVID. 804(b)(2); *see, e.g., Sternhagen v. Dow Co.*, 108 F. Supp. 2d 1113, 1117 (D.Mont. 1999) (individual's statement that he believed his illness was caused by chemicals produced by defendant concerned the cause or circumstances of the illness and death); *United States v. Etheridge*, 424 F.2d 951, 966–67 (6th Cir. 1970) (statement of a gunshot victim describing assailant and the reason for the shooting held to be a dying declaration); *United States v. Lemonakis*, 485 F.2d 941 (D.C. Cir. 1973) (statement in handwritten suicide note exculpating defendant accused of robberies held unrelated to cause or circumstances of death).

The government contends that Roger Angleton's jail notes do not qualify as dying declarations under Rule 804(b)(2), because there is insufficient evidence that they were written when he believed his death was "imminent" and because the notes contain a large amount of material unrelated to the cause or circumstances of his suicide. The government argues that some of the notes were written weeks before Roger Angleton committed suicide and the other, undated notes cannot be shown to have been written in the belief that death was "imminent." The notes cover many topics unrelated to the cause or circumstances of the suicide, including statements about Robert Angleton; about Roger Angleton's relationships with various people; and instructions for funeral arrangements and property disposal and distribution.

Robert Angleton responds that there is evidence to show that the notes were written or presented when Roger Angleton had the intent to commit suicide. Angleton cites the fact that the notes were found together in a plastic envelope on the floor of Roger Angleton's jail cell, protected from damage by the blood from the self-inflicted razor wounds, as evidence that Roger Angleton intended these notes to be his last statements. Robert Angleton contends that whether these statements were made in the belief that death was "imminent" does not depend on when the statements were written, but rather on the fact that Roger Angleton gathered and placed the notes for discovery with his body. Angleton argues that Roger Angleton "made" the statements contained in the notes when he placed them in preparation for suicide.

1. The Case Law as to When a Dying Declaration Must be Made

Dying declarations must be made in the belief that death is "imminent." There is little case law examining the proof necessary to show that a writing made sometime prior to suicide is a statement made in the belief that death is "imminent," so as to be admissible as a dying declaration. In *State v. Satterfield*, 193 W.Va. 503, 457 S.E.2d 440 (1995), the court admitted a suicide note under the state dying declaration rule, which mirrored the federal rule. In *Satterfield*, a witness in a murder trial was "aggressively questioned" in a way that implied his participation in the murder. After the court day ended and before proceedings began the following day, the witness committed suicide. The witness left a note proclaiming his innocence and stating that he "just [couldn't] take the pressure of going through a trial." The trial court admitted the suicide note under the dying declaration [exception] to the hearsay rule. The court found that there was evidence that the decedent wrote the suicide note believing that his death was imminent because the suicide occurred soon after the note was written and the note explained the suicide.

The dissent argued that suicide notes should not be treated as dying declarations:

> [The declarant] was in complete control of the timing and circumstances of his death. The majority fails to distinguish the difference between [a] suicide note, and a statement made by a person facing inevitable death due to circumstances beyond his control. If ever there is a time to put one's best face forward, it would be in a note that will literally stand for all eternity as one's last testament. A suicide note is the perfect opportunity to rewrite one's own history in a way calculated to impress one's final audience.

> My objection is not intended to imply [the declarant] was lying: rather, the idea that suicide notes should be viewed as admissible evidence under the dying declaration exception to the hearsay rule is misguided.

The "classic" dying declaration is made by a person near death from fatal wounds or illness, who makes a statement to a third party about who inflicted the wounds or caused the illness. The third party testifies as to the declarant's condition and the circumstances of the statement. If, as here, a suicide is unwitnessed and the declaration is contained in a writing discovered after the suicide, no one can testify as to the making of the declaration. It can be difficult to show when a statement was written or whether it was written in the belief that death was imminent. The Supreme Court's caution in *Mattox* that the circumstances surrounding the dying declaration must be satisfactorily established underscores the need for a sufficient showing that such a note was written when the declarant believed death was imminent.

The aspect of control involved in an intended death clearly diminishes the spontaneity that is a critical part of the dying declaration exception. The lack of spontaneity makes it even more essential that the statement be made in the belief of imminent and certain death. Statements made some time before a suicide have been held inadmissible hearsay and not dying declarations. The *Lemonakis* court in *dicta* stated that a suicide note dated a week before its author committed suicide was "clearly not made with the belief that death was imminent." In *Collums v. Union Planters Bank, N.A.*, 832 So.2d 572 (Miss.App. 2002), an oral statement made twelve days before the declarant committed suicide was inadmissible as a dying declaration, in part because there was no showing that the declarant then "ha[d] no hope of recovery."

2. The Case Law as to What a Dying Declaration Must Contain

Under Rule 804(b)(2), only statements directly related to the cause and circumstances of the declarant's death are admissible. The court may redact portions of a written statement containing inadmissible hearsay while admitting portions of the statement that are admissible.

In *Lemonakis*, the court in *dicta* stated that a suicide note written by a third party exonerating the defendant was inadmissible because it did not concern the causes or circumstances of the declarant's death. The case of *United States v. Layton*, 549 F. Supp. 903 (N.D.Ca. 1982) involved a tape recording by Jim Jones, founder of Jonestown in Guyana, made shortly before his followers committed mass suicide. Jones made the tape after receiving word that a party sent from Jonestown had killed a visiting congressman. Jones stated on the tape that "I don't know who killed the congressman. But as far as I'm concerned, I killed him." The court held that this statement did not concern the cause of his impending suicide and refused to admit the statement as a dying declaration.

3. The Jail Notes

. . . .

ii. The February 1, 1998 Note

One note is dated February 1, 199[8], sixteen days before Roger Angleton committed suicide. It is headed "Houston Chronicle" and contains a direct statement that Roger Angleton shot Doris Angleton "in an attempt to create an extortion situation based on fear to gain money from my brother I had felt he owed me.... Now I know that I was wrong and can't live with myself and my pain any longer. The purpose of this letter is to let the truth be known."

The statement that "I shot Doris Angleton on April 16, 1997" and "[n]ow I know I was wrong and can't live with myself and my pain any longer" relate to the cause of Roger Angleton's death. This is the only statement in this note potentially admissible as a dying declaration. By contrast, Roger Angleton's explanation of why he committed the murder of Doris Angleton—that it was part of a plot to extort money from Robert Angleton— does not speak to the reason for the suicide. It could not be admitted as a dying declaration.

The February 1, 1998 note was written weeks before Roger Angleton took his life. Defendant argues that because Roger Angleton positioned it in his cell to be discovered after his suicide, that date, rather than the date on which the note was written, is the date of the declaration. There is no authority for this proposition. Accepting as a dying declaration a note written two weeks before death and left to be discovered after death further attenuates the connection between the consciousness of imminent death and the specific words that are said or written. Neither the language of the rule, nor the case law, supports such an attenuation. No part of this note is admissible under Rule 804(b)(2).

iii. The "To Whom It May Concern" Note

One undated note is written to "To Whom it May Concern." It has a sentence of explanation for the suicide: "I killed Doris Angleton ... I realize that I was wrong to take a life of especially an innocent & good person. I am in constant emotional agony and so decided to end my life to stop the pain." This is the only statement in this note potentially admissible as a dying declaration. Much of this note deals with an explanation for the murder of Doris Angleton and statements about Robert Angleton's lack of involvement in that murder. Such statements do not directly relate to the cause or circumstances of Roger Angleton's suicide and could not be admitted under this rule.

This note begins with the words "In the event of my death" and gives instructions to call Vanessa Leggett. The words "In the event of my death" do not suggest or convey imminent death. There is no evidence to suggest that this note was written in the belief that death was swift and certain. No part of this note is admissible under Rule 804(b)(2).

iv. The Note to Vanessa Leggett

In the lengthy undated note to Vanessa Leggett, most of what Roger Angleton writes is unrelated to the cause or circumstances of his death. He discusses his relationship with Leggett. He writes several postscripts asking Leggett to inform family and friends of his death and to make funeral arrangements. The only statements relating to the reason for suicide are before the postscripts, as follows:

> I had still a lot of life in me with the best to come, but so did Doris. She was an innocent, I wasn't fighting her for my life, family, wealth etc., she wasn't any sort of adversary, so there is little if any justification to have killed her. And therefore I must be willing & able to pay in like kind if necessary & if became necessary, although I cry I have no right.

No other portion of this note addresses the cause or circumstances of Roger Angleton's death.

The eight postscripts conclude with the statement that "I just took a load of painkillers and Darvons so I past [sic] the point of no return." The handwriting throughout the note is consistent and not shaky.

The note states that "for the last 2 days, I have [recalled] my life—step by step—and I have only just scratched the surface...." The note also states that Roger Angleton kept thinking of things to write because "maybe I am trying to stall." These comments and the eight postscripts suggest strongly that this note may have been written over a period of time rather than in the moments before Roger Angleton committed suicide. The statement that Roger Angleton was "stalling" suggests a lack of belief in imminent death and that parts of the note were written well before the suicide. There is nothing to show that the statement about the suicide was written when death was believed to be imminent. These delays suggest the absence of a "settled hopeless expectation that death [was] near at hand." Even if Roger Angleton believed that his despair would lead to his death, belief that a condition will eventually end in death is not sufficient to make statements dying declarations. *Shepard*, 290 U.S. at 100. No part of this note is admissible under Rule 804(b)(2).

v. The Note to "Mark"

In the note addressed to "Mark," Roger Angleton asks Bennett to "please give attached confession to Judge." The note states:

> I killed Doris Angleton on April 16, I feel very bad, my brother is innocent, he didn't know.

The note then asks "Mark" to "give this letter to court."

The statement in this note excu[lp]ating Robert Angleton cannot qualify as a dying declaration. As in *Lemonakis* and *Layton*, Roger Angleton's statements that Robert Angleton was not involved in Doris Angleton's murder do not relate to the cause of Roger Angleton's suicide. The only statement in this note that is potentially admissible as a dying declaration is Roger Angleton's statement that "I killed Doris Angleton, I feel very bad." This statement, however, does not directly attribute Roger Angleton's suicide to guilt about Doris Angleton's murder. A statement about past events, rather than about the cause or circumstances of death, is not a dying declaration, unless those events explain the predicament that brought the declarant to death's door. *See Lemonakis*, 485 F.2d at 957 n. 24 (suicide note in which author stated that he had previously lied to prosecutors about defendant's role in a crime inadmissible under Rule 804(b)(2) in part because it did not speak to the cause or circumstances of the suicide); Mueller & Kirkpatrick, § 495 (citing *Etheridge*, 424 F.2d at 966–67 (admitting dying declaration by victim naming assailant and saying that he was shot for knowing too much about bank robbery)).

The undated note to "Mark" states that Roger Angleton had taken painkillers to ease the pain of the razors he would use to inflict fatal wounds on himself and that this was affecting his handwriting. The handwriting in that note becomes shakier in the final paragraph. There is no indication in the record as to when Roger Angleton took painkillers or when he inflicted the wounds that caused his death. Although this is the closest case, there is an inadequate basis to conclude that when Roger Angleton wrote the relevant part of the note to "Mark," he believed his death was imminent. The fact that the handwriting in the much longer note to Vanessa Leggett appears the same throughout strongly suggests that Roger Angleton wrote that note before taking any painkillers or inflicting any wounds.

These doubts undermine the inherent "indicia of reliability" that a dying declaration is normally presumed to have as a firmly rooted exception to the hearsay rule. "[T]he evidence must be received with the utmost caution, and if the circumstances do not satisfactorily disclose that the awful and solemn situation in which he is placed is realized by the dying man because of the hope of recovery, it ought to be rejected." *Mattox*, 146 U.S. at 152.

Satterfield is distinguishable from the facts of this case. The *Satterfield* court stated with confidence that the decedent killed himself soon after writing his suicide note. The statements in the suicide note in *Satterfield* responded to accusations made against the decedent less than twenty-four hours before the decedent's suicide. This court cannot confidently say, based on the facts presented, that Roger Angleton committed suicide soon after writing the relevant parts[ ]of the undated notes. There are no events like the cross-examination the day before the suicide in *Satterfield* that would lead to the conclusion that Roger Angleton wrote the jail notes very shortly before suicide. The state of mind of the declarant "must be exhibited in the evidence, and not left to conjecture." *Shepard*, 290 U.S. at 100. This court's need to resort to conjecture to determine whether any part of the notes are dying declarations leads this court to find them inadmissible under Rule [8]04(b)(2).

A declarant need not expressly state that he or she believes that death is imminent. The court may infer the declarant's sense of impending death from "the nature and extent of the wounds inflicted." *United States v. Peppers*, 302 F.3d 120, 137 (3d Cir. 2002) (*citing Mattox*, 146 U.S. at 152). "It is clearly not only permissible, but indeed necessary ... that the trial judge draw and rely on inferences from the facts of the record, including the types of wounds inflicted and the nature of the decedent's injuries." In most dying declaration cases, the dying declaration is made after the wounds have been inflicted, so that a court may infer that a decedent believed death was imminent even if the decedent does not state that fact. *See, e.g., Mattox*, 146 U.S. 140. In this case, the record does not show when Roger Angleton wrote the notes in relation to when he inflicted the wounds on himself. It is evident that some of the jail notes were written weeks before the suicide and most of the notes do not directly concern the cause or circumstances of the suicide. The jail notes do not qualify as dying declarations under Rule 804(b)(2)....

Connecticut Code of Evidence § 8-6

Hearsay Exceptions: Declarant Must Be Unavailable

The following are not excluded by the hearsay rule if the declarant is unavailable as a witness:

....

(2) Dying declaration. In a prosecution in which the death of the declarant is the subject of the charge, a statement made by the declarant, while the declarant was conscious of his or her impending death, concerning the cause of or the circumstances surrounding the death.

....

COMMENTARY

.... Section 8-6 (2) recognizes Connecticut's common-law dying declaration hearsay exception. The exception is limited to criminal prosecutions for homicide. Furthermore, by demanding that "the death of the declarant [be] the subject of the charge," Section 8-6 (2) retains the requirement that the declarant be the victim of the homicide that serves as the basis for the prosecution in which the statement is offered....

Pennsylvania Rule of Evidence 804

Hearsay Exceptions; Declarant Unavailable

....

(b) Hearsay Exceptions. The following statements, as hereinafter defined, are not excluded by the hearsay rule if the declarant is unavailable as a witness:

....

(2) *Statement under belief of impending death.* A statement made by a declarant while believing that the declarant's death was imminent, concerning the cause or circumstances of what the declarant believed to be impending death.

Comment: Pa.R.E. 804(b)(2) is similar to F.R.E. 804(b)(2), except that the Pennsylvania rule applies in all cases, not just in homicide cases and civil actions....

The common law traditionally, but illogically, excepted a dying declaration from the hearsay rule in a criminal prosecution for homicide, but not in a criminal prosecution for another crime, or in a civil case. Prior Pennsylvania case law followed the common law.

Reasoned analysis dictated a change. If a dying declaration is trustworthy enough to be introduced against a defendant charged with murder, it is trustworthy enough to be introduced against a defendant charged with attempted murder, robbery, or rape. It is also trustworthy enough to be introduced against a party in a civil case.

....

Utah Rule of Evidence 804

Hearsay Exceptions; Declarant Unavailable

....

(b) Hearsay exceptions. The following are not excluded by the hearsay rule if the declarant is unavailable as a witness:

....

(b)(2) *Statement under belief of impending death.* In a civil or criminal action or proceeding, a statement made by a declarant while believing that the declarant's death was imminent, if the judge finds it was made in good faith.

....

Notes and Questions

1. There are two historical rationales for the trustworthiness of dying declarations, one religious and the other secular. The religious rationale is that a person who believes himself to be on the verge of death will not lie for fear of supernatural punishment for meeting his maker with a lie upon his lips. The secular or psychological rationale is a belief that people lose all motivation to lie when death is near. *See* Advisory Committee Note to Rule 804(b)(2); 5 Wigmore, Evidence §§ 1438, 1443, at 289, 302 (Chadbourn rev. 1974). How persuasive are either of these rationales? The exception has also historically been justified on the ground of necessity: unavailability is a prerequisite for invoking the exception, and at least in homicide cases, the need for the evidence is usually great, as homicide is often a secret crime and other evidence to prove the crime is often scarce (although the absence of other evidence has never been a prerequisite for invoking the exception). *See* 5 Wigmore, Evidence § 1435, at 284.

2. At common law, the exception to the hearsay rule for dying declarations could be invoked only if the declarant was unavailable because he was dead. 5 Wigmore, Evidence § 1431, at 276–77. But Rule 804(b)(2) requires only that the declarant be "unavailable" as defined in Rule 804(a), coupled with a statement made by the declarant "while *believing* the declarant's death to be imminent." Fed. R. Evid. 804(b)(2) (emphasis added); *see also* Advisory Committee Note to Rule 804(b)(2) ("Unavailability is not limited to death"). Do you see why a requirement of death is not required to assure the trustworthiness of the statement?

3. Why is the exception limited to homicide cases and civil cases? Originally at common law, no such distinction was drawn, but in the 1800s, courts began to limit the exception to homicide cases on the theory that the need for such evidence was most significant in such cases. *See* 5 Wigmore, Evidence § 1431, at 277–78; Advisory Committee Note to Rule 804(b)(2). The Advisory Committee's original proposal would have extended it to all cases, reasoning that "the theory of admissibility applies equally in civil cases and in prosecutions for crimes other than homicide." Advisory Committee Note to Rule 804(b)(2). However, the House Committee added the limiting language, explaining:

> The Committee did not consider dying declarations as among the most reliable forms of hearsay. Consequently, it amended the provision to limit their admissibility in criminal cases to homicide prosecutions, where exceptional need for the evidence is present. This is existing law. At the same time, the Committee approved the expansion to civil actions and proceedings where the stakes do not

involve possible imprisonment, although noting that this could lead to forum shopping in some instances.

Report of House Committee on the Judiciary, House Report No. 93-650.

4. At common law, the exception applied only in homicide cases in which the subject of the indictment was the declarant's death. Under the common law, then, if A and B were shot at the same time, B's declaration was not admissible in a prosecution for A's murder. *See* 5 Wigmore, Evidence § 1433, at 281–82. Does Federal Rule 804(b)(2) incorporate this common law limitation?

5. How does one demonstrate the declarant's belief that death was imminent? In addition to the methods indicated in the cases excerpted above, this can be demonstrated from the individual's own statements, circumstantial evidence, or the opinion of physicians or others around him. *E.g., Vazquez v. National Car Rental System, Inc.*, 24 F. Supp. 2d 197, 201 (D.P.R. 1998).

6. What of the argument in *Angleton* that the notes could qualify as dying declarations because the statements contained therein were "made" when the notes were placed next to him before he committed suicide? Consider the following:

> It follows, on the one hand, that a *subsequent change* of this expectation of death, by the recurrence of a hope of life, does not render inadmissible a prior declaration made while the consciousness prevailed, although a repetition of the declaration during the subsequent inadequate state of mind would not be admissible; and on the other hand, that a declaration made during an inadequate state of mind may become admissible by a subsequent affirmance of it made when the realization of impending death had supervened.

5 Wigmore, Evidence § 1439, at 292.

7. For an overview of the history of the dying declaration exception, as well as a comparison of the various ways in which current state versions of the exception differ from Federal Rule 804(b)(2), *see* Peter Nicolas, *"I'm Dying to Tell You What Happened": The Admissibility of Testimonial Dying Declarations Post-*Crawford, 37 Hastings Const. L.Q. 487 (2010).

8. The dying declaration has a long history, not just in law but also in literature:

> O but they say the tongues of dying men
> Enforce attention like deep harmony;
> Where words are scarce, they are seldom spent in vain,
> For they breathe truth that breathe their words in pain.

William Shakespeare, *Richard II*, act 2, scene 1.

4. Statements against Interest

Rule 804(b)(3) creates an exception to the hearsay rule for:

A statement that:

(A) a reasonable person in the declarant's position would have made only if the person believed it to be true because, when made, it was so contrary to the declarant's proprietary or pecuniary interest or had so great a tendency to invalidate the declarant's claim against someone else or to expose the declarant to civil or criminal liability; and

(B) is supported by corroborating circumstances that clearly indicate its trustworthiness, if it is offered in a criminal case as one that tends to expose the declarant to criminal liability.

Such statements are viewed as reliable based on a general assumption regarding human nature:

> The circumstantial guaranty of reliability for declarations against interest is the assumption that persons do not make statements which are damaging to themselves unless satisfied for good reason that they are true.

Advisory Committee Note to Rule 804(b)(3).

Of course, to the extent that the statements are made by an individual who is a party to the action, those statements are already admissible against him under Rule 801(d)(2)(A). Rule 804(b)(3)'s utility, then, is in circumstances in which the declarant is *not* a party to the action or when a party is trying to get his *own* statement admitted into evidence.

At common law, only those statements that were against the declarant's pecuniary or proprietary interests were admissible as an exception to the hearsay rule. *See* Advisory Committee Note to Rule 804(b)(3); 5 Wigmore, Evidence § 1476, at 349–350 (Chadbourn rev. 1974). Thus, statements against penal interest, in other words, those, such as confessing to a crime, that tended to subject the declarant to criminal liability, were not admissible. Finding the common law rule to be "indefensible in logic," Advisory Committee Note to Rule 804(b)(3), the Advisory Committee recommended, and Congress ultimately accepted, an expanded version of the common law exception to include statements against penal interest. The Advisory Committee's proposal sought to expand the exception to its "full logical limit" by also including a provision that would have allowed for the admission of statements that tended to expose the declarant to "hatred, ridicule, or disgrace," but Congress decided to delete that provision.

The materials that follow explore the application of Rule 804(b)(3) in a variety of contexts. As it turns out, perhaps the most significant difficulties in applying the exception have resulted from its expansion to include statements against penal interest.

Problem 7-39: The Injured Passenger

Pam is riding as a passenger in a car driven by Anna. Dave's car collides with Anna's car, causing personal injuries to all three of them. Pam sues Dave for damages, claiming that Dave ran the red light. Dave defends, asserting that it was Anna who ran the red light.

At trial, Dave calls Anna to the stand, but she refuses to testify, even after the judge holds her in contempt of court. Dave then seeks to call Wilma, a close friend of Anna's, who would testify that two weeks after the accident, Anna told her that the accident with Dave was all her fault because she (Anna) "ran the red light." Pam raises a hearsay objection.

How should Dave respond, and how will the court likely rule?

Problem 7-40: Herpes

Sally brings a tort action against Roger, claiming that she contracted herpes from him, and that he negligently failed to inform her that he was infected with herpes when they had sexual relations.

Roger defends, contending that Sally probably contracted herpes from David, with whom she had a sexual relationship prior to meeting Roger. David is "unavailable" within the meaning of FRE 804(a), and thus is unable to testify at the trial. Roger seeks to call Wendy as a witness, who would testify that at the time Sally and David's relationship was ongoing, David said to her:

"I've got herpes, but it doesn't bother me. They have drugs for it now."

Sally raises a hearsay objection.

How should Roger respond, and how will the court likely rule?

Heddings v. Steele
496 A.2d 1166 (Pa. Super. 1985)

WICKERSHAM, Judge:

John and Edith Steele appeal from the orders of the Court of Common Pleas of Lycoming County denying them primary custody of their grandchildren, Heidi and Jason Gatz, presently ages ten and five, respectively....

Having decided the procedural issues, we now move to the main substantive issue in these appeals: whether the trial court erred in admitting, and basing certain of its factual findings upon, hearsay evidence that appellant John Steele had conducted an incestuous relationship with his daughter Janet Steele Gatz, when Janet was between the ages of 8 and 16. Appellants argue that the evidence of incest, which consisted of the presentation of seven witnesses who testified as to statements allegedly made to them by Janet in her lifetime, was hearsay not falling within any exception to the hearsay rule and, as such, was improperly admitted and considered. On the other hand, the Gatzes argue that the testimony, while hearsay, was properly admitted as a statement against interest....

Whether a statement of a decedent is admissible when it is not against the declarant's pecuniary, proprietary, or penal interest, but rather is against the declarant's social interest, is a question of first impression in this court. There appear to be no decisions of this court or of our supreme court holding that declarations against societal interest are either admissible or inadmissible. Therefore, no precedent inhibits our adopting, as part of our common law of evidence, the views urged upon us by either appellants or appellees and the lower court.

The law of this Commonwealth has historically been that declarations against pecuniary or proprietary interest are admissible as an exception to the hearsay rule. While our courts have rarely expounded on the nature of the "interest" required to make the exception operable, our state has followed the historical tendency nationwide to define "interest" as pecuniary or proprietary.

Recently, however, many courts and/or legislatures have recognized that statements made against interests which are not pecuniary or proprietary in nature can be uttered under reliable circumstances that indicate trustworthiness.... [O]ur courts now recognize that declarations made against penal interests are also admissible as an exception to the hearsay rule....

Appellees urge us to find that a declarant's assertion made against his or her social interest likewise merits exception to the hearsay rule. Appellees are not the first persons to espouse this social interest exception. As expressed in the Model Code of Evidence and in the Uniform Rules of Evidence, a statement which was at the time of its making so far contrary to the declarant's interest that it would tend "to make him an object of hatred, ridicule, or disgrace, that a reasonable man in his position would not have made the statement unless he believed it to be true," would not be excluded by the hearsay rule.

Following in the pattern of the Uniform Rule, Federal Rule of Evidence No. 804(b), as promulgated by the Supreme Court, included statements tending to make the declarant "an object of hatred, ridicule, or disgrace." This provision was deleted from the rule, however, when enacted by Congress.

Despite the absence of a societal interest exception in the federal rules, some states have expanded their common law "declarations against interest" exception to include an assertion against a declarant's social interest; moreover, several states have modernized their codified rules of evidence to admit declarations against social interest.[1]

While the federal courts and the majority of state courts that have considered the issue refused to recognize an assertion against a declarant's social interest as an exception to the hearsay rule, upon careful consideration we find appellees' arguments to be persuasive. A declarant's assertion made against his or her social interests may merit exception to the hearsay rule, depending, of course, upon the individual circumstances of each case. For example, "a person is not likely to assert that he is afflicted with genital herpes unless it is true. Such assertion is exceptionally trustworthy and merits exception to the hearsay rule." D. Binder, *Hearsay Handbook*, § 29.05 (2d ed. 1983). Similarly, a statement made to a third party by an unmarried woman who later underwent an abortion that she was pregnant was admitted as a declaration against her social interests, because the "declaration was against the interests of the deceased. It tended to show a state of facts inconsistent with her observance of the rules of chastity. No beneficial purpose of the deceased could be served by the declaration." *State v. Alcorn*, 7 Idaho 599, 609 (1901).

Examining (and later rejecting) reasons supporting a social interest exception to the hearsay rule, the *Dovico* court stated:

> [D]eclarations of facts which would *tend to* make the declarant an object of hatred, ridicule, or social disapproval, should on reason be admissible as against the social interest of the declarant * * *. This is particularly so if the notion of untrustworthiness provides the major rationale for the exclusion of hearsay:
>
> > * * * a person will not concede even to himself the existence of a fact which will cause him substantial harm unless he believes that the fact does exist. *If this theory is plausible* there seems no valid reason for not extending the exception to include statements against penal interest and those which would subject the declarant to hatred, ridicule, contempt or *social ostracism.*

Human nature being what it is, people are not likely to concede the existence of facts which would make them objects of social disapproval in their community unless the facts are true. The realization of such a consequence is generally a much more powerful influence upon conduct than the realization of legal responsibility for a sum of money, which has long been accepted as a declaration against interest. As one commentator has stated:

---

1. *See, e.g.*, Arkansas Uniform Rules of Evidence 804(b)(3); California Evidence Code § 1230; Kansas Code of Civil Procedure § 60-460(j); Maine Rules of Evidence 804(b)(3); Montana Rules of Evidence 804(b)(3); Nevada Revised Statutes § 51.345; New Jersey Evidence Rule [803(c)(25)]; North Dakota Rules of Evidence 804(b)(3); Texas Rules of Evidence [8]03(24); Wisconsin Statutes Annotated § 908.045(4).

[T]he restriction to material interests, ignoring as it does other motives just as influential upon the minds and hearts of men, should be more widely relaxed. Declarations against social interests, such as acknowledgements of facts which would subject the declarant to ridicule or disgrace, or facts calculated to arouse in the declarant a sense of shame or remorse, seem adequately buttressed in trustworthiness and should be received under the present principle.

McCormick on Evidence, § 278 (2d ed. 1972).

In summary, the reason for admitting declarations against interests of any type is that people do not make statements that are disadvantageous to themselves without substantial reason to believe that the statements are true. The question is this: Would a reasonable person in declarant's position have made the assertion against interest unless he or she believed it to be true? If not, we see no logical reason, assuming that it is relevant, to forbid its use as an exception to the hearsay rule, whether the personal interest that is imperiled is classified as pecuniary, proprietary, penal, or social. In other words, we find a declaration against interest to be an out-of-court statement that was made by a non-party who has since died or has become unavailable as a witness; that concerned facts of which declarant had personal knowledge; that involved an interest (whether pecuniary, proprietary, penal, or social) of declarant that was so palpable that it would naturally have been present in the declarant's mind; and finally, that was against such interest....

In the case at bar, Janet Steele Gatz made various statements concerning numerous incidents of incest and sexual abuse by her father, one of the appellants herein. She also related to numerous witnesses that this conduct resulted in an unwanted pregnancy, which was ultimately terminated by abortion. Upon close examination, we have no doubt that these statements were made against Janet's social interest. The incidents Janet described to the various witnesses were surrounded by such shame, embarrassment, and disgrace that there could have been no self-serving purpose of the statements when made....

The decedent was 18 years old or older when she described these events to her friends. Thus, she presumably had knowledge of the adverse societal impact that could result upon her revelation of such experiences to other individuals....

[The concurring opinion of Judge Cavanaugh is omitted.]

Notes and Questions

1. There are a number of ways in which the exception for statements of an opposing party and that for statements against interest differ from one another. First, the former applies only if the declarant is the party against whom the statement is offered (or associated with the party under Rules 801(d)(2)(B)–(E)), while the latter applies without regard to the relationship of the declarant to a party. Second, the former applies without regard to whether the declarant is available, while the latter applies only if there is a showing of unavailability. Third, the latter applies only if the statement is found to be against the declarant's interest, while the former imposes no such requirement. Finally, the former applies without regard to whether the declarant has personal knowledge of the matter, while the latter applies only if the declarant is speaking from personal knowledge.

2. The decision in *Heddings* with respect to expanding the statement against interest exception to the hearsay rule was eventually overturned by the Pennsylvania Supreme Court, which explained its decision to do so as follows:

Its use would require a trial judge to first determine the habits, customs and mores of the community within which the declarant lives. An utterance made by a member of a motorcycle gang while in the company of his peers does not tend to make the declarant an object of hatred, ridicule or disgrace in his community whereas the identical statement proffered by a member of this Court may subject him to social disapproval among his brethren. This difficulty does not arise when the statement against pecuniary/proprietary interest and the statement against penal interest are employed. The statement "it was not your fault" by a tort victim is *a fortiori* against his pecuniary interest. To determine what is against one's penal interest, a trial judge need only consult the Crimes Code, which defines criminal conduct.

Heddings v. Steele, 526 A.2d 349, 353 (Pa. 1987).

3. Although statements against social interest do not fall within the scope of Federal Rule 804(b)(3), what if disclosure of the fact contained in the statement might cause the declarant to lose his job or to lose business? Wouldn't that then be a statement against pecuniary interest? *See United States v. Hsia*, 87 F. Supp. 2d 10, 14 (D.D.C. 2000) ("A statement is admissible under Rule 804(b)(3) as being against pecuniary or proprietary interest 'when it threatens the loss of employment, or reduces the chances for future employment.'").

4. Is the test under Rule 804(b)(3) a subjective or an objective one? In other words, is the question whether this *particular* declarant, when making the statement, was aware of its against-interest nature, or only whether a *typical* person would be aware of a statement's against-interest nature? Wouldn't a subjective test be more consistent with the trustworthiness rationale that underlies Rule 804(b)(3)? *But see United States v. Turner*, 475 F. Supp. 194, 198 (E.D. Mich. 1978) (relying on the rule's reference to a "reasonable person" to conclude that the test under Rule 804(b)(3) is an objective one). *See also United States v. Mitchell*, 175 Fed. Appx. 524, 527 (3d Cir. 2006) ("[T]he Rule 804(b)(3) standard is objective so that [the declarant's] lack of knowledge that his possession of ammunition was illegal is not controlling.").

5. Is a statement assuming responsibility for a criminal act against a declarant's penal interest if he cannot be prosecuted for it? *See Hanan v. United States*, 402 F. Supp. 2d 679, 686 (E.D. Va. 2005) (holding that a statement does not qualify as one against penal interest if the statute of limitations has expired, if double jeopardy bars prosecuting him for the offense, or if he lives beyond the jurisdiction of this country's legal system). In this regard, consider the court's discussion of the defendant's alternative argument in *United States v. Angleton*, 269 F. Supp. 2d 878 (S.D. Tex. 2003), that his brother's "jail notes" were admissible as statements against interest:

In arguing that the jail notes qualify as dying declarations, defendant contends that the notes were written just before Roger Angleton's suicide. If that was true, then the statements would not, as a practical matter, subject Roger Angleton to criminal liability. Defendant's argument that the jail notes were written in the belief of imminent death is inconsistent with the argument that the notes are against penal interest.

Id. at 890. *See also United States v. Crowder*, 848 F. Supp. 780, 781–82 (M.D. Tenn. 1994) (statement inadmissible under 804(b)(3) when spoken by a declarant terminally ill with cancer).

6. The theory behind the hearsay exception for statements against interest is that they are reliable because "persons do not make statements which are damaging to themselves

unless satisfied for good reason that they are true." Advisory Committee's Note to Rule 804(b)(3). Given that rationale, why condition admissibility on the unavailability of the declarant? In this regard, consider Texas Rule of Evidence 803(24), which provides as follows:

> The following are not excluded by the hearsay rule, even though the declarant is available as a witness:
>
> ....
>
> **(24) Statement Against Interest.** A statement which was at the time of its making so far contrary to the declarant's pecuniary or proprietary interest, or so far tended to subject the declarant to civil or criminal liability, or to render invalid a claim by the declarant against another, or to make the declarant an object of hatred, ridicule, or disgrace, that a reasonable person in declarant's position would not have made the statement unless believing it to be true. In criminal cases, a statement tending to expose the declarant to criminal liability is not admissible unless corroborating circumstances clearly indicate the trustworthiness of the statement.

What other differences are there between Federal Rule 804(b)(3) and its Texas counterpart?

7. Can an argument be made that in Problem 7-40, Sally might be able to invoke Rule 412?

Problem 7-41: "I Killed That S.O.B."

Donna is on trial on charges of murdering Victor. Donna seeks to call Wallace as a witness. If permitted, he would testify that on a recent trip to Mexico, about two weeks after Donna's arrest, one Richard said to him in a very calm voice, "It's funny that they arrested that Donna woman; I'm the one who killed that s.o.b. Victor, and I did it all by myself." The government raises a hearsay objection.

How should Donna respond? How should the court ultimately rule? Of what relevance would it be to the determination if Richard was Donna's father? If Richard was currently serving a life sentence for another crime?

Williamson v. United States
512 U.S. 594 (1994)

Justice O'CONNOR delivered the opinion of the Court, except as to Part II-C.

In this case we clarify the scope of the hearsay exception for statements against penal interest. Fed.Rule Evid. 804(b)(3).

I

A deputy sheriff stopped the rental car driven by Reginald Harris for weaving on the highway. Harris consented to a search of the car, which revealed 19 kilograms of cocaine in two suitcases in the trunk. Harris was promptly arrested.

Shortly after Harris' arrest, Special Agent Donald Walton of the Drug Enforcement Administration (DEA) interviewed him by telephone. During that conversation, Harris said that he got the cocaine from an unidentified Cuban in Fort Lauderdale; that the cocaine belonged to petitioner Williamson; and that it was to be delivered that night to a particular dumpster. Williamson was also connected to Harris by physical evidence....

Several hours later, Agent Walton spoke to Harris in person. During that interview, Harris said he had rented the car a few days earlier and had driven it to Fort Lauderdale to meet Williamson. According to Harris, he had gotten the cocaine from a Cuban who was Williamson's acquaintance, and the Cuban had put the cocaine in the car with a note telling Harris how to deliver the drugs. Harris repeated that he had been instructed to leave the drugs in a certain dumpster, to return to his car, and to leave without waiting for anyone to pick up the drugs.

Agent Walton then took steps to arrange a controlled delivery of the cocaine. But as Walton was preparing to leave the interview room.... Harris told Walton he had lied about the Cuban, the note, and the dumpster. The real story, Harris said, was that he was transporting the cocaine to Atlanta for Williamson, and that Williamson was traveling in front of him in another rental car. Harris added that after his car was stopped, Williamson turned around and drove past the location of the stop, where he could see Harris' car with its trunk open. Because Williamson had apparently seen the police searching the car, Harris explained that it would be impossible to make a controlled delivery.

Harris told Walton that he had lied about the source of the drugs because he was afraid of Williamson. Though Harris freely implicated himself, he did not want his story to be recorded, and he refused to sign a written version of the statement. Walton testified that he had promised to report any cooperation by Harris to the Assistant United States Attorney. Walton said Harris was not promised any reward or other benefit for cooperating.

Williamson was eventually convicted of possessing cocaine with intent to distribute, conspiring to possess cocaine with intent to distribute, and traveling interstate to promote the distribution of cocaine. When called to testify at Williamson's trial, Harris refused, even though the prosecution gave him use immunity and the court ordered him to testify and eventually held him in contempt. The District Court then ruled that, under Rule 804(b)(3), Agent Walton could relate what Harris had said to him....

Williamson appealed his conviction, claiming that the admission of Harris' statements violated Rule 804(b)(3) and the Confrontation Clause of the Sixth Amendment. The Court of Appeals for the Eleventh Circuit affirmed without opinion, and we granted certiorari.

II

A

....

To decide whether Harris' confession is made admissible by Rule 804(b)(3), we must first determine what the Rule means by "statement".... One possible meaning, "a report or narrative," Webster's Third New International Dictionary 2229, defn. 2(a) (1961), connotes an extended declaration. Under this reading, Harris' entire confession—even if it contains both self-inculpatory and non-self-inculpatory parts—would be admissible so long as in the aggregate the confession sufficiently inculpates him. Another meaning of "statement," "a single declaration or remark," *ibid.*, defn. 2(b), would make Rule 804(b)(3) cover only those declarations or remarks within the confession that are individually self-inculpatory.

Although the text of the Rule does not directly resolve the matter, the principle behind the Rule, so far as it is discernible from the text, points clearly to the narrower reading. Rule 804(b)(3) is founded on the commonsense notion that reasonable people, even reasonable people who are not especially honest, tend not to make self-inculpatory statements unless they believe them to be true. This notion simply does not extend to the broader definition of "statement." The fact that a person is making a broadly self-inculpatory confession does not make more credible the confession's non-self-inculpatory parts. One of the most effective ways to lie is to mix falsehood with truth, especially truth that seems particularly persuasive because of its self-inculpatory nature.

In this respect, it is telling that the non-self-inculpatory things Harris said in his first statement actually proved to be false, as Harris himself admitted during the second interrogation. And when part of the confession is actually self-exculpatory, the generalization on which Rule 804(b)(3) is founded becomes even less applicable. Self-exculpatory statements are exactly the ones which people are most likely to make even when they are false; and mere proximity to other, self-inculpatory, statements does not increase the plausibility of the self-exculpatory statements.

We therefore cannot agree with Justice KENNEDY's suggestion that the Rule can be read as expressing a policy that collateral statements—even ones that are not in any way against the declarant's interest—are admissible. Nothing in the text of Rule 804(b)(3) or the general theory of the hearsay Rules suggests that admissibility should turn on whether a statement is collateral to a self-inculpatory statement. The fact that a statement is self-inculpatory does make it more reliable; but the fact that a statement is collateral to a self-inculpatory statement says nothing at all about the collateral statement's reliability. We see no reason why collateral statements, even ones that are neutral as to interest, should be treated any differently from other hearsay statements that are generally excluded.

Congress certainly could, subject to the constraints of the Confrontation Clause, make statements admissible based on their proximity to self-inculpatory statements. But we will not lightly assume that the ambiguous language means anything so inconsistent with the Rule's underlying theory. In our view, the most faithful reading of Rule 804(b)(3) is that it does not allow admission of non-self-inculpatory statements, even if they are made within a broader narrative that is generally self-inculpatory. The district court may not just assume for purposes of Rule 804(b)(3) that a statement is self-inculpatory because it is part of a fuller confession, and this is especially true when the statement implicates someone else. "[T]he arrest statements of a codefendant have traditionally been viewed with special suspicion. Due to his strong motivation to implicate the defendant and to exonerate himself, a codefendant's statements about what the defendant said or did are less credible than ordinary hearsay evidence." *Lee v. Illinois*, 476 U.S. 530, 541 (1986).

Justice KENNEDY suggests that the Advisory Committee's Notes to Rule 804(b)(3) should be read as endorsing the position we reject—that an entire narrative, including non-self-inculpatory parts (but excluding the clearly self-serving parts), may be admissible if it is in the aggregate self-inculpatory....

Without deciding exactly how much weight to give the Notes in this particular situation, we conclude that the policy expressed in the Rule's text points clearly enough in one direction that it outweighs whatever force the Notes may have. And though Justice KENNEDY believes that the text can fairly be read as expressing a policy of admitting collateral statements, for the reasons given above we disagree.

B

We also do not share Justice KENNEDY's fears that our reading of the Rule "eviscerate[s] the against penal interest exception," or makes it lack "meaningful effect." There are many circumstances in which Rule 804(b)(3) does allow the admission of statements that inculpate a criminal defendant. Even the confessions of arrested accomplices may be admissible if they are truly self-inculpatory, rather than merely attempts to shift blame or curry favor.

For instance, a declarant's squarely self-inculpatory confession — "yes, I killed X" — will likely be admissible under Rule 804(b)(3) against accomplices of his who are being tried under a co-conspirator liability theory. See *Pinkerton* v. *United States*, 328 U.S. 640, 647 (1946). Likewise, by showing that the declarant knew something, a self-inculpatory statement can in some situations help the jury infer that his confederates knew it as well. And when seen with other evidence, an accomplice's self-inculpatory statement can inculpate the defendant directly: "I was robbing the bank on Friday morning," coupled with someone's testimony that the declarant and the defendant drove off together Friday morning, is evidence that the defendant also participated in the robbery.

Moreover, whether a statement is self-inculpatory or not can only be determined by viewing it in context. Even statements that are on their face neutral may actually be against the declarant's interest. "I hid the gun in Joe's apartment" may not be a confession of a crime; but if it is likely to help the police find the murder weapon, then it is certainly self-inculpatory. "Sam and I went to Joe's house" might be against the declarant's interest if a reasonable person in the declarant's shoes would realize that being linked to Joe and Sam would implicate the declarant in Joe and Sam's conspiracy. And other statements that give the police significant details about the crime may also, depending on the situation, be against the declarant's interest. The question under Rule 804(b)(3) is always whether the statement was sufficiently against the declarant's penal interest [that a reasonable person in the declarant's position would have made the statement only if the person believed it to be true,] and this question can only be answered in light of all the surrounding circumstances.*

C

In this case, however, we cannot conclude that all that Harris said was properly admitted. Some of Harris' confession would clearly have been admissible under Rule 804(b)(3); for instance, when he said he knew there was cocaine in the suitcase, he essentially forfeited his only possible defense to a charge of cocaine possession, lack of knowledge. But other parts of his confession, especially the parts that implicated Williamson, did little to subject Harris himself to criminal liability. A reasonable person in Harris' position might even think that implicating someone else would decrease his practical exposure to criminal liability, at least so far as sentencing goes. Small fish in a big conspiracy often get shorter sentences than people who are running the whole show, especially if the small fish are willing to help the authorities catch the big ones.

Nothing in the record shows that the District Court or the Court of Appeals inquired whether each of the statements in Harris' confession was truly self-inculpatory. As we explained above, this can be a fact-intensive inquiry, which would require careful exami-

---

* Of course, an accomplice's statements may also be admissible under other provisions of Rules 801–804. For instance, statements made in furtherance of the conspiracy may be admissible under Rule 801(d)(2)(E), and other statements that bear circumstantial guarantees of trustworthiness may be admissible under ... the catchall hearsay exception.

nation of all the circumstances surrounding the criminal activity involved; we therefore remand to the Court of Appeals to conduct this inquiry in the first instance.

In light of this disposition, we need not address Williamson's claim that the statements were also made inadmissible by the Confrontation Clause....

Justice SCALIA, concurring.

I join the Court's opinion, which I do not understand to require the simplistic view of statements against penal interest that Justice KENNEDY attributes to it....

Employing the narrower definition of "statement," so that Rule 804(b)(3) allows admission of only those remarks that are individually self-inculpatory, does not, as JUSTICE KENNEDY states, "eviscerate the against penal interest exception." A statement obviously can be self-inculpatory (in the sense of having so much of a tendency to subject one to criminal liability that a reasonable person would not make it without believing it to be true) without consisting of the confession "I committed X element of crime Y." Consider, for example, a declarant who stated: "On Friday morning, I went into a gunshop and (lawfully) bought a particular type of handgun and particular type of ammunition. I then drove in my 1958 blue Edsel and parked in front of the First City Bank with the keys in the ignition and the driver's door ajar. I then went inside, robbed the bank, and shot the security guard." Although the declarant has not confessed to any element of a crime in the first two sentences, those statements in context are obviously against his penal interest, and I have no doubt that a trial judge could properly admit them.

Moreover, a declarant's statement is not magically transformed from a statement against penal interest into one that is inadmissible merely because the declarant names another person or implicates a possible codefendant. For example, if a lieutenant in an organized crime operation described the inner workings of an extortion and protection racket, naming some of the other actors and thereby inculpating himself on racketeering and/or conspiracy charges, I have no doubt that some of those remarks could be admitted as statements against penal interest. Of course, naming another person, if done, for example, in a context where the declarant is minimizing culpability or criminal exposure, can bear on whether the statement meets the Rule 804(b)(3) standard. The relevant inquiry, however—and one that is not furthered by clouding the waters with manufactured categories such as "collateral neutral" and "collateral self-serving,"—must always be whether the particular remark at issue (and *not* the extended narrative) meets the standard set forth in the Rule.

Justice KENNEDY, with whom THE CHIEF JUSTICE and Justice THOMAS join, concurring in the judgment....

The rationale of the hearsay exception for statements against interest is that people seldom "make statements which are damaging to themselves unless satisfied for good reason that they are true." Advisory Committee's Notes on Fed.Rule Evid. 804. Of course, the declarant may make his statement against interest (such as "I shot the bank teller") together with collateral but related declarations (such as "John Doe drove the getaway car"). The admissibility of those collateral statements under Rule 804(b)(3) is the issue we must decide here.

There has been a long-running debate among commentators over the admissibility of collateral statements. Dean Wigmore took the strongest position in favor of admissibility, arguing that "the statement may be accepted, not merely as to the specific fact against interest, but also as to every fact contained in the same statement." 5 J. Wigmore, Evidence § 1465, p. 271 (3d ed. 1940). According to Wigmore, because "the statement is made under circumstances fairly indicating the declarant's sincerity and accuracy," the entire statement should be admitted. 5 J. Wigmore § 1465, p. 271 (3d ed. 1940). Dean McCormick's approach regarding collateral statements was more guarded. He argued for the admissibility of collateral statements of a neutral character, and for the exclusion of collateral statements of a self-serving character. For example, in the statement "John and I robbed the bank," the words "John and" are neutral (save for the possibility of conspiracy charges). On the other hand, the statement "John, not I, shot the bank teller" is to some extent self-serving and therefore might be inadmissible. See C. McCormick, Law of Evidence § 256, pp. 552–553 (1954) (hereinafter McCormick). Professor Jefferson took the narrowest approach, arguing that the reliability of a statement against interest stems only from the disserving fact stated and so should be confined "to the proof of the fact which is against interest." Jefferson, Declarations Against Interest: An Exception to the Hearsay Rule, 58 Harv. L. Rev. 1, 62–63 (1944). Under the Jefferson approach, neither collateral neutral nor collateral self-serving statements would be admissible....

The Court resolves the issue, as I understand its opinion, by adopting the extreme position that no collateral statements are admissible under Rule 804(b)(3)....

II

Because the text of Rule 804(b)(3) expresses no position regarding the admissibility of collateral statements, we must determine whether there are other authoritative guides on the question. In my view, three sources demonstrate that Rule 804(b)(3) allows the admission of some collateral statements: the Advisory Committee's Note, the common law of the hearsay exception for statements against interest, and the general presumption that Congress does not enact statutes that have almost no effect.

First, the Advisory Committee's Note establishes that some collateral statements are admissible. In fact, it refers in specific terms to the issue we here confront: "Ordinarily the third-party confession is thought of in terms of exculpating the accused, but this is by no means always or necessarily the case: it may include statements implicating him, and under the general theory of declarations against interest they would be admissible as related statements." This language seems a forthright statement that collateral statements are admissible under Rule 804(b)(3), but the Court reasons that "the policy expressed in the Rule's text points clearly enough in one direction that it outweighs whatever force the Notes may have." Again, however, that reasoning begs the question: What is the policy expressed in the text on the admissibility of collateral statements? As stated above, the text of the Rule does not answer the question whether collateral statements are admissible. When as here the text of a Rule of Evidence does not answer a question that must be answered in order to apply the Rule, and when the Advisory Committee's Note does answer the question, our practice indicates that we should pay attention to the Advisory Committee's Note....

Second ... [a]bsent contrary indications, we can presume that Congress intended the principles and terms used in the Federal Rules of Evidence to be applied as they were at common law. Application of that interpretive principle indicates that collateral statements should be admissible. "From the very beginning of this exception, it has been held that a declaration against interest is admissible, not only to prove the disserving fact stated, but also to prove other facts contained in collateral statements connected with the disserving statement." Jefferson, 58 Harv. L. Rev., at 57; see also McCormick § 256; 5 J. Wigmore, Evidence § 1465 (3d ed. 1940)....

There is yet a third reason weighing against the Court's interpretation, one specific to statements against penal interest that inculpate the accused. There is no dispute that the text of Rule 804(b)(3) contemplates the admission of those particular statements. Absent a textual direction to the contrary, therefore, we should assume that Congress intended the penal interest exception for inculpatory statements to have some meaningful effect. That counsels against adopting a rule excluding collateral statements. As commentators have recognized, "the exclusion of collateral statements would cause the exclusion of almost all inculpatory statements."

....

To be sure, under the approach adopted by the Court, there are some situations where the Rule would still apply. For example, if the declarant said that he stole certain goods, the statement could be admitted in a prosecution of the accused for receipt of stolen goods in order to show that the goods were stolen. See 4 J. Weinstein & M. Berger, Weinstein's Evidence § 804(b)(3)[04], p. 804-164 (1993). But as the commentators have recognized, it is likely to be the rare case where the precise self-inculpatory words of the declarant, without more, also inculpate the defendant. I would not presume that Congress intended the penal interest exception to the Rule to have so little effect with respect to statements that inculpate the accused.

I note finally that the Court's decision applies to statements against penal interest that exculpate the accused as well as to those that inculpate the accused. Thus, if the declarant said, "I robbed the store alone," only the portion of the statement in which the declarant said "I robbed the store" could be introduced by a criminal defendant on trial for the robbery. That seems extraordinary. The Court gives no justification for such a rule and no explanation that Congress intended the exception for exculpatory statements to have this limited effect....

[The concurring opinion of Justice Ginsburg is omitted.]

Notes and Questions

1. Lurking behind the decision in *Williamson* is a concern that statements by a third party that implicate the accused may raise problems under the Confrontation Clause. Because *Williamson* involved a question of statutory interpretation, it was not binding on states, which were free after *Williamson* to interpret their versions of Rule 804(b)(3) more broadly. The last section of this chapter examines the Confrontation Clause question reserved in *Williamson*.

2. In *Williamson*, the statements at issue were made when the declarant was in police custody. Does the setting in which a statement is made have an impact on its admissibility under Rule 804(b)(3)? If so, why? *See, e.g., United States v. Moses*, 148 F.3d 277, 280–81 (3d Cir. 1998) (holding that the context in which a statement is made sheds light on whether or not it is self-inculpatory, and that while making a reference to a third person's involvement in a crime may be an effort to shift blame when made in a custodial setting, and thus not self-inculpatory, it is more likely to be viewed as self-inculpatory when made in a non-custodial setting, such as to friends and acquaintances); *accord United States v. Barone*, 114 F.3d 1284, 1295–96 (1st Cir. 1997).

3. What is the rationale for Rule 804(b)(3)(B), which requires that the statement be "supported by corroborating circumstances that clearly indicate its trustworthiness, if it is offered in a criminal case as one that tends to expose the declarant to criminal liability"? *See* Advisory Committee Note to Rule 804(b)(3) ("one senses in the decisions a distrust of evidence of confessions by third persons offered to exculpate the accused arising from suspicions of fabrication either of the fact of the making of the confession or in its

contents"); *United States v. Silverstein*, 732 F.2d 1338, 1346 (7th Cir. 1984) ("such statements are suspect because of a long-standing concern — whether or not well-founded — that a criminal defendant might get a pal to confess to the crime the defendant was accused of, the pal figuring that the probability of his actually being prosecuted either for the crime or for perjury was slight"). Although originally, such corroboration was only required when such statements were offered to *exculpate* the accused, the rule was amended in 2010 to impose the requirement on all such statements in criminal cases.

4. What factors do courts take into account in determining the trustworthiness of a statement offered under Rule 804(b)(3)? The following is a representative list of the factors considered:

> Although the precise nature of the corroboration required by Rule 804(b)(3) cannot be fully described, the courts have identified several factors which are relevant to determining whether sufficient corroboration exists to justify admitting a statement under the rule, including (1) whether the declarant had at the time of making the statement pled guilty or was still exposed to prosecution for making the statement, (2) the declarant's motive in making the statement and whether there was a reason for the declarant to lie, (3) whether the declarant repeated the statement and did so consistently, (4) the party or parties to whom the statement was made, (5) the relationship of the declarant with the accused, and (6) the nature and strength of independent evidence relevant to the conduct in question.

United States v. Bumpass, 60 F.3d 1099, 1102 (4th Cir. 1995).

5. In applying the trustworthiness proviso in Rule 804(b)(3)(B), is the court to assess the trustworthiness of the declarant or the witness who is testifying to what the declarant allegedly said, or both? *See* Advisory Committee Note to 2010 Amendment to Rule 804(b)(3) ("In assessing whether corroborating circumstances exist, some courts have focused on the credibility of the witness who relates the hearsay statement in court. But the credibility of the witness who relates the statement is not a proper factor for the court to consider in assessing corroborating circumstances. To base admission or exclusion of a hearsay statement on the witness's credibility would usurp the jury's role of determining the credibility of testifying witnesses.")

6. What do you make of Justice Kennedy's claim in *Williamson* that, under the majority's interpretation of Rule 804(b)(3), if the statement "I robbed the store alone," made by a third party, is offered to exculpate the excused, the word "alone" cannot be admitted because it is not inculpatory? In *United States v. Paguio*, 114 F.3d 928 (9th Cir. 1997), the defendant sought to offer into evidence the absent declarant's statement taking full responsibility for the crime, including the part in which he said that the defendant had "nothing to do with it." The prosecution invoked *Williamson*, but the court responded as follows:

> *Williamson* does not mean that the trial judge must always parse the statement and let in only the inculpatory part. It means that the statement must be examined in context, to see whether as a matter of common sense the portion at issue was against interest and would not have been made by a reasonable person unless he believed it to be true. Sometimes that requires exclusion of part of the statement, sometimes not. A reasonable man caught with a trunk full of cocaine, like the unavailable declarant in *Williamson*, might well imagine that he could advance his own penal interest by fingering someone else. But Paguio Sr.'s statement that "my son had nothing to do with it" was not an attempt to "shift blame or curry favor." *Williamson*, 512 U.S. at 603.

Paguio Sr.'s statement is like Justice Kennedy's hypothetical in his *Williamson* concurrence, where the unavailable declarant said "I robbed the store alone," and a defendant charged with the robbery is only allowed to put in "I robbed the store," and not "alone." *Id.* at 617. Wigmore, citing Holmes, characterized as "barbarous" exclusion of an unavailable declarant's confession, because exclusion increases the risk of convicting the innocent. When the prosecution attempts to take advantage of the rule, as in *Williamson*, the statement is typically in the form, "I did it, but X is guiltier than I am." As a matter of common sense, that is less likely to be true of X than "I did it alone, not with X." That is because the part of the statement touching on X's participation is an attempt to avoid responsibility or curry favor in the former, but to accept undiluted responsibility in the latter.

Id. at 934.

7. Although *Williamson* involved a statement against penal interest, its rationale has been extended to statements against pecuniary interest as well. *Silverstein v. Chase*, 260 F.3d 142, 146–148 (2d Cir. 2001).

5. Forfeiture by Misconduct

Problem 7-42: The Grand Jury Witness

Daniel is on trial in federal court on charges of murdering Valerie. Before the grand jury that indicted Daniel, Wanda testified that she saw Daniel shoot Valerie. Between Daniel's indictment and his trial, Wanda is found dead in her apartment with a gunshot wound to the head. The prosecution has some evidence suggesting that Daniel hired someone to kill Wanda, although not enough to prove it beyond a reasonable doubt. The prosecution seeks to offer into evidence the transcript, created by a stenographer employed by the federal government, of Wanda's testimony before the grand jury, but Daniel's attorney objects on hearsay grounds.

How should the prosecution respond, and how will the court likely rule?

United States v. Cherry
217 F.3d 811 (10th Cir. 2000)

LUCERO, Circuit Judge.

This interlocutory appeal from the district court's grant of a motion to suppress out-of-court statements made by a murdered witness requires us to address the difficult question of how the doctrine of waiver by misconduct and Fed.R.Evid. 804(b)(6) apply to defendants who did not themselves directly procure the unavailability of a witness, but allegedly participated in a conspiracy, one of the members of which murdered the witness....

I

The government charged five defendants with involvement in a drug conspiracy: Joshua Price ("Joshua"), Michelle Cherry, LaDonna Gibbs, Teresa Price ("Price"), and Sonya

Parker. Much of the evidence in their case came from a cooperating witness, Ebon Sekou Lurks. Prior to trial, however, Lurks was murdered. The government moved to admit out-of-court statements by Lurks, pursuant to Fed.R.Evid. 804(b)(6), on the grounds that the defendants wrongfully procured Lurks's unavailability.

In support of their motion, the government offered the following evidence. Lurks's ex-wife told Joshua of Lurks's cooperation with the government in retaliation for his obtaining custody of the Lurks' children. After this, Lurks reported being followed by Joshua and by Price. Approximately one week later, Price arranged to borrow a car from a friend, Beatrice Deffebaugh, explaining that she wanted to go on a date with another man without attracting her steady boyfriend's notice by using her usual car. So that Deffebaugh could pick up her children after work, Price loaned her another car, one that Deffebaugh described to an investigating agent as belonging to Gibbs. Joshua picked up Deffebaugh's car, which a witness noticed near Lurks' home at around 10 p.m on January 28, 1998. One of Joshua's girlfriends, Kenesha Colbert, testified to receiving a call from him around 10:40 p.m. and hearing Price's voice singing in the background.

Around 11 p.m., several shots were fired in the vicinity of Lurks's home. Two witnesses saw a tall, thin black man (a description consistent with Joshua Price's appearance) chasing a short, stout black man (a description consistent with Lurks's appearance). Another witness stated she saw a car in the vicinity of Lurks's home, resembling the one borrowed by Joshua and Price, immediately after hearing shots fired. Additionally, one witness reported a license plate for the vehicle identical to that of the vehicle borrowed from Deffebaugh, save for the inversion of two digits. Police found Lurks's body not long after midnight. Price returned the borrowed car to her friend between midnight and 12:30 a.m on January 29, 1998. Further investigation discovered physical evidence linking Joshua to the murder: "debris" on Joshua's tennis shoes matching Lurks's DNA.

The district court held that Joshua procured the absence of Lurks and hence Lurks's statements were admissible against him.[1] It held, however, that there was insufficient evidence that Price procured Lurks's absence and "absolutely no evidence [that Cherry, Gibbs, and Parker] had actual knowledge of, agreed to or participated in the murder of ... Lurks." The district court therefore refused to find that those defendants had waived their Confrontation Clause and hearsay objections to the admission of Lurks's statements.

II

....

A. Rule 804(b)(6) and the Waiver by Misconduct Doctrine

The Confrontation Clause of the Sixth Amendment protects a criminal defendant's "fundamental right" to confront the witnesses against him or her, including the right to cross-examine such witnesses....

The Supreme Court has held repeatedly that a defendant's intentional misconduct can constitute waiver of Confrontation Clause rights....

The recently-promulgated Rule 804(b)(6) of the Federal Rules of Evidence represents the codification, in the context of the federal hearsay rules, of this long-standing doctrine of waiver by misconduct....

Rule 804(b)(6) provides that the rule excluding hearsay does not apply to the following:

---

1. Subsequent to this ruling, the district court severed Joshua's case from the cases of Price, Cherry, Gibbs, and Parker.

> **Forfeiture by wrongdoing.** A statement offered against a party that has engaged
> or acquiesced in wrongdoing that was intended to, and did, procure the un-
> availability of the declarant as a witness.

Fed.R.Evid. 804(b)(6).* Although prior to Rule 804(b)(6), there was disagreement as to
the proper burden of proof in making a showing of waiver by misconduct, it was established in this Circuit that, "before permitting the admission of grand jury testimony of
witnesses who will not appear at trial because of the defendant's alleged coercion, the
judge must hold an evidentiary hearing in the absence of the jury and find by a preponderance of the evidence that the defendant's coercion made the witness unavailable." *Balano*, 618 F.2d at 629. The district court was correct in applying the same burden—
preponderance of the evidence—and procedure in a case under the similar terms of Rule
804(b)(6). *See* Fed.R.Evid. 804(b)(6) advisory committee's note ("The usual Rule 104(a)
preponderance of the evidence standard has been adopted in light of the behavior new
Rule 804(b)(6) seeks to discourage.").

At issue in the instant case is whether Rule 804(b)(6) and the Confrontation Clause permit a finding of waiver based not on direct procurement but rather on involvement in a
conspiracy, one of the members of which wrongfully procured a witness' unavailability.
The government argues that under the principle of conspiratorial liability articulated in
Pinkerton v. United States, 328 U.S. 640 (1946), defendants-appellees are responsible for
the murder of Lurks as a foreseeable result of the drug conspiracy in which they were allegedly involved, and they thereby waive their Confrontation Clause and hearsay objections to his out-of-court statements....

Turning to the language of Rule 804(b)(6), the use of the words "engaged or acquiesced
in wrongdoing"** lends support to the government's assertion that, at least for purposes
of the hearsay rules, waiver can be imputed under an agency theory of responsibility to
a defendant who "acquiesced" in the wrongful procurement of a witness' unavailability but
did not actually "engage[ ]" in wrongdoing apart from the conspiracy itself. Fed.R.Evid.
804(b)(6). The proper scope of such imputed waiver as applied to a criminal defendant
is best defined in the context of the Confrontation Clause doctrine of waiver by misconduct. While the Confrontation Clause and the hearsay rules are not coextensive, *see California v. Green*, 399 U.S. 149, 155–56 (1970), it is beyond doubt that evidentiary rules
cannot abrogate constitutional rights. We therefore read the plain language of Rule
804(b)(6) to permit the admission of those hearsay statements that would be admissible
under the constitutional doctrine of waiver by misconduct, and hold that, in the context
of criminal proceedings, the Rule permits the admission of hearsay statements by unavailable witnesses against defendants if those statements are otherwise admissible under
the doctrine of waiver by misconduct. Our analysis of whether and under what circumstances waiver can be imputed under that doctrine and the acquiescence prong of the
Rule is guided by two important but sometimes conflicting principles: the right to confrontation is "a fundamental right essential to a fair trial in a criminal prosecution," *Pointer*,
380 U.S. at 404; and "courts will not suffer a party to profit by his own wrongdoing,"
Houlihan, 92 F.3d at 1279; *see also Balano*, 618 F.2d at 629.

---

  * Editor's Note: Rule 804(b)(6) was restyled in 2011 to read as follows:
    Statement Offered Against a Party That Wrongfully Caused the Declarant's Unavailability.
    A statement offered against a party that wrongfully caused—or acquiesced in wrongfully
    causing—the declarant's unavailability as a witness, and did so intending that result.
  ** Editor's Note: When the rule was restyled in 2011, this phrase was replace with the phrase
"wrongfully caused—or acquiesced in wrongfully causing."

b. Pinkerton Conspiratorial Liability

The government urges us to adopt the principles of conspiratorial liability enunciated in *Pinkerton v. United States*, 328 U.S. 640 (1946), in the context of Rule 804(b)(6) and the Confrontation Clause waiver-by-misconduct doctrine. The *Pinkerton* Court held that evidence of direct participation in a substantive offense is not necessary for criminal liability under the principles holding conspirators liable for the substantive crimes of the conspiracy....

[W]e have described *Pinkerton* liability as follows:

> During the existence of a conspiracy, each member of the conspiracy is legally responsible for the crimes of fellow conspirators. Of course, a conspirator is only responsible for the crimes of the conspirators that are committed in furtherance of the conspiracy. As stated by the Supreme Court, conspirators are responsible for crimes committed "within the scope of the unlawful project" and thus "reasonably foreseen as a necessary or natural consequence of the unlawful agreement."

United States v. Russell, 963 F.2d 1320, 1322 (10th Cir. 1992) (quoting *Pinkerton*, 328 U.S. at 646–648)....

Pinkerton's formulation of conspiratorial liability is an appropriate mechanism for assessing whether the actions of another can be imputed to a defendant for purposes of determining whether that defendant has waived confrontation and hearsay objections. It would make little sense to limit forfeiture of a defendant's trial rights to a narrower set of facts than would be sufficient to sustain a conviction and corresponding loss of liberty. Therefore, we conclude that the acquiescence prong of Fed.R.Evid. 804(b)(6), consistent with the Confrontation Clause, permits consideration of a *Pinkerton* theory of conspiratorial responsibility in determining wrongful procurement of witness unavailability, and we turn to waiver-by-misconduct case law to define the precise contours of such responsibility.

C. Conspiratorial Responsibility and "Acquiescence" Under Rule 804(b)(6)

. . . .

By analogy to *Pinkerton*, mere participation in a conspiracy does not suffice—yet participation may suffice when combined with findings that the wrongful act at issue was in furtherance and within the scope of an ongoing conspiracy and reasonably foreseeable as a natural or necessary consequence thereof.

Failure to consider *Pinkerton* conspiratorial responsibility affords too much weight to Confrontation Clause values in balancing those values against the importance of preventing witness tampering. By recognizing the applicability of agency concepts and permitting admission of the testimony of an unavailable witness against a co-conspirator involved in, but not necessarily immediately responsible for, procuring that witness' unavailability, a *Pinkerton* theory strikes a better balance between the conflicting principles at stake. This is particularly so considering the potential windfall to defendants and the fundamental principle that "courts will not suffer a party to profit by his own wrongdoing." *Houlihan*, 92 F.3d at 1279. We therefore hold that a co-conspirator may be deemed to have "acquiesced in" the wrongful procurement of a witness' unavailability for purposes of Rule 804(b)(6) and the waiver by misconduct doctrine when the government can satisfy the requirements of *Pinkerton*, 328 U.S. at 647–48.

We are mindful of the district court's solicitude for confrontation rights, and its hesitancy to embrace a novel application of *Pinkerton* liability, as well as the relative paucity of case law in this area. We therefore will attempt to articulate as clearly as possible the proper inquiry, so as to provide guidance to the district court on remand and to future courts faced with similar circumstances. Based on our balancing of the aims of the Confrontation Clause with the grave evil the well-established waiver-by-misconduct rule aims to prevent, we hold that the following interpretation of the "acquiescence" prong of Rule 804(b)(6) is consistent with the Confrontation Clause:

A defendant may be deemed to have waived his or her Confrontation Clause rights (and, a fortiori, hearsay objections) if a preponderance of the evidence establishes one of the following circumstances: (1) he or she participated directly in planning or procuring the declarant's unavailability through wrongdoing; or (2) the wrongful procurement was in furtherance, within the scope, and reasonably foreseeable as a necessary or natural consequence of an ongoing conspiracy.

D. Application of Rule 804(b)(6)

We therefore examine the district court's order in light of our newly-elucidated standard. We conclude the district court did not abuse its discretion in holding that the government failed to show by a preponderance of the evidence that any of the defendants directly participated in the execution of the murder, but remand for application of the planning and *Pinkerton* tests. We take this opportunity to note that, even if the district court finds the standard for waiver by acquiescence to be met for some or all appellees, and thereby their Confrontation Clause and hearsay objections to be forfeited, the district court is still free to consider concerns of weighing prejudice against probative value under Fed.R.Evid. 403.

1. Scope of Conspiracy, Furtherance, and Reasonable Foreseeability as a Necessary and Natural Consequence

... [T]he district court concluded that "the mere fact [that defendants] may have participated in the drug conspiracy did not constitute a waiver of [their] constitutional confrontation rights." This statement is correct, as far as it goes. However, today we hold that participation in an ongoing drug conspiracy *may* constitute a waiver of constitutional confrontation rights if the following additional circumstances are present: the wrongdoing leading to the unavailability of the witness was in furtherance of and within the scope of the drug conspiracy, and such wrongdoing was reasonably foreseeable as a "necessary or natural" consequence of the conspiracy. We therefore remand to the district court for findings on the *Pinkerton* factors as to Lurks's murder: whether it was in furtherance and within the scope of the conspiracy, and whether it was reasonably foreseeable as a necessary or natural consequence of that conspiracy. We note that the scope of the conspiracy is not necessarily limited to a primary goal — such as bank robbery — but can also include secondary goals relevant to the evasion of apprehension and prosecution for that goal — such as escape, or, by analogy, obstruction of justice. We further reiterate that, under *Pinkerton*, a defendant is not responsible for the acts of co-conspirators if that defendant meets the burden of proving he or she took affirmative steps to withdraw from the conspiracy before those acts were committed.

We note that the district court found "there is absolutely no evidence" that defendants Cherry, Gibbs, and Parker (although not Teresa Price) "had actual knowledge of, agreed to or participated in the murder of Ebon Sekou Lurks." After complete review of the record, we conclude that this finding of fact is not clearly erroneous. It does not, however, foreclose the possibility of waiver under a *Pinkerton* theory. Actual knowledge is not required for conspiratorial waiver by misconduct if the elements of *Pinkerton* — scope, furtherance, and reasonable foreseeability as a necessary or natural consequence — are satisfied. A defendant's actual knowledge of a co-conspirator's intent to murder a witness in order to prevent discovery or prosecution of the conspiracy may prove relevant to those elements.

2. Planning

Although the district court found the evidence was "insufficient to show that by a preponderance of the evidence the Defendant Teresa Price procured the absence of Ebon Sekou Lurks," it did not discuss whether the evidence that she obtained the car used in Lurks's murder under false pretenses, combined with her apparent proximity to Joshua around the time of the murder, would be sufficient circumstantial evidence to support a finding that she participated in the planning of the murder. We therefore remand for specific findings on whether the government can meet its burden of showing that Price participated in the planning of Lurks's murder so as to permit a finding of waiver by misconduct....

[The opinion of Judge Holloway, dissenting in part, is omitted.]

People v. Geraci
85 N.Y.2d 359 (N.Y. 1995)

TITONE, Judge.

Defendant was convicted of first degree manslaughter and two counts of first degree assault, primarily on the basis of an eyewitness's Grand Jury testimony, which was admitted over vigorous defense objection. Although the witness had initially come forward and accused defendant, the witness subsequently left the State and refused to give trial testimony consistent with his earlier story. The issue on this appeal is whether there was sufficient evidence establishing that the witness had been intimidated by defendant to warrant the use of that witness's Grand Jury testimony as part of the People's direct case....

As a general rule, the Grand Jury testimony of an unavailable witness is inadmissible as evidence-in-chief. However, the lower courts of this State, as well as the Federal courts, have adopted an exception to this rule where it has been shown that the defendant procured the witness's unavailability through violence, threats or chicanery. In such situations, the courts have held, the defendant may not assert either the constitutional right of confrontation or the evidentiary rules against the admission of hearsay in order to prevent the admission of the witness's out-of-court declarations....

Like all of the other courts that have adopted and applied the rule, we conclude that out-of-court statements, including Grand Jury testimony, may be admitted as direct evidence where the witness is unavailable to testify at trial and the proof establishes that the witness's unavailability was procured by misconduct on the part of the defendant.

The more difficult question is what standard of proof should be required to establish a foundation for the admission of hearsay evidence under this rule. The Second and Sixth Circuits apply the relatively undemanding "preponderance of the evidence" standard. In contrast, the Fifth Circuit and the lower courts of this State have used the "clear and convincing evidence" standard. We conclude that the latter, more exacting standard, which is the one most protective of the truth-seeking process, should be adopted in this State.

Because human fact finders lack the quality of omniscience, the process of determining the truth in adjudicative proceedings necessarily involves some margin of error. The size of the margin of error that the law is willing to tolerate varies in inverse proportion to the importance to the party or to society of the issue to be resolved. On one end of the spectrum are most civil disputes, where, from a societal standpoint, "a mistaken judgment for the plaintiff is no worse than a mistaken judgment for the defendant". On the other end are criminal determinations of guilt or innocence, "[w]here one party has at stake an interest of transcendent value". The rules governing how persuasive the proof must be "[represent] an attempt to instruct the factfinder concerning the degree of confidence our society thinks ... should [be had] in the correctness of factual conclusions for a particular type of adjudication". Viewing the issue in light of this fundamental principle, we deem the "clear and convincing evidence" standard to be the test that best recognizes the gravity of the interest at stake and most effectively balances the need to reduce the risk of error against the practical difficulties of proving witness tampering.

A determination that the defendant has procured a witness's unavailability results in the admission of hearsay statements and the forfeiture of the right to cross-examine about the substance of those statements. Obviously, a defendant's loss of the valued Sixth Amendment confrontation right constitutes a substantial deprivation. Additionally, and even more significantly, society has a weighty investment in the outcome, "[b]ecause of the intimate association between the right to confrontation and the accuracy of the fact-finding process".

In this regard, it is significant that, unlike most exceptions to the rule against hearsay, the exception at issue here is justified not by the inherent reliability of the evidence, but rather by the public policy of reducing the incentive to tamper with witnesses. Indeed, hearsay evidence such as the Grand Jury testimony at issue here is especially troubling because "although given under oath, [it] is not subjected to the vigorous truth testing of cross-examination". Furthermore, Grand Jury testimony is often obtained through grants of immunity, leading questions and reduced attention to the rules of evidence—conditions which tend to impair its reliability.

These factors militate in favor of a standard of proof that is high enough to assure a great degree of accuracy in the determination of whether the defendant was, in fact, involved in procuring the witness's unavailability for live testimony. While we recognize the need for the use of this less trustworthy class of evidence when necessitated by the defendant's misconduct, we also believe that such use should be authorized only to the extent that the misconduct is clearly and convincingly shown....

Notes and Questions

1. Although Rule 804(b)(6) most clearly applies in the situation in which someone kills a witness to make them unavailable, it also applies in many other situations in which less violent forms of silencing a witness are involved. *See* Advisory Committee Note to Rule 804(b)(6) ("The wrongdoing need not consist of a criminal act."); *United States v. Scott*, 284 F.3d 758, 763–764 (7th Cir. 2002) ("The [advisory committee] notes make clear that the rule applies to all parties, including the government. Although, in the ugliest criminal cases, murder and physical assaults are all too possible on the defendant's side, it seems unlikely that the rule was needed to curtail government murder of potential witnesses. Rather, it contemplates application against the use of coercion, undue influence, or pressure to silence testimony and impede the truth-finding function of trials. We think that applying pressure on a potential witness not to testify, including by threats of harm and suggestions of future retribution, is wrongdoing.")

2. Like the Tenth Circuit in *Cherry*, the Seventh Circuit has also applied principles of *Pinkerton* liability to Rule 804(b)(6), reasoning that it is just one more potential adverse consequence of joining a conspiracy:

[A] defendant who joins a conspiracy risks many things—*e.g.* the admission of his coconspirator's statements at trial under Federal Rule of Evidence 801(d)(2)(E), the potential conviction for substantive offenses committed in furtherance of the conspiracy, and the inclusion of his coconspirator's acts in the computation of his relevant conduct at sentencing. We see no reason why imputed waiver should not be one of these risks, particularly when the waiver results from misconduct designed to benefit the conspiracy's members.

United States v. Thompson, 286 F.3d 950, 965 (7th Cir. 2002).

3. It is clear enough that under Rule 804(b)(6), hearsay statements made by a witness who is killed before he is able to testify can be offered against the party responsible for the witness' death in the proceeding in which the witness would have testified in had he not been killed. But can the exception be invoked to admit the witness' statements in a subsequent prosecution for murder of the witness? Consider the following:

By its plain terms, Rule 804(b)(6) refers to the intent of a party to procure the unavailability of the *witness*, and does not, as [the defendant] contends, limit the subject matter of the witness' testimony to past events or offenses the witness would have testified about had he been available. This interpretation is supported by the underlying purpose of the waiver-by-misconduct doctrine—"that a defendant may not benefit from his or her wrongful prevention of future testimony from a witness or potential witness." ... Further, we have declined to read in such a limitation in our pre-Rule 804(b)(6) decisions ... permitting statements made by the declarant to be admitted where the murder of the declarant was one of the charged offenses. Because Rule 804(b)(6) was intended to codify the waiver-by-misconduct rule as it was applied by the courts at that time, it is reasonable to conclude that Rule 804(b)(6) did not intend to create a subject matter limitation where one did not previously exist.

In sum, based on the plain language of Rule 804(b)(6) and the strong policy reasons favoring application of the waiver-by-misconduct doctrine to prevent a party from profiting from his wrongdoing, we hold that Rule 804(b)(6) places no limitation on the subject matter of the declarant's statements that can be offered against the defendant at trial to prove that the defendant murdered the declarant.

United States v. Dhinsa, 243 F.3d 635, 652–53 (2d Cir. 2001); *accord United States v. Emery*, 186 F.3d 921 (8th Cir. 1999). *But see United States v. Lentz*, 58 Fed. Appx. 961 (4th Cir. 2003) (Traxler, J., concurring) ("I interpret the Rule 804(b)(6) exception as being generally limited to the introduction of hearsay statements in the proceeding at which the deceased was expected by the assailant to testify."); *United States v. Mikos*, 2004 WL 1631675, at *5 (N.D. Ill. July 16, 2004) ("Allowing otherwise inadmissible evidence to prove a defendant's guilt in a capital case based upon a judge's pretrial conclusion that the defendant is in fact guilty of that very crime appears to us to be a slippery slope.... The relaxation of the rules of evidence based upon the Court's pretrial determination of the defendant's probable guilt carries with it the very real possibility of someday substantially eroding the defendant's right to be presumed innocent.... This issue is not necessarily encountered when the wrongful conduct which the defendant is accused of in connection with the witness' unavailability is not also the very crime for which he will be tried.").

4. Could an argument be made that whenever a defendant is on trial on charges of murder, any hearsay statements by the victim are admissible against the defendant under Rule 804(b)(6), on the theory that he "wrongfully caused ... the declarant's unavailabil-

ity as a witness, and did so intending that result"? If not, what distinguishes such a case from cases like *Dhinsa*? *See United States v. Natson*, 469 F. Supp. 2d 1243, 1250–51 (M.D. Ga. 2006) ("The Court can discern no reason that a homicide victim's statements should not be admissible if the party against whom the statements are to be used committed the homicide, at least in part, to prevent the victim's testimony.... The Government must show more than the Defendant killed [the victim], but that he killed her *to make her unavailable as a witness*."); *United States v. Jordan*, 2005 WL 513501, at *6 (D. Colo. Mar. 3, 2005) ("The government's unsupported premise is that Defendant killed Stone to make sure Stone was not able to testify that Jordan was the one who stabbed him.... The government proffered no evidence that Jordan decided to silence potential-witness Stone during the assault as a witness to the assault.... The government construes the Doctrine and Rule 804(b)(6) broadly to apply in any murder case. Such a broad construction is not consonant with the Doctrine's policy and not within the intent of the drafters of Fed.R.Evid. 804(b)(6).").

H. The Residual Exception

Problem 7-43: The Grand Jury Witness II

Daniel is on trial in federal court on charges of murdering Valerie. Before the grand jury that indicted Daniel, Wanda testified that she saw Daniel shoot Valerie. Between Daniel's indictment and his trial, Wanda dies, and there is no reason to believe that she died as a result of foul play. The prosecution seeks to offer into evidence the transcript, created by a stenographer employed by the federal government, of Wanda's testimony before the grand jury, but Daniel's attorney objects on hearsay grounds.

How should the court dispose of the hearsay objection?

United States v. Laster
258 F.3d 525 (6th Cir. 2001)

SILER, Circuit Judge.

Defendants Jerry Lear and James M. Laster appeal their convictions and sentences for drug offenses....

In 1993 James Acquisto, a detective for a state drug task force, received information from Universal Testing Incorporated ("UTI"), that one of its employees, Laster, had ordered hydriodic acid, a component of methamphetamine, from Wilson Oil Company using the UTI company name without its permission.

After reviewing the Wilson Oil Company documents confirming these purchases, Acquisto contacted Drug Enforcement Special Agent Gary Tennant. Together they approached Laster on July 8, 1993. Laster stated that approximately four or five months prior, he was contacted by an "unnamed older man" seeking certain chemicals including hydriodic acid, red phosphorous, and sulfuric acids through UTI. Laster stated he was acting under the assumption that he would be paid for securing these chemicals which he believed were to be used to make methamphetamine.

In a second statement provided on July 20, 1993, Laster admitted to making three trips with Lear to Illinois to pick up hydriodic acid and receiving $300 per bottle for it. On July 21, 1993, Lear gave a statement to Acquisto and Tennant corroborating these trips with Laster. He also admitted traveling alone to Illinois on two other occasions to pick up bottles of hydriodic acid. According to Lear, all of these chemicals were picked up for the "older man." Laster's admissions were consistent with the information contained in the Wilson Oil Company purchase documents admitted as exhibits at the 1998 trial.

A meeting was held in September 1993 between government agents, Lear, Laster, and their respective counsel whereby the defendants agreed to assist the government in its investigation of methamphetamine manufacturing in Kentucky.

In August 1994, Officer Richard Derks of the Sturgis City Police Department stopped Lear driving a truck in a reckless manner. Laster exited the passenger side of the vehicle carrying a container and placed it on the bed of the truck. A 9mm semi-automatic pistol was removed from Lear's waistband. An additional magazine for the pistol was found in the cab of the truck along with a .32 caliber semi-automatic pistol. Draino, coffee filters, plastic tubing, Mason jars, towels, lye, an aspiration mask, a funnel, and three plaster-encased glass jars containing liquid were found in the containers in the truck bed. The liquid in the jars was later determined to be 58.2 grams of pure D-methamphetamine. This liquid also contained red phosphorous and iodine, which are consistent with the use of hydriodic acid to manufacture methamphetamine.

A bag inside the cab of the truck contained four other bags of methamphetamine weighing a total of 7.44 grams, razors, razor blades, a vial, a spoon, a lighter, pH strips, corners of plastic bags, and rubber bands. Also seized was a notebook on the dash of the truck which contained, in addition to other non-incriminating pages, references to gram quantities next to dollar figures and initials, as well as fourteen entries of drug sales totaling $2,000. Motions to suppress some of the items taken from Lear's vehicle were denied by the district court....

The defendants argue that the district court improperly admitted purchase records from Wilson Oil Company under the business records exception of Fed.R.Evid. 803(6)....

The records from Wilson Oil Company included four invoices dated March 24, 1993, April 14, 1993, April 30, 1993, and May 14, 1993 which respectively reflected the sale on each date of one 500 milliliter bottle of hydriodic acid, except for the May 14, 1993 invoice wherein two bottles were sold in addition to two bottles of sulfuric acid and one plastic barrel. An additional order for six 500 milliliter bottles had been sought by Laster, but was canceled by the supplier to Wilson Oil Company. Also included in these records was the chemical diversion letter signed by Laster which referenced the sale of hydriodic acid to UTI by Wilson Oil Company. The district court held that the Wilson Oil Company records were admissible under either the business records hearsay exception of Fed.R.Evid. 803(6) or the residual exception of Fed.R.Evid. 807. Acquisto was determined to be a qualified witness under Fed.R.Evid. 803(6), and was permitted to lay the foundation upon which the records were admitted....

Defendants attack the admissibility of the records on the grounds that Acquisto was not qualified to admit these records under the business records exception. Acquisto did not examine the books or ledger sheets of Wilson Oil Company, nor did he know whether Wilson had an accountant or bookkeeper. Neither did Acquisto ask Wilson whether these documents were prepared simultaneously with the transactions reflected thereon. Defendants thus argue that Acquisto had no personal knowledge or any familiarity with the record-keeping practices of Wilson Oil Company.

United States v. Hathaway, 798 F.2d 902 (6th Cir. 1986), holds that a foundation for the application of Fed.R.Evid. 803(6) may be laid, in whole or in part, "by the testimony of a government agent or other person outside the organization whose records are sought to be admitted." *Id.* at 906. The only requirement is that the "witness be familiar with the record keeping system." *Id.* Other than a few conversations between Acquisto and Wilson, there is no evidence that Acquisto was familiar with the record-keeping system of Wilson Oil Company. Therefore, the evidence was not admissible under Fed.R.Evid. 803(6).

However, the district court did not err in admitting the purchase orders and other related documents under the residual hearsay exception of Fed.R.Evid. 807 as there was "no indication" that the records were not reliable. This rule finds an equally trustworthy statement "not specifically covered by [a hearsay exception in] Rule 803 or 804," admissible if it is "material," "more probative on the point for which it is offered than any other evidence [that] the proponent can [obtain] through reasonable efforts," and its admission best serves the interests of justice. Fed.R.Evid. 807.

Although some courts have held that if proffered evidence fails to meet the requirements of the Fed.R.Evid. 803 hearsay exception, it cannot qualify for admission under the residual exception, the court declines to adopt this narrow interpretation of Fed.R.Evid. 807 as suggested by defendants. Rather, this court interprets Fed.R.Evid. 807, along with the majority of circuits, to mean that "if a statement is admissible under one of the hearsay exceptions, that exception should be relied on instead of the residual exception." 5 Jack B. Weinstein & Margaret A. Berger, *Weinstein's Federal Evidence* § 807.03(4) (2d ed. 2000).[3] We endorse the reasoning in *United States v. Earles*, 113 F.3d 796 (8th Cir. 1997), which held that "the phrase 'specifically covered' [by a hearsay exception] means only that if a statement is *admissible* under one of the [803] exceptions, such [ ] subsection should be relied upon" instead of the residual exception. *Id.* at 800....

MOORE, Circuit Judge, dissenting.

Laster and Lear argue that the district court erred in admitting certain business records into evidence. The majority agrees with Lear and Laster that these business records were not properly admitted into evidence under the business records exception to the hearsay rule, Fed.R.Evid. 803(6), because the government failed to lay a proper foundation. The majority concludes, however, that the court below properly admitted these records under the residual exception to the hearsay rule, Fed.R.Evid. 807. For the reasons explained below, I respectfully dissent from this holding....

Despite the plain language of the rule, which states that it applies only to statements "*not specifically covered* by [a hearsay exception in] Rule 803 or [] 804," some courts have applied Rule 807 to statements *not admissible* under either Rule 803 or 804. Under this approach, out-of-court statements inadmissible under either Rule 803 or 804 may still be admissible under Rule 807, even when they are of a sort "specifically covered" by Rule 803 or 804, if they possess "equivalent circumstantial guarantees of trustworthiness." Thus, for example, although grand jury testimony is arguably former testimony, and thus specifically covered (and inadmissible) under Rule 804(b)(1), a number of circuits, including this one, have held that the grand jury testimony of an unavailable witness is admissible under the residual exception when it bears the "equivalent circumstantial guarantees of trustworthiness." *See United States v. Barlow*, 693 F.2d 954, 961–63 (6th Cir. 1982). *See*

---

3. *See also United States v. Ismoila*, 100 F.3d 380, 393 (5th Cir. 1996); *United States v. Deeb*, 13 F.3d 1532, 1536–37 (11th Cir. 1994); *United States v. Clarke*, 2 F.3d 81, 84 (4th Cir. 1993); *United States v. Guinan*, 836 F.2d 350, 354 (7th Cir. 1988); *United States v. Marchini*, 797 F.2d 759, 763 (9th Cir. 1986).

also, e.g., United States v. Earles, 113 F.3d 796, 800 (8th Cir. 1997) (holding that grand jury testimony, although inadmissible under other hearsay exceptions, "may ... be considered for admission under the catch-all exception"), *cert. denied*, 522 U.S. 1075 (1998); *United States v. Marchini*, 797 F.2d 759, 764 (9th Cir. 1986) (holding that grand jury testimony was admissible under the residual exception), *cert. denied*, 479 U.S. 1085 (1987). *But see United States v. Vigoa*, 656 F. Supp. 1499, 1506 (D.N.J. 1987) (concluding "that admission of grand jury testimony under [the residual exception] is a perversion of the Federal Rules of Evidence and should not be condoned"), *aff'd*, 857 F.2d 1467 (3d Cir. 1988).

The contrary (minority) view of the residual exception is that the residual exception means what it says—i.e., that it applies to those exceptional cases in which an established exception to the hearsay rule does not apply but in which circumstantial guarantees of trustworthiness, equivalent to those existing for the established hearsay exceptions, are present. *See Conoco Inc. v. Dep't of Energy*, 99 F.3d 387, 392–93 (Fed. Cir. 1997) (holding that summaries by certain purchasers, made long after the purchases had been made, were not admissible under the residual exception because such summaries were not as trustworthy as either business records, which are covered by Fed.R.Evid. 803(6), or market reports and commercial publications, covered by Fed.R.Evid. 803(17)). Not only is this minority approach consistent with the plain language of the rule, *see United States v. Dent*, 984 F.2d 1453, 1465–66 (7th Cir.) (Easterbrook, J., concurring, joined by Bauer, C.J.) ("Rule [807] reads more naturally if we understand the introductory clause to mean that evidence of a kind specifically addressed ("covered") by one of the ... other [exceptions] must satisfy the conditions laid down for its admission, and that other kinds of evidence not covered (because the drafters could not be exhaustive) are admissible if the evidence is approximately as reliable as evidence that would be admissible under the specific [exceptions]."), *cert. denied*, 510 U.S. 858 (1993), but it is also consistent with the legislative history of the residual exception, *see* S.Rep. No. 93-1277, at 20 (1974) ("It is intended that the residual hearsay exceptions will be *used very rarely, and only in exceptional circumstances. The committee does not intend to establish a broad license for trial judges to admit hearsay statements that do not fall within one of the other exceptions* contained in rules 803 and 804 [ ].") (emphasis added) and the original Advisory Committee Note to Rule 807's predecessors, *see* Fed.R.Evid. 803(24), Advisory Committee Note (1975 Adoption) (repealed 1997) ("It would ... be presumptuous to assume that all possible desirable exceptions to the hearsay rule have been catalogued.... Exception (24) and its companion provision ... are accordingly included. They do not contemplate an unfettered exercise of judicial discretion, but they do provide for treating *new and presently unanticipated situations* which demonstrate a trustworthiness within the spirit of the specifically stated exceptions.") (emphasis added).[1]

This plain-language interpretation of the residual exception is sometimes described by its detractors as the "near-miss theory" of the residual exception: "[t]he doctrine that

---

1. *See also* 3 Stephen A. Saltzburg, Michael M. Martin, & Daniel J. Capra, Federal Rules of Evidence Manual 1931 (7th ed. 1998) ("Unfortunately, the intent of the drafters has often been ignored.... A broad application of the residual exception could permit the case-by-case exception to swallow the categorical rules."); Daniel J. Capra, *Case Law Divergence from the Federal Rules of Evidence*, 197 F.R.D. 531, 534, 543 (2000) ("Rule [807] permits the admission of residual hearsay only if that hearsay is 'not specifically covered' by another exception. This might seem to indicate that hearsay that 'nearly misses' one of the established exceptions should not be admissible as residual hearsay, because it is specifically covered by, and yet not admissible under, another exception. In fact, however, most courts have construed the term 'not specifically covered' by another hearsay exception to mean 'not admissible under' another hearsay exception.") (citing the majority view as an "Example[ ] of Case Law in Conflict with the Text of the Rule, the Committee Note, or Both").

a 'near miss' under a specified exception … renders evidence inadmissible under [the] residual exception." *United States v. Clarke*, 2 F.3d 81, 84 (4th Cir. 1993). In the same vein, however, the majority approach might be called the "close-enough" theory of the residual exception, i.e., the doctrine that hearsay is admissible under the residual exception even when it just misses admissibility under an established exception. Such an approach makes little sense given the listing of explicit hearsay exceptions in Rules 803 and 804, exceptions that the drafters of the residual exception thought sufficient to cover anticipated (in other words, common) hearsay situations. *See United States v. Turner*, 104 F.3d 217, 221 (8th Cir. 1997) ("Allowing Turner to introduce the medical texts under [the residual exception], when Federal Rule of Evidence 803(18) specifically deals with the admissibility of this type of evidence, would circumvent the general purposes of the rules.").

The majority today rejects, in sweeping fashion, the plain-language interpretation of the residual exception. In doing so, it goes far beyond this circuit's prior holding in *Barlow*. For present purposes, *Barlow* stands for the rather narrow proposition that grand jury testimony may be admissible, in certain circumstances, under the residual hearsay exception. *Barlow*, 693 F.2d at 961–63. In the present case, the majority adopts, as a general rule apparently covering every hearsay exception, the "close-enough" reasoning of *Earles* and similar cases. It does so without discussion of the structure of the hearsay exceptions, the legislative history of the residual exception, or the specific hearsay exception at issue in the present case, the business records exception.

Given the plain language of Rule 807, the language and structure of Rules 803 and 804, and the legislative history of the Federal Rules of Evidence, this holding is badly flawed. Moreover, special considerations counsel against holding that the business records in this case were admissible under the residual hearsay exception. The business records at issue here were improperly admitted under the business records exception because, as the majority correctly concludes, Acquisto was unable to lay the proper foundation for their admission. The government, in short, did not produce a sponsoring witness satisfying the already low standard of *United States v. Hathaway*, 798 F.2d 902, 906 (6th Cir. 1986) ("[A]ll that is required is that the [sponsoring] witness be familiar with the record keeping system.").

This lack of a foundation for the admission of the business records is irrelevant, however, under the majority's holding. The residual exception, after all, is always available under the majority's theory for the admission of hearsay evidence inadmissible under the other specific hearsay exceptions, including the business records exception. The majority's holding thus appears to make it unnecessary ever to call a sponsoring witness to establish the admissibility of business records, at least so long as there is "'no indication' that the records [are] not reliable." This cannot be squared with the language of Rule 803(6), which requires "the testimony of the custodian [of the records] or [an]other qualified witness" to vouch for the existence of the other elements of the business records exception. Nor is it clear how, as a general matter, business records introduced without the testimony of a qualified sponsoring witness can be said to have "circumstantial guarantees of trustworthiness" equivalent to those that exist when a qualified sponsoring witness testifies to the trustworthiness of the records in question.

In sum, under the majority's "close-enough" approach, the residual exception swallows all the other exceptions, as well as the rule. This court should not join the other circuits in expanding the residual hearsay exception to cover hearsay situations clearly anticipated by the drafters of the Federal Rules of Evidence. It should certainly not do so in the present case, in which an established hearsay exception clearly applied but rendered the documents inadmissible.

New Jersey Rule of Evidence 803

....

COMMENT

....

(24) Other exceptions—not adopted. *Fed.R.Evid.* 803(24), which creates a general hearsay exception for statements not covered by a specific hearsay rule, provided they are attended by "equivalent circumstantial guarantees of trustworthiness" and are the most probative evidence reasonably available, and provided further that other stated criteria are met, was not adopted. The adoption of the federal rule was attended by substantial controversy and its application since its adoption has been disparate among the federal courts. See A.B.A. Section of Litigation, *Emerging Problems Under the Federal Rules of Evidence* 279–281 (1983). The adoption of *Fed.R.Evid.* 803(24), construable as a general relaxation rule, would represent a radical departure from New Jersey practice. The advantages and disadvantages of this departure are debatable. For the same reason, *Fed.R.Evid.* 804(b)(5) was not adopted....

Washington Evidence Rule 803
Judicial Council Task Force Comment

....

Subsection (b). Federal Rule 803(24) is deleted. The drafters decided not to adopt any catch-all provision. Despite purported safeguards, there is a serious risk that trial judges would differ greatly in applying the elastic standard of equivalent trustworthiness. The result would be a lack of uniformity which would make preparation for trial difficult. Nor would it be likely that an appellate court could effectively apply corrective measures. There would be doubt whether an affirmance of an admission of evidence under the catch-all provision amounted to the creation of a new exception with the force of precedent or merely a refusal to rule that the trial court had abused its discretion.

Flexibility in construction of the rules so as to promote growth and development of the law of evidence is called for by Rule 102. Under this mandate there will be room to construe an existing hearsay exception broadly in the interest of ascertaining truth, as distinguished from creating an entirely new exception based upon the trial judge's determination of equivalent trustworthiness, a guideline which the most conscientious of judges would find extremely difficult to follow.

Notes and Questions

1. Originally, there were two separate catchall hearsay exceptions: one for unrestricted hearsay, set forth in Rule 803(24), and one for restricted hearsay, set forth in Rule 804(b)(5). In 1997, the two rules were combined into a single rule and codified as Rule 807.

2. To invoke Rule 807, a party must demonstrate that the proffered evidence is reliable. How does a court go about determining whether a statement has "circumstantial guarantees of trustworthiness" equivalent to those statements covered by the various hearsay exceptions set forth in Rules 803 and 804?

Some circuits suggest a variety of factors that should be taken into account:

> In determining whether a statement is sufficiently reliable ... a court should examine, among other factors: (1) "the probable motivation of the declarant

in making the statement;" (2) "the circumstances under which it was made;" and (3) "the knowledge and qualifications of the declarant.".. . [O]ther factors which are relevant ... include: (1) the character of the declarant for "truthfulness and honesty and the availability of evidence on the issue;" (2) "whether the testimony was given voluntarily, under oath, subject to cross[-]examination and a penalty for perjury;" (3) "the extent to which the witness' testimony reflects his personal knowledge;" (4) "whether the witness ever recanted his testimony;" and (5) whether the declarant's statement was insufficiently corroborated. Although these factors are neither exhaustive nor necessary prerequisites for admissibility ... they shed light on the sort of considerations a district court should take into account when evaluating the "trustworthiness" of a hearsay statement.

United States v. Hall, 165 F.3d 1095, 1110–11 (7th Cir. 1999). In contrast, other circuits suggest that the trial court focus on the extent to which the evidence poses any of the classic hearsay risks:

> The hearsay rule is generally said to exclude out-of-court statements offered for the truth of the matter asserted because there are four classes of risk peculiar to this kind of evidence: those of (1) insincerity, (2) faulty perception, (3) faulty memory and (4) faulty narration, each of which decreases the reliability of the inference from the statement made to the conclusion for which it is offered. The hearsay rule ordinarily prohibits the admission of out-of-court statements by declarants on the theory that cross-examination can help test for these four classes of error, thus allowing the fact-finder to weigh the evidence properly and to discount any that is too unreliable.
>
> The traditional exceptions to the hearsay rule, in turn, provide the benchmark against which the trustworthiness of evidence must be compared in a residual hearsay analysis. It is thus important to recognize that the trustworthiness of these exceptions is a function of their ability to minimize some of the four classic hearsay dangers.... [As with other hearsay exceptions,] a hearsay statement need not be free from all four categories of risk to be admitted under Rule 807.
>
> Courts deciding whether evidence is sufficiently trustworthy to be admitted under the residual hearsay rule should therefore be aware of these facts and of the relative degree to which the evidence offered is prone to risks like those under discussion.

Schering Corp. v. Pfizer, Inc., 189 F.3d 218, 232–33 (2d Cir. 1999).

3. Rule 807 requires not only a showing that the evidence is reliable, but also that it is necessary. In particular, Rule 807(a)(3) requires that the proponent demonstrate that "it is more probative on the point for which it is offered than any other evidence that the proponent can obtain through reasonable efforts." Obviously, necessity may arise when, for example, the only witness with first-hand knowledge is deceased or otherwise unavailable. However, necessity may also be shown where the alternative would require bringing large numbers of witnesses into court. *See Schering*, 189 F.3d at 236 (fact that survey summarized the views of more than 1000 people with first-hand knowledge could satisfy the necessity prong of Rule 807). *But see Larez v. City of Los Angeles*, 946 F.2d 630, 644 (9th Cir. 1991) (concluding that this provision "essentially creates a 'best evidence' requirement," and refusing to admit newspaper articles containing quotations of what someone allegedly said on the ground that testimony from the reporters themselves, who were available to testify, would be the best evidence of what that person had said).

4. Suppose that a party offers evidence that satisfies the requirements of one of the exceptions to the hearsay rule set forth in Rule 804, except that the declarant is *not* unavailable as a witness. Can such evidence nonetheless be offered under Rule 807? How would the *Laster* majority answer the question? How about the *Laster* dissent? *See Kamara v. United States*, 2005 WL 2298176, at *6–*7 (S.D.N.Y. Sept. 20, 2005) (holding that deposition testimony of a witness who is not unavailable as a witness is inadmissible under Rule 807, reasoning that "[t]hat Rule only applies to '[a] statement not specifically covered by Rule 803 or 804….' and that "[d]eposition testimony is covered by Rule 804, and the requirements for the admission of such testimony have not been satisfied").

5. Rule 807(b) contains a notice requirement, which provides that

> The statement is admissible only if, before the trial or hearing, the proponent gives an adverse party reasonable notice of the intent to offer the statement and its particulars, including the declarant's name and address, so that the party has a fair opportunity to meet it.

Consistent with this requirement, appellate courts do not entertain for the first time on appeal arguments that the evidence might be admissible under Rule 807. *E.g., Rowland v. American General Finance, Inc.*, 340 F.3d 187, 195 (4th Cir. 2003).

Does Rule 807(b) require only notice of an intent to use the *statement*, or does it instead require notice of an intent to *rely on the residual exception* as a means of admitting the statement into evidence? *Compare S.E.C. v. 4NExchange*, 2005 WL 1518838, at *4 n.6 (10th Cir. June 28, 2005) (suggesting that it is the latter that is required), *with Limone v. United States*, 497 F. Supp. 2d 143, 162 n. 31 (D.Mass. 2007) (holding that it is only the former that is required).

I. Hearsay and the Confrontation Clause

1. Background

The Confrontation Clause of the Sixth Amendment to the U.S. Constitution provides that "[i]n all criminal prosecutions, the accused shall enjoy the right … to be confronted with the witnesses against him." This right to confront is understood to provide criminal defendants with a right to cross-examine, before the trier of fact, "witnesses against him." But what does the phrase "witnesses against" mean, and how does the definition of that phrase affect the admissibility of hearsay evidence when offered against defendants in criminal cases?

At its narrowest, the phrase could be understood as referring only to *live* witnesses who are called by the government to testify against the defendant. Under this interpretation, the Confrontation Clause only guarantees the defendant a right to cross-examine any witnesses who actually appear on the stand and testify. So understood, the Confrontation Clause would have no impact whatsoever on the admissibility of hearsay evidence.

At its broadest, the phrase could be understood to refer to *any* person whose statements are used against the defendant, including declarants whose out-of-court written or verbal statements are introduced into evidence against the defendant, either as documentary evidence or through the testimony of another person. So understood, in criminal cases the Confrontation Clause would bar *all* hearsay evidence, even when it falls within an exception to the rule against hearsay, at least where the declarant does not appear in the court proceedings.

Yet about the only thing that one can say with certainty about the Supreme Court's evolving interpretation of the Confrontation Clause is that it has never accepted either of these two extreme definitions of the phrase "witnesses against." Whatever the phrase means, it neither forbids all uses of hearsay evidence against criminal defendants, nor does it permit all uses of hearsay evidence against criminal defendants.

Prior to 1980, the Supreme Court issued a series of cases that addressed whether specific categories of hearsay evidence could be admitted over a Confrontation Clause objection, none of which provided an overarching theory of admissibility.

In 1980, the Supreme Court, in *Ohio v. Roberts*, set forth for the first time a theory for determining when hearsay evidence could overcome a Confrontation Clause objection when offered against the accused.

Ohio v. Roberts
448 U.S. 56 (1980)

Mr. Justice BLACKMUN delivered the opinion of the Court.

This case presents issues concerning the constitutional propriety of the introduction in evidence of the preliminary hearing testimony of a witness not produced at the defendant's subsequent state criminal trial.

I

Local police arrested respondent, Herschel Roberts, on January 7, 1975, in Lake County, Ohio. Roberts was charged with forgery of a check in the name of Bernard Isaacs, and with possession of stolen credit cards belonging to Isaacs and his wife Amy.

A preliminary hearing was held in Municipal Court on January 10. The prosecution called several witnesses, including Mr. Isaacs. Respondent's appointed counsel had seen the Isaacs' daughter, Anita, in the courthouse hallway, and called her as the defense's only witness. Anita Isaacs testified that she knew respondent, and that she had permitted him to use her apartment for several days while she was away. Defense counsel questioned Anita at some length and attempted to elicit from her an admission that she had given respondent checks and the credit cards without informing him that she did not have permission to use them. Anita, however, denied this. Respondent's attorney did not ask to have the witness declared hostile and did not request permission to place her on cross-examination. The prosecutor did not question Anita.

A county grand jury subsequently indicted respondent for forgery, for receiving stolen property (including the credit cards), and for possession of heroin....

Between November 1975 and March 1976, five subpoenas for four different trial dates were issued to Anita at her parents' Ohio residence. The last three carried a written instruction that Anita should "call before appearing." She was not at the residence when these were executed. She did not telephone and she did not appear at trial.

In March 1976, the case went to trial before a jury in the Court of Common Pleas. Respondent took the stand and testified that Anita Isaacs had given him her parents' checkbook and credit cards with the understanding that he could use them. Relying on Ohio Rev. Code Ann. §2945.49 (1975), which permits the use of preliminary examination testimony of a witness who "cannot for any reason be produced at the trial," the State, on rebuttal, offered the transcript of Anita's testimony.

Asserting a violation of the Confrontation Clause and, indeed, the unconstitutionality thereunder of §2945.49, the defense objected to the use of the transcript....

[The trial court rejected Roberts' challenge, but both the intermediate appellate court and the state supreme court held that the admission of the transcript violated the Confrontation Clause.]

We granted certiorari to consider these important issues under the Confrontation Clause.

II

A

The Court here is called upon to consider once again the relationship between the Confrontation Clause and the hearsay rule with its many exceptions. The basic rule against hearsay, of course, is riddled with exceptions developed over three centuries. These exceptions vary among jurisdictions as to number, nature, and detail. But every set of exceptions seems to fit an apt description offered more than 40 years ago: "an old-fashioned crazy quilt made of patches cut from a group of paintings by cubists, futurists and surrealists." Morgan & Maguire, Looking Backward and Forward at Evidence, 50 Harv. L. Rev. 909, 921 (1937).

The Sixth Amendment's Confrontation Clause, made applicable to the States through the Fourteenth Amendment, provides: "In all criminal prosecutions, the accused shall enjoy the right ... to be confronted with the witnesses against him." If one were to read this language literally, it would require, on objection, the exclusion of any statement made by a declarant not present at trial. But, if thus applied, the Clause would abrogate virtually every hearsay exception, a result long rejected as unintended and too extreme.

The historical evidence leaves little doubt, however, that the Clause was intended to exclude some hearsay. Moreover, underlying policies support the same conclusion. The Court has emphasized that the Confrontation Clause reflects a preference for face-to-face confrontation at trial, and that "a primary interest secured by [the provision] is the right of cross-examination." *Douglas* v. *Alabama*, 380 U.S. 415, 418 (1965). In short, the Clause envisions

> "a personal examination and cross-examination of the witness, in which the accused has an opportunity, not only of testing the recollection and sifting the conscience of the witness, but of compelling him to stand face to face with the jury in order that they may look at him, and judge by his demeanor upon the stand and the manner in which he gives his testimony whether he is worthy of belief." *Mattox* v. *United States*, 156 U.S., at 242–243.

These means of testing accuracy are so important that the absence of proper confrontation at trial "calls into question the ultimate 'integrity of the fact-finding process.'"

The Court, however, has recognized that competing interests, if "closely examined," may warrant dispensing with confrontation at trial. See *Mattox* v. *United States*, 156 U.S., at 243 ("general rules of law of this kind, however beneficent in their operation and valuable to the accused, must occasionally give way to considerations of public policy and the necessities of the case"). Significantly, every jurisdiction has a strong interest in effective law enforcement, and in the development and precise formulation of the rules of evidence applicable in criminal proceedings.

This Court, in a series of cases, has sought to accommodate these competing interests. True to the common-law tradition, the process has been gradual, building on past decisions, drawing on new experience, and responding to changing conditions. The Court has not sought to "map out a theory of the Confrontation Clause that would determine the validity of all ... hearsay 'exceptions.'" *California v. Green*, 399 U.S., at 162. But a general approach to the problem is discernible.

B

The Confrontation Clause operates in two separate ways to restrict the range of admissible hearsay. First, in conformance with the Framers' preference for face-to-face accusation, the Sixth Amendment establishes a rule of necessity. In the usual case (including cases where prior cross-examination has occurred), the prosecution must either produce, or demonstrate the unavailability of, the declarant whose statement it wishes to use against the defendant. See *Mancusi v. Stubbs*, 408 U.S. 204 (1972); *Barber v. Page*, 390 U.S. 719 (1968). See also *Motes v. United States*, 178 U.S. 458 (1900); *California v. Green*, 399 U.S., at 161–162, 165, 167, n. 16.[7]

The second aspect operates once a witness is shown to be unavailable. Reflecting its underlying purpose to augment accuracy in the factfinding process by ensuring the defendant an effective means to test adverse evidence, the Clause countenances only hearsay marked with such trustworthiness that "there is no material departure from the reason of the general rule." The principle recently was formulated in *Mancusi v. Stubbs*:

> "The focus of the Court's concern has been to insure that there 'are indicia of reliability which have been widely viewed as determinative of whether a statement may be placed before the jury though there is no confrontation of the declarant,' *Dutton v. Evans, supra*, at 89, and to 'afford the trier of fact a satisfactory basis for evaluating the truth of the prior statement,' *California v. Green, supra*, at 161. It is clear from these statements, and from numerous prior decisions of this Court, that even though the witness be unavailable his prior testimony must bear some of these 'indicia of reliability.'"

The Court has applied this "indicia of reliability" requirement principally by concluding that certain hearsay exceptions rest upon such solid foundations that admission of virtually any evidence within them comports with the "substance of the constitutional protection." *Mattox v. United States*, 156 U.S., at 244.[8] This reflects the truism that "hearsay rules and the Confrontation Clause are generally designed to protect similar values," *California v. Green*, 399 U.S., at 155, and "stem from the same roots," *Dutton v. Evans*, 400 U.S. 74 (1970). It also responds to the need for certainty in the workaday world of conducting criminal trials.

In sum, when a hearsay declarant is not present for cross-examination at trial, the Confrontation Clause normally requires a showing that he is unavailable. Even then, his statement is admissible only if it bears adequate "indicia of reliability." Reliability can be inferred without more in a case where the evidence falls within a firmly rooted hearsay exception. In other cases, the evidence must be excluded, at least absent a showing of particularized guarantees of trustworthiness.

[The Court concludes that both the "unavailability" and "reliability" requirements were satisfied. The dissenting opinion of Justice Brennan is omitted.]

---

7. A demonstration of unavailability, however, is not always required. In *Dutton v. Evans*, 400 U.S. 74 (1970), for example, the Court found the utility of trial confrontation so remote that it did not require the prosecution to produce a seemingly available witness.

8. See, *e. g.*, *Pointer v. Texas*, 380 U.S., at 407 (dying declarations); *Mattox v. United States*, 156 U.S., at 243–244 (same); *Mancusi v. Stubbs*, 408 U.S. 204, 213–216 (1972) (cross-examined prior-trial testimony); Comment, 30 La. L. Rev. 651, 668 (1970) ("Properly administered the business and public records exceptions would seem to be among the safest of the hearsay exceptions").

2. A New Approach: *Crawford v. Washington*

At first glance, *Roberts* appeared to set forth a two-pronged test for determining the admissibility of hearsay evidence against criminal defendants that required *both* a showing of unavailability *and* reliability. That immediately raised the question whether unavailability was *always* a prerequisite for admitting hearsay evidence against the accused, which would effectively transform all hearsay exceptions into *restricted* ones when offered against the accused in a criminal case.

It soon became clear, however, that the Supreme Court did not intend to take the unavailability prong of *Roberts* too seriously. In *United States v. Inadi*, 475 U.S. 387 (1986), the Supreme Court held that the Confrontation Clause did not require a showing of unavailability to admit hearsay declarations of a co-conspirator under Rule 801(d)(2)(E). The *Inadi* Court justified its conclusion, in part, by reference to footnote 7 of the *Roberts* opinion, which indicated that a "demonstration of unavailability ... is not always required." The *Inadi* decision was followed six years later by *White v. Illinois*, 502 U.S. 346 (1992). In *White*, the Supreme Court held that a showing of unavailability was not required to invoke either the excited utterance exception or the exception for statements made for purposes of medical diagnosis or treatment.

So far as reliability was concerned, separate bodies of precedent developed under the "firmly rooted" and "particularized guarantees of trustworthiness" prongs. Whether a hearsay exception was "firmly rooted" or not appeared to turn on its longevity as well as the extent to which it had received widespread acceptance in the states. *See White v. Illinois*, 502 U.S. 346, 355 n.8 (1992). In contrast, where a hearsay exception was not "firmly rooted," the Court identified a variety of factors that a court could balance—factors that in many ways were similar to those used under Rule 807 in determining whether hearsay has "circumstantial guarantees of trustworthiness"—to determine whether a statement had "particularized guarantees of trustworthiness." *See Idaho v. Wright*, 497 U.S. 805, 821–22 (1990).

The Court's unwillingness to require a showing of unavailability in most instances, coupled with the flexibility of the reliability prong of the *Roberts* test, resulted in the Confrontation Clause rarely serving as a barrier to admitting hearsay against the accused. Over time, Justices began to express concerns with the *Roberts* test. *E.g., Lilly v. Virginia*, 527 U.S. 116, 140 (1999) (Breyer, J., concurring); *White v. Illinois*, 502 U.S. 346, 358 (1992) (Thomas, J., concurring in part and concurring in judgment).

In 2004, the Supreme Court revisited the issue in *Crawford v. Washington*, where it set forth a new theory regarding the relationship between hearsay evidence and the Confrontation Clause.

Problem 7-44: *Confronting the Confrontation Clause*

Which of the following, upon proper objection, would likely be *excluded* on Confrontation Clause grounds under *Crawford v. Washington*?

1. Grand jury testimony admitted pursuant to the requirements of Federal Rule of Evidence 801(d)(1)(A) offered into evidence against a criminal defendant at trial to prove the truth of the matter asserted therein (as in Problem 7-13(b)).

2. Grand jury testimony admitted pursuant to the requirements of Federal Rule of Evidence 807 offered into evidence against a criminal defendant at trial to prove the truth of the matter asserted therein (as in Problem 7-43).

3. Testimony by a witness about what someone else said that does not fit into any exception to the hearsay rule but that is offered into evidence against a criminal defendant for some reason other than to prove the truth of the matter asserted therein (as in Problem 7-2).

4. A recorded recollection admitted pursuant to the requirements of Federal Rule of Evidence 803(5) offered into evidence against a criminal defendant to prove the truth of the matter asserted therein (as in Problem 7-26).

5. Testimony given at a previous criminal trial of the same matter (that ended in a hung jury) by a witness who dies before the subsequent re-trial, admitted pursuant to the requirements of Federal Rule of Evidence 804(b)(1) and offered into evidence against the accused at the subsequent re-trial to prove the truth of the matter asserted therein.

6. Testimony given at a previous criminal trial of the same matter (that ended in a hung jury), admitted pursuant to a state version of Federal Rule of Evidence 804(b)(1) that does not require a showing of unavailability (and for which no such showing was made) offered into evidence against the accused at the subsequent re-trial to prove the truth of the matter asserted therein.

7. Testimony given at a previous criminal trial that ended in a guilty verdict by a witness who died shortly thereafter, offered against the accused in a civil action based on the same underlying facts pursuant to the requirements of Federal Rule of Evidence 804(b)(1) to prove the truth of the matter asserted therein (as in Problem 7-36).

Crawford v. Washington

541 U.S. 36 (2004)

Justice SCALIA delivered the opinion of the Court....

I

On August 5, 1999, Kenneth Lee was stabbed at his apartment. Police arrested petitioner [Michael Crawford] later that night. After giving petitioner and his wife [Sylvia] *Miranda* warnings, detectives interrogated each of them twice. Petitioner eventually confessed that he and Sylvia had gone in search of Lee because he was upset over an earlier incident in which Lee had tried to rape her. The two had found Lee at his apartment, and a fight ensued in which Lee was stabbed in the torso and petitioner's hand was cut.

[During police questioning, petitioner gave an account of the fight in which he asserted that he thought Lee drew a weapon just before petitioner assaulted him.]

Sylvia generally corroborated petitioner's story about the events leading up to the fight, but her account of the fight itself was arguably different — particularly with respect to whether Lee had drawn a weapon before petitioner assaulted him....

The State charged petitioner with assault and attempted murder. At trial, he claimed self-defense. Sylvia did not testify because of the state marital privilege, which generally bars a spouse from testifying without the other spouse's consent. In Washington, this privilege does not extend to a spouse's out-of-court statements admissible under a hearsay exception, so the State sought to introduce Sylvia's tape-recorded statements to the police as evidence that the stabbing was not in self-defense. Noting that Sylvia had admitted she led petitioner to Lee's apartment and thus had facilitated the assault, the State invoked the hearsay exception for statements against penal interest, Wash. Rule Evid. 804(b)(3) (2003).

Petitioner countered that, state law notwithstanding, admitting the evidence would violate his federal constitutional right to be "confronted with the witnesses against him." According to our description of that right in *Ohio v. Roberts*, 448 U.S. 56 (1980), it does not bar admission of an unavailable witness's statement against a criminal defendant if the statement bears "adequate 'indicia of reliability.'" To meet that test, evidence must either fall within a "firmly rooted hearsay exception" or bear "particularized guarantees of trustworthiness." The trial court here admitted the statement on the latter ground, offering several reasons why it was trustworthy: Sylvia was not shifting blame but rather corroborating her husband's story that he acted in self-defense or "justified reprisal"; she had direct knowledge as an eyewitness; she was describing recent events; and she was being questioned by a "neutral" law enforcement officer. The prosecution played the tape for the jury and relied on it in closing.... The jury convicted petitioner of assault.

[After being reversed by an intermediate appellate court, the decision was ultimately affirmed by the Washington Supreme Court.][1]

We granted certiorari to determine whether the State's use of Sylvia's statement violated the Confrontation Clause.

II

The Sixth Amendment's Confrontation Clause provides that, "[i]n all criminal prosecutions, the accused shall enjoy the right ... to be confronted with the witnesses against him." We have held that this bedrock procedural guarantee applies to both federal and state prosecutions. *Pointer v. Texas*, 380 U.S. 400 (1965). As noted above, *Roberts* says that an unavailable witness's out-of-court statement may be admitted so long as it has adequate indicia of reliability—*i.e.*, falls within a "firmly rooted hearsay exception" or bears "particularized guarantees of trustworthiness." Petitioner argues that this test strays from the original meaning of the Confrontation Clause and urges us to reconsider it.

A

The Constitution's text does not alone resolve this case. One could plausibly read "witnesses against" a defendant to mean those who actually testify at trial, those whose statements are offered at trial, or something in-between. We must therefore turn to the historical background of the Clause to understand its meaning.

The right to confront one's accusers is a concept that dates back to Roman times. The founding generation's immediate source of the concept, however, was the common law. English common law has long differed from continental civil law in regard to the manner in which witnesses give testimony in criminal trials. The common-law tradition is one of live testimony in court subject to adversarial testing, while the civil law condones examination in private by judicial officers.

Nonetheless, England at times adopted elements of the civil-law practice. Justices of the peace or other officials examined suspects and witnesses before trial. These examinations were sometimes read in court in lieu of live testimony, a practice that "occasioned frequent demands by the prisoner to have his 'accusers,' *i.e.* the witnesses against him, brought

---

1. The court rejected the State's argument that guarantees of trustworthiness were unnecessary since petitioner waived his confrontation rights by invoking the marital privilege.... The State has not challenged this holding here. The State also has not challenged the Court of Appeals' conclusion ... that the confrontation violation, if it occurred, was not harmless. We express no opinion on these matters.

before him face to face." 1 J. Stephen, History of the Criminal Law of England 326 (1883). In some cases, these demands were refused.

Pretrial examinations became routine under two statutes passed during the reign of Queen Mary in the 16th century....

The most notorious instances of civil-law examination occurred in the great political trials of the 16th and 17th centuries. One such was the 1603 trial of Sir Walter Raleigh for treason. Lord Cobham, Raleigh's alleged accomplice, had implicated him in an examination before the Privy Council and in a letter. At Raleigh's trial, these were read to the jury. Raleigh argued that Cobham had lied to save himself.... Suspecting that Cobham would recant, Raleigh demanded that the judges call him to appear.... The judges refused, and, despite Raleigh's protestations that he was being tried "by the Spanish Inquisition," the jury convicted, and Raleigh was sentenced to death.

One of Raleigh's trial judges later lamented that "'the justice of England has never been so degraded and injured as by the condemnation of Sir Walter Raleigh.'" Through a series of statutory and judicial reforms, English law developed a right of confrontation that limited these abuses.... Courts, meanwhile, developed relatively strict rules of unavailability, admitting examinations only if the witness was demonstrably unable to testify in person. Several authorities also stated that a suspect's confession could be admitted only against himself, and not against others he implicated.

One recurring question was whether the admissibility of an unavailable witness' pretrial examination depended on whether the defendant had had an opportunity to cross-examine him. In 1696, the Court of King's Bench answered this question in the affirmative, in the widely reported misdemeanor libel case of *King* v. *Paine*, 5 Mod. 163. The court ruled that, even though a witness was dead, his examination was not admissible where "the defendant not being present when [it was] taken before the mayor ... had lost the benefit of a cross-examination." *Id.*, at 165....

Paine had settled the rule requiring a prior opportunity for cross-examination as a matter of common law, but some doubts remained over whether the Marian statutes prescribed an exception to it in felony cases.... Many who expressed this view acknowledged that it meant the statutes were in derogation of the common law. Nevertheless, by 1791 (the year the Sixth Amendment was ratified), courts were applying the cross-examination rule even to examinations by justices of the peace in felony cases....

B

Controversial examination practices were also used in the Colonies....

Many declarations of rights adopted around the time of the Revolution guaranteed a right of confrontation. The proposed Federal Constitution, however, did not. At the Massachusetts ratifying convention, Abraham Holmes objected to this omission precisely on the ground that it would lead to civil-law practices ... Similarly, a prominent Antifederalist writing under the pseudonym Federal Farmer criticized the use of "written evidence" while objecting to the omission of a vicinage right.... The First Congress responded by including the Confrontation Clause in the proposal that became the Sixth Amendment.

Early state decisions shed light upon the original understanding of the common-law right. *State* v. *Webb*, 2 N.C. 103 (Super. L. & Eq. 1794) (*per curiam*), decided a mere three years after the adoption of the Sixth Amendment, held that depositions could be read against an accused only if they were taken in his presence. Rejecting a broader reading of the English authorities, the court held: "[I]t is a rule of the common law, founded on natural justice, that no man shall be prejudiced by evidence which he had not the liberty to cross examine."...

Many other decisions are to the same effect. Some early cases went so far as to hold that prior testimony was inadmissible in criminal cases *even if* the accused had a previous opportunity to cross-examine. Most courts rejected that view, but only after reaffirming that admissibility depended on a prior opportunity for cross-examination....

III

This history supports two inferences about the meaning of the Sixth Amendment.

A

First, the principal evil at which the Confrontation Clause was directed was the civil-law mode of criminal procedure, and particularly its use of *ex parte* examinations as evidence against the accused. It was these practices that the Crown deployed in notorious treason cases like Raleigh's; that the Marian statutes invited; that English law's assertion of a right to confrontation was meant to prohibit; and that the founding-era rhetoric decried. The Sixth Amendment must be interpreted with this focus in mind.

Accordingly, we once again reject the view that the Confrontation Clause applies of its own force only to in-court testimony, and that its application to out-of-court statements introduced at trial depends upon "the law of Evidence for the time being." 3 Wigmore § 1397, at 101; accord, *Dutton v. Evans*, 400 U.S. 74, 94 (1970) (Harlan, J., concurring in result). Leaving the regulation of out-of-court statements to the law of evidence would render the Confrontation Clause powerless to prevent even the most flagrant inquisitorial practices. Raleigh was, after all, perfectly free to confront those who read Cobham's confession in court.

This focus also suggests that not all hearsay implicates the Sixth Amendment's core concerns. An off-hand, overheard remark might be unreliable evidence and thus a good candidate for exclusion under hearsay rules, but it bears little resemblance to the civil-law abuses the Confrontation Clause targeted. On the other hand, *ex parte* examinations might sometimes be admissible under modern hearsay rules, but the Framers certainly would not have condoned them.

The text of the Confrontation Clause reflects this focus. It applies to "witnesses" against the accused—in other words, those who "bear testimony." 2 N. Webster, An American Dictionary of the English Language (1828). "Testimony," in turn, is typically "[a] solemn declaration or affirmation made for the purpose of establishing or proving some fact." *Ibid.* An accuser who makes a formal statement to government officers bears testimony in a sense that a person who makes a casual remark to an acquaintance does not. The constitutional text, like the history underlying the common-law right of confrontation, thus reflects an especially acute concern with a specific type of out-of-court statement.

Various formulations of this core class of "testimonial" statements exist: "*ex parte* in-court testimony or its functional equivalent—that is, material such as affidavits, custodial examinations, prior testimony that the defendant was unable to cross-examine, or similar pretrial statements that declarants would reasonably expect to be used prosecutorially," Brief for Petitioner 23; "extrajudicial statements ... contained in formalized testimonial materials, such as affidavits, depositions, prior testimony, or confessions," *White v. Illinois*, 502 U.S. 346, 365 (1992) (THOMAS, J., joined by SCALIA, J., concurring in part and concurring in judgment); "statements that were made under circumstances which would lead an objective witness reasonably to believe that the statement would be available for use at a later trial," Brief for National Association of Criminal Defense Lawyers et al. as

Amici Curiae 3. These formulations all share a common nucleus and then define the Clause's coverage at various levels of abstraction around it. Regardless of the precise articulation, some statements qualify under any definition—for example, *ex parte* testimony at a preliminary hearing.

Statements taken by police officers in the course of interrogations are also testimonial under even a narrow standard. Police interrogations bear a striking resemblance to examinations by justices of the peace in England. The statements are not *sworn* testimony, but the absence of oath was not dispositive. Cobham's examination was unsworn, yet Raleigh's trial has long been thought a paradigmatic confrontation violation....

That interrogators are police officers rather than magistrates does not change the picture either. Justices of the peace conducting examinations under the Marian statutes were not magistrates as we understand that office today, but had an essentially investigative and prosecutorial function. England did not have a professional police force until the 19th century, so it is not surprising that other government officers performed the investigative functions now associated primarily with the police. The involvement of government officers in the production of testimonial evidence presents the same risk, whether the officers are police or justices of the peace.

In sum, even if the Sixth Amendment is not solely concerned with testimonial hearsay, that is its primary object, and interrogations by law enforcement officers fall squarely within that class.[4]

B

The historical record also supports a second proposition: that the Framers would not have allowed admission of testimonial statements of a witness who did not appear at trial unless he was unavailable to testify, and the defendant had had a prior opportunity for cross-examination. The text of the Sixth Amendment does not suggest any open-ended exceptions from the confrontation requirement to be developed by the courts. Rather, the "right ... to be confronted with the witnesses against him," Amdt. 6, is most naturally read as a reference to the right of confrontation at common law, admitting only those exceptions established at the time of the founding. See *Mattox* v. *United States*, 156 U.S. 237, 243 (1895); cf. *Houser*, 26 Mo., at 433–435. As the English authorities above reveal, the common law in 1791 conditioned admissibility of an absent witness' examination on unavailability and a prior opportunity to cross-examine. The Sixth Amendment therefore incorporates those limitations. The numerous early state decisions applying the same test confirm that these principles were received as part of the common law in this country.

We do not read the historical sources to say that a prior opportunity to cross-examine was merely a sufficient, rather than a necessary, condition for admissibility of testimonial statements. They suggest that this requirement was dispositive, and not merely one of several ways to establish reliability. This is not to deny, as THE CHIEF JUSTICE notes, that "[t]here were always exceptions to the general rule of exclusion" of hearsay evidence. Several had become well established by 1791. But there is scant evidence that exceptions were invoked to admit *testimonial* statements against the accused in a *criminal* case.[6] Most

---

4. We use the term "interrogation" in its colloquial, rather than any technical legal, sense. Just as various definitions of "testimonial" exist, one can imagine various definitions of "interrogation," and we need not select among them in this case. Sylvia's recorded statement, knowingly given in response to structured police questioning, qualifies under any conceivable definition.

6. The one deviation we have found involves dying declarations. The existence of that exception as a general rule of criminal hearsay law cannot be disputed. Although many dying declarations may not be testimonial, there is authority for admitting even those that clearly are. We need not decide in

of the hearsay exceptions covered statements that by their nature were not testimonial—for example, business records or statements in furtherance of a conspiracy. We do not infer from these that the Framers thought exceptions would apply even to prior testimony. Cf. *Lilly v. Virginia*, 527 U.S. 116, 134 (1999) (plurality opinion) ("[A]ccomplices' confessions that inculpate a criminal defendant are not within a firmly rooted exception to the hearsay rule").

IV

Our case law has been largely consistent with these two principles. Our leading early decision, for example, involved a deceased witness' prior trial testimony. *Mattox v. United States*, 156 U.S. 237 (1895). In allowing the statement to be admitted, we relied on the fact that the defendant had had, at the first trial, an adequate opportunity to confront the witness....

Our later cases conform to *Mattox*'s holding that prior trial or preliminary hearing testimony is admissible only if the defendant had an adequate opportunity to cross-examine. Even where the defendant had such an opportunity, we excluded the testimony where the government had not established unavailability of the witness. See *Barber v. Page*, 390 U.S. 719, 722–725 (1968).... In contrast, we considered reliability factors beyond prior opportunity for cross-examination when the hearsay statement at issue was not testimonial. See *Dutton v. Evans*, 400 U.S., at 87–89 (plurality opinion).

Even our recent cases, in their outcomes, hew closely to the traditional line. *Ohio v. Roberts*, 448 U.S., at 67–70, admitted testimony from a preliminary hearing at which the defendant had examined the witness. *Lilly v. Virginia, supra,* excluded testimonial statements that the defendant had had no opportunity to test by cross-examination. And *Bourjaily v. United States*, 483 U.S. 171, 181–184 (1987), admitted statements made unwittingly to a Federal Bureau of Investigation informant after applying a more general test that did *not* make prior cross-examination an indispensable requirement.[8]

....

Our cases have thus remained faithful to the Framers' understanding: Testimonial statements of witnesses absent from trial have been admitted only where the declarant is unavailable, and only where the defendant has had a prior opportunity to cross-examine.[9]

---

this case whether the Sixth Amendment incorporates an exception for testimonial dying declarations. If this exception must be accepted on historical grounds, it is *sui generis*.

8. One case arguably in tension with the rule requiring a prior opportunity for cross-examination when the proffered statement is testimonial is *White v. Illinois*, 502 U.S. 346 (1992), which involved, *inter alia*, statements of a child victim to an investigating police officer admitted as spontaneous declarations. *Id.*, at 349–351. It is questionable whether testimonial statements would ever have been admissible on that ground in 1791; to the extent the hearsay exception for spontaneous declarations existed at all, it required that the statements be made "immediat[ely] upon the hurt received, and before [the declarant] had time to devise or contrive any thing for her own advantage." *Thompson v. Trevanion*, Skin. 402 (K.B.1693). In any case, the only question presented in *White* was whether the Confrontation Clause imposed an unavailability requirement on the types of hearsay at issue. See 502 U.S., at 348–349. The holding did not address the question whether certain of the statements, because they were testimonial, had to be excluded *even if* the witness was unavailable. We "[took] as a given ... that the testimony properly falls within the relevant hearsay exceptions." *Id.*, at 351, n. 4.

9. .... [W]e reiterate that, when the declarant appears for cross-examination at trial, the Confrontation Clause places no constraints at all on the use of his prior testimonial statements. See *California v. Green*, 399 U.S. 149, 162 (1970). It is therefore irrelevant that the reliability of some out-of-court statements "'cannot be replicated, even if the declarant testifies to the same matters in court.'" *Post*, at 1377 (quoting *United States v. Inadi*, 475 U.S. 387, 395 (1986)). The Clause does not bar admission of a statement so long as the declarant is present at trial to defend or explain it. (The

V

Although the results of our decisions have generally been faithful to the original meaning of the Confrontation Clause, the same cannot be said of our rationales. *Roberts* conditions the admissibility of all hearsay evidence on whether it falls under a "firmly rooted hearsay exception" or bears "particularized guarantees of trustworthiness." This test departs from the historical principles identified above in two respects. First, it is too broad: It applies the same mode of analysis whether or not the hearsay consists of *ex parte* testimony. This often results in close constitutional scrutiny in cases that are far removed from the core concerns of the Clause. At the same time, however, the test is too narrow: It admits statements that *do* consist of *ex parte* testimony upon a mere finding of reliability. This malleable standard often fails to protect against paradigmatic confrontation violations.

Members of this Court and academics have suggested that we revise our doctrine to reflect more accurately the original understanding of the Clause. They offer two proposals: First, that we apply the Confrontation Clause only to testimonial statements, leaving the remainder to regulation by hearsay law — thus eliminating the overbreadth referred to above. Second, that we impose an absolute bar to statements that are testimonial, absent a prior opportunity to cross-examine — thus eliminating the excessive narrowness referred to above.

In *White*, we considered the first proposal and rejected it. Although our analysis in this case casts doubt on that holding, we need not definitively resolve whether it survives our decision today, because Sylvia Crawford's statement is testimonial under any definition. This case does, however, squarely implicate the second proposal.

A

Where testimonial statements are involved, we do not think the Framers meant to leave the Sixth Amendment's protection to the vagaries of the rules of evidence, much less to amorphous notions of "reliability." Certainly none of the authorities discussed above acknowledges any general reliability exception to the common-law rule. Admitting statements deemed reliable by a judge is fundamentally at odds with the right of confrontation. To be sure, the Clause's ultimate goal is to ensure reliability of evidence, but it is a procedural rather than a substantive guarantee. It commands, not that evidence be reliable, but that reliability be assessed in a particular manner: by testing in the crucible of cross-examination. The Clause thus reflects a judgment, not only about the desirability of reliable evidence (a point on which there could be little dissent), but about how reliability can best be determined.

The *Roberts* test allows a jury to hear evidence, untested by the adversary process, based on a mere judicial determination of reliability. It thus replaces the constitutionally prescribed method of assessing reliability with a wholly foreign one. In this respect, it is very different from exceptions to the Confrontation Clause that make no claim to be a surrogate means of assessing reliability. For example, the rule of forfeiture by wrongdoing (which we accept) extinguishes confrontation claims on essentially equitable grounds; it does not purport to be an alternative means of determining reliability. See *Reynolds* v. *United States*, 98 U.S. 145, 158–159 (1879).

The Raleigh trial itself involved the very sorts of reliability determinations that *Roberts* authorizes. In the face of Raleigh's repeated demands for confrontation, the prosecution

---

Clause also does not bar the use of testimonial statements for purposes other than establishing the truth of the matter asserted. See *Tennessee* v. *Street*, 471 U.S. 409, 414 (1985).)

responded with many of the arguments a court applying *Roberts* might invoke today: that Cobham's statements were self-inculpatory, 2 How. St. Tr., at 19, that they were not made in the heat of passion, *id.*, at 14, and that they were not "extracted from [him] upon any hopes or promise of Pardon," *id.*, at 29. It is not plausible that the Framers' only objection to the trial was that Raleigh's judges did not properly weigh these factors before sentencing him to death. Rather, the problem was that the judges refused to allow Raleigh to confront Cobham in court, where he could cross-examine him and try to expose his accusation as a lie.

Dispensing with confrontation because testimony is obviously reliable is akin to dispensing with jury trial because a defendant is obviously guilty. This is not what the Sixth Amendment prescribes.

B

The legacy of *Roberts* in other courts vindicates the Framers' wisdom in rejecting a general reliability exception. The framework is so unpredictable that it fails to provide meaningful protection from even core confrontation violations.

Reliability is an amorphous, if not entirely subjective, concept. There are countless factors bearing on whether a statement is reliable; the nine-factor balancing test applied by the Court of Appeals below is representative. Whether a statement is deemed reliable depends heavily on which factors the judge considers and how much weight he accords each of them. Some courts wind up attaching the same significance to opposite facts....

The unpardonable vice of the *Roberts* test, however, is not its unpredictability, but its demonstrated capacity to admit core testimonial statements that the Confrontation Clause plainly meant to exclude. Despite the plurality's speculation in *Lilly*, 527 U.S., at 137, that it was "highly unlikely" that accomplice confessions implicating the accused could survive *Roberts*, courts continue routinely to admit them.... Courts have invoked *Roberts* to admit other sorts of plainly testimonial statements despite the absence of any opportunity to cross-examine. [The Court here cites to lower court cases admitting grand jury testimony, prior trial testimony, and plea allocution testimony.]

To add insult to injury, some of the courts that admit untested testimonial statements find reliability in the very factors that *make* the statements testimonial.... [O]ne court relied on the fact that the witness's statement was made to police while in custody on pending charges—the theory being that this made the statement more clearly against penal interest and thus more reliable. Other courts routinely rely on the fact that a prior statement is given under oath in judicial proceedings. That inculpating statements are given in a testimonial setting is not an antidote to the confrontation problem, but rather the trigger that makes the Clause's demands most urgent. It is not enough to point out that most of the usual safeguards of the adversary process attend the statement, when the single safeguard missing is the one the Confrontation Clause demands.

C

Roberts' failings were on full display in the proceedings below. Sylvia Crawford made her statement while in police custody, herself a potential suspect in the case. Indeed, she had been told that whether she would be released "depend[ed] on how the investigation continues." In response to often leading questions from police detectives, she implicated her husband in Lee's stabbing and at least arguably undermined his self-defense claim. Despite all this, the trial court admitted her statement, listing several reasons why it was reliable. In its opinion reversing, the Court of Appeals listed several *other* reasons why the statement was *not* reliable. Finally, the State Supreme Court relied exclusively on the interlocking character of the statement and disregarded every other factor the lower courts had considered. The case is thus a self-contained demonstration of *Roberts'* unpredictable and inconsistent application....

We readily concede that we could resolve this case by simply reweighing the "reliability factors" under *Roberts* and finding that Sylvia Crawford's statement falls short. But we view this as one of those rare cases in which the result below is so improbable that it reveals a fundamental failure on our part to interpret the Constitution in a way that secures its intended constraint on judicial discretion. Moreover, to reverse the Washington Supreme Court's decision after conducting our own reliability analysis would perpetuate, not avoid, what the Sixth Amendment condemns. The Constitution prescribes a procedure for determining the reliability of testimony in criminal trials, and we, no less than the state courts, lack authority to replace it with one of our own devising.

We have no doubt that the courts below were acting in utmost good faith when they found reliability. The Framers, however, would not have been content to indulge this assumption. They knew that judges, like other government officers, could not always be trusted to safeguard the rights of the people; the likes of the dread Lord Jeffreys were not yet too distant a memory. They were loath to leave too much discretion in judicial hands. By replacing categorical constitutional guarantees with open-ended balancing tests, we do violence to their design. Vague standards are manipulable, and, while that might be a small concern in run-of-the-mill assault prosecutions like this one, the Framers had an eye toward politically charged cases like Raleigh's—great state trials where the impartiality of even those at the highest levels of the judiciary might not be so clear. It is difficult to imagine *Roberts*[] providing any meaningful protection in those circumstances.

* * *

Where nontestimonial hearsay is at issue, it is wholly consistent with the Framers' design to afford the States flexibility in their development of hearsay law—as does *Roberts*, and as would an approach that exempted such statements from Confrontation Clause scrutiny altogether. Where testimonial evidence is at issue, however, the Sixth Amendment demands what the common law required: unavailability and a prior opportunity for cross-examination. We leave for another day any effort to spell out a comprehensive definition of "testimonial."[10] Whatever else the term covers, it applies at a minimum to prior testimony at a preliminary hearing, before a grand jury, or at a former trial; and to police interrogations. These are the modern practices with closest kinship to the abuses at which the Confrontation Clause was directed.

In this case, the State admitted Sylvia's testimonial statement against petitioner, despite the fact that he had no opportunity to cross-examine her. That alone is sufficient to make out a violation of the Sixth Amendment. *Roberts* notwithstanding, we decline to mine the record in search of indicia of reliability. Where testimonial statements are at issue, the only indicium of reliability sufficient to satisfy constitutional demands is the one the Constitution actually prescribes: confrontation....

[The concurring opinion of Chief Justice Rehnquist is omitted.]

---

10. We acknowledge THE CHIEF JUSTICE's objection that our refusal to articulate a comprehensive definition in this case will cause interim uncertainty. But it can hardly be any worse than the status quo. The difference is that the *Roberts* test is *inherently*, and therefore *permanently*, unpredictable.

Notes and Questions

1. To admit prior out-of-court testimonial statements without having the declarant appear as a witness and be subject to cross-examination, the *Crawford* opinion — unlike *Roberts* — pretty clearly requires *both* prior cross-examination *and* unavailability. Only one hearsay exception, that for former testimony (804(b)(1)) requires both of those, and so statements that satisfy that exception should also satisfy *Crawford*. *See United States v. Avants*, 367 F.3d 433, 445 (5th Cir. 2004). That means, does it not, that testimonial statements that satisfy the *minimum* requirements of any other hearsay exception (save for those that *require* the declarant to appear as a witness and be subject to cross-examination) will *not* satisfy *Crawford*?

2. Although *Crawford* indicates that evidence fitting the business records exception and the exception for statements made in furtherance of a conspiracy would not be barred by the Confrontation Clause under its holding, that is so because the *nature* of statements fitting those exceptions is such that they would not be likely to fall within the *Crawford* Court's definition of "testimonial." In most instances, for example, a statement that fits *Crawford*'s definition of "testimonial" is unlikely to satisfy Rule 801(d)(2)(E)'s requirement that the statement be "in furtherance of the conspiracy." *See United States v. Holmes*, 406 F.3d 337, 348 (5th Cir. 2005) ("Statements made by a co-conspirator during the course and in furtherance of a conspiracy are by their nature generally nontestimonial."). But in applying *Crawford*, what matters is not the particular exception invoked but rather the circumstances in which the statement is made, and even, say, a statement falling within the scope of an exception such as that for statements made in furtherance of a conspiracy might be deemed "testimonial." *See United States v. Logan*, 419 F.3d 172, 178–79 (2d Cir. 2005) (holding that false alibi statements made to police by defendant's co-conspirators would be testimonial under *Crawford* if offered to prove the truth of the matter asserted, but nonetheless admissible because not offered to prove the truth of the matter asserted); *accord Holmes*, 406 F.3d at 348–49 (distinguishing between a "run-of-the-mill co-conspirator's statement made unwittingly to a confidential government informant or made casually to a partner-in-crime" and "a co-conspirator's statement that is derived from a formalized testimonial source"). *See also Melendez-Diaz v. Massachusetts*, 129 S.Ct. 2527, 2539–40 (2009) ("Respondent also misunderstands the relationship between the business-and-official-records hearsay exceptions and the Confrontation Clause. . . . Business and public records are generally admissible absent confrontation not because they qualify under an exception to the hearsay rules, but because — having been created for the administration of an entity's affairs and not for the purpose of establishing or proving some fact at trial — they are not testimonial.").

3. Footnote 9 of the *Crawford* opinion re-affirms the Court's holding in *California v. Green*, 399 U.S. 149 (1970), that the Confrontation Clause poses no barrier to the admission of even testimonial statements when the declarant appears for cross-examination.

Footnote 9 also reaffirms the Supreme Court's prior holding in *Tennessee v. Street*, 471 U.S. 409 (1985). In *Street*, the Court held that when a statement is offered for some reason other than to prove the truth of the matter asserted, it "raises no Confrontation Clause concerns," and that a limiting instruction would suffice to prevent the substantive use of the evidence by the jury. *Id.* at 414–16. Is that consistent with the Court's prior holding in *Bruton* that the Confrontation Clause is violated when a confession by one co-defendant that implicates (and is not admissible against) the other is introduced at their joint trial along with a limiting instruction? In both situations, isn't there a risk that the evidence will be misused by the jury in a way that will violate a defendant's Confrontation Clause rights? *See id.* (explaining that in the *Bruton* situation, there are alternatives, such as severance and redaction, that are not available in the *Street* context).

Moreover, what if something is deemed not to be hearsay because it involves an *implied* assertion, as in *Zenni*, and thus falls outside of the definition of hearsay set forth in Rule 801? Recall that at common law, such evidence was sometimes treated as hearsay when offered as evidence of the declarant's belief in a fact sought to be proved. By excluding such evidence from the definition of hearsay in Rule 801, did the drafters of the federal rules also insulate such evidence from scrutiny under the Confrontation Clause? Would that be consistent with the approach the Court has espoused in *Crawford*? *See generally* James L. Kainen & Carrie A. Tendler, *The Case for a Constitutional Definition of Hearsay: Requiring Confrontation of Testimonial, Nonassertive Conduct and Statements Admitted to Explain an Unchallenged Investigation*, 93 Marq. L. Rev. 1415 (2010).

4. Can a criminal defendant invoke *Crawford* to prevent testimonial hearsay from being offered against him during the *sentencing* phase of his trial? *See United States v. Powell*, 2011 WL 1797893, at *2–*4 (4th Cir. 2011) (collecting cases across the circuits holding that the Confrontation Clause does not apply during the sentencing phase).

5. If a defendant's trial ended before *Crawford* was decided, but his case was still pending *direct* appellate review at the time *Crawford* was decided, is he entitled to invoke *Crawford* on appeal with respect to evidence admitted at trial that would have been admissible under *Roberts* but that is inadmissible under *Crawford*? *See United States v. Sandles*, 469 F.3d 508, 516 n.5 (6th Cir. 2006) (holding that he can). If instead, he had exhausted all direct appellate review before *Crawford* was decided, can he invoke *Crawford* on collateral (habeas) review? *See Whorton v. Bockting*, 549 U.S. 406, 416–21 (2007) (holding that *Crawford* does not apply retroactively to cases on collateral review).

6. What does it mean to be "unavailable" for Confrontation Clause purposes? In *Barber v. Page*, 390 U.S. 719, 724–25 (1968), the Supreme Court held that if a witness fails to appear at trial, he will be deemed "unavailable" for Confrontation Clause purposes so long as the government has made a "good-faith effort" to obtain the declarant's testimony at trial. Recognized categories of unavailability for Confrontation Clause purposes generally track the categories of unavailability listed in Federal Rule 804(a), and include death, extended illness, failed memory, a claim of privilege, or a refusal to testify, in addition to the failure to appear despite good-faith efforts by the prosecution to procure his attendance. *See Ohio v. Roberts*, 448 U.S. 56, 74 (1980); *California v. Green*, 399 U.S. 149, 165–68 (1970); *United States v. Jacobs*, 97 F.3d 275, 282 (8th Cir. 1996). Do these pre-*Crawford* decisions survive *Crawford*? *See United States v. Tirado-Tirado*, 563 F.3d 117, 123 n.3 (5th Cir. 2009) (so holding). *See also Crawford*, 541 U.S. at 57 (citing, with approval, *Barber* and *Green*).

3. Refining the Doctrine: The Meaning of "Testimonial" and Possible Exceptions to *Crawford*

Problem 7-45: Confront This!

On December 5, 2011, Barbara Thompson, a 911 operator, received a call in which the caller screamed, "Oh my God! You have to get down here right away! My sister's former husband, David Peterson, just shot her!" The caller identified her sister as Maria Vallencia. Thompson dispatched an ambulance and the police to Vallencia's apartment.

Moments later, Vallencia's next-door neighbor, Kathy Willis, entered Vallencia's apartment and yelled, "Are you OK?" She then discovered Vallencia on the floor, who said to her, "David just shot me! I don't feel very well, but I think I'll survive."

Shortly thereafter, Tom Burrows, an emergency medical technician, arrived at the Vallencia residence, where he found Vallencia on the floor in a pool of blood. After examining her, he said "Ma'am, your situation is quite serious, and there is a good chance that you won't survive more than a few hours. Do you have any loved ones that you would like me to call?"

At that moment, Lana Fredericks, a police officer, entered the apartment. While Burrows moved Vallencia onto a stretcher, Vallencia said to Fredericks, "My ex-husband, David, shot me after I told him I was going to move out-of-state and take the children with me. Oh God, I can't believe that I won't see my children again!"

Shortly thereafter, Vallencia is taken to the hospital. Lana Fredericks searches the apartment and finds Vallencia's daughter, Nina Peterson, hiding in a closet. When Lana Fredericks asks Nina Peterson what she saw, Nina responds "my daddy shot my mommy with a gun."

Vallencia dies in the hospital, and her ex-husband, David Peterson, is eventually indicted on charges of murder.

At trial, the prosecution seeks to call as witnesses Barbara Thompson, Kathy Willis, and Lana Fredericks. If permitted, Thompson would testify to what Vallencia's sister said to her, while Willis and Fredericks would testify to what Vallencia said to them. Peterson's attorney objects on hearsay and Confrontation Clause grounds.

In addition, the prosecution calls Nina Peterson as a witness, but she refuses to answer any questions. At that point, the prosecution informs the judge that they have evidence—in the form of testimony by Nina's psychologist—that Nina told her that David Peterson threatened to kill her if he testified against her. Accordingly, the prosecution seeks to have Lana Fredericks testify to what Nina said to her in the apartment. Peterson's attorney objects to this testimony on hearsay and Confrontation Clause grounds.

How should the government respond to Peterson's hearsay and Confrontation Clause objections, and how will the court likely rule?

Davis v. Washington
547 U.S. 813 (2006)

Justice SCALIA delivered the opinion of the Court.

These cases require us to determine when statements made to law enforcement personnel during a 911 call or at a crime scene are "testimonial" and thus subject to the requirements of the Sixth Amendment's Confrontation Clause.

I

A

The relevant statements in *Davis* v. *Washington*, No. 05-5224, were made to a 911 emergency operator on February 1, 2001. When the operator answered the initial call, the connection terminated before anyone spoke. She reversed the call, and Michelle Mc-Cottry answered. In the ensuing conversation, the operator ascertained that McCottry was involved in a domestic disturbance with her former boyfriend Adrian Davis, the petitioner in this case:

"911 Operator: Hello.

"Complainant: Hello.

"911 Operator: What's going on?

"Complainant: He's here jumpin' on me again.

"911 Operator: Okay. Listen to me carefully. Are you in a house or an apartment?

"Complainant: I'm in a house.

"911 Operator: Are there any weapons?

"Complainant: No. He's usin' his fists.

"911 Operator: Okay. Has he been drinking?

"Complainant: No.

"911 Operator: Okay, sweetie. I've got help started. Stay on the line with me, okay?

"Complainant: I'm on the line.

"911 Operator: Listen to me carefully. Do you know his last name?

"Complainant: It's Davis.

"911 Operator: Davis? Okay, what's his first name?

"Complainant: Adrian

"911 Operator: What is it?

"Complainant: Adrian.

"911 Operator: Adrian?

"Complainant: Yeah.

"911 Operator: Okay. What's his middle initial?

"Complainant: Martell. He's runnin' now."

As the conversation continued, the operator learned that Davis had "just r[un] out the door" after hitting McCottry, and that he was leaving in a car with someone else. McCottry started talking, but the operator cut her off, saying, "Stop talking and answer my questions." She then gathered more information about Davis (including his birthday), and learned that Davis had told McCottry that his purpose in coming to the house was "to get his stuff," since McCottry was moving. McCottry described the context of the assault, after which the operator told her that the police were on their way. "They're gonna check the area for him first," the operator said, "and then they're gonna come talk to you."

The police arrived within four minutes of the 911 call and observed McCottry's shaken state, the "fresh injuries on her forearm and her face," and her "frantic efforts to gather her belongings and her children so that they could leave the residence."

The State charged Davis with felony violation of a domestic no-contact order. "The State's only witnesses were the two police officers who responded to the 911 call. Both officers testified that McCottry exhibited injuries that appeared to be recent, but neither officer could testify as to the cause of the injuries." McCottry presumably could have testified as to whether Davis was her assailant, but she did not appear. Over Davis's objection, based on the Confrontation Clause of the Sixth Amendment, the trial court admitted the recording of her exchange with the 911 operator, and the jury convicted him. The Washington Court of Appeals affirmed. The Supreme Court of Washington, with one dissenting justice, also affirmed, concluding that the portion of the 911 conversation in which McCottry identified Davis was not testimonial, and that if other portions of the conversation were testimonial, admitting them was harmless beyond a reasonable doubt. We granted certiorari.

B

In *Hammon* v. *Indiana*, No. 05-5705, police responded late on the night of February 26, 2003, to a "reported domestic disturbance" at the home of Hershel and Amy Hammon. They found Amy alone on the front porch, appearing "'somewhat frightened,'" but she told them that "'nothing was the matter'". She gave them permission to enter the house, where an officer saw "a gas heating unit in the corner of the living room" that had "flames coming out of the ... partial glass front. There were pieces of glass on the ground in front of it and there was flame emitting from the front of the heating unit."

Hershel, meanwhile, was in the kitchen. He told the police "that he and his wife had 'been in an argument' but 'everything was fine now' and the argument 'never became physical.'" By this point Amy had come back inside. One of the officers remained with Hershel; the other went to the living room to talk with Amy, and "again asked [her] what had occurred." Hershel made several attempts to participate in Amy's conversation with the police, but was rebuffed. The officer later testified that Hershel "became angry when I insisted that [he] stay separated from Mrs. Hammon so that we can investigate what had happened." After hearing Amy's account, the officer "had her fill out and sign a battery affidavit." Amy handwrote the following: "Broke our Furnace & shoved me down on the floor into the broken glass. Hit me in the chest and threw me down. Broke our lamps & phone. Tore up my van where I couldn't leave the house. Attacked my daughter."

The State charged Hershel with domestic battery and with violating his probation. Amy was subpoenaed, but she did not appear at his subsequent bench trial. The State called the officer who had questioned Amy, and asked him to recount what Amy told him and to authenticate the affidavit. Hershel's counsel repeatedly objected to the admission of this evidence. At one point, after hearing the prosecutor defend the affidavit because it was made "under oath," defense counsel said, "That doesn't give us the opportunity to cross examine [the] person who allegedly drafted it. Makes me mad." Nonetheless, the trial court admitted the affidavit as a "present sense impression," and Amy's statements as "excited utterances" that "are expressly permitted in these kinds of cases even if the declarant is not available to testify." The officer thus testified that Amy

> "informed me that she and Hershel had been in an argument. That he became irrate [sic] over the fact of their daughter going to a boyfriend's house. The argument became ... physical after being verbal and she informed me that Mr. Hammon, during the verbal part of the argument was breaking things in the living room and I believe she stated he broke the phone, broke the lamp, broke the front of the heater. When it became physical he threw her down into the glass of the heater.

> ....

"She informed me Mr. Hammon had pushed her onto the ground, had shoved her head into the broken glass of the heater and that he had punched her in the chest twice I believe."

The trial judge found Hershel guilty on both charges, and the Indiana Court of Appeals affirmed in relevant part. The Indiana Supreme Court also affirmed, concluding that Amy's statement was admissible for state-law purposes as an excited utterance; that "a 'testimonial' statement is one given or taken in significant part for purposes of preserving it for potential future use in legal proceedings," where "the motivations of the questioner and declarant are the central concerns"; and that Amy's oral statement was not "testimonial" under these standards. It also concluded that, although the affidavit was testimonial and thus wrongly admitted, it was harmless beyond a reasonable doubt, largely because the trial was to the bench. We granted certiorari.

II

.... In *Crawford v. Washington*, we held that [the Confrontation Clause] bars "admission of testimonial statements of a witness who did not appear at trial unless he was unavailable to testify, and the defendant had had a prior opportunity for cross-examination." A critical portion of this holding, and the portion central to resolution of the two cases now before us, is the phrase "testimonial statements." Only statements of this sort cause the declarant to be a "witness" within the meaning of the Confrontation Clause. It is the testimonial character of the statement that separates it from other hearsay that, while subject to traditional limitations upon hearsay evidence, is not subject to the Confrontation Clause.

Our opinion in *Crawford* set forth "[v]arious formulations" of the core class of " 'testimonial' " statements, but found it unnecessary to endorse any of them, because "some statements qualify under any definition". Among those, we said, were "[s]tatements taken by police officers in the course of interrogations". The questioning that generated the deponent's statement in *Crawford*—which was made and recorded while she was in police custody, after having been given *Miranda* warnings as a possible suspect herself—"qualifies under any conceivable definition" of an " 'interrogation' ". We therefore did not define that term, except to say that "[w]e use [it] ... in its colloquial, rather than any technical legal, sense," and that "one can imagine various definitions..., and we need not select among them in this case." The character of the statements in the present cases is not as clear, and these cases require us to determine more precisely which police interrogations produce testimony.

Without attempting to produce an exhaustive classification of all conceivable statements—or even all conceivable statements in response to police interrogation—as either testimonial or nontestimonial, it suffices to decide the present cases to hold as follows: Statements are nontestimonial when made in the course of police interrogation under circumstances objectively indicating that the primary purpose of the interrogation is to enable police assistance to meet an ongoing emergency. They are testimonial when the circumstances objectively indicate that there is no such ongoing emergency, and that the primary purpose of the interrogation is to establish or prove past events potentially relevant to later criminal prosecution.[1]

---

1. Our holding refers to interrogations because, as explained below, the statements in the cases presently before us are the products of interrogations—which in some circumstances tend to generate testimonial responses. This is not to imply, however, that statements made in the absence of any interrogation are necessarily nontestimonial. The Framers were no more willing to exempt from cross-examination volunteered testimony or answers to open-ended questions than they were to exempt answers to detailed interrogation. (Part of the evidence against Sir Walter Raleigh was a letter from Lord Cobham that was plainly *not* the result of sustained questioning.) And of course even when interrogation ex-

III

A

In *Crawford*, it sufficed for resolution of the case before us to determine that "even if the Sixth Amendment is not solely concerned with testimonial hearsay, that is its primary object, and interrogations by law enforcement officers fall squarely within that class."... The *Davis* case today does not permit us this luxury of indecision. The inquiries of a police operator in the course of a 911 call[2] are an interrogation in one sense, but not in a sense that "qualifies under any conceivable definition." We must decide, therefore, whether the Confrontation Clause applies only to testimonial hearsay; and, if so, whether the recording of a 911 call qualifies.

The answer to the first question was suggested in *Crawford*, even if not explicitly held:

"The text of the Confrontation Clause reflects this focus [on testimonial hearsay]. It applies to 'witnesses' against the accused—in other words, those who 'bear testimony.' 1 N. Webster, An American Dictionary of the English Language (1828). 'Testimony,' in turn, is typically 'a solemn declaration or affirmation made for the purpose of establishing or proving some fact.' *Ibid*. An accuser who makes a formal statement to government officers bears testimony in a sense that a person who makes a casual remark to an acquaintance does not."

A limitation so clearly reflected in the text of the constitutional provision must fairly be said to mark out not merely its "core," but its perimeter.

We are not aware of any early American case invoking the Confrontation Clause or the common-law right to confrontation that did not clearly involve testimony as thus defined. Well into the 20th century, our own Confrontation Clause jurisprudence was carefully applied only in the testimonial context.

Even our later cases, conforming to the reasoning of *Ohio* v. *Roberts*, never in practice dispensed with the Confrontation Clause requirements of unavailability and prior cross-examination in cases that involved testimonial hearsay, see *Crawford*, 541 U. S., at 57–59 (citing cases), with one arguable exception, *see id.*, at 58, n. 8 (discussing *White* v. *Illinois*). Where our cases did dispense with those requirements—even under the *Roberts* approach—the statements at issue were clearly nontestimonial.

Most of the American cases applying the Confrontation Clause or its state constitutional or common-law counterparts involved testimonial statements of the most formal sort—sworn testimony in prior judicial proceedings or formal depositions under oath—which invites the argument that the scope of the Clause is limited to that very formal category. But the English cases that were the progenitors of the Confrontation Clause did not limit the exclusionary rule to prior court testimony and formal depositions. In any event, we do not think it conceivable that the protections of the Confrontation Clause can readily be evaded by having a note-taking policeman *recite* the unsworn hearsay testimony of the declarant, instead of having the declarant sign a deposition. Indeed, if there is one point for which no case—English or early American, state or federal—can be cited, that is it.

---

ists, it is in the final analysis the declarant's statements, not the interrogator's questions, that the Confrontation Clause requires us to evaluate.

2. If 911 operators are not themselves law enforcement officers, they may at least be agents of law enforcement when they conduct interrogations of 911 callers. For purposes of this opinion (and without deciding the point), we consider their acts to be acts of the police. As in *Crawford* v. *Washington*, therefore, our holding today makes it unnecessary to consider whether and when statements made to someone other than law enforcement personnel are "testimonial."

The question before us in *Davis*, then, is whether, objectively considered, the interrogation that took place in the course of the 911 call produced testimonial statements. When we said in *Crawford* that "interrogations by law enforcement officers fall squarely within [the] class" of testimonial hearsay, we had immediately in mind (for that was the case before us) interrogations solely directed at establishing the facts of a past crime, in order to identify (or provide evidence to convict) the perpetrator. The product of such interrogation, whether reduced to a writing signed by the declarant or embedded in the memory (and perhaps notes) of the interrogating officer, is testimonial. It is, in the terms of the 1828 American dictionary quoted in *Crawford*, "'[a] solemn declaration or affirmation made for the purpose of establishing or proving some fact.'" (The solemnity of even an oral declaration of relevant past fact to an investigating officer is well enough established by the severe consequences that can attend a deliberate falsehood. See, *e.g., United States* v. *Stewart*, 433 F.3d 273, 288 (CA2 2006) (false statements made to federal investigators violate 18 U.S.C. § 1001); *State* v. *Reed*, 2005 WI 53, ¶ 30, 695 N.W.2d 315, 323 (state criminal offense to "knowingly giv[e] false information to [an] officer with [the] intent to mislead the officer in the performance of his or her duty").) A 911 call, on the other hand, and at least the initial interrogation conducted in connection with a 911 call, is ordinarily not designed primarily to "establis[h] or prov[e]" some past fact, but to describe current circumstances requiring police assistance.

The difference between the interrogation in *Davis* and the one in *Crawford* is apparent on the face of things. In *Davis*, McCottry was speaking about events *as they were actually happening*, rather than "describ[ing] past events," *Lilly* v. *Virginia*, 527 U. S. 116, 137 (1999) (plurality opinion). Sylvia Crawford's interrogation, on the other hand, took place hours after the events she described had occurred. Moreover, any reasonable listener would recognize that McCottry (unlike Sylvia Crawford) was facing an ongoing emergency. Although one *might* call 911 to provide a narrative report of a crime absent any imminent danger, McCottry's call was plainly a call for help against bona fide physical threat. Third, the nature of what was asked and answered in *Davis*, again viewed objectively, was such that the elicited statements were necessary to be able to *resolve* the present emergency, rather than simply to learn (as in *Crawford*) what had happened in the past. That is true even of the operator's effort to establish the identity of the assailant, so that the dispatched officers might know whether they would be encountering a violent felon. And finally, the difference in the level of formality between the two interviews is striking. Crawford was responding calmly, at the station house, to a series of questions, with the officer-interrogator taping and making notes of her answers; McCottry's frantic answers were provided over the phone, in an environment that was not tranquil, or even (as far as any reasonable 911 operator could make out) safe.

We conclude from all this that the circumstances of McCottry's interrogation objectively indicate its primary purpose was to enable police assistance to meet an ongoing emergency. She simply was not acting as a *witness*; she was not *testifying*. What she said was not "a weaker substitute for live testimony" at trial, *United States* v. *Inadi*, 475 U. S. 387, 394 (1986), like Lord Cobham's statements in *Raleigh's Case*, 2 How. St. Tr. 1 (1603), or Jane Dingler's *ex parte* statements against her husband in *King* v. *Dingler*, 2 Leach 561, 168 Eng. Rep. 383 (1791), or Sylvia Crawford's statement in *Crawford*. In each of those cases, the *ex parte* actors and the evidentiary products of the *ex parte* communication aligned perfectly with their courtroom analogues. McCottry's emergency statement does not. No "witness" goes into court to proclaim an emergency and seek help.

Davis seeks to cast McCottry in the unlikely role of a witness by pointing to English cases. None of them involves statements made during an ongoing emergency. In *King* v.

Brasier, 1 Leach 199, 168 Eng. Rep. 202 (1779), for example, a young rape victim, "immediately on her coming home, told all the circumstances of the injury" to her mother. The case would be helpful to Davis if the relevant statement had been the girl's screams for aid as she was being chased by her assailant. But by the time the victim got home, her story was an account of past events.

This is not to say that a conversation which begins as an interrogation to determine the need for emergency assistance cannot, as the Indiana Supreme Court put it, "evolve into testimonial statements," once that purpose has been achieved. In this case, for example, after the operator gained the information needed to address the exigency of the moment, the emergency appears to have ended (when Davis drove away from the premises). The operator then told McCottry to be quiet, and proceeded to pose a battery of questions. It could readily be maintained that, from that point on, McCottry's statements were testimonial, not unlike the "structured police questioning" that occurred in *Crawford*. This presents no great problem. Just as, for Fifth Amendment purposes, "police officers can and will distinguish almost instinctively between questions necessary to secure their own safety or the safety of the public and questions designed solely to elicit testimonial evidence from a suspect," trial courts will recognize the point at which, for Sixth Amendment purposes, statements in response to interrogations become testimonial. Through *in limine* procedure, they should redact or exclude the portions of any statement that have become testimonial, as they do, for example, with unduly prejudicial portions of otherwise admissible evidence. Davis's jury did not hear the *complete* 911 call, although it may well have heard some testimonial portions. We were asked to classify only McCottry's early statements identifying Davis as her assailant, and we agree with the Washington Supreme Court that they were not testimonial. That court also concluded that, even if later parts of the call were testimonial, their admission was harmless beyond a reasonable doubt. Davis does not challenge that holding, and we therefore assume it to be correct.

B

Determining the testimonial or nontestimonial character of the statements that were the product of the interrogation in *Hammon* is a much easier task, since they were not much different from the statements we found to be testimonial in *Crawford*. It is entirely clear from the circumstances that the interrogation was part of an investigation into possibly criminal past conduct — as, indeed, the testifying officer expressly acknowledged. There was no emergency in progress; the interrogating officer testified that he had heard no arguments or crashing and saw no one throw or break anything. When the officers first arrived, Amy told them that things were fine, and there was no immediate threat to her person. When the officer questioned Amy for the second time, and elicited the challenged statements, he was not seeking to determine (as in *Davis*) "what is happening," but rather "what happened." Objectively viewed, the primary, if not indeed the sole, purpose of the interrogation was to investigate a possible crime — which is, of course, precisely what the officer *should* have done.

It is true that the *Crawford* interrogation was more formal. It followed a *Miranda* warning, was tape-recorded, and took place at the station house. While these features certainly strengthened the statements' testimonial aspect — made it more objectively apparent, that is, that the purpose of the exercise was to nail down the truth about past criminal events — none was essential to the point. It was formal enough that Amy's interrogation was conducted in a separate room, away from her husband (who tried to intervene), with the officer receiving her replies for use in his "investigat[ion]." What we called the "striking resemblance" of the *Crawford* statement to civil-law *ex parte* examinations is shared by Amy's statement here. Both declarants were actively separated from the defendant—officers forcibly prevented Hershel from participating in the interrogation. Both statements deliberately recounted, in response to police questioning, how potentially criminal past events began and progressed. And both took place some time after the events described were over. Such statements under official interrogation are an obvious substitute for live testimony, because they do precisely *what a witness does* on direct examination; they are inherently testimonial.[5]

Both Indiana and the United States as *amicus curiae* argue that this case should be resolved much like *Davis*. For the reasons we find the comparison to *Crawford* compelling, we find the comparison to *Davis* unpersuasive. The statements in *Davis* were taken when McCottry was alone, not only unprotected by police (as Amy Hammon was protected), but apparently in immediate danger from Davis. She was seeking aid, not telling a story about the past. McCottry's present-tense statements showed immediacy; Amy's narrative of past events was delivered at some remove in time from the danger she described. And after Amy answered the officer's questions, he had her execute an affidavit, in order, he testified, "[t]o establish events that have occurred previously."

Although we necessarily reject the Indiana Supreme Court's implication that virtually any "initial inquiries" at the crime scene will not be testimonial, we do not hold the opposite—that *no* questions at the scene will yield nontestimonial answers. We have already observed of domestic disputes that "[o]fficers called to investigate ... need to know whom they are dealing with in order to assess the situation, the threat to their own safety, and possible danger to the potential victim." Such exigencies may *often* mean that "initial inquiries" produce nontestimonial statements. But in cases like this one, where Amy's statements were neither a cry for help nor the provision of information enabling officers immediately to end a threatening situation, the fact that they were given at an alleged crime scene and were "initial inquiries" is immaterial.[6]

---

5. The dissent criticizes our test for being "neither workable nor a targeted attempt to reach the abuses forbidden by the [Confrontation] Clause". As to the former: We have acknowledged that our holding is not an "exhaustive classification of all conceivable statements—or even all conceivable statements in response to police interrogation," but rather a resolution of the cases before us and those like them. For *those* cases, the test is objective and quite "workable." The dissent, in attempting to formulate an exhaustive classification of its own, has not provided anything that deserves the description "workable"—unless one thinks that the distinction between "formal" and "informal" statements qualifies. And the dissent even qualifies that vague distinction by acknowledging that the Confrontation Clause "also reaches the use of technically informal statements when used to evade the formalized process" and cautioning that the Clause would stop the State from "us[ing] out-of-court statements as a means of circumventing the literal right of confrontation". It is hard to see this as much more "predictable" than the rule we adopt for the narrow situations we address. (Indeed, under the dissent's approach it is eminently arguable that the dissent should agree, rather than disagree, with our disposition in *Hammon* v. *Indiana*, No. 05-5705.)

As for the charge that our holding is not a "targeted attempt to reach the abuses forbidden by the [Confrontation] Clause," which the dissent describes as the depositions taken by Marian magistrates, characterized by a high degree of formality: We do not dispute that formality is indeed essential to testimonial utterance. But we no longer have examining Marian magistrates; and we do have, as our 18th-century forebears did not, examining police officers—who perform investigative and testimonial functions once performed by examining Marian magistrates. It imports sufficient formality, in our view, that lies to such officers are criminal offenses. Restricting the Confrontation Clause to the precise forms against which it was originally directed is a recipe for its extinction.

6. Police investigations themselves are, of course, in no way impugned by our characterization of their fruits as testimonial. Investigations of past crimes prevent future harms and lead to necessary arrests. While prosecutors may hope that inculpatory "nontestimonial" evidence is gathered, this is

IV

Respondents in both cases, joined by a number of their *amici*, contend that the nature of the offenses charged in these two cases—domestic violence—requires greater flexibility in the use of testimonial evidence. This particular type of crime is notoriously susceptible to intimidation or coercion of the victim to ensure that she does not testify at trial. When this occurs, the Confrontation Clause gives the criminal a windfall. We may not, however, vitiate constitutional guarantees when they have the effect of allowing the guilty to go free. But when defendants seek to undermine the judicial process by procuring or coercing silence from witnesses and victims, the Sixth Amendment does not require courts to acquiesce. While defendants have no duty to assist the State in proving their guilt, they *do* have the duty to refrain from acting in ways that destroy the integrity of the criminal-trial system. We reiterate what we said in *Crawford*: that "the rule of forfeiture by wrong-doing ... extinguishes confrontation claims on essentially equitable grounds." That is, one who obtains the absence of a witness by wrongdoing forfeits the constitutional right to confrontation.

We take no position on the standards necessary to demonstrate such forfeiture, but federal courts using Federal Rule of Evidence 804(b)(6), which codifies the forfeiture doctrine, have generally held the Government to the preponderance-of-the-evidence standard. State courts tend to follow the same practice. Moreover, if a hearing on forfeiture is required, *Edwards*, for instance, observed that "hearsay evidence, including the unavailable witness's out-of-court statements, may be considered." The *Roberts* approach to the Confrontation Clause undoubtedly made recourse to this doctrine less necessary, because prosecutors could show the "reliability" of *ex parte* statements more easily than they could show the defendant's procurement of the witness's absence. *Crawford*, in overruling *Roberts*, did not destroy the ability of courts to protect the integrity of their proceedings.

We have determined that, absent a finding of forfeiture by wrongdoing, the Sixth Amendment operates to exclude Amy Hammon's affidavit. The Indiana courts may (if they are asked) determine on remand whether such a claim of forfeiture is properly raised and, if so, whether it is meritorious....

Justice THOMAS, concurring in the judgment in part and dissenting in part.

In *Crawford* v. *Washington*, we abandoned the general reliability inquiry we had long employed to judge the admissibility of hearsay evidence under the Confrontation Clause, describing that inquiry as "*inherently*, and therefore *permanently*, unpredictable." Today, a mere two years after the Court decided *Crawford*, it adopts an equally unpredictable test, under which district courts are charged with divining the "primary purpose" of police interrogations. Besides being difficult for courts to apply, this test characterizes as "testimonial," and therefore inadmissible, evidence that bears little resemblance to what we have recognized as the evidence targeted by the Confrontation Clause. Because neither of the cases before the Court today would implicate the Confrontation Clause under an appropriately targeted standard, I concur only in the judgment in *Davis* v. *Washington*, No. 05-5224, and dissent from the Court's resolution of *Hammon* v. *Indiana*, No. 05-5705.

---

essentially beyond police control. Their saying that an emergency exists cannot make it be so. The Confrontation Clause in no way governs police conduct, because it is the trial *use* of, not the investigatory *collection* of, *ex parte* testimonial statements which offends that provision. But neither can police conduct govern the Confrontation Clause; testimonial statements are what they are.

I

A

.... We have recognized that the operative phrase in the [Confrontation] Clause, "witnesses against him," could be interpreted narrowly, to reach only those witnesses who actually testify at trial, or more broadly, to reach many or all of those whose out-of-court statements are offered at trial. Because the narrowest interpretation of the Clause would conflict with both the history giving rise to the adoption of the Clause and this Court's precedent, we have rejected such a reading.

Rejection of the narrowest view of the Clause does not, however, require the broadest application of the Clause to exclude otherwise admissible hearsay evidence. The history surrounding the right to confrontation supports the conclusion that it was developed to target particular practices that occurred under the English bail and committal statutes passed during the reign of Queen Mary, namely, the "civil-law mode of criminal procedure, and particularly its use of *ex parte* examinations as evidence against the accused."...

In *Crawford*, we recognized that this history could be squared with the language of the Clause, giving rise to a workable, and more accurate, interpretation of the Clause. "'[W]itnesses,'" we said, are those who "'bear testimony.'" And "'[t]estimony'" is "'[a] solemn declaration or affirmation made for the purpose of establishing or proving some fact.'" Admittedly, we did not set forth a detailed framework for addressing whether a statement is "testimonial" and thus subject to the Confrontation Clause. But the plain terms of the "testimony" definition we endorsed necessarily require some degree of solemnity before a statement can be deemed "testimonial."

This requirement of solemnity supports my view that the statements regulated by the Confrontation Clause must include "extrajudicial statements ... contained in formalized testimonial materials, such as affidavits, depositions, prior testimony, or confessions." Affidavits, depositions, and prior testimony are, by their very nature, taken through a formalized process. Likewise, confessions, when extracted by police in a formal manner, carry sufficient indicia of solemnity to constitute formalized statements and, accordingly, bear a "striking resemblance" to the examinations of the accused and accusers under the Marian statutes.[1]

Although the Court concedes that the early American cases invoking the right to confrontation or the Confrontation Clause itself all "clearly involve[d] testimony" as defined in *Crawford*, it fails to acknowledge that all of the cases it cites fall within the narrower category of formalized testimonial materials I have proposed.[2] Interactions between the police and an accused (or witnesses) resemble Marian proceedings — and these early cases — only when the interactions are somehow rendered "formal." In *Crawford*, for example, the interrogation was custodial, taken after warnings given pursuant to *Miranda* v. *Arizona*. *Miranda* warnings, by their terms, inform a prospective defendant that "'anything he says can be used against him in a court of law.'" This imports a solemnity to the

---

1. Like the Court, I presume the acts of the 911 operator to be the acts of the police. Accordingly, I refer to both the operator in *Davis* and the officer in *Hammon*, and their counterparts in similar cases, collectively as "the police."

2. Our more recent cases, too, nearly all hold excludable under the Confrontation Clause materials that are plainly highly formal. The only exceptions involve confessions of codefendants to police, and those confessions appear to have either been formal due to their occurrence in custody or to have been formalized into signed documents.

process that is not present in a mere conversation between a witness or suspect and a police officer.[3]

The Court all but concedes that no case can be cited for its conclusion that the Confrontation Clause also applies to informal police questioning under certain circumstances. Instead, the sole basis for the Court's conclusion is its apprehension that the Confrontation Clause will "readily be evaded" if it is only applicable to formalized testimonial materials. But the Court's proposed solution to the risk of evasion is needlessly overinclusive. Because the Confrontation Clause sought to regulate prosecutorial abuse occurring through use of *ex parte* statements as evidence against the accused, it also reaches the use of technically informal statements when used to evade the formalized process. That is, even if the interrogation itself is not formal, the production of evidence by the prosecution at trial would resemble the abuses targeted by the Confrontation Clause if the prosecution attempted to use out-of-court statements as a means of circumventing the literal right of confrontation. In such a case, the Confrontation Clause could fairly be applied to exclude the hearsay statements offered by the prosecution, preventing evasion without simultaneously excluding evidence offered by the prosecution in good faith.

The Court's standard is not only disconnected from history and unnecessary to prevent abuse; it also yields no predictable results to police officers and prosecutors attempting to comply with the law. In many, if not most, cases where police respond to a report of a crime, whether pursuant to a 911 call from the victim or otherwise, the purposes of an interrogation, viewed from the perspective of the police, are *both* to respond to the emergency situation *and* to gather evidence. Assigning one of these two "largely unverifiable motives" primacy requires constructing a hierarchy of purpose that will rarely be present—and is not reliably discernible. It will inevitably be, quite simply, an exercise in fiction.

The Court's repeated invocation of the word "objectiv[e]" to describe its test, however, suggests that the Court may not mean to reference purpose at all, but instead to inquire into the function served by the interrogation. Certainly such a test would avoid the pitfalls that have led us repeatedly to reject tests dependent on the subjective intentions of police officers. It would do so, however, at the cost of being even more disconnected from the prosecutorial abuses targeted by the Confrontation Clause. Additionally, it would shift the ability to control whether a violation occurred from the police and prosecutor to the judge, whose determination as to the "primary purpose" of a particular interrogation would be unpredictable and not necessarily tethered to the actual purpose for which the police performed the interrogation.

B

Neither the 911 call at issue in *Davis* nor the police questioning at issue in *Hammon* is testimonial under the appropriate framework. Neither the call nor the questioning is itself a formalized dialogue.[5] Nor do any circumstances surrounding the taking of the statements render those statements sufficiently formal to resemble the Marian examinations; the statements were neither Mirandized nor custodial, nor accompanied by any similar indicia of formality. Finally, there is no suggestion that the prosecution attempted

3. The possibility that an oral declaration of past fact to a police officer, if false, could result in legal consequences to the speaker may render honesty in casual conversations with police officers important. It does not, however, render those conversations solemn or formal in the ordinary meanings of those terms.

5. Although the police questioning in *Hammon* was ultimately reduced to an affidavit, all agree that the affidavit is inadmissible *per se* under our definition of the term "testimonial."

to offer the women's hearsay evidence at trial in order to evade confrontation. Accordingly, the statements at issue in both cases are nontestimonial and admissible under the Confrontation Clause.

The Court's determination that the evidence against Hammon must be excluded extends the Confrontation Clause far beyond the abuses it was intended to prevent. When combined with the Court's holding that the evidence against Davis is perfectly admissible, however, the Court's *Hammon* holding also reveals the difficulty of applying the Court's requirement that courts investigate the "primary purpose[s]" of the investigation. The Court draws a line between the two cases based on its explanation that *Hammon* involves "no emergency in progress," but instead, mere questioning as "part of an investigation into possibly criminal past conduct," and its explanation that *Davis* involves questioning for the "primary purpose" of "enabl[ing] police assistance to meet an ongoing emergency". But the fact that the officer in *Hammon* was investigating Mr. Hammon's past conduct does not foreclose the possibility that the primary purpose of his inquiry was to assess whether Mr. Hammon constituted a continuing danger to his wife, requiring further police presence or action. It is hardly remarkable that Hammon did not act abusively towards his wife in the presence of the officers, and his good judgment to refrain from criminal behavior in the presence of police sheds little, if any, light on whether his violence would have resumed had the police left without further questioning, transforming what the Court dismisses as "past conduct" back into an "ongoing emergency."[6] Nor does the mere fact that McCottry needed emergency aid shed light on whether the "primary purpose" of gathering, for example, the name of her assailant was to protect the police, to protect the victim, or to gather information for prosecution. In both of the cases before the Court, like many similar cases, pronouncement of the "primary" motive behind the interrogation calls for nothing more than a guess by courts....

Giles v. California
554 U.S. 353 (2008)

Justice SCALIA delivered the opinion of the Court, except as to Part II-D-2.

We consider whether a defendant forfeits his Sixth Amendment right to confront a witness against him when a judge determines that a wrongful act by the defendant made the witness unavailable to testify at trial.

I

On September 29, 2002, petitioner Dwayne Giles shot his ex-girlfriend, Brenda Avie, outside the garage of his grandmother's house.... Giles fled the scene after the shooting. He was apprehended by police about two weeks later and charged with murder.

At trial, Giles testified that he had acted in self-defense.... He said that Avie charged at him, and that he was afraid she had something in her hand. According to Giles, he closed his eyes and fired several shots, but did not intend to kill Avie.

Prosecutors sought to introduce statements that Avie had made to a police officer responding to a domestic-violence report about three weeks before the shooting. Avie, who

---

6. Some of the factors on which the Court relies to determine that the police questioning in *Hammon* was testimonial apply equally in *Davis*. For example, while Hammon was "actively separated from the [victim]" and thereby "prevented ... from participating in the interrogation," Davis was apart from McCottry while she was questioned by the 911 operator and thus unable to participate in the questioning. Similarly, "the events described [by McCottry] were over" by the time she recounted them to the 911 operator.

was crying when she spoke, told the officer that Giles had accused her of having an affair, and that after the two began to argue, Giles grabbed her by the shirt, lifted her off the floor, and began to choke her. According to Avie, when she broke free and fell to the floor, Giles punched her in the face and head, and after she broke free again, he opened a folding knife, held it about three feet away from her, and threatened to kill her if he found her cheating on him. Over Giles' objection, the trial court admitted these statements into evidence....

A jury convicted Giles of first-degree murder....

II

.... The State does not dispute here, and we accept without deciding, that Avie's statements accusing Giles of assault were testimonial. But it maintains (as did the California Supreme Court) that the Sixth Amendment did not prohibit prosecutors from introducing the statements because an exception to the confrontation guarantee permits the use of a witness's unconfronted testimony if a judge finds, as the judge did in this case, that the defendant committed a wrongful act that rendered the witness unavailable to testify at trial....

A

We have previously acknowledged that two forms of testimonial statements were admitted at common law even though they were unconfronted. The first of these were declarations made by a speaker who was both on the brink of death and aware that he was dying. Avie did not make the unconfronted statements admitted at Giles' trial when she was dying, so her statements do not fall within this historic exception.

A second common-law doctrine, which we will refer to as forfeiture by wrongdoing, permitted the introduction of statements of a witness who was "detained" or "kept away" by the "means or procurement" of the defendant. The doctrine has roots in the 1666 decision in *Lord Morley's Case*, at which judges concluded that a witness's having been "detained by the means or procurement of the prisoner," provided a basis to read testimony previously given at a coroner's inquest. Courts and commentators also concluded that wrongful procurement of a witness's absence was among the grounds for admission of statements made at bail and committal hearings conducted under the Marian statutes, which directed justices of the peace to take the statements of felony suspects and the persons bringing the suspects before the magistrate, and to certify those statements to the court....

The terms used to define the scope of the forfeiture rule suggest that the exception applied only when the defendant engaged in conduct *designed* to prevent the witness from testifying. The rule required the witness to have been "kept back" or "detained" by "means or procurement" of the defendant. Although there are definitions of "procure" and "procurement" that would merely require that a defendant have caused the witness's absence, other definitions would limit the causality to one that was *designed* to bring about the result "procured." Similarly, while the term "means" could sweep in all cases in which a defendant caused a witness to fail to appear, it can also connote that a defendant forfeits confrontation rights when he uses an intermediary for the purpose of making a witness absent.

Cases and treatises of the time indicate that a purpose-based definition of these terms governed. A number of them said that prior testimony was admissible when a witness was kept away by the defendant's "means and contrivance." This phrase requires that the defendant have schemed to bring about the absence from trial that he "contrived." Contrivance is commonly defined as the act of "inventing, devising or planning," "ingeniously endeavoring the accomplishment of anything," "the bringing to pass by planning, scheming, or stratagem," or "[a]daption of means to an end; design; intention."

An 1858 treatise made the purpose requirement more explicit still, stating that the forfeiture rule applied when a witness "had been kept out of the way by the prisoner, or by some one on the prisoner's behalf, *in order to prevent him from giving evidence against him.*" The wrongful-procurement exception was invoked in a manner consistent with this definition. We are aware of no case in which the exception was invoked although the defendant had not engaged in conduct designed to prevent a witness from testifying, such as offering a bribe.

B

The manner in which the rule was applied makes plain that unconfronted testimony would *not* be admitted without a showing that the defendant intended to prevent a witness from testifying. In cases where the evidence suggested that the defendant had caused a person to be absent, but had not done so to prevent the person from testifying—as in the typical murder case involving accusatorial statements by the victim—the testimony was excluded unless it was confronted or fell within the dying-declaration exception. Prosecutors do not appear to have even *argued* that the judge could admit the unconfronted statements because the defendant committed the murder for which he was on trial....

Judges and prosecutors also failed to invoke forfeiture as a sufficient basis to admit unconfronted statements in the cases that did apply the dying-declarations exception. This failure, too, is striking. At a murder trial, presenting evidence that the defendant was responsible for the victim's death would have been no more difficult than putting on the government's case in chief. Yet prosecutors did not attempt to obtain admission of dying declarations on wrongful-procurement-of-absence grounds before going to the often considerable trouble of putting on evidence to show that the crime victim had not believed he could recover.

The State offers another explanation for the above cases. It argues that when a defendant committed some act of wrongdoing that rendered a witness unavailable, he forfeited his right to object to the witness's testimony on confrontation grounds, but not on hearsay grounds. No case or treatise that we have found, however, suggested that a defendant who committed wrongdoing forfeited his confrontation rights but not his hearsay rights. And the distinction would have been a surprising one, because courts prior to the founding excluded hearsay evidence in large part *because* it was unconfronted....

C

Not only was the State's proposed exception to the right of confrontation plainly not an "exceptio[n] established at the time of the founding"; it is not established in American jurisprudence *since* the founding. American courts never—prior to 1985—invoked forfeiture outside the context of deliberate witness tampering.

This Court first addressed forfeiture in *Reynolds v. United States*, 98 U.S. 145 (1879), where, after hearing testimony that suggested the defendant had kept his wife away from home so that she could not be subpoenaed to testify, the trial court permitted the government to introduce testimony of the defendant's wife from the defendant's prior trial. On appeal, the Court held that admission of the statements did not violate the right of the defendant to confront witnesses at trial, because when a witness is absent by the defendant's "wrongful procurement," the defendant "is in no condition to assert that his constitutional rights have been violated" if "their evidence is supplied in some lawful way." *Reynolds* invoked broad forfeiture principles to explain its holding. The decision stated, for example, that "[t]he Constitution does not guarantee an accused person against the legitimate consequences of his own wrongful acts," and that the wrongful-procurement rule "has its foundation" in the principle that no one should be permitted to take advantage of his wrong, and is "the outgrowth of a maxim based on the principles of common honesty."

Reynolds relied on these maxims (as the common-law authorities had done) to be sure. But it relied on them (as the common-law authorities had done) to admit prior testimony in a case where the defendant had engaged in wrongful conduct designed to prevent a witness's testimony. The Court's opinion indicated that it was adopting the common-law rule. It cited leading common-law cases ... described itself as "content with" the "long-established usage" of the forfeiture principle, and admitted prior confronted statements under circumstances where admissibility was open to no doubt under *Lord Morley's Case.*

If the State's rule had an historical pedigree in the common law or even in the 1879 decision in *Reynolds*, one would have expected it to be routinely invoked in murder prosecutions like the one here, in which the victim's prior statements inculpated the defendant. It was never invoked in this way. The earliest case identified by the litigants and *amici curiae* which admitted unconfronted statements on a forfeiture theory without evidence that the defendant had acted with the purpose of preventing the witness from testifying was decided in 1985.

In 1997, this Court approved a Federal Rule of Evidence, entitled "Forfeiture by wrongdoing," which applies only when the defendant "engaged or acquiesced in wrongdoing that was intended to, and did, procure the unavailability of the declarant as a witness." Fed. Rule of Evid. 804(b)(6).* We have described this as a rule "which codifies the forfeiture doctrine." *Davis v. Washington*, 547 U.S. 813 (2006). Every commentator we are aware of has concluded the requirement of intent "means that the exception applies only if the defendant has in mind the particular purpose of making the witness unavailable."[2] The commentators come out this way because the dissent's claim that knowledge is sufficient to show intent is emphatically *not* the modern view.

In sum, our interpretation of the common-law forfeiture rule is supported by (1) the most natural reading of the language used at common law; (2) the absence of common-law cases *admitting* prior statements on a forfeiture theory when the defendant had not engaged in conduct designed to prevent a witness from testifying; (3) the common law's uniform exclusion of unconfronted inculpatory testimony by murder victims (except testimony given with awareness of impending death) in the innumerable cases in which the defendant was on trial for killing the victim, but was not shown to have done so for the purpose of preventing testimony; (4) a subsequent history in which the dissent's broad forfeiture theory has not been applied. The first two and the last are highly persuasive; the third is in our view conclusive....

---

* Editor's Note: This phrase was restyled in 2011 to read "wrongfully caused — or acquiesced in wrongfully causing — the declarant's unavailability as a witness, and did so intending that result."

2. Only a single state evidentiary code appears to contain a forfeiture rule broader than our holding in this case (and in *Crawford*) allow.... The lone forfeiture exception whose text reaches more broadly than the rule we adopt is an Oregon rule adopted in 2005.

E

The dissent closes by pointing out that a forfeiture rule which ignores *Crawford* would be particularly helpful to women in abusive relationships—or at least particularly helpful in punishing their abusers. Not as helpful as the dissent suggests, since only *testimonial* statements are excluded by the Confrontation Clause. Statements to friends and neighbors about abuse and intimidation, and statements to physicians in the course of receiving treatment would be excluded, if at all, only by hearsay rules, which are free to adopt the dissent's version of forfeiture by wrongdoing. In any event, we are puzzled by the dissent's decision to devote its peroration to domestic abuse cases. Is the suggestion that we should have one Confrontation Clause (the one the Framers adopted and *Crawford* described) for all other crimes, but a special, improvised, Confrontation Clause for those crimes that are frequently directed against women? Domestic violence is an intolerable offense that legislatures may choose to combat through many means—from increasing criminal penalties to adding resources for investigation and prosecution to funding awareness and prevention campaigns. But for that serious crime, as for others, abridging the constitutional rights of criminal defendants is not in the State's arsenal.

The domestic-violence context is, however, relevant for a separate reason. Acts of domestic violence often are intended to dissuade a victim from resorting to outside help, and include conduct designed to prevent testimony to police officers or cooperation in criminal prosecutions. Where such an abusive relationship culminates in murder, the evidence may support a finding that the crime expressed the intent to isolate the victim and to stop her from reporting abuse to the authorities or cooperating with a criminal prosecution-rendering her prior statements admissible under the forfeiture doctrine. Earlier abuse, or threats of abuse, intended to dissuade the victim from resorting to outside help would be highly relevant to this inquiry, as would evidence of ongoing criminal proceedings at which the victim would have been expected to testify. This is not, as the dissent charges, nothing more than "knowledge-based intent."

The state courts in this case did not consider the intent of the defendant because they found that irrelevant to application of the forfeiture doctrine. This view of the law was error, but the court is free to consider evidence of the defendant's intent on remand....

Justice Thomas, concurring.

I write separately to note that I adhere to my view that statements like those made by the victim in this case do not implicate the Confrontation Clause. The contested evidence is indistinguishable from the statements made during police questioning in response to the report of domestic violence in *Hammon v. Indiana*, decided with *Davis v. Washington*, 547 U.S. 813 (2006). There, as here, the police questioning was not "a formalized dialogue"; it was not "sufficiently formal to resemble the Marian examinations" because "the statements were neither Mirandized nor custodial, nor accompanied by any similar indicia of formality"; and "there is no suggestion that the prosecution attempted to offer [Ms. Avie's] hearsay evidence at trial in order to evade confrontation."

Nonetheless, in this case respondent does not argue that the contested evidence is nontestimonial; the court below noted "no dispute" on the issue; and it is outside the scope of the question presented. Because the Court's opinion accurately reflects our Confrontation Clause jurisprudence where the applicability of that Clause is not at issue, I join the Court in vacating the decision below.

[The concurring opinions of Justices Alito and Souter, and the dissenting opinion of Justice Breyer, are omitted.]

Michigan v. Bryant

131 S. Ct. 1143 (2011)

Justice SOTOMAYOR delivered the opinion of the Court.

....

I

Around 3:25 a.m. on April 29, 2001, Detroit, Michigan police officers responded to a radio dispatch indicating that a man had been shot. At the scene, they found the victim, Anthony Covington, lying on the ground next to his car in a gas station parking lot. Covington had a gunshot wound to his abdomen, appeared to be in great pain, and spoke with difficulty.

The police asked him "what had happened, who had shot him, and where the shooting had occurred." Covington stated that "Rick" shot him at around 3 a.m. He also indicated that he had a conversation with Bryant, whom he recognized based on his voice, through the back door of Bryant's house. Covington explained that when he turned to leave, he was shot through the door and then drove to the gas station, where police found him.

Covington's conversation with the police ended within 5 to 10 minutes when emergency medical services arrived. Covington was transported to a hospital and died within hours. The police left the gas station after speaking with Covington, called for backup, and traveled to Bryant's house. They did not find Bryant there but did find blood and a bullet on the back porch and an apparent bullet hole in the back door. Police also found Covington's wallet and identification outside the house.

At trial, which occurred prior to our decisions in *Crawford* and *Davis*, the police officers who spoke with Covington at the gas station testified about what Covington had told them. The jury returned a guilty verdict on charges of second-degree murder, being a felon in possession of a firearm, and possession of a firearm during the commission of a felony....

Before the Supreme Court of Michigan, Bryant argued that Covington's statements to the police were testimonial under *Crawford* and *Davis* and were therefore inadmissible.... The court concluded that the circumstances "clearly indicate that the 'primary purpose' of the questioning was to establish the facts of an event that had *already* occurred; the 'primary purpose' was not to enable police assistance to meet an ongoing emergency." The court explained that, in its view, Covington was describing past events and as such, his "primary purpose in making these statements to the police ... was ... to tell the police who had committed the crime against him, where the crime had been committed, and where the police could find the criminal. Noting that the officers' actions did not suggest that they perceived an ongoing emergency at the gas station, the court held that there was in fact no ongoing emergency. The court distinguished the facts of this case from those in *Davis,* where we held a declarant's statements in a 911 call to be nontestimonial. It instead analogized this case to *Hammon v. Indiana,* which we decided jointly with *Davis* and in which we found testimonial a declarant's statements to police just after an assault. Based on this analysis, the Supreme Court of Michigan held that the admission of Covington's statements constituted prejudicial plain error warranting reversal and ordered a new trial. The court did not address whether, absent a Confrontation Clause bar, the statements' admission would have been otherwise consistent with Michigan's hearsay rules or due process.[1]

---

1. The Supreme Court of Michigan held that the question whether the victim's statements would have been admissible as "dying declarations" was not properly before it because at the preliminary

....

We granted certiorari to determine whether the Confrontation Clause barred admission of Covington's statements.

II

....

Davis did not "attemp[t] to produce an exhaustive classification of all conceivable statements — or even all conceivable statements in response to police interrogation — as either testimonial or nontestimonial." *Id.*, at 822.[3] The basic purpose of the Confrontation Clause was to "targe[t]" the sort of "abuses" exemplified at the notorious treason trial of Sir Walter Raleigh. *Crawford*, 541 U.S., at 51. Thus, the most important instances in which the Clause restricts the introduction of out-of-court statements are those in which state actors are involved in a formal, out-of-court interrogation of a witness to obtain evidence for trial. Even where such an interrogation is conducted with all good faith, introduction of the resulting statements at trial can be unfair to the accused if they are untested by cross-examination. Whether formal or informal, out-of-court statements can evade the basic objective of the Confrontation Clause, which is to prevent the accused from being deprived of the opportunity to cross-examine the declarant about statements taken for use at trial. When, as in *Davis*, the primary purpose of an interrogation is to respond to an "ongoing emergency," its purpose is not to create a record for trial and thus is not within the scope of the Clause. But there may be *other* circumstances, aside from ongoing emergencies, when a statement is not procured with a primary purpose of creating an out-of-court substitute for trial testimony. In making the primary purpose determination, standard rules of hearsay, designed to identify some statements as reliable, will be relevant. Where no such primary purpose exists, the admissibility of a statement is the concern of state and federal rules of evidence, not the Confrontation Clause.

Deciding this case also requires further explanation of the "ongoing emergency" circumstance addressed in *Davis*. Because *Davis* and *Hammon* arose in the domestic violence context, that was the situation "we had immediately in mind (for that was the case before us)." 547 U.S., at 826. We now face a new context: a nondomestic dispute, involving a victim found in a public location, suffering from a fatal gunshot wound, and a perpe-

---

examination, the prosecution, after first invoking both the dying declaration and excited utterance hearsay exceptions, established the factual foundation only for admission of the statements as excited utterances. The trial court ruled that the statements were admissible as excited utterances and did not address their admissibility as dying declarations. This occurred prior to our 2004 decision in *Crawford v. Washington*, 541 U.S. 36, where we first suggested that dying declarations, even if testimonial, might be admissible as a historical exception to the Confrontation Clause. *Id.*, at 56, n. 6; see also *Giles v. California*, 554 U.S. 353, 358–359 (2008). We noted in *Crawford* that we "need not decide in this case whether the Sixth Amendment incorporates an exception for testimonial dying declarations." 541 U.S., at 56, n. 6. Because of the State's failure to preserve its argument with regard to dying declarations, we similarly need not decide that question here. See also *post*, p. 1177 (GINSBURG, J., dissenting).

3. *Davis* explained that 911 operators "may at least be agents of law enforcement when they conduct interrogations of 911 callers," and therefore "consider[ed] their acts to be acts of the police" for purposes of the opinion. 547 U.S., at 823, n. 2. *Davis* explicitly reserved the question of "whether and when statements made to someone other than law enforcement personnel are 'testimonial.'" *Ibid.* We have no need to decide that question in this case either because Covington's statements were made to police officers. The dissent also claims to reserve this question, see *post*, at 1169, n. 1 (opinion of SCALIA, J.), but supports one of its arguments by relying on *King v. Brasier*, 1 Leach 199, 200, 168 Eng. Rep. 202, 202–203 (K.B.1779), which involved statements made by a child to her mother — a private citizen — just after the child had been sexually assaulted.

trator whose location was unknown at the time the police located the victim. Thus, we confront for the first time circumstances in which the "ongoing emergency" discussed in *Davis* extends beyond an initial victim to a potential threat to the responding police and the public at large. This new context requires us to provide additional clarification with regard to what *Davis* meant by "the primary purpose of the interrogation is to enable police assistance to meet an ongoing emergency." *Id.*, at 822.

III

To determine whether the "primary purpose" of an interrogation is "to enable police assistance to meet an ongoing emergency," *Davis*, 547 U.S., at 822, which would render the resulting statements nontestimonial, we objectively evaluate the circumstances in which the encounter occurs and the statements and actions of the parties.

A

The Michigan Supreme Court correctly understood that this inquiry is objective. *Davis* uses the word "objective" or "objectively" no fewer than eight times in describing the relevant inquiry. "Objectively" also appears in the definitions of both testimonial and nontestimonial statements that *Davis* established.

An objective analysis of the circumstances of an encounter and the statements and actions of the parties to it provides the most accurate assessment of the "primary purpose of the interrogation." The circumstances in which an encounter occurs—*e.g.*, at or near the scene of the crime versus at a police station, during an ongoing emergency or afterwards—are clearly matters of objective fact. The statements and actions of the parties must also be objectively evaluated. That is, the relevant inquiry is not the subjective or actual purpose of the individuals involved in a particular encounter, but rather the purpose that reasonable participants would have had, as ascertained from the individuals' statements and actions and the circumstances in which the encounter occurred.

B

As our recent Confrontation Clause cases have explained, the existence of an "ongoing emergency" at the time of an encounter between an individual and the police is among the most important circumstances informing the "primary purpose" of an interrogation. See *Davis*, 547 U.S., at 828–830; *Crawford*, 541 U.S., at 65. The existence of an ongoing emergency is relevant to determining the primary purpose of the interrogation because an emergency focuses the participants on something other than "prov[ing] past events potentially relevant to later criminal prosecution."[8] *Davis*, 547 U.S., at 822. Rather, it focuses them on "end[ing] a threatening situation." *Id.*, at 832. Implicit in *Davis* is the idea that because the prospect of fabrication in statements given for the primary purpose of resolving that emergency is presumably significantly diminished, the Confrontation Clause does not require such statements to be subject to the crucible of cross-examination.

This logic is not unlike that justifying the excited utterance exception in hearsay law. Statements "relating to a startling event or condition made while the declarant was under the stress of excitement caused by the event or condition," Fed. Rule Evid. 803(2); see

---

8. The existence of an ongoing emergency must be objectively assessed from the perspective of the parties to the interrogation at the time, not with the benefit of hindsight. If the information the parties knew at the time of the encounter would lead a reasonable person to believe that there was an emergency, even if that belief was later proved incorrect, that is sufficient for purposes of the Confrontation Clause. The emergency is relevant to the "primary purpose of the interrogation" because of the effect it has on the parties' purpose, not because of its actual existence.

also Mich. Rule Evid. 803(2) (2010), are considered reliable because the declarant, in the excitement, presumably cannot form a falsehood. An ongoing emergency has a similar effect of focusing an individual's attention on responding to the emergency.[9]

Following our precedents, the court below correctly began its analysis with the circumstances in which Covington interacted with the police. But in doing so, the court construed *Davis* to have decided more than it did and thus employed an unduly narrow understanding of "ongoing emergency" that *Davis* does not require.

First, the Michigan Supreme Court repeatedly and incorrectly asserted that *Davis* "defined" "'ongoing emergency.'" In fact, *Davis* did not even define the extent of the emergency in that case. The Michigan Supreme Court erroneously read *Davis* as deciding that "the statements made after the defendant stopped assaulting the victim and left the premises did *not* occur during an 'ongoing emergency.'" We explicitly explained in *Davis*, however, that we were asked to review only the testimonial nature of Michelle McCottry's initial statements during the 911 call; we therefore merely *assumed* the correctness of the Washington Supreme Court's holding that admission of her other statements was harmless, without deciding whether those subsequent statements were also made for the primary purpose of resolving an ongoing emergency.

Second, by assuming that *Davis* defined the outer bounds of "ongoing emergency," the Michigan Supreme Court failed to appreciate that whether an emergency exists and is ongoing is a highly context-dependent inquiry. *Davis* and *Hammon* involved domestic violence, a known and identified perpetrator, and, in *Hammon*, a neutralized threat. Because *Davis* and *Hammon* were domestic violence cases, we focused only on the threat to the victims and assessed the ongoing emergency from the perspective of whether there was a continuing threat *to them*.

Domestic violence cases like *Davis* and *Hammon* often have a narrower zone of potential victims than cases involving threats to public safety. An assessment of whether an emergency that threatens the police and public is ongoing cannot narrowly focus on whether the threat solely to the first victim has been neutralized because the threat to the first responders and public may continue.

The Michigan Supreme Court also did not appreciate that the duration and scope of an emergency may depend in part on the type of weapon employed. The court relied on *Davis* and *Hammon*, in which the assailants used their fists, as controlling the scope of the emergency here, which involved the use of a gun. The problem with that reasoning is

---

9. Many other exceptions to the hearsay rules similarly rest on the belief that certain statements are, by their nature, made for a purpose other than use in a prosecution and therefore should not be barred by hearsay prohibitions. See, *e.g.,* Fed. Rule Evid. 801(d)(2)(E) (statement by a co-conspirator during and in furtherance of the conspiracy); 803(4) (Statements for Purposes of Medical Diagnosis or Treatment); 803(6) (Records of Regularly Conducted Activity); 803(8) (Public Records and Reports); 803(9) (Records of Vital Statistics); 803(11) (Records of Religious Organizations); 803(12) (Marriage, Baptismal, and Similar Certificates); 803(13) (Family Records); 804(b)(3) (Statement Against Interest); see also *Melendez-Diaz v. Massachusetts*, 129 S.Ct., at 2539–2540 ("Business and public records are generally admissible absent confrontation not because they qualify under an exception to the hearsay rules, but because—having been created for the administration of an entity's affairs and not for the purpose of establishing or proving some fact at trial—they are not testimonial"); *Giles v. California*, 554 U.S., at 376 (noting in the context of domestic violence that "[s]tatements to friends and neighbors about abuse and intimidation and statements to physicians in the course of receiving treatment would be excluded, if at all, only by hearsay rules"); *Crawford*, 541 U.S., at 56 ("Most of the hearsay exceptions covered statements that by their nature were not testimonial—for example, business records or statements in furtherance of a conspiracy").

clear when considered in light of the assault on Amy Hammon. Hershel Hammon was armed only with his fists when he attacked his wife, so removing Amy to a separate room was sufficient to end the emergency. If Hershel had been reported to be armed with a gun, however, separation by a single household wall might not have been sufficient to end the emergency.

The Michigan Supreme Court's failure to focus on the context-dependent nature of our *Davis* decision also led it to conclude that the medical condition of a declarant is irrelevant. But *Davis* and *Hammon* did not present medical emergencies, despite some injuries to the victims. Thus, we have not previously considered, much less ruled out, the relevance of a victim's severe injuries to the primary purpose inquiry.

Taking into account the victim's medical state does not, as the Michigan Supreme Court below thought, "rende[r] non-testimonial" "all statements made while the police are questioning a seriously injured complainant." The medical condition of the victim is important to the primary purpose inquiry to the extent that it sheds light on the ability of the victim to have any purpose at all in responding to police questions and on the likelihood that any purpose formed would necessarily be a testimonial one. The victim's medical state also provides important context for first responders to judge the existence and magnitude of a continuing threat to the victim, themselves, and the public.

... [N]one of this suggests that an emergency is ongoing in every place or even just surrounding the victim for the entire time that the perpetrator of a violent crime is on the loose. As we recognized in *Davis*, "a conversation which begins as an interrogation to determine the need for emergency assistance" can "evolve into testimonial statements." This evolution may occur if, for example, a declarant provides police with information that makes clear that what appeared to be an emergency is not or is no longer an emergency or that what appeared to be a public threat is actually a private dispute. It could also occur if a perpetrator is disarmed, surrenders, is apprehended, or, as in *Davis*, flees with little prospect of posing a threat to the public. Trial courts can determine in the first instance when any transition from nontestimonial to testimonial occurs, and exclude "the portions of any statement that have become testimonial, as they do, for example, with unduly prejudicial portions of otherwise admissible evidence."

Finally, our discussion of the Michigan Supreme Court's misunderstanding of what *Davis* meant by "ongoing emergency" should not be taken to imply that the existence *vel non* of an ongoing emergency is dispositive of the testimonial inquiry. As *Davis* made clear, whether an ongoing emergency exists is simply one factor—albeit an important factor—that informs the ultimate inquiry regarding the "primary purpose" of an interrogation. Another factor the Michigan Supreme Court did not sufficiently account for is the importance of *informality* in an encounter between a victim and police. Formality is not the sole touchstone of our primary purpose inquiry because, although formality suggests the absence of an emergency and therefore an increased likelihood that the purpose of the interrogation is to "establish or prove past events potentially relevant to later criminal prosecution," informality does not necessarily indicate the presence of an emergency or the lack of testimonial intent. The court below, however, too readily dismissed the informality of the circumstances in this case in a single brief footnote and in fact seems to have suggested that the encounter in this case was formal. As we explain further below, the questioning in this case occurred in an exposed, public area, prior to the arrival of emergency medical services, and in a disorganized fashion. All of those facts make this case distinguishable from the formal station-house interrogation in *Crawford*.

C

In addition to the circumstances in which an encounter occurs, the statements and actions of both the declarant and interrogators provide objective evidence of the primary purpose of the interrogation....

As the Michigan Supreme Court correctly recognized, *Davis* requires a combined inquiry that accounts for both the declarant and the interrogator.[11] In many instances, the primary purpose of the interrogation will be most accurately ascertained by looking to the contents of both the questions and the answers. To give an extreme example, if the police say to a victim, "Tell us who did this to you so that we can arrest and prosecute them," the victim's response that "Rick did it," appears purely accusatory because by virtue of the phrasing of the question, the victim necessarily has prosecution in mind when she answers.

The combined approach also ameliorates problems that could arise from looking solely to one participant. Predominant among these is the problem of mixed motives on the part of both interrogators and declarants. Police officers in our society function as both first responders and criminal investigators. Their dual responsibilities may mean that they act with different motives simultaneously or in quick succession.

Victims are also likely to have mixed motives when they make statements to the police. During an ongoing emergency, a victim is most likely to want the threat to her and to other potential victims to end, but that does not necessarily mean that the victim wants or envisions prosecution of the assailant. A victim may want the attacker to be incapacitated temporarily or rehabilitated. Alternatively, a severely injured victim may have no purpose at all in answering questions posed; the answers may be simply reflexive. The victim's injuries could be so debilitating as to prevent her from thinking sufficiently clearly to understand whether her statements are for the purpose of addressing an ongoing emergency or for the purpose of future prosecution. Taking into account a victim's injuries does not transform this objective inquiry into a subjective one. The inquiry is still objective because it focuses on the understanding and purpose of a reasonable victim in the circumstances of the actual victim—circumstances that prominently include the victim's physical state....

IV

As we suggested in *Davis*, when a court must determine whether the Confrontation Clause bars the admission of a statement at trial, it should determine the "primary purpose of the interrogation" by objectively evaluating the statements and actions of the parties to

---

11. Some portions of *Davis*, however, have caused confusion about whether the inquiry prescribes examination of one participant to the exclusion of the other. *Davis'* language indicating that a statement's testimonial or nontestimonial nature derives from "the primary purpose *of the interrogation*," 547 U.S., at 822 (emphasis added), could be read to suggest that the relevant purpose is that of the interrogator. In contrast, footnote 1 in *Davis* explains, "it is in the final analysis the declarant's statements, not the interrogator's questions, that the Confrontation Clause requires us to evaluate." *Id.*, at 822–823, n. 1. Bryant draws on the footnote to argue that the primary purpose inquiry must be conducted solely from the perspective of the declarant, and argues against adoption of a purpose-of-the-interrogator perspective. But this statement in footnote 1 of *Davis* merely acknowledges that the Confrontation Clause is not implicated when statements are offered "for purposes other than establishing the truth of the matter asserted." *Crawford*, 541 U.S., at 60, n. 9. An interrogator's questions, unlike a declarant's answers, do not assert the truth of any matter. The language in the footnote was not meant to determine *how* the courts are to assess the nature of the declarant's purpose, but merely to remind readers that it is the statements, and not the questions, that must be evaluated under the Sixth Amendment.

the encounter, in light of the circumstances in which the interrogation occurs. The existence of an emergency or the parties' perception that an emergency is ongoing is among the most important circumstances that courts must take into account in determining whether an interrogation is testimonial because statements made to assist police in addressing an ongoing emergency presumably lack the testimonial purpose that would subject them to the requirement of confrontation. As the context of this case brings into sharp relief, the existence and duration of an emergency depend on the type and scope of danger posed to the victim, the police, and the public.

Applying this analysis to the facts of this case is more difficult than in *Davis* because we do not have the luxury of reviewing a transcript of the conversation between the victim and the police officers. Further complicating our task is the fact that the trial in this case occurred before our decisions in *Crawford* and *Davis*. We therefore review a record that was not developed to ascertain the "primary purpose of the interrogation."

We first examine the circumstances in which the interrogation occurred. The parties disagree over whether there was an emergency when the police arrived at the gas station. Bryant argues, and the Michigan Supreme Court accepted, that there was no ongoing emergency because "there ... was no criminal conduct occurring. No shots were being fired, no one was seen in possession of a firearm, nor were any witnesses seen cowering in fear or running from the scene." Bryant, while conceding that "a serious or life-threatening injury creates a medical emergency for a victim," further argues that a declarant's medical emergency is not relevant to the ongoing emergency determination.

In contrast, Michigan and the Solicitor General explain that when the police responded to the call that a man had been shot and found Covington bleeding on the gas station parking lot, "they did not know who Covington was, whether the shooting had occurred at the gas station or at a different location, who the assailant was, or whether the assailant posed a continuing threat to Covington or others."

The Michigan Supreme Court stated that the police asked Covington, "what had happened, who had shot him, and where the shooting had occurred." The joint appendix contains the transcripts of the preliminary examination, suppression hearing, and trial testimony of five officers who responded to the scene and found Covington. The officers' testimony is essentially consistent but, at the same time, not specific. The officers basically agree on what information they learned from Covington, but not on the order in which they learned it or on whether Covington's statements were in response to general or detailed questions. They all agree that the first question was "what happened?" The answer was either "I was shot" or "Rick shot me."

As explained above, the scope of an emergency in terms of its threat to individuals other than the initial assailant and victim will often depend on the type of dispute involved. Nothing Covington said to the police indicated that the cause of the shooting was a purely private dispute or that the threat from the shooter had ended. The record reveals little about the motive for the shooting. The police officers who spoke with Covington at the gas station testified that Covington did not tell them what words Covington and Rick had exchanged prior to the shooting. What Covington did tell the officers was that he fled Bryant's back porch, indicating that he perceived an ongoing threat. The police did not know, and Covington did not tell them, whether the threat was limited to him. The potential scope of the dispute and therefore the emergency in this case thus stretches more broadly than those at issue in *Davis* and *Hammon* and encompasses a threat potentially to the police and the public.

This is also the first of our post-*Crawford* Confrontation Clause cases to involve a gun. The physical separation that was sufficient to end the emergency in *Hammon* was not necessarily sufficient to end the threat in this case; Covington was shot through the back door of Bryant's house. Bryant's argument that there was no ongoing emergency because "[n]o shots were being fired," surely construes ongoing emergency too narrowly. An emergency does not last only for the time between when the assailant pulls the trigger and the bullet hits the victim. If an out-of-sight sniper pauses between shots, no one would say that the emergency ceases during the pause. That is an extreme example and not the situation here, but it serves to highlight the implausibility, at least as to certain weapons, of construing the emergency to last only precisely as long as the violent act itself, as some have construed our opinion in *Davis*.

At no point during the questioning did either Covington or the police know the location of the shooter. In fact, Bryant was not at home by the time the police searched his house at approximately 5:30 a.m. At some point between 3 a.m. and 5:30 a.m., Bryant left his house. At bottom, there was an ongoing emergency here where an armed shooter, whose motive for and location after the shooting were unknown, had mortally wounded Covington within a few blocks and a few minutes of the location where the police found Covington.

This is not to suggest that the emergency continued until Bryant was arrested in California a year after the shooting. We need not decide precisely when the emergency ended because Covington's encounter with the police and all of the statements he made during that interaction occurred within the first few minutes of the police officers' arrival and well before they secured the scene of the shooting—the shooter's last known location.

We reiterate, moreover, that the existence *vel non* of an ongoing emergency is not the touchstone of the testimonial inquiry; rather, the ultimate inquiry is whether the "primary purpose of the interrogation [was] to enable police assistance to meet [the] ongoing emergency." *Davis*, 547 U.S., at 822. We turn now to that inquiry, as informed by the circumstances of the ongoing emergency just described. The circumstances of the encounter provide important context for understanding Covington's statements to the police. When the police arrived at Covington's side, their first question to him was "What happened?" Covington's response was either "Rick shot me" or "I was shot," followed very quickly by an identification of "Rick" as the shooter. In response to further questions, Covington explained that the shooting occurred through the back door of Bryant's house and provided a physical description of the shooter. When he made the statements, Covington was lying in a gas station parking lot bleeding from a mortal gunshot wound to his abdomen. His answers to the police officers' questions were punctuated with questions about when emergency medical services would arrive. He was obviously in considerable pain and had difficulty breathing and talking. From this description of his condition and report of his statements, we cannot say that a person in Covington's situation would have had a "primary purpose" "to establish or prove past events potentially relevant to later criminal prosecution." *Davis*, 547 U.S., at 822.

For their part, the police responded to a call that a man had been shot. As discussed above, they did not know why, where, or when the shooting had occurred. Nor did they know the location of the shooter or anything else about the circumstances in which the crime occurred. The questions they asked—"what had happened, who had shot him, and where the shooting occurred"—were the exact type of questions necessary to allow the police to "'assess the situation, the threat to their own safety, and possible danger to the potential victim'" and to the public, *Davis*, 547 U.S., at 832 (quoting *Hiibel v. Sixth Judicial Dist. Court of Nev., Humboldt Cty.*, 542 U.S. 177, 186 (2004)), including to allow them to ascertain "whether they would be encountering a violent felon," *Davis*, 547 U.S., at 827. In other words, they solicited the information necessary to enable them "to meet an ongoing emergency." *Id.*, at 822.

Nothing in Covington's responses indicated to the police that, contrary to their expectation upon responding to a call reporting a shooting, there was no emergency or that a prior emergency had ended. Covington did indicate that he had been shot at another location about 25 minutes earlier, but he did not know the location of the shooter at the time the police arrived and, as far as we can tell from the record, he gave no indication that the shooter, having shot at him twice, would be satisfied that Covington was only wounded. In fact, Covington did not indicate any possible motive for the shooting, and thereby gave no reason to think that the shooter would not shoot again if he arrived on the scene. As we noted in *Davis*, "initial inquiries" may "*often ...* produce nontestimonial statements." The initial inquiries in this case resulted in the type of nontestimonial statements we contemplated in *Davis*.

Finally, we consider the informality of the situation and the interrogation. This situation is more similar, though not identical, to the informal, harried 911 call in *Davis* than to the structured, station-house interview in *Crawford*. As the officers' trial testimony reflects, the situation was fluid and somewhat confused: the officers arrived at different times; apparently each, upon arrival, asked Covington "what happened?"; and, contrary to the dissent's portrayal, they did not conduct a structured interrogation. The informality suggests that the interrogators' primary purpose was simply to address what they perceived to be an ongoing emergency, and the circumstances lacked any formality that would have alerted Covington to or focused him on the possible future prosecutorial use of his statements.

Because the circumstances of the encounter as well as the statements and actions of Covington and the police objectively indicate that the "primary purpose of the interrogation" was "to enable police assistance to meet an ongoing emergency," *Davis*, 547 U.S., at 822, Covington's identification and description of the shooter and the location of the shooting were not testimonial hearsay. The Confrontation Clause did not bar their admission at Bryant's trial....

Justice THOMAS, concurring in the judgment.

I agree with the Court that the admission of Covington's out-of-court statements did not violate the Confrontation Clause, but I reach this conclusion because Covington's questioning by police lacked sufficient formality and solemnity for his statements to be considered "testimonial."

In determining whether Covington's statements to police implicate the Confrontation Clause, the Court evaluates the "'primary purpose'" of the interrogation. The majority's analysis which relies on, *inter alia,* what the police knew when they arrived at the scene, the specific questions they asked, the particular information Covington conveyed, the weapon involved, and Covington's medical condition illustrates the uncertainty that this test creates for law enforcement and the lower courts. I have criticized the primary-purpose test as "an exercise in fiction" that is "disconnected from history" and "yields no predictable results." *Davis v. Washington*, 547 U.S. 813, 839, 838 (2006) (opinion concurring in judgment in part and dissenting in part).

Rather than attempting to reconstruct the "primary purpose" of the participants, I would consider the extent to which the interrogation resembles those historical practices that the Confrontation Clause addressed. As the majority notes, Covington interacted with the police under highly informal circumstances, while he bled from a fatal gunshot wound. The police questioning was not "a formalized dialogue," did not result in "formalized testimonial materials" such as a deposition or affidavit, and bore no "indicia of solemnity." *Davis, supra*, at 840, 837 (opinion of THOMAS, J.); see also *Giles v. California*, 554 U.S.

353, 377–378 (2008) (THOMAS, J., concurring). Nor is there any indication that the statements were offered at trial "in order to evade confrontation." *Davis, supra,* at 840. This interrogation bears little if any resemblance to the historical practices that the Confrontation Clause aimed to eliminate. Covington thus did not "bea[r] testimony" against Bryant, and the introduction of his statements at trial did not implicate the Confrontation Clause. I concur in the judgment.

Justice SCALIA, dissenting.

. . . .

I

A

. . . .

Crawford and *Davis* did not address whose perspective matters—the declarant's, the interrogator's, or both—when assessing "the primary purpose of [an] interrogation." In those cases the statements were testimonial from any perspective. I think the same is true here, but because the Court picks a perspective so will I: The declarant's intent is what counts. In-court testimony is more than a narrative of past events; it is a solemn declaration made in the course of a criminal trial. For an out-of-court statement to qualify as testimonial, the declarant must intend the statement to be a solemn declaration rather than an unconsidered or offhand remark; and he must make the statement with the understanding that it may be used to invoke the coercive machinery of the State against the accused.[1] That is what distinguishes a narrative told to a friend over dinner from a statement to the police. The hidden purpose of an interrogator cannot substitute for the declarant's intentional solemnity or his understanding of how his words may be used.

A declarant-focused inquiry is also the only inquiry that would work in every fact pattern implicating the Confrontation Clause. The Clause applies to volunteered testimony as well as statements solicited through police interrogation. An inquiry into an officer's purposes would make no sense when a declarant blurts out "Rick shot me" as soon as the officer arrives on the scene. I see no reason to adopt a different test—one that accounts for an officer's intent—when the officer asks "what happened" before the declarant makes his accusation. (This does not mean the interrogator is irrelevant. The identity of an interrogator, and the content and tenor of his questions, can bear upon whether a declarant intends to make a solemn statement, and envisions its use at a criminal trial. But none of this means that the interrogator's purpose matters.)...

The Court claims one affirmative virtue for its focus on the purposes of both the declarant and the police: It "ameliorates problems that ... arise" when declarants have "mixed motives." I am at a loss to know how. Sorting out the primary purpose of a declarant with mixed motives is sometimes difficult. But adding in the mixed motives of the police only compounds the problem. Now courts will have to sort through two sets of mixed motives to determine the primary purpose of an interrogation. And the Court's solution creates a mixed-motive problem where (under the proper theory) it does not exist—viz., where the police and the declarant each have one motive, but those motives conflict. The Court does not provide an answer to this glaringly obvious problem, probably because it does not have one.

---

1. I remain agnostic about whether and when statements to nonstate actors are testimonial. See *Davis v. Washington,* 547 U.S. 813, 823, n. 2 (2006).

The only virtue of the Court's approach (if it can be misnamed a virtue) is that it leaves judges free to reach the "fairest" result under the totality of the circumstances. If the dastardly police trick a declarant into giving an incriminating statement against a sympathetic defendant, a court can focus on the police's intent and declare the statement testimonial. If the defendant "deserves" to go to jail, then a court can focus on whatever perspective is necessary to declare damning hearsay nontestimonial. And when all else fails, a court can mix-and-match perspectives to reach its desired outcome. Unfortunately, under this malleable approach "the guarantee of confrontation is no guarantee at all." *Giles v. California*, 554 U.S. 353, 375 (2008) (plurality)....

D

A final word about the Court's active imagination. The Court invents a world where an ongoing emergency exists whenever "an armed shooter, whose motive for and location after the shooting [are] unknown, ... mortally wound[s]" one individual "within a few blocks and [25] minutes of the location where the police" ultimately find that victim. Breathlessly, it worries that a shooter could leave the scene armed and ready to pull the trigger again. Nothing suggests the five officers in this case shared the Court's dystopian view of Detroit, where drug dealers hunt their shooting victim down and fire into a crowd of police officers to finish him off, or where spree killers shoot through a door and then roam the streets leaving a trail of bodies behind. Because almost 90 percent of murders involve a single victim, it is much more likely—indeed, I think it certain—that the officers viewed their encounter with Covington for what it was: an investigation into a past crime with no ongoing or immediate consequences.

The Court's distorted view creates an expansive exception to the Confrontation Clause for violent crimes. Because Bryant posed a continuing threat to public safety in the Court's imagination, the emergency persisted for confrontation purposes at least until the police learned his "motive for and location after the shooting." It may have persisted in this case until the police "secured the scene of the shooting" two-and-a-half hours later. (The relevance of securing the scene is unclear so long as the killer is still at large—especially if, as the Court speculates, he may be a spree-killer.) This is a dangerous definition of emergency. Many individuals who testify against a defendant at trial first offer their accounts to police in the hours after a violent act. If the police can plausibly claim that a "potential threat to ... the public" persisted through those first few hours (and if the claim is plausible here it is always plausible) a defendant will have no constitutionally protected right to exclude the uncross-examined testimony of such witnesses. His conviction could rest (as perhaps it did here) solely on the officers' recollection at trial of the witnesses' accusations....

The 16th- and 17th-century English treason trials that helped inspire the Confrontation Clause show that today's decision is a mistake. The Court's expansive definition of an "ongoing emergency" and its willingness to consider the perspective of the interrogator and the declarant cast a more favorable light on those trials than history or our past decisions suggest they deserve. Royal officials conducted many of the *ex parte* examinations introduced against Sir Walter Raleigh and Sir John Fenwick while investigating alleged treasonous conspiracies of unknown scope, aimed at killing or overthrowing the King. Social stability in 16th- and 17th-century England depended mainly on the continuity of the ruling monarch, so such a conspiracy posed the most pressing emergency imaginable. Presumably, the royal officials investigating it would have understood the gravity of the situation and would have focused their interrogations primarily on ending the threat, not on generating testimony for trial. I therefore doubt that under the Court's test English officials acted improperly by denying Raleigh and Fenwick the opportunity to confront their accusers "face to face."

Under my approach, in contrast, those English trials remain unquestionably infamous. Lord Cobham did not speak with royal officials to end an ongoing emergency. He was a traitor! He spoke, as Raleigh correctly observed, to establish Raleigh's guilt and to save his own life. Cobham's statements, when assessed from his perspective, had only a testimonial purpose. The same is true of Covington's statements here.

II

A

. . . .

According to today's opinion, the *Davis* inquiry into whether a declarant spoke to end an ongoing emergency or rather to "prove past events potentially relevant to later criminal prosecution," is *not* aimed at answering whether the declarant acted as a witness. Instead, the *Davis* inquiry probes the *reliability* of a declarant's statements, "[i]mplicit[ly]" importing the excited-utterances hearsay exception into the Constitution. A statement during an ongoing emergency is sufficiently reliable, the Court says, "because the prospect of fabrication ... is presumably significantly diminished," so it "does not [need] to be subject to the crucible of cross-examination."

. . . .

The Court announces that in future cases it will look to "standard rules of hearsay, designed to identify some statements as reliable," when deciding whether a statement is testimonial. *Ohio v. Roberts,* 448 U.S. 56 (1980) said something remarkably similar: An out-of-court statement is admissible if it "falls within a firmly rooted hearsay exception" or otherwise "bears adequate 'indicia of reliability.'" We tried that approach to the Confrontation Clause for nearly 25 years before *Crawford rejected* it as an unworkable standard unmoored from the text and the historical roots of the Confrontation Clause. . . .

The Court attempts to fit its resurrected interest in reliability into the *Crawford* framework, but the result is incoherent. Reliability, the Court tells us, is a good indicator of whether "a statement is ... an out-of-court substitute for trial testimony." That is patently false. Reliability tells us *nothing* about whether a statement is testimonial. Testimonial and nontestimonial statements alike come in varying degrees of reliability. An eyewitness's statements to the police after a fender-bender, for example, are both reliable and testimonial. Statements to the police from one driver attempting to blame the other would be similarly testimonial but rarely reliable. . . .

Is it possible that the Court does not recognize the contradiction between its focus on reliable statements and *Crawford's* focus on testimonial ones? Does it not realize that the two cannot coexist? Or does it intend, by following today's illogical roadmap, to resurrect *Roberts* by a thousand unprincipled distinctions without ever explicitly overruling *Crawford?* After all, honestly overruling *Crawford* would destroy the illusion of judicial minimalism and restraint. . . .

B

The Court recedes from *Crawford* in a second significant way. It requires judges to conduct "open-ended balancing tests" and "amorphous, if not entirely subjective," inquiries into the totality of the circumstances bearing upon reliability. Where the prosecution cries "emergency," the admissibility of a statement now turns on "a highly context-dependent inquiry," into the type of weapon the defendant wielded; the type of crime the defendant committed; the medical condition of the declarant; if the declarant is injured, whether paramedics have arrived on the scene; whether the encounter takes place in an "exposed public area"; whether the encounter appears disorganized; whether the declarant is capable of forming a purpose; whether the police have secured the scene of the crime; the formality of the statement; and finally, whether the statement strikes us as reliable. This is no better than the nine-factor balancing test we rejected in *Crawford*. I do not look forward to resolving conflicts in the future over whether knives and poison are more like guns or fists for Confrontation Clause purposes, or whether rape and armed robbery are more like murder or domestic violence....

For all I know, Bryant has received his just deserts. But he surely has not received them pursuant to the procedures that our Constitution requires. And what has been taken away from him has been taken away from us all.

Justice GINSBURG, dissenting.

I agree with Justice SCALIA that Covington's statements were testimonial and that "[t]he declarant's intent is what counts." Even if the interrogators' intent were what counts, I further agree, Covington's statements would still be testimonial.... Today's decision, Justice SCALIA rightly notes, "creates an expansive exception to the Confrontation Clause for violent crimes." In so doing, the decision confounds our recent Confrontation Clause jurisprudence, which made it plain that "[r]eliability tells us nothing about whether a statement is testimonial".

I would add, however, this observation. In *Crawford v. Washington*, 541 U.S. 36, 56, n. 6 (2004), this Court noted that, in the law we inherited from England, there was a well-established exception to the confrontation requirement: The cloak protecting the accused against admission of out-of-court testimonial statements was removed for dying declarations. This historic exception, we recalled in *Giles v. California*, 554 U.S. 353, 358 (2008); see *id.*, at 361–362, 368, applied to statements made by a person about to die and aware that death was imminent. Were the issue properly tendered here, I would take up the question whether the exception for dying declarations survives our recent Confrontation Clause decisions. The Michigan Supreme Court, however, held, as a matter of state law, that the prosecutor had abandoned the issue. The matter, therefore, is not one the Court can address in this case.

Notes and Questions

1. After *Crawford* was decided, lower courts continued to apply the *Roberts* test to nontestimonial hearsay, reasoning that the Court in *Crawford* had not expressly addressed the question whether the Confrontation Clause places any limits on the admissibility of nontestimonial hearsay. *See, e.g., United States v. Holmes*, 406 F.3d 337, 348 n.14 (5th Cir. 2005); *United States v. Hendricks*, 395 F.3d 173, 179 n.7 (3d Cir. 2005). As the Court's subsequent decision in *Davis*, however, seemed to make clear, the Confrontation Clause is concerned only with testimonial hearsay, and places no limits at all on the admissibility of nontestimonial hearsay. Nonetheless, even after *Davis*, courts continued to hold that the *Roberts* test applies to non-testimonial hearsay. *See, e.g., United States v. Mooneyham*, 473 F.3d 280, 287 (6th Cir. 2007). *But see United States v. Tolliver*, 454 F.3d 660, 665 n.2 (7th Cir. 2006); *Hodges v. Commonwealth*, 272 Va. 418, 433–35 (2006).

Any doubt as to the applicability of *Roberts* to non-testimonial hearsay was clarified by the Supreme Court's decision in *Whorton v. Bockting*, 549 U.S. 406, 419–20 (2007), in which it stated "[w]ith respect to *testimonial* out-of-court statements, *Crawford* is more restrictive than was *Roberts*, and this may improve the accuracy of fact-finding in some criminal cases.... But whatever improvement in reliability *Crawford* produced in this respect must be considered together with *Crawford's* elimination of Confrontation Clause protection against the admission of unreliable out-of-court nontestimonial statements."

2. Is Justice Thomas right to criticize the majority in *Davis* for drawing a line between testimonial and nontestimonial hearsay that is as unpredictable and malleable as the *Roberts* reliability inquiry that the Court rejected in *Crawford*? Is Justice Thomas' distinction between formal and informal statements — which he reiterates in *Giles* and *Bryant* — any less subjective than the majority's "primary purpose" inquiry? Is some degree of uncertainty and malleability inherent in anything other than the narrowest and broadest interpretations of the phrase "witnesses against" as used in the Confrontation Clause?

3. *Bryant* is the first opinion by the Supreme Court dealing with the relationship between the Confrontation Clause and hearsay evidence since *Crawford* was decided in which Justice Scalia — the author of *Crawford*, *Davis*, and *Giles* — is in the minority. Is he correct in his assertion that the majority is reverting to the *Roberts* approach?

4. At the end of its opinion, the *Davis* Court reminds us that a criminal defendant can forfeit his rights under the Confrontation Clause through wrongdoing, such as by threatening a witness. The Court hints, but does not hold, that a court need only find by a preponderance of the evidence that the defendant engaged in wrongdoing, and that in making that determination, a court may consider hearsay evidence, including the statement whose admissibility is at issue. Does the *Giles* Court resolve this issue?

5. Return to the facts of *Crawford* for a moment to see what forced the State in *Crawford* to resort to hearsay evidence. Can an argument be made that the defendant in *Crawford* forfeited his right to confront by procuring his wife's unavailability? Do *Davis* and *Giles* provide support for such an argument?

6. Can a criminal defendant invoke *Crawford* to prevent his *own* "testimonial" statements from being offered into evidence against him as individual admissions under Rule 801(d)(2)(A), on the theory that he has a right to confront himself? *See United States v. Brown*, 441 F.3d 1330, 1358–59 (11th Cir. 2006) (quoting 4 Jack B. Weinstein & Margaret A. Berger, Weinstein's Federal Evidence § 802.05[3][d] at 802–25 (2d ed. 2005)) ("a party cannot seriously claim that his or her own statement should be excluded because it was not made under oath or subject to cross-examination"); *State v. Snow*, 282 Kan. 323, 333 (2006) ("the Confrontation Clause does not grant [the accused] the right to confront himself"); *Johnson v. Renico*, 314 F. Supp. 2d 700, 707 (E.D. Mich. 2004) (holding that admitting such statements does not violate the Confrontation Clause); *State v. Lloyd*, 2004 WL 2445224, at *2 (Ohio Oct. 22, 2004) (holding that "the Confrontation Clause is simply inapplicable when the 'witness' is the accused himself"). To the extent that the government's inability to call the defendant to the stand to have him confront himself is based on the defendant's invocation of his privilege against self-incrimination, do *Crawford*, *Davis*, and *Giles* provide an answer to this question?

Some courts have extended the reasoning of cases regarding Rule 801(d)(2)(A) to evidence admitted under Rules 801(d)(2)(B), (C) or (D). *E.g., United States v. Petraia Mar-*

itime Ltd., 489 F. Supp. 2d 90, 95 n.4 (D. Me. 2007); *United States v. Lafferty*, 387 F. Supp. 2d 500, 510–12 (W.D. Penn. 2005); *People v. Jennings*, 237 P.3d 474, 507–09 (Cal. 2010). Is such an extension sound, or are there important ways in which individual admissions differ from adoptive or vicarious ones so far as the Confrontation Clause is concerned?

7. Together, *Crawford*, *Giles*, and *Bryant* rather strongly hint that dying declarations — *even if* testimonial — might *possibly* be admitted consistent with the Confrontation Clause even in the absence of prior or subsequent cross-examination. That means, does it not, that a dying declaration made by a dying victim to police officers in a situation that would be deemed testimonial under *Davis* and *Bryant* could overcome a Confrontation Clause objection, even though made in circumstances that would normally cause a hearsay statement to be excluded? What is the justification for treating dying declarations differently?

To date, lower courts have, with virtual uniformity, relied on these hints in *Crawford*, *Giles*, and *Bryant* to hold that there is a dying declaration exception to the Confrontation Clause. *E.g.*, *State v. Beauchamp*, 796 N.W.2d 780, 788–95 (Wis. 2011) (collecting cases). Assuming that such an exception to the Confrontation Clause exists, does anything falling within the scope of a state's hearsay exception for dying declarations thereby avoid Confrontation Clause scrutiny, or is there a uniform definition of a dying declaration for Confrontation Clause purposes, and if so, what is its scope? *See* Peter Nicolas, *'I'm Dying to Tell You What Happened': The Admissibility of Testimonial Dying Declarations Post-*Crawford, 37 Hastings Const. L.Q. 487 (2010) (arguing that to avoid dilution of the Confrontation Clause right there must be a uniform constitutional definition of "dying declaration," and relying on historical materials to suggest its scope).

8. *Crawford*, *Davis*, *Giles*, and *Bryant* all involve statements made by a declarant to a government official, such as a police officer. Thus, in none of these cases has the Court been squarely presented with the question whether the Confrontation Clause applies to statements made by a declarant to a non-governmental actor, such as a friend, family member, doctor, nurse, or psychologist. Do they nonetheless hint at an answer to the question? *See United States v. Wright*, 536 F.3d 819, 823 (8th Cir. 2008) ("in *Giles*, the Court recently observed in dicta that '[s]tatements to friends and neighbors about abuse and intimidation, and statements to physicians in the course of receiving treatment,' are not testimonial"); *People v. Duhs*, 947 N.E.2d 617, 619–20 (N.Y. 2011) (relying on *Giles* and *Bryant* for proposition that statements to non-governmental actors are non-testimonial).

4. A Fragile Majority and the Future of *Crawford*

As the post-*Crawford* cases above demonstrate, there is a sharp and growing division amongst the Justices regarding the meaning of *Crawford*. Nonetheless, the decisions excerpted above were all decided by significant majorities. The two cases that follow, however, were decided by narrow 5–4 majorities. The narrowness of that majority is compounded by the fact that Justice Thomas — who stands by his distinction between formal and informal statements — was part of the majority in each of these cases, and Justice Sotomayor — who arguably re-shaped *Crawford* somewhat in *Bryant* — was part of the majority in one (she was not on the Court when the other case was decided). It is thus worth paying close attention to their separate opinions in these two cases, since their perspectives could very well be decisive in a future case.

Melendez-Diaz v. Massachusetts

129 S. Ct. 2527 (2009)

Justice SCALIA delivered the opinion of the Court.

. . . .

I

In 2001, Boston police officers received a tip that a Kmart employee, Thomas Wright, was engaging in suspicious activity. The informant reported that Wright repeatedly received phone calls at work, after each of which he would be picked up in front of the store by a blue sedan, and would return to the store a short time later. The police set up surveillance in the Kmart parking lot and witnessed this precise sequence of events. When Wright got out of the car upon his return, one of the officers detained and searched him, finding four clear white plastic bags containing a substance resembling cocaine. The officer then signaled other officers on the scene to arrest the two men in the car—one of whom was petitioner Luis Melendez-Diaz. The officers placed all three men in a police cruiser.

During the short drive to the police station, the officers observed their passengers fidgeting and making furtive movements in the back of the car. After depositing the men at the station, they searched the police cruiser and found a plastic bag containing 19 smaller plastic bags hidden in the partition between the front and back seats. They submitted the seized evidence to a state laboratory required by law to conduct chemical analysis upon police request.

Melendez-Diaz was charged with distributing cocaine and with trafficking in cocaine in an amount between 14 and 28 grams. At trial, the prosecution placed into evidence the bags seized from Wright and from the police cruiser. It also submitted three "certificates of analysis" showing the results of the forensic analysis performed on the seized substances. The certificates reported the weight of the seized bags and stated that the bags "[h]a[ve] been examined with the following results: The substance was found to contain: Cocaine." The certificates were sworn to before a notary public by analysts at the State Laboratory Institute of the Massachusetts Department of Public Health, as required under Massachusetts law.

Petitioner objected to the admission of the certificates, asserting that our Confrontation Clause decision in *Crawford v. Washington*, 541 U.S. 36 (2004), required the analysts to testify in person. The objection was overruled, and the certificates were admitted pursuant to state law as "prima facie evidence of the composition, quality, and the net weight of the narcotic ... analyzed."

The jury found Melendez-Diaz guilty. He appealed, contending, among other things, that admission of the certificates violated his Sixth Amendment right to be confronted with the witnesses against him. The Appeals Court of Massachusetts rejected the claim.... The Supreme Judicial Court denied review. We granted certiorari.

II

. . . .

Our opinion [in *Crawford*] described the class of testimonial statements covered by the Confrontation Clause as follows:

> "Various formulations of this core class of testimonial statements exist: ex parte in-court testimony or its functional equivalent—that is, material such as affidavits, custodial examinations, prior testimony that the defendant was unable to cross-

examine, or similar pretrial statements that declarants would reasonably expect to be used prosecutorially; extrajudicial statements ... contained in formalized testimonial materials, such as affidavits, depositions, prior testimony, or confessions; statements that were made under circumstances which would lead an objective witness reasonably to believe that the statement would be available for use at a later trial."

There is little doubt that the documents at issue in this case fall within the "core class of testimonial statements" thus described. Our description of that category mentions affidavits twice. The documents at issue here, while denominated by Massachusetts law "certificates," are quite plainly affidavits: "declaration[s] of facts written down and sworn to by the declarant before an officer authorized to administer oaths." Black's Law Dictionary 62 (8th ed. 2004). They are incontrovertibly a "'solemn declaration or affirmation made for the purpose of establishing or proving some fact.'" *Crawford, supra*, at 51 (quoting 2 N. Webster, An American Dictionary of the English Language (1828)). The fact in question is that the substance found in the possession of Melendez-Diaz and his codefendants was, as the prosecution claimed, cocaine—the precise testimony the analysts would be expected to provide if called at trial. The "certificates" are functionally identical to live, in-court testimony, doing "precisely what a witness does on direct examination." *Davis v. Washington*, 547 U.S. 813, 830 (2006).

Here, moreover, not only were the affidavits "'made under circumstances which would lead an objective witness reasonably to believe that the statement would be available for use at a later trial,'" *Crawford, supra*, at 52, but under Massachusetts law the *sole purpose* of the affidavits was to provide "prima facie evidence of the composition, quality, and the net weight" of the analyzed substance. We can safely assume that the analysts were aware of the affidavits' evidentiary purpose, since that purpose—as stated in the relevant state-law provision—was reprinted on the affidavits themselves.

In short, under our decision in *Crawford* the analysts' affidavits were testimonial statements, and the analysts were "witnesses" for purposes of the Sixth Amendment. Absent a showing that the analysts were unavailable to testify at trial *and* that petitioner had a prior opportunity to cross-examine them, petitioner was entitled to "'be confronted with'" the analysts at trial.[1]

III

Respondent and the dissent advance a potpourri of analytic arguments in an effort to avoid this rather straightforward application of our holding in *Crawford*....

A

Respondent first argues that the analysts are not subject to confrontation because they are not "accusatory" witnesses, in that they do not directly accuse petitioner of wrongdoing; rather, their testimony is inculpatory only when taken together with other evidence link-

---

1. Contrary to the dissent's suggestion, we do not hold, and it is not the case, that anyone whose testimony may be relevant in establishing the chain of custody, authenticity of the sample, or accuracy of the testing device, must appear in person as part of the prosecution's case. While the dissent is correct that "[i]t is the obligation of the prosecution to establish the chain of custody," this does not mean that everyone who laid hands on the evidence must be called. As stated in the dissent's own quotation, from *United States v. Lott*, 854 F.2d 244, 250 (C.A.7 1988), "gaps in the chain [of custody] normally go to the weight of the evidence rather than its admissibility." It is up to the prosecution to decide what steps in the chain of custody are so crucial as to require evidence; but what testimony is introduced must (if the defendant objects) be introduced live. Additionally, documents prepared in the regular course of equipment maintenance may well qualify as nontestimonial records.

ing petitioner to the contraband. This finds no support in the text of the Sixth Amendment or in our case law.

The Sixth Amendment guarantees a defendant the right "to be confronted with the witnesses *against him*" (emphasis added). To the extent the analysts were witnesses (a question resolved above), they certainly provided testimony *against* petitioner, proving one fact necessary for his conviction—that the substance he possessed was cocaine....

It is often, indeed perhaps usually, the case that an adverse witness's testimony, taken alone, will not suffice to convict. Yet respondent fails to cite a single case in which such testimony was admitted absent a defendant's opportunity to cross-examine....

B

Respondent and the dissent argue that the analysts should not be subject to confrontation because they are not "conventional" (or "typical" or "ordinary") witnesses of the sort whose *ex parte* testimony was most notoriously used at the trial of Sir Walter Raleigh. It is true, as the Court recognized in *Crawford*, that *ex parte* examinations of the sort used at Raleigh's trial have "long been thought a paradigmatic confrontation violation." But the paradigmatic case identifies the core of the right to confrontation, not its limits. The right to confrontation was not invented in response to the use of the *ex parte* examinations in *Raleigh's Case*. That use provoked such an outcry precisely because it flouted the deeply rooted common-law tradition "of live testimony in court subject to adversarial testing."

In any case, the purported distinctions respondent and the dissent identify between this case and Sir Walter Raleigh's "conventional" accusers do not survive scrutiny. The dissent first contends that a "conventional witness recalls events observed in the past, while an analyst's report contains near-contemporaneous observations of the test." It is doubtful that the analyst's reports in this case could be characterized as reporting "near-contemporaneous observations"; the affidavits were completed almost a week after the tests were performed. But regardless, the dissent misunderstands the role that "near-contemporaneity" has played in our case law. The dissent notes that that factor was given "substantial weight" in *Davis*, but in fact that decision *disproves* the dissent's position. There the Court considered the admissibility of statements made to police officers responding to a report of a domestic disturbance. By the time officers arrived the assault had ended, but the victim's statements—written and oral—were sufficiently close in time to the alleged assault that the trial court admitted her affidavit as a "present sense impression." Though the witness's statements in *Davis* were "near-contemporaneous" to the events she reported, we nevertheless held that they could not be admitted absent an opportunity to confront the witness.

A second reason the dissent contends that the analysts are not "conventional witnesses" (and thus not subject to confrontation) is that they "observe[d] neither the crime nor any human action related to it." The dissent provides no authority for this particular limitation of the type of witnesses subject to confrontation. Nor is it conceivable that all witnesses who fit this description would be outside the scope of the Confrontation Clause. For example, is a police officer's investigative report describing the crime scene admissible absent an opportunity to examine the officer? The dissent's novel exception from coverage of the Confrontation Clause would exempt all expert witnesses—a hardly "unconventional" class of witnesses.

A third respect in which the dissent asserts that the analysts are not "conventional" witnesses and thus not subject to confrontation is that their statements were not provided in response to interrogation.... Respondent and the dissent cite no authority, and we are aware of none, holding that a person who volunteers his testimony is any less a "'witness against' the defendant," than one who is responding to interrogation. In any event, the analysts' affidavits in this case *were* presented in response to a police request....

C

Respondent claims that there is a difference, for Confrontation Clause purposes, between testimony recounting historical events, which is "prone to distortion or manipulation," and the testimony at issue here, which is the "resul[t] of neutral, scientific testing." Relatedly, respondent and the dissent argue that confrontation of forensic analysts would be of little value because "one would not reasonably expect a laboratory professional ... to feel quite differently about the results of his scientific test by having to look at the defendant."

This argument is little more than an invitation to return to our overruled decision in *Roberts*.... Respondent and the dissent may be right that there are other ways—and in some cases better ways—to challenge or verify the results of a forensic test. But the Constitution guarantees one way: confrontation. We do not have license to suspend the Confrontation Clause when a preferable trial strategy is available.

Nor is it evident that what respondent calls "neutral scientific testing" is as neutral or as reliable as respondent suggests. Forensic evidence is not uniquely immune from the risk of manipulation.... A forensic analyst responding to a request from a law enforcement official may feel pressure—or have an incentive—to alter the evidence in a manner favorable to the prosecution.

Confrontation is one means of assuring accurate forensic analysis.... Like the eyewitness who has fabricated his account to the police, the analyst who provides false results may, under oath in open court, reconsider his false testimony. And, of course, the prospect of confrontation will deter fraudulent analysis in the first place.

Confrontation is designed to weed out not only the fraudulent analyst, but the incompetent one as well.... Like expert witnesses generally, an analyst's lack of proper training or deficiency in judgment may be disclosed in cross-examination....

D

Respondent argues that the analysts' affidavits are admissible without confrontation because they are "akin to the types of official and business records admissible at common law." But the affidavits do not qualify as traditional official or business records, and even if they did, their authors would be subject to confrontation nonetheless....

The dissent identifies a single class of evidence which, though prepared for use at trial, was traditionally admissible: a clerk's certificate authenticating an official record—or a copy thereof—for use as evidence. But a clerk's authority in that regard was narrowly circumscribed. He was permitted "to certify to the correctness of a copy of a record kept in his office," but had "no authority to furnish, as evidence for the trial of a lawsuit, his interpretation of what the record contains or shows, or to certify to its substance or effect." The dissent suggests that the fact that this exception was "'narrowly circumscribed'" makes no difference. To the contrary, it makes all the difference in the world. It shows that even the line of cases establishing the one narrow exception the dissent has been able to identify simultaneously vindicates the general rule applicable to the present case. A clerk could by affidavit *authenticate* or provide a copy of an otherwise admissible record, but could not do what the analysts did here: *create* a record for the sole purpose of providing evidence against a defendant.

Far more probative here are those cases in which the prosecution sought to admit into evidence a clerk's certificate attesting to the fact that the clerk had searched for a partic-

682   7 · THE RULE AGAINST HEARSAY

ular relevant record and failed to find it. Like the testimony of the analysts in this case, the clerk's statement would serve as substantive evidence against the defendant whose guilt depended on the nonexistence of the record for which the clerk searched. Although the clerk's certificate would qualify as an official record under respondent's definition — it was prepared by a public officer in the regular course of his official duties — and although the clerk was certainly not a "conventional witness" under the dissent's approach, the clerk was nonetheless subject to confrontation.

Respondent also misunderstands the relationship between the business-and-official-records hearsay exceptions and the Confrontation Clause. As we stated in *Crawford*: "Most of the hearsay exceptions covered statements that by their nature were not testimonial—for example, business records or statements in furtherance of a conspiracy." Business and public records are generally admissible absent confrontation not because they qualify under an exception to the hearsay rules, but because—having been created for the administration of an entity's affairs and not for the purpose of establishing or proving some fact at trial—they are not testimonial. Whether or not they qualify as business or official records, the analysts' statements here—prepared specifically for use at petitioner's trial—were testimony against petitioner, and the analysts were subject to confrontation under the Sixth Amendment.

E

Respondent asserts that we should find no Confrontation Clause violation in this case because petitioner had the ability to subpoena the analysts. But that power—whether pursuant to state law or the Compulsory Process Clause—is no substitute for the right of confrontation. Unlike the Confrontation Clause, those provisions are of no use to the defendant when the witness is unavailable or simply refuses to appear. Converting the prosecution's duty under the Confrontation Clause into the defendant's privilege under state law or the Compulsory Process Clause shifts the consequences of adverse-witness no-shows from the State to the accused. More fundamentally, the Confrontation Clause imposes a burden on the prosecution to present its witnesses, not on the defendant to bring those adverse witnesses into court. Its value to the defendant is not replaced by a system in which the prosecution presents its evidence via *ex parte* affidavits and waits for the defendant to subpoena the affiants if he chooses.

F

Finally, respondent asks us to relax the requirements of the Confrontation Clause to accommodate the "'necessities of trial and the adversary process.'" It is not clear whence we would derive the authority to do so. The Confrontation Clause may make the prosecution of criminals more burdensome, but that is equally true of the right to trial by jury and the privilege against self-incrimination. The Confrontation Clause—like those other constitutional provisions—is binding, and we may not disregard it at our convenience.

We also doubt the accuracy of respondent's and the dissent's dire predictions....

Perhaps the best indication that the sky will not fall after today's decision is that it has not done so already. Many States have already adopted the constitutional rule we announce today, while many others permit the defendant to assert (or forfeit by silence) his Confrontation Clause right after receiving notice of the prosecution's intent to use a forensic analyst's report. Despite these widespread practices, there is no evidence that the criminal justice system has ground to a halt in the States that, one way or another, empower a defendant to insist upon the analyst's appearance at trial....

The dissent finds this evidence "far less reassuring than promised." But its doubts rest on two flawed premises. First, the dissent believes that those state statutes "requiring the defendant to give early notice of his intent to confront the analyst," are "burden-shifting statutes [that] may be invalidated by the Court's reasoning." That is not so. In their simplest form, notice-and-demand statutes require the prosecution to provide notice to the defendant of its intent to use an analyst's report as evidence at trial, after which the defendant is given a period of time in which he may object to the admission of the evidence absent the analyst's appearance live at trial. Contrary to the dissent's perception, these statutes shift no burden whatever. The defendant *always* has the burden of raising his Confrontation Clause objection; notice-and-demand statutes simply govern the time within which he must do so. States are free to adopt procedural rules governing objections. It is common to require a defendant to exercise his rights under the Compulsory Process Clause in advance of trial, announcing his intent to present certain witnesses. There is no conceivable reason why he cannot similarly be compelled to exercise his Confrontation Clause rights before trial. Today's decision will not disrupt criminal prosecutions in the many large States whose practice is already in accord with the Confrontation Clause.[12]

. . . .

Defense attorneys and their clients will often stipulate to the nature of the substance in the ordinary drug case. It is unlikely that defense counsel will insist on live testimony whose effect will be merely to highlight rather than cast doubt upon the forensic analysis. Nor will defense attorneys want to antagonize the judge or jury by wasting their time with the appearance of a witness whose testimony defense counsel does not intend to rebut in any fashion.... Given these strategic considerations, and in light of the experience in those States that already provide the same or similar protections to defendants, there is little reason to believe that our decision today will commence the parade of horribles respondent and the dissent predict....

Justice THOMAS, concurring.

I write separately to note that I continue to adhere to my position that "the Confrontation Clause is implicated by extrajudicial statements only insofar as they are contained in formalized testimonial materials, such as affidavits, depositions, prior testimony, or confessions." I join the Court's opinion in this case because the documents at issue in this case "are quite plainly affidavits". As such, they "fall within the core class of testimonial statements" governed by the Confrontation Clause.

Justice KENNEDY, with whom THE CHIEF JUSTICE, Justice BREYER, and Justice ALITO join, dissenting.

The Court sweeps away an accepted rule governing the admission of scientific evidence. Until today, scientific analysis could be introduced into evidence without testimony from the "analyst" who produced it. This rule has been established for at least 90 years....

It is remarkable that the Court so confidently disregards a century of jurisprudence. We learn now that we have misinterpreted the Confrontation Clause—hardly an arcane or seldom-used provision of the Constitution—for the first 218 years of its existence.

---

12. As the dissent notes, *some* state statutes, "requir[e] defense counsel to subpoena the analyst, to show good cause for demanding the analyst's presence, or even to affirm under oath an intent to cross-examine the analyst." We have no occasion today to pass on the constitutionality of every variety of statute commonly given the notice-and-demand label. It suffices to say that what we have referred to as the "simplest form [of] notice-and-demand statutes," is constitutional; that such provisions are in place in a number of States; and that in those States, and in other States that require confrontation without notice-and-demand, there is no indication that the dire consequences predicted by the dissent have materialized.

The immediate systemic concern is that the Court makes no attempt to acknowledge the real differences between laboratory analysts who perform scientific tests and other, more conventional witnesses—"witnesses" being the word the Framers used in the Confrontation Clause.

Crawford and *Davis* dealt with ordinary witnesses—women who had seen, and in two cases been the victim of, the crime in question. Those cases stand for the proposition that formal statements made by a conventional witness—one who has personal knowledge of some aspect of the defendant's guilt—may not be admitted without the witness appearing at trial to meet the accused face to face. But Crawford and Davis do not say— indeed, could not have said, because the facts were not before the Court—that anyone who makes a testimonial statement is a witness for purposes of the Confrontation Clause, even when that person has, in fact, witnessed nothing to give them personal knowledge of the defendant's guilt.

Because *Crawford* and *Davis* concerned typical witnesses, the Court should have done the sensible thing and limited its holding to witnesses as so defined....

I

A

1

The Court says that, before the results of a scientific test may be introduced into evidence, the defendant has the right to confront the "analyst." One must assume that this term, though it appears nowhere in the Confrontation Clause, nevertheless has some constitutional substance that now must be elaborated in future cases. There is no accepted definition of analyst, and there is no established precedent to define that term.

Consider how many people play a role in a routine test for the presence of illegal drugs. One person prepares a sample of the drug, places it in a testing machine, and retrieves the machine's printout—often, a graph showing the frequencies of radiation absorbed by the sample or the masses of the sample's molecular fragments. A second person interprets the graph the machine prints out—perhaps by comparing that printout with published, standardized graphs of known drugs. Meanwhile, a third person—perhaps an independent contractor—has calibrated the machine and, having done so, has certified that the machine is in good working order. Finally, a fourth person—perhaps the laboratory's director-certifies that his subordinates followed established procedures.

It is not at all evident which of these four persons is the analyst to be confronted under the rule the Court announces today. If all are witnesses who must appear for in-court confrontation, then the Court has, for all practical purposes, forbidden the use of scientific tests in criminal trials. As discussed further below, requiring even one of these individuals to testify threatens to disrupt if not end many prosecutions where guilt is clear but a newly found formalism now holds sway.

It is possible to read the Court's opinion, however, to say that all four must testify. Each one has contributed to the test's result and has, at least in some respects, made a representation about the test....

And each of the four has power to introduce error....

The Court offers no principles or historical precedent to determine which of these persons is the analyst. All contribute to the test result. And each is equally remote from the scene, has no personal stake in the outcome, does not even know the accused, and is concerned only with the performance of his or her role in conducting the test.

It could be argued that the only analyst who must testify is the person who signed the certificate. Under this view, a laboratory could have one employee sign certificates and appear in court, which would spare all the other analysts this burden. But the Court has already rejected this arrangement. The Court made clear in *Davis* that it will not permit the testimonial statement of one witness to enter into evidence through the in-court testimony of a second.... Under this logic, the Court's holding cannot be cabined to the person who signs the certificates. If the signatory is restating the testimonial statements of the true analysts—whoever they might be—then those analysts, too, must testify in person.

Today's decision demonstrates that even in the narrow category of scientific tests that identify a drug, the Court cannot define with any clarity who the analyst is. Outside this narrow category, the range of other scientific tests that may be affected by the Court's new confrontation right is staggering.

2

It is difficult to confine at this point the damage the Court's holding will do in other contexts. Consider just two—establishing the chain of custody and authenticating a copy of a document.

It is the obligation of the prosecution to establish the chain of custody for evidence sent to testing laboratories—that is, to establish "the identity and integrity of physical evidence by tracing its continuous whereabouts." Meeting this obligation requires representations—that one officer retrieved the evidence from the crime scene, that a second officer checked it into an evidence locker, that a third officer verified the locker's seal was intact, and so forth. The iron logic of which the Court is so enamored would seem to require in-court testimony from each human link in the chain of custody. That, of course, has never been the law.

It is no answer for the Court to say that "[i]t is up to the prosecution to decide what steps in the chain of custody are so crucial as to require evidence." The case itself determines which links in the chain are crucial—not the prosecution. In any number of cases, the crucial link in the chain will not be available to testify and so the evidence will be excluded for lack of a proper foundation.

Consider another context in which the Court's holding may cause disruption: The long-accepted practice of authenticating copies of documents by means of a certificate from the document's custodian stating that the copy is accurate. *See, e.g.,* Fed. Rule Evid. 902(4) (in order to be self-authenticating, a copy of a public record must be "certified as correct by the custodian"); Rule 902(11) (business record must be "accompanied by a written declaration of its custodian"). Under one possible reading of the Court's opinion, recordkeepers will be required to testify. So far, courts have not read Crawford and Davis to impose this largely meaningless requirement. But the breadth of the Court's ruling today, and its undefined scope, may well be such that these courts now must be deemed to have erred. The risk of that consequence ought to tell us that something is very wrong with the Court's analysis....

II

. . . .

The Court's fundamental mistake is to read the Confrontation Clause as referring to a kind of out-of-court statement—namely, a testimonial statement—that must be excluded from evidence. The Clause does not refer to kinds of statements. Nor does the Clause contain the word "testimonial." The text, instead, refers to kinds of persons, namely, to "witnesses against" the defendant. Laboratory analysts are not "witnesses against" the defendant as those words would have been understood at the framing. There is simply no authority for this proposition.

Instead, the Clause refers to a conventional "witness"—meaning one who witnesses (that is, perceives) an event that gives him or her personal knowledge of some aspect of the defendant's guilt. Both *Crawford* and *Davis* concerned just this kind of ordinary witness—and nothing in the Confrontation Clause's text, history, or precedent justifies the Court's decision to expand those cases.

A

....

The Court today expands the Clause to include laboratory analysts, but analysts differ from ordinary witnesses in at least three significant ways. First, a conventional witness recalls events observed in the past, while an analyst's report contains near-contemporaneous observations of the test. An observation recorded at the time it is made is unlike the usual act of testifying. A typical witness must recall a previous event that he or she perceived just once, and thus may have misperceived or misremembered. But an analyst making a contemporaneous observation need not rely on memory; he or she instead reports the observations at the time they are made....

Second, an analyst observes neither the crime nor any human action related to it. Often, the analyst does not know the defendant's identity, much less have personal knowledge of an aspect of the defendant's guilt. The analyst's distance from the crime and the defendant, in both space and time, suggests the analyst is not a witness against the defendant in the conventional sense.

Third, a conventional witness responds to questions under interrogation. But laboratory tests are conducted according to scientific protocols; they are not dependent upon or controlled by interrogation of any sort....

The Court assumes, with little analysis, that *Crawford* and *Davis* extended the Clause to any person who makes a "testimonial" statement....

It is true that *Crawford* and *Davis* employed the term "testimonial," and thereby suggested that any testimonial statement, by any person, no matter how distant from the defendant and the crime, is subject to the Confrontation Clause. But that suggestion was not part of the holding of *Crawford* or *Davis*. Those opinions used the adjective "testimonial" to avoid the awkward phrasing required by reusing the noun "witness." The Court today transforms that turn of phrase into a new and sweeping legal rule, by holding that anyone who makes a formal statement for the purpose of later prosecution—no matter how removed from the crime—must be considered a "witness against" the defendant....

B

No historical evidence supports the Court's conclusion that the Confrontation Clause was understood to extend beyond conventional witnesses to include analysts who conduct scientific tests far removed from the crime and the defendant. Indeed, what little evidence there is contradicts this interpretation.

Though the Framers had no forensic scientists, they did use another kind of unconventional witness—the copyist. A copyist's work may be as essential to a criminal prosecution as the forensic analyst's. To convict a man of bigamy, for example, the State often requires his marriage records. But if the original records cannot be taken from the archive, the prosecution must rely on copies of those records, made for the purpose of introducing the copies into evidence at trial. In that case, the copyist's honesty and diligence are just as important as the analyst's here. If the copyist falsifies a copy, or even misspells a name or transposes a date, those flaws could lead the jury to convict. Because so much depends on his or her honesty and diligence, the copyist often prepares an affidavit certifying that the copy is true and accurate.

Such a certificate is beyond question a testimonial statement under the Court's definition: It is a formal out-of-court statement offered for the truth of two matters (the copyist's honesty and the copy's accuracy), and it is prepared for a criminal prosecution.

During the Framers' era copyists' affidavits were accepted without hesitation by American courts. And courts admitted copyists' affidavits in criminal as well as civil trials. This demonstrates that the framing generation, in contrast to the Court today, did not consider the Confrontation Clause to require in-court confrontation of unconventional authors of testimonial statements.

The Court attempts to explain away this historical exception to its rule by noting that a copyist's authority is "narrowly circumscribed." But the Court does not explain why that matters, nor, if it does matter, why laboratory analysts' authority should not also be deemed "narrowly circumscribed" so that they, too, may be excused from testifying. And drawing these fine distinctions cannot be squared with the Court's avowed allegiance to formalism. Determining whether a witness' authority is "narrowly circumscribed" has nothing to do with *Crawford*'s testimonial framework....

By insisting that every author of a testimonial statement appear for confrontation, on pain of excluding the statement from evidence, the Court does violence to the Framers' sensible, and limited, conception of the right to confront "witnesses against" the defendant....

III

....

A

....

The Court surmises that "[i]t is unlikely that defense counsel will insist on live testimony whose effect will be merely to highlight rather than cast doubt upon the forensic analysis." This optimistic prediction misunderstands how criminal trials work. If the defense does not plan to challenge the test result, "highlight[ing]" that result through testimony does not harm the defense as the Court supposes. If the analyst cannot reach the courtroom in time to testify, however, a *Melendez-Diaz* objection grants the defense a great windfall: The analyst's work cannot come into evidence. Given the prospect of such a windfall (which may, in and of itself, secure an acquittal) few zealous advocates will pledge, prior to trial, not to raise a *Melendez-Diaz* objection. Defense counsel will accept the risk that the jury may hear the analyst's live testimony, in exchange for the chance that the analyst fails to appear and the government's case collapses. And if, as here, the defense is not that the substance was harmless, but instead that the accused did not possess it, the testimony of the technician is a formalism that does not detract from the defense case....

B

As further reassurance that the "sky will not fall after today's decision," the Court notes that many States have enacted burden-shifting statutes that require the defendant to assert his Confrontation Clause right prior to trial or else "forfeit" it "by silence." The Court implies that by shifting the burden to the defendant to take affirmative steps to produce the analyst, these statutes reduce the burden on the prosecution.

The Court holds that these burden-shifting statutes are valid because, in the Court's view, they "shift no burden whatever." While this conclusion is welcome, the premise appears flawed. Even what the Court calls the "simplest form" of burden-shifting statutes do impose requirements on the defendant, who must make a formal demand, with proper service, well before trial. Some statutes impose more requirements.... In a future case, the Court may find that some of these more onerous burden-shifting statutes violate the Confrontation Clause because they "impos[e] a burden ... on the defendant to bring ... adverse witnesses into court."

. . . .

Bullcoming v. New Mexico
131 S. Ct. 2705 (2011)

Justice GINSBURG delivered the opinion of the Court, except as to Part IV and footnote 6.*

. . . .

In the case before us, petitioner Donald Bullcoming was arrested on charges of driving while intoxicated (DWI). Principal evidence against Bullcoming was a forensic laboratory report certifying that Bullcoming's blood-alcohol concentration was well above the threshold for aggravated DWI. At trial, the prosecution did not call as a witness the analyst who signed the certification. Instead, the State called another analyst who was familiar with the laboratory's testing procedures, but had neither participated in nor observed the test on Bullcoming's blood sample. The New Mexico Supreme Court determined that, although the blood-alcohol analysis was "testimonial," the Confrontation Clause did not require the certifying analyst's in-court testimony. Instead, New Mexico's high court held, live testimony of another analyst satisfied the constitutional requirements.

The question presented is whether the Confrontation Clause permits the prosecution to introduce a forensic laboratory report containing a testimonial certification—made for the purpose of proving a particular fact—through the in-court testimony of a scientist who did not sign the certification or perform or observe the test reported in the certification. We hold that surrogate testimony of that order does not meet the constitutional requirement. The accused's right is to be confronted with the analyst who made the certification, unless that analyst is unavailable at trial, and the accused had an opportunity, pretrial, to cross-examine that particular scientist.

I

. . . .

C

While Bullcoming's appeal was pending before the New Mexico Supreme Court, this Court decided *Melendez-Diaz*....

In light of *Melendez-Diaz*, the New Mexico Supreme Court acknowledged that the blood-alcohol report introduced at Bullcoming's trial qualified as testimonial evidence....

---

* Justice SOTOMAYOR and Justice KAGAN join all but Part IV of this opinion. Justice THOMAS joins in all but Part IV and footnote 6.

Nevertheless, for two reasons, the court held that admission of the report did not violate the Confrontation Clause.

First, the court said certifying analyst Caylor "was a mere scrivener," who "simply transcribed the results generated by the gas chromatograph machine." Second, SLD analyst Razatos, although he did not participate in testing Bullcoming's blood, "qualified as an expert witness with respect to the gas chromatograph machine." "Razatos provided live, in-court testimony," the court stated, "and, thus, was available for cross-examination regarding the operation of the ... machine, the results of [Bullcoming's] BAC test, and the SLD's established laboratory procedures." Razatos' testimony was crucial, the court explained, because Bullcoming could not cross-examine the machine or the written report. But "[Bullcoming's] right of confrontation was preserved," the court concluded, because Razatos was a qualified analyst, able to serve as a surrogate for Caylor....

II

.... In a pathmarking 2004 decision, *Crawford* v. *Washington*, we overruled *Ohio* v. *Roberts*, 448 U. S. 56 (1980), which had interpreted the Confrontation Clause to allow admission of absent witnesses' testimonial statements based on a judicial determination of reliability. Rejecting *Roberts*' "amorphous notions of 'reliability,'" *Crawford* held that fidelity to the Confrontation Clause permitted admission of "[t]estimonial statements of witnesses absent from trial ... only where the declarant is unavailable, and only where the defendant has had a prior opportunity to cross-examine." *Melendez-Diaz*, relying on *Crawford*'s rationale, refused to create a "forensic evidence" exception to this rule. An analyst's certification prepared in connection with a criminal investigation or prosecution, the Court held, is "testimonial," and therefore within the compass of the Confrontation Clause.[6]

The State in the instant case never asserted that the analyst who signed the certification, Curtis Caylor, was unavailable. The record showed only that Caylor was placed on unpaid leave for an undisclosed reason. Nor did Bullcoming have an opportunity to cross-examine Caylor. *Crawford* and *Melendez-Diaz*, therefore, weigh heavily in Bullcoming's favor. The New Mexico Supreme Court, however, although recognizing that the SLD report was testimonial for purposes of the Confrontation Clause, considered SLD analyst Razatos an adequate substitute for Caylor....

A

The New Mexico Supreme Court held surrogate testimony adequate to satisfy the Confrontation Clause in this case because analyst Caylor "simply transcribed the resul[t] generated by the gas chromatograph machine," presenting no interpretation and exercising no independent judgment. Bullcoming's "true 'accuser,'" the court said, was the machine, while testing analyst Caylor's role was that of "mere scrivener. Caylor's certification, however, reported more than a machine-generated number.

Caylor certified that he received Bullcoming's blood sample intact with the seal unbroken, that he checked to make sure that the forensic report number and the sample

---

6. To rank as "testimonial," a statement must have a "primary purpose" of "establish[ing] or prov[ing] past events potentially relevant to later criminal prosecution." *Davis* v. *Washington*, 547 U.S. 813, 822 (2006). See also *Bryant*, 131 S. Ct., at 1155. Elaborating on the purpose for which a "testimonial report" is created, we observed in *Melendez-Diaz* that business and public records "are generally admissible absent confrontation ... because—having been created for the administration of an entity's affairs and not for the purpose of establishing or proving some fact at trial—they are not testimonial." 131 S. Ct., at 1155.

number "correspond[ed]," and that he performed on Bullcoming's sample a particular test, adhering to a precise protocol. He further represented, by leaving the "[r]emarks" section of the report blank, that no "circumstance or condition ... affect[ed] the integrity of the sample or ... the validity of the analysis." These representations, relating to past events and human actions not revealed in raw, machine-produced data, are meet for cross-examination.

The potential ramifications of the New Mexico Supreme Court's reasoning, furthermore, raise red flags. Most witnesses, after all, testify to their observations of factual conditions or events, *e.g.*, "the light was green," "the hour was noon." Such witnesses may record, on the spot, what they observed. Suppose a police report recorded an objective fact—Bullcoming's counsel posited the address above the front door of a house or the readout of a radar gun. Could an officer other than the one who saw the number on the house or gun present the information in court—so long as that officer was equipped to testify about any technology the observing officer deployed and the police department's standard operating procedures? As our precedent makes plain, the answer is emphatically "No." See *Davis* v. *Washington*, 547 U. S. 813, 826 (2006) (Confrontation Clause may not be "evaded by having a note-taking police[officer] recite the ... testimony of the declarant"); *Melendez-Diaz*, 129 S. Ct., at 2546 (KENNEDY, J., dissenting) ("The Court made clear in *Davis* that it will not permit the testimonial statement of one witness to enter into evidence through the in-court testimony of a second.").

The New Mexico Supreme Court stated that the number registered by the gas chromatograph machine called for no interpretation or exercise of independent judgment on Caylor's part. We have already explained that Caylor certified to more than a machine-generated number. In any event, the comparative reliability of an analyst's testimonial report drawn from machine-produced data does not overcome the Sixth Amendment bar. This Court settled in *Crawford* that the "obviou[s] reliab[ility]" of a testimonial statement does not dispense with the Confrontation Clause. Accordingly, the analysts who write reports that the prosecution introduces must be made available for confrontation even if they possess "the scientific acumen of Mme. Curie and the veracity of Mother Teresa." *Melendez-Diaz*, 129 S. Ct., at 2357, n. 6.

B

Recognizing that admission of the blood-alcohol analysis depended on "live, in-court testimony [by] a qualified analyst," the New Mexico Supreme Court believed that Razatos could substitute for Caylor because Razatos "qualified as an expert witness with respect to the gas chromatograph machine and the SLD's laboratory procedures." But surrogate testimony of the kind Razatos was equipped to give could not convey what Caylor knew or observed about the events his certification concerned, *i.e.*, the particular test and testing process he employed.[7] Nor could such surrogate testimony expose any lapses or lies on the certifying analyst's part. Significant here, Razatos had no knowledge of the reason why Caylor had been placed on unpaid leave. With Caylor on the stand, Bullcoming's counsel could have asked questions designed to reveal whether incompetence, evasiveness, or dishonesty accounted for Caylor's removal from his work station. Notable in this

---

7. We do not question that analyst Caylor, in common with other analysts employed by SLD, likely would not recall a particular test, given the number of tests each analyst conducts and the standard procedure followed in testing. Even so, Caylor's testimony under oath would have enabled Bullcoming's counsel to raise before a jury questions concerning Caylor's proficiency, the care he took in performing his work, and his veracity. In particular, Bullcoming's counsel likely would have inquired on cross-examination why Caylor had been placed on unpaid leave.

regard, the State never asserted that Caylor was "unavailable"; the prosecution conveyed only that Caylor was on uncompensated leave. Nor did the State assert that Razatos had any "independent opinion" concerning Bullcoming's BAC....

More fundamentally, as this Court stressed in *Crawford*, "[t]he text of the Sixth Amendment does not suggest any open-ended exceptions from the confrontation requirement to be developed by the courts." Nor is it "the role of courts to extrapolate from the words of the [Confrontation Clause] to the values behind it, and then to enforce its guarantees only to the extent they serve (in the courts' views) those underlying values." *Giles v. California*, 554 U. S. 353, 375 (2008). Accordingly, the Clause does not tolerate dispensing with confrontation simply because the court believes that questioning one witness about another's testimonial statements provides a fair enough opportunity for cross-examination....

In short, when the State elected to introduce Caylor's certification, Caylor became a witness Bullcoming had the right to confront. Our precedent cannot sensibly be read any other way....

IV

The State and its *amici* urge that unbending application of the Confrontation Clause to forensic evidence would impose an undue burden on the prosecution. This argument, also advanced in the dissent, largely repeats a refrain rehearsed and rejected in *Melendez-Diaz*. The constitutional requirement, we reiterate, "may not [be] disregard[ed] ... at our convenience," and the predictions of dire consequences, we again observe, are dubious.

New Mexico law, it bears emphasis, requires the laboratory to preserve samples, which can be retested by other analysts, and neither party questions SLD's compliance with that requirement. Retesting "is almost always an option ... in [DWI] cases," and the State had that option here: New Mexico could have avoided any Confrontation Clause problem by asking Razatos to retest the sample, and then testify to the results of his retest rather than to the results of a test he did not conduct or observe.

Notably, New Mexico advocates retesting as an effective means to preserve a defendant's confrontation right "when the [out-of-court] statement is raw data or a mere transcription of raw data onto a public record." But the State would require the defendant to initiate retesting. The prosecution, however, bears the burden of proof. Hence the obligation to propel retesting when the original analyst is unavailable is the State's, not the defendant's.

Furthermore, notice-and-demand procedures, long in effect in many jurisdictions, can reduce burdens on forensic laboratories....

Even before this Court's decision in *Crawford*, moreover, it was common prosecutorial practice to call the forensic analyst to testify. Prosecutors did so "to bolster the persuasive power of [the State's] case[,] ... [even] when the defense would have preferred that the analyst did *not* testify."

We note also the "small fraction of ... cases" that "actually proceed to trial." *Melendez-Diaz*, 129 S. Ct., at 2540 (citing estimate that "nearly 95% of convictions in state and federal courts are obtained via guilty plea"). And, "when cases in which forensic analysis has been conducted [do] go to trial," defendants "regularly ... [stipulate] to the admission of [the] analysis." "[A]s a result, analysts testify in only a very small percentage of cases," for "[i]t is unlikely that defense counsel will insist on live testimony whose effect will be merely to highlight rather than cast doubt upon the forensic analysis." *Melendez-Diaz*, 129 S. Ct., at 2542.

Tellingly, in jurisdictions in which "it is the [acknowledged] job of ... analysts to testify in court ... about their test results," the sky has not fallen. State and municipal laboratories "make operational and staffing decisions" to facilitate analysts' appearance at trial. Prosecutors schedule trial dates to accommodate analysts' availability, and trial courts liberally grant continuances when unexpected conflicts arise. In rare cases in which the analyst is no longer employed by the laboratory at the time of trial, "the prosecution makes the effort to bring that analyst ... to court." And, as is the practice in New Mexico, laboratories ordinarily retain additional samples, enabling them to run tests again when necessary....

Justice SOTOMAYOR, concurring in part.

I agree with the Court that the trial court erred by admitting the blood alcohol concentration (BAC) report. I write separately ... to emphasize the limited reach of the Court's opinion.

....

II

Although this case is materially indistinguishable from the facts we considered in *Melendez-Diaz*, I highlight some of the factual circumstances that this case does *not* present.

First, this is not a case in which the State suggested an alternate purpose, much less an alternate *primary* purpose, for the BAC report. For example, the State has not claimed that the report was necessary to provide Bullcoming with medical treatment. See *Bryant*, 131 S. Ct., at n. 9 (listing "Statements for Purposes of Medical Diagnosis or Treatment" under Federal Rule of Evidence 803(4) as an example of statements that are "by their nature, made for a purpose other than use in a prosecution"); *Melendez-Diaz*, 129 S. Ct., at 2533, n. 2 ("[M]edical reports created for treatment purposes ... would not be testimonial under our decision today"); *Giles* v. *California*, 554 U. S. 353, 376 (2008) ("[S]tatements to physicians in the course of receiving treatment would be excluded, if at all, only by hearsay rules").

Second, this is not a case in which the person testifying is a supervisor, reviewer, or someone else with a personal, albeit limited, connection to the scientific test at issue. Razatos conceded on cross-examination that he played no role in producing the BAC report and did not observe any portion of Curtis Caylor's conduct of the testing. The court below also recognized Razatos' total lack of connection to the test at issue. It would be a different case if, for example, a supervisor who observed an analyst conducting a test testified about the results or a report about such results. We need not address what degree of involvement is sufficient because here Razatos had no involvement whatsoever in the relevant test and report.

Third, this is not a case in which an expert witness was asked for his independent opinion about underlying testimonial reports that were not themselves admitted into evidence. See Fed. Rule Evid. 703 (explaining that facts or data of a type upon which experts in the field would reasonably rely in forming an opinion need not be admissible in order for the expert's opinion based on the facts and data to be admitted). As the Court notes, the State does not assert that Razatos offered an independent, expert opinion about Bullcoming's blood alcohol concentration.... Here the State offered the BAC report, including Caylor's testimonial statements, into evidence. We would face a different question if asked to determine the constitutionality of allowing an expert witness to discuss others' testimonial statements if the testimonial statements were not themselves admitted as evidence.

Finally, this is not a case in which the State introduced only machine-generated results, such as a printout from a gas chromatograph. The State here introduced Caylor's statements, which included his transcription of a blood alcohol concentration, apparently copied from a gas chromatograph printout, along with other statements about the procedures used in handling the blood sample. Thus, we do not decide whether, as the New Mexico Supreme Court suggests, a State could introduce (assuming an adequate chain of custody foundation) raw data generated by a machine in conjunction with the testimony of an expert witness.

This case does not present, and thus the Court's opinion does not address, any of these factual scenarios....

[The dissenting opinion of Justice KENNEDY is omitted.]

Notes and Questions

1. Recall that Rule 803(10) creates an exception for either testimony *or a certification* by an official of a public agency that a diligent search failed to uncover a record of a matter within its records to prove the nonoccurrence or nonexistence of a matter for which a record is normally made. When invoked by the government in a criminal case, is Rule 803(10) constitutionally suspect?

Since *Melendez-Diaz* has been decided, courts have uniformly held (or prosecutors have conceded) that offering certifications of the sort offered pursuant to Rule 803(10) violates the Confrontation Clause. *See United States v. Orozco-Acosta*, 607 F.3d 1156, 1161 & n.3 (9th Cir. 2010); *United States v. Martinez-Rios*, 595 F.3d 581, 584–86 (5th Cir. 2010); *United States v. Madarikan*, 356 Fed. Appx. 532, 534 (2d Cir. 2009); *Tabaka v. District of Columbia*, 976 A.2d 173, 175–76 (D.C. 2009).

Indeed, a pending, proposed amendment to Rule 803(10) would require a prosecutor seeking to offer a certification under Rule 803(10) to provide advance notice to the accused, and would allow it to be admitted only if the accused failed to object. The Advisory Committee explains the reason for the proposed amendment as follows:

> Rule 803(10) has been amended in response to *Melendez-Diaz v. Massachusetts*.... The *Melendez-Diaz* Court declared that a testimonial certificate could be admitted if the accused is given advance notice and does not timely demand the presence of the official who prepared the certificate. The amendment incorporates, with minor variations, a "notice-and-demand" procedure that was approved by the *Melendez-Diaz* Court.

2. Under Rule 803(6) — the hearsay exception for business records — the foundation necessary for invoking the exception may be "shown by the testimony of the custodian or another qualified witness, or by a *certification* that complies with Rule 902(11) or (12) or with a statute permitting certification." As Justice Kennedy notes in his dissent, the logic of the majority's opinion in *Melendez-Diaz* arguably casts doubt on the constitutionality of that procedure. However, is there language in the majority opinion suggesting that certificates *authenticating* evidence are somehow different? *See United States v. Yeley-Davis*, 632 F.3d 673, 678–81 (10th Cir. 2011) (so holding); *United States v. Mallory*, 709 F. Supp. 2d 451, 453–54 (E.D. Va. 2010) (same).

3. Rule 703 provides:

> An expert may base an opinion on facts or data in the case that the expert has been made aware of or personally observed. If experts in the particular field would reasonably rely on those kinds of facts or data in forming an opinion on the subject, they need not be admissible for the opinion to be admitted. But if

the facts or data would otherwise be inadmissible, the proponent of the opinion may disclose them to the jury only if their probative value in helping the jury evaluate the opinion substantially outweighs their prejudicial effect.

Suppose that a prosecution expert in a criminal case, in forming her opinion, relies upon a lab report that would be testimonial under *Melendez-Diaz* and *Bullcoming* if offered into evidence. Suppose further that the lab report itself is disclosed to the jury under the last sentence of Rule 703 for the purpose of helping the jury evaluate the expert's opinion. If the author of the lab report fails to appear as a witness, do either of these actions violate the Confrontation Clause? The U.S. Supreme Court recently granted certiorari to address the question. *See People v. Williams*, 939 N.E.2d 268 (Ill. 2010), *cert. granted*, 131 S. Ct. 3090 (2011). Are there hints in Justice Sotomayor's concurring opinion in *Bullcoming* as to how she might answer that question?

Chapter 8

Judicial Notice

In civil and criminal trials alike, the trier of fact is, generally speaking, required to decide the issues in the case based only on the information that is brought before it during the course of the trial. And the normal process of bringing information before the trier of fact involves the formal introduction of testimonial, documentary, or physical evidence in accordance with the rules of evidence discussed in the preceding chapters. Part and parcel of this formal process is the ability of parties to cross-examine one another's witnesses and to introduce their own evidence to refute facts allegedly established by the opposing party's evidence.

Yet this formal process can be cumbersome and time-consuming, and it would thus seem to be worth dispensing with it in the case of facts that one can say with a high degree of certainty are not reasonably subject to dispute. For example, it seems silly to follow formal procedures to prove what day of the week January 15, 2011 fell on if that were somehow important in a case.

It is for just such reasons that the doctrine of judicial notice developed at common law. Based in part on the maxim *manifesta non indigent probatione* ("that which is known need not be proved"), the doctrine provides a method by which facts can be established in a case without going through the formal process normally associated with proving facts.

In the federal system, the doctrine of judicial notice is codified in Rule 201. Because formal trial-type procedures such as cross-examination and the introduction of rebuttal evidence are thought to be the best way to resolve issues, Rule 201(b) expressly limits the doctrine to facts that are "not subject to reasonable dispute." Rule 201(c)(1) gives trial courts discretion to invoke the doctrine on their own, while Rule 201(c)(2) requires the trial court to take judicial notice of a fact when a party makes a request and supplies it with the information necessary to satisfy the requirements of Rule 201(b). And while judicial notice is typically taken during a trial, Rule 201(d) provides that it may be taken at any stage of a proceeding, which — according to the Advisory Committee Note — includes the appellate stage.

In civil cases, once the court decides to take judicial notice of a fact, Rule 201(f) provides that it is to instruct the jury to accept as conclusive the fact judicially noticed. Although as originally proposed by the Advisory Committee, the rule would have required the same instruction in criminal cases, as amended by Congress it requires that in criminal case the jury be instructed that it *may*, but is *not* required to, accept as conclusive the fact judicially noticed. Because of the ramifications of such instructions, Rule 201(e) ensures parties a right to an opportunity to be heard on the question whether judicial notice should be taken.

The doctrine in practice is less straightforward than it at first glance appears. Three questions in particular are worth close attention. First, Rule 201(a) provides that the rule only regulates judicial notice of an "adjudicative fact," and the question thus arises, what is an "adjudicative fact" and how does it differ from other facts? Second, how does the court go about determining whether something is "not subject to reasonable dispute" so as to permit the taking of judicial notice? Finally, the special treatment of criminal cases in Rule 201(f) raises special challenges, particularly when the doctrine is invoked for the first time on appeal.

Problem 8-1: The Alibi

Tom is on trial on charges of armed robbery of several banks, including First National Bank. The evidence at trial shows that the robbery of First National Bank took place at 4:25 p.m. on January 10, 2012. Tom offers into evidence Joe's testimony that he was at the Salut Saloon with Tom until 4:20 p.m. on January 10, 2012. Tom asks the trial court to take judicial notice of the fact that (a) the shortest driving distance between the Salut Saloon and First National Bank is 15 miles and (b) that Tom could not have been the person who robbed the bank.

How should the prosecution respond, and how will the court likely rule?

Problem 8-2: The Sweltering Heat

Richard is on trial on charges of murder. At trial, among other things, the prosecution calls as a witness Detective Jones, who stopped and questioned Richard near the vicinity of the murder shortly after it took place. Jones testified as to what Richard said to him, and also testified that he "looked nervous; his hands were shaking and he was sweating profusely." Richard's attorney asks the court to take judicial notice of (a) the fact that the official temperature at the time when and in the area where Richard was stopped was 101 degrees; and (b) that the high temperature was the cause of Richard's sweating.

How should the prosecution respond, and how will the court likely rule?

United States v. Marvin P. Jones
29 F.3d 1549 (11th Cir. 1994)

ALBRITTON, District Judge....

In 1980, [Marvin] Jones applied for and received a scholarship/loan from the NHSC scholarship program to assist him in attending medical school at the Medical College of Georgia. From 1980 through 1984, he received funds totaling $33,543.50, which covered tuition, fees, and other costs. After finishing medical school, Jones was granted a three-year deferment of his repayments so that he could pursue a residency in internal medicine.

In 1987, Jones entered into a "Private Practice Assignment Agreement" ("the Agreement") with the United States Department of Health and Human Services. Under the Agreement, he promised to serve as a physician for four years, from July 8, 1987 to July 7, 1991, at Westside in Savannah, Georgia in return for a write-off of his debt to the NHSC. The Agreement provided that in the event ... Jones failed to satisfy his service requirement, he would have to pay up to three times the amount owed, less credit for partial service performed.

The Agreement provides in relevant part:

> If this assignment is terminated by the Entity [Westside] or the NHSC prior to the expiration of the period specified in this agreement, the Individual will be reassigned to another entity for the remaining period of his or her scholarship service obligation unless the termination is due to the Individual's failure to fulfill the employment requirements of the Entity or the requirements of the Private Practice Assignment. Termination by the Individual or termination due to the Individual's failure to fulfill the employment requirements of the Entity or the requirements of the Private Practice Assignment will subject the Individual to the financial repayment provisions described in paragraph 4.

. . . .

In June 1990, Jones was terminated by Westside after serving three years of his obligation. Shortly after his termination, a NHSC official contacted Jones by telephone, and inquired whether he needed assistance in relocating to another site. At this time Jones was engaged in a suit against Westside and referred the official to his attorney.[2] In a letter dated December 20, 1990, Jones was notified that he was in default of his obligation to the NHSC.

On September 3, 1992, the Government filed suit in federal district court to recover the outstanding loans made to Jones. Subsequently, it filed a motion for summary judgment arguing that it was not obligated to reassign Jones to another hospital because he was dismissed due to poor attendance and interpersonal difficulties, which constituted a failure to fulfill Westside's "employment requirements." In support of its motion, the Government submitted a certified copy of an order dated June 5, 1991 issued by United States District Judge Anthony A. Alaimo in Jones' action against Westside.[3] On May 3, 1993, the district court granted the Government's motion. This appeal followed. . . .

A motion for summary judgment may be granted only if no genuine dispute remains as to any material fact and the moving party is entitled to judgment as a matter of law. Summary judgment may be based on any evidence which would be admissible at trial.

In the instant case, the district court determined that Westside terminated Jones because of a salary dispute. . . .

At oral arguments, the Government conceded that the Agreement did not preclude Jones from requesting an increase in salary. Thus, a "salary dispute" in and of itself did not constitute either a breach of the Agreement or violation of Westside's "employment requirements." Accordingly, in order for the district court to find that Jones' termination because of the salary dispute constituted either a breach of the Agreement or termination for violation of Westside's "employment requirements," it would have had to have reviewed evidence establishing the precise nature of the salary dispute, i.e., did Jones merely request a raise or did he refuse to work unless he received a raise. The only evidence before the district court which provided insight into the nature of the salary dispute was Judge Alaimo's order.

---

2. Jones filed suit against Westside under the Equal Pay Act of 1963, 29 U.S.C. §§ 206 and 215(a)(3), alleging sex discrimination and retaliatory discharge. A jury subsequently found for Westside on both claims.

3. Judge Alaimo's order addressed Jones' motion for judgment notwithstanding the verdict or, in the alternative, for a new trial. It concluded that Jones' attendance and interpersonal problems were the reasons for his termination.

The district court noted that it was not aware of any special interrogatories by Judge Alaimo to the jury requiring it to find the specific reason Jones was fired.

Jones contends that the findings of fact and references to witnesses' testimony contained in Judge Alaimo's order were inadmissible and therefore a genuine issue of fact exists as to whether the Government was obligated under the Agreement to reassign him to another health care facility. In response, the Government argues that the portions of the order in question are admissible under Fed.R.Evid. 201....

In order for a fact to be judicially noticed under Rule 201(b), indisputability is a prerequisite. Since the effect of taking judicial notice under Rule 201 is to preclude a party from introducing contrary evidence and in effect, directing a verdict against him as to the fact noticed, the fact must be one that only an unreasonable person would insist on disputing. If it were permissible for a court to take judicial notice of a fact merely because it has been found to be true in some other action, the doctrine of collateral estoppel would be superfluous. Moreover, to deprive a party of the right to go to the jury with his evidence where the fact was not indisputable would violate the constitutional guarantee of trial by jury.

In *Liberty Mut. Ins. Co. v. Rotches Pork Packers, Inc.*, 969 F.2d 1384, 1388–89 (2d Cir. 1992), the Second Circuit concluded that the district court erred in granting summary judgment based on a finding of fact within a bankruptcy court order. It recognized that a "court may take judicial notice of a document filed in another court 'not for the truth of the matters asserted in the other litigation, but rather to establish the fact of such litigation and related filings.'" Accordingly, a court may take notice of another court's order only for the limited purpose of recognizing the "judicial act" that the order represents or the subject matter of the litigation....

United States v. Bello
194 F.3d 18 (1st Cir. 1999)

LIPEZ, Circuit Judge.

Jesús Bello appeals his conviction and sentence for assaulting a fellow prisoner in the Metropolitan Detention Center in Guaynabo, Puerto Rico ("MDC-Guaynabo") in violation of 18 U.S.C. § 113(a)(6). Bello claims that the court erred in taking judicial notice of the jurisdictional element of the offense, namely, that MDC-Guaynabo was within the territorial jurisdiction of the United States....

I.

Factual background

At the time of the events in question, Bello was a prisoner confined at MDC-Guaynabo where he worked as a food service orderly, serving food to other prisoners. In this capacity, he was responsible for ensuring that food was distributed to all inmates. The victim of Bello's assault, Domingo Santana-Rosa, was also a prisoner in MDC-Guaynabo....

On July 25, 1996, at around 11:30 AM, Santana was playing dominoes with other inmates in the recreational yard.... Bello hit him in the back of the head with [a] push broom head....

Bello was indicted on one count of assault within the jurisdiction of the United States (as defined in 18 U.S.C. §7(3)), in violation of 18 U.S.C. §113(a)(6). Pursuant to Fed.R.Evid. 201 ("Rule 201"), the government filed a pretrial motion requesting that the court take judicial notice that MDC-Guaynabo is located within Fort Buchanan, a military base on lands "reserved or acquired for the use of the United States, and under the exclusive or concurrent jurisdiction thereof," and thus is within the "special maritime or territorial jurisdiction of the United States." The pretrial motion was accompanied by documenta-tion[1] tending to prove the requisite elements. The court deferred making a ruling on the motion until trial.

At trial, the government presented before the jury the testimony of Alma López, the legal advisor to the warden of MDC-Guaynabo, who stated that the land on which the prison was located was owned by the federal Bureau of Prisons and was formerly part of Fort Buchanan, but was transferred to the Bureau by the Department of Defense. After cross-examining López, defense counsel objected to the court taking judicial notice of the fact that MDC Guaynabo is under the exclusive jurisdiction of the United States. Because López was not in a position to authenticate the documentation submitted with the pre-trial motion, the documents were not admitted into evidence. However, the court ex-amined the documents outside the presence of the jury and concluded that it could take judicial notice (based on both the testimony in evidence and the documents) that the MDC-Guaynabo facility was within the jurisdiction of the United States. The court an-nounced to the jury that it was taking judicial notice of this jurisdictional fact, but informed them that they were "not required to accept as conclusive any fact that the Court has ju-dicially noticed." The jury was similarly instructed before it retired to deliberate.... The jury found Bello guilty of assault.

The court subsequently denied an oral motion by Bello to set aside the verdict on the ground that there was insufficient proof of the jurisdictional element of which the court took judicial notice.... Bello was subsequently sentenced to a term of imprisonment of 120 months, 60 months of which was to be served concurrently with the remainder of a previous federal criminal sentence. A supervised release term of 3 years and a special monetary assessment of $100 were also imposed. This appeal ensued.

II.

Judicial notice

Bello argues that the court improperly took judicial notice that the assault occurred "within the special maritime and territorial jurisdiction of the United States."[2] In so doing, the Court took judicial notice of an element of the offense for which Bello was convicted.[3] That fact lends particular significance to the judicial notice issue.

---

1. This documentation consisted of maps and letters from Army officials documenting the trans-fer to the Department of Justice/Bureau of Prisons, a letter from the Secretary of War confirming the transfer of the land from Puerto Rico to the federal government, and Puerto Rico legislative acts re-lating to the transfer.

2. The term "special maritime and territorial jurisdiction of the United States," as used in this title, includes:

   ....

   (3) Any lands reserved or acquired for the use of the United States, and under the exclusive or concurrent jurisdiction thereof, or any place purchased or otherwise acquired by the United States by consent of the legislature of the State in which the same shall be, for the erection of a fort, magazine, arsenal, dockyard, or other needful building.
18 U.S.C. §7(3).

3. Title 18 of the United States code provides that:

   (a) Whoever, *within the special maritime and territorial jurisdiction of the United States*, is guilty of an assault shall be punished as follows:

   ....

   (6) Assault resulting in serious bodily injury, by a fine under this title or imprisonment for not more than ten years, or both.
18 U.S.C. §113(a)(6) (emphasis provided).

Since the government petitioned, and the trial court ruled, pursuant to Rule 201, we address the conformity of the court's judicial notice determination with that rule....

By its terms, Rule 201 applies only to adjudicative facts, and the parties and the court assumed that the jurisdictional element at issue here involved an adjudicative rather than a legislative fact. They assumed correctly. Whether a fact is adjudicative or legislative depends not on the nature of the fact—e.g., who owns the land—but rather on the use made of it (*i.e.*, whether it is a fact germane to what happened in the case or a fact useful in formulating common law policy or interpreting a statute) and the same fact can play either role depending on context. *See* Fed.R.Evid. 201, Advisory Committee's note ("Adjudicative facts are simply the facts of the particular case. Legislative facts, on the other hand, are those which have relevance to legal reasoning and the lawmaking process...."). Where the prison sits is an element of the offense and unquestionably an adjudicative fact[4] ....

MDC-Guaynabo's location within the jurisdiction of the United States is the "kind of fact" judicially recognizable under Rule 201(b). To qualify for judicial notice, a fact [must be one that is not subject to reasonable dispute because it: (1) is generally known within the trial court's territorial jurisdiction; or (2) can be accurately and readily determined from sources whose accuracy cannot reasonably be questioned]. The Advisory Committee's note to Rule 201 explains:

> The usual method of establishing adjudicative facts is through the introduction of evidence, ordinarily consisting of testimony of the witnesses. If particular facts are outside the area of reasonable controversy, this process is dispensed with as unnecessary. A *high degree of indisputability* is an essential prerequisite.

Rule 201, Advisory Committee's note (emphasis provided).

The trial court based judicial notice on both prongs of Rule 201(b), finding that MDC-Guaynabo's presence within the jurisdiction of the United States is of such common knowledge and can be so accurately and readily determined that it cannot reasonably be disputed. By "generally known" Rule 201(b)(1) "must refer to facts which exist in the unaided memory of the populace; if the fact is one that a reasonable person would not know from memory but would know where to find, it falls within subdivision (2)," not (1). 21 Wright & Graham, *Federal Practice and Procedure* § 5105, at 407 (1977). Although the label "federal penitentiary" might suggest to the average person that MDC-Guaynabo is under the jurisdiction of the United States, it is unlikely that the "reasonable person" has any familiarity with MDC-Guaynabo at all, let alone its jurisdictional status. Hence, Rule 201(b)(1) cannot supply a basis for judicially noticing the jurisdictional fact in this case.

However, judicial notice was proper pursuant to Rule 201(b)(2), based on "sources whose accuracy cannot reasonably be questioned." Indeed, "[g]eography has long been peculiarly susceptible to judicial notice for the obvious reason that geographic locations are facts which are not generally controversial and thus it is within the general definition contained in Fed.R.Evid. 201(b)...." *United States v. Piggie*, 622 F.2d 486, 488 (10th Cir. 1980);

---

4. Some other Courts of Appeals have held that Rule 201 is not applicable to judicial notice that a place is within the "special maritime and territorial jurisdiction of the United States," finding this to be a "legislative fact" beyond the scope of Rule 201. *See United States v. Hernandez-Fundora*, 58 F.3d 802, 811 (2d Cir. 1995); *United States v. Bowers*, 660 F.2d 527, 531 (5th Cir. 1981); *see also* II Kenneth Culp Davis & Richard J. Pierce, *Administrative Law Treatise*, § 10.6, at 155 (3d. ed. 1994). *But see* Wright & Graham, *Federal Practice & Procedure* § 5103 n. 16 (1999 Supp.) ("One court has resolved the problem by a dubious holding that the fact that Fort Benning is under the jurisdiction of the United States is a legislative fact," citing *Bowers*).

see also United States v. Blunt, 558 F.2d 1245, 1247 (6th Cir. 1977). Moreover, "official government maps have long been held proper subjects of judicial notice." *Government of Canal Zone v. Burjan*, 596 F.2d 690, 694 (5th Cir. 1979). The government submitted to the court official government maps, letters from Army officials, and various legislative acts of Puerto Rico, all tending to show that MDC-Guaynabo was within the jurisdiction of the United States. Although the defense cross-examined López, the legal advisor to the warden of MDC-Guaynabo, suggesting some "dispute" over López's testimony,[5] it is clear from the record that the trial court based its decision to take judicial notice largely on the maps and other documents submitted by the government whose accuracy was not questioned by the defense. To be sure, the trial court's decision to judicially recognize a fact upon which testimony had already been presented and subjected to cross-examination before the jury was unusual. Nonetheless, the existence of independent and undisputed documentary evidence in the form of government maps, official letters, and public laws provided a sufficient basis for judicial notice under Rule 201(b)(2), irrespective of López's testimony.

Concluding that the trial court properly exercised its discretion in taking judicial notice of the jurisdictional fact, we must decide next whether the trial court correctly adhered to Rule 201's procedures for instructing the jury. Rule 201([f]) provides that: "In a civil [case], the court [must] instruct the jury to accept [the noticed fact] as conclusive []. In a criminal case, the court [must] instruct the jury that it may [or may not] accept [the noticed fact] as conclusive []." Fed.R.Evid. 201([f]). "Congress intended to ... create one kind of judicial notice for criminal cases and another for civil cases." 21 Wright & Graham, *Federal Practice and Procedure* § 5111, at 274 (1999 Supp.). "In a criminal case, Rule 201([f]) treats judicial notice like a presumption; it relieves one party of the need to produce evidence but does not prevent the other party from contesting" the noticed fact with evidence and argument to the jury. *Id.* at 534.[8]

The instruction offered by the court was as follows:

> Even though no evidence has been introduced about it in your presence, I believe that the fact that the Metropolitan Detention Center is within a land reserved for the use of the United States and under its exclusive jurisdiction ... is of such common knowledge and can be so accurately and readily determined from the Metropolitan Detention Center officials that it cannot reasonably be disputed. You may, therefore, reasonably treat this fact as proven even though no evidence has been presented on this point before you.

> As with any fact presented in the case, however, the final decision whether or not to accept it is for you to make and you are not required to agree with me.

This instruction was based on a nearly identical instruction from the Eighth Circuit, Model Crim. Jury Instr. 8th Cir. § 2.04 (1989); *see also* 1 *Weinstein's Federal Evidence* § 201.34[3] (1999) (quoting Federal Judicial Center Pattern Criminal Jury Instructions, no. 7 (commentary), which is itself based on one of the few opinions treating the appli-

---

5. López testified that MDC-Guaynabo houses federal prisoners, the Federal Bureau of Investigation investigates criminal offenses within the facility, and the prison is owned by the United States. The defense cross-examined López, eliciting her admissions that state prisoners were sometimes housed at the prison and that she had not actually conducted a title search to determine the ownership of the property.

8. There is, however, "one fundamental difference between presuming a fact and taking judicial notice of it. A presumption must be based on admissible evidence, but a judge can consult materials not otherwise admissible in order to take judicial notice." 21 Wright and Graham, *Federal Practice and Procedure* § 5102, at 465.

cation of Rule 201([f]), *United States v. Deckard*, 816 F.2d 426, 428 (8th Cir. 1987)). As in *Deckard*, "[h]ere the trial court meticulously followed the command of Rule 201([f]). After having instructed the jury generally on presumption of innocence and burden of proof," the court issued an instruction that complied entirely with the dictates of the rule....

United States v. Lewis
833 F.2d 1380 (9th Cir. 1987)

ALARCON, Circuit Judge:

The government appeals from the district court's order suppressing a confession on motion of defendant Jerri C. Lewis (Lewis) in this bank robbery prosecution. We reverse....

On October 10, 1986, Michael E. Degnan, a Special Agent of the Federal Bureau of Investigation (Degnan), identified Lewis as the person depicted in photographs taken during the robbery of a bank on October 9, 1986.... Lewis was arrested on October 20, 1986.

On October 21, 1986, Degnan and Special Agent Fujita went to the prison ward of the San Francisco General Hospital to interview Lewis. When the agents arrived, they learned for the first time from the hall nurse that Lewis had just returned from surgery for removal of an abscess on her left shoulder caused by the injection of narcotics. The nurse granted them permission to see Lewis. The agents decided to enter and tell her that they had come to interview her but would return the next day because she had just undergone surgery.

Lewis was asked if she remembered Degnan. She replied that she did. Agent Fujita then inquired whether Lewis knew him. She replied that he was "the individual who couldn't run." On October 15, 1986, Agent Fujita had attempted to catch up with Lewis.

Lewis appeared to be in pain. Special Agent Degnan remarked: "you look kind of rough." He asked her how she was feeling. She replied: "O.K."

Degnan told her that they had come to talk to her upon learning that she had finally been arrested. Degnan advised her that he had found out that she had just come out of surgery. Lewis was told that the agents would come back the next day to talk to her about the robberies. Degnan asked her whether she was going to "come clean." Lewis said that she would. Degnan asked her how many they would talk about. She responded, "three." Degnan asked her about the number of robberies to find out if she had committed more than those known by the authorities. If Lewis had stated that she had committed additional robberies, they would have searched their files prior to the interview the next day. The entire period of time spent with Lewis was approximately two minutes.

The agents returned the next day, October 22, 1986, to the hospital prison ward to question Lewis. The hall nurse informed them that Lewis was alert and not under any medication which would affect her ability to be interviewed. [The agents proceeded to interview Lewis.]

....

Lewis filed a motion to suppress the statements she made on October 21, 1986 and October 22, 1986. She argued in her memorandum of points and authorities filed in support of her motion that her October 21, 1986 statement was involuntary because she was a "heroin addict suffering from the effects of drug withdrawal [and] was questioned in her hospital bed hours after she had awakened from a general anesthetic administered during surgery." She also claimed that suppression of the October 22, 1986 statement was compelled because it was obtained through "exploitation of the involuntary admission made the previous day."

The court scheduled argument on the motion to suppress the statements for December 18, 1986. Prior to hearing argument on that date from counsel, the court stated that "the first statement was not knowing and voluntary." Before stating its conclusion that the confession was involuntary, the court said: "Now, anybody that has ever been under a general anesthetic following an operation knows that as you come out of a general anesthetic you are not accountable for what you say and do."

. . . .

The government counsel began his argument by stating that the evidence contained in Degnan's declaration showed that during the first statement on October 21, 1986, Lewis "was at the time aware of what was going on and was able to talk to the agents." The court interrupted the prosecutor's argument regarding the legal effect of the brief conversation on October 21, 1986, on the admissibility of the confession obtained the following day, to inquire whether it was his contention that the earlier statement was voluntary or involuntary. The prosecutor replied: "My contention is that the first statement was voluntary." The court then made the following comment:

> Well, you see, I can't go with you on that. One of the reasons why, and I am frank to say, I am influenced by personal experience. I mean, I represent to you that I have never been a heroin addict and I have never experienced what it is like to come out from under heroin, but I have come out from under an anesthetic. And people have told me that—and I seem to be perfectly all right—and people have told me that I said the most incredible things during the few first six hours or so after I came out of a general anesthetic. And I have had the same experience related by other people.

> You are not accountable for what you do or say for quite a number of hours after you come out of a general anesthetic. So I cannot find that a person who is both withdrawing from heroin and coming out from under a general anesthetic and is under arrest and confronted by FBI agents is in a position to make a voluntary and knowing statement at that time. . . .

We begin our discussion of the applicable law with the statement of an obvious principle. The trial judge in this matter was not a competent witness to Lewis' condition. "The judge presiding at the trial may not testify in that trial as a witness. No objection need be made in order to preserve the point." Fed.R.Evid. 605.*

Furthermore, Rule 602 of the Federal Rules of Evidence prohibits a witness from testifying "[unless] evidence is introduced sufficient to support a finding that the witness has personal knowledge of the matter." No evidence was presented that the trial judge has personal knowledge of Lewis' actual condition at the time she spoke to the agents on October 21, 1986. Thus, had the trial judge been sworn as a witness to testify to the effect of a general anesthetic on Lewis' ability to make a knowing and voluntary statement, his testimony would have been incompetent because of his role as presiding judge in this matter and his lack of percipiency.

Lewis contends for the first time on appeal that the trial judge properly relied on his personal experience based on the court's power to take judicial notice of adjudicative facts under Rule 201 of the Federal Rules of Evidence. This argument is unpersuasive.

---

* Editor's Note: Rule 605 was restyled in 2011 to read as follows:
The presiding judge may not testify as a witness at the trial. A party need not object to preserve the issue.

A trial judge is prohibited from relying on his personal experience to support the taking of judicial notice. "It is therefore plainly accepted that the judge is not to use from the bench, under the guise of judicial knowledge, that which he knows *only as an individual observer outside of court*." 9 J. Wigmore, Evidence in Trials at Common Law § 2569, at 723 (J. Chabourn rev. ed. 1981) (emphasis in original).

In relying on his "personal knowledge" the trial judge did not advise the parties he was taking judicial notice of Lewis' condition at the time she spoke to the agents on October 21, 1986. Furthermore, the trial judge did not rely on facts "generally known within the [trial court's] territorial jurisdiction [] or ... [] accurate[ly] and read[ily] determin[able from] sources whose accuracy cannot reasonably be questioned." Fed.R.Evid. 201(b). Instead, he looked solely to his own reaction to an anesthetic....

Notes and Questions

1. Examples of facts that are deemed to be "generally known" within the meaning of Rule 201(b)(1) include facts regarding local geography, local events—both current and historical—and other similar matters. Although some authorities state that "generally known" is synonymous with universally known within the territorial jurisdiction of the court, others indicate that it need only be known by most people or most "well-informed" people. *See generally* Wright & Miller, 21 Fed. Prac. & Proc. Evid. § 5105.

2. What sources are of the sort that their "accuracy cannot reasonably be questioned" within the meaning of Rule 201(b)(2)? Precedent has established that this includes such things as almanacs, dictionaries, encyclopedias, government records, and official maps, and the provision has been invoked to take judicial notice of facts regarding geography, the economy (such as historical interest rates and stock prices), and history.

3. Can a court take judicial notice of the distance between two points by relying on information contained on websites such as maps.google.com or mapquest.com? *See Bose Corp. v. Sunshine Electronics of New York, Inc.*, 2006 WL 1027684, at *8 n.12 (N.D. Tex. Apr. 12, 2006) (yes); *Green v. Burlington Northern and Santa Fe Ry. Co.*, 2006 WL 154329, at *1 n.3 (N.D. Tex. Jan. 19, 2006) (same). Do you agree that these are sources the accuracy of which cannot reasonably be questioned? *See generally The Great Disappearing Act*, 9 Green Bag 2d 3 (2005) (raising questions about whether material on the Internet satisfies the requirements of Rule 201).

4. As the *Lewis* case indicates, a judge is not supposed to take judicial notice based purely on his personal knowledge. Of course, is there not a fuzzy line among the personal knowledge of the judge, evaluative facts, and facts that are "generally known"?

> There is a real but elusive line between the judge's *personal knowledge* as a private man and these matters of which he takes judicial notice as a judge. The latter does not necessarily include the former; as a judge, indeed, he may have to ignore what he knows as a man and contrariwise....
>
> Where to draw the line between knowledge by notoriety and knowledge by personal observation may sometimes be difficult but the principle is plain.

9 Wigmore, Evidence § 2569, at 722–23. In this regard, consider the following explanation of the relationship between Rule 605 and Rule 201:

> Rule 605 prohibits the judge presiding at the trial from testifying in that trial as a witness. Rule 201 permits a judge to take judicial notice of certain types of facts. Logically, then, if a fact is of a kind that a judge may properly take judi-

cial notice of it, then he is not improperly "testifying" at trial by noting that fact. Any other conclusion would lead to Rule 605 effectively subsuming Rule 201. If, after all, a judge was improperly testifying at trial each time he took judicial notice of a fact, it would be effectively impermissible to take judicial notice of any fact. Accordingly, we must first consider whether the judge was taking permissible judicial notice of a fact, pursuant to Rule 201. If he could not have taken judicial notice of that fact within the bounds of Rule 201 — because, for example, it was not a "matter[ ] of common knowledge" — then we consider whether the judge violated Rule 605.

United States v. Bari, 599 F.3d 176, 179 n.4 (2d Cir. 2010).

Problem 8-3: Currency Exchange

Darnell is indicted and tried in federal court on charges of knowingly transporting stolen merchandise with a value of $5,000 or more in interstate commerce in violation of 18 U.S.C. § 2314. An element of that offense is that the merchandise stolen in fact has a value of $5,000 or more. Because the merchandise originated in Canada, evidence of its value in Canadian dollars was introduced, and that evidence showed that the coats were worth $13,690. No evidence was introduced at trial as to the U.S.-Canadian exchange rate. Darnell was convicted, and on appeal argued that his conviction should be set aside because of the failure to introduce sufficient evidence that the stolen merchandise had a value of $5,000 or more. The government argues that the appeals court can take judicial notice of the official exchange rate.

How should Darnell respond, and how will the court likely rule? How, if at all, would the result differ had the government made its request at trial?

United States v. Gould
536 F.2d 216 (8th Cir. 1976)

GIBSON, Chief Judge.

Defendants, Charles Gould and Joseph Carey, were convicted of conspiring to import (Count I) and actually importing (Count II) cocaine from Colombia, South America, into the United States in violation of the Controlled Substances Import and Export Act. 21 U.S.C. § 951 *et seq.* (1970). Both defendants received five-year sentences on each count to run concurrently, as well as a special parole term of three years....

Defendants do not challenge the sufficiency of the evidence but contend that the District Court erred in ... improperly taking judicial notice and instructing the jury that cocaine hydrochloride is a schedule II controlled substance....

[D]efendants contend that evidence should have been presented on the subject of what controlled substances fit within schedule II for the purpose of establishing a foundation that cocaine hydrochloride was actually within that schedule. Schedule II controlled substances, for the purpose of the Controlled Substances Import and Export Act, [include] the following:

(a) Unless specifically excepted or unless listed in another schedule, any of the following substances whether produced directly or indirectly by extraction from substances of vegetable origin, or independently by means of chemical synthesis, or by a combination of extraction and chemical synthesis:

* * *

(4) Coca leaves and any salt, compound, derivative, or preparation of coca leaves, and any salt, compound, derivative, or preparation thereof which is chemically equivalent or identical with any of these substances, except that the substances shall not include decocainized coca leaves or extraction of coca leaves, which extractions do not contain cocaine or ecgonine.

21 U.S.C. §812 (1970); *see* 21 C.F.R. §1308.12 (1975).

At trial, two expert witnesses for the Government testified as to the composition of the powdered substance removed from Ms. Kenworthy's platform shoes at the Miami airport. One expert testified that the substance was comprised of approximately 60 percent cocaine hydrochloride. The other witness stated that the white powder consisted of 53 percent cocaine. There was no direct evidence to indicate that cocaine hydrochloride is a derivative of coca leaves. In its instructions to the jury, the District Court stated:

> If you find the substance was cocaine hydrochloride, you are instructed that cocaine hydrochloride is a schedule II controlled substance under the laws of the United States.

Our inquiry on this first assignment of error is twofold. We must first determine whether it was error for the District Court to take judicial notice of the fact that cocaine hydrochloride is a schedule II controlled substance. Secondly, if we conclude that it was permissible to judicially notice this fact, we must then determine whether the District Court erred in instructing the jury that it must accept this fact as conclusive.

The first aspect of this inquiry merits little discussion. In *Hughes v. United States*, 253 F. 543, 545 (8th Cir. 1918), this court stated:

> It is also urged that there was no evidence that morphine, heroin, and cocaine are derivatives of opium and coca leaves. We think that is a matter of which notice may be taken. In a sense the question is one of the definition or meaning of words long in common use, about which there is no obscurity, controversy, or dispute, and of which the imperfectly informed can gain complete knowledge by resort to dictionaries within reach of everybody. * * * Common knowledge, or the common means of knowledge, of the settled, undisputed, things of life, need not always be laid aside on entering a courtroom.

It is apparent that courts may take judicial notice of any fact which is "capable of such instant and unquestionable demonstration, if desired, that no party would think of imposing a falsity on the tribunal in the face of an intelligent adversary." IX J. Wigmore, *Evidence* §2571, at 548 (1940). The fact that cocaine hydrochloride is derived from coca leaves is, if not common knowledge, at least a matter which is capable of certain, easily accessible and indisputably accurate verification. *See Webster's Third New International Dictionary* 434 (1961). Therefore, it was proper for the District Court to judicially notice this fact....

Our second inquiry involves the propriety of the District Court's instruction to the jurors that this judicially noticed fact must be accepted as conclusive by them. Defendants, relying upon Fed.R.Ev. 201([f]), urge that the jury should have been instructed that it could discretionarily accept or reject this fact....

It is clear that the reach of rule 201 extends only to adjudicative, not legislative, facts. Fed.R.Ev. 201(a). Consequently, the viability of defendants' argument is dependent upon our characterization of the fact judicially noticed by the District Court as adjudicative, thus invoking the provisions of rule 201([f]). In undertaking this analysis, we note at the outset that rule 201 is not all-encompassing. "Rule 201 * * * was deliberately drafted to cover only a small fraction of material usually subsumed under the concept of 'judicial notice.'" 1 J. Weinstein, *Evidence* ¶ 201[01] (1975).

The precise line of demarcation between adjudicative facts and legislative facts is not always easily identified. Adjudicative facts have been described as follows:

> When a court * * * finds facts concerning the immediate parties—who did what, where, when, how, and with what motive or intent—the court * * * is performing an adjudicative function, and the facts are conveniently called adjudicative facts. * * *
>
> Stated in other terms, the adjudicative facts are those to which the law is applied in the process of adjudication. They are the facts that normally go to the jury in a jury case. They relate to the parties, their activities, their properties, their businesses.

2 K. Davis, *Administrative Law Treatise* § 15.03, at 353 (1958).

Legislative facts, on the other hand, do not relate specifically to the activities or characteristics of the litigants. A court generally relies upon legislative facts when it purports to develop a particular law or policy and thus considers material wholly unrelated to the activities of the parties.

> Legislative facts are ordinarily general and do not concern the immediate parties. In the great mass of cases decided by courts * * *, the legislative element is either absent or unimportant or interstitial, because in most cases the applicable law and policy have been previously established. But whenever a tribunal engages in the creation of law or of policy, it may need to resort to legislative facts, whether or not those facts have been developed on the record.

2 K. Davis, *Administrative Law Treatise, supra* at § 15.03.

Legislative facts are established truths, facts or pronouncements that do not change from case to case but apply universally, while adjudicative facts are those developed in a particular case.

Applying these general definitions, we think it is clear that the District Court in the present case was judicially noticing a legislative fact rather than an adjudicative fact. Whether cocaine hydrochloride is or is not a derivative of the coca leaf is a question of scientific fact applicable to the administration of the Comprehensive Drug Abuse Prevention and Control Act of 1970. 21 U.S.C. § 801 *et seq.* (1970). The District Court reviewed the schedule II classifications contained in 21 U.S.C. § 812, construed the language in a manner which comports with common knowledge and understanding, and instructed the jury as to the proper law so interpreted. It is undisputed that the trial judge is required to fully and accurately instruct the jury as to the law to be applied in a case. When a court attempts to ascertain the governing law in a case for the purpose of instructing the jury, it must necessarily rely upon facts which are unrelated to the activities of the immediate parties. These extraneous, yet necessary, facts fit within the definition of legislative facts and are an indispensable tool used by judges when discerning the applicable law through interpretation.[6] The District Court, therefore, was judicially noticing such a legislative

---

6. The Notes of the Advisory Committee to rule 201 offer support for the proposition that courts utilize legislative facts when they interpret a statute[:]

> While judges use judicial notice of "propositions of generalized knowledge" in a variety of situations: *determining the validity and meaning of statutes,* formulating common law rules, deciding whether evidence should be admitted, assessing the sufficiency and effect of evidence, *all are essentially nonadjudicative in nature* (emphasis added).

fact when it recognized that cocaine hydrochloride is derived from coca leaves and is a schedule II controlled substance within the meaning of § 812.

Through similar reasoning, this judicially noticed fact simply cannot be appropriately categorized as an adjudicative fact. It does not relate to "who did what, where, when, how, and with what motive or intent," nor is it a fact which would traditionally go to the jury. See 2 K. Davis, *Administrative Law Treatise*, supra at § 15.03. The fact that cocaine hydrochloride is a derivative of coca leaves is a universal fact that is unrelated to the activities of the parties to this litigation. There was no preemption of the jury function to determine what substance was actually seized from Ms. Kenworthy at the Miami airport. The jury was instructed that, if it found that the confiscated substance was cocaine hydrochloride, the applicable law classified the substance as a schedule II controlled substance.

It is clear to us that the District Court took judicial notice of a legislative, rather than an adjudicative, fact in the present case and rule 201([f]) is inapplicable. The District Court was not obligated to inform the jury that it could disregard the judicially noticed fact. In fact, to do so would be preposterous, thus permitting juries to make conflicting findings on what constitutes controlled substances under federal law.[7]

United States v. William Allen Jones
580 F.2d 219 (6th Cir. 1978)

ENGEL, Circuit Judge.

Appellee William Allen Jones, Jr. was convicted by a district court jury of illegally intercepting telephone conversations of his estranged wife and of using the contents of the intercepted communications, in violation of 18 U.S.C. §§ 2511(1)(a) and (d) (1976). The proofs at trial showed only that the telephone which Jones had tapped was furnished by South Central Bell Telephone Company. Other than this fact, the government offered no evidence to show that South Central Bell was at the time a "person engaged as a common carrier in providing or operating ... facilities for the transmission of interstate or foreign communications." 18 U.S.C. § 2510(1).

Following the jury verdict of guilty on three of the five counts of the indictment, Jones' counsel moved the court for a new trial on the ground that the government had altogether failed to prove that the wire communication which the defendant tapped came within the definition of Section 2510. Upon a careful review of the evidence, United States District Judge Frank Wilson agreed and entered a judgment of acquittal. The government has appealed.

It is not seriously disputed that an essential element of the crimes charged, and one which the government was obligated to prove beyond a reasonable doubt, was that the conversation which was tapped was a "wire communication" as defined in the Act. Instead, the issue is whether the abbreviated proof offered by the government was minimally sufficient for the *prima facie* case which the government was obligated to place before the jury. In other words, was the proof that the tapped telephone was installed and furnished by

---

7. Common sense dictates that the construction urged upon us by defendants is not well-taken. The fact that cocaine hydrochloride is derived from coca leaves is scientifically and pharmacologically unimpeachable. It would be incongruous to instruct the jurors on this irrefutable fact and then inform them that they may disregard it at their whim. It would be similarly illogical if we were to conclude that trial judges could rely upon generally accepted, undisputed facts in interpreting the applicable statutory law, yet obligate them to instruct the jury that it could disregard the factual underpinnings of the interpretation in its discretion.

"South Central Bell Telephone Company," without more, sufficient to enable the jury to find as a matter of fact that South Central Bell was a common carrier which provided facilities for the transmission of interstate or foreign communications? The government contends that, construing that evidence in the light most favorable to it, these facts could be permissibly inferred by the jury without any other proof....

[T]he government urges that such a fact is the proper subject of judicial notice which may be taken at any stage of the proceeding, including appeal, under Federal Rule of Evidence 201([d])....

The government did not at any time during the jury trial specifically request the district court to take judicial notice of the status of South Central Bell. Nevertheless, it relies upon the provisions of Rule 201([d]) which state that [the court may take judicial notice at any stage of the proceeding]. It is true that the Advisory Committee Note to 201([d]) indicates that judicial notice is appropriate "in the trial court *or on appeal.*" It is also true that the language of 201([d]) does not distinguish between judicial notice in civil or criminal cases. There is, however, a critical difference in the manner in which the judicially noticed fact is to be submitted to the jury in civil and criminal proceedings.... under subsection ([f]) judicial notice of a fact in a civil case is conclusive while in a criminal trial the jury is not bound to accept the judicially noticed fact and may disregard it if it so chooses.

It is apparent from the legislative history that the congressional choice of language in Rule 201 was deliberate. In adopting the present language, Congress rejected a draft of subsection ([f]) proposed by the Supreme Court, which read:

> The judge shall instruct the jury to accept as established any facts judicially noticed.

The House Report explained its reason for the change:

> Rule 201([f]) as received from the Supreme Court provided that when judicial notice of a fact is taken, the court shall instruct the jury to accept that fact as established. Being of the view that mandatory instruction to a jury in a criminal case to accept as conclusive any fact judicially noticed is inappropriate because contrary to the spirit of the Sixth Amendment right to a jury trial, the Committee adopted the 1969 Advisory Committee draft of this subsection, allowing a mandatory instruction in civil actions and proceedings and a discretionary instruction in criminal cases.

H.Rep. No. 93-650, 93d Cong., 1st Sess. 6–7 (1973), U.S.Code Cong. & Admin.News 7075, 7080 (1974). Congress intended to preserve the jury's traditional prerogative to ignore even uncontroverted facts in reaching a verdict. The legislature was concerned that the Supreme Court's rule violated the spirit, if not the letter, of the constitutional right to a jury trial by effectively permitting a partial directed verdict as to facts in a criminal case.

As enacted by Congress, Rule 201([f]) plainly contemplates that the jury in a criminal case shall pass upon facts which are judicially noticed. This it could not do if this notice were taken for the first time after it had been discharged and the case was on appeal. We, therefore, hold that Rule 201([d]), authorizing judicial notice at the appellate level, must yield in the face of the express congressional intent manifested in 201([f]) for criminal jury trials. To the extent that the earlier practice may have been otherwise, we conceive that it has been altered by the enactment of Rule 201.

Accordingly, the judgment of the district court is affirmed.

United States v. Amado-Núñez
357 F.3d 119 (1st Cir. 2004)

BOUDIN, Chief Judge.

This is an appeal by José Amado-Núñez following his conviction for transporting counterfeit tax stamps in interstate or foreign commerce. 18 U.S.C. § 2314 (2000). The appeal presents two issues, one evidentiary and the other of statutory construction. The background is as follows.

On November 25, 1999, Amado went through the primary customs screening point at the Luis Muñoz Marin International Airport in San Juan, Puerto Rico. The later indictment described Amado as arriving on a flight from the Dominican Republic, but the prosecutor neglected to prove the origin point at trial. The inspector at the primary customs point randomly chose Amado for a more thorough examination and he was directed to a second inspector.

In the bottom of Amado's bag, the second inspector found packages of stamps that purported to be issued by the Puerto Rico Department of the Treasury. The inspector summoned a criminal investigator assigned to the customs service who, on examining what she believed to be tax stamps for coin-operated machines, noticed that many had duplicate serial numbers — which she did not think would occur if the stamps were genuine.

Questioned by the agent, Amado said that he owned coin machines for his business in Puerto Rico but gave inconsistent answers as to how many machines he owned. He did not answer directly when asked about the origin of the stamps. Nor, when requested, did he provide any proof of purchase or other documents regarding the origin of the stamps. The agent took custody of 887 stamps, which were later determined to be counterfeit.

A federal grand jury indicted Amado for violating 18 U.S.C. § 2314 (2000). The third paragraph of this statute pertinently provides:

> Whoever, with unlawful or fraudulent intent, transports in interstate or foreign commerce any falsely made, forged, altered, or counterfeited securities or tax stamps, knowing the same to have been falsely made, forged, altered, or counterfeited … [s]hall be fined under this title or imprisoned not more than ten years, or both. …

Amado was tried for this offense in a bench trial, consented to by both sides.… At the close of the case, the district judge determined that Amado was guilty of the offense charged.… Thereafter Amado was sentenced to two years imprisonment. Amado now appeals, raising two arguments: that the evidence does not establish the interstate or foreign commerce element of the offense, and that the statute does not apply to the stamps in question.

The evidentiary issue is easily framed. The prosecutor failed to offer direct evidence that Amado had arrived at the airport from the Dominican Republic or, indeed, from any foreign point. So … the question is whether, from other fragments of evidence, a trier of facts could rationally conclude beyond a reasonable doubt that Amado had arrived from outside Puerto Rico.

The issue can be narrowed further. In describing the initial inspection of Amado's luggage, the inspector who found the stamps explained that her duties consisted of interviewing passengers and searching their luggage. She also made clear that she was talking about *arriving* passengers, saying: "We have to ask them where they come from, how long they stayed in whatever place they went, if they acquired any items in the place where they were visiting."

She also made it clear that Amado had gone through this process. After describing the primary and secondary inspection points, she said that Amado had presented himself at her secondary point and, when asked what she did when coming in contact with him, she described in generic terms the process of requesting the customs declaration card, asking the regular questions (such as "where are you coming from"), and searching the luggage. She then described the search of Amado's luggage and discovery of the stamps.

Based on this evidence, we think a trier could rationally conclude beyond a reasonable doubt that Amado had gone through this process as an arriving passenger from whom a customs declaration form is requested, who is asked about his origin point, and whose luggage is often or ordinarily searched upon arrival. The only remaining link in the chain is the proposition that passengers arriving from a foreign origin go through the customs process while domestic passengers do not; without this link Amado could have been arriving from a flight originating elsewhere in Puerto Rico, defeating the interstate or foreign commerce requirement.

That routine customs checks are done for foreign but not domestic flights is known to anyone who has done even a modicum of air travel; it is also known to many others who have merely met arriving friends and relatives or who have watched films or television programs or read books or newspapers that touch on air travel....

A federal court can take judicial notice of "adjudicative facts"—facts about the parties or events involved in the case—if one of two tests is met and if the parties are given notice, Fed.R.Evid. 201. But that rule is irrelevant here because the practice of customs searches for foreign but not domestic arrivals is not an adjudicative fact, and Rule 201(b)'s limits do not apply to the vast array of "background" facts commonly considered by judges and juries in deciding cases. *See* Fed.R.Evid. 201(a) & advisory comm. note to 201(a).

These "background" or "evaluative" facts cover the whole range of human experience from the rough meaning of common terms ("city") to science (a full moon illuminates a scene) to human psychology (a witness who is related to one of the parties might be biased). *Id.* For example:

> When a witness says "car," everyone, judge and jury included, furnishes, from non-evidence sources within himself, the supplementing information that the "car" is an automobile, not a railroad car, that it is self-propelled, probably by an internal combustion engine, that it may be assumed to have four wheels with pneumatic rubber tires, and so on. The judicial process cannot construct every case from scratch, like Descartes creating a world based on the postulate *Cogito, ergo sum*. These items could not possibly be introduced into evidence, and no one suggests that they be.

Fed.R.Evid. advisory comm. note to 201(a).

Fact-finders rely upon such background references or propositions all the time in deciding whether something did or did not happen; and this is permissible, without resort to the machinery for noticing adjudicative facts. The background facts may be quite important, but by contrast to adjudicative facts, the parties do not have an advantage over the jury in access to evidence about them. This does not, of course, preclude the possibility of parties' seeking to offer evidence about them when they are important.

The level of reliability required is not often discussed in the cases; only rarely can an appeals court be sure (as we are here) that a specific background proposition was employed or, in the alternative, was logically necessary to the result. But refinement of the standard is unnecessary in this case, because we are certain enough that the proposition in this case—formal customs inspections are only for passengers arriving from foreign countries — is both familiar and true. So, there is no reason to worry here about whether and when a more vulnerable alleged background fact might be subject to attack.

Thus, the ultimate fact (that Amado arrived from a foreign country) did not need to be "judicially noticed" under Rule 201; rather, it could (quite easily) be inferred by the fact-finder from the background fact of general customs-service practice coupled with trial evidence that, on this occasion, Amado was interviewed at the secondary arrival customs inspection point and then was questioned and searched in the fashion described by the inspector and agent (both adjudicative facts but amply proved by evidence).

The same process of reasoning disposes of a variant theory offered by Amado to raise a reasonable doubt as to the commerce element, namely, that he might have been searched, regardless of whether he had traveled at all, by a customs-service represen-tative patrolling the airport. There are other problems with this competing explana-tion but the evidence already described disposes of it without more: the testimony of the agent at the secondary arrival point makes clear that Amado was searched as an arriving passenger at a formal checkpoint and not through some random stop in the concourse.

Amado's second claim of error is of a different character. He argues that the items seized from his suitcase were not tax stamps within the meaning of 18 U.S.C. § 2314 (2000)....

The language dealing with tax stamps was added separately to the federal statute in 1961.... The amendment was accompanied by a companion section defining "tax stamp" as including "any tax stamp ... or any other form of evidence of an obligation running to a State, or evidence of the discharge thereof."

Even without the statutory definition, we would readily construe "tax stamp" as a stamp evidencing the discharge of a tax obligation. A conventional dictionary definition of rev-enue stamp describes it as "[a] stamp used as evidence that a tax has been paid." *Black's Law Dictionary* 1320 (7th ed. 1999). This is just what the testimony showed Amado's stamps to be, or more precisely to resemble, since they were counterfeit versions....

Notes and Questions

1. Are *Bello* and *Gould* consistent with one another with respect to distinguishing be-tween adjudicative facts and legislative facts? Couldn't the logic of *Bello* be applied to the facts of *Gould* to conclude that the latter case involved an adjudicative fact? And could-n't the logic of *Gould* be applied to the facts of *Bello* to conclude that the latter case in-volved a legislative fact? In *United States v. Hernandez-Fundora*, 58 F.3d 802 (2d Cir. 1995), the court did the latter:

> [T]he court removed from the jury's consideration the issue whether Raybrook was within the special maritime and territorial jurisdiction of the United States, but reserved for the jury the question whether the assault occurred at Raybrook....

> The question presented in this case is whether, in a criminal case, the disposi-tion of a geographical/jurisdictional issue is premised upon the determination of "adjudicative facts" within the meaning of Rule 201(a), thus bringing into play the procedural requirements of Rule 201([f])....

> The Eighth Circuit applied this distinction in *United States v. Gould*, 536 F.2d 216 (8th Cir. 1976)....

Professor Davis has also addressed this issue very recently, stating:

> Whether 123 C Street is inside or outside the city is a question about 123 C Street, not about a party. The question whether X lives in the city is a question of adjudicative fact, but, even though X lives at 123 C Street, the fact that that address is within the city is not an adjudicative fact.

II Kenneth Culp Davis & Richard J. Pierce, Jr., *Administrative Law Treatise* § 10.6, at 155 (3d ed. 1994).

Hernandez-Fundora, 58 F.3d at 810–12.

Indeed, under the logic of *Bello*, wouldn't the *second* question raised in *Amado-Núñez*, to wit, whether something fell within the definition of the phrase "tax stamp," be an adjudicative fact? Yet after addressing the question whether the fact that only passengers arriving from a foreign country go through customs is an adjudicative fact, the *Amado-Núñez* court refers to the second question as being "of a different character." Note that *Bello* and *Amado-Núñez* were both decided by the First Circuit.

2. Why are legislative facts not regulated by Rule 201 or any comparable rule? Consider the following defense by the Advisory Committee:

> Legislative facts are quite different. As Professor Davis says:
>
> "My opinion is that judge-made law would stop growing if judges, in thinking about questions of law and policy, were forbidden to take into account the facts they believe, as distinguished from facts which are 'clearly ... within the domain of the indisputable.' Facts most needed in thinking about difficult problems of law and policy have a way of being outside the domain of the clearly indisputable."
>
> An illustration is *Hawkins v. United States*, 358 U.S. 74 (1958), in which the Court refused to discard the common law rule that one spouse could not testify against the other, saying, "Adverse testimony given in criminal proceedings would, we think, be likely to destroy almost any marriage." This conclusion has a large intermixture of fact, but the factual aspect is scarcely "indisputable." If the destructive effect of the giving of adverse testimony by a spouse is not indisputable, should the Court have refrained from considering it in the absence of supporting evidence?
>
> "If the Model Code or the Uniform Rules had been applicable, the Court would have been barred from thinking about the essential factual ingredient of the problems before it, and such a result would be obviously intolerable. What the law needs at its growing points is more, not less, judicial thinking about the factual ingredients of problems of what the law ought to be, and the needed facts are seldom 'clearly' indisputable."

Advisory Committee Note to Rule 201(a).

3. Do you agree with the court in *Amado-Núñez* that the fact that people only go through customs screening when they have arrived from a foreign country is a basic evaluative fact akin to the meaning of the word "car"? Can a satisfactory line be drawn between evaluative and adjudicative facts? Wigmore stressed that the scope of the former is narrow, albeit hard to define with precision, but did not think that it was worth worrying too much about:

> [T]he scope of this doctrine is narrow; it is strictly limited to a few matters of elemental experience in human nature, commercial affairs, and everyday life.... The range of such general knowledge is not precisely definable. But in these days when too much emphasis is placed in the selection of jurors on the blankness of

their mental tablets, there can be no harm in the liberal application of the present principle.

9 Wigmore, Evidence § 2570, at 728–31 (Chadbourn rev. 1981)

4. Should the holding in *William Allen Jones*, barring the taking of judicial notice in a criminal case for the first time on appeal, apply if the defendant was convicted after a bench trial? *See Government of Canal Zone v. Burjan*, 596 F.2d 690, 694 (5th Cir. 1979) ("considerations that led the Sixth Circuit to its conclusion in *Jones* are not applicable when, as here, the right to jury trial has been waived").

5. The Advisory Committee Note to Rule 201(f) indicates that once the court has decided to take judicial notice of an adjudicative fact, a party cannot introduce evidence before the trier of fact designed to cast doubt on the fact noticed:

> Within its relatively narrow area of adjudicative facts, the rule contemplates there is to be no evidence before the jury in disproof. The judge instructs the jury to take judicially noticed facts as established. This position is justified by the undesirable effects of the opposite rule in limiting the rebutting party, though not his opponent, to admissible evidence, in defeating the reasons for judicial notice, and in affecting the substantive law to an extent and in ways largely unforeseeable. Ample protection and flexibility are afforded by the broad provision for opportunity to be heard on request, set forth in subdivision (e).

Advisory Committee Note to Rule 201(f).

Does that mean that even in a criminal case, where the jury is not required to accept as conclusive any fact judicially noticed, a defendant is not free to introduce evidence before the jury to cast doubt on the fact judicially noticed? In considering this question, keep in mind that under the version of Rule 201(f) originally proposed by the Advisory Committee, judicially noticed facts were conclusive even in criminal cases, and that this comment is a note to the *original* proposal. *See United States v. Horn*, 185 F. Supp. 2d 530, 549 n.34 (D.Md. 2002) ("Implicitly, the rule would permit a defendant in a criminal case to offer evidence to rebut any adjudicative fact noticed by the Court.").

6. Although the rationale for Congress' amendment to Rule 201(f), to wit, the letter or spirit of a criminal defendant's Sixth Amendment right to a jury trial, would only require that the jury be given a permissive instruction when it is the government who requests that judicial notice be taken, Rule 201(f) is worded broadly to apply in all criminal cases. *Compare* Fed. R. Evid. 803(8)(A)(ii). Could this partly reflect the fact that Rule 201(c)(1) permits the court to take judicial notice *sua sponte* even if not requested by either party, and that in any event it isn't always clear whether a "fact" favors one side or the other? *Compare* Oregon R. Evid. 201(g)(2) ("In a criminal case, the court shall instruct the jury that it may, but is not required to, accept as conclusive any fact judicially noticed *in favor of the prosecution*.") (emphasis added).

7. Consider the following criticism of Rule 201(f) as amended by Congress:

> With deference the (Rule as it emerged from Congress) is irrational. Actual application of the Congressional version makes fools of the judge, the law and the jury.... Under the Congressional rule, in the morning when the judge tries a civil case the world is round. That afternoon when he tries a criminal case the world is flat.

United States v. Piggie, 622 F.2d 486, 489–90 (10th Cir. 1980) (quoting 10 Moore's Federal Practice § 201.70).

Chapter 9

Burdens of Proof and Presumptions

A. Burdens of Proof in Civil Cases

As you no doubt have learned by this point in law school, any given claim typically consists of a number of elements. Consider, for example, a tort claim for battery, which consists of two elements. The first is that the defendant acted with the intent of causing a harmful contact with the plaintiff or a third person, and the second is that a harmful contact with the plaintiff directly or indirectly resulted. *See* Restatement (2d) Torts § 13 (1965).

In addition, there are usually defenses to most claims. The successful establishment of a defense will defeat a claim, even if the elements of the claim have been proved. In the case of a tort claim for battery, self-defense on the defendant's part is just such a defense.

Whether liability for battery will result can be expressed in mathematical form:

If E_1 and E_2 are proved, and unless D_1 is proved, then the defendant is liable for battery.

In this formula, E_1 represents the defendant causing harmful contact, E_2 represents the defendant intending to cause harmful contact, and D_1 represents the defendant acting in self-defense. The formula can be stated more generally:

If E_1 and E_2 and ... E_n are proved, and unless D_1 or D_2 or ... D_n is proved, then the defendant is liable.

In this formula, the "E" variables refer to the elements of the claim, while the "D" variables refer to the affirmative defenses to liability. As demonstrated by the formula, liability will be found only if *all* elements are proved *and* if *none* of the defenses are proved. If even one element is not proved, liability will not be found, and even if all elements are proved, liability will not be found if even a single affirmative defense is proved. Note that it is possible that any given defense, like a claim, may consist of multiple elements. If so, each element of that defense must be proved in order to defeat liability.

Note that at the outset, a decision has to be made whether to denominate any given factor as an element of the claim or instead as an affirmative defense. That is not a question of evidence law, but rather a question of the underlying substantive law, and can only be determined by reference to the legislative enactment creating the claim (and the judicial decisions interpreting it), or in the case of common law claims, by examining precedent. In making that determination, policymakers are guided by a number of considerations, including considerations of which party is likely to be in a better position to prove or disprove a given point and a policy determination as to who should lose in the face of uncertain evidence on a given point.

At trial, two types of burdens arise with respect to the elements of a claim and any defenses thereto, the burden of persuasion and the burden of production. To say that a party bears the burden of persuasion on a claim or defense is to say that she can succeed on that claim or defense only if the trier of fact is persuaded of the elements of that claim or defense by the requisite degree of certainty (in civil cases, usually a preponderance of the evidence, or more likely than not, but in some instances by a greater showing of clear and convincing proof). The party who bears the burden of persuasion is sometimes referred to as the party who bears the risk of nonpersuasion: that is because the party who bears this burden need not be the *source* of all the evidence used to satisfy that burden—the trier of fact can use evidence introduced by the opposing party—and this latter formulation more clearly encompasses that possibility.

The burden of production is different. To say that a party bears the burden of production with respect to an element of a claim or a defense at a given point in time is to say that he must come forward with ("produce") sufficient evidence on that element such that the trier of fact reasonably could find in his favor on that element, with the consequence of a verdict being directed against him on that element if he fails to do so.

In the ordinary case, the party who bears the burden of persuasion with respect to a claim or defense also bears the initial burden of production. Consider as an example a civil action brought for battery. Such a case can be illustrated as follows:

A	B	C
Judge (directs verdict for defendant)	Jury	Judge (directs verdict for plaintiff)
E_1 (harm) ——➤ E_2 (intent) ——➤		◄— D_1 (self-defense)

The extremes of the diagram, columns A and C, represent the zones where the trial court will take an issue away from the jury and direct a verdict on that issue in favor of a particular party, with column A representing a directed verdict in the defendant's favor and column C representing a directed verdict in the plaintiff's favor. At the start of a case, the elements of the claim, for which the plaintiff bears the burden of persuasion, are in column A. If the plaintiff does nothing—in other words, if in the battery action the plaintiff comes forward with no evidence of harm caused by the defendant and no evidence of an intent to do the same—the trial court will direct a verdict in the defendant's favor, and the case will come to an end (indeed, the case will come to an end if he fails to come forward with evidence on even one of the two elements). Thus, in addition to bearing the ultimate burden of persuasion, the plaintiff also bears the initial burden of production with respect to those elements: he must produce sufficient evidence to move those elements at least into column B. Similarly, the defendant, if he wishes to pursue his affirmative defense of self-defense, likewise bears the burden of producing evidence to support that defense sufficient to move that defense at least into column B.

The standard for moving an element or defense from either extreme column into column B is the same: sufficient evidence that the trier of fact reasonably *could* find in favor of the party seeking to move that element or defense into column B by the requisite degree of certainty (again, usually a preponderance of the evidence in civil cases). Thus, the plaintiff must produce sufficient evidence that the trier of fact reasonably could find that the defendant harmed the plaintiff and that the defendant intended to do so. The defendant, if he chooses to invoke the claim of self-defense, must produce sufficient evidence that the trier of fact reasonably could find that he acted in self-defense.

It is conceivable, albeit rare, that a party could produce such overwhelming evidence on a particular element that the element moves not just to the center column, but clear across to the other extreme. Thus, the plaintiff might produce such overwhelming evidence of harm caused by the defendant such that no reasonable jury could fail to find the element of harm established in the absence of counterproof. At this point, the burden of *production* (but *not* the burden of persuasion) would shift to the defendant: if he fails to produce sufficient evidence such that a reasonable jury could find in his favor on that element, he will suffer a directed verdict on that element. But if he does produce sufficient evidence on that point, the element moves to column B, and the question is one for the jury.

After both parties have concluded presenting all of their evidence, any element or defense that remains in column B is a jury question, since everything in column B involves an element or defense for which the evidence is such that a reasonable jury could go either way. Whether a party ultimately meets her burden of persuasion depends on whether the trier of fact is persuaded of the elements of that party's claims or defenses by the requisite degree of certainty.

B. Presumptions in Civil Cases

The allocation of the burdens of persuasion and production are initially determined by reference to what the underlying substantive law, be it statutory or common law, denominates as an element of the claim and what it denominates as an affirmative defense. However, the matter is complicated by a device known as a "presumption."

A "presumption" is a rule of law, created by statute or common law, that requires the trier of fact to draw a particular conclusion (the "presumed fact") if some other fact, or set of facts, (the "basic fact") is proved, in the absence of counterproof. For example, upon proof that a letter has been properly addressed and placed in the mail ("basic fact"), a presumption arises that the letter was received by the addressee ("presumed fact"). Or upon proof that a person has been absent for a certain period of time (typically seven years) without tidings ("basic fact"), a presumption arises that the person is dead ("presumed fact"). Or upon proof that goods are delivered by a bailor to a bailee in good condition, but damaged upon return ("basic fact"), a presumption arises that the bailee was negligent ("presumed fact"). Or upon proof of a death that is consistent with both suicide and accident ("basic fact"), a presumption arises that the death was an accident ("presumed fact").

Several different types of considerations underlie the creation of presumptions. Often, presumptions reflect statistical probabilities, thus minimizing the risk of error on a point for which direct proof may be difficult to obtain. For example, in most instances, a letter that his been properly addressed and dropped in the mail does reach the addressee.

Other times, presumptions are designed to force the party with superior access to evidence on a point to come forward with evidence on that point. For example, in a bailment scenario, the bailee has superior knowledge of what happened to the item while it was in his possession.

Other presumptions reflect a policy judgment as to which party should lose in the face of uncertain evidence. For example, the presumption that death is accidental and not a result of suicide typically arises in suits by survivors on life insurance policies, and is designed to stack the deck in favor of the survivors and against the insurance companies in such cases (most policies exclude coverage when death is the result of suicide).

At one extreme, the party seeking to enlist the aid of a presumption might produce such compelling evidence of the basic fact that no reasonable jury could fail to find that the basic facts have been established. In that situation, if the party against whom the presumption is invoked fails to produce evidence to counter the presumed fact, the presumption compels the trier of fact to find that the presumed fact has likewise been established, and to the extent that the presumed fact is also an element, a verdict will be directed as to that element. Thus, if such compelling evidence is introduced that a letter was addressed and placed in the mail, the trier of fact must find that the letter was received by the addressee, unless the party against whom the presumption is invoked introduces evidence to counter the presumed fact, in other words, evidence that the letter was not received by the addressee.

Consider with regard to this first extreme scenario the battery example. Suppose that there is a presumption that, upon proof that the harm was caused by an illegal weapon, a presumption arises that the defendant intended to cause harm. Suppose further that such overwhelming evidence is introduced that the defendant injured the plaintiff using an illegal weapon that no reasonable jury could find otherwise. Under those circumstances, the presumption has the effect of moving element E_2 from column A to column C, and in the absence of counterproof on the element of intent, a verdict on that element would be directed against the defendant. At the very least, then, the presumption acts to shift the burden of production from one party to the other.

At the other extreme, after a party has invoked a presumption by introducing evidence of the basic facts, the party against whom the presumption is invoked can produce such compelling evidence that the presumed fact is not so that the presumption's effect is completely eliminated. For example, even if overwhelming evidence is introduced that a person has been absent for seven years without tidings, so as to require the jury to find that the person is deceased in the absence of counterproof, if the party against whom the presumption has been invoked introduces such compelling evidence that the presumed fact just is not so — such as by calling the allegedly deceased person as a witness (!) — the presumption's effect is completely undone. To the extent that the presumed fact, death, is also an element of the claim, a directed verdict on that element (and indeed the entire claim) will result.

The typical case, of course, is somewhere in between, both with respect to proof of the basic facts and with respect to the counterproof of the presumed fact. In the ordinary case, proof of the basic facts will be such that a reasonable jury *could* find that the basic facts have been established, but need not necessarily so find. If so, the jury is instructed that it must find the presumed fact if it is persuaded (usually by a preponderance of the evidence) that the basic facts have been proved. In this instance, a failure of the defendant to counter with evidence negating either the basic facts or the presumed fact is not necessarily fatal, as the jury is still free to disbelieve the basic facts, and thus the presumed fact as well.

Finally, without regard to the strength of the evidence of the basic facts, an important question arises as to the effect of the presumption once the party against whom it is invoked responds with counterproof of the presumed fact, not so overwhelming that no reasonable trier of fact could find that the presumed fact has been proved, but enough that he could find either way on that score. Consider again the battery example. Suppose that the plaintiff introduces evidence that the defendant used an illegal weapon to commit the battery sufficient to invoke the presumption that the defendant intended to commit battery. Suppose that the defendant takes the stand and, while conceding that he harmed the plaintiff, testifies that he did so by accident. What is the effect of the presumption once the defendant has met it with this sort of counterproof?

As originally proposed by the Advisory Committee, Rule 301 would have addressed this issue as follows:

> In all cases not otherwise provided for by Act of Congress or by these rules a presumption imposes on the party against whom it is directed the burden of proving that the nonexistence of the presumed fact is more probable than its existence.

In other words, under the version of Rule 301 proposed by the Advisory Committee, a presumption, where it overlapped with an element, would have the effect of shifting the burden of *persuasion* on that element and not merely the burden of production. Under this approach, if the party against whom the presumption was directed failed to produce any evidence, he would of course suffer a directed verdict on that element for failing to meet his burden of production. But beyond that, the party would lose even if he *did* meet his burden of production, if the trier of fact was not persuaded by a preponderance of the evidence of the *opposite* of the element. Thus, the effect in our battery example would be the equivalent of eliminating E_2 as an element of the claim and creating an affirmative defense, D_2, that would be the equivalent of "not E_2":

A	B	C
Judge (directs verdict for defendant)	**Jury**	**Judge** (directs verdict for plaintiff)
E_1 (harm) $\longrightarrow$		$\longleftarrow$ D_1 (self-defense) $\longleftarrow$ D_2 (no intent)

The Advisory Committee explained its rationale as follows:

> Presumptions governed by this rule are given the effect of placing upon the opposing party the burden of establishing the nonexistence of the presumed fact, once the party invoking the presumption establishes the basic facts giving rise to it. The same considerations of fairness, policy, and probability which dictate the allocation of the burden of the various elements of a case as between the prima facie case of a plaintiff and affirmative defenses also underlie the creation of presumptions. These considerations are not satisfied by giving a lesser effect to presumptions.

> The so-called "bursting bubble" theory, under which a presumption vanishes upon the introduction of evidence which would support a finding of the nonexistence of the presumed fact, even though not believed, is rejected as according presumptions too "slight and evanescent" an effect.

Advisory Committee Note to Rule 301. The House Judiciary Committee amended Rule 301 to provide as follows:

> In all civil actions and proceedings not otherwise provided for by Act of Congress or by these rules, a presumption imposes on the party against whom it is di-

rected the burden of going forward with the evidence, and, even though met with contradicting evidence, a presumption is sufficient evidence of the fact presumed, to be considered by the trier of the facts.

The amendment was explained as follows:

> With respect to the weight to be given a presumption in a civil case, the Committee agreed with the judgment implicit in the Court's version that the so-called "bursting bubble" theory of presumptions, whereby a presumption vanishes upon the appearance of any contradicting evidence by the other party, gives to presumptions too slight an effect. On the other hand, the Committee believed that the Rule proposed by the Court, whereby a presumption permanently alters the burden of persuasion, no matter how much contradicting evidence is introduced—a view shared by only a few courts—lends too great a force to presumptions. Accordingly, the Committee amended the Rule to adopt an intermediate position under which a presumption does not vanish upon the introduction of contradicting evidence, and does not change the burden of persuasion; instead it is merely deemed sufficient evidence of the fact presumed, to be considered by the jury or other finder of fact.

House Judiciary Committee, House Report No. 93-650. The Senate Judiciary Committee amended the provision yet again to provide as follows:

> In all civil actions and proceedings not otherwise provided for by Act of Congress or by these rules, a presumption imposes on the party against whom it is directed the burden of going forward with evidence to rebut or meet the presumption, but does not shift to such party the burden of proof in the sense of the risk of nonpersuasion, which remains throughout the trial upon the party on whom it was originally cast.

The Senate explained its reasons for rejecting the House proposal as follows:

> The committee feels the House amendment is ill-advised. . . . "Presumptions are not evidence, but ways of dealing with evidence." This treatment requires juries to perform the task of considering "as evidence" facts upon which they have no direct evidence and which may confuse them in performance of their duties. . . .
>
> The effect of the rule as adopted by the committee is to make clear that while evidence of facts giving rise to a presumption shifts the burden of coming forward with evidence to rebut or meet the presumption, it does not shift the burden of persuasion on the existence of the presumed facts. The burden of persuasion remains on the party to whom it is allocated under the rules governing the allocation in the first instance.
>
> The court may instruct the jury that they may infer the existence of the presumed fact from proof of the basic facts giving rise to the presumption. However, it would be inappropriate under this rule to instruct the jury that the inference they are to draw is conclusive.

Senate Judiciary Committee, Report No. 93-1277. The Conference Committee, in adopting the Senate amendment, provided further explanation of the rule as ultimately adopted:

> The Senate amendment provides that a presumption shifts to the party against whom it is directed the burden of going forward with evidence to meet or rebut

the presumption, but it does not shift to that party the burden of persuasion on the existence of the presumed fact.

> Under the Senate amendment, a presumption is sufficient to get a party past an adverse party's motion to dismiss made at the end of his case-in-chief. If the adverse party offers no evidence contradicting the presumed fact, the court will instruct the jury that if it finds the basic facts, it may presume the existence of the presumed fact. If the adverse party does offer evidence contradicting the presumed fact, the court cannot instruct the jury that it may *presume* the existence of the presumed fact from proof of the basic facts. The court may, however, instruct the jury that it may infer the existence of the presumed fact from proof of the basic facts.

House-Senate Conference Committee, House Report No. 93-1597.

In its present form, the rule retains the substance of the Senate amendment, providing as follows:

> In a civil case, unless a federal statute or these rules provide otherwise, the party against whom a presumption is directed has the burden of producing evidence to rebut the presumption. But this rule does not shift the burden of persuasion, which remains on the party who had it originally.

The materials that follow explore several questions regarding the application of Rule 301. First, under Rule 301, what sort of showing must the party against whom a presumption is invoked make in order to meet the presumption? Second, does Rule 301 adopt the "bursting bubble" theory, and if so, does it have the "slight and evanescent" effect that the Advisory Committee feared? Third, what is the distinction between presumptions addressed in the text of Rule 301 and inferences addressed in the notes thereto? And finally, in federal court, can a presumption ever shift the burden of *persuasion*, and if so, when?

Problem 9-1: Proving Discrimination

Juan Peña, who lives and works in New Mexico, brings suit in federal court against his employer under a federal statute, the Age Discrimination in Employment Act (ADEA), as well as under the New Mexico Anti-Discrimination Act (NMADA). Both ADEA and NMADA provide a civil action for employees who have been discharged or otherwise discriminated against with respect to compensation or terms and conditions of employment because of the employee's age. Moreover, under both statutes, if an employee produces evidence that (a) he was at least 40 years old; (b) he met the employer's legitimate job expectations; (c) he was terminated or constructively discharged; and (d) employees under 40 years old were not fired, that gives rise to a presumption that the employee was discriminated against on account of his age.

Peña introduces sufficient evidence to give rise to the presumptions under ADEA and NMADA. Peña argues that under both statutes, the presumption shifts to the employer the burden of persuading the trier of fact that the employee was *not* discriminated against because of his age. Peña's employer responds that in federal court, a presumption can never shift the burden of persuasion, and that the presumption at most shifts the burden of production.

Who is correct, Peña, his employer, or neither one? If more information is needed to answer the question, what sort of information is required?

In re Yoder Company
758 F.2d 1114 (6th Cir. 1985)

CORNELIA G. KENNEDY, Circuit Judge.

In this Chapter 11 proceeding the Bankruptcy Court, affirmed by the District Court, held that Mark S. Bratton's products liability claim for the loss of four fingers was barred for failure to timely file a proof of claim. Bratton contends that his claim should not be barred because he did not receive notice of the latest date for filing proofs of claim.

In 1981, Yoder filed a petition requesting relief under Chapter 11 of the Bankruptcy Code. At that time Bratton's products liability suit against Yoder was pending in a Michigan state court. Bratton's claim was listed as a "contingent, unliquidated and disputed" claim in the amended schedule of assets and liabilities filed by Yoder. The Bankruptcy Court issued an order setting July 13, 1981 at the last date for creditors to file proofs of claim against Yoder (the "bar date").

Bratton filed a proof of claim on March 15, 1982, about eight months after the bar date. Yoder applied to the Bankruptcy Court for an order expunging certain products liability claims, including Bratton's. Following a hearing on Yoder's application, at which Bratton was represented, the Bankruptcy Court found that Bratton had been sent sufficient notice of the bar date and that Bratton's failure to file timely proof of claim was not due to excusable neglect. Bratton's claim was therefore barred. The District Court affirmed, and Bratton appeals.

Rule 3001 of the Interim Bankruptcy Rules (which are applicable to this proceeding) provides that: "A proof of claim may be filed at any time prior to the approval of the disclosure statement unless a different time is fixed by the court on notice as provided in Rule 2002." Interim Bankruptcy Rule 2002 provides that "the clerk of the bankruptcy court shall give notice by mail to the debtor, all creditors, equity security holders and indenture trustees of ... the time allowed for filing claims pursuant to Rule 3001." It is undisputed that Bratton's proof of claim was filed after the court-ordered bar date but before approval of the disclosure statement. The remaining question is whether notice of the bar date was sent to Bratton....

The Bankruptcy Court heard evidence concerning the procedure used to mail notices of the bar date. An employee of Yoder testified that he supervised a procedure through which an address label was prepared at Yoder for each creditor listed in Yoder's amended schedule of assets and liabilities, and that the employee and an accountant proofread the address labels to make sure that all listed creditors were included. The address labels and corresponding notices were taken to the clerk of the Bankruptcy Court. Using labels and envelopes it received from the Bankruptcy Court, the Cleveland Letter Service then prepared and mailed the notices. No record of the address labels actually prepared was kept by Yoder, the Bankruptcy Court clerk, or the Cleveland Letter Service; and neither the clerk's office nor the Cleveland Letter Service checked the labels against any list of creditors. Bratton's name and address did not appear on the matrix of creditors that was filed earlier with the Bankruptcy Court. The courtroom deputy docket clerk testified that she did not know whether the labels sent to the Cleveland Letter Service were the labels prepared by Yoder or labels prepared from the matrix in the court's file.

Bratton's address on the amended schedule of assets and liabilities, the list which Yoder's employee testified was used to prepare the labels, was that of his attorney, A.T. Ornstein. Ornstein testified that he had not received notice of the bar date. Attorneys for two other listed products liability claimants also represented that they and their clients had not received notices of the bar date.

[The Bankruptcy Court's decision was based on its finding that Bratton's attorney received the notice of the bar date.]

. . . .

The Bankruptcy Court relied mainly on a presumption of receipt that it held arose from evidence that the notice was properly mailed. The common law has long recognized a presumption that an item properly mailed was received by the addressee. *Hagner v. United States*, 285 U.S. 427 (1932). The presumption arises upon proof that the item was properly addressed, had sufficient postage, and was deposited in the mail. *Simpson v. Jefferson Standard Life Insurance Co.*, 465 F.2d 1320, 1323 (6th Cir. 1972). For purposes of this discussion, we will assume that the presumption of receipt did arise.

The District Court held that the presumption had not been rebutted, reasoning that "testimony amounting to a mere denial that a properly mailed notice was not received is insufficient to rebut the presumption of receipt." This statement is inconsistent with prior decisions of this Circuit. In *McKentry v. Secretary of HHS*, 655 F.2d 721 (6th Cir. 1981), the plaintiff and her attorney both filed affidavits that they had not received a notice of reconsideration from the Department of HHS. This Court held that this would have been sufficient evidence of non-receipt to rebut the presumption of mailing, had it arisen.[6] In *Baldwin v. Fidelity Phenix Fire Insurance Co.*, 260 F.2d 951, 953 (6th Cir. 1958), there was evidence that a notice had been sent to an insurance company and to one of its agents. The agent testified that he had not received the notice. This Court held that the evidence was sufficient to support the jury's finding that notice was not received by the insurance company or the agent. These decisions are in consonance with the general proposition that a presumption is rebutted "upon the introduction of evidence which would support a finding of the nonexistence of the presumed fact." 10 *Moore's Federal Practice* § 301.04[2] (2d ed.). Testimony of non-receipt, standing alone, would be sufficient to support a finding of non-receipt; such testimony is therefore sufficient to rebut the presumption of receipt.

The next question is whether the presumption, once rebutted, retains any effect. The Bankruptcy Court found that it was "entitled to presume that notice has been received once a proper mailing is made, even though the intended recipient testifies that the notice never really came." The Bankruptcy Court reasoned as follows:

> According to the note of the Advisory Committee on Proposed Rules, Federal Rule 301 rejects the so-called "bursting bubble" theory, under which a presumption vanishes upon the introduction of evidence that negates the existence of the presumed fact. According to the Federal Rule, when evidence is put forth negating the fact that the presumption tends to support, the presumption still continues and is evidence to be weighed and considered with all of the other evidence in the case.

. . . .

A brief review of the history of [Federal Rule of Evidence 301] will aid in evaluating the Bankruptcy Court's reasoning. Before adoption of the Federal Rules of Evidence there were two major theories concerning the effect of a presumption once rebuttal evidence is admitted. Under the Thayer or "bursting bubble" theory a presumption vanishes entirely once rebutted, and the question must be decided as any ordinary question of fact.[8]

---

6. The Court also held that a copy in the file of a notice addressed to the plaintiff was not sufficient evidence of mailing to give rise to the presumption.

8. The facts giving rise to the presumption often give rise to an inference that remains and may still be considered by the factfinder. *See* IX *Wigmore on Evidence* § 2491 (Chadbourn rev. 1981) ("[T]he

Under a later theory, proposed by Morgan, a presumption shifts the burden of proving the nonexistence of the presumed fact to the opposing party.

The version of Rule 301 that was proposed by the Advisory Committee, accepted by the Supreme Court, and submitted to Congress adopted the Morgan view. That rule, however, was not enacted by Congress. The Advisory Committee notes, on which the Bankruptcy Court relied, that reject the "bursting bubble" theory pertain to the proposed rule, which was not enacted, and are thus of little help in interpreting the final rule.

The House of Representatives adopted a rule espousing an intermediate view, which would allow a rebutted presumption to be considered evidence of the fact presumed. The Senate criticized the House rule on the ground that it made no sense to call a presumption evidence, and adopted the present language of Rule 301, which was adopted by the Conference Committee and enacted into law.

Most commentators have concluded that Rule 301 as enacted embodies the Thayer or "bursting bubble" approach. *See, e.g.,* 10 *Moore's Federal Practice* § 301.04[4.-1] (2d ed.); 1 *Weinstein's Evidence* 301–12; IX *Wigmore on Evidence* § 2493h (Chadbourn rev. 1981). *Contra* 21 C. Wright & K. Graham, *Federal Practice and Procedure* §§ 5121, 5122, 5126.[13] At least two other circuit courts have expressly agreed. *Reeves v. General Foods Corp.,* 682 F.2d 515, 522 n. 10 (5th Cir. 1982); *Legille v. Dann,* 544 F.2d 1, 6–7 (D.C. Cir. 1976). The Thayer view is consistent with the language of Rule 301, which provides only that a presumption shifts "the burden of [producing] evidence to rebut [] the presumption." Accordingly, we hold that a presumption under Rule 301 has no probative effect once

---

legal consequence [of the presumption] being removed, the inference, as a matter of reasoning, may still remain....").

13. Professors Wright and Graham interpret Rule 301 as providing that a rebutted presumption still suffices to carry the issue to the jury, which should be instructed that it may infer the presumed fact. 21 C. Wright & K. Graham, *Federal Practice and Procedure* § 5122 at p. 572. This interpretation differs from the bursting bubble theory only in the effect given an "illogical" presumption, i.e., one where the facts giving rise to the presumption do not logically give rise to an inference that the presumed fact exists. *See id.* § 5126 at pp. 609–11, 609 n. 22. According to Wright and Graham, once an illogical presumption was rebutted the presumption would still have the effect of requiring that the question be sent to the jury with instructions that it may infer the presumed fact. Under the bursting bubble theory a rebutted illogical presumption would have no effect and the only evidence on the question would be the rebuttal evidence, which would be conclusive. However, in the case of a "logical" presumption, such as the presumption of receipt involved here, the jury would be allowed to consider the inference naturally drawn from the facts establishing the presumption whether or not the presumption is given any effect after rebuttal. Wright and Graham's interpretation would therefore have no effect on the present case.

Wright and Graham's conclusion that Rule 301 rejects the bursting bubble theory is based primarily on the Conference Committee's statement that:

> If the adverse party does offer evidence contradicting the presumed fact, the court cannot instruct the jury that it may presume the existence of the presumed fact from proof of the basic facts. *The court may, however, instruct the jury that it may infer the existence of the presumed fact from proof of the basic facts.*

Id. § 5121 n. 27 (emphasis added). The emphasized portion of this quotation is not inconsistent with the bursting bubble theory. Nothing in the legislative history indicates that Congress was concerned with the distinction between "logical" and "illogical" presumptions. The statement that the jury *may* be instructed to consider an inference is most naturally read as permitting such an instruction when called for by the existence of a logical inference. An "inference" not based on logic is not an inference at all, but a presumption. Jurors would have no way to decide how much weight to give an "inference" drawn from a fact that their own logic tells them has no relevance to the question to be decided. The sentence immediately preceding the emphasized portion of the Conference Committee's report clearly indicates that the jury should not be allowed to apply a presumption once rebutted.

rebutted. The Bankruptcy Court therefore erred in considering the presumption as evidence of receipt....

Legille v. Dann
544 F.2d 1 (D.C. Cir. 1976)

SPOTTSWOOD W. ROBINSON, III, Circuit Judge:

An application for a United States patent filed within twelve months after filing of an application for a foreign patent on the same invention is statutorily accorded the filing date of the foreign application and the effect thereof. If, however, the interval between the filings exceeds twelve months, patent protection in the United States may not be available. The practice of the Patent Office, unchallenged in this litigation, is to file the duplicating United States application upon receipt.

This appeal, by the Commissioner of Patents, brings to this court a controversy as to the filing date properly to be given four applications domestically mailed to the Patent Office in time for normal delivery before expiration of the twelve-month period but allegedly received thereafter. On cross-motions for summary judgment, the District Court, utilizing the familiar presumption of regularity of the mails, ruled in favor of the applicants. Our examination of the record, however, discloses potential evidence capable of dispelling the presumption and generating an issue of fact as to the date on which the applications arrived. We accordingly reverse the judgment and remand the case for trial.

I

From affidavits submitted in support of the motions for summary judgment, we reconstruct the facts apparently undisputed. On March 1, 1973, appellees' attorney mailed from East Hartford, Connecticut, to the Patent Office in Washington, D. C., a package containing four patent applications. Each of the applications had previously been filed in the Grand Duchy of Luxembourg, three on March 6, 1972, and the fourth on the following August 11. The package was marked "Airmail," bore sufficient airmail postage and was properly addressed. Delivery of air mail from East Hartford to Washington at that time was normally two days.[7]

The applications were date-stamped "March 8, 1973," by the Patent Office. Each of the four applications was assigned that filing date on the ground that the stamped date was the date of receipt by the Patent Office. If the action of the Patent Office is to stand, three of appellees' applications, on which Luxembourg patents had been granted, fail in this country.

Appellees petitioned the Commissioner of Patents to reassign the filing date. The petition was denied. Appellees then sued in the District Court for a judgment directing the Commissioner to accord the applications a filing date not later than March 6, 1973. Both sides moved for summary judgment on the basis of the pleadings and affidavits respectively submitted. Not surprisingly, none of the affidavits reflected any direct evidence of the date on which the applications were actually delivered to the Patent Office.

---

7. An affidavit by the postmaster whose district includes East Hartford states that items sent by airmail therefrom on March 1, 1973, should have been received in Washington on March 3, and certainly before March 6, and that the affiant knew of no reason why such items were not received until March 8.

The District Court correctly identified the central issue: "whether there exists a genuine issue of fact as to when these applications were received by the Patent Office." By the court's appraisal, appellees' suit was "predicated upon the legal presumption that postal employees discharge their duties in a proper manner and that properly addressed, stamped and deposited mail is presumed to reach the addressee in due course and without unusual delay, unless evidence to the contrary is proven." The court believed, however, that the Commissioner's position rested "primarily upon a presumption of procedural regularity based upon the normal manner, custom, practice and habit established for the handling of incoming mail at the Patent Office and upon the absence of evidence showing that the subject applications were not handled routinely in accordance with those established procedures." On this analysis, the court "concluded that the presumption relied upon by the [Commissioner] is insufficient to overcome the strong presumption that mails, properly addressed, having fully prepaid postage, and deposited in the proper receptacles, will be received by the addressee in the ordinary course of the mails." "This latter presumption," the court held, "can only be rebutted by proof of specific facts and not by invoking another presumption"; "the negative evidence in this case detailing the manner, custom, practice and habit of handling incoming mail by the Patent Office fails to overcome or rebut the strong presumption that the applications were timely delivered in the regular course of the mails to the Patent Office."

. . . .

II

Proof that mail matter is properly addressed, stamped and deposited in an appropriate receptacle has long been accepted as evidence of delivery to the addressee. On proof of the foundation facts, innumerable cases recognize a presumption to that effect. Some presume more specifically that the delivery occurred in due course of the mails. The cases concede, however, that the presumption is rebuttable. We think the District Court erred in adhering to the presumption in the face of the evidentiary showing which the Commissioner was prepared to make.

Rebuttable presumptions[24] are rules of law attaching to proven evidentiary facts certain procedural consequences as to the opponent's duty to come forward with other evidence. In the instant case, the presumption would normally mean no more than that proof of proper airmailing of appellees' applications required a finding, in the absence of countervailing evidence, that they arrived at the Patent Office within the usual delivery time. There is abundant authority undergirding the proposition that, as a presumption, it did not remain viable in the face of antithetical evidence. As Dean Wigmore has explained, "the peculiar effect of a presumption 'of law' (that is, the real presumption) is merely to invoke a rule of law compelling the [trier of fact] to reach a conclusion in the absence of evidence to the contrary from the opponent. If the opponent does offer evidence to the contrary (sufficient to satisfy the judge's requirement of some evidence), the presumption disappears as a rule of law, and the case is in the (factfinder's) hands free from any rule." As more poetically the explanation has been put, "[p]resumptions . . . may be looked on

---

24. We . . . differentiate presumptions from inferences, a dissimilarity which "is subtle, but not unreal. A presumption, sometimes called a presumption of law, is an inference which the law directs the [trier of fact] to draw if it finds a given set of facts; an inference is a conclusion which the [trier of fact] is *permitted*, but not compelled, to draw from the facts."

as the bats of the law, flitting in the twilight, but disappearing in the sunshine of actual facts."

We are aware of the fact that this view of presumptions—the so-called "bursting bubble" theory—has not won universal acclaim. Nonetheless, it is the prevailing view, to which jurists preponderantly have subscribed; it is the view of the Supreme Court, and of this court as well. It is also the approach taken by the Model Code of Evidence and, very importantly, by the newly-adopted Federal Rules of Evidence. These considerations hardly leave us free to assume a contrary position. Beyond that, we perceive no legal or practical justification for preferring either of the two involved presumptions over the other.[39] In light of the Commissioner's showing on the motions for summary judgment, then, we conclude that the District Court should have declined a summary disposition in favor of a trial.

III

[The court summarizes the evidence regarding the procedures that the Patent Office follows in dealing with incoming mail.]

We cannot agree with the District Court that an evidentiary presentation of this caliber would do no more than raise "a presumption of procedural regularity" in the Patent Office. Certainly it would accomplish that much; it would cast upon appellees the burden of producing contradictory evidence, but its effect would not be exhausted at that point. The facts giving rise to the presumption would also have evidentiary force, and as evidence would command the respect normally accorded proof of any fact. In other words, the evidence reflected by the affidavit, beyond creation of a presumption of regularity in date-stamping incoming mail, would have probative value on the issue of date of receipt of appellees' applications; and even if the presumption were dispelled, that evidence would be entitled to consideration, along with appellees' own evidence, when a resolution of the issue is undertaken.[54] And, clearly, a fact-finder convinced of the integrity of the Patent Office's mail-handling procedures would inexorably be led to the conclusion that appellees' applications simply did not arrive until the date which was stamped on them.

In the final analysis, the District Court's misstep was the treatment of the parties' opposing affidavits as a contest postulating a question of law as to the relative strength of the two presumptions rather than as a prelude to conflicting evidence necessitating a trial. Viewed as the mere procedural devices we hold that they are, presumptions are incapable of waging war among themselves....

[The dissenting opinion of Judge Fahy is omitted.]

---

39. The presumption of due delivery of the mails is predicated upon the fixed methods and systematic operation of the postal service. 1 J. Wigmore, Evidence §94 at 524 (3d ed. 1940). The presumption of regularity of the Patent Office's handling of incoming mail, rests on exactly the same phenomena. In sum, both presumptions have a common origin in regularity of action. *Id.* §92. We see nothing suggesting that the methodology buttressing the one is any more or less foolproof than that underpinning the other. We are mindful that some presumptions are founded in part upon exceptionally strong and visible policies, which have been said to persist despite proof rebutting the factual basis for the presumption. See, *e.g.*, C. McCormick, Evidence §345 at 822–823 (2d ed. 1972). The answer here is that from aught that appears the policy reflections are in equilibrium.

54. And, of course, proven facts sufficient to raise initially a presumption of arrival in due course of the mails are entitled to like value as evidence tending to show such an arrival.

St. Mary's Honor Center v. Hicks

509 U.S. 502 (1993)

Justice SCALIA delivered the opinion of the Court....

I

Petitioner St. Mary's Honor Center (St. Mary's) is a halfway house operated by the Missouri Department of Corrections and Human Resources (MDCHR). Respondent Melvin Hicks, a black man, was hired as a correctional officer at St. Mary's in August 1978 and was promoted to shift commander, one of six supervisory positions, in February 1980.

In 1983 MDCHR conducted an investigation of the administration of St. Mary's, which resulted in extensive supervisory changes in January 1984.... Prior to these personnel changes respondent had enjoyed a satisfactory employment record, but soon thereafter became the subject of repeated, and increasingly severe, disciplinary actions.... [O]n June 7, 1984, he was discharged for threatening Powell during an exchange of heated words on April 19.

Respondent brought this suit in the United States District Court for the Eastern District of Missouri, alleging that petitioner St. Mary's violated § 703(a)(1) of Title VII of the Civil Rights Act of 1964.... After a full bench trial, the District Court found for petitioners. The United States Court of Appeals for the Eighth Circuit reversed and remanded, and we granted certiorari.

II

Section 703(a)(1) of Title VII of the Civil Rights Act of 1964 provides in relevant part:

"It shall be an unlawful employment practice for an employer—

"(1) ... to discharge any individual, or otherwise to discriminate against any individual with respect to his compensation, terms, conditions, or privileges of employment, because of such individual's race...."

With the goal of "progressively ... sharpen[ing] the inquiry into the elusive factual question of intentional discrimination," *Texas Dept. of Community Affairs v. Burdine*, 450 U.S. 248, 255, n. 8 (1981), our opinion in *McDonnell Douglas Corp. v. Green*, 411 U.S. 792 (1973), established an allocation of the burden of production and an order for the presentation of proof in Title VII discriminatory-treatment cases. The plaintiff in such a case, we said, must first establish, by a preponderance of the evidence, a "prima facie" case of racial discrimination. *Burdine, supra*, at 252–253. Petitioners do not challenge the District Court's finding that respondent satisfied the minimal requirements of such a prima facie case (set out in *McDonnell Douglas, supra*, at 802) by proving (1) that he is black, (2) that he was qualified for the position of shift commander, (3) that he was demoted from that position and ultimately discharged, and (4) that the position remained open and was ultimately filled by a white man.

Under the *McDonnell Douglas* scheme, "[e]stablishment of the prima facie case in effect creates a presumption that the employer unlawfully discriminated against the employee." *Burdine, supra*, at 254. To establish a "presumption" is to say that a finding of the predicate fact (here, the prima facie case) produces "a required conclusion in the absence of explanation" (here, the finding of unlawful discrimination). 1 D. Louisell & C. Mueller, Federal Evidence § 67, p. 536 (1977). Thus, the *McDonnell Douglas* presumption places upon the defendant the burden of producing an explanation to rebut the prima facie case—*i.e.*, the burden of "producing evidence" that the adverse employment actions were taken "for a legitimate, nondiscriminatory reason." *Burdine*, 450 U.S., at 254. "[T]he defendant must clearly set forth, through the introduction of admissible evidence," reasons for its actions which, *if believed by the trier of fact*, would support a finding that unlawful discrimination was not the cause of the employment action. *Id.*, at 254–255, and n. 8. It is important to note, however, that although the *McDonnell Douglas* presumption shifts the burden of *production* to the defendant, "[t]he ultimate burden of persuading the trier of fact that the defendant intentionally discriminated against the plaintiff remains at all times with the plaintiff." 450 U.S., at 253. In this regard it operates like all presumptions, as described in Federal Rule of Evidence 301.... Respondent does not challenge the District Court's finding that petitioners sustained their burden of production by introducing evidence of two legitimate, nondiscriminatory reasons for their actions: the severity and the accumulation of rules violations committed by respondent. Our cases make clear that at that point the shifted burden of production became irrelevant: "If the defendant carries this burden of production, the presumption raised by the prima facie case is rebutted," *Burdine*, 450 U.S., at 255, and "drops from the case," *id.*, at 255, n. 10. The plaintiff then has "the full and fair opportunity to demonstrate," through presentation of his own case and through cross-examination of the defendant's witnesses, "that the proffered reason was not the true reason for the employment decision," *id.*, at 256, and that race was. He retains that "ultimate burden of persuading the [trier of fact] that [he] has been the victim of intentional discrimination." *Ibid.*

The District Court, acting as trier of fact in this bench trial, found that the reasons petitioners gave were not the real reasons for respondent's demotion and discharge. It found that respondent was the only supervisor disciplined for violations committed by his subordinates; that similar and even more serious violations committed by respondent's co-workers were either disregarded or treated more leniently; and that Powell manufactured the final verbal confrontation in order to provoke respondent into threatening him. It nonetheless held that respondent had failed to carry his ultimate burden of proving that *his race* was the determining factor in petitioners' decision first to demote and then to dismiss him. In short, the District Court concluded that "although [respondent] has proven the existence of a crusade to terminate him, he has not proven that the crusade was racially rather than personally motivated."

The Court of Appeals set this determination aside on the ground that "[o]nce [respondent] proved all of [petitioners'] proffered reasons for the adverse employment actions to be pretextual, [respondent] was entitled to judgment as a matter of law." The Court of Appeals reasoned:

> "Because all of defendants' proffered reasons were discredited, defendants were in a position of having offered no legitimate reason for their actions. In other words, defendants were in no better position than if they had remained silent, offering no rebuttal to an established inference that they had unlawfully discriminated against plaintiff on the basis of his race."

That is not so. By producing *evidence* (whether ultimately persuasive or not) of nondiscriminatory reasons, petitioners sustained their burden of production, and thus placed themselves in a "better position than if they had remained silent."

In the nature of things, the determination that a defendant has met its burden of production (and has thus rebutted any legal presumption of intentional discrimination) can involve no credibility assessment. For the burden-of-production determination necessarily *precedes* the credibility-assessment stage. At the close of the defendant's case, the court is asked to decide whether an issue of fact remains for the trier of fact to determine. None does if, on the evidence presented, (1) any rational person would have to find the existence of facts constituting a prima facie case, and (2) the defendant has failed to meet its burden of production—*i.e.*, has failed to introduce evidence which, *taken as true*, would *permit* the conclusion that there was a nondiscriminatory reason for the adverse action. In that event, the court must award judgment to the plaintiff as a matter of law under Federal Rule of Civil Procedure 50(a)(1) (in the case of jury trials) or Federal Rule of Civil Procedure 52(c) (in the case of bench trials). If the defendant has failed to sustain its burden but reasonable minds could *differ* as to whether a preponderance of the evidence establishes the facts of a prima facie case, then a question of fact *does* remain, which the trier of fact will be called upon to answer.[3]

If, on the other hand, the defendant has succeeded in carrying its burden of production, the *McDonnell Douglas* framework—with its presumptions and burdens—is no longer relevant. To resurrect it later, after the trier of fact has determined that what was "produced" to meet the burden of production is not credible, flies in the face of our holding in *Burdine* that to rebut the presumption "[t]he defendant need not persuade the court that it was actually motivated by the proffered reasons." 450 U.S., at 254. The presumption, having fulfilled its role of forcing the defendant to come forward with some response, simply drops out of the picture. *Id.*, at 255. The defendant's "production" (whatever its persuasive effect) having been made, the trier of fact proceeds to decide the ultimate question: whether plaintiff has proven "that the defendant intentionally discriminated against [him]" because of his race, *id.*, at 253. The factfinder's disbelief of the reasons put forward by the defendant (particularly if disbelief is accompanied by a suspicion of mendacity) may, together with the elements of the prima facie case, suffice to show intentional discrimination. Thus, rejection of the defendant's proffered reasons will *permit* the trier of fact to infer the ultimate fact of intentional discrimination,[4] and the Court of Appeals was correct when it noted that, upon such rejection, "[n]o additional proof of discrimination is *required*." But the Court of Appeals' holding that rejection of the defendant's proffered reasons *compels* judgment for the plaintiff disregards the fundamen-

---

3. If the finder of fact answers affirmatively—if it finds that the prima facie case *is* supported by a preponderance of the evidence—it *must* find the existence of the presumed fact of unlawful discrimination and *must*, therefore, render a verdict for the plaintiff. See *Texas Dept. of Community Affairs v. Burdine*, 450 U.S. 248, 254, and n. 7 (1981). Thus, the *effect* of failing to produce evidence to rebut the *McDonnell Douglas Corp. v. Green*, 411 U.S. 792 (1973), presumption is not felt until the prima facie case has been *established*, either as a matter of law (because the plaintiff's facts are uncontested) or by the factfinder's determination that the plaintiff's facts are supported by a preponderance of the evidence. It is thus technically accurate to describe the sequence as we did in *Burdine*: "First, the plaintiff has the burden of proving by the preponderance of the evidence a prima facie case of discrimination. Second, if the plaintiff succeeds in proving the prima facie case, the burden shifts to the defendant to articulate some legitimate, nondiscriminatory reason for the employee's rejection." 450 U.S., at 252–253. As a practical matter, however, and in the real-life sequence of a trial, the defendant *feels* the "burden" not when the plaintiff's prima facie case is *proved*, but as soon as evidence of it is *introduced*. The defendant then knows that its failure to introduce evidence of a nondiscriminatory reason will cause judgment to go against it *unless* the plaintiff's prima facie case is held to be inadequate in law or fails to convince the factfinder. It is this practical coercion which causes the *McDonnell Douglas* presumption to function as a means of "arranging the presentation of evidence," *Watson v. Fort Worth Bank & Trust*, 487 U.S. 977, 986 (1988).

4. Contrary to the dissent's confusion-producing analysis, there is nothing whatever inconsistent between this statement and our later statements that (1) the plaintiff must show "*both* that the reason was false, *and* that discrimination was the real reason," and (2) "it is not enough ... to *dis*believe the employer". Even though (as we say here) rejection of the defendant's proffered reasons is enough at law to *sustain* a finding of discrimination, *there must be a finding of discrimination*.

tal principle of Rule 301 that a presumption does not shift the burden of proof, and ignores our repeated admonition that the Title VII plaintiff at all times bears the "ultimate burden of persuasion." ...

[The dissenting opinion of Justice Souter is omitted.]

Alabama By-Products Corporation v. Killingsworth
733 F.2d 1511 (11th Cir. 1984)

TUTTLE, Senior Circuit Judge:

Alabama By-Products Corporation ("ABC") petitions for review of the Benefits Review Board's (the "Board") decision awarding benefits under Title IV of the Federal Coal Mine Health and Safety Act of 1969, as amended (the "Act"), to Charles B. Killingsworth, a former employee of the corporation. We affirm the award.

I. BACKGROUND

Killingsworth worked as a coal miner for thirty-nine years, the first thirty-five years underground and the last four on the surface as a shop electrician. He voluntarily retired in 1978 at age sixty-two. Killingsworth filed a claim for benefits under the Act on May 22, 1978 for alleged total disability due to pneumoconiosis. Pneumoconiosis, which is commonly known as "black lung," is a dust disease of the lungs arising from coal mine employment. The Department of Labor approved the claim, holding the coal mine operator, ABC, liable. ABC contested its potential liability and a formal hearing was held on February 11, 1980 before an Administrative Law Judge (the "ALJ"), who awarded benefits to Killingsworth.

Before the ALJ, Killingsworth testified that he retired because he did not feel he was doing a good job for his employer due to his shortness of breath and some problems with his knees. The medical evidence presented to the ALJ included findings from three doctors who examined Killingsworth....

The ALJ found that the evidence was sufficient to invoke the presumption of total disability due to pneumoconiosis under 20 C.F.R. §727.203(a)(1). The ALJ then determined that ABC had failed to rebut the presumption under 20 C.F.R. §§727.203(b)(2) and (b)(3)....

II. DISCUSSION

A. The Nature of Employer's Burden

We first address ABC's contention that the ALJ improperly construed the effect of the presumption at 20 C.F.R. §727.203(a)(1)[5] by giving it independent evidentiary weight and by finding that the presumption, once invoked, shifted the burden of proof to the employer. ABC claims that under the "bursting bubble" theory of presumptions, once the employer offers some rebuttal evidence, the presumption falls out of the case. In other words, ABC asserts that to rebut the presumption, the employer has only the burden of production, not the burden of persuasion. According to ABC, the burden of proof or persuasion remains with the claimant. We disagree with ABC's analysis.

---

5. 20 C.F.R. §727.203(a)(1) provides:
   (a) *Establishing interim presumption.* A miner who engaged in coal mine employment for at least 10 years will be presumed to be totally disabled due to pneumoconiosis ... if one of the following medical requirements is met:
   (1) A chest roentgenogram (x-ray), biopsy, or autopsy establishes the existence of pneumoconiosis (see §410.428 of this title)....

The burden of persuasion may be judicially or legislatively assigned to a specific party to establish a particular fact. *NLRB v. Transportation Management Corp.*, 462 U.S. 393, __, n. 7 (1983). The plain meaning of the regulatory language of 20 C.F.R. § 727.203(b)[6] demonstrates that the burden of persuasion shifts to the employer on rebuttal. Under section 727.203(b), the employer is required to "establish" the elements of rebuttal. "Establish" is clearly synonymous with "prove." Furthermore, under section 727.203(b), the factfinder must consider "all relevant medical evidence" to determine if the presumption has been rebutted, thus indicating that the factfinder must consider evidence introduced by both sides and that the operator must persuade the factfinder.…

ABC also argues that Rule 301 of the Federal Rules of Evidence applies. Rule 301, however, controls only if an act of Congress has not provided otherwise. Here, the regulation specifically states that the operator must "establish" the rebutting factor and therefore, Rule 301 does not apply.

We conclude that the burden of persuasion or proof shifts to the operator on rebuttal. Therefore, the ALJ acted properly in the case at hand.…

Notes and Questions

1. What do the cases suggest about the amount of evidence that a party against whom a presumption is invoked must produce in order to meet the presumption? In the battery example, wouldn't the defendant's testimony denying that he acted with the intent to harm the plaintiff suffice to defeat the force of the illegal weapons presumption under Rule 301? The dissent in *Hicks* criticized the majority decision on the ground that its "scheme places any employer who lies in a better position than the employer who says nothing." *St. Mary's Honor Center v. Hicks*, 509 U.S. 502, 540 n.13 (1993) (Souter, J., dissenting). Is the dissent's point well taken?

2. If, as the cases suggest, the presumption drops out of the picture once it is met even with what has a good chance of being a perjured denial of the presumed fact, what, exactly, does the presumption accomplish?

Asked somewhat differently, suppose that the plaintiff's *only* evidence of discrimination in a case such as *Hicks* consists of the required elements of the "prima facie" case. Would that evidence, in the absence of a presumption, be sufficient to get his case out of column A, in other words, would it be sufficient to avoid having a verdict directed against him? If it would not be (and it is hard to believe that it would be sufficient), then the effect of the presumption is to force the defendant to produce evidence of a legitimate, nondiscriminatory reason for taking the adverse employment action *that he otherwise would not have produced* (since the case would come to an end at the close of the plaintiff's case-in-chief). According to *Hicks*, "[t]he factfinder's disbelief of the reasons put

---

6. 20 C.F.R. § 727.203(b) provides:

(b) *Rebuttal of interim presumption.*

In adjudicating a claim under this subpart, all relevant medical evidence shall be considered. The presumption in paragraph (a) of this section shall be rebutted if:

(1) The evidence establishes that the individual is, in fact, doing his usual coal mine work or comparable and gainful work (see § 410.412(a)(1) of this title); or

(2) In light of all relevant evidence it is established that the individual is able to do his usual coal mine work or comparable and gainful work (see § 410.412(a)(1) of this title); or

(3) The evidence establishes that the total disability or death of the miner did not arise in whole or in part out of coal mine employment; or

(4) The evidence establishes that the miner does not, or did not, have pneumoconiosis.

forward by the defendant … may, together with the elements of the prima facie case, suffice to show intentional discrimination." That means, does it not, that the *net* effect of the presumption is to move the plaintiff's case from column A to column B?

3. Footnote 13 of the *Yoder* opinion as well as the congressional reports on Rule 301 discuss the possibility that, even if the presumption disappears, the trial court may instruct the jury that it may nonetheless infer proof of the presumed fact from proof of the basic fact(s). Unlike a presumption, which is a rule of law and is mandatory, an inference is a rule of logic, and is permissive. How is an instruction that the trier of fact may infer the presumed fact from proof of the basic fact different from the House's proposed version of Rule 301?

4. If in *Legille*, one of the two competing presumptions was indeed deemed to be weightier, what would be the result under Rule 301?

5. The constitutional limitations on the use of presumptions in civil cases are modest. The Supreme Court has held that neither the due process nor the equal protection clauses are offended by a presumption so long as

> there shall be some rational connection between the fact proved and the ultimate fact presumed, and that the inference of one fact from proof of another shall not be so unreasonable as to be a purely arbitrary mandate.

Mobile, J. & K. C. R. Co. v. Turnipseed, 219 U.S. 35, 43 (1910).

Given this standard, is there much force to the distinction, raised in footnote 13 of *Yoder*, between logical and illogical presumptions? Or is it possible to be "rational" for constitutional purposes without being "logical" for intellectual purposes?

6. As the text of Rule 301 indicates, it applies "unless a federal statute or these rules provide otherwise." But who decides whether a federal statute has otherwise provided? Are you persuaded, as *Killingsworth* holds, that the use of the word "establish" was intended to "provide otherwise" with respect to the burden-shifting effect of a presumption? *Killingsworth* is hardly unique in this regard. *See, e.g., Hood v. Knappton Corp. Inc.*, 986 F.2d 329, 331–32 (9th Cir. 1993) (Rule 301 does not alter pre-existing common law drifting vessel presumption that provided for shifting burden of persuasion in admiralty cases). Is it possible that the federal judiciary has found a way to get the version of Rule 301 that it originally preferred?

7. Many states have adopted rules that differ substantially from Federal Rule 301. In some states, the default rule is that a presumption shifts the burden of persuasion. *See, e.g.*, Arkansas Rule of Evidence 301(a) ("In all actions and proceedings not otherwise provided for by statute or by these rules, a presumption imposes on the party against whom it is directed the burden of proving that the nonexistence of the presumed fact is more probable than its existence."). In other states, some presumptions shift the burden of production while others shift the burden of persuasion, with the evidence rules detailing the effect of different types of presumptions. *See e.g.*, Rhode Island Rule of Evidence 302 ("In all civil proceedings not otherwise provided for by statute or rule, a presumption imposes on the party against whom it is directed either (A) the burden of producing evidence (Rule 303) or (B) the burden of persuasion (Rule 305).")

8. Rule 302, like its counterparts in Rules 501 and 601, provides for the application in civil cases of state law with respect to the effect of a presumption in a case in which the claim or defense is grounded in state law. Accordingly, not only would the content of presumptions to be used in such a case be determined by state law, but so would their effect, in other words, whether they shift the burden of production or the burden of persuasion. Do you see why a different result might run up against problems under *Erie*?

Rule 302 applies only as to "the effect of a presumption regarding a claim or defense for which state law supplies the rule of decision." The Advisory Committee Note indicates that Rule 302 thus "does not apply state law when the presumption operates upon a lesser aspect of the case, i.e. 'tactical' presumptions." Advisory Committee Note to Rule 302. What does this mean? *See Kokins v. Teleflex, Inc.*, 621 F.3d 1290, 1302 n.8 (10th Cir. 2010) (describing tactical presumptions as rules of convenience — such as the presumption establishing receipt of a mailed letter — and distinguishing them from substantive presumptions that favor either the plaintiff or defendant in a particular situation).

9. Does Rule 302 require a federal court to look to state law when what is involved is not a presumption but rather an inference? *See Herbert v. Wal-Mart Stores, Inc.*, 911 F.2d 1044, 1047 (5th Cir. 1990) (no); *In re Groggel*, 333 B.R. 261, 304 n.22 (W.D. Pa. 2005) (same).

10. As demonstrated in the introduction, the effect of a presumption that shifts the burden of persuasion can at times be the equivalent of removing a factor as an element of the plaintiff's claim and converting it into an affirmative defense. Why would a policymaker choose to make something an element of the plaintiff's claim, but provide for a presumption that would shift the burden of persuasion, instead of just making that factor an affirmative defense in the first instance?

C. Burdens of Proof and Presumptions in Criminal Cases

The previous sections examined the burdens of production and persuasion in the context of civil claims, as well as the effect of presumptions and inferences in the civil context. We saw that civil claims consist of elements that must be proved by the plaintiff, as well as affirmative defenses that defendants can sometimes invoke and prove in an effort to defeat liability, and that typically the proof must persuade the trier of fact by a preponderance of the evidence. We also saw that policymakers have a large degree of freedom to decide whether to denominate a factor as an element of a claim or instead as an affirmative defense. Finally, we saw that, although not the default norm, presumptions could be created that shift the burden of persuasion, and that the effect of such presumptions under certain circumstances is the equivalent of removing a factor as an element of the plaintiff's case and making it instead an affirmative defense. Moreover, even if a presumption doesn't shift the burden of persuasion, it at the very least shifts the burden of production to the opposing party.

The materials that follow explore all of these issues in the context of criminal cases, which are not covered by Rule 301 and indeed are not regulated by any of the federal rules of evidence. Two questions are of particular importance in the criminal context. First, what restrictions, if any, exist on the ability of a policymaker to remove a factor as an element of a criminal offense and instead to denominate it as an affirmative defense? And second, what role can presumptions and inferences play in the criminal context?

Problem 9-2: Proving Hate

Within weeks of one another, two young men are found murdered, Vladimir Abramov in Oregon and Robert Tildon in Washington. Both men, it turns out, were gay, and police believe that both victims were targeted because of their sexual orientation. Eventually, Dario Green is indicted and separately tried in criminal proceedings in state courts in both Washington and Oregon.

In the Washington case, one of the charges against Green is under a statute that provides in pertinent part as follows:

> A person is guilty of murder in the first degree when, with the intent to cause the death of another person, he causes the death of such person … and the victim was selected because of his or her actual or perceived race, color, gender, handicap, religion, sexual orientation, or ethnicity.

In the Oregon case, Green is charged under two statutes that provide in pertinent part as follows:

> A person is guilty of murder in the first degree when, with the intent to cause the death of another person, he causes the death of such person … except that in any prosecution under this subdivision, it is an affirmative defense that the victim was not selected because of his or her actual or perceived race, color, gender, handicap, religion, sexual orientation, or ethnicity.

> A person is guilty of murder in the second degree when, with the intent to cause the death of another person, he causes the death of such person … under circumstances which do not constitute murder in the first degree because the victim was not selected because of his or her actual or perceived race, color, gender, handicap, religion, sexual orientation, or ethnicity. The fact that homicide was committed without selecting the victim because of his or her actual or perceived race, color, gender, handicap, religion, sexual orientation, or ethnicity constitutes a mitigating circumstance reducing murder in the first degree to murder in the second degree and need not be proved in any prosecution initiated under this subdivision.

Assume that under Oregon law, first-degree murder is punishable by life in prison, and that second-degree murder is punishable by 30 years in prison.

Assume further that at both trials, sufficient evidence is produced at trial that a jury could find (a) that the victims in each case were gay; and (b) that Dario Green had made derogatory statements about gay people in the recent past.

In the Washington case, the prosecution proposes the following alternative jury instructions:

A. "If you find that the victim was gay and that the defendant made anti-gay statements in the past, you must find that he selected his victim because of his actual or perceived sexual orientation, unless the defendant persuades you by a preponderance of the evidence that he did not select his victim for that reason."

B. "If you find that the victim was gay and that the defendant made anti-gay statements in the past, you must find that he selected his victim because of his actual or perceived sexual orientation, unless the defendant produces some evidence to suggest that he did not select his victim for that reason."

C. "If you find that the victim was gay and that the defendant made anti-gay statements in the past, you may, if you choose, infer that he selected his victim because of his actual or perceived sexual orientation."

Which, if any, of the proposed jury instructions in the Washington case are constitutionally valid? Is the Oregon statute constitutional?

Patterson v. New York
432 U.S. 197 (1977)

Mr. Justice WHITE delivered the opinion of the Court.

The question here is the constitutionality under the Fourteenth Amendment's Due Process Clause of burdening the defendant in a New York State murder trial with proving the affirmative defense of extreme emotional disturbance as defined by New York law.

I

After a brief and unstable marriage, the appellant, Gordon Patterson, Jr., became estranged from his wife, Roberta. Roberta resumed an association with John Northrup, a neighbor to whom she had been engaged prior to her marriage to appellant. On December 27, 1970, Patterson borrowed a rifle from an acquaintance and went to the residence of his father-in-law. There, he observed his wife through a window in a state of semiundress in the presence of John Northrup. He entered the house and killed Northrup by shooting him twice in the head.

Patterson was charged with second-degree murder. In New York there are two elements of this crime: (1) "intent to cause the death of another person"; and (2) "caus[ing] the death of such person or of a third person." N.Y.Penal Law § 125.25 (McKinney 1975). Malice aforethought is not an element of the crime. In addition, the State permits a person accused of murder to raise an affirmative defense that he "acted under the influence of extreme emotional disturbance for which there was a reasonable explanation or excuse."

New York also recognizes the crime of manslaughter. A person is guilty of manslaughter if he intentionally kills another person "under circumstances which do not constitute murder because he acts under the influence of extreme emotional disturbance." Appellant confessed before trial to killing Northrup, but at trial he raised the defense of extreme emotional disturbance.

The jury was instructed as to the elements of the crime of murder....

The jury was further instructed, consistently with New York law, that the defendant had the burden of proving his affirmative defense by a preponderance of the evidence. The jury was told that if it found beyond a reasonable doubt that appellant had intentionally killed Northrup but that appellant had demonstrated by a preponderance of the evidence that he had acted under the influence of extreme emotional disturbance, it had to find appellant guilty of manslaughter instead of murder.

The jury found appellant guilty of murder. Judgment was entered on the verdict, and the Appellate Division affirmed. While appeal to the New York Court of Appeals was pending, this Court decided *Mullaney v. Wilbur*, 421 U.S. 684 (1975), in which the Court declared Maine's murder statute unconstitutional. Under the Maine statute, a person accused of murder could rebut the statutory presumption that he committed the offense with "malice aforethought" by proving that he acted in the heat of passion on sudden provocation. The Court held that this scheme improperly shifted the burden of persuasion from the prosecutor to the defendant and was therefore a violation of due process. In the Court of Appeals appellant urged that New York's murder statute is functionally equivalent to the one struck down in *Mullaney* and that therefore his conviction should be reversed.

The Court of Appeals rejected appellant's argument.... We affirm.

II

....

[I]t is normally "within the power of the State to regulate procedures under which its laws are carried out, including the burden of producing evidence and the burden of persuasion," and its decision in this regard is not subject to proscription under the Due Process Clause unless "it offends some principle of justice so rooted in the traditions and conscience of our people as to be ranked as fundamental."

In determining whether New York's allocation to the defendant of proving the mitigating circumstances of severe emotional disturbance is consistent with due process, it is therefore relevant to note that this defense is a considerably expanded version of the common-law defense of heat of passion on sudden provocation and that at common law the burden of proving the latter, as well as other affirmative defenses—indeed, "all ... circumstances of justification, excuse or alleviation"—rested on the defendant. 4 W. Blackstone, Commentaries. This was the rule when the Fifth Amendment was adopted, and it was the American rule when the Fourteenth Amendment was ratified.

In 1895 the common-law view was abandoned with respect to the insanity defense in federal prosecutions. *Davis v. United States*, 160 U.S. 469 (1895). This ruling had wide impact on the practice in the federal courts with respect to the burden of proving various affirmative defenses, and the prosecution in a majority of jurisdictions in this country sooner or later came to shoulder the burden of proving the sanity of the accused and of disproving the facts constituting other affirmative defenses, including provocation. *Davis* was not a constitutional ruling, however, as *Leland v. Oregon* made clear.

At issue in *Leland v. Oregon* was the constitutionality under the Due Process Clause of the Oregon rule that the defense of insanity must be proved by the defendant beyond a reasonable doubt. Noting that *Davis* "obviously establish[ed] no constitutional doctrine," 343 U.S., at 797, the Court refused to strike down the Oregon scheme, saying that the burden of proving all elements of the crime beyond reasonable doubt, including the elements of premeditation and deliberation, was placed on the State under Oregon procedures and remained there throughout the trial. To convict, the jury was required to find each element of the crime beyond a reasonable doubt, based on all the evidence, including the evidence going to the issue of insanity. Only then was the jury "to consider separately the issue of legal sanity *per se*...." *Id.*, at 795. This practice did not offend the Due Process Clause even though among the 20 States then placing the burden of proving his insanity on the defendant, Oregon was alone in requiring him to convince the jury beyond a reasonable doubt.

In 1970, the Court declared that the Due Process Clause "protects the accused against conviction except upon proof beyond a reasonable doubt of every fact necessary to constitute the crime with which he is charged." *In re Winship*, 397 U.S. 358, 364 (1970). Five years later, in *Mullaney v. Wilbur*, 421 U.S. 684 (1975), the Court further announced that under the Maine law of homicide, the burden could not constitutionally be placed on the defendant of proving by a preponderance of the evidence that the killing had occurred in the heat of passion on sudden provocation. THE CHIEF JUSTICE and Mr. Justice REHNQUIST, concurring, expressed their understanding that the *Mullaney* decision did not call into question the ruling in *Leland v. Oregon* with respect to the proof of insanity....

III

We cannot conclude that Patterson's conviction under the New York law deprived him of due process of law. The crime of murder is defined by the statute, which represents a recent revision of the state criminal code, as causing the death of another person with intent to do so. The death, the intent to kill, and causation are the facts that the State is required to prove beyond a reasonable doubt if a person is to be convicted of murder. No further facts are either presumed or inferred in order to constitute the crime. The statute does provide an affirmative defense—that the defendant acted under the influence of extreme emotional disturbance for which there was a reasonable explanation—which, if proved by a preponderance of the evidence, would reduce the crime to manslaughter, an offense defined in a separate section of the statute. It is plain enough that if the intentional killing is shown, the State intends to deal with the defendant as a murderer unless he demonstrates the mitigating circumstances.

Here, the jury was instructed in accordance with the statute, and the guilty verdict confirms that the State successfully carried its burden of proving the facts of the crime beyond a reasonable doubt. Nothing in the evidence, including any evidence that might have been offered with respect to Patterson's mental state at the time of the crime, raised a reasonable doubt about his guilt as a murderer; and clearly the evidence failed to convince the jury that Patterson's affirmative defense had been made out. It seems to us that the State satisfied the mandate of *Winship* that it prove beyond a reasonable doubt "every fact necessary to constitute the crime with which [Patterson was] charged." 397 U.S., at 364.

In convicting Patterson under its murder statute, New York did no more than *Leland* ... permitted it to do without violating the Due Process Clause. Under [*Leland*], once the facts constituting a crime are established beyond a reasonable doubt, based on all the evidence including the evidence of the defendant's mental state, the State may refuse to sustain the affirmative defense of insanity unless demonstrated by a preponderance of the evidence.

The New York law on extreme emotional disturbance follows this pattern. This affirmative defense, which the Court of Appeals described as permitting "the defendant to show that his actions were caused by a mental infirmity not arising to the level of insanity, and that he is less culpable for having committed them," does not serve to negative any facts of the crime which the State is to prove in order to convict of murder. It constitutes a separate issue on which the defendant is required to carry the burden of persuasion; and unless we are to overturn *Leland* ... New York has not violated the Due Process Clause, and Patterson's conviction must be sustained....

Here, in revising its criminal code, New York provided the affirmative defense of extreme emotional disturbance, a substantially expanded version of the older heat-of-passion concept; but it was willing to do so only if the facts making out the defense were established by the defendant with sufficient certainty. The State was itself unwilling to undertake to establish the absence of those facts beyond a reasonable doubt, perhaps fearing that proof would be too difficult and that too many persons deserving treatment as murderers would escape that punishment if the evidence need merely raise a reasonable doubt about the defendant's emotional state. It has been said that the new criminal code of New York contains some 25 affirmative defenses which exculpate or mitigate but which must be established by the defendant to be operative. The Due Process Clause, as we see it, does not put New York to the choice of abandoning those defenses or undertaking to disprove their existence in order to convict of a crime which otherwise is within its constitutional powers to sanction by substantial punishment....

We thus decline to adopt as a constitutional imperative, operative countrywide, that a State must disprove beyond a reasonable doubt every fact constituting any and all affirmative defenses related to the culpability of an accused. Traditionally, due process has required that only the most basic procedural safeguards be observed; more subtle balancing of society's interests against those of the accused have been left to the legislative branch. We therefore will not disturb the balance struck in previous cases holding that the Due Process Clause requires the prosecution to prove beyond a reasonable doubt all of the elements included in the definition of the offense of which the defendant is charged. Proof of the nonexistence of all affirmative defenses has never been constitutionally required; and we perceive no reason to fashion such a rule in this case and apply it to the statutory defense at issue here.

This view may seem to permit state legislatures to reallocate burdens of proof by labeling as affirmative defenses at least some elements of the crimes now defined in their statutes. But there are obviously constitutional limits beyond which the States may not go in this regard. "[I]t is not within the province of a legislature to declare an individual guilty or presumptively guilty of a crime." *McFarland v. American Sugar Rfg. Co.*, 241 U.S. 79, 86 (1916). The legislature cannot "validly command that the finding of an indictment, or mere proof of the identity of the accused, should create a presumption of the existence of all the facts essential to guilt." *Tot v. United States*, 319 U.S. 463, 469.

Long before *Winship*, the universal rule in this country was that the prosecution must prove guilt beyond a reasonable doubt. At the same time, the long-accepted rule was that it was constitutionally permissible to provide that various affirmative defenses were to be proved by the defendant. This did not lead to such abuses or to such widespread redefinition of crime and reduction of the prosecution's burden that a new constitutional rule was required.[12] This was not the problem to which *Winship* was addressed....

IV

It is urged that *Mullaney v. Wilbur* necessarily invalidates Patterson's conviction. In *Mullaney* the charge was murder, which the Maine statute defined as the unlawful killing of a human being "with malice aforethought, either express or implied." The trial court instructed the jury that the words "malice aforethought" were most important because "malice aforethought is an essential and indispensable element of the crime of murder." Malice, as the statute indicated and as the court instructed, could be implied and was to be implied from "any deliberate, cruel act committed by one person against another suddenly ... or without a considerable provocation," in which event an intentional killing was murder unless by a preponderance of the evidence it was shown that the act was committed "in the heat of passion, on sudden provocation." The instructions emphasized that "'malice aforethought and heat of passion on sudden provocation are two inconsistent things'; thus, by proving the latter the defendant would negate the former." 421 U.S., at 686–687.

Wilbur's conviction, which followed, was affirmed. The Maine Supreme Judicial Court held that murder and manslaughter were varying degrees of the crime of felonious homicide and that the presumption of malice arising from the unlawful killing was a mere policy presumption operating to cast on the defendant the burden of proving provocation if he was to be found guilty of manslaughter rather than murder—a burden which the Maine law had allocated to him at least since the mid-1800's.

---

12. Whenever due process guarantees are dependent upon the law as defined by the legislative branches, some consideration must be given to the possibility that legislative discretion may be abused to the detriment of the individual. See *Mullaney v. Wilbur*, 421 U.S., at 698–699. The applicability of the reasonable-doubt standard, however, has always been dependent on how a State defines the offense that is charged in any given case; yet there has been no great rush by the States to shift the burden of disproving traditional elements of the criminal offenses to the accused.

The Court of Appeals for the First Circuit then ordered that a writ of habeas corpus issue, holding that the presumption unconstitutionally shifted to the defendant the burden of proof with respect to an essential element of the crime....

This Court ... unanimously agreed with the Court of Appeals that Wilbur's due process rights had been invaded by the presumption casting upon him the burden of proving by a preponderance of the evidence that he had acted in the heat of passion upon sudden provocation.

Mullaney's holding, it is argued, is that the State may not permit the blameworthiness of an act or the severity of punishment authorized for its commission to depend on the presence or absence of an identified fact without assuming the burden of proving the presence or absence of that fact, as the case may be, beyond a reasonable doubt.[15] In our view, the *Mullaney* holding should not be so broadly read....

Mullaney surely held that a State must prove every ingredient of an offense beyond a reasonable doubt, and that it may not shift the burden of proof to the defendant by presuming that ingredient upon proof of the other elements of the offense. This is true even though the State's practice, as in Maine, had been traditionally to the contrary. Such shifting of the burden of persuasion with respect to a fact which the State deems so important that it must be either proved or presumed is impermissible under the Due Process Clause....

As we have explained, nothing was presumed or implied against Patterson; and his conviction is not invalid under any of our prior cases....

Mr. Justice Powell, with whom Mr. Justice Brennan and Mr. Justice Marshall join, dissenting....

Mullaney held invalid Maine's requirement that the defendant prove heat of passion. The Court today, without disavowing the unanimous holding of *Mullaney*, approves New York's requirement that the defendant prove extreme emotional disturbance. The Court manages to run a constitutional boundary line through the barely visible space that separates Maine's law from New York's. It does so on the basis of distinctions in language that are formalistic rather than substantive.

This result is achieved by a narrowly literal parsing of the holding in *Winship*: "[T]he Due Process Clause protects the accused against conviction except upon proof beyond a reasonable doubt of every fact necessary to constitute the crime with which he is charged." The only "facts" necessary to constitute a crime are said to be those that appear on the face of the statute as a part of the definition of the crime. Maine's statute was invalid, the Court reasons, because it "defined [murder] as the unlawful killing of a human being 'with malice aforethought, either express or implied.'" "(M)alice," the Court reiterates, "in the sense of the absence of provocation, was part of the definition of that crime."

---

15. There is some language in *Mullaney* that has been understood as perhaps construing the Due Process Clause to require the prosecution to prove beyond a reasonable doubt any fact affecting "the degree of criminal culpability." It is said that such a rule would deprive legislatures of any discretion whatsoever in allocating the burden of proof, the practical effect of which might be to undermine legislative reform of our criminal justice system. Carried to its logical extreme, such a reading of *Mullaney* might also, for example, discourage Congress from enacting pending legislation to change the felony-murder rule by permitting the accused to prove by a preponderance of the evidence the affirmative defense that the homicide committed was neither a necessary nor a reasonably foreseeable consequence of the underlying felony. The Court did not intend *Mullaney* to have such far-reaching effect.

Winship was violated only because this "fact" — malice — was "presumed" unless the defendant persuaded the jury otherwise by showing that he acted in the heat of passion. New York, in form presuming no affirmative "fact" against Patterson, and blessed with a statute drafted in the leaner language of the 20th century, escapes constitutional scrutiny unscathed even though the effect on the defendant of New York's placement of the burden of persuasion is exactly the same as Maine's.

This explanation of the *Mullaney* holding bears little resemblance to the basic rationale of that decision.[6] But this is not the cause of greatest concern. The test the Court today establishes allows a legislature to shift, virtually at will, the burden of persuasion with respect to any factor in a criminal case, so long as it is careful not to mention the nonexistence of that factor in the statutory language that defines the crime. The sole requirement is that any references to the factor be confined to those sections that provide for an affirmative defense.[7]

. . . .

With all respect, this type of constitutional adjudication is indefensibly formalistic. A limited but significant check on possible abuses in the criminal law now becomes an exercise in arid formalities. What *Winship* and *Mullaney* had sought to teach about the limits a free society places on its procedures to safeguard the liberty of its citizens becomes a rather simplistic lesson in statutory draftsmanship. Nothing in the Court's opinion prevents a legislature from applying this new learning to many of the classical elements of the crimes it punishes.[8] . . . .

The Court understandably manifests some uneasiness that its formalistic approach will give legislatures too much latitude in shifting the burden of persuasion. And so it issues a warning that "there are obviously constitutional limits beyond which the States may not go in this regard." The Court thereby concedes that legislative abuses may occur and that they must be curbed by the judicial branch. But if the State is careful to conform to the drafting formulas articulated today, the constitutional limits are anything but "obvious." This decision simply leaves us without a conceptual framework for distinguishing

---

6. In *Mullaney* we made it clear that *Winship* is not "limited to a State's definition of the elements of a crime." 421 U.S., at 699 n.24.

7. Although the Court never says so explicitly, its new standards appear to be designed for application to the language of a criminal statute on its face, regardless of how the state court construes the statute. The Court, in explaining *Mullaney*, persistently states that in Maine malice "was part of the definition of that crime [murder]," even though the Maine Supreme Judicial Court, construing its own statute, had ruled squarely to the contrary.... The result, under the Court's holding, is that only the legislature can remedy any defects that come to light as a result of the Court's decision. No matter how clear the legislative intent that defendants bear the burden of persuasion on an issue — an ultimate result the Court approves — state courts may not effectuate that intent until the right verbal formula appears in the statute book.

8. For example, a state statute could pass muster under the only solid standard that appears in the Court's opinion if it defined murder as mere physical contact between the defendant and the victim leading to the victim's death, but then set up an affirmative defense leaving it to the defendant to prove that he acted without culpable *mens rea*. The State, in other words, could be relieved altogether of responsibility for proving *anything* regarding the defendant's state of mind, provided only that the fact of the statute meets the Court's drafting formulas.

To be sure, it is unlikely that legislatures will rewrite their criminal laws in this extreme form. The Court seems to think this likelihood of restraint is an added reason for limiting review largely to formalistic examination. But it is completely foreign to this Court's responsibility for constitutional adjudication to limit the scope of judicial review because of the expectation — however reasonable — that legislative bodies will exercise appropriate restraint.

abuses from legitimate legislative adjustments of the burden of persuasion in criminal cases.[9]

....

Careful attention to the *Mullaney* decision reveals the principles that should control in this and like cases.... In *Mullaney* we concluded that heat of passion was one of the "facts" described in *Winship*—that is, a factor as to which the prosecution must bear the burden of persuasion beyond a reasonable doubt. We reached that result only after making two careful inquiries. First, we noted that the presence or absence of heat of passion made a substantial difference in punishment of the offender and in the stigma associated with the conviction. Second, we reviewed the history, in England and this country, of the factor at issue. Central to the holding in *Mullaney* was our conclusion that heat of passion "has been, almost from the inception of the common law of homicide, the single most important factor in determining the degree of culpability attaching to an unlawful homicide."

Implicit in these two inquiries are the principles that should govern this case. The Due Process Clause requires that the prosecutor bear the burden of persuasion beyond a reasonable doubt only if the factor at issue makes a substantial difference in punishment and stigma. The requirement of course applies *a fortiori* if the factor makes the difference between guilt and innocence. But a substantial difference in punishment alone is not enough. It also must be shown that in the Anglo-American legal tradition the factor in question historically has held that level of importance. If either branch of the test is not met, then the legislature retains its traditional authority over matters of proof. But to permit a shift in the burden of persuasion when both branches of this test are satisfied would invite the undermining of the presumption of innocence....

The *Winship/Mullaney* test identifies those factors of such importance, historically, in determining punishment and stigma that the Constitution forbids shifting to the defendant the burden of persuasion when such a factor is at issue. *Winship* and *Mullaney* specify only the procedure that is required when a State elects to use such a factor as part of its substantive criminal law. They do not say that the State must elect to use it. For example, where a State has chosen to retain the traditional distinction between murder and manslaughter, as have New York and Maine, the burden of persuasion must remain on the prosecution with respect to the distinguishing factor, in view of its decisive historical importance. But nothing in *Mullaney* or *Winship* precludes a State from abolishing the distinction between murder and manslaughter and treating all unjustifiable homicide as murder.[13] In this significant respect, neither *Winship* nor *Mullaney* eliminates the substantive flexibility that should remain in legislative hands.

Moreover, it is unlikely that more than a few factors—although important ones—for which a shift in the burden of persuasion seriously would be considered will come within the *Mullaney* holding.... New ameliorative affirmative defenses, about which the Court

---

9. I have no doubt that the Court would find some way to strike down a formalistically correct statute as egregious as the one hypothesized in n.8, *supra*. But today's ruling suggests no principled basis for concluding that such a statute falls outside the "obvious" constitutional limits the Court invokes.

13. ... Even if there are no constitutional limits preventing the State, for example, from treating all homicides as murders punishable equally regardless of mitigating factors like heat of passion or extreme emotional disturbance, the *Winship/Mullaney* rule still plays an important role. The State is then obliged to make its choices concerning the substantive content of its criminal laws with full awareness of the consequences, unable to mask substantive policy choices by shifts in the burden of persuasion. The political check on potentially harsh legislative action is then more likely to operate.

expresses concern, generally remain undisturbed by the holdings in *Winship* and *Mullaney*—and need not be disturbed by a sound holding reversing Patterson's conviction....

County Court of Ulster v. Allen
442 U.S. 140 (1979)

Mr. Justice Stevens delivered the opinion of the Court.

A New York statute provides that, with certain exceptions, the presence of a firearm in an automobile is presumptive evidence of its illegal possession by all persons then occupying the vehicle....

Four persons, three adult males (respondents) and a 16-year-old girl (Jane Doe, who is not a respondent here), were jointly tried on charges that they possessed two loaded handguns, a loaded machinegun, and over a pound of heroin found in a Chevrolet in which they were riding when it was stopped for speeding on the New York Thruway shortly after noon on March 28, 1973. The two large-caliber handguns, which together with their ammunition weighed approximately six pounds, were seen through the window of the car by the investigating police officer. They were positioned crosswise in an open handbag on either the front floor or the front seat of the car on the passenger side where Jane Doe was sitting. Jane Doe admitted that the handbag was hers. The machine gun and the heroin were discovered in the trunk after the police pried it open. The car had been borrowed from the driver's brother earlier that day; the key to the trunk could not be found in the car or on the person of any of its occupants, although there was testimony that two of the occupants had placed something in the trunk before embarking in the borrowed car. The jury convicted all four of possession of the handguns and acquitted them of possession of the contents of the trunk.

Counsel for all four defendants objected to the introduction into evidence of the two handguns, the machinegun, and the drugs, arguing that the State had not adequately demonstrated a connection between their clients and the contraband. The trial court overruled the objection, relying on the presumption of possession created by the New York statute. Because that presumption does not apply if a weapon is found "upon the person" of one of the occupants of the car, the three male defendants also moved to dismiss the charges relating to the handguns on the ground that the guns were found on the person of Jane Doe. Respondents made this motion both at the close of the prosecution's case and at the close of all evidence. The trial judge twice denied it, concluding that the applicability of the "upon the person" exception was a question of fact for the jury.

At the close of the trial, the judge instructed the jurors that they were entitled to infer possession from the defendants' presence in the car. He did not make any reference to the "upon the person" exception in his explanation of the statutory presumption, nor did any of the defendants object to this omission or request alternative or additional instructions on the subject....

A party has standing to challenge the constitutionality of a statute only insofar as it has an adverse impact on his own rights. As a general rule, if there is no constitutional defect in the application of the statute to a litigant, he does not have standing to argue that it would be unconstitutional if applied to third parties in hypothetical situations. A limited exception has been recognized for statutes that broadly prohibit speech protected by the First Amendment.... That justification, of course, has no application to a statute that enhances the legal risks associated with riding in vehicles containing dangerous weapons.

In this case, the Court of Appeals undertook the task of deciding the constitutionality of the New York statute "on its face." Its conclusion that the statutory presumption was arbitrary rested entirely on its view of the fairness of applying the presumption in hypothetical situations — situations, indeed, in which it is improbable that a jury would return a conviction, or that a prosecution would ever be instituted. We must accordingly inquire whether these respondents had standing to advance the arguments that the Court of Appeals considered decisive. An analysis of our prior cases indicates that the answer to this inquiry depends on the type of presumption that is involved in the case.

Inferences and presumptions are a staple of our adversary system of factfinding. It is often necessary for the trier of fact to determine the existence of an element of the crime — that is, an "ultimate" or "elemental" fact — from the existence of one or more "evidentiary" or "basic" facts. The value of these evidentiary devices, and their validity under the Due Process Clause, vary from case to case, however, depending on the strength of the connection between the particular basic and elemental facts involved and on the degree to which the device curtails the factfinder's freedom to assess the evidence independently. Nonetheless, in criminal cases, the ultimate test of any device's constitutional validity in a given case remains constant: the device must not undermine the factfinder's responsibility at trial, based on evidence adduced by the State, to find the ultimate facts beyond a reasonable doubt.

The most common evidentiary device is the entirely permissive inference or presumption, which allows — but does not require — the trier of fact to infer the elemental fact from proof by the prosecutor of the basic one and which places no burden of any kind on the defendant. In that situation the basic fact may constitute prima facie evidence of the elemental fact. When reviewing this type of device, the Court has required the party challenging it to demonstrate its invalidity as applied to him. Because this permissive presumption leaves the trier of fact free to credit or reject the inference and does not shift the burden of proof, it affects the application of the "beyond a reasonable doubt" standard only if, under the facts of the case, there is no rational way the trier could make the connection permitted by the inference. For only in that situation is there any risk that an explanation of the permissible inference to a jury, or its use by a jury, has caused the presumptively rational factfinder to make an erroneous factual determination.

A mandatory presumption is a far more troublesome evidentiary device. For it may affect not only the strength of the "no reasonable doubt" burden but also the placement of that burden; it tells the trier that he or they *must* find the elemental fact upon proof of the basic fact, at least unless the defendant has come forward with some evidence to rebut the presumed connection between the two facts.[16] In this situation, the Court has gener-

---

16. This class of more or less mandatory presumptions can be subdivided into two parts: presumptions that merely shift the burden of production to the defendant, following the satisfaction of which the ultimate burden of persuasion returns to the prosecution; and presumptions that entirely shift the burden of proof to the defendant. The mandatory presumptions examined by our cases have almost uniformly fit into the former subclass, in that they never totally removed the ultimate burden of proof beyond a reasonable doubt from the prosecution.

To the extent that a presumption imposes an extremely low burden of production — e. g., being satisfied by "any" evidence — it may well be that its impact is no greater than that of a permissive inference, and it may be proper to analyze it as such.

In deciding what type of inference or presumption is involved in a case, the jury instructions will generally be controlling, although their interpretation may require recourse to the statute involved and the cases decided under it. . . .

The importance of focusing attention on the precise presentation of the presumption to the jury and the scope of that presumption is illustrated by a comparison of *United States v. Gainey*, 380 U.S. 63, with *United States v. Romano*. Both cases involved statutory presumptions based on proof that

ally examined the presumption on its face to determine the extent to which the basic and elemental facts coincide. To the extent that the trier of fact is forced to abide by the presumption, and may not reject it based on an independent evaluation of the particular facts presented by the State, the analysis of the presumption's constitutional validity is logically divorced from those facts and based on the presumption's accuracy in the run of cases. It is for this reason that the Court has held it irrelevant in analyzing a mandatory presumption, but not in analyzing a purely permissive one, that there is ample evidence in the record other than the presumption to support a conviction.

Without determining whether the presumption in this case was mandatory, the Court of Appeals analyzed it on its face as if it were. In fact, it was not, as the New York Court of Appeals had earlier pointed out.

The trial judge's instructions make it clear that the presumption was merely a part of the prosecution's case, that it gave rise to a permissive inference available only in certain circumstances, rather than a mandatory conclusion of possession, and that it could be ignored by the jury even if there was no affirmative proof offered by defendants in rebuttal. The judge explained that possession could be actual or constructive, but that constructive possession could not exist without the intent and ability to exercise control or dominion over the weapons. He also carefully instructed the jury that there is a mandatory presumption of innocence in favor of the defendants that controls unless it, as the exclusive trier of fact, is satisfied beyond a reasonable doubt that the defendants possessed the handguns in the manner described by the judge. In short, the instructions plainly directed the jury to consider all the circumstances tending to support or contradict the inference that all four occupants of the car had possession of the two loaded handguns and to decide the matter for itself without regard to how much evidence the defendants introduced.

Our cases considering the validity of permissive statutory presumptions such as the one involved here have rested on an evaluation of the presumption as applied to the record before the Court. None suggests that a court should pass on the constitutionality of this kind of statute "on its face." ....

As applied to the facts of this case, the presumption of possession is entirely rational.... The argument against possession by any of the respondents was predicated solely on the fact that the guns were in Jane Doe's pocketbook. But several circumstances— which, not surprisingly, her counsel repeatedly emphasized in his questions and his argument—made it highly improbable that she was the sole custodian of those weapons.

Even if it was reasonable to conclude that she had placed the guns in her purse before the car was stopped by police, the facts strongly suggest that Jane Doe was not the only person able to exercise dominion over them. The two guns were too large to be concealed in her handbag. The bag was consequently open, and part of one of the guns was in plain

---

the defendant was present at the site of an illegal still....

In *Gainey*, the judge had explained that the presumption was permissive; it did not require the jury to convict the defendant even if it was convinced that he was present at the site.... As we emphasized, the "jury was thus specifically told that the statutory inference was not conclusive." In *Romano*, the trial judge told the jury that the defendant's presence at the still " 'shall be deemed sufficient evidence to authorize conviction.' " Although there was other evidence of guilt, that instruction authorized conviction even if the jury disbelieved all of the testimony except the proof of presence at the site. This Court's holding that the statutory presumption could not support the Romano conviction was thus dependent, in part, on the specific instructions given by the trial judge. Under those instructions it was necessary to decide whether, regardless of the specific circumstances of the particular case, the statutory presumption adequately supported the guilty verdict.

view, within easy access of the driver of the car and even, perhaps, of the other two re-spondents who were riding in the rear seat.

Moreover, it is highly improbable that the loaded guns belonged to Jane Doe or that she was solely responsible for their being in her purse. As a 16-year-old girl in the com-pany of three adult men she was the least likely of the four to be carrying one, let alone two, heavy handguns. It is far more probable that she relied on the pocketknife found in her brassiere for any necessary self-protection. Under these circumstances, it was not unreasonable for her counsel to argue and for the jury to infer that when the car was halted for speeding, the other passengers in the car anticipated the risk of a search and attempted to conceal their weapons in a pocketbook in the front seat. The inference is surely more likely than the notion that these weapons were the sole property of the 16-year-old girl.

Under these circumstances, the jury would have been entirely reasonable in reject-ing the suggestion—which, incidentally, defense counsel did not even advance in their closing arguments to the jury—that the handguns were in the sole possession of Jane Doe. Assuming that the jury did reject it, the case is tantamount to one in which the guns were lying on the floor or the seat of the car in the plain view of the three other occupants of the automobile. In such a case, it is surely rational to infer that each of the respondents was fully aware of the presence of the guns and had both the ability and the intent to exercise dominion and control over the weapons. The application of the statutory presumption in this case therefore comports with the standard laid down in *Tot v. United States*, 319 U.S., at 467, and restated in *Leary v. United States*, 395 U.S., at 36. For there is a "rational connection" between the basic facts that the prosecution proved and the ultimate fact presumed, and the latter is "more likely than not to flow from" the former.

Respondents argue, however, that the validity of the New York presumption must be judged by a "reasonable doubt" test rather than the "more likely than not" standard em-ployed in *Leary*. Under the more stringent test, it is argued that a statutory presumption must be rejected unless the evidence necessary to invoke the inference is sufficient for a rational jury to find the inferred fact beyond a reasonable doubt. Respondents' argument again overlooks the distinction between a permissive presumption on which the prose-cution is entitled to rely as one not necessarily sufficient part of its proof and a manda-tory presumption which the jury must accept even if it is the sole evidence of an element of the offense.

In the latter situation, since the prosecution bears the burden of establishing guilt, it may not rest its case entirely on a presumption unless the fact proved is sufficient to sup-port the inference of guilt beyond a reasonable doubt. But in the former situation, the pros-ecution may rely on all of the evidence in the record to meet the reasonable-doubt standard. There is no more reason to require a permissive statutory presumption to meet a rea-sonable-doubt standard before it may be permitted to play any part in a trial than there is to require that degree of probative force for other relevant evidence before it may be ad-mitted. As long as it is clear that the presumption is not the sole and sufficient basis for a finding of guilt, it need only satisfy the test described in *Leary*.

The permissive presumption, as used in this case, satisfied the *Leary* test. And, as al-ready noted, the New York Court of Appeals has concluded that the record as a whole was sufficient to establish guilt beyond a reasonable doubt....

[The concurring opinion of Chief Justice Burger and the dissenting opinion of Justice Powell are omitted.]

Sandstrom v. Montana

442 U.S. 510 (1979)

Mr. Justice BRENNAN delivered the opinion of the Court....

I

On November 22, 1976, 18-year-old David Sandstrom confessed to the slaying of Annie Jessen. Based upon the confession and corroborating evidence, petitioner was charged on December 2 with "deliberate homicide," Mont. Code Ann. §45-5-102 (1978), in that he "purposely or knowingly caused the death of Annie Jessen." At trial, Sandstrom's attorney informed the jury that, although his client admitted killing Jessen, he did not do so "purposely or knowingly," and was therefore not guilty of "deliberate homicide" but of a lesser crime....

The prosecution requested the trial judge to instruct the jury that "[t]he law presumes that a person intends the ordinary consequences of his voluntary acts." Petitioner's counsel objected, arguing that "the instruction has the effect of shifting the burden of proof on the issue of" purpose or knowledge to the defense, and that "that is impermissible under the Federal Constitution, due process of law." He offered to provide a number of federal decisions in support of the objection, including this Court's holding in *Mullaney v. Wilbur*, 421 U.S. 684 (1975), but was told by the judge: "You can give those to the Supreme Court. The objection is overruled." The instruction was delivered, the jury found petitioner guilty of deliberate homicide, and petitioner was sentenced to 100 years in prison.

Sandstrom appealed to the Supreme Court of Montana, again contending that the instruction shifted to the defendant the burden of disproving an element of the crime charged, in violation of *Mullaney v. Wilbur, supra, In re Winship*, 397 U.S. 358 (1970), and *Patterson v. New York*, 432 U.S. 197 (1977). The Montana court conceded that these cases did prohibit shifting the burden of proof to the defendant by means of a presumption, but held that the cases "do not prohibit allocation of *some* burden of proof to a defendant under certain circumstances." Since in the court's view, "[d]efendant's sole burden under instruction No. 5 was to produce *some* evidence that he did not intend the ordinary consequences of his voluntary acts, not to disprove that he acted 'purposely' or 'knowingly,' ... the instruction does not violate due process standards as defined by the United States or Montana Constitution...."

....

II

The threshold inquiry in ascertaining the constitutional analysis applicable to this kind of jury instruction is to determine the nature of the presumption it describes. See *Ulster County Court v. Allen*, 442 U.S. 140, 157–163 (1979). That determination requires careful attention to the words actually spoken to the jury, see *ante*, at 157–159, n. 16, for whether a defendant has been accorded his constitutional rights depends upon the way in which a reasonable juror could have interpreted the instruction.

Respondent argues, first, that the instruction merely described a permissive inference—that is, it allowed but did not require the jury to draw conclusions about defendant's intent from his actions—and that such inferences are constitutional. These arguments need not detain us long, for even respondent admits that "it's possible" that the jury believed they were required to apply the presumption. Sandstrom's jurors were told that "[t]he law presumes that a person intends the ordinary consequences of his voluntary acts." They were not told that they had a choice, or that they might infer that conclusion; they were told only that the law presumed it. It is clear that a reasonable juror could easily have viewed such an instruction as mandatory.

In the alternative, respondent urges that, even if viewed as a mandatory presumption rather than as a permissive inference, the presumption did not conclusively establish intent but rather could be rebutted. On this view, the instruction required the jury, if satisfied as to the facts which trigger the presumption, to find intent *unless* the defendant offered evidence to the contrary. Moreover, according to the State, all the defendant had to do to rebut the presumption was produce "some" contrary evidence; he did not have to "prove" that he lacked the required mental state. Thus, "[a]t most, it placed a *burden of production* on the petitioner," but "did not shift to petitioner the *burden of persuasion* with respect to any element of the offense...." Again, respondent contends that presumptions with this limited effect pass constitutional muster.

We need not review respondent's constitutional argument on this point either, however, for we reject this characterization of the presumption as well. Respondent concedes there is a "risk" that the jury, once having found petitioner's act voluntary, would interpret the instruction as automatically directing a finding of intent. Moreover, the State also concedes that numerous courts "have differed as to the effect of the presumption when given as a jury instruction without further explanation as to its use by the jury," and that some have found it to shift more than the burden of production, and even to have conclusive effect. Nonetheless, the State contends that the only authoritative reading of the effect of the presumption resides in the Supreme Court of Montana. And the State argues that by holding that "[d]efendant's sole burden under instruction No. 5 was to produce *some* evidence that he did not intend the ordinary consequences of his voluntary acts, not to disprove that he acted 'purposely' or 'knowingly,'" the Montana Supreme Court decisively established that the presumption at most affected only the burden of going forward with evidence of intent—that is, the burden of production.[5]

The Supreme Court of Montana is, of course, the final authority on the legal weight to be given a presumption under Montana law, but it is not the final authority on the interpretation which a jury could have given the instruction. If Montana intended its presumption to have only the effect described by its Supreme Court, then we are convinced that a reasonable juror could well have been misled by the instruction given, and could have believed that the presumption was not limited to requiring the defendant to satisfy only a burden of production. Petitioner's jury was told that "[t]*he law presumes* that a person intends the ordinary consequences of his voluntary acts." They were not told that the presumption could be rebutted, as the Montana Supreme Court held, by the defendant's simple presentation of "some" evidence; nor even that it could be rebutted at all. Given the common definition of "presume" as "to suppose to be true without proof," Webster's New Collegiate Dictionary 911 (1974), and given the lack of qualifying in-

---

5. For purposes of argument, we accept respondent's definition of the production burden when applied to a defendant in a criminal case. We note, however, that the burden is often described quite differently when it rests upon the prosecution. See *United States v. Vuitch*, 402 U.S. 62, 72 n. 7 (1971) ("evidence from which a jury could find a defendant guilty beyond a reasonable doubt"). We also note that the effect of a failure to meet the production burden is significantly different for the defendant and prosecution. When the prosecution fails to meet it, a directed verdict in favor of the defense results. Such a consequence is not possible upon a defendant's failure, however, as verdicts may not be directed against defendants in criminal cases. *United States v. Martin Linen Supply Co.*, 430 U.S. 564, 572–573 (1977); *Carpenters v. United States*, 330 U.S. 395, 408 (1947).

structions as to the legal effect of the presumption, we cannot discount the possibility that the jury may have interpreted the instruction in either of two more stringent ways.

First, a reasonable jury could well have interpreted the presumption as "conclusive," that is, not technically as a presumption at all, but rather as an irrebuttable direction by the court to find intent once convinced of the facts triggering the presumption. Alternatively, the jury may have interpreted the instruction as a direction to find intent upon proof of the defendant's voluntary actions (and their "ordinary" consequences), unless *the defendant* proved the contrary by some quantum of proof which may well have been considerably greater than "some" evidence — thus effectively shifting the burden of persuasion on the element of intent....[7]

We do not reject the possibility that some jurors may have interpreted the challenged instruction as permissive, or, if mandatory, as requiring only that the defendant come forward with "some" evidence in rebuttal. However, the fact that a reasonable juror could have given the presumption conclusive or persuasion-shifting effect means that we cannot discount the possibility that Sandstrom's jurors actually did proceed upon one or the other of these latter interpretations. And that means that unless these kinds of presumptions are constitutional, the instruction cannot be adjudged valid.[8] It is the line of cases urged by petitioner, and exemplified by *In re Winship*, 397 U.S. 358 (1970), that provides the appropriate mode of constitutional analysis for these kinds of presumptions.

III

. . . .

The petitioner here was charged with and convicted of deliberate homicide, committed purposely or knowingly, under Mont.Code Ann. §45-5-102(a) (1978). It is clear that under Montana law, whether the crime was committed purposely or knowingly is a fact necessary to constitute the crime of deliberate homicide. Indeed, it was the lone element of the offense at issue in Sandstrom's trial, as he confessed to causing the death of the victim, told the jury that knowledge and purpose were the only questions he was controverting, and introduced evidence solely on those points. Moreover, it is conceded that proof of defendant's "intent" would be sufficient to establish this element. Thus, the question before this Court is whether the challenged jury instruction had the effect of relieving the State of the burden of proof enunciated in *Winship* on the critical question of petitioner's state of mind. We conclude that under either of the two possible interpretations of the instruction set out above, precisely that effect would result, and that the instruction therefore represents constitutional error.

We consider first the validity of a conclusive presumption.... In *Morissette v. United States*, 342 U.S. 246 (1952), the defendant was charged with willful and knowing theft of

---

7. The potential for these interpretations of the presumption was not removed by the other instructions given at the trial. It is true that the jury was instructed generally that the accused was presumed innocent until proved guilty, and that the State had the burden of proving beyond a reasonable doubt, that the defendant caused the death of the deceased purposely or knowingly. But this is not rhetorically inconsistent with a conclusive or burden-shifting presumption. The jury could have interpreted the two sets of instructions as indicating that the presumption was a means by which proof beyond a reasonable doubt as to intent could be satisfied. For example, if the presumption were viewed as conclusive, the jury could have believed that, although intent must be proved beyond a reasonable doubt, proof of the voluntary slaying and its ordinary consequences constituted proof of intent beyond a reasonable doubt.

8. Given our ultimate result in this case, we do not need to consider what kind of constitutional analysis would be appropriate for other kinds of presumptions.

Government property. Although his attorney argued that for his client to be found guilty, "'the taking must have been with felonious intent,'" the trial judge ruled that "'[t]hat is presumed by his own act.'" After first concluding that intent was in fact an element of the crime charged, and after declaring that "[w]here intent of the accused is an ingredient of the crime charged, its existence is ... a jury issue," *Morissette* held:....

> *A conclusive presumption which testimony could not overthrow would effectively eliminate intent as an ingredient of the offense.... [T]his presumption would conflict with the overriding presumption of innocence with which the law endows the accused and which extends to every element of the crime. Id., at 274–275 (emphasis added.)*

....

[A] conclusive presumption in this case would "conflict with the overriding presumption of innocence with which the law endows the accused and which extends to every element of the crime," and would "invade [the] factfinding function" which in a criminal case the law assigns solely to the jury. The instruction announced to David Sandstrom's jury may well have had exactly these consequences. Upon finding proof of one element of the crime (causing death), and of facts insufficient to establish the second (the voluntariness and "ordinary consequences" of defendant's action), Sandstrom's jurors could reasonably have concluded that they were directed to find against defendant on the element of intent. The State was thus not forced to prove "beyond a reasonable doubt ... every fact necessary to constitute the crime ... charged," 397 U.S., at 364, and defendant was deprived of his constitutional rights as explicated in *Winship*.

A presumption which, although not conclusive, had the effect of shifting the burden of persuasion to the defendant, would have suffered from similar infirmities. If Sandstrom's jury interpreted the presumption in that manner, it could have concluded that upon proof by the State of the slaying, and of additional facts not themselves establishing the element of intent, the burden was shifted to the defendant to prove that he lacked the requisite mental state. Such a presumption was found constitutionally deficient in *Mullaney v. Wilbur*, 421 U.S. 684 (1975).... As we recounted just two Terms ago in *Patterson v. New York*, "[t]his Court ... unanimously agreed with the Court of Appeals that Wilbur's due process rights had been invaded by the presumption casting upon him the burden of proving by a preponderance of the evidence that he had acted in the heat of passion upon sudden provocation." And *Patterson* reaffirmed that "a State must prove every ingredient of an offense beyond a reasonable doubt, and ... may not shift the burden of proof to the defendant" by means of such a presumption.

Because David Sandstrom's jury may have interpreted the judge's instruction as constituting either a burden-shifting presumption ... or a conclusive presumption ... and because either interpretation would have deprived defendant of his right to the due process of law, we hold the instruction given in this case unconstitutional....

[The concurring opinion of Justice Rehnquist is omitted.]

Notes and Questions

1. In criminal cases, the Due Process Clause requires that the prosecution bear the burden of persuasion with regard to every element of the offense, and that it prove each of those beyond a reasonable doubt. No such requirement, however, is imposed on criminal defendants who invoke affirmative defenses. Thus, policymakers are free to denominate a given factor as an affirmative defense, but to only require the defendant to bear

the burden of *production* with respect to that defense (after which the burden of persuasion shifts to the prosecution), or to require the defendant to persuade the trier of fact on that issue only by a preponderance of the evidence, or by some other showing that is less than beyond a reasonable doubt. Nonetheless, as *Patterson* indicates, cases such as *Leland* approve of criminal laws that place on a criminal defendant the burden of persuading the trier of fact beyond a reasonable doubt with respect to a particular affirmative defense.

2. Recall that in the civil context, policymakers are free to shift the burden of persuasion to a defendant with respect to a given factor either by denominating that factor as an affirmative defense, or by denominating it as an element of the plaintiff's case and creating a presumption that has the effect of shifting the burden of persuasion to the defendant with respect to a given element. Yet *Patterson* and *Mullaney* together hold that these two methods are not interchangeable in the criminal context. Couldn't an argument be made that the greater power to denominate something as an affirmative defense includes the lesser power to denominate it as an element of the offense but to make use of a burden-shifting presumption?

3. Notwithstanding the *Patterson* majority's efforts to distinguish *Mullaney*, the *Patterson* decision is at the very least inconsistent with some of the language in *Mullaney*:

> [I]f *Winship* were limited to those facts that constitute a crime as defined by state law, a State could undermine many of the interests that decision sought to protect without effecting any substantive change in its law. It would only be necessary to redefine the elements that constitute different crimes, characterizing them as factors that bear solely on the extent of punishment.... Maine could impose a life sentence for any felonious homicide—even one that traditionally might be considered involuntary manslaughter—unless the *defendant* was able to prove that his act was neither intentional nor criminally reckless.

Mullaney v. Wilbur, 421 U.S. 684, 698–99 (1975).

4. Does the *Patterson* majority place any limits on the ability of legislative bodies to remove factors as elements of an offense and denominate them as affirmative defenses? What would the majority say about the hypothetical that Justice Powell raises in footnote 8 of his dissent? Is part of the majority's theory that no legislative body would enact such an extreme measure? If that is their theory, do you see why, as Justice Powell notes in footnote 7 of his dissent, that the majority decision implies that it must be the statute itself and not a court's strained interpretation of a statute that makes the factor an affirmative defense? Doesn't Justice Powell's theory, which permits legislative bodies to eliminate mitigating factors, to some degree rely on the same theory as does the majority?

5. Do *Patterson* and *Mullaney* together mean nothing more than that legislative bodies can shift the burden of persuasion to criminal defendants only by means of an affirmative defense and not through the use of a presumption? The *Patterson* majority states that "there are obviously constitutional limits beyond which the States may not go in this regard," but is less than clear on what those limits are.

More recent Supreme Court decisions have, albeit in *dicta*, discussed *Patterson*. First, in *Jones v. United States*, 526 U.S. 227 (1999), a case involving the interpretation of the federal carjacking statute, the majority wrote:

> With one caveat, therefore, *Patterson* left the States free to choose the elements that define their crimes, without any impediment from *Winship*. The caveat was a stated recognition of some limit upon state authority to reallocate the traditional

burden of proof, which in that case was easily satisfied by the fact that "at common law the burden of proving" the mitigating circumstances of severe emotional disturbance "rested on the defendant." While a narrow reading of this limit might have been no more than a ban on using presumptions to reduce elements to the point of being nominal, a broader reading was equally open, that the State lacked the discretion to omit "traditional" elements from the definition of crimes and instead to require the accused to disprove such elements.

Id. at 241–42.

The Court again discussed *Patterson* in *Apprendi v. New Jersey*, 530 U.S. 466 (2000), a case involving the constitutionality of a state law giving judges the authority to enhance sentences based on a finding that the crime was a hate crime:

> While a State could, hypothetically, undertake to revise its entire criminal code in the manner the dissent suggests—extending all statutory maximum sentences to, for example, 50 years and giving judges guided discretion as to a few specially selected factors within that range—this possibility seems remote. Among other reasons, structural democratic constraints exist to discourage legislatures from enacting penal statutes that expose *every* defendant convicted of, for example, weapons possession, to a maximum sentence exceeding that which is, in the legislature's judgment, generally proportional to the crime. This is as it should be. Our rule ensures that a State is obliged "to make its choices concerning the substantive content of its criminal laws with full awareness of the consequences, unable to mask substantive policy choices" of exposing all who are convicted to the maximum sentence it provides. *Patterson v. New York*, 432 U.S., at 228–229, n. 13 (Powell, J., dissenting). So exposed, "[t]he political check on potentially harsh legislative action is then more likely to operate." *Ibid.*
>
> In all events, if such an extensive revision of the State's entire criminal code were enacted for the purpose the dissent suggests, or if New Jersey simply reversed the burden of the hate crime finding (effectively assuming a crime was performed with a purpose to intimidate and then requiring a defendant to prove that it was not), we would be required to question whether the revision was constitutional under this Court's prior decisions. *See Patterson*, 432 U.S., at 210; *Mullaney v. Wilbur*, 421 U.S. 684, 698–702 (1975).

Id. at 490–491 n.16.

6. Suppose that the elements of an offense and an affirmative defense overlap, in the sense that evidence that proves the latter also tends to some degree to negate the former. Under those circumstances, is it unconstitutional under the *Winship-Mullaney-Patterson* line of cases to assign to the defendant the burden of persuasion with respect to the affirmative defense, on the theory that this is tantamount to shifting to the defendant the burden of disproving an element of the offense? In *Martin v. Ohio*, 480 U.S. 228 (1987), the Supreme Court considered and rejected such a claim:

> We are thus not moved by assertions that the elements of aggravated murder and self-defense overlap in the sense that evidence to prove the latter will often tend to negate the former. It may be that most encounters in which self-defense is claimed arise suddenly and involve no prior plan or specific purpose to take life. In those cases, evidence offered to support the defense may negate a purposeful killing by prior calculation and design, but Ohio does not shift to the defendant the burden of disproving any element of the state's case. When the prosecution has made out a prima facie case and survives a motion to acquit, the jury may

> nevertheless not convict if the evidence offered by the defendant raises any reasonable doubt about the existence of any fact necessary for the finding of guilt. Evidence creating a reasonable doubt could easily fall far short of proving self-defense by a preponderance of the evidence. Of course, if such doubt is not raised in the jury's mind and each juror is convinced that the defendant purposely and with prior calculation and design took life, the killing will still be excused if the elements of the defense are satisfactorily established.

Id. at 234. In so holding, however, the Court did take pains to point out that "the jury was here instructed that to convict it must find, in light of all the evidence, that each of the elements of the crime of aggravated murder has been proved by the State beyond reasonable doubt, *and that the burden of proof with respect to these elements did not shift.*" *Id.* (emphasis added).

7. Together, the *Allen* and *Sandstrom* decisions clearly seem to hold that in criminal cases, inference instructions (referred to in *Allen* as a "permissive inference or presumption") are permissible; in other words, instructions to the jury that it *may*, but need not, find the presumed fact upon proof of the basic fact. This, of course, is subject to two requirements. First, the requirement of *Allen* that the presumed fact "more likely than not" follows from proof of the basic fact, and second, the requirement of *Sandstrom* that the instructions to the jury be sufficiently clear that jurors understand that they are free to ignore the invited inference.

8. Although *Sandstrom* makes clear that any presumption that shifts to a criminal defendant the burden of persuasion is impermissible under *Winship*, *Mullaney*, and *Patterson*, it, along with *Allen*, leaves open the door, does it not, to a presumption that only shifts the burden of *production*? Yet as the court points out in footnote 5, the effect of such a presumption would be limited by the fact that a verdict could not be directed against a defendant in a criminal case. What would such an instruction look like? If it was an instruction that the jury *may* infer a particular fact if the defendant fails to come forward with evidence on a particular point, that is really no different than an inference, right? And if the instruction is that the jury *must* infer a particular fact if the defendant fails to come forward with evidence on a particular point, doesn't it run into some of the same problems raised by a mandatory presumption that shifts the burden of persuasion? *Cf. McCandless v. Beyer*, 835 F.2d 58,60–62 (3d Cir. 1987) (upholding as constitutional in a prosecution for possessing a handgun without a permit, an instruction that the jury *may* infer from proof that defendant knowingly possessed a handgun, coupled with the defendant's failure to come forward with *any* evidence that he had a permit, that the defendant lacked a permit). *See also Boulware v. United States*, 552 U.S. 421, 438 n.14 (2008) ("we decline to consider the more general question whether the Second Circuit's rule in *Bok*, which places on the criminal defendant the burden to produce evidence in support of a return-of-capital theory, is … consistent with *Sandstrom* … and related cases"); *Francis v. Franklin*, 471 U.S. 307, 315 n.3 (1985) ("We are not required to decide in this case whether a mandatory presumption that shifts only a burden of production to the defendant is consistent with the Due Process Clause, and we express no opinion on that question."); *Davis v. Allsbrooks*, 778 F.2d 168, 172–74 (4th Cir. 1985) (holding that a presumption that shifts the burden of production to a criminal defendant is permissible). *But see People v. Watts*, 181 Ill. 2d 133, 147 (1998) ("mandatory rebuttable presumptions which shift the burden of production to the defendant are unconstitutional. A production-shifting presumption places a burden on the defendant to come forward with a certain quantum of evidence to overcome the presumption. If the defendant does not satisfy that burden, the judge is required, in effect, to direct a verdict against the defendant on the element

which is proved by the use of the presumption. This result conflicts with the longstanding rule that a verdict may not be constitutionally directed against a defendant in a criminal case.").

9. What does the *Allen* Court rely upon to determine that the inferred fact of possession by everyone within a vehicle more likely than not follows from proof of the basic fact that the weapon was present within the passenger compartment of the vehicle? Had the jury not acquitted the defendants of possession of the items in the trunk, the Court would have had to determine whether the inference of possession more likely than not followed from proof of the basic fact that certain items were in the trunk of the car. Would the presumption be constitutional as applied to those facts?

Chapter 10

Impeachment and Rehabilitation of Witnesses

A. Introduction

The lion's share of the evidence presented at trial is in the form of testimony by lay and expert witnesses. Such testimony can greatly advance the cause of one party at the expense of the other: a witness who testifies that she saw the accused stabbing the victim to death can have a much more persuasive effect on the jury than can physical evidence linking the accused to the scene of the crime.

But just as the value of documentary or physical evidence turns on a determination by the trier of fact that the evidence is authentic—in the words of Rule 901(a), "a finding that the item is what the proponent claims it is"—so the value of testimonial evidence depends largely on a finding by the trier of fact that the witness is "authentic," in the sense that his testimony is a truthful and accurate account of what happened.

In Chapter 7, you previewed one method of impeaching a witness' credibility, namely, impeachment by prior inconsistent statement. Other methods of impeaching a witness's credibility include showing that the witness is biased or motivated in a way that might affect his testimony, that the witness's sensory or mental capacities impaired her ability to accurately perceive the events in question, or that the witness has an untruthful character. In addition, a witness's credibility can be impeached by introducing evidence that specifically contradicts a portion or all of his testimony.

In addition, a number of methods exist for rehabilitating the credibility of a witness whose credibility has been impeached. In Chapter 7, you also previewed one such method, namely, rehabilitation by prior consistent statement. Other methods of rehabilitating a witness include re-examination of the witness designed to put the impeaching evidence in context and showing that the witness has a truthful character.

A critical distinction amongst the various methods of impeachment is whether the party seeking to impeach a witness is limited to raising the impeaching matter in the course of examining the witness, or whether she may also introduce "extrinsic" evidence of the impeaching matter. For example, if the claim is that a witness is biased in favor of the plaintiff, is the party seeking to impeach the witness on that ground limited to raising the issue of bias on cross-examination of the witness, or may she also introduce evidence in the form of documents or testimony by other witnesses to demonstrate the alleged bias?

Some of the methods of impeachment and rehabilitation are specifically regulated in the rules of evidence—in particular Rules 607, 608, 609, 610, 613, and 806—while others are governed more generally by Rules 401 through 403. The materials that follow examine the prerequisites for invoking and limitations of the various methods of impeachment and rehabilitation of witnesses.

B. Character for Untruthfulness

Recall that under Rule 404, the general rule is that evidence of a person's character, whether in the form of opinion or reputation testimony or by way of an inference drawn from prior conduct, is not admissible to prove that the person acted in conformity therewith on a particular occasion. Yet Rule 404(a)(3) recognizes an exception to this general rule, providing that "[e]vidence of a witness's character may be admitted under Rules 607, 608, and 609."

Together, Rules 608 and 609 provide for three methods by which the testimony of a witness can be impeached by showing that the witness has a character for untruthfulness. First, Rule 608(a) permits an attack on a witness's credibility by calling a second witness to give opinion or reputation testimony as to the first witness's character for truthfulness. Second, Rule 608(b) provides for a means by which the trier of fact can infer from evidence of specific instances of the witness's prior dishonest conduct that the witness has a character for untruthfulness. Finally, Rule 609 provides for a means by which the trier of fact can infer that the witness has a character for untruthfulness from evidence that the witness has previously been convicted of certain offenses.

1. Untruthful Character and Conduct

Problem 10-1: Lying for Beer, Lying for Jobs

David is on trial on charges of murder. David raises an alibi defense, and calls Molly as a witness, who testifies that David was at her house helping her rearrange furniture at the time the murder took place.

On cross-examination, the prosecution seeks, over David's objection, to ask Molly the following questions: (1) Isn't it true that when you applied for a job three years ago, you submitted a résumé that falsely stated that you had graduated from college with honors?; (2) Isn't it true that in college, you used a false ID card to purchase alcohol when you were underage?

How should the court rule on David's objection? If the questions are permitted and Molly answers them in the negative, may the prosecution introduce evidence to prove that Molly committed the alleged acts? How, if at all, would your answer differ under the Pennsylvania and Texas versions of Rule 608, excerpted below?

United States v. Whitmore
359 F.3d 609 (D.C. Cir. 2004)

KAREN LeCRAFT HENDERSON, Circuit Judge....

On June 20, 2002, Whitmore was charged with one count of unlawful possession of a firearm and ammunition by a felon, in violation of 18 U.S.C. §922(g)(1), and simple possession of a controlled substance (cocaine base), in violation of 21 U.S.C. §844(a). On November 5, 2002, a jury convicted him on both counts....

Viewed in the light most favorable to the government, the evidence at trial established that on the evening of November 1, 2001, Officer Bladden Russell of the District of Columbia Metropolitan Police Department (MPD), while patrolling the Fort Davis neighborhood in Southeast Washington, directed a crowd gathered at a bus stop to disperse. The crowd, with the exception of Whitmore, complied. Russell exited his car to approach Whitmore and Whitmore fled. Russell pursued him on foot and noticed that Whitmore, while running, held his right hand close to his body at his waist and the right side pocket of his jacket.

Whitmore successfully eluded Russell but MPD Officer Efrain Soto, Jr., who was also patrolling the neighborhood in his police cruiser, spotted Whitmore and gave chase, first in his car and then on foot. Soto also noticed Whitmore's right hand holding the right side of his jacket. While still in the cruiser, Soto saw Whitmore throw a gun towards an apartment building next to an alley Whitmore ran into. Shortly thereafter, Soto apprehended Whitmore. Once Russell caught up to assist, Soto found a gun in a window well of the apartment building. The weapon (with four rounds of ammunition, one of which was chambered) showed signs that it had been recently thrown against the building: a piece of brick was stuck in its sight, there were scuff marks on it and it was covered with masonry dust. The police found nothing in the right pocket of Whitmore's jacket but did discover a small bag of cocaine base in his left pocket.

At trial Whitmore defended on the ground that Soto had fabricated the story about the gun and had planted the gun in the window well. Soto provided, almost exclusively, the evidence connecting Whitmore to the gun and Whitmore therefore sought to attack Soto's credibility in several ways. He first attempted to call three defense witnesses—Jason Cherkis, Bruce Cooper and Kennith Edmonds—to testify regarding Soto's "character for truthfulness" under Fed.R.Evid. 608(a). Cherkis, a reporter with the City Paper, wrote an article in January 2000 reporting that Soto and three other MPD officers were the target of multiple complaints from residents of the MPD's Sixth District, the district in which Whitmore was arrested. According to Whitmore, Cherkis would testify, based on conversations he had with his sources for the article, that Soto had a reputation as a liar.... Before trial, the court excluded Cherkis's testimony under Fed.R.Evid. 608(a) because Cherkis was not personally acquainted with Soto and because the foundation of Cherkis's testimony—interviews that he conducted for the 2000 article—was too remote in time to be relevant.

Bruce Cooper was a local criminal defense counsel who, Whitmore claimed, would testify regarding both Soto's reputation for untruthfulness within what he called the "court community" and Cooper's own opinion that Soto was untruthful. Whitmore proffered that Cooper would testify that several defense counsel thought Soto was a liar and that Cooper had the same opinion based on having tried many cases in which Soto was a government witness. The district court excluded Cooper's reputation testimony because, even assuming the "court community" constituted a recognized community, Cooper did not know Soto's reputation within the entire "court community" and did not live in Soto's neighborhood. The court also rejected Cooper's opinion testimony under Fed.R.Evid. 403 because it was "inherently biased," and unduly prejudicial in that Cooper's contacts with Soto arose from his representation of criminal defendants against whom Soto testified and because Cooper's testimony would lead to additional delay—that is, the court would have to allow the government to explore the circumstances underlying Soto's testimony in the other cases about which Cooper intended to testify.

Kennith Edmonds, whom Whitmore also sought to call as both a reputation and opinion witness, was an acquaintance of Soto who used to live in the neighborhood where Soto worked and who saw Soto regularly until roughly five years before the trial, when Edmonds moved away. Whitmore proffered that Edmonds would say that he still saw Soto a few times each week when Edmonds returned to his old neighborhood to visit his mother and still maintained contacts with others in the neighborhood who knew Soto. Edmonds's proffered opinion evidence was based on two incidents: (1) Soto had participated in the arrest of a friend of his and, when Edmonds attempted to collect his friend's property from the police, Edmonds was told that there was no property to collect; and (2) Soto and other officers wrongly arrested Edmonds for drug possession in 1995. The court excluded Edmonds's reputation testimony because he had not lived in the neighborhood where Soto worked for some time; it excluded his opinion testimony because it questioned whether Soto was involved in the events on which Edmonds based his opinion. It also excluded Edmonds's testimony in its entirety under Fed.R.Evid. 403, concluding that the minimal probative value of Edmonds's evidence was outweighed by unfair prejudice, including the government's resulting need to examine the events underlying Edmonds's testimony.

In addition to these three character witnesses, Whitmore also sought to impeach Soto by cross-examining him on three subjects: (1) a D.C. Superior Court judge's finding that Soto had lied when Soto testified before him in a 1999 criminal trial; (2) the suspension of Soto's driver's license and Soto's failure to report the suspension to his supervisors; and (3) Soto's failure to pay child support. Regarding the first, the Superior Court judge had rejected Soto's testimony that he had seen a bag of drugs with a blue line in the defendant's hand. The judge found that testimony "palpably incredible," and concluded that "Officer Soto lied." The judge therefore granted the defendant's motion for acquittal. The U.S. Attorney's Office subsequently investigated Soto for perjury but declined to prosecute him. It did, however, put Soto on a "*Lewis* list," a watch list for officers under investigation.

The government moved *in limine* to exclude cross-examination on the subject under Fed.R.Evid. 608(b) as well as Fed.R.Evid. 403.... The district court ... barred cross-examination under Fed.R.Evid. 403, noting that the finding was not a perjury *conviction*, that the present jury might rely too heavily on the finding in making its own credibility determination regarding Soto and, finally, that any cross-examination would delay the trial and could confuse the jury because the government would have to be given the opportunity to explore the finding before the jury.

Whitmore's other attempted impeachment matters involved the alleged suspension of Soto's driver's license and his alleged failure to pay child support. Whitmore sought to cross-examine Soto from a state document manifesting that Soto's Maryland driver's license had been suspended from 1998 to 2000 for failure to pay child support. MPD regulations require all officers to maintain a valid driver's license and to notify their supervisor of any change in status. Whitmore invoked ... Fed.R.Evid. 608(b) ... [arguing that] Soto's alleged failure to report his suspended license and to make child support payments would reveal his inclination to dissemble and evade the law.... The district court prohibited cross-examination on both subjects, concluding the document Whitmore intended to cross-examine from was hearsay....

In light of the trial court's rulings, Whitmore presented no evidence in his defense and was limited to cross-examining the government witnesses about inconsistencies in their trial testimony....

1. Character Witnesses

Fed.R.Evid. 608(a) allows a party to attack the credibility of a witness through reputation and opinion evidence of his character for truthfulness....

In order to offer reputation evidence under Fed.R.Evid. 608(a), a party must establish that the character witness is qualified by having an "acquaintance with [the witness]," his "community," and "the circles in which he has moved, as to speak with authority of the terms in which generally [the witness] is regarded." *Michelson v. United States*, 335 U.S. 469, 478 (1948). With regard to Cherkis, Whitmore relied on the interviews that Cherkis had conducted for the 2000 article and on the holding in *Wilson v. City of Chicago*, 6 F.3d 1233, 1239 (7th Cir. 1993), in which the Seventh Circuit reversed a district court's exclusion of a reporter's reputation testimony. The reporter in *Wilson*, however, had personally interviewed the principal witness while Cherkis had never met Soto. Furthermore, neither Cherkis nor Edmonds had had direct contact with Soto or his community for some time. The district court found the proposed testimony of both Cherkis and Edmonds as to Soto's alleged reputation for truthfulness "too remote" in time from the time of trial. *See United States v. Watson*, 669 F.2d 1374, 1381 (11th Cir. 1982) (reputation witness not qualified where he knew witness only "for a short period of time" and his "testimony was to a reputation that existed at a time remote from both the time of [the events in controversy] and the time of trial"); *United States v. Lewis*, 482 F.2d 632, 640 n. 44 (D.C. Cir. 1973) (witness' "reputation for testimonial honesty ... is to be established by evidence of his community reputation at the time of trial and during a period not remote thereto"). Finally, with regard to Cooper's testimony—and leaving aside the troublesome issue whether the "court community" represents a cognizable community for the purpose of a law enforcement officer's reputation—the district court found the foundation for his testimony weak because it relied on Cooper's conversations with only a few other criminal defense counsel, a subset of the proposed "community." *See Williams v. United States*, 168 U.S. 382, 397 (1897) (reputation evidence inadmissible because foundation was few individuals in one building and Court noted community cannot be so narrowly drawn as to ignore "general reputation in the community"). We conclude that the district court did not abuse its discretion in excluding the reputation evidence of these witnesses.[3]

While recognizing that the foundational requirement for *opinion* evidence regarding a witness' character for truthfulness is less stringent than that for *reputation* evidence, the district court nonetheless rejected both Cooper's and Edmonds's proposed opinion evidence. It concluded that both opinions lacked sufficiently supportive factual information to be credible and thus would be unfairly prejudicial under Fed.R.Evid. 403. The foundation for Cooper's opinion that Soto was untruthful was limited to his observation that Soto had testified falsely against his clients; the facts underlying Edmonds's opinion did not provide a reasonable basis from which the jury could conclude that Soto was even directly involved in the events, much less indicate that he was untruthful about them.

---

3. The district court also excluded Cherkis's and Cooper's testimony because neither lived in Soto's community. Courts have rejected the notion, however, that reputation testimony is confined to the witness' residential community or that the character witness must physically reside in that community. *See, e.g., Wilson*, 6 F.3d at 1239 (admitting reporter's testimony about witness' reputation among people with whom he had worked and among his family because "a community doesn't have to be stable in order to qualify under the rule"); *United States v. Mandel*, 591 F.2d 1347, 1370 (4th Cir. 1979) (noting that expansion of community to include witness' professional environment reflects "the realities of our modern, mobile, impersonal society").

Whitmore contends that the foundational defects could have been highlighted by the government in cross-examining his character witnesses but were not severe enough to exclude the evidence altogether. The foundation required by Fed.R.Evid. 608(a), however, is designed to keep unreliable evidence from being heard by the jury at all. The district court did not abuse its discretion in excluding this evidence under Fed.R.Evid. 608 — the foundational defects *were* serious — and Fed.R.Evid. 403, on the ground that its value would have been substantially outweighed by the unfair prejudice to the government and by needlessly occupying the time of the jury and the court.

2. Cross-Examination of Soto

Fed.R.Evid. 608(b) allows a party to attack the credibility of a witness by cross-examining him on specific instances of past conduct. Cross-examination pursuant to Fed.R.Evid. 608(b) is not confined to prior criminal convictions — they are governed by Fed.R.Evid. 609 — but the conduct must be probative of the witness' character for truthfulness. *See* Fed.R.Evid. 608(b). It may not, however, be proven by extrinsic evidence. *Id.*; *United States v. Morrison*, 98 F.3d 619, 628 (D.C. Cir. 1996); *see also United States v. Bynum*, 3 F.3d 769, 772 (4th Cir. 1993) (noting that under Fed.R.Evid. 608(b) "cross-examiner may inquire into specific incidents of conduct, but does so at the peril of not being able to rebut the witness'[s] denials" and that "[t]he purpose of this rule is to prohibit things from getting too far afield — to prevent the proverbial trial within a trial")....

Here the district court first determined that the probative value of any cross-examination regarding Soto's testimony before the Superior Court judge would be slight because it involved an unrelated and dated matter and fell short of a perjury conviction. It then concluded ... that cross-examination on the subject presented a "grave risk that the jury might abdicate" its role in weighing Soto's testimony and that both the cross-examination and the government's inevitable rehabilitation of Soto's testimony would "divert the jury from the facts in this case and from the assessment that they need to make in this case."

For his part, Whitmore contends that the proposed cross-examination was strongly probative of Soto's character for untruthfulness and that, given the critical nature of Soto's evidence against Whitmore, the district court should have allowed it. We agree. Nothing could be more probative of a witness' character for untruthfulness than evidence that the witness has previously lied under oath. Indeed, as the Second Circuit observed — in a remarkably similar case (before the enactment of Fed.R.Evid. 608(b)) in which a party sought to cross-examine a "key witness" regarding a finding by another court that the witness had "'intentionally g[iven] false testimony'": "the rule seems to be well settled that although the opponent is not permitted to adduce extrinsic evidence that a witness lied on a previous occasion, he may nonetheless ask questions to that end." *Walker v. Firestone Tire & Rubber Co.*, 412 F.2d 60, 63–64 (2d Cir. 1969)....

Furthermore, the government's suggestion that inquiry under Fed.R.Evid. 608(b) should be limited to a prior perjury conviction would make Fed.R.Evid. 609 superfluous. Fed.R.Evid. 608(b) allows a witness' credibility to be attacked based on misconduct that, while not constituting a criminal conviction, nevertheless tends to show that the witness is untruthful....

In *Morrison* we rejected the defendant's claim that he was entitled to cross-examine a government witness regarding the fact that the latter had been sued in state court, noting that "the mere *filing* of a complaint" — "regardless of whether the allegations in the complaint [were] true" — did not meet Fed.R.Evid. 608(b)'s requirement that cross-examination be confined to conduct that is "'probative of [...] truthfulness or untruthfulness.'" 98 F.3d at 628. We did not address what difference it might have made had the defendant sought to cross-examine the witness about the *substance* of the complaint....

We also believe the district court erred in excluding the entire line of cross-examination on the ground that its probative value was substantially outweighed by the risk that the jury might blindly follow the prior judge's lead or be otherwise distracted from the substance of Whitmore's trial.... The district court here could have adequately guarded against any risk of unfair prejudice or undue delay by limiting cross-examination, by giving limiting instructions to the jury and by setting reasonable parameters on the government's rehabilitation of Soto. Instead, by prohibiting cross-examination of the only witness who testified to Whitmore's unlawful possession of the gun, we believe the district court abused its discretion.

Turning to the district court's denial of cross-examination regarding Soto's suspended driver's license and failure to pay child support, we also find error. The trial court precluded cross-examination on those matters on the ground that there was "no basis" for the cross-examination because Whitmore's only support for them—the record from the Maryland Motor Vehicle Administration—was inadmissible hearsay. Counsel, however, need only have "'a reasonable basis for asking questions on cross-examination which tend to incriminate or degrade the witness,'" and "the general rule in such situations is that 'the questioner must be in possession of some facts which support a genuine belief that the witness committed the offense or the degrading act to which the question relates.'" *United States v. Lin*, 101 F.3d 760, 768 (D.C. Cir. 1996). The copy of Soto's Maryland driving record provided sufficient basis for such cross-examination and defense counsel readily acknowledged that he did not seek to admit the record itself and would be bound by Soto's answers. The court apparently assumed, however, that Soto would simply deny that his license had been suspended, leaving the jury with a bare denial of a damaging accusation. We pass over the fact that this assumption implied that Soto would intentionally lie under oath. The court lacked a basis for such an assumption, however, because it failed to conduct any voir dire. The knowledge that he could be charged with perjury would encourage Soto to respond truthfully, even if he thought that Whitmore's counsel could not impeach him further. Accordingly, in excluding cross-examination on these matters as well, the district court abused its discretion....

United States v. Manske
186 F.3d 770 (7th Cir. 1999)

FLAUM, Circuit Judge....

The defendant was indicted as part of an ongoing investigation of cocaine trafficking in northern Wisconsin. Before Manske's trial, the government had persuaded Stephen Pszeniczka and Daniel Knutowski to plead guilty to charges including distribution of cocaine, and, with their cooperation, successfully prosecuted Patrick Menting and Dennis Tushoski for similar crimes. Pszeniczka and Knutowski fingered Manske as their drug source—a contention Manske vigorously denied. At Manske's trial, both men testified that between 1993 and 1996, the defendant was their primary supplier of cocaine....

This testimony made up the bulk of the government's case, with the remainder supplied by tertiary witnesses....

Manske testified on his own behalf, acknowledging that he knew Knutowski and Pszeniczka.... Like the government, Manske's case relied on oral testimony; he had no physical or documentary evidence with which to exonerate himself. Thus, his defense strategy hinged entirely on destroying the credibility of the witnesses against him. Manske was able to impeach Knutowski, Pszeniczka, Colburn and Campbell with the fact that they were receiving leniency from the government in return for their testimony, and with their extensive history of drug use and drug dealing. Manske also sought to cross-examine Pszeniczka about past acts of witness intimidation which the government acknowledged had taken place, arguing that these acts were probative of Pszeniczka's truthfulness.... Pursuant to a pre-trial motion in limine the district court barred the defendant from inquiring into these areas, thus keeping this evidence from the jury. Thus, the defendant was not able to delve into acts of witness intimidation and potential subornation of perjury which Pszeniczka had previously engaged in....

After a three day trial, the jury retired for deliberations ... it eventually convicted the defendant. Manske appealed, primarily on the grounds that the district court's limitations on his cross-examination of government witnesses were improper....

What the government sought to keep out was mention of roughly half a dozen incidents where Pszeniczka, or people acting on his behalf, allegedly threatened potential witnesses in an effort to keep them from incriminating him....

The government's argument for limiting cross-examination of Pszeniczka was that under Fed.R.Evid. 608(b), this evidence related to specific instances of conduct not probative of truthfulness or untruthfulness. Rather than dealing with truthfulness (or a lack thereof), the government argued that the threat evidence only went to show Pszeniczka's propensity for violence, and therefore could not be admitted. Manske responded by asserting that threats calculated to encourage people to break the law were in fact probative of Pszeniczka's truthfulness or untruthfulness....

The district court granted the government's motion in limine. The trial judge observed that FRE 608(b) did not allow Manske to use the threat evidence to cross-examine Pszeniczka because the threats "[did] not impact upon his credibility." The court also stated that "the fact that there was a threat offered by Pszeniczka does not go to his character for truthfulness," but rather, to the "character [for] violence and [Pszeniczka's] threatening nature." Viewed in this light, the district court held that the evidence Manske wished to use to cross-examine Pszeniczka was irrelevant....

Federal Rule of Evidence 608(b) is a rule of limited admissibility. Other than certain criminal convictions allowed into evidence by FRE 609, a witness' specific instances of conduct may only be raised on cross-examination if they are probative of truthfulness or untruthfulness. As noted, the district court felt that the threat evidence was probative of Pszeniczka's tendencies toward violence, and had no bearing on his probity or lack thereof. The defendant argues that these threats deal with more than mere violence—Pszeniczka's willingness to threaten violence was a means to achieve an end of dissuading people from testifying truthfully in legal proceedings—and thus clearly implicates Pszeniczka's truthfulness.

As a leading treatise notes, there are three ways of looking at 608(b): a broad one, a narrow one, and a middle one. *See* Christopher B. Mueller & Laird C. Kirkpatrick, Federal Evidence, 154–55 (2d ed.1994). The broad view holds that "virtually any conduct indicating bad character indicates untruthfulness, including robbery and assault." This view is untenable, as it would open the door to a potentially mind-numbing array of questions on every cross-examination. It would also "pave the way to an exception [to 608(b)'s limitations] that swallows the rule ... [because it] adopts the hypothesis that all bad people are liars, which is an unverifiable conclusion." The narrow reading of the rule, which the government essentially urges on us, considers a crime as bearing on veracity only if it involves falsehood or deception, such as forgery or perjury. The middle view "is that behavior seeking personal advantage by taking from others in violation of their rights reflects on veracity." While this generally does not cover "personal crimes" involving violence, it does not necessarily exclude all such acts. The threat evidence would clearly be allowed in under the broad view, and probably excluded under the narrow one. Whether it would fit under the middle view is a more vexing question.

Mueller and Kirkpatrick note that "[u]nder some circumstances, it seems wise to allow questions that would not be embraced by the more focused view but would pass muster under the middle view, and there appears to be a trend in this direction [among courts]." Their treatise discusses a circumstance nearly identical to this one, where although the specific instance of conduct may not facially appear relevant to truthfulness, closer inspection reveals that it bears on that issue. "[W]hen [a party's question is] specific and well-founded, the cross-examiner should be allowed to ask ... questions on acts better described as dishonest than false ... [including questions related to] *concealing or frightening off witnesses* or suborning perjury (even in unrelated cases.)"

We have not had many occasions to address the scope of 608(b); however, when we have our approach has been closest to the middle view. For example, in *Varhol v. National RR Pass. Corp.*, we rejected the plaintiff's contention that 608(b) only allowed questioning about acts involving fraud or deceit, such as perjury, subornation of perjury, false statements, embezzlement and false pretenses. 909 F.2d 1557, 1566 (7th Cir. 1990) (en banc) (per curiam). We held that although "receiving stolen goods [fell] into a gray area," the plaintiff could be questioned about buying stolen railroad tickets because "people generally regard stealing (and receiving and using stolen property) as acts that 'reflect adversely on a [person's] honesty and integrity.'" *Id.* (quoting *Gordon v. United States*, 383 F.2d 936, 940 (D.C. Cir. 1967)); *see also United States v. Smith*, 80 F.3d 1188, 1193 (7th Cir. 1996) (under 608(b) witness could be cross-examined regarding prior thefts for which he was not charged because "acts of theft ... are, like acts of fraud or deceit, probative of a witness' truthfulness or untruthfulness."); *United States v. Zizzo*, 120 F.3d 1338, 1355 (7th Cir. 1997) (cross-examination about defendant's receipt of stolen tires not precluded under 608(b)); *United States v. Wilson*, 985 F.2d 348, 351 (7th Cir. 1993) (allowing questions on defendant's failure to file federal income tax returns and bribery as probative of untruthfulness under 608(b)); *United States v. Fulk*, 816 F.2d 1202, 1206 (7th Cir. 1987) (improper for district court to prevent questioning on whether defendant lost his chiropractor's license because of deceptive practices). In *Varhol*, the full court observed that "if the witness has no compunctions against stealing another's property ... it is hard to see why he would hesitate to obtain an advantage for himself or a friend in trial by giving false testimony.... As a practical matter, it is difficult to distinguish between untruthfulness and dishonesty."

Although the factual context of *Varhol* differs, the relationship between the specific acts of misconduct and truthfulness is, if anything, more compelling in this case. Threatening to cause physical harm to a person who proposes to testify against you is at least as probative of truthfulness as receiving stolen tires or a stolen railroad ticket. Also, because Stephen Pszeniczka had no compunction about intimidating potential witnesses in previous legal proceedings, "it is hard to see" why he would hesitate to obtain an advantage for himself in Manske's trial by giving false testimony against Manske. The advantage he hoped to obtain, it appears, was leniency from the government in return for his testimony. Pszeniczka had already been given ten years off of his sentence for cooperation in a prior prosecution, and acknowledged that if the remaining thirty years of his sentence was not reduced, he would likely die in prison. Because of the sum of these facts, we conclude it was legally erroneous for the district court to conclude that the threat evidence was irrelevant under 608(b)....

Pennsylvania Rule of Evidence 608
Evidence of character and conduct of witness

(a) Reputation evidence of character. The credibility of a witness may be attacked or supported by evidence in the form of reputation as to character, but subject to the following limitations:

(1) the evidence may refer only to character for truthfulness or untruthfulness; and

(2) evidence of truthful character is admissible only after the character of the witness for truthfulness has been attacked by reputation evidence or otherwise.

(b) Specific instances of conduct. Except as provided in Rule 609 (relating to evidence of conviction of crime),

(1) the character of a witness for truthfulness may not be attacked or supported by cross-examination or extrinsic evidence concerning specific instances of the witness' conduct; however,

(2) in the discretion of the court, the credibility of a witness who testifies as to the reputation of another witness for truthfulness or untruthfulness may be attacked by cross-examination concerning specific instances of conduct (not including arrests) of the other witness, if they are probative of truthfulness or untruthfulness; but extrinsic evidence thereof is not admissible.

> *Comment*: Pa.R.E. 608(a)(1) and (2) differ from F.R.E. 608(a) in that they permit character for truthfulness or untruthfulness to be proven only by reputation evidence. Opinion evidence is not admissible....
>
> Pa.R.E. 608(b) differs from F.R.E. 608(b). Both ban all use of extrinsic evidence of specific instances of conduct for the purpose of attacking or supporting a witness' credibility, except for evidence of conviction of crime (Pa.R.E. 609 and F.R.E. 609). The two rules diverge, however, in their treatment of cross-examination concerning specific instances of conduct.
>
> Under the F.R.E. 608(b), the court has discretion to permit cross-examination of a witness about specific instances of conduct in two situations: when the specific instances are probative of the witness' own character for truthfulness and when they concern the character for truthfulness of another witness and the witness being cross-examined has testified about the truthfulness of that witness. In the latter case, cross-examination about specific instances of conduct may undermine the credibility of the witness being cross-examined (the "character witness") and the credibility of the other witness (the "principal witness").
>
> Unlike F.R.E. 608(b), Pa.R.E. 608(b)(1) prohibits the use of specific instances of a witness' own conduct for the purpose of attacking the witness' character for truthfulness....
>
> Like F.R.E. 608(b), however, Pa.R.E. 608(b)(2) permits a character witness to be cross-examined, in the discretion of the court, concerning specific instances of conduct of the principal witness. However, unlike the Federal Rule, Pa.R.E. 608(b)(2) makes it clear that although the cross-examination concerns the specific acts of the principal witness, those specific acts affect the credibility of the character witness only....
>
> Finally, Pa.R.E. 608 does not include the last paragraph of F.R.E. 608(b), which provides that the giving of testimony by an accused or any other witness is not

a waiver of the privilege against self-incrimination when the examination concerns matters relating only to credibility. Pa.R.E. 608(b)(1) bars cross-examination of any witness concerning specific acts of the witness' own conduct; thus, the provision is not needed.

Texas Rule of Evidence 608
Evidence of Character and Conduct of a Witness

(a) Opinion and Reputation Evidence of Character. The credibility of a witness may be attacked or supported by evidence in the form of opinion or reputation, but subject to these limitations:

(1) the evidence may refer only to character for truthfulness or untruthfulness; and

(2) evidence of truthful character is admissible only after the character of the witness for truthfulness has been attacked by opinion or reputation evidence or otherwise.

(b) Specific Instances of Conduct. Specific instances of the conduct of a witness, for the purpose of attacking or supporting the witness' credibility, other than conviction of crime as provided in Rule 609, may not be inquired into on cross-examination of the witness nor proved by extrinsic evidence.

Notes and Questions

1. The foundation requirement for giving opinion or reputation testimony under Rule 608(a) is similar to that for giving opinion or reputation testimony under Rule 404(a), but with one critical difference. Under Rule 404(a), evidence of a character trait of the accused or the victim is being introduced to show that the individual acted in conformity with that character trait *at the time the event at issue took place*, and thus the character witness must have been familiar with the individual (or his reputation) *at the time the event at issue took place. See United States v. Curtis,* 644 F.2d 263, 268–269 (3d Cir. 1981); *United States v. Lewis,* 482 F.2d 632, 641 (D.C. Cir. 1973). By contrast, under Rule 608(a), evidence of the witness's character for truthfulness is being introduced to show that the individual is acting in conformity with that character trait *at the time of trial*, and thus the character witness must be familiar with the individual (or his reputation) *at the time of trial. See Cooper v. Asplundh Tree Expert Co.,* 836 F.2d 1544, 1552 (10th Cir. 1988); *United States v. Watson,* 669 F.2d 1374, 1382 n.5 (11th Cir. 1982).

2. A character witness who testifies that another witness has a character for untruthfulness under Rule 608(a) is himself subject to impeachment to show that he has a character for untruthfulness! Thus, a character witness can be impeached by asking him on cross-examination about his own prior misconduct under Rule 608(b). In addition, yet another character witness could be called to testify that the first character witness has a character for untruthfulness.

3. Do you agree with the *Whitmore* court that the trial court was justified in excluding the testimony of some of the character witnesses on the ground that they had not been in contact with Soto for an extended period of time? *Compare United States v. Tedder,* 403 F.3d 836, 839 (7th Cir. 2005) ("Tedder's brothers ... testified that they had low opinions of his honesty. He contends that the family had been estranged for so long that the brothers' views were out of date, but honesty is more like climate than like weather: it is a stable attribute even though subject to daily variability. Rule 608(a) does not contain a time limit, so the fact that Tedder had not spoken with his brothers for a decade

did not compel the judge to block them from testifying. The long break in family relations was a subject for cross-examination and argument by counsel.").

4. Under Rule 608(b), the questions asked of the witness must focus on the alleged conduct *itself*, and not on the consequences of that conduct:

> It should be noted that the extrinsic evidence prohibition of Rule 608(b) bars any reference to the consequences that a witness might have suffered as a result of an alleged bad act. For example, Rule 608(b) prohibits counsel from mentioning that a witness was suspended or disciplined for the conduct that is the subject of impeachment, when that conduct is offered only to prove the character of the witness.

Advisory Committee Note to 2003 Amendment to Rule 608(b).

Does this in any way limit the extent to which Whitmore can cross-examine Soto with respect to his allegedly false testimony before the D.C. Superior Court Judge, and if so, how? *Compare United States v. Whitmore*, 384 F.3d 836, 836–37 (D.C. Cir. 2004) (per curiam) ("According to the government, this note so limits the scope of cross-examination of Soto regarding his prior testimony that the opinion must be amended to further set the parameters on such questioning on retrial…. it is appropriate for us to call the district court's attention to the new Advisory Committee note because that note would apply to the scope of cross examination on retrial."), *with United States v. Dawson*, 434 F.3d 956, 957–59 (7th Cir. 2006) (rejecting an argument that Rule 608(b) limits a party in such a circumstance to asking a witness only whether he had previously lied in court proceedings, and holding that a party is likewise permitted to ask the witness whether a judge has ever found that he lied on the stand).

5. Under Rule 608(b), it is not necessary that the prior conduct be unlawful; all that matters is that it represent dishonest behavior on the witness's part. *E.g.*, *United States v. Elliott*, 89 F.3d 1360, (8th Cir. 1996) (misrepresentation of educational and employment history on resume submitted with job application). And as *Manske* demonstrates, the mere fact that conduct is unlawful does not necessarily mean that it can be inquired about under Rule 608(b), as not all prior criminal conduct is deemed to be probative of truthfulness.

6. Can a witness be asked on cross-examination about conduct for which he has been tried and *acquitted*? Consider the following holding by one court:

> Whether or not an acquittal technically estops the prosecution from eliciting the fact of prior misconduct, it will normally alter the balance between probative force and prejudice…. Moreover, there is the blunt reality that a witness who has been acquitted will almost certainly deny the misconduct…. Thus, the only purpose served by permitting the inquiry is to place before the jury the allegation of misconduct contained in the prosecutor's question, an allegation the jury will be instructed has no evidentiary weight. To permit the inquiry risks unfair prejudice, which is not justified by the theoretical possibility that the witness, though acquitted, will admit to the misconduct. When the witness is the defendant, the significance of the prejudice is magnified.

United States v. Schwab, 886 F.2d 509, 513 (2d Cir. 1989).

7. Rule 608(b) is qualified by the proviso that "the court *may*, on cross-examination, allow" questions concerning the prior conduct of a witness (emphasis added). Factors that weigh against permitting questioning under Rule 608(b) include the remoteness in time of the alleged misconduct and the extent to which the prior misconduct is probative of veracity. *E.g.*, *Johnson v. Elk Lake School Dist.*, 283 F.3d 138, 145 n.2 (3d Cir. 2002).

8. Although often confused with one another, it is important to distinguish between the use of evidence of prior misconduct under Rules 404(b) and 608(b):

> First, the misconduct may be relevant to an issue in the case, such as intent or identity. When offered for that purpose, prior misconduct is governed by Fed.R.Evid. 404(b). Second, the misconduct may be relevant to impeachment of a witness, including the defendant, because it tends to show the character of the witness for untruthfulness. When offered for that purpose, prior misconduct is governed by Fed.R.Evid. 608(b), which precludes proof by extrinsic evidence and limits the inquiry to cross-examination of the witness.

United States v. Schwab, 886 F.2d 509, 511 (2d Cir. 1989).

2. Prior Convictions

Recall from Chapter 4 that at common law, persons convicted of felonies and crimes that involved fraud or deceit were deemed incompetent to testify based on a view that the fact that they committed such conduct in the past meant that they had demonstrated themselves to be untrustworthy and were thus unworthy of belief. Yet over time, this form of incompetency, like most others, disappeared and was replaced with a rule that permitted the witness to testify, but permitted the use of his prior convictions to impeach his credibility as a witness.

The use of prior convictions to impeach a witness' credibility, which is governed by Rule 609, raises a number of challenging questions that were the source of much debate when the federal rules of evidence were adopted and that make the rule challenging to apply in practice. First, some prior convictions are surely more probative of veracity than are others, either because of the *type* of crime for which the person was convicted or because of how old the conviction is. Should the rule distinguish amongst different convictions based on their probative worth, and if so, how? Second, where the witness is a criminal defendant testifying on his own behalf, there is a risk that the trier of fact may draw *two* inferences from proof of the defendant-witness's prior criminal convictions. The first, permitted by Rule 609, is an inference from the defendant-witness's prior convictions to a conclusion that he has a character for untruthfulness to a conclusion that he is probably lying on the stand. Yet the second, prohibited by Rule 404, is an inference from his prior convictions to a conclusion that he has a character for engaging in criminal conduct to a conclusion that he probably committed the crime for which he is now charged.

As originally proposed by the Advisory Committee, Rule 609(a) provided as follows:

> For the purpose of attacking the credibility of a witness, evidence that he has been convicted of a crime is admissible but only if the crime (1) was punishable by death or imprisonment in excess of one year under the law under which he was convicted or (2) involved dishonesty or false statement regardless of the punishment.

The House Committee on the Judiciary narrowed the proposed rule, limiting it only to those prior convictions that involved dishonesty or false statement. The Committee explained its reasons as follows:

> While recognizing that the prevailing doctrine in the federal courts and in most States allows a witness to be impeached by evidence of prior felony convictions without restriction as to type, the Committee was of the view that, because of the danger of unfair prejudice in such practice and the deterrent effect upon an

accused who might wish to testify, and even upon a witness who was not the accused, cross-examination by evidence of prior conviction should be limited to those kinds of convictions bearing directly on credibility, i.e., crimes involving dishonesty or false statement.

House Committee on the Judiciary, Report No. 93-650.

Eventually, Congress settled on a version of the Rule which sought to balance competing concerns in Congress and which is similar to the version that exists today. In its present form, Rule 609(a) provides as follows:

(a) **In General.** The following rules apply to attacking a witness's character for truthfulness by evidence of a criminal conviction:

(1) for a crime that, in the convicting jurisdiction, was punishable by death or by imprisonment for more than one year, the evidence:

(A) must be admitted, subject to Rule 403, in a civil case or in a criminal case in which the witness is not a defendant; and

(B) must be admitted in a criminal case in which the witness is a defendant, if the probative value of the evidence outweighs its prejudicial effect to that defendant; and

(2) for any crime regardless of the punishment, the evidence must be admitted if the court can readily determine that establishing the elements of the crime required proving—or the witness's admitting—a dishonest act or false statement.

In addition, Rule 609(b) provides a special rule for older convictions:

(b) **Limit on Using the Evidence After 10 Years.** This subdivision (b) applies if more than 10 years have passed since the witness's conviction or release from confinement for it, whichever is later. Evidence of the conviction is admissible only if:

(1) its probative value, supported by specific facts and circumstances, substantially outweighs its prejudicial effect; and

(2) the proponent gives an adverse party reasonable written notice of the intent to use it so that the party has a fair opportunity to contest its use.

As is apparent from the legislative history of Rule 609, this complex regulatory scheme, with its many different balancing tests, is designed to serve two purposes. The first is to distinguish prior convictions based on how probative they are of veracity, with the balance tipped in favor of admitting those convictions for crimes that involve dishonesty or false statement and against those convictions that are remote in time. The second is to impose a more stringent requirement of probative worth when the witness is the accused in a criminal case, in recognition of the greater risk that prior convictions of the accused may be misused by the jury.

Understanding the regulatory scheme of Rule 609 is important, but very tricky. The materials that follow are designed to help you master the nuances of the rule.

Problem 10-2: The Criminal Résumé

Paul is on trial on charges that he murdered Tom on the evening of May 4, 2011. Paul is indicted on July 1, 2011, the trial begins August 15, 2011, and he testifies on August 20, 2011. On cross-examination, over objection, the government seeks to ask Paul the following questions:

(1) Isn't it true that on January 15, 2010, you were convicted of petit larceny (a crime punishable by up to 2 years' imprisonment for which Paul received and served a three-month sentence)?

(2) Isn't it true that on March 3, 2005, you were convicted of first-degree manslaughter (a crime punishable by up to twenty years' imprisonment for which Paul received and served a four-year sentence)?

(3) Isn't it true that on February 3, 2004, you were convicted of fraudulent passing of a bad check (a crime punishable by up to 10 months' imprisonment for which Paul received and served a six-month sentence)?

(4) Isn't it true that on July 15, 1999, you were convicted for possession of cocaine with intent to distribute (a crime punishable by up to five years' imprisonment for which Paul received and served a two-year sentence, with a release date of July 15, 2001)?

How should the court rule on the objections? If the objections are overruled, and Paul answers the questions in the negative, can the prosecution introduce evidence to prove that Paul was convicted for these offenses? How, if at all, would your answers differ under the Illinois, Michigan, and Montana versions of Rule 609, excerpted below?

United States v. Jefferson
623 F.3d 227 (5th Cir. 2010)

EDITH BROWN CLEMENT, Circuit Judge:

[Mose Jefferson is indicted on charges of conspiracy to violate the Racketeer Influenced and Corrupt Organizations (RICO) Act. At issue is the admissibility of Jefferson's prior convictions for bribery and obstruction of justice.]

Federal Rule of Evidence 609 governs the admissibility of evidence of convictions for impeachment purposes. Relevant here, the rule provides that "[f]or the purpose of attacking the character for truthfulness of a witness ... evidence that any witness has been convicted of a crime shall be admitted regardless of the punishment, if it readily can be determined that establishing the elements of the crime required proof or admission of an act of dishonesty or false statement by the witness." FED. R. EVID. 609(a)(2).* "Crimes qualifying for admission under Rule 609(a)(2) are not subject to Rule 403 balancing and must be admitted." *United States v. Harper*, 527 F.3d 396, 408 (5th Cir.2008). Rule 609(a)(2) contains "mandatory language [and] *requires* that a trial court admit evidence of such crimes to allow a party to impeach an adversary witness's credibility." *Coursey v. Broadhurst*, 888 F.2d 338, 341–42 (5th Cir.1989).

---

* Editor's Note: Rule 609(a)(2) was restyled in 2011 to provide as follows: "The following rules apply to attacking a witness's character for truthfulness by evidence of a criminal conviction.... for any crime regardless of the punishment, the evidence must be admitted if the court can readily determine that establishing the elements of the crime required proving—or the witness's admitting—a dishonest act or false statement."

Jefferson's prior convictions for bribery are crimes involving dishonesty. "[B]ribery is a *crimen falsi* in that it involves dishonesty.... Hence, it is automatically admissible [under] FED. R. EVID. 609(a)(2)." *United States v. Williams,* 642 F.2d 136, 140 (5th Cir.1981).

Jefferson's prior convictions for obstruction of justice in violation of 18 U.S.C. § 1512(b)(3) are admissible under Rule 609(a)(2) "if it readily can be determined that establishing the elements of the crime required proof or admission of an act of dishonesty or false statement by the witness." FED. R. EVID. 609(a)(2). Section 1512 provides:

> (b) Whoever knowingly uses intimidation, threatens or corruptly persuades another person, or attempts to do so, or engages in misleading conduct toward another person, with intent to—
>
> ....
>
> (3) hinder, delay, or prevent the communication to a law enforcement officer or judge of the United States of information relating to the commission or possible commission of a Federal offense or a violation of conditions of probation, supervised release, parole, or release pending judicial proceedings.

"Ordinarily, the statutory elements of the crime will indicate whether it is one of dishonesty or false statement." FED. R. EVID. 609, advisory committee's note to 2006 amendments. A defendant can be convicted of § 1512(b)(3) for intimidating or threatening another person—actions which do not involve acts of dishonesty or false statement. The statutory elements of § 1512(b)(3) therefore do not indicate whether Jefferson's convictions thereunder are crimes of dishonesty or false statement warranting automatic admission under Rule 609(a)(2). However, "[w]here the deceitful nature of the crime is not apparent from the statute and the face of the judgment ... a proponent may offer information such as an indictment ... or jury instructions to show that the factfinder had to find ... an act of dishonesty or false statement in order for the witness to have been convicted." *Id.*

We turn to the indictment in the earlier case and conclude that Jefferson's convictions for obstruction of justice involve dishonesty or false statement. The obstruction of justice charges contained therein, counts 6 and 7, read, in relevant part, as follows:

> Count 6: On or about May 21, 2007, in the Eastern District of Louisiana, defendant MOSE JEFFERSON did knowingly and corruptly attempt to persuade Ellenese Brooks-Simms to lie to federal law enforcement authorities....
>
> Count 7: On or about May 25, 2007, in the Eastern District of Louisiana, defendant MOSE JEFFERSON did knowingly and corruptly attempt to persuade Ellenese Brooks-Simms to lie to federal law enforcement authorities....

Because counts 6 and 7 each charge that Jefferson knowingly and corruptly attempted to persuade another to lie to the authorities, we hold that the indictment shows that "the factfinder had to find ... an act of dishonesty or false statement in order for [Jefferson] to have been convicted." FED. R. EVID. 609, advisory committee's note to 2006 amendments. Accordingly, we hold that evidence of Jefferson's obstruction of justice convictions must be admitted for impeachment purposes under Rule 609(a)(2) should he choose to testify....

"The admission of prior convictions involving dishonesty and false statement is not within the discretion of the Court." FED. R. EVID. 609, advisory committee's note to subsection (a). "Such convictions are peculiarly probative of credibility and, under this rule, are always to be admitted. Thus, judicial discretion granted with respect to the admissibility of other prior convictions is not applicable to those involving dishonesty or false statement." *Id.* Accordingly, we hold that the district court abused its discretion in excluding evidence of Jefferson's convictions for impeachment purposes....

United States v. Browne

829 F.2d 760 (9th Cir. 1987)

CYNTHIA HOLCOMB HALL, Circuit Judge....

I.

On September 18, 1985, Browne was indicted by the grand jury for armed bank robbery, carrying a firearm during the commission of a crime of violence, and possession of a weapon by a felon. On September 19, 1985, Browne was arraigned and entered pleas of not guilty. Subsequently, the district court granted Browne's motion to sever the possession charge, and on December 3 through December 5, 1985, Browne was tried on the remaining two counts.

On December 5, after receiving detailed instructions from the court, the jury found Browne guilty of both armed bank robbery and carrying a firearm during the commission of a crime of violence. On March 3, 1986, the district court denied Browne's motion for a new trial and sentenced Browne to thirty-years imprisonment, twenty-five years for the armed bank robbery and five consecutive years for carrying a firearm during the commission of the robbery....

III.

The next issue we address is whether the district court's ultimate decision to admit evidence of Browne's prior robbery conviction pursuant to Rule 609 was erroneous....

Rule 609 provides that evidence of prior felony convictions is admissible for the purpose of attacking the credibility of a witness if the prejudicial effect of the evidence is outweighed by its probative value. In *United States v. Cook*, 608 F.2d 1175, 1185 n. 8 (9th Cir. 1979) (en banc), we outlined five factors which a district court should consider in balancing the probative value of evidence of a defendant's prior convictions against that evidence's prejudicial effect: (1) the impeachment value of the prior crime; (2) the point in time of the conviction and the witness' subsequent history; (3) the similarity between the past crime and the charged crime; (4) the importance of the defendant's testimony; and, (5) the centrality of the defendant's credibility....

Here, the district court applied each of the five factors and then ruled that the government had met its burden. We note first that the time factor tips the balance in favor of admissibility: Browne had been out of jail after serving his sentence for the prior bank robbery conviction for less than one year at the time of the Farwest Federal Bank robbery. By its terms, Rule 609 allows for admissibility of such a prior conviction even where the defendant has been released for up to ten years.

The district court found that the similarity of the crimes was the only *Cook* factor which weighed against admissibility. In *Bagley*, we held that the trial court abused its discretion in allowing evidence of two prior bank robberies to be admitted to impeach a defendant who was on trial for bank robbery. There, we dismissed the argument that evidence of the prior bank robberies had probative value which substantially outweighed the prejudice to Bagley, reasoning as follows:

> [W]here, as here, the prior conviction is sufficiently similar to the crime charged, there is substantial risk that all exculpatory evidence will be overcome by a jury's fixation on the human tendency to draw a conclusion which is impermissible in law: because he did it before, he must have done it again. Such a risk was clearly present in this case.

Moreover, the government's need for the robbery convictions for impeachment purposes was nil. Most certainly, the government would have impeached Bagley's credibility by the introduction of his two forgery convictions. Thus, the only purpose served by the robbery convictions would be to plant in the minds of the jury the spectre that Bagley did it before and he did it again.

Bagley, 772 F.2d at 488.

Certainly, given *Bagley*, the similarity of Browne's prior conviction did counsel against admissibility. But a prior "bank robbery conviction [is] not inadmissible per se, merely because the offense involved was identical to that for which [the defendant] was on trial." *United States v. Oaxaca*, 569 F.2d 518, 527 (9th Cir.), *cert. denied*, 439 U.S. 926 (1978). If a prior bank robbery conviction serves a proper impeachment purpose, it, like evidence of other crimes, may be admissible in spite of its similarity to the offense at issue.

Based on the importance of the defendant's testimony and the centrality of his credibility to the defense, the district court found our rulings admitting evidence of prior robberies in *Givens* and *Cook* more apropos than our ruling excluding such evidence in *Bagley*. So do we.

In *Givens*, the defendant was on trial for armed robbery. The government sought to admit evidence of Givens' prior robbery and assault with a deadly weapon convictions. Givens' "proposed testimony, in which he would have denied committing the offense, would have placed his credibility directly at issue." We therefore held that the district court "reasonably ... concluded that the impeachment value of the prior convictions would outweigh their admitted prejudicial effect." Givens' prior robbery conviction, being "probative of veracity," was properly admissible to impeach his proposed testimony.

In *Cook*, we held that the government should not be prevented from providing the jury with information which undercuts the defendant's trustworthiness as a witness. In that bank robbery case, we upheld the use of a prior bank robbery conviction to impeach a defendant who proposed to represent himself to be of stellar character. We stated that in such a context the government is not required to "sit silently by, looking at a criminal record which, if made known, would give the jury a more comprehensive view of the trustworthiness of the defendant as a witness."

In this case, the district court relied on *Givens* and *Cook* to justify its finding that three of the relevant factors—the evidence's impeachment value, the importance of the defendant's testimony, and his credibility's centrality to the case—strongly tipped the balance in favor of admissibility. Its reliance was well-placed. Browne had testified that he did not commit the crime and that he had an alibi. No other witness could confirm or disprove the alleged alibi. Browne's credibility was certainly central to his defense. And since Browne had already admitted that he had been convicted of forgery, the government was left with only the prior bank robbery conviction with which to impeach him.

Bagley is certainly distinguishable. There, the court stated that "the record is devoid of any evidence that Bagley intended to misrepresent his character or to testify falsely as to his prior criminal record." Moreover, the government had two prior unadmitted forgeries with which to impeach Bagley. Here, Browne represented his character to be unimpeachable by testifying about his war record, his artistic nature, and his photographic memory, and by testifying that he gave his secretary money when she needed it, while openly admitting to his one, fifteen-year-old, prior forgery conviction. Browne also detailed an alibi for the day and time of the crime which hinged almost entirely on his credibility. Since the government was left with no avenue of impeachment other than use of the prior bank robbery conviction, the jury was properly allowed to consider it. *Cf. Oax-*

aca, 569 F.2d at 527 ("in light of [defendant's] alibi defense" his credibility "was a key issue in the case" and the prior similar convictions were properly held admissible)....

United States v. Cathey
591 F.2d 268 (5th Cir. 1979)

GODBOLD, Circuit Judge:

Frank Cathey was convicted by a jury on three counts of willful attempt to evade or defeat his federal income tax due for the years 1970, 1971 and 1972, in violation of 26 U.S.C. §7201. He was sentenced to one year imprisonment on each count, the sentences to run concurrently, and a $5,000 fine on each count....

The defendant testified, and on cross-examination the prosecution impeached his credibility by eliciting the fact of his prior military conviction for larceny. The defendant has raised several objections to this use of his prior military conviction. Because we conclude that under Fed.R.Evid. 609(b) the trial judge abused his discretion in admitting Cathey's 16-year-old conviction, we do not reach his other objections.

While stationed in Turkey, Cathey was convicted by general court-martial of five specifications of theft of Air Force Exchange merchandise. He was sentenced to two years hard labor, was released from military confinement June 31, 1961, and called to testify in October 1977. The prior conviction was therefore a little more than 16 years old when offered into evidence as measured by the standards of Rule 609(b). *See U. S. v. Cohen*, 544 F.2d 781, 784 (CA5), *cert. denied*, 431 U.S. 914 (1977).[13] Accordingly Rule 609(b)'s standard of admissibility for convictions over 10 years old applies....

As originally presented to Congress, Rule 609(b) made inadmissible all convictions over 10 years old. Although Congress amended the Rule to allow for the use of prior convictions over 10 years old in some circumstances, the legislative history makes clear that "convictions over 10 years old will be admitted very rarely and only in exceptional circumstances." Sen.Rep. No. 1277, 93d Cong. 2d Sess. 4. Rule 609(b) must be interpreted in light of the gloss Congress placed on the Rule's standard of admissibility. We conclude that by use of the term exceptional circumstances Congress intended the courts to take account of the need for using a prior conviction as an essential element of the probative value-prejudicial effect balancing test mandated by Rule 609(b)....[14]

Before analyzing the factors that go into the balancing of the probative value against the prejudicial effect of a prior conviction under 609(b), we emphasize this court's conclusion in *Mills v. Estelle*, 552 F.2d 119, 120 (CA5), *cert. denied*, 434 U.S. 871 (1977), that 609(b) establishes a presumption against the use of more than 10-year-old convictions. The court's conclusion is supported by both the language of the Rule as well as the leg-

---

13. In *Cohen* we computed the age of the prior conviction from the time of the defendant's release from prison to the commencement of the trial. We see no reason to suggest departing from that approach, except to add a caveat that since the concern is the defendant's credibility when he testifies the correct point from which to measure backwards in time may be the date when he testifies rather than the date when the trial commences, which in a protracted trial might be considerably earlier. We have some doubt that *Cohen* intended to focus upon this difference.

14. The other possible interpretation of the legislative history is that Congress was prophesying that as an empirical matter courts will rarely conclude that the probative value of an over-age conviction substantially outweighs its prejudicial effect. This interpretation accounts for the "very rarely" language of the passage, but leaves unexplained what the "exceptional circumstances" are that justify the use of an over-age conviction.

islative history. Rule 609(b) makes over-age convictions inadmissible unless the court makes the required finding of probative value. The general rule, therefore, is inadmissibility. Moreover, in the Senate Report on the Rules of Evidence, the Senate noted that "convictions over ten years old generally do not have much probative value." Sen.Rep. No. 1277, 93d Cong. 2d Sess. 4. The presumption against admissibility is, therefore, founded on a legislative perception that the passage of time dissipates the probative value of a prior conviction....

The prior convictions of a witness may only be used by the jury to evaluate the witness' credibility. In spite of the legal rule limiting the use of prior conviction evidence to impeachment purposes, when the witness is the accused the evidence is subject to improper use. The jury may misuse the evidence by considering the defendant a person of criminal tendencies and, therefore, more likely to have committed the crime for which he is being tried, or if the prior conviction is similar to the new charges, the jury may misuse the prior conviction as evidence of guilt, or the jury may just be more willing to convict a person who already has been convicted for a different crime....

We now turn to the probative value portion of Rule 609(b)'s equation. The probative value of a prior conviction is a function of at least two factors, the nature of the past crime and the remoteness of the conviction. Crimes involving dishonesty or false statement are often more probative of the witness' lack of credibility than even more serious crimes involving violence. Rule 609(a) incorporates this distinction between types of crimes. Whether this defendant's military conviction was for a crime involving dishonesty or false statement is a matter of dispute between the parties. On the view we take of this case, it is not necessary to resolve this dispute. Assuming that the military conviction was for a crime involving dishonesty, that is insufficient justification, by itself, for use of the prior conviction. The presumption against the use of an over-age conviction is not so weak that it falls before a finding that the prior conviction was for a crime involving dishonesty. Judge Tuttle in *Mills v. Estelle*, noted that Rule 609(b)'s 10-year limit on prior convictions "could be conceptualized as a policy statement that if an offender keeps his record unblemished for ten years, he will be presumed to be as truthful as a normal citizen, i. e., that the ten-year period is evidence that the inference supporting use of prior crime impeachment evidence (a lawbreaker is likely to lie) can no longer be drawn about a certain person." A crime involving dishonesty is more likely to overcome Rule 609(b)'s presumption, but more than that bare conclusion must be shown....

In the context of admissibility of over-age convictions exceptional circumstances includes, though it is not limited to, the need of the party offering the evidence to use it. This concept of necessity is relevant to the district judge's evaluation of the probative value of the conviction. Our recent en banc decision in *Beechum*, interpreting Fed.R.Evid. 404, provides us with guidance. Rule 404 like 609(b) calls on the judge to balance the probative value of the proffered evidence against its prejudicial effect.[18] In *Beechum*, the court stated that

> Probity in this context is not an absolute; its value must be determined with regard to the extent to which the defendant's unlawful intent is established by other evidence, stipulation, or inference. It is the incremental probity of the evidence

---

18. The balancing test mandated by the two rules is different in one important respect. Under Rule 403, the court may exclude Rule 404 evidence "if its probative value is *substantially outweighed* by [a] danger of [...] unfair prejudice...." Fed.R.Evid. 403. Under Rule 609(b), on the other hand, an over-age conviction is admissible only if the conviction's "probative value ... *substantially outweighs* its prejudicial effect." The test in Rule 609(b) is the mirror image of the test under Rule 403.

that is to be balanced against its potential for undue prejudice. Thus, if the Government has a strong case on the intent issue, the extrinsic offense may add little and consequently will be excluded more readily.

Therefore, when a party wishes to use an over-age conviction, the trial judge must consider whether the witness already has been impeached, and if so, the probative value of the prior conviction decreases accordingly.

In this case nothing suggests exceptional circumstances justifying the use of Cathey's prior conviction. The defendant's credibility had already been well impeached by the government's cross-examination during which he had been caught in various contradictions and numerous misstatements. There was little need to add the icing of his military conviction. The district court mentioned that on direct examination Cathey had testified to his accumulation of a cash hoard during his military career, and, of course, the court-martial for stealing occurred during his military service. Possibly the court considered the conviction as bearing on the credibility of defendant's claim that he had accumulated a cash hoard. If anything, the conviction of stealing at the time Cathey claimed he was accumulating his cash hoard, bolsters his credibility with respect to a hoard rather than impeaches it. Absent some additional factor justifying the use of the prior conviction, there is no basis for concluding that it falls within the exceptional circumstances caveat to the general prohibition against the use of a conviction more than 10 years old....

[The dissenting opinion of Judge Fay is omitted.]

Illinois Rule of Evidence 609
IMPEACHMENT BY EVIDENCE OF CONVICTION OF CRIME

(a) General Rule. For the purpose of attacking the credibility of a witness, evidence that the witness has been convicted of a crime, except on a plea of nolo contendere, is admissible but only if the crime, (1) was punishable by death or imprisonment in excess of one year under the law under which the witness was convicted, or (2) involved dishonesty or false statement regardless of the punishment unless (3), in either case, the court determines that the probative value of the evidence of the crime is substantially outweighed by the danger of unfair prejudice.

(b) Time Limit. Evidence of a conviction under this rule is not admissible if a period of more than 10 years has elapsed since the date of conviction or of the release of the witness from confinement, whichever is the later date.

....

Michigan Rule of Evidence 609
IMPEACHMENT BY EVIDENCE OF CONVICTION OF CRIME

(a) General Rule. For the purpose of attacking the credibility of a witness, evidence that the witness has been convicted of a crime shall not be admitted unless the evidence has been elicited from the witness or established by public record during cross-examination, and

    (1) the crime contained an element of dishonesty or false statement, or

    (2) the crime contained an element of theft, and

        (A) the crime was punishable by imprisonment in excess of one year or death under the law under which the witness was convicted, and

(B) the court determines that the evidence has significant probative value on the issue of credibility and, if the witness is the defendant in a criminal trial, the court further determines that the probative value of the evidence outweighs its prejudicial effect.

....

Montana Rule of Evidence 609

Impeachment by evidence of conviction of crime

For the purpose of attacking the credibility of a witness, evidence that the witness has been convicted of a crime is not admissible.

COMMISSION COMMENTS

This rule is unlike either the Federal or Uniform Rules (1974) Rule 609 in that they provide that evidence of conviction of a crime is admissible for the purpose of attacking credibility....

However, the Commission rejects the rule allowing impeachment by evidence of conviction of a crime ... because of its low probative value in relation to credibility. The Commission does not accept as valid the theory that a person's willingness to break the law can automatically be translated into willingness to give false testimony. Advisory Committee Note to Federal Rule 609. The Commission does believe that conviction of certain crimes is probative of credibility; however, it is the specific act of misconduct underlying the conviction which is really relevant, not whether it has led to a conviction. Allowing conviction of crime to be proved for the purpose of impeachment merely because it is a convenient method of proving the act of misconduct (Advisory Committee Note, Id.) is not acceptable to the Commission, particularly in light of Rule 608(b) allowing acts of misconduct to be admissible if they relate to credibility....

Notes and Questions

1. Rule 609 includes not only those convictions that follow a jury trial, but also those that are based on a plea of guilty or a plea of *nolo contendere*. Rule 410 poses no bar to the latter type of conviction, as that Rule bars only evidence of a *plea* of *nolo contendere*, not evidence of a *conviction* that follows from such a plea. *E.g., United States v. Williams*, 642 F.2d 136, 138–40 (5th Cir. 1981).

2. Under Rule 609, a party seeking to impeach an opposing party through the use of a prior conviction normally does so by asking the witness to verify that he was convicted of that offense, akin to inquiries under Rule 608(b). But unlike Rule 608(b), if the witness denies the prior conviction or claims that he cannot remember, the party seeking to impeach him can introduce extrinsic evidence of the conviction, which is normally done through the use of a written record of conviction. In addition, a party is free to bring out the prior convictions of his own witness in order to "remove the sting" of impeachment. *See generally* Advisory Committee Note to 1990 Amendment to Rule 609.

3. Note that under Rule 609(a)(1), the key is not the *actual* sentence imposed or served but only the *potential* sentence: the rule provides that it applies to any crime "*punishable by death or by imprisonment for more than one year*" (emphasis added). However, the offense must be punishable by a sentence *in excess* of one year; an offense with a maximum prison sentence of *exactly* one year is *not* admissible under Rule 609(a)(1). *See Rah-*

maan v. Lisath, 2006 WL 3306430, at *2 (S.D. Ohio Nov. 13, 2006); *United States v. Harris*, 512 F. Supp. 1174, 1176 (D. Conn. 1981).

4. As the *Jefferson* court indicates, prior convictions falling within the scope of Rule 609(a)(2) are not subject to exclusion under Rule 403 or any other balancing test:

> The admission of prior convictions involving dishonesty and false statement is not within the discretion of the Court. Such convictions are peculiarly probative of credibility and, under this rule, are always to be admitted. Thus, judicial discretion granted with respect to the admissibility of other prior convictions is not applicable to those involving dishonesty or false statement.

House-Senate Conference Committee, House Report No. 93-1597. *Accord United States v. Collier*, 527 F.3d 695, 700 (8th Cir. 2008); *United States v. Kiendra*, 663 F.2d 349, 353–355 (1st Cir. 1981).

5. When Rule 609 was amended in 1990, the Advisory Committee declined to amend the language of Rule 609(a)(2) to clarify its scope, but offered these comments:

> The Committee recommended no substantive change in subdivision (a)(2), even though some cases raise a concern about the proper interpretation of the words "dishonesty or false statement." These words were used but not explained in the original Advisory Committee Note accompanying Rule 609. Congress extensively debated the rule, and the Report of the House and Senate Conference Committee states that "[b]y the phrase 'dishonesty and false statement,' the Conference means crimes such as perjury, subornation of perjury, false statement, criminal fraud, embezzlement, or false pretense, or any other offense in the nature of *crimen falsi*, commission of which involves some element of deceit, untruthfulness, or falsification bearing on the accused's propensity to testify truthfully." The Advisory Committee concluded that the Conference Report provides sufficient guidance to trial courts and that no amendment is necessary, notwithstanding some decisions that take an unduly broad view of "dishonesty," admitting convictions such as for bank robbery or bank larceny.

Advisory Committee Note to 1990 Amendment to Rule 609.

6. Rule 609(a)(2) was amended, effective December 1, 2006, to encompass any conviction for which the court can readily determine that establishing the elements of the crime required proof (or the admission of) an act of dishonesty or false statement. The Advisory Committee Note to the 2006 amendment indicates in pertinent part:

> The amendment requires that the proponent have ready proof that the conviction required the factfinder to find, or the defendant to admit, an act of dishonesty or false statement. Ordinarily, the statutory elements of the crime will indicate whether it is one of dishonesty or false statement. Where the deceitful nature of the crime is not apparent from the statute and the face of the judgment—as, for example, where the conviction simply records a finding of guilt for a statutory offense that does not reference deceit expressly—a proponent may offer information such as an indictment, a statement of admitted facts, or jury instructions to show that the factfinder had to find, or the defendant had to admit, an act of dishonesty or false statement in order for the witness to have been convicted. But the amendment does not contemplate a "mini-trial" in which the court plumbs the record of the previous proceeding to determine whether the crime was in the nature of *crimen falsi*.

How good of a job does the amendment do of clarifying the scope of Rule 609(a)(2)? Does it clarify the question whether crimes of robbery or larceny are encompassed within its scope?

7. The relevant *start* date for calculating the ten-year period under Rule 609(b) for a conviction that includes a period of parole or probation following imprisonment is the date on which the person is released from prison. In other words, for purposes of Rule 609(b), a person is not deemed to be in "confinement" when she is on parole or probation. *See United States v. Rogers*, 542 F.3d 197, 198–201 (2008); *United States v. Daniel*, 957 F.2d 162, 168 & n.3 (5th Cir. 1992). But does the relevant start date for purposes of Rule 609(b) change if the person is *re-confined* for violating the terms of his parole or probation? *Compare United States v. Gray*, 852 F.2d 136, 139 (4th Cir. 1988) (holding that it changes to the date on which the person is subsequently re-released from prison), *with United States v. Wallace*, 848 F.2d 1464, 1472–1473 (9th Cir. 1988) (holding that it changes to the date on which the person is subsequently re-released from prison if it involves a substantial probation or parole condition that closely parallels the initial criminal activity, but remains the original release date for other types of probation or parole violations).

8. Suppose that a defendant is sentenced on September 9, 1991 to one year in prison for charge A, to be served *concurrently* with a sentence of seven to twenty-one years in prison for charge B. He is ultimately released from prison on December 3, 2004. In determining the admissibility of his conviction for charge A, what is the relevant start date for calculating the ten-year period under Rule 609(b)? *See United States v. Pettiford*, 238 F.R.D. 33, 39–40 (D.D.C. 2006) (holding that confinement for one conviction has no effect on calculating the ten year period applicable to another conviction, and thus that the relevant start date for calculating the ten-year period for charge A would be the date that he would have been released from prison *"but for* the contemporaneous" charge, which would fall "sometime in 1992").

9. A question on which the courts have divided is the relevant *end* date for calculating the ten-year period under Rule 609(b). Unfortunately, there are almost as many answers to this question as there are cases addressing the issue. *Compare United States v. Rogers*, 542 F.3d 197, 201 (7th Cir. 2008) (date trial starts); *United States v. Cathey*, 591 F.2d 268, 274 n.13 (5th Cir. 1979) (same), *with Trindle v. Sonat Marine Inc.*, 697 F. Supp. 879, 881 (E.D. Pa. 1988) (date witness testifies), *with United States v. Foley*, 683 F.2d 273, 277 n.5 (8th Cir. 1982) (date of offense).

10. If a crime is one that involves dishonesty or false statement, but it is more than 10 years old, which test controls, the admit-without-balancing test of Rule 609(a)(2), or the almost-never-admit test of Rule 609(b)? Does *Cathey* provide an answer to that question? *See United States v. Orlando-Figueroa*, 229 F.3d 33, 46 (1st Cir. 2000) (Rule 609(b) governs); *United States v. Payton*, 159 F.3d 49, 56–58 (2d Cir. 1998) (same). Of course, as *Cathey* indicates, the fact that the crime was one involving dishonesty or false statement would enhance its probative worth under the Rule 609(b) balancing test.

11. In balancing probative worth against prejudicial effect under the various balancing tests set forth in Rule 609, are the only options to admit or exclude *all* information regarding a given conviction? *See Perryman v. H & R Trucking, Inc.*, 135 Fed.Appx. 538, 541 (3d Cir. 2005) (approving of trial court's decision to only allow the jury to be informed of the fact of conviction and the duration of imprisonment but not the specific nature of the crime).

12. If a corporate official testifies in his capacity as such, can he be impeached with evidence that not he, but the *corporation*, has a prior criminal conviction? *Compare Walden v. Georgia-Pacific Corp.*, 126 F.3d 506, 523–24 (3d Cir. 1997) ("Criminal acts are relevant to a witness' credibility only if that witness actually participated in the criminal conduct.

It strains logic to argue that an employee's credibility is properly brought into question by the mere fact that he or she is presently employed by a corporation that in some unrelated manner was guilty of dishonest acts"), *with Hickson Corp. v. Norfolk S. Ry. Co.*, 227 F. Supp. 2d 903, 907 (E.D. Tenn. 2002) ("Because a corporation speaks through its officers, employees, and other agents ... it stands to reason a corporation can be a vicarious witness.... therefore, Rule 609 allows the use of a corporation's felony conviction to impeach the corporation's vicarious testimony").

13. When a witness is impeached with a prior conviction under Rule 609, how much information regarding the prior conviction is the impeaching party entitled to introduce? In other words, are they limited to only informing the jury of the *fact* that the witness has previously been convicted of a crime, or are they also entitled to bring to introduce the date of the offense, the specific type of crime, and the details of the prior offense? *See United States v. Estrada*, 430 F.3d 606, 614–17 (2d Cir. 2005) (holding that under Rule 609, the "essential facts" of the offense — including the statutory name of the offense, the date of conviction, and the sentence imposed — are presumptively admissible but the underlying facts or details of the offense are not). *Accord United States v. Commanche*, 577 F.3d 1261, 1270–71 (10th Cir. 2009); *United States v. Osazuwa*, 564 F.3d 1169, 1175 (9th Cir. 2009).

14. Can a witness be impeached under Rule 609 with evidence that he was convicted of a crime in another country? What if that country does not guarantee criminal defendants rights comparable to those guaranteed under the U.S. Constitution? *Compare United States v. Wilson*, 556 F.2d 1177, 1178 (4th Cir. 1977) (holding that witness can be impeached with foreign criminal conviction even though there was no right to a trial by jury, so long as system was not "fundamentally unfair"), *with United States v. Brito-Hernandez*, 996 F.2d 80, 82 (5th Cir. 1993) (leaving open question whether witness can be impeached with conviction imposed by a country that does not guarantee right to a jury trial and right to be free of Double Jeopardy).

15. Suppose that evidence of a prior conviction is not admissible under Rule 609, either because it is punishable by one year or less imprisonment and does not involve dishonesty or false statement, or because it is more than 10 years old and does not pass the balancing test in Rule 609(b), or for some other reason. Could a party nonetheless impeach the opposing party by instead *inquiring* about the underlying *conduct* in accordance with Rule 608(b)? *See United States v. Weichert*, 783 F.2d 23, 26 n.3 (2d Cir. 1986) (holding that the two rules are independent, and thus that the inadmissibility of the conviction under Rule 609 does not bar inquiry into the underlying conduct under Rule 608(b)). *Accord United States v. Barnhart*, 599 F.3d 737,747 (7th Cir. 2010). *But see United States v. Osazuwa*, 564 F.3d 1169, 1173–75 (9th Cir. 2009) (describing this as a "back door" way to circumvent Rule 609, and concluding that Rule 608(b) "permits impeachment *only* by specific acts that have *not* resulted in a criminal conviction") (emphasis added).

Alternatively, if the person failed to disclose that conviction on a job application or other form that required disclosure of prior convictions, may that failure to disclose be inquired into on cross-examination under Rule 608(b), even if the underlying conviction that the person failed to disclose is not admissible under Rule 609? *Cf. United States v. Smith*, 191 Fed. Appx. 383, 388 (6th Cir. 2006) (holding inquiry into failure to disclose conviction on firearms application proper under Rule 608(b)); *United States v. Redditt*, 381 F.3d 597, 601–02 (7th Cir. 2004) (holding inquiry into failure to disclose conviction on job application proper under Rule 608(b) in a case also upholding the admissibility of the underlying conviction under Rule 609).

16. Rule 609(c)(2) provides that a conviction that has been the subject of a pardon, annulment, or similar procedure based on a finding of *innocence* cannot be used to impeach a witness's credibility under Rule 609. A conviction that has been the subject of a pardon, annulment, certificate of rehabilitation, or similar procedure based on a finding of *rehabilitation* likewise cannot be used to impeach a witness's credibility under Rule 609, *unless* the person has been convicted of a subsequent crime punishable by death or imprisonment in excess of one year. *See* Rule 609(c)(1).

17. As a general rule, convictions based on juvenile adjudications are inadmissible, but in criminal cases, the trial court has discretion to admit such evidence when the witness is someone other than the accused if the conviction would otherwise be admissible under Rule 609 and the court finds that its admission is "necessary to fairly determine guilt or innocence." Rule 609(d).

18. A conviction that has been reversed on appeal is not admissible under Rule 609. *See United States v. Van Dorn*, 925 F.2d 1331, 1337 (11th Cir. 1991). However, the mere fact that a conviction is pending appeal does not render it inadmissible under Rule 609, although the fact that an appeal is pending is also admissible. *See* Rule 609(e).

19. Like Rule 608(b), Rule 609 is often confused with Rule 404(b):

> In a criminal setting, evidence offered under Rule 404(b) is substantive evidence against the accused, i.e., it is part of the government's case offered to prove his guilt beyond a reasonable doubt. Rule 609 evidence on the other hand has to do with the accused's ability to tell the truth when testifying on his or her own behalf. While both rules speak of "probative value" and "prejudice," it is critical to note that evidence offered under the respective rules is probative as to different matters. The probative character of evidence under Rule 609 has to do with credibility of a witness, while 404(b) "probativeness" essentially goes to the question of whether or not the accused committed the crime charged. Any similarity or overlap in the standards of admissibility under the respective rules is irrelevant because the rules apply to completely distinct situations.

United States v. Valencia, 61 F.3d 616, 619 (8th Cir. 1995). *But see United States v. Lattner*, 385 F.3d 947, 961 (6th Cir. 2004) (holding that the fact that court has already determined that prior conviction is admissible under Rule 404(b) reduces the prejudicial effect of the evidence when also offered to impeach defendant-witness's credibility under Rule 609).

20. Lurking in the background of Rule 609 is a subtle hearsay problem. Under Rule 609, proof that the witness has been previously convicted of a crime is admitted to impeach his credibility as a witness. Yet the significance of the prior conviction lies not in the mere *fact* that the witness was convicted, but rather in crediting the *truth* of the matter asserted by the trier of fact in that case, to wit, that the witness committed the offense for which he was convicted. *See* Michael H. Graham, 4 Handbook of Fed. Evid. § 803:8 (6th ed. 2006 & Supp. 2010); Roger C. Park, Trial Objections Handbook 2d § 4:58 (2004).

Because evidence of a prior conviction is thus offered under Rule 609 to prove the truth of the matter asserted therein, it is hearsay. Indeed, it is hearsay within hearsay if what is offered is an official record reporting the trier of fact's verdict (as contrasted with the testimony of a person who has first-hand knowledge of the trier of fact's verdict). In most cases, evidence of the previous judgment of conviction would fall within the scope of Rule 803(22), which creates an exception to the hearsay rule for certain judgments of conviction to prove any fact essential to sustain the judgment. Rule 803(22), however, specifically *excludes* judgments of conviction for crimes punishable by one year or less imprisonment, as well as judgments of conviction based on a plea of *nolo contendere*.

How, then, can one offer evidence of a previous judgment of conviction for a crime of dishonesty or false statement punishable by one year or less imprisonment, which is clearly contemplated by Rule 609(a)(2)'s proviso indicating that evidence of such convictions is admissible "regardless of the punishment"? And how can a judgment of conviction based on a plea of *nolo contendere* be offered under Rule 609? The answer given by most commentators is that Rule 609 *itself*, by commanding that evidence of certain prior convictions *shall* be admitted, creates an implicit hearsay exception for judgments offered under that rule. *See* Christopher B. Mueller and Laird C. Kirkpatrick, 4 Federal Evidence § 8:106 (3rd ed. 2007 & Supp. 2011); Michael H. Graham, 2 Handbook of Fed. Evid. § 609:2 (6th ed. 2006 & Supp. 2010); Roger C. Park, Trial Objections Handbook 2d § 4:58 (2004).

C. Impeachment for Bias or Motivation

United States v. Abel
469 U.S. 45 (1984)

Justice REHNQUIST delivered the opinion of the Court....

Respondent John Abel and two cohorts were indicted for robbing a savings and loan in Bellflower, Cal., in violation of 18 U.S.C. §§ 2113(a) and (d). The cohorts elected to plead guilty, but respondent went to trial. One of the cohorts, Kurt Ehle, agreed to testify against respondent and identify him as a participant in the robbery.

Respondent informed the District Court at a pretrial conference that he would seek to counter Ehle's testimony with that of Robert Mills. Mills was not a participant in the robbery but was friendly with respondent and with Ehle, and had spent time with both in prison. Mills planned to testify that after the robbery Ehle had admitted to Mills that Ehle intended to implicate respondent falsely, in order to receive favorable treatment from the Government. The prosecutor in turn disclosed that he intended to discredit Mills' testimony by calling Ehle back to the stand and eliciting from Ehle the fact that respondent, Mills, and Ehle were all members of the "Aryan Brotherhood," a secret prison gang that required its members always to deny the existence of the organization and to commit perjury, theft, and murder on each member's behalf.

Defense counsel objected to Ehle's proffered rebuttal testimony as too prejudicial to respondent. After a lengthy discussion in chambers the District Court decided to permit the prosecutor to cross-examine Mills about the gang, and if Mills denied knowledge of the gang, to introduce Ehle's rebuttal testimony concerning the tenets of the gang and Mills' and respondent's membership in it. The District Court held that the probative value of Ehle's rebuttal testimony outweighed its prejudicial effect, but that respondent might be entitled to a limiting instruction if his counsel would submit one to the court.

At trial Ehle implicated respondent as a participant in the robbery. Mills, called by respondent, testified that Ehle told him in prison that Ehle planned to implicate respondent falsely. When the prosecutor sought to cross-examine Mills concerning membership in the prison gang, the District Court conferred again with counsel outside of the jury's presence, and ordered the prosecutor not to use the term "Aryan Brotherhood" because it was unduly prejudicial. Accordingly, the prosecutor asked Mills if he and respondent were members of a "secret type of prison organization" which had a creed requiring members to deny its existence and lie for each other. When Mills denied knowledge of such an organization the prosecutor recalled Ehle.

Ehle testified that respondent, Mills, and he were indeed members of a secret prison organization whose tenets required its members to deny its existence and "lie, cheat, steal [and] kill" to protect each other. The District Court sustained a defense objection to a question concerning the punishment for violating the organization's rules. Ehle then further described the organization and testified that "in view of the fact of how close Abel and Mills were" it would have been "suicide" for Ehle to have told Mills what Mills attributed to him. Respondent's counsel did not request a limiting instruction and none was given.

The jury convicted respondent. On his appeal a divided panel of the Court of Appeals reversed....

We hold that the evidence showing Mills' and respondent's membership in the prison gang was sufficiently probative of Mills' possible bias towards respondent to warrant its admission into evidence. Thus it was within the District Court's discretion to admit Ehle's testimony, and the Court of Appeals was wrong in concluding otherwise.

Both parties correctly assume, as did the District Court and the Court of Appeals, that the question is governed by the Federal Rules of Evidence. But the Rules do not by their terms deal with impeachment for "bias," although they do expressly treat impeachment by character evidence and conduct, Rule 608, by evidence of conviction of a crime, Rule 609, and by showing of religious beliefs or opinion, Rule 610. Neither party has suggested what significance we should attribute to this fact. Although we are nominally the promulgators of the Rules, and should in theory need only to consult our collective memories to analyze the situation properly, we are in truth merely a conduit when we deal with an undertaking as substantial as the preparation of the Federal Rules of Evidence. In the case of these Rules, too, it must be remembered that Congress extensively reviewed our submission, and considerably revised it.

Before the present Rules were promulgated, the admissibility of evidence in the federal courts was governed in part by statutes or Rules, and in part by case law. This Court had held in *Alford v. United States*, 282 U.S. 687 (1931), that a trial court must allow some cross-examination of a witness to show bias. This holding was in accord with the overwhelming weight of authority in the state courts as reflected in Wigmore's classic treatise on the law of evidence. Our decision in *Davis v. Alaska*, 415 U.S. 308 (1974), holds that the Confrontation Clause of the Sixth Amendment requires a defendant to have some opportunity to show bias on the part of a prosecution witness.

With this state of unanimity confronting the drafters of the Federal Rules of Evidence, we think it unlikely that they intended to scuttle entirely the evidentiary availability of cross-examination for bias. One commentator, recognizing the omission of any express treatment of impeachment for bias, prejudice, or corruption, observes that the Rules "clearly contemplate the use of the above-mentioned grounds of impeachment." E. Cleary, McCormick on Evidence § 40, p. 85 (3d ed. 1984). Other commentators, without mentioning the omission, treat bias as a permissible and established basis of impeachment under the Rules.

We think this conclusion is obviously correct. Rule 401 defines as "relevant evidence" evidence having any tendency to make the existence of any fact that is of consequence to the determination of the action more probable or less probable than it would be without the evidence. Rule 402 provides that all relevant evidence is admissible, except as otherwise provided by the United States Constitution, by Act of Congress, or by applicable rule. A successful showing of bias on the part of a witness would have a tendency to make the facts to which he testified less probable in the eyes of the jury than it would be without such testimony.

The correctness of the conclusion that the Rules contemplate impeachment by showing of bias is confirmed by the references to bias in the Advisory Committee Notes to Rules 608 and 610, and by the provisions allowing any party to attack credibility in Rule 607, and allowing cross-examination on "matters affecting the [witness's] credibility[]" in Rule 611(b). The Courts of Appeals have upheld use of extrinsic evidence to show bias both before and after the adoption of the Federal Rules of Evidence.

We think the lesson to be drawn from all of this is that it is permissible to impeach a witness by showing his bias under the Federal Rules of Evidence just as it was permissible to do so before their adoption. In this connection, the comment of the Reporter for the Advisory Committee which drafted the Rules is apropos:

> "In principle, under the Federal Rules no common law of evidence remains. 'All relevant evidence is admissible, except as otherwise provided....' In reality, of course, the body of common law knowledge continues to exist, though in the somewhat altered form of a source of guidance in the exercise of delegated powers." Cleary, Preliminary Notes on Reading the Rules of Evidence, 57 Neb.L.Rev. 908, 915 (1978).

Ehle's testimony about the prison gang certainly made the existence of Mills' bias towards respondent more probable. Thus it was relevant to support that inference. Bias is a term used in the "common law of evidence" to describe the relationship between a party and a witness which might lead the witness to slant, unconsciously or otherwise, his testimony in favor of or against a party. Bias may be induced by a witness' like, dislike, or fear of a party, or by the witness' self-interest. Proof of bias is almost always relevant because the jury, as finder of fact and weigher of credibility, has historically been entitled to assess all evidence which might bear on the accuracy and truth of a witness' testimony. The "common law of evidence" allowed the showing of bias by extrinsic evidence, while requiring the cross-examiner to "take the answer of the witness" with respect to less favored forms of impeachment.

Mills' and respondent's membership in the Aryan Brotherhood supported the inference that Mills' testimony was slanted or perhaps fabricated in respondent's favor. A witness' and a party's common membership in an organization, even without proof that the witness or party has personally adopted its tenets, is certainly probative of bias....

Respondent argues that even if the evidence of membership in the prison gang were relevant to show bias, the District Court erred in permitting a full description of the gang and its odious tenets. Respondent contends that the District Court abused its discretion under Federal Rule of Evidence 403, because the prejudicial effect of the contested evidence outweighed its probative value. In other words, testimony about the gang inflamed the jury against respondent, and the chance that he would be convicted by his mere association with the organization outweighed any probative value the testimony may have had on Mills' bias.

Respondent specifically contends that the District Court should not have permitted Ehle's precise description of the gang as a lying and murderous group. Respondent suggests that the District Court should have cut off the testimony after the prosecutor had elicited that Mills knew respondent and both may have belonged to an organization together. This argument ignores the fact that the *type* of organization in which a witness and a party share membership may be relevant to show bias. If the organization is a loosely knit group having nothing to do with the subject matter of the litigation, the inference of bias arising from common membership may be small or nonexistent. If the prosecutor had elicited that both respondent and Mills belonged to the Book of the Month Club, the jury probably would not have inferred bias even if the District Court had admitted the testimony. The attributes of the Aryan Brotherhood—a secret prison sect sworn to perjury and self-protection—bore directly not only on the *fact* of bias but also on the *source* and *strength* of Mills' bias. The tenets of this group showed that Mills had a powerful motive to slant his testimony towards respondent, or even commit perjury outright.

A district court is accorded a wide discretion in determining the admissibility of evidence under the Federal Rules. Assessing the probative value of common membership in any particular group, and weighing any factors counseling against admissibility is a matter first for the district court's sound judgment under Rules 401 and 403 and ultimately, if the evidence is admitted, for the trier of fact.

Before admitting Ehle's rebuttal testimony, the District Court gave heed to the extensive arguments of counsel, both in chambers and at the bench. In an attempt to avoid undue prejudice to respondent the court ordered that the name "Aryan Brotherhood" not be used. The court also offered to give a limiting instruction concerning the testimony, and it sustained defense objections to the prosecutor's questions concerning the punishment meted out to unfaithful members. These precautions did not prevent *all* prejudice to respondent from Ehle's testimony, but they did, in our opinion, ensure that the admission of this highly probative evidence did not *unduly* prejudice respondent. We hold there was no abuse of discretion under Rule 403 in admitting Ehle's testimony as to membership and tenets.

Respondent makes an additional argument based on Rule 608(b). That Rule allows a cross-examiner to impeach a witness by asking him about specific instances of past conduct, other than crimes covered by Rule 609, which are probative of his veracity or "character for truthfulness or untruthfulness." The Rule limits the inquiry to cross-examination of the witness, however, and prohibits the cross-examiner from introducing extrinsic evidence of the witness' past conduct.

Respondent claims that the prosecutor cross-examined Mills about the gang not to show bias but to offer Mills' membership in the gang as past conduct bearing on his veracity. This was error under Rule 608(b), respondent contends, because the mere fact of Mills' membership, without more, was not sufficiently probative of Mills' character for truthfulness. Respondent cites a second error under the same Rule, contending that Ehle's rebuttal testimony concerning the gang was extrinsic evidence offered to impugn Mills' veracity, and extrinsic evidence is barred by Rule 608(b)....

It seems clear to us that the proffered testimony with respect to Mills' membership in the Aryan Brotherhood sufficed to show potential bias in favor of respondent; because of the tenets of the organization described, it might also impeach his veracity directly. But there is no rule of evidence which provides that testimony admissible for one purpose and inadmissible for another purpose is thereby rendered inadmissible; quite the contrary is the case. It would be a strange rule of law which held that relevant, competent evidence which tended to show bias on the part of a witness was nonetheless inadmissible because it also tended to show that the witness was a liar.

We intimate no view as to whether the evidence of Mills' membership in an organization having the tenets ascribed to the Aryan Brotherhood would be a specific instance of Mills' conduct which could not be proved against him by extrinsic evidence except as otherwise provided in Rule 608(b). It was enough that such evidence could properly be found admissible to show bias....

Firemen's Fund Ins. Co. v. Thien

63 F.3d 754 (8th Cir. 1995)

MAGILL, Circuit Judge....

On September 11, 1989, a small aircraft, en route from Kansas City, Missouri, to Springdale, Arkansas, crashed near Bentonville, Arkansas. The airplane was owned and operated by Mid-Plains Corp., an air courier business based in Kansas City, and both the pilot, a Mid-Plains employee, and the passenger, Charles Benedict, were killed. Benedict was associated with Mid-Plains as an employee who ran errands and did "odd jobs" for the company, reporting to Michael Thien, director of operations.

Benedict's parents, Kenneth and Hallowgene Benedict, and his son, Chad Benedict (the Benedicts), brought a wrongful death action in a Missouri circuit court against Mid-Plains, Thien, and Richard Lund, defendant ad litem for the pilot. Mid-Plains was dismissed from the suit, and Benedict's widow and other son, Martina and Chris Benedict, did not join the suit.

Firemen's Fund Insurance Company, Mid-Plains' liability insurer, denied coverage to Thien and Lund because, at the time of the accident, Benedict was a Mid-Plains employee acting within the scope of his employment and thus fell under an exclusionary clause in the liability policy. Subsequently, Firemen's Fund brought an action against Thien and Lund in federal district court seeking declaratory judgment that the exclusionary clause applied to liability coverage of Thien and Lund for Benedict's death. The Benedicts intervened as defendants....

Thien and Lund ... are ... not covered under this policy if Benedict was an employee of Mid-Plains at the time of the accident, and if Benedict was on the airplane acting within the scope of his employment....

The parties agreed that Benedict was a Mid-Plains employee until at least August 31, 1989, but at trial presented conflicting evidence as to his status at the time of the accident. Conflicting evidence was also presented as to whether Benedict was traveling on the Mid-Plains airplane for business or personal purposes. After trial, the jury found that Benedict was an employee acting within the scope of his employment when the accident happened, and that Firemen's Fund therefore was not obliged to indemnify Thien and Lund for any liability arising from Benedict's death. The Benedicts now appeal....

[T]he Benedicts argue that the district court erred in excluding evidence of Martina and Chris Benedict's religious beliefs, offered to show that Martina and Chris were biased witnesses. Martina and Chris were both members of "Zion's Endeavor," a religious group of which Thien was the pastor.

Under Rule 610 of the Federal Rules of Evidence, [evidence of a witness's religious beliefs or opinions is not admissible to attack or support the witness's credibility]. However,

> [w]hile the rule forecloses inquiry into the religious beliefs or opinions of a witness for the purpose of showing that his character for truthfulness is affected by their nature, an inquiry for the purpose of showing interest or bias because of them is not within the prohibition. Thus disclosure of affiliation with a church which is a party to the litigation would be allowable under the rule.

Fed.R.Evid. 610 advisory committee's notes. The court admitted testimony that the church consisted of "a group of folks who met in [Thien's] basement, about 30 people...." The court further admitted testimony that Chris and Martina were members of the church of which Thien was the pastor, and that Chris worked for a company owned by Thien and was "close" to Thien. This evidence was properly admitted for the purpose of showing that Chris and Martina may have been biased in favor of Thien through their religious affiliation with him.

The evidence excluded by the court, however, was not probative of Martina's and Chad's bias in favor of Thien. All of the evidence cited in appellant's brief as improperly excluded under Rule 610 concerns a specific tenet of Zion's Endeavor that participation in civil litigation is in violation of biblical law. The Benedicts proposed to introduce testimony regarding this specific tenet as the reason why Martina and Chris were not parties to the state court wrongful death action brought by the Benedicts, and why Chad delayed in joining that action. We fail to see the relevance of this issue to the instant case, and we fail to see how showing that Martina and Chris had religious reasons to decide not to join the wrongful death action shows that they were biased witnesses in the insurance action. The fact that Martina and Chris were members of a small religious group led by Thien, and that met regularly in Thien's basement, was before the jury. This fact is probative of bias, and was admitted. The reasons why Martina and Chris did not join the wrongful death action, and why Chad was late in joining, do not add to a showing of bias, and appear to us to be an attempt to undermine Martina's and Chris's credibility, and to prejudice the jury against them, by painting them as religious extremists.

The district court did not abuse its discretion in excluding detailed examination of the nature of Martina and Chris Benedict's religious beliefs....

Notes and Questions

1. Impeachment based on the witness's bias or motivation is extremely broad, covering not only evidence of a close or hostile relationship between a witness and a party, but virtually *anything* that might cause a witness to shade his testimony. Thus, for example, a witness, such as an expert witness, can be impeached by proof that he is being paid a fee for testifying. Similarly, a witness who testifies pursuant to a plea agreement with the government can be impeached by proof of the agreement. Indeed, the category is bounded only by the breadth of emotions and temptations that exist in life. Consider, as an example, the following:

> The government argues that evidence of the movie contract had no bearing on Freeman's veracity as a witness. It is true that there was no evidence that the movie contract was in any way contingent on the outcome of the trial. Nevertheless, it seems likely that it was. The market value of a story that ends in acquittal is unlikely to be the same as the market value of a story that ends in conviction. If Freeman was swindled, then there is grist for the cinematic mill; if she was just disappointed, then there is pathos but no movie....

> If Freeman stood to gain more from a conviction than an acquittal, then the movie contract was relevant as to bias. The movie contract might have affected Freeman's testimony both because of the pecuniary benefit to her of a guilty verdict, and because of the nonpecuniary benefit to her of a favorable portrayal in the movie.

United States v. Dees, 34 F.3d 838, 844 (9th Cir. 1994).

2. Note that in cases such as *Thien*, what is relevant is not the particular religious *denomination* that the party and the witness belong to, but instead the fact that they are affiliated with the *same* religious denomination. Thus, to avoid the potential risk of prejudice

against a party because of his *specific* religion, courts sometimes hold that only evidence of common membership and not the name of the religious denomination should be introduced. *See Finch v. Hercules Inc.* 1995 WL 785100, at *5 (D. Del. Dec. 22, 1995).

3. Note that Rule 610 bars evidence of a person's religious beliefs not only when offered to impeach a witness' credibility, but also when offered to suggest that those beliefs enhance a witness's credibility. *See, e.g., United States v. Tsosie,* 288 Fed. Appx. 496, 502 (10th Cir. 2008); *Tisdale v. Federal Express Corp.,* 415 F.3d 516, 536 (6th Cir. 2005).

4. Would the tenets of a person's religion be admissible over a Rule 610 objection if they included a requirement that members of the religion "lie, cheat, steal [and] kill" to protect one another? Stated somewhat differently, in *Abel,* could the defense have argued that the "Aryan Brotherhood" was a religion, and that it thus violates Rule 610 to introduce its tenet that members "lie, cheat, steal [and] kill" to protect one another? *See* Karl R. Moor & Jennifer M. Busby, *Cacotheism and the False Witness: A Modest Proposal for Amending the Federal Rules of Evidence,* 19 Cumb. L. Rev. 75, 94–95 (1989) (proposing that Rule 610 be amended to make clear that it does not bar inquiry into religious beliefs for the purpose of showing adherence to a tenet or membership in a group that requires, sanctions, or encourages the making of false statements).

D. Sensory Perception

United States v. Pryce
938 F.2d 1343 (D.C. Cir. 1991)

STEPHEN F. WILLIAMS, Circuit Judge....

On December 20, 1988 the police raided Marguerite Briscoe's apartment in Southwest Washington. There they found Thomas and Pryce, along with much crack, a little over $2000 in cash, and a nine-millimeter pistol. They also found, among other people, Briscoe's son Reginald Chandler and Reginald's cousin Anthony Chandler. Several weeks later, the police arrested the other two defendants (Antonio and Gaskins) in a nearby apartment and charged them with involvement in the drug ring.

At trial, the government offered as its principal witnesses the police officers who conducted the December 20 raid, and—for an insider's view of the drug ring—Briscoe and the two Chandlers.... The testimony generally suggested that Thomas and Pryce were the leaders of the operation, while Gaskins and Antonio were, by comparison, bit players with look-out and perhaps enforcement roles.

* * *

Our first—and most important—issue concerns the trial court's decision to prohibit defense counsel from cross-examining Anthony Chandler on his past hallucinations. Just before his cross-examination, Gaskins's lawyer told the court that he had access to a psychiatric report, dated September 26, 1988, stating that Anthony had been seeing and hearing nonexistent events. After some preliminary discussion, the court and the lawyer had this colloquy:

> THE COURT: I would say this. I will let you ask him if he suffered any during the relevant time frame, but you may not go into that report or anything he may have told a psychiatrist.
>
> MR. HAND: Very well.

THE COURT: I think, as I said, you can test the credibility of the witness and you can test the ability of the witness to observe. So you can ask him, if you want to take that risk, because it is risky.

MR. HAND: Well, may I ask him, "Do you suffer from"—

THE COURT: No.

MR. HAND: "Do you ever hear things and see things that aren't really there?"

THE COURT: Only during the time frame that he has discussed, December 1 through December 20. You can run the risk if you wish.

MR. HAND: Very well.

The trial court effectively ruled that any cross-examination of Anthony on his mental condition would have to begin and end with questions about that condition as it existed *in December*. The court thus apparently barred defense counsel from asking *any* questions about Chandler's hallucinations in September as a foundation for questions about his condition in December, much less as a basis for impeaching his responses about December. The court gave no explanation for its ruling.

This restriction was an abuse of the trial court's discretion to limit cross-examination on matters affecting credibility, and violated the confrontation clause of the sixth amendment. Hallucinations in September are obviously relevant to a witness' ability to discern reality in December. Physical impairments—a witness' being blind or deaf, or just myopic or hard of hearing—have long been proper subjects of impeachment. Courts have extended that principle to evidence of mental illnesses that do not directly impair a witness' perception, reasoning that such evidence also affects a witness' credibility, though more obliquely. We do not appear to have specifically addressed that extension, and we do not do so here. For even if we assume that evidence of some kinds of mental illness is generally inadmissible for impeachment purposes, we think that a tendency to hallucinate is so like a direct physical impairment as to fall well within the old-fashioned rule. Normally, therefore, a court must not keep such evidence from the jury....

[The concurring opinion of Judge Randolph and the dissenting opinion of Judge Silberman are omitted.]

United States v. DiPaolo
804 F.2d 225 (2d Cir. 1986)

OAKES, Circuit Judge:

While not contesting the sufficiency of the evidence, Nick DiPaolo, Edward Weather, and Paul Snyder all appeal their convictions for conspiracy to intimidate witnesses and prevent communication to law enforcement officers of information relating to a Postal Service robbery in violation of 18 U.S.C. § 371 (1982), and the substantive crimes of using intimidation and physical force against Lucille Barone and against her sister-in-law, Joanne Barone, in violation of 18 U.S.C. § 1512 (1982)....

Appellants claim that their cross-examinations of Joanne Barone were overly restricted because the trial court, after an in camera hearing, declined to permit them to cross-examine her regarding her use of alcohol. She testified in camera that although she has had a drinking problem for two years, there were long periods of time in which she did not drink, including the day Nick DiPaolo assaulted her. Indeed, she testified that she had consumed alcohol on only one occasion between January 1985 and April 15, and that was in the middle of March. After she was beaten by DiPaolo, however, she started drinking again on April 19 and after the second assault experienced a relapse, finally seeking professional help in June 1985. Joanne Barone further testified that she was not under the influence of alcohol at the time she was testifying and in fact had not consumed any alcohol for five months. The court ruled that counsel would not be permitted to impeach the witness solely on the basis of having a drinking problem.

It is, of course, within the proper scope of cross-examination to determine whether a witness was under the influence of drugs or narcotics or alcohol at the time of observation of events in dispute, or at the time the witness is testifying. *See generally* 3A J. Wigmore, *Evidence* §§ 933–934 (Chadbourne rev. 1970). As Wigmore points out, however, "a general *habit of intemperance* tells us nothing of the witness' testimonial incapacity [unless it involves] actual intoxication at the time of the event observed or at the time of testifying." Hence, because its bearing on moral character "does not involve the veracity trait ..., it will usually not be admissible." *Id.* § 933 at 762. No foundation was laid here to permit evidence of alcohol consumption to come before the jury; there was no indication that the witness was under the influence of alcohol or drugs either at the times she observed the events in dispute or at the time she was testifying. As to the relapse that she suffered after the assaults upon her, it was well within the discretion of the district court to exclude such evidence, *see* Fed.R.Evid. 611(a)(3)....

Notes and Questions

1. Recall that at common law, the mentally incapacitated were deemed incompetent to testify. Under modern practice, they are deemed competent to testify, with the fact of their mental incapacity going to the weight rather than the admissibility of their testimony. *See* Advisory Committee Note to Rule 601.

2. Do you agree with the *DiPaolo* court that evidence of chronic alcohol abuse tells you nothing about the witness's ability to perceive if he was not intoxicated at the time he perceived the events or at the time he testified? Isn't it possible that, over time, chronic alcohol abuse can impair a witness's ability to perceive accurately?

3. Should a witness be subject to impeachment merely because he has been treated by a psychologist or a psychiatrist? In considering the use of such evidence to impeach a witness, courts focus on the likely effect that the witness's illness has on her ability to perceive, recall, and report their observations:

> For over forty years, federal courts have permitted the impeachment of ... witnesses based on their mental condition at the time of the events testified to. Evidence about a prior condition of mental instability that "provide[s] some significant help to the jury in its efforts to evaluate the witness's ability to perceive or to recall events or to testify accurately" is relevant....
>
> Despite this precedent, we are aware of no court to have found relevant an informally diagnosed depression or personality defect. Rather, federal courts appear to have found mental instability relevant to credibility only where, during the time-frame of the events testified to, the witness exhibited a pronounced disposition to lie or hallucinate, or suffered from a severe illness, such as schizophrenia, that dramatically impaired her ability to perceive and tell the truth.

United States v. Butt, 955 F.2d 77, 82–83 (1st Cir. 1992). *Accord United States v. Kohring*, 637 F.3d 895, 910–11 (9th Cir. 2011).

4. Just as with evidence of alcohol use and mental illness, courts limit the admissibility of evidence of drug use to situations in which it is shown that the drug use impacted the witness's ability to perceive, recall, and report his observations:

> Evidence of a witness' prior drug use may be admitted insofar as it relates to his possible inability to recollect and relate. However, we have recognized that "there is considerable danger that evidence that a witness has used illegal drugs may so prejudice the jury that it will excessively discount the witness' testimony." Thus, a district court may refuse cross-examination on the issue where memory or mental capacity is not legitimately at issue and the evidence is offered solely as a general character attack.

United States v. Mojica, 185 F.3d 780, 788–789 (7th Cir. 1999).

E. Impeachment by Contradiction

United States v. Beauchamp

986 F.2d 1 (1st Cir. 1993)

LEVIN H. CAMPBELL, Senior Circuit Judge....

I.

On December 4, 1991, defendant was indicted and charged with uttering and publishing a forged treasury check and aiding and abetting others in uttering and publishing the check in violation of 18 U.S.C. § 510(a)(2) and 2. After defendant's first trial ended in a mistrial, the case proceeded to trial again on May 18, 1992.

The evidence indicated that on May 4, 1990, the Internal Revenue Service mailed a tax refund check in the amount of $2006.20 to Francisca and Domingo Franco of Central Falls, Rhode Island. The Francos never received their check. Instead, on May 17, 1990, defendant deposited the Francos' refund check in a checking account he had opened two days earlier at a Fleet Bank branch in Lincoln, Rhode Island. The back of the refund check was endorsed "Domingo Franco" and "Francisco (sic) D. Franco." Underneath the endorsements, which were forged, defendant signed his own name and address. No other deposits were made to the account, which reached a zero balance on June 5, 1990. The account was closed on July 16, 1990.

In May of 1991, the Providence office of the United States Secret Service began an investigation into possible fraud in the negotiation of the Francos' refund check. As defendant's name and address were on the back of the check, Special Agent Rudolph Rivera contacted him. Defendant admitted to having signed his name on the back of the check, but stated that he had been handed the check by a Hispanic man as partial payment for a car. According to defendant, an acquaintance of his, named Joseph Massey, had brought the Hispanic man to defendant to buy the car. Defendant claimed that the Hispanic man had identified himself as the payee on the refund check....

Massey testified for the government at trial.... Massey testified that on August 1, 1991, defendant went to Massey's wife's house and told Massey that he was in trouble about a check....

Defendant was denied permission to call as a witness Zelmare Amaral, the landlady of 101 Carpenter Street, Pawtucket, Rhode Island. Defendant sought to introduce Mrs.

Amaral's testimony primarily to impeach Massey's testimony that he lived at the 101 Carpenter Street address. Mrs. Amaral had testified at the first trial that Massey's brother and sister, not Massey, resided at 101 Carpenter Street, although she acknowledged having seen Massey there. The court would not allow Mrs. Amaral to testify, saying defendant was merely seeking to impeach Massey on a "very collateral" matter.

The jury returned a guilty verdict and defendant was sentenced to 11 months imprisonment. This appeal followed.

II.

A. *Impeachment on Collateral Matters*

Defendant contends the district court abused its discretion when it precluded Mrs. Amaral from taking the stand to contradict Massey's testimony that he lived at 101 Carpenter Street.... Defendant concedes, as he must, that the district court permitted him to cross-examine Massey on his address. Defendant contends, however, that the value of his right to ask Massey where he lives for the purpose of "exposing falsehood" is vastly diminished if defendant cannot also present extrinsic evidence demonstrating that Massey has lied....

It is well established that a party may not present extrinsic evidence to impeach a witness by contradiction on a collateral matter. Thus, it is often said that when a witness testifies to a collateral matter, the examiner "must take [the] answer," i.e., the examiner may not disprove it by extrinsic evidence. A matter is considered collateral if "the matter itself is not relevant in the litigation to establish a fact of consequence, i.e., not relevant for a purpose other than mere contradiction of the in-court testimony of the witness." 1 *McCorm[i]ck on Evidence* § 45, at 169. Stated another way, extrinsic evidence to disprove a fact testified to by a witness is admissible when it satisfies the Rule 403 balancing test and is not barred by any other rule of evidence. To the extent Mrs. Amaral's testimony merely went to Massey's credibility by demonstrating a contradiction on an immaterial matter, it was clearly excludible....

[The opinion of Judge Bownes, concurring in part and dissenting in part, is omitted.]

Notes and Questions

1. Consider the following explanation of the collateral matter rule:

> A collateral contradiction is typically one on a point not related to the matters at issue, but designed to show that the witness' false statement about one thing implies a probability of false statements about the matters at issue.

United States v. Higa, 55 F.3d 448, 452 (9th Cir. 1995).

Why shouldn't you be able to introduce extrinsic evidence to contradict a witness on a collateral matter? Isn't the fact that what the witness said about a minor point was untrue relevant to determining his overall veracity?

2. Note that the collateral matter rule does not prevent a party from cross-examining a witness in an effort to expose the contradiction; it merely bars the use of extrinsic evidence to contradict the witness's testimony. *See Simmons, Inc. v. Pinkerton's, Inc.*, 762 F.2d 591, 604 (7th Cir. 1985) ("while the accuracy of a witness' perception or memory can always be tested through traditional cross-examination techniques, the collateral evidence rule limits the extent to which the witness' testimony about non-essential matters may be contradicted by extrinsic proof"). In this sense, it is akin to evidence of specific acts bearing on trustworthiness under Rule 608(b).

3. Consider the following defense of the rule:

> The laws of evidence on this subject, as to what ought and what ought not to be received, must be considered as founded on a sort of comparative consideration of the time to be occupied in examinations of this nature and the time which it is practicable to bestow upon them. If we lived for a thousand years, instead of about sixty or seventy, and every case were of sufficient importance, it might be possible and perhaps proper to throw a light on matters in which every possible question might be suggested, for the purpose of seeing by such means whether the whole was unfounded, or what portion of it was not, and to raise every possible inquiry as to the truth of the statements made. But I do not see how that could be; in fact, mankind find it to be impossible. Therefore some line must be drawn.

Attorney-General v. Hitchcock, 1 Exch. 91, 104 (1847).

4. Some authorities recognize an exception to the collateral matter rule — described as "concededly vague" — to contradict a witness's testimony about a "linchpin" fact, one that "as a matter of human experience, he could not be mistaken about that fact if the thrust of his testimony on the historical merits was true." *See, e.g., Rowland v. United States*, 840 A.2d 664, 680 (D.C. 2004) (quoting McCormick on Evidence § 49, at 203 (5th ed. 1999)).

5. What is the *source* of the collateral matter rule? *Must* a trial court always exclude evidence deemed to be collateral? *See United States v. Libby*, 475 F. Supp. 2d 73, 98–99 (D.D.C. 2007) ("although the rule permitting a trial court to exclude extrinsic evidence of a prior statement offered solely to impeach a witness on a collateral issue predates the Federal Rules of Evidence by well over a century, it now finds its source in Rule 403. Accordingly, the Court can, in an exercise of its discretion under Rule 403, exclude the extrinsic evidence the defendant wishes to introduce ... if it concludes that it relates to only a collateral issue.").

6. If a witness testifies on direct that he has never committed any crime (or any category of crimes), is evidence that he was convicted of certain crimes governed by Rule 609 or is it instead governing by the common law rules governing impeachment by contradiction? *See United States v. Gilmore*, 553 F.3d 266, 270–73 (3d Cir. 2009) (holding that Rule 609, including its restrictive balancing test for older convictions, is inapplicable in this situation, reasoning that "Rule 609 controls the use of prior felony convictions to impeach a witness' general character for truthfulness, but impeachment by contradiction concerns the use of evidence to impeach a witness' specific testimony.").

F. Impeachment by Prior Inconsistent Statement

Recall from Chapter 7 that, under certain circumstances, a witness' prior inconsistent statement can be admitted at trial as *substantive* proof of the matter asserted within that prior inconsistent statement. Rule 801(d)(1)(A) provides that a statement is not hearsay if:

> The declarant testifies and is subject to cross-examination about a prior statement, and the statement ... is inconsistent with the declarant's testimony and was given under penalty of perjury at a trial, hearing, or other proceeding or in a deposition....

As demonstrated by the *Goodman* case in Chapter 7, use can be made of a witness' prior inconsistent statement even when the statement does not satisfy the requirements of Rule 801(d)(1)(A) because it was not made in a trial, hearing, deposition, or "other proceeding." Upon learning that the witness' current testimony contradicts his earlier statements, the jury will inevitably question his credibility, concluding that "he either lied then, is lying now, or that he lied both then and now." *United States v. Bednar*, 776 F.2d 236, 239 (8th Cir. 1985).

Whether a party wishes to use a prior inconsistent statement merely to impeach a witness, or also as substantive evidence under Rule 801(d)(1)(A), she must comply with the requirements of Rule 613. First, Rule 613(a) provides that when a witness is examined concerning her prior statement, the statement, on request, shall be shown or disclosed to opposing counsel. Second, Rule 613(b) provides that, as a general rule, *extrinsic* evidence of a witness' prior inconsistent statement is not normally admissible unless "the witness is given an opportunity to explain or deny the statement and an adverse party is given an opportunity to examine the witness about it."

Rule 613 represents a relaxing of the common law rule governing the use of prior inconsistent statements. The common law rule, grounded in *The Queen's Case*, 2 Brod. & B. 284 (1820), imposed two requirements. First, the examining lawyer was required to warn the witness about the possible inconsistency between his current testimony and a prior statement of his by showing him the prior inconsistent statement, if written, or alluding to the prior statement, if oral. Second, extrinsic evidence of the prior inconsistent statement could not be introduced until *after* the witness was given a chance to explain or deny the statement.

The common law requirements were thought to give too great a benefit to the dishonest witness who, forewarned of his prior inconsistency, could re-shape his testimony, and generally diminish the impeaching effect of the use of prior inconsistent statements. Accordingly, the first common law requirement is explicitly eliminated by Rule 613(a), which, while requiring disclosure to opposing counsel upon request, provides that "a party need not show it or disclose its contents to the *witness*" (emphasis added). Moreover, while Rule 613(b) maintains the common law requirement that the witness be given an opportunity to explain or deny the statement, the rule contains "no specification of any particular time or sequence." Advisory Committee Note to Rule 613(b).

While Rule 613 contains the only explicit restrictions on the use of prior inconsistent statements to impeach witnesses, there are additional, implicit limitations. The materials that follow explore these limitations.

Problem 10-3: The Turn-Coat Witness

Paula and Donald collide at a busy intersection. As a result of the accident, Paula loses consciousness. Paula was driving a yellow Volkswagen New Beetle and Donald was driving a blue Cooper Mini. At the scene of the accident, William, who witnessed the accident, says to John, an ambulance driver, "I saw the accident, and the blue car ran the red light."

When Paula regains consciousness, she can remember nothing about the accident. Upon speaking with John, however, she learns about what William said. Paula later speaks with William, who says to her, "I saw the accident, and the blue car ran the red light."

Paula sues Donald for negligence. At trial, Paula calls William as a witness and asks him if he saw what happened. William testifies, "My head was turned away, and I don't know who ran the light."

Paula, surprised by this response, asks William about his prior statement in which he said that "the blue car ran the red light." William denies having made the prior statement. Paula then takes the stand, and over Donald's hearsay objection, testifies that William had previously said to her that "the blue car ran the light."

Paula introduces no more evidence, and rests her case, and Donald moves for a directed verdict.

Should Paula have been permitted to testify? How should the court dispose of Donald's motion for a directed verdict? How, if at all, would your answer differ if, at trial, William instead testified that "the yellow car ran the light"? How, if at all, would your answer differ under the Ohio version of Rule 607, excerpted below?

United States v. Ince
21 F.3d 576 (4th Cir. 1994)

MURNAGHAN, Circuit Judge:

Appellant Nigel D. Ince was convicted by a jury for assault with a dangerous weapon, with intent to do bodily harm. Because the United States' only apparent purpose for impeaching one of its own witnesses was to circumvent the hearsay rule and to expose the jury to otherwise inadmissible evidence of Ince's alleged confession, we reverse.

I

Late on the evening of September 4, 1992, a rap concert and dance at the Sosa Recreation Center at Fort Belvoir, Virginia ended abruptly when members of two of the bands performing there got in a scuffle. Shortly thereafter, a black male wearing an orange shirt or jacket fired a nine millimeter pistol twice at trucks leaving the Recreation Center's parking lot. Defendant-appellant Nigel Ince, Angela Neumann, and two of their friends hopped in their van and headed for Pence Gate, Fort Belvoir's nearest exit. The military police pulled the van, as well as other vehicles leaving the parking lot, over to the side of the road and asked the drivers and passengers to stand on the curb.... As part of the investigation that followed, Military Policeman Roger D. Stevens interviewed and took a signed, unsworn statement from Neumann. She recounted that Ince had admitted to firing the shots, but said he no longer had the gun.

The United States indicted Ince for violating 18 U.S.C. § 113(c), assault with a dangerous weapon, with intent to do bodily harm. At Ince's trial the Government called Neumann to the stand. When her memory supposedly failed her, the prosecution attempted to refresh her recollection with a copy of the signed statement that she had given Stevens on the night of the shooting. Even with her recollection refreshed, she testified that she could no longer recall the details of her conversation with Ince. Following Neumann's testimony, the Government excused her and called Stevens, who testified (over the objection of defense counsel) as to what Neumann had told him shortly after the shooting. The trial ended with a deadlocked jury.

At the second trial, the Government again called Neumann. She again acknowledged that she had given the military police a signed statement describing what Ince had told her immediately after the shooting. But she repeatedly testified that she could no longer recall the details of Ince's remarks, despite the prosecution's effort to refresh her recollection with a copy of the statement....

Over defense counsel's repeated objections, the Government again called MP Stevens to the stand, supposedly to impeach Neumann as to her memory loss. He testified that, within hours of the shooting, Neumann had told him that Ince had confessed to firing the gun....

The second time around, the jury convicted Ince. The district judge sentenced him to forty-one months in prison, plus two years of supervised release. Ince now appeals, requesting a reversal of his conviction and a new trial.

II

Appellant Ince argues that the testimony of MP Stevens was inadmissible hearsay because the Government offered it to prove the truth of the matter asserted in Neumann's out-of-court statement (*i.e.*, that Ince confessed to the crime). The United States counters that Stevens's testimony was admissible because the Government offered it only to impeach Neumann's credibility. Ince responds that the prosecution, having already seen Neumann's performance on the stand at the *first* trial, was fully aware that she would not testify as to Ince's alleged confession at the *second* trial either. Nevertheless, the prosecution put her on the stand a second time to elicit testimony inconsistent with her prior statement to Stevens, so as to provide a foundation to offer Stevens's so-called "impeaching" evidence and thereby to get Ince's confession before the jury. Thus, the sole question presented on appeal is whether the admission of Stevens's testimony constituted reversible error.

A

Rule 607 of the Federal Rules of Evidence provides that [a witness's credibility may be attacked by any party, including the party that called the witness]. One method of attacking the credibility of (*i.e.*, impeaching) a witness is to show that he has previously made a statement that is inconsistent with his present testimony. Even if that prior inconsistent statement would otherwise be inadmissible as hearsay, it may be admissible for the limited purpose of impeaching the witness. At a criminal trial, however, there are limits on the Government's power to impeach its own witness by presenting his prior inconsistent statements. *See United States v. Morlang*, 531 F.2d 183 (4th Cir. 1975). In *Morlang*, we reversed the defendant's conviction for conspiracy to bribe and bribery because the Government had employed impeachment by prior inconsistent statement "as a mere subterfuge to get before the jury evidence not otherwise admissible."

At Morlang's trial the Government had called Fred Wilmoth, an original codefendant who had subsequently pleaded guilty, as its first witness despite the fact that his previous statements to the Government suggested he would be hostile. The real purpose for calling Wilmoth was apparently to elicit a denial that he had ever had a conversation with a fellow prisoner in which he had implicated Morlang. Having obtained the expected denial, the Government then called Raymond Crist, another prisoner, to impeach Wilmoth with the alleged prior inconsistent statement. As expected, Crist testified that his fellow inmate Wilmoth had made a conclusory statement from which one could only infer Morlang's guilt. As expected, the jury delivered a guilty verdict.

In reversing Morlang's conviction, Judge Widener explained that courts must not "permit the government, in the name of impeachment, to present testimony to the jury by indirection which would not otherwise be admissible." "To permit the government in this case to supply testimony which was a naked conclusion as to Morlang's guilt in the name of impeachment," he explained, would be tantamount to convicting a defendant on the basis of hearsay:

Foremost among [the notions of fairness upon which our system is based] is the principle that men should not be allowed to be convicted on the basis of unsworn testimony....

We must be mindful of the fact that prior unsworn statements of a witness are mere hearsay and are, as such, generally inadmissible as affirmative proof. The introduction of such testimony, even where limited to impeachment, necessarily increases the possibility that a defendant may be convicted on the basis of unsworn evidence, for despite proper instructions to the jury, it is often difficult for [jurors] to distinguish between impeachment and substantive evidence.... Thus, the danger of confusion which arises from the introduction of testimony under circumstances such as are presented here is so great as to upset the balance and [to] warrant continuation of the rule of exclusion.

Federal evidence law does *not* ask the judge, either at trial or upon appellate review, to crawl inside the prosecutor's head to divine his or her true motivation. Rather, in determining whether a Government witness' testimony offered as impeachment is admissible, or on the contrary is a "mere subterfuge" to get before the jury substantive evidence which is otherwise inadmissible as hearsay, a trial court must apply Federal Rule of Evidence 403 and weigh the testimony's impeachment value against its tendency to prejudice the defendant unfairly or to confuse the jury.

When the prosecution attempts to introduce a prior inconsistent statement to impeach its own witness, the statement's likely prejudicial impact often substantially outweighs its probative value for impeachment purposes because the jury may ignore the judge's limiting instructions and consider the "impeachment" testimony for substantive purposes. That risk is multiplied when the statement offered as impeachment testimony contains the defendant's alleged admission of guilt. Thus, a trial judge should rarely, if ever, permit the Government to "impeach" its own witness by presenting what would otherwise be inadmissible hearsay if that hearsay contains an alleged confession to the crime for which the defendant is being tried.

B

In the case at bar, MP Stevens testified that Ince had *admitted* to firing the gun — the critical element of the crime for which he was being tried. It is hard to imagine any piece of evidence that could have had a greater prejudicial impact than such a supposed naked confession of guilt....

Given the likely prejudicial impact of Stevens's testimony, the trial judge should have excluded it absent some extraordinary probative value. Because evidence of Neumann's prior inconsistent statement was admitted solely for purposes of impeachment, its probative value must be assessed solely in terms of its impeaching effect upon Neumann's testimony or overall credibility. Our review of the record below, however, shows that the probative value of Stevens's testimony *for impeachment purposes* was nil. Unlike the classic "turncoat" witness, Neumann certainly had not shocked the Government with her "loss of memory" at the second trial, as she had made it plain during the first trial that she would not readily testify to the alleged confession of her friend, Nigel Ince.[6]

---

6. The prosecution claims, for the first time at oral argument on appeal, that Neumann had cooperated with the prosecution *between* the two trials and that it therefore had reason to believe that her testimony at the second trial would be entirely different from her testimony at the first trial. Even if we were to credit the Government's account, we would reach the same result. The prosecution's supposed uncertainty about how Neumann would testify on direct examination at the second trial does

Furthermore, Neumann's actual in-court testimony did not affirmatively damage the Government's case; she merely refused to give testimony that the Government had hoped she would give. Thus, the prosecution had no need to attack her credibility....

Because Stevens's so-called "impeachment" testimony was both highly prejudicial and devoid of probative value as impeachment evidence, the trial judge should have recognized the Government's tactic for what it was—an attempt to circumvent the hearsay rule and to infect the jury with otherwise inadmissible evidence of Ince's alleged confession....

Ohio Rule of Evidence 607

Impeachment

(A) Who may impeach

The credibility of a witness may be attacked by any party except that the credibility of a witness may be attacked by the party calling the witness by means of a prior inconsistent statement only upon a showing of surprise and affirmative damage....

STAFF NOTES

....

This rule is a modification of Federal Evidence Rule 607 and constitutes a departure from prior Ohio law. Under prior law, a party ordinarily could not attack the credibility of his own witness. This principle was referred to as the "voucher rule" and the rule reflected the notion that the party who called a witness presented him as a truthful person. Since parties do not select their witnesses, but must take those persons who have perceived the operative facts, the voucher rule rests on an incorrect assumption....

Rule 607 abolishes the general principle, preserving the "voucher rule" in those limited cases in which impeachment by the party calling the witness is predicated upon a prior inconsistent statement unless surprise and affirmative damage can be shown. Otherwise, the party would be entitled to call a known adverse witness simply for the purpose of getting a prior inconsistent statement into evidence by way of impeachment, thus doing indirectly what he could not have done directly.

Requiring a showing of affirmative damage is intended to eliminate an "I don't remember" answer or a neutral answer by the witness as a basis for impeachment by a prior inconsistent statement.

Notes and Questions

1. Under Rule 613(b), a witness can testify, and then after he leaves the stand, extrinsic evidence of the prior inconsistent statement can be introduced, and the witness can later be recalled to the stand to explain or deny the statement. *See United States v. Della Rose,* 403 F.3d 891, 903 (7th Cir. 2005); *Rush v. Illinois Cent. R. Co.,* 399 F.3d 705, 723 (6th Cir. 2005); *United States v. Hudson,* 970 F.2d 948, 955 (1st Cir. 1992). Nonetheless, trial courts have broad discretion to require that the witness first be confronted with the state-

---

not affect whether the jury was misled, confused, or unfairly prejudiced by Stevens's subsequent testimony.

ment while she is on the witness stand to avoid the risk that she will become unavailable for recall. *See Hudson*, 970 F.2d at 955–56 & n.2 (collecting cases); Advisory Committee Note to Rule 613(b). *See also United States v. Surdow*, 121 Fed. Appx. 898, 899–900 (2d Cir. 2005) (holding that trial court can require counsel to indicate intention to introduce inconsistent statement before witness leaves stand, and can further require its use while the witness is on the stand or immediately after).

2. Rule 613(b) is subject to two exceptions: when the statement is that of an opposing party under Rule 801(d)(2), "or if justice so requires." The latter exception is applicable only in narrow circumstances, such as where the examining attorney did not learn of the inconsistent statement until after the witness left the stand, and the witness is no longer available to be recalled. *See, e.g., United States v. Stewart*, 179 Fed. Appx. 814, 821–22 (3d Cir. 2006).

3. Although the caselaw and the Advisory Committee Note to Rule 801(d)(1)(A) make clear that prior inconsistent statements that fail to satisfy the requirements of Rule 801(d)(1)(A) can nonetheless be used to impeach a witness, that can only get a party so far: a statement admitted for impeachment purposes only is *not* substantive evidence, and if a party has no other evidence to prove the point addressed in the statement, he will not be able to overcome a motion for summary judgment or for a directed verdict. *E.g., Santos v. Murdock*, 243 F.3d 681, 683–84 (2d Cir. 2001).

4. Although both *Ince* and *Morlang* involve the *government* impeaching its own witness in a *criminal* case, the principle has been extended to any case, civil or criminal, in which impeachment by prior inconsistent statement is "employed as a mere subterfuge to get before the jury evidence not otherwise admissible." *Whitehurst v. Wright*, 592 F.2d 834, 839–40 (5th Cir. 1979) (civil case). *But see United States v. Buffalo*, 358 F.3d 519, 525 (8th Cir. 2004) ("The vast majority of cases on the issue of impeaching one's own witness with a prior inconsistent statement speak to the government's use of the statements to impeach its witnesses where the statements inculpate the defendant.... When the defendant seeks to introduce a prior inconsistent statement for impeachment purposes, the dangers identified above are not implicated. Simply put, the prejudicial impact of the statement does not endanger the defendant's liberty by risking a conviction based on out-of-court statements that are not subject to confrontation by way of cross-examination.").

5. Under *Ince* and *Morlang*, is it necessary that the party calling the witness be *surprised* by his testimony at trial in order to impeach him with a prior inconsistent statement? Consider the following:

> Webster [citing Professor Graham] urges us ... to go beyond the good-faith standard and hold that the government may not impeach a witness with his prior inconsistent statements unless it is surprised and harmed by the witness's testimony. But we think it would be a mistake to graft such a requirement to Rule 607.... Suppose the government called an adverse witness that it thought would give evidence both helpful and harmful to it, but it also thought that the harmful aspect could be nullified by introducing the witness's prior inconsistent statement. As there would be no element of surprise, Professor Graham would forbid the introduction of the prior statements; yet we are at a loss to understand why the government should be put to the choice between the Scylla of forgoing impeachment and the Charybdis of not calling at all a witness from whom it expects to elicit genuinely helpful evidence. The good-faith standard strikes a better balance; and it is always open to the defendant to argue that the probative value of the evidence offered to impeach the witness is clearly outweighed by the prej-

udicial impact it might have on the jury, because the jury would have difficulty confining use of the evidence to impeachment.

United States v. Webster, 734 F.2d 1191, 1193 (7th Cir. 1984).

6. If surprise is not a necessary prerequisite for impeaching a witness with a prior inconsistent statement, is it a sufficient one? In other words, is surprise *alone* sufficient, or does *Ince* require surprise *plus* something else?

7. Note that a witness who testifies can be impeached by his prior inconsistent statements even if evidence of such prior inconsistent statements would otherwise be inadmissible as substantive evidence because obtained in violation of the *Miranda* rule:

> Every criminal defendant is privileged to testify in his own defense, or to refuse to do so. But that privilege cannot be construed to include the right to commit perjury. Having voluntarily taken the stand, petitioner was under an obligation to speak truthfully and accurately, and the prosecution here did no more than utilize the traditional truth-testing devices of the adversary process. Had inconsistent statements been made by the accused to some third person, it could hardly be contended that the conflict could not be laid before the jury by way of cross-examination and impeachment.
>
> The shield provided by *Miranda* cannot be perverted into a license to use perjury by way of a defense, free from the risk of confrontation with prior inconsistent utterances.

Harris v. New York, 401 U.S. 222, 225–26 (1971).

Similarly, although a witness cannot be impeached by his silence following *Miranda* warnings, a witness *can* be impeached by his silence before those warnings were given. *See Jenkins v. Anderson*, 447 U.S. 231, 235–40 (1980); *Fletcher v. Weir*, 455 U.S. 603, 604–07 (1982).

8. Impeachment by prior inconsistent statement is in point of fact merely a subset of the broader category of impeachment by contradiction, for it is impeachment by self-contradiction. Accordingly, the use of extrinsic evidence to prove a prior inconsistent statement is, like impeachment by contradiction generally, subject to the collateral matter rule. *See United States v. Roulette*, 75 F.3d 418, 423 (8th Cir. 1996).

9. If a witness testifies, and after leaving the court proceedings, makes a statement that is inconsistent with her testimony at trial, can her trial testimony be impeached by introducing evidence of her *subsequent* inconsistent statement? *See United States v. Bibbs*, 564 F.2d 1165, 1168–1170 (5th Cir. 1977) (holding that such testimony is permissible, and that its introduction is not subject to Rule 613(b)'s requirement of an opportunity to deny or explain).

10. Rule 608(b), which governs impeachment using specific instances of conduct, bars the use of extrinsic evidence to prove that the impeaching conduct occurred, while Rule 613(b) permits the use of extrinsic evidence of a witness's prior inconsistent statement to impeach him. Where the "conduct" at issue involves the making of a statement (such as engaging in perjury or making a false statement), can one circumvent the restrictions of Rule 608(b) by recourse to Rule 613(b)? Consider the following effort to distinguish the two:

> Rule 613(b) applies when two statements, one made at trial and one made previously, are irreconcilably at odds. In such an event, the cross-examiner is permitted to show the discrepancy by extrinsic evidence if necessary — not to

demonstrate which of the two is true but, rather, to show that the two do not jibe (thus calling the declarant's credibility into question). In short, comparison and contradiction are the hallmarks of Rule 613(b). As one treatise puts it:

> The theory of attack by prior inconsistent statements is not based on the assumption that the present testimony is false and the former statement true but rather upon the notion that talking one way on the stand and another way previously is blowing hot and cold, and raises a doubt as to the truthfulness of both statements.

> In contrast, Rule 608(b) addresses situations in which a witness's prior activity, whether exemplified by conduct or by a statement, in and of itself casts significant doubt upon his veracity. Thus, Rule 608(b) applies to, and bars the introduction of, extrinsic evidence of specific instances of a witness's *misconduct* if offered to impugn his credibility. So viewed, Rule 608(b) applies to a statement, as long as the statement in and of itself stands as an independent means of impeachment without any need to compare it to contradictory trial testimony.

United States v. Winchenbach, 197 F.3d 548, 558 (1st Cir. 1999).

G. Rehabilitation of Witnesses

While the party who is harmed by the testimony of a witness has an interest in casting doubt on the witness' credibility, the party who is helped by the testimony has just the opposite interest. However, a party is not permitted to "bolster" the credibility of a witness by offering evidence designed to enhance the witness's credibility before it has been attacked. Thus, in the absence of such an attack, a party cannot introduce evidence of a witness' *truthful* character or evidence of the witness' prior consistent statements in an effort to support the witness' credibility.

However, a party anticipating an attack need not sit on pins and needles waiting for the attack to occur. Although he cannot bolster his witness's credibility, he can "remove the sting" of an anticipated impeaching attack by bringing up the impeaching matter himself. Thus, for example, an attorney who knows that his witness has several prior convictions can bring those convictions out on direct examination. Similarly, the proponent of a witness can bring out on direct the fact that the witness is being paid a fee, that he has entered into a plea bargain, or other matters that might imply bias.

Once an attack on a witness' credibility has occurred, the opposing party is generally free to rehabilitate the witness. This can be accomplished by re-examination of the witness in an effort to refute or explain the impeaching fact. Consider, for example, an expert witness who on cross-examination is asked, and answers in the affirmative, "Isn't it true that you are being paid $200 per hour to testify here today?" On re-direct examination, the proponent of the witness can bring out the fact that this amount merely covers the lost earnings that the expert would have earned in his regular job had he not taken the day off to come to court.

While the types of evidence used to rehabilitate a witness' credibility are normally subject only to the restrictions of relevancy and Rule 403, *see generally United States v. Lindemann*, 85 F.3d 1232, 1243–1244 (7th Cir. 1996), the use of at least one type of evidence to rehabilitate a witness—evidence of character for truthfulness—is subject to additional restrictions. These restrictions are explored in the materials that follow.

United States v. Dring

930 F.2d 687 (9th Cir. 1991)

CHOY, Circuit Judge:

OVERVIEW

....

Alan J. Dring was convicted of importing marijuana, possession with intent to distribute, and related conspiracy charges....

FACTUAL AND PROCEDURAL BACKGROUND

At approximately 2:30 a.m. on May 22, 1986, a fishing boat carrying 13,000 pounds of marijuana, docked at Pier 3 in San Francisco Harbor. The marijuana had been transferred to the fishing boat a few miles offshore from a larger vessel, the Panamco II....

Stationed aboard the fishing boat and on the pier were undercover United States Customs agents, who witnessed the unloading of the marijuana. The agents saw an unidentified white male step out of a blue pickup truck parked on the pier.... He supervised the transfer of the marijuana from the boat to the trailer....

At trial, the Government presented considerable circumstantial evidence and five eyewitnesses who placed Dring at the pier that night....

Dring presented a defense of mistaken identity. Mark Lawrence, the tugboat caretaker who lived on Pier 3, testified that Dring was not the man he had spoken to on the pier. Two alibi witnesses testified that Dring had spent the night in question at his home in Napa Valley. Finally, Dring took the stand and denied any involvement in the drug-smuggling operation.

The Government attacked Dring's defense with contradiction evidence and one rebuttal witness. The district court precluded Dring from introducing character evidence of his veracity....

I. EVIDENCE OF DRING'S TRUTHFUL CHARACTER

Dring argues that the district court erred by barring the introduction of evidence as to his truthful character....

Federal Rule of Evidence 608(a)[] provides that "[e]vidence of truthful character is admissible only after the character of the witness for truthfulness has been attacked by opinion or reputation evidence or otherwise."* Dring concedes that the Government did not use opinion or reputation evidence against him, but still maintains that the Government "otherwise" attacked his character for truthfulness.

The first exchange cited by Dring was the response of a Government witness to cross-examination by Dring's counsel. We hold that defense-initiated "attacks" on the character of a defense witness do not trigger rehabilitative testimony under Rule 608(a). To hold otherwise would enable defense attorneys to manufacture attacks on the truthful character of their own witnesses.

The other statements cited by Dring are also insufficient to trigger rehabilitative testimony. The purpose of Rule 608(a)[] is to encourage direct attacks on a witness' veracity

---

* Editor's Note: Federal Rule 608(a) was restyled in 2011 to read in pertinent part: "evidence of truthful character is admissible only after the witness's character for truthfulness has been attacked."

in the instant case and to discourage peripheral attacks on a witness' general character for truthfulness.[2] To this end, the Rule prohibits rehabilitation by character evidence of truthfulness after direct attacks on a witness' veracity in the instant case. However, the Rule permits rehabilitation after indirect attacks on a witness' general character for truthfulness.

The Advisory Committee's Note to Rule 608(a) provides that "[o]pinion or reputation that the witness is untruthful specifically qualifies as an attack under the rule, and evidence of misconduct, including conviction of crime, and of corruption[3] also fall within this category. Evidence of bias or interest does not. McCormick § 49; 4 Wigmore §§ 1106, 1107. *Whether evidence in the form of contradiction is an attack upon the character of the witness must depend upon the circumstances.* McCormick § 49. Cf. 4 Wigmore §§ 1108, 1109" (emphasis added).

Thus, evidence of a witness' bias for or against a party in the instant case, or evidence of a witness' interest in the outcome of the instant case, constitutes a direct attack that does not trigger rehabilitation under Rule 608(a). For example, it would be permissible to imply that, because of *bias* due to *family relationship*, a father is lying to protect his son. Such evidence directly undermines the veracity and credibility of the witness in the instant case, without implicating the witness as a liar in general. By way of contrast, indirect attacks on truthfulness include opinion evidence, reputation evidence, and evidence of corruption, which require the jury to infer that the witness is lying at present, simply because he has lied often in the past.[4]

It is for the trial court, exercising its discretion, to determine whether given conduct constitutes a direct or indirect attack on a witness' character for truthfulness. On the one hand, the presentation of contradiction evidence, in the form of contravening testimony by other witnesses, does not trigger rehabilitation.[5] Vigorous cross-examination, including close questioning of a witness about his version of the facts and pointing out inconsistencies with the testimony of other witnesses, does not necessarily trigger rehabilitation.

---

2. The Advisory Committee's Note to Rule 608(a) states that "[c]haracter evidence in support of credibility is admissible under the rule only after the witness' character has first been attacked, as has been the case at common law. Maguire, Weinstein, et al., Cases on Evidence 295 (5th ed. 1965); McCormick § 49, p. 105; 4 Wigmore § 1104. The enormous needless consumption of time which a contrary practice would entail justifies the limitation." Analogously, by admitting character evidence only pertaining to truthfulness, "the result [of Rule 608(a)] is to sharpen relevancy, to reduce surprise, waste of time, and confusion, and to make the lot of the witness somewhat less unattractive. McCormick § 44."

3. "Evidence of corruption," refers to evidence of prior corrupt conduct including but not limited to forgery, fraud, perjury, bribery, false pretenses, cheating, and embezzlement. *United States v. Medical Therapy Sciences, Inc.*, 583 F.2d 36, 40–41 (2d Cir. 1978), *cert. denied*, 439 U.S. 1130 (1979); 3 Weinstein, ¶ 608 [05] at 608–45 (enumerating crimes indicating lack of truthfulness under Rule 608(b)).

4. On occasion, a single piece of evidence may serve a dual purpose, both as evidence of bias and corruption. We need not decide whether evidence of this dual nature triggers rehabilitation under Rule 608(a).

5. By calling the jury's attention to inconsistencies in testimony, the attorney may simply intend to question the ability of the witness to perceive or recall certain facts due to excitement, fatigue, poor eyesight, poor lighting, great distance from the event in question, or fading memory affected by the passage of time. 4 Wigmore, Evidence § 1109 (Chadbourn rev. 1972).

Even where an attorney points out inconsistencies to attack a witness' *truthfulness*, the attack is direct and relevant because it focuses on the credibility of the witness *in the present case* without relying on prior acts of corruption or bad character.

Nor is rehabilitation in order when an attorney maintains in her closing argument that a witness' testimony is not credible, given inconsistencies with other witnesses' testimony.

On the other hand, "[a] slashing cross-examination may carry strong accusations of misconduct and bad character, which the witness' denial will not remove from the jury's mind. If the judge considers that fairness requires it, he may permit evidence of good character, a mild palliative for the rankle of insinuation by such cross-examination." Mc-Cormick § 49 at 117.

Thus, vigorous cross-examination or the presentation of contradiction evidence can and should trigger rehabilitation where such evidence amounts to the kind of indirect attack on truthfulness embodied by "evidence of bad reputation, bad opinion of character for truthfulness, conviction of crime, or eliciting from the witness on cross-examination acknowledgment of misconduct which has not resulted in conviction." McCormick, § 49 at 116–17.

In this light, the statements cited by Dring constituted direct attacks on Dring's credibility in the instant case. The Government did not introduce opinion or reputation testimony to attack Dring's general character for truthfulness.[6] Nor did it present evidence of prior misconduct or corruption. The Government merely emphasized inconsistencies between Dring's testimony and that of other witnesses. It observed that Dring, a criminal defendant testifying on his own behalf, had a distinct pro-defense bias and a compelling interest in the outcome of the case. Therefore, the district court's denial of rehabilitative testimony was proper....

Notes and Questions

1. Although a party can anticipate an attack on his witness' credibility and defuse the attack by bringing up the impeaching fact himself, the party cannot, by so impeaching his own witness, turn around and rehabilitate him by introducing evidence designed to enhance his credibility. *United States v. Allen*, 579 F.2d 531, 532 (9th Cir. 1978). But the fact that the proponent initially raised the impeaching fact on direct does not bar him from subsequently introducing evidence to rehabilitate the witness if the opposing party subsequently pursues that line of impeachment. *United States v. Montague*, 958 F.2d 1094, 1097–98 (D.C. Cir. 1992).

2. When a character witness testifies that the target witness has an untruthful character under Rule 608(a), a party seeking to blunt the character witness' attack on the target witness' credibility can ask the character witness on cross-examination about his familiarity with particular acts of the target witness that bear on his trustworthiness. The ability to do so is provided by Rule 608(b)(2), which provides in pertinent part:

> extrinsic evidence is not admissible to prove specific instances of a witness's conduct in order to attack or support the witness's character for truthfulness. But the court may, on cross-examination, allow them to be inquired into if they are pro-

---

6. ... it is not merely attacks on *truthfulness* which trigger rehabilitation, but rather attacks on a witness' prior history or general *character for truthfulness*. Far from attempting to prove that Dring was generally a liar, the Government merely suggested that Dring was lying in the instant case about his degree of involvement in the crime. The Government placed Dring's veracity in the instant case at issue, but not his reputation for veracity.

bative of the character for truthfulness or untruthfulness of ... another witness whose character the witness being cross-examined has testified about.

Like cross-examination of character witnesses generally under Rule 405(a), the theoretical purpose of such cross-examination is to test the soundness of the character witness' opinion or reputation testimony. Thus, if the character witness on cross-examination says that he is familiar with the target witness' various acts of trustworthiness, it casts doubt on the soundness of his testimony that the target witness is untrustworthy. And if he says he isn't familiar with the various acts of trustworthiness, it suggests that his testimony is uninformed.

Note that Rule 608(b)(2) also means that when a character witness is called, after an attack, to testify to the target witness' character for truthfulness, the character witness may be asked on cross-examination about his familiarity with certain of the target witness' acts that demonstrate untrustworthiness.

In both instances, the risk of abuse is substantial. Although the questions elicited on cross-examination are supposed to be for the sole purpose of testing the soundness of the character witness' testimony, there is the risk that the process will be abused and the information misused, and so courts have a great deal of discretion to limit the questioning under Rule 608(b)(2). *See* Advisory Committee Note to Rule 608(b)(2).

3. Does Rule 608(b)(1) permit a party to rehabilitate the credibility of his witness on re-direct examination by asking him about specific instances of his prior, honest conduct that are probative of his *truthfulness*? To be sure, Rule 608(b)(1) does allow for inquiry about "specific instances of a witness's conduct ... if they are probative of the character for truthfulness or untruthfulness of ... the witness." But Rule 608(b) also provides that such instances may only be inquired into "on *cross*-examination" of the witness, which would appear to make it unavailable for use on *re-direct* examination. That would mean—would it not—that this method of rehabilitation would be available only in the unusual circumstance in which one party calls someone as a witness and attacks that witness' credibility on direct examination, at which point the opposing party could rehabilitate that witness by asking him about specific instances of his prior, honest conduct? Of course, in that situation, the party is not rehabilitating his *own* witness, but rather is rehabilitating the credibility of the opposing party's witness after the opposing party has attacked his own witness' credibility! Does that strike you as the likely intent of the drafters of Rule 608(b)? *See* Michael H. Graham, 2 Handbook of Federal Evidence § 608.4 (6th ed. 2006 & Supp. 2010) (contending that if a witness' character for truthfulness is attacked on cross-examination, re-direct is treated as cross-examination for purposes of Rule 608(b)).

4. Recall from Chapter 7 that evidence of prior consistent statements cannot be introduced as substantive evidence under Rule 801(d)(1)(B) except to rebut a charge of recent fabrication or improper influence or motive. Moreover, the Supreme Court has interpreted Rule 801(d)(1)(B) as applying only to those prior consistent statements that were made *before* the alleged improper influence or motive occurred. *See Tome v. United States*, 513 U.S. 150 (1995). Left open by *Tome* is whether prior consistent statements can be used for *rehabilitative* purposes in circumstances *other than* those provided for under Rule 801(d)(1)(B). In other words, just as prior inconsistent statements that fall outside the scope of Rule 801(d)(1)(A) can be used for impeachment purposes, so prior consistent statements that fall outside the scope of Rule 801(d)(1)(B) can be used for rehabilitative purposes, a position endorsed by most of the lower courts that have considered the matter. *See United States v. Simonelli*, 237 F.3d 19, 25–28 (1st Cir. 2001); *United States v. Ellis*, 121 F.3d 908, 919 (4th Cir. 1997).

H. Impeachment and Rehabilitation of Hearsay Declarants

Problem 10-4: The Dead Witness

David Smith is indicted on charges of stabbing his wife, Lisa Smith, to death. The prosecution's theory is that David killed Lisa on the evening of January 1, 2012 when Lisa told David that she was planning to leave him.

At David's preliminary hearing, William—the next-door neighbor of David and Lisa—testified that on the evening in question, he saw through an open window David stabbing Lisa. Several weeks later, William dies of a heart attack.

At David's trial, the prosecution seeks to offer into evidence a transcript of William's testimony at the preliminary hearing. David's attorney objects, but the objection is overruled. David's attorney then seeks to offer, over the prosecution's objection, the following testimony into evidence:

(a) Testimony by Marie, a bartender at a bar one block away from the Smiths' house. Marie would testify that about one hour before Lisa was killed, William staggered out of the bar after having imbibed a dozen glasses of beer.

(b) Testimony by Robert, one of William's close friends. Robert would testify that two days after William testified at David's preliminary hearing, William said "when I looked into the window, I saw Tom (Lisa's boyfriend) stabbing Lisa alone."

(c) Testimony by John, William's former employer. John would testify that during his job interview, William falsely stated that he had a law degree.

Was the court correct to overrule David's hearsay objection? Assuming that it was, how should the court rule on the prosecution's objections?

United States v. Saada
212 F.3d 210 (3d Cir. 2000)

HARRIS, District Judge....

A jury convicted Isaac Saada and his son, Neil Saada (collectively "appellants" and sometimes identified by their first names), of one count of conspiracy to defraud an insurance company in violation of 18 U.S.C. § 371, two counts of mail fraud in violation of 18 U.S.C. § 1341, and one count of wire fraud in violation of 18 U.S.C. § 1343. The District Court sentenced Isaac to concurrent prison terms of 36 months, and Neil to concurrent prison terms of 30 months....

Appellants owned and operated a business named Scrimshaw Handicrafts ("Scrimshaw") in New Jersey that purchased, manufactured, and sold items made from ivory, jewels, gold, and other materials....

The government's evidence at trial showed that, in 1990, appellants contacted Ezra Rishty, Isaac's cousin, for help in an insurance fraud scheme.... Rishty agreed to assist Isaac in filing a fraudulent insurance claim, and enlisted the help of Morris Beyda, a former employee who by then owned his own business....

The basis of the fraudulent insurance claim was a staged flooding in Scrimshaw's warehouse caused by a broken sprinkler head. Beyda testified that, on November 28, 1990, he went to the warehouse and, with the assistance of Neil, broke a sprinkler head located above a caged area containing Scrimshaw's most valuable merchandise. When Neil and Beyda broke the sprinkler head, Isaac was in his office with Tom Yaccarino, a vice-president of Scrimshaw and former New Jersey state court judge. Breaking the sprinkler head caused a flood of dirty water to fall on the boxes in the cage, which triggered an automatic alarm and prompted police and fire fighters to go to the Scrimshaw warehouse....

Appellants contend that the District Court improperly admitted evidence of specific instances of misconduct by Yaccarino to impeach his credibility. The impetus for the admission of this evidence was the prior admission of a statement made by Yaccarino at the time of the water damage. Linda Chewning, a Scrimshaw employee, testified that she was working in the warehouse on the night in question. During cross-examination by defense counsel, she testified that Yaccarino had run into the office kitchen screaming words to the effect of "oh my God, Neil did something stupid, [threw] something, now he has got a mess.... I can't believe it. He is so stupid. He threw it. He is stupid, he is dumb." Yaccarino was deceased at the time of trial. The District Court admitted his statement as hearsay under the excited utterance exception in Fed.R.Evid. 803(2).

Yaccarino's statement was important to appellants' defense because it purportedly provided contemporaneous evidence supporting their claim that Neil accidentally had broken the sprinkler head. Accordingly, the government sought to attack the statement by impeaching Yaccarino's credibility. The government asked the District Court to take judicial notice of two New Jersey Supreme Court decisions ordering Yaccarino's removal from the bench and disbarment for unethical conduct, as well as the factual details supporting those decisions, which reflected his unethical conduct. Appellants objected to that evidence on the grounds that the credibility of a hearsay declarant may not be impeached with extrinsic evidence of bad acts, and that the danger of unfair prejudice from this evidence substantially outweighed its probative value. Overruling these objections, the District Court took judicial notice of the two New Jersey Supreme Court decisions and their factual underpinnings. Appellants renew their objections to this evidence, and raise new challenges on the grounds that judicial notice of the facts in the two court opinions was not proper, and that the District Court conveyed an unfavorable assessment of Yaccarino's credibility to the jury in taking such judicial notice.

Appellants first argue that the judicially noticed evidence was admitted improperly because, although Federal Rule of Evidence 806 provides for the impeachment of a hearsay declarant, it limits that impeachment to "any evidence [that] would be admissible for [impeachment purposes] ... if [the] declarant had testified as a witness." Here, the judicially noticed evidence involved specific instances of Yaccarino's misconduct and, as the government acknowledged at trial, constituted extrinsic evidence....

Appellants argue that if Yaccarino had testified, Rule 608(b) would have prevented the government from introducing extrinsic evidence of his unethical conduct, and would have limited the government to questioning him about that conduct on cross-examination. Thus, appellants argue, judicial notice of the evidence constituted improper impeachment of a hearsay declarant. The government correctly avers that it would have been allowed to inquire into Yaccarino's misconduct on cross-examination if he had testified at trial because Rule 806 allows a party against whom a hearsay statement is admitted to call the declarant as a witness and "[to] examine the declarant on the statement as if [on] cross-examination." Because Yaccarino's death foreclosed eliciting the facts of his misconduct in this manner, the government argues that it was entitled to introduce extrinsic evidence of his misconduct. In effect, the government argues that, read in concert, Rules 806 and 608(b) permit the introduction of extrinsic evidence of misconduct when a hearsay declarant is unavailable to testify....

At the outset, we note that the issue of whether Rule 806 modifies Rule 608(b)'s ban on extrinsic evidence is a matter of first impression in this circuit, and a matter which the majority of our sister courts likewise has not yet addressed. Indeed, there are only two circuit court opinions construing the effect of Rule 806's intersection with Rule 608(b). Those cases are themselves in conflict. In *United States v. Friedman*, 854 F.2d 535 (2d Cir. 1988), the Second Circuit ... suggested that extrinsic evidence of such misconduct would have been admissible had the misconduct been probative of truthfulness: "[Rule 608(b)] limits such evidence of 'specific instances' to cross-examination. Rule 806 applies, of course, when the declarant has not testified and there has by definition been no cross-examination, and resort to extrinsic evidence may be the only means of presenting such evidence to the jury." *Id.* at 570 n. 8. The Second Circuit's position in *Friedman* conflicts with the District of Columbia Circuit's more recent statement in *United States v. White*, 116 F.3d 903 (D.C. Cir. 1997).... [I]n contrast to the Second Circuit in *Friedman*, the D.C. Circuit in *White* took the position that the ban on extrinsic evidence of misconduct applies in the context of hearsay declarants, even when those declarants are unavailable to testify.

We agree with the approach taken by the court in *White*, and conclude that Rule 806 does not modify Rule 608(b)'s ban on extrinsic evidence of prior bad acts in the context of hearsay declarants, even when those declarants are unavailable to testify. We perceive our holding to be dictated by the plain—albeit imperfectly meshed—language of Rules 806 and 608(b). As discussed, Rule 806 allows impeachment of a hearsay declarant only to the extent that impeachment would be permissible had the declarant testified as a witness, which, in the case of specific instances of misconduct, is limited to cross-examination under Rule 608(b). The asserted basis for declining to adhere to the clear thrust of these rules is that the only avenue for using information of prior bad acts to impeach the credibility of a witness—cross-examination—is closed if the hearsay declarant cannot be called to testify. We are unpersuaded by this rationale ... even if a hearsay declarant's credibility may not be impeached with evidence of prior misconduct, other avenues for impeaching the hearsay statement remain open. For example, the credibility of the hearsay declarant ... may be impeached with opinion and reputation evidence of character under Rule 608(a), evidence of criminal convictions under Rule 609, and evidence of prior inconsistent statements under Rule 613. The unavailability of one form of impeachment, under a specific set of circumstances, does not justify overriding the plain language of the Rules of Evidence.

We also read the language of Rule 806 implicitly to reject the asserted rationale for lifting the ban on extrinsic evidence. Rule 806 makes no allowance for the unavailability of a hearsay declarant in the context of impeachment by specific instances of misconduct, but makes such an allowance in the context of impeachment by prior inconsistent statements. Rule 613 requires that a witness be given the opportunity to admit or deny a prior inconsistent statement before extrinsic evidence of that statement may be introduced. If a hearsay declarant does not testify, however, this requirement will not usually be met. Rule 806 cures any problem over the admissibility of a non-testifying declarant's prior inconsistent statement by providing that evidence of the statement [may be admitted regardless of whether the declarant had an opportunity to explain or deny it]. *See generally* Fed.R.Evid. 806 advisory committee's notes. The fact that Rule 806 does not provide a comparable allowance for the unavailability of a hearsay declarant in the context of Rule

608(b)'s ban on extrinsic evidence indicates that the latter's ban on extrinsic evidence applies with equal force in the context of hearsay declarants.

In reaching this conclusion, we are mindful of its consequences. Upholding the ban on extrinsic evidence in the case of a hearsay declarant may require the party against whom the hearsay statement was admitted to call the declarant to testify, even though it was the party's adversary who adduced the statement requiring impeachment in the first place. And, as here, where the declarant is unavailable to testify, the ban prevents using evidence of prior misconduct as a form of impeachment.... Nevertheless, these possible drawbacks may not override the language of Rules 806 and 608(b), and do not outweigh the reason for Rule 608(b)'s ban on extrinsic evidence in the first place, which is "to avoid minitrials on wholly collateral matters which tend to distract and confuse the jury ... and to prevent unfair surprise arising from false allegations of improper conduct." *Carter v. Hewitt*, 617 F.2d 961, 971 (3d Cir. 1980)....

Notes and Questions

1. Note that Rule 806 is applicable only when a statement is admitted for a hearsay purpose. When a statement is instead admitted for some reason other than to prove the truth of the matter asserted, Rule 806 does not apply. *E.g., United States v. Arthur Andersen, LLP*, 374 F.3d 281, 292 (5th Cir. 2004), *reversed on other grounds*, 544 U.S. 696 (2005).

2. The use of a prior inconsistent statement to impeach a hearsay declarant under Rule 806 differs from its use to impeach a witness who testifies in person at trial. First, under Rule 806, "[t]he court may admit evidence of the declarant's inconsistent statement or conduct, regardless of ... whether the declarant had an opportunity to explain or deny it." Second, under Rule 806, it may with some frequency be the case that the inconsistent statement was made *after* the hearsay statement with which it is alleged to be inconsistent, and the rule makes clear that the statement may be admitted "regardless of when it occurred." The Advisory Committee explained the reason for this as follows:

> The principal difference between using hearsay and an actual witness is that the inconsistent statement will in the case of the witness almost inevitably of necessity in the nature of things be a *prior* statement, which it is entirely possible and feasible to call to his attention, while in the case of hearsay the inconsistent statement may well be a *subsequent* one....

Advisory Committee Note to Rule 806.

3. Do you see why Rule 806 is inapplicable to statements admitted pursuant to Rules 801(d)(2)(A) (individual admissions) and 801(d)(2)(B) (adoptive admissions)? What would be the effect of including such statements within the scope of Rule 806, particularly in light of Rule 607? *See* Margaret Meriwether Cordray, *Evidence Rule 806 and the Problem of Impeaching the Nontestifying Declarant*, 56 Ohio St. L. J. 495, 533 (1995) (arguing that such a rule would create a backdoor that allows the government in a criminal case to introduce evidence to impeach the defendant's credibility even if he chooses not to testify).

Chapter 11

Appellate Review of Evidentiary Rulings

A. Introduction

As you have no doubt come to appreciate by this point, the federal rules of evidence are complicated, and at times can befuddle even the most skilled attorneys. It should thus come as no surprise that, in the course of a trial, the judge herself may err in applying the rules of evidence, resulting in the exclusion of admissible evidence or the admission of excludable evidence. Indeed, it would be far more of a surprise if the trial judge were to make *no* errors in applying the rules of evidence during the course of any given trial. And despite the best efforts of the attorney arguing for the admission or exclusion of a given piece of evidence to persuade the judge otherwise, the judge may nonetheless persist in her erroneous interpretation or application of the rules of evidence.

The question that thus arises is, what remedy does a party have by way of appeal when the trial court errs in its application of the federal rules of evidence? This in turn raises several other questions. First, what must a party's attorney do to preserve for appeal a claim that the trial court erred in admitting or excluding an item of evidence? Second, at what point in time can the appeal be taken? Third, in reviewing claims of error, what deference will the appellate court give to the trial court's rulings? Fourth, if the appellate court determines that the trial court did make a mistake, what are the consequences of that determination?

Rule 103 provides the starting point for answering the first and fourth of these questions, providing in part as follows:

> (a) **Preserving a Claim of Error.** A party may claim error in a ruling to admit or exclude evidence only if the error affects a substantial right of the party and:
>
> > (1) if the ruling admits evidence, a party, on the record:
> >
> > > (A) timely objects or moves to strike; and
> > >
> > > (B) states the specific ground, unless it was apparent from the context; or
> >
> > (2) if the ruling excludes evidence, a party informs the court of its substance by an offer of proof, unless the substance was apparent from the context.
>
> (b) **Not Needing to Renew an Objection or Offer of Proof.** Once the court rules definitively on the record—either before or at trial—a party need not renew an objection or offer of proof to preserve a claim of error for appeal.
>
> ....
>
> (e) **Taking Notice of Plain Error.** A court may take notice of a plain error affecting a substantial right, even if the claim of error was not properly preserved.

Rule 103 in turn raises several more questions. First, how soon must an objection be made to be considered "timely" within the meaning of Rule 103(a)(1)(A)? Second, what sort of detail does Rule 103(a)(1)(B) require that an objection include? Third, what sort of detail does Rule 103(a)(2) require that an offer of proof include? Fourth, what qualifies as a "definitive[]" ruling by the trial court under Rule 103(b)? Fifth, what sorts of errors affect "substantial right[s]" within the meaning of Rule 103(a)? And finally, what constitutes a "plain error" within the meaning of Rule 103(e)? These questions, as well as the ones raised above, are explored in the materials that follow.

Problem 11-1: A Second Bite at the Apple

Larry Jones is indicted in federal court for the attempted murder of Whitney Wu by way of a stabbing which allegedly took place in a national park. The government seeks to offer the testimony of Dawn Drake. If permitted, Drake, an emergency medical technician (EMT), would testify that on the evening in question, she arrived at the scene of the crime and spoke to Whitney, who said to her in an excited tone "Oh God, Larry Jones stabbed me, and I'm dying!" The attorney for Jones objects on hearsay grounds, but the prosecution contends that the statement qualifies as a dying declaration under Rule 804(b)(2), and that Whitney is "unavailable as a witness" because she was called as a witness but testified that she could not remember the incident. The defense rebuts by arguing that the exception does not apply in attempted murder cases, and that in any event it would not apply because the factual prerequisites for invoking Rule 804(b)(2) were not satisfied.

The trial court overrules each aspect of the defense's objection, Dawn is permitted to testify, and the jury finds Jones guilty of attempted murder. Jones appeals the case to the appropriate circuit of the U.S. Court of Appeals. On appeal, Jones renews his claim that the trial court erred in holding that Drake's testimony qualifies as a dying declaration under Rule 804(b)(2). In addition, Jones claims for the first time on appeal that the admission of Drake's testimony violates Jones' Confrontation Clause rights.

Will the appellate court consider Jones' claims, and if so, under what standard(s) of review? If the appellate court concludes that Drake's testimony does not qualify as a dying declaration, but that it would qualify as an excited utterance, can it affirm the decision on that ground? If the appellate court concludes that Drake's testimony is hearsay not falling within any hearsay exception and/or that the admission of the testimony violated Jones' Confrontation Clause rights, must it reverse Jones' conviction? How, if at all, would the result differ if Jones had raised his Confrontation Clause claim at trial?

B. Preserving Claims of Error for Appellate Review and the Timing of Appellate Review

United States v. Meserve
271 F.3d 314 (1st Cir. 2001)

YOUNG, District Judge.

Brian Eugene Meserve ("Meserve") appeals from his conviction for robbery and firearms offenses in the United States District Court for the District of Maine. On appeal, Meserve claims four errors occurred during the course of his two-day trial; specifically that (A) the district court allowed a witness to repeat the out-of-court statement of a third party in violation of Federal Rule of Evidence 802.... (C) the government used a stale conviction to impeach a defense witness in violation of Federal Rule of Evidence 609(b), and (D) the government cross-examined a defense witness about his character for violence and his prior convictions in violation of Federal Rules of Evidence 608 and 609....

Meserve argues that the district court committed reversible error by permitting the government to cross-examine his brother, Kevin, about his disorderly person and assault convictions and about his alleged violent reputation in the community. The challenged portion of Kevin's cross-examination is as follows:

Q: Now, Mr. McKee asked you questions about your conviction for unlawful sexual contact in '94 and '95, but that's not your only conviction, is it?

A: I have a couple of assaults on my record.

Q: 1999–1979, disorderly conduct.

MR. McKEE: I object, Your Honor, That's improper cross-examination under Rule 609. It specifically precludes that. A disorderly conduct?

MR. McCARTHY: I can lay a foundation for it.

THE COURT: Go ahead....

Q: Been in a lot of fights in your day?

MR. McKEE: I object, improper character evidence, impeachment.

THE COURT: Just a minute. Objection's overruled.

A: How many would you classify as a lot?

BY MR. McCARTHY:

Q: More than one?

A: Yeah, I've been in more than one, probably two.

Q: Okay. And as a result of that, people in the community are afraid of you, aren't they?

A: No.

Mr. McKEE: Object, Your Honor. A continuing objection to my client's—excuse me—this witness' alleged behavior in the past as not being relevant, as not being permissible character evidence under Rule 608 or any other rule....

Meserve objects to this entire line of questioning, asserting that the questions about Kevin's disorderly person and assault convictions were improper because these convictions were not permissible subjects of cross-examination under Rule 609(a) and that the questions about Kevin being a "tough guy" and having been in a lot of fights in his day were improper character evidence under Rule 608. The government counters that Meserve failed to preserve these issues for review and that any errors that may have occurred were harmless, given the cumulative weight of the evidence against Meserve....

The government devoted a great deal of space in its brief and time at oral argument to defending the untenable position that the issues raised by Meserve on appeal were not preserved for review because the defense failed to make *both* contemporaneous objections *and* motions to strike.... Because of the vehemence with which the government argues a position with no seeming support in the law, this court pauses to discuss the obligations placed on each of the parties to a trial by the Federal Rules of Evidence.

It is a basic tenet of our law that in order to preserve an evidentiary issue for review, the party opposing the admission of the evidence must make a timely objection. Fed.R.Evid. 103(a)(1)[(A)]; *see also United States v. Taylor*, 54 F.3d 967, 972 (1st Cir. 1995) ("In general, the law ministers to the vigilant, not to those who sleep upon perceptible rights."). Thus, the government argues that the defense's failure immediately to object when Kevin was asked about convictions in addition to his unlawful sexual contact convictions constrains this court from considering the matter on appeal absent plain error. Examination of the transcript, however, reveals that Meserve's attorney objected as soon as it became obvious that the government's line of questioning was in violation of Rule 609, i.e., when the government indicated that the conviction about which it was asking was a twenty-year-old disorderly conduct conviction. To be timely, an objection must be "made as soon as the ground of it is known, or reasonably should have been known to the objector." *United States v. Check*, 582 F.2d 668, 676 (2d Cir. 1978). The general principle that an objection should be made after a question has been asked but before an answer has been given, *Hutchinson v. Groskin*, 927 F.2d 722, 725 (2d Cir. 1991), is flexible in deference to the "heat of a hotly contested criminal trial," *Check*, 582 F.2d at 676. Thus, the defense was not required to anticipate the government's line of questioning in order for the objection to be timely. *Compare Hutchinson*, 927 F.2d at 725 (holding that objection was timely, even though objection was not made until after question was answered), *and Inge v. United States*, 356 F.2d 345, 350 n. 17 (D.C. Cir. 1966) (holding that defense counsel's failure to object until after he learned the nature of the document being used to refresh the defendant's recollection did not render objection nugatory), *with United States v. Benavente Gomez*, 921 F.2d 378, 385 (1st Cir. 1990) (holding that because at least three pages of transcript were recorded before the defendant objected, the objection came too late to preserve the objection for appeal), *and W. Fire Ins. Co. v. Word*, 131 F.2d 541, 543–44 (5th Cir. 1942) ("It is a rule of law so old that the memory of man runneth not to the contrary that one may not sit by without objection to rulings or instructions, and then after verdict and judgment, and when it is too late for the court to change its rulings or charge, come forward with objections on appeal and seek to put the court in error."). Meserve's objection, although delayed, was sufficiently contemporaneous to comport with the Federal Rules of Evidence.

The government attempts to place an additional onus on parties opposing the admission of such evidence, however, by arguing that the defense was further obligated to move to strike Kevin's answers to the government's questions in order to preserve Meserve's right to review. According to the government, once a question has been answered, even if that answer was provided pursuant to a district court's evidentiary ruling, the proper procedural vehicle to preserve rights for appeal is the motion to strike. The government was able to cite no authority for this proposition during oral argument and the court has found none.

The rule governing objections to evidence states that [a timely objection *or* motion to strike must appear on the record]. Fed.R.Evid. 103(a)(1). Because Rule 103 is written in the disjunctive, the right to review may be preserved either by objecting or by moving to strike and offering specific grounds in support of that motion. The rule is intended to ensure that the nature of an error was called to the attention of the trial judge, so as to "alert him to the proper course of action and enable opposing counsel to take proper corrective measures." Fed.R.Evid. 103(a) advisory committee's note. Thus, both the plain language and underlying goals of Rule 103(a) indicate that a party opposing the admission of evidence may do so through *either* a timely objection *or* motion to strike.[3]

Moreover, the position espoused by the government is contrary to logic. According to the government, even if a witness' answer was given pursuant to a district court's order overruling an objection, the party opposing admission of the evidence must move to strike the witness' answer to escape plain error review. Modern trial practice is unreceptive to such procedural redundancies, and were this court to adopt the government's view, it would take several steps back from the streamlining that the Judicial Conference, the Supreme Court, and the Congress attempted to accomplish through the enactment of the Federal Rules of Evidence in 1975. Because the law imposes no obligation on a party opposing the admission of evidence *both* to object *and* to move to strike, Meserve's timely objections were sufficient to preserve his rights for review....

United States v. Wynn
845 F.2d 1439 (2d Cir. 1988)

FLAUM, Circuit Judge.

Ronald Wynn appeals from his conviction on one count of embezzling a letter in the course of his job as a postal service employee, in violation of 18 U.S.C. § 1709, and one count of knowingly and without authority opening mail not directed to him, in violation of 18 U.S.C. § 1703(b). The letter that Wynn improperly opened contained $100 in food stamps. The sole issue on appeal is whether the district court erred under Federal Rule of Evidence 404(b) in admitting certain evidence relating to previous reports of missing food stamps and a prior investigation of Wynn....

To preserve an issue for appellate review, a party must make a proper objection at trial that alerts the court and opposing party to the specific grounds for the objection. *United States v. Laughlin*, 772 F.2d 1382, 1391–92 (7th Cir. 1985). An objection is proper only if [a party timely objects or moves to strike, and states the specific ground, unless it was apparent from the context]. Fed.R.Evid. 103(a)(1).[6] Neither a general objection to the evidence nor a specific objection on other grounds will preserve the issue for review. *Laughlin*, 772 F.2d at 1392 (defendant's objection at trial that certain photographs were not relevant or alternatively were more prejudicial than probative did not preserve for appeal the claim that the evidence should have been excluded under Federal Rule of Evidence 404(b)). "The specific ground for reversal of an evidentiary ruling on appeal must also be the same as that raised at trial." *United States v. Taylor*, 800 F.2d 1012, 1017 (10th Cir. 1986).

---

3. If a party does not challenge the evidence in a timely manner, however, an after-the-fact motion to strike usually cannot "repair the forfeiture that flows from the failure to interpose a contemporaneous objection." *A.J. Faigin v. Kelly*, 184 F.3d 67, 83 n. 10 (1st Cir. 1999).

6. The defendant does not argue that it is apparent from the context of Hanson's testimony that he was objecting under Rule 404(b); this argument is therefore waived.

At trial Wynn objected that Hanson's testimony about the reports of missing food stamps and the prior investigation was impermissible hearsay and lacked a sufficient foundation. The district court overruled both of these objections and Wynn does not contest those rulings on appeal. Instead, on appeal Wynn raises an entirely new objection to the admission of this evidence—Rule 404(b). Because Wynn did not object under Rule 404(b), the district court never considered whether this evidence was inadmissible on these grounds. As a result, Wynn has waived this issue on appeal unless the admission of Hanson's testimony was plain error....

United States v. Adams
271 F.3d 1236 (10th Cir. 2001)

PAUL KELLY, Jr., Circuit Judge.

Defendant-Appellant Dale L. Adams was found guilty by a jury of possession of a firearm by a felon in violation of 18 U.S.C. § 922(g)(1), and sentenced to 51 months and three years supervised release.... On appeal, he contends that the district court's exclusion of expert testimony by a clinical psychologist [was erroneous]....

At the outset we are faced with the question of whether Mr. Adams made an offer of proof to the trial court adequate to preserve the claimed error of excluding the psychologist's testimony. "Error may not be based on a ruling excluding evidence unless 'the substance of the evidence was made known to the court by offer [of proof] or was apparent from the context within which questions were asked.'" *Inselman v. S & J Operating Co.*, 44 F.3d 894, 896 (10th Cir. 1995). On numerous occasions we have held that "'merely telling the court the content of ... proposed testimony' is not an offer of proof." *Polys v. Trans-Colorado Airlines, Inc.*, 941 F.2d 1404, 1407 (10th Cir. 1991). In order to qualify as an adequate offer of proof, the proponent must, first, describe the evidence and what it tends to show and, second, identify the grounds for admitting the evidence. *Phillips v. Hillcrest Med. Ctr.*, 244 F.3d 790, 802 (10th Cir. 2001); *Polys*, 941 F.2d at 1407. If the proponent's offer of proof fails this standard, then this court can reverse only in instances of plain error that affected appellant's substantial rights.

A twofold purpose underlies these required showings. First, an effective offer of proof enables the trial judge to make informed decisions based on the substance of the evidence. *Polys*, 941 F.2d at 1406. Second, an effective offer of proof creates "a clear record that an appellate court can review to 'determine whether there was reversible error in excluding the [testimony].'" *Id.* at 1407.

Federal Rule of Evidence 103(a)(2) does not mandate a particular form for offers of proof. Instead, the rule invests the trial judge with discretion in determining the form of the offer. Fed.R.Evid. 103([c]). There are at least four ways to make an offer of proof of testimony and achieve the purposes underlying the rule. First, and most desirable from all standpoints except cost, the proponent may examine the witness before the court and have the answers reported on the record. The question and answer method necessitates excusing a jury, but this concern is not present when the offer of proof is made, as here, at a pretrial motion hearing. When the proponent proffers testimony in this manner, opposing counsel may be permitted "to cross-examine the witness to develop any factors which would put the preferred testimony in its true light."

The second, and least favorable, method for making an offer of proof of testimony is a statement of counsel as to what the testimony would be. In this case, the colloquy between counsel and the district court was so lacking in detail that it is difficult to decipher why exclusion of the evidence might be error. During the hearing on the motion in limine, defense counsel stated that he had asked the examining psychologist to "look into whether or not [Mr. Adams's] personality, mental makeup, however you want to put it, would he be so inclined—given the testing that's done, would there be a possibility that he would give a false statement to the police." Counsel then proffered that the examining psychologist had "suggested in one of the paragraphs [of the report] ... that his personality certainly is one that could have been—statements to the police could have been false."

An offer of proof of testimony by counsel is the least favored method because of its potential to fall short of the standard required by the rules of evidence as well as the standard set out in *Phillips* and *Polys*. Defense counsel's offer of proof made during the colloquy with the judge illustrates the potential pitfalls of this method. Specificity and detail are the hallmarks of a good offer of proof of testimony, and conclusory terms, especially when presented in a confused manner, mark poor ones. Defense counsel hardly met the baseline requirement of "'merely telling the court the content of ... [the] proposed testimony.'" *Polys*, 941 F.2d at 1407. As for the additional requirements set out in *Phillips* and *Polys*, counsel did not explain the significance of the proposed evidence or what he expected the evidence to show. *Phillips*, 244 F.3d at 802; *Polys*, 941 F.2d at 1407. Nor did counsel clearly identify "the grounds for which [he] believes the evidence to be admissible." *Id.*

Documentary offers of proof comprise the third and fourth proper forms of proffering anticipated testimony. The first of these, and least common, is a statement written by examining counsel describing the answers the proposed witness would give if permitted to testify. More common, and relevant to this case, the proponent of the evidence may introduce a "written statement of the witness's testimony signed by the witness and *offered as part of the record*." In using either method of documentary proffer for anticipated testimony, "[i]t is suggested ... that the writing be marked as an exhibit and introduced into the record for proper identification on appeal." Indeed the primary, formal reason for an offer of proof is "to preserve the issue for appeal by including the proposed answer and expected proof *in the official record of trial*."

On the morning of the pretrial hearing, counsel for Mr. Adams apparently sent a facsimile of the psychologist's report directly to the district court judge, who referred to the report during the hearing. The report was not marked as an exhibit. "Documents and other exhibits are usually marked for identification and become part of the record on appeal, even if excluded." Nor was it filed as an exhibit to a pleading. The report is not part of the record below.

Merely sending a facsimile of the psychologist's report to the judge on the morning before the hearing unfortunately does not guarantee that the faxed item will actually be marked as an exhibit or filed and become part of the record. Our rules anticipate that when an appeal is based upon the challenge to the admission or exclusion of evidence, we be furnished not only with pertinent transcript excerpts, but also with pertinent trial exhibits that are part of the record.

Mr. Adams has moved to supplement the record. The appellate rules allow supplementation of the record on appeal in instances where "anything material ... is omitted from or misstated in the record by error or accident." Fed. R.App. P. 10(e)(2). Because the district court judge did make passing reference to a recently faxed psychologist's report, and because counsel as an officer of the court represents that this is the same report that was before the district court, and because the government does not oppose it, we will grant the motion. We remind counsel, however, of the importance of a valid, properly presented, detailed, and recorded offer of proof when testimony is involved and of the importance of insuring that supporting documentary evidence be made part of the record.…

Crowe v. Bolduc
334 F.3d 124 (1st Cir. 2003)

LYNCH, Circuit Judge.

[In a pre-trial motion in limine, the trial court held that certain witnesses could not be asked certain questions aimed at exposing their bias on cross-examination.]

….

There is a question as to whether our standard of review for the in limine exclusion should be for abuse of discretion or for plain error. Our rule as to motions in limine is that a party must renew at trial its motion to offer or exclude evidence if there has been an earlier provisional ruling by motion in limine and a clear invitation to offer evidence at trial. If, by contrast, the in limine ruling is final and unconditional, the issue was preserved for appeal and no further steps need be taken to preserve the issue. Here there was no attempt at trial to introduce the evidence which was the subject of the in limine exclusion. Our circuit rule has now been codified in a 2000 amendment to Rule 103, Federal Rules of Evidence. The Rule provides in part: "Once the court [rules definitively on the record—either before or at trial—] a party need not renew an objection or offer of proof to preserve a claim of error for appeal." Fed.R.Evid. 103([b]).

As the commentary to the Rule makes clear: "The amendment imposes an obligation on counsel to clarify whether an in limine or other evidentiary ruling is definitive when there is doubt on that point." Fed.R.Evid. 103 advisory committee's note, 2000 Amendment. Unfortunately, the trial court left doubt on the point in its ruling:

> And, if you feel at any point during the trial that despite this ruling, which is in the nature of an in limine ruling and is therefore by definition tentative, if you feel that you have an argument based on the circumstances of the record as it has developed to press again this issue, then you may do so, of course, but at sidebar. In other words, you are not to be asking any questions of witnesses in cross-examination that seeks to elicit this kind of information until we address the issue again at sidebar. I'm not inviting you to do that, you understand, but I just want to be clear that obviously if you think there is something significant about the way that the evidence has gone in and has not been taken into account by way of analysis, then you can raise it again.

It is not true, as the trial court assumed, that in limine rulings are "by definition tentative." *See Black's Law Dictionary* 791 (7th ed. 1999) (defining "in limine" as "preliminarily; presented to only the judge, before or during trial"). Some in limine rulings may be final, and whether the ruling is final or tentative has important consequences for counsel. The trial court's ruling can be read either way: that the ruling was only tentative, or that it was final unless circumstances at trial changed and warranted a new effort to introduce the evidence. Formulations such as the one used by the trial court here are not uncommon but are inadvisable because of the ambiguity created.

The burden, though, was on Bolduc to clarify whether the in limine ruling was final or not, and he did not.…

[The Court goes on to conclude that the outcome of the case would be the same without regard to the standard employed to review the trial court's decision.]

Luce v. United States

469 U.S. 38 (1984)

Chief Justice BURGER delivered the opinion of the Court....

Petitioner was indicted on charges of conspiracy, and possession of cocaine with intent to distribute, in violation of 21 U.S.C. §§ 846 and 841(a)(1). During his trial in the United States District Court for the Western District of Tennessee, petitioner moved for a ruling to preclude the Government from using a 1974 state conviction to impeach him if he testified. There was no commitment by petitioner that he would testify if the motion were granted, nor did he make a proffer to the court as to what his testimony would be. In opposing the motion, the Government represented that the conviction was for a serious crime—possession of a controlled substance.

The District Court ruled that the prior conviction fell within the category of permissible impeachment evidence under Federal Rule of Evidence 609(a). The District Court noted, however, that the nature and scope of petitioner's trial testimony could affect the court's specific evidentiary rulings; for example, the court was prepared to hold that the prior conviction would be excluded if petitioner limited his testimony to explaining his attempt to flee from the arresting officers. However, if petitioner took the stand and denied any prior involvement with drugs, he could then be impeached by the 1974 conviction. Petitioner did not testify, and the jury returned guilty verdicts....

It is clear, of course, that had petitioner testified and been impeached by evidence of a prior conviction, the District Court's decision to admit the impeachment evidence would have been reviewable on appeal along with any other claims of error. The Court of Appeals would then have had a complete record detailing the nature of petitioner's testimony, the scope of the cross-examination, and the possible impact of the impeachment on the jury's verdict.

A reviewing court is handicapped in any effort to rule on subtle evidentiary questions outside a factual context. This is particularly true under Rule 609(a)(1)[(B)], which directs the court to weigh the probative value of a prior conviction against the prejudicial effect to the defendant. To perform this balancing, the court must know the precise nature of the defendant's testimony, which is unknowable when, as here, the defendant does not testify.[5]

Any possible harm flowing from a district court's *in limine* ruling permitting impeachment by a prior conviction is wholly speculative. The ruling is subject to change when the case unfolds, particularly if the actual testimony differs from what was contained in the defendant's proffer. Indeed even if nothing unexpected happens at trial, the district judge is free, in the exercise of sound judicial discretion, to alter a previous *in limine* ruling. On a record such as here, it would be a matter of conjecture whether the District Court would have allowed the Government to attack petitioner's credibility at trial by means of the prior conviction.

When the defendant does not testify, the reviewing court also has no way of knowing whether the Government would have sought to impeach with the prior conviction. If, for example, the Government's case is strong, and the defendant is subject to impeachment by other means, a prosecutor might elect not to use an arguably inadmissible prior conviction.

Because an accused's decision whether to testify "seldom turns on the resolution of one factor," *New Jersey v. Portash*, 440 U.S. 450, 467 (1979) (BLACKMUN, J., dissenting),

---

5. Requiring a defendant to make a proffer of testimony is no answer; his trial testimony could, for any number of reasons, differ from the proffer.

a reviewing court cannot assume that the adverse ruling motivated a defendant's decision not to testify. In support of his motion a defendant might make a commitment to testify if his motion is granted; but such a commitment is virtually risk free because of the difficulty of enforcing it.

Even if these difficulties could be surmounted, the reviewing court would still face the question of harmless error. Were *in limine* rulings under Rule 609(a) reviewable on appeal, almost any error would result in the windfall of automatic reversal; the appellate court could not logically term "harmless" an error that presumptively kept the defendant from testifying. Requiring that a defendant testify in order to preserve Rule 609(a) claims will enable the reviewing court to determine the impact any erroneous impeachment may have had in light of the record as a whole; it will also tend to discourage making such motions solely to "plant" reversible error in the event of conviction....

We hold that to raise and preserve for review the claim of improper impeachment with a prior conviction, a defendant must testify....

[The concurring opinion of Justice Brennan is omitted.]

Ohler v. United States
529 U.S. 753 (2000)

Chief Justice Rehnquist delivered the opinion of the Court.

Petitioner, Maria Ohler, was arrested and charged with importation of marijuana and possession of marijuana with the intent to distribute. The District Court granted the Government's motion *in limine* seeking to admit evidence of her prior felony conviction as impeachment evidence under Federal Rule of Evidence 609(a)(1). Ohler testified at trial and admitted on direct examination that she had been convicted of possession of methamphetamine in 1993. The jury convicted her of both counts....

On appeal, Ohler challenged the District Court's *in limine* ruling allowing the Government to use her prior conviction for impeachment purposes. The Court of Appeals for the Ninth Circuit affirmed, holding that Ohler waived her objection by introducing evidence of the conviction during her direct examination. We granted certiorari to resolve a conflict among the Circuits regarding whether appellate review of an *in limine* ruling is available in this situation. We affirm.

Generally, a party introducing evidence cannot complain on appeal that the evidence was erroneously admitted....

Ohler argues that it would be unfair to apply such a waiver rule in this situation because it compels a defendant to forgo the tactical advantage of pre-emptively introducing the conviction in order to appeal the *in limine* ruling. She argues that if a defendant is forced to wait for evidence of the conviction to be introduced on cross-examination, the jury will believe that the defendant is less credible because she was trying to conceal the conviction. The Government disputes that the defendant is unduly disadvantaged by waiting for the prosecution to introduce the conviction on cross-examination. First, the Government argues that it is debatable whether jurors actually perceive a defendant to be more credible if she introduces a conviction herself. Second, even if jurors do consider the defendant more credible, the Government suggests that it is an unwarranted advantage because the jury does not realize that the defendant disclosed the conviction only after failing to persuade the court to exclude it.

Whatever the merits of these contentions, they tend to obscure the fact that both the Government and the defendant in a criminal trial must make choices as the trial progresses. For example, the defendant must decide whether or not to take the stand in her own behalf. If she has an innocent or mitigating explanation for evidence that might otherwise incriminate, acquittal may be more likely if she takes the stand. Here, for example, Ohler testified that she had no knowledge of the marijuana discovered in the van, that the van had been taken to Mexico without her permission, and that she had gone there simply to retrieve the van. But once the defendant testifies, she is subject to cross-examination, including impeachment by prior convictions, and the decision to take the stand may prove damaging instead of helpful. A defendant has a further choice to make if she decides to testify, notwithstanding a prior conviction. The defendant must choose whether to introduce the conviction on direct examination and remove the sting or to take her chances with the prosecutor's possible elicitation of the conviction on cross-examination.

The Government, too, in a case such as this, must make a choice. If the defendant testifies, it must choose whether or not to impeach her by use of her prior conviction. Here the trial judge had indicated he would allow its use,[3] but the Government still had to consider whether its use might be deemed reversible error on appeal. This choice is often based on the Government's appraisal of the apparent effect of the defendant's testimony. If she has offered a plausible, innocent explanation of the evidence against her, it will be inclined to use the prior conviction; if not, it may decide not to risk possible reversal on appeal from its use.

Due to the structure of trial, the Government has one inherent advantage in these competing trial strategies. Cross-examination comes after direct examination, and therefore the Government need not make its choice until the defendant has elected whether or not to take the stand in her own behalf and after the Government has heard the defendant testify.

Ohler's submission would deny to the Government its usual right to decide, after she testifies, whether or not to use her prior conviction against her. She seeks to short circuit that decisional process by offering the conviction herself (and thereby removing the sting) and still preserve its admission as a claim of error on appeal.

But here Ohler runs into the position taken by the Court in a similar, but not identical, situation in *Luce v. United States*, 469 U.S. 38 (1984), that "[a]ny possible harm flowing from a district court's *in limine* ruling permitting impeachment by a prior conviction is wholly speculative." *Id.*, at 41. Only when the Government exercises its option to elicit the testimony is an appellate court confronted with a case where, under the normal rules of trial, the defendant can claim the denial of a substantial right if in fact the district court's *in limine* ruling proved to be erroneous. In our view, there is nothing "unfair," as Ohler puts it, about putting her to her choice in accordance with the normal rules of trial....

[The dissenting opinion of Justice Souter is omitted.]

---

3. The District Court ruled on the first day of trial that Ohler's prior conviction would be admissible for impeachment purposes, and the court likely would have abided by that ruling at trial. However, *in limine* rulings are not binding on the trial judge, and the judge may always change his mind during the course of a trial. See *Luce v. United States*, 469 U.S. 38, 41–42 (1984). Ohler's position, therefore, would deprive the trial court of the opportunity to change its mind after hearing all of the defendant's testimony.

Mohawk Industries, Inc. v. Carpenter

130 S. Ct. 599 (2009)

Justice SOTOMAYOR delivered the opinion of the Court.

Section 1291 of the Judicial Code confers on federal courts of appeals jurisdiction to review "final decisions of the district courts." 28 U.S.C. § 1291. Although "final decisions" typically are ones that trigger the entry of judgment, they also include a small set of pre-judgment orders that are "collateral to" the merits of an action and "too important" to be denied immediate review. *Cohen v. Beneficial Industrial Loan Corp.*, 337 U.S. 541, 546 (1949). In this case, petitioner Mohawk Industries, Inc., attempted to bring a collateral order appeal after the District Court ordered it to disclose certain confidential materials on the ground that Mohawk had waived the attorney-client privilege. The Court of Appeals dismissed the appeal for want of jurisdiction.

The question before us is whether disclosure orders adverse to the attorney-client privilege qualify for immediate appeal under the collateral order doctrine....

II

A

By statute, Courts of Appeals "have jurisdiction of appeals from all final decisions of the district courts of the United States, ... except where a direct review may be had in the Supreme Court." 28 U.S.C. § 1291. A "final decisio[n]" is typically one "by which a district court disassociates itself from a case." *Swint v. Chambers County Comm'n*, 514 U.S. 35, 42 (1995). This Court, however, "has long given" § 1291 a "practical rather than a technical construction." *Cohen*, 337 U.S., at 546. As we held in *Cohen*, the statute encompasses not only judgments that "terminate an action," but also a "small class" of collateral rulings that, although they do not end the litigation, are appropriately deemed "final." *Id.*, at 545–546. "That small category includes only decisions that are conclusive, that resolve important questions separate from the merits, and that are effectively unreviewable on appeal from the final judgment in the underlying action." *Swint*, 514 U.S., at 42.

In applying *Cohen*'s collateral order doctrine, we have stressed that it must "never be allowed to swallow the general rule that a party is entitled to a single appeal, to be deferred until final judgment has been entered."

....

The justification for immediate appeal must therefore be sufficiently strong to overcome the usual benefits of deferring appeal until litigation concludes. This requirement finds expression in two of the three traditional *Cohen* conditions. The second condition insists upon "*important* questions separate from the merits." More significantly, "the third *Cohen* question, whether a right is 'adequately vindicable' or 'effectively reviewable,' simply cannot be answered without a judgment about the value of the interests that would be lost through rigorous application of a final judgment requirement."

....

In making this determination, we do not engage in an "individualized jurisdictional inquiry." Rather, our focus is on "the entire category to which a claim belongs." As long as the class of claims, taken as a whole, can be adequately vindicated by other means, "the chance that the litigation at hand might be speeded, or a 'particular injustic[e]' averted," does not provide a basis for jurisdiction under § 1291.

B

In the present case, the Court of Appeals concluded that the District Court's privilege-waiver order satisfied the first two conditions of the collateral order doctrine-conclusiveness and separateness—but not the third—effective unreviewability. Because we agree with the Court of Appeals that collateral order appeals are not necessary to ensure effective review of orders adverse to the attorney-client privilege, we do not decide whether the other *Cohen* requirements are met....

We readily acknowledge the importance of the attorney-client privilege, which "is one of the oldest recognized privileges for confidential communications." *Swidler & Berlin v. United States*, 524 U.S. 399, 403 (1998). By assuring confidentiality, the privilege encourages clients to make "full and frank" disclosures to their attorneys, who are then better able to provide candid advice and effective representation. *Upjohn Co. v. United States*, 449 U.S. 383, 389 (1981). This, in turn, serves "broader public interests in the observance of law and administration of justice."

The crucial question, however, is not whether an interest is important in the abstract; it is whether deferring review until final judgment so imperils the interest as to justify the cost of allowing immediate appeal of the entire class of relevant orders. We routinely require litigants to wait until after final judgment to vindicate valuable rights, including rights central to our adversarial system....

In our estimation, postjudgment appeals generally suffice to protect the rights of litigants and assure the vitality of the attorney-client privilege. Appellate courts can remedy the improper disclosure of privileged material in the same way they remedy a host of other erroneous evidentiary rulings: by vacating an adverse judgment and remanding for a new trial in which the protected material and its fruits are excluded from evidence.

Dismissing such relief as inadequate, Mohawk emphasizes that the attorney-client privilege does not merely "prohibi[t] use of protected information at trial"; it provides a "right not to disclose the privileged information in the first place." Mohawk is undoubtedly correct that an order to disclose privileged information intrudes on the confidentiality of attorney-client communications. But deferring review until final judgment does not meaningfully reduce the *ex ante* incentives for full and frank consultations between clients and counsel.

One reason for the lack of a discernible chill is that, in deciding how freely to speak, clients and counsel are unlikely to focus on the remote prospect of an erroneous disclosure order, let alone on the timing of a possible appeal. Whether or not immediate collateral order appeals are available, clients and counsel must account for the possibility that they will later be required by law to disclose their communications for a variety of reasons—for example, because they misjudged the scope of the privilege, because they waived the privilege, or because their communications fell within the privilege's crime-fraud exception. Most district court rulings on these matters involve the routine application of settled legal principles. They are unlikely to be reversed on appeal, particularly when they rest on factual determinations for which appellate deference is the norm. The breadth of the privilege and the narrowness of its exceptions will thus tend to exert a much greater influence on the conduct of clients and counsel than the small risk that the law will be misapplied.[2]

---

2. Perhaps the situation would be different if district courts were systematically underenforcing the privilege, but we have no indication that this is the case.

Moreover, were attorneys and clients to reflect upon their appellate options, they would find that litigants confronted with a particularly injurious or novel privilege ruling have several potential avenues of review apart from collateral order appeal. First, a party may ask the district court to certify, and the court of appeals to accept, an interlocutory appeal pursuant to 28 U.S.C. § 1292(b). The preconditions for § 1292(b) review—"a controlling question of law," the prompt resolution of which "may materially advance the ultimate termination of the litigation"—are most likely to be satisfied when a privilege ruling involves a new legal question or is of special consequence, and district courts should not hesitate to certify an interlocutory appeal in such cases. Second, in extraordinary circumstances—*i.e.*, when a disclosure order "amount[s] to a judicial usurpation of power or a clear abuse of discretion," or otherwise works a manifest injustice—a party may petition the court of appeals for a writ of mandamus. While these discretionary review mechanisms do not provide relief in every case, they serve as useful "safety valve[s]" for promptly correcting serious errors.

Another long-recognized option is for a party to defy a disclosure order and incur court-imposed sanctions.... Such sanctions allow a party to obtain postjudgment review without having to reveal its privileged information. Alternatively, when the circumstances warrant it, a district court may hold a noncomplying party in contempt. The party can then appeal directly from that ruling, at least when the contempt citation can be characterized as a criminal punishment....

In short, the limited benefits of applying "the blunt, categorical instrument of § 1291 collateral order appeal" to privilege-related disclosure orders simply cannot justify the likely institutional costs. Permitting parties to undertake successive, piecemeal appeals of all adverse attorney-client rulings would unduly delay the resolution of district court litigation and needlessly burden the Courts of Appeals....

[The concurring opinion of Justice Thomas is omitted.]

Notes and Questions

1. Unlike Rule 103(a)(1), nowhere does Rule 103(a)(2) specifically state that the offer of proof must be specific and timely. Nonetheless, the latter provision has been so interpreted by the federal courts. *See Beech Aircraft Corp. v. Rainey*, 488 U.S. 153, 177–178 (1988) (Rehnquist, J., concurring in part and dissenting in part) ("Most courts and treatises have interpreted the need for an 'offer of proof' as requiring a specific and timely defense of the evidence"); *International Land Acquisitions, Inc. v. Fausto*, 39 Fed. Appx. 751, 755–56 (3d Cir. 2002) ("Read literally, this rule tends to suggest that there is no requirement that the offeror state the grounds relied upon for admissibility or that the offer of proof be timely, on the record, or stated with specificity. However, this rule has been applied differently in practice. 'If in the trial court the offeror fails to specify any ground for admissibility, or specifies the wrong ground, he is [in] trouble on appeal.'").

2. A rule requiring a timely objection serves several purposes. First, it brings any potential error to the trial court's attention so that the court can prevent the error from occurring by ruling on the admissibility of the proffered evidence before it is admitted. Second, it gives opposing counsel an opportunity to cure the potential problem, such as by laying the necessary foundation, rephrasing the question, or calling a different witness. Third, it promotes finality by minimizing the need for re-trials by preventing errors from occurring in the first place. A rule requiring a timely offer of proof serves these

same purposes, and also ensures that a record is created that enables the appellate court effectively to review the trial court's decision on appeal.

3. Rule 103(d) provides that

> To the extent practicable, the court must conduct a jury trial so that inadmissible evidence is not suggested to the jury by any means.

The Advisory Committee explains the rationale for this provision as follows:

> This subdivision proceeds on the supposition that a ruling which excludes evidence in a jury case is likely to be a pointless procedure if the excluded evidence nevertheless comes to the attention of the jury.... The judge can foreclose a particular line of testimony and counsel can protect his record without a series of questions before the jury, designed at best to waste time and at worst "to waft into the jury box" the very matter sought to be excluded.

Advisory Committee Note to Rule 103(d).

4. Trial court judges can be temperamental, and it is possible that on occasion a trial court judge will refuse to let a party make an offer of proof. Under such circumstances, the failure to make the offer of proof at trial will not be held against a party. *E.g., Moss v. Ole South Real Estate, Inc.*, 933 F.2d 1300, 1310–11 (5th Cir. 1991).

5. Note that in a case involving multiple parties, such as a criminal prosecution with multiple defendants, an objection by one defendant will not necessarily preserve that claim of error on appeal for another defendant. *See United States v. Ray*, 370 F.3d 1039, 1044 (10th Cir. 2004), *vacated on other grounds*, 543 U.S. 1109 (2005). However, it is convenient in such cases to avoid having every attorney get up and repeat the same objection, and attorneys representing multiple parties with common interests can avoid any problems on appeal by getting the trial court to agree on the record that an objection by one attorney is an objection by all. *See United States v. Pinillos-Prieto*, 419 F.3d 61, 70 n.9 (1st Cir. 2005); *United States v. Westerbrook*, 119 F.3d 1176, 1183 (5th Cir. 1997).

6. In *Meserve*, counsel for the defendant requested a "continuing objection." Such an objection, *if granted by the trial court*, alleviates the need to object to every question that follows in that line of questioning. However, such an objection, like any other objection, preserves only an objection for the *specific grounds* raised. *United States v. Gomez-Norena*, 908 F.2d 497, 500 n.2 (9th Cir. 1990).

7. As the *Wynn* court indicates, a specific objection to the admissibility of evidence on one ground does not preserve a claim that admitting the evidence was error on some other ground, even if the two grounds are closely related to one another. *See, e.g., United States v. Chau*, 426 F.3d 1318, 1321–22 (11th Cir. 2005) (hearsay objection does not preserve Confrontation Clause objection); *United States v. Price*, 418 F.3d 771, 779 (7th Cir. 2005) (relevance objection does not preserve objections based on Rules 403 or 404).

8. Note that appellate courts give themselves substantial flexibility to *affirm* a trial court's decision to admit or exclude evidence. Suppose, for example, that a party claims on appeal that the trial court erred in admitting evidence under a particular hearsay exception. The appellate court agrees that the evidence would not fit that hearsay exception, but concludes that the evidence would have been admissible anyway, either because it would have fit some other hearsay exception or because the evidence is not hearsay because not offered for the truth of the matter asserted. Under these circumstances, the ap-

pellate court would affirm the decision to admit the evidence, for it is a settled rule that an "appellate court will affirm the rulings of the lower court on any ground that finds support in the record, even where the lower court reached its conclusions from a different or even erroneous course of reasoning." *Abuan v. Level 3 Communications, Inc.*, 353 F.3d 1158, 1171 n.3 (10th Cir. 2003). *Accord United States v. Montgomery*, 635 F.3d 1074, 1089 (8th Cir. 2011).

9. A motion *in limine* is a procedural device that a party may use to obtain an advance ruling on the admissibility of evidence. It can be made both before trial and during trial, and is typically made with respect to evidence that a party intends to offer and that she anticipates may be objected to, or with respect to evidence that she anticipates will be offered by opposing counsel and that she finds to be objectionable. Such motions can be particularly useful when the question is complex and ill-suited for an on-the-spot ruling, or where the ruling may help a party to determine trial strategy.

10. The Advisory Committee Note to the 2000 Amendment to Rule 103 provides in pertinent part as follows:

> When the ruling is definitive, a renewed objection or offer of proof at the time the evidence is to be offered is more a formalism than a necessity. On the other hand, when the trial court appears to have reserved its ruling or to have indicated that the ruling is provisional, it makes sense to require the party to bring the issue to the court's attention subsequently.

> The amendment imposes the obligation on counsel to clarify whether an *in limine* or other evidentiary ruling is definitive when there is doubt on that point.

> Even where the court's ruling is definitive, nothing in the amendment prohibits the court from revisiting its decision when the evidence is to be offered. If the court changes its initial ruling, or if the opposing party violates the terms of the initial ruling, objection must be made when the evidence is offered to preserve the claim of error for appeal. The error, if any, in such a situation occurs only when the evidence is offered and admitted.

> A definitive advance ruling is reviewed in light of the facts and circumstances before the trial court at the time of the ruling. If the relevant facts and circumstances change materially after the advance ruling has been made, those facts and circumstances cannot be relied upon on appeal unless they have been brought to the attention of the trial court by way of a renewed, and timely, objection, offer of proof, or motion to strike. Similarly, if the court decides in an advance ruling that proffered evidence is admissible subject to the eventual introduction by the proponent of a foundation for the evidence, and that foundation is never provided, the opponent cannot claim error based on the failure to establish the foundation unless the opponent calls that failure to the court's attention by a timely motion to strike or other suitable motion.

Given these qualifications, do you suspect that many attorneys will take advantage of the 2000 Amendment?

11. The Advisory Committee Note to the 2000 Amendment to Rule 103 states that:

> The amendment does not purport to answer whether a party who objects to evidence that the court finds admissible in a definitive ruling, and who then offers the evidence to "remove the sting" of its anticipated prejudicial effect, thereby waives the right to appeal the trial court's ruling.

As you can see, *Ohler* settled that question. Moreover, the Advisory Committee Note made clear that the amendment had no effect on *Luce*, and also noted that *Luce* applies outside the context of Rule 609 determinations:

> Nothing in the amendment is intended to affect the rule set forth in *Luce v. United States*, 469 U.S. 38 (1984), and its progeny. The amendment provides that an objection or offer of proof need not be renewed to preserve a claim of error with respect to a definitive pretrial ruling. *Luce* answers affirmatively a separate question: whether a criminal defendant must testify at trial in order to preserve a claim of error predicated upon a trial court's decision to admit the defendant's prior convictions for impeachment. The *Luce* principle has been extended by many lower courts to other situations.

Advisory Committee Note to 2000 Amendment to Rule 103. *See also United States v. McConnel*, 464 F.3d 1152, 1162 (10th Cir. 2006) (applying *Ohler* to evidence offered under Federal Rule 608(b)).

12. The combined effect of *Ohler* and *Luce* is that a criminal defendant must make one of several choices, each of which involves some risk. If he opts not to testify, evidence of his prior crimes doesn't get before the jury, but he also loses both the ability to get his own testimony before the jury and loses his right to appeal the trial court's decision. Alternatively, he can choose to testify, and anticipate the government's impeachment by bringing out the impeaching evidence himself. In doing so, he gets his testimony before the jury, and removes the potential "sting" of impeachment, but he loses the ability to appeal the trial court's decision, and the jury is exposed to evidence of his prior crimes. Finally, he can choose to testify without bringing out the impeaching evidence himself. In doing so, he gets his testimony before the jury, and preserves his right to appeal the trial court's decision, but suffers the sting of impeachment. In most cases, isn't it likely that a risk-averse defendant will choose either the first or second options, meaning that he will almost always forfeit his right to an appeal?

13. As illustrated by *Mohawk Industries*, the general rule is that decisions by a trial court judge admitting or excluding evidence are not subject to immediate appellate review. Rather, the parties must wait until a final judgment has been rendered, and raise the claims along with any other claims that they might have. *See* 28 U.S.C. § 1291.

In at least one narrow instance, however, it may be possible to obtain appellate review of an evidentiary ruling prior to final judgment. In criminal cases, the government has the ability to seek interlocutory review of pretrial decisions suppressing or excluding evidence. *See* 18 U.S.C. § 3731. Do you understand the rationale for granting the government, but not the defendant, this option?

C. Standards of Review of Claimed Errors in Interpreting and Applying Rules of Evidence

Assuming that a timely and specific objection or offer of proof is made at trial sufficient to preserve the claim for appeal, the next question that arises is the standard by which the appellate court will review the trial court's interpretation and application of the rule of evidence at issue. As it turns out, appellate courts give different degrees of deference to trial courts, depending on the *type* of error involved. The following excerpt explores this issue.

De Novo Review in Deferential Robes?: A Deconstruction of the Standard of Review of Evidentiary Errors in the Federal System

Peter Nicolas
54 Syracuse L. Rev. 531 (2004)

....

Traditionally, decisions by trial judges have been divided into three categories for purposes of appellate review: questions of law, reviewable "de novo"; questions of fact, reviewable for "clear error"; and matters of discretion, reviewable for "abuse of discretion."

The first category, "de novo review[,] is review without deference," or review that is "independent and plenary." Under de novo review, the appellate court will thus "look at the matter anew, as though it had come to the courts for the first time."

The other two categories involve different degrees of deference to the trial court, with abuse of discretion usually thought to be the more deferential of the two. A finding of fact is said to be "'clearly erroneous' when although there is evidence to support it, the reviewing court on the entire evidence is left with the definite and firm conviction that a mistake has been committed." Under clear error review, the appellate court *cannot* reverse the trial court's determination merely because it would have found the facts differently had it been sitting as the trier of fact: "[w]here there are two permissible views of the evidence, the fact finder's choice between them cannot be clearly erroneous."

A district court vested with discretion on a matter "is not required by law to make a *particular* decision ... [but instead] is empowered to make a decision—of *its* choosing—that falls within a range of permissible decisions." Sometimes, the trial court's exercise of its discretion is based on a weighing of factors, in which case an abuse of discretion will be found only if the trial court failed to consider the appropriate factors, considered improper factors, or made a "'clear error of judgment'" in weighing the correct factors. The appellate court cannot under this standard of review merely substitute its own judgment for that of the trial court. In general, an abuse of discretion will be found only if the trial court's decision is "arbitrary," "irrational," "capricious," "whimsical," "fanciful," or "unreasonable." Furthermore, the trial court's exercise of its discretion will not be disturbed unless it can be said that "'no reasonable person would adopt the district court's view.'"

The rationales for exercising different standards of review for questions of fact and law and for exercises of discretion turn on, inter alia, the relative expertise and institutional structure of trial and appellate courts, the nature of the questions involved, and public policy. Thus, questions of law are reviewed de novo because an appellate court has more time for research and consideration of such issues than does a trial court, which must preside over "fast-paced trials," and also because appellate courts sit in multi-judge panels, permitting "reflective dialogue and collective judgment." Findings of fact by a trial court are reviewed with deference because the trial judge is believed to have greater expertise in finding facts, has the ability to observe the testimony of witnesses live (and is thus better able to judge demeanor than an appellate court reviewing a cold record), and because allowing for plenary review of facts at the appellate level is thought to be a tremendous waste of private and judicial resources. The rationale for limiting review of a particular issue to abuse of discretion is a determination that the trial court is better positioned than the appeals court to decide the issue because it involves "'multifarious, fleeting, special, narrow facts that utterly resist generalization.'"

So what standard of review applies when a trial court is said to have erred in admitting or excluding an item of evidence? Does a decision to admit or exclude evidence in applying the Federal Rules of Evidence involve a question of law, a question of fact, an exercise of discretion, or a combination of all of these?

In every federal circuit, one can find a panel decision stating in general terms that a decision to admit or exclude evidence by the trial court is reviewed only for "abuse of discretion," suggesting that the application of the Federal Rules of Evidence is committed to the sound discretion of the trial court. Does this mean, then, that trial courts have broad discretion in how they interpret the rules of evidence, such as the determination whether the hearsay exception for statements for purposes of medical diagnosis or treatment covers statements made to psychologists, or whether a federal physician-patient testimonial privilege exists? Either these appellate panels cannot mean what they say, or "abuse of discretion" review means something different than has been traditionally understood, or the traditional tripartite standard of review (and the policies underlying it) has been thrown out the window when it comes to review of decisions admitting or excluding evidence.

A review of the cases demonstrates that the traditional tripartite standard of review is alive and well when it comes to reviewing evidentiary errors. Only the First Circuit explicitly delineates the tripartite standard of review in this context. Yet many circuits, such as the Second Circuit, have re-defined "abuse of discretion" review in this context as incorporating a combination of de novo, clear error, and traditional abuse of discretion review....

Under this "peculiar lexicon," there are thus three prongs to this new "abuse of discretion" review that mirror the traditional tripartite law-fact-discretion standard of review. A claim that the trial court erred in admitting or excluding evidence based on an erroneous interpretation of a rule of evidence is reviewed under the de novo prong of the "abuse of discretion" standard. A claim that the trial court erred in admitting or excluding evidence based on an erroneous factual finding is reviewed under the clear error prong of the "abuse of discretion" standard. And a claim that the trial court erred in admitting or excluding evidence in exercising its discretionary authority is reviewed under the abuse of discretion prong of the "abuse of discretion" standard.

Why on earth, one might ask, would the appellate courts replace the traditional tripartite standard of review in this context with "abuse of discretion" review, only to re-define "abuse of discretion" review as wholly encompassing the traditional tripartite standard of review? Part of the story appears to be a misreading of the Supreme Court's decision in *General Electric Co. v. Joiner*, in which the Supreme Court held that the trial court's determination of the reliability of expert witness testimony is subject only to review for abuse of discretion. In *Joiner*, there is a sentence that reads "[a]ll evidentiary decisions are reviewed under an abuse-of-discretion standard." In context, it seems clear that this sentence refers to an argument attributed to one of the parties before the Court. Yet, it has been misinterpreted as being part of its holding by some appellate courts, thus causing them to feel bound to review all claims of evidentiary error under an abuse of discretion standard. At the same time, these appellate courts remain wed to the policies that underlie the traditional tripartite standard of review, and thus find it hard to believe that the Supreme Court would mean that a trial court has "discretion" over how to construe the text of a rule of evidence. They thus resolve their dilemma by re-interpreting the "abuse of discretion" standard to include de novo review of errors of law, with such errors deemed to be an "abuse of discretion."

....

[The article goes on to examine these principles with respect to each rule of evidence. What follow are a few representative samples.]

Consider a trial in which an attorney claims that the evidence he seeks to offer into evidence is not subject to exclusion under the hearsay rule because it is being offered for some reason other than to prove the truth of the matter asserted, such as to impeach a witness or to show the effect on the person who heard it. Suppose the trial judge nonetheless excludes the evidence on the ground that it is hearsay. By what standard should a court of appeals review this determination? This involves an interpretation of the meaning of the text of the hearsay rule, to wit, what it means for something to be "offered to prove the truth of the matter asserted," and thus is a question of law that should be reviewed de novo....

Consider instead a trial in which the dispute centers on whether or not something falls within the definition of the word "statement." In most cases, the parties are unlikely to dispute this issue, yet in the case of nonverbal conduct, a determination must be made whether the conduct was "intended by the person as an assertion." This finding of intent is clearly a factual finding, as the official commentary to Rule 801(a) notes, thus making it appropriate to be reviewed only for clear error. Yet consider instead the question whether the word "conduct" includes non-affirmative conduct, such as silence (in the sense of an absence of complaints). This raises a question of law as to the meaning of the term "conduct," subject to de novo review....

The determination of the existence and scope of a federal evidentiary privilege under Rule 501 is a question of law reviewed de novo, although the application of such a recognized privilege to a particular factual scenario is subject to deferential review. Thus, for example, the existence and scope of a federal marital confidence privilege is a question of law subject to de novo review, but the factual determination that the prerequisites to invoking such a privilege exist — a valid marriage and a communication made in confidence — would be reviewed for clear error....

Notes and Questions

1. Rule 403 is a paradigmatic example of a rule whose application is reviewed solely for abuse of discretion in the traditional sense of the word. *See Old Chief v. United States,* 519 U.S. 172, 183 & n.7 (1997). Another example is the trial court's application of *Daubert* to determine the reliability of scientific evidence. *See General Elec. Co. v. Joiner,* 522 U.S. 136, 146 (1997). Do you see why deference is so high in reviewing such decisions?

2. As the journal article excerpted above indicates, the First Circuit has most clearly delineated the standards by which claims of evidentiary error are reviewed:

> It is commonly said that a trial judge's decision regarding the admissibility of expert testimony will not be disturbed absent a clear abuse of discretion. This formulation is adequate to our case which involves judgments of balancing and degree as to relevance, prejudice and the like. It is useful to note, however, that admissibility of evidence issues can also turn on abstract questions of law, where review is de novo, or on findings by the judge of specific facts, where review is for clear error.

Baker v. Dalkon Shield Claimants Trust, 156 F.3d 248, 251–52 (1st Cir. 1998).

By contrast, the following is an example of the "peculiar lexicon" used by other courts:

> It is plain from our analysis of these evidentiary issues that a trial court has no "discretion" to disregard the explicit foundational requirements of the hearsay rule

as codified in the Federal Rules of Evidence.... When a federal court admits or rejects evidence in violation of the requirements of these rules, it errs as a matter of law, sometimes harmlessly, sometimes harmfully. But in the peculiar lexicon of our precedentially binding federal evidence jurisprudence, an evidentiary error of law has been held to be an "abuse of discretion"; that, and our obedience to the Supreme Court's command in *Joiner*, are the only explanations we can offer for analyzing the district court's rulings under Rule 801(d)(2) using an abuse of discretion standard.

United States v. Brown, 2000 WL 876382, at *9 (6th Cir. June 20, 2000). *See also United States v. Wheaton*, 517 F.3d 350, 364 (6th Cir. 2008) ("We review a district court's evidentiary determinations under the abuse-of-discretion standard, mindful that 'it is an abuse of discretion to make errors of law or clear errors of factual determination.'").

3. A properly preserved claim that hearsay evidence is "testimonial" and thus that its admission violated a criminal defendant's rights under the Confrontation Clause is deemed a question of law subject to de novo review. *See United States v. Lamons*, 532 F.3d 1251, 1261 n.15 (11th Cir. 2008); *United States v. Brito*, 427 F.3d 53, 59 (1st Cir. 2005).

4. A claim of evidentiary error or an offer of proof that would normally be reviewed de novo, for clear error, or for an abuse of discretion will only be reviewed, if at all, for "plain error" if a timely and specific objection or offer of proof was not made. The ability of courts to review a decision under the plain error standard in the absence of an objection or offer of proof is provided in Rule 103(e), which states that "[a] court may take notice of a plain error affecting a substantial right, even if the claim of error was not properly preserved."

An appellate court's invocation of the plain error doctrine is within its discretion, and the doctrine, when invoked, allows for reversal only where the trial court made an error that was "clear" or "obvious" and that affected the outcome of the case. *United States v. Olano*, 507 U.S. 725, 734–35 (1993). The burden of proving that the error affected the outcome is on the party invoking the plain error doctrine: thus, in a criminal case, a criminal defendant invoking the plain error doctrine bears the burden of proof. *Id.*

The relevant time period for determining whether an error is "plain" is at the time of appellate review, not at the time of the original trial. Thus, the question is whether the error is so obvious that a trial judge and prosecutor would be derelict in permitting it in a trial held *at the time the case is being reviewed on appeal. See United States v. Hardwick*, 523 F.3d 94, 98 (2d Cir. 2008); *United States v. Thomas*, 274 F.3d 655, 667 (2d Cir. 2001).

D. Harmless Error Doctrine

Even if a party takes the appropriate steps to preserve a claim of evidentiary error, and even if, after applying the appropriate standard of review, the appellate court determines that the trial court made an error, that does not mean—even in a criminal case—that the decision will be overturned. Indeed, there is a very high likelihood that the decision will be affirmed, the error notwithstanding. That is because of the opening sentence of Rule 103(a), which provides that "[a] party may claim error in a ruling to admit or exclude evidence only if the error affects a substantial right of the party," a codification of the so-called "harmless error" doctrine. The following is an illustration of the application of the doctrine.

United States v. Piper
298 F.3d 47 (1st Cir. 2002)

SELYA, Circuit Judge.

Following his conviction for both distributing cocaine and conspiring to engage in distribution, defendant-appellant Stanley M. Piper challenges the district court's admission of certain tape-recorded conversations between an alleged coconspirator, Anthony Stilkey, and various third parties. The court admitted these statements under Evidence Rule 801(d)(2)(E) (the so-called coconspirator hearsay exception)....

[The Court concludes that six audiotapes admitted by the trial court satisfied Rule 801(d)(2)(E), but that the seventh one did not, because it did not satisfy the "in furtherance" element of that exception.]

....

We have concluded, to this point, that the April 22 conversation between Stilkey and Shafir was improvidently allowed into evidence, but that no error attended the admission of the conversations captured on the six other audiotapes. The question thus becomes whether the erroneous admission of the April 22 conversation requires a new trial.

A non-constitutional evidentiary error is harmless (and, therefore, does not require a new trial) so long as it is highly probable that the error did not influence the verdict. Under this test, the government bears the burden of establishing harmlessness. *United States v. Rose*, 104 F.3d 1408, 1414 (1st Cir. 1997). Because the inquiry is fact-specific, each case must be treated separately. As we have written:

> There is no bright-line rule for divining when particular errors that result in a jury's exposure to improper evidence are (or are not) harmless. Rather, a harmlessness determination demands a panoramic, case-specific inquiry considering, among other things, the centrality of the tainted material, its uniqueness, its prejudicial impact, the uses to which it was put during the trial, the relative strengths of the parties' cases, and any telltales that furnish clues to the likelihood that the error affected the factfinder's resolution of a material issue.

Sepulveda, 15 F.3d at 1182.

Here, the appellant asserts that Stilkey's April 22 statements go to the heart of the matter and that the government's case, stripped of those statements, collapses like a ruined soufflé. To highlight the importance of the erroneously admitted evidence, he points to the final portion of the prosecutor's closing argument. There, the prosecutor, referring to the fact that the seven secretly recorded audiotapes were to be sent to the jury along with a Panasonic tape recorder, stated:

> The best witness in this case, ladies and gentlemen of the jury, is Mr. Panasonic.

> What I ask you to do, if you want to get what this case is all about, if you want to really find out what was going on back in April of 1999, go back in the jury room during your deliberations and pay attention to everything you recall, everything you can that you heard during the course of this trial, harken to some particularity, listen closely to Mr. Panasonic. And the answer is right in front of you.

It is always dangerous to focus on rhetorical flourishes at the expense of the big picture. The appellant's argument runs afoul of this precept. Notwithstanding the hyperbole contained in the prosecutor's impassioned summation, the record shows quite plainly that the statements made during the April 22 conversation were cumulative of other evidence. Accordingly, their admission constituted harmless error. We explain briefly.

At trial, the government sought to establish that the appellant (1) distributed cocaine on April 13, and (2) conspired with Stilkey to traffic in drugs during April 1999. The government's case was very strong. Stilkey's testimony made out the essential elements. He testified that on three separate occasions — April 8, 13, and 20 — he handed the appellant money, received cocaine, and proceeded to effect a retail sale. He also vouchsafed that these transactions were within the purview of a drug-trafficking scheme hatched by the two men. This, then, was the foundation of the government's case.

The government built on this foundation throughout the trial, corroborating Stilkey's testimony in a myriad of ways. One way was through the testimony of Shafir, who gave a detailed account of his drug purchases on April 13 and April 20. Another was through the testimony of Jennifer Stilkey, who testified that the appellant was at the Stilkey residence on the afternoon of April 13; that he balked when Stilkey mentioned that the prospective customer (Shafir) wanted "to try [the cocaine] first"; and that, when Stilkey gave him the money that Shafir had paid, he counted it. A third source of corroboration was the eye-witness testimony of two detectives who functioned as members of the surveillance team. These witnesses provided cogent circumstantial evidence that Stilkey met with the appellant, as he had claimed, on April 8 and April 13.

Last — but surely not least — the six properly admitted audiotapes contained statements that not only bolstered Stilkey's trial testimony but also furnished independent evidence of the appellant's guilt. To cite one example, Stilkey told Rodney on April 8 that his supplier — "Stanley" — traveled to New Hampshire to purchase drugs. The jury certainly could have credited Stilkey's trial testimony that "Stanley" was Stanley Piper (the appellant), especially since Jennifer Stilkey testified that the appellant mentioned that he had purchased cocaine from a New Hampshire supplier. To cite another example, Stilkey told Shafir on April 13 that his source had agreed to show up at Stilkey's house that evening at 6:00 p.m. When linked with the testimony of several witnesses who placed the appellant at the Stilkeys' home on April 13, this statement was highly probative.

It would serve no useful purpose to recount other examples. The short of it is that the details related by Stilkey about his source in the six properly admitted conversations were internally consistent, jibed with the other evidence in the case, and functioned to identify the appellant and place him at the center of the charged conspiracy.

Against this backdrop, the statements made by Stilkey on April 22 do not seem to add very much to the mix. The most damning aspect of that conversation was Stilkey's clear identification of "Stanley" as his original drug source — yet he had made the same identification in the secretly recorded conversation of April 8, and that identification was already before the jury. Moreover, Stilkey, from the witness stand, had made an unambiguous identification of the appellant as his original supplier, and the other evidence in the case tended to verify Stilkey's claim. In the last analysis, then, the most powerful aspect of the April 22 conversation was merely cumulative of other identity-related evidence adduced by the government. Cumulative evidence is typically regarded as harmless, and there is no sound reason to doubt its harmlessness here.

Nor do we believe that the prosecutor's "Mr. Panasonic" reference is a particular cause for concern. That soliloquy was part and parcel of the government's rebuttal to the appellant's closing argument, which strenuously attacked Stilkey's credibility. By emphasizing the *collective* importance of the taped statements, the government sought to rehabilitate its witness. For this purpose, the six properly admitted tapes bore much of the load; the April 22 conversation, in and of itself, was of no special import.

That ends this aspect of the matter. Given the overwhelming evidence indicating that the appellant was Stilkey's original supplier, we deem it highly unlikely that the improvident admission of the April 22 conversation had a significant impact on the jury's evaluation of the evidence or contributed in any way to the jury's verdict. It follows that the error was harmless....

Notes and Questions

1. The harmless error and plain error doctrines are similar in one respect: both allow for reversal only when the error can be shown to have affected the outcome of the proceedings. But in this regard, they differ with respect to who bears the burden of proof. In a criminal case, a defendant who tries to invoke the plain error standard bears the burden of proving that the error affected the outcome, but in a criminal case in which the government wishes to invoke the harmless error doctrine, the government bears the burden of proving that the error did not affect the outcome. *See generally United States v. Olano*, 507 U.S. 725, 734 (1993).

2. The *Piper* case described the harmless error standard for non-constitutional errors, requiring that the government show that it is "highly probable" that the error was harmless. Other courts use a slightly different standard, requiring a showing by a preponderance of the evidence that the error was harmless. *E.g., United States v. Marshall*, 432 F.3d 1157, 1162 (10th Cir. 2005).

Most constitutional errors, such as admitting evidence in violation of the Confrontation Clause, are likewise subject to harmless error analysis, but the government's showing in such instances is higher: it must prove beyond a reasonable doubt that the error in admitting the evidence did not affect the outcome. *E.g., United States v. Williams*, 632 F.3d 129, 143 (4th Cir. 2011).

Index